THE CAMBRIDGE HISTORY OF
LATINA/O AMERICAN LITERATURE

The Cambridge History of Latina/o American Literature emphasizes the importance of understanding Latina/o literature not simply as a U.S. ethnic phenomenon but more broadly as a trans-American tradition extending from the sixteenth century to the present. Engaging with the dynamics of transculturation, linguistic and cultural difference, and the uneven distribution of power across the Americas that characterize Latina/o literature, the essays in this History provide a critical overview of key texts, authors, themes, and contexts as discussed by leading scholars in the field. This book demonstrates the relevance of Latina/o literature for a world defined by legacies of coloniality, the imposition of militarized borders, and the transnational migration of people, commodities, and cultural practices.

JOHN MORÁN GONZÁLEZ is Professor of English and Director of the Center for Mexican American Studies at The University of Texas at Austin. He is the author of *Border Renaissance: The Texas Centennial and the Emergence of Mexican American Literature* and *The Troubled Union: Expansionist Imperatives in Post-Reconstruction American Novels*. His articles and reviews have appeared in *American Literature, American Literary History, Aztlán, Nineteenth-Century Contexts, Symbolism, Western Historical Quarterly*, and *Western American Literature*. He edited *The Cambridge Companion to Latina/o American Literature* (2016).

LAURA LOMAS is Associate Professor in English and American Studies at Rutgers University-Newark, where she teaches Latina/o and comparative American literature. Her first book, *Translating Empire: José Martí, Migrant Latino Subjects and American Modernities*, won the MLA Prize for Latina/o and Chicana/o literature and an honorable mention from the Latin American Studies Association's Latina/o Studies Section. She has published essays in *Small Axe, The Latino Nineteenth Century, Translation Review, Cuban Studies,* the *Journal of American Studies, Comparative American Studies* and *American Literature*.

THE CAMBRIDGE
HISTORY OF
LATINA/O AMERICAN LITERATURE

*

Edited by
JOHN MORÁN GONZÁLEZ
The University of Texas at Austin

LAURA LOMAS
Rutgers University-Newark

CAMBRIDGE
UNIVERSITY PRESS

CAMBRIDGE
UNIVERSITY PRESS

University Printing House, Cambridge CB2 8BS, United Kingdom

One Liberty Plaza, 20th Floor, New York, NY 10006, USA

477 Williamstown Road, Port Melbourne, VIC 3207, Australia

314–321, 3rd Floor, Plot 3, Splendor Forum, Jasola District Centre, New Delhi – 110025, India

79 Anson Road, #06–04/06, Singapore 079906

Cambridge University Press is part of the University of Cambridge.

It furthers the University's mission by disseminating knowledge in the pursuit
of education, learning, and research at the highest international levels of excellence.

www.cambridge.org
Information on this title: www.cambridge.org/9781107183087
DOI: 10.1017/9781316869468

© Cambridge University Press 2018

First published 2018

Printed in the United States of America by Sheridan Books, Inc.

A catalogue record for this publication is available from the British Library.

Library of Congress Cataloging-in-Publication Data
NAMES: González, John Morán, 1966 June 30- editor. | Lomas, Laura, 1967- editor.
TITLE: The Cambridge history of Latina/o American literature / edited by
John Morán González, Laura Lomas.
DESCRIPTION: Cambridge ; New York, NY : Cambridge University Press, 2018. |
Includes bibliographical references and index.
IDENTIFIERS: LCCN 2017032440 | ISBN 9781107183087 (Hardback)
SUBJECTS: LCSH: Latin American literature–History and criticism.
CLASSIFICATION: LCC PQ7081.A1 C353 2018 | DDC 860.9/98–dc23
LC record available at https://lccn.loc.gov/2017032440

ISBN 978-1-107-18308-7 Hardback

A Patricia, Angelita, y Santiago, siempre en mi corazón — JMG

A Amaru, Marta Zabina, el futuro; y a Rubén, mi cielo — LAL

Contents

Contents

Contents

Contents

Contents

Contributors

JESSE ALEMÁN is Professor of English at The University of New Mexico, where he teaches nineteenth-century American and Chicana/o literatures. He has published over a dozen articles in venues such as *Aztlán*, *American Literary History*, *MELUS*, and *Arizona Quarterly*. He edited Loreta Janeta Velazquez's *The Woman in Battle*. In addition, he has coedited two anthologies, *Empire and the Literature of Sensation* with Shelley Streeby (2007) and *The Latino Nineteenth Century* with Rodrigo Lazo (2016).

LORENA ALVARADO holds a Ph.D. in Culture and Performance from the University of California, Los Angeles. Her book project, *Playing with Feeling: Musical Performances of Mexican Sentimiento*, develops a theory of *sentimiento*, the ability to convey and inspire emotion as it circulates through twentieth- and twenty-first-century U.S. Mexican and Latina/o vocal and musical practices. She is Assistant Professor at University of California, Merced, Global Arts program, and has previously taught at University of California, Riverside, Northwestern University, and the University of Houston.

ARTURO ARIAS is John D. and Catherine T. MacArthur Foundation Professor in the Humanities at the University of California, Merced. He has published *Taking Their Word: Literature and the Signs of Central America* (2007), *The Rigoberta Menchú Controversy* (2000), *The Identity of the Word: Guatemalan Literature in Light of the New Century* (1998), and *Ceremonial Gestures: Central American Fiction 1960-1990* (1998), as well as a critical edition of Miguel Angel Asturias's *Mulata* (2000). From 2001 to 2003 he was president of the Latin American Studies Association. He also cowrote the film *El Norte* (1984) and has published six novels in Spanish, two of which have been translated to English (*After the Bombs*, 1990, and *Rattlesnake*, 2003). Twice winner of the Casa de las Américas Award, and winner of the Ana Seghers Award for fiction in Germany, he was given the Miguel Angel Asturias National Award for Lifetime Achievement in Literature in 2008 in his native Guatemala. At present he is working on a three-volume analysis of indigenous literatures in Latin America.

ELIANA ÁVILA is Professor of English-Language Literatures at Federal University of Santa Catarina at Florianopolis, Brazil. Her doctoral research on Elizabeth Bishop's Brazilian writings led her to explore the relations among postcolonial studies, queer temporality, disability studies, and translation studies in the volume she edited for *Ilha do Desterro*

(2005) as well as in her articles and book chapters published in Brazil – such as "Pode o tradutor ouvir?" in *Tradução e Relações de Poder* (2013), partially based on Gayatri Chakravorty Spivak's "Translation as Culture" (2000) which she co-translated (with Liane Schneider) into Brazilian Portuguese. She received a visiting research grant to complete a translation of Gloria Anzaldúa's *Borderlands / La frontera* into Brazilian Portuguese, based on her research on decolonial queer criticism, while affiliated with the Latin American and Latino Studies Department and the Chicano Latino Research Center at the University of California at Santa Cruz.

María del Pilar Blanco is Associate Professor of Spanish American Literature at the University of Oxford and Fellow of Trinity College. Author of *Ghost-Watching American Modernity: Haunting, Landscape, and the Hemispheric Imagination* (2012), she is currently coediting the first volume of *The Oxford Critical and Cultural History of Global Modernist Magazines*, which comprehensively explores the print cultures of South America, Central America, and the Caribbean from the late nineteenth to mid-twentieth centuries. Her second monograph project explores the intersections of science and literature in Spanish American print cultures from 1870 to 1910.

Marta Caminero-Santangelo is the Director of the Center for Latin American and Caribbean Studies and Professor in the English Department at the University of Kansas. Her books include *The Madwoman Can't Speak, or Why Insanity Is Not Subversive* (1998), *On Latinidad: U.S. Latino Literature and the Construction of Ethnicity* (2007), and *Documenting the Undocumented: Latino/a Narrative and Social Justice in the Era of Operation Gatekeeper* (2016).

Norma Elia Cantú currently serves as the Norine R. and T. Frank Murchison Endowed Professor in the Humanities at Trinity University in San Antonio, Texas. The twentieth anniversary expanded edition of her award-winning *Canícula: Snapshots of a Girlhood en la Frontera* (1995) was published in 2015. Her collaborative project *Transcendental Train Yards* presents her poetry and the artwork of Marta Sanchez. Cofounder of CantoMundo, a workshop for Latina/o poetry and poets, she has also edited or coedited important works in Chicana/Latina literature and folklore including the recently published *Entre Guadalupe y Malinche: Tejanas in Literature and Art* and *Barrio Dreams: Selected Plays by Silviana Wood*.

David A. Colón is Associate Professor of English and Director of the Latina/o Studies Program at Texas Christian University. He is the editor of *Between Day and Night: New and Selected Poems, 1946–2010 by Miguel González-Gerth* (2013) and author of numerous essays for publications such as *The Princeton Encyclopedia of Poetry and Poetics, The Routledge Companion to Latina/o Popular Culture, Critical Insights: Contemporary Immigrant Short Fiction, The Journal of Latino/Latin American Studies, Cultural Critique,* and *Jacket2.* He has held fellowships from the Woodrow Wilson National Fellowship Foundation, the Social Science Research Council, the Stanford Humanities Center, and the University of California, Berkeley.

PEDRO GARCÍA-CARO is Associate Professor of Spanish at the University of Oregon, where he is currently directing the Latin American Studies Program. His most recent work concentrates on the cultural history of mining (literature, film, and photography) in the Western hemisphere throughout the nineteenth and twentieth centuries. His published books include *After the Nation: Postnational Satire in the Works of Carlos Fuentes and Thomas Pynchon* (2014), a translation into Spanish of Wallace Shawn's *The Fever* (2012) in collaboration with Rafael Spregelburd, and a critical edition of the first secular play performed in California in the late eighteenth century, *Astucias por heredar un sobrino a un tío* (1789) by Fermín de Reygadas (2017).

JOHN MORÁN GONZÁLEZ is Professor of English and Director of the Center for Mexican American Studies at the University of Texas at Austin. He is author of *Border Renaissance: The Texas Centennial and the Emergence of Mexican American Literature* and *The Troubled Union: Expansionist Imperatives in Post-Reconstruction American Novels*. His articles and reviews have appeared in *American Literature, American Literary History, Aztlán, Nineteenth-Century Contexts, Symbolism, Western Historical Quarterly*, and *Western American Literature*. He edited *The Cambridge Companion to Latina/o American Literature* (2016).

KIRSTEN SILVA GRUESZ is Professor of Literature at the University of California, Santa Cruz, where she directs the Latino Literary Cultures Project. She is the author of *Ambassadors of Culture: The Transamerican Origins of Latino Writing* (2002) and numerous essays on Spanish-language print culture in the United States. Her new book, *Cotton Mather's Spanish Lessons: Language, Race, and American Memory*, is forthcoming from Harvard University Press, and she is also preparing an edition of translated material from nineteenth-century New Orleans, including E.J. Gómez's novel *A Marriage Like Many Others*.

LAURA G. GUTIÉRREZ is Associate Professor in the Department of Mexican American and Latina/o Studies at the University of Texas at Austin, of which she is also Interim Chair. She is a scholar of Latin American and Latina/o performance studies and visual culture and is the author of *Performing Mexicanidad: Vendidas y Cabareteras on the Transnational Stage*, winner of the ninth Modern Languages Association Prize in United States Latina and Latino and Chicana and Chicano Literary and Cultural Studies. Gutiérrez has published essays and book chapters on topics such as Latina/o performance, border art, Mexican video art, and Mexican political cabaret.

JUANITA HEREDIA is Professor of Spanish at Northern Arizona University. Her scholarly interests include U.S. Latina/o and Latin American literary and cultural studies. She is the editor of *Mapping South American Latina/o Literature in the United States* (2018), author of *Transnational Latina Narratives in the Twenty-first Century: The Politics of Gender, Race and Migrations* (2009) and coeditor of *Latina Self-Portraits: Interviews with Contemporary Women Writers* (2000). During her time as a post-doctoral Fellow and Visiting Scholar at the Institute of American Cultures/Chicano Studies Research Center at UCLA, she advanced work on her monograph, *Transnational Latinas/os and the City: Negotiating Urban Experiences in Twenty-first Century Literature and Culture*. She has also published widely on U.S.

Latina/o literature and culture in *Aztlán, Hispania, Journal of American Studies in Turkey*, and *Latino Studies* as well as edited collections.

LUZ ANGÉLICA KIRSCHNER is Assistant Professor in the Department of Modern Languages and Global Studies at South Dakota State University. She is the editor and author of the volume *Expanding Latinidad: An Inter-American Perspective* (2012). Her most recent publication appeared in *The Routledge Companion to Literature and Human Rights* (2015), and she has a forthcoming chapter in the *The Routledge Companion to InterAmerican Studies* (2017). Kirschner is currently completing her single-authored monograph, *The Persistence of Racialization: Literature, Gender, and Ethnicity*.

CRYSTAL M. KURZEN earned her Ph.D. at the University of Texas at Austin in English with a concentration in Mexican American and ethnic American literatures. She is at work on her manuscript, *Literary Nepantla: Genre and Method in Contemporary Chicana/o Life Narratives*. Her project focuses on how contemporary Chicanas/os relate self and community from the alter-Native spaces of *nepantla* through multigeneric storytelling techniques based primarily in strategies of reconceptualizing conventional autobiography. She has published on Pat Mora and Native American women's autobiographies and teaches courses in composition as well as American, Chicana/o, and Latina/o literatures at Columbus State Community College.

CARMEN E. LAMAS is Assistant Professor of English and American Studies at the University of Virginia. Her research examines Latinas/os in the United States during the nineteenth century from a hemispheric perspective. She is a cofounder of the Latina/o Studies Association, an academic organization that brings together scholars, students, and activists in the study of Latina/o concerns. Her work has appeared in *Revista Hispánica Moderna, Latin American Research Review*, and *Latino Studies*, and she has articles in the edited collections *The Latino Nineteenth Century* and *OUP Bibliographies*. Her book project is titled *The Latina/o Continuum: Rethinking American and Latin American Studies*.

RODRIGO LAZO is Associate Professor of English and an affiliate in the Chicano/Latino Studies Department at the University of California, Irvine. He is the coeditor of *The Latino Nineteenth Century* and has published numerous articles on the relationship between archive theory and the historical recovery of Latino literature. He is completing a book-length study on Philadelphia and the hemispheric movement of Latino writers in the early nineteenth century.

LAURA LOMAS (Ph.D., Columbia University, 2001) is Associate Professor of English and American Studies at Rutgers University-Newark. Her first book, *Translating Empire: José Martí, Migrant Latino Subjects and American Modernities* (2008), received the Modern Languages Association Prize for Latina and Latino and Chicana and Chicano Literature and an honorable mention from the Latin American Studies Association Latina/o Studies section. Lomas has published essays most recently in *Cuban Studies, Small Axe, Review: Literature and Arts in the Americas, Translation Review, Journal of American Studies*,

Comparative American Studies and *American Literature*. She is co-editing *Against Dichotomies: The Collected Writings of Lourdes Casal*, and completing a book on Casal and bilingual, feminist, interdisciplinary forms of knowledge that arose in the borderlands of New York and the Caribbean in the twentieth century.

Antonio López is Associate Professor of English at George Washington University and author of *Unbecoming Blackness: The Diaspora Cultures of Afro-Cuban America* (2012).

Milagros López-Peláez Casellas is Associate Professor and Designated Researcher at Coventry University. Her research interests include border studies, Chicana/o, Latina/o, and multiethnic American literatures and cultural studies. She has previously worked at the University of Leeds and at Arizona State University, where she also obtained her M.A. and Ph.D. She has a single-authored monograph, *What about the Girls?: estrategias narrativas de resistencia en la primera literatura chicana* (2011), and has published articles and book chapters on Chicana/o and Hispanic literature, film, and cultural studies in national and international peer-reviewed journals.

William Luis is the Gertrude Conaway Vanderbilt Professor of Spanish at Vanderbilt University. He has authored, edited, and coedited fourteen books, including *Literary Bondage: Slavery in Cuban Narrative* (1991), *Dance Between Two Cultures* (1997), *Looking Out, Looking In: Anthology of Latino Poetry* (2013), and *The AmeRícan Poet: Essays on the Works of Tato Laviera* (2014). Luis was the recipient of a Guggenheim Fellowship for 2012. He is the Director of Latino and Latina Studies at Vanderbilt University and editor of the *Afro-Hispanic Review*. Born and raised in New York City, Luis is widely regarded as a leading authority on Latin American, Caribbean, Afro-Hispanic, and Latino literatures.

Sophie Maríñez is Associate Professor of French and Spanish at Borough of Manhattan Community College, City University of New York, and a 2016-2017 Faculty Fellow at the Center for Place, Culture, and Politics, Graduate Center (CUNY). She is the author of the NEH-funded monograph *Mademoiselle de Montpensier: Writings, Châteaux, and Female Self-Construction in Early Modern France* (Brill/Rodopi, 2017), and the co-editor of *J'essaie de vous parler de ma patrie* (Mémoire d'encrier, 2018), a translation into French of Jacques Viau Renaud's poetry. She has published numerous essays on Haitian and Dominican relations and is currently working on a book-length monograph on the French Caribbean and the dynamics between Haiti and the Dominican Republic.

Yolanda Martínez-San Miguel teaches Latino and Caribbean Studies and Comparative Literature at Rutgers University-New Brunswick. During 2017-2018, she is the Martha S. Weeks Chair in Latin American Studies at the University of Miami and visiting professor in the Department of Modern Languages and Literatures. Her M.A. (1991) and Ph.D. (1996) are from the University of California, Berkeley. She is the author of *Saberes americanos: subalternidad y epistemología en los escritos de Sor Juana* (1999), *Caribe Two Ways: cultura de la migración en el Caribe insular hispánico* (2003); *From Lack to Excess: 'Minor' Readings of Colonial Latin American Literature* (2008); and *Coloniality of Diasporas: Rethinking*

Intra-Colonial Migrations in a Pan-Caribbean Context (Palgrave, 2014). She recently finished a co-edited anthology titled *Critical Terms in Caribbean and Latin American Thought* (2016).

José Antonio Mazzotti is King Felipe VI of Spain Professor of Spanish Culture and Civilization and Professor of Latin American Literature in the Department of Romance Studies at Tufts University. He is also Director and chief editor of the *Revista de Crítica Literaria Latinoamericana* since 2010. He has published *Coros mestizos del Inca Garcilaso: resonancias andinas* (1996), *Poéticas del flujo: migración y violencia verbales en el Perú de los 80* (2002), *Incan Insights: El Inca Garcilaso's Hints to Andean Readers* (2008), *Encontrando un inca: ensayos escogidos sobre el Inca Garcilaso de la Vega* (2016), *Lima fundida: épica y nación criolla en el Perú* (2016), eleven volumes of poetry, and more than eighty articles on Latin American colonial literature and contemporary poetry. He has also edited several collective volumes on colonial and contemporary Latin American and Latino studies.

Claudia Milian is Associate Professor in the Department of Romance Studies and Director of the Program in Latino/a Studies in the Global South at Duke University, where she works between and among the intellectual traditions of Latina/o studies, African American studies, southern studies, and hemispheric American studies. She is the author of *Latining America: Black-Brown Passages and the Coloring of Latino/a Studies* (2013).

Urayoán Noel is Associate Professor of English and Spanish at New York University and the author of *In Visible Movement: Nuyorican Poetry from the Sixties to Slam* (2014), winner of the Latin American Studies Association Latina/o Studies Section Book Award, and recipient of an honorable mention in the Modern Language Association Prize in Latina and Latino and Chicana and Chicano Literary and Cultural Studies. A contributing editor of *NACLA Report on the Americas* and *Obsidian: Literature & Arts in the African Diaspora*, Noel has been a fellow of the Ford Foundation and CantoMundo and is also the author of several books of poetry, including *Buzzing Hemisphere/Rumor Hemisférico* (2015).

William Orchard is Assistant Professor of English at Queens College, the City University of New York. He is the coeditor of two volumes: *The Plays of Josephina Niggli* (2007) and *Bridges, Borders, and Breaks: History, Narrative, and Nation in Twenty-First Century Chicana/o Literary Criticism* (2016). He is currently completing a book entitled *Drawn Together: Politics, Pedagogy, and the Latina/o Graphic Novel*.

Ricardo L. Ortíz is Chair and Associate Professor of Literary and Cultural U.S. Latinidades in the Department of English at Georgetown University. His first book, *Cultural Erotics in Cuban America*, was published in 2007 by the University of Minnesota Press; his second book, *Testimonial Fictions: Cold War Geopolitics and the U.S. Latin-x Literary Imagination*, is nearing completion. Professor Ortiz has also published scholarly work in numerous journals, including *Social Text, Modern Drama, Contemporary Literature*, and *GLQ*.

YOLANDA PADILLA is on the faculty of the School of Interdisciplinary Arts and Sciences at the University of Washington, Bothell. She is currently completing a book entitled *Revolutionary Subjects: The Mexican Revolution and the Transnational Emergence of Mexican American Literature and Culture, 1910–1959*. She has published essays related to this project in *CR: New Centennial Review* and in the volume *Open Borders to a Revolution*. She is the coeditor of two volumes: *Bridges, Borders and Breaks: History, Narrative, and Nation in Twenty-First-Century Chicana/o Literary Criticism* (2016) and *The Plays of Josefina Niggli: Recovered Landmarks of Latina Literature* (2007).

RICHARD PEREZ is Associate Professor of English at John Jay College, City University of New York. He is currently concluding a book project entitled *Towards a Negative Aesthetics: U.S. Latino/a Fiction and the Remaking of American Literature* and is the coeditor of two critical anthologies: *Contemporary U.S. Latino/a Criticism* (2007) and *Moments of Magical Realism in U.S. Ethnic Literatures* (2012), both published by Palgrave Macmillan. Dr. Perez cofounded the Biennial U.S. Latina/o Literary Theory and Criticism Conference. His work has also appeared in the *Centro Journal for Puerto Rican Studies*, *Women Studies Quarterly*, *Latino Studies Journal*, and *MELUS Journal*.

VANESSA PÉREZ-ROSARIO is Associate Professor of Latino Studies at Brooklyn College, City University of New York. She is author of *Becoming Julia de Burgos: The Making of a Puerto Rican Icon* (2014) and editor of *Hispanic Caribbean Literature of Migration: Narratives of Displacement* (2010). Vanessa recently completed a translation of Mayra Santos-Febres's collection of poetry *Boat People* and has edited and translated a manuscript titled *I am My Own Path: A Bilingual Anthology of the Collected Writings of Julia de Burgos*. She is managing editor of *Small Axe: A Caribbean Journal of Criticism*.

RAFAEL PÉREZ-TORRES has authored three books: *Movements in Chicano Poetry: Against Myths, Against Margins* (1995), *Mestizaje: Critical Uses of Race in Chicano Culture* (2006), and *To Alcatraz, Death Row, and Back: Memories of an East L.A. Outlaw*, written with Ernest López (2005). With Chon Noriega, Eric Avila, Mary Karen Davilos, and Chela Sandoval, he coedited *The Chicano Studies Reader: An Anthology of Aztlán 1970–2000*, now entering its third edition. His recent research examines the formation of historical memory and futurity in Chicana/o culture.

ANA PATRICIA RODRÍGUEZ is Associate Professor in the Department of Spanish and Portuguese and U.S. Latina/o Studies at the University of Maryland, College Park, where she teaches classes on Latin American, Central American, and U.S. Latina/o literatures and cultures. She is the author of *Dividing the Isthmus: Central American Transnational Histories, Literatures, and Cultures* (2009) and coeditor of *De la hamaca al trono y al más allá: Lecturas críticas de la obra de Manlio Argueta* (2013). Rodríguez was elected president of the Latina/o Studies Association (LSA) (2017–2019) and serves on the advisory boards of the Smithsonian Latino Gallery, Washington History, Central American Resource Center (CARECEN), and Casa de Cultura de El Salvador (Washington, DC).

Contributors

CÉSAR A. SALGADO is Associate Professor of Spanish and Portuguese and Comparative Literature at the University of Texas at Austin. He is the author of *From Modernism to Neobaroque: Joyce and Lezama Lima* (2001) and articles in *Revista Iberoamericana, Centro, The New Centennial Review, Casa de las Américas*, and other journals. He is the coeditor of *Latina and Latino Writers* (2004), *Cuba* (2011), and *TransLatin Joyce: Global Transmissions in Ibero-American Literature* (2014). He teaches seminars on New World Baroque genealogies; archival fashioning, visual culture, and journal history in the Caribbean; Joyce and the Global South; and critical theory. *Unsovereign Custodies: Archival Fashioning in Colonial Puerto Rico (1852–1952)* is his next book.

MARÍA JOSEFINA SALDAÑA-PORTILLO is Professor in the Department of Social and Cultural Analysis and the Center for Latin American and Caribbean Studies at New York University. She is the author of two monographs: *Indian Given: Racial Geographies across Mexico and the United States* (2016) and *The Revolutionary Imagination in the Americas and the Age of Development* (2003). Saldaña-Portillo coedited *Des/posesión: Género, territorio, y luchas por la autodeterminación* with Marisa Belausteguigoitia Rius on indigenous women's leadership roles in the global struggle to defend their territories (2015). She has published more than twenty-five articles in the United States and Latin America on revolutionary subjectivity, subaltern politics, indigenous peoples, racial formation, and Latin American and Latino cultural studies.

SILVIO TORRES-SAILLANT is Professor of English and Dean's Professor of the Humanities at Syracuse University. A former director of the Latino-Latin American Studies Program, he has served as the William P. Tolley Distinguished Teaching Professor in the Humanities and was the 2015 recipient of the Frank Bonilla Public Intellectual Award from the Latin American Studies Association (LASA). In addition to collaborative works, his publications include *Caribbean Poetics* (1997; 2013), *El tigueraje intelectual* (2002; 2011), *Introduction to Dominican Blackness* (1999; 2010), *An Intellectual History of the Caribbean* (2006), *Diasporic Disquisitions: Dominicanists, Transnationalism, and the Community* (2000), and *El retorno de las yolas: Ensayos sobre diaspora, democracia y dominicanidad* (1999).

ELISA SAMPSON VERA TUDELA is Associate Professor in the Department of Spanish, Portuguese and Latin American Studies, King's College London. Her publications include *Colonial Angels* (2000) and *Ricardo Palma's Tradiciones: Illuminating Gender and Nation* (2012). She teaches colonial and post-colonial Latin American literature and cultural and gender studies and her research, which has the interrogation of historiography and the historical imagination at its center, has ranged from seventeenth-century women's writing through the nineteenth century and on to contemporary Peruvian literature.

Acknowledgements

We would like to thank Ray Ryan, our editor at Cambridge University Press, for encouraging this volume along to fruition. Thanks also to the editorial and production staff of Cambridge University Press for their efforts in making this volume a reality; in particular, Emma Collison, Divya Mathesh, and Jane Voodikon lent their expertise. We also extend our appreciation to Sandra Spicher for compiling the index.

As this critical anthology would be nothing without the essays, we would like to thank all the contributors for their wonderful efforts in creating this collaborative critical overview of Latina/o literary studies.

Finally, we would like to acknowledge Juan Flores and José Esteban Muñoz, two inspiring and engaged scholars who helped make the field what it is today. They had each agreed to contribute an essay but passed away during the volume's elaboration. For us, they will always be ¡Presente!

Chronology

This chronology sets out dates and events that have informed Latina/o American literary history. While not comprehensive, it is intended to illustrate connections among and across the disparate, heterogeneous histories discussed herein. The geographical scope is transnational and includes salient points of contact between Latin America, the Caribbean, and the United States as these interactions shaped the trans-American and Latina/o literary imagination. Insofar as the latinidades of the Americas have been formed through the dynamics of European colonization, African slavery and emancipation, and indigenous resistance and survival, this chronology highlights these processes as they have found expression in the cultural practices and productions across the Americas. The goal is to offer a sense of a present defined by migration and empire; to provide reference points for entangled routes; to map transculturation rather than national assimilation; to explain the impossibility of return to a single point of departure. The event of textual publication offers but one index of historicity, often belated, so this chronology also references processes, performance, movements, and cultural work peculiar to Latina/o literature, both emergent and recovered.

1492	Columbus's small fleet accidentally runs across inhabited Caribbean islands; Columbian Viceroyalty of the Indies lasts until 1526. Reconquista of Iberian Peninsula terminates with the fall of the Emirate of Granada; the expulsion of Jews from all Spanish territories generates numerous *nuevos cristianos*.
1494	The Kingdoms of Portugal and Spain divide the Americas between themselves in the Treaty of Tordesillas.
1500	The Kingdom of Portugal claims the area of what is now Brazil.
1510	King Ferdinand of Spain authorizes the beginning of systematic transport of Africans to the new world, beginning with fifty taken to Santo Domingo.

1519	Spanish conquest of Mexica Empire aided by indigenous allies. Malinali, Doña Marina, or la Malinche was given as spoils of war to the Spanish, and she gave birth to her son Martín by conquistador Hernán Cortés, after the fall of Tenochtitlán in 1522.
1524	*Popul Wuj* transcribed into Spanish.
1528–1536	Black navigator Esteban joins Pánfilo de Narvaez's expedition to explore Florida, Georgia, Alabama, Louisiana, Mississippi, New Mexico, Arizona, and Texas; Núñez Cabeza de Vaca publishes narrative of said disastrous expedition entitled *Naufragios* in 1542.
1532	Francisco Pizarro massacres Incas in Caxamarca and captures the Inca, Atahualpa.
1535	Viceroyalty of New Spain, established in what would become Mexico, lasts until 1821.
1542	Viceroyalty of New Castilla, set down in what would be Peru, Ecuador, Bolivia, and Chile, lasts until 1824.
1565	Pedro Menéndez de Avilés claims San Augustine, Florida, in the land of the Seminole.
1591	Juan de Cárdenas describes the Mexican Spanish *criollos* in *Problemas y maravillos secretos de los Indios*.
1609	Expulsion of Muslims from Spain. Mestizo writer Inca Garcilaso de la Vega publishes the *Comentarios reales de los Incas*.
1610	Gaspar Pérez de Villagrá writes *Historia de la Nueva México*, with a first-hand account of the massacre of 800 Acoma by Spanish troops under Juan de Oñate, who imprisoned hundreds in addition to ordering the amputation of the right foot of male survivors and enslavement of the rest of the Acoma Pueblo in the oldest continuously inhabited city in what is now the United States.
1615	Felipe Guaman Poma de Ayala sends to King Phillip III of Spain his handwritten manuscript, *El primer nueva crónica y buen gobierno*, which documents Andean civilization and the effects of the Spanish conquest. The manuscript resurfaced in 1908 and published in 1936.
1680	Pueblo Revolt unites indigenous groups throughout the Upper Rio Grande basin and ends Spanish rule in New Mexico for twelve years.
1680–1688	Sor Juana Inés de la Cruz, or Juana Ramírez de Asbaje, becomes the most prominent unofficial poet of the court of Mexico City, having published in Spain her poems, theater, and other writings while living cloistered in the convent of San Francisco de Paula.

1717	Viceroyalty of New Granada in what would become Panama, Colombia, and Venezuela established, lasts until 1819.
1769	City of New Orleans under Spanish rule until 1802.
1776	Viceroyalty of Rio de la Plata established, lasts until 1814.
1776–1783	U.S. Revolution: thirteen British North American colonies successfully revolt to establish the United States. Haitian, Dominican, and Havana's Batallónes de Pardos y Morenos fight in decisive battles against the British forces.
1780–1781	Túpac Amaru II and Micaela Bastidas lead an indigenous and black revolt against Spanish colonial rule in Peru.
1790	Fermín de Reygadas submits *Astucias por heredar un sobrino a un tío* to be considered for the stage at the Mexican Coliseum. But the play is banned by the censor, and not performed until 1796 in the secular settlement Villa de Branciforte, next to the Mission Santa Cruz in California.
1791–1804	Slave revolts, beginning in Bois Caiman and led by Jamaican Dutty Boukman and Cécile Fatiman, spark revolution against Napoleon led by Toussaint L'Ouverture. Founding of the Republic of Haiti.
1799	Juan Pablo Vizcardo y Guzmán, "Carta a los Hispanos Americanos" proposes criollo rights to territories of the Americas dominated by the Spanish.
1803	United States acquires Louisiana.
1808	Under Napoleon, France invades Spain. In what would become Texas and other parts of the Spanish empire in the Americas, this attack on the Spanish monarchy makes it possible to redefine sovereignty locally. *El Misisípi*, the first Spanish-language newspaper in the United States, is published through 1810.
1810–1829	Wars of Independence across Latin America.
1812	José Antonio Aponte, free black artisan and leader of a black military battalion, uses an infamous book of paintings to plot a black-led revolt in Havana. Aponte and other leaders are detained, and he is decapitated.
1816	Manuel Torres publishes *An Exposition of the Commerce of Spanish America; With Some Observations Upon Its Importance to the United States.*
1819	United States acquires Florida from Spain in the Adams-Onís Treaty.
1823	Proclamation of the Monroe Doctrine by the United States.
1824–1826	Father Félix Varela edits *El Habanero* in Philadelphia.

1826	The anonymously authored Spanish-language historical novel *Jicoténcal* is published in Philadelphia. Simón Bolivar hosts the Congreso Anfictiónico de Panamá.
1836	Texas revolt and the formation of the Republic of Texas.
1845	United States annexes the Republic of Texas as a state; Eusebio José Gómez publishes a Spanish-language paper, *El Hablador/La Patria/La Unión* in New Orleans, through 1851, in which is serialized what may be the first Latino novel, *Un matrimonio como hay muchos* (1848–1849).
1846	U.S.-Mexican War begins as border dispute.
1848	Treaty of Guadalupe Hidalgo ends U.S.-Mexican War, transferring Mexico's northern provinces to the United States.
1848–1860s	*La Verdad* and *La Crónica* are published in New York City.
1851	Guatemalan-born Antonio José de Irisarri's *El cristiano errante* is serialized in *La Patria* of New Orleans.
1854	Periodical *El Mulatto* is published in New York City.
1855	Many Spanish-language journalists of the annexed portion of Mexico denounce the 1851 Land Act and Manifest Destiny. Francisco P. Ramirez defends "la raza latina" in *El Clamor Público*, a Los Angeles newspaper that is published until 1859.
1855–1857	Filibuster by William Walker in Nicaragua.
1858	Exiled Cuban poets publish *El laúd del desterrado* in New York. Juan Nepomuceno Seguin, a native of San Antonio de Bexar, describes himself "a foreigner in my native land" in *Personal Memoirs of John N. Seguin*, published in San Antonio, Texas.
1861–1864	U.S. Civil War.
1861–1867	French military occupies Mexico until driven out by Republican forces under Benito Juárez.
1868–1878	Ten Years War in Cuba and a strike for independence in Puerto Rico leads to the migration of thousands of Cubans and Puerto Ricans to the United States, many of whom are tobacco workers who contribute significantly to the creation of the cities of Key West, Tampa, and migrant communities in New York.
1872	María Amparo Ruiz de Burton publishes *Who Would Have Thought It?*
1873	U.S. ship *Virginius* is captured and filibuster Narciso López is put to death.

1875	Mariano Guadalupe Vallejo completes an unpublished manuscript, *Recuerdos históricos y personales, tocantes a la alta California*, in five volumes; excerpts published in 1994, 1997, and 2001.
1876	Loreta Janeta Velazquez publishes *The Woman in Battle: The Civil War Narrative of Loreta Janeta Velazquez, Cuban Woman and Confederate Soldier*.
1881	José Martí publishes "Coney Island" in Bogotá, Colombia.
1885	María Amparo Ruiz de Burton publishes *The Squatter and the Don*.
1887	Spanish General Romualdo Palacios represses advocates of social equality in the Autonomist Party during the "compontes," which disproportionately affects Afro-Puertorriqueños; Lucy Gonzalez Parsons helps lead hundreds of thousands in demanding the eight-hour workday.
1888–1889	José Antonia Fernández de Trava edits the newspaper *El Moro de Paz* and later becomes the first professor of Spanish at Tulane.
1889–1891	International American Conference in Washington, D.C. convenes leaders of Latin American and Caribbean nations to lower tariffs, obtain concessions for industry, and establish a single hemispheric currency; Latin American leaders travel to various U.S. cities and attend meetings and ultimately refuse the proposal.
1891	José Martí's "Nuestra América" published in Mexico City and New York.
1892	Arturo Schomburg participates in founding with José Martí of Partido Revolucionario Cubano in New York. Francisco Gonzálo Marín publishes "Nueva York desde adentro" in New York's *La Gaceta del Pueblo*, and his book of poetry, *Romances*. Eusebio Chacón publishes *El hijo de la tempestad* and *Tras la tormenta*.
1893	Lola Rodríguez de Tío publishes *Mi Libro de Cuba;* Aurelia Castillo de González attends and writes about the World's Columbian Exhibition in Chicago.
1894	Manuel Zeno Gandía publishes *La charca*.
1895–1898	Cubans and Puerto Ricans fight in the Cuban War of Independence, led by Dominican Máximo Gómez, Antonio Maceo, and José Martí.

1898–1901 U.S.-Cuban-Spanish War results in the transfer of Cuba, Puerto Rico, Guam, and the Philippines to U.S. control. Justo Sierra publishes *En tierra yankee (notas a todo vapor)* in Mexico City.

1899 Incorporation of United Fruit Company; Máximo Soto Hall publishes *El Problema*.

1900–1938 Flores Magón brothers, anarchist opponents of Porfirio Díaz regime, moved publication of their major newspaper from Mexico, upon the editors' imprisonment and exile, to Texas, Missouri and California. The paper continues to circulate in the United States, with interruptions, to 30,000 readers.

1901 In *Downes vs. Bidwell*, Supreme Court justice Edward E. White declares Puerto Rico and other annexed territories "foreign in a domestic sense." The Platt Amendment reserves the right of the United States to intervene in the affairs of a nominally independent Cuba, beginning in 1902.

1904–1910 Sara Estela Ramírez, revolutionary Mexicana in exile, contributes to *La Crónica* and *El Demócrata fronterizo*, in addition to founding and directing two literary magazines, *La Corregidora* and *Aurora*.

1906–1909 U.S. military occupies Cuba for a second time.

1908 New Mexican ex-confederate James Santiago Tafolla writes his memoir in Spanish, which will not be published until 2009, after being translated and edited by his great-granddaughters Carmen and Laura Tafolla, as *A Life Crossing Borders*.

1910s María Cristina Mena's short stories are published in U.S. magazines. Aurora Lucero White Lea's "Plea for the Spanish Language," published in New Mexican press.

1910–1920 The Mexican Revolution forces up to a million Mexicans to migrate to the United States as war refugees.

1911–1927 *El Mercurio* (New Orleans) includes prose by Salvadoran born Máximo Soto Hall and poetry by Peruvian José Santos Chocano. Luisa Capetillo publishes *Mi Opinión Sobre las Libertades, Derechos y Deberes de la Mujer* (1911).

1912 New Mexico Territory admitted to the Union as a state; Several thousand members of the Partido Independient de Color, are massacred by the Cuban military under President José Miguel Gómez, whose government had declared any political parties organized by racial groups to be illegal and "racist"; Arturo Schomburg publishes "Gen. Evaristo Estenoz," in *The Crisis*.

1912–1933   U.S. military occupies Nicaragua.

1914   Alirio Díaz Guerra publishes *Lucas Guevara*.

1914–1918   First World War.

1915   Armed uprising of *los sediciosos* in South Texas; Mariano Azuela publishes *Los de abajo*.

1915–1934   U.S. military occupies Haiti.

1916–1924   U.S. military occupies the Dominican Republic.

1917   United States imposes citizenship upon Puerto Ricans through the Jones-Shafroth Act. Puerto Ricans drafted for military service.

1918   Salomón de la Selva publishes *Tropical Town and Other Poems*.

1920   Merchant Marine Act forces Puerto Rico to become dependent on shipping from U.S. ports.

1925   William Carlos Williams publishes *In the American Grain*.
             Arturo Schomburg publishes "The Negro Digs up His Past," in Alaine Locke's anthology of the Harlem Renaissance, *The New Negro*.

1926   The Schomburg Collection of Negro Literature and Art is established in Harlem.

1926–1929   The Cristero Rebellion in Mexico sends a new wave of migrants to the United States.

1927–1933   Augusto César Sandino leads guerilla war against the U.S. military in Nicaragua.

1928   Daniel Venegas publishes *Las adventuras de Don Chipote*.

1929–1939   Worldwide Great Depression; tens of thousands of Mexican nationals and Mexican American citizens alike are deported to Mexico by the U.S. government.

1932   Agustín Farabundo Martí organizes peasants to challenge exploitative conditions in El Salvador, to which the military government of Maximiliano Hernández Martínez responds with *La Matanza*, a massacre of between 10,000 and 30,000, nearly eradicating the Pipil culture.

1932–1939   Mexican-American labor leader Emma Tenayuca inspires thousands at Finck Cigar Company, garment workers, and 1938 Pecan Shellers strike, and helps write *The Mexican Question* with Homer Brooks in 1939.

1933   U.S. president Franklin Roosevelt announces the "Good Neighbor Policy."

1935	María Elena Zamora O'Shea publishes *El Mesquite*.
1936	Texas centennial of independence from Mexico; Miguel Antonio Otero publishes *The Real Billy the Kid; With New Light on the Lincoln County War*.
1936–1940	Américo Paredes drafts *George Washington Gómez*, although it is not published until 1990.
1937	Massacre of nationalists by state authorities in Ponce, Puerto Rico; dictator Rafael Leonides Trujillo orders the massacre of 10,000 Haitians in the Dominican Republic.
1938	Julia de Burgos publishes *Poema en veinte surcos*, to be followed by *Canción de la verdad sencilla* in 1939; Eusebia Cosme performs *poesía negra* in U.S. cities.
1937–1941	Jovita González and Margaret Eimer collaborate to write *Caballero*.
1938–1945	Second World War; up to 500,000 "Hispanics" serve in the U.S. military.
1943	Zoot Suit Riots in Los Angeles.
1942–1964	In response to wartime labor shortages in U.S. agriculture, the bracero program admits hundreds of thousands of Mexican agricultural workers into the United States.
1945	Josefina Niggli publishes *Mexican Folk Plays*.
1948	Operation Bootstrap initiated in Puerto Rico and consequent industrialization leads tens of thousands to migrate to New York City.
1950	National Party president Pedro Albizu Campos calls for coordinated militant attacks for independence in eight Puerto Rican cities and an attempted attack on President Harry Truman in Washington, D.C. Albizu Campos is held political prisoner of the United States from 1936 to 1947 and again from 1950 to 1965.
1951	Guillermo Cotto-Thorner publishes *Trópico en Manhattan*.
1952	Puerto Rico becomes a U.S. Commonwealth, or Estado Libre Asociado.
1954	Puerto Rican nationalists led by Lolita Lébron open fire in the U.S. House of Representatives; Operation Wetback implemented to deport undocumented Mexican migrants in the United States; René Marqués publishes *La carreta*.
1954	The CIA topples democratically elected government of Guatemala's president Jacobo Arbenz, who had implemented

Decree 900, an ambitious land-reform program that benefited 500,000 poverty-stricken Guatemalans.

1955–1975   U.S.-Vietnam War; 170,000 "Hispanics" serve in the U.S. military.

1956   Pedro Juan Soto publishes *Spiks*.

1958   Américo Paredes publishes doctoral dissertation at University of Texas at Austin, about *El corrido de Gregorio Cortez*, as *With a Pistol in his Hand*.

1959   The Cuban Revolution overthrows U.S.-backed dictator Fulgencio Batista, initiating the first wave of the Cuban diaspora to the United States. José Antonio Villareal publishes *Pocho*; William Carlos Williams publishes *Yes, Mrs. Williams: A Personal Record of My Mother*.

1960   The United States imposes trade and travel embargos on Cuba in the wake of nationalization of industries; through Operation Pedro Pan, Catholics cooperate with U.S. government to airlift 14,000 unaccompanied minors from Cuba to the United States.

1961   Failed military invasion by CIA-sponsored paramilitary group of Cuban exiles at Playa Girón, or Bay of Pigs Invasion. Jesús Colón publishes *A Puerto Rican in New York, and other sketches*.

1962   Cuban Missile Crisis; César Chavez and Dolores Huerta organize the United Farm Workers Association.

1963   John Rechy publishes *City of Night*.

1964–1985   Brazil under military dictatorship.

1965   U.S. military occupies the Dominican Republic after period of civil unrest following Trujillo's assassination in 1961; Immigration and Nationality Reform Act shifts future immigration to the United States away from Europe and to Asia; Hart-Cellar Act imposes quota restriction upon Latin American and Caribbean migration for the first time and thus generates the category of the "deportable" or "illegal" alien. Luis Valdez founds Teatro Campesino as the cultural arm of the United Farm Workers Association in conjunction with the grape strike (1965–1970), with support of César Chávez.

1966–1978   Severe repression during Joaquin Balaguer's "Twelve Years" initiates mass migration from the Dominican Republic to the

United States. Max Ferrá founds INTAR Theater as part of the Hispanic American Arts Center.

1967   Rodolfo "Corky" Gonzales publishes *I am Joaquin*; Piri Thomas publishes *Down These Mean Streets*; Luis Valdez publishes *Los Vendidos*. Miriam Colón and Roberto Rodríguez found Puerto Rican Travelling Theater in New York City.

1968   In tandem with strikes across the globe, the Third World Liberation Front student strike leads to the establishment of the Department of Ethnic Studies at San Francisco State University. Pedro Pietri publishes "Puerto Rican Obituary"; Victor Hernández Cruz publishes *Snaps*; George Romero releases film *Night of the Living Dead*.

1969–1970   Young Lords active in Spanish Harlem.

1970   José Montoya publishes *El Louie*; Luis Valdez publishes "Notes on Chicano Theatre." U.S .Census begins to count "Hispanics"; Chicano Studies Research Center at UCLA founds *Aztlán: A Journal of Chicana/o Studies*.

1971   Tomás Rivera publishes . . .*y no se lo tragó la tierra*; Alurista publishes *Floricanto en Aztlán*; Pedro Pietri records live album, *Aquí Se Habla Español*.

1972   Oscar Zeta Acosta publishes *Autobiography of a Brown Buffalo*; Rodolfo Anaya publishes *Bless Me, Ultima*; Ernesto Galarza publishes *Barrio Boy*; Eddie Palmieri features Felipe Luciano on *Live at Sing Sing* album; Jesus Papoleto Meléndez publishes *Street Poetry and Other Poems*.

1972–1987   Asco art performance collective is active.

1973   With CIA backing, General Augusto Pinochet overthrows the democratically elected president Salvador Allende, installing a dictatorship in Chile that lasts until 1990 and prompting Chilean exile. Oscar Zeta Acosta publishes *Revolt of the Cockroach People*; Rolando Hinojosa publishes *Estampas del Valle y otras obras*; Nicholasa Mohr publishes *Nilda*; Lourdes Casal publishes *Los Fundadores: Alfonso y otros cuentos*; Miguel Algarín and others found the first Nuyorican Poet's Café; Nicolás Kanellos and Luis Dávila found *La Revista Chicano-Riqueña*, which becomes *Americas Review*.

1974   Miguel Piñero publishes *Short Eyes*; Puerto Rican Riots break out throughout New Jersey; Isabelo Zenón Cruz publishes *Narciso descubre su trasero: El negro en la cultura puertorriqueña*;

Lourdes Casal et al. edit *Areíto*, a Cuban diaspora quarterly that lasts for a decade.

1975 Miguel Algarín and Miguel Piñero edit *Nuyorican Poetry: An Anthology of Puerto Rican Words and Feelings;* Lorraine Sutton publishes *SAYcred LAYdy.*

1976 Victor Hernández Cruz publishes *Tropicalizations;* Rosario Ferré publishes *Papeles de Pandora.*

1977 César Andreu Iglesias's edition and transformation of Bernardo Vega's 800-page, five-volume manuscript into a first-person *memoria* is published twelve years after Vega's death; Juan Flores's translation into English appears seven years later. María Irene Fornés publishes *Fefu and Her Friends;* Gary Soto publishes *The Elements of San Joaquin.*

1978 Luis Valdez publishes *Zoot Suit.*

1979 Tato Laviera publishes *La Carreta Made a U-Turn;* Anani Dzidzienyo and Lourdes Casal publish *The Position of Blacks in Brazil and Cuba;* Norma Alarcón founds Third Woman Press and the Latina feminist journal *Third Woman.* Jimmy Santiago Baca publishes *Immigrants in Our Own Land.*

1980s Responding to endemic poverty, a socialist revolution in Nicaragua and the U.S.-sponsored counterrevolutionary intervention across the region, civil wars in Guatemala (dating to 1944) and El Salvador (beginning in 1979), initiate the great Central American diasporas to the United States. Sandra María Esteves publishes *Yerba Buena* (1980).

1980 Mariel boatlift brings 125,000 Cubans to U.S. soil; Raúlrsalinas publishes *Un trip through the mind jail;* Miguel Piñero publishes *La Bodega Sold Dreams.*

1981 Gloria Anzaldúa and Cherríe Moraga edit *This Bridge Called My Back*; Alurista publishes *Spik in Glyph;* Lorna Dee Cervantes publishes *Emplumada;* Richard Rodriguez publishes *Hunger of Memory;* Rodolfo Acuña publishes *Occupied America: A History of Chicanos;* Lourdes Casal publishes *Palabras juntan revolución.*

1982 Edward Rivera publishes *Family Installments;* Gilbert and Jaime Hernández commence publication of comic book series *Love and Rockets.*

1983 Cherríe Moraga publishes *Loving in the War Years/ lo que nunca pasó por sus labios.*

1984   Sandra Cisneros publishes *The House on Mango Street*; Arturo Islas publishes *The Rain God*; Tato Laviera publishes *La Carreta Made a U-Turn*.

1985   Miguel Algarín publishes *Time's Now*; Helena María Viramontes publishes *The Moths and Other Stories*.

1986   Immigration and Control Reform Act provides path to citizenship for 2.7 million undocumented workers in the United States while enacting more stringent border controls. Ana Castillo publishes *The Mixquiahuala Letters*; Cherríe Moraga publishes *Giving Up the Ghost*.

1987   Gloria Anzaldúa publishes *Borderlands/ La Frontera*; Sandra Cisneros publishes *My Wicked, Wicked Ways*; Martín Espada publishes *Trumpets from the Islands of Their Eviction*; Luz Maria Umpierre publishes *The Margarita Poems*.

1988   Ana Castillo publishes *My Father Was a Toltec*; Roberto Fernández publishes *Raining Backwards*.

1989   U.S. military invades Panama; Lucha Corpi publishes *Delia's Song*; Virgil Suárez publishes *Latin Jazz*; Julio Ramos publishes *Desencuentros de la modernidad en América Latina*.

1990   Oscar Hijuelos's *The Mambo Kings Play Songs of Love* awarded the Pulitzer Prize for fiction; Judith Ortiz Cofer publishes *Silent Dancing*.

1990–1991   First U.S.–Iraq War.

1991   Julia Alvarez publishes *How the García Girls Lost Their Accents*; Sandra Cisneros publishes *Woman Hollering Creek and Other Stories*.

1992   Columbian Quincentenary; Los Angeles riots; Recovering the U.S. Hispanic Literary Heritage Project is founded. Reinaldo Arenas publishes *Antes que anochezca*; Cristina García publishes *Dreaming in Cuban*; Alejandro Morales publishes *The Rag Doll Plagues*; Luisa Valenzuela publishes *Black Novel with Argentines*; launch of InSite, a network of contemporary art programs and commissioned projects that maps the dynamics of permeability and blockage that characterize the liminal border zone of San Diego-Tijuana.

1992–1994   Coco Fusco and Guillermo Gómez-Peña perform *The Year of the White Bear and Two Undiscovered Amerindians Visit the West*;

Abraham Rodriguez, Jr. publishes *The Boy without a Flag*; Maria Negroni publishes *Ciudad gótica*.

1993   Juan Flores publishes *Divided Borders: Essays on Puerto Rican Identity*; Dagoberto Gilb publishes *The Magic of Blood*; Gloria Vando publishes *Promesas: Geographies of the Impossible*; Graciela Limón publishes *In Search of Bernabé*; Luis Rodríguez publishes *Always Running*; Tino Villanueva publishes *Scenes from the Movie GIANT*; Esmeralda Santiago publishes *When I Was Puerto Rican*.

1994   NAFTA Treaty lowers barriers to capital while restricting labor's movements. Zapatista movement responds with a military insurrection in Mexico. Influx of U.S. agribusiness displaces small farmers and prompts a new wave of Mexican migration to the United States. United States further intensifies policing of the border with Operation Gatekeeper. Tens of thousands of Haitian and Cuban *balseros* depart their islands due to Special Period and political violence. Rafael Campo publishes *The Other Man was Me*; Gustavo Pérez-Firmat publishes *Life on the Hyphen: the Cuban American Way*; Edwidge Danticat publishes *Breath, Eyes, Memory*; Demetria Martínez publishes *Mother Tongue*; Alina Troyano performs *Milk of Amnesia* as Carmelita Tropicana at PS122 in New York City.

1995   Norma E. Cantú publishes *Canícula: Snapshots of a Girlhood en la Frontera*; Helena María Viramontes publishes *Under the Feet of Jesus*; Aline Helg publishes *Our Rightful Share: The Afro-Cuban Struggle for Equality, 1886–1912*; Selena Quintanilla's death generates a mass vigil in Texas.

1996   U.S. president Bill Clinton signs into law the Illegal Immigration Reform and Immigrant Responsibility Act, which eliminates key defenses against deportation and subjects many immigrants, including legal permanent residents, to detention and deportation; Achy Obejas publishes *Memory Mambo*; Junot Díaz publishes *Drown*; Willie Perdomo publishes *Where a Nickel Costs a Dime: Poems*; Esmeralda Santiago publishes *America's Dream*; Coco Fusco and Nao Bustamante perform *Stuff*.

1997   Francisco Goldman publishes *The Ordinary Seaman*.

1998   Mario Bencastro publishes *Odyssey to the North*; Giannina Braschi publishes *Yo-yo Boing!*; Héctor Tobar publishes *The Tattooed Soldier*; Edwidge Danticat publishes *The Farming of Bones*;

Caridad de la Luz "La Bruja" performs one-woman show *Brujalicious;* Frances Aparicio publishes *Listening to Salsa.*

1998–
2000   Guillermo Gómez-Peña and La Pocha Nostra's "Ethno-Techno: A Virtual Museum of Radical Latino Imagery and Fetishized Identities" active on the Internet (1998–2000).

1999   Loida Maritza Pérez publishes *Geographies of Home;* Los Cybrids active on the Internet until 2003.

2000   U.S. Census Bureau declares "Hispanic/Latino" the largest minority group; Ernesto Quiñonez publishes *Bodega Dreams;* Evelio Grillo publishes memoir, *Black Cuban, Black American;* Julia Alvarez publishes *In the Name of Salomé;* Josefina Baez publishes *Dominicanish.*

2001   Terrorist attacks of September 11; U.S. military operations commence in Afghanistan; Ana Menendez publishes *In Cuba I Was a German Shepherd;* Angie Cruz publishes *Soledad; Telling to Live: Latina Feminist Testimonios* is published; Denise Chávez publishes *Loving Pedro Infante;* Marie Arana publishes *American Chica.*

2002   Nicolás Kanellos et al. publish *Herencia: The Anthology of Hispanic Literature of the United States.* Kirsten Silva Gruesz publishes *Ambassadors of Culture: The Transnational Origins of Latino Writing;* Karin Rosa Ikas publishes *Chicana Ways: Conversations with Ten Chicana Writers;* Sandra Cisneros publishes *Caramelo;* Leticia Hernández-Linares publishes *The Razor Edges of My Tongue.*

2003   Nilo Cruz's *Anna in the Tropics* is awarded the Pulitzer Prize for drama; Oscar Cásares publishes *Brownsville;* Manuel Muñoz publishes *Zigzagger;* Alisa Valdes-Rodriguez publishes *The Dirty Girls Social Club;* Juana María Rodríguez publishes *Queer Latinidad: Identity, Practices, Discursive Spaces.*

2004   Marta Moreno Vega publishes *When the Spirits Dance Mambo.*

2005   Javier Téllez performs *One flew Over the Void (Bala perdida)* ; Sesshu Foster publishes *Atomik Aztex;* Nina Marie Martínez publishes *¡Caramba!;* Salvador Plascencia publishes *The People of Paper;* Alicia Gaspar de Alba publishes *Desert Blood: The Juarez Murders.*

2006   Millions protest against proposed anti-immigrant federal legislation that would criminalize immigration violations; Martín Espada publishes *The Republic of Poetry;* Angie Cruz publishes *Let it Rain Coffee;* Reyna Grande publishes *Across a*

Hundred Mountains; Kathleen de Azevedo publishes *Samba Dreamers.*

2007   José Luis Falconi and José Antonio Mazotti, edit *The Other Latinos: Central and South Americans in the United States;* Daniel Alarcón publishes *Lost City Radio;* Jaime Manrique publishes *Our Lives are the Rivers;* Dominican Republic-Central American Free Trade Agreement passes; Alex Rivera directs the film *Sleep Dealer.*

2008   Junot Díaz's *The Brief Wondrous Life of Oscar Wao* awarded the Pulitzer Prize for fiction; Lin-Manuel Miranda's *In the Heights*, opens on Broadway; Arlene Dávila publishes *Latino Spin.*

2009   Jennine Capó Crucet publishes *How to Leave Hialeah;* Sonia Sotomayor becomes first Latina U.S. Supreme Court justice.

2010   Juan Flores and Miriam Jiménez Román publish *The Afro-Latin@ Reader;* Oscar Martínez publishes *Los migrantes que no importan* Josefina López publishes *Detained in the Desert;* Luis Negrón publishes *Mundo Cruel.*

2011   Ilan Stavans et al. publish *The Norton Anthology of Latino Literature;* Ecuadorean-born, New Orleans-based Gabriel Alemán publishes post-Katrina short story, "Jam Session." Quiara Alegría Hudes publishes *Water by the Spoonful;* Robert Henry Moser and Antonio de Andrade Tosta co-edit *Luso-American Literature: Writing by Portuguese-Speaking Authors in North America;* José L. Torres-Padilla and Carmen Haydée Rivera, co-edit *Writing off the Hyphen: New Critical Perspectives on the Literature of the Puerto Rican Diaspora.*

2012   U.S. President Barack Obama institutes Deferred Action for Childhood Arrivals (DACA); Arizona lawmakers ban schools from teaching "ethnic studies" classes, and works of Latina/o literature are banned from public libraries; Justin Torres publishes *We the Animals;* Junot Díaz publishes *This Is How You Lose Her;* Cristy C. Road publishes *Spit and Passion.*

2013   Richard Blanco publishes *One Today* and is the first Latino poet to recite at a U.S. Presidential Inauguration; Raquel Cepeda publishes *Bird of Paradise: How I Became Latina;* Alanna Lockward publishes *Marassa y la Nada;* Carmen Giménez Smith publishes *Milk and Filth;* Ito Romo publishes *The Border is Burning;* Rigoberto Gonzalez publishes *Unpeopled Eden.*

2013–2015　　Approximately 80,000 unaccompanied minors from Central America are detained along the U.S.-Mexico border, representing a small percentage of those child migrants who actually reach the United States.

2014　　Barack Obama and Raul Castro reestablish diplomatic relations between Cuba and the United States; Daisy Hernández publishes *A Cup of Water under My Bed;* Cristina Henríquez publishes *The Book of Unknown Americans;* John Chávez and Carmen Giménez Smith co-edit *Angels of the Americlypse: New Latin@ Writing;* Fredy Roncalla publishes *Hawansuyo ukun words.*

2015　　Juan Felipe Herrera becomes U.S. Poet Laureate; Lin-Manuel Miranda debuts the musical *Hamilton,* which is awarded the Pulitzer Prize for drama in 2016; Jennine Capó Crucet publishes *Make Your Home Among Strangers.*

Introduction

JOHN MORÁN GONZÁLEZ AND LAURA LOMAS

Having grown substantially over the past two decades as an institutional presence and in methodological sophistication, the field of Latina/o American literature has coalesced sufficiently to require its own literary history. By this adjective "Latina/o" American, we refer to literature by writers of Latin American and Caribbean origin who find themselves annexed or incorporated into the United States (as in the case of Puerto Rico and the formerly northern half of Mexico), or who have migrated or descended from exiled or immigrant Hispanic, Latin American, and/or Caribbean peoples residing outside their place of origin. Initially starting as disparate community-supported research staking claims to institutional resources through literary manifestoes during the 1960s (e.g., Chicano studies and Puerto Rican studies), what now circulates as Latina/o American literary history has not only expanded to include the writing of numerous and influential Latina/o groups such as Cuban Americans, Dominican Americans, and U.S.-based Central and South Americans, but has also shifted from its originally narrow national foci into new critical conversations with American, Latin American, and other interdisciplinary and diasporic literary histories. The scholarly conversations across these fields have raised questions about the "when" and "where" of any ethno-racial literary history and the nationalist or idealist narratives that have tended to organize them.

The long-awaited chicken to the egg of Latina/o literary anthologies that began to circulate in the last two decades (*Herencia*, published by Oxford University Press in 2002 and the *Norton Anthology of Latino Literature* (2011)), this first major Latina/o literary history of its kind has a sustained focus on the categories of race, class, gender, and sexuality that came to the fore in struggles for representation, and that remain urgent for this field. Their intersections generate a significant imperative for inquiry as bodies classified as "Hispanic or Latina/o" now constitute the largest, economically, and politically disenfranchised "minority" in the United States. This rapidly growing U.S. demographic is set to displace a longstanding "non-Hispanic white" majority in the pecking order of ethno-racial groups by the mid-twenty-first century. "Hispanic or Latina/o" remains the problematic label for a multilingual, multiracial, and mobile force with a long history in the Americas that has required the development of distinct analytics and methodologies for bringing into focus a new literary history.

What is in a name? Like historical circumstances transmitted from the past, and not of our choosing, names form part of the inherited conditions with which we make literary histories such as this one. Given that counting "Spanish surnamed" individuals functioned in the 1970s as one method of assembling a disparate group that has historically included descendants of the colonizers and of the colonized, of the enslavers and the enslaved, of those who write history and those whose history is unwritten, of those who do not remember and those who do or are in the process of remembering and redefining, we recognize that a variety of terms have emerged to refer to the changing object of study that necessitates this volume. As editors, we have permitted different labels to coexist and circulate according to the interpretive commitments of each contributor. If "Latina/o" represents a gender-inclusive adjective that refers to the persistence of Latin-ness or *latinidad* as it moves outside its place of origin, the "Latina/o American" of our title should not be confused with the "Latin American" that refers to the region proper, which another multivolume literary history published by Cambridge over a decade ago has already addressed. Nonetheless, these fields intersect and overlap in crucial ways, as we discuss below. Breaking the rule of Spanish grammar that makes the collective masculine-ending term speak as the natural universal, the term we use in this Introduction – "Latina/o" – calls attention to the persistent material effects of a male/female gender binary, and acknowledges long-standing feminist transgression of breaking grammatical rules to inscribe difference within the tradition. The limits of the binary form have given rise to the newer term "Latinx," which conveys both gender neutrality and creates another ending to stand in for polymorphous forms of sexual and gender presentation in excess of a male/female and normalized-as-straight binary. By abandoning an inherited patronymic as Malcolm X did, and by making the last syllable of the non-Anglicized term an "x" (or *equis*), this still-novel term might suggest a post-feminist latinidad. All these terms emphasize a mobile and displaced latinidad, a term that itself evokes the violence of the Iberian Peninsula's colonial projects while coming to represent a more inclusive descriptor. Rather than the term "Hispanic," which fetishizes linguistic purity and tends to lump together Spain with its former colonies, often further subordinating non-European cultural forms, Latina/o calls attention to Francophone, Lusophone, and other intermingling among variegated migrant communities outside Latin America and the Caribbean.

The field's methods and heterogeneous object of study render both a nation-based, monolingual or mono-ethno-racial framework insufficient. While this literary history does not offer a single, overarching, developmental narrative, it articulates how this emergent literary field has begun to periodize – drawing on distinct interrelated regional conjunctures – and to theorize the relationships among texts across space and time. In four parts that reach from the colonial period to the twenty-first century, this volume demonstrates how the fixed space of what is now the United States does not offer the geographic criteria for inclusion in this history. These chapters acknowledge cultural *herencias* or persistent colonial deformations deriving from Latin America, the Caribbean, the United States and beyond, all of which continue to shape Latina/o literary imagination and aesthetic form.

In large measure, the "transnational turn" in American Studies can be attributed to the introduction of the "border" as a key concept through scholarship in Latina/o literature, history, and criticism. This multivalent term refers to more than geographic borders, and includes the zones of contact among languages, cultures, and differently racialized or gendered groups. Likewise, Latin American Studies has benefited from a Latina/o studies interpretation of the cultural and political effects of people, capital, and culture moving across national borders from the Global South to the Global North and back again, with particular attention to how migrants negotiate competing national, economic, political, and cultural transitions, from the nineteenth century to a post–Cold War moment. In turn, interaction with American and Latin American studies has "worlded" Latina/o literary history. This volume foregrounds literary comparison, contact with multiple languages and cultures, the effects of shifting political borders and contexts, in and beyond this hemisphere, all of which have pushed the field to recognize its broader implications.

The methodological turn to comparative frameworks in Latina/o literary history has remained grounded in specific cultural expressions, practices, and relationships, thus countering the trend among transnational approaches to globalize everything and thus decontextualize, in an uncritically celebratory fashion, the dynamics of power that operate locally and globally, below, through, and above nation-states. The essays of *The Cambridge History of Latina/o American Literature* situate trans-American articulations within texts, writers, communities, and historical moments. Rather than seek a continuous, unbroken literary genealogy, this history rehearses particular scenes of struggle, the changing significance of central terms (such as "Latina/o" itself), disparate and discontinuous literary genres, variably structured by the institutions of governmentality, the flow of transmigrant communities and cultural forms, mobilized largely by the dominant systems of colonization and capitalism.

The deepening of temporal dimensions complements the new spatial and linguistic dimensions of Latina/o literary studies. When first founded in the 1960s and 1970s, Chicano and Puerto Rican studies were hard-pressed to locate literary texts written or published prior to 1959. Thanks to the archival research and methodological insights about the archive made possible by the Recovering the U.S. Hispanic Literary Heritage Project, scholars have convincingly demonstrated how Spanish colonial-era texts dating to the sixteenth century may be considered as antecedents to Latina/o literature with regard to its origins in hemispheric coloniality, and Spanish-language texts previously read as only part of a Latin American literary history have acquired new significance in representing or informing the perspectives, narratives, and literary forms that have emerged. The constellation of texts that figure in these chapters thus mediate the displacement and transculturation, or two-directional influence, due to asymmetrical contact in the border zones created by colonization, annexation, and migration. In particular, research into the eighteenth and nineteenth centuries has greatly expanded the number and scope of Latina/o literary texts, the majority of which were written in Spanish.

In effect, what had been previously considered to be a minor, late twentieth-century subset of U.S. ethnic literature has become a literature that predates and unseats monolingual and Anglo-cultural origin narratives. Latina/o literary history reconceptualizes U.S. literature and extends beyond it as a multilingual, multiple assemblage that often emerges from spaces in between nations, through creative remaking of official languages and dissenting from dominant national cultural discourses. Without the ostensible unity of a single racial category, this extensive and variegated Latina/o American literary history is marked by the minor use of globally dominant languages (predominantly Spanish, English, and Portuguese), as enriched by hundreds of suppressed or surviving indigenous Amerindian, African, and Asian languages, by the stubborn adherence to a reworked or hybridized mother tongue, or even by an untranslatable bilingualism in the face of pressures to assimilate and standardize. Different languages imply widely dispersed readerships, punctilious wit aimed specifically at bilinguals and transnational print-communities constantly engaged in translation.

Introduction

The Recovering the U.S. Hispanic Literary Heritage Project, a multidisciplinary initiative directed by Nicolás Kanellos since 1991, has made many of these texts and much of the criticism about them available to a wide range of readers either through literary anthologies or reprints through Arte Público Press, providing a critical apparatus and widespread accessibility for adoption in college and university courses. International scholarly initiatives (such as Casa de las Américas in Cuba where Rolando Hinojosa's narratives and Juan Flores's critical work on Puerto Rican literature and the Nuyorican diaspora have each received international recognition, or the teaching of these texts in British, European, Latin American, and other universities) have launched research and scholarly inquiry that opens the conversations around Latina/o literary and cultural history far beyond the United States.

The Cambridge History of Latina/o American Literature makes this cutting-edge research accessible to a wide scholarly audience interested in the global emergence of this field of study. Written by eminent scholars from the Americas and Europe, the essays in this volume highlight key texts and contexts for a wide range of literary genres, especially narrative prose, poetry, and performance. The chapters are arranged to orient researchers to the most current developments in the field, with close readings, intertextual connections, and case studies giving sense to historical and methodological debates. As such, *The Cambridge History of Latina/o American Literature* complements other titles in Cambridge University Press's History series such as *The Cambridge History of African American Literature, The Cambridge History of Asian American Literature, The Cambridge History of American Women's Literature*, and the multivolume histories of *American* and *Latin American Literature*.

This very complementarity raises the question: what points of tension distinguish Latina/o American literature from what we may think of as the parent fields of Latin American and (U.S.) American literary histories? If Latin American literary history focuses on the relationships among literary works by people who share a language and conceive of themselves in relation to a shared geographic space, Latina/o American literary history refers to works by and relating to minor groupings, geographically dispersed, which share neither a single language nor a single territorial, regional, or cultural reference point. Much more than a cultural origin or single region, movements and forms in response to historical processes of displacement and transculturation define this literature. Rather than a narrative or epic recounting of a singular origin or cumulative national project, this field is marked by disjointed processes of European colonization, the genocide of indigenous

5

peoples, the uprooting of slavery, the exploitation of migrant labor, and the violent mestizaje introduced by rape and border-crossing, all of which shatter any narrative of incorporation, belonging, or wholeness.

Diverging from Latin American and U.S. interpretive frameworks, this literary history emerges from its activist origins in the 1960s to name the experience of a mainly working-class, minoritized group that must necessarily creatively engage displacement. As the history of a minor perspective from within the bowels of a still aggressive empire, and yet nevertheless still in contact and communication with distant *patrias*, Latina/o American literature bears an oblique subaltern relation to the unmarked "American" or U.S. literature that, until the mid-twentiethcentury, considered itself a branch of British literature. Betraying the trenchant residue of the colonial conditions from which it emerges, Latina/o American literature plays a crucial role in pressing dominant forms of North American literary studies to recognize its complicity with empire and to define itself more precisely as a literature of the United States and/or Canada. Latina/o American literary history similarly challenges its Latin American counterpart to acknowledge the extent to which the area studies framework through which it entered the academy originally did not fully consider the cultural politics of representation – especially persistent problematics of race, gender, sexuality, language, class, and coloniality – within light-skinned, Creole-dominant, masculinist Latin American, North American, and indeed, even Latina/o forms of nationalism or regionalism.

Latina/o American literary history is in dialogue with and intersects with African, Asian, and indigenous or Amerindian diaspora literary histories, which afford it indispensable theoretical resources, many of which are on display in this volume. The notion of diaspora as a heterogeneous field of entanglement without the possibility of return to a single origin, relevant especially to Afro-Latina/o but also to other diasporic writing, and the concept of intersectionality, are directly indebted to scholars of African American literature and culture, even as queer, Chicana and Caribbean feminism have also contributed to the groundwork of thinking through multiple, intersecting categories. At the edges of these fields, we glimpse the future work not included in this volume, such as, for example, an Asian and or Muslim Latina/o literary history, which will become increasingly relevant in light of expanding U.S. empire and ongoing historical research on Asians and Islam in the Americas. From Boukman Dutty and Cécile Fatima's role in presiding over a syncretized Islamic and Afro-Caribbean religious ceremony in Bois Caiman to launch the Haitian revolution to discussions of the misrecognition and solidarity among Arabs or Muslims and Latinas/os in the context of U.S. global imperial engagements as documented by Moustafa Bayoumi, these avenues of inquiry will only grow alongside examinations of Filipina/o and other forms of Asian-latinidad). Similarly, we expect this research to expand in the direction of international literatures of latinidades in the sites where Latina/o migrants move, including Canada, Europe, Asia, Africa, and even Latin America and the Caribbean, which have become sites of return migration and landing points post-deportation.

Part and Chapter Descriptions

The Cambridge History of Latina/o American Literature is structured into four parts and an epilogue. The four parts offer a comprehensive overview of the development of Latina/o American literature from the Spanish colonial era to the contemporary moment, with particular care to move beyond stale debates over identity politics and thematic concerns to more productive ones over periodization, the impact of coloniality and authoritarian regimes, and the complexities of multidirectional transculturation at moments of unequal exchange.

Part I revisits the relationship between colonial-era expressive practices throughout the Americas and the Latina/o American texts they inform. Starting with the long colonial era between Columbus's arrival to Hispaniola and the historical events that prompted a rethinking of sovereignty, and subsequent independence movements in the Spanish American colonies Latina/o literary history works to initiate a process of decolonization in its very methodology. Previous theoretical frameworks of Latina/o literature focused upon finding genealogies of resistance in Spanish colonial texts in those parts of the Spanish Empire that would later become the United States, but this section departs from those models by offering not a literary lineage, traceable by unbroken links deep into a specific territory's colonial past, but rather a proleptic and contingent articulation of specific cultural productions, emergent literary genres, and singular authors whose influence extends from the colonial period to the present. At the literary level, towering intellectuals such as Sor Juana Inés de la Cruz, indigenous texts such as Aztec codices, and performative practices such as the *Requerimiento* or *Las Pastorelas*, continue to inform the imaginary of subsequent Latina/o American literature.

As in all American literatures, Latina/o literary history begins with the texts of the original inhabitants of this hemisphere. Indigenous texts – such as the *Popul Vuj*, transcribed from an oral recitation in 1524 – languages, woven forms, and signs inscribed upon other material objects besides books have survived despite distortion, misunderstanding, and misinterpretation. Arturo Arias underscores the often disavowed or underestimated significance of the relations of power between the *ego conquiro* (Dussel and Mignolo) and the indigenous women and men who bore the brunt of this violence. These relations of power take shape in the context of a genocide (killing some 86 percent of the indigenous inhabitants during the colonial period) that peaked between the fifteenth century and the twentieth. Late into the latter century, migrants from South and Central America of indigenous background have continued to be affected as a result of colonialism and anti-indigenous racialization; the film *El Norte* (1983), on which Arias collaborated as a screen writer, depicts the dangerous border-crossing journey of two Guatemalan migrants to the United States after they flee the Guatemalan government's persecution during that nation's civil war. Arias's chapter calls for the acknowledgement of this history of colonial violence, including sexual violence affecting male- and female-gendered bodies, as a point of departure for interpreting the literature of the descendants of the colonizers and of the colonized in Latina/o literary history. Gloria Anzaldúa pioneered decolonial research that led her to coin the concept of *nepantla* from a Nahuatl word that articulated the subjective experience of invasion from the perspective of Mexicas (Aztecs). Arias suggests that Latina/o criticism might also usefully bring the tools of European theory to bear on the "phantasmic presence of indigenity," in order to consider representations of the repercussions of this psychic and physical violence.

Pedro García-Caro follows the clues of a previous generation of "recovery" scholarship to uncover a new archive of the colonial period that includes secular and religious theater and spectacle among many other performance genres that circulated in Hispanic colonial territories of what is now the United States. García-Caro's research drives home the point that the indigenous audience of this performative tradition is "captive," i.e., imprisoned, within a colonial matrix and subject to performances that celebrate the extirpation and banishing of that audience's pre-Columbian practices and beliefs. This chapter reveals how this literary tradition emerges out of, and has long been fully complicit with, a project of violent incorporation of this captive indigenous audience into a Latina/o sphere.

At the methodological level, the insights into "the coloniality of power" developed within Latin American literary and cultural theory have provided a crucial vocabulary through which to examine gendered subject formation under conditions of coloniality, thus vexing dominant narratives about how literary theory "travels" in Latina/o literary scholarship. While the dominant narrative posits a trickling down of Continental philosophy, filtered by the mainstream U.S. academy into a pre-theoretical, identitarian academic backwater, this volume's reimagining of colonization indicates that Latina/o literature is itself a creative point of departure. Elsa Sampson Vera Tudela shows how a wide range of creative and interpretive representations of Sor Juana Inés de la Cruz reveal a long-standing tradition of Latina feminist readings that claim the erudite Mexican nun as a theoretical and performative precursor and influence. Notable elements of sorjuanian tricks of the weak and performative practice include material and gendered embodiment as a foundational contingency of all intellectual and creative work. Sor Juana writes as a gendered subaltern subject with canny insight about how coloniality is also always gendered. Early twentieth-century Chicana feminist Jovita González and contemporary Latina performance artists and writers alike acknowledge and celebrate Sor Juana's revolutionary sexual difference, and as a woman with no husband to "tuck in." She critically engages the gatekeepers of the patriarchal Roman Catholic Church, from within spaces such as the convent, where women enjoyed opportunities to practice alternatives to maternal, heterosexual reproduction. Above all, Sor Juana's powerful, unfinished posthumous lyric "Romance 51" affirms her writings' irreducible difference from existing colonial knowledge, and illegibility through any of the limiting labels or interpretive systems derivative therefrom.

Yolanda Martínez-San Miguel's chapter acknowledges the significance of the colonial period, which does not end in the nineteenth century, but continues, in some cases, into the present. With caveats about how narratives of the colonial period in Latina/o literary history often problematically elide thousands of years of indigenous civilizations or ignore the significance of black struggles for self-emancipation and self-government, Martínez-San Miguel interrogates how the emphasis on a Spanish "antecedence" to English colonizers problematically recenters European-descended Creole settler protagonists. Through a generative reading of foundational anthologies and histories of Latina/o literature, she notes the relevance of colonial period texts for understanding the matrix that forged contemporary Latina/o identities, especially for an increasingly heterogeneous Latina/o population that includes South, Central, and Caribbean migrants in the United States. This reading observes the persistent effects of coloniality that continue to isolate Latina/o literary studies from relevant theoretical work in Native American, colonial Latin American, Caribbean, or decolonial U.S. American studies. Martínez-San Miguel's comparative and decolonial approach reads against the grain of the colonial archive in order to perceive the limits of what we know of this period, and emphasizes the need to listen for the multiple and often conflicting voices in the archive. She calls our attention to asymmetrical relationships of power within and among the intersecting fields of Latina/o, Latin American, Caribbean, Native, and U.S. American studies, and calls for vigilance about the persistent blind spots of Latina/o studies. Drawing on Edward Said, Martínez-San Miguel suggests that we read for secular affiliations rather than organicist and triumphalist assumptions of genealogical descent from the colonizers to the present day.

José Antonio Mazzotti documents the circulation of Spanish-language terms dating to the seventeenth century – such as "criollo," "mestizo," and "Latino" – that are fundamental to Latina/o literature and likewise inform a Latina/o American literary imaginary. He sets them in contrast to terms that have emerged in subaltern writings and social protest texts as alternatives to such European-derived terms. These counter-terms, such as "Anahuac," "Abya-Yala," and "Aztlán," also circulated contemporaneously within subaltern communities. Even a seemingly neutral term like "mestizo," carried a derogatory meaning in most written texts through the mid-nineteenth century despite being revindicated as early as 1609 by the Andean writer Inca Garcilaso de la Vega, himself a mestizo. According to Mazzotti, the term "Latina/o" cannot pretend to designate an oppositional group within the United States or other contexts where migrants from Latin America create minor oppositional cultures, without full acknowledgment of how it is always also marked by the trauma of colonial violence and by the internal exclusions of Creole-led nationalisms that formed in the wake of colonization. Mazotti offers us a deep historical sense of "Latina/o" and "latinidad," noting their loaded, Eurocentric significance. Indeed, all these chapters excavate aspects of a long, incomplete Latina/o literary history in which the struggle over the meaning of a discontinuous past informs contemporary definition of the field's scope, key terms, and its relation to subjugated or submerged knowledges, often available only through the filter of the colonial archive.

Part II focuses on the hemispheric aspects of Latina/o literature as it mapped out the possibilities of republican interactions between and coalitions among the nations of the Americas. Already in this period it is possible to see the limits of these visions once the United States turned increasingly imperialistic. This section covers the period from the late eighteenth century until the early twentieth century, and includes key historical moments, such as the dismembering aftermath of the Tupac Amaru II and Micaela Bastidas rebellion of 1780–1781, the end of the Revolution of the Thirteen Colonies in 1783, the Haitian Revolution 1791–1804, the four-decade-long Spanish occupation of New Orleans beginning in 1769, the wars of Spanish American independence between 1810–1821, the U.S.–Mexican War of 1846–1848, the wars of Cuban and Puerto Rican independence 1868–1878, the U.S.–Spanish-Cuban War of 1895–1902, and the Cuban Race War of 1912, in order to suggest their relevance for periodizing Latina/o literary history.

Emphasizing the blurred and mutually contaminating space between Latin American and Latina/o literary histories, Maria del Pilar Blanco brings into focus specific uses and inflections of the adjective "Latin," as it derives from Latin American literature, and then examines specific late nineteenth-century uses of this term in writing outside of the region. Her chapter traces the emergence of this term in travel writings that reflect on the different meanings that latinidad acquires inside the United States. While Blanco revisits the foundational border regions between the United States and Mexico or among Caribbean and Latin American writers traveling or residing in the north, she provocatively invites us to consider Latina/o literary history not simply as it interacts with the cultures of the United States, but rather as a force that increasingly transculturates literatures across the globe.

Carmen Lamas recuperates exiled Cuban Roman Catholic priest Félix Varela's near thirty-year residence in New York City, and in particular his writings in *Cartas a Elpidio* (1835–1838) and in numerous U.S.-based, English-language Catholic periodicals as an early instance of Latina/o writing. Complicating the prevailing focus on Varela's supposed authorship of the historical novel *Jicotencál* (1826), Lamas depicts him as an activist community leader in New York who fostered coalitional politics across cultural lines for the protection of civil rights. Varela mobilized a largely Irish Catholic minority to critique Protestant denigration of the Roman Catholic Church and fight discrimination against immigrant Catholics while contributing to the secularization of the Protestant-biased public-school curriculum. According to Lamas Varela's activism reveals how cross-cultural alliances against discriminatory practices became available under certain circumstances of mutual respect.

Kirsten Silva Gruesz, who has influentially raised the question of what *was* Latina/o literature, reveals a long history of Latina/o writing in the trans-American contact zone of New Orleans, Louisiana, and the Gulf of Mexico. Bringing into focus three distinct historical nodes of writing that merit further research and investigation – mid-nineteenth-century serialized romances, early twentieth-century modernist fiction, and contemporary

Latina/o writing that has become more visible in the post-Katrina era – Gruesz interrogates the elision of the long-standing Spanish cultural influence (a slippery, wide adjective that includes large contingents of Canary Islanders, Hondurans, Cubans, and Mexicans, among many others), which led to a widespread misreading of New Orleans's Latin-ness as primarily French. She also meticulously documents a long-standing bi- or trilingual print culture in this port city and border region that plots the city as a part of the circum-Caribbean region, within Latin American, Caribbean, and U.S. literary traditions, thus marking the nexus as a key point of departure for Latina/o literary history.

Rodrigo Lazo reminds us that this volume has the significant task of providing a literary history for a body of writing that since its inception has not had one. He reflects on the task of explaining the relationships between the historical periods that anthologies have introduced, sui generis, without the benefit of a literary history that would explain the logic – imposed or imagined – of the relationship between historically, geographically, and formally disparate literary texts. Revisiting the definition of literary history, outlined by René Wellek, as contingent upon history and criticism, Lazo calls upon this and future literary histories to theorize the relationships between periods and texts in a field without uncritically mapping Latina/o literary history onto literary periods that derive strictly from U.S. or Latin American histories. Lazo acknowledges the significance of recovery and mobile archives that often move "in unexpected directions," including the biographical narratives and transnational routes of many "recovered" or long-marginalized Latina/o writers. He proposes criteria for explaining the connections across time – print culture and economic conditions – that in turn reveal the influence of a theoretical framework that attends to the material and economic forces shaping superstructural forms such as literature. Lazo offers periods for the nineteenth century that reflect the role of print culture, exilic political movements, and economic interests in the emergence of writing by racially and economically privileged Latina/o Creoles. One such case in point is María Amparo Ruiz de Burton, a scion of the declining formerly Mexican landowning elite of Alta California, who takes up fiction writing in English during the 1870s and 1880s as a way to sustain her family when she finds herself widowed and facing economic necessity in the wake of California's annexation by the United States.

Continuing this focus on the long cultural, economic, and political aftermath of the U.S.–Mexican War of 1846–1848, Jesse Alemán underscores the unique regional contribution of the states that once constituted the northern half of Mexico and teases out the genres – the testimonio, the corrido, and the memoir – and the material conditions through which these regional Latina/o forms articulated a collective Mexican American critique of U.S. aggression as a creative response to the trauma of displacement and racialization. This chapter usefully recuperates the struggles, starting as early as 1855, to retain Spanish and the Spanish-language press, including the long-standing press of New Mexico, where early working-class Chicana feminist writers defended the preservation of Spanish-language literature and journalism as a means to preserve the cultural livelihood and identity of *nuevomejicanos* and *californios*, surrounded as they were by a domineering Anglo presence.

Milagros López-Peláez Casellas surveys nineteenth-century women writers from throughout Latin America and the Caribbean who overcame gendered barriers to publish novels, poetry, and political prose, and who, in some cases, lived or sojourned far from home in Paris, Madrid, Chicago, Washington, D.C., or New York. As most of these writers came from elite Creole backgrounds, their feminism is distorted by a possessive investment in whiteness. This chapter usefully glosses the limits of a liberal "Creole" tradition while acknowledging these early pioneers' contributions to articulating a female-gendered subjectivity and authorship in overlapping traditions of Latin American and Latina literature.

During the 1880s, Latina/o literature adopted a new form of literary prose, la crónica, in an effort to translate the culture and politics of U.S. modernity for Spanish-language readers. A distinctly Latina/o modernist aesthetic emerges in New York-based Cuban José Martí's poetic manifestoes, essays, and unpublished fragments, not unlike those of his French contemporaries Baudelaire and Flaubert. As such, Latina/o modernity critically dissented from the reigning literary aesthetic (realism), from the emerging instrument of U.S. hemispheric domination (Pan-Americanism), and from the increasingly virulent segregation and violence that characterized U.S. racism. Laura Lomas highlights the writings of Martí in establishing connections among Hispanic Caribbean and Latin American migrants, dispossessed people of Mexican descent, excluded Chinese migrants, Jim-Crowed African Americans, the militarily embattled Sioux, and non-English-speaking European migrant workers stigmatized for their anarchist political views.

This section's end date of 1912 gestures toward the violent foreclosure of Martí's idealized post-racial republic that occurred with "el Doce," a "race war" in which a U.S.-backed white criollo elite (including José Martí's only son) massacred several thousand Afro-Cuban men, women, and children, including many veterans of the Wars for Independence, after accusing the

Partido Independiente de Color (PIC) of being "racist." The leaders of this uprising, in particular Evaristo Estenoz and Pedro Ivonnet, had associations with U.S.-based activists such as W. E. B. DuBois and Arturo Alfonso Schomburg, and asserted Afro-Cubans' right to full democratic and economic equality, including recognition of their contributions to the long struggle for national liberation. The history of this black-led social movement has largely remained repressed under both liberal capitalist and socialist Creole-led regimes. Diasporic treatment of this and other histories of Latin American and Caribbean black insurgencies has expanded space for critical theorizing and historical memory of such black-affirming and violently repressed movements for liberation.

As Silvio Torres-Saillant demonstrates in his essay on the emergence of Afro-latinidad, the point is that the hemisphere's racist flames equally derive from Latin American, Caribbean, and U.S.-styled racisms, all of which continue to burn in the diaspora. This hemispheric racism has called into being ethnic sub-traditions that will remain urgent and necessary as long as violence directed against people of color persists. This chapter, which closes Part II, examines the emergence of "Afro-Latino" as a site of critical inquiry within the field of Latina/o studies that critically redefines the historical Latin American tradition by acknowledging its entrenched and persistent negro-phobic racism. As the experience of living at the intersections of major racial, economic, and cultural discourses has defined the lives of African-descended people within Latin American and Caribbean diasporas to the United States, the field centers representations of these experiences in the writings of Afro-Latina/o authors. Doubly marginalized by hoary U.S. and Latin American traditions of anti-black theory and practice, and by the failure of dominant discourses of blackness within the United States to acknowledge fully the heterogeneous practices of blackness with roots in the Hispanophone Caribbean and Latin America, these authors offer a rich counter-tradition of Afro-Latina/o writing.

Part III centers on the gradual emergence of Latina/o American literature onto a global stage as the dynamics of modernity unleash large-scale military conflicts and consequent migrations. Aggressive U.S. interventions in the Caribbean and Central America, alongside the outbreak of the Mexican Revolution during the early twentieth century, created massive displacements and migrations northward, resulting in a literature that criticized the exclusion of Latinas/os from the U.S. national imaginary. U.S. military occupations of Cuba (1906–1909), Nicaragua (1912–1933), Haiti (1915–1934), and the Dominican Republic (1916–1924) disrupted self-governance and inscribed U.S. security forces into subsequent generations of diaspora writing. The Jones-Shafroth Act of 1917 granted U.S. citizenship to Puerto Ricans, but this was perceived as an unwelcome imposition to forestall the possibility of independence while allowing the U.S. military to draft Puerto Ricans to serve in the First World War. Puerto Rican writers chronicled their community's continued exclusion, and often remained committed to national liberation struggles or other forms of cultural independence. Depression-era deportations of tens of thousands of Mexican nationals and Mexican American citizens alike by the U.S. government contributed to the constructions of Latina/o migrants and citizens as "illegal" and "deportable." By mid-century, violent industrialization programs such as "Operation Boot-strap" had displaced tens of thousands who migrated to New York and other East Coast cities. The tropicalization of New York and the eventual develop-ment of a vibrant Nuyorican literary scene, starting in the 1940s with Julia de Burgos and others, found fulsome expression during the 1960s and 1970s and continues to the present day.

As decolonization proceeded on a global scale after the Second World War, Latina/o writers, some inspired by the Cuban Revolution, turned toward revolutionary art even as Cuban American exiles arrived to form strongly anticommunist communities in south Florida and New Jersey. First propelled by the Chicano and Puerto Rican movements of the late 1960s and early 1970s, Latina/o literature underwent a cultural nationalist renaissance in formal aesthetic terms, articulating a militant imperative to represent the radicalized Latina/o community in a deep critical engagement with the cultural dynamics of the United States during the U.S.–Vietnam War. Brown power groups such as the Chicano Brown Berets and the Puerto Rican Young Lords – inspired by Black Panthers – sought to address problems of economic redlining, govern-mental neglect, and racial discrimination through direct-action strategies such as street protests, takeovers of governmental and university offices, and mass boycotts. The purpose of aesthetics became increasingly and directly politi-cized: to instruct the masses about their untaught histories, to instill pride in their suppressed cultural practices (especially the use of Spanish), and to mobilize them to agitate for state resources and social respect. Throughout this period, anticolonial and decolonial imaginaries remained vital aspects of Latina/o literature even as the United States initiated and consolidated its role as global hegemon, with particularly devastating results for the Americas.

In his essay, Antonio López explores the possibility of accessing the seemingly elusive and intangible elements of everyday moments of the past – sights, sounds, smell, and touch – that inform the labor and political movements of early-twentieth-century Latinas/os through the writings and voices of Emma Tenayuca, Luisa Capetillo, Eusebia Cosme, and Alberto O'Farrill. Each of these figures – Mexicana, Boricua, Afro-Cubana, and Afro-Cubano respectively – engaged various sites of performance that left affective and sensory traces upon the written page. Whether on the picket lines (Tenayuca), as a *lectora* on the tobacco-rolling factory floor (Capetillo), in front of audiences performing *declamaciones* (Cosme), or performing in *teatro bufo* (O'Farrill), these historical actors imprinted the powerful affect of their vernacular performances for subsequent generations, defined a Latina/o public sphere and pioneered Latina feminist perspectives dating to the early twentieth century. As such, they advanced the critique of colonial capitalism that would continue as a through-line of Latina/o thought throughout the rest of the twentieth century.

The impact of the Mexican Revolution on the history of the Americas cannot be underestimated. As the first major civil war of the twentieth century, the Revolution not only shaped Latin American nationalism for decades to come but also initiated the century's first great wave of migration from south to north in the Americas as nearly a million Mexican war refugees fled to the United States. The U.S. government, responding to fears of non-white migration from Mexico and Eastern Europe, enacted the Johnson-Reed Immigration Act in 1924, creating the Border Patrol, a racialized immigration quota system, and the conceptual framework for the "illegal alien."[1] While the 1924 Immigration Act was replaced by the less restrictive Immigration and Nationality Act of 1965, the former continues to expand its militarized presence on the U.S.–Mexico border. Revisiting the consequences of the Mexican Revolution for subsequent generations, Yolanda Padilla reframes scholarly conversations about the literary impact of transnationally situated border writers for post-Revolutionary projects of Mexican national consolidation. Arguing against a Mexican nationalist interpretation of the novel of the Mexican Revolution as the nation's entry into modernity, Padilla makes the U.S.–Mexico border region and its inhabitants key figures not only in the history of the Revolution but also in its literary legacies. The Revolutionary-era and post-Revolution works of fronteriza/o and migrant writers such as Mariano Azuela, Leonor Villegas de Magnón, Sara Estela Ramírez, María Cristina Mena, Conrado Espinoza, and Daniel Venegas suggest that the meaning of the Revolution begins outside, and continues to exceed the national boundaries

---

[1] See Mae Ngai, *Impossible Subjects: Illegal Aliens and the Making of Modern America* (Princeton: Princeton University Press, 2004).

of the Mexican state. Padilla's readings point to the role of actors whose concerns lay elsewhere than the creation of a coherent Mexican state but rather in the fostering of fluid transnational fronteriza/o subjectivities.

Responding to the dominant conceptualization of modernity as a Western European, metropolitan experience that eventually diffused across the rest of the world, recent scholarship in Latina/o literary studies has examined how Latina/o writers of the first half of the twentieth century engaged the question of modernity not as a deferred or belated experience but rather as a contemporary one. David Colón's work on modernist poets from the first decades of the twentieth century reveals the ligaments that bind together traditions and shows how such interrelationships came to be ignored. Revisiting the question of latinidades and modernism, Colón argues for an approach that does not view these experiential analytics as separate or even antithetical but rather mutually constitutive. William Carlos Williams, a "high" modernist and associate of Ezra Pound, drew inspiration from the Caribbean and Spanish-speaking environment of his mother's home, and from constant contact with the working-class immigrant New Jersey communities of Paterson and East Rutherford. Salomón de la Selva, the Nicaraguan-born Nobel Prize nominee, translated into unaccented English the hard rhymes made famous by the great poet of modernismo, Rubén Darío, after serving as his translator. Julia de Burgos's intimate poetry irrupts during her nomadic travels outside of her island of birth, and echoes de la Selva's critique of dollar diplomacy in Nicaragua and the Caribbean. The modernist poetics of Williams, de la Selva, and de Burgos challenge conventional narratives about modernism as a European phenomenon that diffused to the global peripheries. Rather, the works of these poets identify the proliferation of modernisms across the Americas through the transculturation, travel, and colonial displace- ment that characterizes the experiences of latinidad in the early twentieth century.

If the Puerto Rican roots of William Carlos Williams have been over- looked in discussions of literary modernism in the United States, so too have been the Puerto Rican roots of Arturo Alfonso Schomburg, one of the key figures in African American literary history. Latina/o voices have often been absent from discussions of the modernism of the Harlem Renaissance, despite Schomburg's Afro-Latinidad. Schomburg, who spent his youth in Puerto Rico before migrating to New York City in 1891, later anglicized his first name to "Arthur" as part of his affiliation with English-speaking African- American and West Indian historians, Masons, and bibliophiles. The conten- tious scholarly debate over how to interpret Arturo/Arthur Schomburg's allegiances and legacies is addressed by César Salgado in his essay. Arguing against the two main interpretations of Schomburg as primarily engaged in either an Anglophone African American intellectual project or a Hispanophone Caribbean Latino one, Salgado makes the case for a third possibility that reimagines Africanity in a trans-American context: Afro-Latinidad. In particular, Schomburg's Spanish-language correspondence with Langston Hughes suggests that, far from abandoning his Puerto Rican roots, Schomburg strategically redeploys it to influence another of the Harlem Renaissance's key figures in a trans-American, bilingual direction. As such, Salgado suggests that Africanity dating to the period of the Spanish colonialism and the Renaissance offers the key missing term from the scholarly debate that would otherwise define Schomburg solely within U.S. terms of black and white.

The Second World War and its consequences – the Cold War and global decolonization movements – form the contextual framework for the Latina/o literature of the second half of the twentieth century. The latter in particular informs the Chicano and Puerto Rican cultural nationalist movements of the 1960s and 1970s, the focus of the next two chapters on Latina/o poetics. Even as Chicanos – the self-adopted term to denote a Mexican-American community acting according to decolonial principles – mobilized en masse against the U.S.–Vietnam War and racial discrimination and for cultural, economic, and political autonomy, artists mobilized to enact a revolution in aesthetics. Rafael Pérez-Torres analyzes the aesthetic imperatives of Chicano poetry in floricanto (flower and song) to represent the struggles of the Chicano *raza* (people) against U.S. racism and to revalorize the indigenous practices and knowledges otherwise lost to colonial domination. Drawing upon the concept of Aztlán, the mythical geographic origin of the Aztecs and imagined community of a Chicano nation, Chicano Movement poets such as Alurista, Rodolfo "Corky" Gonzales, José Montoya, Ricardo Sánchez, and raúlrsalinas formulated alternative epistemologies through complex multilingual performances that mixed English, Spanish, caló (Chicano street vernacular), and sometimes Amerindian languages. But, as Chicana activists and poets noted at the time, the Chicano Movement also replicated heterosexist and patriarchal modes of domination while criticizing racial and class hierarchies. While central to the creation of a Chicano collectivity, the poetry of the movimiento often created heteronormative and masculinist narratives of cultural nationalist inclusion that Chicana poets such as Lorna Dee Cervantes and Bernice Zamora challenged in their poetry.

In his chapter on the rise of Nuyorican poetry, Urayoán Noel proposes that this literature should be read less as an expression of an essential Puerto Rican identity or a single location, and more as the instantiation of a Puerto Rican diasporic poetics in constant motion, less about the fixity of such identities, and more as the fluid processes that mark their contingent yet critical production through both roots and routes. Nuyorican or Nuyorico poets such as Miguel Algarín, Victor Hernández Cruz, Pedro Pietri, Miguel Piñero, Sandra María Esteves, Tato Laviera, Willy Perdomo, Lorraine Sutton, Caridad de la Luz, Lydia Cortés, and Nancy Mercado established a polyvalent, multilingual intersectional site of the Boricua diaspora-in-motion, challenging both hegemonic representations of "a culture of poverty" as well as cultural nationalist imaginaries of authenticity. Spanning a period from the late 1960s through the contemporary moment, Noel considers the multiple legacies and future directions of this performative, irreverent, and mobile tradition into the present as it continues to negotiate neoliberalism, militarism, and gentrification, from Chinese American Martin Wong's 1980s paintings of Miguel Piñero in *La Vera de Nuyorico* to Li Yun Alvarado's *Nuyorico, CA* (2013).

Unlike Puerto Ricans who entered with citizenship but still felt like second-class citizens, Cubans seeking entry into the United States after the Cuban Revolution encountered a much more welcoming reception from the U.S. government than most other migrants from Latin America.[2] William Luis examines the complexities of exile, language, and diaspora in Cuban American literature before and especially after the Cuban Revolution. The particularities of the Cold War diaspora created, on one hand, distinct advantages for those Cubans fleeing communism to the United States, but, on the other, fomented the politics of exilic nostalgia that defined a significant portion of the Cuban American literary output post-1959; Luis includes Carlos Eire, Roberto Fernández, Pablo Medina, Carolina Hospital, and Gustavo Pérez-Firmat in this category. Other Cuban American writers, mostly notably those not associated with the exilic Miami community such as Oscar Hijuelos and

---

[2] In the waning days of his administration, U.S. President Barack Obama ended the twenty-two-year-old policy – also known as the "wet foot, dry foot" rule – that allowed unauthorized Cuban nationals to remain in the United States and gain legal residency upon reaching U.S. territory. A part of the normalization of relations between Cuba and the United States, the revocation of this exemption means apprehended Cuban nationals without proper authorization are subject to the same deportation procedures as others so apprehended. See Julie Hirschfeld Davis and Frances Robles, "Obama Ends Exemption for Cubans Who Arrive Without Visas," *New York Times*, January 12, 2017. Accessed online at www.nytimes.com/2017/01/12/world/americas/cuba-obama-wet-foot-dry-foot-policy.html.

Cristina García, examined the diaspora experience of transculturation in the United States and the vexed possibilities for freedom of expression in sexual and racial terms. Writing outside Miami opened up space particularly for gays and lesbians (Achy Obejas, Reinaldo Arenas, Richard Blanco) and for Afro-Cubans (Lourdes Casal, Evelio Grillo, Adrián Castro).

Performance art from high drama to improvised street theater has formed an important aspect of Latina/o literature since the mid-twentieth century. In his essay, Ricardo Ortíz traces the emergence of a properly "Latino" theater from its origins during the Brown Power movements of the 1960s and 1970s. Even as Chicano and Puerto Rican theater of this period – as typified by Luis Valdez and Miguel Piñero respectively – mobilized a largely realist aesthetics in the service of the cultural nationalist movements, Cuban American playwright María Irene Fornés articulated a Latina presence within mainstream institutions of U.S. theatrical production through award-winning plays such as *Fefu and Her Friends* (1977). However, the general exclusion of Latinas/os from institutional venues led to the rise of performance art as a key genre, as witnessed by the emergence of artists such as Henry Gamboa, Coco Fusco, Carmelita Tropicana, and Guillermo Gómez-Peña during the 1980s and 1990s. In the twenty-first century, Latina/o dramatists such as Nilo Cruz, Quiara Alegría Hudes, Quíque Avila, and, most recently, Lin-Manuel Miranda, have reinvigorated mainstream theater with their critical examinations of the United States from the perspective of latinidades. In particular, Miranda's award-winning hip-hop reimagining of the origins of the United States as a Caribbean immigrant story in *Hamilton* suggests the profundity of the coming transformation of U.S. theater in Latina/o literature.

Part IV of the volume highlights key literary developments of contemporary Latina/o literature within the context of the massive transformations in Latina/o communities wrought by the last decade of the Cold War during the 1980s and the rise of neoliberalism during the 1990s. Significant Latina/o diasporas from Central America and the Dominican Republic came into existence as a result of Cold War policies, while massive population displacements, due to neoliberalist economic policies implemented at the behest of the United States in Mexico as well as Central and South America, intensified the migrant streams *al Norte*. Developing and maintaining transnational ties via air corridors, electronic media, and the Internet, Latina/o communities in the United States expanded as a major supply of cheap labor, an ethnic community with deep-seated social problems, and a political scapegoat for anti-immigration nativists. Responding to this triangulation as a pathological "problem," Latina/o literature asserted a prominent position for Latinas/os in the impending demographic and cultural remaking of the contemporary United States, especially in light of official recognition in the 2000 Census of Latinas/os as a group larger than that of African Americans and projected to become numerically more significant than any other "minor" grouping by 2040. In other words, Latina/o literature foresees a time in the not-too-distant future when the United States may at last embrace itself as a Latina/o American nation. The essays in this section trace this trajectory of Latina/o literature as it exits the cultural nationalist movements of the 1960s and 1970s, and emerges into post- or critically nationalist reconfigurations. During this period, Latina/o critics pioneered border theory that became influential across the globe, and in particular in Latina feminist, queer, postcolonial and postmodern Latina/o theory. This section historicizes the current moment of cultural conflict in which difference and discontinuity has replaced identity and unity as the connective tissues that explain a minor literature. The emphasis on difference includes new genres and media, and cultural responses to intensified local policing and global violence that explain the scope of this heterogeneous literary history.

As migration from the southern half to the northern half of the Americas parallels a global migratory shift where the majority of the globe now dwells in urban centers, the question of migration's effects looms ever more significantly as a defining characteristic of the world's economic, political, and cultural systems. In this period, Latina/o literature has provided the aesthetic basis to reimagine said migration beyond U.S. nationalist concerns about terrorism, job loss, and undesired cultural change. Even as the 1965 immigration reforms did away with racially biased annual national quotas, subsequent major changes in immigration policy and enforcement (1986, 1990, 1996, and post–September 11, 2001) have increasingly restricted documented migration and virulently criminalized undocumented migration, creating in the latter what historian Mae Ngai has termed "impossible subjects," or non-citizens who embody a crisis of governability for nation-states. Latina/o literature has increasingly represented this condition, both as a reflection of the substantial presence of unauthorized migrants from Mexico, Central America, and the Hispanophone Caribbean within Latina/o communities and as an extended metaphor for the racialized condition of latinidades within the United States. As Marta Caminero-Santangelo writes in her essay, Latina/o literature traces the increasingly felt ethical imperative on the part of Latina/o writers to address the injustices encountered by migrants in their translation to the United States while also combatting the white nationalisms that render even U.S. citizens of color as undesirable aliens.

Part of the groundswell of feminist and nationalist movements of the 1970s, and also a critical reaction to them, Latina feminism has been a key influence upon Latina/o literary studies, especially since the publication of *This Bridge Called My Back: Writings by Radical Women of Color*, edited by Chicana lesbian feminists Gloria Anzaldúa and Cherríe Moraga in 1981. Vanessa Pérez Rosario makes the case that contributions by Chicana, Puerto Rican, and other Latin American and Caribbean diaspora feminists powerfully define current Latina feminist methodological concerns. Tracing the precursors of this decolonial feminist practice to anarchist and nationalist activists such as Luisa Capetillo and Lolita Lebrón, Pérez Rosario indicates how the contemporary Latina feminist approaches owe much to the interrogation of mind/body hierarchy, and to a critique of heterosexist and masculinist cultural nationalism by Anzaldúa and Moraga during the 1980s. The theorization of the Latina feminist subject through intersectionality is further developed in more recent memoirs of cultural and familial survival by Puerto Ricans Aurora Levins Morales and Irene Vilar, and by the Colombian-Cuban Daisy Hernández. As such, Latina feminism remains a vibrant, central force within Latina/o literary studies.

Just as Latina feminism has changed the conceptual framework of Latina/o literary studies, so too has the influx of migrants from the Central American nations of the Northern Triangle (El Salvador, Guatemala, Honduras) changed the idea of latinidad within the United States since the 1980s. The literature of U.S. Central Americans points to a vexed history of diasporic migration initiated in large part by U.S. Cold War policies in Central America during the 1970s and 1980s and continued by neoliberal trade policies and U.S. deportation policies. In 1979, the Frente Sandinista de Liberación Nacional (FSLN) overthrew the U.S.-supported dictator Anastasio Somoza Debayle, in conjunction with civil wars in Guatemala and El Salvador. Afraid of a Central American domino effect in which "backyard" nations would turn communist, the United States supported the repression of organized working-class and indigenous groups who demanded human and labor rights in an effort to undermine leftist guerrilla movements in Guatemala and El Salvador. The resultant flow of Central American war refugees (who were, for political reasons, classified largely as economic migrants) to the United States increased the Central American-origin population nine-fold between 1980 and 2013, to over 3.1 million, including some 80,000 unaccompanied Central American minors released from detention between 2013 and 2015.[3]

---

[3] See Jie Zong and Jeanne Batalova, "Central American Immigrants in the United States," September 2, 2015. Accessed online at www.migrationpolicy.org/article/central-ameri can-immigrants-united-states.

In her essay, Ana Patricia Rodríguez outlines how these dynamics have led to contrasting generational outcomes in terms of U.S. Central American literature. First-generation U.S. Central Americans writers such as Mario Bencastro, Horacio Castellanos Moya, and Martivón Galindo, dealing with trauma of state repression, attempt to address the diasporic impasse of seeking justice back home through testimonio while quietly surviving in the United States. The 1.5-generation writers such as Tanya María Barrientos, Francisco Goldman, and Héctor Tobar, whom Rodríguez terms "postmemorial," negotiate the difficult terrain of familial and communal memory in the diaspora as they did not experience the violence of the civil wars firsthand, but nonetheless still feel the effects upon their parents and other older relatives that extend down to them. Second-generation authors, more acculturated to the United States and more comfortable in English, address issues of the lack of communal political visibility cultivated by the first generation as part of its survival strategy. These authors, often women who explore hierarchies of race, gender, and sexual identity, include Maya Chinchilla, Lorena Duarte, and Leticia Hernández-Linares.

In her essay, Crystal Kurzen examines Latina/o life writing – or "self-writing," as she terms it – as a key discursive site for the development of Latina/o literature. While always in conversation with the self-reflexive Western European tradition of writing the self into individual subjectivity since the Renaissance, Latina/o life writing, as expressed through the sub-genres of autobiography, memoir, testimonio, and even novels, differs from the normative trajectory of Western life-writing through its introduction of communal as well as individual subjectivities, especially in the testimonio. This turn to the communal is out of necessity, as Kurzen writes, as structural conditions of colonial, racial, and gender domination did not allow for the same experience of subject-making to be realized for non-white, non-male, non-literate groups. When conditions did allow, Latina/o life writing turned to collective subject-making to register resistance to abject subjectification; some mid-twentieth-century Chicano writers such as José Antonio Villareal (*Pocho*, 1959) and Ernesto Galarza (*Barrio Boy*, 1971) attempted to meld individualist and communal concerns even as Richard Rodriguez's *Hunger of Memory* (1982) attempted to fully privilege the individual over the communal. Kurzen notes that life writing has assumed particular importance for queer Chicana feminists Cherríe Moraga and Norma Elia Cantú, who move between literary genres in their life-writing texts (*Loving in the War Years: lo que nunca pasó por sus labios*, 1983 and *Canícula: Snapshots of a Girlhood en la frontera*, 1995, respectively) to assert themselves into patriarchal and heteronormative (cultural) nationalist narratives that would otherwise silence their voices. Similarly, life writing has become a vehicle for gay Latino writers such as Cuban American Richard Blanco (*The Prince of Los Cocuyos*, 2014) seeking to dismantle heteronormative parameters of agency.

The focus of Norma Elia Cantú's contribution is the intersection of poetry, the historical core of Latina/o literature with deep roots in the literary and oral traditions of pre-Columbian and colonial-era communities, and the largely grassroots institutions that Latina/o communities have created to preserve and advance this art form. As such, Latina/o communities have a long tradition of supporting poetry. Poems were a mainstay of Spanish-language periodicals since the mid-nineteenth century and the preferred aesthetic idiom of the Puerto Rican and Chicano literary renaissance of the late 1960s and early 1970s. Since then, community-origin workshops such as Macondo and Canto Mundo have fostered the next generations of poets and writers in continuance of that tradition. As Cantú relates, poetry retains an important role in the articulation of latinidades today, particularly insofar as Latina/o poets choose the Spanish language or bilingual code-switching to construct ties to the literary traditions of Latin America and the lived experiences of the borderlands respectively.

As is the case with U.S. Central Americans, Dominican Americans have fundamentally altered the sense of latinidad in the United States, further pluralizing it into latinidades. Sophie Maríñez expands the definition of what diasporic experiences shall be encompassed by latinidades in her essay on "The Quisqueya Diaspora." While the Republic of Haiti and the Dominican Republic have sent significant numbers of migrants to the United States since the 1970s, literary scholars have regarded the diasporic writers from these migrations solely in relation to national and distinct linguistic literary traditions (when they are considered at all). But given that the two countries share not only the island of Hispaniola (also known as Quisqueya in the indigenous Taíno language) but also a long, tortuously intertwined history, Maríñez suggests that a new literary methodology that moves beyond national literary frameworks and linguistic divisions in favor of a composite approach better accounts for the complexities of Quisqueyan diaspora literature. Arguing that a too-narrow focus on the diaspora from the Hispanophone Caribbean has obscured the historic literary ties between Haiti and the Dominican Republic, Maríñez calls for an analytic framework that recognizes not only the deep historical imbrication of the twinned nations but also how the common diasporic experience of their migrant writers have created coalitional opportunities not otherwise available within their respective nationalist discourses. In this sense, the tropes of state violence that manifest themselves in the diaspora in works of Haitian American Edwidge Danticat and Dominican American Junot Díaz are less about distinct national histories and more about the racialized definition of each nation in relation to each other.

Lorena Alvarado reminds us that Latina/o literature is deeply enmeshed within specific sonic contexts that define and refine its otherwise logocentric presentation. Afro-Caribbean rhythms, Amerindian tonalities, transculturated Western traditions, and the performative aspects of music in the Americas form a central experiential soundtrack of everyday life for Latinas/os. Focusing upon the presence of various kinds of popular music, both Latin and non-Latin, in Latina/o literary works since the 1980s, Alvarado discusses the sonic presence of the mambo, the Afro-Cuban dance craze in the United States during the 1950s, in several contemporary Latina/o novels. In Mary Helen Ponce's *The Wedding* (1989), the presence of the mambo indicates not only how a Caribbean Latino sound travels into Chicano Los Angeles, but also how gender roles are negotiated in the act of dancing. In Marta Moreno Vega's *When the Spirits Dance Mambo* (2004), the mambo provides working-class Puerto Ricans such as Cotito the opportunity to luxuriate in the splendor of an Afro-Boricua tradition that extended from the local botanica to the Palladium in New York City. Meanwhile, in the Chicago of Achy Obejas's *Memory Mambo* (1996), the signature grunt of famed Cuban bandleader Pérez Prado, uttered while singing the mambo, becomes the key to understanding the familial dynamics of the novel. Finally, Oscar Hijuelos's *The Mambo Kings Play Songs of Love* (1989) offers up a Pulitzer Prize-winning example of a nostalgic, libidinous, and excessively stereotypical Latino masculinity. Indexing a particular kind of experiential knowledge ("earwitnessing"), Alvarado signals exegetic audio elements of Latina/o literature that point beyond the printed page to a fuller account of the audible sensorium of latinidades. The inclusion of sound studies within Latina/o literary studies opens up possibilities of contextualization and understanding to a major aspect of Latina/o cultural production that goes beyond the often exclusive space of print-culture.

While migrants from all over the Hispanophone Americas have gained acceptance under the umbrella of latinidad, this has not always been true for migrants from South America's largest nation, Brazil. Because of historic linguistic balkanization and the historic division between the Lusophone and Hispanic Americas, *Brazuca* (Brazilian American) literature has only recently begun to figure within Latina/o literary studies. Luz Angélica Kirschner examines the case for, and against, including this body of writing in Latina/o literary history. Cultural pride in a specifically Luso-American, rather than Spanish-American, tradition, along with the marked tendency of Latin American literary schools to marginalize Brazilian literature, have contributed to a Brazuca disidentification from diasporic Hispanophone latinidades. Added to this, as Kirschner relates, was the U.S. Census Bureau's explicit rejection of Portuguese and the Lusophone diaspora from the definition of "Hispanic" as a disadvantaged minority group in 1973. Yet simultaneously, Kirschner argues, latinidad in its mid-twentieth-century configuration becomes popularized through two key figures: Desi Arnaz of Cuba and Carmen Miranda of Brazil, suggesting a historical precedent for Brazilians as Latinas/os within the U.S. national imaginary. In the present moment, authors such as Kathleen de Azevedo and Luana Monteiro are among a new generation of Brazuca writers reclaiming this genealogy of latinidades through their works, thus reminding us to take into account the complex history of the Brazilian diaspora's contact with other Latina/o migrants, along with the legacies of plantation slavery that Brazil shares with the United States and Caribbean, as undeniable aspects of Latina/o literary history.

Laura G. Gutíerrez examines how Latina/o cultural production has played a crucial role in interrogating the neoliberal reconfiguration of hemispheric relations since the 1990s, particularly the relationship between Mexico and the United States as redefined by the North American Free Trade Agreement (NAFTA), first implemented in 1994. As Gutíerrez writes, a major preoccupation of contemporary Latina/o performance is the effects of neoliberalism upon bodies as subjected to its disciplining through labor exploitation and the privatization of welfare-state safety mechanisms. Even as Latina/o labor became crucial for the contingent manufacturing and assembly work done in maquiladoras along the U.S.-Mexico border, these bodies themselves became more disposable in this exploitative environment. Nowhere else was this more apparent during the first two decades of NAFTA than in Ciudad Juárez, the twin border city of El Paso, Texas. Several hundred young women were victims of *femicidio*, or brutally murdered through forms of gendered violence, while hundreds of others "disappeared." Border performance artists and theorists such as Venezuelan-born Javier Téllez, Chicana Nao Bustamante, Cuban-born Coco Fusco, Mexican-born artists Astrid Hadad Jesusa Rodriguez and Lorena Wolffer offer critiques of neoliberalist discourses and practices, especially as they impact the well-being of women, even as they acknowledge how their own craft is in part enabled by them.

In his essay, William Orchard explores the contemporary impact of the fast-growing areas of Latina/o genre fiction and graphic novels by contextualizing the production and reception of these academically margin-alized popular forms within the creation of a "Latino" market starting in the 1990s. While thoroughly enmeshed within the neoliberalist individualism of commodity relations, these texts also offer the utopian possibility of imagin-ing other forms of social relations not entirely defined by their market matrix. Orchard provides a useful historical context for the emergence of genre fiction outside the literary mainstream: the ascendency of MFA pro-grams in creative writing often privileged a stylistic realism, while cultural nationalist movements narrowed the character palate to working-class, resist-ant types. Genre fiction offered possibilities outside those demands on both counts, providing an autodidactic, other commercial space to experiment in what literary scholar Ramón Saldívar terms "post-race aesthetics." Chica lit, typified by Alisa Valdes-Rodriguez's *The Dirty Girls Social Club* (2003), allowed for the exploration of upwardly mobile characters but often at the expense of defining them mostly through their relation to consumer goods. Other genres, such as horror or detective fiction, allow for an analysis of the Latina/o condition as the return of the suppressed subaltern/working class or as the difficult search for knowledge in a world of deliberately obscured power relations. Similarly, science fiction, and various forms of speculative fiction, have come to the fore for Latina/o literary studies thanks to Junot Díaz's *The Brief Wondrous Life of Oscar Wao* (2006) and the graphic novels of Los Bros Hernandez. Ultimately, Orchard argues that the antirealist aesthetic of these marginalized genres make them fruitful for reimagining latinidades in the twenty-first century.

Much as previous essays have opened the concept of latinidades to Haitian American and Brazuca writing, the contributions of Latina/o authors whose roots lie in South America is taken up in the chapter by Juanita Heredia. Although not as numerous as those from Central America or the Caribbean, Latina/o writers from Peru, Colombia, Argentina, Chile, Uruguay and other Latin American nations have made significant contributions to expanding the forms, histories, and languages of latinidades, whether depicting the traumas of dictatorship, the effects of civil wars and dirty wars, or the trials of exile in the United States. Writers such as Majorie Agosín, Sergio Waisman, Maria Negroni, Ariel Dorfman, Marie Arana, Luisa Valenzuela, Walter Ventosilla, Patricia Engel, Daniel Alarcón, Daisy Hernández, Jaime Manrique, Carmen Giménez, Fredy Amilcar Roncalla and Carolina de Robertis draw on the diversity of South America from its northern Caribbean shore to the South-ern Cone, from Andean indigenous cultural forms to Borgesian aesthetics, from tango to Quechua, from the role of radio in locating the disappeared to the task of translating between South and North America. Heredia offers a capacious and detailed account of how the complex histories of these distinct, yet intimately interrelated regions have marked contemporary Latina/o literary history.

Claudia Milian theorizes the production of the abject Central American American subject in her contribution. Beginning with a reading of Oscar Martínez's *The Beast: Riding the Rails and Dodging Narcos on the Migrant Trail*, Milian maps out the spatial and temporal transformation of Central American bodies from non-agential citizens of their home countries to paradoxically crucial sources of "migradollars" upon becoming stateless and undocumented in the United States. This transformation occurs via the experience of the "Beast," the grim moniker given the freight train through Mexico that migrants use as dangerous, even deadly, transport to the U.S.–Mexico borderlands. Milian outlines how this process of subjectification, violent and exploitative, comes to define the migrant experience of neoliberal capitalism and its production of abjection before and during its reconstitution as "Latina/o" in a U.S. context. Milian reminds us that the contingency of latinidades within the United States depends upon an entire series of social processes that often cross multiple national borders and legal regimes, each with its own social violence attached to it, before a migrant ever becomes "Latina/o" in the United States.

Latina/o literary history's critical resources range from the submerged knowledges of subaltern Latina/o cultures to traditional "high" theory. Richard Perez builds on Juan Flores's major theoretical contributions to this literary history by examining how U.S. Puerto Rican literature demands a transnational hermeneutic that revalues transnational and diaspora subjectivity, and challenges the dominant ontological framings of the subaltern subject. Drawing on a theoretical toolkit ranging from Levinas to Spivak to decode the wild freedom and beautifully strange and often ironic language of U.S. Puerto Rican literature, Perez observes how the writings of Piri Thomas, Pedro Pietri, Esmeralda Santiago, and Justin Torres call into question the colonial and heteropatriarchal discourses that enable domination on the Island and discrimination in the United States within a common capitalist extractive system. From Thomas's *Down these Mean Streets* comes the realization that the *cara palo*, or hard face, that Piri adopts to combat racial discrimination is the very mask that racism forces him to wear but also the mark of his trans-American positioning. In Pietri's classic Nuyorican poem "Puerto Rican Obituary," the dead are resurrected as a critique of the capitalism that exploits them to death. Santiago's *America's Dream* enacts the colonial relationship between the United States and Puerto Rico that is enforced by patriarchal masculinity but resisted by feminist actions. Perez closes his essay with a reading of Torres's *We the Animals*, in which the condition of youthful "animality" comes to figure the utopian possibilities beyond heteronormative patriarchy as situated in the transnational border crossings of Puerto Ricans off the island. In close readings of these major texts extending from the late twentieth century through the first decade of the twenty-first, Perez finds in "trans-ing" – or the ghostly hauntings of the present by the past – a utopian resource to imagine shared aesthetics, alternative ethical practices, and new forms of desire that move beyond exploitation and silence.

Through a reading influenced by recent Latina/o and Caribbean radical philosophy and postcolonial queer theory, Eliana Ávila closes the volume with a call for a decolonial queer critique of racialized anachronism that reveals her South American perspective on Latina/o literary history. Ávila defines how relations of power naturalize hierarchies by plotting peoples and geopolitical regions linearly, as destined to progress from childlike, non-European, disabled backwardness toward heterosexuality, maturity, and consumerism within a white-dominant cultural norm. Given that this volume marks a kind of entrance into global legibility in English for Latina/o literary history, Ávila's vigilance about how narratives of straight temporality naturalize the epistemic annihilation that assimilation demands is especially salient to this section on Latina/o literature as narratives of migration across the Americas. Reframing post-colonial critique to think beyond "straight time" in order to incorporate a critique of anachronism as a racializing and gendering device, Ávila usefully calls attention to the need for coeval relation and coalitions that consider both the standpoint of displacement and that of rootedness. Through a close reading of Latina texts (Daisy Hernández's *A Cup of Water under My Bed* and Felicia Lemus's *Like Son*) that bring into focus the proliferation of "temporal borderlands" occurring with the denaturalizing of borders, Avila takes up Gloria Anzaldúa's creative liminality and José Esteban Muñoz's queer utopia as a means to imagine futurity for all in ways that do not reproduce the straight time of coloniality.

In the volume's epilogue, María Josefina Saldaña-Portillo contextualizes the disparate and discontinuous elements of the intellectual project that is *The Cambridge History of Latina/o American Literature*. For Saldaña-Portillo, the efforts of the scholars in this volume should not be considered as simply yet another academic exercise, but rather a continuation of the long struggle of Latina/o diasporic intellectuals to transform the production of knowledge within the sites where such production has material effect. Although often situated within institutions deeply implicated in the colonial project, these scholars embark upon this transformative project by linking their study of the literary and, more generally, the aesthetic, to the vernacular, organic know-ledges generated from within the various latinidades that have arisen as a result of the trans-American operations of colonial capitalism.

Saldaña-Portillo and others in the volume single out two eminent Latina/o literary scholars who have made just such major contributions to the field: Juan Flores and José Esteban Muñoz. Their untimely deaths will always raise the question of what further transformative concepts they might have contributed otherwise to the field, and even to this volume, to which they had both agreed to contribute. Thanks to their efforts, and those of many less heralded critics–but no less important–past and present, this volume offers a history of the field of Latina/o literary studies as it theorizes the uncertain, yet-to-be-realized future.

PART I

★

REREADING THE COLONIAL ARCHIVE

Transculturation and Conflict, 1492–1808

I

Indigenous *Herencias*

Creoles, Mestizaje, and Nations before Nationalism

ARTURO ARIAS

The earliest inklings of a Latina/o literary imaginary were forged in the colonial encounters between Spanish settlers, subjected Indigenous peoples, and enslaved Africans as they negotiated the social vortex then known as "the West Indies" (Indias Occidentales). This was a phrase used in the sixteenth century to designate the territories encountered by Columbus when he accidentally ran aground in the Bahamas that fateful evening of October 1492 that scarred forever the wellbeing of hemispheric indigeneity. Claimed subsequently by Spain to differentiate the hemisphere from the "East Indies," those British and Dutch colonial enterprises that competed early on with the Philippines, Spain's sole possession in the area, the "West Indies" are in what we presently know in our time as the Americas.[1] José Rabasa conjectures the invention of America as originating in Columbus's gaze, as it injected an intentionality that came to be realized *ex post facto*.[2] Seen as such, the *sui generis* of the Columbian gaze is an epistemological and *settled* way of seeing, as John Berger would creatively underscore. Under this scrutiny, Indigenous thought unsettles the taken-for-granted quality of what has already been seen, all the while bringing Indigenous humanity and the production of Indigenous thought as evidence of what "they" had been cobbling together and continued to manifest before, during, and well after the ("Latin"/ "American") beginning.

As many know, Columbus's mistake in thinking that he had landed in "the Indies" – that is, present-day India – led to his naming the local inhabitants he encountered and enslaved right away as "indios," that is, as Indians, a loaded

---

[1] The phrase is still used to name a region of the Caribbean Basin and North Atlantic Ocean that includes the many islands and island nations of the Antilles and the Lucayan Archipelago.

[2] See "Intencionalidad, invención y reducción al absurdo en la invención de América," especially the last section entitled "Cuatro tesis para pensar la intencionalidad del mundo americano" (Four theses for thinking about the intentionality of the American world).

trope that has remained highly problematic to this day. Columbus also inaugurated the genocide documented by Dominican friar Bartolome Las Casas (1484–1566) in *The Devastation of the Indies: A Brief Account*, originally written in 1542 in Spain and published a decade later. Whereas the rise of northern European protestant powers in the late seventeenth century erased much of this story, it has been narrated consistently since at least the early 1990s by Native American and Indigenous scholars, among others.

Centering the question of how coloniality staged the conceptual clash of peoples and ideas, this chapter locates the first expressions of transculturation in Latin America within the contact zones created by European colonialism and the subaltern responses that ultimately became a critical element in the forging of contemporary Latina/o identities.[3] My main focus within this perspective will be the argument that indigeneity remains a problematically unanalyzed epistemological basis for latinidad, due to the colonial heritage that – with some notable exceptions such as Gloria Anzaldúa – has pushed Latina/o subjectivities to favor their Spanish heritage over their Indigenous one. The claim of European colonialism to uniquely narrate the encounter between Europeans and Indigenous peoples throughout the Americas underwrites the privileging of colonial ways of knowing and the dismissal of Indigenous ones. Asserting the relevance of these geographies and temporalities, this chapter documents the constellation of colonial and postcolonial relationships even as the Viceroyalties of Mexico and of Peru supplanted the Mexica (Aztec) and Inca Empires in order to provide a longer, more sedimented genealogy of categories and concepts such as "creoles," "mestizaje," "hybridity," and "nations."[4] This heritage from colonial Mexico ultimately scarred US Latinas/os, whether they were descendants of Californios, Tejanos, or from Mexicans or Central Americans of Indigenous descent.

Turning to Indigenous systems of representation, manifested as text and graphics (such as Nahuatl codices) or weavings (such as Inca quipus), allows not only for the examination of Indigenous knowledges as counterweights to colonial European discourses, but also helps in understanding present-day social and symbolic imaginaries. These alternative systems of representation

---

[3] The term "contact zone" was, of course, developed by Mary Louise Pratt in her seminal book *Imperial Eyes: Travel Writing and Transculturation*, where she defined it as "social spaces where cultures meet, clash, and grapple with each other, often in contexts of highly asymmetrical relations of power, such as colonialism, slavery, or their aftermaths as they are lived out in many parts of the world today."

[4] "Aztecs" actually called themselves Mexicas. The name "Aztec" is a subsequent colonial imposition resulting from still one more misunderstanding on the part of Spanish friars trying to interpret the symbolic codes of Mexicans.

anticipate what would become a key aspect of Latina/o literature's trans-American forms of knowledge, which retain metaphorical and subliminal traces of this past in its formal elements, whether poetry, prose, or other genre. In the context of unequal social power, this chapter suggests how the discursive conflict between Spanish narratives of invasion, conquest, and control of Indigenous populations and the counter-narratives put forth by the colonized subjects themselves, deemed incapable of Western rationality, models a key epistemological dynamic of Latina/o literature. Needless to say, this purview falls within what Claudia Milian has labeled the economies of racialized Latinities when establishing "a link in the semiotic lines of race, culture, movement, and geography" (123).

David Theo Goldberg has argued in *The Racial State* (2002) that the hier-archy of indigeneity over African descent originated in the 1550s debate between Bartolome de Las Casas and Juan Ginés de Sepúlveda (1489–1573) over Indigenous enslavement. Las Casas insisted on the salvation of Indigenous souls, endorsing African slavery in the Caribbean Basin, an act for which he later felt responsible. Las Casas uncannily acknowledged his guilt in his *Historia de las Indias*, as Antonio Benítez-Rojo addressed in *The Repeating Island* (1996). The original gesture conferred a racialized hierarchy for the Americas, one that also marked the racial configuration and racialization of modern state power.[5]

---

[5] By way of literary example, Brazilian modernism articulated Mário de Andrade's *Macunaíma* as a foundational myth to configure Brazilian subjectivity, rather than the history of Zumbí dos Palmares, the leader of the *quilombo* rebellion. In Cuba, indigenous leader Hatuey still plays a foundational symbolic role in the island's genealogy of being, as opposed to any *cimarrón* leader, and Martí eclipses the figure of Antonio Maceo. Bolívar's mulatto-ness was "whitified" when representations of the Liberator become iconic through the continent during the second half of the nineteenth century. Bolivar's "whitification" established a racial hierarchy in most Andean countries. Brazil's Machado de Assis is perhaps the only Latin American writer who was born black and died as a white man, given the Brazilian understanding that only a "white" man could have been the founder of the Academia Brasileira de Letras (Brazilian Academy of Letters). Machado de Assis's birth certificate says that he was born "black." His death certificate states that he died "white." His whiteness is associated here with rise in social standing, prestige, and recognition that he was the founder of the Academia Brasileira de Letras. The phantasm of Sarmiento's racial hierarchy in *Facundo* (1845) constitutes this world's terms of reference, if we conceive, above all, this phantasm as answering the need to articulate a dispersed cultural tradition on a body, what Cuban novelist Alejo Carpentier calls the *desajuste* between the experienced reality and the interpret-ative grid. Finally, when Cuban poet Roberto Fernández Retamar attempted in *Calibán* (1971) to refute José Enrique Rodó's idealization of a Europeanist Ariel by presenting the "cannibal" figure in *The Tempest* as an African alternative, he did so out of his under-standing that the indigenous subject in Latin America was the West's privileged interlocutor, whereas the African descendant was not. Retamar introduced a reading that linked Caliban primarily to the African presence in the Caribbean vis-à-vis Fanon's deconstruction of this Shakespearean character's Eurocentric readings.

A question that grows out of these historical annotations and that the reader should critically take cognizance of is: what conditions have given rise to creative imaginations from Indigenous perspectives? This is one of the many possible outcomes of Peruvian sociologist Aníbal Quijano's concept of the coloniality of power. The coloniality of power incorporates domination and racialization to the known factor of colonialism as a critical dimension of modernity. Quijano's idea speaks to how colonized peoples were subalternized during the centuries of colonization. A caste system was implemented: Spaniards were originally ranked at the top and those they had conquered at the bottom due to different phenotypic traits and a culture presumed to be inferior.[6]

A case in point would be the naming of the Yucatán Peninsula, as one emblematic example of this process. Dennis Tedlock tracks the origin of Yucatán's name to Francisco Hernández de Córdoba's 1517 expedition (239). Tedlock directs our attention to how Hernández de Córdoba,

> thinking to learn something about the land that lay beyond the shore, he heard the fishermen say something he wrote down as "Yucatán." What they actually said was *k'i ut'an*, which means, "'The way he talks is funny.'" (239)

Regardless of whether Tedlock's narrative is true or apocryphal, bearing in mind that at least two supplemental versions exist, all of these summaries rehash a linguistic misunderstanding on the Spaniards' part.[7] Tedlock's claim about the name, an imaginative though somewhat silly social construction, is emblematic of linguistic misunderstandings and a series of cognate traditions that erase the continent's native names, as Walter Mignolo points out.[8] This speculative topography, combined with Spanish arrogance and recalcitrance, accounts for the geographical denominations of a good portion of the Americas. Geographical names represent the remnants of colonial projects embedded in the Americas' contemporary existence, much as Spanish names in Texas, California, and the rest of the US Southwest operate in analogous fashion, evoking an originary Latina/o presence. All of these are seemingly innocent signs, apparently devoid of signification. But they carry within their semantics the stain and the trace of past (and present) genocidal and imperial

---

[6] See Quijano's "Coloniality and Modernity/Rationality."
[7] The other two versions are that a Spaniard explorer asked a Maya what that land was named, and he responded *Ma'anaatik ka t'ann*, which means, "I don't understand your language, or, how you're speaking." The third, if we were to consider Tedlock's the first, would be that the Maya who was interpellated answered *Ci u t'ann*, which means, "I don't understand."
[8] *The Darker Side of the Renaissance* and *Local Histories/Global Designs*.

campaigns. These gestures cohere with institutionalized hierarchies foreign to the country's reality that evidence the nature of coloniality as a refusal to contest the patterns of knowledge (or silliness) imposed by the West.

For that matter, Peninsular (i.e., Yucatán) Mayas, as was the case of Mayas in Guatemala, had written literature not only prior to the arrival of Spaniards, but also during the colonial period. Crucial to this order is, of course, the *Popol Wuj*, the heart of the Mesoamerican cultural matrix. The *Popol Wuj* creates an alternative macro-narrative to the Western bible. It tells the story of creation in a fashion that conflates the origins of all Mesoamerican peoples in one foundational discourse. During the Spanish Conquest, Indigenous peoples endured the destruction of their cities and their cultures, the rape of their women, and the enslavement of their men; within fifty years following the event, they had lost approximately 86 percent of their total population. Those who survived were forced to accommodate their perception of the world to new cultural and social realities. But the *Popol Wuj* became the foundational manifesto of resistance. It was originally written around the 1540s in K'iche' Maya, but employing a Latin alphabet. A debate continues over the text's authority/authoredness, but one thing is clear: after the holocaust of the Spanish Conquest, surviving Maya-K'iche' leaders/ priests of the Kavek lineage sensed their imminent extermination. The need to leave a trace of their peoples' experience on Earth became urgent. Much as their classic ancestors had done by carving glyphs on stelae to record their deeds and history with astronomical associations, they chose to leave a testimony to explain their origins and their culture. The *Popol Wuj* offers an account of the pre-creation of the world in the twins' victory over the lords of the underworld, Xibalbá. The text continues with the world's creation, the fashioning from maize of the first humans, signaling the emanation of the K'iche' people, followed by the history of their rulers up until the Spaniards' arrival. The *Popol Wuj* empowered those rulers to make claims while under Spanish rule. Most importantly, K'iche' leaders declare that they received the insignia and gifts of Quetzalcoatl/Kukulkán, the feathered serpent, the highest deity in the cosmos, god of arts and culture. In other words, the *Popol Wuj* claims that the K'iche' Maya were the chosen ones, the apogee of human civilization, and that the Spaniards were simply the barbarians who won the war. As a caveat to this statement, we should recall that, as we know it, this text is already born in a colonial semiosis, where the written letter, the Latin alphabet, is employed for the first time both to name a non-Western referent – K'iche'-Maya significations – and to occlude the vaporous condition of the original, an oral text performed before audiences for thousands of years. We have to nuance the quasi-celebratory mantle placed over this seemingly urtext, emerging from a zone where the aura of the other, and of otherness, has been smothered.

The *Books of Chilam Balam* were written as early as the seventeenth century, though most appeared in the eighteenth.[9] William F. Hanks states in *Converting Words* that the *Books of Chilam Balam* were not simply preservations of a mystical past, but texts that were partially shaped by what he labels *Maya reducido*, meaning by this a "revised and reordered language fitted to the discursive practices of an emerging community of Christian Indios" (5–7).[10] However, even if Hanks is right, this did not impede the spread of this colonial variant of Maya language beyond its originary religious purposes, nor its use as a tool of resistance. After all, any language may gesture to multiple points of reference. For example, read alongside doctrinal works, the *Books of Chilam Balam* clearly may be understandable as partial products of the process of *reducción de indios* because repetitive discursive practices bring about the internalization of any new language.[11] However, in the course of iteration and reiteration, linguistic usage, while turning into habit, also becomes self-replicating. At this stage, so do the language's forms of intelligibility. This enables linguistic signs to acquire the capability of moving beyond the confines of religion, reconfiguring meanings in secular life.

After independence from Spain, most Latin American elites mobilized their own biased "understandings" of heroic stories of local Indigenous peoples to highlight the identitary cohesion of their own nation so as to gain the upper hand over pro-Spanish sectors during the nascent power struggles of the emerging nations. Latin American independence ideologues, heavily influenced by French Enlightenment thinking, exercised quasi-total intellectual hegemony, and enjoyed enormous political respect, benefiting from the

---

[9] "Books" appear in the plural, because nine of them are known, all different, though all claim to be the mouthpiece, or to have been written, by a legendary author called, or labeled with the name of, *Chilam Balam*. *Chilam* means a diviner, a religious figure specialized in prophecies. *Balam* denominates a jaguar, a common surname in the Mayab', given that jaguars were the most sacred animals in the Mesoamerican region alongside the snake.

[10] Hanks explores what he labels "commensuration." That is, the process by which Spanish words were brought into alignment with Maya words by missionaries, in such a way that Spanish meanings managed to resignify Maya lexical forms, creating the resulting traits of *Maya reducido*. Hanks traces the creation of this "translanguage," as he codifies it, into morphology and syntax. See *Converting Words*, chapters 5 and 6.

[11] *Indios reducidos* were those native peoples gathered into towns (pueblos) to transform their habits, dispositions, and beliefs so as to turn them into Christian subjects of the Spanish crown.

explicatory power of the "lettered city." The phrase "lettered city" was conceived by Uruguayan critic Angel Rama, to highlight the central role that colonial cities in Latin America played in deploying and reproducing the power of written discourse. In Rama's understanding, the Iberian monarchs planned cities where institutional and legal powers were administered through a specialized cadre of elite men called *letrados*, to impose their hegemonic vision and colonial design on their empire. *Letrados* – which included the journalists, fiction writers, essayists, and political leaders of the nineteenth century – were not competing with ideologues because they were the ideologues themselves, the producers of symbolic capital. *Letrados* were for the most part *criollos*, full-blooded Spaniards born in the Latin American colonies. They were the early protagonists of national public spheres. Described by Román de la Campa as intellectuals whose "lust for power" cohabited with "isolated acts of literary transgression" (74), they intervened to legitimize exemplary narratives of national formation and integration in the process of constructing the nation itself as a symbolic entity, constituting its national imaginaries through discourses, symbols, images, and rites. Nineteenth-century literary production, then, established an ideological hegemony that interpellated individuals and transformed them into subjects who identified with the discursive formation named by the *letrado*. They were the first to imagine Indigenous tropes and traits that articulated the collective imaginaries and symbolic codes framed in variously written cultural manifestations with their political, historical, and social context. It enabled them to combat Spanish colonial discourses and insert Enlightenment ideas – including those of the "noble Savage" – in their place. We could cite Mexico's first novelist José Joaquín Fernández de Lizardi, Venezuelan poet Andrés Bello, and Central American philosopher José Cecilio del Valle as examples of its earliest exponents. All of them incorporated indigenousness – as perceived from an elite Eurocentric perspective – within their literary output and political manifestos. This same model launched Latino writing in Texas, as Raúl Coronado has shown in *A World Not to Come: A History of Latino Writing and Print Culture*, noting how Spanish Americans in Texas used writing as a means to establish new sources of authority, and how a Latino literary and intellectual life was born in the New World. Coronado claims that Texas Mexicans devolved from an elite colonial community to a racialized group whose voices were annihilated by the war of 1848, but he understands this process of racialization as the birth of an emergent Latino culture and literature.

I wish also to underscore that this plotting of Latino literature's Indigenous heritage requires attention to dates and details that are particular to Latin

America's national political alliances and ideologies and their impact on subaltern subjects and literary praxis. The events narrated here allow for intricate openings concerning the cultural role by motley immigrant generations who, becoming "Latino" after settling in the United States, have struggled to voice and preserve Indigenous languages and literary production, and for even more contradictory representations of indigeneities or Indigenous tropes within what we now label Latina/o literatures.

Following this logic, we can rightfully claim that, since the 1800s, Latin American thinkers have produced a certain kind of knowledge that articulates the collective imaginaries and symbolic codes framed in variously written cultural manifestations with their political, historical and social context, in much the way Coronado asserts that *letrados* from throughout Spanish America came together through their "shared language and Spanish-American creole cultural heritage" (369), linked by a "sense of cultural-linguistic solidarity" (392). Thus, we always have to understand Latina/o cultural issues in in a broader trans-American sense, including those implications associated with indigeneity, especially the violence that accompanied the racializing and "othering" of Indigenous subjects throughout North America and Mesoamerica in the 500 years that followed the Spanish invasion of the continent.

Another factor to be considered in this heritage is, inevitably violence. Violence is not random, as we know. All types of violence, national and corporate as well as intra-ethnic, configure the distinctiveness of the United States as a modern nation-state. Consequently, it produces a logic of repression that remains often unsaid, but always traumatic for those who suffer it. Nicole Guidotti-Hernández underlines how "trauma manifests itself in people's behavior, in both the physical body and the psyche," and argues that the inability to reckon with the intertwined histories of the United States and Mexico "forecloses the possibility of reconciliation because individuals and nations on one side of the equation are not willing to take responsibility for the violence" (7). For her, these violent and traumatic events were overdetermined by racialized paradigms. In consequence, it is inevitable that peoples from those countries involved must return to these shared histories to identify both the traces and the practices of violence as the locus reconfiguring white epistemological dominance.

Latin American intellectuals undoubtedly began to focus on continental issues rather than national ones in response to the US expansion into the Caribbean Basin as a result of the US–Spanish War of 1898. This crucial event took place fifty years after Mexico was forced to cede the present-day states of California, Nevada, Utah, and parts of Colorado, Arizona, New Mexico, and Wyoming – losing more than 500,000 square miles, or about 40 percent of its territory – in the US–Mexican War of 1846–1848, an event soon followed by the 1855 occupation of Nicaragua by filibuster William Walker, who invaded that country and proclaimed himself president. The more aggressive entrance of the United States into the Latin American sphere in 1898 initiated a new era of difficult hemispheric North–South relations. US President Theodore Roosevelt justified this intervention with the Roosevelt Corollary to the Monroe Doctrine, which implied that the United States could step into Latin America at will, on the pretext of preventing interventions by European nations. When Nicaragua threatened to build a trans-isthmus canal to compete with the then-under-construction Panama Canal, the United States occupied the country (1909). The US Marines would stay until 1933 in just one of a series of US military interventions throughout Latin America and the Caribbean, including Cuba, the Dominican Republic, Haiti, Puerto Rico, and Panama.

This foreign policy poisoned US–Latin America relations during most of the twentieth century. José Martí had anticipated this move in *Nuestra América* when he signaled the danger of appropriating knowledges that had not been created to solve the problems of Latin American postcolonial societies as explicatory power for thinking through turn-of-the-century postcoloniality. In the wake of the Spanish-American War, José Enrique Rodó's *Ariel* (1900) emerged as an attempt to explain the cultural and metaphysical differences between North American and Latin American cultures. Warning against *nordomanía*, or the attraction of North America to debilitated, effete souls, this essay associated the Anglo-Saxon subjectivity with the negative, materialist, and utilitarian tendencies embodied by Caliban in Shakespeare's *The Tempest*. By contrast, Latin Americans were represented by the positive, utopian ideals of Ariel. Rodó saw in this symbol the spiritual and intellectual unity of Latin America with Spain and Europe, figured by Ariel, from the same play, a character capable of sacrificing material gain for spiritual concerns. Rodó's critique, flaws notwithstanding, described an articulation of postcoloniality wherein the residues of colonial domination had seeped into the post-independence state. This also created a reclamation of anticolonial resistance, which would frame the grand narrative of Latin American cultural studies' self-constituting genealogy.

Building on this legacy of signifiers as markers of "meaning," Alfonso Reyes attempted in *Visión de Anáhuac* (1917) to reconfigure a fractured post-revolutionary Mexican identity by reconciling and blending pre-Columbian and modern-day Mexican cultures. With the Dominican critic Pedro Henrí-quez Ureña and fellow Mexicans Antonio Caso and José Vasconcelos, Reyes founded the *Ateneo de la Juventud* (Atheneum of Youth). This joint effort would pave the way both for the emerging notion of *mestizaje* and for the elaboration of a cultural aesthetics. The first, originally articulated in *Visión de Anáhuac*, would find its highest expression in Vasconcelos's *La raza cósmica* (1925), where the idealized image of *mestizaje* as an end-of-history "cosmic race" inaugurates a contentious site of nation building and racial politics. The second, prefigured in Reyes's *Cuestiones estéticas* (1911), would be achieved by Henríquez Ureña's systematization of cultural production in *Seis ensayos en busca de nuestra expresión* (1928), *Literary Currents in Hispanic America* (1945), and *Historia de la cultura en la América Hispánica* (1947). In these works, Henríquez Ureña conceives of Latin American literary production, organized for the first time into a coherent whole, in terms of what Mignolo has more recently labeled the history of the modern/colonial world, in an attempt to understand the historical formation and ethno-racial conformation of the continent. Thus, despite appearances, Henríquez Ureña's vast *oeuvre* is not strictly literary criticism, but a mapping of the "frame" of Latin American cultural production and a history of how literature becomes the primary means for the conformation of an epistemological subjectivity within the various nations of the continent. Like many contemporary practitioners of cultural studies, Henríquez Ureña worked, in Julio Ramos's words, "in the interstitial site of the essay, with transdisciplinary devices and ways of knowledge" (36).

In *Notas sobre la inteligencia Americana* (1937) and *Posición de América* (1942), Reyes would return to issues of *mestizo* subjectivity by rearticulating another variable of cultural fusion of Western and Indigenous values. He did not escape the "ethnocentric and reverse-ethnocentric benevolent double bind" (Spivak, 118) that effectively denies Indigenous peoples their own "worlding" as Vasconcelos had not either, though he avoids the latter's missteps. Vasconcelos ultimately re-wove the threads of colonialism into his national narrative, whereas Reyes remained critical of European positionality and argued for an American identity constructed in opposition to what we would presently label "Eurocentrism." If these debates were about Indigenous *herencias* in which Indigenous scholars did not yet participate, we have to remember once more José Rabasa's words that when Indigenous subjects "choose to remain outside the state and history" (4), their own strategies "cannot be comprehended ... by the state" (5), that is, by the implied Western reader. But we should also add that Indigenous scholars emerged in significant numbers only during the second half of the twentieth century, and have begun to be taken seriously, and quoted, only since the turn of the twenty-first century.

It is also in this same logic we should understand Gloria Anzaldúa's concept of *nepantla*, that liminal stage for which the entire Borderlands stand as a trope. Anzaldúa gained primary fame for introducing the concept of *mestizaje* in her book *Borderlands/La Frontera: The New Mestiza* (1987) to US academic audiences, reformulating it with a feminist/queer twist that criticized heteronormativity, colonialism, and male dominance, while calling for a "new mestiza." This foundational text also enfranchised Indigenous *herencias* within Latina/o cultural production. Anzaldúa's work was key in Mignolo's development of decolonial thinking.[12] *Nepantla* is a Nahuatl word often articulated by Mexicas (Aztecs) during the sixteenth century to explain how they felt in their own post-invasion situation, a term to be explained in the next paragraph. The concept was recuperated by the foundational scholar of contemporary Nahua studies, Miguel León-Portilla.[13] It stands for the land in the middle, an in-between space where liminality enables subjects to become aware of issues or perceptions from two different angles. Anzaldúa considered it a space of renovation, a logic derived directly from Indigenous thinking. As a zone where one can reflect critically upon normative belief systems, Anzaldúa labeled it the third eye that is capable of looking inward and outward. Indeed, *Nepantla* is also one of the seven stages of what she called "the path of *conocimiento* – a personal epistemological path based on seven stages of awareness or reflective consciousness" (135).[14] One of the most substantive contributions of Anzaldúa has also been the introduction of Indigenous thought and spirituality into the Latina/o conceptual world.

Regarding the debate of the usage of the term "invasion" as opposed to "conquest," the invasion of the Americas was labeled a "conquest" by the Spaniards themselves. The term became a traditional trope to describe this

---

[12] Mignolo uses Anzaldúa's categories to develop his own concept of border gnosis in *Local Histories/Global Designs: Coloniality, Subaltern Knowledges and Border Thinking* (1999), and briefly coedited an academic journal titled *Nepantla: Views From the South*.

[13] See "Introduction to Part III: The Intersection of Contemporary Latin American Art and Religion" (2014) by Charlene Villasenor Black and *Conquests and Historical Identities in California, 1769–1936* (1996) by Lisbeth Haas. The latter adds that Leon-Portilla describes how conquered indigenous peoples created their own "in between" culture.

[14] "Nepantla, Spiritual Activism, New Tribalism: Chicana Feminist Transformative Pedagogies and Social Justice Education."

tragic episode during the colonial period as a victory, and simply survived on its own momentum after independence from Spain in the nineteenth century. However, Bolivian Aymara intellectual Fausto Reinaga (1906–1994) produced an enormous body of literature addressing the critical themes of twentieth-century indigeneities: race, nation, and colonialism, emphasizing non-Western perspectives. *La revolución india* (1969; Indian Revolution) argued – among other things – that Indigenous peoples of the Americas should stop using the Spanish triumphalist term "conquest," and label it for what it was: an invasion of their nations and territories. Bolivian Aymara leader Takir Mamani, who founded the Tupaj Katari Indigenous Movement in 1978, suggested Indigenous and decolonial thinkers use the term "invasion" instead of the Spanish term "conquest." This trend became dominant in the first decade of the twenty-first century and was adopted by Indigenous political organizations at the II Continental Meeting of the Peoples and Nations of Abya Yala in Quito, Ecuador, in 2004.[15] Decolonial studies mark the Spanish invasion of the Americas in 1492 as the initial assertion of the centrality and supremacy of European knowledge. It is the first marker and constitutive element of modernity. In the wake of the Spanish invasion of the Americas, native peoples were required, if possible, or if it was legal, to gain knowledge of European languages to obtain minimum rights and articulate basic claims.

Yet, colonialization's effects have lingered, explaining the cultural imprint of negative tropes of indigeneity among elite Latin Americans, such as the infamous "Mongolian spot" that marked the center of *mestizo* literariness in countries with sizable Indigenous populations such as Guatemala, Peru, Bolivia, and southern Mexico, during the end of the nineteenth and early twentieth centuries as an epistemic metaphor of the trace of indigeneity among *mestizos*, a visible sign of their inferiority complex in relation to "whiteness," inevitably marking an Indigenous inheritance that they would prefer to hide and deny.[16] It was this entire problematical package that informs the framework of Latina/o literature in the United States.

[15] See "Abya Yala" in *Clubensayos*, May 27, 2014. www.clubensayos.com/Historia/Abya-Yala/1749360.html. The name "Abya Yala" for the Latin American continent was adopted in the same meeting. The phrase, from the Kuna language, means "land in its full maturity," or "land of vital blood."

[16] Regarding the Mongolian spot in question, Dr. Erwin Bälz (1849–1913) was a German internist, anthropologist, and personal physician of the Japanese Imperial family. In 1885 he published a paper in a German anthropological journal calling attention to an unrecorded feature among Japanese babies. They are often born with a dark blue stain, low down on the back that gradually fades and disappears after about a year. Bälz called

There is no need to reproduce in this chapter the history of *mestizo* violence against Indigenous populations in Mesoamerica. Enough has been said by many critics, myself included. Ongoing racism against Indigenous migrants in the United States, remains, however, very understudied. This is why emerging contributions by academics who have studied this phenomenon, such as sociologists Nancy Wellmeier, Cecilia Menjívar, and Eric Popkin, among others, or by young Central American–American scholars of Maya origin such as Giovanni Batz, are invaluable. Indeed, testimonies or collected memoirs from Guatemalan migrants in the Southern California area and those academic articles or books addressing Maya immigrant issues in the United States are indicative of a problematic trend.[17] Whereas it is well known that Mayas are migrating at least in equal proportion to *mestizo* Guatemalans, the de facto apartheid between both groups is reproduced when they settle in the United States. *Mestizos* and Mayas rarely, if at all, socialize in this country, even when acquainted with members of the other ethnic group in the workplace. In a recent article, US Maya scholar Giovanni Batz states, "Being Maya in Los Angeles has less severe consequences but is still marked by marginalization, repression, and discrimination" (195).[18] Batz adds that migrant Mayas face pressure to adapt to a dominant Latino environment that discriminates against Maya customs, making Indigenous presence in the area – and elsewhere in the United States – virtually invisible in public spaces and institutions:

> Despite the presence of many indigenous communities in Los Angeles, indigenous identity is almost nonexistent in many public spaces and

the stain *Mongolische Flecken*, Mongolian spots, and associated it with all peoples he thought were of Mongolian origin. This label stuck with indigenous peoples, who indeed were born with a purplish spot in the small of the back. In Guatemala, this led to a widespread fear of being born with one. The Mongolian spot has, thus, remained an invisible scar, a phantasm of an ethnic inferiority complex on the part of Mestizos to this day, pointing to their difficulty in constituting themselves as a hegemonic class. Racial inferiority complexes such as this one continue to mark Mestizos' everyday lives, as witnessed by the importance of "looking European" in many of these same societies to this day.

[17] The publications are too numerous to list. Books alone include *Guatemala-U.S. Migration: Transforming Regions* (2014) by Susanne Jonas and Nestor Rodríguez; *The Maya of Morganton: Work and Community in the Nuevo New South* (2003) by Leon Fink; *The Maya Diaspora: Guatemalan Roots, New American Lives* (2000) by James Loucky and Marilyn M. Moors; *Deciding to Be Legal: A Maya Community in Houston* (1994) by Jacqueline Maria Hagan; and *Maya in Exile: Guatemalans in Florida* (1993) by Allan Burns. This list does not exhaust the topic in question.

[18] "Maya Cultural Resistance in Los Angeles: The Recovery of Identity and Culture among Maya Youth."

institutions. Discrimination against the Maya by their compatriots and other Latinos, coupled with high rates of undocumented immigration, has contributed to this invisibility. Some Maya parents view the lack of a strong indigenous identity among their children as the source of a lack of respect for elders, violence, individualism, and misbehavior. (195)

He adds that derogatory expressions "such as *no seas indio* (don't be an Indian) or *cara de indio* (Indian-face) are still heard" (198). Wellmeier mentions that Q'anjob'ales from Santa Eulalia created the Fraternidad Ewulense Maya Q'anjob'al (FEMAQ') in the late 1980s in order to incorporate Maya spirituality in their religious practices as a mechanism to resist the dilution of their ethnic identity (100). This sociological evidence has yet to translate into significant Latina/o cultural production, but it is most certainly a trace that haunts most of the latter. *El Norte* (1983) featured two Maya leading characters, brother and sister Enrique and Rosa, yet the plot's emphasis falls more on the need to flee from military repression in Guatemala. More recently, *La jaula de oro* (2013) includes a Maya Tsotsil teenager named Chauk joining Ladino Guatemalans in their effort to reach the US border, but the film's focus is on their bonding as individuals as they pursue their immigrant dream. These are all evidence of the "internal multiple Souths and their crossovers to other contexts, communities, and maps" (125) in Milian's terms. Indeed, most Latinas/os in the United States continue to perceive Indigenous subjects, and their cultural heritage, as if they were Fanon's *damnés de la terre*.

In this logic, Puerto Rican scholar Nelson Maldonado-Torres has named as the *ego conquiro*, a category he attributes to Mignolo.[19] Maldonado-Torres argues:

> Enrique Dussel states that Hernán Cortés gave expression to an ideal of subjectivity that could be defined as the *ego conquiro*, which predates René Descartes's articulation of the *ego cogito* ... The certainty of the self as a conqueror, of its tasks and missions, preceded Descartes's certainty about the self as a thinking substance (*res cogitans*) ... The *ego conquiro* is not questioned, but rather provides the ground for the articulation of the *ego cogito*. (244–45)

Racialized and subalternized, Indigenous peoples began to live under a permanent suspicion regarding their very humanity. This sixteenth-century articulation rendered an imperial attitude that promoted a genocidal mindset,

[19] See "On the Coloniality of Being: Contributions to the Development of a Concept," note 3.

marking colonialized and racialized subjects as dispensable (246). Modern colonialism can thus be understood as a damnation, a living hell characterized by the naturalization of slavery:

> Coloniality is an order of things that put people of color under the murderous and rapist sight of a vigilant ego. And the primary targets of rape are women. But men of color are also seen through these lenses. Men of color are feminized and become for the *ego conquiro* fundamentally penetrable subjects.   (247–48)

Maldonado-Torres characterizes this attitude as the beginning of a certain form of violence, because it constitutes a "racist/imperial Manichean misanthropic skepticism," that is, the imperial attitude that configures the Eurocentric modern Imperial Man. This attitude, in turn, will point in the direction of "a fundamentally genocidal attitude in respect to colonized and racialized peoples. Through this process, he adds, "colonial and racial subjects are marked as dispensable" (246). This attitude naturalizes war, conquest, and slavery. In the process, it also naturalizes the form of violence justified as a means for disposing of that which originally belonged to others. That is, the West creates an ontological differentiation as a nested set of abstractions to justify imperial goals, differentiating qualitatively between conquering European men, in opposition to those others situated outside of the purview of allegedly superior Christian religion and culture, and attributes to the latter's lack, or absence, an "innate" inferiority. Under these premises, violence became normative in the modern world. However, as Maldonado-Torres notes, before it became "constitutive of a new reigning episteme" (247), it normalized relations between colonizers, Indigenous peoples, and black slaves, because war-like behavior emerged as the norm, without observing, needless to say, the codes of ethics that governed inter-European wars.

The justification for violence was anchored on the fact that colonialism enables the conceptualization of Indigenous peoples and African slaves as inferior to conquering European subjects. This ontological naturalization of racism operated at the center of the everyday violence that governed even the smallest of domestic events. Colonialism radicalized and naturalized the exercise of everyday violence. Indeed, Richard Trexler (1995: 60–81) had already pointed out in *Sex and Conquest* that Spaniards feminized their enemies in warfare, and they often raped both the men and the women they conquered. Racialization thus also naturalizes the daily exercise of violence in relation to gender, sex, and color.

In this logic, Latina/o literatures bring, in Andreotti, Ahenakew, and Cooper's words, "a temporary state of cognitive dissonance and destabilization"

(46) with the phantasmatic presence of indigeneity. Ultimately, Latina/o literatures evidence that those sites under construction in the US Latina/o imaginary still remain – as well they should – as approximations to a vast and complex challenge that still requires multiple strategies and interventions. As Indigenous subjects move toward nomadic and migrant spaces, they continue to be racialized, clearly marking the end of any remnant of multiculturalism. Indigenous migrants are exposed to the racism manifested by other Latino a/o communities as well. Latina/o literatures dramatically shift those cartographies always in need of being redrafted, as Milian states when speaking of "Central Americanness as a site of neglected multiple subjectivities and geographies that move and alter" (148). Identitarian categories inevitably mutate in manifold directions, however evanescent these may be. They can slide beyond latinidad itself, toward other identitary directions whose shared connectivity is still the heritage of colonialism. Indigenous subjects remain ever more vulnerable to US sovereign power but also to its deployment by racialized others as a form of structuring violence that has become internal to the ontological naturalization of racism by virtue of colonialism's enabling even those others located at the bottom of the heap – "brown Guatepeorians" in Milian's terms – to conceive of themselves as residual non-subjects condemned to social forms of nonexistence, abandoned by the law, exposed, and threatened on the threshold of entering the political body, treated as mere biological residues bereft of legal protections of citizenship in Agamben's terms (28–29). Indigenous migrants are indeed "bare life without bare habitance" as Mark Rifkin labels this in "Indigenizing Agamben" (94). Their very existence enables Latinas/os to articulate that other common Mesoamerican saying, "*mejor pobre que indio*" (better a poor *mestizo* than an Indian). This is because, as Mary Weismantel has observed in a different context, the allegedly "white" elites "pull the circle of whiteness inwards towards themselves" (326). Coloniality thus remains at play when *mestizo* subjects feel shame at embodying indigeneity, resent it, and do their best to hide its heritage. Transforming these racialized attitudes remains the great challenge of the present and the future.

WORKS CITED

Agamben, Giorgio. *Homo Sacer: Sovereign Power and Bare Life*. Daniel Heller Roazen (Trans.). Stanford, CA: Stanford University Press, 1998.

Andreotti Vanessa, Cash Ahenakew and Garrick Cooper. "Epistemological Pluralism: Ethical and Pedagogical Challenges in Higher Education." *AlterNative: An International Journal of Indigenous Peoples* 7, 1 (2011): 40–50.

Anonymous. *Chilam Balam of Chumayel*. México DF: UNAM, 1941.

Anzaldúa, Gloria. *Borderlands/La Frontera: The New Mestiza*. San Francisco: Aunt Lute Books, 1987.

Batz, Giovanni. "Maya Cultural Resistance in Los Angeles: The Recovery of Identity and Culture among Maya Youth." *Latin American Perspectives* 41, 3 (May 2014): 194–207.

Benítez-Rojo, Antonio. *The Repeating Island: The Caribbean and the Postmodern Perspective*. Durham, NC: Duke University Press, 1996.

Berger, John. *Ways of Seeing*. London: Penguin, 1972.

Casas, Bartolome de las. *The Devastation of the Indies: A Brief Account*. Herma Briffault (Trans.). Bill M. Donovan (Intro.). Baltimore: Johns Hopkins University Press, 1992.

Coronado, Raúl. *A World Not to Come: A History of Latino Writing and Print Culture*. Cambridge, MA: Harvard University Press, 2013.

De la Campa, Román. *Latin Americanism*. Minneapolis: University of Minnesota Press, 1999.

Goldberg, David Theo. *The Racial State*. Oxford: Blackwell, 2002.

Guidotti-Hernández, Nicole M. *Unspeakable Violence: Remapping U.S. and Mexican National Imaginaries*. Durham, NC: Duke University Press, 2011.

Hanks, William F. *Converting Words: Maya in the Age of the Cross*. Berkeley: University of California Press, 2010.

Henríquez Ureña, Pedro. *Seis ensayos en busca de nuestra expresión. Obra Crítica*. Ed. Emma S. Speratti Piñero. Mexico: Fondo de Cultura Económica, 1960.

Literary Currents in Hispanic America. Cambridge, MA: Harvard University Press, 1945.

Las corrientes literarias en la América Hispánica. Mexico: Fondo de Cultura Económica, 1945.

Historia de la cultura en la América Hispánica. Mexico: Fondo de Cultura Económica, 1947.

Maldonado-Torres, Nelson. "On the Coloniality of Being: Contributions to the Development of a Concept." *Cultural Studies* 21, 2 (2007): 240–70.

Martí, José. *Nuestra América*, Volumen 15. Caracas: Biblioteca Ayacucho, 1977.

Menjívar, Cecilia. "Living in Two Worlds? Guatemalan-Origin Children in the United States and Emerging Transnationalism." *Journal of Ethnic and Migration Studies* 28 (2002): 531–52.

Mignolo, Walter D. *The Darker Side of the Renaissance: Literacy, Territoriality, & Colonization*. Ann Arbor: University of Michigan Press, 1995.

Milian, Claudia. *Latining America: Black-Brown Passages and the Coloring of Latino/a Studies*. Athens: University of Georgia Press, 2013.

Popkin, Eric. "The Emergence of Pan-Mayan Ethnicity in the Guatemalan Transnational Community Linking Santa Eulalia and Los Angeles." *Current Sociology* 53 (2005): 675–706.

Pratt, Mary Louise. *Imperial Eyes: Travel Writing and Transculturation*. London: Routledge, 1992.

Quijano, Aníbal. "Colonialidad y Modernidad/Racionalidad." *Perú Indígena* 13, 29 (1991): 11–20.

Rabasa, José. "Intencionalidad, invención y reducción al absurdo en la invención de América." *Nuevo Mundo Mundos Nuevos*. Workshops 2012: 2. Réinvention de l'histoire coloniale. http://nuevomundo.revues.org/63440?lang=en

Without History: Subaltern Studies, The Zapata Insurgency, and the Spectre [?] of History. Pittsburgh, PA: University of Pittsburgh Press, 2010.

Rama, Angel (1984). *La ciudad letrada*. Hanover, NH: Ediciones del Norte.

Ramos, Julio. "The Trial of Alberto Mendoza: Paradoxes of Subjectification." *Journal of Latin American Cultural Studies* 7, 1 (1998): 36–54.

Reinaga, Fausto. *La revolución india*. La Paz: Ediciones PIB, 1969.

Reyes, Alfonso. *Visión de Anáhuac*. Mexico: Fondo de Cultura Económica, 1956.
  Notas sobre la inteligencia Americana. Mexico: Fondo de Cultura Económica, 1955.
  Posición de América. Mexico: Nueva Imagen, 1982.

Rifkin, Mark. "Indigenizing Agamben: Rethinking Sovereignty in Light of the 'Peculiar' Status of Native Peoples." *Cultural Critique* 74 (Fall 2009): 88–124.

Rodó, José Enrique. *Ariel*. Mexico: Porrúa, 1968.

Spivak, Gayatri. (1999). *A Crtique of Postcolonial Reason: Toward a History of the Vanishing Present*. Cambridge, MA: Harvard University Press.

Tedlock, Dennis. *2000 Years of Mayan Literature*. Berkeley: University of California Press, 2010.

Trexler, Richard. *Sex and Conquest: Gendered Violence, Political Order, and the European Conquest of the Americas*. Ithaca, NY: Cornell University Press, 1995.

Vasconcelos, José. *La raza cósmica. Obras Completas, t. II* (pp. 903–42). México: Libreros Mexicanos, 1958.

Weismantel, Mary J. (2001). *Cholas and Pishtacos: Stories of Race and Sex in the Andes*. Chicago: University of Chicago Press, 2001.

Wellmeier, Nancy J. "Santa Eulalia's People in Exile: Maya Religion, Culture, and Identity in Los Angeles." Ed. R. Stephen Warner and Judith G. Wittner. *Gatherings in Diaspora: Religious Communities and the New Immigration*. Philadelphia: Temple University Press, 1998.

2

Performing to a Captive Audience

Dramatic Encounters in the Borderlands of Empire

PEDRO GARCÍA-CARO

Hispanic settlers throughout the Americas deployed religious performances and dramatic acts to signify and to impose a sense of spiritual and cultural bond-age to a new audience: the people they were seeking to conquer and subjugate. This enforced Western aesthetic staged novel cultural displays of newfangled hierarchies of power. Colonial performances displaced, replaced, repressed, and criminalized the cultural practices of the colonized native inhabitants after casting them first as pagan, and then increasingly as demonic.[1] In many areas now incorporated into the United States, from Puerto Rico to California, the cultural patterns of an emerging latinidad were fraught with the original sin of this bondage, a captivity presented as the cultural bond of a new community where colonial hierarchies of race, class, and gender determined the legitimacy of aesthetic knowledge(s) and practices.

Throughout this chapter, I trace a number of performative acts in the long history of the colonization of the North American continent by evoking a fragmented narrative of cultural encounters. In this narrative, Hispanic colonizers and a diversity of indigenous peoples engaged in the tense production of mutual knowledge through corporal performance art ranging from military spectacle to religious acts to pantomime and drama. This framing of Hispanic/Latina/o culture in the colonial period and beyond as performed to a captive audience, for a public incarcerated within the matrix of colonial power, seated within the confines of the Western episteme and defined as a passive spectator in need of cultural and religious conversion, allows me to critically reflect on the ethos of performance and the archives of

---

[1] Fernando Cervantes describes this process of demonization as an evolving concept: "By the middle of the sixteenth century ... a negative, demonic view of the Amerindian cultures had triumphed" (Cervantes 8). Jorge Cañizares-Esguerra traces the similarities between Iberian Catholic and Anglo-Protestant settlers and how they conceived of the occupation of space in the Americas as a battle "that pitted them against demons" (Cañizares-Esguerra 117).

the public stage to further disclose this literature's foundational epistemic violence. While the scattered archival records of over 300 years of settlement and contact highlight the wide use of music, dance, and drama, as tools for the theatricalization of the colonial regime, the records also confirm these arts' relevance as a precious space for cultural survival and resistance for the colonized (Burkhart 16; Ramos Smith 28). A predominantly Western and characteristically modern bifurcation between two spheres of power, church and state, offers a first set of liminal performances that underscore the long brewing divide between secular and religious spectacles (Viqueira Albán 33–35). These tenuous but widespread practices attest to an open competition over the captive audience of indigenous peoples on their way to becoming Hispanicized and Latinized. The fragmentary surviving archive of these performances confirms the potency of aesthetics to parade and to realize a fractured cultural hegemony, but also to contest that very enforced epistemic order and to open up a threshold of knowledge, or what Walter Mignolo has called a "border gnosis."[2]

In what follows, I plan to consider four sets of records in the colonial archive of the Interior Provinces of New Spain, specifically throughout those northern border territories of the viceroyalty annexed into the United States after the treaty of Guadalupe-Hidalgo in 1848, Alta California, New Mexico, and Texas. These cultural records, which have not been considered side by side before, evoke a series of performances that range from military parades to religious acts to formal comedies, and they configure a provisional, partial historiography of heterogeneous dramatic presentations in the pre–US Hispanic colonial borderlands. One of the central objectives of this narrative is to outline the colonial history of performative practices and to understand the competing discourses of religious and secular settlement, colonization, and the projected incorporation of the colonized into the Hispanic/Latina/o sphere. Here emerges what I refer to as a captive audience.

One of the foundational acts in this narrative is the grand proclamation of the legal *Requerimiento*, formally uttered as a request for submission to

---

[2] The concept of "border gnosis" refers to the knowledges produced in the overwrought, violent encounters between the West and other cultures. It is a "knowledge that takes form at the margins of the modern Western world" (Irwin 509). First proposed by Walter Mignolo, border gnosis elicits a decentering of the power relations established by the colonial epistemic regime of classification, expropriation, and settlement by recognizing "subaltern reason striving to bring to the foreground the force and creativity of knowledges subalternized during a long process of colonization of the planet, which was at the same time the process in which modernity and the modern Reason were constructed" (Mignolo 13).

Hispanic rule by the incoming troops. As an edict of territorial possession, the *Requerimiento* conjoined secular and religious narratives in its substantiation, citing the entangled claims of crown and church over lands and souls. While this dramatic apostrophic text of territorial allocation appeared after the second decade of Spanish colonization in 1512, by the end of the sixteenth century the *Requerimiento* had been superseded by more specialized and sophisticated dramatic acts, such as *Moros y Cristianos* [Moors and Christians] (Ramos Smith 25–27), open-air battle reenactments, and related festive conquest dance-dramas such as the *Danza de los Matachines* in northern New Mexico (Sponsler 17–41; Harris 237–50); all aimed to capture the imagination, the minds, and the bodies, of the native inhabitants. These subtler performative acts inaugurated a new calendar of public parades and festivities that competed with the well-established traditions of indigenous dance-dramas and sought to replace them as part and parcel of the colonizing project.

Franciscan missionaries staged a panoply of religious performances throughout their ample sphere of influence from Florida to California, ranging from Yuletide *pastorelas* to Corpus Christi celebrations and other liturgical processions (Mann 69–99; Lozano 116–227). I will claim in this chapter that we need to consider the production of an alleged miracle – the purported transatlantic bilocation of a nun from Soria (north-central Spain) to New Mexico in the 1620s – as part of the repertoire of religious performances staged by the Franciscan order in northern New Spain. This type of miraculous intervention highlighted the divine mandate of the Spanish conquest which, together with the many other spectacular religious acts, public pageants, sung masses, and constant bell ringing, were intended to discipline and foment conversions among those apprehended as future Hispanics – the Amerindian population. At the same time that the Roman Catholic Church produced these ritualized narratives of religious participation in the transnational enclaves of the missions, it simultaneously extirpated and banished the old rituals, masks, dances, and performative traditions that had constituted local native American spiritual and aesthetic customs over the preceding era (Morrow 41; Schaafsma, 121–22).

As a way of contrast with the religious obsession with conversion and acculturation, I will briefly discuss the evolution of Creole and Spanish proto-scientific ethnographies dealing with Native American performance by looking at the account of José Mariano Moziño (Temascaltepec, 1757– Barcelona, 1820) of the outermost northern enclave of Hispano-Mexican influence: the island of Nootka in what is now British Columbia. Literary and cultural criticism around native performance arts became a device by which

Moziño – an enlightened *letrado* – embarked in a large-scale botanical exped-ition and other early ethnographers translated and relocated the cultural practices of indigenous peoples by contrasting them with Western traditions and by defining them within the secular parameters of public decency as morally inappropriate, licentious, or pagan. However, despite the ambivalence between the perfunctory censoring tone and his romanticizing of indigenous culture, Moziño's *Noticias de Nutka* allows us to understand indigenous ritual dances within their own cultural logic rather than as a mere devious ancient custom in need of dramatic conversion (Moziño 59; Weber *Bárbaros* 180).

Finally, I will recapitulate some of my research on *Astucias por heredar, un sobrino a un tío* (*Tricks to Inherit: a Nephew and His Uncle*) a secular play smuggled into California and performed there by Catalán and Mexican soldiers – and quite possibly by some of the female settlers that came with them – in the public space of the newly founded Villa de Branciforte in present-day Santa Cruz, California, an event that marks another important break in the secular-religious colonial compact circa 1797. Much like the clerical Creole censor who had banned the play in Mexico City at the beginning of that decade, the Basque and Balearic Franciscan missionaries across the Saint Lawrence River in Santa Cruz must have balked at the sight of their native Costanoan and Yokut neophytes watching an Italianate satirical play unsympathetic to the mores of the faraway imperial capital, Madrid. The old colonial antagonism between the mission, with its clear divisions of spiritual and physical labors and the mixed-race, socially complex *pueblo* became increasingly more visible in the closing decades of the eight-eenth century, and it culminated with the Mexican secularization of all remaining missions by 1834 and the distribution of their lands to townships and ranchers (Weber *Mexican Frontier* 66–67). Before that, these two comple-mentary institutions of colonial settlement had been characterized by often-conflicting cultural performances for a commonly held captive audience: the religious spectacles necessitated by Catholic doctrine and liturgy, with their ample and well-documented use of music, devotional rituals, miracles, *pastorelas*, and mystery plays; and the emerging practices of the secular settlements with alternate practices of music, dance, and surprisingly, even contraband modern satirical drama, as is the case of *Astucias por heredar*.

A Forceful Opening Scene: The Requerimiento

From the outset, colonialism in the Americas was as much a remapping, a renaming, an armed evacuation, and a forcible occupation of territory, as it was a performance of formidable power, cultural and material prestige, and religious righteousness. As early as 1513, violent material grafts of goods, land, and people throughout the Caribbean, the Gulf of Mexico, and the coasts of Central America and Florida were accompanied by a "new" fundamental political act predicated on a theatricalization of metropolitan power: the *Requerimiento* (Adorno 265). Crafted on the mold of the old Muslim battle-cry of religious submission to the jihad (Seed 72–87), this official edict was a carefully scripted notarized performance of possession, a public overture to the native inhabitants as a prelude to military intervention and thus accompanied by drum and horn marches, salvos, and other fanfare.[3] From the very beginning of the colonial encounter, the practice of hostile theatrics around the Spanish legal *Requerimiento* to advance the lines of imperial expansion and assimilation offered an inaugural keynote to the violent aesthetics of Hispanicity, while its Oriental origins also denoted for European observers the peripheral, unique practices of Spanish colonialism throughout the Americas with a performance that sounded "a little foreign, *umheimlich, morisco* or *marrano*" (Sherwood 35).[4] Such was the power attributed to the mere public reading and performance of the possession edict, that at times the *Requerimiento* appears as a kind of formulaic cultural soliloquy, read out of arrow shot, and without even an actual native audience in attendance, eliciting some famous reactions on the part of European commentators such as Michel de Montaigne, but also Fray Bartolomé de las Casas.[5]

And yet, notwithstanding its purported Oriental origins, the dramatic proposition publicly enacted in the *Requerimiento* epitomizes what Aníbal Quijano has called the "pattern of global power" or the "colonial power matrix," a "coloniality of power" which casts out otherness into the category

---

[3] For Patricia Seed this heavily armed "context in which it [the Requisition] was delivered" added to the absurdity of the text itself (Seed 71).

[4] Félix Padilla suggests Ponce de León took possession of Florida with a similar formula as early as 1513 (Padilla 261). In contrast, José Rabasa locates the first performance of the *Requerimiento* in what is today Panamá in the Darién by Pedrarias Dávila the following year in 1514, by Cortés in México in 1519, and then by Pánfilo Narváez in his 1527 expedition to Florida (Rabasa 42). Ponce de León's second and fatal visit to Florida is also likely to have included the *Requerimiento* (Quinn 134).

[5] The French founder of the modern essay writing discussed the flimsiness of the *Requerimiento* in his "Des coches" (Of Coaches) (1588), by empathically echoing an indigenous response with a detailed logical contestation of all the claims of the Spanish edict: from right to possess to religious supremacy (Montaigne 172). Bartolomé de las Casas commented on the absurdity, hypocrisy, and tragicomic quality of this possessive recital. Evoking the text of the *Requerimiento*, Las Casas famously stated that upon witnessing its performance, he did not know whether to laugh or to cry (Seed 71; Adorno 81).

of *casta* or race in order to incorporate its heretofore non-space into the new geopolitical globe (Quijano 533, 553). Farcically staging the incoming occupation of the territory and its implied redefinition of the political body as an enactment of Western freedom through the scheme of the "required choice," the *Requerimiento* confirms Enrique Dussel's suspicion of the central hollowness in the overarching conceptual motif of Western hegemonic ethics: freedom (Dussel 141). The *Requerimiento* forecloses the legitimacy of resistance or of an outside (or an underside) to the matrix, i.e., freedom *from* the Western matrix does not exist. Citing Derrida on the sacred source of law, Jill Lane has described the enactment of the *Requerimiento* as a founding moment "that institutes law as performative force" (56). Cried out loud in legalistic, formal, and incomprehensible Latin and Castilian – though often translated by an interpreter, as in the case of Cortés in Yucatán through Aguilar, or with Doña Marina in Tenochtitlán – the *Requerimiento* proposed two alternatives to the newly branded "Indians" as children of god gone astray: yield or die. There are many examples of the practice of *Requerimiento* in Cortés's *Cartas de relación* in which the captain asks his proxies to use this very formula: "mandé de parte de Vuestra Majestad que **requiriese** a los naturales de aquellas provincias que viniesen de paz a se dar por vasallos de Vuestra Majestad como antes lo habían hecho, y que tuviese con ellos toda la templanza que fuese posible; y que si no quisiesen recibirle de paz, que les hiciese la guerra. . ." My emphasis ("ordering him, on the part of Your Majesty, **to require** the natives of those provinces to submit peaceably as vassals of Your Majesty, as they had done heretofore, and to use all possible moderation with them; but, if they would not receive him peaceably, to make war upon them") (Seed 98–99; Cortés 6). Cortés's account reveals the naturalized logic of the *Requerimiento* and its militarized compulsion to bondage.

From the outset of European colonization, indigenous identities had been put under suspicion, rebranded, and relocated into the colonial matrix of power through an obstinate reassertion of the imagined remapping of the hemisphere as the "Indias Occidentales," an epistemic ploy that preceded wholesale expropriation. In the *Requerimiento*, the "options" of Native Americans were falsely cast as a choice between exercising a legal and religious submission to the new rightful owners of the land, or to face the wrath of god on earth: i.e. the terrors of gunpowder, hounds, horses, enslavement, or certain death.[6] The language was quite explicit: "if you do not do this . . . we

---

[6] By virtue of the Papal donation to the Catholic monarchs of Spain: "Spain relied in that document as the official legitimizing basis of its right to conquer and rule throughout

shall do you all the mischief and damage that we can, as vassals who do not obey."[7] The corollary to these first Western assertions of manifest destiny and Christian entitlement to the land and its inhabitants not only contained a dramatic falsification of freedom, but they already also charged the victims and survivors of colonialism themselves with full responsibility for their own violent fate: "the deaths and losses that shall accrue from this are your fault" (Helps 266). As Jill Lane has posited: "This writerly performance does not ceremonially seal the victories of warfare: it enacts and initiates the founding violence of conquest itself" (56). This sense of narrative predestination is key in the early configuration of colonial space, and it pervades the spiritual rhetoric undergirding the concept of race. Colonization was predicated on at least two concomitant plots: an epic account for the advance of the Christian West, and a tragic drama for the Indians and their seemingly disposable histories, marked bodies, and illicit, pagan artifacts and demonic rituals. The destiny of these indispensable communities – the earliest inhabitants of the coveted territory – had already been determined by their oppositional externality to divine (i.e., the West's) plans. Their resistance to the imposed Western destiny corroborated their constant representation as tragic characters (Sayre 5) in chronicles from the time of Columbus onward, which included the informal staging of *Los comanches* from New Mexico (Lamadrid 207–26), through the many other conquest reenactments that were performed throughout the entire American hemisphere.

In *The Archive and the Repertoire*, Diana Taylor has pointed out how "performing the act of possession makes the claim; the witnessing and writing down legitimates it" (Taylor 61). For Taylor the *Requerimiento* constituted a central part of the repertoire of performances that were in turn

---

the Americas" (Williams 92). As an added layer of juridical justification to the earliest diplomatic documents on America, the (Aragonese) papal bull *Inter caetera* (1493) and the Treaty of Tordesillas (1494) between Spain and Portugal, this formal process of territorial allocation allowed Spaniards to legitimize their conquests and their active conversion of the Indians (Hanke, *The Spanish Struggle* 33).

[7] "But, if you do not do this ... we shall powerfully enter into your country, and shall make war against you in all ways and manners that we can, and shall subject you to the yoke and obedience of the Church and of their Highnesses; we shall take you and your wives and your children, and shall make slaves of them, and as such shall sell and dispose of them as their Highnesses may command; and we shall take away your goods, and shall do you all the mischief and damage that we can, as to vassals who do not obey, and refuse to receive their lord, and resist and contradict him; and we protest that the deaths and losses which shall accrue from this are your fault, and not that of their Highnesses, or ours, nor of these knights who come with us." (Helps 266)

Written at the request of Ferdinand of Aragon, the standardized 1512 text of the *Requerimiento* was authored by Juan López de Palacios Rubios (Hanke 29; Williams 93).

archived through written accounts, chronicles, and even later representations of the event (64). Regardless of their understanding of the performance, the captive audience of indigenous bodies was implied in its address: "interpolated as the indispensable, though backgrounded, guarantors of its efficacy" (63). The repeated performance of the interpolation is the one-sided legalistic act bolstering the right to conquest, a dramatic encounter subsequently archived and restaged as a form of historical reminder of the "legal" origins of the colonial status quo.

North America was not exempt from this Hispanic ritual performance of possession and its later recitations over time. Traveling with the 1527 Narváez expedition to Florida, Cabeza de Vaca confirms in his *Naufragios* the imperative moment of staging the ritual possession of the land by governor Narváez upon arrival with the planting and unfurling of the royal standards.[8] Later on in the extensive captivity narrative of his survival and nine-year trip throughout the territories of Appalachia, Texas, and New Mexico, Cabeza de Vaca performs the act of the *Requerimiento* in all but name. Rolena Adorno has traced the underlying conceptual notions of vassalage and formal Christian conversion in Cabeza de Vaca's description of two of his last encounters with indigenous groups in the area of the Sinaloa River toward the end of his long travels. Vaca's perfunctory performance of settlement and incorporation is accompanied by an impressive account of the utter diversity and variety of landscapes and peoples in precolonial North America. Adorno characterizes Cabeza de Vaca and his alleged resettlement of native people in their own lands through their implicit acceptance of Christianism – and thus their fulfillment of the *Requerimiento* – as "one of the founding works of the Latin American literary tradition" (269). In contrast, while acknowledging Cabeza de Vaca's active participation in the colonial venture, Bruce-Novoa and others have pointed out the relevance of his cultural transformation as a stranded migrant to place him as a forerunner of the Chicano experience and as "an alternative to the egocentrism and arrogance of the conqueror" (Bruce-Novoa 17). Cabeza de Vaca's ambivalent program of (self)acculturation is thus one of many archival records that crisscross and constitute the shared colonial tradition of both Chicano and Latin American letters: a captivity narrative of shipwrecks and pilgrimage, observation and reciprocated wonderment that revels in the sheer humanity of its many encounters.

[8] Steele and Rhoden 4.

Many later enactments of conquest would contain and stage a more theatrical version of the *Requerimiento* within their storyline as a formal narrative requirement and as a justification of the colonial takeover (Lane 61). Describing how the 1598 conquest of New Mexico was orchestrated by Juan de Oñate's troops in the form of a "spectacular theatrical performance" echoing the conquest of Tenochtitlán – in which Cortés had been able to communicate the *Requerimiento* through his two famous interpreters Aguilar and Doña Marina – adapted now for an audience of Pueblo Indians, Ramón Gutiérrez explores the deployment of "conquest drama" in the northern border of New Spain as a "political and pedagogical instrument" (Gutiérrez 55). This elaborate instrument was intended to forge an historical consciousness of defeat among the natives (62). Gutiérrez argues that while conquest narratives and dramas, such as *Los Comanches*, had "disciplinary powers" (62) seeking to "fix and perpetuate humiliations," native populations used veiled humor, mockery, and other burlesque coded gestures in their performance of Western culture to subvert the hegemony Spanish conquerors had so fiercely sought to impose.

One example of a traditional conquest drama enacted over hundreds of years in New Mexico and elsewhere is *Moors and Christians*, an open-air performance that restages the *conquista* of the Iberian Peninsula and grafts it onto the history of the conquest over indigenous peoples, in this case, Puebloans. These performances, however, could be interpreted quite radically by an audience self-aware of its captivity within the new cultural frame of Hispanic *Latinitas*, Spain's universalist imperial project. For Max Harris, the plot of the Christian liberation and Reconquista of their former peninsular territory in *Moors and Christians* allowed indigenous observers and participants to imagine the possibility of liberating themselves from the invading Moors/Spaniards. According to Harris, "it was this image of liberation rather than that of Spanish victory that attracted indigenous Mexicans to the imported tradition. In colonial festivals of Moors and Christians, a public transcript of Catholic triumph masked a hidden transcript of native reconquest" (Harris 67). In the end, we should perhaps read the *Requerimiento* and the other theatrical representations of conquest and incorporation it spawned as the first explicit – but not always successful – attempts by the Hispanic crown in the space that would be renamed as the Americas, to secure a people and a (re)public, to create a captive audience. While these dramatic acts of incorporation grew more sophisticated and complex as empire turned from exploration and conquest to settler colonialism to become a multilayered historical reality over many generations and localities, so too grew the possibilities for the newly Latinized public – the proto-Latinos and Latinas of the colonial period – to interpret and incorporate these acts into a native performance of emancipation and deliverance, thus breaking away from their captivity into a new role as critical interpreters of the script.

Dea ex Machina: The Lady in Blue

If the *Requerimiento* implied a subservient audience of silent spectators soon to be absorbed and slowly acculturated into the Latinate empire of the Hispanic monarchy as vassals, inaugurating the future conflicts and contradictions within a hybrid Latino ethnic practice, the religious incorporation of indigenous populations necessitated a more proactive conversion and a performance of Christian ritual on the part of the neophytes *as if* they converted out of their own will. Priests and inquisitors, monks and observers, all policed the new Christians and their performance of rituals to try and prevent the survival of their "pagan-demonic" indigenous traditions (Gruzinski 186; Cervantes 5–39). In the second of the performative moments that I want to evoke in this study into the fractured formation of a forcibly Hispanicized captive audience, indigenous requests for baptism uttered in the native tongue are configured as the central motifs of the story.

This performance represents a production of transatlantic dimensions governed by the innovative principle of colonial bilocation. Bilocation is a phenomenon that first and foremost can be accounted for by looking at the historical context of the diminished legitimacy of the Spanish *Requerimiento*.[9] As the Pope's authority had been questioned by Lutheran Protestant Reformists throughout the sixteenth century, a redefinition of the sacred right to colonial expropriation had to be enacted through direct divine intervention. Such intervention came in the form of apparitions of the virgin Mary – such as the virgin of Guadalupe in 1531 (León Portilla and Valeriano) – saints – Santiago, the patron saint of Spain "James the Moor-killer" [Santiago Matamoros] turned "James the Indian-slayer" [Santiago Mataindios] (Domínguez García 67) – and other such miracles, including an innovative type of apparition: psycho-physical bilocation (Pueyo Zoco 22). In the 1620s, during the early colonization of Nuevo México, the northernmost reaches of the Viceroyalty of New Spain at the time, a territory comprising western Texas, New Mexico, and northern Chihuahua, members of a large group of people

---

[9] It was progressively abolished between 1556 and 1573 as a "useless legalism" and replaced with the concept of empire as a "missionary enterprise" (Williams 93).

living near one of the branches of the Colorado River in Texas known as the *jumani* or *humana* nation approached the Isleta missionaries to relate the puzzling presence of a lady in blue.[10] The mysterious, caped lady – the blue cape is a central part in the Franciscan *attrezzo* of this miracle play – had come to preach the Christian gospel to them in their own language and asked them to seek baptism in the nearby missions. The spiritual portage of a cloistered nun, María de Jesús de Ágreda (María Coronel de Arana, Ágreda, 1602– Ágreda, 1665), who from her convent in faraway Soria in upper Castile, could be beamed in through unknown coordinates of time and space into New Mexico and Texas, makes Spanish metaphysics at the time of Descartes all that much more ingenious and theatrical.

As a departure from the emerging Western regime of Renaissance rationality at the very time in which modernity was being constituted, bilocation can be explained from within the Spanish counterreformist thought system through religious zeal – what Colahan has defined as a "radical supernatural epistemology" (Colahan 5) – or through a critical, materialist historical understanding of the very need for miracles and religious legitimacy for colonial rule in the wake of anti-papal disobedience. The *Requerimiento* and the pope's geographic distribution of the Indies had indeed become *papel mojado*, irrelevant, with its authority increasingly eroded after the Reformation.[11] We thus need to locate this purported miracle within the propaganda wars that raged throughout Western Europe between the Protestant North and the Catholic South, more specifically, between the dislocated puritanical Reformed Protestant churches that were settling Plymouth Bay among the Massachusetts during that very decade (1620s) and the more powerful but intellectually besieged Counter Reformation theocracy and its already overextended missionary network. By the early seventeenth century, the interests of the Spanish crown and the colonizing Catholic orders were intimately and reciprocally invested in the business of empire building: more controllable than the military entrepreneurial conquistadores of the chaotic first half of the sixteenth century, the missionaries extended the king's realm unquestioningly, while the king's purse was the

---

[10] Nancy Hickerson and others identify the ethnic group of the Jumanos as Eastern New Mexican Pueblo belonging to the Tanoan language group closely associated with the Piro and Tompiro linguistic groups of the southern Pueblos (Hickerson 67).

[11] For Greengrass, throughout the sixteenth and seventeenth centuries "Papal and imperial legitimation for 'world empire' became, however, increasingly irrelevant" (Greengrass 152).

ultimate benefactor and beneficiary, as legal guardian and sole financer, of the missionary regime.

The bilocation of a Spanish nun in the midst of Texan and New Mexican indigenous groups is shrouded in much more mystery than the other dramatic performances studied here, even though its archival documentation is perhaps more exhaustive. The representation of mystery – and by association, of faith – is of the essence in the phenomenology of Catholic bilocation. In order to attempt to disentangle the mysteries of this rather well-documented and intensely investigated apparition, we would need to exercise a measure of hypothetical reasoning and interrogate biased archival records.

This orchestrated apparition of a lonely young Franciscan nun in the midst of unconverted indigenous groups invigorates the theatrical concept of the "deus ex machina," while it defies the tradition of captivity narratives of Western women and men captured by distrustful demonic natives, such as Mary Rowlandson's well-known North American narrative of captivity and "restoration." Bilocation reveals itself as a dramatic demand from the indigenous captive audience, a "logical" demand for conversion and incorporation into the Catholic empire. This miraculous apparition and subsequent mass conversion unsurprisingly coincided in time with the very authorized presence of a unique witness in New Mexico: the new *custodio* or director of the Franciscan Missions, the Portuguese friar Alonso de Benavides, whose *Memorial* (1630) is a central record in the archival documentation of early New Mexico and the purported miracles surrounding its Christian conquest. Only on returning to Spain after his long stay in New Mexico and Texas was Benavides able to "identify" Sister María de Ágreda as the bilocated preacher. As a custodian, Benavides was in charge of fomenting the missionary network, exploring its material conditions, documenting the number of conversions, as well as detailing for his chief patron, the king, the socioeconomic makeup of this newly incorporated vast territory. Thus, Benavides's *Memorial* is one of the earliest detailed ethnographic descriptions of recognizable ethno-linguistic groups – Hopi, Zuni, and Apache to name just a few – throughout what is today the US Southwest. Perhaps what partly accounts for the ongoing appreciation of the veracity of this phantom apparition is the fact that its narrative is couched within such early ethnohistorical descriptions.

For Benavides, as Nancy Hickerson has put it, "spiritual and secular objectives [were] inseparable" (Hickerson 80). Benavides broadly defines one of his central ideological categories, the term "miracle," and makes apparent the sheer materiality of his "supernatural epistemology" in a section of his *Memorial* entitled "What that Kingdom Owes to Your Majesty" (Morrow 41–42). Here Benavides exalts the direct intervention of the Hispanic monarch in developing and funding straight from the royal coffers the expansion of the missionary network in the recently settled province, a material and spiritual investment that also takes the form of a virtual transatlantic visitation: "Your Majesty should bask in the glory of having been the source of all this transformation. Your Majesty should also enjoy the fruits of all these conversions, in which we have snatched so many thousands of souls from the claws of the devil. Nothing but a miracle can explain it" (42).

Thus the monarch himself – like his close confidante and protegée, the nun from Ágreda – miraculously appears under the condition of bilocation not merely transported into the political persona of the viceroy, the socio-historical avatar of the monarch on the earthier land of the colony, but astoundingly he now is also the author of a miracle: dramatized colonization as a double-edged form of salvation. Perhaps bilocation then should be read more as a colonial symptom or as a dramatic projection of metropolitan desires over the colonial territory, a projection that took different forms, but that ultimately was supposed to happen in one direction only: the Western trajectory of empire. In the meantime, the captive audience of newly converted natives could perhaps exult in their marginal centrality within the performance of the transatlantic virtual miracle, their souls imaginatively claimed by the king and his missionaries. It is perhaps in that confirmation that they were able to perform their own (captive) symbolic bilocation.

Dirty Dancing and Colonial Ethnographies

If Benavides's *Memorial* could be salvaged beyond the counterreformist rhetoric of the miraculous, it is perhaps due to his rich accounts not only of indigenous customs and peoples, but also to its testimony of cultural and performative devices set in motion by the clergy to immerse the neophytes in the musical and liturgical traditions of Spain and Roman Catholic *Latinitas*. His comments on the proliferation of musical workshops throughout the territory of New Mexico, and the many well-attended musical schools within the missions there, have been constantly cited as evidence of a material culture of performance and its unarchived repertories (Morrow 23; Lozano 608–609). Fast forward to the end of the eighteenth century, the 1790s, a decade in which the Pacific Northwest had become the new frontier of the overstretched

Hispanic empire and the secular scientific projects of colonization and exploration were rapidly replacing and even ideologically challenging the missionary impulse (Weber *Bárbaros* 103). Returning to Mexico City from his research trip to the island of Nootka in the far northern reaches of the Spanish empire, the distinguished Creole enlightened botanist and ethnographer José Moziño speculated about the literary, musical, and performative customs of the indigenous inhabitants of the coast of what is today the province of British Columbia in Canada. The fort of Santa Cruz de Nootka was one of the last settlements of (New) Spain in the northern hemisphere. As an embedded scientist within the 1792 military expedition led by Bodega to investigate the Spanish "Limits to the North of California," a controversial diplomatic issue with Great Britain at the time, Moziño was a first-row spectator, and indeed an important player, in one of the last acts of Spanish colonialism in the Americas.

Like many Western explorers before him, Moziño witnessed a wide repertoire of Native American performances that ranged from martial warrior dance dramas to sexual pantomimes. Paradoxically, Moziño offered some meticulously described examples of what these dances entailed after mentioning his inability to record a "detailed description" on the grounds of a respect for "decency" (Moziño 59). Referring to these sexualized performances as making use of "brilliant expressions" and giving "vivid and witty portrayals," Moziño traces these pantomimes with a carefully crafted imprecision. Moziño's proposed ethnography was safely placed behind a moral and cultural filter that contained these acts within the realm of the obscene. Moziño's account is torn between providing a meaningful insight into these artistic customs and also foreclosing the possibility of a future expurgation at the hands of a discerning ecclesiastical or governmental reader. Due to this explicit self-censorship exercised by the author in his consideration of the lasciviousness of these acts (the "most lascivious that one can imagine" 59), the contemporary reader is left to speculate about the specific forms deployed in these performances and their social function. Interestingly, while proscribing these accounts, the ethnographer sketched them out in enough detail to allow us to glimpse at a lesson in indigenous sexual lore, a communal performance of a multiplicity of sexual practices, which included the inexperienced single man and the impotent elderly: "Decency compels me to omit the detailed description of the obscene dances of the *meschimes* because the movements with which they carry them out are extremely scandalous, especially in the dance of the man impotent because of age and of the poor man who has not been able to marry" (60). The detail of these aesthetic acts is thus outlined while safely put under lock, allowing for a speculative gnoseology of the meaning and practice of these dances for the Nootkans as a performance of social types in the margins of Western prudery.

One of the methods deployed by Moziño to circumvent the strictures of the censor was to compare these dances with the sexually explicit pantomimes of classical antiquity, thus locating them in a contrast with the more familiar archive of paganism, while constantly claiming his inability to provide a more explicit account on the grounds of public decency:

> One night they presented a spectacle for us which surely exceeded the indecent pantomimes of the ancient Greeks and Romans; and I have information that they spend all the nights in Tasis during the winter in this kind of recreation. Many times the spectators of this dissolute opera are these same *taises* [chiefs], who scruple only not to mingle their voices in the obscene songs. (59)

Moziño's ambivalence and his ability to both inscribe these practices within a familiar landscape of performance art ("opera," "pantomime"), while putting them sous-rature ("indecent," "dissolute," "obscene") permeates his entire "Article 7" devoted to "the rhetoric and poetry of the Nootkans, and of their dances." This ambivalent mode tests the charges of a "romanticized" vision that his *indigenista* study has received (Weber *Bárbaros* 180). Characteristically, his article briefly sketches out the dramatic and literary exchanges that took place between the Western visitors, British and Spanish, and the Nootkans. The opinions voiced by the Nootkans on the cultural performances offered by the Europeans whose songs and poetry – for the most part love songs, and a eulogy to wine and beautiful women – offer an insight into the way in which Western culture could be perceived from the other side of the stage. The judgments voiced by one of the native chiefs offer a remarkable rejoinder to Moziño's own ethnography of native paganism: "Do not the Spanish or the English have a God, since they celebrate only fornication and drunkenness? The *taises* of Nootka sing only to praise Qua-utz and ask for his help" (58). By revealing Europeans in their base humanity, and by denying their claims to theological or cultural superiority through a critique of their dramatic and literary arts, the native Nootkan chief undermined and resisted European efforts to demonize his people and capture his audience.

This example allows us to reflect on a lost archive and a missing repertoire. Many similar though unrecorded dramatic encounters occurred throughout the hemisphere as it was being explored and settled. The dramatic acts that took place at the borderlands of the Spanish empire were never one-sided: throughout the three centuries of colonial expansion and settlement, well-established Native American and African traditions of religious, dramatic, and musical performance became subjected to the demands of intercultural contact in the context of territorial encroachment, conquest, displacement, resettlement, enslavement, and colonial everyday life. As they were transformed and transcultured, so too were the European performances gradually subjected to open criticism, discussion, and adaptation by a community of increasingly "emancipated spectators," to borrow Rancière's terms.

Performing Satire in Colonial California

A banned and smuggled neoclassic play, *Astucias por heredar* (1789), illustrates well the complexity of Hispanic settlements in the *Provincias Internas* – Alta California, New Mexico, and Texas among them – during the eighteenth century as the growing tensions between secular and religious communities were punctuated by their competing artistic performances. *Astucias por heredar, un sobrino a un tío (Tricks to Inherit a Nephew and His Uncle)* is manuscript MSS CE 120 at the Bancroft Library, University of California, Berkeley. No other copies of this important dramatic text appear to have survived, and until 2017 it had never been given to the press, nor is there any evidence that the work has been performed at any time in the last 200 years. Handwritten in Mexico in 1789, and signed by a Spanish colonist devoted to mining and science in New Spain, all we know for sure is that it somehow made its way up to the Alta California territory. There is no evidence that this work circulated or was ever performed at the Coliseo in Mexico City, the largest colonial theatre for which it had been written, or in the metropolitan capital, Madrid, where the action of the drama was set. Its author, Fermín de Reygadas, lived for much of his life between Mexico City and several mining sites, prominently in Temascaltepec where he became a deputy for the Real Colegio de Minería. One of the fundamental and demonstrable facts about this play is that its only audience appears to have been the small secular circuit of military garrisons and townships, which were still being developed after the third decade of Spanish colonization of California (Vallejo).

After the censor's damning report had banned it from the Mexican stage (Olavarría y Ferrari 78–79), the dislocated play traveled north to Alta California in the 1790s with a group of settlers headed to what would soon become a ghost town – the failed utopian project of the Villa de Branciforte. This town was to be the last secular settling project within the Spanish imperial designs to reassert Spanish claims to the territory of Alta California as pressure by explorers, merchants, and potential settlers from Great Britain, Russia, and the emerging United States was mounting. In this context, a banned neoclassical satirical play was shored up in the furthest reaches of the empire in the wake of the French Revolution of 1789. Starting in 1796, a diverse group of families, veteran Catalán soldiers, and Mexican prisoners received the invitation to settle across the San Lorenzo River and the Franciscan Mission of Santa Cruz in what is today the town of Santa Cruz, California. Spanish colonial administrators were intent on creating a villa of the Enlightenment: a small agricultural township that would inevitably enter into immediate competition with the parallel model of colonization represented by the neighboring feudal Misión Santa Cruz across the river. In the archival documentation of the period, there are many traces of the rivalry between the mission and the secular settlement as a way of situating the scandalous performance of a forbidden play at the inauguration in California of modern political divides. It is also very likely that the play was performed not just for the community of secular settlers, but also in front of a "captive audience" of neophyte Costanoan and Yokut indigenes from the nearby Mission Santa Cruz.

These secular settlers brought with them cultural artifacts that characterized eighteenth-century Spanish American leisure, such as musical instruments, gambling games, and books, including this banned manuscript play (Viqueira Albán). This displaced text has remained in California to this day largely due to the cultural zeal shown by the descendants of those first settlers who smuggled the manuscript, read, and performed it in this newly established colonial territory. Yet despite its literary and historical intrinsic value, *Astucias* has received almost no attention until now: its obscurity is the result of several historical dislocations.[12] Signed by a Spaniard emigrated to Mexico, who lived there into old age after Mexican independence in 1821, it is a satirical work of secular theater that was never printed; officially censored in Mexico City in the spring of 1790, it was nevertheless performed in the tiny secular colony of California some years later, preserved there in private archives, and later rescued among the papers of the debacle of the Spanish-Mexican colonizing project after the annexation of Alta California to the United States (War of 1846–1848), just to be filed away again by Hubert Howe Bancroft.

---

[12] Nicolás Kanellos is one of the few critics who had mentioned *Astucias* as one of the earliest proofs of secular drama in the northern provinces. (Kanellos 1–2).

One of the obvious reasons for the lack of consideration for this piece is the greater narrative of the Spanish colonization of California, dominated by the study of the Franciscan missionary network. In the context of the highly regulated and scrutinized missionary space of early California, the appearance of a work of secular drama, questioning property, inheritance, and the social order, is an indisputable rarity, difficult both to understand and to explain. Its ultimate neglect also derives from the fact that its author, Fermín de Reygadas, does not exist as such. That is, he is not recognized as a literary author in the poetic and dramatic historiography of Spain or Mexico for this turbulent period (1789–1821). So, *Astucias* is a fitting precedent for Latino drama: it is a homeless, rootless text; but it is also, surprisingly, a polished play, already revised and prepared for its theatrical performance. It has remained, until now, however, dislocated and secluded within the archive as a rare specimen of an interrupted literary tradition. Despite its unique and penetrating dramatic quality that links it directly to the performing strategies of *commedia dell'arte* in its neoclassical version, it is a migrant literary text deprived of a national literary canon willing to claim it for itself. It is perhaps this migrant origin, its smuggled nature, and its suppressed past, that most enduringly make it a prime example of colonial Latino drama. Due to the invisibility to which it has been exposed first by the colonial censor in Mexico City and then eighty years later by the suspicious silence of Bancroft, the earliest historiographer of California, this play does not yet belong to any national literary tradition.[13] Given its linguistic complexity and the sagacity of this dramatic text, all cultural spaces to which in one way or another this play belongs – Spain, Mexico, California (and the US more broadly) – are reconfigured and expanded as they begin to include it within their eighteenth-century literary heritage. The publication of this play as part of the Recovering the US Hispanic Literary Heritage Series by Arte Público Press (University of Houston), its contemporary literary and performative reenactment in the original Spanish by Teatro Milagro of Portland (February 2018), and in English by the University of Oregon Theatre Department under the direction of Olga Sánchez Saltveit (May-June 2018), expands the range of the colonial literary archive and its repertoire in the northern Mexican border and can be reclaimed for contemporary Latina/o culture and literary history to illustrate its diverse and extended dramatic traditions.

---

[13] It is surprising that Bancroft, who had already received the manuscript and an accompanying letter from Mariano Vallejo describing the importance of this first secular performance, omitted any references in his seven volumes of the *History of California*. (Bancroft et al.)

The subject matter of *Astucias por heredar* is both traditional and provocative: the rights to inherit a fortune. Its linguistic and dramatic modernity is both surprising and refreshing. In this *comedia* the language flows; social satire and drama are very much alive. The plot of the play revolves around the will of a rich old man, Don Lucas, an archetypal icon of a provincial settled at court. A *montañés* (from Cantabria), this landowner living in Madrid resembles a stock character of Spanish drama at the time, the "figurón" (or big shot), a generally exaggerated, pedantic, dislocated, or displaced provincial living in the capital, whose lack of nobility is compensated by his large fortune, resulting from "sudor y trabajo" (3696) ("sweat and toil"). His wealth is said to be higher than the income provided by many noble titles "en esta corte / hay algunos mayorazgos / que no tienen tanta renta" (3681–83) ("there are in this court / some noble houses / without such income"). Not surprisingly, Don Lucas is surrounded by probable and improbable family relatives and their servants who all wish to grab a share of his inheritance: "Catorce mil son ya los herederos / que sé constan listados y aún nos faltan / de sobrinos y primos dos millones / que están dando en el reino su probanza" (95–98). ("Fourteen thousand are listed heirs / already and that's not counting / two million nephews and cousins / all attesting lineage throughout the kingdom"). Lucía, the maid; Don Pedro, the nephew of the title; his servant, Crispín; Isabel, the nephew's girlfriend; and Doña Teresa, her mother, all make up a cast of characters that circulate around the old sick man trying to make sure he does not die without leaving a written will, preferably with their names on it. This is a comedy in which the servants are much more than the typical *gracioso* of traditional Spanish *comedia*. Both Lucía – a cunning *criada*, described as having a degree ("bachillera") – and her dramatic partner, Crispín – ironically a shrewd rake and a declared rogue – are subaltern characters who aspire to make their job both dignified and rewarded, even if they have to put up various "tricks" to inherit, including disguise, deception, forgery, and moral argumentation. Similarly, the nephew Don Pedro, whose only known goal seems to be to become *the* heir, sharpens his wit and his rhetoric to achieve Isabel's love while competing with his uncle Don Lucas, and while trying to stay on the will with the tricks and ruses of his servant Crispín.

The ethical argument hurled by the shrewd maid, Lucía, about the (im)possibility of transferring wealth beyond this life, complements the servant's attacks on the old rich miser. Lucía reminds Don Lucas that the origin of his fortune is arbitrary, reviewing the fortuitous direction of the money "flow" (caudal/caudales) while relativizing its moral or metaphysical value: whereas money is of no use in the afterlife, it can however assist the misery of the poor on earth. By the same token, his donation of wealth could help to save the rich man's soul.[14]

These elements of social-class conflict between landowners and hardworking servants exploited by the "tyrant misery," but also between patriarchal ownership versus female unfettered wisdom, belongs to a wider debate about the correlation of tradition, material heritage, generosity, greed, and spiritual salvation with which the work culminates into a comprehensive comedy of errors, fake or falsified identities, and selfish desires that can be easily adapted to address social injustices and inequalities in other times and places. Inheritance and social class, privilege and the arbitrariness of fortune, are interwoven themes that provide a particularly rich site for the discussion of key questions within the larger philosophical debates of the Enlightenment: tyranny and democracy, social mobility and serfdom, equality and gender, and the possibility of amending the social contract through a new constitutional text, in this case, a testament. This progressive secular agenda allows us to evoke the contrast and indeed the open fracture between the different projects and discourses at the end of the colonial experience in the Hispanic Southwest.

What had started with the apparently neat, compact performance of the *Requerimiento* threatening to uniformly roll out the universal empire of Catholic Spain, was progressively performing its own fractures and tensions. The competing models of feudal mission and "modern" *pueblo* were obviously facing off at the two shores of the Saint Lawrence River – a satirical play that must have exacerbated an already dire competition for hegemony over the colonial discourse of public performance. In *Astucias*, the carefully rehearsed teachings of the church about the sacredness of the social order and its archival inscription in sacramental records and texts is challenged by the malleable scripture of the will that servants and relatives can edit and

---

[14] The maid explains with daring clarity:

"Si el grueso caudal que Dios	If the heavy bounty that God
os dio porque fue su agrado,	Gave you because it pleased him,
os sirviera en la otra vida	Were to serve you in the next life
justo fuera conservarlo	It would be right to preserve it
para transportarlo allá;	To transport it there;
pero si habéis de dejarlo	But if you have to leave it
aunque os pese, ¿por qué no	Even though it hurts, why not
con franca y piadosa mano,	With an honest and pious hand,
de la tirana miseria	From tyrannous misery
no rescatáis dos criados . . .?"	Rescue two servants...?

(Translated by Olga Sánchez Saltveit) (3746–55)

alter. The performance of such a radically satirical text in a debated settlement built very close to a mission offers an insight into the competing projects over the captive audience – and troop – of mestizos, Native Americans, and other "castas" who populated these colonial spaces. The fracture of the Hispanic West can be perceived in these separate and increasingly entrenched billboards of secular and religious bilocations performed in front of an ever more self-aware and defiant captive audience.

WORKS CITED

Adorno, Rolena. *The Polemics of Possession in Spanish American Narrative*. New Haven, CT and London: Yale University Press, 2008.

Bancroft, Hubert Howe, et al. *History of California*. San Francisco: History Co., 1884.

Beebe, Rose Marie, and Robert M. Senkewicz. *Junípero Serra: California, Indians, and the Transformation of a Missionary*. Norman: University of Oklahoma Press, 2015.

Bruce-Novoa, Juan. "Shipwrecked in the Seas of Signification: Cabeza de Vaca's *Relación* and Chicano Literature." *Reconstructing a Chicano/a Literary Heritage: Hispanic Colonial Literature of the Southwest*. Ed. Herrera-Sobek, María. Tucson: University of Arizona Press, 1993. 3–23.

Burkhart, Louise M. *Aztecs on Stage: Religious Theater in Colonial Mexico*. Norman: University of Oklahoma Press, 2011.

Cañizares-Esguerra, Jorge. *Puritan Conquistadors: Iberianizing the Atlantic, 1550–1700*. Stanford, CA: Stanford University Press, 2006.

Cervantes, Fernando. *The Devil in the New World: the Impact of Diabolism in New Spain*. New Haven, CT and London: Yale University Press, 1994.

Colahan, Clark A. *The Visions of Sor María de Agreda: Writing Knowledge and Power*. Tucson: University of Arizona Press, 1994.

Cortés, Hernán. *Letters of Cortés: the Five Letters of Relation from Fernando Cortés to the Emperor Charles V*. Ed. MacNutt, Francis Augustus. Vol. 2. 2 vols. New York: G. P. Putnam, 1908.

Domínguez García, Javier. *De Apóstol matamoros a Yllapa mataindios: dogmas e ideologías medievales en el (des)cubrimiento de América*. Salamanca: Ediciones Universidad de Salamanca, 2008.

Dussel, Enrique D. *Beyond Philosophy: Ethics, History, Marxism, and Liberation Theology*. Ed. Mendieta, Eduardo. Lanham, MD: Rowman & Littlefield Publishers, 2003.

Greengrass, Mark. *Christendom Destroyed: Europe 1517–1648*. New York: Viking, 2014.

Gruzinski, Serge. *La colonización de lo imaginario: sociedades indígenas y occidentalización en el México español, siglos XVI-XVIII*. Ed. Ferreiro, Jorge. México: Fondo de Cultura Económica, 1991.

Guest, Florian. "The Establishment of the Villa de Branciforte." *California Historical Society Quarterly* 41.1 (1962): 29–50.

Gutiérrez, Ramón. "The Politics of Theater in Colonial New Mexico: Drama and the Rhetoric of Conquest." *Reconstructing a Chicano/a Literary Heritage: Hispanic Colonial*

Literature of the Southwest. Ed. Herrera-Sobek, María. Tucson: University of Arizona Press, 1993. 49–67.

Hanke, Lewis. *The Spanish Struggle for Justice in the Conquest of America*. Philadelphia: University of Pennsylvania Press, 1949.

    All Mankind is One: A Study of the Disputation Between Bartolomé de las Casas and Juan Ginés de Sepúlveda on the Religious and Intellectual Capacity of the American Indians. DeKalb: Northern Illinois University Press, 1974.

Harris, Max. *Aztecs, Moors, and Christians*. Austin: University of Texas Press, 2010.

Helps, Arthur. *The Spanish Conquest in America: and Its Relation to the History of Slavery and to the Government of Colonies*. 1855. Ed. Oppenheim, M. Vol. 1. 4 vols. London: J.W. Parker and Son, 1900.

Hickerson, Nancy P. "The Visits of the 'Lady in Blue': An Episode in the History of the South Plains, 1629." *Journal of Anthropological Research* 46.1 (1990): 67–90.

Irwin, Robert McKee "Toward a Border Gnosis of the Borderlands: Joaquin Murrieta and Nineteenth-Century U.S.-Mexico Border Culture." *Nepantla: Views from South* 2.3 (2001): 509–37.

Kanellos, Nicolás. *A History of Hispanic Theatre in the United States: Origins to 1940*. Austin: University of Texas Press, 1990.

Lamadrid, Enrique R. *Hermanitos comanchitos: Indo-Hispano Rituals of Captivity and Redemption*. Albuquerque: University of New Mexico Press, 2003.

Lane, Jill. "On Colonial Forgetting: The Conquest of New Mexico and Its *Historia*." *The Ends of Performance*. Eds. Phelan, Peggy and Jill Lane. New York: New York University Press, 1998. 52–69.

León Portilla, Miguel, and Antonio Valeriano. *Juan Diego Cuauhtlatoatzin*. Ciudad de México: DGE/Equilibrista, 2005.

Lozano, Tomás. *Cantemos al alba: Origins of Songs, Sounds, and Liturgical Drama of Hispanic New Mexico*. Ed. Montoya, Rima. Albuquerque: University of New Mexico Press, 2007.

Mann, Kristin Dutcher. *The Power of Song: Music and Dance in the Mission Communities of Northern New Spain, 1590–1810*. Stanford, CA: Stanford University Press, 2010.

Mignolo, Walter. *Local Histories/Global Designs: Coloniality, Subaltern Knowledges, and Border Thinking*. Princeton, NJ: Princeton University Press, 2000.

Montaigne, Michel de. *Essais III*. Paris: Folio, 1965.

Morrow, Baker H. *A Harvest of Reluctant Souls: Fray Alonso de Benavides's History of New Mexico, 1630*. Trans. by Claton Butcher. Albuquerque: University of New Mexico Press, 1996.

Moziño, José Mariano. *Noticias de Nutka; an Account of Nootka Sound in 1792*. Trans. and ed. by Iris H. Wilson. Seattle: University of Washington Press, 1970.

Núñez Cabeza de Vaca, Alvar. *Naufragios*. Ed. Maura, Juan Francisco. Madrid: Cátedra, 1989.

Olavarría y Ferrari, Enrique de. *Reseña histórica del teatro en México: 1538–1911*. Vol. 1. 6 vols. México, DF: Editorial Porrúa, 1961.

Padilla, Felix, ed. *Handbook of Hispanic Cultures in the United States: Sociology*. Vol. 3. 4 vols. Houston, TX and Madrid: Arte Público Press and Instituto de Cooperación Iberoamericana, 1993.

Pueyo Zoco, Victor. "Cuerpos imaginarios e imágenes corporales. La producción del sujeto femenino en el espacio místico de la bilocación (1570–1670)." *Letras Femeninas* 40.1 (2014): 21.

Quijano, Aníbal. "Coloniality of Power, Eurocentrism, and Latin America." *Nepantla: Views from South* 1.3 (2000): 533–580.

Quinn, David B. *Explorers and Colonies: America, 1500–1625.* London: Hambledon Press, 1990.

Rabasa, José. *Writing Violence on the Northern Frontier: The Historiography of Sixteenth Century New Mexico and Florida and the Legacy of Conquest.* Durham, NC: Duke University Press, 2000.

Ramos Smith, Maya. *La danza en México durante la época colonial.* 1979. México: Conaculta, 1990.

Rancière, Jacques. *The Emancipated Spectator.* London: Verso, 2011.

Reygadas, Fermín de. *Astucias por heredar, un sobrino a un tío [1789].* Recovering the U.S. Hispanic Literary Heritage. Ed. Pedro García-Caro. Houston, TX: Arte Público Press, 2017.

   Astucias por heredar, un sobrino a un tío. Ciudad de México, 1789. MS-CE120, Bancroft Library.

Russell, Craig H. *From Serra to Sancho: Music and Pageantry in the California Missions.* New York: Oxford University Press, 2009.

Sayre, Gordon M. *The Indian Chief as Tragic Hero Native Resistance and the Literatures of America, from Moctezuma to Tecumseh.* Chapel Hill: University of North Carolina Press, 2005.

Schaafsma, Polly. *Kachinas in the Pueblo World.* Albuquerque: University of New Mexico Press, 1994.

Seed, Patricia. *Ceremonies of Possession in Europe's Conquest of the New World, 1492–1640.* Cambridge and New York: Cambridge University Press, 1995.

Sherwood, Yvonne. "Comparing the "Telegraph Bible" to the Chaotic Bible." *In the Name of God: the Bible in the Colonial Discourse of Empire.* Eds. Crouch, C. L. and Jonathan Stökl. Leiden: Brill, 2014. 5–62.

Sponsler, Claire. *Ritual Imports: Performing Medieval Drama in America.* Ithaca, NY: Cornell University Press, 2004.

Steele, Ian Kenneth, and Nancy L. Rhoden. *The Human Tradition in Colonial America.* Wilmington, DE: SR Books/Scholarly Resources, Inc., 1999.

Taylor, Diana. *The Archive and the Repertoire: Performing Cultural Memory in the Americas.* Durham, NC: Duke University Press, 2003.

Vallejo, José Guadalupe. "Carta a H.H. Bancroft." Feb. 9, 1875. Bancroft Library.

Viqueira Albán, Juan Pedro. *Propriety and Permissiveness in Bourbon Mexico.* Trans. Lipsett-Rivera, Sonya and Sergio Rivera Ayala. Wilmington, DE: Scholarly Resources, 1999.

Weber, David J. *Bárbaros: Spaniards and Their Savages in the Age of Enlightenment.* New Haven, CT: Yale University Press, 2005.

   The Mexican Frontier, 1821–1846: the American Southwest under Mexico. Albuquerque: University of New Mexico Press, 1982.

Williams, Robert A. *The American Indian in Western Legal Thought.* New York: Oxford University Press, 1993.

3

The Tricks of the Weak

Sor Juana Inés de la Cruz and the Feminist Temporality of Latina Literature

ELISA SAMPSON VERA TUDELA

Cualquier semejanza con la vida real es virtual.
(Any resemblance to real life is purely coincidental.)[1]

[Part of a message displayed on Sor Juana's laptop and projected on a giant onstage screen to the audience. Jesusa Rodríguez, "Sor Juana en Almoloya" (395)]

Latina readings of Sor Juana are not immune to the illusions of the field, but they have been some of the most lucid and reflective interventions both in terms of academic writing and more creative contributions in the form of poetry, drama, and fiction. This essay sets out to trace some of these and to delineate the genesis and shape of this ongoing fascination with Sor Juana as well as to describe the directions in which such fascination is now taking scholars and writers.

The ubiquity of Sor Juana in Hispanic culture is given – she appears on money, in magazines and on TV as well as at school (Poot Herrera, Hind). For Latina thinkers (that is, the female-gendered Latin American diaspora located worldwide but outside the region of origin) this ubiquity has been made even more complex by the intervention of perhaps one of the most significant patriarchs of Hispanic culture, Octavio Paz. Paz's biography of Sor Juana, *Las trampas de la fé* (1980) can be thought of as a continuation of his project to explain Mexican identity begun in *El laberinto de la soledad* (1950) and as such his interpretation of the nun's life and work has become

---

[1] All translations from Spanish are mine. The humor and nuance of the Spanish is lost somewhat here by using the terms of the "all persons fictitious disclaimer" in English. *Virtual* means both "virtual" and "partial" in this context.

completely enmeshed in the polemic surrounding his more general pronouncements. The interventions about Sor Juana examined here seek to
wrest her from the arms of this and various other grandfathers, however
benign they appear. As such, they participate in what Eduardo Santí has
described as the politics of "restitution" surrounding the nun, which began
almost the moment she died with the publication of Calleja's first autobiography in the edition of Sor Juana's *Fama y Obras Póstumas* (Madrid, 1700).
According to Santí, the various personae of the nun constructed by the
critical canon have been created "in order to domesticate the radical otherness of her work" (104). Glantz makes a similar observation, commenting on
the desire (implicit or explicit) in sorjuanian criticism to use Sor Juana "as a
fundamental element in a theory, in spite of the fact that the complexity of
her figure means that it is unclear exactly where she should be located"
(*Figure* 175).

The Latina readings of Sor Juana form part of a longer struggle over
meaning and methodology. There is, however, no need to import theory
when the subject has apparently anticipated it: "three hundred years before
postmodernism, feminist theory, deconstructive praxis and decolonial theory
Sor Juana was writing about not only the social construction of gender and
the gendered construction of knowledge but also about representation,
subjectivity, fragmented identities, and the power of the imaginary" (Gaspar
de Alba, [*Un*]*framing* 270). The temporal issues this kind of understanding
raises have centrally informed the definition and scope of Latina/o studies
itself, suggesting a long Latina history in which the struggle over the
meaning of the discontinuous past is central. Perhaps the most obvious and
central reason Sor Juana has become a key figure for Latina thought is that
she provides a way of thinking about the two key legacies of colonialism –
patriarchy and race – are intimately related to the historically central concerns of Latina/o studies: hybrid identities and social injustice. Sor Juana is
the prototype of the gendered subaltern (Ludmer, Clarmurro, Glantz
Hagiografía).

If we turn first to the feminist criticism of Sor Juana and her writing, the
various emphases, from the identification of feminine themes to readings of
feminist theology, all coalesce around the notion of Sor Juana as a feminist
precursor (Merrim, *Feminist Perspectives* 11–37). Sor Juana herself in the
Respuesta a Sor Filotea begins the construction of this genealogy (Ludmer 48).
However, the problematic nature of invoking exemplarity (the most
common way of understanding Sor Juana's relation to tradition) is apparent
as much to the nun herself as it is to her most recent critics. The strategic

exemplarity deployed by certain feminist projects for example that have attempted to discover their own genealogies leading back to Sor Juana rely on her biography, a set of non-facts that has dogged sorjuanian criticism from the very first publication of the nun's works.[2] From Calleja in 1700 through to Schons in the 1920s, Pfandl in the 1950s and Paz in 1980, these biographies have innocently (and not so innocently) confused "life" with "text" to such a degree that the vignettes their plots turn on (the not eating cheese, the hair cutting, the competition against the learned men) have become utterly disarticulated from their historical context and instead form floating elements of a number of narratives of self-destruction or liberation, murder mystery, or romance, depending on the author's stance.[3] Linda Egan concludes that critics appear intent on pursuing this line of investigation that she calls "criticism by séance" in which scholars seek to give Sor Juana the "full and fair hearing that history denied her" (206, 216). Women biographers have not been immune to the production of fantastical personae for Sor Juana. Perelmuter describes how early Latina readings by Luisi, Alfau de Solalinde, Sarre, Mistral, and Castellanos bear the marks of a similar obsession with the biographical however much they might have been arguing for a different (often feminist) interpretation of the life described (116). Luciani's corrective, pointing out the possibility that these "facts" are rhetorical constructions and not scraps of "real life" strikes at the heart of the biographers' project for it replaces "real life" with "a morass of texts and contexts from which the biographer cannot emerge with his authority intact" (10, 16).[4]

In Alicia Gaspar de Alba's "sapphic diary" of Sor Juana, the position of the biographer is occluded and instead the nun speaks for herself in a cache of letters to the dead Leonor Carreto, a vicereine of New Spain, to whom she

---

[2] For how the relatively little verifiable information on Sor Juana's life has been interpreted see Emir Rodríguez Monegal quoted in Bergmann; "con lo que se sabe (de la vida de Sor Juana) se pueden escribir toda clase de novelas biográficas, todas ellas falsas, todas ellas verdaderas. Pero solo en el terreno de la ficción" (174) (All kinds of biographical novels – all of them false, all of the true - can be written with what we know about the life of Sor Juana).

[3] See Moraña's interpretation of the "love" of the censor cited in Glantz *Sor Juana y sus contemporáneos* for another way of thinking about the distortions of biography (320–21). For a more extreme description of the biographer's actions, see Glantz's own assessment of Octavio Paz's biography of Sor Juana, which she calls an "anthropophagical ceremony," saying that he "has swallowed" Sor Juana and "has written her back in history and literature through a sacrificial act in which her whole being belongs to him: he has labeled her silence" (*Posthumous Fame*, 137).

[4] Luciani sees Octavio Paz's biography as characterized by "repeated slippage from the biocritical high ground into a precarious space marked by the desire to recover reality through the sign, to conjure up the lost original, to incarnate the metaphor" (8).

describes her love for Maria Luisa Manrique de Lara y Gonzaga, the new vicereine of the colony. In this imagined epistolary exchange Gaspar de Alba confronts the challenges of essentialism and historicity head-on, her recreation of Sor Juana's words resonating with contextual knowledge about the nun and her works while foregrounding an exoticism and sensuality (the *mole* is spicy, the lesbianism explicit, the letters are in English with some codeswitching) that speaks directly to the contemporary. It is in this kind of creative reading and writing of Sor Juana that we see Latina feminists negotiating the challenges of understanding the life and texts of the nun in a way that acknowledges the impossibility of talking about her in a linear biographical narrative. For as Catherine Boyle argues, "all her complex being seems to be alive in each act of her life and writing, epitomized in the labyrinthine intrigue of the endgame, and she has to be read through the complex edifice she constructed to create a space for her devotion to letters" (3).

These kinds of self-reflective Latina projects, which question the notions of antecedence and of lineage even as they gesture toward them, represent a radical rereading of exemplarity, stressing its proleptic and contingent character. Sor Juana becomes then utterly generative, her work representing a "swerve" from tradition in the Bloomian sense, where writers "modify, complete or selectively reject" the courses set by strong precursors (Merrim, *Feminist Perspectives* 23). The heart of this challenge lies in heeding the need to recognize the alterity of the past and thus, as Molloy warns, avoiding "impoverish[ing]" Sor Juana by taking her out of context (quoted in *Early Modern Women's Writing* xlii).[5]

Recent work on Sor Juana's *Neptuno Alegórico* (a complex piece of Baroque art that comprised both a physical triumphal arch and several texts interpreting its construction and decoration) is an excellent example of how critics have sought to complicate ahistoricizing portrayals of the nun as speaking for the subaltern (Bokser, *Reading and Writing*). According to Bokser, "the Neptune allegory depicts a utopian state and supports a conservative one. It also attempts to alter the status quo" and such complexity is poorly served by an interpretation exclusively fixed on establishing Sor Juana as working undercover against the dominant ideology (*Reading and Writing* 161).[6] Understanding

---

[5] Jean Franco issues a similar warning that although debates about rationality in Sor Juana's texts may resonate with contemporary feminist concerns, the context should be recognized as entirely different (25).

[6] See Arenal and Martin for how the Arch is now recognized as a colonial manifestation of the Early Modern genre of manuals on kingship and so how Sor Juana's version allows us to reexamine how we think women took part in this tradition.

colonial relations as "more than gendered" and engaging in a "more fully textured" encounter with the historical Sor Juana allows us to appreciate her "both/and" position (both critic and ideologue) according to Bokser and so produce a more robust feminist approach (*Reading and Writing* 144).[7] It is indeed by radically historicizing their understanding of the nun that Latina writers are able to follow Sor Juana's "lessons" in literary and ideological criticism, namely that "[d]ogmatic truths and hierarchical systems, she says, erase the traces of history in the text" (Merrim paraphrasing Ludmer, *Early Modern Women's Writing* xxii). Through this understanding, the radical potential of exemplarity is realized and as a result, it is possible to easily imagine Sor Juana and her texts as sympathetic to the "agendas" of Chicana activism and queer studies (*Angels of History* 63, 79).

The difficulties surrounding the use of Sor Juana's figure as exemplary in terms of race/culture/ethnicity are very similar to those outlined regarding gender. According to Alatorre, from Calleja's first invocation of Sor Juana's birthplace of Amecameca – a small town between the two volcanoes Iztacci-huatl and Popocatepl that dominate Mexico City – place has instantly been associated with the nun in a process of "metaphorization" where she becomes a specifically American product (glossed by Glantz in *Figure of Genius* 181). Sor Juana's American identity generally and most specifically her *mexicanidad* have obviously been of central concern in criticism. Octavio Paz's reading of Sor Juana is a key example of this emphasis and, according to Merrim, actually displaces gender concerns with ones of national identity (Merrim *Feminist Perspectives* 11). So, where feminist critics would interpret solitude and silence in Sor Juana's work as speaking to her position as a writing woman, Paz understands these themes as key attributes of a Mexican rather than a female poetic identity. Paz's elaboration of Sor Juana as his own poetic predecessor should be understood in the context of the rehabilitation of the colonial period more generally in Mexican culture and Paz's book can therefore be thought of as a key part of this cultural politics (Allatson 4). This means that in particular Chicana, but also more generally Latina, reinventions of Sor Juana have necessarily had to engage with the nun "through" Octavio Paz. Gaspar de Alba sees such an engagement with Paz as part of her "decolonizing" of Sor Juana in a formulation that explicitly conflates the feminist and postcolonial agendas (she characterizes Paz as marked by his

---

[7] John Beverley's description of the effect of the Baroque in Latin American culture as a kind of "cultural neurosis" linked to what Aníbal Quijano calls the "coloniality of power" is apposite in relation to these new readings of Sor Juana's arch (150).

"self-righteous upper-class, heteronormative Mexicanness").[8] Gaspar de Alba feels literally haunted by Paz, whose ghost she runs into wherever she goes to talk about her Sor Juana novel (*[Un]framing* 261). The ghostly presence of Paz also haunts Rodríguez's "pastorela virtual" *Sor Juana en Almoloya*, a pastiche of contemporary politics, historical texts, and Sor Juana's own writing. Offstage, a voice that could be Paz's own, reads the passages from *Las trampas de la fé* that dismiss the suspected lesbianism of Sor Juana while on stage the nun and the vicereine (disguised as a boy) kiss passionately (401–403). Simultaneously citing and questioning Paz, Rodríguez's haunting is less earnest than Gaspar de Alba's and manages to stress same-sex desire "but always with a playful uncertainty; is it a joke on Paz or is it the 'true' relationship between the two women we see on stage?"(Gladhart 221).

In Rodríguez's play, Paz is not the only problematic man. Our nun heroine finds herself imprisoned and censured in the imagined future by a catalog of patriarchal authority figures that dress up as nuns (following in the footsteps of Núñez de Miranda, the infamous Sor Filotea) the better to harass her under the guise of false humility. The play riotously weaves very specific political satire and critique of contemporary twentieth-century Mexican politics with rewritings of Sor Juana's own works in a way that suggests the reinvention and imprisonment of the iconic nun has been used as a smokescreen to distract from contemporary issues and scandals (Gladhart 218). Dismissed as an "enemiga de México," her stance (and that of all unamenable women) is summed up by the character of Emilio Azcárraga (the Chairman of Televisa, a huge multimedia conglomerate and one of the richest businessmen in Latin America): "Todas son iguales, pinches viejas" (409, 411) (They're all the same – a load of old bags). Rodríguez unmistakably maps a feminist critique onto her politics and sees in Sor Juana a figure through which to explore the workings of a corrupt capitalist patriarchy and the constraints it places on her own writing and that of other Latina artists (Gladhart 218).[9] Rodríguez's balancing of a feminist and mexicanist reinterpretation of Sor Juana demonstrates the fruitful polivalency of the nun's

---

[8] See also fn 50 where Paz, though credited as "such a good poet," and having said some "remarkably accurate things" about fiestas and the Day of the Dead, is described as "homophobic in the extreme" and "dangerous" to those who fit the categories he maligns – "women, Mexican Americans and lesbians" (261).

[9] The stakes in terms of freedom to write could not have been higher for Sor Juana of course and Franco, glossing a metaphor of Moses in his reed bed that Sor Juana uses for her writing, comments that "creation, for Sor Juana, is precariously forged with the full knowledge of the unhappy prospect of choosing between institutionality and 'child murder'" (45).

figure. Sor Juana's historical and geographical context as a colonial subject of the Spanish crown in the Viceroyalty of New Spain (a space which today is partly Mexico and partly the United States) calls effortlessly and effectively into question notions of national identity and has proved inspiring to Latina thinkers and artists.

Contemporary Latina rewritings then invoke the historical figure of Sor Juana and cite her texts, but do so in a self-reflexive way that is determinedly political and connects them to wider liberatory aims. Karen Zacarías's play is available both in English (with elements of codeswitching) and Spanish and raises themes relevant to Latina feminist culture through the strategies of juxtaposition, anachronism, and collage. Iris Zavala's novel *Nocturna mas no funesta* (1987) which tells the story of a Sor Juana alter ego – an imaginary Puerto Rican nun – is constructed around a series of juxtaposed inquisition files and interviews as well as letters from the nun to a number of correspondents (Georges Sand, Ruben Darío as well as some imaginary ones – the Dark Lady of Shakespeare's sonnets for example – and Sor Juana herself). The displacement of the historical Sor Juana is perhaps most emphatic in Rodríguez's play where she is an "explicitly *virtual* representation, doubly, even triply distanced in that we see a performer acting the role of a computer projection of a historical person. We are not seeing the 'real thing'"(Gladhart 222). All the texts that appear in the play – spoken, written, and projected – merge into a hypertext that is characterized by its continual cross-referencing and linking but also by its discontinuity (Gladhart 224). In marked contrast, in her interview with Sor Juana, Gaspar de Alba could be mistaken for indulging quite literally in Egan's "criticism by séance" (*[Un]framing* 54–63). It quickly becomes apparent, however, in questions ranging from what does Sor Juana think of Simone de Beauvoir and Monique Wittig to whether her *negra inclinación* was exclusively intellectual or perhaps sexual that Gaspar de Alba, if she can be thought of as participating in a "restitution" of the nun, is doing so with an explicitly political agenda that complicates ideas of temporality and causality.[10] The reader of the interview is forced to jettison notions of chronological specificity and purity of source material and form – Sor Juana's prose and verse answers in the academic interview are from her own texts, but in English, and come from a variety of translations, some from translators canonized by sorjuanian studies, some Gaspar de Alba's own.

---

[10] Very difficult to translate out of context, negra inclinación allows for interpretations ranging from "willfull stubbornness" to "evil will."

The methods of fragmentation and collage evident in these Sor Juana projects align them with the radical agenda of Latina historians and philosophers very closely. Emma Pérez, for example, theorizes a "third space feminist revision" where the recovery of historical figures and their connection to the contemporary can be made radical through an explicit articulation of the "liberatory consciousness" of history. Pérez values particularly the construction of stories in such a project, stressing their value in making temporality supremely complex: "[a]ll at once we live the past, present, and future" (127). Jean Franco signals the value of a similar approach, rooted in Wittgenstein's idea of language games, which would allow critics to avoid "impos[ing] a false unity on the corpus" (25).

Latina reinterpretations of Sor Juana, however they might complicate notions of subjectivity, notably focus on the nun herself. Her cloistered community, presented very ambivalently in various texts by Sor Juana herself, figures much less prominently, but it is possible to detect opportunities for a radical rereading of this too from a Latina perspective. The convent as a feminist space has been a key area of research in Sor Juana studies, and Merrim in *Early Modern Women's Writing* provides both a good overview of specific research on Sor Juana and more general research about the convent in the Early Modern world as an alternative "feminine" space. The convent community, in its admission of the nun through the ceremony of profession could be considered as providing an alternative lineage to that of patriarchy (Glantz *Hagiografía* X). It certainly provided Sor Juana a room of her own in which she constructed for herself an intellectual community of dead female scholars through her reading and writing. However, critics have also begun to reevaluate the gossipy and noisy community of real-life nuns outside the cell that Sor Juana complains bitterly about. Bokser for example sees in Sor Juana's famous *Respuesta* the reconstruction of the "non-dominant, disruptive, and potentially resistant" voices of these nuns: "Sor Juana reconstructs the nuns' interruptive behaviour into a 'female' rhetorical model of resistance and challenge" (*Silence* 15). The reappropriation of women who seem to safeguard the patriarchal status quo for any feminist project is obviously complex and approaches that attempt it range from condemnation to consciousness raising. Latina writers' engagement with these figures (known as "gatekeepers") is an important feature of their texts, and in the examination of the wider convent community it is possible to also rethink the role of these women as "cultural censors and guides into the prison house of adult womanhood in a dystopic patriarchy" (Kafka 12).

One illuminating entry into this field comes in studies that examine female "work" in the convent and writing specifically. Margo Glantz describes a hierarchy where texts produced by nuns at the behest of confessors were at the bottom. Of course, the notion that Sor Juana used the confinement of her writing to "minor" genres in a strategic way is a cornerstone of feminist interpretations of her work (Martínez-San Miguel *Saberes americanos* 80; Ludmer 54). However, it is Glantz's insight into how this women's writing was considered on a par with other female handiwork carried out in the convent (embroidery, baking, gardening, etc.) that enables an interpretation going beyond Sor Juana to her sisters. The habitual dismissal of their own writing as scribblings constantly needing correction (a metaphor used by Sor Juana herself) allied with the fragility of these texts which did not belong to their authors and so were never usually archived and certainly only ever printed in the most exceptional of cases, makes the vulnerable status of this writing (and of its authors) absolutely evident. The precariousness of women's writing is, as we have seen, also central to the Latina interpretations of Sor Juana and clearly marks a point of political intervention where issues of censorship and expression can be explored.

However, it is in the emphasis on the sexed nature of this writing through the category of "handiwork" that more radical interpretation is possible. According to Glantz, women wrote with their hands while men wrote with their heads (*Labores de manos* 28). In this respect, the contemporary art of Amalia Mesa-Bains, which works to define a Chicana aesthetic by recovering neglected or devalued Mexican American traditions, is instructive. In her domestic altars, Mesa-Bains reconstructs the various icons of Latina and specifically Chicana identity but subjects them to a purposefully gendered reduction: they are at once quotidian and ephemeral. Her 1994 recreation of Sor Juana's library (an installation/collage of the familiar representation of the library that appears in portraits of the nun and in the frontispieces of her published texts with some significant modern additions in the form of eyelash curlers, for example) is placed in a small sitting room and appears makeshift in the extreme. It makes a pointed comment on the vulnerability of the "real thing" which Sor Juana was ordered to dismantle and disperse by her confessor, as well as on the limited space and rooms of their own given to many contemporary women.

This carving out of a feminist space from unlikely materials – the fact that, as Jean Franco says "in the struggle for interpretive power, women are forced to bring practical life into the realm of knowledge" (47) – is a theme that critics have frequently read back into and from Sor Juana's texts. Most famously her assertion that had Aristotle cooked more he would have also been able to write more, has become something of a feminist mantra.

Ludmer categorizes this rhetorical move on Sor Juana's part as archetypal subaltern behavior, accepting the dictates of power but transforming their reach (99).[11] Recent feminist research into these writing hierarchies and spaces has meant a concentrated focus on the female body that inhabits them and not only the practices performed within them. Bokser for example sees Sor Juana as embodying learning through her *sexed* experience of these domestic spaces (*Silence* 11). Similarly, Glantz emphasizes that what sets the texts written by female hands apart is the sex of the body that writes them and not any other circumstance. And this body, according to Glantz, is impossible to evade (*Hagiografía* X). In an environment where the female body was most explicitly present only to be disciplined – a tradition sanctioned in the ultimate form of discourse available to women, that of mysticism – Sor Juana's masculine writing was a threat. This reevaluation of the body in Sor Juana's work presents something of a challenge to established scholarship on the nun that has tended to align her with philosophical schools that oppose body to soul. Harvey, however, argues that "the body is neither absent nor rejected in her works" and sees in Sor Juana's poem *Primer Sueño* a challenge to ideas about the inferiority of women's bodies, with Sor Juana affirming that the female body is functional and necessary (55). Yolanda Martínez-San Miguel also questions the supposed absence of the body in Sor Juana's writing and hypothesizes that the nun's choice not to follow the path of mysticism can be considered as a project to enter the masculine sphere and then truly de-sex it by writing a female body into it.

Martínez-San Miguel makes explicit how such a reading offers a lesson and corrective for contemporary post-modernity that she characterizes as reductively skeptical and destructive of meaning. For her, Sor Juana's practice shows that the subject "siempre ha vivido en un mundo en el cual negocia su espacio y, por más viajes que el Alma emprenda, siempre tendrá que regresar al cuerpo" (*Sujeto femenino* 278) ([Sor Juana] has always lived in a world in which she has to negotiate her own space and, however many voyages her Soul undertakes, it will always have to return to her body). Many contemporary interpretations of Sor Juana precisely engage the political traction offered by embodiment and figure the body as a lesbian one, employing a strategic essentialism in order to assert historical visibility. For Gaspar de Alba, the imperative was compelling and yet utterly proverbial – she had to "call a spade a spade" and thus "the spade that her critics and biographers

---

[11] Rosario Castellanos literally locates lessons from Sor Juana on how to contest patriarchy in the kitchen in her *Lección de cocina* (1972).

have called everything but a spade" is named as Sor Juana's lesbianism. Gaspar de Alba's project then is to "reconfigure" Sor Juana "not as a Hispanic, but as a Chicana lesbian feminist" (*[Un]framing* 46). The multiple incarnations of the queer ghostly Sor Juana in contemporary writing would appear to attest to the desire, summed up movingly by Caroline Dinshaw as "the possibility of touching across time, collapsing time through affective contact between marginalized people now and then" and suggesting that with "such queer historical touches we could form communities across time" (178).[12] Dinshaw's allusion to the queering of history marks yet another development in historical projects to explore sexuality across time with McCabe summing up the shift thus: "queer studies has veered from a monolithic model of historicism (and its concomitant modes of nomination) to one that depends on a paradox: the trans-historical existence of erotic pluralism" (120). In a way similar to that in which feminist readings of Sor Juana are seen to draw away from unified notions of feminine subjectivity, readings of sexuality also withdraw from the category of identity (naming the lesbian) toward that of "orientations" – and thus illustrate the need to fuse the work of excavation with recognition that identities and sexualities are socially and temporally constructed and can take multiple forms.

Setting aside its sexuality, the body of Sor Juana that is imagined by Latina writers is a specifically mestiza one. Identifying with the nun's illegitimacy, criollo ethnicity, and her colonial status, Latina literature reads her catachrestically as embodying its own predicament. According to Paul Allatson, Sor Juana thus becomes a resource for transforming the field of "transfrontera Chicana feminist traditions" (23). For Norma Alarcón, Chicana identities must be understood as "imbricated in the historical *and* imaginary shifting national borders of Mexico and the United States" (198) and so the mobilization of Sor Juana in the project to construct them is driven by a very precise notion of history and place. The artist Katia Fuentes (born in Mexico but living in the United States) who works by projecting images of iconic Mexican figures onto her body has produced a series of artworks where Sor Juana appears in a "tattoo of light" on her own body. Fuentes's description of her art stresses the element of personal discovery but roots its power in location – it allows her to define self in relation to a "now-foreign" Mexican culture and from the "negativity of America" (Fuentes 3).

---

[12] See also Maria Luisa Bemberg *Yo la peor de todas* (1990) for a filmic interpretation of Sor Juana's lesbianism.

This here and there, *allá* and *acá*, invoked by Fuentes, are reminiscent of a key romance (*Diversa de mi misma*) by Sor Juana that has become the cornerstone not only of Chicana interpretations of the nun's work, but more broadly of hemispheric ones. The apparently unfinished poem, also known as "Romance 51" is believed to be if not the last, then certainly one of the last works by the nun, written in the months before her death in 1695. The poem was published for the first time in *Fama y Obras Póstumas* (1700) and is essentially a reply to her European readers and the praise they have heaped on her work. The first part of the poem, structured as a number of rhetorical questions, has Sor Juana suggesting that her European fans have misunderstood her writing because of the difference between their two contexts: the *aquí* (here) of the poem and the *allá* (there) of the readers. Falsely modest (as many critics interpret her to be) Sor Juana goes on in the second part of the poem to discuss explicitly the "differences" at stake – from her place as a woman and a nun to her situation as an autodidact and colonial subject.

Contemporary critics have celebrated Sor Juana's invocation of the *"mágicas infusiones/de los Indios herbolarios/de mi Patria"* (Cruz, I 159–60) (magical infusions of the Indian herbalists from my country) in this second part of the poem as a reappropriation of indigenous elements that are then put to use in a subtle but devastating reproach from the nun that questions the idea of any cultural or poetic continuity between Spain and America. The romance has thus become a privileged text in which it is possible to read signs of two-directional transculturation under circumstances of unequal exchange. For Zamora for example, the key moment in the poem is that of "el paisaje lírico de la Patria" (the lyrical landscape of Nation) (*América* 141). Zamora argues that this recollection, while certainly a Baroque invocation of the exotic, exceeds this and intimate remembering of place and indigenous specificity becomes "una actividad diferenciadora no solo de dos lugares, nuevo y viejo mundo, sino sobre todo de la posición del sujeto mnemónico" (an action that differentiates not only two places, new and old world, but above all marks the position of the remembering subject) (*América* 147). Zamora elaborates this insight in a way that makes perfectly apparent its relevance to contemporary Latina constructions of self: "[e]l sujeto americano, sea indio, mestizo, criollo o inmigrante" (the American subject, be they Indian, criollo, mestizo, or immigrant), constructs the coherence and meaning of her life from her memory of *acá* (*América* 147).

Martínez-San Miguel has a similar reading of the romance as radical, but she places the emphasis on what she sees as Sor Juana's refusal of the role of mediator between *acá* and *allá* (here and there). Sor Juana doesn't so much reject a transatlantic reading as ask under which conditions it becomes possible. It is this question that reveals how the transatlantic context may function simultaneously as "límite y espacio posibilitador" (limit and enabling space) for the colonial condition (*Otra vez Sor Juana* 61, 62). Both these readings of the hemispheric in the poem coalesce around the astonishingly complex colonial subjectivity that it produces (*Otra vez Sor Juana* 63). Recognizing this asymmetric and dissonant identity means there is little need to conjure a Sor Juana who speaks exclusively for the subaltern. It is enough, as Martínez-San Miguel says, that we see "en su *performance* del discurso criollo las múltiples sinuosidades que explican lo que Quijano ha denominado como la 'colonialidad del poder' . . . o la pervivencia de las estructuras coloniales en los imaginarios criollos americanos" (in her performance of criollo discourse the multiple intricacies of what Quijano calls the "coloniality of power" . . . or the persistence of colonial structures in the *criollo* imaginary) (*Otra vez Sor Juana* 66–67).

A strong reading precisely in this vein comes from Merrim in her assessment of Sor Juana's use of the figure of la Virgen de Guadalupe. Merrim describes sorjuanian scholarship's consternation at the near absence of this illustrious foremother in Sor Juana's texts and then goes on to trace how the Virgin's "trademark features" are diffused by Sor Juana and reinscribed onto the Virgin Mary. According to Merrim, "Sor Juana in fact absorbs the Mexican icon into her universalizing, syncretic, transatlantic modus operandi" (*Angels of History* 75). Resonantly, Merrim characterizes this absorption as a refusal to translate or bridge cultures and offers it as a model of contemporary relevance for how to live life on the border. She argues that it is possible to understand Sor Juana's "bold, wilful, and syncretic campaign" as a template that has inspired Chicana reappropriations of la Virgen de Guadalupe, most notably Gloria Anzaldúa's (*Angels of History* 63).

For Martínez-San Miguel, work on Sor Juana's figure and texts constitutes a response to the central difficulty of hemispheric studies – its notion of modernity as the exclusive "marco de referencia epistemológico" (*Otra vez Sor Juana* 56) (epistemological frame of reference). Here it would be possible to make an analogy between the radical force of this critical work and García Canclini's "transdisciplinary gaze" in that they both acknowledge the need for any critique of modernity to be itself temporally hybrid and nomadic (Kraniauskas 143). The hybridized nomadic critique, in its refusal to translate or bridge, does not, however, negate the notion of community. Quite the reverse. Merrim, for example, identifies Gaspar de Alba's novel as meeting the challenge of Sor Juana's "pursuing gaze" about how to represent icons (herself included one assumes) for "both Américas, and for the past and present".

This instrumentalized interpretation and critique of history responds absolutely to the need for creating "imagined communities when 'most exigent or most meaningful'" (*Angels of History* 76, 79, 70). The notion of a "usable" past as articulated in Latina readings of Sor Juana allow us for example to rethink gender across time in the way that Maria Lugones advocates. Her project on what she calls the "colonial/modern gender system" attempts to articulate the link between two frameworks of analysis – the work done by feminist scholars on race and colonialism and that of Anibal Quijano on the "coloniality of power" with the intention of making visible "the instrumentality of the colonial/modern gender system in subjecting ... both women and men of color" (1). Lugones's project, in its thinking through feminist and postcolonial agendas shares many points of contact with the readings of Sor Juana we have examined. Perhaps the most salient is the "real world" concern for the project's potential to heal communities by making visible "the crucial disruption of bonds of practical solidarity inherent in the colonial/modern gender system" (1).

How the legacy of Sor Juana studies can facilitate an alternative understanding of Latina modernity is perhaps best illustrated in the way the most obvious hemispheric pairing of Sor Juana with Anne Bradstreet has been interpreted. The opportunity afforded for hemispheric analysis of these near contemporaries, Tenth Muses, and first two published female poets of the New World appears obvious and tempting. However, Merrim enumerates the more profound and seemingly unbreachable differences: Bradstreet moving from frontier town to frontier town, Sor Juana enclosed, Bradstreet mother and wife, Sor Juana nun, Bradstreet Puritan, Sor Juana Catholic, Bradstreet exponent of "plain style," Sor Juana expert technician of the Baroque (*Early Modern Women's Writing* 139). Given these obvious differences between the women, Merrim suggests that Electa Arenal's play *This Life Within Me Won't Keep Still* (which features both women and dramatizes the tension between difference and commonality) is a model for any hemispheric project. In the play, the tensions between commonality and difference are dramatized but not resolved – the audience is left to interpret and provide an "ending" – a strategy Merrim recommends for any hemispheric project to align colonial discourses from the Americas.

The agency of the audience/reader is similarly central to Jovita González's story *Shades of the Tenth Muses* (circa 1935) that also imagines an encounter between the two poets. Although the dramatic tension hinges on differences,

González's story conjures an extraordinary moment of multi-temporal community as the culmination of a number of exchanges where Sor Juana, speaking English, has performed colonial Catholic Mexican culture for Bradstreet. Bradstreet prepares to leave explaining she needs to tend to her husband by preparing his pipe and "tucking him in." Sor Juana's response is gently mocking, aligning the reader with her irony and yet also extending the possibility of a continued relationship to Bradstreet:

> "Simon must be tucked in," giggled the nun to herself, and aloud to Anne she said, "It has been a great honor and a pleasure to know another Tenth Muse. I thought I had the monopoly to the title. Come up and see me again." (González, 370)

The invitation issued by Sor Juana is spoken through the trademark pickup line of Mae West from the 1933 film *She Done Him Wrong*, which at the time of the story's publication would have been at the height of its fame and which has subsequently become an iconic tagline of dominant female sexuality.

This frankly sexual invitation by the Mexican nun, ventriloquizing a North American and now global icon, demonstrates how even very early twentieth-century Latina interpretations of Sor Juana are able to articulate a modernity that is represented not as alien or dominant but that works through a temporally heterogeneous movement between the Americas. González's early twentieth-century Chicana appropriation of Sor Juana chooses to emphasize the explicit articulation of desire by the nun. In doing so, it reveals the power that later creative and critical Latina interventions into Sor Juana will accrue through their reworking and questioning of key ideas in the nun's work and life – from the constructedness of gender roles to the problem of exemplarity and the impact of material life on the realm of knowledge and learning. Sor Juana's wink to the male narrator of the frame story (an itinerant worker on the ranches of northern Texas but also a collector of folklore) demonstrates how this haunting on the border constituted by Latina interventions on Sor Juana involves so much more than history inhabiting the text, and thus offers a seductive alternative to bland discussions of hemispheric modernity that tend to downplay ethnicity, sexual orientation, and gender.

WORKS CITED

Alarcón, Norma. "Cognitive Desires. An Allegory of/for Chicana Critics." *Chicana (W)rites: On Word and Film*. Eds. Maria Herrera-Sobek and Helena Maria Viramontes. Berkeley, CA: Third Woman Press, 1992.

Alatorre, Antonio. "La Carta de Sor Juana al P. Núñez." *Revista de Filología Hispánica* 35 (1987): 591–673.

Alatorre, Antonio and Martha Lilia Tenorio. *Serafina y Sor Juana (Con tres apéndices).* Mexico: Colegio de México, 1998.

Alfau de Solalinde, Jesusa. "El barroco en la vida de Sor Juana." *Humanidades* México: Facultad de Filosofía y Letras, UNAM I. 1, 1943. (Reproduced by *Claustro de Sor Juana*, Cuaderno no. 8, 1981).

Allatson, Paul. "A Shadowy Sequence: Chicana Textual/Sexual Reinventions of Sor Juana." *Chasqui* 33.1 (May 2004): 3–27.

Anzaldúa, Gloria. *Borderlands/La Frontera: The New Mestiza.* San Francisco: Aunt Lute Books, 1987.

Arenal, Electa. "This Life Within Me Won't Keep Still." *Reinventing the Americas: Comparative Studies of Literature of the United States and Spanish America.* Eds. Bell Gale Chevigny and Gari Laguardia. Cambridge: Cambridge University Press, 2009: 158–202.

Arenal, Electa and Vincent Martin. *Sor Juana Inés de la Cruz. Neptuno alegórico.* Madrid: Cátedra, 2009.

Bemberg, Maria Luisa, Dir. *Yo la pero de todas.* 1990.

Bergmann, Emilie L. "Ficciones de Sor Juana: poética y biografía." *Y diversa de mí misma entre vuestras plumas ando. Homenaje internacional a Sor Juana Inés de la Cruz.* Ed. Sara Poot Herrera. Mexico: El Colegio de México, 1993. 171–83.

Bergmann, Emile L. and Stacey Schlau. *Approaches to Teaching the Works of Sor Juana Inés de la Cruz.* New York: The Modern Language Association of America, 2007.

Beverley, John. *Essays on the Literary Baroque in Spain and Spanish America* London: Tamesis, 2008.

Bokser, Julia A. "Sor Juana's Rhetoric of Silence." *Rhetoric Review* 25 (2006): 5–21.

"Reading and Writing Sor Juna's Arch: Rhetorics of Belonging, Criollo Identity and Feminist Histories." *Rhetoric Society Quarterly* 42 (2012): 144–63.

Boyle, Catherine. "Sor Juana Inés de la Cruz. The Tenth Muse and the Difficult Freedom to Be." *Cambridge History of Mexican Literature.* Cambridge: Cambridge University Press, Forthcoming.

Calleja, Diego. "«Aprobación» en *Fama y obras póstumas*". Facsimile of 1700 Madrid Edition. Introduction by Antonio Alatorre. México: Universidad Nacional Autónoma de México, 1995.

Castellanos, Rosario. "Asedio a Sor Juana." *Juicios Sumarios.* Xalapa: Universidad Veracruzana, 1966. 19–25.

"Otra vez Sor Juana." *Juicios Sumarios.* Xalapa: Universidad Veracruzana, 1966. 26–30.

"Lección de cocina." *Album de familia.* México: Joaquín Moniz, 1972.

Clamurro, William H. "Sor Juana Inés de la Cruz Reads her Portrait." *Revista de Estudios Hispánicos* January 20.1 (1986): 27–43.

Dinshaw, Carolyn. "Theorizing Queer Temporalities: A Roundtable Discussion." *GLQ: A Journal of Lesbian and Gay Studies* 13.2.3 (2007): 177–95.

Egan, Linda. "Sor Juana's Life and Work: Open Texts." Review Essay *Mexican Studies/Estudios Mexicanos* 18.1 (Winter 2002): 205–16.

Franco, Jean. *Plotting Women. Gender and Representation in Mexico*. New York: Columbia University Press, 1989.

Fuentes, Katia. "Artist's Statement." *Caveat Lector* 16.1. 4 pages. June 18, 2015. www.caveat-lector.org/1601/html/1601_art_fuentes3.htm.

Gaspar de Alba, Alicia. *[Un]Framing the "Bad Woman." Sor Juana, Malinche, Coyolxauhqui, and Other Rebels with a Cause*. Austin: University of Texas Press, 2014.

Gladhart, Amelia. "Monitoring Sor Juana: Satire, Technology and Appropriation in Jesusa Rodríguez's *Sor Juana en Almoloya*." *Revista Hispánica Moderna* 52.1 (June 1999): 213–26.

Glantz, Margo. "Labores de manos: hagiografía o autobiografía? (el caso de Sor Juana)." *Revista de Estudios Hispánicos* 19 (1992): 293–308.

—— "Octavio Paz and Sor Juana Inés de La Cruz's Posthumous Fame." *Pacific Coast Philology* 28. 2 (1993): 129–37.

—— *Sor Juana Inés de la Cruz: ¿Hagiografía o autobiografía?* Mexico: Grijalbo-Universidad Nacional Autónoma de México, 1995.

—— "The Construction of a Figure of Genius." *Journal of Latin American Cultural Studies* 4 (1995): 175–89.

—— ed. *Sor Juana Inés de la Cruz y sus contemporáneos*. Mexico: Facultad de Filosofía y Letras Universidad Autónoma de México, 1998.

González, Jovita. "Short Fiction: Shades of the Tenth Muses." *Women's Studies: An Inter-Disciplinary Journal* 43.3 (2014): 363–71.

Hind, Emily. "Sor Juana, an Official Habit: Twentieth-Century Mexican Culture." *Approaches to Teaching the Works of Sor Juana Inés de la Cruz*. Eds. Emilie L. Bergmann and Stacey Schlau. New York: The Modern Language Association of America, 2007. 245–55.

Kafka, Philippa. "Saddling la Gringa: Major Themes in the Works of Latina Writers." *Latina Writers (The Ilan Stavans Library of Latino Civilization)* Ilan Stavans, Intro. West Port, CT: Greenland Press, 2008. 3–15.

Kraniauskas, John. "Nestor García Canclini's *Culturas híbridas: Estrategias para entrar y salir de la modernidad* (1990)." *Journal of Latin American Cultural Studies* 1. 2 (1992): 143–51.

Luciani, Frederick. "Recreaciones de Sor Juana en la narrativa y teatro hispano/norteamericano, 1952–1988." *Y diversa de mí misma entre vuestras plumas ando. Homenaje internacional a Sor Juana Inés de la Cruz*. Ed. Sara Poot Herrera. Mexico: El Colegio de México, 1993. 395–408.

Ludmer, Josefina. "Las tretas del débil." *La sartén por el mango. Encuentro de escritoras latinoamericanas*. Eds. Patricia González and Eliana Ortega. Río Piedras, Puerto Rico: Ediciones Huracán, 1984. 47–55.

Lugones, Maria. "The Coloniality of Gender." *Worlds and Knowledges Otherwise* Vol. 2 Dossier 2. On the De-colonial(II): Gender and Decoloniality (2008): 1–17.

Luisi, Luisa. "Sor Juana Inés de la Cruz. *Contemporáneos* 9. (1929): 130–60.

Martínez-San Miguel, Yolanda. "El sujeto femenino del saber o las estrategias para la construcción de una conciencia epistemológica colonial en Sor Juana." *Revista de Crítica Literaria Latinoamericana XX*. 40 (1994): 259–80.

"Saberes Americanos: contitución de una subjetividad intellectual femenina en la poesía lírica de Sor Juana." *Revista de Crítica Literaria Latinoamericana* XXIV.49 (1999): 79–98.

"Otra vez Sor Juana: leer la heterogeneidad colonial en un contexto transatlántico." *Revista de Crítica Literaria Latinoamericana* XXXI.62 (2005): 53–71.

McCabe, Susan. "To Be and Not to Have: The Rise of Queer Historicism." *GLQ: A Journal of Lesbian and Gay Studies* 11.1. (2005): 119–34.

Merrim, Stephanie, ed. *Feminist Perspectives on Sor Juana Inés de la Cruz.* Detroit, MI: Wayne State University Press, 1991.

Early Modern Women's Writing and Sor Juana Inés de la Cruz. Nashville, TN: Vanderbilt University Press, 1999.

"Angels of History and Colonial Hemispheric Studies." *Letras Femeninas* 35.1 número especial: Mujeres alborotadas: Early Modern and Colonial Women's Cultural Production. A Festscrift für Electa Arenal (2009): 63–84. Mesa-Bains, Amalia. Home Page. June 18, 2015. http://v1.zonezero.com/magazine/essays/distant/ymesa2.html

Mistral, Gabriela. "Silueta de Sor Juana Inés de la Cruz." *Lecturas para mujeres.* [1923.] 1924. 2nd ed. Intro. by Sara Sefchovich. Mexico (1987): 176–79.

Paz, Octavio. *Sor Juana Inés de la Cruz o Las trampas de la fé.* Barcelona: Seix Barral, 1982.

El laberinto de la soledad. Mexico: Fondo de Cultura Económica, 1950.

Perelmuter, Rosa. *Los límites de la femineidad en Sor Juana Inés de la Cruz.* Madrid: Universidad de Navarra-Iberoamericana-Vervuert, 2004.

Perez, Emma. "Queering the Borderlands: The Challenges of Excavating the Invisible and Unheard." *Frontiers: A Journal of Women's Studies* 24.2 & 3 (2003): 122–31.

Pfandl, Ludwig. *Sor Juana Inés de la Cruz, la décima Musa de México, su vida, so poesía, su psique.* Ed. Franciso de la Maza. Mexico: UNAM, 1963.

Poot Herrera, Sara. "Traces of Sor Juana in Contemporary Mexicana and Chicana/Latina Writers." *Approaches to Teaching the Works of Sor Juana Inés de la Cruz.* Eds. Emilie L. Bergmann and Stacey Schlau, New York: The Modern Language Association of America, 2007. 256–64.

Rodríguez, Jesusa. "Sor Juana en Almoloya." *Debate Feminista* 1.2 (September 1990): 395–411.

Santí, Enrico Mario. "Sor Juana, Octavio Paz and the Poetics of Restitution." *Indiana Journal of Hispanic Literatures* 1.2 (1993): 101–39.

Sarre, Alicia. "Gongorismo y conceptismo, en la poesía lírica de Sor Juana." *Revista Iberoamericana* XVII33 (1951): 33–52.

Schons, Dorothy. "Some Obscure Points in the Life of Sor Juana Inés De La Cruz." *Modern Philology* 24.2 (1926): 141–62.

"Nuevos datos para la biografia de Sor Juana." *Contemporáneos* 9 (1929): 161–76.

Sor Juana Inés de la Cruz. *Obras completas de Sor Juana.* Eds. Alfonso Méndez Plancarte and Alberto G Salceda. Mexico: Fondo de Cultura Económica, 1951–57.

Enigmas ofrecidos a la Casa del Placer. Edición y estudio de Antonio Alatorre. Mexico: El Colegio de México, 1994.

The Divine Narcissus. El Divino Narciso. Translated and annotated by Patricia A. Peters and Renée Domeier, O.S.B. Albuquerque: University of Mexico Press, 1998.

Veintiún sonetos de amor y otros poemas. Introduction by Cesce Esteve and edited by Georgina Sabat de Rivers and Elias Rivers. Cordoba: Almuzara, 2008.

Quijano, Anibal and Michael Ennis. "Coloniality of Power, Eurocentrism, and Latin America." *Nepantla: Views from South* 1.3 (2000): 533–80.

Zacarías, Karen. *The Sins of Sor Juana.* Woodstock, IL: Dramatic Publishing, 2000.

Zamora, Margarita. "América y el arte de la memoria." *Revista de crítica literaria latinoamericana* 21.41 (1995): 135–48.

Zavala, Iris. *Nocturna mas no funesta.* Barcelona: Montesinos, 1987.

4

Rethinking the Colonial Latinx
Literary Imaginary

A Comparative and Decolonial Research Agenda

YOLANDA MARTÍNEZ SAN MIGUEL

Colonizing and Decolonizing the Latinx Archive

In this essay I analyze how two Latinx histories, as well as three anthologies, reclaim the Spanish colonial period as part of their archive to theorize how to undertake a decolonial reading of colonial texts within Latinx literary history.[1] Conceiving the colonial period is a problematic endeavor in Latinx studies. Some scholars claim that this category and periodization does not apply at all to Latinxs in the United States. Other scholars want to recognize certain iconical Latin American and Hispanic writers and artists as a point of departure for the Latinx literary traditions in the United States and beyond. This debate in many ways reflects the hybrid nature of Latinx studies as a result of this field's multiple affiliations with Caribbean, Latin American, and US American literary and cultural traditions. I join this debate as a scholar trained in Colonial Latin American studies who recognizes the political and symbolical power of the constitution and definitions of origins in literary manifestations.

I would like to take as my point of departure the inflections of this debate among Latin American and Latinx studies scholars. My colleagues José Rabasa (from Colonial Latin American studies) and Lázaro Lima (from Latinx studies) both critically evaluate the postulation of Álvar Núñez Cabeza de Vaca as a point of origin for Latinx and Chicanx literature and thus shed light on the sometimes fluid boundaries between Latin America and Latinx histories and cultural artifacts. On the one hand, José Rabasa calls for a

---

[1] In this essay, I have adopted the most recent usage of Latinx, over Latina/o, Latin@, or Latin, to insist on the importance of using gender-neutral critical language, whenever possible. I also use Chicanx in this essay, for the same reasons.

decolonization of the field of colonial Latin American studies that has chosen to read Cabeza de Vaca, author of *Naufragios* (1542), as a "critic of empire . . . advocate of peaceful conquest . . . first Chicano . . . [and] first Spanish transculturator of Indian culture" (2000, 35). Rabasa ends his chapter inviting Latin American and Latinx scholars and readers of colonial narratives more broadly to recognize our complicity with the colonial legacies of these texts when we choose to privilege a subversive agenda over the imperial motives that were central in most of the *relaciones* (chronicles), diaries, and travel narratives that were produced by European and *criollo* authors during the sixteenth and seventeenth centuries.[2]

Lázaro Lima, on the other hand, reads the embrace of Cabeza de Vaca as an effect of the 1990s of academic multiculturalism, along with the institutionalization of Latinx studies as a field, which called for textual foremothers and forefathers for Latinx identities and discourses. Luis Leal and Juan Bruce-Novoa identified a genealogy by claiming that Chicanx literature is "that literature written by Mexicans and their descendants living or having lived in what is now the United States" (Leal 1979, 21), and by proposing Cabeza de Vaca as the founder of Chicanx literature (Bruce-Novoa, 1990). Nicolás Kanellos's founding of the Recovering the US Hispanic Literary Heritage project in 1992 fleshes out this effort to claim colonial precursors for a long-standing Spanish-speaking presence – one that antedates the English colonial presence – in what is now the United States. It may be evident by now that the issue of origins and colonialism is crucial for the articulation of Latinx studies as a field. As a consequence, although I recognize the problematic nature of the inclusion of writers from the colonial period as defining the principle origins of *latinidad*, I also see how this invention of origins responds to a political need to create a tradition that can serve as the point of departure for what HBO has described in a documentary as the *Latin Explosion* (2015).

The main goal of this chapter is to revisit this debate about the colonial dimensions of the US Latinx archive and to acknowledge its richness and complexities. The archive for latinidad has been constituted in a hybrid and transnational context that requires critics and scholars to be vigilant about the ways in which archives often reproduce the logic of national, imperial and/or colonial imaginaries. In the national logic informing most of the official archives, Latinxs embody a cultural formation that emerges as a result of a

[2] *Criollo*, in the Spanish tradition, usually refers to a descendant of Spaniards, but it applies more generally to anybody born and raised in the Americas. See discussion in José Antonio Mazzotti's chapter 4 in *Critical Terms in Caribbean and Latin American Thought*.

complex array of colonial and postcolonial contexts that transcend nationality. This corpus of texts constantly encourages us to question the frameworks that we use to identify the genealogies, origins, or affiliations of a particular tradition or identity. I will attempt to analyze the recovery and inclusion of the colonial dimension of latinidad while insisting on the importance of developing a decolonial perspective that will read these archives at face value and against the grain simultaneously.

Claiming the first Spanish settlements in what today is the United States, and even in the rest of Latin America, as the single source of Latinx literary history is problematic because it locates the origins of an identity in the imperial/colonial context of occidentalism and modernity. Furthermore, such claims sometimes conflate colonial European, *criollo*, and *mestizo*[3] writers with Latinx narrative subjects, and anachronistically assume the existence of the United States as a region even before the actual constitution of the Anglo-American colonies. Such a recovery parallels the generative claim that Latin American literature begins to take shape in the globalized colonial interactions between European, Asian, and African populations and the indigenous populations of the region. What are the advantages and challenges of these kinds of claims? And what is the role that Europe and the United States play in the validation of a Latinx and/or Latin American identities?

Latinx literary histories provide one argument for the historical basis for the inclusion of the colonial period in the Latinx literary archive. The framework of Latinx literature anthologies privileges the texts that will be included as foundational for a genealogy of Latinx literature. I propose that scholars incorporate the colonial archive, while keeping a critical distance from anachronistic interpretations of these texts. By proposing this kind of reading I want to take into account the reservations both José Rabasa and Lázaro Lima have about the validation of Latinx and Latin American identities through the assimilation of voices, discourses, and texts that were produced *before* latinidad existed as a cultural, social, ethnic, and political formation, while recognizing the intense political value of recovering indigenous, criollo, mestizo, and mulatto discourses through reading against the grain of colonial archives and in order to vindicate the alterity of identity formations that were not totally displaced or assimilated by the conquest and

---

[3] *Mestizo* often refers in the colonial context to the offspring of a European man and an indigenous woman, but also refers to any person whose ancestors are of different "racial" backgrounds.

colonization of Latin America and the Caribbean. I will attempt to illustrate the tense and contradictory path of this inclusion of the colonial period in the "Latino Literary Imagination" by reviewing how some Latinx histories and anthologies have dealt with this issue.[4] I will conclude this essay by returning to the question of colonial origins and by proposing a decolonial agenda that would ideally enrich Latinx and Colonial Latin American studies as fields of knowledge production.

Latinx Colonialities in the Historical Imagination

In *Latino U.S.A.: A Cartoon History* by Ilán Stavans and illustrated by Lalo Alcaraz, the colonial period launches the section of the book entitled "Conquest and Exploration: 1492–1890." The book opens with a discussion of the different meanings of the concept of America, and how the river demarcating the border between Latin America and the United States is known as the Río Bravo in the United States and as the Río Grande in Mexico (3). In this narrative, Christopher Columbus's "discovery" of the Americas marks the unification of Spain (right after the expulsion of the Moors and the Jews) and Spain's eventual expansion into the New World as an originary moment for Latinx literature. However, even though Columbus's arrival to the Americas marks the constitution of the world as we know it today, according to Stavans, "the history of Latinos doesn't actually begin until early in the sixteenth century, when the first Spanish explorers set foot in Florida and other unknown territories" (14). This is an interesting assertion, since it establishes a continuity between contemporary Latinx communities and the indigenous inhabitants of the Americas. At the same time, Stavans is displacing the foundational moment of latinidad to a time period that predates the constitution of the Americas through the contact with European conquerors. This history does not provide its readers with a framework that would allow them to interpret this time period as relevant to latinidad, Latin Americanness, or even Americanness.

Stavans proposes a critical review of the colonization and conquest of the Americas by showcasing the exploitation and cruelty of the Spaniards against the indigenous populations of the Americas that formed part of this

---

[4] I am using here a notion proposed in "The Latino Literary Imagination: East Coast/ South West Dialogue on Narrative Voices and the Spoken Word," a conference organized as a collaboration between Rutgers University and the University of New Mexico in April 2011. For more information see http://news.unm.edu/news/latino-literary-imagination-features-authors-and-artists-at-unm-and-rutgers

"civilizing" and "evangelizing" enterprise (20). Stavans makes references to expeditions to Florida by Juan Ponce de León (1474–1521), Hernando de Soto (1496–1542), and Alvar Núñez Cabeza de Vaca (1490–1560), as well as to Cabeza de Vaca's close interaction with the indigenous populations of what is today Florida, Georgia, Alabama, Louisiana, Mississippi, New Mexico, Arizona, and Texas in his relación *Naufragios* (*Shipwrecks*, 1542). *Latino U.S.A.* also mentions Francisco Vázquez de Coronado's two-year expedition (1540–1542) through what today is known as Arizona, Oklahoma, and Kansas; Fray Marco de Niza's expedition to the legendary Seven Cities of Cibola; and the conquest and colonization of the New Spain by Cortés. Likewise, it includes Gaspar Pérez de Villagrá's and Juan de Oñate's coloniza-tion of New Mexico, as depicted in Villagrá's epic poem the *History of New Mexico* (1610). The foundation of cities like St. Augustine in Florida, the first Spanish city in North America, and Santa Fé (1610), the oldest state capital in the Southwest, are also identified as key historical events in a colonial period that is claimed for narrating the origins of latinidad .

Stavans devotes particular attention to several Spanish dissidents who questioned the exploitation of the indigenous populations in the Americas, such as Bartolomé de Las Casas (1488–1566) and father Junípero Serra (1713–1784). The historical account presented in *Latino U.S.A.* also describes some of the racial types of the New World – such as *mestizo* and *criollo* – that would become central in racial debates and definitions of Latinx identities. Interestingly enough, the text narrates using a double voice that is constantly second guessing the epic narrative of conquest and colonization of the Americas by asking if the New World was really "new" and by arguing that "to colonize is to subdue, to rename, to redefine" (Stavans 19).

The first part of *Latino U.S.A.* refers to the arrival of the British pilgrims in New England in 1607 and the eventual constitution of the United States as an autonomous nation in 1776. This section also refers to the war of independ-ence of México lead by white criollos (1810–1821) that took place at the same time in which the United States was expanding its territorial control with the purchase of Louisiana from the French in 1803, the cession of Florida in 1819, and the loss of British control over Oregon in 1846. US expansion culminated with the annexation of Texas in 1845 after the Texas Revolution (1836) and the Mexican American War that ended with the signing of the Guadalupe-Hidalgo Treaty in 1848, which forced Mexico to sell two-thirds of its terri-tory. Mexican inhabitants of these regions were supposed to "be free to continue where they now reside, or to return at any time to the Mexican Republic, retaining the property which they possess in the said territories"

(Article VIII, Stavans 37). However, after the incorporation of the Southwest to the United States, Anglo inhabitants, who were in control of the courts and the law, were able to dispossess *tejanos* and *californios* and make them marginal subjects in the same places they had been living for at least two centuries. Stavans identifies this moment as *another* possible origin of US Latinx identity "when a considerable number of Mexicans suddenly found themselves living within the geographical boundaries of the United States" (36). Here Stavans's narrative touches upon a central motive in Mexican American and Chicanx historical imaginaries, which argue that the first inhabitants of the Anglo American region were originally tejanos, californios, and other Mexican Americans. The illegitimacy of the occupation of the Southwest, both as a result of the Mexican American War and as a consequence of the illegal displacement of Mexican inhabitants protected under the terms of the Guadalupe-Hidalgo Treaty are two motives that permeate the foundation of Mexican American and Chicanx identity in the United States. In this imaginary, the border – legally and illegally displaced – plays a central role. Yet this is a problematic assertion because it dismisses the longstanding presence of Native American populations in the region.

Stavans also tries to include a narrative that is specific for the Latinxs of Hispanic Caribbean descent. In order to trace the history of the Caribbean previous to US intervention, *Latino U.S.A.* goes back to the colonial period to describe the colonization and conquest of the insular overseas possessions. US intervention in the Caribbean as a defining moment in Latinx literary history emerges only in the second part of the narrative entitled "Into the Cauldron 1891–1957." This recovery of the colonial period includes references to piracy and to the African slave trade (46). The year 1898 is crucial in US-Caribbean relations, since the Spanish American War culminates with the cession of Cuba, Puerto Rico, Guam, and the Philippines to the United States as stipulated in the Treaty of Paris.

Although this historical account implicitly expands the colonial period until the end of the nineteenth century, there are several problematical choices in the historical narrative proposed in this book. First, the end of the "colonial" period is not as clear cut when we take into account the sociopolitical histories of the Caribbean and Latin America. This narrative contradiction allows us to identify different colonial periods for Latinxs in the United States, depending on the populations under study. Second, Stavans establishes an implicit distinction between *mestizaje* or the miscegenation taking place between Europeans and Native Americans in the continental Americas and *mulataje*, or the racial mixing between Africans, Europeans, and indigenous populations in the Caribbean. Yet scholars have documented African and Asian immigration to the Mexican and Andean regions, and Asians and Yucatecans to the Caribbean, so as to question an impermeable border between mestizaje and mulataje (Bennett, Brewer-García, Bulmer-Thomas). However, this historical account does not dwell on the implications of these different colonial temporalities. Another angle of history that remains unexplored in this text is the comparative study between Native American and indigenous studies in North and South America respectively.

Juan González's *Harvest of Empire* (2000) incorporates the colonial period to latinidad using a different time frame. The book begins with a section entitled "Roots/Las raíces" that includes three chapters that cover historical events taking place between 1500 and 1950. The first chapter, "Conquerors and Victims: The Image of America Forms (1500–1800)," proposes a history that would trace the presence of Spanish and Anglo Europeans in relation to the original inhabitants of the Americas. This approach displaces the role African – including Muslim – and Asian immigrants had in the formation of New World American identities (Bennett, López) and circumscribes the origins of Latinx culture to the interaction between Spanish, Anglo, and indigenous cultures. Yet González takes advantage of this particular approach to engage in a comparative analysis of the indigenous and Native American populations in South and North America (4–6) – a topic not developed by Stavans in his text.

González, like Stavans, emphasizes the antecedence of Spanish-speaking cultures to the Anglo cultures dominant after 1848: "Spanish *conquistadores* crisscrossed and laid claim to much of the southern and western United States nearly a century before the first English colonies were founded in Jamestown and Massachusetts Bay" (8). This affirmation of having Spanish presence in the region *before* Anglo presence continues to be a central tenet in the articulation of Latinx studies that most likely derives from central strategies in the definition of Chicanx/Mexican American identity. This argument elides the influence of the Native American inhabitants in the Americas before the arrival of the Spanish. Furthermore, this claim to legitimacy through arriving first also marginalizes immigrant Latinx groups that did not arrive in the United States before the Anglos.

Like Stavans, González refers to Juan Ponce de León, Francisco Vázquez de Coronado (1510–1554), and Hernando de Soto as foundational figures in their attempts to conquer present-day Florida, Arizona, New Mexico, Texas, Oklahoma, and Kansas. Cabeza de Vaca figures here as conducting "the first crossing of North America by Europeans" (9). González also chronicles Las

Casas's struggle to protect American Indians from slavery (even as he urged the importation of African slaves). In *Harvest of Empire*, we encounter interesting additions to the Latinx canon, such as the figure of La Malinche, who influentially shapes indigenous, Mexican, and Chicana/o imaginaries, and the Inca Garcilaso de la Vega, one of the best known sixteenth-century mestizo narrators of the colonization and conquest of the Andean region, who also writes an account of Hernando de Soto's expedition to Florida. Some of these additions are problematic, since they embody the contradictions and tensions that transform *mestizaje* into what Cornejo Polar defined in the title of an article published in 1993 as "the discourse of impossible harmony." Moreover, they do not necessarily represent Anglo-Spanish interaction and contact. The inclusion of Malinche, Inca Garcilaso, and Hernando de Soto does, however, assert the relevance of Latin American imaginaries for increasingly heterogeneous Latinx communities that migrated to the United States after the 1980s and 1990s. The question here, again, is how to frame this colonial corpus to allow us as readers to recover discursive strategies and imaginaries that are relevant to some sectors of contemporary latinidad without conflating Latin American and Latinx interpretations of these texts.

González compares Spanish mestizaje colonial practices with English and US colonial segregation practices (14). Sometimes, the comparison between the racial mixing taking place in the Spanish colonies displaces the violence that informs the creation of the first mestizo populations. González tries to give an account of the violent contradictions of Spanish conquest and colonization through the discussion of the evangelization work done by Bartolomé de las Casas in Venezuela in 1520, and the establishment of *misiones* in Central Mexico by Vasco de Quiroga (15–16). The Spanish evangelical *misiones* (missions), the *encomiendas*,[5] and the repression of the Inquisition are compared to Indian segregation and the Puritan witch trials in Salem in the late 1680s. This is one of Gonzalez's main contributions, since he suggests the need for comparative studies on American indigenieties, by focusing on the ways in which colonialism and dispossession were common denominators in the conquest and colonization of Anglo and Latin America.

The second chapter, entitled "Spanish Borderlands and the Making of an Empire (1810–1898)," proposes a comparative study of Latin America's

---

[5] *Encomiendas* were granted by the Spanish crown and gave the right to Spanish colonizers to extract tributes in the form of labor or gold in exchange for "protection" and evangelization of the Indians under their control.

economic and political stagnation as a direct result of the US imperial expansion (28). This chapter also analyzes the ambivalent position white Latin American criollos had toward Spain, most of the time claiming reforms instead of revolution, with the goal of independence (31). The movement of independence in Latin America emerged as a result of the French usurpation of the Spanish crown in 1808, and the failure of Spain to include the American provinces in the structure of representation of the Spanish empire. In that context, Latin American criollos began their struggle for independence, at times conceiving the United States as a model for a democratic republic, and at other times proposing Latin American and Caribbean models of government as an alternative to that of the United States.

The most interesting part of the chapter meditates on the relationship between people of Hispanic and Anglo descent. González locates the "first Latinxs" as people of Spanish descent who interacted with Anglo settlers and neighbors after the Louisiana Purchase, the cession of Florida through the Adams-Onís Treaty (1819), and the resulting expansion of the United States into northern Mexico during the struggle for Texas independence and throughout the US–Mexico War. In this geographical relocation of the origins of Latinx culture to the Gulf region, Gonzalez provides a historical antecedent to US expansion through filibustering expeditions that took place throughout much of the nineteenth century. Filibusters, as "a band of newcomers or mercenaries simply captured a town or territory and proclaimed their own republic" (37), took into their hands the enactment of the policies of the Monroe Doctrine 1823,[6] and later Manifest Destiny (1829–1837).[7] Anglos displaced tejanos, californios, and other Mexican inhabitants from the Southwest, as they colonized the Mexican American imaginary by representing cowboys as the heroic protagonists of westward expansion that displaced *vaqueros* and other Mexican cultural references.[8] González usefully relates this nineteenth-century history to twentieth-century US interventions in Central America and the Caribbean as part of the same

---

[6] The Monroe Doctrine refers to President James Monroe's proclamation in 1823, "America for Americans." The United States committed to not interfere in European nations and in exchange European nations would not intervene in American nations.

[7] The Manifest Destiny, advanced under Andrew Jackson's presidency (1829–1837), justified US American expansion from the Atlantic to the Pacific coasts as a matter of destiny.

[8] I am using here Serge Gruzinski's illuminating notion of the "colonization of the imaginary" as one of the most powerful ways in which imperial expansion displaces local ways of knowing and conceiving the world to replace them with the history and culture of the colonizers.

project of territorial expansion, initially accomplished by assuming control over Spanish settlements in these regions. According to Gonzalez, the "climax" of this violent process of territorial expansion takes place with the occupation and claim of the Spanish Caribbean in 1898 rather than – as Frederick Jackson Turner claimed – with the closing of the western frontier (González 56).

These two historical accounts share certain features that are worth noting. First, they both include the colonial period in the Americas as a significant element to understand some of the contemporary racial formations and political contexts of latinidad. Second, they all distinguish the Mexican-American experience from the diasporic Spanish Caribbean experience, but still define colonialism using the prevalent historical periodizations deriving from US and Latin American histories (1776–1810), which ignore the major significance of Haiti's successful emergence as a republic built on struggles of black self-emancipation. Third, the nineteenth century occupies a liminal space in which the Spanish Caribbean was still trying to become independent while the United States was engaging in expansion at the expense of the Native American and Hispanic populations already present in this region. During the nineteenth century the United States became a hemispheric imperial power, reconfiguring the Mexican American, Central American, and Spanish Caribbean political and historical borderlands. I would like to argue that it is precisely this context of late or extended colonialism[9] that we should focus on to define the colonial dimensions of latinidad in the United States.

In the next section I analyze how these Latinx histories translate into the archival project behind US Latinx literary anthologies. Some of the questions I consider are: How does the rise of the United States as hemispheric imperial power reconfigure the borderlands and thus underscore the relevance of colonial and imperial formation for Latinx literature? And in what ways does the recuperation of archives shaping Latinx anthologies reinforce, interrogate, and/or reconfigure the current imperial borders of the US American cultural and historical imaginaries?

---

[9] I use *extended colonialism* to refer to colonialism "that began in the sixteenth and seventeenth centuries and lasted until the twentieth century (and sometimes until today), and that frequently includes the coexistence of more than one colonial system (Spanish and French in Martinique; Spanish and US American in Cuba, Puerto Rico, and the Philippines; Spanish, French, and English in many islands of the Anglo-Caribbean)" (Martínez-San Miguel 6). I am expanding the term here to include the Mexican American experiences in the US Southwest.

Latinx Literature Anthologies

Literary anthologies have a different relationship to historical foundations than historical accounts. Literary anthologies tend to trace what I would like to denominate as literary and cultural "beginnings," following Edward Said's secularization and humanization of this term: "The state of mind that is concerned with origins is, I have said, theological. By contrast, . . . beginnings are eminently secular, or gentile, continuing activities. . . . A beginning intends meaning, but the continuities and methods developing from it are generally *orders of dispersion,* of *adjacency,* and of *complementarity*" (372–73). Anthologies redefine the notion of latinidad by proposing literary canons in which continuity and contiguity with colonialism and coloniality are crucial points of departure to imagine and understand the indigenous, Spanish, US American, mestizo, and mulatto dimensions of Latinx ethnic discourses. I consider here how three literary anthologies frame the incorporation of the colonial period as a hybrid point of departure against and from which Latinx identities are forged. The following meditation on the framework the editors provide for each of these anthologies highlights how this colonial history is a crucial yet problematical beginning for latinidad.

From the title to its celebratory analysis, *The Latino Reader: Five Centuries of American Literary Tradition from Cabeza de Vaca to Oscar Hijuelos* (1997) claims a direct link between the conquistador and the contemporary Chicanx / Latinx, and thus highlights the violent tensions between these two identities. Harold Augenbaum and Margarite Fernández-Olmos link Spanish conquerors and Latinxs through their common experience with imperial expansion:

> From the Hispanic soldiers and missionaries in former Spanish territories, to the *hispanos, californios,* and Mexicans in lands invaded later and occupied by Anglo Americans before and after the Mexican-American War, to the Caribbean (im)migrants affected by US political and economic incursions, the destinies of Latino peoples have been intricately linked to imperial territorial expansion and the vagaries of geopolitics. (xi)

The editors use previous scholarship by Ramón Gutiérrez, Genaro Padilla, Juan Bruce-Novoa, and Luis Leal, among many others, to justify the identification of Alvar Núñez Cabeza de Vaca and Gaspar Pérez de Villagrá (1555–1620) as the foundation of Chicanx literature (xiv). But this anthology does not clearly develop how these depictions of colonial experiences in the Southwest of the United States illuminate Latinx literature, and in particular Chicanx subjectivity. In the introduction, the editors argue that Alvar Núñez Cabeza de Vaca undergoes a transformation after which he is neither European, nor Indian, [he is] a cultural hybrid created by the American experience, [that] converts the explorer into a symbolic precursor of the Chicano/a. Not entirely identified with either Mexican or Anglo society, the Chicano/s, like Cabeza de Vaca, undergoes a cultural adaptation and transformation that makes him or her the ideal New World American. (xv)

There are several questionable assumptions in the reading proposed here. On the one hand, this interpretation takes Alvar Núñez Cabeza de Vaca's account at face value, without contextualizing the multiple goals of his *relación*. Cabeza de Vaca's hybridity must be read with suspicion, since the *Naufragios* are a *relación de méritos* [chronicle of merits] (Bauer, *Cultural Geography*, 36–37, Adorno y Pautz 2003, 25) or a text that was written to report services that should be recognized by the Spanish Crown. Furthermore, the introduction assumes a US-centric definition of the New World American (Lima 97–98). In the Latin American-centric definitions of *Americanismo*, the ideal New World American would be the *mestizo* or the fifth race as described by José Vasconcelos in *La raza cósmica* (published in 1925), and not necessarily an inhabitant of the United States who probably identifies neither as Spanish nor Anglo. Augenbraum and Fernández Olmos implicitly recognize the complication of the inclusion of Spanish colonial texts by referring to Ray Padilla's classification of all works written before 1848 as "Pre-Chicano Aztlanese materials" (xv). Yet Padilla's proposal is also questionable, because it assumes Chicanidad again as the *single site of origin* for all latinidad (Calderón and Saldívar, quoted in Lima 97). Given that Cabeza de Vaca began his expedition in Florida, if we are going to claim him as a foundational Latinx writer, he may as well represent both Chicanx and Spanish Caribbean beginnings.

The first section of Augebraum and Fernández-Olmos's book is entitled "Encounters," a term that displaces "discovery" as a misnomer for the European exploitation of the Americas. The term "Encounters" euphemistically characterizes the origins of Latinx culture and literature as "the encounter between the Spanish sensibility and that of the natives peoples" (3). The notion of "encounter" displaces the political asymmetry that informs the understanding of both colonial Latin American and Latinx identities. This first part of the anthology is organized around Spanish imperial narratives that take place in regions that today we identify as part of the United States: Alvar Núñez Cabeza de Vaca (Florida and the Southwest), Inca Garcilaso de la Vega (Florida), Gaspar Pérez de Villagrá (New Mexico), Fray Mathias Sáenz de San Antonio (Texas), the Comanches (New Mexico), and Fray

Junípero Serra (California). Yet the question remains: How are we to conduct a reading that focuses on the specific questions of a US Latinx archive? In what ways can we propose readings of these texts that would allow us to propose or understand the decolonial gestures in writings and artistic depictions of latinidad?

The second part of the anthology, entitled "Prelude," includes a combination of nineteenth-century texts from Texas and the Southwest along with some texts from the Caribbean written in the late nineteenth and early twentieth centuries. As the title of the section implies, these texts are not identified as pertaining to Latinx literature, but as precursors of this tradition. The notion of a precursor is simultaneously thought provoking and challenging, since at times it would seem that links to latinidad in these texts are a result of a presentist reading. How can we recover these rich reappropriations of the colonial period in the present without proposing an anachronistic conceptualization of the colonial period? Interestingly enough, a Caribbean author is presented as the founder of Latinx literature: "José María Heredia's depictions of romantic longing for the natural beauty of Cuba and his literary efforts on behalf of New York's Spanish speaking community mark the establishment of Latino literature (as opposed to Spanish colonial literature) in the United States" (64–65). Can we comfortably claim that a nationalist Cuban text written from exile in New York effectively "made New York the second city of the Caribbean" (65)? My answer to this question would be two-pronged. Historically, these beginnings are inaccurate, since Heredia, like Martí and other Cuban writers, do not primarily conceive of themselves as Latinxs. But politically speaking, these nationalist discourses that became possible in exile serve as ideological precursors to the Latinx voices that will emerge in the second half of the twentieth century.

The second part of the anthology focuses on the late-nineteenth-century texts produced by Mexican Americans and Chicanxs, and Hispanic Caribbean writers without fully exploring the colonial connections between the Caribbean and the US–Spanish borderlands during the nineteenth century. The introduction to the second part of the anthology identifies the 1880s and 1890s as the years in which the first Mexican American and Chicanx autobiographies and novels emerged simultaneously with diasporic Spanish Caribbean texts. It is not clear in the framework provided by the anthology which kinds of continuities and/or discontinuities exist between late-nineteenth-century texts and the colonial corpus from the sixteenth, seventeenth, and eighteenth centuries. This section closes with the *corridos* or border ballads narrating the tensions between Mexican Americans and Anglos through the life stories of legendary popular heroes – or bandits, for the Anglos – like Joaquín Murrieta from California and Gregorio Cortez from Texas. The anthology then includes texts from three Caribbean authors: Heredia's poem dedicated to the Niagara Falls, José Martí's letter "A Vindication of Cuba" and a selection of poems from "Simple Verses," and Pachín Marín's fictional chronicle of Latinx migrant life in New York in the 1890s, as well as a couple of his poems. These texts meditate on the colonial condition of Cuba and Puerto Rico, and express concern with the increasing political and economic presence of the United States in the Caribbean. The Mexican American writers include Eulalia Perez's memoir of her life in a California mission; María Amparo Ruiz de Burton's now-canonical narrative about the struggle of Mexican landowners after the signing of the Treaty Guadalupe-Hidalgo, *The Squatter and the Don* (1885); Eusebio Chacón's novel *The Son of the Storm* (1892), a novella about Mexican American traditions in New Mexico; and the "Ballad of Gregorio Cortez" (1901). It would have been useful if this particular section of the anthology had explored in more detail the Mexican and Puerto Rican annexation to the United States with a particular focus on their specific and sometimes similar conditions of coloniality in the United States, a comparison that could explain later Latinx initiatives like the *Revista Chicano-Riqueña* (1973–1985), or the productive alliances between the Young Lords, the Black Panthers, and the Brown Berets in the 1960s.

The second anthology that I would like to analyze here is *Herencia: The Anthology of Hispanic Literature in the United States* (2002), edited by Nicolás Kanellos and a group of coeditors. It is part of the "Recovering the US Hispanic Literary Heritage" project, founded by Kanellos together with a group of leading scholars and funded by the Rockefeller Foundation.[10] This anthology – along with Kanellos's broader recovery process – may be the first to showcase the antecedence of Spanish to US Anglo domination. The problem of this claim is that it needs to be further developed to capture a more nuanced understanding of the Hispanic roots of latinidad. On the one hand, Kanellos's work clearly unseats claims of English as the major or only language in US American literatures. Based on a similar idea, José David Saldívar and others developed this argument further in their proposal for a multilingual and multiethnic American studies (*Border Matters* and

---

[10] This project's history and significance is discussed in Kenya Dworkin y Méndez and Agnes Lugo-Ortiz's editorial introduction to Volume 5: *Recovering the US Hispanic Literary Heritage* (2006), upon the fifteenth anniversary. A forthcoming volume of essays celebrating the twenty-fifth anniversary of the Recovery Project similarly reflects on the project's history and significance.

Trans-Americanity). On the other hand, Spanish and Spanish-ness also represent an imperial ideology that displaced indigenous, African, and Asian languages and cultures in the definition of *Americanidad*. So as we can see, what may function as a revolutionary argument in one field (English and American Studies) can be an almost reactionary position in the case of Latin American, Caribbean, Native American, and indigenous studies. Hispanidad can simultaneously index multilingualism, multiculturalism, and multiethnicity in American studies and monolongualism, monoculturalism, and *criollismo* or whiteness in Latin American and Hispanic studies. Therefore, these anthologies should develop further Gloria Anzaldúa's critical stance vis-à-vis Spanish and English as imperial languages and cultures that displaced indigenous, mestiza, and creolized voices and identities.

Three characteristics make *Herencia* different from the other two anthologies. First, it defines Hispanics and Latinxs in such a way as to justify the inclusion of colonial texts written in Spanish:

> Historically, the diverse ethnic groups that we conveniently lump together as "Hispanics" or "Latinos" created a literature in North America even before the founding of the United States. The sheer volume of their writing over 400 years is so overwhelming that it would take thousands of scholars researching for many years to fully recover, analyze, and make accessible all that is worthy of study and memorializing. (1)

Second, the definition of literature used by Kanellos and the rest of the editors goes beyond the printed book and includes newspapers and other serial publications, as well as folklore and oral traditions. This archival project also emphasizes the value of translating literary, periodical, and oral texts originally available in Spanish into English, or from English into Spanish, in order to make them available for monolingual readers of English or Spanish.

Finally, this anthology makes a compelling argument for the specificity of a Hispanic or Latinx identity that is different from other forms of immigrant literature based on the fact that Latinxs often identify the United States as their primary homeland. The editors also make a clear distinction between including texts from the colonial period and acknowledging the very specific colonial experience of some of the groups currently identified as part of the Latinx community:

> Native Hispanic literature develops first out of the experience of colonialism and racial oppression. . . . The Hispanics were subsequently conquered and/ or incorporated into the United States through territorial purchase and then treated as colonial subjects. . . . Unlike immigrant literature, it does not have

one foot in the homeland and one in the United States. For native Hispanic people of the United States, the homeland is the United States; there is no question of a return to the ancestors' Mexico, Puerto Rico, or Cuba. (5)

The selection of texts themselves then includes colonial *relaciones* and travel narratives by Alvar Núñez Cabeza de Vaca and Fray Marcos de Niza that took place in what today is known as part of the US continental territories, epic poems that refer to the colonization of New Mexico (Gaspar Pérez de Villagrá) and Florida (Alonso Gregorio de Escobedo), letters that refer to the conquest of Texas (Fray Matías Sáenz de San Antonio), and oral accounts and traditions included in the *indita* ballads[11] and *alabado* songs,[12] as well as the *corridos fronterizos*. The anthology distinguishes between a literature of exploration and colonization (written between 1500 and 1700) and a mestizo literature, produced in the nineteenth century before the Treaty of Guadalupe-Hidalgo (1848). Although the introduction makes a compelling case in its distinction between colonial texts and colonialism as experienced by Mexicans, Puerto Ricans, and Cubans in the United States, the brief introductory remarks presenting the texts written by Spanish conquistadors lack a specific framework for reading these colonial / imperial accounts as specifically part of a US Latinx tradition.

I would like to conclude this section with a commentary on *The Norton Anthology of Latino Literature* (2011), edited by Ilán Stavans. This volume is a monumental editorial project that was thirteen years in the making (liii). The preface opens with the assumption that the anthology was published at the moment in which Latinx literature celebrated five centuries of existence. The main editor collaborated with a team of coeditors who chose the 201 authors included in the 2,600-page volume. This anthology is the testimony of the actual institutionalization of Latinx literature and provides this working definition:

> the editors have defined Latinx literature in elastic terms, as the artistic, written manifestations, in Spanish, English, Spanglish, or any combination of these three, by an author of Hispanic ancestry who has either lived most of his or her existence in the United States or, while having only some

---

[11] *Inditas* are a common folk song from New Mexico: "the term connotes a song in which Indian influence is apparent. In other words, it is the type of song which might result when Hispanic people adopt an Indian song and, though aural transmission gradually transform it into a form neither purely Indian nor entirely Hispanic" (Robb 2).

[12] *Alabados* are "a repertory of hymns of praise sung by the Hermandad de Nuestro Padre Jesús Nazareno, a lay Catholic penitential brotherhood. . . . The dominant themes of the *alabados* are the Passion of Jesus and the suffering of Mary" (Kanellos, 67)

tangential connection to the Latinx community, has helped define that community through his or her work.   (lvii)

The Norton Anthology of Latino Literature includes an interesting selection of texts that acknowledges the complex location of Latinx literature between US American and Latin American literatures. A unique element of this anthology is that the selection of authors to be included is not only based on self-identification, but it also takes into account authors and historical figures who may resonate in the Latinx literary imaginary (lxvi). In this regard, the editors recognize the agency of Latinx artists and communities to appropriate particular works and historical icons to forge their own identities. They also recognize the critical work of Anglo and Latinx scholars who argued in favor of a broader definition of latinidad, in order to be able to manage a hemispheric archive that includes texts from many different locations and cultural traditions.

Evidently, the *Norton Anthology* takes advantage of the rich archival work conducted by Nicolas Kanellos and his team, and it emerged after mainstream presses began to "discover" and publish Latinx authors in the 1990s. What is interesting here, however, is how the apparent fluidity in language usage and in the definition of latinidad adopts a decidedly presentist perspective that is not necessarily based on a historical concern with the actual constitution and emergence of a distinct Latinx discourse or perspective in the United States. Residence in the United States takes precedence over actual identification with the historical experiences and cultural formations of latinidad. By the same token, figures that have become significant for Latinx identity formations are included even "while having only some tangential connection to the Latinx community." In many regards, then, the elasticity of latinidad in this anthology runs the risk of negating the ethnic and historical specificity of Latinxs in the United States.

The framework for the inclusion of the texts from the colonial period – included in a section entitled "Colonization, 1537–1810" – is to claim Hispanic identity as existing before Anglo identity in the United States:

> More than a century before the appearance of John Smith's *A Description of New England* (1616), William Bradford's *Of Plymouth Plantation* (1608–47), and Anne Bradstreet's poems of 1660s – that is, long before the foundational works of present-day American literature were created – accounts of the Iberian conquest, exploration, and colonization of the Americas were published in Spain. These narratives are the origin of the Latino literary tradition.   (1)

Claiming accounts of Iberian conquest and colonization of the Americas as the "origin" of latinidad, although apparently radical, can be construed as a very conservative and problematic argument. This historical framework elides the layers of colonialism that inform Latinx identity in relation with the Spanish and the United States. Furthermore, claiming these texts as the origin – instead of the secular beginnings proposed by Said – presupposes a definitive teleology in which Spanish and Anglo imperialism engenders Latinx identity.

Stavans complicates this argument when he reflects on the concrete historical experience of colonialism and imperial expansion in the Southwest of the United States and the Caribbean as elements in the articulation of a contemporary definition of Latinx literature. Finally, in the introductory remarks for the section on colonization, the editors link the emergence of native voices and perspectives with Latin American literary and cultural *indigenismo*[13] that were later recovered during the Chicano movement in the United States (1960–1970). This particular link between *indigenismo*, mestizaje, and latinidad adds another layer to the articulation of a Latinx colonial archive that merits further study. On the one hand, it recognizes the importance of indigeneity in the articulation of some alternative identities in the United States and Latin America, while it also showcases indigeneity as an ethnic element that takes latinidad beyond the black and white racial matrix that reductively served to define the United States. Whereas indigeneity marks a fundamental difference between Chicanx and Hispanic Caribbean literatures, it problematically has served to displace the study of Afro-Latinidad in insular and diasporic Caribbean cultures. Yet recently, indigeneity has been analysed through a more nuanced discussion within Caribbean studies (Newton, Jackson), and among diasporic Caribbean communities as a result of the theorizing of several Neo-Taíno movements.

The section entitled "Colonization: 1537–1810" follows spatial and temporal frameworks that are similar to the ones used for colonial Latin American studies. As principal associate editor of this section, María Herrera-Sobek selected and framed most of the texts defined as colonial precursors to Latinx literature. According to the editors, Luis Leal (1970s–1990s), and Herbert Eugene Bolton (1932–1950s) were also important figures in the configuration of the hemispheric colonial archive included in the anthology. This section

---

[13] *Indigenismo* is a literary movement in Latin American literature that took place from the 1870s to the 1950s and made the indigenous populations the protagonists of a Latin American Creole imaginary.

includes fourteen authors from the colonial period, that can be roughly divided in the following categories: 1. accounts of indigenous colonization and evangelization in the Americas (Las Casas, Núñez Cabeza de Vaca); 2. conquest and colonization of New Mexico and Arizona (Fray Marcos de Niza, Juan de Oñate, Gaspar Pérez de Villagrá, Juan Bautista de Anza); 3. colonization of Florida (Hernando de Soto, Inca Garcilaso de la Vega); 4. expeditions in the Southwest (Pedro Castañeda de Nájera); 5. Spanish domination in the Hispanic Caribbean (Juan de Castellanos); 6. imperial expansion to California (Sebastián Vizcaíno); and 7. missionary accounts in Arizona and California (Fray Eusebio Francisco Kino, Fray Junípero Serra, Fray Juan Crespí). Perhaps the most questionable choice in this section is Bartolomé de Las Casas, who may have defended Native American populations in the Americas, yet never settled in any region close to the United States. The common denominator for all of the texts included here is that they have been or have become important in contemporary definitions of latinidad.

The second section of the book, entitled "Annexations: 1811–1898," is again relevant to our analysis, since it includes texts written by Spanish Caribbean writers who meditate on their countries' independence from Spain and who were participating in separatist political organizations based in New York. The title of the second section refers simultaneously to the US American territorial expansion at the expense of Mexican American communities, as well as the eventual cession of Cuba and Puerto Rico (along with the Philippines and Guam) to the United States after the Spanish American War that ended in 1898. Internal and external colonialism[14] functions as a powerful link between the Spanish Caribbean and Mexican Americans authors and shows the limits of nation-building discourses prevalent in many of the countries of the Latin American *tierra firme*. Moreover the thirty authors included in this section write in the United States, or refer to the United States as the new imperial power, showcasing in this way links that transcend any previous subordination to Spain. This second section of the anthology does in fact include many foundational texts that depict the tensions between Anglos and Hispanics in the articulation of regional and hemispheric identities during the nineteenth century.

---

[14] The notion of "internal colonialism" was originally proposed in Latin America by Stavenhagen and González-Casanova, to refer to the complex class and ethnic relations in post-independence Latin America. Allen, Blauner, Barrera et al. bring this conversation to the United States, to conceptualize the marginalization of African Americans and Latinxs. Rodolfo Acuña's *Occupied America* makes an early argument along these lines.

The selection of texts included in this anthology reveals the editors' desire to be as broad and inclusive as possible. This represents an important effort to validate latinidad as a source of a rich literary and cultural tradition. Yet at times, the inclusion of many authors who do not conceive themselves as Latinx writers blurs the boundaries and elides the specificity of Latinx identities and discourses. This is an ironic outcome, since the *Norton Anthology* wants to celebrate and validate latinidad, but at times the lack of specificity of what is defined as Latinx literature detracts from the institutional impulse behind the important canonization of this literary tradition.

I would like to conclude this essay by meditating on ways to read the colonial archive from a Latinx perspective that would take advantage of interdisciplinary collaborations and methodologies that have successfully reframed the terms of this conversation about the beginnings of an ethnic literary tradition.

Decolonizing Latinx Literary Imaginaries

The review I have proposed in this essay focuses on an important moment for Latinx cultural studies that takes place after the recent emergence of ethnic studies as a new methodology to produce knowledge about US American culture and before the actual institutionalization of these fields into distinct disciplines. I have identified in my analysis some of the conflictive strategies used in the articulation of a Latinx colonial archive. The inclusion of texts written by Spanish conquistadors, religious figures, and colonial functionaries requires a new framework that would allow the reader to focus on early historical periods that are relevant for the understanding of the Latinx literary and cultural imaginary.

One of the possible strategies to design this framework is to forge closer collaborations with the scholars working on Colonial Latin American studies, as well as with researchers conducting comparative early Ibero/American early modern studies (Bauer). This collaboration does not presuppose that Latinx studies scholars need merely to learn from colonialists, but it also implies an exchange of knowledges and discursive analysis strategies that should eventually transform both fields. Colonial Latin American studies problematizes the essentialization of Spanish as a crucial marker for the origins of latinidad, by showcasing how Spanish has also been an imperial language that has displaced and is working to displace numerous indigenous languages in the Americas. Latinx and American studies invigorate and question the analysis of what Bolton denominated as the "Spanish Borderlands" (1921) in order to propose an Americanism that conceives latinidad from the colonial period to the present without imposing a US-centric perspective that eventually elides the shared conditions of Latinx, Latin American, and Caribbean mestizaje, mulataje, creolization, and indigeneity. As I have mentioned before, several theoretical and critical moves that may seem radical in American studies (e.g. the Hispanization of the colonial period or the borderlands proposed by Bolton) appear conservative in Latin American and Latinx Studies (the definition of Hispanidad as the legitimate beginnings of latinidad proposed by *criollismo* and *hispanismo*). I propose instead to forge a new collaborative research agenda that recognizes the complex genealogies that criss-cross the Spanish and Anglo colonial periods and extend into post-colonial cultural formations like latinidad, mestizaje, mulataje or creolization.

A truly comparative framework – that is based in a solid historical grounding that recovers the multiple connections among the many layers of human experience in the Americas – could also open a space for a serious consideration about the real relationship between the colonial period and the postcolonial/national period in the Americas. I opened this essay by arguing that assuming that the texts from the colonial archive are the origins of a Latinx tradition is as organic and as artificial as advancing the same assumption in the case of contemporary Latin American or US American studies. This does not mean that the colonial archive is totally disconnected from the contemporary cultural imaginaries. It means that we should question the frameworks that we use to identify the foundations, origins, or roots of a particular tradition or identity.

Instead of proposing a genealogical relationship that presupposes a relationship of direct descent between the colonial and contemporary texts, we should consider adopting the alternative framework of affiliation, as proposed by Edward Said in his foundational essay "Secular Criticism." This would allow scholars in Latinx studies, American studies, and Latin American studies to identify the particular affiliations that have been constructed and imagined among overlapping corpuses of texts in light of contemporary cultural imaginaries in the Americas. Such a secularizing gesture would also explain why the same set of texts could have more than one particular affiliation. This kind of framework would allow us to analyze the work that we do as cultural critics when we define the "beginnings" of Latinx, Latin American, and American studies by using the colonial discourses produced by European conquerors and colonial functionaries about the New World.

Another question that remains unanswered after the consolidation of this colonial US Latinx archive is how to read these texts from a perspective that showcases the particular urgencies of Latinx identities. The histories and anthologies I have reviewed in this essay seem to have reached some sort of general consensus in terms of the texts to be included in the colonial archive. Most of these texts were written by European colonizers and/or criollo, and – to a much more minimal extent – indigenous or mestizo voices inhabiting regions that today we identify as part of the United States. These texts provide us with ethnographic and historical information about past historical discourses and racial and social formations that inform contemporary latinidad. Yet these anthologies still need to promote interpretations of the colonial texts that open up these imperial accounts of Spanish colonization, to recognize them as complex beginnings for identities that emerge in Eurocentric contexts of conquest and modernization. We need to prepare the reader of this archive to answer the following questions: What is the specifically Latinx content of these texts? How is the reading advanced by scholars in Latinx studies different from readings articulated by Latin American or American studies scholars?

Perhaps the first step to answer these questions would be to identify a series of debates that we as scholars and readers want to elucidate by turning to the colonial archive. Issues of racialization, colonialism, and the complex interactions among Anglo or Spanish settlers and "autochtonous" inhabitants – that must include indigenous communities and/or Hispanic communities established in the region before the arrival of Anglos – can be a useful point of departure to engage the asymmetrical relationships that characterized imperial expansion and colonization. Another kind of reading could focus on a comparative study of the interactions among Hispanics and Anglos with the indigenous populations that were originally settled in the region. María Josefina Saldaña-Portillo does some of this work for Native American and indigenous studies in the United States and Mexico in her book *Indian Given*, but more needs to be done focusing on early colonial indigenous studies in the Americas (including the Caribbean), as well as in the Pacific. This same colonial archive should allow us to better understand the different historical trajectories of diverse Latinx communities. As we have noted in our analysis of histories and anthologies of Latinx literatures and cultures, the primary texts included in the colonial archive already refer to distinctions between colonial discourses of the sixteenth and seventeenth centuries about the colonization of the Americas and narratives of late, extended, and internal colonialism as experienced by Mexican Americans in the Southwest or diasporic Spanish Caribbean people in the nineteenth century. Likewise, many of these texts allow us to understand contemporary distinctions between mestizaje and mulataje that translate into the ambivalent inclusion of black and Asian identities within latinidad. Finally, the narrative of continuous identification with the native land, or of arrival to the United States before the Anglos, refers to a powerful foundational indigenous and Chicanx narrative that does not resonate among diasporic (and translocal[15]) Spanish Caribbean subjects, nor with Latinxs of South American descent.[16]

Therefore, in addition to reading colonial texts against the grain to uncover their gestures of resistance – a common strategy in colonial Latin American and postcolonial studies – we should begin to read these texts from a *decolonial* perspective. This means that in the analysis of this archive we must not only recognize the colonial legacies that distinguish some Latinx experiences from others, but we must also make a critical intervention to open up Latinx studies scholarship to its blind spots. Some of these blind spots are well known in the field: the lack of substantive collaboration between Chicanx and Puerto Rican or other Spanish Caribbean studies scholars; the erasure of Central America and many South American countries in our conceptualization of the main frameworks to study contemporary latinidad; the unreadability of Afro-Latinidad; and the aporetic invisibility of Brazilians, West Indians, and contemporary diasporic indigenous or Asian, (particularly Muslim) cultures from our conceptualization of the field. This archive should also allow us to identify and analyze the different temporalities and timelines that inform US American, Latin American, and Latinx studies, as well as Mexican American and diasporic Caribbean studies and their experiences of early, late, and extended colonialism.

Another complex blindspot for latinidad is its active and passive engagements with Americanness, sometimes understood as US American

---

[15] Agustín Lao-Montes defines a translocal nation as "the tailoring of a formation of peoplehood that, though hyperfragmented and dispersed, is netted by a web of coloniality (subordinate citizenship, racialization) and intertwined by multiple networks (political organizations, professional associations, town club) and flows (phone, faxes, salsanet) to constitute a deterritorialized-reterritorialized 'imagined community' and a 'social space'" (176). I use it to refer to communities that are defined beyond the national, but that are linked to more than one national state or cultural tradition through colonial networks.

[16] Although in South America several communities claim a heritage relationship to autochtonous civilizations with millennial histories preceding European colonization, migrants to the US often do not identify with similar claims based on continuity with the Native American populations based in the United States. This lack of connection between Latin America's indigenous and US Native American imaginaries is also a result of the impact of colonialism and nationalism in the Americas.

or Anglo-American identity, other times conceived as a reference to the global and imperial United States, and still others as the complex hemispheric field of the Americas. The colonial Latinx archive should prompt us to engage in hemispheric and transnational indigeneity studies to compare the experience of indigenous populations in North and South America during the colonial period as Saldaña and Brotherston have proposed, as well as the contemporary experiences of displacement and dispossession among indigenous diasporic communities in the United States and Latin America.

The combined reading of the colonial and Latinx archives must diversify and complicate our definition of latinidad. The US colonial Latinx archive includes a wide array of voices, often more diverse than any of our narratives had previously imagined. Some of the texts showcase a voice of resistance that identifies a distinct Latinx identity that is defined against the grain of US Americanism. Other texts preserve the voices of those who wanted to assimilate to US American culture, and of those who considered their latinidad as a critical rearticulation of dominant narratives of homogeneous US American identity. To decolonize the US Latinx archive also means to visibilize these internal tensions that also inform contemporary Latinx literature and discourses of self-representation. Only when we are willing to imagine a latinidad that embraces the glaring differences and tensions between Gloria Anzaldúa's problematization of the multiple dimensions of racialized and sexualized coloniality enmeshed in the Latinx archive and Richard Rodriguez's affirmation of Latinxs as an identity that falls within US Americanness, we may be ready to fully engage colonial and modern Latinx archives from a decolonial perspective.

WORKS CITED

Acuña, Rodolfo. *Occupied America: the Chicano's Struggle toward Liberation*. San Francisco: Canfield Press, 1972.

Adorno, Rolena and Patrick Charles Pautz. "Introduction." *The Narrative of Cabeza de Vaca*. Lincoln and London: University of Nebraska Press, 2003. 1–42.

Allen, R. *Black Awakening in Capitalist America: An Analytic History*. Garden City, NY: Doubleday, 1969.

Alpert, Jonathan and Mathew O'Neill, director and producer. *The Latin Explosion: A New America*. New York: HBO, 2015.

Anzaldúa, Gloria. *Borderlands/La Frontera*. San Francisco: Aunt Lute Books, 1987.

Barrera, M., C. Muñoz, and C. Ornelas. "The Barrio as Internal Colony." *Urban Affairs Annual Review* 6 (1972): 465–98.

Bauer, Ralph. "Notes on the Comparative Study of the Colonial Americas: Further Reflections on the Tucson Summit." *Early American Literature* 38.2 (2003): 281–304.

The Cultural Geography of Colonial American Literatures: Empire, Travel, Modernity. Cambridge: Cambridge University Press, 2003.

Bennett, Herman. *Colonial Blackness. A History of Afro-Mexico.* Bloomington: Indiana UniversityPress, 2009.

Blauner, R. *Internal Colonialism and Ghetto Revolt.* Indianapolis, IN: Bobbs Merrill, 1969.

Bolton, Herbet E. *The Spanish Borderlands: A Chronicle of Old Florida and the Southwest.* New Haven, CT: Yale University Press, 1921.

Wider Horizons of American History. New York: D-Appleton Century, 1939.

Brewer-García, Larissa. Beyond Babel: Translations of Blackness in Colonial Peru and New Granada. Doctoral Dissertation, University of Pennsylvania, 2013.

Brotherston, Gordon. *The Book of the Fourth World: Reading the Native Americas through their Literature.* New York: Cambridge University Press, 1995.

Bruce-Novoa, Juan. "Naufragios en los mares de la significación: de *La Relación* de Cabeza de Vaca a la literatura chicana." *Plural* 19.5 (February 1990): 12–21.

Bulmer-Thomas, Victor. *The Economic History of the Caribbean since the Napoleonic Wars.* New York: Cambridge University Press, 2012.

Calderón, Héctor and José David Saldívar. "Introduction: Criticism in the Borderlands." *Criticism in the Bordrlands: Studies in Chicano Literature, Culture and Ideology.* Durham, NC: Duke University Press, 1991. 1–7.

Cornejo Polar, Antonio. "El discurso de la armonía imposible: (el Inca Garcilaso de la Vega: discurso y recepción social)." *Revista de crítica literaruia latinoamericana* 19.38 (1993): 73–80.

Escribir en el aire. Ensayo sobre la heterogeneidad sociocultural en las literaturas andinas. Lima: Centro de Estudios Literarios "Antonio Cornejo Polar," Latinoamericana Editores, 2003.

González, Juan. *Harvest of Empire. A History of Latinos in America.* New York: Viking, 2000.

González-Casanova, Pablo. 1965. "Internal Colonialism and National Development." *Studies in Comparative International Development* 1.4 (1965): 27–37.

Gutiérrez, Ramón and Genaro Padilla. *Recovering the US Hispanic Literary Heritage.* Houston, TX: Arte Público Press, 1993.

Gruzinski, Serge. *La colonisation de l'imaginaire: societés indigènes et occidentalisation dans le Mexique espagnol, XVIe-XVIIe siècle.* Paris: Gallimard, 1988.

Jackson, Shona. *Creole Indigeneity: Between Myth and Nation in the Caribbean.* Minneapolis: University of Minnesota Press, 2012.

Kanellos, Nicolás, et al. *Herencia: The Anthology of Hispanic Literature of the United States.* New York: Oxford University Press, 2002.

Laó-Montes, Agustin. "Islands at the Crossroads: Puerto Ricanness Traveling between the Translocal Nation and the Global City." *Puerto Rican Jam: Rethinking Nationalism and Colonialism.* Eds. Frances Negrón-Muntaner and Ramón Grosfoguel. Minneapolis: University of Minnesota Press, 1997. 169–88.

"Latino Literary Imagination: East Coast/South West Dialogue on Narrative Voices and the Spoken Word." Conference and writer's residence organized as a collaboration between Rutgers University and the University of New Mexico. April 7–8 and 15–16, 2011.

Leal, Luis. "Mexican American Literature: A Historical Perspective." *Modern Chicano Writers: A Collection of Essays.* Eds. Joseph Sommers and Tomás Ybarra Frausto. Englewood Cliffs, NJ: Prentice Hall, 1979. 18–30.

Lima, Lázaro. "The Institutionalization of Latino Literature in the Academy: Cabeza de Vaca's *Castaways* and the Crisis of Legitimation." *The Latino Body: Crisis Identities in American Literary and Cultural Memory*. New York: New York University Press, 2007. 91–126.

Martínez-San Miguel, Yolanda. *Coloniality of Diasporas: Rethinking Intra-colonial Migrations in a Pan Caribbeann Context*. New York: Palgrave, 2014.

Mazzotti, José Antonio. "Criollismo, Creole and Créolité." *Critical Terms in Caribean and Latin American Thought: Historical and Institutional Trajectories*. Eds. Yolanda Martínez-San Miguel, Ben. Sifuentes-Jáuregui and Marisa Belausteguigoitia. New York: Palgrave, 2016. 87–100.

Newton, Melanie. "Returns to a Native Land: Indigeneity and Decolonization in the Anglophone Caribbean." *Small Axe* 41 (2013): 108–22.

Rabasa, José. "Reading Cabeza de Vaca, or How We Perpetuate the Culture of Conquest." *Writing Violence on the Northern Frontier. The Historiography of Sixteenth Century New Mexico and Florida and the Legacy of Conquest*. Durham, NC: Duke University Press, 2000. 31–83.

Robb, John Donald. *Hispanic Folk Songs of New Mexico*. Albuquerque: University of New Mexico Press, 2008.

Rodriguez, Richard. *Hunger of Memory*. Boston, MA: D. R. Godine, 1982.

Said, Edward. *Beginnings: Intention and Method*. New York: Columbia University Press, 1985.

"Secular Criticism." *The World, the Text, and the Critic*. Cambridge, MA: Harvard University Press, 1983. 1–30.

Saldaña-Portillo, María Josefina. *Indian Given: Racial Geographies across Mexico and the United States*. Durham, NC: Duke University Press, 2016.

Saldívar, José David. *Border Matters: Remapping American Cultural Studies*. Berkeley: University of California Press, 1997.

Trans-Americanity: Subaltern Modernities, Global Coloniality, and the Cultures of Greater Mexico. Durham, NC: Duke University Press, 2012.

Stavans, Ilán, et al. *The Norton Anthology of Latino Literature*. New York: W. W. Norton & Company, 2011.

Stavenhagen, R. Classes, Colonialism and Acculturation. *Studies in Comparative International Development* 1.6 (1965): 53–77.

Stavans, Ilans and Lalo Alcaraz. *Latino U.S.A.: A Cartoon History*. New York: Bascis Books, 2012.

Turner, Frederick Jackson. *The Frontier in American History*. University of Virginia, [1893] 1996. http://xroads.virginia.edu/~HYPER/TURNER.

Vasconcelos, José. *La raza cósmica*. México: Espasa-Calpe, 1966.

5

The Historical and Imagined Cultural Genealogies of Latinidad

JOSÉ ANTONIO MAZZOTTI

Genealogy of the Term "Latino"

The importance of the term "Latina/o" cannot be overlooked in any approach to the diversity and the richness of what is now Latin America, the United States, and those parts of the world where Spanish and Portuguese languages and cultures have some long-standing presence. However, the term is still subject to debate and is charged with conceptual inconsistencies, an imperialist origin, and, consequentially, a discriminatory effect on the indigenous and African-descended people who do not identify themselves as "Latinos" but were born and raised in "Latin" America. To understand the complexity of the term, it may be useful to trace its genealogy and some of the first uses it has had in over 2,500 years of history.

As is well known, the Romans appeared as a new civilization sometime in the eighth century BCE on the central-western area of the Italic peninsula called "Latium" or Latio (a possible meaning is "plain" or "flat zone," from the verb latere). Therefore, their language and their culture, Latin, refers to a specific region of origin, but became a synonym of "Roman" with the expansion of the Republic and then the Empire in the following centuries. The Latin language spread through vast territories in Northern Africa, the Middle East, southeastern Europe, the Mediterranean world, and parts of northern Europe, including southern England. In some areas of such a large dominion, the influence of local languages determined the appearance of regional variables that would later become the so-called Romance languages because of their origin in the Roman language.

When the Western Roman Empire decayed in the fifth century CE, the language of Cicero and Virgil kept its prestige as a lingua franca among cultured individuals and, of course, as the official language of the Catholic church. To know Latin in the Middle Age was equivalent to being a refined, educated person. With the appearance of Humanism in the fourteenth century, the prestige of Latin only increased and was an unavoidable tool to access the classical writers. In his *Tesauro de la lengua castellana* (1611), Spanish lexicographer Sebastián de Covarrubias presents two etymologies of "Latín," the name of "el lenguaje del Lacio" (the language of Latium): the first from Ovid, "latendo, quod illic latuerit Saturnus dum Iouem fugeret," in reference to the myth in which Saturn escapes from his son Jupiter and takes refuge in the region known as Latium; and the second from a legendary "Rey Latino. Y de alli Latinos los de aquella prouincia y ſu lenguaje" (King Latino, and therefore Latinos [are] those from that province and its language).

The names "Latino" and "Ladino" became interchangeable. To be a "Latino" or "Ladino" was a sign of social and cultural superiority. Rome still kept its reputation as a great civilization with incomparable architectonic, artistic, and literary prowess over later European cultures. To be a true Humanist involved being a "Latino," and vice versa: "al que sabia en aquellos tiempos [medievales] la lengua Latina, le teniã por hombre auiſado y discreto: y de alli nacio llamar oy en dia Ladino, al hombre que tiene entendimiento y diſcurſo, auiſado, y corteſano" ("whoever knew the Latin language in those [Medieval] times, was regarded as a discrete and well-informed man: and from there a man is called Ladino when he has good understanding and speech, is alert, and behaves politely") (Covarrubias f. 516r). The 1734 *Diccionario de Autoridades* confirms this meaning of Latino as someone versed in the Latin language: "LATINO, NA. adj. El que era natural, o gozaba los privilegios y exenciones de la Provincia de Lacio en Italia. Oy se entiende por el que habla o sabe el idioma Latíno, o por cosa perteneciente a él" (He who was natural or enjoyed the privileges and exemptions of the Province of Latium in Italy. Today it is understood as someone who speaks or knows the Latin language, or anything that belongs to it) (http://web.frl.es/DA.html).

Thus, the word "Latino" referred to a specific linguistic skill and a sound knowledge of classical cultures. However, sometime in the sixteenth century, a new meaning was applied to "Ladino," the synonym of "Latino." The "discovery" and conquest of the New World generated a radical and unseen transformation of cultural conceptions about humankind and the globe. Indigenous peoples of the Americas constituted an enigma to Europeans, who debated about the humanity of those peoples and their capacity to understand and behave within the cultural and religious paradigms of Europe. In Spain, the 1550–1551 debate between Bartolomé de las Casas and Juan Ginés de Sepúlveda summarizes two opposite positions toward the Amerindians: Las Casas from a condescending perspective, giving credit to the natural, benevolent, and innocent features of the natives; Sepúlveda from an Aristotelian stand that classified human beings as masters and slaves, giving the Europeans the right to dominate and exploit the indigenous peoples of the Americas. Both Las Casas and Sepúlveda, however, departed from a common ground: the Indians needed to be transformed in order to enter a new and more advanced form of life under Christianity. The logic of this first wave of European colonialism relied on the belief that Amerindians should be assimilated to a single, homogeneous identity as Roman Catholics in order to save their souls.

Decolonial studies in Latin America have explained the abrupt and brutal epistemological rupture that Europeans inflicted on the indigenous peoples by creating a system of cultural domination that justified the colonization of their lands and the exploitation of their labor force. Since the accidental arrival of Christopher Columbus in 1492, the treatment of the natives was far from ideal. During the following decades, and despite many protective laws issued by the Spanish Crown, conquerors and settlers tended to see in the Indians a quick opportunity to get rich and to acquire unprecedented power. The system of the *encomienda* became common in the annexed territories. *Encomienda* literally translates as "commission" or "charge" and refers to a grant by the Spanish Crown to a colonist in America conferring upon a conqueror the right to demand tribute and forced labor from the Indian inhabitants of an area in exchange for military protection and, overall, evangelization. Conquerors came to represent a new local aristocracy with immense privileges and wealth. Las Casas denounced their abuse against the Indians, and the Crown decreed the New Laws of 1542 that limited the *encomenderos'* tenure for more than one life, i.e., many of them were either dispossessed of their privileges or prevented from passing their lands and indigenous servants (who paid mandatory tribute) to their offspring.

The implementation of the New Laws provoked an immediate resentment among the *encomenderos* and their descendants against the Crown and its officials. This phenomenon contributed to the formation of a Creole group (descendants of Europeans, born and raised in the New World) with a collective identity and a common agenda that after many generations would contend against Spain for independence.[1] However, this precedent should

---

[1] The Spanish word *criollo*, translated as "Creole" in English, derives from the Portuguese *crioulo*, which in turn comes from the verb *criar* (to raise, both in Portuguese and in Spanish). Both crioulo and criollo were originally used to refer to the offspring of African slaves born outside Africa. This meaning is still preserved in some non-Spanish-speaking

not be understood in a teleological way, as if Creoles of the sixteenth and seventeenth centuries were already a national formation in the modern sense of the word. In their specific cities of residence, they became a "nation" only in the archaic sense, i.e., as an ethnic group that privileged their own European roots and their collective superiority vis-à-vis the majority of indigenous and African-descended groups (see Mazzotti 2005).

This complex process of new social formations enabled a practical genocide of the indigenous population by means of forced labor and the abandonment of the existing advanced Amerindian agricultural systems of production in order to privilege mining and diseases. In only one century, for example, the Andean population decreased 90 percent, from 12 million people to 1.5 million by 1650. The Crown and the church, however, continued their project to create a Christian society by imposing Catholic values and rituals, principally through a campaign called extirpation of idolatry (see Duviols, Gareis, Greenleaf). In order to make their plans more effective, missionaries trained a number of indigenous individuals as translators. These Indians were called "indios ladinos," precisely because of their knowledge of the Romance language of Spanish.

Thus, the words "Latino" and "Ladino" coexisted for a long time, although in colonial Spanish America they began to refer to different things. A "Latino" was someone well versed in the Latin language and, therefore, of superior social and cultural status. A "Ladino" was an indigenous individual who knew Spanish and could likely serve as translator. Curiously, "Ladino" is also

areas of Latin America (e.g., Brazil, the French and English Caribbean islands, and in Louisiana). It also refers to cultural mixture. However, it has become traditional since the sixteenth century in Spanish America that criollos are the descendants of Europeans born in the New World. One of the first appearances of the term criollo in its Spanish American, white-related meaning dates from 1560 (see Martínez-San Miguel 404). This use probably derives from the insulting connotation of the same name originally used for the children of African slaves born outside Africa, as Bernard Lavallé explains (15–25), reflecting the scorn that some Spanish peninsulares felt toward the American-born children of the conquerors. The election of "criollo" as the main term used to refer to that group had two reasons: (1) many of the conquerors who were dispossessed of their lands and *encomiendas* after the New Laws of 1542 represented an emerging social stratum that threatened the power and hegemony of the Spanish Crown in the new territories; they were seen as "new rich" people of lower origins, and therefore undeserving of the political and economic power they had acquired; their children were also seen as suspicious and undeserving of trust; and, (2) up to 40 percent of "criollos" of the first generations may have had indigenous blood (see Schwartz; Kuznesof). In addition, they were raised by Indian or African nannies, and had contact with indigenous and African-descent children while growing up in the New World, not to mention the climatic and dietary influences that supposedly made them a sort of "degenerate" Spaniards. These criollos defended their blood purity during the successive generations, denying they were "contaminated" in any form.

the name of the particular kind of Spanish spoken by the Sephardic community before and after their expulsion from Spain in 1492. In Latin America, a more modern derivation of the meaning of "Ladino" is anyone who belongs to a Spanish/European tradition (even a *mestizo*) and has Spanish as their mother tongue, as opposed to the indigenous individuals who mainly speak an Amerindian language. This is at least the meaning of the word "Ladino" in Central America today, where Ladino became associated with a landed, conservative elite (*Diccionario de la Real Academia de la Lengua Española*, third entry). In other parts of the Spanish-speaking world, particularly in South America, a related meaning of "Ladino" is someone tricky and sleazy, an untrustworthy individual.

Going back to the colonial period, it is worth mentioning that in the eighteenth century the Spanish possessions in the Americas experienced a dramatic change in the way the Crown organized them. A series of reforms took place under the Bourbon administration, which had replaced the Hapsburg dynasty in 1700. Among others, the reforms consisted of the creation of two new viceroyalties, dividing the Viceroyalty of Peru into three new administrations: the reduced Viceroyalty of Peru, the Viceroyalty of New Granada (what is now Venezuela, Colombia, Panama, and Ecuador) in 1739, and the Viceroyalty of River Plate (Argentina, Bolivia, Chile, Uruguay, and Paraguay) in 1774. The original Viceroyalty of Peru was left with a fourth of its former territory. More importantly, the Crown implemented a system of "Intendencias" or small administrative units within each viceroyalty to better control the collection of tribute. Monopoly in commerce and high taxation were also some of the changes that Creoles felt as a direct aggression from the Crown. The tension between Creoles and Spaniards only grew, and the discontent against the Crown nurtured an already existing feeling of belonging to the native land. This feeling of differences of the Creoles from the Spaniards did not, however, prevent Creoles from assuming the Spanish cultural tradition as their own. And this feeling was not new either. Since the late sixteenth century, Creoles had expressed a strong patriotism with respect to the New World, a natural sentiment of appreciation for the place in which they were born, for its beauty, climate, and abundance. The exaltation of the New World nature and the grandeur of the Spanish cities founded in it translated into an eloquent defense of the virtues and high qualities of the offspring of the Spaniards in the New World. Creolism (or "criollismo" in Spanish), as this trend is known, with its allegiance to both the local and the metropolitan, would become in time a substantial precedent to a "Latin" definition of the new republics created in the nineteenth century, as we will see.

To better understand the phenomenon of Creolism and define it as a precedent of the "Latin" American identity, it may prove useful to trace its origins since the sixteenth century. For example, in describing Mexican Creoles, Juan de Cárdenas, in Book 3 of his *Problemas y secretos maravillosos de las Indias* (*Problems and Marvelous Secrets of the Indies*, 1591) affirms that "los Eſpañoles nacidos en las Indias [ſon] por la mayor parte de ingenio biuo, tracendido y delicado" ("Spaniards born in the Indies [are] for the most part, of a live, transcendent, and delicate mind"), and that they speak Spanish "tan pulido, corteſano y curioso" ("in a very polished, courteous, and distinct manner") (f. 176v). In Peru, Creole Friar Buenaventura de Salinas exclaimed in 1630 that Creoles "son con todo estremo agudos, viuos, sutiles, y profundos en todo genero de ciencias . . . [y] este cielo y clima del Pirú los leuanta, y ennoblece en animos" ("they are extremely intelligent, shrewd, subtle and well-grounded in all kinds of sciences . . . [and] this sky and weather of Peru elevates and ennobles their spirit") (246). Before Salinas, Francisco Fernández de Córdoba, an admired Creole scholar from Huánuco, in Peru, described Creoles as "hijos de la nobleza mejorada con su valor, . . . siendo más aventajados en esta transplantación, [de lo] que fueron en su nativo plantel" ("children of the [Spanish] nobility, [but] improved by their valor . . . for they are more advantaged in this new setting than they were in their native soil [i.e. Spain]") (Fernández de Córdoba 8). Creole Friar Antonio de la Calancha praised Peruvian Creoles in such a way that he placed them above the Spaniards and any other human group (see his *Crónica moralizada* of 1638).

It is not strange that the Bourbon reforms of the eighteenth century caused such an opposition among Creoles, forcing them to embrace their own sense of identity. After all, they had proclaimed themselves a "nation" (in the archaic sense of the word) even before the eighteenth century. This concept was not unusual and generally referred to what we now understand as an ethnic group, a concept that was applicable to both the Europeans and their descendants. In 1680, Mexican savant Carlos de Sigüenza y Góngora spoke of Creoles as "nuestra criolla nación" (our Creole nation) in his *Teatro de virtudes políticas* (19). That same year, in Lima, Spanish priest Francisco Antonio de Montalvo wrote in his *El Sol del Nuevo Mundo*:

> Los hombres y mugeres que cria eſte nueuo Mundo, por mas proporcionados a la participacion de los beneuolos influjos de ſus aſtros gozan de excelentes calidades, y de todos aquellos dones con que la naturaleza iluſtra a ſus muy fauorecidos, los cuerpos de las mugeres tienen mucha alma, las almas de los hombres mucho entendimiento, y todos en comun, buenos talles, hermoſas caras, afables condiciones, y liberales animos. Aun donde la

agudeza es muy natural ſe gaſtan ſeys y ocho años para eſtudiar la grammatica, y los criollos del Perù en menos tiempo acaban todos ſus eſtudios, de que ſe infiere no ſer inferiores à otras algunas naciones en la habilidad, y que exceden à muchas en la aplicación.

(Because they are more adapted to partake in the benevolent influences of their stars, the men and women of this New World enjoy excellent qualities; and as a result of all the gifts with which nature has favored them, women's bodies have plenty of soul, men's souls are filled with understanding, and everyone has nice figures, beautiful faces, kind manners, and generous spirits. Even in those parts of the world where intelligence comes naturally, people spend six or eight years studying grammar; however, since the Creoles of Peru finish all their studies in less time, it can be inferred that Peruvian Creoles are not inferior to other nations in their abilities, and that they surpass many others in their diligence.) (f. 16r)

Thus, even some Spaniards perceived Creoles as a "nación" with superior qualities to those of other nations within the Spanish Empire and elsewhere. Almost a century later, in 1778, and in a similar way, José Joaquín Granados y Gálvez, a Spanish priest who lived in Mexico for several decades, published his *Tardes americanas*, a curious dialogue between an Indian and a Spaniard who described life and institutions in Mexico. About Mexican Creoles, Granados stated: "no hay facultad, ciencia o arte donde no se hayan distinguido con especial aclamación de todo el orbe los hijos de Españoles de esta América Septentrional" ("there is no capacity, science, or art where the offspring of Spaniards in this Northern region [i.e., Mexico] have not distinguished themselves with special acclamation from the entire world"] (in Gil Amate 110). Granados also advocated for an equal treatment to Creoles within the Spanish Empire, recognizing their merits and granting them high offices usually reserved for Peninsular aristocrats. In an effort to strengthen the ties between Creoles and Peninsulars, Granados affirmed the cultural identity of both kinds of Spaniards: the Spanish Americans were as good and as Spanish as the Peninsular ones.

This defense of Creoles had an important precedent in jurist Juan de Solórzano Pereira, who in his *Política Indiana* of 1640 had stated similar ideas. The term "españoles americanos" (Spanish Americans) figures frequently in works by Peralta y Barnuevo and Vizcardo y Guzmán, among many other writers of the eighteenth century. It was preferred to that of Creoles and it was the immediate precedent to that of "Latin Americans." It implied a cultural preference for Europe, an elitist background, and a sense of local patriotism that did not necessarily entail an appreciation for indigenous and black people. On the contrary, Creoles or "Spanish Americans" based their alleged superiority on their capacity to keep their biological and cultural distinctiveness away from their subalterns' blood and daily practices. Even though many Spaniards thought since the sixteenth century that Creoles were somehow "contaminated" by their proximity to Indians and blacks, Creoles once and again denied any form of spiritual and corporeal impurity. They also distinguished themselves from *mestizos* (half Indian, half Spanish), a group considered suspicious because of their indigenous blood. While Spaniards accused Creoles of also being mixed or becoming Indians due to the influence of climate (see López de Velasco 37–38), Creoles always underlined their racial purity. The term *mestizo* was derogative in general; it referred to animals of mixed breeding ("mixtos"), and it entailed a negative cultural connotation, given that religious inclination was based on the "purity" of blood, according to Spanish conceptions at that time. Admitting to having indigenous blood was not strategic for Creoles if they wanted to achieve moral and administrative authority in their place of origin. Despite the bad reputation of *mestizos* in general, Inca Garcilaso de la Vega vindicates the use of the term and takes pride in it at the end of his masterful *Royal Commentaries of the Incas* of 1609.[2] But with the development of Linnaean classifications of vegetal species and the definition of "castes" or groups of mixed blood in the eighteenth century, Creoles gave a rational and "scientific" foundation to their early practice of modern racism.

The Independence, New Imperialisms, and the Invention of "Latin" America

As is common knowledge, Creoles led the Spanish American independence wars taking advantage of a series of historical circumstances, among which were – but not alone – the aforementioned Bourbon Reforms. When Napoleon invaded Spain in 1808, he created a power vacuum that Creoles interpreted according to an ancient medieval tradition, well established by King Alfonso X in his *Siete partidas*. This tradition consisted in the recognition of a *pactum subjectionis* or pact of subjection between the king and his vassals. The people or *vecinos* (nobles and free owners of a property in a given town) delegated their sovereignty to the king, who was a legitimate ruler as long as he took care of the common good and acted in the interest of his vassals, both in the spiritual and the material realms. The lack of a king or his

---

[2] See also Mazzotti, "Epic, Creoles and Nation in Spanish America."

tyrannical conduct automatically meant the return of the principle of sovereignty to the people.

This medieval Spanish legal tradition inspired the political philosophy of neo-Sscholasticism in the sixteenth century. Jesuits such as Francisco Suárez and Juan de Mariana proclaimed the need to keep an eye on the royal authority if the king violated any fundamental Christian principles (see Stoetzer). Rebellious Creoles of the early nineteenth century also found inspiration in the writings of late eighteenth-century Jesuits such as Francisco Javier Clavijero and Juan Pablo Vizcardo y Guzmán, who were expelled from the Spanish possessions along with the entire Jesuit order in 1767 for their opposition to the Crown. Clavijero, a Mexican priest, wrote extensively about the prowess of the Aztec culture and the greatness of the Mexican land, consolidating the pride of Creoles over their place of birth. Vizcardo, a Peruvian Jesuit, wrote his famous "Letter to the Spanish Americans" (1799), a document in which he assumed the heritage of the early conquerors and explained that their descendants, the Creoles, had the legitimate right to take over the administration of the vast Spanish possessions in the New World.

In addition, Creoles used some of the arguments from the Enlightenment and the American and French revolutions to justify their rebellion against the Crown. Declaring war against tyranny, oppression, the Inquisition, and all forms of political and economic subjugation became the only means to preserve their welfare and their dignity. In contrast, earlier strikes for independence like the failed rebellion of Tupac Amaru II in 1780–1781, along with the Haitian revolution, beginning with the successful revolt led by the Jamaican Boukman in 1791, did not declare their allegiance to a European cultural matrix as a sign of their identity.

Creoles carried out simultaneous revolutionary movements in Buenos Aires, Caracas, and Mexico in 1810. Fourteen years of bloody war followed until the final expulsion of the Spanish army from the continental Americas after the Creole victory of Ayacucho in Peru on December 9, 1824. Although there was some participation of indigenous, black, and, particularly, mestizo soldiers and low-ranking officers, Creoles from wealthy families constituted the core and leadership of the rebellion. Simón Bolívar, one of the most outstanding revolutionaries, was a wealthy landowner himself. These Spanish Americans founded the new republics under the notion of a common ancestry, a shared language (different in pronunciation, vocabulary, and some grammatical features from the Spanish spoken in the Iberian Peninsula) and their clear sense of difference vis-à-vis the majority of indigenous,

African-descent, and mestizo peoples in their vast territories. In many ways, they behaved as if the new political situation and their independent states were just a natural derivation of their sense of Creole nationhood.

Bolívar foresaw the need to create a union of American republics that could confront the growing power of the United States. In 1824, he called for a conference in Panama (Congreso Anfictiónico de Panamá), which finally took place in 1826. The conference failed because of the regional interests of each specific Creole group, the indifference of Chile, Argentina, and Brazil, and the growing opposition of the United States. This was the first political attempt to form a Spanish American community of nations with a common agenda. Bolívar's predecessor, Francisco de Miranda, had also proposed the creation of a single large nation under the name of "Colombia." Both Miranda's and Bolívar's initiatives were soon forgotten after Bolívar's death in 1830.

Meanwhile, it was clear to the world that Spain had already become a decadent empire. Taking advantage of this situation, the new imperial powers of the moment made an easy prey of the new Spanish American republics, infested as they were with civil wars and political chaos. After the defeat of Napoleon in 1815, some European countries signed a treaty known as the Holy Alliance by which they supported reestablishing the Bourbon domain over the former Spanish colonies in the Americas. England did not second this initiative because it would have affected its commercial interests in the region. More importantly – at least on a symbolic level – the Holy Alliance was decisively rejected by US president James Monroe and John Quincy Adams through the so-called Monroe Doctrine in 1823. The phrase "America for the Americans" resounded all over the continent and announced the larger project of the Manifest Destiny, by which the United States justified the occupation of western North America and its foreign interventions according to its political and economic needs, in the name of "civilization" and "democracy."

From one empire or another, the weak Spanish American countries began to suffer, thus, a series of military interventions: the British occupation of the Argentine Falkland Islands (islas Malvinas) in 1833, the French blockade of Buenos Aires and other Argentine ports from 1839–1840, another blockade by the British between 1845 and 1850, the US–Mexico war between 1846 and 1848 (which resulted in the appropriation of almost half of the Mexican territory), the tensions in 1850 over Panama generated by France and the United States to control the area for a future transoceanic canal, the British occupation of the eastern part of Venezuela or Guyanne Ezequiba in 1855, the incursions of

US filibuster William Walker in Nicaragua in the 1850s, the Spanish attempt to recover its former colonies in several points of the Americas in the 1860s (with the actual occupation of the Dominican Republic between 1861 and 1865), the French invasion of Mexico between 1862 and 1865, the British invasion of the eastern coast of Nicaragua (now called Bluefields), etc.

At the cultural level, both in France and in Spanish America, the notion of "race" as synonym of culture began to permeate the debates about the identity of those countries with a historical link to the Roman Empire and a Romance language as a national tongue. A "Germanic race" from northern Europe versus a "Latin race" from southern Europe were the two poles of historical tension for future imperialist plans from the European powers. France presented itself as the new leader of the "Latin race" in order to confront the growing power of England and the United States. French historian Michel Chevalier established in 1836 a comparison between a Germanic or Teutonic Protestant Europe and an Anglo-Saxon, also Protestant, North America. Likewise, a southern, Catholic, and "Latin" Europe had its direct inheritor in a "Latin," also Roman Catholic, South America. Through this conceptual configuration, French imperialist ambitions would find a perfect historical and cultural justification to seek an economic and political hegemony over Spanish and Luso America, given that Spain and Portugal were no longer capable of balancing the geopolitical map vis-à-vis the United States and England.

Not too many years later, in 1855, José María Torres Caicedo, a Colombian poet and politician based in Paris, wrote a poem entitled "Las dos Américas" ("The Two Americas"), in which he explicitly defined the opposition between an Anglo America and a Latin America, divided by religion, language, race, and historical trajectory. The expression "Latin America" began to circulate among Spanish American intellectuals who embraced a larger, Mediterranean cultural tradition than that of Spain alone. "Latin America" entailed a recognition of the French, the Italian, and other "Latin" or Romance cultures as part of the identity of the Creole elite. It entailed a project of modernity with peculiar and idiosyncratic features and became an effective conceptual tool to pursue a distinctive identity before the threatening and overpowering "Anglo America" (see Ardao). The fact that the label "Latin America" implicitly silenced and denied the majority of indigenous, black, and mestizo peoples of the continent was very revealing of its Creole, pro-European nature.

During the same years, and in a similar way, Chilean intellectual Francisco Bilbao published *Iniciativa de América. Idea de un Congreso Federal de las Repúblicas* (*Initiative of America. Idea of a Federal Congress of Republics*) in

1856, in which he resumed Bolívar's initiative to unify the South American republics in one single front in order to define their common destiny under the "modern" ideals of liberalism and progress, without the intervention or tutelage of the United States or any European power. For Bilbao, the bottom line was to "unificar el alma de América" (unify the soul of America) (*Iniciativa de América* 5). For that purpose, the new republics had to "unificar el pensamiento, unificar el corazón, unificar la voluntad de la América" (unify the thought, unify the heart, unify the will of America) (6). His agenda consisted of determining the common features of the new republics and how they could leave behind the traditional dependency on Europe and its "civilizing" mission. Walter Mignolo (68–71) has clearly explained that Bilbao was reasoning from an original standpoint that questioned the validity of European and US models of modernity because, when translated into the Latin American reality, these imported models meant a prolongation of the old colonialism against Indians and blacks. However, Bilbao did not question the validity of a Republican and secular political model, very much inspired in the original ideals of the French revolution. In no way did he propose to delegate power to subaltern groups; much less did he propose to adopt any political system derived from indigenous forms of organization.

In another important book, *América en peligro (America in Danger)* (1862), Bilbao argued against the imminent threat of French imperialism over Mexico. He also criticized those defenders of "civilization" who proclaimed that progress should follow European paradigms of society, at the expense (intended or not) of the native and African-descent groups: "Los partidos *civilizados* piden la dictadura, para combatir, dominar y civilizar a las masas. Es la dictadura de las clases privilegiadas" (*Civilized* parties ask for a dictatorship in order to combat, dominate, and civilize the mass. It is the dictatorship of the privileged classes) (italics in the original, 91). Finally, Bilbao proposed that South American countries should adopt "la religion de la república" (the religion of the republic)" (*América en peligro* 7) and unify themselves into a "United States of the South" (126) as the only possible choice to confront foreign interventions. Despite his defense of a genuine American political system against foreign intervention, Bilbao's underlying idea that Latin America should recognize its own identity as different from that of Europe and the United States was not matched by a full appreciation of indigenous and black cultural contributions, except in a condescending way. Bilbao still calls them "barbarians" who should be redeemed, naming them "masas brutas" (brute masses) (*América en peligro* 17) that nonetheless constitute the foundation of national sovereignty, but need guidance.

Intellectuals of the early twentieth century prolonged this gesture in their repeated assertion that the national and continental essence of Spanish and Portuguese ex-colonies of Spain and Portugal was Latin, by which they referred to a Mediterranean cultural matrix. For example, José de la Riva-Agüero, a prominent Peruvian intellectual of aristocratic background, when examining the oeuvre of the seventeenth-century emblematic mestizo writer Inca Garcilaso de la Vega, found in him "la más palmaria demostración del tipo literario peruano" (the most evident demonstration of the Peruvian literary type) (XXXVIII). When defining that type and, by extension, the entire Peruvian cultural identity, he affirmed that "nuestras aptitudes, por conformación y coincidencia espirituales, mucho más que por derivación de sangre, se avienen sorprendentemente con la tradicional cultura mediterránea que denominamos **latinismo**" (our aptitude, by form and spiritual coincidence, more than because of blood, are compatible with the most traditional Mediterranean culture called **Latinism**) (XXXIX, emphasis in the original). In 1926, another prominent intellectual, Pedro Henríquez Ureña, from the Dominican Republic, published his *Seis ensayos en busca de nuestra expresión* (*Six essays in Search of Our Expression*), in which he advocated for the enforcement of a Latin American cultural community and identity under the name of "Romania." The reference to the old Roman and Mediterranean tradition was obvious, and it seemed not to represent any problem for such brilliant scholars.

Nonetheless, the name "Latin America" was not always accepted in all cultural and political circles. In 1924, a young Peruvian politician, Víctor Raúl Haya de la Torre created an anti-imperialist political party, APRA ("Alianza Popular Revolucionaria Americana" or Popular Revolutionary American Alliance) defending the denomination of "Indoamérica" for Latin America. His agenda was to create a "single class front," including workers, peasants, and bourgeoisie to develop a national capitalism that could resist the economic domination of the United States over the region. The term "Indoamérica," however, did not have much fortune, except for a few sporadic uses among intellectuals.[3]

---

[3] "Indoamérica" figures in a title to José María Arguedas's *Formación de una cultura indoamericana*, following José Carlos Mariategui's essay with this term. Arguedas's volume was edited by Angel Rama in 1975. José Martí uses the term "la América indohispánica" in 1894 in a letter to José María Mayorga Rivas, rpt. in Miguel Gutiérrez Corrales, published in *Archivo José Martí*, La Habana 1943, 83–88 and 190–91. More recently, Mexican writer Carlos Fuentes proposes the use of "Indo-Afro-Ibero América" in his book *Valiente Mundo Nuevo* (1990).

"Latin America" and Latinos/as Today

Other names for the region, like "Iberoamérica" or "Hispanoamérica" are still popular in Spain, but not so much in "Latin America." The reason is that both "Iberoamérica" and "Hispanoamérica" immediately refer to the Iberian Peninsula and to Spain, respectively. "Iberoamérica" is useful only when it means a community of Latin American countries together with Spain and Portugal. "Hispanoamérica" makes sense only for the Spanish-speaking countries of the Americas, and leaves out Brazil and other countries or political formations in the Caribbean where Spanish does not predominate. To refer only to "Latin America" as a community of countries that have a different tradition and destiny than their former colonizers is not only more accurate, but it also has a political connotation. Given that Brazil and other countries share many of the same problems of colonialism and neocolonialism of the Spanish-speaking countries in the Americas, and that Spain and Portugal are former colonizing empires, it would be illogical to refer to the entire region exclusively as "Hispanoamérica" or "Iberoamérica."

Here is, then, where the name "Latin America" takes us back to the debate about the exclusions it supposes. Its origin, as stated before, is elitist and pro-European. It erases the very rich tradition and contributions from the large indigenous, black, and mestizo groups. Particularly in the case of the indigenous population, with more than 600 languages still spoken today, to be called "Latino" or "Latinoamericano" may even seem offensive. Those groups were historically oppressed, exploited, and massacred by the Europeans and their descendants. Even today, Creole states continue to advance an agenda for the exploitation of natural resources that takes into very little consideration the well-being of the surviving indigenous communities.

However, a similar argument can be made from the opposite point of view: "Indoamérica" excludes the white, the black, and the mestizo communities (not to mention the population of Asian origin, like the Chinese and Japanese in Brazil, Peru, and other countries). Even when the asymmetry is obvious in terms of the "coloniality of power" that both names (Latinoamérica and Indoamérica) entail, neither of them represent the variety and complexity of "Latin American" societies. Far from being a homogeneous and uniform region of the world, "Latin America" is the space of failed national projects and heterogeneous societies where nation-states do not represent or even include vast portions of their population.

Nonetheless, the name "Latin America" makes sense – in a resignified way – as a political tool to denounce the continuous foreign intervention it has suffered since 1492. Particularly since the Cuban Revolution in 1959, the term has been used within a progressive agenda to oppose the region's interest to those of the United States and other imperial powers. Several organizations such as the "Asociación Latinoamericana de Integración" (ALADI), the "Comisión Económica para América Latina" (CEPAL), the "Facultad Latinoamericana de Ciencias Sociales" (FLACSO), and the "Consejo Episcopal Latinoamericano" (CELAM), among others, have taken the name to identify their agendas with the region's common problems and interests.

When the category of "Hispanic" was included in the 1970 census in the United States, many celebrated that there was some recognition of the existence of this long-standing minority. However, not too long after, the category of "Latino" began to prevail, in part because of its political anti-imperialist connotation today and because it is more inclusive than "Hispanic" – it permits the possibility of considering the Brazilian-descent, and potentially Haitian and Dutch-descent, population. At the same time, the term "Latino" works as an umbrella to include a variety of very different groups that may have in common only some ancestry located in "Latin America": Chicanos, Puerto Ricans, Cuban Americans, and, in increasing numbers since the 1980s, Dominicans, Central Americans, and South Americans (also called "the other Latinos," who today constitute about 25 percent of the total of 50 million Latinas/os in the United States; see Falconi and Mazzotti).

In conjunction with ongoing struggles for civil and human rights by subaltern groups within emerging American nations, Latina/o writers since the 1970s have drawn on pre-Columbian terminology to refer to this region otherwise: the Nahuatl terms "Anahuac" (a country by the waters, and a pseudonym José Martí adopts in letters he publishes while living in Mexico), "Nepantla" (a space-in-between, by Gloria Anzaldúa), and "Aztlán" (a legendary home of Nahuatl or Aztec peoples, by poet Alurista – see Acuña), the Quechua term "Tawantinsuyo" to refer to the four regions that made up the Incan Empire, or the Kuna term "Abya-Yala" (land of abundance, by Takir Mamani – see López Hernández) from Panama's original inhabitants. Critically assessing the violent introduction of European cultures and languages and asserting a postcolonial Latina/o subjectivity, these terms figuratively evoke modes of cultural history and geography that antedate and look beyond European colonial domination. Indigenous movements in "Latin America" have achieved an important presence in the political spectrum of the region and have questioned the validity of the "Latin American" denomination, with good reason. In part, this is due to the fact that "Latin America," despite its anti-imperialist connotation at an international level, still works as a reminder of the internal colonialism that takes place within most of its countries. Therefore, in the U.S. context, the term "Latina/o" is also controversial. It works as a general denomination for statistical purposes, but it erases the profound differences between the different "Latino" groups. Indeed, part of the new waves of "Latin American" immigrants in the United States are people of indigenous origin who primarily speak a native American language. That is the case of Zapotec and Quechua-speaking peasants, whose allegiance with the Spanish language is many times remote.

Nonetheless, the term latinidad, meaning the condition of being "Latina/ o" is gaining consensus in current struggles around culture, immigration, education, and economic rights. Just as "Latina/o" may not represent the enormous variety of identities, languages, and subjectivities within this large minority in the United States, "latinidad" has a strategic use that may prove to unify political goals against discrimination and toward more recognition and active citizenship in years to come.

WORKS CITED

Acuña, Rodolfo F. *The Making of Chicana/o Studies: In the Trenches of Academe*. New Brunswick, NJ: Rutgers University Press, 2011.

Anzaldúa, Gloria. *Borderlands/La Frontera: The New Mestiza*. San Francisco: Aunt Lute Books, 1987.

Ardao, Arturo. *Génesis de la idea y el nombre de América Latina*. Caracas: Centro de Estudios Latinoamericanos Rómulo Gallegos, 1993.

Bilbao, Francisco. *Iniciativa de América. Idea de un congreso federal de las repúblicas* [1856]. México, DF: Universidad Nacional Autónoma de México, 1978.

La América en peligro. Buenos Aires: Bernheim y Boneo, 1862.

Calancha, Antonio de la. *Chronica Moralizada del Orden de San Agustín en el Perú con sucesos exemplares vistos en esta Monarchia*. Barcelona: por Pedro de Lacavalleria, 1638.

Cárdenas, Juan de. *Problemas y secretos maravillosos de las Indias* [1591]. Edición facsimilar. Madrid: Ediciones Cultura Hispánica, 1945.

Covarrubias, Sebastián de. *Tesauro de la lengua castellana o española* [1611]. Martín de Riquer, ed. Madrid: S.A. Horta, I.E., 1943.

Duviols, Pierre. "La idolatría en cifras: una relación peruana de 1619". *Études Latino-Américaines* 3 (Aix-en-Provence, 1967): 87–100.

La lutte contre les religiones autochtones dans le Pérou colonial. L'extirpation de l'idolâtrie entre 1532 et 1660. (Travaux de l' Institut Français d'Etudes Andines 13). Lima-Paris: Institut Français d'Etudes Andines, 1971.

Falconi, José Luis, and José Antonio Mazzotti, eds. *The Other Latinos: Central and South Americans in the United States*. Cambridge, MA: Harvard University Press, 2007.

Fernández de Córdoba, Francisco. "Prólogo al lector" (dated September 8, 1620). In Alonso Ramos Gavilán, *Historia de Nuestra Señora de Copacabana*. La Paz: Academia Boliviana de la Historia, [1621] 1976, 2nd. ed., 7–9.

Gareis, Iris. "Repression and Cultural Change: the "Extirpation of Idolatry" in Colonial Peru." In *Spiritual Encounters. Interactions between Christianity and Native Religions in Colonial America*. Nicholas Griffiths and Fernando Cervantes, eds. Birmingham: The University of Birmingham Press, 1999. 230–54.

Gil Amate, Virginia. *Sueños de unidad hispánica en el siglo XVIII. Un estudio de Tardes americanas de José Joaquín Granados y Gálvez*. Alicante: Centro de Estudios Mario Benedetti, Universidad de Alicante, 2012.

Greenleaf, Richard E. (1985). *Inquisición y sociedad en el México colonial* (Colección "Chimalistac" de libros y documentos acerca de la Nueva España, 44). Madrid: Porrúa Turanzas, 1985.

Kuznesof, Elizabeth Anne. "Ethnic and Gender Influences on 'Spanish' Creole Society in Colonial Spanish America." *Colonial Latin American Review* 4, 1 (1995): 153–76.

Lavallé, Bernard. *Las promesas ambiguas. Ensayos sobre el criollismo colonial en los Andes*. Lima: Fondo Editorial de la Pontificia Universidad Católica del Perú, 1993.

López de Velasco, Juan. *Geografía y descripción universal de las Indias*. Edición de Don Marcos Jiménez de la Espada. Estudio preliminar de Doña María del Carmen González Muñoz. Madrid: Atlas, [1571–1574] 1971.

López Hernández, Miguel Ángel. *Encuentros por los senderos de Abya-Yala*. Quito: Editorial Abya-Yala, 2004.

Martínez-San Miguel, Yolanda. "Poéticas caribeñas de lo criollo: creole/criollo/creolité". In *Poéticas de lo criollo. La transformación del concepto "criollo" en las letras hispanoamericanas (siglo XVI al XIX)*. Juan M. Vitulli and David Solodkow, eds. Buenos Aires: Corregidor, 2009. 403–41.

Mazzotti, José Antonio. "Epic, Creoles and Nation in Spanish America." In *A Companion to the Literatures of Colonial America*. Susan Castillo and Ivy Schweitzer, eds. Oxford: Blackwell Publishing Ltd., 2005. 480–99.

Mignolo, Walter. *The Idea of Latin America*. Malden, MA: Blackwell, 2005.

Riva Agüero, José de la. "Elogio del Inca Garcilaso." In *Comentarios reales de los Incas*. Lima: Librería e Imprenta Sanmarti y Cía., [1916]1918, vol. 1.

Salinas y Córdova, Fray Buenaventura de. *Memorial de las historias del Nuevo Mundo Piru*. Lima: por Geronimo de Contreras, 1630.

Schwartz, Stuart. "Colonial Identities and Sociedad de Castas." *Colonial Latin American Review* 4, 1 (1995): 185–201.

Sigüenza y Góngora, Carlos de. *Theatro de Virtudes Politicas que conſtituyen à un Principe: advertidas en los monarchas antiguos del Mexicano Imperio, con cuyas efigies ſe hermoseó el Arco Triumphal que la muy noble, muy leal, imperial Ciudad de Mexico erigió para el digno recivimiento en ella del Excelentiſſimo Señor Virrey Conde Paredes, Marqués de la Laguna, & c*. México: por la Viuda de Bernardo Calderón, 1680.

Stoetzer, O. Carlos. *The Scholastic Roots of the Spanish American Revolution*. New York: Fordham University Press, 1979.

PART II

★

THE ROOTS AND ROUTES OF
LATINA/O LITERATURE

*The Literary Emergence of a Trans-American
Imaginary, 1783–1912*

6

Whither Latinidad?

*The Trajectories of Latin American, Caribbean,
and Latina/o Literature*

MARÍA DEL PILAR BLANCO

Like virtually any question related to identity, defining *latinidad*, or "Latin-ness," is difficult business. To speak of a latinidad is to embrace the idea that, in a modern world full of races, languages, and cultures, Latin American or Latina/o exceptionality is visible through identifiable traits and unique modes of expression. This particular nomenclature asks us to consider *how* these qualities have been manifested throughout history within the regions of "Latin" America and the Spanish Caribbean, in the United States, and, increasingly, other parts of the planet. However, as a doggedly unstable term, latinidad requires a multiplicity of interpretations, given the many sites – both chronological and geographic – of its enunciation, and the many racial, social, and cultural realities that abound in the movements from Latin America and the Caribbean to other parts of the world. Latinidad, as Marta Caminero-Santangelo has argued, "suggests a contrast" between Latina/o groups and non-Latina/o groups; it is inherently a term of comparison, one that is dynamic and bound to be transformed with each locale, and each interpretation.[1]

As networks of migration have intensified throughout the post/colonial history of Latin America, and – in the academic context – as the fields of Latin American and Latina/o studies have gone through different cycles of (dis)unity, "latinidad" has become a fractured and fractious term. Debates about assimilation and transculturation as byproducts of migration, and of how these phenomena manifest themselves in different cultural areas – especially language – have led to a variety of conundrums about canon

---

[1] Marta Caminero-Santangelo. "Latinidad." *The Routledge Companion to Latino/a Literature.* Eds. Suzanne Bost and Frances R. Aparicio (New York: Routledge, 2015), 13.

development and demarcation. The questions that have occupied scholars within Latin American and Latina/o studies have been varied: Can a Latina/o writer claim to also be Latin American? Are the categories of "Latina/o" and "Latin American" self-appointed, or are they identities that are designated from outside the group? Are they both? Can US Latina/o subjects claim a Latin American text as part of their heritage? An increasingly important question in today's global context is what significance the label "Latina/o" has beyond the academic centers of the United States.

A recent (anecdotal) example captures the difficulty of pinpointing latinidad's concreteness, not to mention its location(s): On August 22, 2012, Dominican-American author Junot Díaz spoke to a packed audience in Foyles bookstore in London's West End. All over the venue were copies of the UK edition of the Pulitzer-winning *The Brief Wondrous Life of Oscar Wao* (2007), published in the country by Faber & Faber; the front cover of the novel, rather more referential than the US version (a brown-skinned boy wearing a superhero mask and reading comic books) featured a blurb from a *Guardian* review, which deemed the work "exotic." In a relatively small venue, the first two rows of seats were reserved for a group of people from the Dominican embassy. In that particular European forum, the Dominican government representatives looking on, Díaz unquestionably appeared as a national treasure, not least because he had received one of the most important accolades in the international literary scene. But cultural affinity and belonging happen differently in different geographies; they have their limits. Over a year later, in a *Los Angeles Times* article from November 10, 2013, Díaz, together with US journalist Mark Kurlansky, Dominican-American writer Julia Alvarez, and Haitian-American novelist Edwidge Danticat, denounced the Dominican high court's decision (known as Sentencia 168-13) to strip the citizenship from those born after 1929 and whose parents were not native to the country. (The Sentencia is being carried out to disastrous effect at the moment I write this.) As the writers explained, "The ruling affects an estimated 250,000 Dominican people of Haitian descent, including many who have had no personal connection with Haiti for several generations."[2] They deemed the court's decision a blatantly racist act redolent of the 1937 massacre of Haitians ordered by dictator Rafael Leonidas Trujillo. The article prompted some intellectuals in the Dominican Republic to

---

[2] Mark Kurlansky, Julia Alvarez, Edwidge Danticat, and Junot Díaz. "In the Dominican Republic, Suddenly Stateless." November 10, 2013: http://articles.latimes.com/2013/nov/10/opinion/la-oe-kurlansky-haiti-dominican-republic-citizensh-20131110.

attack the writers, particularly Junot Díaz. One such invective came in the shape of a widely disseminated e-mail written to Díaz by José Santana, executive director of the country's International Advisory Committee on Science and Technology, who accused the author of *Oscar Wao* of being an "overrated pseudo intellectual" who "should learn first to speak Spanish before coming to this country to speak nonsense."[3] In this context, Díaz ceased to be a source of national pride and became a kind of impostor whose comments on domestic policy in the Dominican Republic were both unwelcome and out of place; indeed, Santana's open letter explicitly slates the novelist as a "pseudo intellectual" and implicitly as a pseudo-Dominican, given his status as a Latino writer living outside the country. The questioning of Díaz's Spanish skills here is a classic strategy of dismissiveness in which subjects from the native land attempt to strip those on the outside of their right and of a medium in which to speak about the political realities in the "home" country. Santana's condemnation of Díaz was not an isolated opinion: in October 2015 Eduardo Selman, the Dominican Republic's consul in New York, revoked the Order of Merit medal awarded to the novelist in 2009.

These two separate anecdotes about one of the best known Latino figures on the contemporary international literary scene illustrate how the concept of latinidad is kaleidoscopic in the sense that it is unstable, shifting, and morphing depending on the position from which it is observed or within which it announces itself. In the Santana-Díaz debate, the novelist's status as a hyphenated subject – a Dominican-American – who dares to pose an open critique to domestic policy on the island immediately cancels out any stake he may have as a "true" islander. Ironically, Santana tries to deny Díaz the capacity and right to speak of internal racial politics, despite race being such a fundamental factor in the unleashing of the Dominican diaspora to which Díaz belongs. And yet, far away from the back-and-forth between two locations in the American hemisphere (one north and another south), in a city like London where Latinos are not (yet) an organized ethnic group in the way they are in the United States, we see how the contemplation of Latino subjectivity is pointedly different: there, an audience would be inclined to deem Díaz a Latin American or Caribbean writer before thinking of using the "Latino" category, with all the implications that it has amassed in the United States since the second half of the twentieth century. (The fact that the novel

[3] www.latinorebels.com/2013/12/03/dominican-govt-officials-email-to-junot-diaz-youre-a-fake-and-overrated-pseudo-intellectual-who-needs-to-speak-spanish-better/

was deemed "exotic," I would argue, also aligns it with the kind of Latin American literary works that have been so successfully marketed globally in the twentieth and twenty-first centuries, namely the magical realist novels of the post–Second World War "Boom" period.) However, the myriad locations from which latinidad can be witnessed and expressed are not just demarcated by national borders; the notion changes within a variety of institutional sites, from the governmental to the academic. The claim to a singular "Latino" identity has succeeded in mobilizing an ethnically and nationally diverse minority group in the political as well as the cultural realm; but it is also a performative term, as Pedro Cabán noted in the 1990s, for the label can be "readily shed when Latin American and Caribbean people are among themselves, an arena in which we identify ourselves on the basis of country of origin."[4]

Latinidad's Canons

To understand and locate a Latina/o American literary corpus entails a parallel consideration of the historical development of the Latin American and US canons, and the extent to which these two disciplinary fields have engaged with texts that emerge out of the experience of exile and diaspora. When does a text cease to be part of a Latin American canon to become part of a Latina/o corpus? What does it mean to engage in the study of Latina/o literature, as opposed to Latin American literature? Are they separate entities, or could we consider Latina/o literature an outcropping of Latin American literature? Aside from presenting a disciplinary dilemma, this second question signals the challenge of periodicity, of where one begins to trace a Latina/o literature that could theoretically stand on its own in terms of a canon, possibly even extricating itself from the aegis of Latin American literature. As Kirsten Silva Gruesz notes in her review of *The Norton Anthology of Latino Literature*, edited by Ilan Stavans, Latina/o literature does not yet have a set literary history, therefore making the claim to a canon a difficult, if not controversial, move.[5] Much of the most interesting recent scholarship on Latino literature (e.g., Raúl Coronado's *A World Not to Come*) has devoted itself to tracing an archive of Latino literature in the United States into the

---

[4] Pedro Cabán. "The New Synthesis of Latin American and Latino Studies," in *Borderless Borders: U.S. Latinos, Latin Americans, and the Paradox of Interdependence*. Eds. Frank Bonilla, Edwin Meléndez, Rebecca Morales, and María de los Ángeles Torres. Philadelphia: Temple University Press, 1998: 195–215; 212.
[5] Kirsten Silva Gruesz. "What Was Latino Literature?" *PMLA* 127.2 (2012): 335–41; 336.

early nineteenth century, in forgotten sites where enlightened subjects came together to fight against subordination by the Spanish. The *Recovering the U.S. Hispanic Literary Heritage* project, which began in 1992, has tirelessly sought to trace a literary lineage that goes back to the sixteenth century, in an effort to furnish a sense of US colonial literary history that puts texts like Alvar Núñez Cabeza de Vaca's *Relación* (1542) on equal pegging to William Bradford's *Of Plymouth Plantation* (1630–1651).[6] Ilan Stavans's *Norton Anthology* includes a translation of Cabeza de Vaca's narrative alongside several others from the colonial period (more on this collection below).

This body of literature from the colonial period to the beginning of the Latin American republican moment offers meanings and ramifications to the term "Latino" that are different from those used in the second half of the twentieth century. Moreover, it is a nomenclature pronounced by subjects whose politics (whether in such periods as the US–Mexican War of 1846–1848, the Pan-American Conferences that took place from 1889 to 1891, or the US–Spanish War of 1898) can often be distinct from, if not intensely opposed to, those of contemporary Latina/o literature scholars, whose analytical impetus reflects the spirit of resistance exemplary of the Chicano and Puerto Rican movements that began in the 1960s and continue to this day. The opening of the archive, as Coronado posits in his book, involves a suspension of our expectations as scholars, because we must learn to "read history from the unsure, unfolding perspective of its makers."[7] Gruesz also explains what is at stake for archival scholars of the Latina/o literary imagination: they must "risk anachronism in order to pose larger questions about how the anxiety of a Latino future drives readings of its past."[8] In studying expressions of latinidad as they manifest themselves in different points of the American hemisphere, it is crucial to entertain both the contact points and the digressions between past and present histories, and also to understand such enunciations of identity as open-ended, often contradictory narratives.

Speaking in terms of the institutionalization of literary study, we see how the establishment of "Latin" American and Caribbean literatures – as

---

[6] See José F. Aranda, Jr.. "Recovering the US Hispanic Literary Heritage," in *The Routledge Companion to Latino/a Literature*. Eds. Suzanne Bost and Frances Aparicio. New York and London: Routledge, 2015: 476–84.

[7] Raúl Coronado. *A World Not to Come: A History of Latino Writing and Culture*. Cambridge, MA and London: Harvard University Press, 2013: 393.

[8] Kirsten Silva Gruesz. *Ambassadors of Culture: The Transamerican Origins of Latino Writing*. Princeton, NJ and Oxford: Princeton University Press, 2002: xi.

analytical fields that assume, to greater or smaller degrees, a regional homo-geneity – enables an understanding of their role as countering other (North-ern) American literatures; to borrow Gruesz's terminology, their past as well as their future are always and already engaged in a productive anxiety about hemispheric identity. Latina/o literature illustrates a similar anxiety, but from within the smaller-scale (i.e., not continental) theaters of immigration and exile in the United States. While "Latin" American literature has so often engaged in a discourse of differentiation from its northern neighbors, Latina/o literature is an expression of singular identities resisting being subsumed into dominant cultures of the north. In academia, scholars of Latina/o literature – and, more recently, those who are devoted to the formation of an archive that stretches further into the past – seek to rewrite North American literary history through a demonstration of the presence of Latino voices embedded in that history. These activities are testaments of the anxiety of ethnic/racial/cultural preservation in local, regional, and global contexts. That anxiety is a productive response to the specter of colonialism, and a direct engagement with the contradictions spawned by that same colonization.

Rather than offer a set of demarcations that would artificially separate Latin American from Latina/o literature, in what follows I focus on a set of examples from the fin de siècle – one of many climactic points in inter-American relations – that perform and question latinidad as a collective opposition against new forms of colonialism. Taking as inspiration Josefina Ludmer's call to build a "máquina para leer el siglo XIX" (a machine to read the nineteenth century), through which literature and politics are read together to produce a history that takes into account hegemonic structures and its subalterns, my aim here is not to see the *fin de siglo* (with the events of 1898 as a centerpiece) as a species of ground zero of the production of latinidad north and south.[9] As already mentioned and as numerous critics of Latina/o literature have shown, we can and should continue digging further into the past to continue building a literary history of this identity formation. Rather, I offer this example as just one pathway – a confluence of ideas about coloniality, race, and autochthony – in which texts that could be artificially construed as belonging to different fields (Latin American, as opposed to Latina/o literature) can be read together as commentaries on trans-American pasts and presents. Studying these texts in their specificity can

[9] Josefina Ludmer. "Una máquina para leer el siglo XIX." *Revista de la Universidad Autónoma de México* 530 (1995): 65–66.

facilitate further reflection on the limits and promises of bodies of work we have come to identify as belonging to national literary traditions, or to "Latina/o" or "Latin" American" textual bodies, while allowing us to retain a sense of the specific histories and geographies of a polyvalent latinidad.

The Problem of Naming "Latin" America

As established in this chapter, terms like "Latina/o," "Hispanic," and "Spanish American" are as intensely problematic as they are heavily contested. They are simultaneously markers of a community with shared interests, histories, and desires, and of the perseverance of labels created by colonial powers that have the luxury of naming their subaltern others. However, the category of "Latina/o" refers to the assumption that there is such a thing as "Latin" America or a "Spanish" Caribbean as a starting point of migration and movement – and that there is a recognizable and cohesive geography to and out of which subjects can appeal for to a common identity. But the difficulty of assigning labels rears its head yet again, alluding as it does to colonialism's steady hold on our choice of nomenclatures. Indeed, as John Beverley remarks, "*Latin* America" is "a doubly colonial double misnomer (first, for the name of the Italian navigator, and second, for the idea of 'Latinity' promulgated by the French Foreign Office in the nineteenth century to try to displace US and British hegemony)."[10] Pointing to the contiguity of nineteenth-century exoticist epistemes, Walter Mignolo notes how "the very idea of Latin America was born at the same time that the idea of the Orient was being produced in Europe."[11] Furthermore, to embrace this "misnomer" that is "Latin" America is, as Beverley warns, an affirmation of a homogeneous and univocal entity that stands against "a foreign other" – one that nevertheless runs the risk of eliding "the relations of exclusion and inclusion, subordination and domination that operate *within*" the nations that form part of the Latin American region (68). The qualifiers "Spanish" or "Hispanic" used to denote the communities of Latino subjects in the United States pose a similar conundrum, as they gloss over the complexities of the internal racial and class divisions that are ingrained in the histories of Latin American nations, and of the many migrations into the northern country. As Suzanne

---

[10] John Beverley. *Latinamericanism after 9/11*. Durham, NC: Duke University Press, 2011: 18.

[11] Walter Mignolo. "Capitalism and Geopolitics of Knowledge: Latin American Social Thought and Latino/a American Studies." *Critical Latin American and Latino Studies.*, Ed. Juan Poblete. Minneapolis: University of Minnesota Press, 2003: 35.

Bost and Frances Aparicio explain, "Hispanic" and "Latino" are "misnomers to the extent that they imply a transplanted European heritage and elide the mixture with indigenous and African peoples that characterized the formation of *mestizaje*... throughout 'Latin' America."[12] The names that huddle around latinidad in the south as in the north, as these recent engagements reflect, are double-edged appropriations and at times even unwitting extensions of the wounds of colonial history. There is therefore a paradox at the very heart of these two adjacent identities, one that must be necessarily embraced in the name of community and cultural unity.

"Latin" America, following Beverley, is a fiction of the (neo-)imperial age. Beginning in the nineteenth-century republican period, it has also served a narrative in which cultural exceptionality is announced for geopolitical reasons. Appropriations of the term "Latin" flourished as a result of mounting hemispheric tensions. Following the wars of independence in the nineteenth century, subjects in the region – José Martí, José Enrique Rodó, and later (though worth mentioning) José Vasconcelos, to name just three examples – have directly or indirectly appropriated an idea of latinidad to describe a set of racial, linguistic, and cultural values that stand in direct opposition to the United States and an "Anglo-Saxon" culture. Eight years before the outbreak of the US–Spanish War of 1898, in his renowned essay "Nuestra América" (by now an ur-text of hemispheric American and Latin American studies), Martí warns of the dangers at bay in the relations between the hemisphere's "dos factores continentales" (two factions) that do not share the same "orígenes, métodos e intereses" (origins, methods, and interests).[13] In this essay, he offers a poignant critique of the paradoxical persistence of colonial thinking even in a republican age, which could eventually spell out a transnational disaster for Latin America and the Caribbean: "La colonia continuó viviendo en la república" (The colony lives on in the republic), he writes (*Obras completas* 21; 293). The antidote to the north's sense of enterprise, and to the internal weaknesses in Latin American nations comes in the shape of an "hombre natural" (natural man) who, unburdening himself from the shackles and masquerades of colonialisms present and future, can attain an autochthony that answers to the specific conditions of the region.

[12] Suzanne Bost and Frances Aparicio. "Introduction." *Routledge Companion to Latino/a Literature*. Eds. Bost and Aparicio. London and New York: Routledge, 2015: 1.
[13] José Martí. "Nuestra América." *Obras completas*, vol. 6. Havana: Editorial de Ciencias Sociales, 1975: 21. Translated version, "Our America." José Martí, *Selected Writings*. Trans. Esther Allen. New York: Penguin, 2002: 295.

At the dawn of the new century, Rodó proposes (via Shakespeare's *Tempest*) that the Hispanic south is the spiritual antidote to the utilitarian Calibans of the north. In this context, the Uruguayan speaks of the "americanos latinos" that are inextricably united by ethnicity and race (not to mention language), and who stand in direct opposition to their neighbors, whose identity is encapsulated in the *"Washington más Edison"* equation.[14] A few decades later, in *La raza cósmica* from 1925, Vasconcelos celebrates Latin America as a territory where "mil puentes" (a thousand bridges) lead to "la fusión sincera y cordial de todas las razas" (the sincere and cordial fusion of all races).[15] Martí, Rodó, and Vasconcelos represent different degrees of engagement with an idea of latinidad that describes a (rather problematic) blood link among all subjects south of the United States. Their goal is ultimately to offer a historical and/or genetic narrative of regional exceptionality that directly contests northern manifest destiny. While Vasconcelos's thesis of the "raza cósmica" relies on a post-positivist celebration of the many *mestizajes* of Iberoamerica, Martí also speaks of the racial and cultural mixing of "nuestra América" in the years leading to the wars of independence: "Con los pies en el rosario, la cabeza blanca y el cuerpo pinto de indio y criollo, vinimos, denodados, al mundo de las naciones" (Our feet upon the rosary, our heads white, and our bodies a motley of Indian and criollo we boldly entered the community of nations) (*Obras completas* 18; 291). For his part, Rodó's attack on what he calls *"nordomanía"* is a warning against an "América *deslatinizada*" (de-latinized America) that forgets its common Hispanic heritage ("Ariel," 34).

In the realm of poetry, Rubén Darío, the figure at the forefront of Spanish American *modernismo*, illustrates in "A Roosevelt" (1904) a post-bellum Latin American exceptionality in verses that speak of the region's common Catholic, Hispanic, and indigenous heritage: "Eres los Estados Unidos, / eres el futuro invasor / de la América ingenua que tiene sangre indígena, / que aún reza a Jesucristo y aún habla español" (You are the United States, / you are the future invader / of the naive América that has Indian blood, / that still prays to Jesus Christ and still speaks Spanish).[16] Similarly, in his "Salutación del optimista" (Madrid, 1905), which Gerard Aching calls "the grandest gesture toward imagining a supranational

---

[14] José Enrique Rodó. *Ariel. Motivos de Proteo*. Caracas: Biblioteca Ayacucho, 1976: 45.
[15] José Vasconcelos. *The Cosmic Race/La raza cósmica*. Trans. Didier Jaén. Baltimore: Johns Hopkins University Press, 1997 (1979): 20; 40.
[16] Rubén Darío. "A Roosevelt." *Azul.../Cantos de vida y de esperanza*. Madrid: Espasa Calpe, 2007: 203.

trans-Atlantic Hispanism,"[17] the poet hails a "latina estirpe" (Latin stock) united by "espíritu y ansias y lengua" (spirit and yearning and language) (193). As Aching explains, Darío read "Salutación" at the Ateneo de Madrid in 1905 as a way of "redress[ing] the lingering 'abulia' or apparent indifference among Spaniards" after their defeat in 1898 (56). Far from being a plea for readmission into the Spanish Empire at a time in which the threat of a US invasion of its southern neighbors loomed ever larger, Darío's poems are willful, strategic admissions of a global latinidad as a reaction to current and future geopolitical shifts in the region. In other words, it is a search for transatlantic cultural and aesthetic (not political) unity at a time of anxiety regarding the political independence of the Latin American region.

Notably, Darío and Vasconcelos – and Martí, to a lesser extent – address latinidad as a *mestizo* identity that results from the mix of Spanish, indigenous, and African blood. Their approach to indigeneity is not without its problems, speaking as they do from within ideological formations that have their basis in nineteenth-century racial discourses. In addition, their perception of Amerindian pasts can rely heavily on a notion of heroic histories rather than the realities of subordination (in the epic "A Roosevelt," Darío writes of an América of the "gran Moctezuma" and "el noble "Guatemoc," for example). But it is nevertheless important to trace the lines that connect such celebrations of *mestizaje* in texts we study under the aegis of Latin American literary studies to the ur-texts of Latina/o studies, like for example Gloria Anzaldúa's *Borderlands/La Frontera* (1987) where she calls for a "new mestiza" consciousness.[18] We should also think critically about the persistence and evolutions of such discourses, and their relation to canon formation within the fields of Latin American and Latina/o studies. The section devoted to "Colonization: 1537–1810" in Stavans's *Norton Anthology of Latino Literature* opens with an introduction that rather problematically marks *modernismo* as the moment in which "a renewed appreciation for aboriginal civilizations took shape south of the Rio Grande," from which *indigenismo* and later Chicana/o celebrations of mestizo identity appear to flow naturally.[19] Without a doubt, an established Latin American literary canon

---

[17] Gerard Aching. *The Politics of Spanish American* modernismo. Cambridge: Cambridge University Press, 1997: 56.

[18] For a discussion of the connections between Vasconcelos and Anzaldúa, see Rafael Pérez-Torres, "Mestizaje." *Routledge Companion to Latino/a Literature*. Eds. Bost and Aparicio. New York and London: Routledge, 2015. 26–27.

[19] Introduction to "Colonization: 1537–1810." *The Norton Anthology of Latino Literature*. Ed. Ilan Stavans. New York: W.W. Norton & Company, 2010: 10.

should be open to cross-fertilizations with bodies of literature that have been cordoned off as belonging to the Latina/o imaginary. This kind of openness acknowledges the impossibility of thinking of a national literary canon as a bordered entity. In the case of the Latina/o imaginary, to think of a tradition that is rooted in but also routed from Latin America, is to envision literature as a body that travels and grows with its migrations. Having said this, and thinking back to Stavans's connection between the budding *indigenismo* of the Latin American *modernistas* and later texts that are firmly located within the Latina/o canon of the twentieth century, it is nevertheless important to ask difficult questions about how we go about this by addressing each text's responsiveness to acts of racial, ethnic, and cultural essentialism. These are instances in which our presents and our pasts as literary scholars productively collide.

As the examples above demonstrate, the sites from/in which latinidad is enunciated are pivotal in our understanding of how identity is articulated for comparative and oppositional purposes. As a Nicaraguan in Madrid in 1905, Darío's celebration of the "latina estirpe" is a strategic enunciation of difference *against* the new imperial threat to an audience whose country had lost an empire but left its culture behind in the American hemisphere. Here, culture – with the Spanish language as its cornerstone – becomes the most powerful tool to achieve solidarity among subjects. Things change once latinidad is named from a different locale where this solidarity is harder to come by. Darío's creative forebear, Martí, wrote a great majority of his oeuvre from within the United States; his position as an exiled colonial subject fighting against an established empire and another one to come is a call to complete independence of the region, given how "ni el libro europeo, ni el libro yanqui" can answer "el enigma hispanoamericano" (No Yankee or European book could furnish the key to the Hispanoamerican enigma) (20; 293–94). Laura Lomas notes how Martí's latinidad is deeply affected by his condition as a non-assimilated migrant and a Latino, whose "America lies in and beyond the United States, both geographically and temporally."[20] As part of a growing community of Hispanic exiles in the northeast of the United States, Martí was an incisive commentator, or, as Lomas notes, an "infiltrative translator" of US matters for audiences in Latin America – one who is "simultaneously inside and outside of imperial modernity's frame" (49).

---

[20] Laura Lomas. *Translating Empire: José Martí, Migrant Latino Subjects, and American Modernities*. Durham, NC and London: Duke University Press, 2008: 35.

Traveling Latinidades

Migration, exile, and other forms of travel narratives between the north and south are important lenses through which to entertain the many twists and turns of oppositional fin-de-siècle latinidad. In his capacity as translator of US culture for Latin American audiences, Martí was also fully attuned to the northern country's perception of their southern neighbors, and regularly reviewed travel narratives by North American travelers in the south (e.g., David Wells's *Study of Mexico* from 1887). As Jason Ruiz has explained, travel between the United States and Mexico began to pick up in the 1880s thanks to the connection of the two countries' rail networks. "So many US citizens entered Mexico during this period," he writes, "that some Mexicans – and even some travelers – referred to the Americans that swarmed train stations and popular destinations as the ruins at Mitla as a foreign invasion."[21] But, countering the exoticising views of US citizens abroad, there are also other narratives, which describe south-north travel, and which represent another site from which to both observe and critique latinidad as it was manifesting itself *within* the United States. In his travel narrative from 1895 *En tierra yankee (notas a todo vapor)*, the Mexican author and statesman Justo Sierra relates his experiences in a series of tableaux that, while redolent of the aestheticizations of Romantic travel writers, reveal an incisive perception of the imposing northern country. One particular episode ("Colón-Cervantes") describes his time in New York City, during which he visits the Círculo Colón-Cervantes, a club whose members are Hispanic men and women from Spain, various South American countries, and Cuba. "Entre los socios," he writes, "los mexicanos están en minoría" (Mexicans were a minority in the membership). Despite the small numbers of fellow countrymen in this company, Sierra celebrates how "todos parecen compatriotas; á nosotros todos nos parecieron mexicanos, con todos fraternizamos" (all seem to be compatriots; to us, they all appeared to be Mexicans, and we fraternized with all of them).[22] He then says, poignantly: "Es muy bello esto de creer, durante ese largo espacio de la vida de un mortal que se llama una noche de baile, que todos los hombres somos hermanos, que todos los latinos formamos un pueblo, que de nuestras patrias particulares podemos remontarnos, al compás de una habanera, á una patria ideal que nos es común" (It's all very beautiful to think that, during

---

[21] Jason Ruiz. "Desire among the Ruins: The Politics of Difference in Visions of Porfirian Mexico." *Journal of American Studies* 46.4 (2012): 919–40; 920–21.

[22] Justo Sierra. *En tierra yankee (notas a todo vapor)*. Mexico City: Palacio Nacional, 1898: III.

that long stretch of time that we call an evening of dance, all men are brothers, that all of us *latinos* comprise a single people (*pueblo*), that from our own homelands, to the rhythm of a habanera, we can rise up to an ideal homeland that is common to all). As we have seen with the nineteenth-century examples cited above, Sierra employs the word *latino* to speak of the expatriate subjects who hailed from the new republics of the southern continent, but he also uses it to speak about the Spaniards in his company, with whom he shared a language. There is an air of skepticism in Sierra's tone, however, as he wonders at the idea of seeing all of this company as a coherent entity. To borrow Raymond Williams's term, Sierra recognizes latinidad as a structure of feeling intensified by distance and that nevertheless would appear to carry an expiration date; its triggers (here, the sounds of a habanera) are as emotionally strong as they can be fleeting.

In this geographical space outside of the patria(s), Sierra discovers a community of debate – a debate that, in the mid-1890s, is concerned with international politics and the intimations of neocoloniality: Britain's advances on Venezuela, but most prominently Cuba's future and the island's precarious position as part of the American hemisphere where, ideally and given its revolutionary history, "no puede haber más que pueblos libres" (only free nations can exist), and which is internally divided between the "raza sajona" (Anglo-Saxon race) and "los latinos" (115). Sierra's visit to the Círculo Colón-Cervantes illustrates the paradoxical situation in which confraternity appears to blossom out of necessity as a product of the circumstance of exile and dispossession. On the eve of the Spanish–American War, the particular latinidad he sees on display is surrounded with questions about the complex relationship between and among the Americas (not to mention Spain and its flailing imperial enterprise), and also about the Latina/o subject's position as s/he enters into the experience and life of that other America north of the Rio Grande.

In Sierra's report, the members of the Colón-Cervantes club display a mentality that echoes Martí's, and (proleptically) Rodó's: they recognize how, while the two Americas are similar in their colonial histories, their respective trajectories and cultures in the late nineteenth century place them in constant opposition to each other. The subjects in the Colón-Cervantes club, feeling more like relocated Latin Americans and liberal Spaniards than transculturated subjects in the United States, represent an interesting point of transition in identity formation vis-à-vis the changing power relations in the American hemisphere. Speaking from a contemporary point of view that is nevertheless relevant here, Walter Mignolo reads this recognition of similarity between northern and southern histories and of geopolitical opposition as the "double bind" within which the Latino population in the United States – and, by extension, Latina/o scholarship – is embedded (36). We thus return to the idea of latinidad as an identity formation that emerges from the efforts of subjects in and out of Latin America to develop what Juan Flores (also speaking about the contemporary moment) has called a "cultural imaginary, a still emergent space or 'community' of memory and desire."[23] Sierra's description of the gathering in fin-de-siècle New York City allows us a glimpse into a Latina/o future in the making – one in which an imagined community emerges out of the active questioning of echoing histories and the possible evolutions of inter-American colonizations.

Of Race and Borders

A transamerican latinidad – one that, like Sierra and his company, travels from south to north, all the while questioning Latin America's relation to the United States – must also engage in a consideration of both international and internal politics of the northern neighbor. While admiring much of what the country has to offer, Sierra nevertheless posits that Mexicans cannot forget "la espantosa injusticia cometida ... hace medio siglo" (the terrible injustice inflicted half a century ago): the US annexation of the territories of Alta California and Santa Fe de Nuevo México and thus the redrawing of US and Mexican borders in 1848. To be sure, the leisurely journey that Sierra makes from his country into the United States is starkly different from the countless crossings of Mexicans and other Central American subjects across that border that has become a *locus classicus* of Latina/o studies. This said, his border crossing brings home a crude reality about social relations in the United States: the contradiction between the northern country's democratic discourse and the deeply ingrained racialization that fractures its citizenry. While on a train that is taking him across Texas, he notices "un wagon que lleva este gran letrero *for whites*, para blancos: primer contacto con la democracia americana. Entramos en ese wagon en nuestra calidad de semiblancos" (a wagon with a large sign that says "for whites": our first contact with American democracy. We walk into that wagon in our status as semi-white) (20–21). In claiming that he is "semi-white" in the United States, Sierra

[23] Juan Flores. "The Latino Imaginary: Meanings of Community and Identity." *The Latin American Cultural Studies Reader*. Eds. Ana del Sarto, Alicia Ríos, and Abril Trigo. Durham, NC: Duke University Press, 2004: 617.

recognizes the delicate and potentially dangerous business of passing in the northern country. As an anonymous, Spanish-speaking traveler within the United States, his position as a member of the white upper class in Mexico is no guarantee for equal treatment. For Sierra there is no question that US democracy relies on a racial exclusivity that extends from local white–black relations to north–south interactions. His impressions of a US landscape riven with Jim Crow laws uncover a poignant, albeit brief, observation about how this country's local racial politics translate onto a wider trans-American arena. His reaction to the racial inequalities in the United States is an admission of the inequalities that haunt – and continue to haunt – the migratory networks between north and south.

Sierra's reported experience in the Pullman car riding through the southern United States is literally and figuratively different from his description of the scenes of camaraderie at the Círculo Colón-Cervantes in New York City. However, read together, we get a sense of the many twists and turns latinidad may take as it manifests itself within the United States: in the racialized spaces of the northern country, it denotes a vulnerable status; in burgeoning cosmopolitan hubs it enjoys the possibility of organized dialogue and confraternity – the opportunity (however imaginary) to develop an imagined transnational collectivity. Sierra maintains an underlying air of doubt about whether the latter can nevertheless be perceived as a necessary examination of both the advantages and limitations of claiming a common identity. These literary sites in which identity undergoes different levels of scrutiny contribute toward a wider understanding of "Latin" American subjects' contact with the foreign, yet-so-close other, and the formation of a latinidad as a cross-border, oppositional iteration in relation to that other.

Latina/o Worlds

Latinidad is progressively becoming a global phenomenon. We are living in a moment in global academia in which there is an increased currency in critical formations like "world" literature.[24] Meanwhile, the political and cultural conception of "Latin" America that gave rise to Latin American studies

---

[24] This erosion of the national is happening simultaneously to large shifts in academic centers in the US and beyond. Citing Samuel Weber, Debra Castillo points to the irony involved in making appeals to the global while also curtailing the amount of foreign-language departments across universities. See Debra Castillo, *Redreaming America: Toward a Bilingual American Culture*. Albany: SUNY Press, 2004: 6.

departments and centers during the Cold War is now changing.[25] As a result, current scholarship on Latin American literature is engaging with these transformations, by considering how this body of texts relates to a much more expansive tradition beyond the American hemisphere. In *Beyond Bolaño* (2015), Héctor Hoyos invites us to "situat[e] Latin American works within a planetary configuration," as it presents a chance to "cross-pollinate Latin Americanism and world literature, without forgetting their dissymmetry" – by which he means regional differences, but also the ways in which the two have been institutionalized in academia and the global market alike.[26] Hoyos sees this cross-pollination as useful because of the very problem at the heart of the total idea of a "Latin America": "There is something of a leap of faith in reading Borges, Gabriel García Márquez, Gabriela Mistral, or Guimarães Rosa as Latin American, but this leap is one that structures a discipline, a praxis, an ethos. It is not unlike trying to understand how works of fiction may belong to a planetary community" (9). As an imagined region, the idea of "Latin" America has enabled the formation of a canon and the production of a body of criticism that is constantly responding to global political and cultural shifts. In this current landscape, the iterations of latinidad to emerge from this imagined region, and from the migrations that take place between this region and the rest of the world, must contend with new developments that transform racial, ideological, and political relations at local and global levels. The study of literature should continue tracing these developments.

To this end, we should broaden Hoyos's proposition regarding the interplay between Latin American literature and world literature by asking how we can envision the cross-fertilization between area studies – and, for the purposes of this volume, Latina/o literary studies – and the current broadening of the category of world literature. How is a body of literature that has addressed migrations, intercultural tensions, and the solidarity that emerges from these dynamics transformed by our contemporary global condition? What new cultural developments will lead us to retrace the trajectories of latinidad? Here again, the idea of the kaleidoscope is useful in visualizing the ways in which an identity is something that is transformed

---

[25] In *Latinamericanism after 9/11*, John Beverley notes a change in US–Latin American relations, most notably with the formation of the strong socialist governments that form part of the *marea rosada*: "Before 9/11, and especially during the Clinton presidency in the 1990s, geopolitically the United States and the neoliberal assumptions of the Washington consensus were hegemonic in every sphere of Latin American life. After 9/11, that hegemony begins to fade" (6).

[26] Héctor Hoyos. *Beyond Bolaño: The Global Latin American Novel*. New York: Columbia University Press, 2015: 8–9.

depending on the vantage point from which it is scrutinized. In present-day London, where Junot Díaz was ceremonially embraced as a Dominican writer, communities of working- and middle-class Latin Americans are growing, and neighborhoods like Seven Sisters and Holloway in the northern part of the city are showing signs of Latinization. This growing presence points to migratory paths that are undoubtedly different from the border crossings that have marked the trajectories of north-south based Latina/o studies. The living and working conditions of members of these communities will also likely be distinctly different in a national context in which such human rights as health care and labor representation have been patently more accessible than in the United States. Nonetheless, the historical evolution of such communities is and will be affected by the long history of the experiences of Latinas/os in the United States, and also by the particular cultural experiences of other immigrant groups (Caribbean, African, South Asian, Middle Eastern) whose arrivals throughout the past two centuries have transformed British society and in turn recalibrated notions of cosmopolitanism and multiculturalism. Latinidad is reshaped by its contacts and affiliations, by its perpetual re-attunement to each new home's ethnic constitution. The evolution from a hemispheric American to a transatlantic history of latinidad thus allows us to understand it as a global development whose trajectories are multiple and shifting. Its creative and political formations have the potential to transform the way old and new readers of Hispanic cultures perceive the shape of the world.

WORKS CITED

Aching, Gerard. *The Politics of Spanish American* modernismo. Cambridge: Cambridge University Press, 1997.

Aranda, José F., Jr. "Recovering the US Hispanic Literary Heritage." *The Routledge Companion to Latino/a Literature*, ed. Suzanne Bost and Frances R. Aparicio. London and New York: Routledge, 2015, 476–84.

Beverley, John. *Latinamericanism after 9/11*. Durham, NC: Duke University Press, 2011.

Bost, Suzanne and Frances R. Aparicio. "Introduction." *The Routledge Companion to Latino/a Literature*, ed. Suzanne Bost and Frances R. Aparicio. London and New York: Routledge, 2015, 1–10.

Cabán, Pedro. "The New Synthesis of Latin American and Latino Studies." *Borderless Borders: U.S. Latinos, Latin Americans, and the Paradox of Interdependence*, ed. Frank Bonilla, Edwin Meléndez, Rebecca Morales, and María de los Angeles Torres. Philadelphia: Temple University Press, 1998, 195–215.

Caminero-Santangelo, Marta. "Latinidad." *The Routledge Companion to Latino/a Literature*, ed. Suzanne Bost and Frances R. Aparicio. New York: Routledge, 2015, 13–24.

Castillo, Debra. *Redreaming America: Toward a Bilingual American Culture.* Albany: SUNY Press, 2004.

Coronado, Raúl. *A World Not to Come: A History of Latino Writing and Culture.* Cambridge, MA and London: Harvard University Press, 2013.

Darío, Rubén. *Azul. . ./Cantos de vida y de esperanza.* Madrid: Espasa Calpe, 2007.

Flores, Juan. "The Latino Imaginary: Meanings of Community and Identity." *The Latin American Cultural Studies Reader,* ed. Ana del Sarto, Alicia Ríos, and Abril Trigo. Durham, NC: Duke University Press, 2004, 606–19.

Gruesz, Kirsten Silva. *Ambassadors of Culture: The Transamerican Origins of Latino Writing.* Princeton, NJ and Oxford: Princeton University Press, 2002.

"What Was Latino Literature?" *PMLA* vol. 127, no. 2 (2012): 335–41.

Hoyos, Héctor. *Beyond Bolaño: The Global Latin American Novel.* New York: Columbia University Press, 2015.

Kurlansky, Mark, Julia Alvarez, Edwidge Danticat and Junot Díaz. "In the Dominican Republic, Suddenly Stateless." November 10, 2013. http://articles.latimes.com/2013/nov/10/opinion/la-oe-kurlansky-haiti-dominican-republic-citizensh-20131110.

Lomas, Laura. *Translating Empire: José Martí, Migrant Latino Subjects, and American Modernities.* Durham, NC and London: Duke University Press, 2008.

Ludmer, Josefina. "Una máquina para leer el siglo XIX," *Revista de la Universidad Autónoma de México,* no. 530 (1995): 65–66.

Martí, José. "Nuestra América." *Obras completas,* vol. 6. Havana: Editorial de Ciencias Sociales, 1975, 13–23.

"Our America." *Selected Writings.* Trans. Esther Allen. New York: Penguin, 2002, 288–95.

Mignolo, Walter. "Capitalism and Geopolitics of Knowledge: Latin American Social Thought and Latino/a American Studies." *Critical Latin American and Latino Studies,* ed. Juan Poblete. Minneapolis: University of Minnesota Press, 2003, 32–75.

Pérez-Torres, Rafael. "Mestizaje." *Routledge Companion to Latino/a Literature,* ed. Suzanne Bost and Frances Aparicio. New York: Routledge, 2015, 25–33.

Rodó, José Enrique. *Ariel. Motivos de Proteo.* Caracas: Biblioteca Ayacucho, 1976.

Ruiz, Jason. "Desire among the Ruins: The Politics of Difference in Visions of Porfirian Mexico." *Journal of American Studies* vol. 46, no. 4 (2012): 919–40.

Sierra, Justo. *En tierra yankee (notas a todo vapor).* Mexico City: Palacio Nacional, 1898.

Stavans, Ilan, ed. *The Norton Anthology of Latino Literature.* New York: W. W. Norton & Company, 2010.

Vasconcelos, José. *The Cosmic Race/La raza cósmica.* Trans. Didier Jaén. Baltimore, MD: Johns Hopkins University Press, 1997 [1979].

7

Father Félix Varela and the Emergence of an Organized Latina/o Minority in Early Nineteenth-Century New York City

CARMEN E. LAMAS

Through a reading of works by the Cuban Catholic priest Father Félix Varela (1788–1853) that were published in New York during his almost thirty years in that city, in this chapter I recover the emergence of Latina/o-led political activism as an identifiable and organized minority in New York City in the 1820s to 1840s. Specifically, I argue that the Protestant/Catholic debates in which Varela participated converted him, and other Latinas/os in New York City at that time, into political agents who confronted anti-immigrant sentiments prevalent in the city. This recovery does not simply mark Varela as an influential figure in US Catholicism, but it prompts contemporary scholars to delve more deeply into the significance of Varela's life and works beyond the "supposed" authorship of *Jicoténcal* (1826), as scholars of Latina/o literature know him, or as one of the first philosophers in Latin America or the first proponent of Cuban independence, as he is studied by scholars of Cuban and Latin American history. Instead, what unfolds from reading Varela's US archive is a Latina/o intervention into US history, including a contribution to the rise of minority politics in the United States and the secularization of public-school curricula. Varela's US archive and wider body of writings, and that of other Latina/os during this period, fundamentally challenge scholars to rethink the still existing divides between American, Latina/o and Latin American studies. More importantly, it locates Latinas/os, such as Varela, as actors at the very heart of US history and the US body politic.

Varela's Life and Works

Born in Havana, Cuba in 1788, Félix Varela was raised in St. Augustine, Florida, which was under Spanish rule until 1821. At the age of thirteen, he returned to Havana, choosing a religious career instead of a military one because "he wished not to kill men but to save their souls."[1] He taught at the *Seminario de San Carlos* and held the chair of philosophy there. He traveled to Spain in 1822 as a Cuban representative to the Spanish Cortes, but had to flee Spain that following year once Ferdinand VII reestablished monarchical rule, disbanded the Cortes, and exiled his opposition. Varela fled to the United States and lived first in Philadelphia (1824–1825), then New York (1825–1850), whereupon he retired permanently to St. Augustine, Florida due to his declining health, residing there until his death in 1853.

In Cuba, Varela wrote philosophical texts that defended the New Science emerging from Europe. While Varela did not reject scholasticism outright – he was an ardent reader of Thomas Aquinas – he advocated for induction in scientific inquiry and the use of the Cartesian method.[2] The first to teach in Spanish instead of Latin at the university level in Cuba, Varela, after arriving in the United States, wrote in both Spanish and English, and translated, for example, Thomas Jefferson's *Manual on Parliamentary Procedures* into Spanish in 1826. In these early years, he also published *El Habanero* (1824–1826), a political newspaper he founded in Philadelphia that espoused independence for Cuba and cautioned against US intervention in Latin American affairs. For this reason he has been considered one of the first advocates for Cuba's political independence.[3] He also published US editions of his early philosophical writings, *Lecciones de filosofía* (*Philosophical Lessons*) and *Miscelánea filosófica* (*Philosophical Miscellanea*) which were originally published in Havana in

---

[1] Rodríguez, José Ignacio. *Vida del Presbítero Don Félix Varela*. New York: Imprenta de "O Novo Mundo," 1878. Rodríguez cites a eulogy published in the *New York Freeman's Journal and Catholic Register* 13.38 March 19, 1856.

[2] Scholasticism argued that there were God-decreed universal truths that governed the cosmos, a cosmos in which everything was in perfect balance. Catholicism was at the core of their structuring and understanding of the universe. While scholasticism in Western Europe was debunked during the Renaissance, the Protestant Reformation and the Enlightenment, late scholasticism continued to structure philosophical and political arguments in Spain and its colonies into the late eighteenth and early nineteenth centuries. The new science, meanwhile, privileged reason over faith in understanding the cosmos and promoted the scientific method in the "natural sciences," by which they referred to experiments and empirical observation in scientific investigations and philosophical argumentation that served to explain reality.

To understand Varela's position in relation to scholasticism and the new science emerging from Europe, see Travieso (1942), Vitier (1970) and Leal (1971), among others. See also Coronado (2013), who addresses the impact of the emergence of the new science on early nineteenth-century Hispanic America and Latina/o communities in the United States.

[3] See Hernández's introduction ("Félix Varela: el primer cubano") to the compilation *El Habanero: papel político, científico, y literario* (1997).

1818 and 1819, respectively. Finally, he coedited with his student José Antonio Saco *El Mensajero Semanal* (1829–1831).[4]

To understand the significance of Varela for New York City and for Latina/o literary history, we must be aware that a large portion of his extant writings are preserved in English in US Catholic newspapers and magazines of the era, periodicals that in many instances he founded and edited himself, all in New York. For example, he edited and published many dozens of articles in the *Catholic Expositor and Literary Magazine* (1841–1844) and *The Protestant Abridger and Annotator* (1830), which he founded and edited in response to the publication of *The Protestant*, an anti-Catholic weekly in New York City, and its arguments against Catholicism. Similarly, he published articles in the *Truth Teller* (1825–1855), a Catholic newspaper in New York that responded to the accusations of popery published in *The Protestant*, cited above. He published and contributed to the first bilingual magazine in New York: *El Amigo de la Juventud/The Youth's Friend* (1825). And he was the founder and editor of the *New York Weekly Register and Catholic Diary* (1834–1835) and the *New York Catholic Register* (1839–1840). The latter was absorbed by the *New York Freeman's Journal*, which ran until 1918. This newspaper became *the* voice of Archbishop John Hughes in his successful fight against the New York Public School Society, which ultimately led to the removal of religious teaching from the public-school curriculum in New York City.[5]

Varela was a critical early figure in these debates. In fact, he had started the *Catholic Register* in order to keep Archbishop Hughes apprised of the status of the public-school debate while the latter traveled to Europe. During

---

[4] José Saco was one of the anti-annexationist editors of the influential *Revista Bimestre Cubana* (1831–1834). Exiled to Spain as of 1834 because of his political beliefs – he was a reformist who rejected absolutist monarchical rule – Saco is the well-known author of *Historia de la esclavitud desde los tiempos más remotos hasta nuestros días* (1875–1877). Varela and Saco held different views on slavery. Saco advocated for the end of the slave trade and pushed for an increase in white immigration and white labor to the island in order to counter the large number of Africans who were brought to Cuba as slaves in the early nineteenth century. Varela wanted to end the slave trade but also called for a gradual abolition coupled with indemnification to slave holders, citing a fear of slave revolts due to the large number of slaves already on the island as the reason for abolition. Both Varela's and Saco's positions regarding the end of the slave trade and slavery are deplorable at best, but Varela, in particular, was an early advocate for abolition. A more detailed analysis of Varela's views of slavery and abolition is yet to be completed. However, Luis (1990), Williams (1994), Reid-Vázquez (2011), and Aching (2015) provide introductory explanations and comparisons of these two authors' respective positions.

[5] Ravitch (1947), Shea (2004), and Gjerde (2012) offer useful summaries of the New York public-school debates of 1840–1842.

Hughes's absence, Varela asked the Public School Society to bring all of their textbooks to him, so he could highlight the parts that misrepresented Catholics or Catholicism. Varela's critical readings required the Society to then change the books in order to make education more inclusive. According to his US biographers, Joseph and Helen McCadden, Varela, like the editors of the *Truth Teller*, wished for religion to be taught in schools but opposed the demonization of Catholics. Varela's early advocacy led to the end of the use of the King James Bible as a text in the public schools (106–107). Although Varela and the other editors sought to collaborate with the Public School Society, General Vicar John Powers and Archbishop John Hughes intervened to excise religion from public schools altogether while obtaining access to state funds for Catholic education. The latter – but not necessarily the former – was a position Varela also advocated. The cumulative effect of this debate contributed to the secularization of the US public-school system.[6]

So, if Varela was so prolific and so key to US Catholic history, why have so few US historians heard of or written about him? The answer lies in how scholars approach the archive. Recovering Varela requires the transnational, multilingual approach to archival research that has characterized Latina/o studies scholarship. In my work, the "archive" refers to the physical archives found throughout the United States, in Spain, and in Latin American countries and especially Cuba (in this case), which house texts that are usually thought to be field- and nation-specific, due to their being recorded in certain languages, and/or their authors or publishers being of that national origin. For example, while a Cuban author's work might be housed in a US location – Yale University, the Cuban Heritage Collection at the University of Miami, or the New York Public Library – that author and his or her work regularly figure only in Latin American or Caribbean historical narratives.

The archive for me also includes the historiographical sources that have been written by area studies scholars who have a more nationalist bent. These sources are built around academic fields and disciplines such as American studies or Latin American and Latina/o studies. Such secondary works create their own historical record – that is, they may be read

---

[6] The McCaddens' biography (1969) provides a positive picture of Archbishop Hughes and his role in the New York public school debates; however, they stress the tactical differences between Hughes and Varela, noting Hughes's polarizing position and Varela's more conciliatory approach (106–110). Meanwhile, Travieso in *Biografía* (1949) presents Hughes as an individual who marginalized Varela's more conciliatory strategy altogether (409–433).

themselves as primary sources that illustrate the views of their authors and record the trends and biases in their respective historiographies.

The contribution of Latina/o literary history and the argument at hand is that scholars in American, Latin American, and Latina/o studies must enter all of these archives and conduct a rereading of texts, both primary and secondary, a rereading that is transnational, trans-American, and transatlantic in scope. This approach, located at the intersection of these archives, invites scholars to ask different questions about the material emerging therefrom; and it allows the reader, in this case, scholars and students of Latina/o history and literature, to bring forth a new and more complex narrative of the Latina/o experience and of the parent disciplines of American and Latin American studies. Entering Father Félix Varela's Americas archive from this perspective forces an epistemological shift in how we study Latina/o literature, not merely as a bridge traversing the American and Latin American studies divide, but as an integral part of both histories, the exclusion of which has led to the formation of dangerous lacunae in those histories.[7]

Varela's Reception in Latina/o, Latin American, and American Studies

Most Latina/o studies scholars know of Father Félix Varela from Luis Leal's 1960 article *"Jicoténcal,* primera novela histórica en castellano."[8] This article claimed that it was Varela himself who wrote this work, what is often regarded as the first historical novel in Latin America, and that was, provocatively enough, published in "la Famosa Filadelfia" in 1826, a site we know through Rodrigo Lazo and others' work as key to nineteenth-century Latina/o literary history. As such, while Father Varela had previously been regarded as a key figure in Latin American philosophy by Latin American intellectuals, Leal's article placed Varela at the very center of both American and Latin American literary history, at a key juncture for Latina/o studies: the first historical novel in Latin America – a novel that condemned the conquest of Mexico by Hernán Cortés – now could also be claimed as part of Latina/o literary history.

---

[7] My current book project, *The Latina/o Continuum: Rethinking American and Latin American Studies* (in progress), addresses these concerns at length.

[8] The preface to the Spanish edition of *Jicoténcal* published by Arte Público Press includes an extended introduction by Luis Leal and Rodolfo Cortina regarding the authorship of the novel. However, Leal first published his findings in the academic journal *Revista Iberoamericana* (vol 25. no 4. pages 9–31) in 1960.

Although it took nearly forty years following the publication of Leal's article for *Jicoténcal* to be published in the United States, first in Spanish in 1995, and then in English, in 1999,[9] the novel today is a staple work in anthologies of Latina/o literature and in introductory Latina/o literature courses, its authorship invariably attributed to Félix Varela. And yet, while this attribution guarantees Varela's name is at least known in Latina/o studies, it is the novel's narrative/contents – its critique of the conquest of Mexico and the abuse of the indigenous at the hands of the conquerors – that take center stage. Its anonymous production continues to relegate its supposed author, and the balance of his writings, to a certain obscurity.

Take, for example, the manner in which Varela is treated in the 2014 edition of the *Heath Anthology of American Literature*. While the importance of including *Jicoténcal* in the anthology must not be dismissed, Varela, as in other anthologies that include him, is literally an aside: no effort is made there to consider the biography of the author in relation to his significance in Latina/o or US history. That is, the *Heath* finds importance in the book only in its arguments regarding the conquest of Mexico and its depiction of *La Malinche* as the mother of the mestizo nation in particular, as this is the section of the novel they choose to anthologize. What this means, in other words, is that the *Heath* highlights the presence in the narrative of a key symbol for the Chicana/o movement of the 1960s and 1970s in the United States, and does little to explore the significance of the Cuban identity of the text's supposed author, within his US context. Yet, regardless of the manner in which Varela is approached, one must laud the *Heath* editors for including *Jicoténcal* in their anthology,[10] and Raúl Coronado, the author of the entry, for selecting such a representative excerpt from the novel. However, the lack of contextualization of Varela's life and works creates a need for wider reading and theorizing to address the lacunae surrounding Varela, which I undertake here.

The Norton Anthology of Latino Literature (2010), in turn, moves closer to giving Varela his rightful place in Latina/o literary history, since the editors anthologize excerpts from *Cartas a Elpidio*, a work by Varela that speaks

---

[9] It was not until 1995 that Arte Público Press – the press for the *Recovering the US Hispanic Literary Heritage Project* – published *Jicoténcal* in Spanish. Four years later, the University of Texas Press published an English translation for wider use in the university classroom. With these publications, the anonymously written *Jicoténcal* was canonized in Latina/o studies, appearing in the emerging market of anthologies of Latina/o literature of the 1990s.

[10] *The Norton Anthology of American Literature*, for example, does not include Latina/o writing in its nineteenth-century compilation.

directly to his US experience and ministry. However, they also frame Varela as an exile who happened to be "an insightful observer of American life" (173) and thereby not as an integral part of it. Perhaps it was because Varela chose not to return to Cuba when a general amnesty was offered in 1832 for those who had been exiled in 1823, and also because he refused to take US citizenship, even while remaining in the United States, that scholars labeled Varela an exile. This ascription, which only partially captures his lived and political experience, has also augmented the aforementioned lacunae.

My point is this: nowhere in the showcasing of *Jicoténcal* or of *Cartas a Elpidio* is any measured consideration given to Varela's *entire* body of written work, nor to the significance of his biography. In the final part of this chapter I will remedy this omission.

Turning now to the reception of *Jicoténcal* in Latin American studies, we find Latin American studies scholars unanimously unsupportive of the ascription of authorship to Varela. Shortly after the publication of the first Spanish-language edition of *Jicoténcal* in the United States in 1995, González Acosta dedicated an entire book to what he called *El enigma de Jicoténcal* (1997), attributing the authorship of the text to the Cuban romantic poet José María Heredia and debunking the classification of the work as the first historical novel in Latin America. In turn, Anderson Imbert, the well-known Argentinian anthologist of Latin American literature, went so far as to ask, "¿Es legítimo incluir *Jicoténcal* en una historia de la literatura hispanoamericana?" (Is it legitimate to include *Jicoténcal* in a history of Hispano-American literature?) (221). Anderson Imbert agrees to do so, because it is in his anthology of Latin American literature, but justifies its inclusion by listing the reasons that the novel resembles European literary productions of the time, thereby suggesting a Spaniard may have authored the piece.[11]

In the field of Cuban studies, *Jicoténcal* is simply nonexistent. Instead, both before and after the 1959 revolution, scholars of Varela on the island have concentrated almost exclusively on his early philosophical works.[12] And his US

---

[11] One of Imbert's rationales (among several) for questioning the Mexican and/or Latin American origins of the writer is that the novel is discursive instead of descriptive and that the discourse itself translates the conquest of Mexico into "*términos europeos*" (222).

[12] As early as 1862, Mestre writes of the importance of Varela's philosophical texts for Cuban history in *De la Filosofía en la Habana*, but excludes Varela's US works. Likewise Rexach (1950), Roig de Leuchsenring (1957), Vitier (1970), Serpa (1983), and Piqueras (2007) concentrate almost exclusively on Varela's philosophical texts not addressing *Cartas a Elpidio* or Varela's political activism found in US newspapers. While his Cuban biographer, Travieso (1949), who combed through US sources in DC, Philadelphia, and New York, speaks to Varela's US activism and writings, he dedicates most of his biography to his Cuban writings. His previous book, *Varela y la reforma filosófica en*

archive is generally excluded from Cuban historiography, which is a shame given that the socially progressive ideology of the Cuban Revolution would have found resonances with the ideas Varela develops in his US publications[13] (although, Varela, as a Catholic priest, would have denounced how the revolution has approached religion, Catholicism in particular, and the state).

Finally, American studies, generally speaking, does not consider *Jicoténcal* to be a part of the US literary heritage, except insofar as it figures in the Latina/o studies curriculum.[14] It is not a work counted in the canon as integral to our understanding of American history, as is the case when we read Washington Irving or William Prescott and their respective histories of the discovery and conquest of the New World, for example. This exclusion is problematic, since, after all, Varela (assuming he is the author of *Jicoténcal*) also wrote about the conquest of the New World in this historical novel, and he lived in the United States for more than thirty years. Couldn't his historical novel also count as a relevant colonial narrative for American history, but from a Latina/o perspective?

In sum, the above discussion offers one example that illustrates how the segmentation we see – in Cuba, in Latin America, and in the United States – in the reading and study of the writings of a Latina/o intellectual and historical figures obscures the greater links that exist across these geographic and cultural regions. The methodological approach I propose illuminates the role of Latinas/os not only in US politics and history but in Cuban and Latin American cultural and political histories, as well.

Cuba (1942), concentrates on the latter's philosophical works. Meanwhile, *El Habanero* (1824–1826) has become a resource for scholars since a complete compilation of its articles was published in 1997 by Editorial Universal in Miami, Florida. This edition includes the once-lost seventh issue of the newspaper. The introduction to this important compilation does not include a review of the significance of Varela in a US context. Moreover, his US biographers, José Ignacio Rodríguez (1878) and Joseph and Helen McCradden (1969) speak to Varela's importance in relation to US Catholicism but do not contextualize his life from a Latina/o perspective. The former dedicates most of his book to Varela's work originally published and/or written in Cuba and Spain.

[13] The University of Havana, under the direction and editorship of Torres-Cuevas et al., published Varela's *Obras* in three volumes in 1997. Unfortunately, due to lack of access to US sources, the editors were not able to compile and include Varela's articles from US Catholic newspapers, thereby providing an incomplete compilation and limited assessment of Varela's importance.

[14] Two scholars that have given attention to *Jicoténcal* but have not concentrated on Varela's other works are Silva Gruesz (2001) and Brickhouse (2004). While they do not speak in detail as to Varela's wider significance in Latina/o literature and history, their books are essential reading for those interested in Latina/o studies from a hemispheric perspective.

The Protestant/Catholic Debates of the
1830s and 1840s

When we understand that Varela's life and ministry took place over the course of some thirty years in the infamous and mainly Irish Five Points neighborhood of New York City, referred to as such because Cross, Orange, and Anthony Streets came together to form a five-point intersection in what is now between SoHo and Chinatown in Manhattan, it is hard to discount his importance, and by extension that of other Latinas/os, to US and New York history.[15] For example, Varela is credited with founding a Catholic school for children in 1828 at Christ Church as well as a vocational school for women, mostly for Irish immigrants who populated the Five Points area, in order to help them enter the workforce and support their families; he was the founder of the *Half Orphan Asylum* (1835–1852), a refuge for children who had only one parent or relative; and he established the New York Catholic Temperance Society (1840), the first of its kind in the city. As vicar-general of New York, he pastored and/or founded St. Peter's, St. Patrick's (the first cathedral), Christ Church, St. Mary's, and the Church of the Transfiguration, which is serving parishioners to the present, though at a different location than where Varela first founded the church. His dedication to his mainly Irish parishioners has led him to be called the "Father of the Irish," and he is today considered to be the founder of New York Catholicism.[16]

Varela was also an apologist for the place of the Catholic Church in American life. In his day, various Protestant groups held public meetings that called on Catholics to defend the church, demanding they prove that the church was not the "whore of Babylon," was not religiously intolerant, and was not calling for a new Inquisition in the US (in a move parallel to that of the Carlists, who at that time were advocating for the Inquisition's return to Spain). Varela addressed moral and religious themes in his little-studied *Cartas a Elpidio*, a series of letters written to a friend, "Elpidio." Written in Spanish in New York and published there in two separate volumes in 1835 and 1838 respectively, the *Cartas* record his prominent role in these debates. The volumes, respectively entitled *Irreligiosity* and *Superstition*, speak to events in Spain, as well as the growing despotism of Cuba's governor and

---

[15] Tyler Anbinden's book titled *Five Points* (2001) concentrates on this neighborhood and its importance for Irish-American and US history. Yet, Varela is absent from his book.

[16] These biographical details and many others are compiled from Varela's three book-length biographies (Rodríguez [1878], Travieso [1949] and McCadden [1969]) as well as the introduction of *Letters to Elpidio* by Estévez (1989). The latter is the first English translation of *Cartas* in its entirety.

the concurrent repression on the Island. Yet, its main theme is religious intolerance in the United States.[17]

Specifically, in the second volume, he describes in detail his confrontation with the Presbyterian Nativist W. C. Brownlee in a public debate in which Brownlee's monologue forestalled Varela's participation in the debate by interrupting him repeatedly, when Varela attempted to respond to Brownlee's monologue. Remembering the farcical nature of the encounter, in which he was hardly permitted even to speak, Varela says:

> Not accepting the theological existence of any religion, they [the Protestants] cannot admit to true tolerance that necessarily presupposes the existence of things tolerated. We would not have argued on this matter if there would have been a true belief in religious tolerance. I mean, if there would have been [by Protestants] more charity and less arrogance. (151)[18]

We must stop here and ponder the word "arrogance." Varela expresses a theological concern. Varela understood that, in his day, the Catholic Church saw itself as the one and only church, the only path to salvation. He also knew that the Catholic Church admitted that exceptions would be made for non-Catholics who, in their ignorance or incapacities, could not see or properly know the church. They, although not Catholic, could also attain salvation. Furthermore, Varela also understood his Protestant opponents to maintain the same theological view, just as he knew that they also were aware of the theological parallels between Protestant and Catholic views of salvation.

Yet, as Varela notes in *Cartas*, his Protestant (primarily Presbyterian) opponents hypocritically attacked Catholicism for its intolerance, while ignoring the exceptions Catholics allowed for non-Catholics to attain salvation. More than this, Varela lamented that his Protestant opponents ignored the existence of their own theological exceptions, because they could not recognize the existence of his differing beliefs. Instead, as he objected in *Cartas*, they repeatedly sought to convert him to Protestantism. Simply, he felt they could not tolerate a Catholic remaining Catholic in their midst, even though their theology could tolerate just that. And, he lamented that, despite the known parallels in their theologies, his Protestant interlocutors could not tolerate his Catholicism precisely because they wrongly demonized the

---

[17] Volume 1 of *Cartas a Elpidio* was also published in Madrid in 1836. In the twentieth century, it was published in Cuba in 1944. In 1997, it was included in volume 3 of Varela's complete works, published by the University of Havana and edited by Torres Cuevas, et al.

[18] All translations are mine.

Catholic Church as exclusivist. He concludes ironically by saying, "Believe me, the strongest argument against tolerance is the mere act of having to argue so much about it" (*Superstition* 151).

Varela's indictment in *Cartas* and in his newspaper articles followed from his experience with religion in the United States, since he wished to warn his readers against erroneously praising the pluralism of Protestant denominations, as if they reflected a concomitant tolerance for diverse political or even religious views. Though noting that religious pluralism was enshrined as a legal right in the US Constitution, in *Cartas* he argued that, in practice, no concomitant social or theological tolerance accompanied this legal right.

And Varela warns his readers in the United States and Latin America not to see the North American model as a foundation for their democratic projects. He says:

> You may have heard a lot about the religious liberty in this country accompanied by social harmony and an admirable peace... I fear that men may not have acquired correct ideas on this point, and that you may have allowed yourself to be taken up by the exaggerations of some and the injustice of others. (*Irreligiosity* 100)

In order to impress upon his readers the serious nature of his warning in *Cartas*, Varela concludes:

> I have known the impious for a long time, but here I have come to know Protestants. One and the other accuse the [Catholic] Church of being intolerant, and one and the other exceed themselves in their intolerance. (*Superstition* 136)

Directly linking his discussion of religion to political and social concerns, including discrimination, Varela also explicitly cautioned that it was not his identity as a Catholic priest that led him to write about Protestantism; rather, it was the eminently political nature of religion in the United States that led him to write about politics by way of discussing religion. He decries the veracity of judgments formed in haste by short-term visitors who perceived the United States as a model for Latin American republics:

> The experience I have of the human heart warns me that my examples [of religious intolerance] will be passed over as the delirious rantings of religious interest, simply because the language I am using for my argument is different than what is found in books of mere political calculations. That language used to praise the democratic project [of the US] is used by many who believe they know this country, simply because they have strolled through some of its cities and attended one or another social gathering. (*Superstition* 171)

Given his views of the limits of US tolerance, it is no surprise that Varela supported Cuban independence over annexation, and by doing so as early as 1823, is regarded, as mentioned earlier, as one of the first Cubans to do so.[19]

But perhaps most notable in the last quotation is Varela's distinction between the casual visitor to the United States, specifically to New York (here he may be referring to the likes of Domingo del Monte, etc.), and the experience of others, such as himself, who had come to know the country intimately as a resident over the course of decades. Indeed, he was more than merely a Cuban exile in New York, as most anthologists and biographers have called him, but rather an actor integral to US history.

Varela also recorded a similar absence of religious tolerance not in debate but in everyday social practice. Most poignantly, I wish to highlight his role in events surrounding the burning of the Ursuline Catholic Convent outside of Boston in 1834, which in turn triggered rioting in New York. While both Protestants and Catholics criticized the violence perpetrated against the young women who studied in this convent school, mostly populated by daughters of Congregationalists, the perpetrators were never convicted. In *Cartas*, Varela notes the significance of the event:

> Experience has shown that the beliefs of the city of Boston are opposed to the Catholic religion and very foreign to that supposed tolerance of which so much is spoken but so little is practiced. A fire always incites compassion ... but the Bostonians were happy with their expressions of grief and condolences (*lamentaciones de gazeta*) and did not believe they should do anything else for a place of education reduced to ashes due to religious hatred ... which was proven by the newspapers themselves, as a universal fact. (*Superstition* 155–6)

Varela here criticizes the fact that, while Bostonian newspapers spoke against the anti-Catholic sentiments that fueled the fire, Bostonians publicly celebrated when those accused of the arson were exonerated for the crime (*Superstition* 157–58).[20]

---

[19] His presentation to the Spanish Cortes (1822–1823), but primarily his articles in *El Habanero*, speak to his call for Latin American and Cuban independence.

[20] Oxx (2013) dedicates an entire chapter to the Ursuline Convent burning and cites primary sources that signal the rise of Nativism in the US in its religious context in the early nineteenth century. Franchot (1994) provides a detailed account of the newspaper coverage of the arson case as well as the court proceedings surrounding the case. Her endnotes (398–401) are particularly useful for those wishing to read primary sources related to this event. Billington (1938) also offers a useful summary from a religious perspective.

Moreover, Varela objected to the fact that the state of Massachusetts denied the convent reparation funds to rebuild it, which were set aside specifically for such purposes (*Superstition* 155). Franchot contextualizes the significance of this denial when she highlights that the convent was situated close to Bunker Hill, and that writings of the time stressed that it was inappropriate for a Catholic institution ever to have been built so close to such an essential American historical site. In the end, the convent was never rebuilt (Franchot 135–54).[21]

In another event that led to Varela's indictment of the so-called religious freedom in the United States, Varela mobilized the Catholic community to resist a planned attack in 1835 against New York's St. Patrick's Cathedral. In *Cartas* he describes the manner in which he helped to thwart the attack. The attackers claimed that the Pope was sending Catholics to the United States in order to take over the country and that the Inquisition was being secretly administered in St. Patrick's Cathedral. Varela tells the reader how one of his parishioners overheard the would-be arsonists. A group of Protestant butchers at the local market allegedly had described their plan to destroy the cathedral. Varela warned the church trustees, who reached out to the governor for protection in response. According to *Cartas*, he then joined 500 Catholics in surrounding St. Patrick's to greet the arrival of the 200 to 300 rioters, who were turned back by the sheer numbers of parishioners present who were willing to defend the building. This mobilized minority group along with the governor's threat to interfere, stopped the planned arson (*Superstition* 159–61).

Kyle Volk (2014) traces the beginnings of minority politics not to twentieth-century history, but defines it as a reaction to the rise of majority rule in the United States in the 1820s by immigrants, blacks, and Catholics. Varela was key to the rise of minority politics in the United States since he established the first Catholic temperance society in New York. Following Lyman Beecher's role in the Second Great Awakening, as demonstrated by

---

[21] Two important dimensions linked to this event and depicted in *Cartas* are the disenfranchisement of the working class in early America, for the arsonists were Scot-Presbyterian bricklayers who found themselves competing for jobs with the Irish and having to move west in order to subsist and find work (Franchot, 135–154) and the disestablishment of mainstream Protestantism and its impact on US religion and politics. In *Superstición* Varela amply lists and critiques the many Protestant groups (Methodists, Baptists, Quakers, Shakers, et al.) emerging from and populating the US religious landscape. Along with Franchot (1994), see Hatch (1989) and Fessenden (2010) for a full discussion of disestablishment and the secularization of religion in the nineteenth century.

the positive reception acquired by *A Plea for the West* (1835), the reformers of
the period linked moral rectitude with the survival of the American republic.
As such, reformers lobbied to convert their beliefs about observing the Sabbath
and also to legislate temperance. Specifically, Volk notes that in the shift from
minority to majority rule in American politics, reformers used that majority
rule to impose their mandates on the US populace. They did so through
grassroots campaigns that mobilized the masses: "By involving millions of
predominantly middle-class men, women and children, reform associations
emerged alongside political parties as a major force of democratization" (27).
Volk, in the end, claims that this widespread mobilization allowed these
reformers to single out immigrants, blacks, and Catholics as the driving force
behind the moral depravity of the nation that would in turn lead to the collapse
and end of the American republican project (25). He concludes:

> Their exertions would continue to transform public life in the nineteenth
> century, not least by giving rise to popular debates about American democ-
> racy's central postulate—that the majority should rule—and by rousing a
> range of new grass-roots political action on behalf of minority rights. (35)

These mass mobilizations in turn led to minorities organizing themselves
against this type of morality-based legislation.

One example cited by Volk was the reaction by minorities after the
election won by the nativist James Harper in 1844, as mayor of New York.
Harper wanted to impose Sunday laws, proposed the exclusive use of the
Protestant King James Bible in public schools, opposed the funding of
Catholic Schools, and sought tougher naturalization legislation (43). These
attempts to regulate morality via majority rule were seen by minority groups
as opposing working-class and immigrant rights and culture as well as
hindering the religious freedom established in the constitution:

> Countering Sabbath reformers and other advocates of Sunday legislation,
> these critics advanced cultural pluralism and religious liberty as cornerstones
> of American democracy. In their view, governmental protection of religious
> worship would ruin the republican experiment. The implication of their
> position reflected not only the diversifying ethno-religious order but also the
> everyday changes accompanying the ascension of market capitalism. (43–44)

Varela was integral in these debates and events, as evidenced from his
arguments against the supposed "Blue Laws of Connecticut" (*Superstition*
127–29). He protested against temperance societies that were totalitarian in
nature (Travieso 421–23), and played an active role in the public-school

debates. As such, he was at the very heart of and integral to the very rise of minority politics in the United States.[22]

Varela, moreover, is but one figure, an exemplar of the many Latinas/os who were actively integrated into American life in the nineteenth century, yet who continued simultaneously to be a part of the Cuban, Latin American, and Spanish imaginaries.[23] He presents us with a series of intersections and flows, networks and relations, that are within yet also move beyond space and time and ultimately structure the Latina/o experience.[24] But these intersections are in fact set out on a continuum that is obscured by the siloed reading of the evidence, housed as it is in what are restrictively imagined as national archives that are often separated by linguistic divides.

Conclusion

Félix Varela and his thirty years in the United States speak to his deep engagement in US life, as an agent in important events in the life of the American Catholic Church and in US history more generally. But, I would also suggest that the Protestant/Catholic debate in which he took part speak beyond the limits of a US context.

One must recall that the engagements of Varela with American social, political, and religious life summarized in this article were at times written in Spanish. And that he self-consciously targeted *Cartas* to a Cuban audience – Cubans settled in New York and those visiting the United States, as well as Cubans in Cuba. His narrative about American Protestantism, that is, also offered another narrative. It was a narrative meant to express concern for Cuban understanding of American political, religious, and social life.

Here, I find Varela writing one story in *Cartas*, about American intolerance, while also writing multiple stories simultaneously: American legal tolerance

---

[22] When inaugurating the society in 1840, Varela wrote, "The object of the New York Catholic Temperance Society is to abolish intemperance without imposing unnecessary privations ... each person is solely impelled to avoid intemperance, and not to deprive himself completely of liquor ... We do this in this manner because we consider imprudent the establishment of a general rule when each case is, in its very nature, different. He that during his meals always drinks a glass of wine without feeling the effects of intemperance; we will not force him to break his custom, because others are drunkards" (Qtd. in Travieso, 421–22).

[23] Other Latinas/os who lived extended periods in the US during the Varela's lifetime include Cristobal Madán and Agustín José Morales, among others.

[24] Silva Gruesz (2002) argues for the network of trans-American texts and lives that are part of the Latina/o experience. Brickhouse (2004) address the trans-American relations of which Latina/o and US writers were a part.

did not extend to a theological or social inclusivism in the United States, in Varela's view, as we have seen. And, this erroneously imagined inclusivism also would not extend to Cubans in Cuba, who often read into the legality of religious pluralism in the United States a concomitant tolerance for social and political difference (Travieso, *Biografía* 412). In other words, Varela in his narrative about American intolerance wished to warn Cubans (and Latin Americans more broadly) in Cuba and in the United States that annexation would not bring the sort of inclusivism and social harmony they imagined.

Varela also saw other perils for the United States in annexing Cuba. Varela opposed slavery and did not wish to see the institution reinforced by the incorporation of the island into the United States, given that slavery was so deeply ensconced in Cuba.[25] The theme of intolerance in *Cartas* speaks simultaneously to this concern.[26]

Third, Varela did not wish to see the Catholic church, despite his misgivings with the manner in which its business was sometimes conducted in Cuba, dismissed out of hand for the transgressions of the Cuban Church in particular. Although he chided the Church for siding too closely with Spain and its colonial control of the island, in the Church he believed society could find precisely the sort of charity that he felt the United States needed: service to the poor, including the multitude of immigrants who were deeply in need; the Church's educational missions; and in his view at least, the Church's capacity to imagine itself, not merely theologically superior, but more thoroughly self-conscious and accepting of the possibility of other ways of thinking and believing. The Church, that is, still had something to offer to Cuba and the United States; and Varela's narrative tells this story, as well.

Finally, and, yes, most directly, *Cartas* speaks to a desire to find in the United States the values it was supposed to present, with a place there to be found for the poor, non-white religious minority: the Irish who were not yet "white," at least prior to the Civil War, and other immigrant and minority groups that hailed from across the world and who should have been welcomed in keeping with the values of the US Constitution.[27]

---

[25] In a presentation he drafted for the Spanish Cortes (1822) but never delivered, Varela proposed the abolition of slavery in Cuba. He also drafted a plan for gradual abolition. (*Obras*, 2: 113–27).

[26] See *El ingenio, complejo socioeconomic cubano* (1964) by Manuel Morena Fraginals, a classic for those interested in the topic.

[27] For more information on Irish Americans and their perspectives on slavery during the nineteenth century, see Roediger (1991), Ignatiev (1995), and Murphy (2010).

I wish to suggest that a concerted entry into the intersection of Varela's multiple archives furnishes new information concerning the Latina/o experience, and also impacts our understanding of Latina/os who lived and live their lives constantly crossing multiple borders, both physical and metaphorical. And, his life and biography give voice to those who, like him, refuse or cannot return to their place of origin but who, at the same time, cannot entirely unproblematically find their place in the United States. Varela, after all, both refused to return to Cuba and at the same time decided not to take US citizenship.

What emerges from his decision to live between worlds is an individual who lives and addresses multiple worlds simultaneously. We can recover this figure from the past, and, by way of his example and the company he keeps, consider him a representative of so many who similarly live today across multiple borders. Moving forth into the future, I propose that a recovered Latina/o literary history will help to forge a more inclusive and, to use Varela's term, "hopeful" society.

WORKS CITED

Aching, Gerard. *Freedom from Liberation: Slavery, Sentiment and Literature in Cuba*. Bloomington: Indiana University Press, 2015.

Amigo, Gustavo. *La posición filosófica del Padre Félix Varela (1947)*. Miami, FL: Editorial Cubana, 1991.

Anbinder, Tyler. *Five Points: The 19th-Century New York City Neighborhood that Invented Tap Dance, Stole Elections and Became the World's Most Notorious Slum (2001)*. New York: Free Press, 2010 Reissue.

Billington, Ray. *The Protestant Crusade 1800–1860: A Study of the Origins of American Nativism*. New York: Macmillan, 1938.

Brickhouse, Anna. *Transamerican Literary Relations and the Nineteenth-Century Public Sphere*. Cambridge: Cambridge University Press, 2004.

Coronado, Raúl. *A World Not to Come: A History of Latino Writing and Print Culture*. Cambridge, MA: Harvard University Press, 2013.

Fessenden, Tracy. *Culture and Redemption: Religion, the Secular, and American Literature*. Princeton, NJ: Princeton University Press, 2007.

Franchot, Jenny. *Roads to Rome. The Antebellum Protestant Encounter with Catholicism*. Berkeley: University of California Press, 1994.

Gjerde, Jon. *Catholicism and the Shaping of Nineteenth-Century America*. New York: Cambridge University Press, 2012.

González Acosta, Alejandro. *El enigma de Jicoténcal. Dos estudios sobre el héroe de Tlxacala*. Mexico: Instituto Tlaxcalteca de Cultura, 1997.

Hatch, Nathan. *The Democratization of American Christianity*. New Haven, CT: Yale University Press, 1989.

The Heath Anthology of American Literature. Eds. Paul Latuer, et al. Volume B. *Early Nineteenth Century*. Boston, MA: Wadsworth Publishing, 2013.

Ignatiev, Noel. *How the Irish Became White*. New York: Routledge, 1995.

Imbert, Anderson. *Historia de la literature hispanamerica* (1954). Vol. 1 *La Colonia. Cien años de república*. 9th reprint. Mexico: Fondo de Cultura Económica, 1995. 221–22.

Lazo, Rodrigo. *Writing to Cuba: Filibustering and Cuban Exiles in the United States*. Chapel Hill: University of North Carolina Press, 2005.

Leal, Luis. "Jicoténcal, primera novela histórica en castellano." *Revista Iberoamericana* 25.49 (1960): 9–31.

Luis, William. *Literary Bondage: Slavery in Cuban Narrative*. Austin: University of Texas Press, 1990.

McCadden, Joseph and Helen M. *Félix Varela. Torch Bearer for Cuba*. (1969). 2nd ed. San Juan, Puerto Rico: Ramallo Bros., 1984.

Mestre y Domínguez, José Manuel. *De la filosofía en la Habana*. Havana: Imprenta "La Antilla," 1862.

Moreno Fraginals, Manuel. *El ingenio, complejo socioeconómico cubano*. Havana: Comisión Nacional Cubana del UNESCO, 1964.

Murphy, Angela F. *American Slavery, Irish Freedom: Abolition, Immigrant Citizenship and the Transatlantic Movement for Irish Repeal*. Baton Rouge: Louisiana State University Press, 2010.

The Norton Anthology of Latino Literature. Ed. Ilán Stavans. New York: W. W. Norton & Company, 2010.

Oxx, Katie. *The Nativist Movement in America. Religious Conflict in the Nineteenth Century*. New York: Routledge, 2013.

Ravitch, Diane. *The Great School Wars. New York City (1805–1973): A History of the Public Schools as Battlefield of Social Change*. New York: Basic Books, 1974.

Reid-Vázquez, Michele. *The Year of the Lash: Free People of Color in Cuba and the Nineteenth-Century Atlantic World*. Athens: University of Georgia Press, 2011.

Rodríguez, José Ignacio. *Vida del prebístero Don Félix Varela*. 1878. New York: Imprenta de "O Novo Mundo", 1878.

Roediger, David R. *The Wages of Whiteness: Race and the Making of the American Working Class*. New York: Verso, 1991.

Roig de Leuchsenring, Emilio. *Ideario cubano Félix Varela, precursor de la revolución libertadora cubana*. Havana: Oficina del Historiador de la Ciudad, 1953.

Saco, José. *Historia de la esclavitud desde los tiempos más remotos hasta nuestros días*. 3 vols. Paris, Tipografía Lahure, 1875; Paris: Imprenta de Kugelmann, 1875; Barcelona: Imprenta de Jaime Jepús, 1877.

   Historia de la esclavitud de la raza africana en el nuevo mundo y en especial en los paises hispano-americanos. Vol. 1. Barcelona: Imprenta de Jaime Jepús, 1877.

Serpa, Gustavo. *Apuntes sobre la filosofía de Félix Varela*. Havana: Editorial Ciencias Sociales, 1983.

Shea, William M. *The Lion and the Lamb: Evangelicals and Catholics in America*. New York: Oxford University Press, 2004.

Silva Gruesz, Kirsten. *Ambassadors of Culture. The Transamerican Origins of Latino Writing*. Princeton, NJ: Princeton University Press, 2001.

Travieso, Antonio Hernández. *El Padre Varela. Biografia del forjador de la conciencia cubana*. Havana: Jesus Montero, 1949.

Varela y la reforma filosófica en Cuba. Havana: Jesús Montero, 1942.

Varela, Félix. *Cartas a Elpidio. Sobre la impiedad, la superstición y el fanatismo en sus relaciones con la sociedad*. Ed. Humberto Piñera. Epilogue by Raimundo Lazo. 2 vols. Havana: Universidad de la Habana, 1944.

Jicoténcal. Luis Leal and Rodolfo Cortina, eds. Houston, TX: Arte Público Press, 1995.

Félix Varela. Obras. El que nos enseñó primero a pensar (1997). 3 vols. Eds. Torres-Cuevas, Eduardo, Jorge Ibarra Cuesta and Mercedes García Rodríguez. Havana: University of Havana, 2001 (Digital Reprint).

Letters to Elpidio. Ed. Felipe Estévez. Trans. John Farina, et al. New York: Paulist Press, 1989.

Xicoténcatl. An anonymous historical novel about the events leading up to the conquest of the Aztec empire. Trans. Guillermo I. Castillo-Feliú. Austin: University of Texas Press, 1999.

Vitier, Medardo. *Las ideas y la filosofía en Cuba*. Havana: Editorial Ciencias Sociales, 1970.

Volk, Kyle. *Moral Minorities and the Making of American Democracy*. New York: Oxford University Press, 2015.

William, Lorna V. *The Representation of Slavery in Cuban Fiction*. Columbia: University of Missouri Press, 1994.

8

Transamerican New Orleans

Latino Literature of the Gulf, from the Spanish Colonial Period to Post-Katrina

KIRSTEN SILVA GRUESZ

In "Shake It, Moreno," a story in RC Ortiz's 2013 chapbook *Gutter Beads*, an African American girl invites a young man to play "a Spanish game they taught her at school." The narrator considers his response: "I ain't Spanish, I felt like saying, but then Christoph would've said: 'Oh, yeah, baby, over here you are.'" "Over here," a *moreno* codes casually, vaguely, as "Spanish." "Over here" means New Orleans, described elsewhere in the collection as "the northernmost city of the Caribbean, the Sodom and Gomorrah of the South."[1] That both/and formulation aptly describes the space where the US South dissolves into the Global South, a border one crosses not by land, but by water – the Gulf of Mexico and the Spanish Caribbean. Known as the "Spanish Sea" in colonial times, this heavily trafficked region strategically encircles Florida, Louisiana, and Texas with Veracruz, the Yucatán, and Central America's eastern coast, closing the ring around Cuba, Puerto Rico, and Hispaniola. While this mapping of the Anglo-Latin contact zone by way of the Gulf of Mexico may be less familiar than that of the continental border, it enables us to see the cultural continuities between these spaces – and to think about Latino literary history through points of ocean-going transit and exchange, centered around ports and coastlines.

What Miami has been to the United States since the 1950s, New Orleans was during earlier historical periods: the nearest entry point for Latin American migrants, where Spanish speakers from all over would comingle, compete, and often forge connections across national lines. Linked only by tenuous threads of language, culture, and their general misperception by the

---

[1] Roberto Carlos Ortiz, *Gutter Beads* (2013), 2, 14. Self-published; accessible at www.rcortiz.com/gutterbeads. Ortiz describes himself as a "New Orleans-based Puerto Rican writer."

US-American mainstream, a variety of social groups were thrust into sudden proximity with one another: laborers and elites; students, artists, and merchants; radicals and conservatives. The literary culture of this "Spanish" border city peaked during two periods that I will focus on particularly in this overview – the 1840s through 1850s, and the apogee of *Modernismo* from the 1910s through the 1930s – although the signs of a Latino cultural renaissance are growing in contemporary New Orleans as well, spurred by an influx of migrants after Hurricane Katrina in 2005. Like Miami, New Orleans shares with Cuba in particular a rich, difficult history of attachment, desire, and subjugation, and much of its Latino literary production arose in an effort to describe and reimagine the US–Cuba relationship. But New Orleans both predates the rise of Florida's dominance as a Latino cultural center, and adds its own unique layer to that neocolonial context: since the early twentieth century, the Louisiana economy has been strongly tied to Central America, particularly to Honduras. As a result, New Orleans is the only US city in which Central American-Americans have a plurality over other Latino subgroups; it is home to more Hondurans than any other city besides Tegucigalpa.

The notion of New Orleans as "the northernmost city of the Caribbean" is, to some extent, a touristic cliché: countless travel writers and painters have underscored the striking visual resemblances between New Orleans and cities like Havana, Port-au-Prince, and Cartagena, arising from their parallel Creole architectural styles – all, ultimately, derived from southern Spain. Despite the decoratively tiled signs in the Vieux Carré indicating the Spanish versions of familiar street names, however, most visitors (and many locals) downplay the significance of the nearly four decades of Spanish rule in colonial Louisiana. Whatever Spanish character seeped into the city is assumed to have been fully absorbed by the French Creoles. But recent historiography has shown otherwise.[2] Spain took over the swampy French town at the mouth of the Mississippi in 1769, as part of a master plan to

---

[2] On architecture, see Richard Sexton, *Creole World: Photographs of New Orleans and the Latin Caribbean Sphere* (New Orleans, LA: The Historic New Orleans Collection, 2014). The best integrated histories of the region are Ned Sublette, *The World That Made New Orleans: From Spanish Silver to Congo Square* (Chicago: Chicago Review Press, 2008) and Andrew Sluyter, Case Watkins, James P. Chaney, and Annie M. Gibson, *Hispanic and Latino New Orleans: Immigration and Identity since the Eighteenth Century* (Baton Rouge: Louisiana State University Press, 2015). In my essay "The 'Latinness' of New Orleans and the Gulf of Mexico System," *American Literary History* 18.4 (Fall 2006), 468–95, I argue for seeing the Gulf as a distinct transnational region of cultural exchange and political struggle.

expand its settlements – and check the spread of English power – on the North American continent. The port of New Orleans guarded the territory claimed as northern New Spain (that is: present-day Texas and the trans-Mississippi West), as well as the strategically crucial, but sparsely settled lands of East and West Florida, which changed hands various times during the eighteenth century. Governor Bernardo de Galvez recruited thousands of Canary Islanders to serve in the Revolutionary War army that beat back the British along the Florida frontier; these *isleño* families settled along the Gulf coast and preserved their language until the twentieth century. Spanish rule brought New Orleans the custom of the *lagniappe* and, more importantly, the law of *coartación* by which enslaved Africans could purchase their freedom, which created the city's population of free persons of color. Among the very first Afro-Latino citizens were these carpenters, ironsmiths, and their families, who took advantage of that opening – only to lose most of their liberties when an influx of planters from post-revolutionary Haiti, and a fear of spreading insurrection, brought about much more restrictive racial codes.

Galvez's administration had made some use of the press to communicate with the local French population, but the local print culture exploded when the United States took over Louisiana in 1803. Greater press freedom encouraged not only English newspapers, but French and Spanish ones as well: *El Misisipi*, which included a section in English, was established in 1808 – the first Spanish-language newspaper in the United States – and lasted a respectable two years. Spanish sections continued to appear in French and English papers, and several Spanish weeklies that focused on commerce and news started up routinely in the following decades, with some titles like *El Iris de la Paz* (The Rainbow of Peace) gesturing at the importance of US support for Spain during the Napoleonic Wars, and others like *El Telégrafo* implying that progress and modernity had arrived in the region. Two generations of Louisianans had grown up under Spanish rule, and many intermarried with French Creole families, building a Latin Catholic cultural bulwark against the Anglo-Protestants who settled on the newer side of Canal Street. Yet then, as now, those increasingly assimilated Spanish speakers with roots dating back to the 1770s lived in close proximity to more recent arrivals who followed trade routes into the now-booming city, as regularly scheduled steamships trekked between New Orleans, Veracruz, Havana, New York, and Cádiz. Some trades in particular – manufacturing cigars, selling tobacco products, and running coffeehouses – were considered the province of the "Spanish": this being, as in Ortiz's contemporary story, a casually incorrect omnibus term that could refer equally to Cubans, Puerto Ricans, Dominicans, *isleños*, *peninsulares*, or even Mexicans like Benito Juárez, who supported himself in exile by rolling cigars.

Given its diverse local population and its status as a trade nexus between the Anglo and Latin worlds, mid-nineteenth-century New Orleans was ripe for a major Spanish-language publishing venture. An ambitious man of letters seized the opportunity: Eusebio José Gómez, born in Louisiana in 1820 and perfectly bilingual in English and Spanish. Along with his Spanish immigrant partner, Victoriano Alemán, he established the most significant Spanish-language publication empire in the nation prior to the Civil War, revolving around the newspaper they coedited for six years and extending into ancillary projects like satirical journals and business directories.[3] In addition to journalism and editing, Gómez also wrote fiction, and his *Un matrimonio como hay muchos* (A Marriage Like Many Others), serialized in their newspaper in 1849, stands as the first known novel written by a US-born Latino. "E. J.," as he signed himself, offered English lessons to Spanish speakers, and Spanish lessons to English speakers, in the paper's editorial offices, which also served as a bookstore and community gathering place.

Headed by a nameplate that depicted the interlaced flags of the United States, Spain, and Mexico, *La Patria* benefitted from the outbreak of the war with Mexico in 1846: not only was New Orleans a launching point for troops and supplies, it was linked by telegraphic lines to the Eastern seaboard. The editors scooped the rest of the local press by gathering breaking news from their Spanish-language sources in Mexico itself, and their war coverage was copied and quoted as far as Washington, DC.[4] Shortly after the outbreak of the war, General Winfield Scott arrived in New Orleans and asked local

---

[3] I suggest this based on publication frequency, circulation, longevity, and scale of the publishing enterprise. Begun as *El Hablador* in September 1845, the paper continued uninterrupted as *La Patria* beginning January 1, 1846 through its renaming as *La Unión* on January 1, 1851, lasting until August of that year. Beginning as a semiweekly, from 1847 onward, it was published three times a week. Many newspapers in this era did not survive their first few issues; those that did lasted an average of two years, and did not reach a significant readership outside their locale. The bilingual *Santa Fe Gazette*, which ran from 1859–64, was the most long-lasting of these, and in subsequent decades other local Spanish papers in New Mexico had ten- to fifteen-year runs, without significant national readership. *La Patria*'s only peer in terms of wide circulation outside its region was thus *La Crónica* of New York (1848–67), triweekly for three years, then twice a week. However, *La Crónica*, which went through multiple editors, apparently did not have a bookselling outlet or other spinoff periodicals.

[4] I discuss in more detail the war coverage and poetry published in *La Patria* in *Ambassadors of Culture: The Transamerican Origins of Latino Writing* (Princeton University Press, 2002), 108–44; and Gómez's novel in "Tracking the First Latino Novel: *Un matrimonio como hay muchos* (1849) and Transnational Serial Fiction," in *Transnational Serial Fiction*, ed. Patricia Okker (New York: Blackwell, 2011).

officers to recommend an official Spanish interpreter to accompany the Army to Mexico. The officers named Gómez as a man "of gentlemanly habits," and Scott recommended that he be commissioned as a lieutenant colonel. But *La Patria* – a Whig paper in a heavily Democratic city – had made enemies. Despite being a US citizen, despite his admiring portraits of George Washington and his colorful Fourth of July issues, Gómez was accused in print of being "a Mexican at heart." Scott rescinded the appointment. If one consistent theme of the US Latino experience is being mistaken for something you are not (he was actually descended from settlers of Spanish Florida), Gómez's painful brush with ethno-national bias is a resonant early case of it. As *La Patria* covered the war, its editorial position challenged the seemingly endless thirst among some factions in the United States, especially the South, to acquire new territories. With sales agents from Texas to Alabama, Florida, South Carolina, and up the coastline to New York, the paper promised to defend the interests of Spanish speakers in the whole nation – a group they sometimes addressed as *españoles* and sometimes as *hispano-americanos*. At the same time, its readership extended beyond the United States to Mexico City, the Yucatán, Puerto Rico, and Cuba. The exact scope of the "homeland" of the paper's title, then, is left for its readers, not its editors, to define.

In addition to international, local, and commercial news, *La Patria* published a substantial amount of literary material: poetry, long nonfiction pieces, and fiction. While most were copied from other papers, about one-fifth of the literary works appear to be original: those marked *remitido*, sent into the offices, or signed with initials. The dominant poetic styles were the satirical *letrilla*, a staple since the Baroque period, and the ardent nationalist verse of the Romantics – Espronceda, Larra, Heredia. In one poem, a local *letrilla* writer spread gossip about a Mexican actress then touring the South. A very different, anonymously submitted lyric titled "La Patria" imitated the tropes of Cuban exile that Heredia had made famous: the palm tree, the *colibrí*, the chilling contrast between the tropical homeland and the frozen North. The clearly pro-independence message, reinforced by an imaginative breaking of slaves' chains, indicates that the paper was willing to tolerate a range of political orientations among the writers they published, even as their editorials consistently supported Spain's continuing hold over the islands.

Regular contributors of nonfiction included the anonymous figures who wrote under the pen names "El Observador," "Triboulet," and "Lucas Gómes." They bandied back and forth a series of first-person satirical essays, poking fun at the alcohol-soaked social scene in New Orleans and its corrupt political culture, or mocking their own failed courtship attempts. Some of these humorous sketches were published in installments over three or four issues and labeled *folletín*, a sign of the global dissemination of a new literary fad introduced by the French: the *feuilleton*, or serialized novel. The salacious "mysteries" novel originated by Eugène Sue was so popular in the 1840s that it seemed every city on the globe inspired at least one. *La Patria*, which translated, published, and sold bound copies of Sue's novels, ran its own version in 1846, the anonymous *Los misterios del Cerro en la temporada de 1844 (Historia que parece cuento)* (The Mysteries of Cerro in the 1844 Social Season [A True Story that Seems Like Fiction]). Satirizing wealthy youth in Havana (the mansion-lined Cerro district was a summer retreat for the planter class), and thumbing its nose at the Cuban censor who had supposedly prevented it from being published on the island, the novel abruptly ends after a few suggestive installments.

The Mysteries of Cerro was published anonymously, but Gómez's own novel, *A Marriage Like Many Others*, was prominently advertised with his byline when it was serialized in *La Patria* between December 1848 and April 1849. Subtitled "A Contemporary Novel," it opens in the Havana household of Fernando Mendoza and Luisa Bermúdez, married just one year and coping with their post-honeymoon disappointments. The first third of the novel explores the gap between each partner's expectations and experience of marriage: Fernando wants a well-ordered, hierarchical household; Luisa wants Fernando to worship her as he seemed to do during their courtship. Later, however, the novel veers away from this domestic realism to dip into the sensationalist "Mysteries" tradition, with descriptions of seamy gambling clubs and secret dueling places; and subsequently into a theatrical, preposterous subplot: two predatory cousins, Eduardo and Emilia, befriend Fernando and Luisa, each scheming to seduce one of the married couple. Letters are slipped under doors and kept from their intended recipients. Mothers-in-law get involved in the intrigue. Luisa leaves Fernando, wrongly convinced he has been unfaithful and acquired a disease; Fernando, in despair, leaves Cuba for New Orleans in order to forget his troubles by indulging his "irresistible passion for Business." On the steamship, he meets the New Orleanian narrator. Fernando then "devoted himself to certain branch of commerce between New Orleans and Mexico, which did not work out well, so he decided to move North" to New York. There, in the frigid climate, he takes ill, and although a repentant Luisa rushes to his deathbed, she is too late. Perhaps, the narrator hints in conclusion, some of his female readers know Luisa personally. Underscoring the realism of the novel's beginning, the story ends in 1848, so that its fictional time frame catches up to the point in real time at which the serialization began.

A Marriage borrows much from popular stage productions that feature romantic foursomes in seduction plots, either comic or tragic. Yet other parts of the novel speak to the themes of domestic order and female self-regulation that one sees in Anglo-American sentimental fiction of the period. Although only its final chapter takes place in the United States, the novel features what would become clichés of Cuban American writing: the tearful look back at Havana Harbor; the fear of dying among cold, covetous Northerners; the ambivalent sense that Cuba is a space of deception and disorder. *La Patria* was pro-Spanish, but the introduction to the first installment mocks the strict censorship of the Tacón regime, which so suppressed literary production on the island that no other Cuban novels were published during this period (there are no other known "Mysteries of Havana"). In setting up contrasts between its settings, then, *A Marriage* addressed one of the major political questions of the day in New Orleans: what sort of political relationship might these two culturally symmetrical, economically sutured places have in the future?

In historian Robert May's words, "annexation, intervention, and acquisition of transit rights" preoccupied both policy makers and the general public, particularly in the South, where the Knights of the Golden Circle envisioned a regional slaveholding empire that would swallow Mexico and Central America, as well as the Spanish Caribbean islands.[5] The Cuban flag, designed by a poet, flew first in New Orleans at the head of Narciso López's military expeditions to Cuba in 1850 and 1851, a scene memorialized by a marker on Poydras Street. Gómez and Alemán wrote scathingly against the López filibusters: the war with Mexico had shaped their opposition to any further US acquisition of territory in the Americas, and by the same principle they also rejected the prospect of US intervention in the Yucatán, called out the bad behavior of gold-seekers crossing the isthmus to California, and treated with skepticism the plan of New Orleans investors to dig a canal through the Isthmus of Tehuantepec. (That route, in addition to violating Mexican sovereignty, would have passed through a diffi-cult-to-navigate river: readers at the time might have guessed the "certain branch of commerce between New Orleans and Mexico" that hurt the fictional Fernando Mendoza was the crash of the Tehuantepec Canal bond market).[6]

---

[5] Robert May, *The Southern Dream of a Caribbean Empire, 1854–1861*, 2nd ed. (Gainesville: University Press of Florida, 2002), p. 155.

[6] Gómez shares an in-joke here with his New Orleans readers: the steamship that carries Fernando to the United States is the *Alabama*, one of the regular fleet plying the New Orleans-Havana route whose comings and goings were regularly announced in *La Patria*. The *Alabama* was also one of the ships that made the Tehuantepec passage during the Gold Rush; while *A Marriage* was being serialized, tiny engravings of ships bound for California appeared in advertisement boxes on Page One.

Yet many Spanish speakers in the United States supported either outright independence for Cuba or, as a stopgap, its annexation as a territory or state. Although many members of the López expeditions were white Southerners hoping to profit from bond sales, Gómez and Alemán admitted that the local community was split on the question – that the Spanish cafés and *tabaquerías* also hummed with the talk of would-be liberators. Only a small minority among this group was committed to ending chattel slavery in Cuba. *La Patria* itself did not take an antislavery position, but neither did they engage in a systematic defense of the institution, as other local publications did, nor did they publish slave-auction and runaway ads. (Indeed, the prospectus for their first 1845 paper had promised to appeal to all readers, "man or woman, young or old, white or black.") They also reprinted and sold works by known abolitionists: Orestes Brownson's fiery pamphlet against filibustering, a novel by Gertrudis Gómez de Avellaneda, and many works by the Spanish translator of *Uncle Tom's Cabin*, Wenceslao Ayguals. The newspaper's tendency to skirt the emancipation question reflects a delicate balance between its location in the very heart of the US domestic slave trade, and the variety of feelings among its international readers: slavery had been outlawed by all the young Latin American republics, and it was seen as an embarrassment by many educated Spaniards. Mexico had decried Texas's lapse into a slaveholding economy, welcoming Afro-Texans who fled across the border. As Southern aspirations to expand into the *Seno Mexicano* gave further fuel to sectionalism, the change in the paper's name to *La Unión* at the start of 1851 may be taken as a sign of resistance to the region's rogue politics of filibustering, officially discouraged by Washington.

Gómez and Alemán were joined in 1851 by a third coeditor, the Guatemalan-born Antonio José de Irisarri, and the paper serialized his novel, *El cristiano errante* (The Wandering Christian), previously published in Bogotá. Gómez took an extended sabbatical, and the paper became more singly focused on its defense of Spanish control over Cuba, celebrating the execution of López and some of his Southern co-combatants after the failure of their second attempt. In August of that year, an angry mob stormed the paper's editorial offices, sacked and wrecked the printing equipment and stock, and shot at Alemán, who jumped across the roofs of the *Vieux-Carré*, his leg broken. The mob went on to attack other "Spanish" people and destroy their businesses. Alemán fled to Cuba, then Argentina. Gómez relocated to Key West, where he worked for the remaining decades of his life as an insurance agent and a diplomat – though he did not, apparently, publish any more fiction. Irisarri's stay in filibuster-crazed New Orleans had taught him how development, transit, and colonization companies eyed Central America as part of the South's "Golden Circle," and during the final decades of his life, spent in Brooklyn, he became an important voice of opposition to later US interventions in Guatemala, El Salvador, and Nicaragua. No other print organ in New Orleans would approach the ambition and influence of *La Patria/La Unión* for many decades to come.

The indiscriminate violence unleashed during this ethno-racial riot likely landed on those who opposed Spain's hold on Cuba, as well as those who defended it. All six of the pro-independence Cuban poets whose work would be included in the patriotic anthology *El Laúd del Desterrado* (The Exile's Lute, published in New York in 1858) lived in New Orleans at some point. Some remained there after 1851: Leopoldo Turla and Pedro Angel Castellón eked out meager livings as teachers and writers, and died in penury. Pedro Santacilia met Juárez in New Orleans and followed him to Mexico, where he worked to dismantle Indian peonage. José Agustín Quintero, on the other hand, took the lyrical voice he had brought to the cause of Cuban sovereignty in sentimental poems like "The Exile's Banquet", and lent it to the defense of slavery. After a stint in journalism in Texas and in Mexico as a Confederate spy, Quintero settled in New Orleans, where he wrote editorials in English for the *Picayune*—the very organ that had jingoistically led the march to Mexico.

Although the Civil War seemingly put an end to the vision of a plantation empire that would encircle the Gulf of Mexico, the idea that New Orleans might share cultural and economic interests with this transnational region endured. A new Spanish newspaper, *El Pelayo*, had taken the place of *La Unión* soon after the 1851 riot, but it was carefully nonpolitical. Other publications that came and went during Reconstruction testify to the continuity of a Spanish-speaking community: one surviving example is *El Moro de Paz* (1888–1889), under the editorship of José Antonia Fernández de Trava, who would become the first professor of Spanish at Tulane. The commercial focus of these publications reinforced what had become a general theme among city leaders: that only by shifting the focus of its trade toward Latin America could the port of New Orleans hope to recapture the importance and wealth it enjoyed before the Civil War. Legions of visitors to the Cotton Exposition of 1884–1885, and the Exposition of the Three Americas that followed, heard *mariachi* music for the first time at the popular Mexican Pavilion. Both the music and food of the greater Gulf were increasingly absorbed into the local culture: the African rhythm of the Cuban *contradanza* influenced early jazz, while recipes for *tamales* were appearing in Creole cookbooks by the turn of the century. Even José Martí wrote about New Orleans as a kind of urban estuary, where the Anglo and Latin worlds flowed together and comingled.

Martí stayed with *El Titan de Bronce*, Antonio Maceo, whenever he passed through the city in the early 1890s; Maceo resided in the Tremé neighborhood, with the descendants of Spain's original free people of color. But Cuba had never been far off the radar for other New Orleanians: in 1873, the capture of a US-registered ship that was smuggling arms to Cuban rebels, the *Virginius*, had incited the New Orleans press to cry for war with Spain, rallying around the memory of the López filibusters and glorifying the anti-Spanish riot. Maceo, Martí, and Máximo Gómez, in contrast, organized their revolutionary activities among the local *tabaqueros* along very different political principles. The neocolonial relationship that resulted from the US victory in the War of 1898 did not quite bring that old fantasy of extending the South into Cuba to pass: it was mostly Northern companies who moved in to buy up sugar and tobacco farms and factories on the island. But New Orleans retained its reputation among Cuban laborers and activists as a place one could seek haven from unfavorable conditions – as did, for instance, some cigar makers who lost the so-called Currency Strike against their US corporate employer in 1907.

The closest realization of the original "Golden Circle" vision of regional dominance occurred not in Cuba, but in Central America. Once refrigeration technology made it possible to ship bananas to the United States, New Orleans flowered again as a trade power during the first half of the twentieth century. Standard Fruit, Cuyamel Fruit, and eventually United Fruit were headquartered in the city (later mergers would make these into the still-recognizable brands Chiquita and Dole). In addition to shipping, these corporations owned massive plantation and transportation infrastructures in Jamaica, Ecuador, Colombia, Costa Rica, Guatemala, and especially Honduras. With the banana trade came the "Great White Fleet" (*La Flota Blanca*) of the United Fruit Company, which along with its competitors' ships glamorously ferried passengers along with cargo. New Orleans gloried in becoming the nexus of tourism both to and from Latin America. Logically, given the inter-American theme of the expositions, a municipal booster organization helped fund a glossy, illustrated literary and cultural review in Spanish, *El Mercurio*, published between 1911 and 1927.

A sixty-page monthly featuring cutting-edge printing technologies like full-color rotogravure cover art and photographic news dispatches, and as much original literary and cultural material as it could solicit, *El Mercurio* published some of the most important writers from Spain and Latin America in the early years of its editorship under Josep Branyas. Essays, poems, and stories embraced the new wave of pan-Hispanism, and when war broke out in Europe, it – like other Latin American periodicals – assumed it was the Western Hemisphere's turn to lead the world. There was local content too, promoting New Orleans, yet again, as the meeting place of the Northern and Southern halves of that hemisphere. The Salvadoran-born Máximo Soto Hall, whose short novel *El problema* is considered the first anti-imperialist fiction in Latin America, was a frequent contributor to the first two volumes of *El Mercurio* while he lived in the city. In his dozen or more contributions dated from New Orleans, Soto Hall penned everything from a fluff piece on the history of the Napoleon House bar, to an investigation on the state of tropical medicine, to a poem on the sinking of the Titanic. Similarly, the leftist Peruvian poet José Santos Chocano debuted several poems in *El Mercurio*, including one titled "Pasajera" (In Passing), written and dated aboard a United Fruit boat in the Gulf of Mexico. *El Mercurio* has not yet received the scholarly attention it deserves as an important incubator of *Modernismo* in the Spanish-speaking world – and in particular, for its exploration of the new Central American realities that were being shaped under the influence of the very city in which the magazine was published.

One recovered story, published in 1912 under the pseudonym of "Lapis Lázuli," may be the work of a local writer.[7] Titled "El regenerador de Centro-América: Historia cómico-trágica para llorar cinco minutos" (The Regenerator of Central America: A Tragicomic Story to Cry About for Five Minutes), it features an assimilated, bilingual Latino protagonist, Eladio Pérez. He is approached one night in the French Quarter and recruited to help a wealthy Central American stage a coup in his unnamed native country, and bring democracy and progress to it. After investing a fortune with shady *gringo* types who are vaguely connected to the State Department (with Pérez translating), the would-be revolutionaries are tricked by their suppliers and stranded on the beach with boxes of oysters and crackers, instead of the promised guns and ammunition. The story's hero barely makes it back to New Orleans alive, scrubbing dishes to pay his passage.

---

[7] *El Mercurio* 2.2, March 1912, 13–14. Who was "Lapis Lázuli"? Given the traditional association of editorial work with the blue pencil, we might suspect a member of the editorial staff. For more detail, see my "The Mercurial Space of 'Central' America: New Orleans, Honduras, and the Writing of the Banana Republic," in *Hemispheric American Studies*, eds. Caroline Levander and Robert S. Levine (New Brunswick, NJ: Rutgers University Press, 2007).

The unnamed country in "The Regenerator of Central America" is reminiscent of Honduras, which had just undergone two turbulent years of regime change and occupation by the US Marines under the strong influence of Samuel Zemurray, owner of the Cuyamel Fruit Company – the major landholder on the north coast of Honduras.

Hondurans and other Central Americans came and went frequently on these fruit boats: laborers came in search of work, strivers sent their children to learn English in the Catholic schools, elites came to buy consumer goods. Two young Honduran writers, who came of age together during the general wave of political leftism and anti-imperialism that swept Latin America between the World Wars, gravitated almost inevitably toward New Orleans. Guillermo Bustillo Reina and Arturo Martínez Galindo founded a monthly review, *El Continente*, there in 1928, just after *El Mercurio* folded. It lasted only three issues, but Martínez Galindo's fiction and journalism began to probe the unusually close ties between his country and Louisiana.[8] A few of the stories collected in his posthumous *Sombra* (1940) are set in New Orleans as well as Washington, DC. One begins on the deck of a steamship of the Great White Fleet crossing the Gulf of Mexico, where (says the narrator) "almost all the passengers were originally from those beloved lands that extend, so blue, so blue, from the Rio Grande to the Panama Canal. It was in the good old days, when the steamers weren't completely overwhelmed with flocks of Yankee tourists."[9] Martínez Galindo was assassinated in the Gulf town of Trujillo at the age of forty by agents of the corrupt state governor. His friend Bustillo Reina later memorialized their youth in his poem "Viaje a Nueva Orleans," a recollection of avid wanderings around the historic city that ends in a melancholic goodbye to Old Man Mississippi. The image of the Great White Fleet crossing to New Orleans became bound up in later twentieth-century Central American representations of their neocolonial relationships with the United States: the Salvadoran leftist poet Armando López Muñoz, for instance, imagined his populist speaker in "El Loco de Puertocortés" waiting for a ship from New Orleans that would never arrive to the Honduran port, and Nicaraguan Ernesto Cardenal's documentary poems refer repeatedly to the sphere of influence of the banana oligarchs.

---

[8] It was followed by the monthly magazine *Lucero Latino* – aimed more at women readers – which was edited in Tegucigalpa but published in New Orleans from 1933 to 1934.

[9] Arturo Martínez Galindo, "Aurelia San Martín," in *Sombra* (Tegucigalpa: Imprenta Calderón, 1940), 57–70 at 57 (translation mine).

The major fruit companies ceased their passenger service in the 1950s, as Miami and Houston claimed a greater share of regional traffic, and as moderately successful labor strikes were launched against them. The involvement of United Fruit's Samuel Zemurray and local politicians in the US-backed overthrow of Guatemalan president Jacobo Arbenz in 1954 caused a stir in the New Orleans press. (Fittingly, or ironically, Zemurray's family was a major benefactor of Tulane University's pioneering Latin American Studies program, research center, and library, and these resources remain a powerful draw for Latin American students – not only those from elite families.[10]) Cold War politics like the Arbenz overthrow unsettled the city's Latino population, even as the charismatic Democratic mayor Chep Morrison (who held office from 1946 to 1961) traveled all over Central America, Mexico, and the Caribbean to build regional trade partnerships, and lined Basin Street with statues of Latin American heroes. When Castro's revolution took hold in Cuba, the Morrison administration and the city's Catholic institutions welcomed thousands of exiles with open arms. Some settled near Hondurans in the *barrio lempira* in the Lower Garden District; others went to Mid-City, where they erected their own statue (to Martí, although Maceo might have been a more historically resonant choice).

The violence in Central America in the 1980s brought more displaced persons – right-leaning, left-leaning, and everywhere in between – to New Orleans. So did Hurricane Mitch, which devastated coastal Honduras in 1998. The post-Mitch diaspora included a higher concentration than ever before of *garifunas* of African-Carib descent, adding another component to the submerged population of Afro-Latinos who had been present in the city since the Spanish period. The diversity of national, ethno-racial, and class backgrounds among the city's Latino population, and the lack of a single neighborhood where Latinos congregate, challenges the capacity of "Hispanic Heritage" organizations to represent the population adequately. These socioeconomic factors – along with the stubborn myth that only the French influence made New Orleans "Latin" – made it relatively invisible, at least until the massive influx of migrant workers from Mexico and Central America following

---

[10] The Puerto Rican Luis Adam Nazario recalled his student years there during the 1940s in his *Mi vida estudiantil en Nueva Orleans* (San Juan, Puerto Rico, 1971); more recently, the Ecuadoran-born writer Gabriel Alemán, who received her PhD at Tulane, has made New Orleans a setting in several of her fictional works, such as *Body Time* (2003), *Poso Wells* (2007), and the post-Katrina short story "Jam Session" (2011). R. C. Ortiz was also a Tulane student. Latino students have also built coalitional communities at private universities like Loyola, Dillard, and the University of New Orleans, as well as Louisiana State University.

Hurricane Katrina in 2005. Much was made in the press of the new racial order the disaster had produced, and of the coming "re-Latinization" of New Orleans (which forms, of course, part of a larger demographic reshaping of the entire US South). As this overview has tried to show, however, it is only the perception – not the influence – that is new. The Gulf of Mexico constitutes a trans-American border system in its own right: one that has been crossed regularly, over the centuries, by Latino migrants and settlers with a host of motives, memories, and stories yet to be told.

9

Trajectories of ExChange

Toward Histories of Latina/o Literature

RODRIGO LAZO

The highly anticipated (and somewhat controversial) publication of *The Norton Anthology of Latino Literature* arrived in 2011 with fanfare as commentators noted the fulfillment of crossover dreams across the literary landscape. "With this anthology from Norton, the publisher of all of those authoritative, referenced-till-ragged anthologies of American and British literature, a milestone has been reached. Latinos – and implicitly, Mexican Americans – matter to American literary culture," wrote Oscar Villalon in a short review ("Mainstream"). His enthusiasm was not far from more sober reflection, since critics and the publishers of anthologies themselves have made a case for the institutional force of these tomes. Even a skeptical duo, Raphael Dalleo and Elena Machado, had noted prior to the book's publication that the Norton would presumably "assert, codify, and institutionalize the ascendancy of the field" (2). But in a review of the *Norton*, Kirsten Silva Gruesz pointed to numerous disjunctions between the publication of anthologies and the writing of literary historical studies. Gruesz noted that the *Norton* "occupies the unusual position of presenting an authoritative canon for a body of literature that doesn't yet have a literary history" (336). In response, Gruesz calls for taking account of how periodization complicates continuity and suggests that perhaps "the temporal aspect of ethnoracial identity remains to be fully worked through" (336–37). One of the disconcerting effects of anthological efforts is that they provide an apparatus proposing continuity or points of comparison across hundreds of years without adequately articulating how such continuities emerge or persist. Neither do they delve adequately into the difference of print-culture conditions, historical contexts, or how the organizing term "Latino" travels historically.

Previous anthologies such as *Herencia: The Anthology of Hispanic Literature of the United States* (2002) have initiated a field with broad historical strokes that go back to the colonization of the Americas and move toward contemporary fiction and even pop culture. But the paucity of studies in Latino literature going back centuries raises the question of why Fray Bartolomé de las Casas and Ricky Martin are in the same collection of "literature," in this case the *Norton*. The category of "literature" has become like taffy stretched in a candy-store window, and anthologies of Latino literature cannot escape a historical mix with other forms of culture. My concern is not that las Casas's account of the devastation of Indians is literature while "Livin' la Vida Loca" is not, or vice versa. This will become clear in my argument for histories of Latino *literature* in a capacious sense of that word, but for now let us note that neither the priest nor the pop star is writing in the genres that have become associated with literature (drama, poetry, fiction). The point is that we do not have a rigorous explanation of how and why texts from other centuries necessarily or even purportedly are connected to contemporary texts other than through an imagined imposition.

The default in creating a literary historical panorama is to cast a net into the past, and thus anthologies bring in Alvar Nuñez Cabeza de Vaca and company into a new hybridized field-formation. Rather than a critical understanding of these connections, anthologies offer introductory suggestions such as the following:

> Not every "Latino" author in the anthology has an equally rounded Latino identity. Is Fray Bartolomé de las Casas, whose activism against Spanish abuses of the indigenous population in the Americas made him a hero in some quarters and infamous in others, a proto-Latino, since he did not set foot in any part of what constitutes the United States today?   (Stavans lvi-lvii)

The answer is both no (in the tone of the rhetorical query) and yes (in the table of contents). Nevertheless, my point is not to fault anthologies but to begin thinking how literary histories might offer explications of connections from one period to another and to propose trajectories of textual production across time. At the very least, a consideration of how latinidades differ depending on periods and locations is necessary. An anticolonial intellectual in the early nineteenth-century United States, for example, may call himself *Americano* in an anti-European hemispheric sense, a process that we can retroactively associate with latinidad, whereas by the late nineteenth century a writer in New York may be more engaged with US racial constructions, particularly in relation to blacks, and their effect on Latino/Hispano populations. That particular comparison assumes self-identification as the changing element throughout the century, but my gesture toward literary history is more varied and cognizant that print culture and/or economic conditions may be the most important dimension in an attempt to develop a historical trajectory.

Admittedly, the writing of literary history has not fared well in academic circles in the last twenty-five years. The latter part of the twentieth century saw a series of challenges to historical continuity that turned into skepticism about narratives focused on traditions, nations, and even ethnicity. Literary history saw intense criticism from New Critics and later deconstruction's challenge to a hermeneutics of closure and semiotic certainty. As a result of this interrogation of these categories as an effect of discourse, the mainstays of literary history came into question. The skepticism was best captured in the title of David Perkins's book *Is Literary History Possible?* An answer to that type of question was provided by Robert Johnstone in *PMLA*:

> The comprehensive history must introduce, represent and relate what the anthology need only introduce and present; it must demonstrate case by case what the synthetic essay need only assert. Expectation mirrors ambition, however, and the critical consensus since mid-century has been that it is impossible to construct or imagine a text that is genuinely literary, respectably historical, and satisfactorily comprehensive. (26–27)

It wasn't always so impossible. Perkins reminds us that in the nineteenth-century literary history enjoyed popularity and prestige due to "three fundamental assumptions: that literary works are formed by their historical context; that change in literature takes place developmentally; and that this change is the unfolding of an idea, principle or suprapersonal entity" (1–2). The notion of suprapersonal entities was driven by idealism, and it granted legitimacy to works that were positioned as articulating or representing the spirit of a people.

Another ideal drove a type of literary history that traced changes in literary form from one decade or century to another. René Wellek at one point compares literary history to tracing the "evolution" of artistic forms in music or visual art, "without necessarily paying much attention to the biographies of painters or composers or to the audience for which the paintings and compositions were designed" (Wellek 112). While the emphasis on artistic forms is not the only approach to literary history, the attempt to distance a text from its writer is directly at odds with the goals of Latino literature, which has always focused not only on texts but also on people, not only writers but reading publics, even if sometimes people are read through texts. For Latino literature, particularly in the recovery of historical contexts, biographical accounts of writers and their reasons for publishing have been an important dimension of scholarship. Furthermore, Wellek's notion of artistic forms across time is more pertinent for traditions in which something like the sonnet may be important from one century to another. By contrast, the historical panorama of Latino literature is more likely to confront a multiplicity of forms that do not carry from one century to another.

Arguments against the developmental approach to literary history are not unwarranted. While the tracing of changes does not equate with charting evolution, notions of historical development have too often been linked to teleology, narratives of progress or improvement, and even the Enlightenment's bogeyman: civilization. The critique of development runs from European theory to politically minded critics of area studies. "Chronological ordering of intellectual and scholarly achievements is one of the most damaging principles of modern epistemology, which runs parallel to the modern economy; what is new is better, and the idea of newness is running the market," writes Walter Mignolo (34). Unfortunately, a type of market-driven valorization of newness and experimentation underlies the table of contents of *The Norton Anthology of Latino Literature*, whose chronological account of development culminates in a section on the post-1980 decades titled "Into the Mainstream." Still, the importance of novels, poems, and memoirs published after 1980, which in many ways opened the field, provides a reason to keep an eye on print-culture processes. For historical studies, the importance is in the different functions of markets when one compares earlier centuries to literature of the last three decades.

Criticism, skepticism, or outright dismissal of literary history can come into conflict with attempts to consider new histories of textual production by minority populations. Perkins articulates the issue by noting that in the 1980s, literary history gained new groups of supporters. "The movements for liberation of women, blacks, and gays produce literary histories for the same motives, essentially, that inspired the national and regional literary histories of the nineteenth century. These groups turn to the past in search of identity, tradition, and self-understanding" (Perkins 10). Bracketing his assumptions about motives, Perkins does implicitly call our attention to the problems of marshaling arguments against literary histories across the board. It is one thing to attempt to overturn the terms of national literary development (not only US, written as "American," but also German, French, etc.) but another to turn such arguments on Latino or African American literature, which do not have the same long-standing scholarly production. The writing of literary history privileges certain nations or traditions over others. Even if "American" literature's evolutionary history is out of favor as a scholarly project, library shelves are stocked with books by Perry Miller, F. O. Matthiessen, Alfred Kazin, and their heirs. As such, some critics in US literary studies continue to operate with the assumption of national movements and periods (early American, antebellum, long nineteenth century, Modernism, etc.). The weight of these lingering narratives of historical development is to provide a tradition against which scholars can argue. The same tradition is not always afforded scholars of minority literature. In the case of Latino literature, narratives are in short supply, even as new historical scholarship has emerged.

Historical work in Latino literature in the last three decades has emphasized the recovery and contextualization of writing that until recently had been either neglected completely (e.g., the novels of María Amparo Ruiz de Burton) or considered only in relation to Latin America (e.g., the anonymous novel *Jicoténcal*). Here it is important to note, following Wendell Harris, that historical scholarship does not necessarily entail the type of diachronic consideration afforded by literary history. Historical scholarship may attend to contexts, print-culture conditions, and sociohistorical influences, among other factors, but does not necessarily trace these over time.[1] In its critical volumes, the Recovering the US Hispanic Literary Heritage Project has been at the forefront of historical scholarship, while a range of book-length studies have delimited the scene of analysis by nationality, genre, or topic. Much of the early work was organized around specific dimensions of textual production that introduce a local reference or a transnational readership, including Mexican American autobiography or Cuban exile newspapers.[2] Such specificity has ruled the day with good reason, given the ongoing scholarly need to present writers, print-culture conditions, and particular contexts. More recently, scholars are starting to challenge temporal limits. Raúl Coronado's influential "history of Latino writing and print culture," begins with the eighteenth century and concludes in the mid-nineteenth century. Such a contribution is a necessary step toward a series of studies that might move the field from the Conquest to the present.

Considering that scholars in the historical study of Latino literature continue facing the imperatives of archival excavation – and archives present new texts, modes of distribution, and even media, thus shifting discussions – it has not

---

[1] Harris is unwilling to equate skepticism about narrative with a dismissal of historical access to factual information. He writes in response to critics who emphasize the indeterminacy of meaning, "At a time when commentary on literature seems built on shifting sands, it is well to recognize that historical scholarship treats factual questions that are for the most part open to determinate resolution" (438). This is an important matter for critics in Latino studies committed to considering individual people and populations connected to the historical analysis of texts.

[2] For examples, see books by Padilla, Meléndez, and Lazo.

always been feasible or even practical given the exigencies of academic clocks to move beyond one century. While historical specificity and historical continuity are not mutually exclusive, a single book would be hard-pressed to offer a convincing account of historical change from colonization to the present. The first and still most daring attempt to approach the historical study of Latino writing from various US sites with hemispheric connections, Gruesz's *Ambassadors of Culture*, shows how forceful it can be to remain within a set of decades. That is to say, the shorter period allows for a geographic and generic range to inform the study.

The pre-independence period in the Americas offers Latino literature difficult analytical challenges, including generic difference across centuries and a radically different set of publishing conditions. Some regions did not have printing presses. But in addition, the geographical location of writing and publication raises a variety of questions. If the US Revolution and Spanish America's independence movements, tied as they are to the rise of nation-states, create conditions for the emergence of Latino subjectivities and printing networks, the preceding centuries offer many sites through which conquerors, travelers, and priests move with an intellectual string attached to a colonial fatherland. What texts are claimed as part of Latino literature? The argument for the inclusion of Cabeza de Vaca (c. 1490–c. 1560) was based on his geographic movement through what today can be considered the important Latino territories of Florida and Texas. (Juan Bruce-Novoa also argued that as a result of his transformation in America, Cabeza de Vaca entered "the inherent instability of an identity system" (22), which Bruce-Novoa connected to Chicano culture.) Anthologies have followed suit, claiming texts through a geographic mapping of the present-day United States onto the past, even if the texts were historically written in or about places that were homes to indigenous populations and/or claimed by Spanish colonialism. (Las Casas is included not because he visited territories of the future United States but because of his ethical position in relation to the Spanish treatment of indigenous populations.)

A problem that is at once geographic and conceptual emerges when texts from the sixteenth century pull Latino studies toward colonial conditions that have been the critical terrain of Latin American studies or the scholarship of national South American cultures. El Inca Garcilaso de la Vega (1539–1616) wrote an account of a Florida expedition, but he was born in Peru and lived most of his life in Spain and his best-known writings are about the history of Peru, raising questions as to limitations of Latino literature and its inextricable connections to the United States in approaching this figure. Garcilaso de la Vega, who appears in the *Norton*, is an excellent example of an anthology's option of including a text without making a convincing analytical case for the types of connections necessitated by literary history.

Colonial conditions and contact zones in the fifteenth to seventeenth centuries may pose the greatest challenge for Latino literary history in that the contexts of textual production are so different from the print culture formations that emerged in the nineteenth century and the market-driven publications of the late twentieth century. Even the North/South divide, sometimes written as Anglo/Spanish, may not be operational in that figures like Cabeza de Vaca wrote before the English had established themselves in North America. A literary historical project would have to articulate how the concerns of Latino literature may emerge across a historical panorama; these concerns may include migration and exile, the meeting of Spanish and other cultures, and the textual engagement with two or more countries. But the ways texts cross the Americas, whether in content or circulation, or the way they grapple with a homeland, are not necessarily similar across time. Oscar Hijuelos imagining Cuba in an English-language novel published by a major New York house is on different terrain in terms of print culture and generic expectations than Vicente Pérez Rosales's publishing a memoir in Spanish (in Santiago, Chile) about his trip from Chile to California and back again during the California gold rush. At the very least, the question must be posed as to the difference that emerges from writing and publishing in English versus Spanish, especially in terms of readership and a text's circulation.

In Latino literary history, the hemisphere becomes a site of movement and an influence on textual crossings rather than a geographical area that encapsulates a field. Latino literature cannot account for the entire textual history of a hemisphere, even if the hemisphere as a conception and a material condition is inextricable from Latino literature's terrain of analysis. One of the goals of a literary history should be to articulate the criteria for the inclusion of certain texts with connections to multiple national sites. The criteria may include the crossing of countries and languages, the grappling with European colonialism and US imperialism, and the various ways identity and affiliation emerge historically. It is almost impossible to separate Latino literature from the United States, which is its site of institutional beginnings. As a country that has attracted, conquered, colonized, and categorized populations called Latino/Hispanic, the United States establishes a set of conditions that make it feasible to fashion a Latino literary history from the early nineteenth century to the present. But to demonstrate a trajectory from the pre-national past to the present calls for a rigorous consideration of what exactly is moving across history. This type of work is possible as a result of ongoing work in historical scholarship.

Given the theoretical unraveling of literary history and the emphasis on the present in much Latino studies, scholars in literary historical scholarship under the aegis of Hispanic/Latino studies have been fighting against intellectual trends that attempt to unravel the very project which they undertake. And yet the volumes of *Recovering the US Hispanic Literary Heritage* offer a variety of scenarios that open a conversation into how we might begin piecing together histories of Latino literature. Numerous monographs shed light on specific writers and texts. The collection of essays *The Latino Nineteenth Century* (2016), which I coedited with Jesse Alemán, contains articles that allow us to approach multiple sites of analysis even as they continue the process of introducing new texts. The historical scholarship of the last twenty-five years has started to present the outlines of potential new diachronic histories of Latino literature that retain the complexity of archival challenges: dislocation, destruction, disorganization, and occlusion as well as revelation. The imperative of recovery is still important, and attempts to build narratives across decades or centuries will necessarily have to account for ongoing archival encounters. Latino literary history will need to consider potential gaps and confront the historical erasure of certain writing and the people that produced it; that occlusion is inherent in the deployment of the term "Latino."[3]

I retain the term "literature" in histories of Latino literature rather than use "textual" or "writing" to preclude the type of imbalance by which some traditions or people have literature while others have writing. In my usage, "literature" does not refer solely to the genres of poetry and fiction that are prevalent in many twentieth-century invocations of the term. I start with one of the general definitions – "printed matter of any kind" – but also include unpublished writing, including epistolary writing. A Latino literary history would have to recognize the heterogeneity, even the fragmented nature, of its archival remains. Materials produced over the centuries ranged from broadsides to pamphlets to economic treatises. Many newspapers remain only in partial run or even single issues. The term "literature" also encompasses "letters" not only in the epistolary sense (and there are some interesting letters in archives) but rather a broad range of textual production, from personal writing to published books. The point here is that the historical

---

[3] Following other critics, I use "Latino" rather than the gendered "Latino/a" to complicate the notion that the term can name people historically and in relation to specific genders. See, for example, Beltrán 5.

study of Latino literature scrambles the reliance on genre. In the early nineteenth century, for example, novels and poems were not the mainstay of Latino publishing in the United States.

One of the major challenges of literary history, as already noted, is establishing an account of change across time. How to move from one decade or century to another? In order to begin such a project, I turn to the nineteenth century, a period rich in recent recovery scholarship. Studies by numerous scholars have shown that the Latino nineteenth century is a period rich in a variety of publications that appeared in connection with numerous hemispheric sociopolitical events. Throughout the century, the types of texts published and the emphasis of the writers changed, from the anticolonial arguments by Spanish American exiles and migrants in the Northeast early in the century to the engagement with US racial politics and the importance of the Caribbean in the late century. One major difference between the Latino nineteenth-century and other forms of "American litera-ture" is the importance of the Spanish language. Another difference emerges from the inevitable connections to various sites throughout the hemisphere. While not all US literature has hemispheric dimensions, Latino literature almost always engages other points in the hemisphere, not only in content but sometimes also through histories of circulation.

As we move from the early century to the late, an outline of a history of Latino literature begins to emerge. The century gives us at least three phases: the multiplicity of writing associated with independence movements (1790s–1830s), the rise of newspaper publishing at a time when wars and filibustering expeditions affected inter-American relations (1840s–1860s), and the increased interest in fiction, poetry, and crónicas during years when the US positions itself as an imperialist power in the Americas (1870s–1900). The changes emerge in relation to evolving print culture conditions but more importantly are connected to political and military conditions that offer important con-texts for Latino populations. My outline of phases in the nineteenth century is bound to produce criticism, some of it as a result of complications that are bracketed by the emphasis on certain aspects or historical conditions of the texts produced. But my argument is suggestive rather than proscriptive, and I emphasize the need for a multiplicity of histories rather than a singular narrative. The sheer variety of texts that come under the historical banner of Latino literature can point in various directions, and the archive is not static but rather moving in unexpected directions.

A significant amount of textual production is in dialogue with historical events, as these events prompt the US annexation of populations as well as changing notions of social identity. Technologies of publishing facilitate greater engagement with the issues that emerge as a result of significant events in US–Latin American relations, including the US–Mexico War. In the early nineteenth century, for example, the Spanish American Wars of Independence influenced the production of texts in US cities even as US printers committed to Spanish-language publishing not only for readers in the US but also in other parts of the Americas, thus entering what I would call, to invoke Immanuel Wallerstein, a "world system" that is both transatlantic and hemispheric. As such, war and independence movements became intertwined with print-culture relations that stretched across nation-states; writing published in New York and Philadelphia circulated in other parts of the hemisphere, a process that critics from Gruesz to Anna Brickhouse have referred to as "trans-American."

Literary historical narratives, as well as methodologies for approaching the questions of literary history, would have to contend with at least four theoretical and historical areas, which we can broadly articulate as political context, incorporation of populations, changing notions of communal formation, and print-culture conditions. These are interconnected and even intertwined so that changes in print culture (e.g., the growth of Spanish-language newspapers) cannot be divorced from political developments that sometimes motivated those publications. The question of communal formations and their relationship to textual consumption calls for a theoretical-historical analysis of ethnic labels and self-identification.

In the second part of this chapter, I focus on texts that allow for historical consideration over roughly seventy years. Rather than a definitive narrative, I offer a set of connections that bring together texts produced in the early, mid, and late nineteenth century. I focus on how white Creoles fomented economic relations between the United States and Latin America within a liberal economic frame that did little to redress economic inequality across the hemisphere. Writers in the early century popularized the production of political publications to circulate in Latin America and the Caribbean, and this continued throughout the century, but so did the fostering of macroeconomic relations that benefitted those who were economically powerful. This is by no means the only story to be told about nineteenth-century Latinos, but it is an important one that brings forward how textual production is inextricable from larger economic processes of capital accumulation. It also prompts us to consider the twists of anticolonial thinking, how opponents of Spanish colonial rule who may have conceived of themselves as fighting for liberation turned to conceptions of political economy that were not necessarily beneficial to all Latinos in the United States or abroad. Furthermore, considering the role of race (whiteness) in the textual production of the Latino nineteenth century shows how the historical deployment of the term "Latino" contains racialized hierarchies.

A History of Commercial Connections

The three phases that I have divided roughly into the early, mid-, and late nineteenth century differed in important ways from the contemporary period, which gives us writers producing fiction, poetry, and nonfiction in a marketplace that emphasizes certain genres. By contrast, the early nineteenth century in the United States and Spanish America had not yet seen the emergence of the professional writer devoted to poetry and fiction, and even those who have in retrospect garnered canonical fame as literary artistes (e.g., José María Heredia as poet) did not work exclusively in a literary vein. (Heredia eventually worked as a government functionary in Mexico.) Many of the publications that appeared in the United States before the 1830s are difficult to classify generically, and they ranged from economic arguments to collections of political essays. We see textual variety, for example, in considering two important publications: Vicente Rocafuerte's *Ideas necesarias a todo pueblo americano independiente, que quiera ser libre* (Philadelphia, 1821), a collection of translations of US revolutionary documents, and Felix Varela's *Cartas a Elpidio* (1835–1838), a series of theological reflections. Rocafuerte addressed his book to compatriots in Guayaquil but was also intervening in constitutional debates in Mexico while Varela addressed readers in his home country of Cuba while working as a priest in the United States. These books, like many of their historical counterparts coming out of print shops in Philadelphia and New York in the early century, cannot be extricated from the print culture conditions that inspired US printers to venture into Spanish-language publishing. I refer to them as fragments because it is not easy to place some of them in the literary historical narratives that are available (e.g., history of the novel or poetry).

A book that exemplifies this complicated archive is the 119-page *An Exposition of the Commerce of Spanish America; With Some Observations Upon Its Importance to the United States* (Philadelphia, 1816). Its author was Manuel Torres, a wealthy intellectual who left Colombia after taking part in a movement against Spanish colonialism and went on to settle in Philadelphia from 1796 until his death in 1822. During his years in the United States, Torres worked tirelessly in support of independence movements in

Spanish America. He was very well connected politically and personally, claiming as a close friend William Duane, the influential editor of the Philadelphia *Aurora Commercial Advertiser* newspaper. In the early 1820s, as it became clear that new nations would emerge in South America, Torres met several times with John Quincy Adams, secretary of state in the James Monroe Administration, to advocate for recognition of emerging governments. Shortly before his death, Torres was received by President Monroe himself as the first ambassador from one of the new Spanish American republics ("South America"). In Philadelphia, Torres hosted a growing community of Spanish-speaking intellectuals and became a stopping point for revolutionaries from South America who made their way to the United States. Historians have surmised that Torres may have helped procure support, including arms, for Francisco de Miranda's failed landing in Venezuela in 1806 and, later, for Simón Bolívar via Bolívar's brother (Bowman 30–34). Emily García, whose scholarship has brought Torres to the forefront in Latino literature, has presented Torres as a figure whose political commitments were integral to his moving in elite Anglo-American circles. His prominence is evident in a plaque that García located at St. Mary's Roman Catholic Church in Philadelphia, which commemorates his burial in the church graveyard: "As Minister of the Republic of Colombia he was the first Latin American diplomatic representative in the United States of America. Tribute from the Government of Colombia and from Philadelphia descendants of his friends. July 20, 1926" (García 71).

Torres cannot be separated from Philadelphia, which hosted an important community of exiles and migrants from Spanish America and became the most important site for Hispanophone publication and Spanish American revolutionary activity in the early US republic. Rocafuerte, Heredia, and others referred to the city as "la famosa Filadelfia," a city that brought together the symbolic potential of revolution and the presses to publish books critical of Spanish colonialism, even as it presented a model of liberal economics that writers believed could be transferred to other countries in the Americas. Spanish-language books coming out of Philadelphia ranged from studies of constitutional theory to translations of European philosophy to gift books. Among these books were political and economic tracts that were important to the intellectual circle of Torres and other opponents of Spanish colonialism. By the 1820s, Philadelphia printers entered a network of international publishing and circulation, even as the city hosted a nascent Spanish-speaking community. In other words, the city is an early example of how the nexus of writing/publishing among Spanish speakers in the United States was intertwined with economic and political transformation that spanned the Americas. And thus it was no surprise that Torres in one of his books chose to take up the question of US–Spanish American economic relations as they pertained to the hemisphere's future.

Torres's *An Exposition* was no less than an economic manual promoting investment in Spanish America. It opens with a clear statement about its audience, goals, and perspective on the relationship between government and economics:

> The different matters of this work, destined to guide merchants in their commercial operations, will also be very useful to every one who buys, sells, or exchanges in any way: to the farmer and to the insurer, to the banker and to the statesman. There is such an intimate connexion between political economy and commerce, that no one can become acquainted with the former, without knowing well the latter; and, in order to acquire this knowledge, the different monies, weights, measures, exchanges, and every thing relative to national as well as foreign commerce, must be well known. (Torres 1)

Torres connected the supposition of economic usefulness (for the United States) to trade on an international scale. His use of "political economy" emphasized the relationship of production within nation-states and their trade. The book's emphasis on "monies, weights, measures, exchanges" situated economic interests in the realm of international commerce. To that end, Torres set out not only to present "a precise statement of the articles annually exported from the different departments of Spanish America to foreign countries, and their value" (4) but also to provide an accounting of the measures and weights and rates of exchange in various settings. That exchange would be carried out not only hemispherically but also with England, France, and other European countries.

An Exposition is a serious persuasive attempt to get more US merchants trading with Spanish America. The book's first half argues that Spanish America is a site with resources that can be tapped and also declares that the region is undergoing important political changes. Touting "the rich commerce of that part of the new world" (7), Torres positions Spanish America as a potential market for goods produced in the United States or other countries. Spanish America "consumes yearly, the value of one hundred millions of dollars in articles of foreign manufacturing industry" (11). He also holds out the area's resources as ripe for the taking: "It is there, and only there, that all nations can obtain, with facility, those precious metals, which have become so necessary to trade throughout the world, and particularly

Asia" (11). In other words, Torres is doing the work of global capitalism, situating the United States as an exporter nation in search of markets and offering Spanish America as a resource for raw goods. "The United States, more than other nations, have a powerful interest in an extensive participation of it, in carrying thither foreign or domestic mercantile articles, either from their own ports, or from those of Europe, where suitable assortments could be procured, to be changed in South America for the precious metals, or for raw materials" (11), the latter including cochineal, indigo, logwood, and even medicinal plants. By this logic, the United States would become the dominant (free) trading partner, dislodging Spain's colonial mercantile policies.

Torres argues in the 1810s that trade is becoming easier with Spanish America because of important political changes leading to an end of Spanish colonial protectionist policies. The book praises "the efforts of its inhabitants to shake off the yoke of the Spanish government" and "the extraordinary progress of their revolution" (7). Torres anticipated that they would become fully independent and saw the potential for an increase in North–South trade as a result of that change. In a curious phrase that echoes Bolívar's dream of a united Spanish America, Torres ventures that it is only a matter of time for complete emancipation and "the establishment of a new, powerful, and independent empire, (probably) under the form of a representative and central government" (7).

Torres's enthusiasm for US merchants to trade with other parts of the Americas shows his investment in a global capitalist system. He was an upper-class white man whose distance from South America's indigenous populations was expressed most clearly in a paternal benevolence toward the laborers on his plantation in Colombia. His position in the United States cannot be extricated from the racialized economic hierarchies of Spanish America, or North America, and he was connected to the intellectual elite in Philadelphia. *An Exposition*, replete with commercial information, is a reminder that Torres moves in the world of bankers and investors rather than financially strapped immigrants, and the dominant mode of thinking for him is commercial exchange and capital accumulation across the hemisphere.

Torres's enthusiasm for US investment in the Americas opens a trajectory that allows us to consider the production of the newspaper *La Verdad*, which appeared in New York as a group of Cuban exiles became enamored with the possibility of Cuba's annexation to the United States. Published between 1848 and 1860, *La Verdad* is one of many Spanish-language newspapers that circulated in the United States in the mid-nineteenth century, sometimes with the goal of reaching other countries.[4] Eastern cities, particularly New Orleans and New York, saw a variety of periodicals emerge. In the Western United States, the number of presses increased after the US annexation of territories following the Treaty of Guadalupe Hidalgo, although that historical event did not immediately lead to an independent Latino press. In some cases, Anglo Americans controlled bilingual papers with Spanish-language pages (Meléndez 22–23). New York in the 1850s became a crucible of Cuban-exile publications, including periodicals that sometimes lasted a few issues. And it is in the context of this print-culture activity that *La Verdad* became an influential and constant attempt to reach readers both in the USA and Cuba. One of its stated goals was to bypass colonial censorship on the island and offer "the truth" to Cubans in Cuba.

Funded in part by wealthy Cuban exiles, *La Verdad* featured a colorful masthead with a drawing of the island of Cuba and the phrase "El Patriotismo Cubano Sostiene Este Periódico Para Circularlo Gratis" (Cuban patriotism ensures the free circulation of this newspaper). *La Verdad* featured an almost never-ending stream of political articles about conditions on the island and the need to bring an end to Spanish colonialism. It included some English-language articles, presumably written by Anglo Americans in conjunction with Cubans (most are unsigned). The newspaper veered from a proto-national Cuban position to support of the island's annexation to the United States, making it a multivocal textual production. In truth, *La Verdad* was the product of a marriage of convenience between US-based expansionists and Cuban exiles. Among proponents of US expansion into Cuba supporting the newspaper were Moses Yale Beach, editor of the New York *Sun*, which printed the paper on its presses; the journalist Jane McManus Storm Cazneau, who wrote under the pen name Cora Montgomery; and John L. O'Sullivan, the activist editor who coined the term "Manifest Destiny"; among the Cuban group were writers and journalists such as Miguel Teurbe Tolón and the novelist Cirilo Villaverde, who tended more toward a Cuban nationalist position, as well as Cuban businessmen who believed annexation would help the island avoid potential turmoil and a slave insurrection. This meant that sometimes articles and even poems were closer to the aspirations of the writers from Cuba, who wanted to liberate the island, whereas at other times the newspaper seemed to speak for the expansionist US cause.

---

[4] For a bibliography of newspapers, see Kanellos and Martell.

La Verdad is exemplary of historical challenges presented by periodicals in that they do not abide by the contemporary byline connecting a published article to a name. The notion of a unitary writing subject who owns his or her work is not operative in conditions where what the paper says (not to mention the ads it prints) is more important than who is saying it. For scholars of Latino literature this has meant delving into a terrain that is disconnected from notions of authorial presence. While we can connect Torres to *An Exposition*, it is more difficult to connect Latino writers to the articles they published or even the newspapers they edited. In the case of *La Verdad*, Cuban exiles became associated with the paper's expansionist politics, even though they may have harbored individual positions that broke from that position.

In its enthusiasm for promoting commercial exchange between Cuba and the United States, *La Verdad* picked up where Manuel Torres's *An Exposition* had left off. The paper appealed directly to commercial interests, and it made a case for Cuba's separation from Spain and annexation to the United States: "Cuba seems placed by the finger of a kindly Providence, between the Atlantic and the Mexican seas at the crossing point of all the great lines of our immense coasting trade, to serve as the centre of exchange for a domestic commerce as extensive as our territory, and as free as our institutions," one article argued ("Series" 10). Here the perspective of expansionists emerges in the language of Manifest Destiny, as the piece claims a providential reason for annexation. Furthermore, it made the case that annexation would open the island to trade with other US states without the tariffs imposed by Spanish colonial authorities.

> Official documents show that out of the 20 or 22 millions of dollars of annual exportations into Cuba, fifteen millions are in provisions, fabrics, lumber and materials which one or the other of the United States could better supply than any other country; but through the multitude of taxes and restrictions imposed by European policy not more than a third of it comes from our fields and factories ("Series" 11).

While Torres's *An Exposition* made a case that US merchants should find ways to increase trade with Spanish America, *La Verdad* situated annexation as the machination that would clear the way for such exchange to emerge outside of the fetters of Spain's protectionist policies. With Hispanisms such as "22 millions of dollars," the passage above shows the participation of native Spanish speakers in the production of *La Verdad*. Furthermore, it shows that these writers viewed individual US states as having independence of trade rather than conceiving of that strictly along national lines. Annex-ation was acceptable because US states presumably had economic autonomy.

Because of its annexationist leanings, *La Verdad* showed the contradictions inherent in the elite *criollo* vision that situated anti-Spanish politics above the potential for Cuba's independence. *Criollo* here is a reference to the racialized economic hierarchies of Latin America, which sometimes transferred over to the United States. The paper's racial politics reflected the positions adopted by its white editors, including the white Cubans involved in the publication. More often than not, the newspaper bracketed the question of slavery or attempted to appeal to readers on both sides of the US North/South debate. But one article spelled out the paper's position on race and slavery by explaining conditions in the following terms: Spain inflected "horrors" on the island, which included ongoing participation in the slave trade and the subjugation of free Mexicans into debt peonage; these conditions could prompt an insurrection that would result in a Haiti-like blood-bath; one of the alternatives, independence for the island, would mean "the whites who are but little inferior in numbers to the blacks, will maintain the ascendancy by their superior intelligence, and slavery will probably be abolished by slow degrees" ("A Series" 4). White supremacist thinking drives the analysis of both of these potential scenarios: a slave revolt or sudden abolition. The article then positions annexation as the best option because supposedly it would bring an end to participation in the slave trade and set free the Mexican people being pressed into bondage; Cuba would then enter the Union as a slave-holding state but be on a course toward "gradual emancipa-tion." Stopping short of calling for abolition, *La Verdad*'s editors also argue that slavery was not sustainable on economic grounds.

These types of racial politics, driven as they are by economic considerations, are an important dimension of Latino literary history. The act of recovery and contextualization, although it adds to creating a more nuanced vision of the past, does not in itself lead to a redemptive literary history. The recovery of historical figures and their texts in light of the privileged economic positions of white *criollos* instead can bring forward an encounter with hierarchies of privilege that can travel across the Americas. In the early years of the Recover-ing the Hispanic Literary Heritage Project, scholars were conscious of how historical scholarship would bump up against the "Spanish ideology of racial superiority" (Gutiérrez and Padilla 19), even as they called for examining the "silence and resistance of female and subaltern voices" (Gutiérrez and Padilla 25). What has become increasingly clear is that both ideology and resistance in Latino history are intertwined with the contradictions of a world capitalist system that privileges white economic elites, both Latino and Anglo. From Torres and others in his group during the early nineteenth century to the annexationist Cubans of the mid century, writers developed an economy of print by which published materials addressed hemispheric economic questions, in a way that sustained criollo economic power. Texts also responded in a contrapuntal way, to use Edward Said's term, to illuminate challenges to the economic hierarchy. For example, the periodical *El Mulato* (New York, 1854), which published an abolitionist serialized novella called *El negro mártir*, characterized itself as socialist and defended both Cuban independence and the elimination of slavery.[5]

Economies of print, intertwined as they were with the elite status of many writers, also emerge in the third phase of the Latino nineteenth century, the three final decades leading to the War of 1898. In this period fiction of varying lengths circulates more widely, and writers publish a number of novels in both English and Spanish. (This change is accompanied with the ongoing importance of periodicals so that newspapers continue to proliferate from one phase to another.) The publication of particular genres, as it should become clear, is not constant over time for Latino literature. *Jicoténcal* (1826) is one of several Hispanophone novels published in the early nineteenth-century USA, including translations of novels by Europeans. But it would be difficult to make a case for fiction as a dominant mode in US Latino literature prior to the 1860s, which presents difficulties for writing histories in relation to literary genres. Wendell Harris referred to accounts of changes in literary genres as "histories of a type," arguing that these literary histories "chronicle the facts of succession and change, the explanations of which changes are understood to lie primarily within the relations between author and author, text and text" (442). But my goal is not to plot the changes in Latino fiction over the century but rather to point out that fiction becomes increasingly popular in the late century, introducing a new dimension of print culture's economic domain.

Latino writers entered a marketplace of fiction that differed in important ways from conditions in the early nineteenth century. For example, Cirilo Villaverde, who had not devoted himself to fiction for almost thirty years in the United States, returned to one of his earlier fictional creations and prepared the final edition of *Cecilia Valdés* in 1882. This publication was connected to the New York commercial newspaper *El Espejo*, which was its

---

[5] On *El Mulato*, see Lazo, *Writing*, 141–67. David Luis-Brown elaborates on Lazo's work in his 2009 article.

publisher and featured advertisements appealing to readers in the United States and the island who may have felt nostalgia for the Cuba of the 1830s. While in this case, the periodical *El Espejo* provided the printing press for a standalone book, in other cases periodicals featured short fiction. As John Alba Cutler has argued, Latino short fiction constitutes a "fugitive" archive that crossed the United States and other parts of the Americas and was connected to newspaper publication (Cutler). (More scholarly work needs to be done on specific works of short fiction as well as the print culture conditions of particular newspapers.) Stories sometimes engaged the political challenges faced by Latinos in the United States, but writers also sought to enter a broader literary discussion, which Cutler ties to a world republic of letters. José Martí, whose publications are predominantly crónicas and poems, wrote *Amistad Funesta* (Baneful friendship), which appeared in serialized form in the New York newspaper *El Latino-Americano* and was later published as the book *Lucía Jerez*. Laura Lomas has argued that Martí published the novel for economic gain under the pseudonym Adelaida Ral so as to capitalize on women readers. "Similarly, the translation project of *Ramona* acknowledges the power of women as writers and consumers of books, insofar as Martí sought to make money through its sales," Lomas writes (247).

The late-century writer whose textual production exemplifies Latino writers' entrance into a marketplace of fiction that included not only Spanish- but also English-language books is María Amparo Ruiz de Burton. Her particular situation shows that a personal stake in making money came to be part of the publication process. While Torres had published *An Exposition* with the goal of promoting commerce in the Americas, writers in the late century intertwined their political viewpoints with the creation of novels and stories that could sell on the marketplace. In Ruiz de Burton's case, her sharp political viewpoints were conveyed in fiction that leaned toward the sensational and the sentimental. This marks a change in the trajectory that I have been outlining here from early-century examples of intellectuals producing works in accordance with the interests of their class to late-century examples of writers driven by a potential market for the writing.

In the last three decades, Ruiz de Burton's work has received more critical attention in the United States than other nineteenth-century Latino writers because she published both of her major novels in English. This has facilitated her inclusion in Anglophone US literature courses and scholarship. Critics have analyzed her subject positions and political perspectives, and many critics have considered the way *Who Would Have Thought It?* (1872) and

The Squatter and the Don (1885) engage with nineteenth-century discourses of sentimentalism and Manifest Destiny.[6] I want to situate Ruiz de Burton in the phases I have outlined of a literary history that is connected to print-culture conditions. Historical events such as the US–Mexico War and the US Civil War cannot be separated from Ruiz de Burton's writing or her personal trajectories. Neither can the biographically important event of her husband's death be omitted from the how and why of her fiction. Add to these changes in the marketplace that lead to a growing number of writers, including women, making a living from fiction in the late nineteenth century, and Ruiz de Burton comes to occupy a trajectory of Latino literature tied to economics.

Ruiz de Burton's economy of print was personal, as her reason for taking up the writing of fiction was tied to ongoing financial problems that plagued her after she became a widow. Letters that she wrote in the early 1870s show her struggling to maintain her standard of living while supporting two children who were studying on the East Coast. She claimed title to the Jamul ranch near San Diego, but that was a contested land that hosted the types of cattle-shooting squatters who made it into her second novel. Ruiz de Burton also had claim to two tracts in Baja California, which she hoped to sell in order to get much-needed cash. This brought her into contact with a lawyer, Samuel Latham Mitchell Barlow, who worked for the Lower California Colonization Company (Sánchez and Pita, "Letters" 207). Letters show that she called on Barlow to help her sell the Baja tracts. Writing from the Grand Hotel in San Francisco in 1872, she told Barlow that she also hoped to travel to the East Coast to see about "a land claim I would like to attend to in Washington" ("Letters" 433). In other words, she turned to her lawyer Barlow for multiple finance-related requests, including favorable reviews of her first book, to obtain revenue. Later in 1872, she followed up with the following request to Barlow related to *Who Would Have Thought It?*:

> Did you get my book? And did you send the copies to the newspapers requesting them to give me "a puff"? . . . I thought that after you had promised and pledged your word to have the book favorably noticed, that you would certainly not fail only because you felt some little irritation at something I said on a very hot day when I was very unsupportable mentally and physically.

[6] For debates on Ruiz de Burton's biography and its connection to politics, see Rosaura Sánchez and Beatriz Pita's introductions to the Arte Público editions of the novels by Ruiz de Burton as well as Aranda's article. For a collection of articles about Ruiz de Burton, see Montes and Goldman.

> Was I mistaken? And did I misjudge your character? As I have not seen any notice of the book I really do not know what to think. ("Letters" 433–34)

Like other writers, Ruiz de Burton allows Spanish words to influence her English prose: "unsupportable" acknowledges she was *insoportable* (unbearable). Later that year she wrote again to Barlow inquiring about the sale of the land in Baja, then took up the book again with a reference to its publisher, J. B. Lippincott, in Philadelphia.

> I will write today to Mr. Lippincott telling him to send *you* a copy, and then you must really do all you can for me. . . . I hope you will give me all the benefit of your influence with the New York Press, for I would like to make the venture a little bit profitable. I did not write for glory. ("Letters" 427–438)

Whatever literary aspirations she may have had, it becomes clear that one of her major concerns was making money from the sale of the book. These letters display a less than romantic approach to literary production: a brutal recognition of publicity as an important factor in the book's financial results.

Amelia María de la Luz Montes has noted that the novel eventually received several reviews, not all positive. Montes writes that in one review Ruiz de Burton "explains her decision to have the publisher omit her name (it was published anonymously) because she felt the book should be criticized solely on the writing – as she feared that a Mexican American would not be considered capable of writing such a book" (Montes, "Introduction" xxi). Ruiz de Burton may have wanted a fair reading, but she may also have worried that prejudice against her as a Mexican American writer could have curtailed sales.

Ruiz de Burton points to an important change. For much of the nineteenth century, Latino literature was written predominantly in Spanish. (Torres was an exception when he wrote in English in Philadelphia.) For the most part, Latino writers sought to reach multiple Hispanophone audiences in the Americas. Ruiz de Burton, whose fiction considers sites outside of the United States and raises questions of hemispheric political conditions, presents a model of a writer who sought to sell her fiction in an Anglophone marketplace. This turn toward English will become increasingly important in the twentieth century and cannot be divorced from changes in economies of print.

The importance of writing for profit is not in what it tells us about Ruiz de Burton. Women writing for money was not unusual by the 1870s, and we know that Ruiz de Burton had financial troubles and as a widow and single mother was constantly looking for economic lifelines. Rather, the importance is that it shows how at this moment in the history of Latino literature, a woman could aspire to enter the publication market with at least the potential for monetary gain. This is a far cry from the publication projects of the early nineteenth century, when writing was an exclusive fraternity for men who had resources to pay for a run of a publication. In early Philadelphia, printers sometimes looked for profits in Spanish-language books, but Latino writers did not turn to fiction for money. By the late century that had changed, and because Ruiz de Burton moved in elite circles in California and the East Coast, she provides another example of the influential role of white *criollos* in the history of Latino literature.

The response of the Latino elite to indigenous populations and blacks is a question that spans the century. In the case of Torres, he considered indigenous populations who had not integrated themselves into Spanish society outside the orbit of governmental reach. He argues that representative government "will procure happiness to nineteen millions of people already civilized, and prepare the same advantage for a vast number of aborigines, who are yet in their primitive state of independence" (7). In this case, the opposition between civilization and barbarism that reappears in Latin American history is framed in relation to US forms of government. In the case of *La Verdad*, the anticolonial position of Creoles is intertwined with support for a Cuban-born white ruling class that would attend to the question of slavery only after the island had separated from Spain. Ruiz de Burton also engages with racial hierarchies, privileging white skin and portraying indigenous and black characters as inferior, even as she criticized New England's racism against people of Latin American descent. Numerous scholars have criticized the racial politics of Ruiz de Burton's work, in some cases noting her affiliation with Southern Confederates.[7]

In the three examples from different parts of the century, historical hierarchies emerge that place white *criollos* with access to financial assets in a position that allows them to publish texts that are important to Latino literary history. Their personal economic and social resources are an important dimension in the production of texts that they believed could cross nations or languages and engage with a reading public situated in multiple sites. In tracing one vein of Latino literature through the nineteenth century, I have focused on white elites driven by economic conditions either at the macro scales of world systems or in relation to an individual household. This is one potential narrative, and an important one. But it is not the only one,

---

[7] See, for example, Aranda and the essays by Jesse Alemán and John M. González in the collection edited by Montes and Goldman.

and histories of Latino literature, rather than one literary history, will have to contend with multiple conditions of publication.

The influence of the trans-American elite on textual production in the nineteenth-century United States reminds us of the need to grapple with the historical dimension of latinidades. Those who saw themselves in a social formation under a Latino/Hispano label in the United States of necessity grappled with and responded to an Anglo-American majority culture, but the turn toward latinidad was affected by geographic and social location as well as the particular historical juncture, as we see in different parts of the century.

The discourse of *la raza Latina* that began to circulate in the 1830s, for example, is at once a response to the growing Anglo-US domination of the hemisphere but also an attempt to emphasize a Francophilic and European element in the history of the Americas. In his influential study *América Latina y la latinidad*, Arturo Ardao traced the use of *la raza Latina* not only to various intellectuals from Latin America (including José María Torres Caicedo and his poem "Las dos Américas") but also to European influences. The Spanish *raza*, closer historically to "lineage" than to the twentieth-century English "race," was deployed at first to highlight the achievements of a people going back to Roman greatness. Among the influences on the conception of *la raza Latina* was the French intellectual Michel Chevalier, a French statesman and economist who sought to build an alliance between Mexico and France as part of "Latin" people. Chevalier positioned Mexico as a site where the greatness of Latin (French-inflected) Catholicism could respond to the Protestant North. Chevalier framed the major questions as follows: "whether the genius of Catholicism, when in close contact with that of Protestantism, can preserve its position, or whether in our times Catholicism can restore a healthy tone to a people struck with the languor of decay" (91). For Chevalier, it was Catholicism that offered a contrast to the Protestant North and to the "decay" that he saw as a potential future for Spanish America. "Let us remember that France has a vaster interest than is generally conceived in this question, for it has ever been and still is the corypheus of Catholic nations; and from this fact derives its chiefest claim to greatness" (91). This connection to France allowed the emergence of a *Latin* America that was not primarily tied to Spain.

Given this kind of Franco-Mexican celebration, it should be no surprise that Ruiz de Burton took a Francophilic turn. In one of her letters, Ruiz de Burton wrote, "La historia no miente y la historia nos dice cuan gloriosa ha sido la carrera de la raza Latina" (History does not lie and history tells us how glorious has been the development of la raza Latina.) (Sánchez and Pita, *Conflicts* 301). As if influenced by Chevalier, Ruiz de Burton emphasized the importance of France: "De las naciones Latinas, ¿cuál es la única que progresa? La

Francia...¿Por qué? porque es la única que adoptando todos los adelantos del siglo...en ideas y materialmente – ha conservado un gobierno que es el único capaz de manejar a los franceses" (Of all the Latin nations which is the only one that progresses? France... Why? Because it is the only one that by adopting all of the advances of the century...in ideas and materially – has maintained a government that is the only one capable of leading the French.) (Sánchez and Pita, *Conflicts* 301). The passage is a response to US Manifest Destiny and attempts to position Latin people along a differential cultural and *historical* lineage than the rising empire of the United States.

Other nineteenth-century writers in the United States also used the phrase *la raza Latina*, including the Cuban Juan Clemente Zenea in one of his final poems. And the newspaper editor Ramón de Contador y Muñiz published a newspaper in San Francisco in the late 1870s with the title *El Eco de la Raza Latina*. Contador's usage was pluralistic, and he attempted to cross national lines and build readership in the Americas and Spain. Contador described his paper as "el organo de los intereses materiales y morales de España y los españoles en particular, y de toda la raza latina en general" or, in his own English description, "the organ of the moral, political and commercial interests of all the latine race." The Francophone adjective "latine" displays his own engagement with France. (Contador was fluent in French and translated texts from French into Spanish for his newspaper.) But by 1878, the year from which we have an issue of his paper, Contador was less interested in France than with a more general Hispanic world market (Lazo, "Introduction" 1–3).

An emphasis on a Frenchified and Catholic *raza Latina* tells one story in the Latino nineteenth century that is connected to white elites. Torres, the contributors to *La Verdad*, and Ruiz de Burton all were part of the upper class of their Latin American societies and thus willing to conceptualize Latinos in the United States as participating in a world economy that was intertwined with their textual production. But that is only one story. Alternate literary trajectories can be traced, particularly in relation to versions of latinidad that consider indigenous, African, and multiracial working-class influences. Scholars such as Nicolás Kanellos, Nancy Mirabal, and Laura Lomas are currently working on latinidades influenced by Afro-Caribbean subjects who contended with racism against blacks in the late nineteenth-century United States. In those contexts, the economic dimensions of US urban conditions become an important factor.

I have outlined a series of problems that are important to the nineteenth century as well as other historical periods: 1) the role of print-culture conditions and the market at both local and international levels 2) how race and class influence writers and their conceptions of commercial processes, and the changing role of gender in the literary marketplace 3) the position exhibited by a text in relation to indigenous and enslaved or post-plantation populations and 4) conceptions of latinidad across time. By analyzing these types of questions it would be possible to underscore racial and economic oppression, two ongoing preoccupations of contemporary Latino studies, as possible connections across time. Ruiz de Burton also alerts us to changes in the participation of women in print culture. Such considerations would move literary history away from an emphasis on literary genre and toward thematic and content-driven analyses, often in hemispheric contexts, that are crucial to the literature under consideration. The question of power and the economic capacity and connections of the participants are at the center of nineteenth-century print culture, and that allows for a possible narrative move into other periods. My suggestions for the writing of histories of Latino literature are not proscriptive, and others may choose to emphasize different aspects of history or even how latinidad is defined historically. But regardless of the route taken, literary history will have to offer an accounting of the common elements that move across time – as opposed to relying on generalities about an amorphous Latino identity.

WORKS CITED

Aranda, José. "Contradictory Impulses: María Amparo Ruiz de Burton, Resistance Theory, and the Politics of Chicano/a Studies." *American Literature* 70 (September 1998): 551–79.

Beltrán, Cristina. *The Trouble with Unity: Latino Politics and the Creation of Identity*. New York: Oxford University Press, 2010.

Bowman, Charles H., Jr., "Manuel Torres: A Spanish American Patriot in Philadelphia, 1796–1822," *The Pennsylvania Magazine of History and Biography* 94: 1 (Jan. 1970): 26–53.

Bruce-Novoa, Juan. "Shipwrecked in the Seas of Signification: Cabeza de Vaca's *Relación* and Chicano Literature." *Reconstructing a Chicano/a Literary Heritage: Hispanic Colonial Literature of the Southwest*. Ed. María Herrera-Sobek. Tucson: University of Arizona Press, 1993. 3–23.

Chevalier, Michel. *Mexico: Before and After the Conquest*. Trans. Fayette Robinson. Philadelphia: Carey and Hart, 1846.

Coronado, Raúl. *A World Not to Come: A History of Latino Writing and Print Culture*. Cambridge, MA: Harvard University Press, 2013.

Cutler, John Alba. "Toward a Reading of Nineteenth-Century Latino/a Short Fiction." *The Latino Nineteenth Century*. Ed. Rodrigo Lazo and Jesse Alemán. New York: NYU Press, 2016.

Dalleo, Raphael and Elena Machado Sáez, *The Latino/a Canon and the Emergence of Post-Sixties Literature*. New York: Palgrave Macmillan, 2007.

García, Emily. "On the Borders of Independence: Manuel Torres and Spanish American Independence in Filadelphia." *The Latino Nineteenth Century*. Eds. Rodrigo Lazo and Jesse Alemán. New York: NYU Press, 2016.

Gruesz, Kirsten Silva. *Ambassadors of Culture: The Transamerican Origins of Latino Writing*. Princeton: Princeton University Press, 2002.

"What Was Latino Literature?" *PMLA* 127 (March 2012): 335–41.

Gutiérrez, Ramon A. and Genaro Padilla, "Introduction." *Recovering the US Hispanic Literary Heritage*. Houston, TX: Arte Público Press, 1993.

Harris, Wendell V. "What Is Literary History?" *College English* 56: 4 (April 1994): 434–51.

Johnstone, Robert. "The Impossible Genre: Reading Comprehensive Literary History," *PMLA* 107: 1 (Jan. 1992): 26–37.

Kanellos, Nicolás, et al., eds. *Herencia: The Anthology of Hispanic Literature of the United States*. New York and Oxford: Oxford University Press, 2002.

Lazo, Rodrigo. "Introduction". *The Latino Nineteenth Century, Ed*. Rodrigo Lazo and Jesse Aleman. New York: NYU Press, 2016.

Lazo, Rodrigo. *Writing to Cuba: Filibustering and Cuban Exiles in the United States*. Chapel Hill: University of North Carolina Press, 2005.

Lomas, Laura. *Translating Empire: José Martí, Migrant Latino Subjects, and American Modernities*. Durham, NC: Duke University Press, 2008.

Luis-Brown, David. "An 1848 for the Americas: The Black Atlantic, "El negro mártir," and Cuban Exile Anticolonialism in New York City." *American Literary History* 21: 3 (Fall 2009): 431–63.

Meléndez, A. Gabriel. *Spanish-Language Newspapers in New Mexico, 1834–1958*. Tucson: University of Arizona Press, 2005.

Mignolo, Walter. "Capitalism and Geopolitics of Knowledge: Latin American Social Thought and Latino/a American Studies." *Critical Latin American and Latino Studies*. Ed. Juan Poblete. Minneapolis: University of Minnesota Press, 2003.

Montes, Amelia María de la Luz. "Introduction." *Who Would Have Thought It?* New York: Penguin Books, 2009. xi–xxiii.

Montes, Amelia María de la Luz and Anne Elizabeth Goldman, eds. *María Amparo Ruiz de Burton: Critical and Pedagogical Perspectives*. Lincoln: University of Nebraska Press, 2004.

Padilla, Genaro. *My History, Not Yours: The Formation of Mexican American Autobiography*. Madison: University of Wisconsin Press, 1993.

Perkins, David. *Is Literary History Possible?* Baltimore and London: Johns Hopkins University Press, 1992.

Sánchez, Rosaura and Beatrice Pita, eds. *Conflicts of Interest: The Letters of María Amparo Ruiz de Burton*. Houston, TX: Arte Público Press, 2001.

A Series of Articles on the Cuban Question. By the Editors of "La Verdad." New York, 1849.

"South America (From the Boston Patriot)," *Aurora General Advertiser*, July 2, 1822, 2.

Stavans, Ilan, et al., eds. *The Norton Anthology of Latino Literature*. New York and London: W. W. Norton, 2011.

Torres, Manuel. *An Exposition of the Commerce of Spanish America; With Some Observations Upon Its Importance to the United States*. Philadelphia: G. Palmer, 1816.

Villalon, Oscar. "Into the Mainstream: An Essay from the American Book Review." *Zyzzyva*. Posted May 2, 2011. www.zyzzyva.org/2011/05/02/into-the-mainstream-an-essay-from-the-american-book-review/.

Wellek, René. "Six Types of Literary History." *English Institute Essays*. New York: Columbia, 1947.

10

Narratives of Displacement in Places that Once Were Mexican

JESSE ALEMÁN

Near the end of his autobiography, James Santiago Tafolla recounts crossing the border at the Rio Grande in Texas:

> We got to the very edge of the water... I took off all my clothes, and picked up a stick to use as a staff. It was February, and the water was very cold. The current was very swift and almost swept me away, but I fought it till I got to an island in the middle of the river. I crossed the island, and got to the river branch on the other side. But it occurred to me that my companions might not be safe, considering that a squad of soldiers might come by since they patrolled the river day and night. I went back and helped them cross to the island, and then I went to check the depth on the other side. It was just as deep and just as strong a current, but when I got to the other side... I went back and brought my companions... As soon as the last man had crossed, I shouted "Qué viva México!"   (78–79)

While Tafolla's account captures the trepidation, militarization, collective effort, and elation of getting to the other side, *al otro lado*, this is no run-of-the-mill border crossing. It occurs in February 1865, and Tafolla and his compatriots – Jose Casillas, Jose Garza, and Francisco Martinez – are deserting the Confederate Army. The soldiers patrolling the river are most likely Confederates, and the greatest irony is that Tafolla and company are not headed north but escaping (back?) to Mexico, though Tafolla admits earlier that "none of them had ever been on Mexican soil" (73). They're a band of *mojados reversos*, with this border crossing figuring as the culmination of Tafolla's geographic dislocations from Santa Fe, New Mexico, to Independence and St. Louis in Missouri, and from there to Washington, DC, Talbotton, Georgia, and back to DC to join the US Army in an attempt to get home. He makes it as far as Texas, where after serving in the US Army, he joins the Confederate Army, deserts it for Mexico, and then settles in the San Antonio area after the Civil War, never to return to New Mexico.

Republished as *A Life Crossing Borders*, Tafolla's narrative, originally penned in Spanish in 1908, maps his multiple regionalisms across the greater southwest but also charts how his mobility deterritorializes him to the point of alienation. To take issue with the published title, let me begin with the fact that Tafolla did not cross the US-Mexico border in September 1848, when as an eleven-year-old waif he ran away from his brothers' home; rather, the border crossed him, as Chicana/o scholars say of the 1848 Treaty of Guadalupe Hidalgo. So when Tafolla mentions that he had never "been on Mexican soil," some kind of historical amnesia has occurred between the time he jumps a wagon from Santa Fe to Washington, DC, in 1848, and the time he deserts the Confederacy in 1865. He was *born* in Mexico, after all – in Santa Fe in 1837. Yet, after Tafolla and his confederates escape to Mexico and meet the mayor of Monclova, Coahuila, who happens to be a relative of Tafolla's wife, they must surrender their guns, because, as Tafolla's relative explains, "no *foreigners* were allowed to carry weapons" (79). In the original Spanish, Tafolla uses the word "desconocida" (196), which his translators render as "foreigner," but "desconocida" is more like someone unknown or much changed, strange, unrecognizable, or not one's usual self. In essence, Tafolla's deterritoralization has left him estranged from the United States and looking even stranger in Mexico, where his Americanization has made him unfamiliar, pocho we might say, without a region to claim.

What historical processes pressure land loss and the concurrent psychological amnesia that erases the fact that, in this instance, Tafolla was born on Mexican soil? A kind of negative nostalgia is at work – it's a longing for a homeland that has been dispossessed from psychological memory. "Autobiographical nostalgia for an idealized and unobtainable past arose," Padilla explains about early Mexican American autobiography, "but nostalgia functioned as opposition to assimilation, while idealizations of prior cultural habitat operated as articulations of resistance to cultural evisceration" (16). Yet, the alienation borne out of geographical dislocation and psychological deterritorialization that occured after the US–Mexican War and the way land and people changed hands from Mexican to American regimes overnight prove that it's possible to be displaced without ever moving. More so for the fugitive, like Tafolla, whose process of dispossession leads him to forget that he was born on Mexican soil; he cannot remember it nostalgically because he's forgotten that he's from it. He's been divested of his sense of belonging to a native land – dispossessed of his home because he's been displaced from it.

After serving in the Union Army, Rafael Chacón, a New Mexican, finds himself in a similar space. He writes in his 1912 memoir, "On writing these memoirs I have nothing, but, nevertheless, in what seems like a paradox, I lack nothing. The God, who has watched over me since I was a child on *foreign soil* and who later allowed me to come out of combat unharmed, watches over me" (326). Chacón uses the phrase "suelo extraño" in the Spanish manuscript, which his editor and translator, Jacqueline Meketa, translates as "foreign soil," but it should read as "strange land" not only to echo Chacón's Biblical sentiment but also because "suelo extraño" registers his social and spiritual deterritorialization. His reference to being a child in "suelo extraño" literally refers to his military school days in Chapultepec in 1844, but for the aged veteran, "suelo exatraño" characterizes the New Mexico territory during the interwar years, when the region was a part of and apart from the Union, a strange de-territory, if you will. Finally, given his feeling of dispossession after his discharge from Union service, his phrase might be more allegorical – the Union being the strange land Chacón inhabits in combat. Facing alienation in all places on the eve of New Mexico statehood, the deterritorialized Chacón remains a stranger in a strange land, writing with(out) nothing from a state of intersticiality.

Narratives of displacement often express this alienation of deterritorialization, a haunting position of not belonging in a place of belonging, of being strange, unrecognizable, uncanny, or foreign in a place that was once home, familiar, and native, of feeling the weight of US empire and the way it cut Mexico's far northern regions into states and territories that bestowed second-class citizenship onto Mexican Americans. *Tejano* Juan N. Seguin captures this sentiment when he says he's a "foreigner in my native land" after Texas's revolution (73), and *Californio* congressman Pablo de la Guerra expressed the same estrangement to characterize Mexicans in California in 1856: "They do not understand the prevalent language of their native soil. They are foreigners in their own land" (Weber vi). This is not just a psychological feeling; it's trauma borne out of historical processes – such as deferred citizenship promised in the Treaty, the 1851 Land Act, and the indeterminate status of the Territory of New Mexico, for instance – that enacted the racial logic of US empire and propelled people and Anglophone print culture west. In fact, one could read Anglo-American sensational fiction of this era as the culture of coloniality that beset Mexican America in the mid nineteenth century. While the literature of the US–Mexican War "reveals that the conflict undermined, at least momentarily, modes of nationalism in both United States and Mexico," as Rodriguez argues (1), the literature itself was "one of the many forms of collective cultural memory that embodies and enacts the desire for and the excitement, confusion, and trepidation about empire" (Alemán and Streeby xv). The war may have been vexed, in other words, but its colonial mission proved more seamless in the way it displaced Mexican Americans.

What emerges out of dispossession, dislocation, and the negative nostalgia of deterritorialization, however, is an alternative expressive culture that resists US empire through history, memory, and transnationality by imagining Mexico and Mexican Americans in the United States despite their displacement from it. This is what Marissa López concludes with her study of Mariano Vallejo's *Recuerdos*, which serve as a corrective to Bancroft's mammoth history of California. "In that dual history of himself and California," López writes, "Vallejo attempts to encompass everything: what happened, what did not happen, and what it means when the two do not match up. The text thus offers not just a narrative of loss but also a narrative of future possibility" (89). The point is pivotal, for while Vallejo's *Recuerdos* narrates the displacement of *Californios*, his writings also imagine surviving colonization through a transnational sensibility best characterized in his response to a Mexican reporter's question:

> I am an American because the treaty of Guadalupe placed me on the other side of the line, dividing the two nations but I was born a Mexican [sic]; my ancestors were Mexican and I have always maintained with my sword the honor of Mexico. I have both Mexican and American children and I desire for *my native land* all the prosperity and progress enjoyed by the country of some of my children and mine by adoption. (Empáran 141; italics added)

Vallejo navigates the negative nostalgia that haunts Tafolla, Seguin, and Chacón through a language of familial genealogy that remembers California under Mexico as his "native land" *within* the United States, with his foster-family analogy leaving it ambiguous as to who "adopted" whom. In Vallejo's response is what John-Michael Rivera terms the emergence of Mexican America: "Although Anglo-Americans played a part in the racial constitution of the political people now ethnically defined as 'Hispanic,'" Rivera explains, "the first Mexicans to engage the public spheres in the United states reinvented their racial and political ontology and therefore refashioned the contours of Mexican peoplehood" (19).

Mexican American narratives of displacement, then, simultaneously critique colonial dispossession and express the right to possessive equality – peoplehood, citizenship, land, and a sense of place – within the United States.[1] Ruiz de Burton's two novels, the 1876 *Who Would Have Thought It?*

---

[1] I am drawing and distinguishing from Macpherson's critique of possessive individualism by rejecting the liberal-democratic investment in individualism but affirming the need for a "possessive quality" (3), which I reframe as the possession of "equality" to resist the very liberal-democratic social, political, and economic apparatuses that initiate, propel, and warrant Mexican American displacement.

and the 1885 *The Squatter and the Don*, enact such a double gesture, with the latter more instructive than the former as a narrative of displacement that insists on Mexican America's right to possess equality in the land from which they have been displaced. A critique of the Treaty of Guadalupe Hidalgo, the 1851 Land Act, and the marriage between monopoly capitalism and the federal government, *Squatter*'s negative nostalgia remembers the conquest of California, the dispossession of *Californios*, and the corrupt politics of Yankee America through a historical romance between a *Californiana*, Mercedes Alamar, and Clarence Darrel, the son of a squatter. With this plot line "Ruiz's critique of republicanism," to borrow from Rivera's reading of *Who Would Have Thought It?*, "reveals that [Ruiz] is participating in a long line of protofeminist thinkers who explored the sexual politics of the gendered body and its significance in people-making" (83). What might at first be dismissed as sentimental fluff, especially in relation to the narrative's historical and legal critiques, actually imagines a structure of possessive equality by which the marriage between Mercedes and Clarence ostensibly keeps the Alamar acres in the family's hands, although now in Clarence's possession. The racial whiteness, class mobility, and genteel gender norms that structure this imaginary marriage of equality, as numerous scholars have shown, is the devil of Ruiz de Burton's dispossession.

If Ruiz de Burton's novel offers the historical romance of displacement, Juan N. Cortina's 1859 Proclamation announces a structure of feeling more kin to Chicana/o critiques of disenfranchisement and Anglo-American oppression. Cortina published almost a dozen Proclamations, but the first one captures the complex way narratives of displacement withstand colonial domination, assert rights to equality, and imagine the collective resistance of Mexican America, calling their "peoplehood" into being, as Rivera has it, to fight against further oppression.

> Our object... has been to chastise the villainy of our enemies, which heretofore has gone unpunished. These have connived with each other, and form, so to speak, a perfidious inquisitorial lodge to persecute and rob us, without any cause, and for no other crime on our part than that of being of Mexican origin... These [enemies], as we have said, form, with a multitude of lawyers, a secret conclave... for the sole purpose of despoiling the Mexicans of their lands and usurp[ing] them afterwards. (Thompson 14–16)

Not one much to rest on words, Cortina waged war across the Brownsville, Texas, area in the First and Second Cortina Wars (1859–1860 and 1873–1875) that, from the start, were about dispossession and its cultural trauma of estrangement: "Our families have returned as strangers to their old country to beg for asylum. Our lands, if they are to be sacrificed to the avaricious covetousness of our enemies, will be rather so on account of our own vicissitudes" (Thompson 17), which, according to Montejano, proved true: "The results of the Cortina War... were the depopulation and laying to waste of the whole country from Brownsville to Rio Grande City, 120 miles" (33).

Cortina's proclamations were themselves print iterations of the most salient form of early Chicana / o aesthetics – *corridos* of border conflict. Border folk balladry offers the earliest expressive resistance to the violence of displacement by recounting the injustices of Anglo oppression and hailing a real and imagined community to critical consciousness and action. "The corridos about Cortina's War," Ramón Saldívar notes, "helped establish a tradition of socially symbolic artforms in the Mexican American communities of the Southwest" (28). Along with *El corrido de Gregorio Cortez*, *El corrido de Juan Cortina* recounts border violence, cultural conflict, and the assertion of Mexican American equality, but unlike the Cortez ballad, the Cortina *corrido* stages land displacement as the historical cause for the symptoms of cultural conflict and racial violence that follow along the border: "Dizque muy serio tratado / de Guadalupe-Hidalgo / y la tierra se han robado. / México sufre un despojo / y dijo Juan Cortina / Ahorita yo me enojo." According to Paredes, "corridos about Cortina date back to the late 1850s and the early 1860s" (*Cancionero* 23), and while only fragments of these early ballads exist, Óscar Chávez's 1983 rendition of the Cortina *corrido* links the "supposedly serious" Treaty of Guadalupe Hidalgo to stolen lands, leaving Mexico to "suffer from dispossession" and Juan Cortina to rise up in "anger."[2]

The *corrido*'s "self-consciously crafted acts of social resistance" (Saldívar 42) find a discursive counterpart in *Californio testimonios*, which give firsthand witness to the dispossession of *Californios* through a mediated form of personal and collective memory. As Sánchez puts it, "For the Californios, conquered and dispossessed as they were by 1875, social exiles within their own homeland, the testimonials are spaces of resistance, refutation, and disavowal, counter-spaces for recentering collective subjectivity" (13). *Californio testimonios* offer the bedrock proof of the trauma of dispossession, but their displacement from Bancroft's seven-volume *History of California* underscores Mexican America's

---

[2] I've incorporated here my translation of the *corrido*'s poetic stanza above, which more literally and awkwardly reads: "Serious supposedly Treaty of Guadalupe Hidalgo, and land has been stolen. Mexico suffers from dispossession and Juan Cortina said, 'Now I get angry.'"

dislocation from the places where Spanish-language memories meet the Anglophone world. The collection of *testimonios*, letters, documents, and manuscripts in the Bancroft Library – most notably Juan Bautista Alvarado's 1876 *Historia de California*, María Angustias de la Guerra Ord's 1878 *Ocurrencias en California*, and Mariano G. Vallejo's aforementioned 1874 *Recuerdos históricos y personales tocante a la Alta California* – offer narratives of displacement that are personal, autobiographical, historical, cultural, linguistic, racial, gendered, and spatial. They are narratives that lay bare the other forms of displacement that occur with land dispossession. "This consciousness of subalternity," Sánchez goes on, "this awareness of having been conquered and displaced, informs (implicitly and explicitly) every narrative" and in turn fosters "the construction of an ethnic identity" aware of collective history, shared racial identity, and political mobilization (271).

Between *corridos* and *testimonios* is another displacement that makes readable the relationship between land, language, and print culture. *Corridos* and *testimonios* are Spanish-language oral forms sung and told that often remain in the archive of cultural memory precisely because English also took over places that were once Mexican. *Testimonios* bear witness to the process of cultural and linguistic exclusion that accompanies territorial displacement, for the initial oral Spanish-language account undergoes transcription into prose and translation into English, and even after such sociolinguistic disarticulation, *testimonios* still didn't warrant inclusion in Bancroft's project. Similarly, because of its specific ethno-folk function, the *corrido* has always been on the cusp of modern cultural production – it is a fugitive, Spanish-language oral form of folk balladry meant to be sung. The advent of recording, print culture, and English acquisition, as Paredes concedes, brought an end to the heroic era of the *corrido* and, by extension, dislocated the *corrido*'s Hispanophone audience from having a voice in the Anglophone world's modernity (*Pistol* 106–107). As narratives of displacement, in other words, *corridos* and *testimonios* express, critique, and remember the history of dispossession; they also call into being a real and imaginary collective racial identity. However, their very forms of personal, literary, and cultural expression in Spanish undergoes linguistic dislocation under Manifest Destiny.

This is not to say that there wasn't a print culture to emerge as a direct response to empire. California newspapers *La Crónica* (San Francisco, 1855) and *El Clamor Público* (Los Angeles, 1855) cropped up more quickly than the 1851 Land Act could dispossess the *Californios*, and the latter organ featured the editorials of Francisco Ramírez, whose criticism of the United States as a model republic gets to the heart of possessive equality:

But here in this fabulous country, he who robs and assassinates the most is he who enjoys freedom. Certain people have no kind of freedom – this freedom, we say, is that which the courts deny to all individuals of color. To buy a man for money, to hang or burn him alive arbitrarily, is another great liberty which any individual has here, according to his likes. This happens in the Unites States, where slavery is tolerated, where the most vile despotism reins unchecked – in the middle of a nation that they call the "Model Republic." It is enough that these institutions are unique in a country that tries to consume everything due to its "Manifest Destiny." (110)

As Nicolás Kanellos teaches us, Ramírez and his *Clamor* were hardly solitary voices in the Spanish-language press. Hispanophone newspapers stretched across the terrain that was once Mexican in the United States, from Nacogdoches, Texas, to San Francisco, California, and points west in between, including San Antonio and El Paso, Texas; Santa Fe and Las Vegas, New Mexico; Trinidad, Colorado; and Tucson, Arizona, to name a few of the Spanish-language print hubs.[3] "Quite often," Kanellos explains, "Hispanic-owned newspapers took on the role of contestation, offering alternative views and reports challenging those published in the English-language press, especially as concerned their own communities and homelands" (6). Nowhere is this more apparent than in New Mexico's print culture.

The greater *Nuevomexicano* region is home to an arguably unique history of print culture that, according to Gabriel Meléndez, "is characterized by a localized pattern of development that precedes, and for a variety of reasons, survives the blow of the American conquest. From its beginning in Santa Fe the *Nuevomexicano* press extended its influence to neighboring regions, linking itself to parallel developments in northern Mexico, West Texas, southern Arizona, and southern Colorado" (5). In this regard, the dissemination of Spanish-language newspapers across *Nuevomexico* operates as a discursive counterpart to the historical forces of displacement that, after the 1848 Treaty, deterritorialized the region by reclassifying it as the Territory of New Mexico. The press's relatively late (1834) emergence in New Mexico didn't curtail Spanish-language print culture from blossoming during the days of territorial conquest, 1848 to 1879, and while the railroad's

---

[3] Hispanophone newspapers extend further when we consider the corpus of print by Latinas/os – exiles, immigrant, or native – in the United States. Boston, Philadelphia, New York, Key West, and New Orleans were transnational hubs of Spanish-language print that, as Kirsten Silva Gruesz argues, shore up the trans-American origins of a literary history "that would unseat the fiction of American literature's monolingual and Anglocentric roots and question the imperial conflation of the United States with America" (4).

1879 arrival brought with it Anglo-American modernity, industrialization, and forms of capitalism that further displaced *Nuevomexicanos*, new print technologies allowed the Spanish-language press to circulate across the Rio Grande corridor. "Paradoxically," Meléndez explains, "Yankee incursions in the West also translated into greater access to Yankee print technologies in the region... In the thirty years since the American conquest, *Nuevomexicanos* had developed a powerful culture of print with the capacity to communicate with the majority of the citizenry in the southwest" (26). On par with other narratives of displacement, the *Nuevomexicano* press critiqued dispossession and (re)constituted the deterritorialized population through expressions of collective rights and resistance. As Enrique Salazar put it in *La Voz de Pueblo* in 1890:

> Our periodical... will continue its watch to protect the interests, honor, and advancement of all the segments of our great Territory. The well-being of the people of New Mexico and principally of the native population will be at every instance the powerful motive that will impel with great vigor our efforts in the publication of our weekly. We are the foot soldiers of the community, guarding its rights; for this reason, believing that the battle nears, we wish to place our batteries where they are most effective and where they will cause the most damage to our enemies. (75, qtd. in Meléndez)

Alongside Salazar's bellicose rhetoric, the Spanish-language press launched a variety of literary forms, including poetry, editorials, essays, forms of short fiction, sketches, serialized writings from across Latin America, and attempts at *belles lettres*, romances, and novels, such as Eusebio Chacón's 1892 novellas, *El hijo de la tempestad* and *Tras la tormenta la calma*, both of which first appeared in the Spanish-language paper *El Boletín Popular*. Admittedly, Chacón's two novellas are not good in the classical sense of aesthetic unity of form, content, character development, or structure. Instead, *El hijo* tells a strange and uneven allegorical tale about the birth and rise of a tempestuous bandit – born in stormy weather – who, on his supernatural wedding night, meets his demise at the hands of soldiers. Not quite a sequel in any formal sense, *Tras la tormenta* reveals that, in "matters of love" (83), there's hardly calm after the storm when it comes to a complicated love triangle that leaves the narrator "to feel like crying" (97).

While not the first Mexican American novelist, as Francisco Lomelí once proclaimed, Chacón nevertheless asserted his attempt at self-consciously producing a specific Mexican American – in this case, *nuevomexicano* – literary history that sets out "to achieve a national literature against a backdrop of relative invisibility" (Lomelí 16). "These novels are a genuine creation of my own fantasy and not stolen or borrowed from Anglos or foreigners," Chacón announced in his introduction to *El hijo*. "I dare lay the foundational seed of an entertaining literature on New Mexican soil so that if other writers with a more felicitous talent can later follow the path I hereby establish, may they look back at the past and single me out as the first to undertake such a rough journey" (49).[4] We can understand his affirmation of literary independence along many lines. It is oppositional to "gabachos" y "extranjeros," as he puts it in the original Spanish, and both categories indicate that Chacón clearly does not see himself as a stranger in his own land but rather finds it inundated by Anglos and foreigners. Second, his statement presents a decolonial stance by which he rejects dominant literary forms of colonial culture for a native literary imagination – "mi propia fantasia," he says in Spanish – that's akin to a psychological terrain of belonging *contra* a feeling of alienation. The understanding that his stories are decolonial expressions of native literary imagination explains the unevenness of both novellas: they are uneven not because they lack artistic merit, as an aesthete might first assume, but because their very aesthetics emerge from the uneven social and psychological colonial tension of displacement and belonging. Chacón's novellas, in other words, narrate displacement by way of their uneven form while their content imagines a native literary terrain free from *gabachos* and other strangers.

By the turn of the twentieth century, the Spanish-language press opened the door for a boom in Mexican American print culture that took issue with years of political, economic, and cultural displacement by way of editorials, memoirs, and other forms of imaginative fiction and nonfiction prose. Chacón himself penned editorials, letters, speeches, and commentaries in New Mexican newspapers on the government, capitalism, corruption, cultural chauvinism, and other pressing political issues, and his rhetoric is far more sharp than his fictional plotlines: "Our system of laws has become an unruly monster," Chacón says in an April 28, 1894, piece published in *El Sol de Mayo*, "given to speculation and fraud. The nation is now no more than one massive banking system where bets are made and money is won or lost. It is a gigantic money market where basic human needs are choked off and the people are left to perish, killed off by hunger and misery" (117). If Chacón's critique of modernity under capitalism rang true in terms of economic displacement, Jovita Idar's editorials in *La Crónica*, her family's Laredo, Texas, newspaper, a decade later heralded an

---

[4] I am following Amy Diane Prince's translation of the text as it appears in the Meléndez and Lomelí edition of Chacón's writings.

alternative to modernity altogether in which possessive equality, a central concern in male narratives of displacement, extends doubly to Mexican American women who resist colonial dispossession and gender inequity from both within and outside of Mexican America. "The working-class woman, recognizing her rights," Idar asserts in a 1911 editorial, "raises her head with pride and confronts the struggle; her period of degradation has passed. She is no longer the slave sold for a few coins, no longer the servant. She is equal to man, his companion" (144).

Idar's editorial voice rings louder in her statement "For Our Race": "What we wanted to suggest," Idar writes, "is that the national language [Spanish] should not be ignored, because it is the stamp that characterizes races and nations. Nations disappear and races sink when they forget their national language" (143). A year before, Aurora Lucero White Lea's 1910 speech, "Plea for the Spanish Language," hit the New Mexico press in English and Spanish and made a very similar case: "We want to learn the language of our country, and we are doing so; but we do not need, on that account, to deny our origin or our race or our language or our traditions or our history or our ancestry, because we are not ashamed of them" (139).[5] For Idar and Lea, a thread of coloniality entwines land displacement and language dispossession and holds together an entire power structure of historical, economic, political, cultural, educational, racial, and gender dislocation. As the editor of *La Crónica* and other organs, Idar also shaped the literary culture and political voice of the Texas–Mexico borderlands, generating a transnational critique of displacement that, as with *corridos* and *testimonios*, reimagined Mexico and Mexicans back into the very places from which they had been dispossessed. Nowhere is this early feminist disentanglement of displacement more prescient than in the life and writings of Idar's contemporary, Sara Estela Ramírez.

Born in Coahuila, Mexico, in 1881, Ramírez arrived in Laredo, Texas, in 1898 as a teacher and soon launched a brief but bright literary career as a poet, essayist, editorialist, and speaker. She published in Idar's *La Crónica* and *El Demócrata Fronterizo*, among other venues, and launched two of her own literary organs, *La Corregidora* and *Aurora* – the first with transnational print and distribution that encompassed Mexico City, San Antonio, and Laredo, and the second, according to Emilio Zamora, "a daily published in Laredo during the last years of her life" (165). Known for her political support of the Partido Liberal Mexicano (PLM) and

---

[5] Idar and Lea prefigure the truth that there's no "taming a wild tongue," as Gloria Anzaldúa has it: "Ethnic identity is twin skin to linguistic identity – I am my language," she asserts more than half a decade after Idar and Lea made the same appeal (59).

her friendship and correspondence with PLM intellectual Ricardo Flores Magón, Ramírez cut a distinct revolutionary voice that called for change in women's roles as much as workers' rights on the eve of the Mexican revolution. "¡Surge!," a 1910 poem dedicated "A la mujer," admonishes women to "Rise up! Rise up to life, to activity, to / the beauty of truly living; but rise up radiant / and powerful, beautiful with qualities, splendid / with virtues, strong with energies" (Hernandez 22). Asked to speak to the Society of Workers, Ramírez used a similar expression of uplift: "I come as a fervent admirer of the mutual benefit movements, to call on all workers, my brothers, and say: Combatants, forward!" (Ramírez 444). With the voice of a poet and a pundit, Ramírez's life and work no doubt "attest to the existence of a poetic tradition in the Mexican American community in Texas long before the Chicano / a movement" (Hernandez 13), and along these lines, her poetry, according to Ben Olguín, precedes the masculine *corrido* tradition. "Instead, through her activism and writing," Olguín argues, "Ramírez proposes the Mexican American borderlands subject as invested with a simultaneously local resonance and global importance that arises from the historical significant wars that are waged there" (112).

Idar and Ramírez were the advance guard of an army of *feministas Mexicanas* who turned to print activism, political agitation, and volunteer action during the heady days of the Mexican Revolution to announce and imagine revolutionary change for women. Along with Idar and Ramírez, the Villarreal sisters Andrea and Teresa, Isidra T. de Cardenas, and Blanca de Moncaleano launched feminist, reform, and anarchist papers such as *La Voz de Mujer, La Mujer Moderna*, and *Pluma Roja* in El Paso, San Antonio, and Los Angeles, respectively. Their participation in feminist leagues, worker societies, and the Mexican Revolution proved them to be "organic intellectuals of their times who revealed different discursive positionings of women within their societies, positionings informed by the master narratives of nationalism, religion and anarchism" (Lomas xvi-xvii). Leonor Villegas de Magnón's mid-twentieth-century memoir, *The Rebel*, captures the fervor of this era and the way newspapers and La Cruz Blanca, a nurse corps Villegas de Magnón founded and for which Idar volunteered, were instrumental venues for women to stage a revolutionary, transnational intervention against gender disenfranchisement, political displacement, and historical dispossession across what Paredes called Greater Mexico.[6]

---

[6] "'Greater Mexico'," Américo Paredes explains in *A Texas-Mexican* Cancionero, "refers to all the areas inhabited by people of Mexican culture – not only within the present limits of the Republic of Mexico but in the United States as well – in a cultural rather than a political sense" (xiv).

Mexican American women writers thus emerged on the literary scene in full force in the early twentieth century, turning the negative nostalgia of early narratives of displacement into prose works that revisit the nineteenth century with the imaginative gaze of repossessing what was historically lost. Adina de Zavala's 1917 *History and Legends of the Alamo*, for instance, turns the Alamo into a battleground of cultural memory and modernity with her public-preservation politics and the way her writings respond to the rapid, uneven capitalist transformation of San Antonio and its symbolic sacred center. Meanwhile, Elena Zamora O'Shea's 1935 *El Mesquite* makes a curious case for the perseverance of Mexican American expressive culture in a narrative told from the point of view of a mesquite tree that witnesses the long history of Spanish, Mexican, and American occupation of south Texas. Zamora O'Shea's *longue durée* story of displacement, according to John Morán González, follows the double logic of critiquing displacement but also affirming Mexican America's right to possess equality within a place that was once Mexico. "Through this novella," González explains, "Zamora O'Shea offered the hope that Texas Mexicans would learn those lessons [of patriarchal land loss and maternal story-telling], reclaim Texas history, and, through that history, the rights of U.S. citizenship" (92).

With *Caballero*, the late-1930s cowritten historical novel by Jovita González and Eve Raleigh, these rights ride the double edge of land dispossession and disenfranchisement under patriarchy. Following María Cotera and John Morán González respectively, *Caballero* wages war against the perseverance of patriarchal codes that situate women and land as two related forms of property to be protected or possessed. "In its unflinching depiction of patriarchal values in Chicano culture, its deconstruction of the idealized male hero, and its thematic use of the issues surrounding Malinchismo, *Caballero* forecasts the cultural production of women of color," Cotera asserts (340). This is indeed the case for González as an early Chicana feminist writer, but the narrative also functions within and against what John Morán González characterizes as a border modernity: "Operating under the twin guises of liberalism – capitalism and democracy – border modernity initiated a profound revolution in class and gender relationships within the Texas-Mexican community and in cultural and racial relations between that community and Anglo-Texas" (191). Such a border modernity might draw a distinction between territorial displacement, on the one hand, and social and political disenfranchisement on the other, with Mexican American women making critical links between gender equality, land stewardship, and the rights to possessive equality that structure the power relations between patriarchy and *la patria*.

The span between the *corrido* to *Caballero* thus charts how Mexican American women writers transformed the terms of earlier narratives of displacement to imagine their enfranchisement as full and equal Mexican American citizens in the United States. Their life and writings, however, remain on the margins of literary history: Idar's and Ramírez's writings, for instance, are largely fugitive, as are critical biographies of their literary, intellectual, and political impact on Mexican America and progressive-era border writing. Theirs is not the negative nostalgia that leads Tafolla to forget he was born in Mexico, or even the sense of alienation that Seguín characterized so well, because women were already displaced in the real and imaginary patriarchal places that were once Mexican. "It's not necessary for me to be enthused about progress on the continent," Ruiz de Burton, *la gran madrina* of all narratives of displacement, once wrote to Mariano Vallejo; "What for? Neither my race nor my gender will get anything from it" (*Conflicts* 280).[7] Yet, she still wrote and published, first under the cover of her husband's name and then under a pseudonym, "C. Loyal," that affirmed her loyal citizenship, ostensibly to the United States and symbolically to Mexico but imaginatively to a Mexican America that cropped up in the place that was once Mexican.

WORKS CITED

Alemán, Jesse and Shelley Streeby. "Introduction." *Empire and the Literature of Sensation: An Anthology of Nineteenth-Century Popular Fiction.* Eds. Jesse Alemán and Shelley Streeby. New Brunswick, NJ: Rutgers University Press, 2007. xii–xxx.

Anzaldúa, Gloria. *Borderlands/La Frontera: The New Mestiza.* 1st ed. San Francisco: Aunt Lute Press, 1987.

Brady, Mary Pat. *Extinct Lands, Temporal Geographies: Chicana Literature and the Urgency of Space.* Durham, NC: Duke University Press, 2002.

Chacón, Rafael. *Legacy of Honor: The Life of Rafael Chacón, A Nineteenth-Century New Mexican.* Ed. Jacqueline Dorgan Meketa. 1st ed. Albuquerque: University of New Mexico Press, 1986.

Chávez, Oscar. "Corrido de Juan Cortina." *16 Éxitos de Oro.* Polygram Latino, 1983. CD.

Cotera, María. "Hombres Necios: A Critical Epilogue." *Caballero: A Historical Novel.* By Jovita González and Eve Raleigh. Eds. José E. Limón and María Cotera. College Station: Texas A&M University Press, 1996. 339–46.

Empáran, Madie Brown. *The Vallejos of California.* San Francisco: Gleeson Library Associates, 1968.

Flores, Richard. "Introduction: Adina de Zavala and the Politics of Restoration." *History and Legends of the Alamo and Other Missions in and around San Antonio.* By Adina de Zavala. Ed. Richard Flores. Houston, TX: Arte Público Press, 1996.

---

[7] Translation my own.

González, John Morán. *Border Renaissance: The Texas Centennial and the Emergence of Mexican American Literature*. Austin: University of Texas Press, 2009.

González, Jovita and Eve Raleigh. *Caballero: A Historical Novel*. Eds. José E. Limón and María Cotera. College Station: Texas A&M University Press, 1996.

Gruesz, Kirsten Silva. *Ambassadors of Culture. The Transamerican Origins of Latino Writing*. Princeton, NJ: Princeton University Press, 2002.

Hernandez, Inés. "Sara Estela Ramirez: Sembradora." *Legacy* 6.1 (1989): 13–26.

Idar, Jovita. "We Should Work." *Herencia: The Anthology of Hispanic Literature of the United States*. Ed. Nicolás Kanellos. New York: Oxford University Press, 2002. 143–44.

Kanellos, Nicolás with Helvetia Martell. *Hispanic Periodicals in the United States, Origins to 1960: A Brief History and Comprehensive Bibliography*. Houston: Arte Público Press, 2000.

Lea Aurora Lucero White. "Plea for the Spanish Language." *Herencia: The Anthology of Hispanic Literature of the United States*. Ed. Nicolás Kanellos. New York: Oxford University Press, 2002. 135–39.

Lomas, Clara. "Introduction: Revolutionary Women and the Alternative Press in the Borderlands." *The Rebel*. By Leonor Villegas de Magnón. Ed. Clara Lomas. Houston, TX: Arte Público Press, 1994. xi–lvi.

López, Marissa K. *Chicano Nations: The Hemispheric Origins of Mexican American Literature*. New York: New York University Press, 2011.

Macpherson, C. B. *The Political Theory of Possessive Individualism: Hobbes to Locke*. New York: Oxford University Press, 1962.

Meléndez, Gabriel A. and Francisco A. Lomelí, eds. *The Writings of Eusebio Chacón*. Albuquerque: University of New Mexico Press, 2012.

Montejano, David. *Anglos and Mexicans in the Making of Texas, 1836–1986*. Austin: University of Texas Press, 1987.

O'Shea, Elena Zamora. *El Mesquite*. [1935]. College Station: Texas A&M University Press, 2000.

Olguín, B. V. "Barrios of the World Unite!: Regionalism, Transnationalism, and Internationalism in Tejano War Poetry from the Mexican Revolution to World War II." *Left of the Color Line: Race, Radicalism, and Twentieth-Century Literature of the United States*. Eds. Bill V. Mullen and James Smethurst. Chapel Hill: University of North Carolina Press, 2003. 107–39.

Padilla, Genaro. *My History, Not Yours: The Formation of Mexican American Autobiography*. Madison: University of Wisconsin Press, 1993. Print.

Paredes, Américo. *A Texas-Mexican Cancionero: Folksongs of the Lower Border*. Austin: University of Texas Press, 1995.

   With His Pistol in His Hand: A Border Ballad and Its Hero. Austin: University of Texas Press, 1958.

Ramírez, Sara Estela. "Speech Read by the Author on the Evening that the 'Society of Workers' Celebrated the Twenty-Fourth Anniversary of Its Founding." *Herencia: The Anthology of Hispanic Literature of the United States*. Ed. Nicolás Kanellos. New York: Oxford University Press, 2002. 444–45.

Rivera, John-Michael. *The Emergence of Mexican America: Recovering Stories of Mexican Peoplehood in US Culture*. New York: New York University Press, 2006.

Rodríguez, Jaime Javier. *The Literatures of the US-Mexican War: Narrative, Time, and Identity*. Austin: University of Texas Press, 2010.

Ruiz de Burton, María Amparo. *Conflicts of Interest: The Letters of María Amparo Ruiz de Burton*. Eds. Rosaura Sánchez and Beatrice Pita. Houston, TX: Arte Público Press, 2001.

Saldívar, Ramón. *Chicano Narrative: The Dialectics of Difference*. Madison: University of Wisconsin Press, 1990.

Sánchez, Rosaura. *Telling Identities: The Californio* testimonio. Minneapolis: University of Minnesota Press, 1995.

Seguín, Juan N. *A Revolution Remembered: The Memoirs and Correspondence of Juan N. Seguín*. Ed. Jesús F. de la Teja. Austin, TX: State House Press, 1991.

Tafolla, Santiago. *A Life Crossing Borders: Memoir of a Mexican-American Confederate/Las memorias de un mexicanoamericano en la Confederación*. Eds. Carmen Tafolla and Laura Tafolla. Trans. Fidel L. Tafolla. Houston, TX: Arte Público Press, 2010.

Thompson, Jerry, ed. *Juan Cortina and the Texas-Mexico Frontier, 1859–1877*. El Paso: Texas Western Press, 1994.

Villegas de Magnón, Leonor. *The Rebel*. Ed. Clara Lomas. Houston, TX: Arte Público Press, 1994.

Weber, David, ed. *Foreigners in Their Native Land: Historical Roots of the Mexican Americans*. Albuquerque: University of New Mexico Press, 1973.

Zamora, Emilio. "Sara Estela Ramírez: Una rosa roja en el movimiento." *Mexican Women in the United States: Struggles Past and Present*. Eds. Magdalena Mora and Adelaida R. Del Castillo. Los Angeles: Chicano Studies Research Center Publications, University of California at Los Angeles, 1980. 163–69.

II

Under the Skin of Latina Feminism and Racism

Travel Narratives, Novels of Reform and Racial Rhetoric

MILAGROS LÓPEZ-PELÁEZ CASELLAS

¡Oh las mujeres! ¡Pobres y ciegas víctimas! Como los esclavos, ellas arrastran pacientemente su cadena ... eligen un dueño para toda la vida.
(*Sab* 271)[1]

In past times, the literary colonial voice of the Latina and Chicana woman was often found tucked away, like an afterthought, in the corner, consigned to a second-class treatment at best, if not simply ignored or silenced altogether. It was a fate that, looking back today, is not hard to understand given the way that gender, as well as race and social class, blocked the access of colonized women to literature.[2] The nineteenth century was a time when Latina women, whatever their social class, were exploited and excluded from all forms of cultural production – never mind the control of that production – and were relegated to their "natural" role of reproduction.

---

[1] Oh women! Poor and blind victims! Like slaves, they drag their chains patiently ... they choose a master for their entire lives (my translation).

[2] By using the term "race" in this chapter, I am not implying the acceptance of its actual existence. The scientific validity of this notion, has been questioned – or directly refuted – in the field of biology mainly. As Todorov explains, the series of biological differences and the groups to which these supposedly belong, do not coincide; groups have intermixed since time immemorial; the differences among individuals are bigger than those found between groups, etc. (68–74). Furthermore, Eliav-Feldon, Isaac, and Ziegler have explained the problem of using these exclusively biological approaches to human diversity, explaining graphically that the use of genetics to explain the notion of race is similar to the action of cutting soup: you can cut as much soup as you like, but soup will always remain mixed (8). On the other hand, to reclaim the fictitious character of the notion of "race" (that is, its existence considered merely as a topic in the history of ideas) does not imply rejecting the reality of social groups, some of them differentiated by their skin color. It will be this concept of "race" that I will be using throughout this essay.

Yet, despite these constraints, the writings left by nineteenth-century Latina women provide valuable insights. They show us how nationalistic discourse in Latin America emerged parallel to the discourse of women, resulting in a hybrid discourse in which the voice of the subaltern – be it women, African slaves, or indigenous peoples – served to construct imagined national identities.[3] Walter Mignolo explains the story of Latin America after independence as "the variegated history of the local elite, willingly or not, embracing 'modernity' while Indigenous, Afro, and poor Mestizo/a communities get poorer and more marginalized" (57–58). The writings of elite Creoles certainly helped to consolidate and increase the political and economic power of these privileged few and within their exemplary discourse – in particular, the works of nineteenth-century Latina women – ambivalent and contradictory ideologies and subject positions echo the contradictions.[4]

It is our wish here to delve into these aspects in the writings of Latina forerunners such as María Amparo Ruiz de Burton, Gertrudis Gómez de Avellaneda, Clorinda Matto de Turner, Mercedes Santa Cruz y Montalvo, Mercedes Cabello de Carbonera, Lola Rodríguez de Tió, Aurelia Castillo de González, and Manuela Sáenz. By critically documenting the writing of some of these foundational nineteenth-century Latina feminists, whose literary work has been largely overlooked until being recovered in the last decades of the twentieth century – we will be able to open a window on the subversive, feminist but sometimes also racist character of their narratives. Their writings include biases and blind spots that are a direct consequence of their elite Creole class and race privilege. Some of their narratives – all of them relevant for their marked and undeniable sociohistoric and artistic value – delve into the theme of gender and racial identity while revealing an entire racist ideology that served to explain as a natural process the segregation, exclusion, and discrimination (at every level) of African and Indigenous peoples in the nineteenth century.

Contemporary Chicana/o narrative – understood as a hybrid literature, formed of at least two cultural traditions and two languages, and originating in what is known today as the US Southwest – needs to be explored within its

---

[3] Benedict Anderson examines the concept of nation in his book *Imagined Communities* where he defines it as: "an imagined political community – and imagined as both inherently limited and sovereign. It is imagined because the members of even the smallest nation will never know most of their fellow members, meet them, or even hear of them, yet in the minds of each lives the image of their communion" (15).

[4] For a study of the role that women characters in nineteenth-century narratives play in symbolizing a national identity and a united Creole feeling, see Mendez Rodenas 2002.

own conflicting specificity, a specificity which by the end of the nineteenth century takes shape as a simultaneous production and reproduction of processes of confrontation and cultural and linguistic syncretism, racial prejudices and discrimination in terms of social class or gender. Ruiz de Burton's novels are hybrid productions positioned in a liminal space, and they provide a deconstructive criticism of American imperialism, imitating – or perhaps parodying – the sentimental and romantic novels written at the end of the nineteenth century – albeit while introducing some key innovations.[5]

Most of the research carried out until now on her two novels, *Who Would Have Thought It?* (1872) and *The Squatter and the Don* (1885), can be divided into two groups. One is based on the premise that there is a subaltern's voice, a resistance narrative, in Ruiz de Burton's two novels. The other points out the author's appropriation of the same imperialist discourse that she is trying to critically unsettle (which takes into account arguments about the author's ideology and class status).[6]

However, these novels cannot be read as simple binarisms but as hybrid productions, positioned in a Lotmanian semiospheric border where the articulation of cultural differences results in imagined national identities.[7] What Ruiz de Burton seems to create in her novels is a fixed cultural identity for the recently annexed Californian/Mexican, with the objective of resisting the Anglo-American colonizer who, as several of her characters point out, was destroying their Mexican culture. Nevertheless, as Hall warned us, the only benefit of using this identity discourse is a "good night's rest."[8] The essentialist identity to which Ruiz de Burton refers in her novels, among

---

[5] See López-Peláez Casellas 2012.

[6] The first view is maintained by Chicana critics Rosaura Sánchez and Beatrice Pita among others, while the second one by critics José F. Aranda and Manuel Martín Rodríguez.

[7] Bhabha's "liminal" concept is similar to Lotman's notion of the semiospheric border. In this sense, the Estonian-Russian semiotician Jüri Lotman theorized the notion of the border as the (liminal) space of interchange, mixing, contamination, bilingualism, and cultural translation. Lotman's semiosphere, a semiotic concept established by analogy with the biosphere, is defined as the semiotic space outside of which no semiosis is possible (123). According to Lotman, the semiosphere is constructed as an abstract yet real and material space at the core of which the most highly codified structures involved in the production of meaning are located. Closer to the periphery (i.e., to the boundary) of the semiosphere reside those structures or mechanisms that lack a complete internal organization, and this provides them with a greater capacity for dynamism.

[8] As Hall explains: "The notion that identity has to do with people that look the same, feel the same, is nonsense. As a process, as a narrative, as a discourse, it is always told from the position of the Other" (45).

other things, impedes the characters' possibility of change or adaptation, in as much as they decline to alter their ways of life on the basis of a series of collective characteristics.[9]

In nineteenth-century Californian society, the class status of Californians and Anglo-Americans was dependent on the exploitation of mestizos, subservient indigenous populations and enslaved Africans, just as it had been during the Mexican and Spanish periods of sovereignty in this region. In *The Squatter and the Don*, when the Creole Don Mariano Alamar realizes that he risks losing his possessions owing to the new legislation imposed by the Anglo-American colonizer, he compares his wretched situation with that of his Indian neighbor: "I am sure I am to be legislated into a ranchería, as there is no poor-house in San Diego to put me into" (214). For the indigenous populations, the Spanish colonial class hierarchy was still very much in force: Creole at the top of the edifice, with the categories of mestizo and Indian occupying a subordinate status. Ruiz de Burton's novels show that discrimination functions at different levels since those elite Californians who are suffering discrimination are, at the same time, discriminating against others. In here, the *gente de razón*, or Californian elite, even though territorially colonized, are also colonizers themselves on the basis of social class and presumed racial hierarchy.

In *The Squatter and the Don*, the common exploitation of the non-whites carried out by both the Anglo-American colonizers and the Californian *dons* puts these two groups, albeit different in racial terms, together. The novel also provides us with a depiction of the Mexicans and Californians as intellectually and morally superior to the Anglo-Americans – who instead wield only political and economic power. However, there is no interrogation of the discrimination that the Mexicans/Creoles inflict on the Indians, something that evidently raises questions about their supposed moral superiority.

In *Who Would Have Thought it?*, Ruiz de Burton reinforces the US position of "cleaning the border of Indians" by presenting the Indian as a savage and dangerous to the Anglo-Americans as well as to the Mexicans (35, 78, 201, 269). With this, she maintains the Manifest Destiny rhetoric based on the

---

[9] Ruiz de Burton first used the term *Spano-Americans* in *The Squatter and the Don* (1885): "they do so quickly enough with us – with us, the Spano-Americans, who were to enjoy equal rights, mind you, according to the treaty of peace" (65). There are other instances in this novel where Ruiz de Burton makes use of the term: Clarence Darrell, an Anglo character, refers to the Mexican Americans as "the most defenseless, the most powerless of our citizens – the orphaned Spano-Americans" (97) while another character, Don Mariano Alamar, refers to them as "the natives of California, the Spano-Americans" (162).

binary of civilization/barbarism. This discourse can be seen in the words of Doña Theresa Medina, who, before dying, gives a bag full of gold and precious stones to the Anglo-American Dr. Norval in return for saving her daughter: "Take my child away from among savages and bring her up as a Christian" (35). We see the same rhetoric in Dr. Norval's description of the Indian pueblo where he found Lola's mother:

> In a miserable Indian hut lay the dying lady. The surroundings were cheerless enough to kill any civilized woman, but the bedclothes, I noticed, were as white as snow, and everything about her was clean and tidy. She ... said, "Thank God, Lolita is away from those horrid savages!" (36)

The *fin-de-siècle* US-Southwest witnessed racial tensions between Chicano and indigenous communities which – as Guidotti-Hernández's research work documents – resulted in the lynching of some Chicanas in this period.[10] In this way, writing from a liberal perspective Latinas contributed to the silencing of stories of lynching, racialized and sexualized violence, and genocide (i.e., Juanita's/Josefa's lynching in 1851; Camp Grant Indian massacre in 1871; and the Yaqui Indian wars of 1880–1910).

One must highlight the racist content in some characters' discourse in Ruiz de Burton's two novels, including that of the narrator, toward the mestizos and the original inhabitants of the region.[11] Indeed, in the way it makes use of a class and caste-based identity, there are echoes of US Southern romances that endorsed enslavement of Africans and their descendants. We find a discourse in favor of including the Indians in a "civilized" society, albeit in the role of subordinated slaves/servants and thus, even though we can speak of the voice of the subaltern in the novel, there exists at the same time a discriminatory tone. For instance, in *Who Would Have Thought It?*, Lola is the focus of racist insults coming from the Anglo-Americans throughout the entire novel and suffers Fanon's epidermalization. Lola manages in part to "whiten" herself both through the loss of the black paint on her skin (the result of a dye the Indians put on her during the time she was kidnapped) and, on a symbolic level, through her marriage to an Anglo-American.[12]

From the very beginning, the novel features the basic racial prejudices found in white society in New England. Once the black paint has disappeared

---

[10] See Guidotti-Hernández 2011.

[11] See *The Nineteenth-Century American Novel* by Gregg Crane for a comparative study of this novel and pro-slavery US Southern romances in general.

[12] As Alarcón states, "whiteness not *mestizaje* has been constructed as the Absolute idea of Goodness and Value" ("Chicana Feminism" 187).

and her skin is white, one of the characters exclaims: "How very pretty that Little girl Lola has got to be! – and so very white! She is superb" (246). This is something that even the narrator emphasizes: "When the doctor met Lola, his kind heart beat with pleasure. The unfortunate spots had almost entirely disappeared; Lola's skin was white and smooth, and she was very pretty" (79). In this way, the belief that contact with the ethnic Other not only provokes fear but denigrates is established and reinforced in the novel, something that is exemplified through Lola's previously blackened skin and the whitening of her skin once she comes into contact with non-Indian society. Furthermore, in the dialogue between Lola and the Anglo-American Julian, Lola helps reinforce the colonial epistemology that has been transmitted as a consequence of the monoculture generated by the European semiosphere (masculine and white):

> I was an object of aversion because my skin was black ... My mother also was made to stain her lovely white skin all black ... I hated to think that you *might* suppose I was Indian or black ... And you were wrong, because my father already told me that you are of pure Spanish descent. (100)

Parallel to the ambiguity that characterizes Ruiz de Burton's ideological discourse, the writings of Gertrudis Gómez de Avellaneda reveal a trenchant investment in racial and class hierarchies. Gómez de Avellaneda toward the end of the nineteenth century gained both admirers and detractors for her literary work.[13] On the one hand, like Ruiz de Burton, she identified herself with European colonial discourse (she lived for many years in Spain), and on the other, she provided a subversive subtext of gendered difference in her work.[14] In this respect, it might be better to refer to her discourse as being "anfibiológico"; that is, one that "is born out of the dominant discourse which at the same time reveals the culture of the periphery" (Garfield 52).

The privileged class position from which Gómez de Avellaneda writes and also that frontier space, which in Lotmanian terms is translated into a semiospheric border – an interstitial space between the Spanish semiosphere and the Cuban one – allows for the creation of a subversive subtext in her

---

[13] In 1839 Gómez de Avellaneda began her literary activity with her first publication in *La Aureola* magazine under the pseudonym *La Peregrina*. In total, as well as *Sab* and *Dos Mugeres*, she published a large number of articles in various newspapers, nineteen plays, seven novels, and a collection of poems.

[14] In Spain, Gómez de Avellaneda was the first woman to edit a newspaper, *La Gazeta de las mujeres, redactada por ellas mismas* (which later became *La Ilustración de las Damas* in 1845). In Cuba she edited the woman's magazine *Album Cubano de lo Bueno y lo Bello* (1860).

novels. One could well assert that in *Sab*, the use of the civilization-barbarism/urban-rural dichotomy allows the writer to alter the fixed meaning in both spaces to later expose the mechanism for constructing the categories of gender, class, and race.[15]

In the case of *Sab*, this novel deals with slavery on two levels – on the basis of race but also gender.[16] An example of sentimental romanticism (a slave falls in love with the master's daughter) with clear and descriptive language and *costumbrista* content, *Sab* offers a crude vision of the slaves' reality while providing some degree of abolitionist sentiment, albeit, as we must point out, the latter was never Gómez de Avellaneda's goal.[17] From the start, there is an evident lack of racial clarity with Sab. The novel does not offer something other than a reading of the slave in terms of black and white,

> No parecía un criollo blanco, tampoco era negro, ni podía creérsele descendencia de los primeros habitantes de las Antillas. Su rostro presentaba un compuesto singular en que se descubría el cruzamiento de dos razas diversas ... la casta africana con ... la europea, sin ser, no obstante, un mulato perfecto. (104)[18]

That said, the ambiguous and "imperfect" identity of Sab ("sin ser ... un mulato perfecto") – which precludes a reading of him within binary European racial parameters – does still allow for the deconstruction of racial and social class parameters by using a subtext of Otherness in the novel. The fact that the slave has been granted access to language and knowledge allows for the transgression of social-class identity. The end product is a forerunner of the indigenous novel and a statement against the injustice of slavery during a crucial moment in Cuban history.[19]

Indeed the strongly subversive antislavery tone of this novel meant that the book was not actually allowed through customs in Cuba and got sent back to Spain.[20] It is worth noting too that this book appeared in print and

[15] See Ibarra 2011.
[16] For a study of the proto-feminist character of the novel, see Méndez Rodenas 2002.
[17] For an analysis of race and gender in *Sab*, see Pastor 57–76.
[18] He did not look like a white Creole but nor was he black and nor could he be considered a descendant of the first inhabitants of the Antilles. His face represented a singular blend of two different races ... the African race with ... the European, but without being a perfect mulatto.
[19] The failed "Conspiración de la Escalera," the first great slave revolution in Cuba, took place three years after the publication of this novel.
[20] *Sab* was not allowed through Cuban customs and was sent back to Spain for "containing doctrines that were subversive and against morality" ("contener doctrinas subversivas y contrarias a la moral." In *Boletín del Archivo Nacional*, La Habana, 1943; cit. in Picon Garfield 183.

encountered censorship ten years before the first publication of *Uncle Tom's Cabin* in 1852. However, the novel is full of contradictions, notably with the unconscious racism found in it. We cannot ignore Sab's comment: "a pesar de su color, era mi madre hermosa" (in spite of her color, my mother was beautiful) nor the fact that the slave could be viewed as a mere conduit through which the novel addresses other themes, specifically social equality and women's rights.[21]

This ideological ambiguity is also characteristic of Peruvian writer Clorinda Matto de Turner for whom writing was a space for liberation and struggle and a resistance mechanism in the face of social inequality.[22] For all that, we must remain cautious when considering the question of social denunciation in her work *Aves sin nido*.[23] While this novel denounces the mistreatment and oppression of the Indians in Peru, it is equally a novel that makes use of the figure of the noble savage and features paternalistic colonial discourses on the protection of the helpless, infantile and innocent Indian.[24] What is more, Matto de Turner provides us with an entirely romanticized indigenous figure who can be saved only by the loss of his identity and conversion into a Creole.

Therefore, because of Matto de Turner's position of class and race-based privilege, she does not criticize Creole land owners in *Aves sin nido* and limits herself to analyzing the problem of the Amerindian in purely moral and legal terms.[25] This problem – seen at all times from the point of view of the foreigner – is thereby simplified and de-historicized. The indigenous community of the Andes enters into the story through its interaction with foreigners who are associated with social progress, morality, and modern values. When the Marín family abandon the Sierra – on the failure

---

[21] See Pastor 97; cited in Girona Fibla 127.

[22] In *Boreales, Miniaturas y Porcelanas* (1902), Matto de Turner asserts that the woman writer: "takes hold of her rights ... women who write (are) real heroines" (251).

[23] Matto de Turner wrote, as well as her great novel *Aves sin nido*, a large number of poems and essays, a historical drama (*Hima-Sumac*), and newspaper articles promoting social equality and women's right to education in *El Heraldo, El Ferrocarril* and *El Eco de los Andes* (the last of which she edited). Like many other contemporary writers (Ruiz de Burton, Gómez de Avellaneda, etc.) Matto de Turner used several pseudonyms when publishing her newspaper articles: Lucrecia, Betsabé, and Rosario.

[24] For a study of the indigenous novel in *Aves sin nido*, see Cornejo Polar 1994; Tauro 1976, and Cruz Leal 2010.

[25] We should emphasize that both this novel and the magazine *El Perú Ilustrado* were strongly criticized by the church, in particular by the bishop of Lima, Antonio Bandini, who prohibited the reading of it and even ordered the burning of an effigy of the writer (Tauro 7).

of their plan to save the Indians – the novel finishes and, with it, their attempt at social reform.[26]

In her novel, Matto de Turner reflects and reinforces the nineteenth-century Peruvian Creole nation and argues for the inclusion of the indigenous people in Peruvian society from a moral rather than socioeconomic stance. *Aves sin nido* serves as a forerunner of the writings of Chicanos about indigenous people, albeit with some differences. In the 1960s, Chicanos highlighted a pre-Columbian indigenous origin as a means to emphasize the unique singularity of their culture and used pre-Hispanic symbolic and mythological elements to give form to a newly defined Chicano essentialized identity (i.e., Alarista's *Plan Espiritual de Aztlan* and Anzaldúa's *Borderlands/La Frontera*).

Aves sin nido clearly displays what Austin has expressed as "the writing subject's ideological psychosis as it is torn between hopeful liberal ideology and the discouraging history of modernization in the Andes" (35). Thus, while this is a precursor of the twentieth-century indigenous novel, it has received considerable criticism for its tepid defense of the indigenous peoples.[27]

Amid such criticism, it is worth noting that in Matto de Turner's work there are strong secondary characters who are indigenous, and also women (albeit white, middle-/upper-class women). Additionally, Matto de Turner succeeds in creating a certain subversive subtext in her novel by showing the myth of education as a tool for the modernization of both subalterns, women and indigenous peoples. So while the woman in *Aves sin nido* is still confined to the domestic sphere she has moved from *angel of the hearth* to *angel of the house*.[28] This new position provides her with more mobility and freedom, even if there is no direct confrontation with the existing patriarchy.

A Creole and aristocrat by birth, Mercedes Santa Cruz y Montalvo – Condesa de Merlin or "la belle créole" – belongs to this same number of writers who, by virtue of their social class, enjoyed the freedom and means to publish their work but, because of this same social class, provided an idealized vision of their colonial world. Condesa de Merlin was one of the first Cuban women to deal with the theme of slavery – understood as oppression both in terms of race and gender. In her *Viaje a la Habana* (1844), an epistolary novel that combines autobiography and travel writing, the system of slavery is criticized in ambiguous terms.[29] In her twentieth

---

[26] See Cornejo Polar 1994.   [27] See Cruz Leal 2010.   [28] See Peluffo 2004.
[29] Gómez de Avellaneda herself wrote a biographical section in the prologue to this work. In it, she highlights the character of the exile that both writers shared: "Nothing, in fact,

letter to baron Charles Dupin, which was published in the *Revue des Deux-Mondes* in 1841, under the title *Les esclaves dans les colonies espagnoles*, Condesa de Merlin writes: "Nothing more just than to abolish the enslavement of blacks; but nothing more unjust than the emancipation of slaves."[30] In her writings, therefore, she revealed herself to be against the slave trade but also in favor of maintaining the ownership of slaves. From her position of privilege as a member of the *sacarocracia*, the countess favored a gradual solution to the problem of slavery and maintained a strategic position. Even though she may have drawn a parallel between the respective situations of slaves and women in the colony, she did not do it in the same convincing and explicit way that Gómez de Avellaneda did a few years later. Conscious of her privileged class status and her belonging to two worlds, her vision is projected from a strategic, semiospheric, hesitant, and nuanced perspective.

There is also ambiguity in Mercedes Cabello de Carbonera's works – as they are marked by a feminist tone and also by a nationalistic rhetoric.[31] In them she calls for the deconstruction of the dualistic patriarchal vision of the role of women in fin de siècle Peruvian society and demands the lay education of women. *Sacrificio y Recompensa* (1887) and *Blanca Sol* (1889) provide an archetypical dual vision. In *Sacrificio y Recompensa* Catalina personifies honor, uprightness, and sacrifice; it is a feminine ideal that cannot be found in Cabello de Carbonera's second novel, *Blanca Sol*, where Blanca symbolizes the type of woman who is a victim of society's wrongs and ends up being the complete opposite of Catalina.[32] The women's roles found in these novels – both the woman of sacrifice and the woman victim – enable the writer to question society's moral codes and to propose to the reader (through their identification with the characters) the need to change the sociopolitical terrain and critique matrimony.

Another common denominator for many of these Latina writers is exile, and it is a particularly formative element in nineteenth-century autobiographical literature and travel writing. Condesa de Merlin, for instance, finds her

---

is so bitter as expatriation ... Just like the famous writer, we have abandoned the land of our birth" (9–10).

[30] "Rien de plus juste que l'abolition de la traite des noirs; rien de plus injuste que l'émancipation des esclaves" (735).

[31] Cabello de Carbonera wrote under the name Enriqueta Pradel before finally deciding to use her birth name. In Ruiz de Burton's case, *Who Would Have Thought It?* was published anonymously while she used "C. Loyal" ("Ciudadano Leal") for *The Squatter and the Don*.

[32] See Goswitz 113–14.

identity as a travel writer and author in exile and because of exile.[33] Having left Havana for Spain aged eight, she lived for most of her life in France and also spent time in New York before finally returning to Cuba in 1840. As Gómez de Avellaneda wrote in the prologue to Merlin's *Viaje a la Habana*: "Nada, en efecto, es tan amargo, como la expatriación"(Nothing is more sour than exile) (9–10).

On the other hand, for those writers of more humble origins, such as Aurelia Castillo de González, her two exiles in Spain (1875–1878 and 1896–1898), her numerous travels in Europe, and in particular her frequent visits to the United States were marked by the strong influence of feminist movements.[34] The travel writing and intellectual activity of Castillo – who published in such diverse newspapers as *El País*, *El Fígaro*, *Revista Habanera*, *Revista Cubana*, *Cuba Contemporánea*, and *La Habana Elegante* and traveled to Europe, Mexico, and the United States (she was correspondent at the 1889 Universal Expo in Paris and later for *El País* at the Colombian Exposition in Chicago in 1893) – allowed her to take the Cuban reader beyond the island and also to criticize life in Cuba and propose alternatives. Her exile and travel writing (her published collection of letters *Un paseo por América. Cartas de México y de Chicago*) enabled her to "write back" to Cuba and through her "exilic view" become a direct interpreter of the supposed modernity of the Paris or Chicago metropolis.

While in exile, Castillo – in her 1878 article, "La mujer cubana" – revealed herself as a supporter of Cuban independence and an opponent of that slavery experienced by women.[35] What is striking about Castillo is her already clearly marked feminist character and we can appreciate in all her work a wish to deconstruct patriarchal constructions while overcoming gender-based obstacles to get published. In 1895, Castillo published a special volume in the newspaper *El Fígaro*, which she dedicated to the Cuban woman and in which she included her article titled "Esperemos." This is rightly considered one of the earliest feminist texts in Cuba, and in it she declared: "la mujer reivindica sus derechos. Ella ha sido la última sierva del

---

[33] See Molloy 1991.

[34] In the fin-de-siècle United States there are numerous examples of feminist writing that was influenced by the workers' movement in newspapers such as the anarchist, Tampa-based *El Esclavo*, where we find a poem from 1896, "El burgués de la casa" by Luz Herrera de Rico, which stands out for its denunciation of patriarchal oppression (Estrada 191).

[35] Her poem titled "Libertad" (Freedom) was composed after the abolition of slavery on the island.

mundo civilizado ... Sus destinos se decidieron sin consultarla para nada y decretada quedó su eterna minoría."[36]

Kanellos has noted that most of the Cuban and Puerto Rican literature published in the United States had a great political component, and the work of the poet and revolutionary Lola Rodríguez de Tió certainly supports this view.[37] Expelled for a second time from Puerto Rico in 1896, she established herself in New York where she soon continued propagating her independent views and her fight for women's suffrage and the improvement of women's education in Puerto Rico.[38] Rodríguez de Tió has a place in history not only for her literary merit – recognized far beyond Puerto Rico's borders, [39] for works such as her 1876 poetry collection *Mis Cantares* – but also for her efforts on behalf of the revolutionary independence movement alongside the likes of Ramón Emeterio Betances and José Martí.[40] Her political activism places her among such figures as Manuela Sáenz, who was a direct witness as well as participant in the official narration of the independence and formation of new republics in Latin America. Sáenz has been reinserted into South American history through more recent literary works such as Denzil Romero's *La esposa del doctor Thorne* (1988); García Márquez's *El general en su laberinto* (1989); Ricardo Palma's *Tradiciones Peruanas* (1893–1896); and Victor Von Hagen's *The Four Seasons of Manuela* (1952). This last work directly influenced contemporary Chicano writer Jaime Manrique's *Our Lives are the Rivers* (2007) – a historical novel that restores Sáenz to her rightful place in history.

In general, the work of these early proto-feminist Latina writers links the narration of historic events – in many instances lived out in the first person (as is the case for Bolivar's partner and strategist in Creole revolutions, Manuela Sáenz) – with the type of sentimental novel and romantic style predominant in nineteenth-century literature.[41]

Apart from the absence of models that could influence these early Latina writers and the difficulty of publication, their literary production was directly

---

[36] "The woman claims her rights. She has been the last servant of the civilised world ... Her destiny was decided without even consulting her and her eternal minority status set in stone" (Campuzano 70–79).

[37] For a study of the marked political element in de Tió's literary work, see Kanellos 2005.

[38] See César González 2003.

[39] The first magazine aimed at women was *Brisas de Borinquen*, published in San Juan in 1864. See Muna Lee 1934.

[40] The first Puerto Rican woman to publicize anticolonial and revolutionary ideas was María de las Mercedes Barbudo. See Figueroa 1979 and Rivera 1997.

[41] For a study of the role that women characters in nineteenth-century narratives play in symbolizing a national identity and a united Creole feeling, see Mendez Rodenas 2002.

discredited on the basis of it being deemed a mere imitation of masculine literary strategies. The bourgeois novel produced precisely a class of women in a state of flux which allowed these writers to create a type of "masculine language" within a phallocentric world. Gómez de Avellaneda, her Cuban compatriot Aurelia Castillo de González, and Manuela Sáenz, among others, were defined as "virile" owing to their collision with the patriarchal prejudices of the time, as well as androcentric conceptions based on the idea that masculine values and experiences were the basis for theoretical constructions.[42] It is interesting to add that in the case of Gómez de Avellaneda, due to an outspoken feminist position – reflected in her life as well as her written work – she was viewed as "masculine" by most contemporary critics. José Martí established that Gómez de Avellaneda was "too much of a man for this woman" and that there was "a proud and fierce man in her poetry" while the nineteenth-century critic Luis Vidart, a contemporary of Gómez de Avellaneda, refers to her as "not ... a poet-woman but a poet" (Pastor 9). If this characterization continued to negate the feminist component in these Latina writers' narratives until recent decades, it was through the aforementioned "state of flux" that they were still able to create a female writer's identity, unearthing the tools that would allow future women to access that sealed patriarchal domain through a strong criticism of the institution of marriage and by defending women's education. Cuban writer Castillo de Gonzalez does the latter in her *Cartas de México* while Gómez de Avellaneda critiques the institution of marriage in her two denunciatory novels, *Sab* (1841) and *Dos mugeres* (1842–1843), the second of which features a defense of the right to divorce.[43]

When it comes to an analysis of these writers, we must be cautious not to ignore the inherent contradictions – racial stereotypes and the existence of a marked Creole discourse – that abound in their narratives. As Arun P. Mukherjee highlights, "writing is not just a matter of putting one's thoughts on paper. Writing is also about social power. How I write depends a lot on who I write for" (13). Women like Gómez de Avellaneda and Matto de Turner do not manage to provide an efficient critique of the abuses and unequal racial situation of the indigenous/slave in their works; instead,

---

[42] See Valdés 87.

[43] In *Sab*, Gómez de Avellaneda provides a vision of marriage as a mere business transaction resulting from the emergent capitalism of the time. As an example, one must consider the dialogue between Enrique and his father who reminds him that "one marries a woman ... for speculation, for convenience" (152).

their narratives remind us of the existence of power relations that are assimilated and transmitted across generations.

One pertinent question is whether we can find the voice of the subaltern – black/indigenous/working-class female – in their narratives. In Ruiz de Burton, for instance, we can refer to what Chicano critic Genaro Padilla has coined as whispers of silence; that is, adopting a position that does not ignore "those flashes in imprisoned discourse that are a textual signal of embryonic consciousness, whispers of antecedent resistance that have provided us the opening for clearly revisionary and resistive utterance" (60). Works such as the *Cartas* to Simón Bolívar as well as the brochure "La Torre de Babel" provide more than an example of Sáenz's mastery of the written word; they serve also as indisputably politico-historical documents and as antidotes to that state of amnesia in which the Latin American historic conscience dwells when it comes to the role played by women over the course of history.[44]

These writers permeated their literature with Positivist ideas that pushed not only for women's emancipation but also their access to education. Unfortunately, they drew criticism for transgressing the tacit rules of patriarchal discourse, even though they had overcome gender obstacles to get published. Yet with regards to a writer like Cabello de Carbonera, her work surely warrants more detailed study, particularly the feminist and sociopolitical character of her work, and her novels deserve to be edited afresh.[45] Condesa de Merlin's legacy owes much to this kind of fresh analysis. Her literary production was strongly criticized in Cuba, where she was accused of providing a foreign-eyed view of Havana, and only recently have her narratives begun to be valued outside of Cuba (Carmen Vásquez and Adriana Méndez Ródenas).[46] The significance of these women can be underlined by the contribution of Gómez de Avellaneda, who laid the foundations for our understanding of later leading Latina writers. In her life she

[44] In Simón Bolívar's letter to Manuela Sáenz in 1824, he acknowledges the significant role played by Sáenz, who was responsible for informing him of events on the battlefield as well as giving orders to his generals on the front. Bolívar tells her: "tu presencia servirá para que te encargues de hacerme llegar informes minuciosos de todo pormenor, que ninguno de mis generales me haría saber" (your presence will help through your taking charge of ensuring that even the most minute details get through to me, something that none of my generals would be able to do) (42).

[45] Her numerous articles have been collected by the critic Cornejo Quesada – in particular those published from 1874–1897 – and her life story told by her most important biographer, Pinto Vargas. For a comprehensive approach to the life of this writer, see Pinto's *Sin perdón y sin olvido: Mercedes Cabello de Carbonera y su mundo* (2003).

[46] Her two works *Mis doce primeros años* and *Historia de Sor Inés* appeared in the Cuba and America volumes from January–April 1902.

disregarded social conventions – she had a tumultuous love affair with the critic Gabriel García Tassara and became pregnant by him – and similarly the heroines in her novels fight against the feminine stereotype of the submissive, quiet, silent woman. It is not only important to study the work of this author, therefore, but also to acknowledge her valuable legacy to contemporary feminist literature.

It is true that these writers wrote from a position of presumed superiority (white/Creole and middle/upper class) and that their narratives offered a romanticized vision – and sometimes racist understanding – of a period that was oppressive in terms of class, race, and gender. Nevertheless, they managed to create a discourse of historical significance. Recovering foundational Latina writings and challenging their narratives can be done only by using a strategic discourse approach characterized by what critic Padilla has deemed as a "rhetoric of duplicity" – that is, restoring the difficult conditions under which these narratives were produced in the first place (34). The narratives discussed in this chapter show the ethnic and gender conflict present in the Hispanic world during the nineteenth century while creating a type of inherently contradictory ideology. They serve to keep us questioning that type of historic amnesia that still characterizes the twenty-first century. Positioned from the border of their own semiosphere, these women translated their experiences in order to end up giving a voice to a muted Latina her-story.

WORKS CITED

Anderson, Benedict. *Imagined Communities*. Norfolk, VA: Verso Editions, 1983.
Austin, Elisabeth. *Exemplary Ambivalence in Late Nineteenth-century Spanish America: Narrating Creole Subjectivity*. Plymouth, NH: Bucknell University Press, 2012.
Back, Les and John Solomos, eds. *Theories of Race and Racism: A Reader*. New York: Routledge, 2009.
Bhabha, Homi. *The Location of Culture*. New York: Routledge, 1994.
Campuzano, Luisa. 'Cuando salí de la Habana.' *Cartas de México, de Aurelia Castillo de González. Casa de las Américas* 20.5 (1996): 70–79.
Castillo de González, Aurelia. *Cartas de México. Escritos de Aurelia Castillo de Gonzalez*. Havana: Imprenta siglo XX, 1914.
Cornejo Polar, Antonio. "Prólogo." *Aves sin nido*. Caracas: Biblioteca Ayacucho, 1994. XIV. *Escribir en el aire. Ensayo sobre la heterogeneidad sociocultural en las literaturas andinas*. Lima: Editorial Horizonte, 1994.
Crane, Gregg. *The Cambridge Introduction to the Nineteenth-Century American Novel*. Cambridge: Cambridge University Press, 2007.
Cruz Leal, Petra-Iraides. "El diluido indigenismo de Aves sin nido." *Cien años después. La literatura de mujeres en América Latina: El legado de Mercedes Cabello de Carbonera y Clorinda Matto de Turner*. Ed. Claire Emilie Martin. Lima: USMP Fondo Editorial, 2010. 125–37.

Figueroa, Loida. *Breve Historia de Puerto Rico*. San Juan: Editorial Edil, 1979.

Gómez de Avellaneda, Gertrudis. *Sab*. Ed. José Servera. Madrid: Cátedra, 1999.

Dos mujeres. Havana: Letras Cubanas, 2000.

"Apuntes biográficos de la Dra. Condesa de Merlin." *Viaje a La Habana*. By Condesa de Merlin. Havana: Imprenta de la Sociedad literaria y tipográfica, 1844.

González, Julio César. *En busca de un espacio: historia de mujeres en Cuba*. Havana: Editorial de Ciencias Sociales, 2003.

Goswitz, María Nelly. "Catalina y Blanca: Un análisis del ideario narrativo de Mercedes Cabello a través de las protagonistas femeninas de Sacrificio y recompensa y Blanca Sol." *Cien años después. La literatura de mujeres en América Latina: El legado de Mercedes cabello de Carbonera y Clorinda Matto de Turner*. Ed. Claire Emilie Martin. Lima: USMP Fondo Editorial, 2010. 111–25.

Hall, Stuart. "Old and New Indentities, Old and New Ethnicities." *Culture, Globalization and the World System: Contemporary Conditions for the Representations of Identity*. Eds. Anthony D. King. Minneapolis: University of Minnesota Press, 1997.

Kanellos, Nicolas. "Hispanic American Intellectuals Publishing in the 19th United States: from Political Tracts in Support of Independence to Commercial Publishing Ventures." *Hispania* 88.4 (2005): 68–92.

Lee, Muna. "Puerto Rican Women Writers: the Record of One Hundred Years." *Books Abroad* 8.1 (1934): 7–10.

López-Peláez Casellas, Milagros. *What about the Girls?: Estrategias narrativas de resistencia en la primera literatura chicana*. Oxford: Peter Lang, 2012.

Lotman, Jüri M. "On the Semiotic Mechanism of Culture." *New Literary History* 9 (1978): 211–32.

Mangini, Shirley. *Las modernas de Madrid: Las grandes intelectuales de la vanguardia*. Barcelona: Ediciones Península, 2001.

Matto de Turner, Clorinda. *Boreales, Miniaturas y Porcelanas*. Buenos Aires: Imprenta de Juan A. Alsina. 1902.

Mendez Rodenas, Adriana. *Cuba en su imagen. Historia e identidad en la literatura cubana*. Madrid: Editorial Verbum, 2002.

Mercedes Cabello de Carbonera. *Sacrificio y Recompensa* (1887). Buenos Aires: Stockcero, 2005.

Blanca Sol (1889). Madrid: Iberoamericana, 2004.

Merlin, Comtesse Mercédès. "Les esclaves dans les colonies espagnoles." *Revue des Deux-Mondes*. 1841: 734–69. Web. April 12, 2015.

Mignolo, Walter. *The Idea of Latin America*. Oxford: Blackwell, 2005.

Minh-ha, Trinh T. "Writing Postcoloniality and Feminism." *The PostColonial Studies Reader*. Ed. Bill Ashcroft, Gareth Griffiths and Helen Tiffin. New York: Routledge, 1995. 264–68.

Molloy, Sylvia. *At Face Value: Autobiographical Writing in Spanish America*. Cambridge: Cambridge University Press, 1991.

Mukherjee, Arun P. *Oppositional Aesthetics: Readings from a Hyphenated Space*. Toronto: TSAR Publications, 1994.

Padilla, Genaro. *My History, Not Yours: The Formation of Mexican American Autobiography*. Madison: University of Wisconsin Press, 1994.

Pastor, Brigida. "A Legacy to the World: Race and Gender in *Sab*." *Revista del CESLA* 9 (2006): 57–76.

Peluffo, Ana. "Why Can't an Indian Be More Like a Man? Sentimental Bonds in Manuel González Prada and Clorinda Matto de Turner." *REH* 38 (2004): 3–21.

Picon Garfield, Evelyn. *Poder y sexualidad. El Discurso de Gertrudis Gómez de Avellaneda.* Rodopi: Amsterdam, 1993.

Pinto Vargas, Ismael. *Sin perdón y sin olvido: Mercedes Cabello de Carbonera y su mundo.* Lima: Universidad San Martín de Porres, 2003.

Rogelia Lily Ibarra, "Gómez de Avellaneda's Sab: A Modernizing Project." *Hispania* 94.3, 2011 (385–95).

Ruiz de Burton, María Amparo. *The Squatter and the Don.* Eds. Rosaura Sánchez y Beatrice Pita. 1885. Houston, TX: Arte Público Press, 1992.

Who Would Have Thought It?. Eds. Rosaura Sánchez y Beatrice Pita. 1872. Houston, TX: Arte Público Press, 1995.

Saénz, Manuela. *Las más hermosas historias de amor entre Manuela y Simón Bolívar acompañadas de los diarios de Quito y Paita, así como de otros documentos.* Caracas: Ediciones de la Presidencia de la República, 2010.

Sánchez, Rosaura y Beatrice Pita. "Introduction." *The Squatter and the Don.* Eds. Rosaura Sánchez y Beatrice Pita. 1885. Houston, TX: Arte Público Press, 1992. 7–49.

Sharpe, Jenny. "The Unspeakable Limits of Rape: Colonial Violence and Counter-Insurgency." *Colonial Discourse and Post-Colonial Theory/A Reader.* Ed. Patrick Williams and Laura Chrismas. New York: Columbia University Press, 1994. 221–43.

Tauro, Alberto. *Clorinda Matto de Turner y la novela indigenista.* Lima: Universidad Nacional Mayor de San Marcos, 1976.

Valdés Estrella, Mercedes. *Aurelia Castillo: Ética y Feminismo.* Havana: Acuario, 2008.

12

José Martí, Comparative Critique, and the Emergence of Latina/o Modernity in Gilded Age New York

LAURA LOMAS

Es claro que la Am. puede crear y está creando, un lenguaje nuevo.
(It is clear that America can create and is creating a new language.)
–José Martí (*Obras completas* 22: 143)

Es de hombres de prólogo y superficie–que no hayan hundido los brazos
en las entrañas humanas, que no vean desde la altura imparcial hervir
en igual horno las naciones, que en el huevo y tejido de todas ellas no
hallen el mismo permanente duelo del desinterés constructor y el odio
inicuo,–el entretenimiento de hallar variedad sustancial entre el egoísta sajón
y el egoísta latino, el sajón generoso o el latino generoso, el latino burómano
o el burómano sajón: de virtudes y defectos son capaces por igual latinos
y sajones. Lo que varía es la consecuencia peculiar de la distinta
agrupación histórica.
–José Martí ("La Verdad sobre los Estados Unidos," *Patria* 23 de
marzo de 1894; *En los Estados Unidos* 1753)

[The entertainment of locating any substantial distinction between the Saxon
egotist and the Latino egotist, the generous Saxon and the generous Latino,
the Saxon bureaucrat and the Latino bureaucrat – for Latinos and Saxons
have an equal capacity for virtues and defects – is only for men of prologue
and surface, men who have not sunk their arms into human entrails,
men who do not, from an impartial height, watch the nations all
boiling on the same stove, men who do not find, in their very germ
and fabric, the same permanent duel between constructive selflessness
and wicked hatred. What varies are the peculiar consequences of the
distinct historical grouping.
–José Martí ("The Truth about the United States," *SW* 329,
translation modified)]

A self-affirmation of latinidad as modern despite being minoritarian, not
beholden to the cultural ideals nor the political dictates of Europe or the

United States, appears in the New York-resident José Martí's writings towards the end of his life, when, after twelve years in the largest US city, he became the "Delegado" of the Partido Revolucionario Cubano and continued to write the torrents of poetry and prose through which he inscribed himself into multiple literary histories. Appearing in the newspaper of the Cuban independence movement and *The North American Review*, the term "Latin" figures in opposition to "Saxon" in political debates about the International American Conference of 1889–1890 and the International Monetary Conference of 1891. This binary refers not to ethnoracial essences, but to a historically determined relation.[1] The original Spanish term –*"latino"*– does not define an essence or a "race," but something more akin to Lisa Lowe's definition of "race as a mark of colonial difference."[2] This anti-essentialist proposal, unusual for the late nineteenth century, attends to differences while underscoring a common humanity in order to undermine the scientific racism that organized a hierarchy of races according to biological or essential causes. To counteract Anglo stereotypes of Latinas/os, and to expose the racial violence that such theories of the period attempted to justify, Martí uses the structure of a print community to expose, through translations from English-language newspapers, "the crude, unequal, and decadent character of the United States, and the continual existence within it of all the violence, discords, immoralities, and disorders of which the Hispanoamerican peoples are accused" ("Truth about the United States," 333). Martí's influential dissent from imitating the United States thus helped open a pathway to a future in which the English-speaking world would come to acknowledge and respect an equal Latina/o creative ingenuity, to which we hope this volume bears witness.

The critical redefining of "America" from a Latina/o perspective inside the United States – a question opened up by Martí's "Nuestra América"(1891) published in New York and Mexico – helps to launch a new phase of both Latina/o and Latin American literatures that underscores the affinity of these distinct traditions. In describing Martí as a Latino migrant, I do not claim Martí exclusively for a multicultural US tradition against a Cuban national tradition, but rather consider his writing also as part of a transnational, multilingual

---

[1] Matías Romero, "The Pan-American Conference," *North American Review* 151 (1890). See Carlos Márquez Sterling's illuminating account of Martí's "brilliant" leadership at the meetings, and his response to the secret attempt to bribe him into submission to the position endorsed by then Secretary of State, James Blaine, in *Martí y la conferencia monetaria de 1891*.

[2] Lisa Lowe, *The Intimacies of Four Continents*, 7.

Latina/o American literary and cultural history that belongs to the border-lands and migratory routes of the Global South. It may be many decades before a hegemonic sector of the United States ceases to speak of American culture, "alluding of course to [their] North America, without thinking that there might be another America" (Martí, *OC*, 22:279). Nonetheless, a critical rejection of US presumption is already palpable in Martí's late nineteenth-century moment. This phase of Latina/o American literature began to envision a decolonized América, characterized by self-determination for the vast majority who speak Spanish or Portuguese. Forged in a crucible of revolutionary struggle in New York's Gilded Age, a Latino writer in the United States invited readers to imagine, in a form far more radical than that of Ralph Waldo Emerson or Walt Whitman, a planet not controlled by modern European or North American empires and their culture of violence.

Cuban-American biographers have at last come to acknowledge Martí's significance not only for Cuba and Latin America, but also specifically for "the forging of Latino/a identities" (Alfred López xiii). Now it is possible to ask: Would the notion of a Latino Martí who associated with blacks and anarchists diminish his status as Cuban nationalist? Does this reading of Martí as "Latino" critical of the United States threaten Cuban-exile status as model minority? Does this claiming of Martí as someone who worked hard to earn a living diminish the great teacher and founder's Cubanía, by dangerously suggesting that he may have been edified by his many years as a migrant living in boarding houses in the United States, a gusano transformed by residing in the guts of empire?[3]

Between the imposition of the US embargo upon Cuba in 1962 and the reestablishment of diplomatic relations between the two nations in 2014, a bitter struggle has persisted between Miami and Havana over the interpretation of Cuba's most influential poet-statesman as, on one hand, the leading ideologue of the socialist revolution forged by Fidel Castro Ruz, where Martí's ideas – ever present in Cuba but especially pronounced as Soviet-inspired Marxist-Leninism has waned; and, on the other, the anticommunist, pro-capitalist US-identified liberal idealized by the Cuban exile community and its supporters. The working-class-identified Latino who dwells in the mined borderlands of these starkly antagonistic positions may become increasingly relevant in the phase of reestablished relations. This version of

---

[3] In "Domingo triste," for example, Martí uses this figure to evoke his own despair as a migrant: "Ni un gusano es más infeliz" (Not even a worm is more unhappy) (*Obras completas, Edición Crítica*, vol. 14, 242).

Martí not only as an exile, but also as a racialized economic migrant, provides a more capacious framework in which to recognize how class, race, and the legacies of empire shape Latina/o literary history. For a Latino Martí, in between Spain, the United States, Mexico, Guatemala, Venezuela, and a future Cuban nation, admits to the great writer's human foibles, secret affiliations or addictions, and productively complicates the sanctimonious received orthodoxies that have often supplanted close readings of Martí's own prolific and startlingly beautiful writings.[4]

In the late nineteenth century, it was possible to perceive the characteristics of modern Latina/o writing at the border of cultures in conflict and engaged in translation, and to read in it an alternative to the dominant, celebratory immigrant narrative of remaking oneself through amnesia, language loss, and assimilation. This chapter examines the conditions of emergence of a self-conscious Latina/o modernity as a discourse that drew on comparative critical readings of other major and minor cultural forms. As a poet, as a public intellectual, and as a statesman, Martí theorized connections between different subgroups with parallels to or direct participation in Latina/o cultures, including intersecting native, black, Asian and European working-class diasporas. This comparative reading placed in contact the subtraditions of Mexican American, Hispanic Caribbean, and Central and South American diaspora writing, thanks to Martí's voracious and omnivorous reading, circle of contacts and trans-American readership. This comparative framing underscored common vulnerability to "democratic masks," which is to say, to false promises of liberty that pretended to distract migrants from the quotidian reality of racial violence and inequality.[5] In journalism or crónicas, in poetry, in his notebooks, Martí conjured a Latina/o American form against the dominant literary schools of realism and romanticism, against monolingualism, against pan-Americanist projects, and against myths of racial hierarchy.

Against Romanticism and Realism

Martí's literary form consciously diverged from the dominant literary genres and aesthetic ideals in the United States and Europe of his time: romanticism

---

[4] See Jossiana Arroyo's work on Martí, René Betancourt, and many others as masons; José Oviedo on Martí's illegitimate daughter María Mantilla; and Alfred López on Martí's swollen testicle or sarcoidosis and his use of the cocaine-laced stimulant beverage Vin Mariani, legally available during this period in New York.

[5] See Angel Rama's posthumous text, *Las Máscaras democráticas del modernismo*.

and realism. As a twice-deported Cuban exile who held diplomatic posts for Argentina, Uruguay, and Paraguay, worked as a translator, and taught Spanish as a second language, Martí's other main source of employment was writing for newspapers. In major Latin American and US-based Spanish-language periodicals with transnational circulation throughout the Spanish-speaking world, he developed *la crónica* – an adaptation of French and Spanish literary nonfiction traditions that became a new hybrid genre and that remains influential in Latina/o literature.[6] These short nonfiction essays for newspapers published elsewhere focused on a range of current events, cultural happenings, or quotidian "North American Scenes" (Martí's title for a compilation unrealized in his lifetime) and profoundly inspired Martí's modernist successor, the exiled Nicaraguan Rubén Darío.[7] The crónicas, in addition to other prose and poetry by Martí and those in his circle, came to articulate distinct aesthetic and political criteria for the region, but also for the diverse subculture of "gente latina" ("Carta a Manuel Mercado" April 12, 1885; *Epistolario* I: 299) who were the US-based readers of *El Latino Americano*, *La América*, *La Revista Ilustrada de Nueva York*, *La Ofrenda de Oro*, and *El Economista Americano*. This Latina/o audience included a lettered diaspora and thousands of tobacco workers – many of whom fled Cuba and Puerto Rico after slavery ended and came to form part of a politically astute mixed-race working class in South Florida, New York, and Philadelphia.[8]

Martí's enunciation of a Latina/o modernist aesthetic outside of Latin America begins by documenting a distinct set of aesthetic criteria as compared to that of the average North American. In his crónica "Coney Island," published in *La Pluma* of Bogota, Colombia in 1881, he announces the

[6] In 1887, Martí reports in his correspondence that his crónicas for Argentina's *La Nación*, and Mexico's *El Partido Liberal*, were being reprinted in over twenty other Latin American newspapers without any royalties coming to him (*Epistolario* I, 397; cf. Hidalgo Paz 114–15). We might read the crónica as the precursor genre to twentieth-century Latina/o nonfiction and journalism by writers such Julia de Burgos, Daniel Venegas, and Jesús Colón, and to contemporary accounts of migration and its effects by Rubén Martínez, Oscar Martínez, Héctor Tobar, Juan González and Susana Chávez-Silverman, among others. Rotker, *La invención de la crónica*.

[7] See Martí's April 1, 1895, letter to Gonzalo de Quesada that has come to be known as Martí's last will and testament, written in the Dominican Republic just before the final embarkment for Cuba (*Epistolario vol 5*). Martí called Rubén Darío "hijo" in 1893 upon meeting him in New York. Rubén Darío begins the process of recuperating Martí as a writer in *Los Raros (The Rare Ones)* where he recalls reading reprints of Martí's prose about the Brooklyn Bridge or the International American Conference in Chile.

[8] See Tony López's chapter in this volume for more on the tabaqueros and the Latina/o culture of public performance. Special thanks to Tony for his generative comments on this chapter.

perspective of "other peoples – ourselves among them – [who] live prey to a sublime inner demon that drives us to relentless pursuit of an ideal of love or glory" ("Coney Island," *Selected Writings* 92). This melancholic and relentless pursuit of an ideal pertains to "the men of our Hispanoamerican peoples who live here," people (for we know there were, of course, a large number of women among them) who become conscious of themselves as such, and critical of their initial bedazzlement by the United States, in the midst of a Coney Island scene of "frenetic multitudes" (*Selected Writings* 89) disturbed only by "their eagerness to possess wealth" (*SW* 92).

Martí's careful reading and response to some of the most influential US writers reveals his inspiration by, and ultimate disappointment with, Ralph Waldo Emerson, Walt Whitman, William Dean Howells, and Frederick Douglass, among others. The first two of these writers received extended treatment and commentary, but Martí ultimately rejected the model of these North Americans.[9] Associating Emerson with a declaration of cultural independence from Europe that nonetheless reproduced a cultural chauvinism inimical to the liberty of his America, Martí identifies Emerson in 1888 with stereotypically Anglo-Saxon blue eyes and an "imperial mien" (*OC* 5:120).

Martí's reading implies that the New Englander's divergence from Europe did not go far enough, as evidenced when Emerson figuratively presides over the ritual of the America's Cup – an annual sailing tournament on the Hudson River adjacent to Manhattan – the description of which precedes a dramatic account of anti-Chinese violence. Martí notes that the principal fallen intellectual heroes of the previous generation have become decorative portraits, whose rebellious ideas did not lead to cultural independence from the former colonizer, England:

> ningún galán neoyorquino se cree bautizado en elegancia si no bebe agua de Londres; a la Londres se pinta y escribe, se viste y pasea, se come y se bebe, mientras Emerson piensa, Lincoln muere, y los capitanes de azul de guerra y ojos claros miran al mar y triunfan.

> (no New York gentleman believes himself baptized in elegance if he does not drink the water of London; just as in London, they paint and write, they dress and strut, they eat and drink, as Emerson thinks, as Lincoln dies

---

[9] See Martí's essays, "Emerson" and "The Poet Walt Whitman," (*SW* 116–29; 183–94). A long critical tradition is profoundly invested in Martí's identification with Emerson and Whitman, but I have argued that this reading ignores Martí's divergence from problematic aspects of Emerson and Whitman's vision of the United States. See chapters 2 and 3 of *Translating Empire* and Julio Ramos, *Divergent Modernities*.

and as the blue-uniformed and blue-eyed captains of war look toward the
sea and triumph)

("Placeres y problemas,"*La Nación*, October 22, 1885;
En los Estados Unidos, 538; my translation).

This post-mortem reference to Emerson and Lincoln's soft echo in the midst of
a Romanesque and militarily aggressive Gilded Age calls attention to persistent
"Anglomania," despite the New Englander's famous exhortations to cast off
the Old World mantle and Lincoln's war to end slavery.[10] The life's work of
the preeminent US philosopher and the assassinated president who issued the
Emancipation Proclamation did not transform the elite citizenry's exploitation
of disenfranchised workers, nor did it curtail a general investment in white
supremacy, nor did it end the imitation of an Anglo imperial prerogative. The
sailboat race for the "Cup" becomes an allegory of the United Kingdom and
the United States fighting for control of Latin American resources.

In conjunction with the race, a ceremonial procession of armaments
gestures to the post-bellum American Union gearing up for overseas wars
under the aegis of the Monroe Doctrine. Emphasizing the connections
between the foreign war and racialized and anti-immigrant violence, Martí's
crónicas in 1885 describe a white mob setting fire to 79 homes and to the
cadavers of dozens of massacred Chinese workers: "Dan los blancos tras
ellos. Pocos escapan. Por donde asoma uno, lo cazan." (The whites go after
them. Few escape. Where one appears, the whites hunt him down) ("El
problema industrial en los Estados Unidos," *La Nación*, October 23, 1885; *En
los Estados Unidos* 542). This historical account in uncharacteristically staccato
sentences disrupts the report on pleasurable festivities of September to
contest the widespread and frankly imperialist notion that the United States
should serve as a model for and administrator of Latin America. A formal
gesture of Latina/o modernity, the crónica juxtaposes effusive baroque
sentences with this formally modernist economy. The distinct tempo jars
the effusive narrative of self-satisfied liberty and momentarily lifts the democratic mask to reveal the brutal enforcement of inequality.

As a literary critic and creative writer, Martí also diverged from natural-
ism, sentimentalism, realism, and from the conventional rhyming lyric.
Moreover, his criticism resisted the segmentation of the literary into a

---

[10] José Ballón reads this 1885 passage as Martí's embrace of Emerson and Whitman's
intellectual and cultural movement with the capacity to respond to the destructive
tendencies of their society. But his argument that Emerson represents the possibility of
an Adamic renewal overlooks the crisis of racial violence in this period.

separate sphere to be consumed by a bourgeois-identified domestic reader.[11] Martí stretched poetic language to express a revolutionary desire and to capture another version of modernity in writing. Adopting the critique of France's bourgeois culture that characterizes the prose of Charles Baudelaire and Gustave Flaubert, albeit from his different vantage point as a colonized Hispanic Caribbean subject, Martí's prose and poetry echoes the effects of Flaubert's unhinging of the categories of European knowledge. Whereas Flaubert offers in his posthumous novel *Bouvard et Pécuchet*, for example, a pessimistic portrayal of bourgeois characters who discover their inability to master or grasp truth or to understand and control the world through Europe's mode of encyclopedic knowledge, Martí's critical reading of Flaubert anticipates a revolutionary fire.[12]

As a contemporary who shared Baudelaire's fascination with the task of capturing modernity, Martí likens these French writers to painters.[13] Martí often referred to Baudelaire and Flaubert in the same breath: "un poeta y un novelista han tenido cincel en las manos en vez de pluma, cuando escribían: el novelista fue Flaubert; el poeta fue Baudelaire, genio rebelde" (one poet and one novelist have wielded a paintbrush in their hands instead of a pen when they were writing: the novelist was Flaubert and the poet was Baudelaire, a rebellious genius) (*OC* 23: 131). Flaubert's *Bouvard et Pécuchet*, which Martí read and reviewed for New Yorkers before it had been translated into English, informs the migrant Cuban's poetic imagery in his *Versos sencillos* (1891), in which Martí evokes the "fuego de la mañana / que tiñe las colgaduras / De rosa, violeta y grana" (fire of morning / that colors the vast draperies / pink, violet and deep red) (*SW* 278–79). The internal rhyme and uncanny juxtaposition of the domestic draperies and the fire of revolution bespeak Martí's modernity. He uses this same allusion to fire to announce to José Dolores Poyo in December 1891 of the imminent rekindling of revolution against Spain and against the imperial expansion of the United States:

---

[11] See Martí's commentary on the city spectator immersed in Buffalo Bill Cody's massive shows, who experienced an ironic awareness of "escualidez de la vida ciudadana (scrawniness of citizen life)," upon merely standing up in the bleachers, and thus "holgando en los estrados de la vida (at leisure in the benches of life)" (*En los Estados Unidos* 708). This critique of a squalid spectator citizen informs Martí's disdain for novels, including his own *Lucía Jérez*, and for the reader/spectator they addressed as passive consumer, rather than as participant.

[12] Carmen Suárez León attributes Martí's difference from Baudelaire to an "acto de soberana voluntad" (161), and to "una inquebrantable posición de fe y una exaltada pasión constructora"(168) in *La sangre y el mármol*.

[13] Martí, "Flaubert's last work," *The Sun* (New York Sun, July 8, 1880. Reprinted in *OC* 15: 203–09).

"Es la hora de los hornos, en que no se ha de ver más que la luz" (It is the hour of the furnaces, when we will see nothing but light) (*OC* 1:275). Martí's oft-cited reference, both uncanny and domestic, depicts the moment of revolution as a furnace, which adapts the image of fire that occurs in Flaubert's novel when the two melancholic copyists lose their home in a blaze. As Michel Foucault notes, Flaubert's late work represents "the illumination of multiplicity itself – with nothing at its center, at its highest point, or beyond it" ("Theatrum Philosophicum," 189). For if Flaubert's humble pair of retired friends observe that Europe is not the center of the world, Martí's reading of Flaubert illuminates an impending and enormous task of decolonization as a result of that insight. The furnace drives the revolutionary possibility of becoming someone or something else, without a clear end in sight. Latina/o modernism is marked by this adaptation of received ideas in the midst of violent contradictions, and by movements for transformation.

The epochal 1887 crónica "Un Drama terrible" (A Terrible Drama), dedicated to the Haymarket anarchists hung by the state of Chicago after a highly publicized trial of anarchists accused of throwing a bomb at the city's police during a demonstration, defines a key moment of radicalization in which Martí gives voice to the rebellious, largely German-speaking migrants who were prosecuted through a trial conducted in English when the majority of the accused did not speak the language. The anarchists – including the imprisoned white Albert Parsons and his wife, the Afro-Latina Lucy Parsons – impressed Martí with their marches of tens of thousands for an eight-hour workday. Already in 1884, Martí categorized a demonstration of 20,000 workers, toting their shining tools down Broadway, as a "modern procession" ("La Procesión moderna," *La Nación* September 5, 1884; *En los Estados Unidos* 376–84). In 1887, the crónica not only studied the workers as "creadores de si propios" (creators of themselves) (idem 376), but voiced their disillusionment with the United States: "¡America es, pues, lo mismo que Europa! (America is, then, the same as Europe!)" (*En los Estados Unidos* 962). Radically, this crónica vindicates a tradition of revolt, from Montezuma and John Brown to Saint-Just and Desmoulins. In answer to the sardonic rhetorical question, "the law protected them, didn't it?" (*SW* 205), the chronicle denounces the complicity of the press with the police and the factory owners: "Every newspaper from San Francisco to New York misrepresents the trial, depicting the seven accused men as noxious beasts, putting the image of the policemen ripped apart by the bomb on every breakfast table" ("A Terrible Drama"; *SW* 212). In casting his lot with "los pobres de la tierra" (the poor of the earth) in the *Versos sencillos* (*SW* 276–77), Martí engages not in a romantic act of charity but attempts to place into writing the coming to consciousness by which a vulnerable group might find it necessary to resort to violent rebellion. Martí's poetic persona and his chronicles anticipate the "flood of the other," a reaction that realists such as William Dean Howells both fear and await.[14]

Martí's modernism addresses and articulates the perspective that belongs to the people whom Stephen Crane associates with this threatening "flood." The Cuban admired the way that Lucy Parsons shot words like "shrapnel" ("A Terrible Drama," *SW* 202). Martí demonstrates sympathy with the anarchists' position by likening it to that of a person like himself "in exile from one's patria" (*SW* 202).[15] The transplanted foreigner from the Caribbean climes on display – like wilting tropical plants in Madison Square Garden, or the exploitable migrant worker – were among the colonial and racializing scripts through which latinidad was becoming legible in Gilded Age New York City.

Modernist Form Against Monolingualism

Cuando se vive en uno como vórtice del mundo, donde se pintan ante los ojos, en horno colosal, lo primitivo y lo heredado, lo burdo y lo culto, es fuerza que el lenguaje se resienta de sobra de peso. . ... De un amaneramiento sí huyo; pero no de aquel que puede resultar y debe resultar, de pretender poner, con las tradiciones de la lengua, las corrientes de la vida moderna y el fuego del mundo.

(When in one lives as something like the vortex of the world, where a colossal furnace, the primitive and the inherited, the rough and the cultured are painted before our eyes, a force too great to bear weighs on language. . ... I flee overstylized form; but not form that results and should result from trying to place within language's traditions the currents of modern life and the fire of the world.)
–José Martí fragments 163 and 166 (*OC* 22: 100)

---

[14] Stephen Crane publishes this interview with Howells as "Fears Realists Must Wait," in the *New York Times* (October 28, 1894): 20; rpt. *Critical Essays on William Dean Howells* 146–47.
[15] See Lomas, "Imperialism, Modernization and Commodification of Identity in José Martí's 'Great Cattle Exposition,'" and Martí's portrayal of himself displaced to a cold urban environment, gesturing to an "estranjero (stranger)" huddled alongside elderly ladies and bespectacled teachers, "desolado como las palmas (desolate as the palm trees)," in 1890, "La exhibición de flores," *La Nación* (Jan 11, 1891); rpt. *En los Estados Unidos*, 1468.

The fragments above and others such as the prologue to Venezuelan Juan Antonio Pérez Bonalde's *Poema al Niágara* (1882) refer to the fundamental role of Latina/o migrants in forging a distinctly modern poetics in Spanish in New York.[16] As someone who migrated as an adult, Martí had a vexed relationship to the English-language-dominant culture in which he generated his major poetry and prose, almost all in Spanish, despite being bilingual and engaging in translation from a young age.[17] As a deported, stateless nomad – a "man without a country, but without a master" (*OC* 16, 100) – Martí never sought U.S. citizenship nor cowed to the pressure to assimilate.

Instead he exposed the trauma apparent in the unwillingness of other Latina/o contemporaries to retain their mother tongue. These former Latin American citizens attempted, like recently weaned children, unsuccessfully to hide the traces of their original Spanish mother tongue:

> Dice 'mi país' cuando habla de los Estados Unidos con los labios fríos como dos monedas de oro, dos labios de que se enjuga a escondidas, para que no se las conozcan sus nuevos compatriotas, las últimas gotas de leche materna.

> (He says "my country" when he refers to the United States, with cold lips like two gold pieces, two lips that he wipes furtively, so as to hide from his new compatriots the remaining drops of his mother's milk.)   (*OC* 6:35).

This scene from Martí's journalism about the International American Conference of 1889–1891 alludes to the temptation faced by transplanted representatives of Latin American countries to cash-in on the benefits of US citizenship and of the language of the new global empire.[18] Like the Mexicans in the annexed portion of California and the Francophone speakers of Quebec in Canada, his disciple, Gonzálo de Quesada, retained Spanish as a Cuban born in the United States, a point Martí makes in his preface to

---

[16] Roosevelt's 1893 article "True Americanism" and makes English language mastery a condition of being 'truly' American.

[17] Martí's literary translations include Shakespeare, *Hamlet*, Victor Hugo, *Mes Fils (Mis hijos)*, attempted translations of Longfellow, Poe, a lost translation of Thomas Moore's *Lalla Rooke*, Helen Hunt Jackson, *Ramona*, and Theuriet's, "Un Idilio de Pascua," which appeared in *La Revista Ilustrada de Nueva York*, May 15, 1892. See de la Cuesta, *Martí, Traductor*, and Suárez León, "Martí Traductor," in *La Alegria de Traducir*.

[18] In contrast, see for example Martí's classmate José Ignacio Rodríguez, who adopted US citizenship upon arriving in Washington, DC, where he married and practiced law before becoming the official translator and staff member of the Bureau of American Republics. See also María Amparo Ruiz de Burton, the California writer who represented the elite class of former Mexicans who tended to intermarry with wealthy Anglos in hopes of preserving their status in opposition to both the thievish "Anglo squatters" and the indigenous who worked for them.

Quesada's book of poetry (*OC* 5: 195). The discomfort – by contrast – with his colleagues' abandonment of the mother tongue looks forward to language politics and language loss as persistent themes in Latina/o literary history.

Even though Martí slowly but surely became completely fluent in English (in addition to French) through his studies and through a decade and a half of living and working in New York, his acquaintances report that he rarely used what he referred to as his "barbarous" English.[19] Martí "trembled" when he first faced the task of writing an article in English, for up until 1882, he claims that "he had never written in English," or had written in it only in "extreme situations" ("momentos extremos") (*OC* 22: 285). This comment underscores the economic necessity that compelled the "friendless" and "fresh Spaniard" (*SW* 33, 32) to undertake numerous articles for *The Hour* and for Charles Dana's *New York Sun* between 1880 and his death in 1895.[20] Unlike his retention of Spanish, which represented a lifeline to another American intellectual tradition and defied pressures to abandon the mother tongue, Martí's English-language writing and a speech in English at the end of his life in Key West reveal a subtle tactical interpretation of the United States from a dissembling insider's position.[21]

Unlike the *Versos sencillos* or some of his unrhymed *Versos libres*, few of Martí's fragmentary texts and notebooks have been translated and anthologized, despite the fact that they represent some of the richest material of all of his projected forty-volume critical edition of complete works, penned on the back of letterhead of import-export firms on Wall Street where Martí worked as a clerk during his early years in New York, or in notebooks he

[19] Miguel Tedín, Argentine delegate to the International American Monetary Commission of 1891, reflects on José Martí's profound knowledge of English and his lack of inclination to speak it in "José Martí," *La Nación*, December 1, 1909; rpt. *Yo conocí a Martí* 163. See also Martí, fragment 411, *OC* 22: 284.

[20] The articles in *The Hour* (1880–1882) cover topics as diverse as Alexander Pushkin and modern Spanish poetry. According to Ivan Schulman's invaluable research, the Cuban may have produced as many as 300 articles in Dana's *The Sun* from 1882–1895 under the pseudonym "M. de S." See Schulman, *Genesis del modernismo*, 83.

[21] A report in the Key West *Equator Democrat* describes Martí's speech to a mixed crowd of 700 in Key West. See Martí, "The Patrick Henry of Cuba," *Equator Democrat* (November 24, 1892); summary in *OC* 28: 341. This printed English summary offers only a guide to the original speech in English, which is not extant. It is likely that Martí spoke extemporaneously. Although Charles Dana clearly admired Martí and was interested in the Cuban efforts to oust Spain, Rubén Darío's description of his meeting with Charles Dana confirms what he describes as the "dictatorial gesture" of the North American editor and publisher, who conducted the conversation in English and barely permitted Darío one or two monosyllables during their meeting, in "Charles A. Dana," 93.

managed to keep throughout his nomadic life.[22] Manuscript fragments 163 and 166 reveal a poet and theorist of literary modernity who dreams of revolutionizing poetic language by forging "the currents of modern life" into literary form, by infusing "the traditions of the tongue" with the "fire of the world." This worldly awareness of the dramatic historical moment in which he lived, together with a sense of his proximity to the vortex of these churning forces, infuses the migrant Cuban's literary and political philosophies.

Specifically, the proximity of multiple languages in the metropolitan center created an acute consciousness of language's plasticity, even as displaced migrants in the cities turned toward the inventiveness of spoken languages and dialects to inspire modern forms. The venue for the debut of what Martí calls "the modern poem" is the multilingual city of New York: "Cities have more tongues now than there are leaves on the trees of the forest; ideas mature in the public square where they are taught and passed from hand to hand" (SW 46). The figure that Martí's generative reader, the exiled Uruguayan Angel Rama, uses for modernism is the "word-suitcase" (palabra-maleta), or a well-worn piece of luggage full of images and phrases, the contents of which the writer-traveler carefully selects and unpacks, interprets, and adds to while away from home, surrounded by another language.[23] Rama's figurative suitcase adapts and translates Friedrich Nietzsche's metaphor of a large standing wardrobe for the costumes and masks of post-monarchical European nations.[24] Martí's association of his historical moment with the cadavers of gods also resonates with Nietzsche's secular vision; as historian Rafael Rojas has noted, Martí references the German philosopher in his notebooks.[25] The modernist suitcase's portability – unlike the standing wardrobe of romanticism – facilitates the contact and translation that gives rise to modernist form through a peripheral perspective that migrants and travelers in the urban metropolis began to introduce.[26]

---

[22] See Carmen Suárez León, *Indagación de universos*. Suárez León is editing Martí's notebooks and fragmentary writings as part of the critical edition prepared by a team of scholars under the direction of Pedro Pablo Rodríguez.

[23] Rama, *Las Máscaras democráticas del modernismo*, 64–65.

[24] Nietzsche, Fragment 223, *Beyond Good and Evil*, 146–47 and Rama, *Las Máscaras democráticas del modernismo*, 80–83.

[25] Martí refers to "cadáveres de los dioses (cadavers of the gods)" (*OC* 10: 226) and cites the "Gaya Scienza" in his notebooks (*OC* 21: 226). See Rafael Rojas, *José Martí: La invención de Cuba* (Edicion Colibri) and Blanca M. Rivera Meléndez, 192.

[26] Williams, *The Politics of Modernism*, 45.

As opposed to the nineteenth-century romantic obsession with a handful of "representative men" as projected by Ralph Waldo Emerson, Martí witnessed a modern "decentralization of intelligence" in which diverse expressions of genius would emerge not in the lifelong work of a single privileged individual, but in fragmentary, democratic, widely accessible, and broadly disseminated printed forms (SW 47). In the chronicler's adduction of the qualities of modern poetry, he notes the evanescence of "individual geniuses," who are beginning to lose "la pequeñez de los contornos que realzaban antes tanto su estatura" (the smallness of the periphery that previously heightened their stature) (OC 7: 228; SW 47, translation modified). As Martí's notebook fragments on Ralph Waldo Emerson suggest, the center loses its privileged superior status without the periphery's subordination.[27] Martí sees genius moving from the individual to the collective, from inaccessible private venues to broadly public and common spaces. The movement of "gente latina" from the place assigned them in Spanish colonial and U.S. imperial discourses threatened a U.S.-led pan-American hierarchy and disrupted forms of class- and race-based exclusion that divided public spaces in the United States. Martí takes stock of a shift palpable at the moment of Emerson's passing in 1882: "Now men are beginning to walk across the whole of earth without stumbling" (SW 45). This early twentieth-century Latina/o writing evokes the massive flux of human beings across borders. Martí's iteration of Latino modernism arises in response to the aesthetic and political insufficiency of one language, of a singular modernity, or of one representative man.

Against Pan-Americanism

Martí's poetry and prose emerge in the United States in spite of, and acutely conscious of, a will to silence or deform a Latina/o aesthetic. The International American Conference during the winter of 1889–1890 provides the backdrop to some of Martí's most influential, most anthologized, and widely cited texts, including his rhyming décimas in the Versos sencillos (1891) and "Madre América," a speech at the Sociedad Literária Hispanoamericana

---

[27] Martí wrote extensive notes on Emerson, only some of which appeared in print on the occasion of Emerson's death. See Ballón Aguirre, Autonomia Cultural Americana: Emerson y Martí (Madrid: Editorial Pliegos, 1986); Anne Fountain, José Martí and US Writers (Gainesville: University Press of Florida, 2003), and Lomas, "José Martí's 'Evening of Emerson' and the United Statesian Literary Tradition," Journal of American Studies 43 (2009): 1–17.

de Nueva York (Hispanic American Literary Society of New York), at which many of representatives of Latin American republics were in attendance.[28] The title derives from the image of a submarine, umbilical connection between the members of the Latin American diaspora and their home region. A book by Charles O'Rourke, a U.S. publicist tasked with offering a full account of that first pan-American meeting, described the sumptuous decor of the train that took delegates to factories, insurance companies, and mines throughout the Northeast.[29] He noted that the delegates attended a special reception at the Sociedad Literaria Hispanoamericana, but did not mention Martí's momentous speech, which contains many of the ideas that appeared in "Nuestra América" the following year.[30] In other words, O'Rourke's publicity book produces an official erasure of Martí's dissent from that of "los panamericanos" (OC 6: 57), a term Martí used with biting sarcasm and alarm. Pro-annexation Cuban and North American merchants such as Fidel S. Pierra and Andrew Carnegie – Martí's political opponents – endorsed the pan-Americanist proposals, so it is problematic to associate Martí with such a movement or vision as thenpresident George Bush did in a speech in celebration of the Free Trade Area of the Americas in 2001.[31]

---

[28] José Martí, "Madre América," discurso pronunciado el 19 de diciembre de 1889, OC 6: 140. Cf. "Our Spanish-American Literary Society," *New York Herald* (February 1, 1891), p. 24. Thanks to Enrique López Mesa for this reference.

[29] See discussion of the failed International American Congress in Oscar Montero's *Introduction to José Martí*, who discovered O'Rourke's propaganda piece for Blaine's project.

[30] O'Rourke, *Congreso Internacional Americano. Paseo de los delegados. Objeto del Congreso* (New York: New York City Press Association, 1890). Promising to be a "crónica fiel de ese viaje" (4), O'Rourke cites Blaine's toast to the perpetual friendship and prosperity of all the nations of the Americas at the Hotel Bijou, and describes a banquet at Delmonicos hosted by the Unión Comercial Hispano-Americana, but elides from the record Martí's speech of December 19. The reader learns only that at the reception at 29th and Madison Avenues, the Colombian journalist and writer, founder "[e]l Sr. Perez Triana pronunció un discurso sobre los objetos y fines de la Sociedad (Mr. Perez Triana pronounced a speech about the goals and objectives of the Society)" (109). As Enrique López Mesa notes, Martí was the "orador predilecto (favorite orator)" of this society where he served as president between 1890 and 1891, to prod the society not to become an irrelevant space of "intellectual narcissism" and "commemorative rhetoric" in New York (11).

[31] Bush cited Martí in his speech on behalf of economic integration at the Summit of the Americas in Quebec, on April 21, 2001 (*New York Times*, April 22, 2001, p. 1). By recalling the historical baggage that this term carries with it, I am responding to a field of comparative or inter-American research where "pan-American" still circulates as a deceptive reference to José Martí's project or as a way to define literature of the Americas. See José Saldívar's reference to a "pan-American consciousness," in *Dialectics of Our America*, xi.

In Martí's crónicas and essays of the 1880s and 1890s, he described his task as one of disenchantment and demystification: he alerted the novice or the unstudied to the seductive trap of the "espejismo de progreso" (mirage of progress) (*OC* 6: 61). The notion of the United States as the pinnacle of modernity emphasizes a "superficie" (surface) that covers over the unspeakable entrails of an emerging empire. Martí's texts point to this untranslatable difference in perspective between "our America" and the "America that is not ours" (*OC* 8: 35). Martí makes the case to his readers that his location in the United States permits him to see what the Latin American looking north and the U.S. writer looking south cannot. This task of translation from a displaced position within the hemisphere has continued to haunt the notion of "America" as "a relational, comparative concept" (Kaplan 9). Untranslatable difference underscores the need for scholars of American and Latina/o studies to be able to work – at the very least – with Spanish- and English-language texts.[32]

At stake in Martí's counternarrative of pan-Americanism is nothing other than the future of Cuba, as sovereign nation or future territory owned by the United States. Although Martí respects the united continent, organized to defend the new republics' freedom from future conquest, he censures what he sees to be the creation, in effect, of "un nuevo despotismo" (a new despotism) (*OC* 6: 62) in the heart of a liberty-loving public. This new despotism threatens to betray and corrode a revolutionary tradition in the Americas. For example, the US encroachment upon Haiti's sovereignty in 1889 becomes a key node in Martí's narration of the corruption of liberty spearheaded by one of the most influential Republican party leaders in the nineteenth century, James Blaine, for whom the International American Congress was a brainchild as early as 1881. Although Martí was erroneously framed as an autonomist with a reformist colonial agenda, he actually never wavered from his commitment to sovereignty and separatism. As a deported exile who upon meeting fellow Caribbean students in Spain would lift the shirt off his back to show the scars of the whipping he received as a political prisoner, Martí viscerally opposed annexation or autonomist reform.[33]

---

[32] Coronado, "The Aesthetics of Our America."

[33] The Puerto Rican novelist and medical doctor Manuel Zeno Gandía recounts this anecdote in his description of meeting Martí when they both were studying in exile in Spain. See his "Cómo conocí a un caudillo," *Yo conocí a Martí*, selección y prólogo de Carmen Suárez León (Santa Clara, Cuba: Ediciones Capiro, 1998): 214. For a fuller discussion of the abiding friendship between Martí and Zeno Gandía, including an

Martí's 1882 review of Frederick Douglass's *Autobiography* celebrates the formerly enslaved writer and politician as an "extraordinary modern man of color," a renowned orator and "ornament of the Senate."[34] But after 1889, when Douglass attempts to implement the Republican party's acquisition of a US military base in Haiti, Martí's estimation of the African-American orator changes. He comes to represent any island's abject possible future if leaders such as he were to become instruments of annexationism. Here Martí paraphrases and translates from the account of Douglass's failed diplomacy in the US press, noting that an openly racist envoy of Republican officials refused to sit with him: "no podían sentarse en la mesa con un mulato" (could not sit down at the table with a mulatto).[35] Exposing this prevailing tendency, Martí paraphrases Douglass with biting irony: "there are no more tender friends than those gentlemen of the ship: those who refused to sit with him."[36] Martí's initial respect and favorable view of Douglass as an exemplary figure of modernity changes to ironic mockery as the heroic escaped slave becomes a lackey who praises the very Republicans using him to subordinate other members of the African diaspora.

In dramatic life-and-death terms, Martí wrote of the significance of the Cuban insurrection that began on the island in 1895 in an open letter translated by Eugene Bryson for the *New York Herald* and published, as history would have it, on the day of his death, May 19, 1895: "[Cuba] has risen that she might emancipate an intelligent and generous people, who have an especial[sic] place in American history."[37] This phrase strategically leaves open the question of the influence of the people of Cuba in the Americas, while conveying to English-speaking U.S. readers a corrective to the common misunderstanding that U.S. history constitutes all of American

account of the *velada* where Martí read aloud his *Versos sencillos*, and the multiple instances where Martí's enemies depicted him as the autonomist he never was, see Enrique López Mesa, *Hipótesis*.

[34] Martí, *La Opinión Nacional*, Caracas, February 25, 1882, rpt. *Obras completas, Edición Crítica* (12; 220), my translation.

[35] Martí, "En los Estados Unidos," *La Nación*, November 22, 1889; *En los Estados Unidos* 1319; see also Martí, "Congreso Internacional de Washington," *La Nación*, December 20, 1889; *En los Estados Unidos* 1341.

[36] Martí, "En los Estados Unidos" *La Nación*, November 22, 1889; *En los Estados Unidos* 1319.

[37] Letter to the Editor of the *New York Herald* ("The Letter from the Cuban Leaders"). English version, May 19, 1895; Spanish version, *Patria*, June 3, 1895. Reprinted in *Epistolario* 5: 205–25; and in Toledo Sande, "José Martí contra *The New York Herald*," 49–72.

history. At the same time, this letter in its Spanish and English versions in a major New York daily and in *Patria*, the newspaper of the Cuban Revolutionary Party, implies what we have come to learn in the twenty-first century: that Latinas/os are likely to play a leading role in shaping the future politics of the United States, in the Americas, and beyond. The phrasing does not exclude the diaspora, of which Martí was a leading member.[38]

Against Racism

En otros... no les parece que haya elegancia mayor que la de beberle al extranjero los pantalones y las ideas, e ir por el mundo erguidos, como en el faldero acariciando el pompón de la cola. En otros es como sutil aristocracia, con la que, amando en público lo rubio como propio y natural, intentan encubrir el origen que tienen por mestizo y humilde, sin ver que fue siempre entre hombres señal de bastardía el andar tildando de ella a los demás ("La Verdad sobre los Estados Unidos," *Patria*, March 23, 1894; *En los Estados Unidos* 1755).

(In others... there is no greater elegance than drinking up both the cut of the foreigner's pants and his ideas, and going about the world like petted lapdogs with the pompoms of their tails sticking up. In others it is a kind of subtle aristocracy whereby, publicly loving all that is fairskinned as if that were natural and proper, they try to cover up their own origin, which they see as mestizo and humble, without seeing that it was always a sign of bastardy in men to go about branding others as bastards). (*SW* 332)

Para el *Herald* el negro no pertenece a la humanidad. Debe privársele de la garantía de los fueros humanos. Son inferiores a los demás. Luego, ¿siendo Cuba un pueblo de negros, al unirse a éste de blancos, qué esperanza de felicidad nos queda cuando ya se nos anuncia la estimación que para los americanos merecemos?

(For the *Herald*, the black does not belong to humanity. They should be deprived of the protections of human rights. They are inferior to all others.

---

[38] Román de la Campa notes that Cuban exiles have been reluctant to see themselves as part of a larger Latino minority in the United States (*Cuba on My Mind* 3, 7). Lisandro Pérez's proposal that the Cuban diaspora should be able to retain Cuban citizenship and participate in the life of the nation as is the case for Mexicans, Peruvians, and residents of many other Latin American countries remains a controversial proposal in light of a long history of organized Cuban exile opposition that has actively participated in US-organized attacks on the current government (July 17, 2016, presentation at Fresa y Chocolate in La Habana, Cuba).

Then, if Cuba is a country of blacks, when it joins this people of whites, what hope for happiness remains for us, when already the Americans announce the esteem that they have for us?)

– Rafael Serra y Montalvo, "Ni Española ni Yankee"[39]

Not an obsequious adherence to a "nordic" racial ideal in vogue in the United States, but an affirmation of an antiracist politics served as an axiom of Martí's aesthetics and politics as a result of his encounter with the U.S. racial system. La Liga, the Afro-Latina/o night school where Martí lectured on historical figures such as the Afro-Cuban organizer and poet Gabriel Concepción de Valdés (Plácido) and the Haitian revolutionary leader Toussaint L'Ouverture, sought to procure "the intellectual advancement of men of color born in Cuba and Puerto Rico" by facilitating access to education by working-class youth with potential for a career in which members of the colored class were underrepresented.[40] The material reality of working as an immigrant in New York to support his economically unstable parents, sisters, and wife and child, afforded the professionally trained lawyer (with additional degrees in philosophy and literature) an affinity with working people, especially Afro-Cubans and Afro–Puerto Ricans who found in Martí a refreshing alternative to the New York Cuban impresarios, many of whom were former slave owners or merchants who sought to preserve their class and color privilege through a possessive investment in whiteness. Many of these affluent Latino annexationists saw Martí as destined to failure because of his association with working-class black and white Cuban migrants.[41]

Enrique Trujillo, Martí's contemporary and editor of a key Spanish-language newspaper in New York, described the differences between the

---

[39] New York, January 30, 1898, *Ensayos Políticos*; rpt. in Oficina del Historiador de la Ciudad de la Habana, 125.

[40] Gonzalez Veranes, *Personalidad de Rafael Serra*, 19.

[41] See José Ignacio Rodríguez, who disparages Martí's antiracist, working-class-based organizing practices in his extensive treatise on annexation: "Todos creyeron que aquel movimiento improvisado, en que no figuraban sino emigrados cubanos, los más de ellos de la clase obrera, blancos y negros, de Cayo Hueso, Tampa, New York, Philadelphia, y alguna otra ciudad de la Unión, que aparentemente no contaban, ni con dinero, ni con los demás elementos que para empresa de esta clase se han creido siempre indispensables, estaba destinado a fracasar miserablemente" (Everyone believed that his improvised movement – in which only Cuban migrants, in the majority working-class whites and blacks of Key West, Tampa, New York, Philadelphia, and other cities of the Union, which apparently had neither the money nor other forms of support that this sort of endeavor had always been thought to be indispensable – was destined to fail miserably) (*Origen de la anexión* 279).

Northern and Southern hubs of the Cuban diaspora in terms of their politics, which also reflect to an extent the prevailing color and class affiliation of each city's Latina/o majority or minority culture:

> The Cuban immigrants in Key West are the most patriotic; those in Philadelphia, the most tranquil; those in New York, the most heterogeneous. In Key West, all are separatists; in Philadelphia, they have not made up their minds; and in New York they range from "ultramontane" to socialist. In New York there is an aristocracy; in Philadelphia, everyone is family; and in Key West, everything is democratic.[42]

The terms "democratic" and "socialist" gesture also to the working-class identified, well-informed tabaqueros, who worked in racially integrated spaces despite their location in the deep U.S. South. The aristocracy in New York included the former slave owners and historic leaders of the Cuban junta, during the period of the pro-annexationist filibustering efforts, alongside the growing constituency of mixed-race, working class, and politically radical groups that included a large number of socialist Puerto Ricans, such as Martí's friend, the Afro–Puerto Rican Francisco Gonzálo "Pachín" Marín.[43]

Martí poetically condenses his relationship to Cuba as an irreparable wound, and indicates on multiple occasions his sense of being indebted to his black compatriots, because of the extreme suffering that white Cubans had inflicted upon them during slavery and after emancipation (SW 275).[44] His *Versos sencillos*, which culls memories and epiphanies from throughout his life, depict a young boy looking up to encounter an African who had been mortally punished and placed on display:

Rojo, como en el desierto,	Red as if it shone from a desert sky
Salió el sol al horizonte:	the sun came out on the horizon
Y alumbró a un esclavo muerto,	and cast its light on a dead slave
Colgado a un seibo del monte.	hanging from a ceibo tree.
Un niño lo vio: tembló	A child saw this and shuddered

---

[42] *El Avisador Cubano* 4.24 (New York, June 1885), p. 3, my translation.

[43] See Lomas, "Migration and Decolonial Politics in Two Afro-Latino Poets: 'Pachín' Marín and 'Tato' Laviera," *REVIEW: Latin American Literature and Arts* 89.48.2 (Fall 2014): 155–63, Special Issue Edited by Nicolás Kanellos, for a fuller discussion of the Marín's socialist affiliations while in exile.

[44] In his notebooks, in English, Martí describes the suffering of blacks as a cause of shame and an inspiration for action: "I wear an iron ring, and I have to do iron deeds.... No suffering as the black men in my country" (Fragment 184 *OC* 22, p. 108) and in Spanish, "Y los negros? ¿Quien que ha visto azotar a un negro no se considera para siempre su deudor? Yo lo vi, lo vi cuando era niño y todavía no se me ha apagado en las mejillas la vergüenza" (Fragment 286 *OC* 22, p. 189).

De pasión por los que gimen;	with passion for those who groan;
Y, al pie del muerto, juró	he stood below the corpse and swore
Lavar con su vida el crimen!	to wash the crime away with his life! (280–81)

Although the metaphor of the nation as a slave has problematically granted white Creoles opportunities to speak on behalf of Afro-Cubans and to render anti-black racism secondary to the project of nation-building, it is possible to see in these stanzas how racism constitutes a wound without suture that informs Martí's activist opposition to the logic of white supremacy as part of his revolutionary labor. This idea of Martí as a critic of racism, as experienced by Cubans of color at home and abroad, tends to unsettle dominant narratives of exilic Cuban self-understanding. Nonetheless, these writings represent a quotidian experience of Latina/o migrants.

Martí acknowledges his position as a Latino migrant who experienced racialization through quotidian interactions or in his denunciation of stereotypes about Latin America and the Caribbean that circulated in the United States, coincident with heightened white, Anglo-supremacist and anti-immigrant violence in the post-Reconstruction Gilded Age.[45] Martí's widely circulated and self-translated Letter to the Editor of the *New York Post* counters stereotypes of Cubans in the United States as "moral pests," "destitute vagrants" accused of having a "distaste for exertion" or of belonging to an "effeminate" people ("A Vindication of Cuba," *New York Evening Post*, March 23, 1889; rpt. *SW* 263–64) and simultaneously interrogates a long-standing discourse about Cuba's imminent annexation to the United States.[46]

Martí articulates this unsettling of a Latino/Saxon binary in part through a controversial antiracism that some have read as having the effect of "silencing" race within the Independence Movement. It is clear that this antiracist discourse was twisted in the Cuban Republic to prevent Afro-Cubans from organizing to bring about social equality in the face of *de facto* white criollo exclusion of blacks (including many decorated veterans of the War of Independence) from government jobs, clubs, and public space.[47]

---

[45] I discuss Martí's racialization and his critique of racism in "'El Negro es tan capaz como el blanco': José Martí, Pachín Marín, Lucy Parsons and the Politics of Late-Nineteenth Century Latinidad," in Rodrigo Lazo and Jesse Alemán, eds. *The Latino Nineteenth Century*.

[46] I should note that some readers in Miami took umbrage at the idea of Martí making a critique of monolingualism and racism. See Lomas, "Martí in las trincheras de papel," *Diario las Américas* (February 4, 2013): 6A.

[47] Lourdes Casal, "Race Relations in Contemporary Cuba," 18. Casal offers the figure of 75 percent black soldiers among Cuba's rank and file during the struggle for Cuban independence, note 18, and calls attention to the very "black look" of the officers, of

A discourse on African culture as "barbaric," immigration policies that fostered European immigration and excluded blacks, the demonization of Afro-Cuban religions and the generalized fear of a Haitian-style black self-emancipation flourished even when the Cuban constitution granted full citizenship and equal rights without respect to color.[48] Indeed the persistence of white monopolization of positions of power and prestige despite claims to have eliminated racism or to have entered a post-racial period remains a key point of contention in Cuba and in the United States.[49] Lourdes Martínez-Echázabal rightly raises the crucial question of whether Martí would have endorsed José Miguel Gómez's 1912 massacre of thousands of black men, women, and children who had joined the Partido Independiente de Color, a black voter's association, to protest lack of equality for Afro-Cubans in the years after independence; or if he would have stood with Afro-Cubans such as his friend and co-conspirator Rafael Serra, who called upon his black compatriots to organize to reclaim their rights.[50] Despite the gruesome repression after independence of what Afro-Cuban and Afro–Puerto Rican supporters referred to in a newspaper with the same title as "la doctrina de Martí," the pre-independence phase of the antiracist critique not only helped mobilize the black-majority Hispanic Caribbean diaspora that raised funds and recruited soldiers for Cuban and Puerto Rican independence; it also offered arguments that Cubans of color used to interrogate the white-supremacist practices that became widespread and reached a dramatic pitch with the so-called "Guerrita" or Race War of 1912.

Martí's critique of the second-class status of Cubans of color in early 1894 is informed by over a decade of comparative study and translations of the experiences of other racialized groups, including Chinese workers facing white working-class violence after the passage of the Chinese Exclusion Act, native Americans massacred after a military struggle with the US Army at Wounded Knee in 1891, African Americans subject to lynch law in the post-Reconstruction period, the immigrant workers attacked by the police and

---

whom 40 percent were black (25). These forces were dismantled and whitened during the US military occupations of Cuba from 1899–1902 and 1906–1909.

[48] Ada Ferrer, "The Silence of Patriots," José Martí's "Our America," *From National to Hemispheric Cultural Studies*, ed. Jeffrey Belnap and Raúl Fernández, Duke (1998): 228–49; Lillian Guerra, *The Myth of Martí*.

[49] See Roberto Zurbano, "For Blacks in Cuba, the Revolution Hasn't Begun," *New York Times* (March 23, 2013).

[50] Indeed one of the most startling photographs in the aftermath of the hunting down and eradication of a political party designed to demand equal rights for black Cubans features José Martí's son Pepé at the feast celebrating the massacre.

hanged as criminals in 1887, and *tejanos* and *californios* in the states that once were Mexican and were subject to abuses after 1848.[51] Institutionalized racial terror under democratic capitalism pertains to the currents of modern life that Martí incorporates into "language's traditions" to which he referred in fragment 166.

In the case of his account of anti-black racial terror, Martí's 1892 chronicle transcribes the speech of African Americans fleeing the United States for Africa to show how racism circumscribed citizenship. In the same *crónica* that depicts a lynching in which 5,000 people witness a white woman lighting the pyre of a black man in Texarkana, a small town on the Texas-Arkansas border, Martí recreates the call-and-response exchange of a group of African Americans en route to Liberia. Martí's version in Spanish mixes the relentless pace of Cuban *choteo* with the subtlety of African-American signifying:

> ¿Conque somos cobardes porque no nos quedamos aquí, donde el que tiene fango, aquí basta que venga el Mesías? pues "los cobardes viven mucho." Conque a Luisiana otra vez, y a Texas y Arkansas?: "¡gato quemado tiene miedo al fuego!" ¿Y que no sabemos adónde vamos a ir? "¡el puerco sabe en qué árbol se frota!" ¡Y para qué nos hemos de quedar aquí, para ser como esos, que no son más que medio caballeros? "el cortarle las orejas a un mulo, no le hace caballo"

> (Are we cowards, then, because we don't stay here, in these muddy waters, until the Messiah comes? Well, "cowards live long lives," they say. It is back to Louisiana or Texas or Arkansas, then? "Once bitten twice shy!" And don't we know where we're going? "The pig knows what tree to scratch against!" For why would we stay here, to be like those who are never more than half gentlemen? "Cutting the ears off a mule doesn't make it a horse."

> ("A Town Sets a Black Man on Fire," *SW* 310–13; "El negro en los Estados Unidos," *En los Estados Unidos* 1506).

Singing, laughing, "thrusting both hands deep in their pockets," the black refugees display their canny common sense and earn the readers' respect for the decision to go "where they do not set fire to our men" (*SW* 310). Not to be confused with the white-led African colonization movement discourse,

---

[51] See his letter: "solo esperan a nuestra tierra las desdichas y el éxodo de Texas, y de que el predominio norteamericano que se intenta en el continente haría el mismo éxodo en las cercanías sumidas, al menos, odioso e inseguro" (what awaits our land are the misfortune and exodus of Texas, for the North American predominance that is being attempted in the continent will likely be reproduced in the subordinated margins, and it will be odious and uncertain) (*Epistolario* t. 2, 160).

this chronicle attempts to bring the reader close to the perspective of those who found life in the United States to be a nightmare.

In the next scene of "A Town Sets a Black Man on Fire," Martí contrasts the measured, persuasive, and respectful language of the black man Coy with members of the white mob. Coy insists upon his innocence by exclaiming: "I offered Mrs. Jewell no offense!" (SW 313). He utters this phrase as the crowd forces him to trot and then binds him to a tree and douses him with petroleum. Before the same Mrs. Jewell touches a match to Coy's jacket, the crowd insults and threatens Coy: "We are going to kill you, Coy, kill you like the dog you are, before the mayor can sic the troops he asked the governor for on us!" (SW 313). The white woman, Mrs. Jewell, also figures as a cooperative instrument in this practice.

Through representations of the lynch mob that would burn a black man or of a massacre of a community of migrant Chinese workers, and crónicas that recorded the responses of the dominated to that violence, Martí – in the late-nineteenth century – imagines the specters that haunt the "freedom" forged through racial and imperial violence. While Martí contributes to Spanish-language modernism in poetry and prose, he writes in New York, as a speaker of what functioned in the North as a minor language. There, his poetry and prose stake out a critique of the prevailing discourses of literary realism and romanticism, of pan-Americanism, and of racism as they functioned in the United States and in Latin American and Caribbean contexts. This modern sensibility and critical Latina/o subjectivity emerge in response to the histor-ical experience of working and writing in the Anglophone-dominant and racialized empire city of New York, where Martí observed the emergence of a people "criado en la esperanza de la dominación continental [a people raised up in the hope of continental domination]" (OC 6:63). In these texts we encounter a Latina/o literary modernity premised not on continental domin-ation, nor on a false claim to originality, but on comparative critique.

WORKS CITED

Ballón, José. *Lecturas Norteamericanas de José Martí: Emerson y el socialismo contemporaneo (1880–1887)*. México: Centro Coordinador y Difusor de Estudios Latinoamericanos, Universidad Nacional Autónoma de México, 1995.

Belnap, Jeffrey, and Raul Fernández, eds. *José Martí's "Our America": From National to Hemispheric Cultural Studies*. Durham, NC: Duke University Press, 1998.

Casal, Lourdes. "Race Relations in Contemporary Cuba." Lourdes Casal and Anani Dzidzienyo, *The Position of Blacks in Brazilian and Cuban Society*. London: Minority Rights Group, 1979.

Collazo, Enrique. *Cuba independiente*. Havana: La Moderna Poesía, 1900.

Coronado, Raúl. "The Aesthetics of Our America: A Response to Susan Gillman." *American Literary History*. 20.1–2 (2008): 210–16.

Crane, Stephen. "Fears Realists Must Wait." *New York Times* Oct. 28, 1894, 20; rpt. *Critical Essays on William Dean Howells (1866–1920)*. Ed. Edwin H. Cady and Norma W. Cady. Boston: G. K. Hall & Co., 1983. 146–47.

Darío, Rubén. "José Martí." *Los raros*, 193–203. 1896. Buenos Aires: Editora Espasa-Calpe, Argentina, 1952.

De la Campa, Román. *Cuba on My Mind: Journeys to Severed Nation*. London: Verso, 2000.

De la Cuesta, Leonel. *Martí, Traductor*. Salamanca: Universidad Pontificia de Salamanca, 1996.

Douglass, Frederick. "Haiti and the United States: The Inside History of the Negotiations for the Môle San Nicholas." *The North American Review* 153 (1891): 337–45.

Ferrer, Ada. "The Silence of Patriots: Race and Nationalism in Martí's Cuba." *José Martí's "Our America."* Ed. Belnap and Fernandez. 228–49.

Foucault, Michel. "Theatrum Philosophicum." *Language, Counter-Memory, Practice*. Ithaca, NY: Cornell University Press, 1977.

González Veranes, Pedro N. *La personalidad de Rafael Serra y sus relaciones con Martí. Conferencia pronunciada en la Institución Cultural "Club Atenas" en la noche del 17 de diciembre de 1942*. Havana: La Veronica, 1943.

Guerra, Lillian. *The Myth of José Martí: Conflicting Nationalisms in Early Twentieth-Century Cuba*. Chapel Hill: University of North Carolina Press, 2005.

Hidalgo Paz, Ibrahim. *José Martí 1853–1895: Cronología*. Havana: Centro de Estudios Martianos, 2003.

International American Conference. *Minutes of the International American Conference, Actas de la Conferencia Internacional Americana*. Washington, DC: Government Printing Office, 1890.

Kaplan, Amy, "Violent Belonging and the Question of Empire Today." Presidential Address to the American Studies Association, October 17, 2003. *American Quarterly* 56.1 (2004): 1–18.

Lazo, Rodrigo and Jesse Alemán, *The Latino Nineteenth Century*. New York: New York University Press, 2016.

Lomas, Laura. *Translating Empire: José Martí, Migrant Latino Subjects and American Modernities*. Durham, NC: Duke University Press, 2008.

"Imperialism, Modernization and Commodification of Identity in José Martí's 'Great Cattle Exposition.'" *Travesía: Journal of Latin American Cultural Studies* 9.2 (2002): 193–212.

"Migration and Decolonial Politics in Two Afro-Latino Poets: 'Pachín' Marín and 'Tato' Laviera." *Review: Literature and Arts of the Americas* 47.2 (2014): 155–63.

"The Unbreakable Voice in a Minor Language: Following José Martí's Migratory Routes." *Hispanic Caribbean Migration: Narratives of Displacement*. Ed. Vanessa Pérez Rosario. London: Palgrave Macmillan, 2010.

López, Alfredo J. *José Martí: An Heroic Life*. Austin: University of Texas Press, 2014.

López Mesa, Enrique. *Hipótesis sobre un elogio: José Martí y Manuel Zeno Gandía*. Havana: Centro de Estudios Martianos, 2015.

Lowe, Lisa. *The Intimacies of Four Continents*. Durham, NC: Duke University Press, 2015.

Márquez Sterling, Carlos. *Martí y la conferencia monetaria de 1891*. Havana: Imprenta "El Siglo XX" A. Muñiz y Hno. Calle Brasil, 1938. 21–23.

Martí, José. *En los Estados Unidos: periodismo de 1881–1892*. Ed. Roberto Fernández Retamar and Pedro Pablo Rodríguez. Havana: Casa de las Américas, 2003.

   Epistolario. 5 vols. Ed. Luis García Pascual and Enrique H. Moreno Plá. Havana: Editorial de Ciencias Sociales, 1993.

   Obras completas. 28 vols. Havana: Editorial de Ciencias Sociales, 1963–65. Page references are to the second edition, 1975.

   Obras completas, edición crítica. 26 vols, incomplete. Havana: Centro de Estudios Martianos, 2003–2016.

   Selected Writings. Ed. and trans. Esther Allen. New York: Penguin, 2002.

Martínez-Echazábal, Lourdes. "'Martí y las Razas': A Re-Evaluation." *Re-Reading Martí, One Hundred Years Later*. Ed. Julio Rodríguez-Luis. Albany: State University of New York Press, 1999. 116–26.

Montero, Oscar. *Introduction to José Martí*. New York: Palgrave Macmillan, 2005.

O'Rourke, Charles. *Congreso Internacional Americano. Paseo de los delegados. Objeto del Congreso*. New York: New York City Press Association, 1890.

Picón-Garfield, Evelyn, and Ivan Schulman. *"Las Entrañas del Vacío": Ensayos sobre la modernidad hispanoamericana*. Mexico City: Ediciones cuadernos americanos, 1984.

Rama, Angel. *La ciudad letrada*. *Prólogo Hugo Achugar*. Montevideo: Arca, 1998.

   Las Máscaras democráticas del modernismo. Montevideo: Fundación Angel Rama, 1985.

   "La dialéctica de la modernidad en José Martí." *Estudios Martianos: Memoria del Seminario José Martí*. Río Piedras: Editorial Universitaria, Universidad de Puerto Rico, 1974.

Ramos, Julio. *Desencuentros de la modernidad: literatura y política en América Latina*. México: Fondo de Cultura Económica, 1989.

   Divergent Modernities: Culture and Politics in Nineteenth-Century Latin America. Durham, NC: Duke University Press, 2001.

   Rosario, Argentina: Beatriz Viterbo Editora, 2002.

Rivera Meléndez, Blanca Margarita. "Poetry and Machinery of Illusion: José Martí and the Poetics of Modernity." Ph.D. dissertation. Cornell University, 1990.

Rodríguez, José Ignacio. *Estudio histórico sobre el origen, desenvolvimiento y manifestaciones prácticas de la idea de la anexión de la isla de Cuba á los Estados Unidos de América*. Havana: Imprenta La Propaganda Literaria, 1900.

Rojas, Rafael. *José Martí: la Invención de Cuba*. Madrid: Editorial Colibri, 2001.

Romero, Matías. "The Pan-American Conference." *North American Review* 151 (1890).

Rotker, Susana. *La invención de la crónica*. Buenos Aires: Ediciones Letra Buena, 1992.

Roosevelt, Theodore. "True Americanism." *The Forum Magazine* (April 1894).

Rotker, Susana. *La invención de la crónica*. Mexico City: Fondo de cultura económica, 2005.

Saldívar, José David. *The Dialectics of Our America: Genealogy, Cultural Critique and Literary History*. Durham, NC: Duke University Press, 1991.

Schulman, Ivan A. *Genesis del modernismo: Martí, Nájera, Silva, Casal*. Mexico City: Colegio de México, 1966.

Serra, Rafael. *Rafael Serra, Patriota y Revolucionario; Fraternal Amigo de Martí* Havana: Oficina del Historiador de la Ciudad de la Habana, 1959.

Suárez León, Carmen. *La Alegría de traducir.* La Habana: Ciencias Sociales, 2007.

Indagación de universos: Los Cuadernos de apuntes de José Martí. Havana: Centro de Estudios Martianos, 2015.

La sangre y el mármol: Martí, el Parnaso, Baudelaire. Havana: Centro de Estudios Martianos, 2001.

ed. *Yo conocí a Martí.* Santa Clara, Cuba: Ediciones Capiro, 1998.

Vega, Bernardo. *Memorias de Bernardo Vega: Contribución a la historia de la comunidad puertorriqueña de Nueva York.* Edición de César Andreu Iglesias. Río Piedras, Puerto Rico: Ediciones Huracán, 1977.

13

Afro-Latinidad

Phoenix Rising from a Hemisphere's Racist Flames

SILVIO TORRES-SAILLANT

The Dark Side of Self-Affirmation

Professional basketball player Charlie Villanueva (born 1984), a native New York who has enjoyed an ascendant career since first joining the National Basketball Association (NBA) league in 2005, remembers a high school photo shoot that occasioned his first serious encounter with racism. As he posed for the camera of the woman photographing him, he recalls a man intruding: "There comes this gentleman, and he says to the lady, right in front of me, 'Why are you taking pictures of this. . .?' And he said the 'N' word!" The athlete remembers the shock and the fear triggered by this act of aggression, which distressed him to the point that he even considered leaving the school. To his credit, before further nurturing that thought, he picked up the phone and called his mother, a Dominican immigrant woman who had a very simple message to convey. She told him that if he harbored any hopes of getting anywhere in life, he could not afford to let insults make him change his course. Villanueva's account forms part of "One Nación: Afro-Latinos," a five-minute ESPN video aired October 8, 2015 that sets out to make viewers aware of African-descended people of Hispanic descent and the challenges they face as a demographically distinct component of the US population. Also featured in the segment, Victoria Benítez of the Office of Communications and Public Affairs at Columbia University, remembers the disappointment she caused her fair-skinned Puerto Rican mother once by describing herself as black.

The other Afro-Latino interviewed in the video, journalist and author Ed Morales, a faculty member in Columbia University's Center for Ethnicity and Race, explained that in Latin America both racism and affirmations of black identity developed distinct traits vis-à-vis their equivalents in the United States. In a review of the ESPN film, Los Angeles-based writer and photographer Walter Thompson-Hernández commended the production's "attempt to package the Afro-Latino experience" in such a brief segment and forgave its

276

inevitable elisions (Thompson-Hernández 2015). Fortunately, the short film does not commit explicitly to answering the implicit question concerning the meaning of Afro-latinidad. Even so, Thompson-Hernández prudently worries about the pervasive presence of music, dance, and sports that visually and sonically frame the piece. Such a frame seems to suggest performance and athletics as constitutive elements of the identity of the group in question, inadvertently validating annoying stereotypes that still plague media coverage of Latinos. Both Benítez and Villanueva adduce bilingual ability as an aspect of their heritage which they treasure, while expressing perhaps inordinate pride at having their particular ancestries. The former praises Puerto Rican music and the latter extols Dominican food, just as they characterize their heritage respectively as a "blessing" and "a beautiful thing."

Celebrations of ancestry for people belonging to the less empowered sectors of the US population – or their marginalized counterparts in the citizenry of other societies in the hemisphere – share their genesis with ethnoracial self-hatred or alienation from their heritage. Both stem from a history that deprived given segments of the human family of the ability to take their ancestry for granted, requiring them to assume a position about it and to politicize its significance. The "black is beautiful" mantra of the 1960s in the United States emerged to offset the self-loathing that had plagued many African Americans. Exposed to centuries of a pernicious white supremacist creed that aimed systematically to dehumanize them, many people of African descent came to see themselves through the demeaning eyes of their Caucasian detractors. Throughout the hemisphere, the vilification of blackness and the attending glorification of whiteness proved effective, damaging the self-concept of those in the African-descended population who lacked vigorous defenses to guard themselves from ongoing psychological aggression. The famous "Doll Test" experiment conducted by psychologists Kenneth and Mamie Clark in the 1940s established the detrimental impact that a racist environment had on the minds of black children. The psychologists presented black children with a choice between a white and a black doll in various scenarios to test their preference. When asked to point to the doll fitting a pejorative term such as "ugly" or "bad," the children in the sample would overwhelmingly select the black doll, just as they would point to the white one when asked to match the doll with a positive term such as "good" or "smart." Malcolm X, in his famous 1963 speech "Message to the Grass Roots," berated those blacks who looked at Africa with contempt or who boasted about being the only blacks living in a white neighborhood. Similarly, Maya Angelou's first autobiography, *I Know Why the Caged Bird Sings* (1969), captures a glimpse of the problem in a scene that evokes the trepidations many black patients felt when putting their health in the hands of a black doctor, having previously learned to associate medical skill with whiteness. Indeed, the prominent nineteenth-century narratives of former slaves, such as those by Frederick Douglass (1845) and Harriet Jacobs (1861), as well as militant antislavery orations such as David Walker's *The Appeal* (1829), tended to devote several pages to condemning the cases they encountered of blacks – enslaved as well as free – who identified with their white masters more deeply than they did with their black brethren. Douglass recalls fellow captives looking down on the slaves of another master who owned fewer slaves or enjoyed lesser power than the master who owned them.

Black affirmation, in the United States as in Latin America, has no other *raison d'être* than that of providing an antidote against the inferiority complex that the architects of the colonial transaction malevolently inculcated in the descendants of enslaved Africans following the conquest and colonization of the Americas. It comes, in short, to combat the enduring effect of the negrophobic doctrine that for centuries informed thinking about race or ethnic difference throughout our hemisphere. In that respect, while allowing Villanueva and Benítez to convey their joy at being Afro-Latinos through citing the musical, linguistic, and culinary virtues of their ancestry, ESPN producers, again, deserve recognition for avoiding the folly of explaining or glorifying Afro-latinidad. The best thing a person of African and Hispanic descent can do for his or her identity is to leave it undefined to avoid unleashing the epistemological pandemonium that might otherwise ensue.

Like any other social-identity stance originating at the losing end of the stick in the tragic history of American societies South and North, the Afro-Latino label emerges as a reactive identity. It reacts against the racist regimes spawned by the particular form that imperialism and slavery took in the region. This form of domination distinguished itself from previous chapters in the history of enslavement in the central role it assigned to ancestry in the measure of a person's worth. That distinction culminated in the birth of societies whose cultural logic structured social relations in accordance with a dogma that upheld the inherent inequality among the various branches of the human species. The material conditions that brought this new ethno-racial reality into being, rather than any metaphysics of identity, ought to take precedence in any sound effort to explain or understand its meaning, but that inquiry, which this author takes up elsewhere, lies outside the scope of this entry. To call oneself an Afro-Latino (or Asian-Latino or Indo-Latino) is to expose the Eurocentric bias at the core of latinidad. Hispanics of African, Indigenous, or Asian heritage find it tempting to uphold a label that marks their distinct segment within the "Latina/o" pan-ethnicity as a way to demand recognition, render themselves visible and legible, before the racially compromised eyes of both the Hispanic and the Anglo worlds. But before moving on to invoke the pan-hemispheric history that produced Afro-latinidad as a distinct identity location that a black person from the Hispanic world might embrace, a note on the currency of the label may come in handy. We use the term *Afro-Latino* in this entry to name the African-descended portion of the US Hispanic population while referring to their counterparts in societies south of the Rio Grande as *Afro-Latin Americans*. Similarly, we use the term *Afro-Hispanic* to speak of dark-skinned people of African origin anywhere in the hemisphere, Spain, or elsewhere in the vast geography where the Spanish Empire held colonial sway irrespective of chronology.

While the chronology of our usage in this entry will correspond to the rise of *Latinos* as an ethnically differentiated segment of the US population in the twentieth century, it behooves us to acknowledge from the outset the presence of Afro-Hispanics in North America several centuries prior to the emergence of the United States. That presence starts with Juan Ponce de León's 1513 exploratory expedition to Florida, whose crew included the Christianized enslaved African Juan Garrido, who had previously accompanied the conquistador in the invasion of Puerto Rico (Alegría 1990; Restall 2000). Also, a North African black servant named Estevan formed part of the ill-fated 1527 voyage to Florida led by Pánfilo de Narváez, figuring as one of only four crew members who survived along with Alvar Núñez Cabeza de Vaca, the treasurer who told the story of the failed enterprise in his 1542 memoir *Naufragios* (Núñez Cabeza de Vaca 1993). In 1539 Estevan appears as the official guide to a reconnaissance mission led by Fray Marcos de Niza from Mexico City into the Zuni territory in western New Mexico, where the missionary thought he would find the legendary Seven Cities of Cibola (Niza 2002). After this, Estevan falls out of the historical record with Father Marcos going back to Mexico City before actually venturing to catch up with him in Zuni territory. The following year a mission sponsored by conquistador Francisco Vázquez de Coronado and Viceroy Antonio de Mendoza would explore the same region, but the sequence of events places the black Estevan as the first non-Native-American explorer of Zuni territory. Concomitantly, on the East Coast "a free mulatto from Santo Domingo" named Juan Rodrigues would in 1613 settle in the territory that subsequently became New York City, preceding the Dutch settlement that would start there nearly a decade later (Torres-Saillant and Hernandez 226).

Insofar as these instances of an Afro-Hispanic presence in the colonial period occurred as individual undertakings, they offer little to a genealogy of Afro-latinidad as a social identity with relevance to us today. Social identities, by definition, have little to do with individuals. When applied to those occupying a lesser rank in the structure of power, they operate as stigmas that brand groups, with individuals serving merely as illustrative samples of the character of the groups. Individuality must step out the moment racializing or ethnic othering comes in. Afro-latinidad emerges as an option for a collective to embrace when historical circumstances enable it, which did not happen until quite recently. The dark-skinned Dominican women who came to Washington, DC, as maids of the diplomats of Rafael Leónidas Trujillo's negrophobic dictatorship had their ethno-racial allegiance determined by Jim Crow, which barred them from seeking residence in the areas that their light-skinned employers could legally inhabit. As Ginetta Candelario has shown, these Afro-Dominicans went to live in mostly African American or – in keeping with the parlance of the day – *Negro* neighborhoods, often embracing the ethno-racial identity of their neighbors (Candelario 2001). The United States did not offer a site of belonging designed for piecing together the Latin and the African components of their ancestry without stress. Perhaps the Afro–Puerto Rican Arturo (Arthur) Schomburg, a full-fledged member of the Harlem Renaissance intelligentsia, deserves credit for articulating via his praxis the search for an Afro-Latino location of identity that he clearly deemed wanting, as we gather from the work of historian Jesse Hoffnung-Garskof (2001: 37–38).

The racial dramas endured by Afro-Cuban Evelio Grillo (1919–2008) and the Afro–Puerto Rican Piri Thomas (1928–2011) merit mention insofar as they offer telling glimpses of the difficult location of Afro-Hispanics in the decades immediately preceding the advent of Afro-latinidad as a readily available site of ethno-racial identity. Grillo's *Black Cuban, Black American: A Memoir* (2000) tells the story of a Cuban of African ancestry who became socially African American by virtue of his inability to find a space of belonging among the predominantly white Cuban community of Tampa. Thomas's *Down These Mean Streets*, on the other hand, dramatizes the difficult existential plight of a New York-born Puerto Rican, the son of a black Cuban father and white Boricua mother, who finds it hard to navigate the complexity of a racially mixed ancestry in a society dominated by the ideology of racial purity. Grillo contends with negrophobia as manifested publically in the Anglo-imposed Jim Crow apartness that dovetailed smoothly with the racial mores of white Cubans in Tampa. Thomas, on the other hand, confronts the unbearable existential discomfort produced by the two distinct legacies of racism that assail him in the neighborhood and in his family home. In his Manhattan apartment Thomas deals with the island-grown bias of the Hispanic world, transmitted to him via his mother's negrophobic lexicon to express maternal love. She treats him to sentiments of endearment contained in disparaging terms when saying, for instance, "I have to love you because only your mother could love you, *un negrito* and ugly" (Thomas 1997: 19). Outside of the home, he must ward off racial insults from members of rival gangs vying for street hegemony, getting a sour taste of the contempt for blackness cultivated on the US mainland over two centuries. Like the historical Schomburg, Piri tries to defect from the Hispanic side of his ancestry in order to seek racial refuge in the African American realm, but, like Schomburg, he too fails to attain a harmonious locus of identity there: "I was a Puerto Rican trying to make a Negro" (Thomas 1997: 177).

The foregoing examples lend credence to the claim that Afro-Latino identity emerges out of the difficulty of achieving a comfortable sense of belonging among regular Latinos who themselves, irrespective of phenotype, have had their perception and desires educated by the Caucasian ideal. Heirs of both Anglo and Iberian histories of worship of whiteness and of vilification of blackness, white and mestizo Latinos rarely display a predisposition to embrace Afro-Latinos without pause. However, with the emergence of the Hispanic/Latino label as the marker of an officially recognized pan-ethnicity that named one of the five ethno-racially differentiated segments of the US population, the necessary conditions became available for US Hispanics of African ancestry to conceptualize for themselves a further segmentation. In that respect, Afro-latinidad as a social identity comes into being on the heels of the widespread circulation of the Hispanic/Latino label to acknowledge Americans who traced their origins to the Iberian world as one of the country's minority populations.

The emergence of this identity category occurred, of course, in the context of the social movements that swept US society from the 1950s through the 1970s. With the African American-led Civil Rights Movement at its center, these instances of massive civic engagement brought about an increased urgency on the part of marginalized groups to assert the right to their difference vis-à-vis the prevailing homogenized ideal of American national identity. US Hispanics, no less than African Americans, Native Americans, and Asian Americans, sought to subvert the dogma of assimilation, which for at least a century had upheld a doctrine of Americanness that required for citizens, irrespective of ancestry, to refashion themselves by shedding the trappings of their origins. As asserting the right to one's difference became a viable cause, one that US Hispanics themselves had embraced, it did not take long for Afro-Hispanics to realize that they had their own additional layer of difference for which to advocate. Because latinidad alone did not suffice to grant them access to an identity space free of misrecognition and exclusion, Afro-Hispanics in the United States have increasingly endeavored to articulate their further differentiated sites of belonging within the larger Latina/o pan-ethnicity.

Over the last two decades Latino and Latin American studies scholars have sought to map the state of knowledge on the conditions of Afro-Latinos and Afro-Latin Americans vis-à-vis their counterparts in the larger non-black US Hispanic pan-ethnicity or the non-black national population in one or another Latin American country. A few of the milestone publications merit mention for their immediate relevance to our emphasis here, beginning with the 1995 collection *No Longer Invisible: Afro-Latin Americans Today* edited by the human-rights advocacy organization Minority Rights Group. Consisting of scholarly overviews of the history and present conditions of people of African descent in sixteen Latin American countries, the volume ends with a comprehensive commentary by Brown University anthropologist Anani Dzidzienyo, who invites readers to consider whether Afro-Latin Americans may retain their sense of national identity unaltered when they cross over to the United States, where a recognition of one's "race" often trumps or at least competes with one's allegiance to the nationality of a given home country. Urging the exploration of the racial identity location of the people involved outside of the national territory as an important field of inquiry, Dzidzienyo presciently asked: "Do Dominicans in the United States hold steadfastly to the single commonality of Dominicanness, irrespective of race or colour?" (Dzidzienyo 353). Via queries of this kind, Dzidzienyo posited a pan-hemispheric framework for the study of issues surrounding Afro-Hispanic heritage.

A decade later, Dzidzienyo paired up with Latino and Latin American studies scholar Suzanne Oboler in assembling the remarkable collection *Neither Enemies nor Friends: Latinos, Blacks, and Afro-Latinos* (2005), a volume whose fifteen chapters encompass the examination of the various experiences of racialization undergone by Afro-Hispanics in the United States as well as in Latin America, the exploration of various telling moments in the history of African American and Latino relations in US society, and the overall emergence of Afro-latinidad. In his solid overview of "black and Latina/o" political collaboration and coalition building, UCLA political scientist Mark Sawyer places particular emphasis on the potential of "diaspora research" to shed light on the political conundrums that draw Blacks and Latina/os together" as well as "to expand identities and create new political possibilities" (Sawyer 276). To cite only one more contribution to the Dzidzienyo and Oboler volume, one might highlight a piece by anthropologist Mark Anderson that considers "the intricacies and ironies of the transnational dimension" in the lives of Garifuna in Honduras and the United States (Anderson 2005). Anderson finds that Garifuna assert their identification with the "black" racial category in Honduras more than they do in the United States, where they seem to find use in accentuating the Hispanic component of their heritage in order to distinguish themselves from African Americans (Anderson 112). In other words, while assertive of their blackness, Garifuna seem no less intent on affirming the distinct culture their ancestors created as African-descended Hondurans.

While inherently invaluable as a compilation of unique materials pertinent to the black experience in the Iberian world from the sixteenth to the nineteenth centuries, the collection *Afro-Latino Voices: Narratives from the Early Modern Ibero-Atlantic World, 1550–1812* (2009), edited by literary scholar Joy McKnight and historian Leo J. Garofalo, serves us here to illustrate the changing face of the academic field wherein many would place the study of Afro-Latinos. The editors have no qualms about borrowing the term *Afro-Latinos* to name the groups and individuals whose experiences their anthology covers, which clearly take place outside the geography of knowledge of Latino studies as a subsection of Ethnic studies in the United States. At this point it would seem fruitless to wish to cordon off the territory of Latino studies or to wish to control the nomenclature produced by scholars in the field to denote the regions and demography of their inquiries. Already by 2000, in a study entitled *Hispanic/Latino Identity: A Philosophical Perspective*, philosopher Jorge J. E. Gracia of the State University of New York at Buffalo explored the ontology of the populations within the Iberian world by means of a capacious lens that encompassed US Hispanics, Iberian-descended Latin Americans, Spaniards, Amerindians, and Africans (Gracia 2000: 61). Gracia reads latinidad as a fluid as well as expansive and inclusive site of ethno-racial identity that exists alongside a pan-ethnic, transnational, and multicultural plane of signification.

Concomitantly, the Field of Latino Studies in the Eyes of Many Has Transcended the Ethnic Contours that Previously Circumscribed It to the United States

The field of "transnational Latino studies" that some scholars now advocate covers a geography of knowledge that can conceivably bring "ethnic" and "area" studies together while straddling the cultural histories of the "old" and the "new" worlds on a common ground of scholarly inquiry (Heiskanen 2009). But, to bring this selective chronology to a close, we may view the collection *The Afro-Latin@ Reader* (2010), edited by Miriam Jiménez Román and Juan Flores (1943–2014) as the natural outcome of a quarter-century of scholarship and thought by multiple authors on various aspects of the black experience in the Americas. Jiménez Román had long occupied herself with the subject of pan-hemispheric Afro-Hispanic identity as researcher and curator of sociohistorical exhibitions at the Schomburg Center for Research in Black Culture. She also had served as managing editor of *Centro: Journal of the Center for Puerto Rican Studies*. Flores, director, at one point, of the Centro de Estudios Puertorriqueños, had achieved distinction as a scholar who excelled in the study of Puerto Rican and pan-Latino cultural discourse, including literature, music, and the arts. In 2006 the couple collaborated with the late George Priestly (1940–2009), a noted Afro-Panamanian political scientist who headed the Latin American and Latino Studies Program at Queens College, CUNY, in a project that sought to disseminate knowledge and foster dialogue about the conditions of Afro-Hispanics in the United States. With Ford Foundation support, they launched an ambitious under-taking that convened an array of scholars who had studied the subject in question as well as civil-rights activists and cultural advocates to fuel the conversation and articulate a vision. Their collaborative initiative bifurcated shortly thereafter, resulting in the Afro-Latino Project, headed by Priestly in Queens and the Afro-Latin@ Forum led by Jiménez Román and Flores in Manhattan. Not unlike their counterparts in Queens, Jiménez Román and Flores convened many fruitful colloquia on various facets of the Afro-Latino experience, but their *Afro-Latin@ Reader* stands as their most tangible contribution. As editors, they used to advantage the legacy inherited from previous scholars, judiciously selecting nearly seventy pieces of moderate length, the majority previously published. The manageable size of the texts included as well as their diversity of topics and approaches renders their volume superbly suited for use in an undergraduate classroom setting. As of this writing the most comprehensive compilation available on the academic market, the *Afro-Latin@ Reader* stands as an eloquent testimony to the remarkable volume of data, resources, and ana-lyses presently available to scholars and educators exploring questions pertinent to the Afro-Latino experience, a subject that has lately elicited increasing attention and which shows signs of emerging as a differentiated field of ethno-racial inquiry.

Two-Way Negrophobia

As a conglomerate of national and ancestral origins, the Hispanic or Latina/o label names a pan-ethnic designation identifying over 50 million members of the US population. With its formal genesis in the 1977 Office of Management and Budget's Statistical Directive 15, which came to address a need for reliable data that would enable the government to implement the mandates of the Voting Rights Act of 1965 and Title VII of the Civil Rights Act, the label survives as a joust between competing desires (Hollinger 1995:33; Oboler 1995). On the one hand, as a factor of political expediency, affiliation to the pan-ethnic Hispanic or Latino heritage attends to a longing of its members for the greater empowerment that the strength of numbers presumably promises. On the other, they still seem to wish for acknowledgement of the multiple national origins that make up their composite pan-ethnicity to account for differences in culture, language, region, religion, and political memory from one country of origin to another. That is, they seem to want to promote a sense of the oneness of their impressive demographic force while simultaneously seeking to fend off the media images and voices of public discourse that would too easily reduce them to a homogeneous mass.

In her highly acclaimed "chick lit" novel *The Dirty Girls Social Club* (2004), the fiction writer Alisa Valdés-Rodríguez achieves an engaging critique of the homogenizing compulsion that plagues American society in matters of race and ethnicity. Her main character, Lauren Fernández, who claims Hispanic heritage on account of her white Cuban father, but who's also "half white trash, born and raised in New Orleans," describes herself as "a pretty good journalist," but "not a good Latina," as judged by her bosses at the *Boston Gazette*, the daily newspaper for which she writes the weekly column "My Life" in the Lifestyle section. She constantly has to check her temper to come up with noncombative ways of answering or deflating the weirdest questions about Latino life. Her Anglo editor, Chuck Spring, asks her about the position of Latinos on a national issue then current in the news. She tells him she does not know but would find out shortly as she has scheduled a conference call "with them" later in the afternoon, and he takes her response seriously. To avoid succumbing to angry outbursts, Lauren takes time off to cool down after Chuck finds fault with her column for not being "Latina" enough (Valdés-Rodríguez 2004: 5, 7, 164).

Dirty Girls intimates that the expectation for Latinas/os to look, think, and behave in keeping with a pan-ethnically preordained script operates internally no less than externally bringing along arbitrary demands that negatively impact the lives of people whether they come from within or without. The novel features the character of a television news anchor named Elizabeth Cruz, a dark-skinned, stunning black woman who migrated from Colombia. Elizabeth "has a hard time" getting dates as a result of the misrecognition that her color produces. Neither black nor white American men can figure her out, nor does her visage fare particularly well in the eyes of Latinos. The narrator tells us that, irrespective of their own color, Hispanic men "want a light girl. You can see it in our soap operas and magazines" (38). The daughter of a white Cuban and an Anglo mother, meaning that she shares the phenotype of her bosses at the paper, Lauren discovers to her astonishment that the promotions department has doctored the color of her face in the publicity picture, making her darker to accentuate her "Latina" appearance (10). The realization that she could look too white to be Latina while her Afro-Colombian friend would not qualify on account of a "deep dark" hue informs Lauren's understanding of the differing delusions of the racial imaginaries operative on both sides of the Rio Grande. She poignantly observes that in the United States "Hollywood pretends that we all look like Penelope Cruz and JLo" whereas representations in the Latin American media seem to emerge out of the belief "that we all look like a Swedish exchange student or Pamela Anderson" (38). Through the "chick lit" genre, a type of fiction that promises readers a time of recreation, *Dirty Girls* treads some delicate ground as it explores the unsettling issues of identity that we see illustrated in the plights of Lauren and Elizabeth.

Perhaps nothing distinguishes Afro-Latinos from other segments of the US population more manifestly than the two-pronged structure of the racist legacy which they must navigate. As people with African ancestry who trace their origins to Latin America, the Caribbean, and other sites of the Hispanic world, they exist at the existential crossroads of two traditions of ethno-racial disparagement: the Iberian on one side of the Western hemisphere and the Anglo on the other. Intra-Latino hyphenation becomes a serious option for people of Hispanic origin whose phenotype, by virtue of ancestral origins outside of Europe or the Middle East, does not match the ideal type that the prevailing image of Latinas/os summons to mind. Intra-Latino hyphenation offers them refuge in alternative locations of identity even while they may feel no need to delink from their affiliation to the Latina/o pan-ethnicity, as the case of the Honduran-American Garifuna mentioned above would illustrate. Overall, an intra-Latina/o hyphenation such as Afro-latinidad becomes a useful identity marker to help Hispanics of African descent overcome the barrier that obstructs their visibility and recognition as "regular" Latinos in the United States or "regular" Latin Americans in countries south of the Rio Grande, precisely the plight that afflicts the Afro-Colombian Elizabeth in the novel by Valdés-Rodríguez. When they look at social and historical phenomena across the hemispheric geography of their heritage, Afro-Latinos cannot avoid encountering negrophobia embedded as a national patrimony in their ancestral homeland no less than in their country of civic belonging. They will recognize this inimical inheritance in official state practices, rules of social relations, differential access to material well-being, cultural biases, and bodies of discourse developed with the purpose of impeding or conditioning their belonging in the citizenry and the body politic. The two traditions of othering may coalesce into composite instances of disqualification to the detriment of black Hispanics in the United States.

We can read the coming together of the Hispanic and Anglo negrophobic traditions in an episode of racial exclusion experienced at the start of the 1960s by an eighteen-year-old Afro–Puerto Rican soldier named Rubén Díaz, today a vocal New York state senator known for the mixture of progressive and conservative positions that have distinguished his legislative platform. His story, in a nutshell, describes the experience of a black Puerto Rican teenager who at one point found himself assailed jointly by two types of Jim Crow law, one in effect legally in the United States and the other a de facto social practice in Díaz's country of origin. Senator Díaz evoked the racial episode in question on January 22, 2014, during the discussion of a motion to honor the legacy of Dr. Martin Luther King, Jr. The seventy-two-year-old senator used his turn in the deliberations to support the motion by settling accounts with current public servants whom he viewed as failing to uphold the values preached by Dr. King ("Senator Rubén Díaz, Sr. Speaks"). Díaz criticized a fellow state senator, a forty-year-old, fair-skinned peer named Gustavo Rivera, who like Díaz, was born in Puerto Rico. Díaz charged Rivera with mocking his faulty command of English. At this point in his harangue, Díaz used the occasion to share with fellow legislators his painful encounter with Hispanic and Anglo racism, of which he became a target nearly sixty years before. A recent recruit in the US Army, stationed at Fort Buchanan, a military installation located in the metropolitan area of San Juan, Díaz formed part of a detachment sent from Puerto Rico to Fort Jackson in South Carolina. A Youtube film of the exchange on the Senate floor shows the level of emotion and lingering bitterness with which Díaz recalled a day when he and his fair-skinned Puerto Rican comrades went to have a drink at a bar nearby. A waiter came and promptly served his companions, but when it was time to serve him, his discernibly negroid features presented a problem. The waiter stood behind him and said plainly: "Whatever you're looking for, we don't got it here" ("Senator Rubén Díaz").

The few details given by Senator Díaz would set the story in 1961, the year when the Confederate rebel flag went up on the South Carolina State House. During the flag hoisting ceremony, among the messages conveyed by dignitaries addressing the white-only crowd on the state grounds, two stand out as particularly memorable. South Carolina state senator John D. Long invoked the heroic contributions of the Ku Klux Klan and the Red Shirts, two extremist white-supremacist organizations that terrorized African Americans from the late nineteenth century onward with their murderous violence and intimidation, in helping restore the "dignity" of the South from its earlier humiliation. By "humiliation" Senator Long was referring to the "dishonor" the South had supposedly endured during the Reconstruction Era, when from 1865 to 1877 the US Civil War's victorious Northern troops occupied the South in order to help implement the terms of the Emancipation Proclamation that gave formerly enslaved blacks their freedom, legally speaking. After the state legislator, the other speaker, US senator Strom Thurmond, was no less disdainful of the idea that blacks deserved treatment as the equals of whites. At that time, on the fifth of forty-eight years he would spend in that office, having previously served in the South Carolina legislature and as governor of the state, Thurmond expressed nothing but contempt for the doctrine of racial equality and inclusion. He cheered his segregationist listeners with the assurance that the US Constitution did not anywhere "hint a purpose to insure equality of man or things" and that the founders meant the country as a republic, not a democracy "where everyone rules and majority rule is absolute" (Bursey n.d.). Thurmond construed equality and inclusion, the goals behind desegregation, as a threat to the survival of the United States, characterizing the goal of "social equality among diverse races" as "the surest method" to destroy "free governments" (Bursey n.d.).

In 1961 South Carolina, the aforementioned waiter could not even have imagined breaking the segregation law by welcoming and serving the young Díaz. A US soldier or not, the customer was still a Negro. Probably for that reason Díaz did not focus on the waiter when recounting the story from the Senate floor in 2014. Instead, he focused emphatically on his compatriots and fellow soldiers who in his view "should have left that place with me, but no, they stayed" ("Senator Rubén Díaz"). Perhaps his white Puerto Rican peers had impediments of their own that kept them from displaying the solidarity that Díaz would have liked to see. While the island of Puerto Rico did not have Jim Crow laws that officially kept the "races" apart, it was not devoid of the long legacy of post-plantation racism that had weakened the ties of solidarity across ancestral differences in the Western hemisphere. In a pathbreaking essay entitled *Narciso descubre su trasero: El negro en la cultura puertorriqueña* (1974), the Afro-Puerto Rican educator and scholar Isabelo Zenón Cruz (1930–2002) captured the cultural history of anti-black sentiment in his homeland by showing the pervasive disparagement of African ancestry and the normalizing of whiteness as a core element of Puerto Rican identity. The author argues that black Puerto Ricans look at their likeness "in the distorted mirror designed" by the commissars of national identity – "the white man" in the author's words – with the result that, thus "alienated" from "the image of Puerto-Ricanness" and, effectively "injured, ill-treated, and repulsed ad nauseam," they have "learned to despise themselves" (Zenon Cruz 1975, II: 17).

Indeed, an emphasis on depicting their people as whiter and more advanced than those in neighboring islands in the Hispanic Caribbean figured prominently among the issues stressed by those Puerto Rican leaders advocating annexation to the United States following the 1898 takeover. The physician and political thinker José Celso Barbosa (1857–1921), himself of African ancestry, advanced the view that the country would lose out by aligning itself with other Caribbean nations in an "Antillean Confederation," and should seek instead an association with "a powerful and well-organized nation" (qtd. in Ramos 1987: 29–30). More pointedly, in 1900 the physician and politician José Julio Henna (1848–1924) made public an open letter that he addressed "to the American people" with the intention of winning support for a proposal to make Puerto Ricans palatable to readers in the north as the US Congress deliberated on the island's suitability for membership in the Union. In his letter, Henna made sure to dispel the doubts he suspected Americans harbored about his people's ancestry. He thus went on to describe the island's population as "a million inhabitants, people of white race and Christian faith, with the refinement, culture, and intelligence of an ancient civilization" (qtd. in Ramos *Las ideas anexionistas* 69).

Perhaps the future state senator Díaz, as a US soldier in late adolescence entering Jim Crow country in South Carolina, was in no position to consider that the light-skinned recruits who traveled with him from Fort Buchanan may have had their consciousness trained by a native sort of color line. Their homegrown color line, while less clearly codified by means of overt segregation laws like those followed by the waiter at the bar, may have had a numbing effect on their solidarity muscle that caused them to condition their response while witnessing a wrong done to a comrade and compatriot in their presence. Conceivably, at that moment, the phenotype of the fellow soldier being denied service and asked to leave the establishment may have made the affront easier to stomach since his blackness perhaps impeded immediate and full identification. His features did not accord with the white Puerto Rican flaunted by Henna in 1900 or other influential voices of later generations. Nor did they accord with the features discernible in the visage of the *jíbaro*, the rustic farmer of European descent who from the 1930s onward gained ascendancy as symbolic representation of the Puerto Rican, becoming the symbol of the Popular Democratic Party founded by Luis Muñoz Marín in 1938. In her study of Puerto Rican women writers in Borinquen and the US mainland, the literary scholar Marisel C. Moreno argues convincingly for this complex engagement whereby, for instance, Esmeralda Santiago's *When I Was Puerto Rican* (1993) endeavors to embrace *"muñocismo*'s quest to cement the *jíbaro* as the foundation of *puertorriqueñidad"* while also breaking with the tenets of "the *jibarista* discourse" by seeming to make room within that cultural synecdoche for a sort of *"Afra-jíbara* experience," thereby making it available to the diverse phenotype of Puerto Ricans in the diaspora (Moreno 2012: 119–122 et passim).

In the Puerto Rico of the 1960s, as everywhere else in the Hispanophone and Lusophone parts of the Americas, blackness remained outside official depictions of the visage of the nation. The citizenry had learned to recognize blackness as circumscribed to differentiated sites of the national experience, such as athletics, popular performing arts, folklore, domestic labor, and unlawful activity. Blackness in fact did inhabit other core sites of the national experience, but it did so without acquiring a normative presence with the capacity to serve as exemplary of the collective Puerto Rican family. It inhabited those sites in a state of alterity vis-à-vis the norm, a norm that insisted upon its whiteness irrespective of the diverse phenotypes prevalent in the population. A pattern had thereby ensued that caused African-descended persons to attain visibility only in those spaces where the national imaginary had learned to notice them thanks to the racial literacy imparted to the citizenry during the period of Spanish colonial domination and its sequel in the period of US hegemony. That the social psychology involved continued to influence the climate of human relations across the generations may be deduced from the present-day practice of law enforcement, which tends to approach the less-valued segments of the population with a predisposition to find them deserving of punishment, corporeal abuse, or summary killing. As a result, in Puerto Rico, for instance, low-income Puerto Ricans and citizens of African descent, along with Dominican immigrants, who stand out in the national Puerto Rican imaginary for their blackness, have long suffered abuse at the hands of the police, who benefit from a prevailing culture of impunity.[1]

The ethno-racial drama that emerges from the foregoing scattered bits of social and intellectual history gains layers of complexity when Puerto Ricans come to inhabit the social margins of the US mainland, their US citizenship notwithstanding. A long history of contact with US blackness, prompted by a long rapport consisting of collaboration, competition, harmony, and acrimony with African Americans after the great exodus from the island in the 1940s, has brought mainland Puerto Ricans into possession of a menu of identity locations to inhabit the intersection of black and Boricua. The speaker in Willie Perdomo's poem "Nigger-Reecan Blues" wrestles with how best to answer the either/or question of belonging: "Hey, Willie, what are you, man? Boricua? Moreno? Que? Are you/Black? Puerto Rican?" (Perdomo 1996: 19). The poem's closing stanza settles for an answer that draws not on a metaphysics of identity but on a historical memory of shared disparagement: the Madison Avenue lady who will tighten the grip on her purse as he approaches her, the cabdriver who will turn the "off-duty" sign on to avoid him as a passenger, or the media that will represent him only in association with violence whether as victim or perpetrator. Thus, his answer to the question simply dismantles the either/or formulation: "I'm a spic! I'm a nigger! / Spic! Spic! Just like a nigger! / Neglected, rejected, oppressed and dispossessed / From banana boats to tenements / Street gangs to regiments / Spic, spic, spic. I ain't nooooo different than a nigger!" (20–21).

An overview of racist pronouncements by the most revered intellects of the hemisphere north and south – a task well beyond the scope of this entry – could easily dispel any lingering view of negrophobia as somehow less widespread or virulent in Hispanic America than in Anglo America. Let us, for the sake of concision, simply draw a parallel between two figures whose legacies have had a comparable influence on the political and intellectual histories of Latin America and the United States respectively. The venerated General Simón Bolívar (1783–1830), one of the most enlightened of the Ibero-American leaders heading the nineteenth-century independence movement from imperial Spain, conceived an emancipation scheme that contemplated the decimation of the enslaved black population by the time military victory

---

[1] An ACLU report entitled *Island of Impunity: Puerto Rico's Outlaw Police Force* that draws its data from 2005 to the time of publication in 2012, has added "non-violent political protestors" among the social sectors suffering police brutality (*Island of Impunity* 2012).

over the Spanish forces was achieved. In an April 20, 1820 memorandum to his comrade General Santander, he explained his order to free "all slaves available for bearing arms" and suitable for enlisting in the independence forces (Bolívar 1951: 222). Understanding that for the slaves there is no "more fitting or proper means by which to win freedom than to fight for it" and thinking it unfair for "free men" to "die for the liberation of the slaves," Bolívar rhetorically poses this chilling question: "Is it not proper that that the slaves should acquire their rights on the battlefield and that their dangerous numbers should be lessened by a process both just and effective?" (Bolívar 1951: 223). As he envisioned upcoming clashes with the Spanish Army in Cundinamarca, the seat of power of New Granada (present-day Colombia), Bolívar proceeded to gloss further by noting that Venezuela had already experienced the undesirable outcome of the free population dying and the unfree surviving: "I know not whether or not this is prudent, but I do know that, unless we employ the slaves in Cundinamarca, they will outlive us again" (Bolívar 1951: 223). Bolívar could simply not bring himself to conceive of free blacks moving about in large numbers as citizens of the new republics that would come out of the independence effort.

When it came to racial thought, then, Bolivar revealed a clear ideological kinship to the no less enlightened Anglo statesman Thomas Jefferson (1743–1826), who decades before had voiced his strong belief that free blacks could not become integrated into US society as citizens due to their moral, intellectual, and spiritual inferiority, no less than to their incapacity for improvement and unsightly phenotype (Jefferson 1984: 264–70). Jefferson did not plan the creation of opportunities for the blacks in bondage to die, as did Bolívar, mostly because the greater success of the slave economy in the US South rendered them highly valuable as producers of wealth and as commodities themselves. To his credit, he had enough foresight to realize that one day blacks in bondage would become free, but he could not fathom their peaceful coexistence with whites. Perhaps more than the possibility of friction due to any rancor the free blacks might harbor against their former white masters, Jefferson found the idea that the two populations might interbreed especially unsettling, hence his conviction that upon emancipation the country would simply have to coordinate the emigration of the free blacks "to such place as the circumstances of the time should render most proper" (Jefferson 264). Because he spent several pages of his only book *Notes on the State of Virginia* (1785) on conceptualizing the inferiority of blacks and going through the trouble of offering a sustained argument to substantiate his case – the poor quality of his reasoning and the odd handling of what he took for data notwithstanding – he stands as the intellectual founding father of US negrophobia. The likes of John C. Calhoun (1782–1950), Woodrow Wilson (1856–1924), and George C. Wallace (1919–1998), to name only three of the most virulent negrophobes in US history, may be thought of as Jefferson's intellectual heirs. It would not work, however, to pursue the parallel further by presenting the likes of José Antonio Saco (1797–1879), Juan Bautista Alberdi (1810–1884), Domingo Faustino Sarmiento (1811–1888), José Vasconcelos (1882–1959), and José Carlos Mariátegui (1894–1930), among other prominent racist thinkers of Latin America, as Bolívar's intellectual heirs. Because the Spanish conquest and colonization of the Americas pioneered the construction of discourses of dehumanization, Iberian-American authors have had an older and richer selection of intellectual ancestors from which to draw their racist dogma, dating back to the first decades of the Conquest. Readers will find, for instance, that the aspersion cast by Juan Ginés de Sepúlveda in his *Democrates Secundus* (1554) against the indigenous peoples of the Americas – as a way to make them unworthy of Christian piety and deserving of the bondage and destitution to which the Spanish invaders had subjected them – remained unmatched even by the most septic negrophobic tirades produced by the apologists of plantation slavery in the US South during the nineteenth century.

Racism by Default

Albeit necessarily schematic, the preceding references to the racial views of leading social theorists, political thinkers, writers, statesmen, literary scholars, and creative writers from both sides of the Rio Grande should suffice to encourage the claim that racism in the Americas operates as a default ideology. For countless generations, respect across ancestral and phenotypical difference in the region came as a result of a personal revelation. One thinks of Cuban ethnologist and sociologist Fernando Ortiz (1881–1969), who delinked from racist paradigms after having started his scholarly career under their powerful spell. His first books, *Los negros brujos* (1906) and *Los negros esclavos* (1916), written while under the influence of theories that looked to heredity as the cause of a person's leaning toward wrongdoing, primarily the teachings of Italian criminologist Cesare Lombroso (1835–1909), attributed to blacks the origin of most criminal and immoral behavior on the island. But he subsequently learned to look at the humanity and the creativity of the African-descended Cuban population. His understanding underwent a transformation, with the result that he became one of the leading pioneers in the study of the black experience in the Americas. His classic monograph *Contrapunteo cubano del tabaco y el azúcar* (1940) grants center stage to the defining role of black creativity in any credible account of Cuban culture. Ortiz mustered the foresight to remove the racist veil that had blurred his vision when looking at the value of the differentiated segments of the Cuban population even though he grew up in a society that adhered fiercely to negrophobic paradigms.

The state of racial thought and feeling among the intelligentsia active in Cuba when Ortiz was a child might be gleaned from the interest of some of the country's most distinguished naturalists, physicians, naturalists, and anthropologists in the skull of the universally admired Afro-Cuban independence warrior Antonio Maceo (1845–1896), as a means to figure him out racially. Intrigued by the puzzling widespread recognition of the "Bronze Titan" as a "superior" human being, which seemed odd in light of the negroid phenotype of the departed hero, scholars José R. Montalvo Covarrubias, Carlos de la Torre Huerta, and Luis Montané Dardé sought the proper permission from the family and exhumed his body his on September 17, 1899. After their detailed study of every crevice of the revolutionary warrior's skull, the scholars could find comfort in their findings. For even though "many anthropological characteristics" would place Maceo in the "black type," he was "closer to the white race," so they now could scientifically affirm that indeed "Maceo may be considered a superior man" (Montalvo Covarrubias, de la Torre Huerta, and Montané Dardé 1997:13). What's more, they now knew the reason: whiteness. They could establish Maceo's closer proximity to "the white race," thereby confirming the premise underlying their study, namely that "the crossing of whites and blacks produces an advantageous group when the influence of the former predominates but an inferior group when the two influences balance each other out, and even more so when the black influence exceeds the white" (1997: 2). With the "Titan" having his blackness toned down by science, a blackness that for all intents and purposes rendered him alien, patriotic white Cubans could now continue to admire his greatness without the interdiction induced by racial otherness. Perhaps nothing other than the radical otherness of blackness can explain the extreme response of the Cuban government forces and the civilian militias that followed the peaceful civil-rights demonstration organized by the Partido Independiente de Color on May 20, 1912. With a galvanizing force one would typically associate with the fervor of a patriotic national resistance and retaliation against dangerous foreign invaders, the country seems to have unified solidly against the black menace, with a heavy toll of blacks killed in a massacre that the establishment press characterized as a "race war" (Helg 1995). The recovery of Maceo's "whiteness" and the unwarranted violence against a peaceful demonstration of Afro-Cubans occurred in a Cuba that since 1898 belonged to the sphere of influence of the United States in a more explicit way than any other Latin American nation. In that Cuba, African-descended people lost many of the social gains they had accrued over generations of struggling for equality.

Afro-Latinidad and Humane Solidarity

Although Cuba obviously did not inherit its racism from the United States, it does offer a glimpse of the change that tends to come about in the sphere of social relations in the hemisphere when the Northern and Southern trad-itions of racial disparagement coincide on the same national space. The Hispanic Caribbean, as the above references to Puerto Rico and Cuba would suggest, offer particularly poignant examples of the confluence of Hispanic and Anglo legacies of negrophobia operating in unison through the history of direct US intervention in those countries as well as through the immigrant and diasporic presence of their populations in the US mainland. The United States played a role in the affairs of the Dominican Republic since the late 1860s, when the Ulysses S. Grant administration obsessed about annexing the country, an objective that did not receive the necessary votes in the US Congress. The decades that followed witnessed the control of Dominican customs revenue by the San Domingo Improvement Company, a private US corporation as of 1893; a State Department arbitration on behalf of the company that would lead to making the Dominican Republic a US protect-orate beginning in 1905; and the military occupation of the country from 1916 to 1924. Occurring under the watch of President Woodrow Wilson, a bona fide negrophobe who resegregated all federal offices the very moment he stepped into the White House, the US occupation had an unsurprising racial dimension as Dominicans belonged among those peoples whom Wilson viewed as "incapable of governing themselves" (García-Peña 2016: 74–75). More specifically, the occupying forces placed a high premium on attacking African-descended rituals and religious practices in the country's rural areas, as the work of Lorgia García-Peña has shown (2016).

Raised in Santo Domingo in those years of frequent US engagement with Dominican society, the literary scholar Pedro Henríquez Ureña (1884–1946) came to the United States in 1901 right after high school, and received his higher-education degrees from the University of Minnesota. Henríquez

Ureña says nothing about race in his much-admired 1936 study entitled *La cultura y las letras coloniales en Santo Domingo*, a book that sets out to document the flourishing of literature and the arts there during the early period of the conquest and colonization of the Americas, which had Hispaniola at the center. His contemporary Américo Lugo, the author of the first extant account of Dominican literature in the twentieth century, evoked the florescence of intellectual life in early Santo Domingo. The creative ebullience at the time earned the colony the epithet, "Athens of the New World," a feat that Lugo credited to the motherland, Spain, "because she weaned us on her breast, and in her arms she lulled us to sleep" (Lugo: 1906: 94–95). Henríquez Ureña evoked the glories of the empire as it passed gradually into the hands of Creoles. His book takes up a narrative bent that by then had become normative when recalling the early history of what, as of February 1844, would become the Dominican Republic. It focused on the former glories of Spain's first colony in the Americas along with the caliber of the families that lived there, many of whom had to emigrate due to the gradual loss of significance of Santo Domingo after newly opened economic possibilities in mainland South America lured them away. By contrast, a study of the island today following the same chronology outlined by Henríquez Ureña, especially if done by a Dominican in the US academy, would probably seek to stress the place of Santo Domingo as the "cradle of blackness in the Americas" (Torres-Saillant 1995).

Indeed, rectifications of key elements of the story of racial relations in the country as issues pertaining to justice, equality, and inclusion now constitute the majority of scholarly efforts conducted by Dominicans in the US academy. Henríquez Ureña came from a society where, by his teens, the national intelligentsia arguably did not even have access to a language with which to speak of equality across ancestry and phenotype. Negrophobia and the white-supremacist imaginary reigned supreme there despite the overwhelmingly dark hue of the majority of the population. A general guide and directory to Dominican society for the benefit of visitors published in 1907 by journalist, educator, and diplomat Enrique Deschamps (1872–1933) offers a telling illustration of racial thinking and feeling then. In the section of his *Guía* that evokes the early years of the colony of Santo Domingo, Deschamps cites the handsomeness of the Tainos found by Christopher Columbus in 1492 on the island. He describes their bodies by means of this problematic praise: "with beautiful and attractive figures, fine and soft skin *despite their dark color*" (Deschamps 1907: 72 emphasis added). Of the imported African workers, he says that "in spite of the abuses to which their captivity made them victims, and although the number of males among them exceeded that of the females, the African race, contrary to the indigenous population, multiplied rapidly, *deriving physical and moral advantages* from their crossing with the European and indigenous races with which they immediately came into contact" (1907: 72 emphasis added). Since Deschamps also indicts the abusive treatment to which the white masters subjected their enslaved blacks as "inhumane and shameful," the reader will find it hard to figure out what could possibly qualify such depraved merchants of human flesh to pass on "moral advantages" to their captives (73). Strange as it may sound, the answer seems to be that whiteness of the skin itself contained the superior morality irrespective of any depraved conduct of the individual whose flesh is under that skin.

In keeping with the flexibility of race, which, as it names nothing concrete, has the power to attach to anything, the government of the Haitian-descended Dominican tyrant Rafael Leónidas Trujillo could use it as a tool of control and as a glue to hold his malevolent regime together. The dictatorship defined the Dominican population as white, Catholic, heterosexual, capitalist, and Spanish-descended. As scribes of the dictatorship, the intelligentsia of the regime made good use of the standard historical narrative that had left over 300 years of Afro-Dominican resistance against oppression out of the story of the nation. Blackness continued to be stigmatized with outrageous passion, including by writers and pundits who themselves had African ancestry. Joaquín Balaguer (1906–2002), a writer and thinker of humble intellectual merits, enjoyed national prestige because of the fifty-two years he spent in positions of power – thirty as scribe of the dictatorship and twenty-two as president of the republic. Balaguer's 1983 negrophobic pamphlet entitled *La isla al revés* attributes the country's insufficient development to the progressive Africanization of the population as a result of the proximity to Haiti and the influx of Haitian immigrants. The self-deluded caudillo went as far as to propose measures to halt "the africanization of the Dominican people" so that, in due time, the population may "gradually improve its anthropological traits" and thereby repair the country's moral decay brought about by "the contact with blacks" even as, oddly, he deemed the influence of Africa on Dominican culture "imperceptible" (Balaguer 1984: 45, 97–98, 211). When he attended the first Ibero-American Summit of Presidents and Heads of State held in Mexico, Balaguer took time to extol "the tremendous vitality of our [Castilian] race" as a key to the survival of Santo Domingo, though in the colonial period its population constantly faced the harassment of pirate ships form Spain's imperial rivals trading in black slaves (Balaguer, "Discurso" 1991).

Whether in Dominican society or in the United States, Afro-Dominicans are likely to respond to their country's pervasive negrophobia in different ways depending on their level of political awakening or their personal agendas. They may inscribe themselves in the long legacy of resistance that is represented today by the likes of Afro-Dominican singer Xiomara Fortuna. They may simply value themselves in their ancestry while managing to numb their ears to surrounding negrophobic discourses. Or they may join the voices of persons who today make a living preaching anti-Haitianism and negrophobia, such as the pundit Manuel Núñez whose services to the status quo typically earn him government jobs and literary prizes. An Afro-Dominican with highly pronounced negroid features, the fifty-nine-year-old Núñez earned notoriety with the publication of an essay entitled *El Ocaso de la nación dominicana* (1990) (The Decline of the Dominican Nation). In many respects a mere rewrite of Balaguer's *Las isla al revés*, *El Ocaso* reads as an invective against progressive scholars and thinkers, especially those affiliated with the Autonomous University of Santo Domingo, who since the 1960s had made headway in discrediting the negrophobic, anti-Haitian, and Eurocentric narrative of the Dominican nation.

A Eurocentric ultranationalist, Núñez took on the task of upholding the theory of national identity promoted by the murderous Trujillo dictatorship and the tyrant's heir Joaquín Balaguer. Balaguer was in power in 1990 when a government-appointed panel of jurors gave that year's National Book Award in nonfiction prose to *El Ocaso de la nación dominicana*. In 2001, Núñez published an expanded edition of *El Ocaso* which retained the ultranationalist, Eurocentric, anti-Haitian, negrophobic, and anti-Dominican diaspora argument of the original. The book offers a benign representation of the genocide of thousands of Haitian immigrants and their Dominican-born children in October 1937 as a "policy of nationalization" that responded to the "denationalizing presence" of Haitian immigrants on the border regions. And the author goes as far as to deny validity to Caribbean culture, which he regards as an invention of Afrocentric advocates taking advantage of their academic jobs for the purpose of advancing a deviant view of history and civilization that insist on foregrounding race as a factor in the story of humanity (Núñez 2001: 531, 546–47, 656, 678). This second edition was oddly accepted as a legitimate submission to the 2002 competition for the "best book," the highest literary distinction in the country bearing the largest monetary award. Handpicked by Minister of Culture Tony Raful, a panel of jurors voted to give the coveted prize to the negrophobic tract by Núñez despites its many typically disqualifying features, not the least of which were the poverty of its writing and its failure to meet an acceptable modicum of academic standards. Minister Raful, a published poet and a liberal politician with former revolutionary sympathies, vigorously defended the prize given to Núñez from the barrage of condemnation that came from numerous writers, journalists, scholars, and artists from Dominican society and the diaspora. The position maintained by Raful reminds us that racism and the white supremacist bias can very well cut across ideological views and party affiliations in our hemisphere.

The Dominican case offers us a good unit of analysis with which to move toward closing this chapter on Afro-latinidad. As Afro-Latinos must come to terms with the two equally vigorous negrophobic legacies that they straddle, perhaps they may have access to a wider lens through which to perceive the fact of injustice both ways, that is, in the society of civic belonging and the ancestral homeland. Afro-Latinos may be uniquely poised to respond to instances of violations of human rights and specifically racial oppression or disempowerment of people on the basis of ancestry in their homelands while continuing to advocate for justice and inclusion in the United States. The possibility that Afro-Latinos might be in possession of a pan-hemispheric field of vision to detect and respond to inequity has to remain tentative since much will depend on the degree to which each individual is politicized as well as the ideological brand of his or her politicization. Too often ethno-national loyalties can make us unconditional allies of governments that we have allowed to be integral to the construction of our identity, as happened in the case of the many US Jews who felt obligated to defend the 2014 Benjamin Netanyahu offensive in Gaza and branded some critics who simply wished for an end to bombardments of children's hospitals and nursery schools as "anti-Israeli" or "anti-Semitic."

Allowing the government of a land of origin an inherent spot in the constitution of our ethnic identity may cause us to default on our human or, more importantly, humane solidarity. We might learn to view the injustice committed by the government or the ruling elite against a vulnerable population *over there* as easier to stomach than one we might see happening against comparable victims over here. We might lose the ability to recognize the resemblance between the abuse perpetrated by Dominican authorities against a group to which we feel no allegiance *over there* and the disempowerment we ourselves might be suffering from corporate or political sectors of power *over here*. At the level of literary and intellectual activity, in many respects the writings of Dominican authors in the United States, the majority of whom own to their African ancestry, can be read holistically as a composite indictment of the Eurocentric, negrophobic, and white-supremacist imaginary that continues to inform the official institutions of cultural promotion in their ancestral homelands. Works such as the novels *Geographies of Home* (1999) by Loida Maritza Pérez, *In the Name of Salomé* (2000) by Julia Alvarez, *Soledad* (2001) by Angie Cruz, *Song of the Water Saints* (2002) by Nelly Rosario, *Erzulie's Skirt* (2006) by Ana-Maurine Lara, and *The Brief Wondrous Life of Oscar Wao* (2007) by Junot Díaz as well as the performance poetry of Josefina Báez and the classical verse of Rhina P. Espaillat all partake in different ways and varied degrees of intensity in subverting the script of official Dominican narratives of national identity in the ancestral homeland simultaneously with their advocacies for social justice and inclusion in their US sites of civic belonging. My own *El tigueraje intelectual* (2011) consists of a collection of essays prompted by the mind-boggling 2002 Núñez award and other assaults on the ideal of equality, justice, and inclusion in Dominican society. The text shows a case of an Afro-Dominican scholar from the diaspora using the occasion to challenge the endurance of cultural *trujillismo* in his land of origin.

The Dominican diaspora, with African-descended compatriots at the forefront, has found itself involved deeply in various activist fora that came into being in response to the September 2013 ruling of the Dominican Republic's Constitutional Court, TC 0163–13, which revoked the citizenship status of Dominican-born people of Haitian ancestry, effective immediately and retroactively reaching back to 1929, with the result that some 250,000 compatriots of all ages became foreigners in their own home and eligible for deportation overnight. Dominican Americans, many of whom have long accepted the burden of diasporic citizenship, namely that of seeing to the enhancement of social relations "in more than one society at the same time," became immediately involved in the condemnation of a legislation that too closely resembled the denationalization of Germans of Jewish ancestry during the Third Reich and the removal of people of Indian origin from the roster of Ugandan citizenship during the Idi Amin dictatorship (Torres-Saillant 2005: 281). Nor can Dominican Americans fail to condemn a law that requires for Haitian Dominicans to demonstrate that their forbears entered the country legally numerous generations ago for them to retain an entitlement to the status of Dominican citizens. Here, the conservative right in the United States, which has so busily engaged in crafting voter-suppression laws since the first decade of the twenty-first century, echoes the Dominican court's disavowals of the principle of *jus solis*, which had previously been consecrated in Dominican jurisprudence. For many Dominican Americans the impulse to challenge the annulment of citizenship for vulnerable populations in the ancestral homeland may stem from a necessarily self-interested altruism.

Afro-latinidad emerges under negrophobic pressure, and as such it comes prepared to *respond to* rather than *initiate* action. As an offspring of racism, it may lack a self-sustaining purpose other than to engage positively or negatively with the historic vilification of blackness that in the United States has occupied the hours of many of the nation's most powerful public figures, whose Iberian-American counterparts have been no less acerbic in their racial disparagement. In the Western Hemisphere, we are racist by default, the heirs of the conquerors as well as the descendants of the vanquished. One would not run the slightest risk of exaggeration by proposing the white-supremacist dogma, pervasive ancestral othering, and radical racialization of populations of origins other than European as central pillars of the civilization born in the Americas through conquest and colonization. We also need to consider that diasporic communities are not exempt from the complexities and contradictions of their counterparts in ancestral homelands. As individuals, they partake of solidarity, betrayal, greed, generosity, selflessness, goodness, and malice in quite comparable proportions. The unjust law that denationalizes a major segment of the Dominican population has not earned universal disapproval of US Dominicans, many of whom find themselves speaking harshly against one another across the ideological divide or speaking harshly against non-Dominican critics of the denationalization ruling for attacking "the Dominican Republic." Just as some German patriots who viewed any criticism of the Third Reich for the denationalization laws of the 1930s as "anti-German," today many Dominican patriots regard the external criticism as "anti-Dominican." Then, just as now, those who view the authorities as the anchor of their national identity will have a hard time realizing that the national victims of state violence too are "Germany" or "the Dominican Republic."

Afro-Dominicans in the United States range in political choices from someone like Carlos Cooks (1913–1966), a black nationalist native of the Samaná Bay who figured among the trusted lieutenants of Marcus Garvey and who kept the banner of Garveyism aloft in Harlem until the 1960s, to someone like the famous baseball player Sammy Sosa, the slugger who after achieving fame and fortune for his athletic prowess came back to the news in 2009 for his concerted effort to alter his phenotype by relaxing his coarse hair, whitening his dark skin, and trading his brown eyes for green ones. Dominicans on and off the island are, therefore, likely to inhabit their blackness as problematically as any other segment of the African diaspora in the Americas. Because racism follows a logic of its own and because race becomes knowable only when it manifests itself in acts of violent racism, it is hard to predict what any Afro-Latino person will do at given junctures when a stance of ethno-racial solidarity might be expected. Afro-Latinos, like all other offspring of the world that Spanish, Dutch, French, and English invasions of conquest and colonization produced in the Americas, are the products of a civilization grounded in abuse, dehumanization, cruelty, and injustice. They too inherit the ethos of the perpetrators, the colonialist creed, and the cultural logic of the conquerors since it was the conquerors who set the terms of socialization in their world. The independent republics that emerged in those sites in the hemisphere that separated from European governance, led, as they were, by descendants of the colonial masters, did not at the moment of independence commit to creating a new ethos of social relations devoid of inequality, injustice, and exclusion. They simply acted on the knowledge of what had worked in the colonial period. The conquerors and their heirs organized a civilization on the backs of indigenous peoples whose lands and labor they robbed as well as on the backs of the coerced African workforce whose servitude they enforced for nearly 400 years.

To become a force of good, Afro-latinidad will need to pass the test of putting to productive use its potential to help dismantle the racist paradigms that continue to impoverish the calibre of human relations on both sides of the Rio Grande, whether those paradigms come from the Anglo or the Hispanic world, while remaining attentive to the need for victims of racism to refrain from replicating racist structures in the name of antiracist causes. Racism has been the primary civilizing force in the Americas. In many respects, it is all we have known except for those who have chanced upon alternative logics of social relations and have sought to acknowledge the worth of their fellow human beings with eyes unobstructed by race, ethnicity, gender, class, religion, sexual orientation, and cultural heritage, among other areas of social identity. We owe to Martin Luther King, Jr., the prescient thought, articulated while fending off the fiercest violence from white negrophobes that we cannot afford the luxury of fighting oppression without at the same time monitoring our own potential to oppress. Convinced that "all life is interrelated" and that people "are caught in an inescapable network of mutuality, tied in a single garment of destiny," King had the foresight to warn against the danger of becoming "victimized with a philosophy of 'black supremacy'"(King 1986:121–22, 200).

To remain viable as an identity location worth taking seriously, Afro-latinidad will need to show its value beyond the mere act of self-affirmation. The field of Latino studies and the Afro-Latino component within it have to face the challenge of articulating a discourse that encourages us to fight for the general even as we focus, if we must, on the specific. Thinking of the new economy that emerged with the conquest and colonization of the Americas, which required ongoing maltreatment and dehumanization as factors of accumulation and development, we will do well to identify and activate our solidarity with the demographic most disempowered by that system at any given time, whether it is *us* or somebody else. The "blessing" Victoria Benítez finds in her Puerto Rican music and the high regard in which Charlie Villanueva holds the "beautiful thing" that he deems Dominican food to be can enrich us all if they serve as links that connect us to other ancestries, other demographic lineages, and other social identities that ancestry and phenotype cannot account for. Afro-latinidad can prosper morally only to the extent that it can muster the humane solidarity required for attending to the needs of those who resemble us in ways unrelated to ancestry or phenotype but whose kinship we recognize in our shared plight, namely the advent of a state of affairs wherein our differences are annulled by the shared history of dispossession traceable to a genesis of newly defined humanity. Perhaps the barber Feidin Santana, a twenty-three-year-old immigrant from the Dominican Republic, has a lesson of hope about humane solidarity that can inspire us, the type that does not depend on tribal allegiance or blood ties. An Afro-Dominican young man in North Charleston, South Carolina, Santana had occasion to witness and film (using his Smartphone) the killing of a fifty-year-old African American man, Walter Scott, by thirty-three-year-old white police officer Michael Slager in April 2015. Eligible for deportation as most immigrants are, he also got scared after he caught the killing on tape for fear of police retaliation, which he knew could happen both in the Dominican Republic or the United Sates. But the sense that the unjustified use of lethal force he had seen "was not right" proved strong enough for Santana "bravely" to bring his video to the press, prompting an investigation that resulted in the police officer having to face a murder charge (Belliard 2015). Afro-latino Santana acted on a humane moral compulsion to respond to an act of severe wrongdoing in which both the victim and the perpetrator were strangers to him. But, though he could claim ethnic kinship with neither officer Slager nor Mr. Scott, he knew one thing for sure: the unwarranted killing was "not right."

WORKS CITED

Alegría, Ricardo E. *Juan Garrido: el conquistador Negro en las Antillas, Florida, México y California, c. 1503–1540*. San Juan: Centro de Estudios Avanzados de Puerto Rico y el Caribe, 1990.

Anderson, Mark. "Bad Boys and Peaceful Garifuna: Transnational Encounters between Racial Stereotypes of Honduras and the United States (and Their Implications for the Study of Race in the Americas)." In Dzidzienyo and Oboler 102–15.

Arias, Arturo, and Claudia Milian. "US Central Americans: Representations, Agency, and Communities." *Latino Studies* 11.2 (Summer 2013): 131–49.

Balaguer, Joaquín. "Discurso." I Cumbre Iberoamericana de Jefes de Estado y de Gobierno. Guadalajara, México, June 18, 1991. http://cumbresiberoamerica.cip.cu.

La isla al revés: Haití y el destino dominicano. 2nd. ed. Santo Domingo: Librería Dominicana, S.A. 1984.

Belliard, Marianella. "From Alejandro Gonzalez Inarritu to Feidin Santana: Colliding Lives, Disrupting Narratives." Latino Rebels, www.latinorebels.com, April 24, 2015. Accessed January 7, 2017.

Bolívar, Simón. *Selected Writings of Bolivar.* 2 vols. Comp. Vicente Lecuna. Ed. Harold A. Bierck, Jr. Trans. Lewis Bertrand. Vol. 1. New York: Colonial Press/Banco de Venezuela, 1951.

Bursey, Brett. "The Day the Flag Went Up." www.scpronet.com n.d. Accessed January 30, 2016.

Cabeza de Vaca, Alvar Núñez. *The Account.* Trans. Martin A. Favata and José B. Fernández. Houston, TX: Arte Público Pres, 1993.

Candelario, Ginetta. "Black Behind the Ears—and Up Front Too? Dominicans in *The Black Mosaic.*" *The Public Historian* 23.4 (Fall 2001): 55–72.

Deschamps, Enrique. *1907. La República Dominicana: directorio y guía general.* Sociedad Dominicana de Bibliófilos. Santo Domingo: Editora de Santo Dominogo, S.A., 1974.

Dzidzienyo, Anani. "Conclusions." *No Longer Invisible: Afro-Latin Americans Today.* Ed. Minority Rights Group. London: Minority Rights Publications, 1995. 345–58.

Dzidzienyo, Anani, and Suzanne Oboler, eds. *Neither Enemies nor Friends: Latinos, Blacks, and Afro-Latinos.* New York and Houndmills: Palgrave Macmillan, 2005.

García-Peña, Lorgia. *Borders of Dominicanidad: Race, Nation, and the Archives of Contradiction.* Durham, NC and London: Duke University Press, 2016.

Gracia, Jorge J. E. *Hispanic/Latino Identity: A Philosophical Perspective.* Malden, MA: Blackwell, 2000.

Grillo, Evelio. *Black Cuban, Black American: A Memoir.* Houston, TX: Arte Público Press, 2000.

Heiskanen, Benita. "Where Are 'We' in Transnational Latino Studies?" *Diálogos Latinoamericanos* 16 (2009): 5–15.

Helg, Aline. *Our Rightful Share: The Afro-Cuban Struggle for Equality, 1886–1912.* Durham, NC: The University of North Carolina Press, 1995.

Henríquez Ureña, Pedro. *1940. El Español en Santo Domingo.* 4th. ed. Santo Domingo: Editora Taller, 1982.

La Utopía de América. Prólogo de Rafael Gutiérrez Girardot. Ed. Angel Rama and Rafael Giardot. Caracas: Biblioteca Ayacucho, 1978.

Hernández, Tanya Katerí. *Racial Subordination in Latin America: The Role of the State, Customary Law, and the New Civil Rights Response.* Cambridge, New York, and Melbourne: Cambridge University Press, 2013.

Hoffnung-Garskoff, Jesse. "The Migrations of Arturo Schomburg: On Being Antillano, Negro, and Puerto Rican in New York, 1891–1938." *Journal of American Ethnic History* 21.1 (2001): 3–49.

Ingenieros, José. "Las ideas sociológicas de Sarmiento." *Conflicto y armonía*. Ed. Sarmiento, 7–40.

Island of Impunity: Puerto Rico's Outlaw Police Force. ACLU: American Civil Liberties Union. New York. American Civil Liberties Union, June 2012.

Jefferson, Thomas. *Works: Selections*. New York: Literary Classics of the United States, 1984.

Jiménez Román, Miriam, and Juan Flores, eds. *The Afro-Latin@ Reader: History and Culture in the United States*. Durham, NC and London: Duke University Press, 2010.

King, Jr., Martin Luther. *A Testament of Hope: The Essential Writings of Martin Luther King, Jr*. Ed. James Melvin Washington. San Francisco: Harper & Row Publishers, 1986.

Lugo, Américo. *Bibliografía*. Santo Domingo: Imprenta La Cuna de América, 1906.

McKnight, Joy, and Leo J. Garofalo, eds. *Afro-Latino Voices: Narratives from the Early Modern Ibero-Atlantic World, 1550–1812*. Indianapolis, IN: Hackett Publishing Company, 2009.

Montalvo Covarrubias, José R., Carlos de la Torre Huerta, and Luis Montané Dardé. "El cráneo de Antonio Maceo." *Ahora*. Sección Dominical, Havana, December 2, 1934; rpt. *Cuaderno de Historia* 82 (1997): 1–13. Online at bvs.sld.cu/his/vol_1_97.

Moreno, Marisel C. *Family Matters: Puerto Rican Women Authors in the Island and the Mainland*. Charlottesville: University of Virginia Press, 2012.

Niza, Marcos de. "Discovery of the Seven Cities of Cibola" (Excerpt). *Herencia: The Anthology of Hispanic Literature in the United States*. Ed. Nicolas Kanellos. Oxford and New York: Oxford University Press, 2002. 39–46.

Núñez, Manuel. *El ocaso de la nación dominicana*. 2nd ed. Santo Domingo: Editorial Letra Gráfica, 2001.

"NYS State Senator Rubén Díaz Rant on MLK, White Puerto Ricans, and Governor Cuomo's Views on Extreme Conservatives." *NiLP*. January 24, 2014. Web.

Perdomo, Willie. *Where a Nickel Costs a Dime: Poems*. New York and London: W. W. Norton & Company, 1996.

Ramos, Aarón Gamaliel, ed. *Las ideas anexionistas en Puerto Rico bajo la dominación norteamericana* (Río Piedras, Puerto Rico: Ediciones Huracán, 1987.

Restall, Matthew. "Black Conquistadors: Armed Africans in Early Spanish America." *The Americas* 57.2 (October 2000): 171–205.

Sawyer, Mark. "Racial Politics in Multiethnic America: Black and Latina/o Identities and Coalitions." In Dzidzienyo and Oboler 265–79.

"Senator Ruben Díaz, Sr. speaks on the Martin Luther King, Jr. Resolution." *Youtube.com*. January 23, 2014.

Thomas, Piri. *Down These Mean Streets*. New York: Vintage Books, 1997.

Thompson-Hernandez, Walter. "What It Means to Be Afro-Latino? The NBA's Charlie Villanueva Explains." *Remezcla*, October 19, 2015. *NiLP Report* October 22, 2015. Web.

Torres-Saillant, Silvio, and Ramona Hernandez. "Community, Culture, and Collective Identity." *One Out of Three: Immigrant New York in the Twenty-First Century*. Ed. Nancy Foner. New York: Columbia University Press, 2013: 223–45.

Torres-Saillant, Silvio. "Racism in the Americas and the Latino Scholar." Ed. Dzidzienyo and Oboler. 281–304.

Zenón Cruz, Isabelo. *Narciso descubre su trasero: El negro en la cultura puertorriqueña*. 2 vols. 2nd ed. Humacao, Puerto Rico: Editorial Fundi, 1975.

PART III

NEGOTIATING LITERARY MODERNITY

Between Colonial Subjectivity and National Citizenship, 1910–1979

14

Oratory, Memoir, and Theater

Performances of Race and Class in the Early Twentieth-Century Latina/o Public Sphere

ANTONIO LÓPEZ

In Memory of Lucy O'Farrill

What becomes of writing, authorship, and audience in the performance spaces of an early twentieth-century latinidad: the factories, picket lines, and streets of Tampa and San Antonio, the theaters of the District of Columbia and New York City? The literary here opens onto the staged, interactive speaking practices of actors, activists, and writers reading aloud from newspapers and poems, novels, and political argument. In public, these early performance and spoken-word artists borrowed and gave body and voice to written words – always a mixture of their own and others' – in ways that transformed elements of genre, style, and publication, producing, in effect, another Latina/o text, one represented in the sonic and heard by many, though often leaving little material trace of itself behind. Venues for these performances include labor protests, *lecturas* (readings) of fiction and the news in cigar factories, routines in Latina/o blackface theater, and recitations of Caribbean poetry in university halls.

Emma Tenayuca, Luisa Capetillo, Eusebia Cosme, and Alberto O'Farrill – the central figures of this chapter – contend in their oratorical and dramatic work with the determinations of race and class, gender, and sexuality. Each practiced and – crucially for a Latina/o literary history – formalized a particular decolonial agency, one always in contact with the predations and accommodations of a settler-postcolonial United States during its period of interwar adjustment to hemispheric hegemony. The literary performance and other labors of these figures signified in multiple ways, sometimes encompassing the possibilities of launching and sustaining activist, writing, and entertainment careers, sometimes involving collaborations with multiethnic and multiracial workers across the industrial zones of the United States. The young *tejana* radical Emma Tenayuca, an adolescent during a period of remarkable political activity in the 1930s, drew on anarchism, communism, and the discourses and lived experiences of the *plaza* and *"lo indio"* (the indigenous) in Mexican America to raise her voice, literally, against capitalism, Anglo-white supremacy, and the state. For Luisa Capetillo, a radical anarchist and workers' advocate in her own right, a job reading aloud in a Florida cigar factory during the summer of 1913 shaped her *boricua* feminist narratives and practices. Time and again, working-class Latinas during the period mastered oral representations of the written word, coming up against the gendered barriers of a literary culture that prized authorship and publication. The Afro-Cuban-American Eusebia Cosme is another such figure in her recitations during the 1930s and 1940s of poems composed by white and mixed-race men imagining an "authentic" Afro-Cuban vernacular. Still another Afro-Cuban in the United States, Alberto O'Farrill, whose story concludes this essay, assumed the prerogatives of Cuban-American blackface in appearances from 1925 to 1935 on the Latina/o Harlem stage, a time and place of performance important for its correspondence with the sidewalk of the strike and the platform of the cigar factory. It is from such spaces that countervailing, though not inimical, words resounded from our speakers, teaching and championing, entertaining, and distracting. The senses mattered a great deal, with the sonic foremost, but also the visual and, as we shall see, even the olfactory. Memoirs make a mark as well: The private and public lives of Bernardo Vega and Evelio Grillo, composed and published in both timely and belated ways over the course of the twentieth century, offer a corroborative reimagination of these oratorical scenes.

I approach Tenayuca, Capetillo, Cosme, and O'Farrill in view of Latina/o literature's binding incommensurabilities: the way in which Mexican-American and US-Caribbean poetics and geographies are articulated in difference, though the matter is meaningful, too, on the basis of a difference internal to the US Caribbean (a construct from which any Cuban, Puerto Rican, or Dominican diasporic archive, each itself already multiple, is always seeping) and the Mexican American (appearing strange unto itself across region, period, and genre). I suggest, then, that speaking voices performing in Spanish and English in the scriptive and audio technologies of (and beyond) the early twentieth century amplify incommensurate, literary-oratorical latinidades that contend with the surfaces and depths, speed and delay, collisions and spectacles – the modernity, in short – of culture in the settler-post/colonial United States.[1]

---

[1] Weheliye (2005) accounts for the constitutive interaction between sound and writing in modern African-American culture, an indispensible point of reference for the Latina/o literary-sonic, particularly in its African-diasporic iterations.

Mary Pat Brady's chronotope of a Douglas, Arizona, mission-style structure that, from 1912 to 1996, went from mining-company railroad depot to border police station is a powerful Chicana intellectual and historiographic statement against Anglo-settler appropriations of the symbolic and material ecologies of a modern Native and Chicana/o Southwest (1). Emma Tenayuca's tone and turns of phrase as an interviewee in late twentieth-century oral histories recall her 1930s San Antonio speeches and hail those long-ago women and men who worked in the agricultural and manufacturing industries of the region; Tenayuca communicates a kind of Chicana reclamation in dialogue with Brady's refashioning of that border building.[2] Playing off the cultures of a Greater Mexico after the Porfirio Díaz dictatorship, the Revolution, and waning, elite *tejana/o* institutions in tension with the violence of ongoing Anglo settlement, Tenayuca's Texas oratory inflects the *topoi* of Chicana/o narrative modernism.[3] One can join Teyanuca with Daniel Venegas's serial novel *Las aventuras de Don Chipote, o cuando los pericos mamen* (1928; 1999) and, in so doing, map Mexican America from San Antonio to Los Angeles via Tenayuca's pro-labor, Chicana Anglophony and the novel's masculinist, Hispanophone vernacular and infrastructural imaginary across which characters at once "productive" and work-averse circulate and labor. This map represents the economic conditions Tenayuca attended to among migrant and US-resident Mexicans.[4]

For US-Caribbean subjects, Lisa Sánchez González's literary history of the Puerto Rican diaspora proposes a forceful *boricua* figure in the "humble exiles and activists jettisoned" (21) to New York City in the aftermath of the revolutionary movements against Spanish colonialism and US empire in Cuba and Puerto Rico after 1898. To see a "jettisoned" Capetillo and, a generation after her, a "jettisoned" Cosme and O'Farrill is moving, in every

---

[2] My approach to Tenayuca's agency in interviews follows Vazquez (2013), who recognizes the genre's performance value in the Afro-Cuban-American musician Graciela's testing, playful interviewee demeanor.

[3] See Saldívar (2006) for the period as a particular *tejana/o* complex in the work of Américo Paredes. Limón (2004) addresses transnational migration and cross-border economic and political repression around the turn of the twentieth century in the constitution, after Paredes, of the "Greater Mexicanness" of Chicana/o cultures. A step back from our period is Coronado (2013), which unpacks pre-1900 *tejana/o* writings in their political and cultural dimensions.

[4] López (2011) explores *Chipote*'s gender and print-culture contexts, among other matters. Indeed, key to that novel, and to a consideration of Chicana/o modernism, is the press's support of narrative fiction (Kanellos [2000]) and Los Angeles's survival as a post-*pueblo* literary and social space (Villa [2000]). The history of the Mexican Players at the Padua Hills Institute is a performance counterpoint (Habell-Pallán [2005]).

sense. Each was abandoned to Manhattan by the national (if not independent nation-state) forms of Cuba and Puerto Rico. A period network of jettisoned US-Caribbean Latina/o writers includes Pura Belpré, William Carlos Williams, Jesús Colón, Arturo Schomburg, Camila Henríquez Ureña, Julia de Burgos, and others.[5]

The peril of evidence for the modernist Latina/o literary-oratorical moment (the specter of little or nothing – a recording, a report – surviving to show how it happened) is also perhaps its saving grace. I appreciate José Muñoz in this regard. His meditations on queer performance and performativity – the acts of hopeful identity and collectivity *doing* into the future – relocate evidence. Apart from its original time and place, Muñoz's evidence is dispersed, appearing elsewhere, otherwise, and so transformed – a process we see in the performances of speeches, recitations, and readings that follow. We note Muñoz "looking after" evidence, as it were, in his stewardship of Elizabeth Bishop's 1976 poem "One Art." He reads, in particular, how the speaker's "parenthetical remarks communicate a queer trace, an ephemeral evidence" (71). To look after evidence in the manner of Muñoz, the invitation goes, is to care for, by forsaking, the possibility of any such evidence, orienting expectations instead toward the trace, the ephemeral, and, as Muñoz says, the residual. Each of these is evidence's subsequence; each performs, and this might be everything we are looking for, Muñoz proposes, because "although we cannot simply conserve a person or a performance through documentation, we can perhaps begin to summon up, through the auspices of memory, the acts and gestures that meant so much to us" (71–72). Latina/o literary oratory "means so much" to itself, to others, and, on this particular occasion, to literary history, whose common logic of period, author, and movement might erroneously sleight the after-effects of Tenayuca, Capetillo, Cosme, and O'Farrill. Against that reduction, their after-effects take center stage in this chapter, and I turn now to the first of those figures.

Emma Tenayuca and the Voice of Labor

Emma Tenayuca (1917–1999) belongs in a line of Latina radicals of the period that includes Manuela Solís Sager, Luisa Moreno, and Josefina Fierro de

---

[5] Lomas (2008) anatomizes the literatures and cultures of José Martí in the 1880s and 1890s, edging toward the Latina/o modernisms of Afro-Cubans (López [2012]) and Dominicans (Torres-Saillant [2000]). Noel (2013) and Pérez Rosario (2014) limn, respectively, Williams's and de Burgos's remarkable US-Caribbean latinidad in and beyond the lyrical. The interwar, African-diasporic networks of translation and publication in Edwards (2003) are a necessary connection.

Bright. Her 1930s speeches, whose social justice and vocal timbre echo in a 1987 audio interview I consider below, inaugurate a career of "hunger marches, protests, and demonstrations to gain relief, obtain jobs on public works, and fight against racial injustice and harassment," an effort that made her, in the words of Zaragosa Vargas, "the era's most celebrated Mexican American champion of labor and civil rights" (124), particularly in her leadership during San Antonio's 1938 pecan shellers' strike. Tenayuca was of indigenous ancestry on her father's side, Spanish on her mother's. Her maternal grandfather took her to see and hear the exchanges of San Antonio's Plaza del Zacate, and he read the newspaper aloud, complementing the reading she was already doing on her own in that Catholic family. Into young adulthood, Tenayuca studied and witnessed the practices of unions and anarchist groups and, at 22, joined the Communist Party. She participated in 1932 and 1933 strikes against the Finck Cigar Company and 1934 strikes in the garment industry, advocating on behalf of women workers, many of them migrant Mexicans and Mexican Americans. She helped establish locals of the International Ladies' Garment Workers Union. Near the end of the decade, Tenayuca became a member of the Executive Committee of the Workers' Alliance of America, which grouped organizations of the unemployed. With Homer Brooks, her then-husband, she published "The Mexican Question in the Southwest" (1939), an example of Chicana/o prose that merits further attention. Tenayuca's commitments during the Popular Front-era drew criticism and hostility from a range of observers, from middle-class organizations and institutions such as the League of United Latin American Citizens (LULAC) and San Antonio's preeminent Spanish-language newspaper *La Prensa* to anticommunist labor. In 1984, the National Association of Chicana and Chicano Studies – then known as NACS – paid tribute to Tenayuca and Solís Sager, recognizing a half-century of links between them and post-movement Chicana and women-of-color activists, artists, and intellectuals.[6]

To imagine Tenayuca, the rhetor, as "San Antonio's West Side Mexicans filled the streets to hear [her] angrily rail against the Southern Pecan Shelling Company and the city bosses" at "open-air meetings drawing an average attendance of 5,000 pecan shellers" (Vargas 151) is to broach the "autonomy" of Chicana radicalism: how a *tejana-mestiza* politics does not reduce to – but,

---

[6] Tenayuca (1987), Vargas (2005), Calderón and Zamora (1986), Ledesma (2004), and Schmidt Camacho (2008).

in fact, articulates – a class politics.[7] The strike involved 10,000 people, with Mexican and Mexican-American women a majority in the leadership and workforce. A reading of *La Prensa* during the strike shows the newspaper pointing to her communism and the fact she herself wasn't a sheller to downplay, if not discredit, the efficacy of Tenayuca's *tejana-mestiza* identification with the workers and, in general, labor. Tenayuca emerged as "honorary strike leader" (Vargas 135), a sign of her contingency and devotion. In the end, however, fellow organizers asked her to step aside lest her "reputation" harm the effort. Even though the strike's effort to stall mechanization and raise wages led to mixed, if not unsuccessful, results, it went on to have enduring power in movement-era politics.[8]

"The Mexican Question" sets in motion another negotiation with Chicana radicalism, coauthored as it was with Brooks, an orthodox communist (Vargas 140). Written while Tenayuca was jailed due to her strike activities (Schmidt Camacho 53), "Mexican" departs from a dialogue with Marxism on nations, minorities, and oppression to account for the histories of Anglo-settler land theft in the invention of "the Southwest." It recognizes a Mexican America inhabited by both Mexican- and US-born people, including cross-border subjects. It foregrounds the public value and effects of Spanish. It refers to histories of comparable struggle among African Americans. And, in outlining its stance against capital, the essay (at sentence and theory levels) imagines a logic other than labor for organizing, or at least recognizing, human potential: "It would, of course, be the greatest mistake to give a purely *labor* aspect to this broad people's movement," Brooks and Tenayuca write. "But to be most effective, this movement must bring about the closest relationship with the labor and democratic forces in the Anglo-American population of the Southwest" (265, emphasis in original).[9]

The audio recording of a February 21, 1987, interview between Tenayuca and the Cuban-American historian Gerald Poyo proffers, I propose, a trace of her oratory – of her voice sounding in the "filled streets" and "open-air meetings" of San Antonio in 1938. The interview genre with its ad hoc, temporizing, and discursive possibilities, not to mention the varying promises – and threats – of its impermanence, archiving, and, often, Anglo-US

---

[7] I am refashioning "autonomous black radicalism" in Edwards (2001). Edwards appreciates how C. L. R. James's midcentury arguments on "the independent Negro struggle" in the era's radicalism implicate "mass insurgency" and "artistic expression" (3), both of which resonate with Tenayuca's political and aesthetic activities.

[8] Vargas (2005) and Schmidt Camacho (2008).

[9] Schmidt Camacho reads "The Mexican Question" in relation to Popular Front projects (54). Vargas associates the essay with *El Plan de San Diego* (1915) and notes the rarefied publication venue that was *The Communist* (144, 145).

endorsement, bears great Chicana meaning, as we know from Rosaura Sánchez's *Telling Identities: The Californio testimonios* and Tey Diana Rebolledo and María Teresa Márquez's *Women's Tales from the New Mexico WPA: La Diabla a Pie*, which explain the dialogic moves toward autonomy and self-representation among Mexican-American women in interview scenes from the 1870s to the period of Tenayuca's arrival in the public sphere.

Sound, affect, and thought find powerful expression in the Chicana literary-oratorical of Tenayuca's 1987 interview.[10] Her English words *about* Spanish turn toward, *into*, and back out of Spanish in remarkable ways. Poyo asks if Spanish was spoken in her maternal family, and Tenayuca says, "El español, yeah" [something falls to the floor, in response to which Tenayuca says, "Let's take some of those things," before resuming], "que yo hablaba era un español que los conquistadores trajeron [sic] aquí, verdad, porque era" [the Spanish I spoke was the Spanish the conquistadors brought here because it was] "vide por vi, ansina por así, and I, I, when I went to school and started to learn Spanish, I had an awful time, because some of these teachers were not from the city or from Texas."[11] The interruptions and "errors" of the interview and its setting in the Tenayuca house, with its noisiness, serve the generative opacity of the text, and they meet the interruptions of a history which is, of course, of Tenayuca's own doing, bilingually: her Spanish, welcomed into the interview with the English "yeah," leads to a veritable performance of Spanish that's coded in – and actually enacts – Spanish-linguistic coloniality and the seeming archaism of early modernity, which itself, seemingly like nothing, yields anew to a modern Latina/o English and critique of the kind of Texan modernities in which someone like Tenayuca would have been "taught" Spanish by non-Texan, Anglo-white "outsiders."[12] Such Spanish effects reappear twenty

---

[10] Available online at http://digital.utsa.edu/cdm/compoundobject/collection/p15125coll4/id/1172/rec/35 (accessed on 6/1/15). The University of Texas-San Antonio library's digital collections also contain a number of photographs of Tenayuca during the period.

[11] The University of Texas-San Antonio library features a transcript of the interview, but I am offering my own transcription, as there are discrepancies between the library's transcript and the actual words of the interviewer and interviewee.

[12] The exchange begins at 9:30 in the audio file. A significant omission in the University of Texas-San Antonio transcript is a digression at this point during which Poyo references his own Spanish-speaking experience as a Cuban American, which leads to a fascinating exchange with Tenayuca on the place of indigenous-origin words in Cuban and Mexican America. For Tenayuca and her peer, Américo Paredes, whose *George Washington Gómez* also recognizes the significance of the *tejana/o* school scene, see Saldívar (2006). Unless otherwise noted, all translations are mine.

minutes later in the interview to accompany the matter of indigeneity: Tenayuca says that "there were certain members of my mother's family who never accepted my father, you see. [She pauses for four seconds.] Para ellos él era un [a two-second pause], era indio, verdad [he was an Indian, right], y – um – of course, no lo aceptaron [they never accepted him]."[13]

Tenayuca's interview poetics also deliver a kind of affective "transport" into the past. Poyo asks if there was a cigar workers' union in San Antonio during the period:

TENAYUCA:	No, no, no.
POYO:	Because there was the, of course, there was the International. . .
TENAYUCA [INTERRUPTING]:	And this guy, this Finck, Finck – F-I-N-C-K – this guy here was a devout Catholic. I don't know where his father is, whether he's up above or down below somewhere, but he was a louse. He was a louse.

Over forty minutes into the interview, Tenayuca's voice here is crisp, and it intensifies and becomes louder as she stops Poyo's follow-up remark, which recalls how the cigar industry existed in Texas, too. She repeats the name of the cigar factory owner, takes it apart, and, finally, folds it into an epithet, all in measured, satisfying time. Tenayuca transports. She voices emotion, "taking us back" to the moment of the strikes. Her anger and disappointment transmit information, and they do more: they stand for Tenayuca acting on behalf of herself and those feelings, then and now, regardless of the interview and its needs, though the interview is supple enough to accommodate this, which makes it "for us," too, and so a performance that allows for the possibility of other publics. With Tenayuca's "F-I-N-C-K," we can remember, through that spelling gesture's insistence on accuracy *for the record*, that Tenayuca was, in fact, around fifteen years old when she participated in the strikes against the Finck Cigar Company. Adolescence and old age course through this exchange. The hopeful doing of incipient young adulthood is also the hopeful doing of the orator delivering her speech on behalf of others, of herself, of a program. The sage Tenayuca was doing this in 1987. She was doing it 1932, as a teenager. In her audio record, she does it still, to this day.[14]

---

[13] The exchange begins at 31:04 in the audio file.

[14] Tenayuca's oratory led to the nickname "La Pasionaria" (Schmidt Camacho 52). The 1987 interview has so many rich moments, including her reading from Menefee and Clark Cassmore's *The Pecan Shellers of San Antonio: The Problem of Underpaid and Unemployed Mexican Labor* (1940) and reflecting on US intervention in Central America.

Luisa Capetillo, Lectora

Moments after the cigar strike reference, Tenayuca asks, "Uh, do you mind if I smoke?" Poyo responds, "No, it doesn't bother me at all. I used to smoke cigars" (Tenayuca 1987). Turning to the cigar factory *lector/a*, we recognize Poyo's scholarship on the island-Cuban and Cuban-exile cigar industries and the latter's role in Cuban independence in Key West and Tampa during the late nineteenth century. This was a world in which the activism and journalism of workers and others flourished, including those of Poyo's great-great-grandfather, José Dolores Poyo, a major figure of the exile community's print and organizing efforts.[15] Luisa Capetillo's (1879–1922) *Influencias de las ideas modernas: notas y apuntes* (Influences of Modern Ideas: Notes and Sketches, 1916) was written, in part, during her *lectora* time in Tampa. A modernist Latina/o text arriving in the post-1898 aftermath of that Cuban-exile moment in Florida, it assembles, after Sánchez González (2001), a *boricua* anarcho-feminist fictional and critical narrative of engagement and desire whose formal "fragmentation and disjuncture" suggest, too, Capetillo's condition as a "working-class woman of her times" (34–40).

Influencias is preoccupied, through its own textual inclinations, with the history of the cigar-factory *lectura*: that unique practice of someone reading to cigar workers in the workspace itself from the pages of local, international, and labor newspapers, from literary works by such figures as Zola, Pérez Galdós, Balzac, Hugo, and Cervantes, as well as from historical and political works by Kropotkin, Marx, and others in the radical tradition, all in their originals and in translations (Pérez 444–46; Colón 11; Rodríguez; Tinajero).[16] From large factories in Tampa to small *chinchales* (workshops) in Manhattan, readers and workers collaborated in cross-racial, proletarian cultures that educated and organized people even as they earned wages. The *lectura* distracted from, even as it drew attention to, the everyday activities of work. It called for collectivity and resistance, and the way it spread critical knowledge and debate was often inseparable from indoctrination and pleasure. The everyday experience of laboring with one's hands and listening to the

---

A video interview (ca. 1988) provides another interview performance and is available online at https://medialibrary.utsa.edu/Play/9046 (accessed on 6/1/15).

[15] See Poyo (1989) and, for José Dolores Poyo, Poyo (2014). Tinajero (2010) identifies J. D. Poyo's role in the cigar *lectura*'s arrival in late nineteenth-century Key West and Tampa (87).

[16] This nineteenth-century *lectura* syllabus touches on Capetillo's own modernism, which reworked romantic and realist configurations of nature on the basis of "revolutionary feminist theory, fiction, and practice" (Sánchez González 37).

words of others happened in a space of intense physical sensations, from the repetitive feel of the leaf on fingers to the leaf's residue in nose and throat, which authored an addictive enjoyment shaped, of course, by that other habit (in narrative) of listening to the oratory of voices that, according to one *lector*, resounded out of laryngitic, swollen throats in ways that made "the page vibrate" (Gálvez y del Monte 190, 192). In this light, the sensuality of Capetillo's text – her committed meditations, for example, on eating and sex – is important. It acknowledges a working-class woman's experience and knowledge of embodied desire and pleasure. Such embodiment appears in the mouths of the *lectora* reading and of the cigar rollers calling in response, not to mention the mouths of inhaling and exhaling smokers. Passages all, these mouths sound out the labor conditions, wages, products, and profits of an international nicotine market circulating among the related ones of caffeine and sucrose.[17] Sound, embodied, was the thing, and it was the silence of the cigar factory, compared to the noise of the sugar mill, that made the *lectura* possible (1978 [1947], 84). In the Tampa setting of *Influencias*, however, the sounds of the radio and, by 1938, machines would drown out the *lector/a* (Ortiz, 1978 [1947], 87; Tinajero 126, 134). In fact, the matter had already been made moot: in 1931, after a strike, the Tampa factory owners abolished the *lectura* (Tinajero 136), ending that tradition of reading aloud – and thus limiting the intellectual, conversational, and productive possibilities of workers making it through their morning and afternoon shifts in the cigar factory.[18]

Capetillo's job as a *lectora* in Tampa during the summer of 1913 is framed by her prior work reading to workers in Puerto Rico and, later, to cigar makers in New York City (Tinajero 144, 150; Hewitt 3; Valle-Ferrer 54). Her trans-Caribbean itinerary of labor, activism, and literary creation aligns with the histories and poetics of the *lectura* itself. In Cuba, where Capetillo also spent time, the nineteenth-century *lectura* influenced and accommodated itself to liberal and radical anticolonial and abolitionist nationalisms among cigar workers who, in a crucial development for the custom, had begun paying their fellow workers to read aloud – a tradition of self-supportive

---

[17] Fernando Ortiz (1978 [1947]) on Cuban tobacco-sugar cultures and Moreno Fraginals (1964) on Cuban sugar's political economy are classics. Cosner (2015) is a history of Cuban tobacco. Ricardo Ortiz (2007) offers a perspective on island and diaspora ideologies with Cuban coffee.

[18] The Tampa *lector* Abelardo Gutiérrez Díaz recalls a loudspeaker system (which never caught on) presaging the radio age (Pérez 447). Manuel Aparicio, a renowned Tampa *lector*, had a thriving radio career after 1931 (Fontanills).

resistance in keeping with the *lectura*'s origins in jails and convents (Ortiz 1978 [1947], 84–86; Tinajero 62; Pérez 443–44). The *lectura* arrived into a late nineteenth-century Floridian exile in Key West, Tampa, Ocala, and Jacksonville with the cigar industry's flight from the political and economic crises of the extended battle for Cuban independence.

Exiled cigar workers and their wages were the engine of the independence movement; José Martí's collaborations with *tabaqueras/os* and readers in Tampa and Key West in late 1891 and early 1892 are two important episodes in that history of cross-racial laborers from the Hispanophone Caribbean using money earned on US soil to fund an island-Cuban military campaign whose forces, often majority of color and with significant Chinese-Cuban participation, sought to expel the last evidence of Spanish colonialism from the hemisphere (Poyo 1989; Tinajero 80–84; Pérez 443; Ferrer; K. López). The 1886 establishment of the Spanish-born, former Cuban resident Vicente Martínez Ybor's cigar factory in Tampa led to the founding nearby of Ybor City. With the development of the industry there over the next fifty years, Latina/o labor activity flourished; anarchism, syndicalism, and communism brought every kind of effect – successful strikes, upward mobility, and management violence (Pérez 443; Tinajero 86–124).

The inventiveness of the *lectura* is notable. Having secured employment by auditioning on a raised platform before the workers, each of whom had a vote, readers were sometimes also writers, spoke multiple languages, and even translated multilingual materials on the spot. Though occupying a position of prestige, readers were under pressure to please an audience that, if unhappy with the *lectura*, might withhold pay in the end. They not only read with feeling; when presenting a fictional text, they spoke in the different voices and accents of its characters – men, for example, learned to speak "like a lady" – a technique heightened in passages of extended dialogue (Gálvez 168, 187; Pérez 448; Rodríguez). (Capetillo's commitment to modifying gender expectations by occasionally dressing in men's clothes embodies the *lectura*'s cross-gender vocal performance.[19]) Readers negotiated matters of taste with workers; if compelled to read from a piece of "bad" writing – the workers voted on the selection of texts to be read – the fact that such a reading happened despite a *lector/a*'s "better taste" only added to the

---

[19] The front pages of the Havana newspaper *El día* for July 26 and 28, 1915, document Capetillo's arrest in Cuba for wearing pants. I thank Laura Lomas for this information and the references. Julio Ramos discusses this image of a gender-crossing Capetillo in his edition of her writings.

performance (Gálvez 168–77).[20] Relations between the *lectura* platform and the theater stage were multiple, and, in the career of the *lector* Manuel Aparicio, director of the Federal Theater Project's Spanish-language efforts in Tampa, definitive (Dworkin y Méndez 1996, 2000). That Latina/o Tampa theater turned on Cuban-American blackface – the *teatro bufo* – shows anew the mutual constitution of racial impersonation and popular entertainment in US-Caribbean Latina/o modernism (Dworkin and Méndez 2000; López 2012). Such *bufo* spaces enjoyed a dependency on race and abjecting blackness whose characteristic disavowal, while simultaneous, refers nevertheless, in our Tampa circumstances, to the sociality of black, white, and mixed-race Cubans, island migrants and US-born, working in cigar factories alongside people of Spanish and Italian descent, these last allowing a shift, in that time and place, in the meanings of "Latin" to include Europeans. Cubans of African descent experienced the different, on occasion overlapping, threats of Cuban-American and Anglo-US white supremacies, which Evelio Grillo meditates on in *Black Cuban, Black American* (2000), a memoir of Tampa during the period and, later, of Oakland, California.[21] Grillo recalls a single Afro-Cuban-American *lector* during his Tampa youth, a man he calls Facundo Acción (7), an unheralded counterpart, perhaps, to Martín Morúa Delgado, the Afro-Cuban novelist, politician, and erstwhile Key West *lector* (Lamas 2015). With the women stemmers of the cigar factory – underpaid, as they were, for very difficult work (Pérez 447; Tinajero 106) – the figure of an Afro-Cuban *lector* in the United States joins that of Capetillo, the *lectora* and author, to inflect the labor space of the cigar factory with the sonic African diasporic and a Latina quality of voice.[22]

Capetillo's *Influencias* traces the Latina/o oratory of the *lectura*; as such, it is a back story for more explicit representations of the tradition in recent Latina/o literature.[23] The text's middle section, "Philosophical, Naturalist,

[20] Gálvez (1897) is a memorable account of coming into the *lector/a* profession, including auditioning. The Ybor City Oral History Project (available at http://digital.lib.usf.edu/ohp-ybor [accessed on 6/1/15]) offers many accounts of the everyday lives of readers from the readers themselves, other cigar workers, and their families. See, in particular, interviews with Fontanills, Rodríguez, Vega Díaz, Medina, López, and Palermo.

[21] On Latina/o Tampa and race, see Mormino and Pozzetta (1998), Mirabal (1998), and Greenbaum (2002).

[22] Hewitt imagines Capetillo, in the Anglo-US gaze, as "not quite white but also not Black" (4), which is to say, along the lines of an ideological feminine latinidad that would signal indeterminate race. Sánchez González identifies Capetillo's French (or French island colonial-born) mother and Spanish father (24).

[23] See, for example, García (1998), Cruz (2003), and Medina (2006). Sporn (2007) is a documentary of the *lectura* in contemporary Cuba. The radio episode "Cigar Stories"

Psychological, and Moralist Notes, Sketches, Thoughts, Concepts, Definitions, Maxims, and Reflections," was "begun in Ybor City, July 24, 1913,"
and it evinces "fragmentation and disjuncture" in its series of brief, though
sometimes extended, fictional and nonfictional narratives on the creative
potential of life against the ideological forces that would otherwise limit it:
a literary convergence of the *lectura* in all its diversity of topics. Indeed, an
explanatory subheading suggestively references the newspapers with which
the *lectora* started her day – "Newssheets [*Gacetilla*]; Gazette; from *Gazzetta*,
newspapers worth a coin so named at the beginning of the seventeenth
century" (51).[24] Thus meta-textualized with the print culture of the period,
a narrative follows whose storytelling rhythms measure the passing of the
workday and plot a disquisition on worms – that is, "lowly" animality – and
food: "One morning, unwrapping a piece of cheese," it begins, "I discovered
in one of its little crevices a white worm" (52). The narrator goes on to delay
her meal, wondering instead, without "disgust," on the state of the worm
and her disposition toward it: one of "compassion" and of wanting to aid in
its feeding, at her own expense. *Influencias* locates the interiority of the *lectora*
here, perhaps her state of mind upon offering up her newspaper reading to
begin her shift before the dozens, sometimes even hundreds of workers who,
heads down, hands to their materials, were experiencing their own internal
streams, tethered to the class, mass, and collective rationalizations of a labor
form from which the *lectora*'s oratory offered both a respite and – in the
worm's allegory of cross-species vulnerabilities and mutual dependence – an
intensification.[25] The *lectora*'s interiority complements memoir representations of the *lectura*'s exteriority. There is Evelio Grillo's in Ybor City, "peek
[ing] into the factory" where his mother worked as a leaf stripper, hearing a
reading of Hugo (21). There is Bernardo Vega's in New York City, noting
how the *lectura*, once finished, sparked conversations "from one worker's
table to another," leading to debate, but also to laughter, a "current of *choteo*
[that] jumped from table to table" (44).[26]

(1999) plays a clip of a sound disc of the period with the voice of the *lector* Manuel
Aparicio. See Klinkenberg (1996).

[24] I am drawing on and modifying the translation of Lara Walker, who translates and
introduces an English version of *Influencias* (Capetillo 2008).

[25] I am inspired and challenged here by the call of Chen (2012) "to explore the insistent
collisions of race, animality, sexuality, and ability, and to probe the syntaxes of their
transnational formations" (104).

[26] Vega (1977) is an important account of the Latina/o cigar-factory cultures of the early
twentieth century in New York City. See Kevane (1999) for the complicated recovery,
editing, and generic history of this mid-twentieth-century text, which was cut down
and "defictionalized" by its editor, César Andreu Iglesias; the late Juan Flores, English

Attuned to its own constitution, *Influencias* is aware of how women, worms, and men are put together, thereby orienting us to the embodiment of the *lectora* herself, sitting above the factory floor, at work with her lips and teeth, tongue and throat. A later passage in that middle section reveals how family history resides in the everyday act, again, of eating. The narrator, still autobiographical, grants that one of her "favorite dishes is julienned potatoes fried in oil: the French style my mother was used to" (98). Maternal memories occasion the gustatory – "I like eating [the fries] right out of the pan with olives and a little piece of sweet red pepper" (98) – and the olfactory: how the *lectura*, to the *lectora*, may have smelled and tasted. James Weldon Johnson, a peer of Capetillo's, pairs well with her. In *The Autobiography of an Ex-Colored Man* (1912), he senses the significance to his narrative of the *lectura*, here as a narrative-driving scent imagined in the setting of Jacksonville, Florida. The African-American narrator, on the verge of passing as white, comes into an Afro-Cuban-American orbit with a job in a cigar factory, remarking, "At first the heavy odor of the tobacco almost sickened me; but when I became accustomed to it I liked the smell" (70). Soon his fluency in Spanish leads to his "being selected as 'reader'" (71). The Latina *lectora* Capetillo and the "ex-colored man" *lector* of Weldon Johnson offer a Floridian prose of *tabaquera/o* culture whose realist-modernist seams perhaps match the spatio-temporal seams of the peninsula itself: the way Florida's pre-statehood "Spanish borderlands," jigsawing the Chicana/o borderlands of the Southwest and California, yields to the peninsula's indigenous people, those Creek-descended Seminoles and Miccosukees who, still residing *there*, despite "Removal," living in league with free and enslaved black people, would soon harbor and traffic in the modernity (tourism, real estate, and anthropology) of their Everglades homeland, a swampland in the midst of drainage.[27] Decades before a 1960s Cuban-exile arrival into South Florida, Capetillo and the ex-colored man collaborated, in and out of fiction, with that earlier Cuban-exile cigar exemplarity of Ybor City and Jacksonville. I foreground how their bodies swallow and smell (of) tobacco and food to conjure, in part, their embodiment atop the *lectura* platform.[28] Floridian *tabaquera/o* figures,

---

translator of Vega, was interested in bringing to light elements of the original manuscript. Laguna (2010) updates the argument on the Cuban comedic form that is the *choteo*.

[27] See Bolton (1921) for a period history of Florida as borderlands and Benson Taylor (2012) and Wiggins Porter (2013) for Southern and Floridian indigeneity and blackness.

[28] Page (2009) considers Weldon Johnson's vexed relations with the U.S. government in the Americas. See Dugan (2011) for scent's cultures and politics.

the historical Capetillo and the fictional ex-colored man read to workers, revolutionary and resigned; they kept body and soul together; and, when the job was over, as it often was, given its temporariness, they moved on, though not without leaving a reminder of the verbal and sonic force of the cultural and political practice that was the transforming *lectura*.

Voicing Poetry: Eusebia Cosme

Eusebia Cosme (1908–1976) introduces to the discussion of Latina/o oratory the practice of *declamación*: the dramatized recital of poetry in theaters and academic halls. The middle-class audiences that attended *declamaciones* contrast with the strikers who heard Tenayuca's speeches and the cigar makers who listened to Capetillo's *lectura*, though Cosme's performances troubled notions of class coherence: authored by and large by white and mixed-race men from the Hispanophone Caribbean, the pieces she voiced depended on an imagined Spanish vernacular whose properties intended to signify – and transform into "culture" – the poor or working-class speech of Afro-Cubans in keeping with the avant-garde discourses of *afrocubanismo* on the island and beyond in the 1930s (Moore 1997). Configured to such an aesthetics of racial and class vocalization was Cosme's own identity as a once-poor, upwardly mobile Afro-Cuban woman who came to New York City in 1938 and spent the next three and a half decades in the country living as an Afro-Latina through the multiple, white-presumptive diasporas of the Cuban-American twentieth century.[29]

Cosme established her career in poetry recital despite a resistance in early twentieth-century Cuba to the literate agency of poor and working-class black women, a legacy of slavery and the island's later "postracial," *mestiza/o* nationalisms (Rubiera Castillo and Martiatu Terry 2011). Cosme's voicing of *"poesía negra"* ("black poetry") encodes that legacy as both consequence and defiance, in particular because performing poetry was, in a sense, compensatory for her: Cosme was not blocked just from a literary career but from an acting one (until very late in life), too. *Poesía negra*'s practitioners

---

[29] Valdés (2014) offers a genealogy of Afro-Latin-American and Afro-Latina writers with which we can identify Cosme, though the significance of Cosme resides in her exclusion from literary authorship, as I say below. On the Cuban diaspora, see Mirabal (2003) on the first half of the twentieth century, Ortiz (2007) on the second. Kunheim (2014) explains the trajectory of poetry performance, including Cosme's, in Latin America. This section draws on the research and ideas of my chapter on Cosme in López (2012), to which I direct readers for a more thorough account of her remarkable career.

from the mid-1920s included the white Puerto Rican Luis Palés Matos, the Afro-Cuban Nicolás Guillén, and the white Cuban Emilio Ballagas, and though the movement emerged in relation to Caribbean literary avant-gardes, by the mid 1930s, a belatedness overshadowed its creations.[30] The point is crucial; after performances in Cuba throughout the mid-1930s, including a well-known presentation at Havana's Lyceum in 1934, Cosme's post-1938 US performances through the end of the war gave *"poesía negra"* a second life – which is to say, Cosme leveraged its waning capital, investing the form with an African-diasporic sensibility in her presentations before middle-class African-American and cross-racial Latina/o audiences.

The *Pittsburgh Courier* offers a view of Cosme's Afro-Latina condition on her arrival into the United States that emphasizes the generative dissonance of her name to a black Anglophone reading public. "Harlem's Spanish-speaking colony is playing host this week to Cuba's premier dramatic artist, Eusebia Cosme (pronounced You-say-bia Cos-may)," the article reads. Later, it adds, "Her one regret right now is that she is unable to digest enough English overnight so as to enjoy the works of Claude McKay, Langston Hughes, Zora Neale Hurston, Paul Laurence Dunbar, Countee Cullen, and others. Someday she hopes to recite in English from their works" ("Harlem's"). The *Courier* imagines Cosme's blackness in striking fashion: that is, as "You-say-bia," a construct bearing her name over from the Spanish into the scriptive logic of an Anglophone pronunciation guide in ways that indicate the primacy of the linguistic and the sonic in Cosme's estranging *afrolatinidad*, her being both black and Latina – and black and Spanish speaking, or black and Spanish-accented English-speaking – in the Anglo-white, African-American, and multiracial Latina/o United States. If "you say" *You-say-bia*, in other words, "you" articulate a black diaspora across differences, especially linguistic difference (Edwards 2003), and the registers are affective, too: the "regret" of not "enjoying" the black literary canon enough just yet, the "hope" of one day reciting from it in the original, a hope we know, at least as far as her archive is concerned, that Cosme never met.[31]

A scene of Cosme around this time in her career was a performance at the Armstrong High School Auditorium in Washington, DC, organized by the Spanish Club of Howard University. Billed as a "Spanish Recital of Afro-Antillean Poems," Cosme performed poems like Guillén's

---

[30] Kutzinski's (1993) literary history uncovers *poesía negra*'s gender politics.
[31] The Cosme Papers are at the Schomburg Center for Research in Black Culture, New York Public Library. I explain the archive's provenance in López (2012).

"Sensemayá," Palés Matos's "Falsa canción de baquiné," and others ("Spanish Recital").[32] A reviewer in the *Washington Afro-American* writes that "Miss Eusebia Cosme, native Cuban girl," received "the thunderous applause of the many hundreds of Spanish-speaking spectators present" ("Cuban Girl"), suggesting a desire for Hispanophone collectivity, presumably of Afro-Latinas/os and African Americans, all gathered under the aegis of a black university, in a black high school, in a segregated District of Columbia.

But the performance of the Latina/o oratorical in Cosme also troubles linguistic understanding. Such an observation was made by the long-time chair of the Romance Languages Department at Howard, V. B. Spratlin. Remarking on Cosme's performances during the DC visit, Spratlin writes of "the enthusiastic response of the audience, despite the fact that the great majority of those present did not understand Spanish" (Spratlin). Spratlin conceptualizes an experience of Cosme's performance among African Americans in which her voice is "oratorical" beyond the traditional signification of her words. The matter opens up a feminist method, for, if Cosme's cultural politics settles on her reciting the poetry of men at the expense of her own words – and at the expense of professionalizing her own literacy – an alternative attends to Cosme's voice against any "proper" signification that would lead back to the words of Guillén, say, or Palés Matos. One way to listen to her, in other words, is as Spratlin's non-Hispanophone black audiences did, within earshot of the unsettling authority of black women's vocality (Griffin 2004).

I have approached an extant recording of Cosme in that spirit (López [2012], 94–98), listening closely to the sound of her voice (and its enabling technologies) reciting "Sensemayá" around the time of a visit to Northwestern University on January 27, 1940 ("United States"). With such an audition, I note that Cosme's performance cracks, hisses, and pops through the layers of its recording, thus signaling a pastness which Cosme's own voice further textures. She speaks, "La culebra tiene los ojos de vidrio" (The snake's eyes are glass) and what sounds is a timbre that is heavy, imparting apprehension, while in "La culebra viene y se enreda en un palo" (The snake comes and tangles itself on a stick), Cosme makes the first word louder than the rest, her throat scratching along the way. Throughout the recording, she repeats a soft, low-pitched, three-tone phrase: "Mayombe, bombe, mayombé." "Mayombe, bombe, mayombé." Each time, the last syllable of the last word rings on. The phrase, in its mutual appearance with

---

[32] "Sensemayá" resists *poesía negra* categorization in its time of publication, 1934, and formal and thematic ambitions (Kutzinski [1987], 136–39).

the cracks, hisses, and pops, sounds beautiful. An Afro-Cuban-American vocal performance in the United States in the tradition of the Chicana Tenayuca and the *boricua* Capetillo, Cosme's vocality is a key text of the Latina/o oratorical of the early twentieth century.

Coda: Alberto O'Farrill and Latina/o Harlem Blackface

More than just implied by the strike sidewalk, *lectura* platform, and *declamación* stage, the "actual" theater stage is, in fact, in dialogue with these, as a history of Latina/o theater of the early twentieth century demonstrates (Kanellos 1990). The lyric imaginary of an Afro-Cuban vernacular in *poesía negra* recitals, for example, mollifies the "black speech" in the Cuban-American *teatro bufo* of the blackface character of the *negrito*, a comedic protagonist both wily and ridiculed (Lane 2–3). I end this chapter with a return to the compelling figure of Alberto O'Farrill (1899–?), an Afro-Cuban-American blackface actor, prose and stage writer, and central figure in the publication history of the New York City newspaper *Gráfico*.[33] On stage, in print, and in film, O'Farrill leaves still another trace of the Latina/o voice, now dramatic. As I show, that trace also touches on the personal in a way that puts the critic – namely, me – face to face with the contemporary O'Farrill family, years after first convening with their forebear in the scholarly archive.

O'Farrill arrived in Key West from Havana in 1925. By 1926, he was appearing on stage in *bufo* productions in Harlem's Teatro Apolo, an important venue in the history of New York City Latina/o theater on 125th Street, a crossroads of Latina/o, African-American, and US ethnic-white popular entertainment cultures (Glasser 112–13). For about five years, O'Farrill appeared on stage in dozens of performances, often as the *negrito*, a role that, as an Afro-Cuban-American man, likened him to Bert Williams and others (Chude-Sokei 2006): that is, to men of African descent in blackface, extending a white-supremacist caricature by challenging the very racist prerogative of whites in such performances, gaining thereby a measure professional viability, if not success, in an industry averse to employing them as black men outside of blackface. O'Farrill's "Afro-Cuban-American-on-*negrito* performance" strained the Latina/o discourse of a *raza hispana* (Hispanic race) – a totalizing,

---

[33] I first learned of O'Farrill in Kanellos (1990, 2000), whose recovery work on O'Farrill's print and stage careers is indispensible. I detail the career of O'Farrill in chapter 1 of López (2012); the work there inspires this conclusion.

culturalist conception of Latina/o belonging beyond indigeneity, blackness, whiteness, or Asianness (Torres-Saillant [2000], 1102; Clara Rodríguez [2000], 123) – with the meaningful slippages of a minstrel performance (already belated in relation to island productions) in which, at any moment, a "real" Afro-Cuban identity might upstage the "ruse" of the personage in what was once burnt cork. In the period's establishment Spanish-language newspaper, *La Prensa*, the word used early on to identify O'Farrill's appearances speaks to such slippages: *moreno*, a term that, despite a lack of "consolidated" *bufo* meaning, indicated *"negrito"* at one and the same time as it signified a euphemism for people of African descent (López [2012], 29). In what I have called a practice of Afro-Cuban-American "blackface print culture," O'Farrill appeared as the pseudonymous "Ofa" – a contraction of his last name – in the Sunday pages of *Gráfico* from the mid to late 1920s, authoring a serial personal-fictional narrative, "Pegas Suaves" (Easy Jobs), whose narrator, bearing the unmistakable traits of the *negrito* (his "shifty" characterization, his thinly veiled association with the well-known O'Farrill), revised the logic of racial performance, moving it from the fictional stage to the fictional narrative streets of Manhattan and Brooklyn, along the way invoking the realism (and reality) of an Afro-Latino protagonist (López [2012], 37–47).

Matching the relative professional success of O'Farrill's Teatro Apolo and *Gráfico* era was his tenure at the Teatro Campoamor on 116th Street and Fifth Avenue in the mid 1930s, where he continued his *bufo* work, now in collaboration with the renowned Afro-Cuban-American flutist Alberto Socarrás, house bandleader. It was at the Campoamor that O'Farrill was "discovered" by the Mexican film director Miguel Contreras Torres, who cast him in a supporting role in *No matarás (Mi hermano es un gangster)* (Thou Shalt Not Kill [My Brother Is a Gangster], 1935). The film sent O'Farrill into a brief moment of stardom, prompting a return to Cuba in 1936 to stage a series of revues (López [2012], 47–60). Decades later, it was a private screening of my copy of that film, mailed to a warm, generous woman and her family in Louisville, Kentucky, that would bring the matter of O'Farrill's scholarly "recovery" into a particular focus, delineating literary history's personal, transtemporal dimensions: the way the O'Farrill of print culture and the archive – of Latina/o literary history – might also be someone's long-lost father, grandfather, and great-grandfather, his face, frame, and gestures finally seen again and, in time, recognized.

On December 6, 2012, I received an e-mail from Erran Michael Huber, a student at the University of Louisville who had read my book and "was taken aback at a very familiar name: Alberto Heliodoro O'Farrill." The reason was simple: the name was also "that of my great-grandfather." Huber continued, "I have strong reason to believe that the man about which you write... and the man who was my great-grandfather were the same person" (Huber 2012). Not only did I reach out to Huber after this; I learned about his grandmother, Lucía (Lucy) Peregrina O'Farrill, and, over subsequent visits to Louisville in 2013 and 2015, I became acquainted with the wonderful woman with the beautiful name who, indeed, was Alberto O'Farrill's daughter.

As Huber puts it in a paper he wrote for a fall 2014 graduate course, the O'Farrill-Huber family sat down one day to watch the DVD of *No matarás* I had sent them. "[D]uring one scene, O'Farrill placed a hat upon his head and was close enough to the camera" (6). That was it: Lucy "instantly recognized the man upon the screen as her father, and all sorts of long-forgotten visuals of him came flooding back. We had found him at last" (6). Lucy's mother, Alberto O'Farrill's ex-wife, Mary Elizabeth "Bette" Spingler Rush, was deceased, and the information she had revealed about Alberto over the years was selective; indeed, as Huber writes, "this man was not to be spoken of," and "[n]o photographs of him remained in the albums." For the O'Farrill-Huber family, the impact of rediscovering – or discovering – O'Farrill was great, and, as "the critic," I continue to reflect on the momentousness of this encounter, appreciative of the family and their generosity toward me and toward those words I put down about a life both theirs and not. Citing the "evidence [for]... O'Farrill as an Afro-Cuban," Huber comments on the "dissonance" that initially marked the family's response, particularly with Lucy, "who had spent nearly 70 years with no reason to suspect anything otherwise than what she 'knew' about her father" – that, in part, he was a Spaniard. "Finding Ofa," as Huber puts it in the title to his paper, is, rather than an ending, a new beginning. Huber says it best: "the question 'Who was my great-grandfather?' still lingers, [and]... to that question, I've been forced to add, 'Who am I?' as well" (Huber 2014).[34]

WORKS CITED

Bolton, Herbert. *The Spanish Borderlands: A Chronicle of Old Florida and the Southwest.* New Haven, CT: Yale University Press, 1921.
Brady, Mary Pat. *Extinct Lands, Temporal Geographies: Chicana Literature and the Urgency of Space.* Durham, NC: Duke University Press, 2002.

---

[34] "Rush Loves Life" (2006), an interview with Alberto O'Farrill's ex-wife, Bette, reveals details of their lives together in South America between the late 1930s, when I lose track of O'Farrill in the New York City Latina/o press, and 1945, when she returned to the United States with Lucy. Lucy never saw O'Farrill again.

Brooks, Homer and Emma Tenayuca. "The Mexican Question in the Southwest." *The Communist* 18 (March 1939): 257–62.

Calderón, Roberto, and Emilio Zamora. "Manuela Solís Sager and Emma Tenayuca: A Tribute." In *Chicana Voices: Intersections of Class, Race, and Gender*, ed. Teresa Córdova, Norma Cantú, Gilberto Cárdenas, Juan García, and Christine Sierra. Austin: University of Texas Center for Mexican American Studies, 1986.

Capetillo, Luisa. *Influencias de las idea modernas: notas y apuntes*. San Juan, Puerto Rico: Tipografía Negrón Flores, 1916.

Absolutely Equality: An Early Feminist Perspective (Influencias de las ideas modernas). Trans. Lara Walker. Houston, TX: Arte Público Press, 2008.

Amor y anarquía: los escritos de Luisa Capetillo, ed. Julio Ramos. San Juan, Puerto Rico: Ediciones Huracán, 1992.

Chen, Mel. *Animacies: Biopolitics, Racial Mattering, and Queer Affect*. Durham, NC: Duke University Press, 2012.

Chude-Sokei, Louis. *The Last "Darky": Bert Williams, Black-on-Black Minstrelsy, and the African Diaspora*. Durham, NC: Duke University Press, 2006.

"Cigar Stories." *Lost and Found Sound*. NPR. WNYC, New York. May 14, 1999. Radio.

Colón, Jesús. *A Puerto Rican in New York and Other Sketches*. New York: International Publishers, 1982 [1961].

Coronado, Raúl. *A World Not to Come: A History of Latino Writing and Print Culture*. Cambidge, MA: Harvard University Press, 2013.

Cosner, Charlotte. *The Golden Leaf: How Tobacco Shaped Cuba and the Atlantic World*. Nashville, TN: Vanderbilt University Press, 2015.

Cruz, Nilo. *Anna in the Tropics*. New York: Theatre Communications Group, 2003.

"Cuban Girl in Recital." *Washington Afro-American*, February 18, 1939: 10.

Dugan, Holly. *The Ephemeral History of Perfume: Scent and Sense in Early Modern England*. Baltimore: Johns Hopkins University Press, 2011.

Dworkin y Méndez, Kenya. "The Tradition of Hispanic Theater and the WPA Federal Theater Project in Tampa-Ybor City, Florida." In *Recovering the US Hispanic Literary Heritage, Vol. 2*, ed. Erlinda Gonzales-Berry and Chuck Tatum. Houston, TX: Arte Público Press, 1996.

"From Factory to Floodlights: Original Spanish-Language Cigar Workers' Theatre in Ybor City and West Tampa, Florida." In *Recovering the US Hispanic Literary Heritage, Vol. 3*, ed. María Herrera-Sobek and Virginia Sánchez Korrol. Houston, TX: Arte Público Press, 2000.

Edwards, Brent. "Introduction: The Autonomy of Black Radicalism." *Social Text* 67 (19.2), Summer 2001: 1–13.

The Practice of Diaspora: Literature, Translation, and the Rise of Black Internationalism. Cambridge, MA: Harvard University Press, 2003.

Ferrer, Ada. *Insurgent Cuba: Race, Nation, and Revolution, 1868–1898*. Chapel Hill: University of North Carolina Press, 1999.

Fontanills, Mary. "Mary Fontanills Oral History Interview." Ybor City Oral History Project, Oral History Program, Florida Studies Center, University of South Florida Library, 1983.

Gálvez y del Monte, Wenceslao. *Tampa: impresiones de emigrado*. Tampa, FL: Establecimiento Tipográfico Cuba: 1897.

García, Cristina. *The Agüero Sisters*. New York: Ballantine, 1998.

Glasser, Ruth. *My Music Is My Flag: Puerto Rican Musicians and Their New York Communities, 1917–1940*. Berkeley: University of California Press, 1997.

Greenbaum, Susan. *More than Black: Afro-Cubans in Tampa*. Gainesville: University of Florida Press, 2002.

Griffin, Farah Jasmine. "When Malindy Sings: A Meditation on Black Women's Vocality." In *Uptown Conversations: The New Jazz Studies*, ed. Robert G. O'Meally, Brent Edwards, and Farah Jasmine Griffin. New York: Columbia University Press, 2004.

Grillo, Evelio. *Black Cuban, Black American: A Memoir*. Houston, TX: Arte Público Press, 2000.

Habell-Pallán, Michelle. *Loca Motion: The Travels of Chicana and Latina Popular Culture*. New York: New York University Press, 2005.

"Harlem's Spanish Section Raves about Cuba's Premier Dramatic Artist, Eusebia Cosme." *Pittsburgh Courier*, September 10, 1938: 13.

Hewitt, Nancy. *Southern Discomfort: Women's Activism in Tampa, Florida, 1880s–1920s*. Champaign: University of Illinois Press, 2001.

Huber, Erran Michael. E-mail correspondence. December 6, 2012.

"Finding 'Ofa': Constructions of Identity, Authenticity, and Homeland." Unpublished paper. 2014.

Kanellos, Nicolás. *A History of Hispanic Theatre in the United States: Origins to 1940*. Austin: University of Texas Press, 1990.

Hispanic Periodicals in the United States, Origins to 1960: A Brief History and Comprehensive Bibliography. Houston: Arte Público Press, 2000.

Kevane, Bridget. "Confessions of an Editor: César Andreu Iglesias and the 'Memorias de Bernardo Vega.'" *Latin American Literary Review* 27.53 (1999): 67–80.

Klinkenberg, Jeff. "His Father's Voice: Henry Aparicio Longs to Hear Again the Voice That Once Brought Words of Life in the Cigar Factories of Ybor City." *Fort Lauderdale Sun-Sentinel*, June 16, 1996: 9.

Kuhnheim, Jill. *Beyond the Page: Poetry and Performance in Spanish America*. Tucson: University of Arizona Press, 2014.

Kutzinski, Vera. *Against the American Grain: Myth and History in William Carlos Williams, Jay Wright, and Nicolás Guillén*. Baltimore: Johns Hopkins University Press, 1987.

Sugar's Secrets: Race and the Erotics of Cuban Nationalism. Charlottesville: University of Virginia Press, 1993.

Laguna, Albert. "*Aquí Está Álvarez Guedes*: Cuban *choteo* and the Politics of Play." *Latino Studies* 8 (2010): 509–31.

Lamas, Carmen. "The Black Lector and Martín Morúa Delgado's *Sofía* (1891) and *La familia Unzúazu* (1901)." *Latino Studies* 13 (Spring 2015): 113–30.

Lane, Jill. *Blackface Cuba, 1840–1895*. Philadelphia: University of Pennsylvania Press, 2005.

Ledesma, Irene. "Texas Newspapers and Chicana Workers' Activism, 1919–1974." In *Women and Gender in the American West*, ed. Mary Ann Irwin and James F. Brooks. Albuquerque: University of New Mexico Press, 2004.

Limón, José. "Greater Mexico, Modernism and New York: Miguel Covarrubias and José Limón." In *The Covarrubias Circle: Nickolas Muray's Collection of Twentieth-Century Mexican Art*, ed. Kurt Heinzleman. Austin: University of Texas Press, 2004.

Lomas, Laura. *Translating Empire: José Martí, Migrant Latino Subjects, and American Modernities*. Durham, NC: Duke University Press, 2008.

López, Antonio. *Unbecoming Blackness: The Diaspora Cultures of Afro-Cuban America*. New York: New York University Press, 2012.

López, Kathleen. *Chinese Cubans: A Transnational History*. Chapel Hill: University of North Carolina Press, 2013.

López, Marissa. *Chicano Nations: The Hemispheric Origins of Mexican American Literature*. New York: New York University Press, 2011.

Medina, Pablo. *The Cigar Roller*. New York: Grove Press, 2006.

Menefee, Selden Cowles and Orin Clark Cassmore. *The Pecan Shellers of San Antonio: The Problem of Underpaid and Unemployed Mexican Labor*. Washington, DC: US Government Printing Office, 1940.

Mirabal, Nancy. "Telling Silences and Making Community: Afro-Cubans and African-Americans in Ybor City and Tampa, 1899–1915." In *Between Race and Empire: African-Americans and Cubans Before the Revolution*, ed. Lisa Brock and Digna Castañeda Fuertes. Philadelphia: Temple University Press, 1998.

"'Ser De Aquí': Beyond the Cuban Exile Model." *Latino Studies* 1.3 (2003): 366–82.

Moore, Robin. *Nationalizing Blackness: Afrocubanismo and Artistic Revolution in Havana, 1920–1940*. Pittsburgh, PA: University of Pittsburgh Press, 1997.

Moreno Fraginals, Manuel. *El ingenio: el complejo económico social cubano del azúcar, Tomo 1, 1760–1860*. Havana: Comisión Nacional Cubana de la UNESCO, 1964.

Mormino, Gary and George Pozzetta. *The Immigrant World of Ybor City: Italians and Their Latin Neighbors in Tampa, 1885–1985*. Gainesville: University of Florida Press, 1998.

Muñoz, José. *Cruising Utopia: The Then and There of Queer Futurity*. New York: New York University Press, 2009.

Noel, Urayoan. "For a Caribbean American Graininess: William Carlos Williams, Translator." *Small Axe: A Caribbean Journal of Criticism* 17.3 (2013): 138–50.

Ortiz, Fernando. *Contrapunteo cubano del tabaco y el azúcar*. Caracas: Biblioteca Ayacucho, 1978 [1947].

Ortiz, Ricardo. *Cultural Erotics in Cuban America*. Minneapolis: University of Minnesota Press, 2007.

Page, Amanda. "The Ever-Expanding South: James Weldon Johnson and the Rhetoric of the Global Color Line." *Southern Quarterly* 46.3 (2009): 26–46.

Pérez, Jr., Louis. "Reminiscences of a Lector: Cuban Cigar Workers in Tampa." *The Florida Historical Quarterly* 53.4 (April 1975): 443–49.

Pérez Rosario, Vanessa. *Becoming Julia de Burgos: The Making of a Puerto Rican Icon*. Urbana: University of Illinois Press, 2014.

Porter, Kenneth Wiggins. *The Black Seminoles: History of a Freedom-Seeking People*. Gainesville: University of Florida Press, 2013.

Poyo, Gerald. "*With All, and for the Good of All: The Emergence of Popular Nationalism in the Cuban Communities of the United States, 1848–1898*. Durham, NC: Duke University Press, 1989.

Exile and Revolution: José D. Poyo, Key West, and Cuban Independence. Gainesville: University Press of Florida, 2014.

Poyo, Jerry. "Audio of Interview with Emma Tenayuca." Institute of Texan Cultures Oral History Collection. University of Texas at San Antonio, 1987.

Rebolledo, Tey Diana and María Teresa Márquez. *Women's Tales from the New Mexico WPA: La Diabla a Pie*. Houston, TX: Arte Público Press, 2000.

Ramos, Julio, ed. *Amor y anarquía: los escritos de Luisa Capetillo*. San Juan: Edictiones Huracán: 1992.

Rodríguez, Clara. *Latinos, the Census, and the History of Ethnicity in the United States*. New York: New York University Press, 2000.

Rodríguez, Wilfredo. "Wilfredo Rodríguez Oral History Interview." Ybor City Oral History Project, Oral History Program, Florida Studies Center, University of South Florida Library, 1984.

Rubiera Castillo, Daisy and Inés María Martiatu, eds. *Afrocubanas: historia, pensamiento y prácticas culturales*. Havana: Editorial de Ciencias Sociales, 2011.

"Rush Loves Life in the Fast Lane." *The Louisville Line*, March 2006: 2.

Saldívar, Ramón. *The Borderlands of Culture: Américo Paredes and the Transnational Imaginary*. Durham, NC: Duke University Press, 2006.

Sánchez, Rosaura. *Telling Identities: The Californio testimonios*. Minneapolis: University of Minnesota Press, 1995.

Sánchez González, Lisa. *Boricua Literature: A Literary History of the Puerto Rican Diaspora*. New York: New York University Press, 2001.

Schmidt Camacho, Alicia R. *Migrant Imaginaries: Latino Cultural Politics in the US-Mexico Borderlands*. New York: New York University Press, 2008.

"Spanish Recital of Afro-Antillean Poems," 2/7/39. Box One, Printed Material, Programs (Concerts), 1930, May to 1958, May, n.d. The Eusebia Cosme Papers, Schomburg Center for Research in Black Culture, New York Public Library.

Sporn, Pamela. *With a Stroke of the Chaveta/Con el toque de la chaveta*. New York: Cinema Guild, 2007.

Spratlin, V. B. Manuscript document, n.d. Box One, Poems and Essay, Folder Four, Written about Cosme, 1937–1952, n.d. The Eusebia Cosme Papers, Schomburg Center for Research in Black Culture, New York Public Library.

Taylor, Melanie Benson. *Reconstructing the Native South: American Indian Literature and the Lost Cause*. Athens: University of Georgia Press, 2012.

Tinajero, Araceli. *El Lector: A History of the Cigar Factory Reader*. Trans. Judith E. Grasberg. Austin: University of Texas Press, 2010. (Translation of *El lector de tabaquería: historia de una tradición cubana*. Madrid: Editorial Verbum, 2007.)

Torres, Luis. "Emma Tenayuca Oral History Interview." José Ángel Gutiérrez Papers, University of Texas at San Antonio Libraries, Manuscript 24, Box 31. Ca. 1988.

Torres-Saillant, "Before the Diaspora: Early Dominican Literature in the United States." In *Recovering the US Hispanic Literary Heritage, Vol. 3*, ed. María Herrera-Sobek and Virginia Sánchez Korrol. Houston: Arte Público Press, 2000.

"United States, Illinois, Evanston, Afro-Antilleans, 1940." Sound recording. Archives of Traditional Music, Indiana University.

Valdés, Vanessa. *Oshun's Daughters: The Search for Womanhood in the Americas*. Albany: SUNY Press, 2014.

Valle-Ferrer, Norma. *Luisa Capetillo, Pioneer Puerto Rican Feminist*. New York: Peter Lang, 2006.

Vargas, Zaragosa. *Labor Rights Are Civil Rights: Mexican American Workers in Twentieth-Century America*. Princeton, NJ: Princeton University Press, 2005.

Vazquez, Alexandra. *Listening in Detail: Performances of Cuban Music*. Durham, NC: Duke University Press, 2013.

Vega, Bernardo. *Memorias de Bernardo Vega: contribución a la historia de la comunidad puertorriqueña en Nueva York*, ed. César Andréu Iglesias. New York: Ediciones Huracán, 1977.

Venegas, Daniel. *Las aventuras de Don Chipote, o cuando los pericos mamen*. Houston, TX: Arte Público Press, 1999 [1928].

Villa, Raúl Homero. *Barrio-Logos: Space and Place in Urban Chicano Literature and Culture*. Austin: University of Texas Press, 2000.

Weheliye, Alexander. *Phonographies: Grooves in Sonic Afro-Modernity*. Durham, NC: Duke University Press, 2005.

15

Literary Revolutions in the Borderlands

Transnational Dimensions of the Mexican Revolution and Its Diaspora in the United States

YOLANDA PADILLA[1]

Mariano Azuela's *Los de abajo* (*The Underdogs*) has long been considered the quintessential "novel of the Mexican Revolution" – the narrative thematic that both initiates and defines Mexico's national literary tradition. Prior to the novel's appearance in 1915, Mexican literature was characterized as derivative of European traditions. Azuela is credited with inaugurating an autochthonous Mexican literary tradition by anchoring his narrative in the cataclysmic events of early twentieth-century Mexican history, and foregrounding the social divisions that led to the peasant rebellion he was chronicling. Strikingly, however, and despite its "hyper" national status, the remarkable conditions of *Los de abajo's* publication have always left open the possibility of its being read *transnationally*. As has been well documented, Azuela joined a band of Pancho Villa's men in 1914, in part because he wanted to write a novel about the war and the insurgent peasants behind it. When the Villistas started to suffer defeats, Azuela fled across the northern border into El Paso, Texas. There he finished the novel that he had been crafting during the hard months of flight throughout central and northern Mexico. Penniless and close to starvation, he published his novel in serial installments with the El Paso Spanish-language newspaper, *El Paso del Norte.*[1]

Mexican literary histories have paid scant attention to the fact that this most national of Mexican novels was published on the much-reviled fringes of the nation, in the US–Mexico borderlands. Instead, *Los de abajo* is read through what Juan Pablo Dabove calls a "nation-state identity paradigm," an interpretive apparatus that underwrites the post-revolutionary Mexican government's nation-building project by enabling the appropriation of the

---

[1] For an account of this episode in the novel's publication history, see Robe.

revolution's meanings through imperatives of centralization, exclusion, and the achievement of modernity (260).[2] This interpretive lens begins by celebrating the narrative's peasant protagonists, led by Demetrio Macías, as the source of Mexican values and identity, crediting them with setting into motion the war that enabled national self-actualization. Ultimately, however, those subjects are seen to be frightfully violent, backward, and anti-modern, qualities putatively indicated in *Los de abajo* by the circular wanderings in which they engage, and which become increasingly aimless as the narrative progresses. That seemingly pointless roaming along with Demetrio's violent and meaningless death at the novel's conclusion are understood to symbolize the masses' lack of plan for the nation and their disconnection to the national center. The novel's meanings, then, are sucked into a "state-centered vortex" (Dabove 252–53), as the dislocated rural insurgents are understood to be narrative *closures*, dead ends that have no generative potential for the national future.

Yet situating the novel in the context of the *fronterizo* print culture from which it emerged pulls us away from that vortex. Instead, we shift toward a transnational optic that emphasizes margins, borders, and migrations, one motivated by but also exceeding Azuela's personal experience of dislocation and border crossing. Of course, margins, borders, and migrations are a constitutive aspect of Chicana/o studies' frameworks, especially in the context of the US–Mexico borderlands. They counter the nation-state's totalizing narratives by understanding the dispossessed to constitute narrative *openings* – their experiences of dislocation and migration are the starting points from which to engage the revolution's meanings. Through this lens, the seemingly aimless movement of Azuela's landless insurgents indicates not a failure of politics, but an alternate register of the political, one that suggests a refusal to be captured or disciplined by the nation and its narratives. Such a reading from the periphery undercuts the state's official and appropriative "misreadings," restoring the popular subjects that inject the novel with its vitality back to their positions as protagonists on the terrain of politics and culture.[3]

I begin with this analysis of a canonical Mexican novel in a chapter on the Mexican diaspora in the United States for several reasons. First, as the above discussion shows, applying a Chicana/o studies framework to *Los de abajo*

---

[2] For more on the Mexican center's "centrifugal" power, see Leal.

[3] Of interest for this discussion is Schedler's reading of *Los de abajo* in the context of works by US writers of color such as Américo Paredes through the concept of "border modernism." He focuses on the formal aesthetic strategies these writers used to critique elite notions of modernism and modernity from their bordered perspectives.

provokes a powerful rereading of the narrative that demonstrates the generative possibilities of incorporating such frameworks into Mexican cultural criticism, which has tended to follow a nation-based logic dictating that Mexican-American cultural expressions, histories, and epistemological interventions be severed from those of Mexico because of their location north of the border. Second, and following from this, such a framework necessarily initiates a geopolitical heuristic informed by the neocolonial relationship between Mexico and the United States, drawing attention to the myriad ways in which Mexicans north of the border engaged the revolution, not only through their direct participation – which was considerable – but also through their literary writings, many of which were published in the vibrant network of Spanish-language newspapers that they produced in this period.[4] This transnational material history and the conceptual apparatus it enables undermines the geopolitical limits imposed by nationalist literary histories in understandings of the revolution, as it foregrounds the perspectives of those migrants, immigrants, and border subjects who were cut loose by the Mexican nationalist project. When read in this light, *Los de abajo* becomes the departure point for an alternate literary current, one that critiques the neocolonial relationship between Mexico and the United States, and consequently emphasizes issues such as US imperial aggression, dispossession, racial and ethnic conflict, and debates about cultural integrity.[5] Put another way, this literary current ignores Demetrio's death at the conclusion of *Los de abajo*, refusing to understand him as the martyred hero who marks the end of the popular class's role as historical protagonist, but rather seeing him as a future migrant, as one whose story continues as a journey to the north.

This chapter begins by providing a brief gloss of the Mexican Revolution and its significance for Mexicans in the United States. It then focuses on a

---

[4] This transnational geopolitical dimension distinguishes the Chicana/o studies framework I describe from one such as the equally generative "regional" framework Parra applies in his study of novels of the revolution. For an overview of the use of transnational approaches in Chicana/o literary studies, see Orchard and Padilla. For an argument about the importance of what he calls Chicana/o studies' "centrifugal" mode of transnationalism and its influence on hemispheric studies, see Luis-Brown.

[5] Elsewhere I have read *Los de abajo* alongside Mexican American literary engagements with the revolution in terms of what I call "the 'other' novel of the Mexican Revolution," indicating "narratives that demand a reckoning with the refuse of nations – those migrants, immigrants, and border subjects who were cut loose by the Mexican nationalist project, and who subsequently probed the cracks in that project from a transnational perspective" (67). See also Parle, who studies novels of the revolution that were published by San Antonio's Casa Editorial Lozano, a press owned by Ignacio Lozano, publisher of the important Spanish-language newspaper *La Prensa*.

small number of exemplary writers in order to chart the widely divergent political spectrum represented by their literary output. These range from poetry calling for revolution produced by members of the anarchist Partido Liberal Mexicano (PLM), to the culturally conservative novels that called for Mexican immigrants to return to their war-torn homeland immediately or risk the cultural corruption of US influence, to feminist writings that argued for the centrality of women in the war's military and political affairs. Taken together, these diverse writings reveal members of the Mexican diaspora in the United States to be producers of knowledge, as they elucidated through engagements with the revolution the place of Greater Mexico at the center of issues encompassing ethnic, national, and transnational concerns.

The Mexican Revolution (1910–1920), the first major revolution of the twentieth century, was a seismic event that transformed Mexico and deeply influenced the United States. Initially, the war was fought to overthrow the regime of Porfirio Díaz, who was held in high regard for his exploits in various wars of the mid-nineteenth century. Backed by the military, he appointed himself president in 1876, and ruled for the next thirty-four years. His regime was marked by great economic prosperity and political stability. It was also marked by violent repression, political surveillance, and economic policies that encouraged the growth of large haciendas at the expense of small farmers and communally owned lands. Previously independent peasants were left landless, and by 1910, the rural masses were on the brink of starvation. Dissatisfaction and anger were also rampant among Mexico's middle classes and industrial workers. Lack of democracy, which meant lack of access to political power and subordination to an all-powerful state bureaucracy, increasing taxation, and resentment at the privileges accorded to foreigners profoundly affected Mexico's middle classes.

These radically different segments of the population came together in a tense alliance in order to overthrow the regime, rallying around the wealthy landowner Francisco Madero. Díaz fled into exile in 1911, and by the end of that year Madero had been elected to the presidency. However, this result did not bring political stability. The historical consensus is that Madero was a weak leader, and that this led to his assassination in February of 1913. While he lost almost all of his support during his brief presidency, in death he instantly became an honored martyr, galvanizing the splintered factions of the revolution into action. Factions led by Venustiano Carranza, Pancho Villa, Emiliano Zapato, and Alvaro Obregón came together and succeeded in overthrowing the counterrevolutionary government of Victoriano Huerta almost immediately. However, their alliance quickly disintegrated due to their differing goals and the desire of several to grab power. The ensuing years were marked by continuing violence and instability that eventually saw the death of one million of Mexico's 15 million citizens, and every major leader of the revolution met a violent death. Many mark the end of the revolution in 1920, the year of Carranza's assassination, but violence continued well into the next decade.[6]

While nation-based histories would contain the story of the revolution within Mexico's borders, in truth the war was a transnational event from its very inception. This is unsurprising when we remember that those who lived on either side of the international boundary had functioned as a cohesive community for decades, moving freely back and forth across the border well into the twentieth century. When the revolution began, the borderline did little to stop Mexicans north of the Rio Grande from partici-pating. On the contrary, significant groundwork for the war was laid in the United States, with ethnic Mexicans working together to plan the overthrow of the Díaz regime. Richard Griswold del Castillo puts this point more starkly: "The Mexican Revolution was launched from the barrios of San Antonio, Laredo, El Paso, and Los Angeles" (42). This does not mean, however, that Mexicans in the United States were unified in their responses to the revolution. They were a diverse group marked by differences in key elements of identity formation, such as class, race, and regional background, and encompassed an array of subject positions as migrants, immigrants, exiles, and deeply rooted residents who traced their family lines back to when the US Southwest was still the Mexican north. Accordingly, they spanned the political spectrum, as they ranged from radical anarchists to conservative counterrevolutionists.[7]

Regeneración, one of the most influential Spanish-language newspapers published in the United States during the revolution, was the principle outlet for the ideas and positions of the PLM, an anarchist party established by Ricardo Flores Magón in 1900. Flores Magón, his brother Enrique, and other key party members were persecuted in Mexico due to their calls for the overthrow of the Díaz regime, and were forced to seek refuge in the United

---

[6] The historiographical literature on the revolution is vast. Examples include Gilly, Knight, and Katz. For a good overview and critique of this literature and the different stages of its development, see Vaughan.
[7] A very partial list of work that examines the role played by Mexicans in the United States in the revolution includes Griswold del Castillo, García, Montejano, Zamora, Pérez, Lomas, and the collection of essays edited by Marroquín Arredondo, Pineda Franco, and Mieri. For an engaging microhistory of the Revolution in El Paso, Texas, see Romo.

States. They settled in Los Angeles in 1910, where they continued publishing their newspaper with great success, reaching a circulation of roughly 30,000 that stretched into Mexico. They used *Regeneración* to promote an anarchist position dedicated to proletarian social justice, championing the total destruction of the existing order, including the capitalist system, the government, and the church. While the party's overriding objective was to unite all oppressed people in a borderless, multinational, multiethnic solidarity, Flores Magón could not ignore the subjection he witnessed of Mexicans in the United States. He wrote articles denouncing the escalating violence perpetrated against border Mexicans, while also voicing vehement opposition to the possibility of US intervention in the Mexican Revolution. As Griswold del Castillo argues, Flores Magón believed that Mexicans struggling against political tyranny and economic exploitation in Mexico were leading the way for the liberation of working-class Mexicans in the United States. Furthermore, though he had little interest in championing nationalist causes, he suggested that US disrespect for the Mexican nation ultimately would lead to negative consequences for Mexicans north of the border (46).

Artistic expression featured prominently in *Regeneración*'s pages, reflecting the PLM's belief that art had a crucial role to play in any social movement. Flores Magón elaborates on such ideas in a 1920 letter to Elena White, in which he assails as "nonsense" a modernist current celebrating the idea of "art for art's sake." He states that such is his "reverence" for the power of art that it "hurts" him to "see it prostituted by persons, who having not the power of making others feel what they feel, nor of making [them] think what they think, hide their impotency" under the "art for art's sake" motto (qtd. in Streeby 5). By implication, true artists are those who have the power to make others feel and think as they do, who can, as Shelley Streeby elaborates in her discussion of this letter, employ a sentimental mode that inspires feeling, thought, and direct action at odds with state and capitalist power, while envisioning an alternate, socially just world (5–6). For the PLM, then, art not only helped the movement define its goals, it also cultivated the "formation of spiritual affinities between strangers who could then reach out and support one another spontaneously" and promoted a "philosophical attitude that led individuals to revolt against what might otherwise have been naturalized as 'their lot'" (Lomnitz, par. 4).

Flores Magón's brother Enrique wrote numerous poems for *Regeneración* that exemplify such principles. Though the PLM was not a nationalist group, Enrique's poetry at times strategically cultivates and mobilizes national sentiment in order to foment a spirit of rebellion. "Tierra y Libertad," which appeared in *Regeneración* on February 14, 1914, appropriates Mexico's national hymn. The official version speaks from the perspective of the bourgeois nation-building project, urging all Mexicans to fight to the death if their homeland is attacked in order to defend the principles of "unity" and "liberty" for which it stands. In contrast, Enrique's version speaks from the perspective of the oppressed, the country's true heroes. Again, the call is for combat, but this time the enemy is not imagined to be a rapacious foreigner, but rather a group of internal foes: the rich, the clergy, and the government. He writes,

> Pues si libres queremos, hermanos,
> Encontrarnos algún bello día,
> Es preciso apretar nuestras manos
> En los cuellos de tal trilogía.
>
> (If one beautiful day in the future, brothers,
> we want to find ourselves free,
> we must tighten our hands with precision
> around the necks of that trilogy.)

Fernándo Grijalva Tapia observes that if the official hymn obscures class divisions through abstract appeals to unity, such divisions explicitly animate Enrique's version, which entreats its audience to "rip off the chains of slavery" in order to "take back the land" and "win liberty" (67). The cry of "land and liberty" that gives the poem its title and that reappears at its conclusion was the PLM's motto, and was famously taken up by Emiliano Zapata and his followers as their rallying call.[8] Thus, Enrique makes specific reference to the revolution, entreating those moved by his message to join the rebellion raging at that moment and to help realize his vision of a Mexico for the people. Moreover, as Louis Mendoza argues, PLM rallying cries around national identity were not directed solely at those within Mexico's borders, "but also at Mexicans in the United States who were being affected by unequal development in the process of expanding capitalism." He further elaborates that "Mexican nationalism need not be Mexico-specific but, rather, a response to a trans-border capitalism that simultaneously prompted

---

[8] The PLM and Zapata's influence continue to be felt in Mexico to this day through the Zapatista Army of National Liberation (Ejército Zapatista de Liberación Nacional, EZLN), an insurgent collection of indigenous and non-indigenous groups fighting for "economic equity and democratic freedoms" (Saldaña-Portillo, 402). The EZLN sees itself as the ideological heir to Zapata, especially with respect to his struggles for land reform and redistribution, among other issues. For analyses of the EZLN in Chicanx and borderlands contexts see Saldaña-Portillo and Martín.

migration from Mexico and forced people into a new relationship with capital in a land that was both foreign and familiar" (107).

Regeneración published at least one essay on the subject of women's equality in each of its issues. Emma Pérez argues, however, that if the PLM's male leaders were visionaries when it came to imagining an alternate world based in economic, social, and political liberation, they fell short when it came to imagining the liberation of women. She singles out Ricardo Flores Magón's essay, "A la mujer" ("To Women"), which appeared in *Regeneración* on September 24, 1910, as representative of PLM views. She credits him with a perceptive analysis of women's social condition ("If men are slaves, you are too. Bondage does not recognize sex"), but draws attention to his flawed conceptualization of women's "natural" roles, of their important but ultimately secondary duty to, in his words, "help the man; to be there when he suffers; to lighten his sorrow" (62). As feminist scholars such as Pérez, Clara Lomas, and Ana Lau and Carmen Ramos have shown, women were an integral part of the PLM network, and their roles went far beyond the "nurturing" of men envisioned by the male leadership. Women were central to the launching of the revolution in numerous ways, not least through their work with the Spanish-language press in the borderlands.

The foremost poet among these revolutionary women was Sara Estela Ramírez. Born in Coahuila in 1881, she moved to Laredo, Texas in 1898 to accept a teaching position. She immediately became an integral part of Laredo's vibrant intellectual and political life, publishing articles and poems in the local Spanish-language newspapers *La Crónica* and *El Demócrata Fronterizo*, and publishing two literary periodicals of her own, *La Corregidora* and *Aurora*, between 1904 and 1910. She was an active member of the PLM, "counting herself amongst the growing numbers of opposition press journalists that were decrying, both North and South of the Rio Grande, the conditions under which Mexican people were living" (Hernández, 16). While her poetry did not appear in *Regeneración*, her writings were published in the PLM's supporting network of local newspapers, which the party considered crucial for the success of its cause (Gómez-Quiñones, 23). Her poem "21 of March: To Juárez," which appeared in *El Demócrata Fronterizo* on May 9, 1908, is one of her more explicit calls for an uprising against the Díaz regime. Perhaps her most well-known piece is her prose poem "¡Surge!," which was published in the April 9, 1910 issue of *La Crónica* just months before her premature death at the age of 29. The poem is a passionate admonishment to women to transcend the narrow roles society prescribes for them, and to embrace "lives of action ... lives dedicated to noble and grandiose tasks" (Hernandez, 22). She writes "Sólo la acción es vida; sentir que se vive, es la más hermosa sensación" (Only action is life; to feel that one lives is the most beautiful sensation). Ramírez does not directly reference political rebellion here. However, Zamora points out that it might not have been socially acceptable for Ramírez to make explicit appeals for women to organize "as women." He teases out the poem's political undertones by focusing on the keyword "action." When she thematizes action in her other works, she is normally urging Mexicans to organize both as Mexicans and as workers. Thus, "when Ramirez remarks that 'only action is life,' she may be suggesting that women can achieve authenticity by participating in struggles for democratic rights" (166). Moreover, and as Lau and Ramos argue, for many of these women, gender rebellion and political rebellion emerged simultaneously, and were mutually constituting. Thus, raising one often necessarily implies the other (23).

Like Ramírez, Leonor Villegas de Magnón played an important role in Laredo's political and intellectual culture through her work as a writer, teacher, and activist. They were both part of the same circle of friends who participated in the revolution. Of particular importance in this circle were Nicasio Idar, his daughter Jovita, and the rest of the Idar family, a number of whom were leading figures in civic organizations, labor organizers, and active in city politics. Most importantly, they published *La Crónica*, a weekly newspaper that ran from at least 1910–1914, and which stood alongside *Regeneración* and San Antonio's *La Prensa* in terms of circulation and influence (Kanellos 2000, 100). Both Ramírez and Magnón published in the newspaper. However, neither Magnón's nor the Idar's politics were as radical as Ramírez's, and they were not members of the PLM. Rather, they were Tejana "progressives," a term used by historian Benjamin Johnson to describe Tejanas/os who supported the revolution but had much more moderate agendas than the PLM anarchists (42).[9]

Magnón was born in Nuevo Laredo, Tamaulipas, Mexico in 1876, the same year that Porfirio Díaz began his thirty-six-year dictatorship of the country. Although born into an affluent and cultured family that was part of the Mexican frontier's "rural aristocracy," her unhappiness with the inequalities of the Mexican social order and the political corruption that undergirded them compelled her to risk her family wealth by participating in the overthrow of the Díaz regime. What followed was a series of remarkable exploits,

---

[9] For more on the women of this circle, especially in terms of their roles as educators, see Enoch.

as she tended to injured revolutionary soldiers, housed political exiles, engaged in numerous acts of political intrigue, and rubbed shoulders with the likes of Pancho Villa, Alvaro Obregón, and Emiliano Zapata. Moreover, she became an important confidante and advisor to Venustiano Carranza, a future Mexican president, and the person who urged her to write down and publish her experiences of the Mexican Civil War.

Magnón wrote the first version of her memoir, entitled *La rebelde* (*The Rebel*), in the 1920s. Writing in Spanish and with Mexican audiences in mind, she had two interrelated objectives: to challenge Mexico's negative view of the northern borderlands, and, following from this, to memorialize and validate the borderlands' female revolutionaries, especially those who were members of the nursing corps she created – *La cruz blanca* – and who played key roles in the war's military and political affairs. The Mexican center historically has regarded the northern frontier with contempt, viewing the region as a "cultural desert" (Zuñiga 19) and, even more, as an untameable zone of rebellion unassimilable into the national body (Alonso 18). María Socorro Tabuenca Córdoba notes that the "barbaric" cultural desert in the Mexican imaginary includes the US Southwest along with northern Mexico (498). As Clara Lomas asserts, *La rebelde's* importance stems in part from the fact that "it is one of the few documents produced between 1910–1920 that challenges the stereotypes of Texas Mexicans held by both Mexican and US dominant societies" ("Introduction" xii). The memoir's key intervention in this regard is to push back against a faulty Mexican historiography that had begun to erase *fronteriza/o* contributions to the war before the last bullets had even been fired. Magnón makes this aim explicit, lamenting that "history has assumed responsibility for documenting the facts, but it has forgotten the important role played by the communities of Laredo, Texas, and Nuevo Laredo, Tamaulipas and other border cities which united themselves in a fraternal agreement" (qtd. in Lomas 1994, xxxix). In contrast to such histories, Magnón positions border Mexicans at the center of the revolution, and thus at the center of the defining event of twentieth-century Mexican history. She chronicles the actions of those *fronterizas/os*, such as the Idars, who dedicated their lives to social change, and who did so in the multiple ways dictated by their positions between nations. Thus, many actively engaged in the revolution at the same time that they worked as labor and political activists seeking to improve the positions of Mexicans in the United States.

Magnón makes clear throughout her historiographical project of revision that border women will take center stage, a strategy she references numerous times in the memoir, as when she writes that "la historia relatará los hechos militares, aquí solo toca hacer vivir y recordar a las heroicas olvidadas" (history will relate military matters, here the concern is to keep alive and remember our forgotten heroines) (73). Lomás explains that Magnón was troubled not only by the erasure of these women from official accounts, but also by the way in which the few females who were recognized were mythified folkloric figures such as "la Adelita" and "la soldadera." These figures were celebrated for nothing more than their beauty and for their roles as the love interests of the male soldiers. In contrast, Magnón's portrayals of "rebel women" run the gamut from rural, destitute soldiers' companions to middle-class teachers, journalists, propagandists, printers, telegraph operators, nurses and to bourgeois socialites, all of which challenge the masculinist official history of the revolution (xxxiii). And of course, the strongest challenge to such histories comes from Magnón's self-portrayal as an "independent, intelligent, and extremely outspoken woman" ("Transborder Discourse" 67).

María Cristina Mena was a contemporary of Magnón's, but her background and experiences as a writer were very different. Born in Mexico City in 1893, she came from an upper-class family with strong ties to the Díaz regime. Sensing that increasing domestic turmoil in the country might explode into all-out violence and retribution against Díaz's supporters, her family sent her to New York City in 1907 to stay with family friends. In 1916 she married the playwright Henry Kellett Chambers, and over time she became friends with major modernist authors such as D. H. Lawrence and Aldous Huxley. Mena was already an accomplished writer by the time she married, having published numerous short stories in some of the most prominent journals of the day, the majority of which appeared in *Century Magazine*. Her timeliness as an "insider" writing about Mexico during the revolution gave her a high level of visibility, which she took full advantage of in order to focus attention on the causes and possible solutions to the problems overwhelming her homeland, while also providing a more balanced portrait of Mexico than her US readers would otherwise be exposed to.

While Mena was not a direct participant in the revolution in the manner of Flores Magón, Ramírez, or Magnón, her stories in *Century* did intervene in US perceptions of Mexico during the revolution, doing so by subtly challenging the periodical's typically denigrating depictions of her homeland. *Century* promoted itself as a cosmopolitan magazine with a focus on political and cultural events, and featured literary pieces, travel narratives, and cultural criticism. Doherty and Tiffany Ana López explain that during the revolution the magazine increasingly portrayed Mexico as a threat to the nation's borders, both because of the mass migration that would result from the war, and because of the revolution's threat to economic and political ties between the two countries. A 1914 editorial by W. Morgan Shuster makes this point, arguing that if Mexico, with its "thousands of ignorant and blameless peons, Indians, and other citizens," did not heed the civilized world's demands for peace, that the "international police power which in the end must reside in the leading civilized nations of the earth" would have to intervene through force (qtd. in Doherty, 168).

At times Mena's stories display a condescension toward their Mexican characters that seems to align them with the *Century* view of Mexico as premodern, exotic, and "other." Yet, as López shows, Mena distinguishes her stories from typical *Century* fare in that she "humanizes her characters, giving them dignity, and portraying them in complex ways rather than as one-dimensional caricatures" (68). Such is the case in "The Gold Vanity Set" (1913), which features a young Mexican "indita" named Petra, who steals a US tourist's makeup compact in order to offer it to the Virgin of Guadalupe in prayer that her husband will remain sober and stop beating her. At first glance, the story might seem simply to reinforce stereotypes of indigenous peoples as quaint and superstitious. However, it shows the indigenous characters resisting the colonizing gaze, most explicitly when Petra staunchly refuses to allow Miss Young to take a picture of her. Marissa López observes that moments such as these "stand as an indictment of the United States's paternalistic and exoticizing view of Mexico" (100). Moreover, they exemplify what Tiffany Ana López has identified as Mena's "trickster discourse," one that purposefully moves between Anglo-American and Mexican perspectives in order to disrupt and challenge dominant US reading practices and under-standings of Mexico.

While Mena's work challenges general US views of Mexico, it can also be read in light of the revolution's impact on the relationship between Mexico and the United States, and Mexican fears of US imperial aggression during the war. One sees such layered meanings in "The Education of Popo," the story of a wealthy US family – the Cherrys – that visits an affluent Mexican family – the Arriolas – in order to initiate a business relationship. Alicia Cherry, the recently divorced daughter of the US family, pursues the four-teen-year-old Popo Arriola, who is enchanted with the attentions of his blond-haired, blue-eyed visitor. Alicia encourages the flirtation until her ex-husband appears and she suddenly breaks off with Popo. At that point, the superficiality of her intentions becomes apparent to the dejected and suddenly more mature Popo. Doherty argues that "this story of a sexually exploitative relationship symbolizes American imperialism south of the border," and that Alicia and Edward indicate the United States' "consume and dispose" stance toward Mexico: "Alicia and Edward are literally products of American capitalism, 'ugly American tourists' who expect to be served . . . and who use the Mexicans for their own pleasure" (2001, 176).[10]

While Mena was critical of the US relationship to Mexico, she seemed happy to live out her life in her adopted home. Such was not the case for a significant number of Mexicans who found themselves in the United States due to the chaos of the revolution, and who were driven by what Nicolás Kanellos identifies as the "dream of return." The resulting literary expressions are marked by a "double-gaze perspective" as these writings "forever compare the past and the present, the homeland and the new country, and see the resolution of these conflicting points of reference only when the author, characters, and/or the audience can return to the patria" (*Hispanic* 7). Such literature opposes the celebration of the American Dream, focusing instead on what the narrators see as the ills of American society, with oppression of the working class and racial discrimination chief among them. They promote the idea that "it is far better to suffer oppression and poverty among one's own people in the homeland than on foreign soil," and, even more, that "it is the patriotic duty of the sons of Mexico not to abandon their native land but to invest in their country's future and to respect its history and culture" (*Hispanic* 68). Consequently, the most despised characters in these writings are those that assimilate into US culture, the "pochos," "agringados," and "renegados" who speak a corrupted Spanish-English hybrid, embrace US materialism, and subscribe to Anglo-America's lax social mores. Such defilement typically is represented most scathingly through female characters that flout their traditional gender roles. As Gabriela Baeza Ventura explains, women were tasked with preserving and transmitting Mexican cultural values and practices through their roles as mothers, and this role was even more crucial in the hostile and corrupting environment of the United States (31). Figures such as the "pelona" – so-called because they adopt the short hairstyles, clothing, and morally corrupt behavior of "flappers" in the United States – always indicate moral and cultural ruination.[11]

---

[10] For an analysis of newly recovered works by Mena housed at the Recovering the US Hispanic Literary Heritage Project at the University of Houston, see Toth.

[11] The underlying ideologies in these immigrant narratives overlap with but are not identical to writings that promoted the idea of "México de afuera," the extreme belief that Mexico had been so transformed by the "bolchevique" hordes spearheading the war that the only true Mexican culture survived in the exiled colonies north of the border.

Conrado Espinoza's *El sol de Texas* (*Under the Texas Sun*) (1926) exemplifies this nationalist ideology of return. Espinoza was active in Mexican politics in the early 1920s, a period that continued to be marked by the violence and political disarray of the revolution. Finding himself in danger due to his political associations, he was forced into exile in the United States, where he worked for numerous Spanish-language newspapers. John Pluecker observes that Espinoza's novel manifests a complicated narrative position with respect to the Mexican immigrant laborers that are its focus. On the one hand, it celebrates their resilience and capacity for resistance in a foreign land that subjects them to racial exploitation at every turn. On the other hand, the author's nationalist stance demands the rejection of those immigrants who fail to return to Mexico as soon as they are able, and who are doomed to lose their cultural and moral integrity under the defiling influence of the United States (114).

Espinoza illustrates the imperative of return through the alternative scenarios presented by two families, both of whom go to the north in search of economic opportunities that their war-torn home cannot provide. In their minds, the United States promises "peace, work, riches, and happiness," and they will no longer have to fear the "villistas or the carrancistas, the government or the rebels" because they have left the revolution behind ("¡Ahora sí que nada habían de temer de villistas ni de carrancistas, de gobierno ni de rebeldes!" 8). The first family, composed of Quico and his wife and children, embraces life in the United States, despite the racism and oppression the members face both in the cotton fields and outside of the work environment. So thoroughly do they take to their new lives that they lose their honor and dignity, with their son becoming a lazy drunk and their daughter a prostitute. In contrast, the second family, made up of Don Serapio and his two sons, is incorruptible. Almost as soon as they reach the United States they realize their mistake, which Espinoza dramatizes through the exploitative conditions under which they are forced to work, and the resulting death of one of the sons. For the rest of the novel the remaining family members strive to return home. The tragedy of the novel is that "the family had to leave home to learn to love their nation, to become patriots" (Kanellos, *Hispanic* 68).

Like Espinoza and Venegas, who I discuss below, these expatriates were culturally conservative, viewed even the slightest gesture toward assimilation as cultural defilement, and demanded that women adhere to traditional gender roles. However, they differed in that they were unsympathetic and even scornful toward the working classes, and refused to return to Mexico until the revolution had been defeated and the Porfirian social order had been restored. For more on this group, see Novoa, Ventura, and Kanellos.

Daniel Venegas's serial novel *Las aventuras de Don Chipote, o, cuando los pericos mamen* (*The Adventures of Don Chipote, or, When Parrots Breast-Feed*) appeared in Los Angeles's Spanish-language daily newspaper *El heraldo de México* in 1928. Little is known of Venegas's life. He ran a vaudeville ensemble from 1924–1933 called Compañía de Revistas Daniel Venegas that performed his plays in theaters catering to the working class, and published a weekly satirical newspaper called *El Malcriado* (*The Brat*) from 1924–1929. The penchant for burlesque and social commentary that characterize his work in the newspaper reach full fruition in *Don Chipote*. The eponymous protagonist leaves his impoverished home after hearing false tales of riches in the United States from a returning migrant. What he finds instead is a corrupt US society, racism, and the dehumanization of immigrants. His wife, Doña Chipote, makes the trek north to retrieve him, and the novel ends with him back in his homeland. His disillusionment with the promise of the United States is made clear in the novel's final line: "Los mexicanos se harán ricos en Estados Unidos: CUANDO LOS PERICOS MAMEN." (Mexicans will make it big in the United States . . . WHEN PARROTS BREAST-FEED).

Don Chipote serves as a remarkable early example of Mexican American working-class literature, communicating its searing criticisms of the treatment of Mexican laborers through the vernacular and cultural expressions of the laborers themselves, with whom Venegas identified (Kanellos, "Introduction" 1). While the novel vilifies Anglo-American culture and society, it offers equally denigrating attacks of Mexicans themselves, as it satirizes the immigrant "greenhorns" who believe that everything about the United States is superior to Mexico. Finally, and as was typical of such "dream of return" stories, the narrative saves its most intense criticism for "assimilated" Mexican women. Thus, the sole purpose of the Mexican female laborers in Venegas's novel, whether they be waitresses, vaudeville performers, or prostitutes, is to take advantage of Don Chipote. These women have embraced US cultural norms by working outside of the home, through their "flapper" way of dressing, and in their morally corrupt behavior. It is left to Don Chipote's wife, Doña Chipota, to act as a counter to these "Americanized" women. Representing the nuclear family and Mexican cultural values, she journeys to the United States to rescue her husband and to "reestablish social order by returning him to Mexico" (Kanellos, "Introduction" 10).[12]

---

[12] See M. López for a discussion of the ways in which *Don Chipote* challenges the class biases inherent in the "México de afuera" ideology.

While scholars have long been interested in fronteriza/o literary engage-ments with the revolution, the extensive mapping I provide here would not have been possible prior to the early 2000s. Many of the texts I cite have been made available over the past twenty-five years by the Recovering the US-Hispanic Literary Heritage Project, based at the University of Houston. With its focus on recovering works by Latinas/os in the United States written before 1960, the project has unearthed a body of writing by authors who were not fully interpellated into US citizenship, and who were still active participants in Latin American political life. This literature has made it possible to alter the geographical imaginary that traditionally organizes Latina/o literary studies as a field. In the cases studied here, fronteriza/o engagements with the revolution raise numerous questions. For example, what Mexican and Latin American cultural and historical coordinates become more evident as influences on Mexican American narratives when viewed through the transnational lens required by this literature? How do Mexican American writers transform these influences to engage their positions as subjects of the United States? How might this literature reshape understandings of Mexican literary history? In what ways have Mexicans in the United States acted as as dynamic parts of multiple nations and of transnational phenomena? Scholars will examine these and other generative questions as they continue to consider fronteriza/o engagements with the Mexican Revolution.

WORKS CITED

Alonso, Ana María. *Thread of Blood: Colonialism, Revolution, and Gender on Mexico's Northern Frontier*. Tucson: University of Arizona Press, 1995.

Azuela, Mariano. *Los de abajo. 1915*. Ed. Jorge Ruffinelli. Buenos Aires: Ministerio Rela-ciones Exteriores, 1988.

    The Underdogs. 1915. Trans. Sergio Waisman. New York: Penguin Books, 2008.

Bruce-Novoa, Juan. "*La Prensa* and the Chicano Community." *The Americas Review* 17.3–4 (1987): 150–56.

Dabove, Juan Pablo. *Nightmares of the Lettered City: Banditry and Literature in Latin America, 1816–1929*. Pittsburgh, PA: University of Pittsburgh Press, 2007.

Doherty, Amy. Introduction to *The Collected Stories of María Cristina Mena*. Houston, TX: Arte Público Press, 1997: vii–l.

    "Redefining the Borders of Local Color Fiction: María Cristina Mena's Short Stories in the *Century Magazine*." *The Only Efficient Instrument: American Women Writers and the Periodical*. Eds. Aleta Feinsod Cane and Susan Alves. Iowa City: University of Iowa Press, 2001: 165–78.

Enoch, Jessica. *Refiguring Rhetorical Education: Women Teaching African American, Native American, and Chicano/a Students, 1865–1911*. Carbondale: Southern Illinois University Press, 2008.

Espinoza, Conrado. *El sol de Texas*. 1926. Bilingual edition with English translation by Ethriam Cash Brammer de González. Houston, TX: Arte Público Press, 2007.

Flores Magón, Enrique. "Tierra y Libertad." *Regeneración* February 14, 1914.

Flores Magón, Ricardo. "To Women." *Dreams of Freedom: A Ricardo Flores Magón Reader*. Eds. Chaz Bufe and Mitchell Verter. Oakland, CA: AK Press, 2005.

García, Mario T. *Desert Immigrants: The Mexicans of El Paso, 1880–1920*. New Haven, CT: Yale University Press, 1981.

Gilly, Adolfo. *The Mexican Revolution*. 1971. Trans. Patrick Camiller. New York: The New Press, 2005.

Gómez-Quiñonez, Juan. *Sembradores, Ricardo Flores Magón y el Partido Liberal Mexicano: A Eulogy and Critique*. Los Angeles, CA: Aztlán, 1973.

Grijalva Tapia, Fernando. "Ideologia y poesia en el exilio: Cuatro poetas mexicanos en el suroeste norteamericano (1900–1920)." Dissertation, University of Arizona. Ann Arbor: ProQuest/UMI, 1991.

Griswold, Richard del Castillo. "The Mexican Revolution and the Spanish-Language Press." *Journalism History* 4.2 (1977): 42–47.

Hernández, Inés. "Sara Estela Ramirez: Sembradora." *Legacy: A Journal of Nineteenth-Century American Women Writers* 6.1 (1989): 13–26.

Johnson, Benjamin Heber. *Revolution in Texas: How a Forgotten Rebellion and Its Bloody Suppression Turned Mexicans into Americans*. New Haven, CT: Yale University Press, 2003.

Kanellos, Nicolás. Introduction to *The Adventures of Don Chipote, or, When Parrots Breast Feed* by Daniel Venegas. Houston, TX: Arte Público Press, 2000: 1–17.

  Hispanic Immigrant Literature: El sueño del retorno. Austin: University of Texas Press, 2011.

Katz, Friedrich. *The Life and Times of Pancho Villa*. Stanford, CA: Stanford University Press, 1998.

Knight, Alan. *The Mexican Revolution*. 2 vols. Cambridge: University of Cambridge Press, 1986.

Lau, Ana, and Carmen Ramos. *Mujeres y revolución, 1900–1917*. Mexico City: Instituto Nacional de Antropología e Historia, 1993.

Leal, Luis. "Mexico's Centrifugal Culture." *Discourse* 18.1–2 (1995–1996): 111–21.

Lomas, Clara. Introduction to *The Rebel* by Leonor Villegas de Magnón. Houston, TX: Arte Público Press, 1994: xi–lvi.

  "Transborder Discourse: The Articulation of Gender on the Borderlands in the Early Twentieth Century." *Frontiers* 24.2–3 (2003): 51–74.

Lomnitz, Claudio. Interview with Javier Sethness Castro. *Counterpunch* March 13–15, 2015. Online.

López, Marissa. *Chicano Nations: The Hemispheric Origins of Mexican American Literature*. New York: New York University Press, 2011.

López, Tiffany Ana. "María Cristina Mena: Turn-of-the-Century La Malinche, and Other Tales of Cultural (Re)Construction." *Tricksterism in Turn-of-the-Century American Literature: A Multicultural Perspective*. Eds. Elizabeth Ammons and Annette White Parks. Hannover, NH: University Press of New England, 1994: 21–45.

  "'A Tolerance for Contradictions': The Short Stories of María Cristina Mena." *Nineteenth-Century American Women Writers: A Critical Reader*. Ed. Karen L. Kilcup. Malden, MA: Blackwell Publishers, 1998: 62–80.

Luis-Brown, David. "The Transnational Imaginaries of Chicano/a Studies and Hemispheric Studies: Polycentric and Centrifugal Methodologies." *Borders, Bridges, and*

Breaks: History, Narrative, and Nation in Twenty-First-Century Chicana/o Literary Criticism. Eds. William Orchard and Yolanda Padilla. Pittsburgh, PA: University of Pittsburgh Press, 2016: 40–62.

Marroquín Arredondo, Jaime, Adela Pineda Franco, and Magdalena Mieri, eds. *Open Borders to a Revolution: Culture, Politics, and Migration.* Washington, DC: Smithsonian Institution Scholarly Press, 2013.

Martín, Desirée A. *Borderlands Saints: Secular Sanctity in Chicano/a and Mexican Culture.* New Brunswick, NJ and London: Rutgers University Press, 2013.

Mena, María Cristina. *The Collected Stories of María Cristina Mena.* Ed. Amy Doherty. Houston, TX: Arte Público Press, 1997.

Mendoza, Louis. *Historia: The Literary Making of Chicana and Chicano History.* College Station: Texas A&M Press, 2001.

Montejano, David. *Anglos and Mexicans in the Making of Texas, 1836–1986.* Austin: University of Texas Press, 1987.

Orchard, William and Yolanda Padilla. "Chicana/o Narratives, Then and Now." *Bridges, Borders and Breaks: History, Narrative, and Nation in Twenty-First-Century Chicana/o Literary Criticism.* Eds. William Orchard and Yolanda Padilla. Pittsburgh, PA: University of Pittsburgh Press, 2016: 1–24.

Padilla, Yolanda. "Mexican Americans and the Novel of the Mexican Revolution." *Open Borders to a Revolution: Culture, Politics, and Migration.* Eds. Jaime Marroquín Arredondo, Adela Pineda, and Magdalena Mieri. Washington, DC: Smithsonian Institute Scholarly Press, 2013: 133–52.

"The 'Other' Novel of the Mexican Revolution." *Bridges, Borders and Breaks: History, Narrative, and Nation in Twenty-First-Century Chicana/o Literary Criticism.* Eds. William Orchard and Yolanda Padilla. Pittsburgh, PA: University of Pittsburgh Press, 2016: 63–79.

Parle, Dennis J. "The Novels of the Mexican Revolution Published by the Casa Editorial Lozano." *The Americas Review* 17.3–4: 163–68.

Parra, Max. *Writing Pancho Villa's Revolution: Rebels in the Literary Imagination of Mexico.* Austin: University of Texas Press, 2005.

Pérez, Emma. *The Decolonial Imaginary: Writing Chicanas into History.* Bloomington: Indiana University Press, 1999.

Pluecker, John. "'One More Texas-Mexican': *Under the Texas Sun* and Conflicts of Nation." Introduction to *Under the Texas Sun* by Conrado Espinoza. Houston, TX: Arte Público Press, 2007: 113–38.

Ramírez, Sara Estela. "¡Surge!" *La Crónica*, April 9, 1910, p. 3.

Robe, Stanley L. *Azuela and the Mexican Underdogs.* Berkeley: University of California Press, 1979.

Romo, David Dorado. *Ringside Seat to a Revolution: An Underground Cultural History of El Paso and Juárez, 1893–1923.* El Paso: Cinco Puntos Press, 2005.

Saldaña-Portillo, María Josefina. "Who's the Indian in Aztlan? Rewriting Mestizaje, Indianism, and Chicanismo from the Lacandon." *The Latin American Subaltern Studies Reader.* Ed. Ileana Rodríguez. Durham, NC and London: Duke University Press, 2001: 402–23.

Schedler, Christopher. *Border Modernism: Intercultural Readings in American Literary Modernism.* New York and London: Routledge, 2002.

Streeby, Shelley. *Radical Sensations: World Movements, Violence, and Visual Culture.* Durham, NC: Duke University Press, 2013.

Tabuenca Córdoba, María Socorro. "Sketches of Identities from the Mexico-US Border (or the Other Way Around)." *Comparative American Studies* 3.4: 495–513.

Toth, Margaret A. "María Cristina Mena, Transnationalism, and Mass Media: Untold Stories in the Archive." *Legacy: A Journal of Nineteenth-Century American Women Writers* 30.2 (2013): 331–54.

Vaughan, Mary Kay. "Cultural Approaches to Peasant Politics in the Mexican Revolution." *Hispanic American Historical Review* 79.2 (May 1999): 269–305.

Venegas, Daniel. *Las aventuras de Don Chipote, o, cuando los pericos mamen. 1928.* Houston, TX: Arte Público Press, 1999.

The Adventures of Don Chipote, or, When Parrots Breast-Feed. 1928. Trans. Ethriam Cash Brammer. Houston, TX: Arte Público Press, 2000.

Ventura, Gabriela Baeza. *La imagen de la mujer en la crónica del "México de afuera."* Juárez, México: Universidad Autónoma de Ciudad Juárez, 2006.

Villegas de Magnón, Leonor. *The Rebel.* Houston, TX: Arte Público Press, 1994.

La rebelde. Houston, TX: Arte Público Press, 2004.

Zamora, Emilio. "Sara Estela Ramírez": Una Rosa Roja en el Movimiento." *Mexican Women in the United States: Struggles Past and Present.* Eds. Magdalena Mora and Adelaida R. del Castillo. Occasional Paper 2. Los Angeles: Chicano Studies Research Center Publications, University of California, 1980: 163–69.

The World of the Mexican Worker in Texas. College Station: Texas A&M University Press, 1993.

Zuñiga, Victor. "El norte de méxico como desierto cultural: anatomía de una idea." *Puentelibre* 1 (1995): 18–23.

16

Making It Nuevo

Latina/o Modernist Poetics Remake High Euro-American Modernism

DAVID A. COLÓN

A key lesson to be taken from the study of modernist literature is that there were many modernisms. One might say there were more modernisms than there were nations participating in the discourse, even if the enterprise was by character transnational and heterolingual. While watersheds like the US–Spanish War of 1898 or Andy Warhol's exhibition of *Campbell's Soup Cans* in 1962 allow the historian to approximate its lifespan, modernism manifested itself on a continuum of literary and philosophical praxis, bleeding far beyond its twentieth-century confines. James Joyce turned to Homer, Ezra Pound to Arnaut Daniel, Velimir Khlebnikov to Stenka Razin, so the looking backward of high modernist writers, in their pursuit of iconoclasm, ought to be remembered as farsighted. Likewise, the dialogue of modernism across linguistic divides was extensive. For example, Jorge Luis Borges's manifesto "Ultraísmo" (1921) virtually plagiarizes Pound's "A Few Don'ts by an Imagiste" (1913), which itself is a pastiche so wide-ranging in principles, from Li Po to Dante to Mallarmé, that it practices its own creed: "Be influenced by as many great artists as you can, but have the decency either to acknowledge the debt outright, or to try to conceal it" (*Essays* 202). It is in its concealment of influence that modernist poetry undermines its most lasting stereotype: that it was a literature of newness. Another stubborn stereotype of modernist poetry and poetics is that it exclusively was the cultural production of select initiates in founding *-isms*: F. T. Marinetti, Aldo Palazzeschi, and Futurism; Hugo Ball, Tristan Tzara, Hans Arp, and Dadaism; Wyndham Lewis, Pound, and Vorticism. Such microhistories of early twentieth-century avant-gardes truncate vital details of the complexity of intellectual interchange that brought high modernism into being. There were many outliers to the salon cultures of the European, British, and expatriate American vanguard who, through various means, participated in the burgeoning of modernist aesthetics, including writers who in retrospect would be identified as Latina/o. As the modernist era spanned most of the twentieth century, there were numerous manifestations of modernisms that allowed for practitioners to remake emergent modernist ideals and principles in the contexts of their own societies and languages. But the term *Latina/o* is a postmodern one; in applying it to modernist writers, it does not fit neatly. It works to encompass communities including Puerto Rican, Mexican American, Chicano, Nuyorican, and all immigrants and their descendants from Hispanophone American countries south of the United States, but the term was not available to these members in their moment, not mobilized for the political intent it has garnered in recent decades. A different cultural dynamic was in play from the turn of the twentieth century to the Cold War. Thus, as a precursor to considering the extent to which Latina/o poets remade high Euro-American modernism, one ought to consider the role Latinas/os had in formulating Euro-American modernist poetics from the beginning, a role that at times dialogued with Spanish, Hispanic-American,[1] and Latin American literary production. These interventions were few by the standard of literary history – that being the measure of first moves and subsequent devotees – but nevertheless there were several innovations that filtered into modernist Anglo-European and Euro-American poetry and poetics that are attributable to Latina/o writers, and close examination of these innovations supports an understanding of Euro-American modernist poetry as influenced by the cultural politics of latinidad.

To that end, this essay will begin by focusing on arguably the major American Anglophone poet of the twentieth century, William Carlos Williams (1883–1963), whose impact on the development of modernist poetry and

---

[1] The philosopher George Santayana (1863–1952), an immigrant to the United States and lifelong Spanish citizen, and the art historian Ernest Fenollosa (1853–1908), the Salem-born son of a Spanish musician, had profound influence on the emergence of Anglo-American modernist poetics. Both were educated at Harvard, where Santayana's opinions on poetry were studied by Wallace Stevens and T. S. Eliot among other important poets. Stevens's famous poem "To An Old Philosopher in Rome" (1954) expresses his deep reverence for Santayana, and Eliot's key aesthetic concept of the "objective correlative," proposed in "Hamlet and His Problems" (1920), is widely accepted as developed from Santayana's chapter, "The Elements and Function of Poetry" (1900). Fenollosa authored the essay, "The Chinese Written Character as a Medium for Poetry" (1919), published posthumously by Pound, which provided the rhetoric for Pound's "ideogrammic method." Pound's Chinese translations in *Cathay* (1915) are rooted in Fenollosa's notebooks, which Pound inherited as literary executor after Fenollosa's death.

poetics is undeniable but whose connection to Latina/o culture and identity is often elided in criticism. I will argue that the aforementioned modernist concealment of influence had unique bearing on Williams's ethnicity: that his aesthetic innovations were largely factored on his cultural experiences and identarian politics. Next, I will turn to the Nicaraguan-born poet Salomón de la Selva (1893–1959), whose years in the Northeast produced the first collection of English poems published in the United States by a Latin American author, *Tropical Town and Other Poems* (1918), and illustrate how his unique perspective of writing *into* the English tradition bears on innovations in poetic and creative translation. Lastly, this essay will consider the Puerto Rican poet Julia de Burgos (1914–1953) and how her political activism and journalism, coupled with her lack of rigid aesthetic doctrine, positioned her as the central forebear of Nuyorican poetry. In discussing these key figures, this essay will contextualize them by intersecting disparate spheres of cultural circumstances, across Spanish and English lines. The ideolinguistic tension between Hispanophone culture and Anglophone culture in the Americas was one that widely affected literary discourse and the paths of inquiry for avant-garde poets throughout the twentieth century. The multiple legacies of Spanish empire and English empire within the broader American context interject pressures, both political and linguistic, at the very center of American literary, and identarian, discourse.

William Carlos Williams: Enter the New World *Desnudo*

Contemporary Williams scholars such as Julio Marzán and Lisa Sánchez González, and more recently Peter Ramos and Jonathan Cohen, have illustrated the extent to which Williams was a "bicultural" writer, examining ways that Williams's Caribbean background contributed to both his thematic preoccupations and his aesthetic.[2] This trend was begun in earnest by

---

[2] In analyzing Williams's experience as a Caribbean-American writer, scholars tend to note this in the context of an inherited, systemic approach to Williams as a non-ethnicized subject. For example: "While some critics continue to ignore Williams's bicultural background – and thus maintain his image as the 'non-ethnic' canonical figure to which we have been accustomed – certain trends in identity-based scholarship and pedagogy have allowed those who teach and write about Williams to feel comfortable enough now to emphasize the poet's multicultural, diverse background" (Ramos 89). The elision of Williams's Puerto Rican background from critical consideration of his work is only recently being reconsidered by many poetry scholars who have avoided the issue. As Mark Rudman noted, in 2008: "In all these years of reading Williams I'd never once paused over his middle name" (53).

Marzán, whose book, *The Spanish American Roots of William Carlos Williams* (1994), is a thorough examination of all the depths of Puerto Rican influence in Williams's poetry and poetics. Williams himself left a considerable record, especially in his *Autobiography* (1951), *Yes, Mrs. Williams: A Personal Record of My Mother* (1959), and *Interviews with William Carlos Williams: "Speaking Straight Ahead"* (1976), that details the circumstances of his upbringing and heritage as a Latino. Williams's British father had a peripatetic childhood, moving from England to New York to St. Thomas to the Dominican Republic and then to Puerto Rico, becoming fluent in Spanish. Williams's mother was born and raised in Mayagüez, Puerto Rico, to a blended West Indian family of Puerto Rican, Martiniquan, and Dutch extraction. Williams has been clear that as a child he "heard Spanish constantly spoken" (*Yes, Mrs. Williams* 4) in his home, an environment steeped in Spanish-Caribbean and Latin-American culture. Marzán claims that "Williams' Latin *half* revealed itself as his spiritual center" (xi), especially arguing that "the free, *jaiba*, underground spirit of" Williams's mother (88) moves through much of his writing: by inspiration, lending idiomatic expression, and present in imagery. Much of the evidence Marzán provides takes the form of deciphering "a stylistic code" employed by Williams to translate "the exotic voice of that core into the voice of an Anglo persona amenable to a reading public that conventionally held in low regard that most important component of his historical person" (xi).

The dialogue Williams established between his Latino subjectivity and Anglo-American avant-gardes centered him as a key innovator of modernist poetry. In 1902, he met Ezra Pound[3] at the University of Pennsylvania, where Pound was studying languages and literatures and Williams studied medicine. At Penn, Pound introduced Williams to many poet and artist friends, including Hilda Doolittle (H. D.) and Charles Demuth, in a flourishing arts scene. But unlike Pound, who spent the years between 1908 and 1945 primarily in England, France, and Italy, or H. D., who lived in England and Europe from 1911 until her death in 1961, Williams's travels abroad were limited and primarily professional or educational, including a stint in Leipzig studying postgraduate pediatrics. Williams practiced medicine for forty years in his native New Jersey and New York, a responsibility that kept him away

---

[3] That Williams's family came from Puerto Rico was a detail not overlooked by Pound. He called Williams "Carlos" for many years, and in a letter to Hubert Creekmore, referred to Williams as "a mere dago immigrant. Finest possible specimen of course" (*Letters* 322).

from the vanguard salons of London and Paris. Nevertheless, his correspondence with Pound included him in the imagist circle, and his early books of verse – *Poems* (1909), *The Tempers* (1913), and *Al Que Quiere!* (1917) – established him as one of the more profound poetic iconoclasts of his time.

Al Que Quiere! was a title borrowed from colloquial Spanish, a Latin American term from the context of playing soccer: one ought to pass the ball to the player who is going to do something with it, the one with *ganas*, the one who wants it (*I Wanted to Write a Poem* 19). The choice signals Williams's Latino self-consciousness as integral to his poetics, a blending of aesthetic principle and personal experience[4] that diverges from the post-imagist path toward academic poetry that Pound, T. S. Eliot, and others would take: a type of poetry Williams once denounced because it "returned us to the classroom just at the moment when I felt we were on a point to escape to matters much closer to the essence of a new art form itself – rooted in the locality which should give it fruit" (*Autobiography* 174). Several poems in *Al Que Quiere!* demonstrate Williams's desire for a new art form, one rooted in a particularly Latino locality. "El Hombre," comprised of a mere four lines, hails "a strange courage" betokened by an "ancient star" (31). "Libertad! Igualdad! Fraternidad!" renders the modern French motto into Spanish while the English text of the poem evokes a distinctly working-class voice to express the sentiment that while "all things turn bitter in the end / ...dreams are not a bad thing" (33). "Mujer," another very short poem, presents a "black Persian cat" that is "cursed with offspring" and is taken to an "old / Yankee farm" for rest (33–34). These three poems – as well as "Divertimiento" (62) – each establish a suggestive and discernibly private connection between title and text; the Spanish titles minimally situate the particulars of the poems in relation to, in Eliotic terms, a Latino objective correlative.

But not all of *Al Que Quiere!* is this subtle. "Dedication for a Plot of Ground," inspired by the life of his paternal grandmother, is more explicit in Williams's poetic attempts "to overcome ... the deliberate exclusion of not only Boricua but also ... other subaltern constituencies in the annals of transamerican history" (Sánchez González 44):

> This plot of ground
> facing the waters of this inlet

---

[4] William Marling has surmised that for Williams, unlike most of his contemporaries, "his 'influences' seem of the simplest, most explicable sort: his brother and his mother, his college classmates, his close friends" (2).

is dedicated to the living presence of
Emily Richardson Wellcome
who was born in England; married;
lost her husband and with
her five year old son
sailed for New York in a two-master;
was driven to the Azores;
ran adrift on Fire Island shoal,
met her second husband
in a Brooklyn boarding house,
went with him to Puerto Rico
bore three more children, lost
her second husband, lived hard
for eight years in St. Thomas,
Puerto Rico, San Domingo, followed
the oldest son to New York,
lost her daughter, lost her "baby,"
seized the two boys of
the oldest son by the second marriage
mothered them – they being
motherless – fought for them
against the other grandmother
and the aunts, brought them here
summer after summer, defended
herself here against thieves,
storms, sun, fire,
against flies, against girls
that came smelling about, against
drought, against weeds, storm-tides,
neighbors, weasles that stole her chickens,
against the weakness of her own hands,
against the growing strength of
the boys, against wind, against
the stones, against trespassers,
against rents, against her own mind.
She grubbed this earth with her own hands,
domineered over this grass plot,
blackguarded her oldest son
into buying it, lived here fifteen years,
attained a final loneliness and –
If you can bring nothing to this place
but our carcass, keep out. (69–70)

The breathless litany of trials endured by Emily is a composition that integrates Williams's poetic ideals with his Puerto Rican sensibility. Williams believed that a poem "formally presents its case and its meaning" simultaneously, and as such must be "an object consonant with [the poet's] day" (*Autobiography* 264, 265). In "Dedication for a Plot of Ground," the indignities that comprise Emily's immigrant experience are conveyed, through an exasperated voice, as exasperating. The lack of reflection and abstraction, replaced by a run-on syntax, allows traction to build in the recitation of particulars, performing Williams's credo of "no ideas but in things" (*Paterson* 6). Even though Williams's imagistic style was justified by avant-garde principle, he suffered an "early reputation as a poetic 'primitive,'" often regarded by his contemporary critics as "an artist not inclined to thinking" (Marling 9). This is due to the fact that, unlike that of Pound, H. D., or Richard Aldington, the palette of Williams's poetry largely replaced erudition with lived experience. His Latino consciousness – in its polyglossia, subalterneity, and sympathy – was elemental to his poetic praxis and the drive behind his remaking of Euro-American modernism.

When Williams published *Kora in Hell: Improvisations* (1920), his old Penn friends Pound and H. D. did not approve. In short, they were not ready for it. While they traveled the world, in body and in mind, to pursue a new *paideuma* predominated by Greek and East Asian classics,[5] Williams remained in the Northeast, practicing medicine in working-class communities and involved in the stateside literary-artistic scene,[6] and therefore his writing began to venture more into Cubist and Dadaist dimensions while borrowing from the dialects of disenfranchised Americans. As a doctor-poet, he blended his experiences of the Lower East Side, Hell's Kitchen, and Rutherford into an experimental prose-poetry collage that evades

---

[5] Certain moments of *Kora in Hell* seem to mock Pound's persistence with the Classics: "Giants in the dirt. The gods, the Greek gods, smothered in filth and ignorance. The race is scattered over the world. Where is its home? Find it if you've the genius ... Homer sat in a butcher's shop one rainy night and smelt fresh meat near him so he moved to the open window. It is infinitely important that I do what I well please in the world. What you please is that I please what you please but what I please is well rid of you before I turn off from the path into the field. What I am, why that they made me. What I do, why that I choose for myself. Reading shows, you say. Yes, reading shows reading. What you read is what they think and what they think is twenty years old or twenty thousand and it's all one to the little girl in the *pissoir*. Likewise to me" (64–65).

[6] Williams was instrumental in establishing and sustaining *Others: A Magazine of the New Verse*, an avant-garde poetry publication founded in 1915 by Alfred Kreymborg and Walter Conrad Arensberg. It was based in the Lower East Side of Manhattan and borrowed its name from "The Others," a group of artists and writers, including Man Ray, associated with the artists' colony started in 1913 in Grantwood, New Jersey.

conventions of narrative and verse, and revels in doing it. Relying on the vibrancy of American idiom, Williams asserts, *"Ay dio!* I could say so much were it not for the tunes changing, changing, darting so many ways" (35). He transcribes the Spanish *dios* as *"dio"* to capture an informal, Puerto Rican pronunciation of the expression, and later in the book invokes the changing tunes of *danzón* to declare, "'N! cha! cha! cha! destiny needs men, so make up your mind" (62). He even includes the following enigmatic passage, squeezing together words to capture a familiar, rapid Latino Spanish cadence: "Baaaa! Ba-ha-ha-ha-ha-ha-ha! *Bebe esa purga.* It is the goats of Santo Domingo talking. *Bebe esa purga!* Bebeesapurga! And the answer is: *Yo no lo quiero beber!* Yonoloquierobeber!" (78).

Williams's reflections on Spanish were vital to his thinking about poetic innovation. He habitually jotted down things his mother would say in Spanish for inspiration because of their richness of expression and detail (*Yes, Mrs. Williams* 23), and his experimentation with the form of the "variable foot" while writing *Paterson* (1963) led to *"versos sueltos,* 'loose verses,' as he called them" (Thirlwall 183). In the introduction to Williams's collected translations, *By Word of Mouth: Poems from the Spanish, 1916–1959* (2011), Jonathan Cohen characterizes the work as "expressions of his Hispanic self" (xxiv), which Peter Ramos has argued led Williams to discover new poetic techniques in English (Ramos 90, 92). His relationship with the Spanish language deepened his allegiance to Spanish-American culture and, by extension, history. Williams's later work in *Paterson* manifested his desire to reconfigure the *modus operandi* of historiography by reclaiming this task for epic poetry as well as localizing the book's scope to the life of a city small enough to be accurately characterized but large enough to reach through the broader context of the United States. His earlier prose work, *In the American Grain* (1925), however, took a much wider view of American history – conceived as a history of and for the Americas, with chapters ranging from Aaron Burr and Daniel Boone to Montezuma and Eric the Red – that defied conventions of history with poetic license. *In the American Grain* is overtly fragmented and yet it all coheres; by switching between fabricated first-person narratives, paraphrases of source texts and transcripts, and personal speculations, "Williams attempts to write and read transamerican history as a sensual and living – as opposed to an essentialized and deadened – experience" (Sánchez González 44). No other book by Williams preserves iconoclastic impact and immediacy as effectively as *In the American Grain*. Providing both a new past and a new manner of articulating that past at once, its revisionist challenge was thoroughly decolonialist decades before the term entered critical parlance. His radical vision of American culture and history as transnational, hemispheric, and multilingual was indigenous to his personal experience as a Latino of diverse origins. In the period of his career when he effected the most change to Euro-American modernist literature, Williams's major contributions were inflected with a Boricua purview.

Salomón de la Selva's Vanguard Vanguard

Whereas many readers of Williams have regarded his writing with little attention to his Latino expression, many readers of Salomón de la Selva have neglected his contribution to Anglo-American poetry. Both poets were defined by the interstitial complexities of their cultural circumstances, but their respective oeuvres predominated in different languages. De la Selva was born in León, Nicaragua, where he was raised until he came to the United States to pursue his education sometime in his early adolescence. Little is reliably known about de la Selva's transition to the United States[7] and the record of his university training (Sirias 4–5), although various accounts say he attended Williams College and taught there before taking a job at Cornell. De la Selva lived about a dozen years in the United States until he enlisted in the British Army[8] in 1918 and served in combat during the First World War. After the War, he stayed briefly in London but lived from 1920 until his death in 1959 in Nicaragua, Mexico, Costa Rica, and Panama (for many years in political exile). His life's work in Latin America was dedicated to political causes, service, and literature, and as a writer in Spanish with ties to several countries, he published numerous well-regarded collections of poems that placed him prominently in the Latin American literary scene – so much so that he was the first Latin American to be nominated for the Nobel Prize in Literature (Rosenstein 61).

In his relatively brief time in the United States, de la Selva established friendships with numerous important writers. He had relationships with

---

[7] In his introduction to *Tropical Town*, Silvio Sirias notes: "Considerable variance exists between the accounts at hand regarding Salomón de la Selva's departure from Nicaragua. Buitrago and Tünnerman state that he left at age eleven. Wallace, writing in the *Dictionary of Mexican Literature* (630), and Pedro Henríquez Ureña (13), state that he left his country at age twelve (632). The *Oxford Compendium to Spanish Literature* (537) and Ernesto Cardenal (35) place de la Selva at age thirteen when he leaves Nicaragua. Arellano seems to suggest that de la Selva was eighteen years of age when he left" (4).

[8] De la Selva's grandmother was a British subject. During the war, he served at the battlefront in Flanders (Sirias 6).

Katherine Anne Porter and Edna St. Vincent Millay, whose poems "Recuerdo" and "Mariposa" are likely inspired by him. He served as Rubén Darío's translator when Darío visited New York in the winter of 1914–1915, and months later he published, with Thomas Walsh, a poetry translation, *Eleven Poems of Rubén Darío*. This engagement with Darío's work would prove crucial to de la Selva's emergence as a poet, for his first book of verse, *Tropical Town and Other Poems* (1918), was composed not in Spanish but in English. In his introduction to the 1999 reprint of *Tropical Town*, Silvio Sirias notes that this book was the first collection of English verse by a Latin American writer published in the United States (6), and since *Tropical Town* closely followed de la Selva's translation of his compatriot Darío – as well as emulated the style and preoccupations of Darío, who died in 1916 – Sirias argues that de la Selva's book is effectively a figurative translation of the aesthetic and sensibility of Darío's poetry (30–44), which had to that point been unknown in English. Sirias's argument is well-founded, and in this vein it could be understood that a dimension of de la Selva's remaking of modernism was in remaking *modernismo*.

De la Selva was not alone in reworking Darío's poetics: Borges identified such poets as the school of "rubenismo." But in doing so outside of the Spanish language, de la Selva's *Tropical Town* poses a curious challenge to its historically contiguous English parallels. Published at the height of the avant-garde era, *Tropical Town* is composed almost entirely of rhymed verse with sustained meters, often employing symbols, espousing political opinion, and expressing nostalgia – aspects true to Darío's *modernismo* but anathema to most of the Anglo and Euro-American avant-gardes of the time. In a material consideration of poetic form, *Tropical Town* is antithetical to the verbal experimentation of imagism, vorticism, dadaism, or futurism and the values these movements proffered in their manifestoes and defenses. But *Tropical Town* is no less an experiment for it. While vanguard poets in the modernist moment were writing against the tradition, de la Selva, as an immigrant from a different language, was writing his way into the tradition. The aesthetic of his English poetry seems stylistically regressive for a writer in his day, but the cultural factors behind his work were, conceptually speaking, avant-garde. His citizenship was foreign, his native language was foreign, and his politics were outspokenly anti-imperialist, ardently against the status quo. Educated and employed in the United States, his nationality as a Nicaraguan distinctly identified him as Latin American, and as Fernando Rosenberg argues: "The various futurisms and primitivisms that European movements displayed in an attempt to articulate a reaction against a bourgeois, conservative order (to express it in blatantly vanguardistic terms) were untenable from the Latin American position. For the Latin American avant-gardes, these alternatives kept referring back to the subaltern situation of Latin Americans themselves vis-à-vis the idea of the West, a concept that neither clearly included nor excluded Latin America" (Rosenberg 2). In other words, the sociopolitical rhetoric vital to avant-garde iconoclasm was endemic to him in his particular condition as a US immigrant, and because of the cultural politics of this condition, its execution in the poetry took an unexpected form.

In retrospect, de la Selva's *Tropical Town* provides a noteworthy challenge to how we think about an avant-garde literary event. Ezra Pound's vanguard poetics sought to escape formal, ontological, and epistemological confines of English, and these are the achievements of his modernism that have stayed with most readers of his work; it takes closer analysis to understand how deeply entrenched in an occidental Romantic mindset Pound was, how it fully shaped his regard of world literature and the poets. De la Selva, on the other hand, wrote *Tropical Town* to conform to English – to conform *into* English – with a concomitant effort to distill subversive ideologies into palatable verse: to say what an other has to say without the trappings of the voice sounding othered. Steven White has suggested that, "while it maintains nineteenth-century verse forms, de la Selva's early poetry in English treats political themes with a twentieth-century awareness" (White 124), and the synthesis of this dichotomy is a by-product of de la Selva's otherness as a Latino in the United States.

The opening poems of *Tropical Town* – "Tropical Town," "Tropical House," "Tropical Park," and "Tropical Morning" – all ease the reader into the setting of de la Selva's homeland, and the tone is decidedly welcoming. Images of "Blue, pink, and yellow houses" (61) and "girls from the river with flowers in their hair" (64) support the pronouncement that, "When the Winter comes, I will take you to Nicaragua, – / You will love it there!" (62). But by the fifth poem, the tenor of the pages takes a stark turn. "The Haunted House of León (Burned by American Filibusters 1860)" (73–74) recalls the history of William Walker's band of Anglo-American mercenaries who fought for the Democratic Party in Nicaragua's civil war. De la Selva is unremorseful in his characterization of the "Yankee filibusters":

> Sons of the Devil
> Who drank to the Devil
> All one night, and burned the house
> After the revel. (73)

A pair of subsequent stanzas reveal that "la Juanita" was raped by those soldiers, her body bruised and abandoned (she is presumably one of the ghosts that haunts the house), and the tone of the poem remains dark until the very end, where it offers a surprising gesture of reconciliation: "I will marry a Yankee girl / And we will dare!" (74).

The next poem, "A Song for Wall Street," reverses this mode of initial condemnation leading toward a promise of vindication. The first three stanzas of "A Song for Wall Street" celebrate Nicaragua as a land of modest riches. Yet the fourth and final stanza makes a dramatic pivot, lambasting "the unjust political relationship between the United States and Latin America" (White 123):

> In Nicaragua, my Nicaragua,
>> What can you buy for a penny there? –
> A basketful of apricots,
>> A water jug of earthenware,
> A rosary of coral beads
>> And a priest's prayer.
> . . .
> And for a nickel? A bright white nickel? –
>> It's lots of land a man can buy,
> . . .
> But for your dollar, your dirty dollar,
>> Your greenish leprosy,
> It's only hatred you shall get
>> From all my folks and me;
> So keep your dollar where it belongs
>> And let us be! (75)

De la Selva's condemnation of US economic exploitation is blatant, and no less denunciatory than Pound's prolific disdain for "the dither of bank-pimps now reigning" (*Kulchur* 242). But whereas Pound typically dressed his ideological dissents in colorful language or bricolage, de la Selva does so here in iambic meter. As a result, certain aspects of the formalism of *Tropical Town* affect a sense of sarcasm, one that is uniquely possible within the context of a Latino immigrant composing traditionally styled poems with politically subversive messages. This might be a distortive effect of historical distance, but reading poems like "Ode to the Woolworth Building" (115–18) in light of de la Selva's openly anti-imperialist sentiments calls into question their sincerity. Sirias claims that de la Selva's conceit of the "Woolworth Building proudly stands as a monument to human redemption" (14), and this ostensibly appears to be true. The poem likens the Woolworth Building to a "knight-worshipped medieval maid," a "Lone Gothic princess," "Mary's handmaiden, garlanded with bells," even "Like Jesus, when He preached in Galilee." The façade of reverence never cracks in the poem and therefore it is hard to justify reading the poem as farcical. But de la Selva manipulated disingenuousness for poetic effect in his later work in Spanish,[9] notably in "Mi primer judío" ("My First Jew") (1969), a nineteen-page prose poem published ten years after his death. In his article, "Nicaraguan Poet as Wandering Jew: Salomón de la Selva and 'Mi primer judío,'" Roy Rosenstein examines the storyteller-ancient mariner trope in regards to de la Selva's biography, especially his extensive travels, and how in "Mi primer judío," de la Selva "traces these lifelong wanderings back to a youthful encounter with a Jew who doubly marked his development. That Wandering Jew taught him the theme of human suffering and prefigured the poet's own career of wanderings" (60). Notwithstanding, the poem opens with the line, "Yo colecciono judíos" ("I collect Jews") (3), and proceeds to narrate how the speaker looks for Jews everywhere he goes: a tension deliberately evoked by the recent memory of the Holocaust and the hunting of Jews by Nazis. It turns out that the speaker is sympathetic rather than predatory, but a layer of intensity persists in the opening pages of the poem before its rhetorical stance is fully established. This manipulation of the listening space by means of incipiently withholding the intentions of the speaker is a dynamic that might be in play in *Tropical Town* more than critics have previously considered. From one poem to the next, *Tropical Town* oscillates between allegiance and antagonism. As true as this book's subversive poems read, one wonders whether duplicity is stowing away in the more somber, reverent verses. Perhaps the extent of de la Selva's remaking of modernism lies in his producing an avant-garde poetry without an avant-garde aesthetic. Yet it is an intriguing proposition to extend the idea and explore whether the verses that excessively celebrate the United States in *Tropical Town* might be read as

---

[9] It is important to note that de la Selva did not adhere as strictly to formalist, inherited forms of verse in his Spanish work as he did in *Tropical Town*. Regarding de la Selva's collection *El soldado desconocido* (*The Unknown Soldier*) (1922), White measures de la Selva's work against the standards of avant-garde modernism: "If we consider the term in the Poundian sense, there is the prosaism of the 'Carta' [Letter] poems, the Chinese presence in 'La trinchera abandonada' [The abandoned church], and the juxtaposition of the modern and the archaic in 'Oda a Safo' [Ode to Sappho], in which the real battle is between elevated beauty ('Oh Safo, ¿tus rosas dónde se abren?') [Oh, Sappho, where do your roses open?] and its opposite ('En el dug-out hermético, / sonoro de risas y de pedos. . .') [In the airtight dug-out, / echoing with laughter and farts. . .]" (132).

a literary wink of sorts, by a Latino with a furtive, deeply subversive agenda heretofore unacknowledged.

Julia de Burgos, Ur-Nuyorican Poet

William Carlos Williams published over twenty volumes of poetry in English; Salomón de la Selva, maybe two.[10] As for Julia de Burgos, her poetry output in English consists of a pair of poems, "Farewell in Welfare Island" and "The Sun in Welfare Island."[11] They were composed in the final months of her life when she was receiving treatment for respiratory disease and liver cirrhosis at Goldwater Memorial Hospital on Roosevelt Island in New York City. Burgos had first moved to New York from Puerto Rico in 1940 at the age of twenty-five, and aside from two stints in Cuba and Washington, DC, she spent most of her adult life there, a period defined by struggle. Both of her marriages ended in divorce, and a partnership with Juan Isidro Jimenes Grullón, a physician and political dissident exiled from the Dominican Republic, ended unceremoniously. In Puerto Rico, she worked as a school teacher in Naranjito and wrote for various local publications in San Juan, including *El Mundo* and *La Acción*, earning a powerful voice in the Puerto Rican independence movement that she would bring to New York. After leaving the island, "Burgos lived in various neighborhoods in Harlem, where she struggled to make a living as a writer" (Pérez Rosario 9). There she worked as a journalist for *Pueblos Hispanos*, a newspaper that "was a vehicle for disseminating news supporting international labor movements and freedom from oppressive governments in Latin America and the Caribbean" (Pérez Rosario 76). Burgos extended this mission by narrativizing the plight of the working poor in New York, and especially of Latinas/os, conveying the rising prominence of the city within the Latin American diaspora. Through these wartime writings,

> Burgos asserts that part of her civic and cultural mission is to work with, among, and for the migrant and immigrant communities that now find themselves in New York. The city acts as a site of transnational intersections,

---

[10] It is rumored that de la Selva published a second collection of poems in English, *A Soldier Sings* (London: The Bodley Head, 1919), but no copy of the book is known to exist (White 125).

[11] Jack Agüeros, in the introduction to his 1997 edition of Burgos's complete poems, suggests that it is possible if not likely that there are still unpublished poems by Burgos yet to be discovered (xxxvii). Most recent available scholarship on Burgos, Li Yun Alvarado's article, "Ambivalence and the Empire City: Julia de Burgos's New York" (2015), confirms the current consideration that "Farewell in Welfare Island" and "The Sun in Welfare Island" are the only known extant poems by Burgos written in English (Alvarado 70).

where diverse cultures and nations . . . from Latin America . . . converge and resist the "cold reality" presented by the metropolis. She is determined to assess the "cold reality" and use those assessments to combat destruction and promote creation.   (Alvarado 62)

Such a treatment of the cold reality of New York is subtext to "Farewell in Welfare Island" and "The Sun in Welfare Island." Although certain works like "A José Martí" (To José Martí) and "Canción a los pueblos hispanos de América y del mundo" (Song to the Hispanic People of America and the World) proffer ideologies that are especially topical, Burgos's Spanish poems (which number over 200) can be generally characterized as not overtly political: focused more on private meditations, emotions, and anxieties. And while her "early political poetry contains numerous images of workers and their connections to the land . . . Burgos never articulates a mythologized *jíbaro* and rejects nostalgia for an idealized past" (Pérez Rosario 24). In the subtler varieties, "the lyrical voice remains connected to the body as a material conscience extended into the social-universal" (Arroyo 144). Political realities saturated with tensions demanding social justice – and cultivated by the expressed agendas of the serial publications in which she first published them – serve as context for her Spanish verses, enabling the poetry to exploit understatement through a style "that asserts itself in specific flights or nothingness" (Arroyo 133).

Nothingness, and "cold reality," govern her two English poems. She was seriously ill at the time that she wrote them. The years of hardship she endured both in New York and Puerto Rico took their toll through alcoholism and what some believe was a suicidal impulse (Rodríguez Pagán 343–45). Her death on July 5, 1953, is famous among Puerto Ricans: discovered unconscious and lying in the street, she was taken to Harlem Hospital where she died, and since she neither possessed identification nor had anyone claim her body, she was buried in the pauper's grave on Hart Island. The English poems read like snapshots of a mind readying itself for such an ignominious demise. "Farewell in Welfare Island" begins with this pair of stanzas:

> It has to be from here,
> right this instance,
> my cry into the world.
>
> Life was somewhere forgotten
> and sought refuge in depths of tears
> and sorrows
> over this vast empire of solitude
> and darkness. (Burgos 357)

"The Sun in Welfare Island" ends with this stanza:

> For my soul asks just
> solitude,
> My smile depends on
> solitude,
> my eyes are full of
> solitude
> and all of me is loneliness
> in a rebellious heart. (359)

The timing of these poems is uncanny; rarely did Burgos explicitly invoke New York in her poetry.[12] And the voice in the poems, though in English, is so recognizable as her own. There are moments in both poems when she uses suggestive words like "freedom," "liberty," "empire," "comrades," and "rebellious," giving hints at a politicized double-entendre, but the overwhelming impact of both poems is an insight into personal suffering.

It is a boon that Burgos left us these English poems. This modest entry into the Anglophone realm of poetry, combined with her rhetorical stance as a vocal *independista*; her disenfranchised socioeconomic status as a writer-activist living in Harlem; and the political symbolism of her undignified death, preserved a legacy that identifies her as the literary common ancestor of all Boricua poets that emerged in the decades that followed. She bridges two important generations of Puerto Rican writers: the *Generación del Treinta* (Generation of the 1930s) and the Nuyorican poets who emerge in the 1970s. Her first collection of poems, *Poema en 20 surcos* (*Poem in 20 Furrows*) (1938), "helped establish her lyrical and deeply personal aesthetic, revealing a strong feminist voice" (Alvarado 56) that subverted the dominant patriarchal and nostalgic attitude of 1930s poets. Jossianna Arroyo has detailed the depths to which Burgos, along with the revolutionary Lolita Lebrón, imposed a "semiotic-feminine" at the heart of Puerto Rican culture and politics in her time (Arroyo 132), and thus the "routes that Burgos creates to escape the heteropatriarchy of the Generación del Treinta nation builders also create spaces in which gay, lesbian, Nuyorican, and Puerto Rican writers on the margins can have fruitful interactions and encounters" (Pérez Rosario 3).

---

[12] See Alvarado: "While she describes New York several times in her writings for *Pueblos Hispanos*, she only makes explicit reference to New York in four poems. The first two she wrote in Spanish – 'Puerto Rico está en ti [tí]' ('Puerto Rico Is in You') and 'Media tarde' ('Mid-Afternoon') – and the final two in English – 'Farewell in Welfare Island' and 'The Sun in Welfare Island'" (Alvarado 63).

Her influence on subsequent Nuyorican writers is immeasurable; she is regarded as a patron saint in certain contemporary literary circles. But Burgos accomplished something else quite extraordinary as a poet of the modernist era. Unlike the poets of imagism, futurism, dadaism, surrealism – or of *ultraísmo, negrismo,* or for that matter *rubenismo* – Burgos was a poet whose work does not lend to a productive close reading or analysis of form. To my mind, her chief contribution to the remaking of Euro-American modernism was in rendering purely formal-aesthetic considerations of her poetry irrelevant. There is no point to analyze her form as a standalone object of scrutiny, in part because there is no poetic doctrine to her form. Jack Agüeros, in his introduction to *Song of the Simple Truth: The Complete Poems of Julia de Burgos* (1997), cites two knowledgeable sources to defend this position. He quotes Armando Rivera Quiñones: "If Julia had a particular 'poetic,' I don't know it. That I can recall Julia never cared for 'schools' or 'isms.'" Agüeros adds that José Emilio González supported this view by saying, "Julia never entered in discussions of aesthetics. She was more interested in social problems. She hardly said anything about her poetry" (qtd. in Agüeros xxvii). In sum, Burgos was of no poetic camp, and she had no stake in establishing a new one. Her contribution to modernism was to take an individualist's role, working away from collectivist thinking about emergent poetry: to unburden herself of the weight of literary influence and the task of the poet to rhetoricize the strategy of her tactics. To be clear, Burgos surely did not write a formless poetry. But sentiment and consciousness are so much more salient in her work, and the balance her poems strike between the personal and the political is one that Latina/o poets have been admiring ever since.

WORKS CITED

Agüeros, Jack. "Julia de Burgos: Una Introducción"/Julia de Burgos: An Introduction." Burgos, ii-xl.

Alvarado, Li Yun. "Ambivalence and the Empire City: Julia de Burgos's New York." *Arizona Quarterly* 71.1 (2015): 53–81.

Arroyo, Jossianna. "Living the Political: Julia de Burgos and Lolita Lebrón." *Centro Journal* 26.2 (2014): 128–55.

Burgos, Julia de. *Song of the Simple Truth: The Complete Poems of Julia de Burgos.* Ed. and trans. Jack Agüeros. Willimantic, CT: Curbstone Press, 1997.

Cohen, Jonathan. "Introduction." Williams, *By Word of Mouth*, xxi-xliii.

Marling, William. *William Carlos Williams and the Painters, 1909–1923.* Athens: University of Georgia Press, 1982.

Marzán, Julio. *The Spanish American Roots of William Carlos Williams.* Austin: University of Texas Press, 1994.

Pérez Rosario, Vanessa. *Becoming Julia de Burgos: The Making of a Puerto Rican Icon*. Urbana: University of Illinois Press, 2014.

Pound, Ezra. *Guide to Kulchur*. New York: New Directions, 1970.

Literary Essays of Ezra Pound. Ed. T. S. Eliot. New York: New Directions, 1954.

The Selected Letters of Ezra Pound, 1907–1941. New York: New Directions, 1950.

Ramos, Peter. "Cultural Identity, Translation, and William Carlos Williams." *MELUS: Multi-Ethnic Literature of the U.S.* 38.2 (Summer 2013): 89–110.

Rodríguez Pagán, Juan Antonio. *Julia en blanco y negro*. San Juan: Sociedad Histórico de Puerto Rico, 2000.

Rosenberg, Fernando J. *The Avant-Garde and Geopolitics in Latin America*. Pittsburgh, PA: University of Pittsburgh Press, 2006.

Rosenstein, Roy. "Nicaraguan Poet as Wandering Jew: Salomón de la Selva and 'Mi primer judío.'" *Latin American Literary Review* 18.35 (1990): 59–70.

Rudman, Mark. "William Carlos Williams in America." *American Poetry Review* 37.2 (2008): 53–62.

Sánchez González, Lisa. *Boricua Literature: A Literary History of the Puerto Rican Diaspora*. New York: NYU Press, 2001.

Selva, Salomón de la. "Mi primer judío." Ed. Manuel Rodríguez Vizcarra, Jr. *Poesía en el mundo 70*. Monterrey: Sierra Madre, 1969.

Tropical Town and Other Poems. Ed. Silvio Sirias. Houston, TX: Arte Público Press, 1999.

Sirias, Silvio. "Introduction." Selva, 1–51.

Thirlwall, John C. "Ten Years of a New Rhythm." Afterword to William Carlos Williams, *Pictures from Brueghel and Other Poems*. New York: New Directions: 1962. 183–84.

White, Steven F. *Modern Nicaraguan Poetry: Dialogues with France and the United States*. Lewisburg, PA: Bucknell University Press, 1993.

Williams, William Carlos. *A Book of Poems: Al Que Quiere!* Boston, MA: The Four Seas Company, 1917.

The Autobiography of William Carlos Williams. New York: Random House, 1951.

Trans. *By Word of Mouth: Poems from the Spanish, 1916–1959*. Ed. Jonathan Cohen. New York: New Directions, 2011.

I Wanted to Write a Poem: The Autobiography of the Works of a Poet. New York: New Directions, 1967.

Kora in Hell: Improvisations. Boston, MA: The Four Seas Company, 1920.

Paterson. New York: New Directions, 1963.

Yes, Mrs. Williams: A Personal Record of My Mother. New York: McDowell, Obolensky, 1959.

17

The Archive and Afro-Latina/o Field-Formation

Arturo Alfonso Schomburg at the Intersection of Puerto Rican and African American Studies and Literatures

CÉSAR A. SALGADO

Overcoming the Dualism of Schomburg's Two Legacies

In 1989, two books dealing with the life and legacy of New York-based Afro-Boricua bibliophile, librarian, and archivist Arturo Alfonso Schomburg appeared in print after years of research by scholars trained in library and information sciences in the United States and Puerto Rico. Despite this shared academic framework, their authors approached Schomburg's work using contrasting field agendas, paradigms of interpretation, and historical assumptions. They thus set off a debate regarding the role that Schomburg's refashioning of the subaltern archive has played in shaping racial, national, transnational, and postcolonial identities and politics in black, Latino, and Puerto Rican communities to this day. Was the epistemic matrix behind Schomburg's career as a collector and race intellectual primordially Anglo-Africanist or was it configured according to decolonizing archival paradigms emerging in Puerto Rico, Cuba, and other non-Anglophone Antilles at the turn of the century? In what follows I will review how the scholarly dispute over Schomburg's two legacies – the Afro-American versus the Latino Caribbean – may have slighted a third zone of identity fashioning that both blends together and bleeds out from those two: the Afro-Latina/o. How can we think beyond this "either black or Latino" dualism to consider Schomburg's achievements as subaltern archivist as constitutive for the acknowledgment and study of *afrolatinidades*, as this field has been defined recently by scholars such as Juan Flores, Miriam Jiménez-Román, and Antonio López? By examining the evolving structures of Latino and African-American mentorship in his career, I will show how Schomburg sought to harmonize the remappings of Pan-Africanist historiography (centered on continental Africa as motherland) with those of a pan-Latino Americanism (focused on Mediterranean-to-New World colonial and postcolonial interconnections) by striving for an archive that could redefine the Renaissance as the *Afro-Latin* cultural outcome of Southern European and North-and-Central African socioeconomic and migratory exchange and integration at the very moment of transatlantic expansion.

Elinor Des Verney Sinnette wrote her biography *Arthur Alfonso Schomburg: Black Bibliophile and Collector* based on her doctoral dissertation for the Columbia University School of Library Service. After a thorough review of Schomburg's publications and manuscripts, as well as his correspondence with John Edward Bruce, John Wesley Cromwell, W. E. B. Du Bois, Alain Roy Locke, and many other foundational Afro-American intellectuals, Sinnette tracks Schomburg's career as a collector of rare books, documents, and artifacts related to the African diaspora in North America and abroad. Sinnette devotes the first chapter to Schomburg's formative years in Puerto Rico and his six-year involvement with Cuban and Afro-Boricua emigré circles of pro-independence activists after his 1891 arrival in New York City at seventeen years of age. The next seven chapters document Schomburg's activism in support of racial uplift through archival recovery in the United States while achieving middle-class respectability working as a mail clerk and manager in a major Wall Street bank and serving as an officer of some of the most outstanding black historical societies and civic institutions in New York until his death in 1938. Sinnette covers Schomburg's partnership with Bruce to direct the Negro Society for Historical Research; his years as member and last president of the American Negro Academy; his regular scholarly collaborations in NAACP's *The Crisis*, the National Urban League's *Opportunity*, UNIA's *Negro World*, and other major black journals and dailies; his support of rising artists and writers of the Harlem Renaissance; his tenure as Curator of Black Studies at the Fisk University Library; and his stewardship of the Division on Negro History at the New York Public Library (NYPL), now known as the Schomburg Center for Research in Black Culture. At the center of all these endeavors is the legendary collection of Afrocentric rare books, manuscripts, and prints that Schomburg acquired with his salary as Foreign Mail division manager at the Bankers Trust Company. Schomburg sold his collection to the NYPL in 1926 for $10,000 furnished by the Carnegie Foundation (at a fifth of its real value, according to Alain Locke); in 1932, he was hired as its curator.

While acknowledging his upbringing in San Juan, family sojourns in St. Thomas and St. Croix, his 1892–1896 stint as secretary of the pro-independence club "Las Dos Antillas," and his travels to Cuba and Hispaniola, Sinnette observes throughout Schomburg's life and career a process of de-Hispanization or deliberate distancing from the Latino community and his Spanish Caribbean background in favor of the Anglophone Afro-American world in New York City and pan-Africanism at large. In 1999, Columbia University historian Winston James made a similar argument, declaring Schomburg an "aberration" (218), "one of a rare breed of Puerto Ricans, if not a species of one" (201) in that, against Jesús Colón and other prominent Afro-Boricua migrants' preference to set down roots and livelihood in New York's mixed-race, Spanish-speaking barrio communities, Schomburg stood out "conspicuous [ly]" in Harlem for being "a black Puerto Rican who actively supported and identified with black nationalist aspirations, and with the struggles of African Americans" (197). Instead of continuing to fight for greater rights in an ostensibly more tolerant or "race-blind" Spanish Caribbean homeland, Schomburg thus opted to fully embrace what scholar Antonio López, in his research on Afro-Cuban Americans pursuing better life opportunities as blacks in the United States, has called an "unbecoming blackness." Rather than undertake the "redemptive return to Cuba" (6), Schomburg chose to stay and refashion his racial and cultural identity into that of an Anglophone U.S. Negro rather than a Hispanocentric Afro-Latino. By contravening nationalist *criollo* myths that portrayed Latin American societies as racially tolerant due to centuries of biological and cultural *mestizaje* and U.S. society as racist and xenophobic to encourage repatriation and gradual social whitening, Schomburg exemplified what López describes as "the unbecoming *desire for* the ways in which African Americans belong in the 'rough and brutal and contemptuous' Anglo United States" (8). Indeed, Sinnette and James account for a radical reduction in Schomburg's interfacing with New York Hispanic circles and his written and spoken use of Spanish from 1898 on. That was the year that saw, as a consequence of U.S. military intervention in the three-year-old anti-Spain guerrilla insurrection in Cuba, the disintegration of the Cuban Revolutionary Party effort, launched in New York City by the poet patriot José Martí in 1892, to win full Cuban and Puerto Rican sovereignty. According to Sinnette, after 1898, Schomburg severed his association with Sotero Figueroa, Rafael Serra, Rosendo Rodríguez, and other outstanding Afro-Antillean organic intellectuals: the emigré blue-collar printers, tobacco workers, journalists, and public educators who had helped mentor and incorporate young Schomburg into the cause of Cuban and Puerto Rican independence led by Martí.

By 1902 these New York Afro-Antillean activists had chosen to relocate to Cuba, aspiring to participate as full citizens in the development of a new multiracial republic. In 1900 Schomburg had become a twenty-six-year-old widower with three children. Instead of following his associates' lead, he remarried and stayed in New York, with aspirations to become a lawyer. For this purpose, Schomburg secured employment from 1901 to 1906 as a clerk in the law firm of Pryor, Mellis, and Harris (Sinnette 35). There he applied to test for a law certificate, but his school transcripts were either unavailable or not certified to allow him further accreditation. In letters to the editor published in the *New York Times* between 1901 and 1905, we see how immersed Schomburg became, while clerking at the firm, in matters of U. S. civil rights and constitutional law and in the racial, electoral, and territorial debates of the day. There he fiercely denounced the myths and practices behind the selling of negro votes (Oct. 31, 1903), declaimed against white preachers that justified lynching as an expeditious form of mob justice (June 28, 1903; Aug. 21, 1904), and decried Jim Crow measures in Southern states that sought to disenfranchise blacks, "depriving the negro from the lawful exercise of their political and natural rights" (Dec. 20, 1903). He also argued strongly against Back-to-Africa Movement advocates in keeping with his view that African descendants should remain and pursue full citizenship in the United States through a vigilant enforcement of the 14th and 15th Amendments (May 24, 1903). He thus sought to express a sense of belonging in a perfectible, multiracial U.S. republic, and endorsed the possibility of a non–white-supremacist, racially inclusive U.S. constitutional covenant.[1]

Schomburg's desire to be part of a multiracial United States turns even more "unbecoming" when he supports U.S. territorial expansion and neocolonial tutorship in Puerto Rico, the Philippines, and Panama as exemplary and progressive. Rather than dispute post-1898 U.S. sovereignty in Puerto Rico and other "possessions," he embraces it to argue in favor of lifting "alien immigrations exams" for territorial natives wishing to move North, entitling them automatically with "the privileges and immunities enjoyed by all citizens" (Aug. 9, 1902). He defends upgrading the "imperishable" Monroe Doctrine with a "Roosevelt Doctrine" that would allow, by "rule of ex-propio vigore," diplomatic maneuvering with an unruly, recently seceded Panama

---

[1] In a letter published on Sept. 3, 1901, Schomburg asks: "Why should we wish the negroes in the U.S. to emigrate to Africa, and what benefit will they derive and gain by emigration? ... I am under the impression that there is much field for improving the existing conditions of the negro in the United States . . .. If he cannot prosper here, then he will nowhere else under the sun." Scholars have not yet analyzed in full Schomburg's early letters to the *New York Times*; more than twelve of these have not been listed so far in the bibliography of major Schomburg studies.

to achieve a Plattist-like supervisory compact for the safe U.S. construction and safeguarding of an interoceanic canal.[2] Thus, vis á vis Latin America, at this stage of his career as a New York Negro intellectual aware of his rights as a U.S. citizen participating in black and white public arenas through the mastering of metropolitan print culture, Schomburg sought to conceive and portray himself as an African-American Anglophone local insider ("Arthur") and not as a Hispanic or Latino immigrant outsider ("Arturo"). At this early stage, Schomburg's break with Martí-inspired, anti-imperial doctrines of latinidad and *nuestraamericanidad* is definitive.[3]

It is not until later that decade, with the beginnings of his correspondence and collaboration with figures such as Booker T. Washington, du Bois, and James Weldon Johnson, that the "existential blending of African American and Caribbean experience" (36) that scholar Kevin Meehan has persuasively analyzed as the epistemological basis for the "decolonizing valance" behind Schomburg's intellectual labor fully evolves.[4] Sinnette marks as a watershed moment Schomburg's attendance in January 1904 at a series of meetings at Carnegie Hall that called upon Washington and Du Bois to resolve their long-standing feud regarding the best educational model for black uplift.[5] According to Sinnette, both leaders "agreed that the collection and dissemination of information about black history and culture would be a beneficial step towards promoting harmony among and between the races of the South as well as the North" (33). The meeting inspired Schomburg to start corresponding with each and offer his services as bibliophile and bibliographer. The success of these exchanges opened to Schomburg the pages of New York's premier black periodicals, *The Crisis* and *Opportunity*, and motivated an important perspectival change in his writing. Schomburg abandoned the

[2] In a letter dated Nov. 19, 1903, published Nov. 22, Schomburg declares: "The American Commonwealth has shown and taught Cuba that she must govern herself in the manner that is expected of civilized countries. The Platt Amendment is a good instrument: it should be extended to offending Republics .... We need the canal and we must have it: it is beyond words an absolute necessity for the defense and integrity of the American nation."
[3] Regarding José Martí's legendary trajectory as a poet, political and cultural thinker, and revolutionary organizer during his 1881–1895 sojourn in New York City and his critical view of U.S. expansionist interests in Latin America see Lomas, Montero, and Rojas.
[4] Keenan finds that, thanks to his working class origins and life-long commitment to the educational betterment of unschooled blacks, Schomburg managed to critically synthesize Du Bois's pan-Africanist vision with Martí's ideals of hemispheric pan-Latino cultural unity while disavowing both Du Bois's preferences for an elitist, "talented tenth" black middle-class hegemony and Martí's false hopes in a race-blind Latin American democracy (52–75).
[5] On the debate between Washington and Du Bois, see Aiello and Moore.

investment-minded, statistically-argued, Plattist-friendly thinking behind pieces such as "Is Hayti Decadent" (*Unique Advertiser* IV, August 1904) and his pro-U.S. expansionism letters to the *Times*. He adopted instead the narrative format of his African-centric biographical vignettes celebrating highly accomplished black cultural and military heroes and martyrs – almost all of Caribbean provenance – that best characterized his writings for the black press, starting with "Placido: an Epoch in Cuba's Struggle for Liberty" (*The New Century*, Dec. 25, 1909) and "General Evaristo Estenoz" (*The Crisis* IV, July 1912). In the latter piece he fully disavowed U.S. Plattist hegemony in Cuba by denouncing President Jose Miguel Gómez's bloody repression of Estenoz and the Afro-Cuban armed followers who protested the outlawing of the Independent Party of Color during the 1912 Race War as a great moral collapse of U.S. stewardship in the young Republic.[6]

Still, after starting work at the Banks Trust Company, through black Freemasonry connections, Schomburg found his most important mentor, the outspoken race journalist, orator, and activist John Edward Bruce. Popularly known as "Bruce Grit," Bruce had fled slavery in Maryland as a child with his mother and studied in integrated schools in New England and briefly at Howard University during Emancipation. He eventually settled in the DC area to become a maverick of the post–Civil War black press and a Republican Party black leader and advocate during Reconstruction. In 1908, he followed the Great Migration to New York City and settled in Yonkers to become a Prince Hall Freemason leader, a militant pan-Africanist, a late-in-life Garveyite, and an indefatigable promoter of Negro historical studies. In 1911 he assisted Schomburg in transforming the mixed-race, Spanish-speaking *El Sol de Cuba* lodge, where Schomburg had risen to the rank of master, into the mainly black and English-speaking Prince Hall lodge No. 38. Schomburg, in turn, assisted Bruce in running the Negro Society for Historical Research that Bruce presided over from his Yonkers residence from 1911 until his death in 1924. In 1914 Bruce would persuade historian John Wesley Crumwell to induct Schomburg into the American Negro Academy (ANA), an erudite research society gathering the top race scholars and opinion makers instituted in 1889 by Bruce's mentor, the pan-Africanist professor, diplomat, and Episcopal minister Alexander Crummell. Schomburg rose to become president in 1920 and, after a period of administrative troubles, oversaw its

---

[6] On the Afro-Cuban independence army general and race leader Evaristo Estenoz, Cuba's suppressed *Partido Independiente de Color*, and the 1912 *Guerra de las razas* in Cuba, see Helg and Fermoselle.

disbandment in 1929. Scholars such as Alfred A. Moss, Jr., author of a history of the ANA, and Ralph L. Crowder and William Serraile, experts on Bruce's career as a pan-Africanist institution builder, have shown how Bruce's and Schomburg's joint efforts were part of a broader trend involving prospering immigrant and minority community and professional groups that established learned societies to foment ethnic pride and civic agency at the turn of the century. According to Crowder, Bruce mentored Schomburg as part of "a cadre of lay historians ... critical to [his] organized effort to popularize African American history" (97).

Thus in the wake of the 1896 Plessy v. Ferguson Supreme Court decision that bolstered Jim Crow segregation for years after the Spanish American War, Schomburg chose to be part of a U.S. Northeast Great Migration network of African-American self-trained researchers. This network was fully engaged in a multiplatform campaign to counter the white supremacist branding of blacks as an "inferior race" with well-documented examples of black progress, respectability, and arts-and-sciences accomplishment in world history. Schomburg transitions into a new group of race associates and publications that were, for the most part, non-Spanish speaking, non-Latino, and militantly pan-Africanist. After interviewing his children, Sinnette argues that Schomburg's immersion into an "English-mostly" African-centric exist-ence seemed calculated as he did not encourage the use of Spanish at home (35–36; 166). In another interview, Afro-Boricua librarian Pura Belpré recalled that Schomburg never spoke with her in Spanish in all their years as colleagues at the Harlem NYPL branch (148). James sees that, rather than the outcome of Schomburg's post-1898 mentorship under Bruce and Crum-well, these choices might have resulted from Schomburg not identifying fully as "Hispanic" in the first place (104–105).

In contrast to Sinnette and James, in *Arturo Alfonso Schomburg: A Puerto Rican's Quest for His Black Heritage*, Flor Piñeiro de Rivera places Schomburg's long-standing Hispanic affiliations at center stage. Rather than a full-fledged biography, this 1989 book is an anthology reuniting articles and essays that Schomburg published in mainland race journals and special editions. Piñeiro purports to collect and annotate Schomburg's principal publications, but the selection is not exhaustive. The twenty-six selected texts are interspersed with photos of family and Harlem Renaissance associates and bookended by a biographical introduction by Piñeiro and an iconographic addendum fea-turing portraits of Schomburg-relevant figures from the Hispanic Antilles and West Indies. This addendum bears as title *Caribbeana*, a play of words that seems to dispute or at least complicate Schomburg's foundational association with *Africana*. The *Centro de Estudios Avanzados del Caribe* – a San Juan–based graduate program and research institute – published the book in twin editions, one in English, another in Piñeiro's Spanish translation. Both start with a foreword by Ricardo E. Alegría, the renowned archeologist of Taíno pre-Columbian sites, architectural restorer of colonial old San Juan, and founding director of the Commonwealth's Institute of Puerto Rican Culture.

While Piñeiro acknowledges the change of heart and cause at the core of Sinnette's work – "he who had dedicated his youth to the Antillean fight for freedom now devoted the rest of his life to the fight for freedom for the Afro-American" (3) –, she holds, against James, that "his identity as a Puerto Rican and his mastery of the Spanish language moved him to commit himself to the mission of discovering and making known the Afro-Caribbean and Afro-Hispanic contribution to civilization" (32). Extrapolating from the scant sources available about Schomburg's earlier years in Puerto Rico, Piñeiro highlights Schomburg's education at San Juan's several *institutos* for public primary and secondary instruction[7]; his friendship with New York Afro-Boricua cigar-trade workers such as Flor Baerga, Bernardo Vega, and Rosendo Rodríguez; his role as secretary of the pro-independence club *Las Dos Antillas*; his acquaintance with the "apostolic" founder of the Cuban Revolutionary Party (PRC), José Martí; and his participation in the PRC's Puerto Rico Section after Martí's death in 1895.[8] Piñeiro does not explore in full the post-1898 career as Negro bibliophile and race leader that most concerns Sinnette.

Piñeiro thus claims that Schomburg deserves remembrance "firstly . . . as a distinguished Puerto Rican" and "secondly, because Schomburg won a lasting place in the hearts of Afro-Americans" (11). She makes the case for the primacy of his Puerto Rican heritage by arguing that Schomburg's celebrated historical vocation was not first inspired by Bruce Grit's

---

[7] There is an alarming lack of consensus among Schomburg scholars regarding his schooling in Puerto Rico. Sinnette was not able to find hard evidence that could confirm which public or private schools Schomburg did attend in the island; she speculates about his education based on Schomburg's personal accounts (13). Piñeiro declares categorically that Schomburg "studied at the Instituto Civil de Segunda Enseñanza and at the Instituto de Enseñanza Popular in San Juan" based, apparently, on unpublished research by Mario Rodríguez León (21).

[8] Schomburg only refers in detail to Martí in "General Antonio Maceo," an article honoring the great Afro-Cuban top officer of the independence army (Crisis XXVII 1931). Schomburg recalls meeting Martí through the mediation of the former's Afro-Boricua mentor, "Dos Antillas" club cofounder, and off-and-on print-shop employer, Sotero Figueroa, one of Martí's closest friends and associates as chief editor of *Patria*, the news organ of the Cuban Revolutionary Party (178–79).

mentorship, but by that of José Julián Acosta, a Puerto Rican white *criollo* historian, politician, printer, scientist, and educator who apparently was Schomburg's history teacher at Acosta's Instituto Civil de Segunda Enseñanza.[9] According to Piñeiro, Schomburg's practice as collector of historical documents followed methods set by Acosta when the latter helped found the Puerto Rican *Sociedad Recolectora de Documentos Históricos*. This historical club was constituted in January 1851 by white Boricua literati – such as Acosta, Alejandro Tapia y Rivera, and Segundo Ruiz Belvis – and aspiring mulatto liberals and radicals – such as Román Baldorioty de Castro and Ramón Emeterio Betances – studying in Madrid between 1847 and 1853. Acknowledging great gaps in Puerto Rico's collective memory due to built-in neglect of the colony's educational system and inspired by a positivist vogue to recuperate and disseminate primary historical sources as a public good, this patriotic society, first led by Baldorioty, worked to seek out and collect through longhand copying a concerted list of foundational documents about Puerto Rican history in state and private collections and libraries. The club met to identify and locate academics, lay historians, and government officers harboring Boricua-related materials; secure access to locked documents and set strategies to circumvent censorship; translate foreign texts; and hire copyists when needed. In 1852, Tapia took over from Baldorioty when he secured a permit to transcribe sealed documents at the National Library in Madrid. Back in Puerto Rico in 1854 and with the authorities' approval and financial support, Tapia published a wide selection of the *Sociedad*'s trove of sixteenth-to-nineteenth-century document copies as the *Biblioteca Histórica de Puerto Rico*.[10]

These young Puerto Ricans thus accomplished seventy-five years before what Schomburg would claim about black history enthusiasts in his famous 1926 essay "The Negro Digs Up His Past." They had felt a "prime social necessity" to "remake [their] past, in order to make [their] future;" that pride

---

[9]   Schomburg refers twice to Acosta as his teacher in two published articles, "In Quest of Juan de Pareja," *The Crisis* XXXIV July 1927 (Piñeiro 139) and "Negroes in Sevilla," *Opportunity* VI March 1928 (Piñeiro 158), and often in his unpublished papers. In a recent article about Acosta's Masonic affiliations, Edgardo M. Vigo-Jorge shows how Acosta was also among Sotero Figueroa's most influential mentors. Figueroa first worked as an apprentice in Acosta's printing shop in San Juan, called Acosta *maestro* in many writings, and dedicated to Acosta his 1888 collection of biographies of Puerto Rican luminaries, *Ensayo biográfico: De los más que han contribuido al progreso de Puerto Rico* (107).

[10] About the accomplishments of the *Sociedad* and the key role most of its members would play in Puerto Rico's abolitionist, reformist, separatist, and revolutionary struggles, see Moscoso and Gutiérrez de Arroyo.

and "a group tradition must supply compensation" for persecution and prejudice (Piñeiro 117); that "history [had] become less a matter of argument and more a matter of record" (118); and that colonial Boricuas had to think "more collectively, more retrospectively than the rest, and apt, out of the very pressure of the present, to become the most enthusiastic antiquarian[s] of them all" (117). Several *Sociedad* members would carry the torch of abolitionism in both the island and the peninsula, starting antislavery clubs and publications and participating in the 1867 drafting of the *Project for the Abolition of Slavery*, thus becoming the intellectual precursors of the 1873 banning of slavery in the island.[11] Thus, according to Piñeiro, the archival strategies to construct a subaltern liberational structure of historical authority that could revoke aspects of white supremacist metropolitan hegemony came down from this group of island *criollos* to Schomburg: "Schomburg advanced the torch he received from Acosta" (45). "May the spirit of pure historical dimension, passed on to Schomburg by José Julián Acosta and Salvador Brau [Acosta's successor in nineteenth century Puerto Rican historiography] be honored," concludes Piñeiro (50).[12]

Since 1989, several scholars of Puerto Rican and Caribbean descent have sought to give a more complex vision of Schomburg as a hybrid or transcultural Afro-Latino rather than apply the either/or choices between Afro-Anglo vs. Boricua-Latino binaries that we see in Sinnette, James, and Piñeiro. Lisa Sánchez González has lucidly and aggressively critiqued what she has called James's and Sinnette's "dismissal" of Schomburg's "Puerto Ricanness," arguing that Schomburg's main motive as a collector was to overcome the "paperless condition" that non- or sub-citizenship imposed on Puerto Rican colonial subjects after the U.S. occupation.[13] Jesse Hoffnung-Garskof sees Schomburg as a Caribbean migrant in the United States who constantly morphed his Afro-diasporic identity while transiting across hemispheric, continental, and national frontiers and through ethnically, racially, and culturally marked New York neighborhoods.[14] Jossianna Arroyo-Martínez

---

[11] Acosta and Ruiz Belvis helped write and submit this proposal to the Spanish government during a Madrid consultation with territorial deputies. For more about the antislavery movement and its leadership, see Schmidtt-Novara and Cancel.

[12] Schomburg references Brau's works in "José Campeche 1752–1809" (Piñeiro 204) and in several instances of his unpublished typescripts.

[13] Sánchez González presents this critique in full in "Arturo Alfonso Schomburg: A Transamerican Intellectual" (143). She elaborates her ideas about Schomburg and Puerto Rican "paperlessness" in *Boricua Literature* (68–69).

[14] Hoffnung-Garskoff makes this case both in his 2001 *JAEH* article and in his 2010 contribution to Jiménez-Román's and Juan Flores's *The Afro-Latin@ Reader*.

speaks about the diverse personas Schomburg tailored for himself writing under the pen names of Arturo, Arthur, and Guarionex as part of a fluid black positionality that Schomburg fashioned thanks to his life-long affiliation with trans-Caribbean Prince Hall Freemasonry.[15] Still, none really has made yet a full case about whether and how Schomburg envisioned Afro-latinidad according to what Flores and Jiménez Román, paraphrasing Du Bois, have discussed as a condition of "triple consciousness" or as a unique cultural and existential ethno-racial zone beyond black or Latino binaries.[16]

Schomburg's singular vision of Afro-latinidad may be better revealed by turning the mentorship genealogy on its head. One of the problems of the either/or paradigm is the assumption that either the Anglo-Afro or Hispanic "side" predominates because one system of subaltern mentorship should prevail over others. If Martí, Figueroa, and Acosta are taken as main mentors, Schomburg figures primarily as a Puerto Rican and a Latino who at one point chose to also identify as Afro-American. If it's Du Bois, Bruce, or Crumwell, Schomburg is first an African American of West Indian ancestry who happened to have been born and partly raised in Puerto Rico. If we instead switch and focus on the older Schomburg's relation as mentor to the younger "New Negro" intellectuals of the Harlem Renaissance, a different ethno-racial cartography emerges with great clarity. With the relocation and economic mobility of Great Migration blacks in the North and the greater expectations for full citizenship brought by U.S. black regiments returning from the First World War, the "New Negro" cultural and intellectual movement that coalesced in 1920s Harlem represented a significant generational shift in post-Reconstruction African-centric militancy. Nurtured by a cosmopolitan ethos that transcended U.S.-centric and narrow black nationalist paradigms, the movement introduced pluralistic and cosmopolitan ideals of blackness and diaspora that were more artistic-minded than statistical,

[15] Arroyo-Martínez makes this case in her 2005 Centro Journal article. In her 2013 book *Writing Secrecy in Caribbean Freemasonry*, she studies how the Prince Hall tradition of Black Masonic lodges originating in the Caribbean and spreading in the Northeastern United States helped Afro-Caribbean migrants such as Serra and Schomburg secure footholds for racial uplift and upper mobility through a spectrum of civic roles and functions.

[16] In *The Diaspora Strikes Back*, Flores also proposes, as one zone of Afro-latinidad especially suitable for Schomburg, that of *anfroantillanía*: "What marks off *caribeños* within the Latino pan-ethnicity as a whole is precisely this interface with blackness and an Afro-Atlantic imaginary. As Afro-Latinos, they embody the compatibility of blackness with the notion of Latino identity in the United States ... the *antillano* perspective instates the continuity and mutuality between them" (64–65).

more cultural than sociological, more creative than prescriptive.[17] In this context, many New Negro thinkers and artists found Schomburg – an eccentric, hard-to-categorize, bilingual and multicultural, self-taught erudite from the Spanish Caribbean – just as inspiring as the better established Washington, Du Bois, Bruce, and Garvey. In turn, the contact with the sophisticated and well-traveled Harlem Renaissance coterie would reenergize Schomburg and inspire him to fully develop a unique Afro-Latino vision of the diaspora beyond the paradigms and frameworks that his previous Puerto Rican, Cuban, or Afro-American mentors had set or expected.

Schomburg's vigorous collaborations with philosopher, critic, editor, and Harlem Renaissance "dean" Alain Locke in the mid-1920s and with the movement's most emblematic poet Langston Hughes in the 1930s show that, in the last stage of his career, Schomburg embarked on a full reconceptualization and recovery of his Afro-Latino roots. For example, Schomburg and Locke partnered to tour Europe's great art museums together in 1926 as part of an evolving project on image fashioning by and about Africans and their descendants throughout Western and non-Western art history. Both envisioned writing ambitious books on the topic while helping spur new African-American artwork by collaborating with the New Jersey-based Harmon Foundation in promoting emerging black artists through yearly prize competitions and multi-city travelling exhibits.[18] Still, while Locke believed in the esthetic valorization of ancestral African tribal art for the modern development of a more authentic African-American visual expression fully conversant with cosmopolitan avant-garde trends, Schomburg focused on the capacity of African-descended "Latin" easel painters (i.e., of Mediterranean, Italian, Andalusian, and Spanish Caribbean heritage) to assimilate and advance the achievements of Renaissance visual and civic culture. In his essays on seventeenth-century School of Seville freedmen black painters Juan de Pareja and Sebastián Gómez and Spanish Caribbean master artists such as José Campeche and Pastor Argudín, Schomburg traced the emergence of a transatlantic Afro-Latino sovereign subject, one that shed his subordinate condition through strategies of Renaissance self-invention and perfectibility available through the mentor-apprentice structure prevalent in gremial

---

[17] I draw from scholarship on the Harlem Renaissance by Nathan Irvin Huggins, Paul Gilroy, Brent Edwards, and Henry Louis Gates and Gene Andre Jarrett for this quick synthesis.
[18] About Locke's visual art criticism and esthetic thought see Calo. About Locke's and Schomburg's collaboration with the Harmon Foundation see Reynolds, esp. 13–25, 65–66, and Harris & Molesworth (258–62).

artisan workshops.[19] Schomburg thus reenvisioned the Renaissance not as a period of white European civilizational dominance, but of dynamic inter-Mediterranean and transatlantic exchange between urban cultures of lower Europe – Spain, Italy, France, and Portugal – and traditions brought there by free and enslaved black migrants from North, West, and Central Africa. The African Mediterranean/Southern Europe/Latin Caribbean genealogical map suggested by Schomburg's periodization and selection of *post-Renaissance Afro-Latin* artists thus diverged significantly from the cartographies informing Garveyism and other Pan-African movements of the Harlem Renaissance era.[20]

Schomburg's 1930s Afro-Latin Correspondence with Langston Hughes

Schomburg's Afro-Latin Renaissance vision also informs how he connected with Langston Hughes throughout their 1930s correspondence. The Schomburg–Hughes correspondence of 1932–1937 represents an exceptional moment of collaboration in both authors' careers. As well-known Afro-American intellectuals during the heyday of the Harlem Renaissance, both Schomburg and Langston Hughes generated and preserved thousands of letters during their lifetimes. Still, each chose to fashion and fully expand their epistolary personas differently and with contrasting casts of correspondents. In fact, Hughes's biographer and scholar Arnold Rampersad does not place Schomburg among Hughes's major interlocutors either in his biography or his coeditions of Hughes's letters.[21] Due to differences in age, temperament, national background, and political inclinations, and in their approaches to blackness, history, and literature, Schomburg and Hughes interacted as correspondents only in their last six years of acquaintance.[22] The exchange I wish to

---

[19] See "Sebastián Gómez" (*Crisis* XI Jan 1916), "In Quest of Juan de Pareja" (*Crisis* XXXIV July 1927), and "José Campeche 18752-1809" (*Mission Fields at Home* VI April 1934) in Piñeiro 99–100, 138–43, and 201–208; and "Pastor Argudín y Pedroso" (*New York Age* Sept. 20, 1934).

[20] I deal at length with Schomburg's and Locke's research projects on Negro art history and esthetics in an article in progress titled "Countervisuality in Arthur A. Schomburg's Writings on Black Atlantic Art."

[21] Schomburg corresponded best with pan-Africanist antiquarians and black Masonic officials such as Bruce, Harry Williamson, and Cromwell. Hughes liked to engage professional editors and writers from both mainstream and black publishing, such as the wealthy white Iowan novelist and photographer, Carl Van Vechten, and the Louisiana-born black anthologist of the Harlem Renaissance, Arna Bontemps.

[22] Indeed, the contrasts between Hughes and Schomburg were many. Whereas Hughes famously adapted popular black "folk" culture in his poetry, Schomburg was more interested in fomenting African-descendent participation in the "fine" arts. Schomburg

examine here took place in the 1930s, when the Depression had dampened the excitement of the Harlem Renaissance years. Starting a new life phase as curator of the NYPL Division of Negro Culture, the cloistered Schomburg struggled to expand a collection he had spent most of his life assembling at a time when funding was scarcer than ever, which frustrated his wishes to do more research overseas (Sinnette 108). Hughes, on the other hand, was taking his wanderlust to a new level. He was being paid to go overseas as a journalist and well-recognized, black-identified author. The established black bibliophile in Harlem and the rising Negro literary star abroad pooled together their prestige for mutual benefit to consolidate a grand archive for the African Diaspora. As we shall see, this partnering was inherently an Afro-Latino one.

Schomburg was fifty-eight years old when he began writing to a thirty-year-old Hughes in a bid to reconnect with Harlem Renaissance writers upon his relocation to New York. As NYPL curator, he had just undertaken a two-week acquisition trip to Cuba in which he met with and interviewed at length the network of Afro-Cuban literati and pro-black-rights activists who had befriended and sponsored Hughes during the latter's eventful 1930–1931 visit to the island. This network included the civic personalities convened at the *Atenas* Afro-Cuban social club and the circle of writers behind the production of the widely-read "Ideales de una raza" (A Race's Ideals), a weekly Sunday feature of the influential newspaper *Diario de la Marina* covering the progress and achievements of African-descendants worldwide. Among the circle's top figures were the white man of letters, businessman, and diplomat José Antonio Fernández de Castro (often called the "Cuban Van Vechten"), Afro-Cuban architect and essayist Gustavo Urrutia, Afro-Cuban historian Lino D'Ou, Afro-Chinese poet Regino Pedroso, and the great communist writer later honored as National Poet by the 1959 Revolution, Nicolás Guillén (often called the "Cuban Langston Hughes"). All regarded Hughes and Schomburg as iconic examples of the New Negro phenomenon in the United States and as important sources for insights about the Anglophone Afro-diaspora. They published articles about both visitors during and after their stay. To encourage further Havana/Harlem rapprochements, they also started an expansive bilingual chain of correspondence with them that often had Hughes and Schomburg working as a team, sharing Havana news, letters, and research tasks.[23]

was an Episcopalian wary of communism while Hughes remained a Soviet-sympathizer who wrote revolutionary poems often deemed as "incendiary."

[23] On the dynamics of solidary and exchange among Afro-Cuban and Afro-American intellectuals and artists in the "Havana-Harlem nexus," see Frank Guridy's exceptional

Ten years before, after laboring in Mexico in his father's farming business in 1920 and dropping out from Columbia University the following year after a feuding with his father, Langston Hughes had begun publishing poems in W. E. B. Du Bois's NAACP journal, *The Crisis*. From 1921 to 1925, Hughes continued submitting poems to Harlem publications while traveling along the western African coast and throughout Europe employed as a mess boy on a tramp steamer and as a dishwasher in a Paris jazz club. Back in the United States, he worked as a waiter and as a research assistant to black historian Carter Woodson while living in Washington, DC. In 1925 Carl Van Vechten encouraged Hughes to submit his poetry to Alfred Knopf, who published Hughes's first two poetry books, *The Weary Blues* (1926) and *Fine Clothes to the Jew* (1927), and first novel, *Not Without Laughter* (1930), making Hughes the most visible living black poet in the United States while he attended Lincoln College in Pennsylvania and spent his summers in Harlem. The Depression found Hughes conflicted about how to revamp his writing and make a living as an author after a falling out with Zora Neale Hurston over the rights to *Mule Bone*, a play on which they had collaborated, and a rough break-up with Charlotte Osgood Mason, his white benefactor. The 1930s thus arrived as a new period for "wandering and wondering." Hughes toured all over the Southern states in poetry recitals; traveled to Cuba, Haiti, and other Caribbean islands where he was welcomed as a prestigious writer; consolidated his leftist outlook and convictions by spending 1933 in Moscow as a script doctor on a film production about U.S. racial prejudice and as a reporter in Soviet Asia; lived and worked in Mexico as a literary translator in 1935; and covered the outbreak of Spanish Civil War as a correspondent for the *Baltimore Afro-American* in Valencia and Madrid in 1937.[24]

Schomburg wrote first on November 21, 1932 when he learned that Hughes was about to depart for Moscow. In the letter, he first asks Hughes to find, while in Moscow, memorabilia related to the Afro-American exile actor Ira Aldridge's stay in Russia and a lithograph of the noted Afro-Russian romantic poet Alexander Pushkin's statue in Leningrad. Then Schomburg recaps his trip to Cuba earlier that year, and expands the web of bilingual Afro-Latin collaboration by passing on greetings from Fernández de Castro,

---

chapter "Blues and *Son* from Harlem to Havana" (107–150). Guridy discusses at length Hughes's and Schomburg's interactions with Guillén and the *Ideales* circle.

[24] I draw from Rampersad's biography and on Hughes's two autobiographies, *The Big Sea* (1940) and *I Wonder as I Wander* (1956), for this profile. On scholarship regarding Hughes's connections to Cuba, Mexico, and the Caribbean and Latin America as a whole I rely on Kutzinski, Guridy, and Mullen.

Urrutia, and Guillén. He asks that Hughes finish translating Guillén's recently issued book *Sóngoro Cosongo* for an edition that Schomburg would contract with a U.S. black press (HPWJC Box 143, folder 2660).[25] In three follow-up letters (Feb. 5 from Meschabpom Film office in Moscow; Aug. 7 and Dec. 7 from Carmel, California), Hughes declines the request to translate Guillén; he would get the job done later, assisted by Ben Frederic Carruthers, with *Cuba Libre: Poems by Nicolas Guillén* (1948). He tells Schomburg to contact the Voka Society for Cultural Relations about the Aldridge materials, shares the address of the Leningrad Pushkin Society, and encloses picture postcards of the statue and other such materials (SCSBC Box 3, Folder 23).[26]

In early 1935, Hughes returned to Mexico to attend his father's funeral. He stayed for six months to collaborate with Fernández de Castro, then Cuban Embassy secretary in Mexico, translating into English an ambitious anthology of stories by up-and-coming writers from Cuba and Mexico with the hope of publishing it in the United States. He writes on April 18 to let Schomburg know about this project; he attaches clips of articles in the Mexican press about his poetry plus news about the stage success of *La Rebambaramba*, Afro-Cuban composer Amadeo Roldán's *Orisha*-themed ballet. This letter triggers a remarkable change in Schomburg's epistolary routine, evidenced in his April 26, 1935 response. Schomburg wrote it exclusively in Spanish, addressing it to "Señor Don Langston Hughes."

Although a good part of the letter deals with routine professional matters, the language switch introduces a warmer, playful tone and a spirit of complicity. Schomburg acknowledges receipt of the attached articles, requests more compositions by Roldán, congratulates Hughes on receiving a Guggenheim, and sends greeting from librarian Ernestine Rose along with Claude McKay's new address in Harlem. But at mid-letter Schomburg moves on to advise Hughes on how he should conduct himself *as a trans-American Afro-Latino* in Mexico and what sort of African-diasporic knowledge he should seek out there. He starts by giving Hughes a mini-history lesson about the role of free blacks in the colonization of Mexico:

[25] I consulted and transcribed Schomburg's letters to Hughes at the James Weldon Johnson Collection in Yale's Beinecke Rare Book and Manuscript Library during research visits in 2004 and 2006. I reference hard copies by box and folder under the abbreviation HPWJC.
[26] I have consulted Schomburg's unpublished papers at the NYPL Schomburg Center during three research trips made over the last ten years. I reference the hard copy of these materials as archived at the Schomburg Center by box and folder under the abbreviation SCSBC.

I . . . hope that Mexico's history will give you means to instruct yourself on how much service the black race has rendered [there]. José Condé was the first comedian sent by Cuba's governor to entertain Hernán Cortés with charming and humorous tales. Juan Garrido was the [first] to plant wheat according to Mexican historians. Historian Bancroft tells us that a Negro Head was found where a milpa was about to be plowed – a great number of Africans thus disembarked in the coast of Vera Cruz. You should serve as our ambassador so that the Mexican people never build a wall against the Negro in the Mexican Republic. Write me once in a while, I'd like to know about your progress in the sister republic . . .. Greetings to all the friends who live there, as well as to our friend Diego Rivera who will tell you about the Negro Head.[27]

Fully aware of Hughes's affective and intellectual interests and affiliations in Cuba and Mexico, Schomburg adopts in this letter the role of Afro-Latino mentor. His historical lesson about the convergence of blackness and *latini-dad* at very start of the transatlantic encounter is part of a meta-narrative quite distinct from those learned from either Acosta or Bruce. It is the story of the service rendered by learned, virtuous, and entrepreneurial African descendants from the Mediterranean Afro-European contact zone in the ascending process of global Old World/New World unification, dating to the Renaissance. According to Schomburg, the first Negroes to arrive in the Americas came from dynamic, racially mixed South European cities who had successfully combined the civilizational legacies of Roman Christendom and Eastern and North African Islam, such as Seville, Granada, and Venice. Either as free men or as slaves, these first Afro-Latinos developed their trades, talents, and aptitudes as part of black *cofradías*, religious societies of both slaves and free people of color who protected and promoted their social and economic interests in a context of Mediterranean *convivencia*. Thus, before the Spanish crown could institute a full-blown African-slave-trade system in the Americas, free Renaissance Afro-Latinos such as the comic actor by trade

---

[27] "Vivo en la esperanza que la historia de Mejico le facilitará para orientarse en lo mucho que tiene del servicio prestado por la raza negra - José Condé fue el primer cómico que el governador de Cuba envió a Hernan Cortez para entretenerlo con cuentos agra-dables y chimosos. Juan Garrido el que sembró trigo según consta en la historia de Mexico. La cabeza de un Negro que el historiador Bancroft nos dice fue encontrada donde se pensaba eregir una milpa – un gran número de africanos que desembarcaron en la costa de Vera Cruz. – Usted debe servir como embajador para que el pueblo mejicano no levante una muralla contra el Negro en la república mejicana – Escríbame de vez en cuando, pues yo quiero saber el progreso que viene haciendo en la república hermana . . . Recuerdos á los amigos . . . como también al amigo Diego Rivera quien le dirá de la Cabeza del Negro" (HPWJC Box Box 143, folder 2660).

Condé and farming pioneer Garrido, recruited at the *cofradías* as indispensable crewmembers for New World expeditions, had already "served with distinction" as accomplished tradesmen in all sorts of artistic, military, agricultural, and commercial matters across the Atlantic. During his 1926 stay in Seville, Schomburg had dug up the names and careers of these "Early Americas" Afro-Latinos at the Archivo General de Indias (Archive of the Indies). He then surveyed the textual and archeological remains of the chapels and neighborhoods that the *cofradías* had built and maintained in fifteenth-, sixteenth-, and seventeenth-century Seville, apex years for Renaissance Humanism and New World travel.[28] Thus, when Schomburg instructs Hughes to *serve* as ambassador against white supremacy in Mexico, he is not asking the latter to just represent U.S. blacks or Anglophone ideals of an Afro-diasporic nation; rather, he is asking Hughes to save from neglect and oblivion the memory and legacy of the Afro-Latino Renaissance migrants who helped lay the foundations of post-Columbian mixed societies.

For Schomburg, the Olmec head or "Cabeza de Negro" that he mentions promised the best possible archeological evidence of the foundational presence of Mediterranean Africans and Afro-Latinos in Early America. Schomburg was refering to the ongoing discovery of colossal basalt Olmec heads at the archeological sites of Tres Zapotes and La Venta near Veracruz between the 1890s and 1920s, later fully excavated by a team lead by Matthew Stirling between 1938 and 1946.[29] The negroid features (full lips; wide, well-defined noses) of the "helmeted African heads" led some anthropologists at the time to speculate whether ships piloted by North Africans had crossed the Atlantic and, as Schomburg appears to assume, disembarked in Veracruz sometime before the Spanish arrival. As scientific findings confirmed the Olmecs as the earliest Mesoamerican civilization, this assumption was disqualified. In any case, what is clear is that Schomburg subscribed to and pursued the thesis of a long-standing presence of African-descended persons in the early modern indigenous-colonial matrix from which emerged the variegated, mixed cultures of Mexico and the rest of the New World. For instance, Schomburg translated into English a 1921 article by Mexican anthropologist Alfonso Toro arguing this vision, "Influence of the Negro Race in the Formation of the Mexican Race" (SCSBC typescript, Box 16, Folder 30). According to Irene

---

[28] See Schomburg's articles "The Negro Brotherhood of Sevilla" (*Opportunity* V, June 1927) and "Negros in Sevilla" (*Opportunity* VI, March 1928) in Piñeiro 145–59.

[29] About the excavation of colossal heads and the history of Olmec archeology, see Coe 40–50.

Vasquez, Toro's article anticipated the vogue of Afro-Mexican studies today. The prescient Schomburg was thus pursuing a research track regarding an Afro-diasporic constitutive presence in both Renaissance Europe and Early Colonial Mexico that contemporary scholars such as Vasquez, T. F. Early, and K. J. P. Lowe are now documenting in its linguistic, cultural, and visual complexity back to the fifteenth and sixteenth centuries.[30] The active participation of African descendants in these enterprises also suggests that up-to-par North African advancements in navigational, cartographical, and representational technologies took part in the bridging of the New World with the Old.

Beside an interest in a prevailing "Afro-Latin" factor in Mexico's racial, cultural, and social history, we also have here a case of intentional Afro-bilingual play in Schomburg's and Hughes's correspondence. In their research, Sánchez González and Guridy have shown that as NYPL curator Schomburg continued to use Spanish regularly in his dealings with fellow Afro-Latinos in the Harlem-Havana nexus and business contacts in many other Spanish and Latin American cities. Still, few of these letters employ the bilingual register that Schomburg assumes with Hughes. With this "code-switching" gesture – writing to Langston Hughes in Spanish and English – Schomburg communicates with the poet-translator in the same "Latino" way Cuban writers such as Guillén, Fernández de Castro, and Urrutia had done. By assuming this new corresponding persona, Schomburg facilitated Hughes's trans-American translation project and prompted him to broaden his use of Spanish as a fully bilingual subject. Schomburg encouraged Hughes not just to sing the mother's vernacular blues, but also to speak in the father's adopted Mexican tongue. Thus Schomburg helps reconfigure Afro-Latino racial identity by way of language politics. Similarly, the act of addressing Hughes in Spanish draws out Schomburg's bilingualism and complicates Sinnette and James's emphasis on his "deliberate loss" of Spanish.

In Schomburg's and Hughes's correspondence, we thus see the opening of an Afro-Anglo-Latino space connected to what critic Vera Kutzinski has recently called, in her study of Hughes and translation in the Americas, Hughes's "perpetual state of heterolingualism" (33). Here the black American

---

[30] In her article, Vasquez reviews how research questions regarding Afro-Mexican identity, ethnography, cultural and social history, demographics, and national formation have burgeoned into a powerful academic field of study since Toro's work. In *Black Africans in Renaissance Europe*, Earle and Lowe gather art scholars, cultural historians, and other Renaissance specialists to reassess the social presence of African and Afro-descendant slaves and freedmen in Renaissance Italy, Portugal, Spain, and England through a close examination of their visual and textual representations in the arts and other trades.

vernacular project sought by Hughes in his exploration of the blues as a source for an Afro-American poetic voice meets Schomburg's search for icons of black freedom and enterprise in the history of post-Renaissance Afro-Latin expansion in the New World. In both Hughes and Schomburg, the end result is a sort of Afro-Latino vision that challenged many of the geopolitical and cultural premises of Garveyite, "English-mostly" pan-Africanism. Schomburg and Hughes agreed that the development of a black consciousness in the Americas had to be rigorously *heterolingual*, operating through the mutual confrontation, contamination, and vernacular inflexion of the two major imperial languages of the continent.

To develop this diasporic, multilingual outlook, Langston Hughes not only translated Nicolás Guillén into English; he also worked on the poetry of Federico García Lorca and Gabriela Mistral, among others. The rhythms and meters of Peninsular and Spanish American poetic speech thus inflected Hughes's transcriptions of the black voice in poetry and prose. These Latino voices are not just circumscribed to the correspondence between the chorus structures of Guillén's *sones* and the refrains of Hughes's blues; through them, Hughes embraced transatlantic Spanish in all of its accents and dialectal variants. Similarly, Schomburg's stubbornly Hispanicized English, the "florid" style that so irked the decorous writerly standards of many major Afro-American intellectuals (W. E. B. Du Bois, Locke, and Bruce among them), was also an exercise in language power and willful hybridity, a way to bend English around and make it fit into an Afro-Latino soundscape. In Hughes's and Schomburg's heterolingual *signifyin'* we find thus an early instance of Spanglish used as an Afro-Latino expressive force.

WORKS CITED

Aiello, Thomas. *The Battle for the Souls of Black Folks: W. E. B. Du Bois, Booker T. Washington, and the Debate that Shaped the Course of Civil Rights.* Santa Barbara, CA: Praeger, 2016.
Arroyo-Martínez, Jossianna. "Technologies: Transculturations of Race, Gender & Ethnicity in Arturo A. Schomburg's Masonic Writings." *Centro Journal* 17(1): 4–25.
Writing Secrecy in Caribbean Freemasonry. New York: Palgrave Macmillan, 2013.
Bontemps, Arna. *Arna Bontemps-Langston Hughes Letters, 1925–1967. Selected and Edited by Charles H. Nichols.* New York: Dodd, Maed, 1980.
Calo, Mary Ann. Race. *Distinction and Denial. Race, Nation, and the Critical Construction of the African American Artist, 1920–40.* Ann Arbor: University of Michigan Press, 2007.
Cancel, Mario R. *Segundo Ruiz Belvis: el prócer y el ser humano (una aproximación crítica a su vida).* Bayamón, Puerto Rico.: Editorial Universidad de América, 1994.

Coe, Michael D. *America's First Civilization: Discovering the Olmec*. New York: American Heritage Press, 1968.

Crowder, Ralph L. *John Edward Bruce. Politician, Journalist, and Self-Trained Historian of the African Diaspora*. New York and London: New York University Press, 2016.

Edwards, Brent Hayes. *The Practice of Diaspora: Literature, Translation, and the Rise of Black Internationalism*. Cambridge, MA: Harvard University Press, 2003.

Earle, T. F. and K. J. P. Lowe, ed. *Black Africans in Renaissance Europe*. Cambridge: Cambridge University Press, 2005.

Fermoselle, Rafael. *Política y color en Cuba: la guerrita de 1912*. Madrid: Editorial Colibrí, 1998.

Flores, Juan. *The Diaspora Strikes Back. Caribeño Tales of Learning and Turning*. London, New York: Routledge, 2009.

Gates, Henry Louis and Gene Andrew Jarrett. *The New Negro: Readings on Race, Representation, and African American Cultures, 1892–1938*. Princeton, NJ: Princeton University Press, 2007.

Gilroy, Paul. *The Black Atlantic. Modernity and Double Consciousness*. Cambridge, MA: Harvard University Press, 1993.

Guridy, Frank Andre. *Forging Diaspora. Afro-Cubans and African-Americans in a World of Empire and Jim Crow*. Chapel Hill: University of North Carolina Press, 2010.

Gutierrez de Arroyo, Isabel. "La Sociedad recoletora de documentos históricos: su colección documental." *Revista del Instituto de Cultura Puertorriqueña* 48 (July–Sept. 1970): 36–44.

Harris, Leonard and Charles Molesworth, *Alain L. Locke: The Biography of a Philosopher*. Chicago and London: Chicago University Press, 2009.

Helg, Aline. *Our Rightful Share: The Afro-Cuban Struggle for Equality*. Chapel Hill: University of North Carolina Press, 1995.

Hoffnung-Garskof, Jesse. "The Migrations of Arturo Schomburg: On Being Antillano, Negro and Puerto Rican in New York 1891–1938." *Journal of American Ethnic History* 21(1): 3–49.

"The World of Arturo Alfonso Schomburg." Ed. Miriam Jiménez Román and Juan Flores. *The Afro-Latin@ Reader: History and Culture in the United States*. Durham, NC: Duke University Press, 2010: 70–91.

Huggins, Nathan Irvin. *Harlem Renaissance*. New York: Oxford University Press, 1971.

Hughes, Langston. *The Collected Poems of Langston Hughes*. New York: Knopf, 1994.

The Big Sea. An Autobiography. New York: Hill and Wang, 1963.

I Wonder as I Wander. An Autobiographical Journey. New York: Hill and Wang, 1964.

Papers. James Weldon Johnson Collection in the Yale Collection of American Literature, Beinecke Rare Book and Manuscript Library, Yale University.

Remember Me to Harlem: The Letters of Langston Hughes and Carl Van Vechten, 1925–1964. Ed. Emily Bernard. New York: Alfred A. Knopf, 2001.

James, Winston. *Holding Aloft the Banner of Ethiopia. Caribbean Radicalism in Early Twentieth Century America*. London; New York: Verso, 1999.

Jiménez Román, Miriam and Juan Flores, eds. "Introduction." *The Afro-Latin@ Reader: History and Culture in the United States*. Durham, NC: Duke University Press, 2010: 1–15.

Kutzinski, Vera M. *The Worlds of Langston Hughes: Modernism and Translation in the Americas*. Ithaca, NY: Cornell University Press, 2012.

Lomas, Laura. *Translating Empire. José Martí, Migrant Latino Subjects, and American Modernities*. Durham, NC and London: Duke University Press, 2008.

Lopez, Antonio. *Unbecoming Blackness: The Diaspora Cultures of Afro-Cuban America*. New York: New York University Press, 2012.

Meehan, Kevin. *People Get Ready. African American and Caribbean Cultural Exchange*. Jackson: University Press of Mississippi, 2009.

Montero, Oscar. *Jose Martí: An Introduction*. New York: Palgrave McMillan, 2004.

Moore, Jacqueline M. *Booker T. Washington, W. E. B. Du Bois, and the Struggle for Racial Uplift*. Wilmington, DE: SR Books, 2003.

Moscoso, Francisco. "Tapia, la Sociedad Recolectora y la Biblioteca Histórica de Puerto Rico (1854)."s *Tapiana 1: Actas del II Congreso*. San Juan: Editorial LEA, 2012: 25–42.

Moss, Alfred A. *The American Negro Academy. Voice of the Talented Tenth*. Baton Rouge and London: Louisiana State University Press, 1981.

Mullen, Edward J., ed. *Langston Hughes in the Hispanic World and Haiti*. Hamden, CT: Archon Books, 1977.

Piñeiro de Rivera, Flor, ed. *Arthur Alfonso Schomburg. A Puerto Rican Quest for His Black Heritage. His Writings Annotated With Appendices*. San Juan: Centro de Estudios Avanzados de Puerto Rico y el Caribe, 1989.

Rampersad, Arnold. *The Life of Langston Hughes. Vols. 1 & 2*. New York: Oxford University Press, 1986–1988.

Reynolds, Gary A., ed. *Against the Odds: African-American Artists and the Harmon Foundation*. Newark, NJ: Newark Museum, 1989.

Rojas, Rafael. *La invención de José Martí*. Madrid: Editorial Colibrí, 2000.

Sánchez González, Lisa. "Arturo Alfonso Schomburg: A Transamerican Intellectual." *African Roots/American Cultures. Africa in the Creation of the Americas*. Sheila S. Walker, ed. Lanham, MD: Rowman & Littlefield, 2001: 139–52.

  Boricua Literature: A Literary History of the Puerto Rican Diaspora. New York and London: New York University Press, 2001.

Schomburg, Arthur Alfonso. "Lynching, a Savage Relic." Signed "Guarionex." *New York Times*. June 28, 1903, p. 8.

  "The Lynchings in Georgia. Thinks They Indicate Influence of Extra Legal and Extra Judicial Theories." Signed "Guarionex." *New York Times*. August 21, 1904, p. 8.

  "The Negro and His Rights." *New York Times*. May 24, 1903, p. 26.

  Papers, including correspondence, clippings, manuscripts, bibliographies, and photographs. Schomburg Center for Research in Black Culture, New York City Public Library.

  "A Philippine Republic Suggested." *New York Times*. November 21, 1901, p. 6.

  "The Philippine Question." *New York Times*. June 8, 1902, p. 6.

  "Questions by a Porto Rican." *New York Times*. August 9, 1902, p. 8.

  "The Roosevelt Doctrine." *New York Times*. November 22, 1903, p. 24.

  "The Selling of Votes." Signed "Guarionex." *New York Times*. October 31, 1903, p. 8.

  "Takes Issue with Bishop Turner." *New York Times*. September 3, 1901, p. 6.

  "Tillman Trial and Verdict." *New York Times*. October 18, 1903, p. 25.

  "Union League Clubs' Action." *New York Times*. December 20, 1903, p. 23.

Schmidt-Nowara, Christopher. *Empire and Antislavery: Spain, Cuba, and Puerto Rico, 1833–1874*. Pittsburgh, PA: University of Pittsburgh Press, 1999.

Serraile, William. *Bruce Grit. The Black Nationalist Writings of John Edward Bruce*. Knoxville: The University of Tennessee Press, 2003.

Toro, Alfonso. "Influencia de la Raza Negra en la Formación del Pueblo Mexicano," *Ethnos* 1.8–12 (1920–1921): 215–18.

Vasquez, Irene. "The *Longue Durée* of Africans in Mexico: The Historiography of Racialization, Acculturation, and Afro-Mexican Subjectivity." *The Journal of African American History* 95.2 (Spring 2010): 183–201.

Vigo-Jorge, Edgardo M. "Un estudio sobre la posible afiliación masónica de José Julián Acosta." *Lumen. Revista Oficial Respetable Logia de Investigación José G. Bloise* 1 (August 2014): 99–111.

18

Floricanto en Aztlán

Chicano Cultural Nationalism and Its Epic Discontents

RAFAEL PÉREZ-TORRES

Floricanto names the poetic expression associated with a particularly urgent moment in Chicano history. It represents a "people's art," merging oral tradition and performance with a revolutionary purpose. The poetry sought to participate in creating a transnational, neo-indigenous, independent, and liberated Chicano identity. Mainly published in the 1970s and often viewed as an articulation of the Chicano movement, *floricanto* poetry often depicts the repressive racist and exploitative realities of *barrio* life while asserting a renewed Chicano identity emerging into a more just future. The poetry served multiple functions: expression of personal despair at ingrained oppression, assertion of an emboldened new race or *raza*, depictions of the day to day life practices of the *barrio*. Collectively, the poems were meant to educate about the roots of injustice, to recuperate lost heroic histories, to preserve forms of knowledge associated with the collective wisdom of Mexican culture, and to inspire its listeners to work collectively toward greater social equality.

The first evocation of the term is the 1971 collection by poet Alurista (Alberto Baltazar Urista Heredia): *Floricanto en Aztlán*, a collection of multilingual, experimental, avant-garde poetic expressions of hope, rage, and playful joy. In the fall of 1973, Alurista and others organized, under the auspices of the Chicano Studies Center at the University of Southern California, a *Festival de Floricanto*, a three-day event whose photos and films are now online via the University of Southern California Digital Library. Over the next few years, participants organized other large festivals held yearly at universities in Austin (1975) and San Antonio, Texas (1976), Albuquerque, New Mexico (1977), and Tempe, Arizona (1978). With the exception of the San Antonio event, the poetry along with prose and critical pieces read at the festival were published in a series of *floricanto* anthologies. Along with Alurista, notable poets among the participants over the years included José Antonio Burciaga, Margarita Cota-Cárdenas, Lorna Dee Cervantes, Abelardo

Delgado, Sergio Elizondo, Juan Felipe Herrera, Angela de Hoyos, Miguel Méndez, José Montalvo, José Montoya, Américo Paredes, Leroy V. Quintana, Omar Salinas, raúlsalinas, Ricardo Sánchez, Carmen Tafolla, Reimundo Tigre-Pérez, Luis Valdez, Tino Villanueva, and Bernice Zamora.

The festivals were conceived democratically as a national forum that would be open to all Chicano writers. Each had about the same amount of time to present their work, professional or not, in order to foster an atmosphere conducive to creative exchange and to make Chicano literature available to all community members (Alurista 1979, 13). While fomenting political action and enacting Chicano liberation were not among the stated goals of the festivals, the thrust of much of the poetry and the underlying assumptions behind the events certainly assert *chicanismo*: the carving out of an empowered self-identity firmly rooted in the cultural, racial, and ethnic grounding of Mexican-American communities emphasizing self-worth, pride, uniqueness, and a feeling of cultural rebirth (Gómez-Quiñones 1990, 103–104).

Alurista notes that the *floricanto* anthologies "materialize the spirit of our people" and are a concrete documentation of a literature that is "a progressive force in our social and intellectual struggle to determine by ourselves and for ourselves the role that we, Chicano people, shall play in U.S. and world history" (1979, 15). Chicano writing, from this perspective, proves more than an expression of *chicanismo*: it becomes its manifestation. The poetry voiced at the *floricanto* festivals enacts the complexities, contradictions, desires, conflicts, and dreams of a newly emerging and empowered Chicano identity.

The term *floricanto* – as critic Cordelia Candelaria points out – has become somewhat synonymous with Chicano poetry as a whole and derives from the Nahuatl expression for incantatory prayer in Aztec times (1986, 34). For the Nahua, the people of the Aztec empire (1428–1521), this prayer or poetry in Nahuatl was called *in xochitl in cuicatl*: in English "flower and song" and in Spanish *flor y canto* or *floricanto*.

The term resonants on a number of levels. "Linguistically," Candelaria explains, "*flor y canto* joins images which, in conjunction, mean something else, and the meaning derives from *both the images and the conjunction*. By yoking the flowers of the earth in their aromatic, colorful, natural beauty to the human created song of the air, the Nahuas demonstrated their recognition of the transcendent quality of poetry" (1986, 34–35 emphasis in original). The transformative power of the word intoned or performed in Aztec religious ceremonies finds new significance in the recuperative strategies of poets affirming the Chicano movement. The juxtaposed image of song and flower in the formation of new meanings resonated with the desire to generate new social relations and foster the growth of an empowered Chicano community.

The calling up of Aztec iconography, religion, and philosophy reflects significant discursive elements of *floricanto* traceable to nationalist discourses of modern Mexico. The Mexican nation state has at once affirmed its *mestizo* mixed racial population as the agents of progress while incorporating indigenous culture and symbology, most centrally that of the militaristic Aztec empire, to construct a story about national development. In this respect, the deployment of Aztec iconography by Chicano writers and artists also evokes a Mexican nationalist discourse that renders the Indian as a noble but tragic symbol of a heroic yet inevitably failed resistance to European dominance (Saldaña-Portillo 2001, 407). *Floricanto*, driven by a liberatory impulse, ironically relies upon the repressive language of Mexican nationalism that values the *mestizo* over the *indio*.

Whereas *floricanto* might now be synonymous with any form of Chicano poetry, as Candelaria avers, during the decade of its development it suggests as much a type of poetry as a cultural, social, and political event. The enacted performances of poems at the *floricanto* festivals clearly influenced the palette and tones of much subsequent Chicano poetry. They helped establish a "classic Chicano poetics" that thematizes social inequalities against Chicano and other historically aggrieved communities, critiques the effects of racist and ethnocentric ideologies, and gives voice to hitherto silenced communities enduring multiple legacies of colonialism (Pérez-Torres 1995, 6). The mission in creating *floricanto* was as much poetical as political, employing the occasion of poetic expression to educate, inspire, and organize mass political action for the betterment of the Chicano community.

Earlier poetic formations like Rodolfo "Corky" Gonzales's epic "I am Joaquín" from 1967 would consequently be understood within a *floricanto* tradition because of its emphasis on orality both in form and content, its invocation of Mexican and Aztec history, and its assertion that the "music of the people stirs the / Revolution" (1972, 97). Moreover, Gonzales's poem was intended as an organizing tool, a verse to be declaimed, mimeographed, and pasted on walls in order to generate activism. The poem seems the expression of an authentic organic intellectual and employs many of the formal techniques associated with *floricanto* poetry.

Formalistically, *floricanto* poetry relies on multilingual expression, with some poems in a single language but more often intermingling standard Spanish, standard English, *caló* (Chicano street patois), and various registers of colloquial forms of both Spanish and English marking particular class or cultural positions. Most of the poetry is written in free verse, and the literary influences (and literary talents) as diverse and varied as the participants.

Drawing upon the iconography and spirit of Aztec religious philosophy in order to name the poetic/political experience of the contemporary Chicano people represents perhaps the most striking but also quirky characteristic of *floricanto*. While rooted in a deeply problematic Mexican nationalist discourse, the evocation of ancient Aztec (or Toltec or Mayan) traditions arises from a desire to embolden and encourage the community through evocations of the heroic and rich indigenous history from whence flows Chicano culture. The poetry seeks to instill a familiarity with and affirm a sense of pride in a Mexican culture firmly secured to its indigenous roots.

While the affirmation of deep historical, cultural, and biological ties to ancient indigenous cultures is significant, a focus on this formal aspect of the poetry may undercut the sustained engagement with American Indian rights movements that Chicano writers, teachers, and educators have historically fostered, and continue to foster. Especially for poets in Arizona and New Mexico (but true for all Chicano poets conscious of demands for Indigenous sovereignty), Chicano culture lives because of its continuing engagement with Indigenous communities and cultures and not because it serves as a reliquary for ancient Aztec icons. Notably, the organizers of the fourth and fifth *Festival de Floricanto* highlight the participation of American Indians from various tribes of the Southwest in order to merge heritages that derive from "similar experiences of subjugation: loss of lands, languages, and liberties" (Armas and Zamora 1980, 10). To which Chicano experience of subjugation the organizers refer – the U.S. colonization of Mexican territory (1846–1848), the Spanish invasion of the Aztec Empire (1519–1521), or the current internal colonization of the *barrio* – seems intentionally unclear. The point being, the fetishization of Aztec imagery may serve to detract from recognizing the overlapping (though certainly unequal) histories and heritages shared by Chicano communities and Indigenous peoples living in history, not entombed amid the ruins of a mystical Aztec past.

On another level, the emphasis upon Aztec iconography erases the multiple manifestations of Chicano culture as one that is fully lived and embodied. Indeed, many of the poems declaimed at the *floricanto* festivals highlight the multiple ways that Chicano expressive culture attempts to embody the wisdom of a people born from a long and conflicted history of multiple colonizations. Many of the poems weave into their lines cultural referents like *dichos* (popular sayings), musical forms such as the *corrido*

(Mexico-Texan ballads) and the *ranchera*, food ways, household traditions, and other aspects of lived Mexican and Chicano daily life.

While certainly affirming Chicano and *Mexicano* popular culture, *floricanto* as text and performance can be seen as descending from specifically U.S. cultural forms as well. The performative dimension of the poetry suggests the improvisational nature of bebop jazz, the exuberance of Beat poetry, and even the cosmic consciousness of New Age spiritualism. In terms of codifying the cultural repertoire that would clearly delineate the unique characteristics of *floricanto* as a Chicano manifestation, the poetry relies upon the familiar litany of iconic Mexican and Chicano imagery.

The emphasis upon the collective "folk" wisdom evident in the anonymous and ubiquitous *dichos*, for example, serves to underscore how the idea of collectivity underpins the cultural elements significant to a classic Chicano poetics. Similarly, representations of the *barrio*, the life in the streets as examples of working-class life, become one locus around which poets cluster their concerns. ("Working in canneries or / picking beets is the / metaphor of being" observes Bernice Zamora [1979, 43].) Several poems are directed specifically to or are recollections of mothers, grandparents, uncles, and other memorable family members.

More often than not, these familial poems serve to point out some level of inequity or injustice that characterizes life in the barrio. Where the poetry expresses a shared sense of communal belonging, a sense of outrage at social inequities also arises. José Montoya in "Until They Leave Us A Loan" reflects humorously on the way the neighborhood took over the pool at the public park after the boys' swimming holes were overtaken by newly constructed freeways. The theme of dislocation resonates with the broader concerns about displacement and colonization representing the historical forces that have shaped Chicano experiences. The poem closes with the speaker reflecting on a rumored freeway that would cut directly through the neighborhood, underscoring continued displacement, exploitation, and marginalization as a legacy of colonization. Similarly, the speaker in Marco Antonio Domínguez's "Mi Hijo" asks his son why he looks so downcast. The boy replies that he is on his way to school, which he doesn't like because it is small and mean and the teacher mistreats him. The poet's intimate exchange with his son reveals the pervasive social persecution and discrimination that Chicanos regularly face. The interpenetration of the social world with its profound inequalities and the intimate world of family and home reflect a central tenant of *floricanto* poetry: one's identity is ever-entwined with a larger collective, be it the family, the barrio, or even *Aztlán*. As an imagined homeland or as an alternate name for the U.S. Southwest, the idea of *Aztlán* foregrounds a representation of Chicano identity in relationship to others. Relational conceptualizations of identity emerge as an abiding concern in *floricanto* and, more broadly, a guiding principle of *chicanismo*.

Because of the focus on collectivity, the community or *barrio* becomes a rich locus of significance for the poets. The poetic representation of the *barrio* involves the inevitable evocation of street figures populating a socially marginal demimonde: gangbangers, winos, and criminals both grand and petty. The *pachuco* or street tough often pictured wearing his zoot suit called a *tacuche*, the *vato loco* or crazy dude, the *tecato* or junky, the *pinto* or convict, the use of *caló* – the street slang associated with a criminal underworld and woven into a multilingual poetics – all become part of its repertoire. *Floricanto* poetry introduces these figures and styles as representative of the marginalized reality lived by Chicanos.

The *pachuco*, with his stylized clothes, gangster image, and coded patois, represents the quintessence of nonconformity and resistance. José Montoya – a participant at several *floricanto* events although this poem is not from one – provides us the most influential poetic portrait of the *pachuco* in his 1969 poem "El Louie," a text literary critic Juan Bruce-Novoa calls the "clearest expression of the paradigm of Chicano literature" (1982, 14). Employing *caló*, the poet sings an elegy at the passing of "un vato de atolle" (a really together dude): the remarkable Louie Rodríguez. El Louie cuts a figure of pachuco cool in the small town of Fowler before being shipped off to the Korean War. After an uneven military career, Louie returns to hock his bronze star "for pisto" in the local cocktail lounges (175) while the "booze and vida dura" do Louie in, leaving him "slim and drawn, / there toward the end" (174). The poet concludes: "The end was a cruel hoax. / But his life had been / remarkable!" – enjambment underscores the extraordinary quality of El Louie – before affirming finally: "Vato de atolle, el Louie Rodríguez" (176). This last phrase, signaling respect and esteem for the departed, becomes Louie's epitaph. Despite neglect, abuse, discrimination, and exploitation, the *pachuco* represents self-empowerment and self-identification on one's own terms. The willful self-creation inherent in the performance of the *pachuco* underscores the importance of self-determination, self-definition, and self-respect that beats at the heart of *chicanismo*.

For this reason, raúlsalinas writes "Homenaje al Pachuco" (Mirrored Reflections), a scathing parody of academic fashion. Addressing the *pachuco*, the poet bemusedly reports how he is described in scholarship: "you are (¡ja-ja, que lucas!): / a non-goal oriented, / alienated being, / sufriendo un

'identity-crisis,' / rejecting conventional modes & mores. / ¡Me la Rayo!"
(1976, 151). The poet expresses his impatience with the objectification of the
pachuco ("ha ha, how crazy! / …. / I swear to it!"), since, in the end,
positioning him as a curious object of study from the past obscures the
present reality of continued Chicano incarceration and the unending social
disavowal of poor Chicano communities. The poet ends by noting that
society doesn't care for hungry children or unemployed migrants, much less
for the "street-corner born, / forlorn fugitives / of the total jail / Hail
Pachuco!" (153). The internal rhyme of these lines draws to a close the poet's
critique of the university's erasure of the living *pachuco* and, significantly,
pachuca "who also bears the brunt" of social exclusion and pressure.

The poet literally hails the *pachuco*, but also hails the subjectivity of the
pachuco as being still present and evident among the young gangsters, the
vatos locos, the lowriders, and anyone else *quien anda en el desmadre*, who
walks amid the bitter chaos and struggle of life on the streets and in the
prisons. The *pachuco* occupies an existential position, stylishly rejecting the
society that refutes him while asserting social alienation as an ethical
response to deeply imbedded injustices and inequalities. Incorporating *caló*,
the language of the *pachuco*, and other forms of colloquial or regional speech,
the poetic switching of linguistic codes becomes another element in the
repertoire of *floricanto*. By evoking the wide variety of linguistic forms
present in Chicano expressive culture, the poetry asserts a self-representation
that valorizes the expressive language of the working poor, of the politically
disenfranchised, of the marginalized both socially and culturally. The use of
caló captures for *floricanto* orality as a privileged and creative form of cultural
expression.

Moreover, the orality *in* the poetry underscores the orality *of* the poetry:
the *floricanto* festivals manifested themselves through recitation and declamation. Through oral expression there "reverberates the spirit and the reality
of Chicanos; and the national character, *Chicanismo*, is the permeating refrain
of each *recitación*" (Armas and Zamora 1980, 10). *Floricanto* as participation
between speaker and auditor generates a moment of Chicano affirmation:
the materialization of the Chicano spirit. The use of *caló* in this context
represents an affirmation of origins and originality, a recognition of socioeconomic inequalities beyond the poem that have been indexed by the lexical
generation of a new language. It affirms the life and presence of the *barrio*
itself as the wellspring of Chicano culture. By employing the language of the
streets as part of its poetic evocation, *floricanto* performs its own status as an
authentic embodiment of *chicanismo*.

At another level, by calling up different forms of linguistic expression – some categorized as standard, others regional, some colloquial, some as dialect – *floricanto* evokes a quality of Chicano expressivity that Juan Bruce-Novoa has usefully termed interlingualism. Where bilingualism implies moving from one language code to another, interlingualism is a literary technique that signifies two (or more) languages in a state of tension within a literary text, generating meaning beyond any one of the linguistic codes set in play (1979, 133). Interlingualism as a distinctly multileveled form of expression manifests the unique, ever improvisatory, fluid, playful, and dynamic creativity of Chicano cultural expression.

While the individual poems performed at different *floricanto* festivals vary in theme, tone, and form, the dominant and most dramatic sensibility shared by many is of the organic intellectual speaking the truths of the streets. Be he or she performing the role of the poetic visionary or the political revolutionary, the poet responds to the colonized conditions of the people, *la gente*. More centrally, the *floricanto* poets were *la gente*: "Many Chicanos have discovered art within the Chicano movement; many have discovered personal truths about the meaning of art on picket lines, at meetings, and at demonstrations. Chicanos have discovered universal truths and meaning when they were most themselves. Some of them, those included in the present anthology and others, are turning the historical experiences of the struggle into literature" (Segade 1976, 4). *Floricanto* poetry arises organically from the people in struggle; the literature becomes the very embodiment of the Chicano movement.

Police surveillance and brutality, imprisonment, drug abuse, and unemployment haunted the community, representing the unjust conditions the movement sought to reverse. It is the voice of the community that speaks through the poet's words to address these issues. Convict or (in *caló*) *pinto* poetry marks the embodied interpenetration between the lives of the authentic *barrio* and the grassy campuses of the poetic festivals. Prisoners who became poets, poets made prisoners, bring to *floricanto* the voice of the street, the voice of the prison yard. They thematize the continuity between injustices in the *barrio* and penal institutions where the inequalities and prejudices of society are brutally laid bare.

The most recognizable *pinto* poets – Ricardo Sánchez and raúlsalinas – contributed to the first *Festival de Flor y Canto* in 1973. In his brief offhand remarks before reading, raúlsalinas chuckles that in two weeks he will have been *"en la libre"* for a year ("Raúl R. Salinas reads"). The prison within Chicano poetic expression comes to represent the embodiment of industrialization, control, and technological emptiness. The violence, rigidity, sterility, and murderous environment of the prison makes it the crystallization of contemporary American society. *Pinto* poetry illuminates and scrutinizes the underside of American power from an experiential perspective. Once, if ever, out of the prison system, the *pinto* remains socially, economically, and educationally marginalized.

Yet the *pinto* is decidedly not a powerless victim. Through the enactment of poetry, the *pinto* comes to perform as an organic intellectual and proto-guerrilla. As an example, raúlsalinas conveys in his poem "Canto (just for the hell of it)" how the convicts hid scared in their jailhouse of terror until the mountains of brick and bars of steel, "were pulverized/internalized/ & CRYSTALIZED" with the help of the voice of rebellion. The jailhouse is at once utterly destroyed but also persistently internalized (1976, 155). It is also "CRYSTALIZED" – in a startlingly effective invocation of concrete poetry – at once conveying the solidity and transparency of the prison-industrial system made an object of critical scrutiny (with the aid of the voice of rebellion). So the *pinto* poet is both emblem of the *barrio* as an index of authenticity and the new voice of rebellion that articulates a poetics of resistance.

Floricanto poets could also become something of Amerindian visionaries. Alurista's 1971 poetry collection *Floricanto en Aztlán* opens with an epigraph from Carlos Castaneda's *The Teachings of Don Juan*, the controversial and popular account of Castañeda's apprenticeship under the tutelage of a Yaqui visionary. As poet, Alurista places the teachings of the mystic Don Juan in a textualized position of authority, foregrounding the spiritually transformative aspects of the Chicano movement in conjunction with its strongly political aspects of social activism. The spiritual dimension of *floricanto* is clearly on Alurista's mind when considering the aesthetic and ethical implications of Chicano poetry: "Flower and song will humanize, teach, and gladden the heart and face of nations, bringing them closer to creation, the Creator, and to themselves through the movement and the measure that cause harmony-periodicity, dialectic relationship among nations giving rise thusly to the unity of all beings." (1977, 56–57). The union of the spirit quest with a successful transformation of national relations signals the depth of possibility envisioned through the transformative powers of *floricanto*.

In another register, the *floricanto* poet could perform less the role of mystical visionary and more the revolutionary bard urging collective struggle. A strong, politically-tinged declamation, consequently, is a regular feature among *floricanto* poetics. Miguel Lerma Macias writes an exhortation in "U.F.W. Sufrir ya no" (U[nited]. F[arm]. W[orkers]. Suffer no more) in which he recognizes that the "pobre raza" suffers and waits but encourages the United Farm Workers leaders César Chávez and Dolores Huerta to continue their efforts on the workers' behalf (1979, 107). Bernice Zamora pens "The Sovereign: For Cesar Chavez" in which she tells us to, "Behold the man whose / bones are pillars that / sustain the world" (1979, 44). Diction and tone stilted, the admiration for Chávez's heroic humility rings sincere.

The poets look beyond struggles for justice in the fields close to home and consider the Chicano condition in an international context. Juan Gómez-Quiñones, academic and once young poet, pens an homage to the Latin American revolutionary hero Che Guevarra, "Octubre, 1967, A Che" (1976, 78). Jorge González writes the memorial "A Salvador Allende," recollecting the Marxist Chilean president who died in a 1973 military coup backed by the U.S. government. González ends his poem with the traditional revolutionary exclamation: "¡Adelante para siempre / y siempre hasta la victoria!" (Always forward / and always to victory!) (1976, 90). The literature makes plain its commitment "to the struggle of the wretched of the earth" (Segade 1976, 3). The poetry of *floricanto* evokes the presence of the political in a number of different registers, be it agribusiness pressures that sustain the exploitation of migrant workers in the fields or imperialist manipulations by the CIA on the international stage. The poet variously plays the role of educator, supporter, visionary, revolutionary, and spirit guide.

Given the numerous pressures exerted on *floricanto* poetry in terms of its ethical, political, critical, and educational intentions, it should not be surprising that the poetry came to reach certain ideological and artistic limitations. The declamatory style, the return to Aztec symbology, the exhausting demands for authenticity of voice limited the range of poetic expression and came, finally, to be seen as stylistically archaic (Binder 1985, 198). Simultaneously, the ideological demands that the poetry must educate about various forms of oppression, recuperate lost forms of knowledge, and inspire social transformation weighed heavily. Artistic expression, in order to be meaningful for *chicanismo*, had to generate a socially relevant form of work. Yet poets as artists and not only activists felt that the insistent clarion call to serve the *barrio* constrained their craft and art. Indirectly addressing this issue, the editors of the third *floricanto* anthology recognize that – while the "national character" of *chicanismo* emerges through oral recitation – "Originality and independence of expression are still within the realm of this national art as it is practiced and enjoyed by Chicanos throughout Aztlán" (Armas and Zamora 1980, 10). The sentence reflects an anxiety about the poetry as a public "national art" that yet allows for individuality in aesthetic expression. The relation of individual art to the collective endeavor of *chicanismo* generated some significant schisms.

Some formulations of *chicanismo* gave voice to patriarchal privilege, *machismo*, and homophobia as well as racism and xenophobia. Critic Angie Chabram-Dernersesian has encapsulated the charge against a certain version of Chicano nationalism that equated revolutionary Chicano power with *machismo* and betrayal, weakness and deception with *malinchismo* (1992, 83). Malinalli, Doña Marina, or La Malinche are names given to Hernán Cortés's indigenous translator. Because she is cast as a traitor to her Mexican people, *malinchismo* is the worst kind of betrayal in Mexican and Chicano culture, a *malinchista* the ultimate traitor.

By associating national betrayal with a female figure and revolutionary power with heterosexual male figures, a form of *chicanismo* generated divisions not easily resolved. In one cantering stanza, raúlsalinas refers to the university-trained career woman as, "la Mujer / de ayer / que se dice ser / my 'sensitive.' Ms. Carrerista / proud Feminista / to you ... RoAcH" (1976, 156). The woman from yesterday who they say is very sensitive – pointedly referring to herself as Ms. Careerist and a proud feminist, while referring to the poet as a roach – embodies a betrayal of *chicanismo* in pursuit of individual independent success through education. Expressing similar distrust toward institutions of higher learning, Ricardo Sánchez sees withdrawing from social struggle, "al estilo / de profesores / de Yale o Stanford" (in the style / of professors / from Yale or Stanford) (1980, 135), as a perversity. Educational institutions as sites that disrupt commitment to *barrio* or *familia* become objects of suspicion. An elaborate discourse about traditional Mexican family structures undergirds the criticism evident in the poems. Consequently, if one dimension of the *floricanto* festivals was to generate the spirit of *chicanismo*, conversations about the contributive role that Chicanas could play in *chicanismo* were not evident.

About a quarter of the presenters at the festivals were Chicana poets; female voices were certainly not absent from the events. However, gender as a contested category does not emerge as a concern and is instead subsumed within other discourses. Juanita Salas, for example, associates in "Voz mestiza" the Indian woman's voice with a passivity and tranquility that lends the night its tenderness. The Chicana, with her mixed *india* and *española* blood, needs to be reminded not to succumb to passivity but rather engage with social struggle. The poet turns to the "indito de mi alma [the little Indian of my soul]" prompting her "not leave for tomorrow what you can do today"

(1979, 102). Rather than address gender as a critical category worthy of analysis, the mestiza poet bespeaks a racist construct of Indigenous women as passive, tranquil, and at one with nature.

Gender, while not a privileged category of inquiry, reveals itself in a number of instances. In Sergio Elizondo's "Ruca Firme Liberated" (Liberated Cool Chick) the male speaker recalls his lover expressing her absolute independence while also proclaiming her unending devotion to him; she wants to be free, but never without her man (1976, 70). Alfredo González in "A la Chicana" addresses a woman he imagines as a cup made not of alabaster or crystal but clay, with the color of her skin drawn from "la tierra madre" that reflects the endurance and strength "de la mujer Chicana" (1976, 83). These constructs of "the Chicana woman" drawn from "mother earth" render her a passive being linked to irrational realms of nature, spirit, and emotion.

The phrase "la mujer Chicana" proves telling. While "Chicano" can stand alone as a noun, the word "Chicana" functions as an adjective. The articulation of Chicana as a subjectivity in *floricanto* does not find voice. Chabram-Dernersesian addresses the manner in which this textualized erasure removes Chicanas from "full-scale participation in the Chicano movement as fully embodied, fully empowered U.S. Mexican female subjects" (1992, 83). Since *floricanto* manifests *chicanismo*, its representation of the Chicano as male, empowered, revolutionary and potent leads to the exclusion of a Chicana subjectivity. Chicano names the radical new subjectivity being born into history by the Chicano movement; but Chicano subsumes "the Chicana into a universal ethnic subject that speaks with the masculine instead of the feminine and embodies itself in a Chicano male." (1992, 82). *Chicanismo*, some felt, needed a way to convey strength and pride while rejecting its more troubling, paternalistic, and patriarchal aspects. Difference within identity becomes a new tenet for *chicanismo*.

Two of the *floricanto* poets who innovatively took up this task were Bernice Zamora and Lorna Dee Cervantes. As participants, they each engaged the *floricanto* repertoire in their poetry, drawing from different colors of its discursive palette. Zamora, for example, contributes in 1977 the engaging narrative poem "Chicana in New York Report" where the Chicana recounts an alienating trip that leaves her "conquered, again, again" (1980, 153). At one point, she finds herself on the street viewing an electronic billboard across which "the Chicana saw flashing pictures / of dead presidents, white women, and white children / of different decades – no Chicanos and only one / black woman in the whole historical panorama"

(1980, 155). The poet thematizes her alienation through a lens of colonization as a historico-social continuum erasing people of color from the national narrative.

Cervantes offers "Self-Portrait" to the 1977 festival. This delightfully self-referential piece deploys familiar Aztec religious iconography, but in a wickedly witty act of appropriation. The poet envisions herself as the female side of Ometeotl, the androgynous supreme creator god associated with duality. The poet claims that Quetzalcoatl, the ancient Mesoamerican plumed serpent god associated with culture and wisdom, "has his sex in me. His long cock / is a soft pink plume of subtle poetry" (1980, 55). The poet transforms the god's long phallus – an extreme manifestation of *chicanismo's* Aztec-themed priapic masculinity – into a soft and pink feather. This feminized phallus becomes a representation of "subtle" poetry. The speaker slyly positions herself the supreme creator in the poem, controlling and feminizing the fetishized Aztec imagery of masculinist Mexican and Chicano nationalisms and countering the aesthetics of the more rhetorically blunt forms of *floricanto* artistry.

Zamora (with yet another *floricanto* alumnus, José Antonio Burciaga) in 1976 published a doubled-sided collection of poetry and drawings titled *Restless Serpents*. The title's oblique reference to Queztalcoatl and the cover design of a stylized plumed serpent reflect a familiar Aztec religious iconography. The poems begin on an appropriately spiritual note, recalling the Easter celebrations of the *penitentes* – a religious brotherhood with practices deriving from the Middle Ages – and trace a renewed though ambiguous spiritual journey (Bruce-Novoa 1982, 182–83). The poet recalls hearing in the ancient Spanish hymns "uncoil wailing tongues / of Nahuatl converts" forced by the conquering Spanish to embrace Christianity (1976, 8). Set against this recollection of colonial violence, the poet expresses a profound spiritual yearning the ceremony has awakened, but conceives of this spirituality in terms of nature, "to swim / arroyos and know their estuaries / where, for one week, all is sacred in the valley" (ibid.). The quest for spiritual renewal, but one not lashed to the bloody history of Catholicism in the new world, drives the poetic imagination through a series of poems, many that resonate with the *floricanto* repertoire. The poet employs this repertoire – a critique of the soullessness of wealth, homages to colorful locals (often powerful women) who populate the poetic *barrio* of the poet's mind – in order to offer a vision of spiritual renewal linked to the sacredness of the valley's natural beauty.

By the last poem, "Restless Serpents," the snakes represent the restless, creative, fecund spirit of creation. This spirit can be soothed through the creation of poetry, but they also bring with them new, transformative, and devastating transformations that lay waste those destructive and delimiting aspects of the poet's journey including patriarchal privilege. A recognition of the duality inherent in the conjoining of destruction and creation echoes the Aztec philosophical underpinnings of *floricanto* itself. Zamora's poetic expression incorporates some of the classic poetics of *floricanto* while asserting an independent Chicana subjectivity and articulating a distinctly Chicana poetic voice.

A similar claim can be made for Lorna Dee Cervantes. She was deeply engaged in various social, labor, and political movements in the 1970s when she realized her poetry could be both an organizing tool and a means by which to explore her personal history (Mish 2012, 201). In 1976, even as she continued crafting her poetry, Cervantes began publishing poems written by other San Francisco Bay Area artists using a small printing press once used to make pizza menus for side money. Inspired by the moral imperative of her political commitments (to the National Organization for Women, to the Chicano Moratorium, to labor unions), Cervantes saw that their creative collective empowerment was possible by publishing the work of artists she admired in addition to her own efforts (Mish 2012, 203). Mango Publications, one of several significant poetic journals, was born.

In 1979 Cervantes and Gary Soto, another young Chicano in the Bay Area poetry scene, combined their literary sensibilities and began to publish the Chicano Chapbook Series. Small but stylish chapbooks printed poems by Orlando Ramirez (who helped with the publication of *Mango*). Other esteemed and influential poets published in the Chapbook series were Luis Omar Salinas, Alberto Ríos, Sandra Cisneros, and Jimmy Santiago Baca. *Mango* published poetry by Ray Gonzalez, Wendy Rose, Bernice Zamora, Ricardo Sanchez, and José Antonio Burciaga (Cervantes 2006). Around Burciaga and his wife Cecilia turned a Chicano poetic world at Stanford University populated by Juan Felipe Herrera, Francisco X. Alarcón, Víctor Martínez (they formed the collective *Poetas Humanos* that produced the literary magazine *Humanizarte*) along with Lucha Corpi, Gary Soto, and many others (Alarcón 2014).

In 1981, Pittsburgh University Press published Cervantes's own profoundly influential book. *Emplumada*, awarded the American Book Award, offers an antipatriarchal vision of Chicana empowerment. Not at all distancing herself from the progressive social or spiritual dimensions of *chicanismo*, Cervantes nevertheless presents an aesthetically challenging, powerfully articulated, Chicana-focused vision profoundly resonant with its message about sexual abuse, exploitation, racial discrimination, and collective survival. Combined, Zamora, Cervantes, and their circles significantly impacted the breadth and depth of Chicano poetry on formal and thematic levels across regions and decades.

Through the collective efforts of many, the moral imperative that served to make *floricanto* the poetic, aesthetic, and cultural manifestation of liberatory social consciousness remains a dynamic and productive impetus for Chicano poetry. The first Latino to serve as the United States Poet Laureate, Juan Felipe Herrera, developed his poetry from the ethical and egalitarian principles of *floricanto*. The cultural traditions embodied by *floricanto* form chains and ribbons for new as yet unimagined Chicana and Chicano poetics. From its own contradictions, *floricanto* continues to grow new, multiple, and innovative forms for expressing critically engaged, aesthetically adventurous, and socially relevant Chicana/o poetry.

WORKS CITED

Alarcón, Francisco X. 2014. "A Poem for Víctor Martínez and Some Rememberances." www.facebook.com/notes/francisco-x-alarcon/a-poem-for-v%C3%ADctor-mart%C3%ADnez-and-some-remembrances-by-francisco-x-alarcón/10152217844345734. Accessed Dec. 14, 2015.

Alurista (Alberto Urista). 1971. *Floricanto en Aztlán*. Los Angeles, CA: Chicano Cultural Center.

1976. *Festival de Flor y Canto: An Anthology of Chicano Literature from the Festival Held March 12–16, 1975, Austin, Texas*. Alberto Urista, ed. Los Angeles: University of Southern California Press.

1977. "La estética indígena a través del floricanto de Nezahualcoyotl." *Revista Chicano-Requeña* 5.2: 48–62.

1979. "Introduction." *Festival de Flor y Canto II: An Anthology of Chicano Literature from the Festival Held March 12–16, 1975, Austin, Texas*. Albuquerque, NM: Pajarito Publications, pp. 13–15.

Armas, José and Beatriz Zamora. 1980. "Introduction." *Festival de Flor y Canto IV and V: An Anthology of Chicano Literature from the Festivals Held in Albuquerque, New Mexico, 1977, and Tempe, Arizona, 1978*. Albuquerque, NM: Pajarito Publications, pp. 10–11.

Binder, Wolfgang. 1985. *Partial Autobiographies: Interviews with Twenty Chicano Poets*. Erlangen, Germany: Palm and Enke.

Bruce-Novoa, Juan. 1979. "The Other Voice of Silence: Tino Villanueva." *Modern Chicano Writers: A Collection of Critical Essays*. Joseph Sommers and Tomás Ybarra-Frausto, eds. Englewood Cliffs, NJ: Prentice-Hall, pp. 133–40.

1982. *Chicano Poetry: A Response to Chaos*. Austin: University of Texas Press.

Candelaria, Cordelia. 1986. *Chicano Poetry: A Critical Introduction*. Westport, CT: Greenwood Press.

Cervantes, Lorna Dee. 1980. "Self-Portrait." *Festival de Flor y Canto IV and V: An Anthology of Chicano Literature from the Festivals Held in Albuquerque, New Mexico, 1977, and Tempe, Arizona, 1978*. Albuquerque, NM: Pajarito Publications.

1981. *Emplumada*. Pittsburgh, PA: University of Pittsburgh Press.

2006. "Mango Publications – 30 Years Ago Today." http://lornadice .blogspot.com/2006/ 07/mango-publications-30-years-ago-today.html. Accessed Dec. 14, 2015.

Chabram-Dernersesian, Angie. 1992. "'I Throw Punches for My Race, but I Don't Want to Be a Man.'" *Cultural Studies*. Lawrence Grossberg, ed. New York: Routledge, 1992, 81–96.

Domínguez, Marco Antonio. 1976. "Mi Hijo." *Festival de Flor y Canto: An Anthology of Chicano Literature from the Festival Held March 12–16, 1975, Austin, Texas*. Alberto Urista, ed. Los Angeles: University of Southern California Press, pp. 66–67.

Elizondo, Sergio. 1976. "Ruca Firme Liberated." *Festival de Flor y Canto: An Anthology of Chicano Literature from the Festival Held March 12–16, 1975, Austin, Texas*. Alberto Urista, ed. Los Angeles: University of Southern California Press, p. 70.

Festival de Flor y Canto II: An Anthology of Chicano Literature from the Festival Held March 12–16, 1975, Austin, Texas. 1979. Albuquerque, NM: Pajarito Publications.

Festival de Flor y Canto IV and V: An Anthology of Chicano Literature from the Festivals Held in Albuquerque, New Mexico, 1977, and Tempe, Arizona, 1978. 1980. Albuquerque, NM: Pajarito Publications.

Gómez-Quiñones, Juan. 1976. "Octubre, 1967, A Che." *Festival de Flor y Canto: An Anthology of Chicano Literature from the Festival Held March 12–16, 1975, Austin, Texas*. Alberto Urista, ed. Los Angeles: University of Southern California Press, p. 78.

1990. *Chicano Politics: Reality and Promise, 1940–1990*. Albuquerque: University of New Mexico Press.

González, Alfredo. 1976. "A la Chicana." *Festival de Flor y Canto: An Anthology of Chicano Literature from the Festival Held March 12–16, 1975, Austin, Texas*. Alberto Urista, ed. Los Angeles: University of Southern California Press, p. 83.

González, Jorge. 1976. "A Salvador Allende." *Festival de Flor y Canto: An Anthology of Chicano Literature from the Festival Held March 12–16, 1975, Austin, Texas*. Alberto Urista, ed. Los Angeles: University of Southern California Press, p. 90.

Gonzales, Rudolfo "Corky." 1972. *I am Joaquín. Yo Soy Joaquín*. New York: Bantam Books.

Lerma Macias, Miguel. 1979. "U.F.W. Sufrir ya no." *Festival de Flor y Canto II: An Anthology of Chicano Literature from the Festival Held March 12–16, 1975, Austin, Texas*. 1979. Albuquerque, NM: Pajarito Publications, p. 107.

Mish, Jeanetta Calhoun. 2012. "A Conversation with Poet Lorna Dee Cervantes." *Stunned into Being: Essays on the Poetry of Lorna Dee Cervantes*. Eliza Rodríguez y Gibson, ed. San Antonio, TX: Wings Press, pp. 196–209.

Montoya, José. 1972. "El Louie." *Literatura Chicana: Texto y Contexto/Chicano Literature: Text and Context*. Antonia Castañeda Shular, Tomás Ybarra-Frausto, and Joseph Sommers, eds. Englewood Cliffs, NJ: Prentice-Hall, 1972, pp. 173–76.

1980. "Until They Leave Us a Loan." *Festival de Flor y Canto IV and V: An Anthology of Chicano Literature from the Festivals Held in Albuquerque, New Mexico, 1977, and Tempe, Arizona, 1978*. Albuquerque, NM: Pajarito Publications, pp. 106–108.

Pérez-Torres, Rafael. 1995. *Movements in Chicano Poetry: Against Myths, Against Margins*. New York: Cambridge University Press.

Salas, Juanita. 1979. "Voz mestiza." *Festival de Flor y Canto II: An Anthology of Chicano Literature from the Festival Held March 12–16, 1975, Austin, Texas*. 1979. Albuquerque, NM: Pajarito Publications, pg. 102.

Saldaña-Portillo, María Josefina. 2001. "Who's the Indian in Aztlán? Re-Writing Mestizaje, Indianism, and Chicanismo from the Lacadón." *The Latin American Subaltern Studies Reader*. Ileana Rodríguez, ed. Durham, NC: Duke University Press, pp. 402–23.

Salinas, Raúl (raúlsalinas). 1973. "Raúl R. Salinas Reads from his Works, 1973." U.S.C Digital Library.

    1976. "Canto (Just for the Hell of It)." *Festival de Flor y Canto: An Anthology of Chicano Literature*. Alurista, et al., eds. Los Angeles: University of Southern California Press, pp. 155–57.

    1976. "Homenaje al Pachuco (Mirrored Reflections)." *Festival de Flor y Canto: An Anthology of Chicano Literature*. Alurista, et al., eds. Los Angeles: University of Southern California Press, pp. 151–53.

Sánchez, Ricardo. 1980. "III." *Festival de Flor y Canto IV and V: An Anthology of Chicano Literature from the Festivals Held in Albuquerque, New Mexico, 1977, and Tempe, Arizona, 1978*. Albuquerque, NM: Pajarito Publications, p. 135.

Segade, Gustavo. 1976. "An Introduction to Floricanto." *Festival de Flor y Canto: An Anthology of Chicano Literature*. Alurista, et al., eds. Los Angeles: University of Southern California Press, pp. 1–5.

U.S.C Digital Library. http://digitallibrary.usc.edu/cdm/collections. Accessed Dec. 14, 2015.

Zamora, Bernice. 1976. *Restless Serpents*. Menlo Park, CA: Diseños Literarios.

    1979. "Metaphor and Reality." *Festival de Flor y Canto II: An Anthology of Chicano Literature from the Festival Held March 12–16, 1975, Austin, Texas*. 1979. Albuquerque, NM: Pajarito Publications, p. 43.

    1979. "The Sovereign: For Cesar Chavez." *Festival de Flor y Canto II: An Anthology of Chicano Literature from the Festival Held March 12–16, 1975, Austin, Texas*. 1979. Albuquerque, NM: Pajarito Publications, p. 44.

    1980. "Chicana in New York Report: To Chicano Fellows Stanford University." *Festival de Flor y Canto IV and V: An Anthology of Chicano Literature from the Festivals Held in Albuquerque, New Mexico, 1977, and Tempe, Arizona, 1978*. Albuquerque, NM: Pajarito Publications, pp. 153–55.

19

"The Geography of Their Complexion"

Nuyorican Poetry and Its Legacies

URAYOÁN NOEL

in memory of Juan Flores (1943–2014)

Nuyorican poetry is written and/or performed by New York Puerto Rican poets affiliated with or in the tradition of the Nuyorican Poets Cafe, a performance space and cultural center on the Lower East Side of Manhattan founded by Miguel Algarín and others circa 1973. Although heterogeneous in form and content, many Nuyorican poems explore the limits of the page and the performed word, often mixing English and Spanish and animated by an irreverent and decolonial sensibility. Its boundaries are porous, as the earliest Nuyorican poems predate the Nuyorican Poets Cafe, and as it has influenced a range of contemporary performance-oriented poetics (such as slam poetry). Nuyorican poems and poets were central to the Puerto Rican Movement of the 1960s and 1970s and to the formation and evolution of Latina/o studies. More recently, they have been crucial to the emergence of diaspora and Afro-latinidad as key terms in Latina/o studies through the widely influential work of the late Juan Flores: a poem such as Felipe Luciano's influential "Jibaro/My Pretty Nigger" (1968) spans these contexts, having been performed in the film *Right On! The Original Last Poets* (1970) and on Eddie Palmieri's *Live at Sing Sing* album (1972) and excerpted in Flores and Miriam Jiménez Román's *The Afro-Latin@ Reader* (2010). Ultimately, the history and legacy of Nuyorican poetry also involve poetry's intimate relationship to music, theater, visual art, fiction, and other expressive cultural forms in mapping the complex and evolving spatial politics of the Puerto Rican diaspora.

In essays such as "Nuyorican Literature" (1981) and in his introduction to the foundational *Nuyorican Poetry: An Anthology of Puerto Rican Words and Feelings* (1975), coedited with Miguel Piñero, Algarín develops a sophisticated poetics and cultural politics of survival and struggle, of a community's evolution and its modes of resistance and healing. Algarín argues for a poetics that can "verbalize the stresses of street experience" ("Introduction" 14), documenting urban struggle in a way that creates a new reality instead of simply reflecting the current one, as is the case with the term "Nuyorican," which was used pejoratively on the island of Puerto Rico to refer to the supposed inauthenticity of New York Puerto Ricans, but which is reclaimed by Algarín, Piñero, and their peers in an act of poetic and political revisionism (Hernandez 39–40). Thus, in Algarín's most famous poem "A Mongo Affair," included in the *Nuyorican Poetry* anthology, the speaker exclaims "I am in the minority everywhere" yet affirms being one of "the original men and women of this island" (*Survival* 42) and eschews a fixed linguistic and/or geographic understanding of identity, instead affirming Nuyorican-ness bilingually in terms of "feelings" (43) and "el poder de realizarme" (the power of fulfilling myself) (44).

Algarín's framing of Nuyorican identity in affect-loaded and translingual/translocal terms dovetails with the spatial politics of *Loisaida*, a term that refers to the Lower East Side of Manhattan as performatively rendered into Nuyorican Spanish/Spanglish by poet Bimbo Rivas and activist Chino García and popularized by Rivas's poem "Loisaida" (1974), which describes the neighborhood in Puerto Rican and transcultural terms: "una mezcla, la perfecta / una gente bien decente / de todas rasas [*sic*]" (a mix, the perfect one / a most decent people / of all races) (361). As a creative response to urban neglect and an affirmation of poor and working-class voices (Ševčenko 296), Rivas and García's Loisaida informs the survivalist poetics of urban struggle of the *Nuyorican Poetry* anthology, where Rivas's poetry is included and García is invoked as a model (24). Specifically, Algarín foregrounds the urban-ecological activism pioneered by García as part of The Real Great Society, a 1960s collective that sought utopian alternatives to hegemonic Great Society liberalism and that prefigured García's leadership of the organization/cultural center CHARAS/El Bohío.

Loisaida arguably provides the spatial logic for a poem that embodies Algarín's survivalist street poetics: Miguel Piñero's "A Lower East Side Poem," included in *Nuyorican Poetry* and in Piñero's *La Bodega Sold Dreams* (1980). In this, Piñero's most famous poem and a landmark of Nuyorican poetry, the speaker locates the Lower East Side "from Houston to 14th Street / from Second Avenue to the mighty D" (*Outlaw* 4), whereas the historical Lower East Side encompasses a larger area, south to around Canal Street. Piñero's Lower East Side thus exemplifies Edward Soja's concept of Thirdspace as "*fully lived* space, a simultaneously real-and-imagined, actual-and-virtual locus of structured individual and collective experience and agency"

(11) distinct from both Firstspace (the "real" inasmuch as mappable urban space of the Nuyorican barrio) and Secondspace (the "imagined" space of the barrio as represented in urban renewal projects or the work of Brooklyn College-based anthropologist Oscar Lewis). Celebrating the "hustlers" and "faggots and freaks" who "get high / on the ashes" scattered throughout the Lower East Side (4), Piñero understands how (as Soja suggests) Firstspace is mediated through Secondspace, inasmuch as the speaker claims to be "a cancer of Rockefeller's ghettocide" (5), a figure of resistance to the centralized urban development initiatives of the 1960s and early 1970s, projects that effectively displaced working-class neighborhoods of color in urban areas across the United States. In embodying a poetic Thirdspace, Nuyorican poets document a mappable space but they also perform a critical revision of urban space as ideologically defined and confined, revealing instead what Pedro Pietri calls in his foundational "Puerto Rican Obituary" (1968), "the geography of their complexion" (Pietri 10). Although typically and understandably read through the lens of 1960s cultural nationalism, Pietri's poem also locates its decolonial politics in an existential and spiritual geography, in a Thirdspace where diasporic Puerto Ricans can "communicate with their latino souls" even in the midst of the "nervous breakdown streets."

While Pietri's poem – first published in the Young Lords Party's newsletter *Palante*, then performed during their 1969 occupation of what would become the People's Church in East Harlem, and included on his 1971 live album *Aqui Se Habla Español: Pedro Pietri en Casa Puerto Rico* and in his first book *Puerto Rican Obituary* (1973) – predates the rise of the Nuyorican Poets Cafe, it is widely regarded as the quintessential Nuyorican epic. Its staging of the death-in-life of Puerto Ricans in Harlem, where Pietri settled with his family as a young child, embodies Nuyorican poetry's complex spatial politics, caustically depicting their spiritual death while memorializing and affirming their struggle:

> Here lies Juan
> Here lies Miguel
> Here lies Milagros
> Here lies Olga
> Here lies Manuel
> who died yesterday today
> and will die again tomorrow
> Always broke
> Always owing
> Never knowing

> that they are beautiful people
> Never knowing
> the geography of their complexion
>
> PUERTO RICO IS A BEAUTIFUL PLACE
> PUERTORRIQUENOS ARE A BEAUTIFUL RACE
> (9–10, uppercase in the original)

The Puerto Rican "race" emerges here not as a biological or "color" category, but rather as an embodied history, and the "place" of Puerto Rico is similarly revised beyond discrete island geographies so as to map the streets of Harlem. "Never knowing" becomes a condition of possibility for Pietri's utopian affirmation of an "aqui" [sic] or "here" where Spanish can be spoken without the interruption of "soap commercials" and "tv dinners" and "where you do not need a dictionary / to communicate with your people" (11). Pietri's utopia is a Thirdspace inasmuch as it seeks to map the Firstspace of Puerto Rican Harlem against the ideological distortions of the capitalist state that maps ethnic communities as consumers, and his poem defines geography affectively, attuned to what geographer E. C. Relph calls "existential insideness" – a deep "immersion" (55) in a place that is "experienced without deliberate and self-conscious reflection yet is full with significances" (14) – as an alternative to the alienation of the immigrant. With its lyric depth, vernacular flow, and seemingly spontaneous succession of urban images, Pietri's poem seems perfectly suited to the production of this existential insideness, this immersion, and as such it marks a critical alternative to contemporary texts that sought to map urban Puerto Rican life from the outside, such as anthropologist Lewis's National Book Award-winning *La Vida; A Puerto Rican Family in the Culture of Poverty – San Juan and New York* (1966). A similar insideness animates Afro-Cuban/Puerto Rican writer and performer Piri Thomas's autobiographical novel/memoir *Down These Mean Streets* (1967), a foundational text of Nuyorican literature that was banned by a number of school districts across the country, ironically including on Long Island, where the book's autobiographical narrator moved with his family, only to realize there is no escaping the existential streets. Thomas's streets are those of the speaker's searing self-scrutiny as much as they are those of Harlem.

Works such as Piñero's Tony-nominated and Obie-winning play *Short Eyes* (1974), written while he was incarcerated at Sing Sing, detail how institutions have failed Puerto Ricans and how the system produces institutionalized subjects. Nuyorican poets eschew the ethnographic instrumentality of Lewis, with his penchant for tape-recorded interviews (xii) and his static and deterministic "culture of poverty," which inscribes Latinos as a permanent subculture or underclass even as it prefigures contemporary structural understandings of poverty. In his 1976 book *Tropicalization*, Victor Hernández Cruz, a foundational Puerto Rico-born and New York-raised Nuyorican poet who lived and worked for many years in California, writes mockingly about finding Lewis's tape recorder "behind a pizza shop in the Bronx" (32) and not being able to pawn it. That Cruz's poem depicts Lewis's tape recorder as anathema opposes Nuyorican deterritorializing poetics to Lewis's obsessive archiving. Cruz's "tropicalization" uses synaesthesias to fuse and confuse tropical and northern landscapes, revealing the complexities of diasporic space, as in these lines from *Tropicalization*'s "Airoplain":

> They can keep Puerto Rico just give us
> the guava of independence depending on no bodies tortures dreams
> of the past or future within the present State no State ever of
> things   (77)

In this passage that sidesteps the statehood question and 'glosses C.L.R. James' essay collection, *The Future in the Present* (1977), Cruz imagines independence against the strictly territorial. Rather, the poem locates culture beyond the nation and in the "guava of independence," at the intersection of taste, sight, touch, smell, and especially, sound, as in the poem's frequent alliterations and the wordplay between plain/plane/playin' and Afro-Puerto Rican *plena* music. "Airoplain" thus references the airplane that brought many Puerto Ricans (Cruz among them) to New York in the mid twentieth century, but it also unsettles the linear logic of migration in favor of what Paul Gilroy calls the "fractal" and "rhizomorphic" (4) logic of diaspora. In Latina/o cultural studies, Cruz inspired Frances Aparicio and Susana Chávez-Silverman's influential concept of "tropicalization," understood as "a polydirectional and multivocal approach to the politics of representation, seeking to avoid the pervading binarism in the field and the colonial gaze that essentializes and fetishizes subaltern cultures and privileges dominant ones" (14). Though *Nuyorican* suggests a binary framing, Nuyorican poets have approached questions of culture, politics, and identity from a "tropicalizing" polydirectional perspective, performing new spatial logics against colonial maps and histories and static/statist understandings of identity.

Nuyorican poetry is central to Juan Flores's theorization of a "diaspora from below" in *The Diaspora Strikes Back* (2007). Influenced by Stuart Hall, Flores understands diaspora as attuned to the "grassroots" and the "vernacular" and as an alternative to the transnational elites that dominate the media, arguing that his approach, "guided by a concern for subaltern and everyday life struggles of poor and disenfranchised people, also allows for special insights into ongoing issues of racial identity and gender inequalities that are so often ignored or minimized in the grand narratives of transnational hegemony" (25). In mapping Caribbean Latina/o diasporas, Flores highlights Nuyorican poems that foreground these raced and gendered perspectives, from Tato Laviera's "nuyorican" (in 1985's *AmeRícan*) to María Teresa Mariposa Fernández's "Ode to the Diasporican" (1993). Already in the 1970s, some of the most potent work produced by Nuyorican poets was animated by such perspectives "from below." Flores has written about Afro–Puerto Rican poet Louis Reyes Rivera's debut *Who Pays the Cost* (1977), emphasizing its working-class "monologues" (*Borders* 137), among them the signature autobiographical poem "A Place I Never Seen," which dramatizes Malcolm X's assassination and evokes the speaker's subsequent spiritual awakening and political evolution:

> I was there
> on a sunny harlem sunday
> in a place I never been
> on the 21st of the 2nd
> in a room I can't forget
> on a stage I never seen
> with a man I barely knew
> I saw the bullet
> cry.
> I heard the man fall. (Rivera 29)

Rivera was a student leader during the 1969 takeover of City College by the Black and Puerto Rican Student Union, and he would go on to found and direct Shamal Books, an independent publisher of radical writers of color, while translating revolutionary Puerto Rican poet Clemente Soto Vélez and publishing essays such as "Inside the River of Poetry" (2002), an Afro-diasporic genealogy of socially engaged poetics. He would also influence a younger generation of poets through his teaching and open readings, and through his role as coeditor, with poet Tony Medina, of the anthology *Bum Rush the Page: A Def Poetry Jam* (2001), which features a number of younger Nuyorican-identified poets, while hewing to an Afro-diasporic genealogy much less evident in other anthologies such as Algarín and Bob Holman's *Aloud: Voices from the Nuyorican Poets Cafe* (1994).

Rivera also provided the foreword to Sandra María Esteves's *Yerba Buena* (1980) – along with Lorraine Sutton's landmark, Black-Arts-feminist-inflected

SAYcred LAYdy (1975), perhaps the key text of Nuyorican feminist poetics – foregrounding the organic poetic and political sensibility of its herbal "cantations" (xvii). As Miriam DeCosta-Willis notes, Esteves's *Yerba Buena* is fueled by a "signifying difference," spanning a holistic and cross-media range of "tactile, auditory, and visual images, as well as the allusions to noted singers, musicians, and poets" (6). Esteves, who was trained as a visual artist and whose drawings of plants, landscapes, and women's bodies are featured in the book, was affiliated with the Taller Boricua in East Harlem, a still-extant art space and cultural center that sought to recover and represent aboriginal cultures, what Yasmin Ramírez calls "Afro-Taino Ricanstructions of Puerto Rican icons" (38).

In her poem "Aguacero Inside 'Agua Que Va Caer [*sic*],'" included in *Undelivered Love Poems* (1997) and performed at the Young Lords Party fortieth anniversary in 2009, Esteves's organic poetics at once extends and revises the Young Lords' decolonial movement politics from a diasporic feminist perspective, rewriting largely male-centered "hiss-stories" (*his*-stories) while celebrating the creolized diaspora theorized by Flores:

> Studyin' hiss-stories
> of some other place
> Conflictin' lyfestyles of an alien race
> Not knowin' our original Borinquen names
> Our common ancestors
> African, Arawak and Quisqueya source
> Salutin' someone else's flag
> Prayin' in someone else's church
> *"Te juro que va llover*
> *Agua que va caer"* [*sic*]
> (I swear to you it's gonna rain /
> That water is going to fall) (42)

Here, mapping the geography of the Nuyorican complexion involves a holistic poetics of recovery and affirmation, including the African and the indigenous Caribbean (Arawak). Esteves, who is of Puerto Rican and Dominican descent, makes clear that a decolonial politics (including a consciousness that Boricuas have been forced, before and after 1898, to be "Salutin' someone else's flag") must involve an engagement with a history of crossings beyond Puerto Rico and encompass broader Caribbean and hemispheric geographies ("Quisqueya" is the Taíno name for the island of Hispaniola, and Arawakan peoples have spanned South America and the Caribbean). Thus, Esteves revises Nuyorican poetics from a multifocal and pan-diasporic perspective, emphasizing that the cultures of the Puerto Rican diaspora cannot be properly represented independently of these (African, Arawak) histories. If Pietri's utopia imagines a "BEAUTIFUL RACE," Esteves confronts "Conflictin' lyfestyles of an alien race" by insisting on "common ancestors," yet her poetics is not so much essentialist as attuned to the multiple spatial logics of diasporic difference.

The syncretism of Afro-diasporic spiritual practices is key to *Yerba Buena* poems such as "Oracion (Prayer)" and to Nuyorican poetry more generally, from the allusions to the Mesa Blanca variety of Spiritualism in Pietri's "Puerto Rican Obituary" to the coding of Afro-Latino musicians as griots or oral storytellers in Cruz's debut *Snaps* (1968). As Marta Moreno Vega notes, the Yoruba tradition of the orishas links the Harlem of Amiri Baraka and the Black Arts movement to Jorge Soto and Taller Boricua (249–50) so that black power becomes "a means of confronting the division between the African American and Latino communities" (249). The Indigenous Taíno/ Arawak elements of Caribbean syncretism should not be overlooked; in addition to Esteves, José-Angel Figueroa's *East 110th Street* (1973), published by Detroit's Broadside Press, an important venue for Black Arts poetry, is marked by an Afro-Taíno sensibility and incorporates a Spanish and Taíno glossary, while newer books like Bobby González's *The Last Puerto Rican Indian* (2006) continue these explorations.

DeCosta-Willis highlights the "synesthetic images" (9) that underpin Esteves's signifying differences, and synaesthesia is key to a Nuyorican poetics of diasporic representation since Cruz's *Snaps*, with its Latin-jazz and Latin-boogaloo-inflected poems about musicians such as Ray Barretto and Joe Bataan, who prefigure and will help shape 1970s salsa. Music's capacity to articulate an embodied alternative history is essential to Nuyorican poetry and its critical reception, from "Salsa, Maracas, and Baile: Latin Popular Music in the Poetry of Victor Hernandez Cruz" (1990), where Frances Aparicio considers the relational yet shape-shifting dimensions of Cruz's poetics, to Juan Flores's influential readings of the work of Tato Laviera, a foundational Nuyorican poet who (along with Cruz) constitutes a pioneer in Spanglish poetics, and a major figure in the emerging U.S. Latina/o canon of poetry.

Writing within and against the zeitgeist that produced Latina/o studies as a field, Flores writes about Laviera at various points over the years, emphasizing how his poetry resists assimilation – in the essay "Qué assimilated, brother, yo soy asimilao" from *Divided Borders* – and how music in Laviera's poetry scores the struggle of poor and working-class people while foregrounding the cultural innovations of a diaspora from below. In his introduction to Laviera's *Enclave* (1982), Flores alludes to the bilingual resonances in the title and to the diasporic nuances of its wordplay (*en clave* is Spanish for "in key" and "in rhythm" and the Afro-Cuban *clave* rhythm is central to salsa); Flores suggests that by asking readers to follow the hidden *clave*, Laviera moves them beyond the legibility of the ethnic enclave and toward a popular counterhistory of diasporic crossings.

In "the salsa of bethesda fountain," from his 1979 debut *La Carreta Made a U-Turn*, Laviera explores the "internal soul of salsa" (67), forging connections in "afro-spanish" language between Puerto Rican bomba and plena, the soul of Marvin Gaye, and Cameroonian fusion musician Manu Dibango, who played with salsa supergroup Fania All Stars. These pan-diasporic spatial connections are echoed in the poem's New York geography: Bethesda Fountain in Central Park was the site of Sunday-afternoon Latin music parties throughout the mid 1970s where, Robert Iulo notes, "jazz station WRVR DJ Rodger Dawson's Sunday Salsa Show was played on boom boxes strategically placed around the fountain plaza" (Carlson). The redeployment of jazz-station programming and of Central Park itself toward a community block party embodies Flores's diaspora from below, inasmuch as music-as-radio-commodity is resignified through the grassroots creativity that turns Central Park into the existential insideness of the lived street:

> the internal feelings we release
> when we dance salsa
> is the song of manu dibango
> screaming africa
> as if it were a night in el barrio
> when the congas are out (67)

The internal feelings summoned by salsa bridge not only the distance between Africa, the Caribbean, and New York, but also that between Loisaida and Central Park, between the Nuyorican "enclave" and the New York mainstream, a mainstream that Laviera (who cofounded the community-based organization Loisaida, Inc. in 1979, paving the way for the present-day Loisaida Center and its yearly Loisaida Festival) will seek to remap from a critically revisionist perspective in his 1988 book *Mainstream Ethics/ética corriente*. As with Esteves, Laviera's concluding lines "well, okay, it is a root called africa / in all of us" (68) are not essentialist inasmuch as they evoke what Paul Gilroy famously called the "roots" and "routes" of diaspora (19) in all its "radically unfinished forms" (105).

The radically unfinished quality of Laviera's vernacular forms is emblematic of Nuyorican poetry and its recasting of poetics as an embodied, process-based art invested in what Flores calls "créolité in the hood" (*Diaspora* 26) that he also finds in 1990s poets such as Willie Perdomo and María Teresa Mariposa Fernández. By identifying as Nuyorican, these younger poets are not only affirming their New York Puerto Rican roots, they are also mapping and remapping the diasporic routes of their poetic forebears across and along the embodied city. Nuyoricanness is, then, not just a social identity but also an aesthetic one, defined through performative and translingual embodied acts that constantly retrace the geography of a complexion in a field of differences.

Aparicio outlines some of these differences in her essay "La vida es un Spanglish disparatero: Bilingualism in Nuyorican Poetry" (1988), which takes its title from Laviera. Aparicio and Laviera understand *disparatero* as a Spanish word suggesting "nonsense" or "absurdity" but also as capturing the disparateness of English and Spanish, whose coexistence results in Spanglish practices: Laviera's is not just any Spanish, it is an explicitly and defiantly Afro-diasporic and vernacular translanguage that draws on urban black English to unsettle standard English *and* Spanish. Laviera and other Nuyorican poets will help inspire Ana Celia Zentella's influential "anthro-political linguistics" (1995) as developed in her classic book *Growing Up Bilingual* (1997), where she maps New York Puerto Rican language practices and their complex relationship to African-American Vernacular English, Puerto Rican Spanish, and beyond. Poets such as Laviera and Cruz are also crucial to Doris Sommer's book *Bilingual Aesthetics* (2004), which argues for the political power of language play in the context of a globalized liberalism. Elsewhere, in a 1998 essay, Sommer explores how Laviera's "AmeRícan accents" help "syncopate the state" and thereby imagine a non-monolingual public sphere. Referencing Laviera's most famous poem "AmeRícan," from his 1985 book of the same name, Sommer suggests that Spanglish marks U.S. American space with an accented (Puerto/Nuyo) "Rícan" difference, again pointing away from the discrete ethnic enclave and toward a rooted/routed translocal/hemispheric polis. Laviera's *La Carreta Made a U-Turn* was the first book published by Arte Público Press, which was crucial in shaping a U.S. Latina/o literary canon during the 1980s, yet his Latina/o sensibility is grounded in diasporic differences: there is a section of the book pointedly titled "Loisaida Streets: Latinas Sing" where Laviera is already exploring the raced and gendered struggles of Loisaida from an intersectional perspective. These poems seek to understand Nuyorican-specific histories both from below and in broader Latina/o terms.

The ways in which raced and gendered performance cultures complexly mark the differences between a diasporic Nuyorican tradition and canonical Latina/o histories are already evident in the work of a poet such as Lorraine Sutton. As I note in *In Visible Movement: Nuyorican Poetry from the Sixties to Slam* (2014), Sutton's landmark book *SAYcred LAYdy* (1975) remains largely unknown and out of print despite its status as a foundational Nuyorican feminist text and its acknowledged influence on major poets such as Esteves and Luz María Umpierre. In my book I also read the radical wordplay in *SAYcred LAYdy* in pan-diasporic terms, alongside the jazz-inflected vernacular, syntactical, and typographical experiments of Black Arts feminist poets/ performers such as Sonia Sanchez, and I quote Sutton's description of her poetry readings as high-energy performances often accompanied by salsa instrumentation. Thus, Esteves's neologism "hiss-stories" also evokes Sutton's at once bold, moving, and irony-laced wordplay in *SAYcred LAYdy*, where "hermanos" (brothers) becomes "HER manos" (HER hands) (22). In the largely homosocial context of both salsa and movement politics, Sutton's irreverent performance of gendered difference represents both a triumph of a Nuyorican poetic performance and a radical feminist critique of that same tradition's political limitations.

The link between live music (especially Latin jazz and salsa), artistic experimentation, and new political visions is evident throughout the Nuyorican 1970s. Notably, poets such as Pietri, Esteves, and Américo Casiano, Jr., – founder and artistic director of the NuyoRican School Original Poetry Jazz Ensemble – organized experimental performances in collaboration with the musicians from the legendary avant-garde salsa group Conjunto Libre at a venue called the New Rican Village, founded by former Young Lord Eddie Figueroa and located on Avenue A near the Nuyorican Poets Cafe on 6th Street. As Ed Morales suggests ("Places"), for Figueroa the live performances were key to the New Rican Village, understood less as a fixed space than as a nomadic and affective one, a place "in the heart." Inspired by Figueroa's concept of a "Puerto Rican Embassy" and his vision of a Nuyorican "Spirit Republic," Pietri and the artist ADÁL (Maldonado) developed El Puerto Rican Embassy into a long-running conceptual art and activist project and onto the digital coordinates of the website ElPuertoRicanEmbassy.org.

A shared investment in diasporic practices of revisionist performance links Laviera, Pietri, and the New Rican Village to the younger poets associated with the current Nuyorican Poets Cafe (the original one had closed in the early 1980s; it reopened in its current location on East 3rd Street toward the end of the decade). As Ed Morales notes (2003), the Nuyorican Poets Cafe renaissance of the 1990s was fueled by poet Bob Holman's importation from Chicago of the competitive poetry events known as poetry "slams," with which the cafe has become synonymous, receiving significant mainstream media during the early 1990s, a period of effervescence culminating with the publication of the aforementioned 1994 anthology *Aloud: Voices from the Nuyorican Poets Cafe*, coedited by Algarín and Holman. The majority of the poets included in this anthology are not Puerto Rican, but rather a mix reflective of the broader (and largely hip-hop-influenced) socially conscious multiculturalism of the era; simultaneously, as Morales (2003) observes, this new Nuyorican scene was decried by some at the time as a problematic whitewashing of Loisaida histories in the name of media mainstreaming (and also, eventually, as a harbinger of the neighborhood's gentrification).

A key 1990s Nuyorican poem included in the *Aloud* anthology is Perdomo's "Nigger-Reecan Blues," where, as Flores argues, the speaker's self-scrutiny harks back to the "interracial dilemmas" ("Nueva York" 73) of Piri Thomas's *Down These Mean Streets*: "Yo soy Boricua! Yo soy Africano! I ain't lyin'. Pero / mi pelo is kinky y curly y mi skin no es negro pero it can pass" (*Aloud* 112). Along with Perdomo's poem, included in his debut *Where a Nickel Costs a Dime* (1996) and performed on HBO's *Def Poetry* (2006), another watershed post-1990 Nuyorican poem is Fernández's "Ode to the Diaspor-ican" (1993); both are included in *The Norton Anthology of Latino Literature* (2011) and are central to Flores's theorization of New York as a "diaspora city" (2003) that aims to resist increasingly market-driven Latina/o imagin-aries. With its already classic refrain, "Yo no naci en Puerto Rico / Puerto Rico nacio en mi" (I wasn't born in Puerto Rico / Puerto Rico was born in me) (Stavans 2424), Fernández's poem reflects what Flores calls "defiance of a territorially and socially confined understanding of cultural belonging" ("Nueva York" 73) and thereby embodies the revisionist spatial politics of the Nuyorican poetic tradition.

Flores, Aparicio ("Ethnicity" 28), Maritza Stanchich, and others have used the term "post-Nuyorican" to account for the work of writers temporally (and sometimes spatially) removed from the foundational Nuyorican scene of the 1970s. In their introduction to the anthology *Open Mic/Micrófono Abierto* (2005), Flores and coeditor Mayra Santos-Febres use the term to refer to a diverse second wave of mainland Puerto Rican writers that "had already been visible since the later 1970s and 1980s in the work of such writers as Tato Laviera, Martín Espada, Judith Ortiz Cofer and others" (xi). Among the writers anthologized there are a number of poets who identify as part of the Nuyorican tradition – including Perdomo, Fernández, Bonafide Rojas,

Shaggy Flores, Edwin Torres, Caridad De la Luz "La Bruja," Flaco Navaja, Sandra García Rivera, and Emanuel Xavier – alongside fiction writers such as Abraham Rodriguez, Jr., and Ernesto Quiñónez, whose influential novel *Bodega Dreams* (2000) revisits Nuyorican barrio poetics (its title echoing Piñero's *La Bodega Sold Dreams*) from the perspective of a gentrifying East Harlem ("El Barrio"). Similarly, Perdomo, in his 2003 book *Smoking Lovely*, decries the signs of commodification and exclusion that mark this white-washed barrio: "Coffee chains, T-shirt clubs and ringing taco bells got the magazines saying that our communities are safe and clean" and "the world is getting baggy with brand names and producers are taking hip-hop speak seminars so they can help us keep it real" (24). Some of these younger writers reflect the new demographics of New York City, as in the case of Quiñónez and Emanuel Xavier – an important openly gay voice and the editor of anthologies such as *Bullets & Butterflies: Queer Spoken Word Poetry* (2005) – who are both of Puerto Rican and Ecuadorian descent.

Although the gentrification of East Harlem and the Lower East Side undoubtedly put new kinds of pressures on a poetics of urban representation, these struggles over urban space are not new. Already in his poems "Canción del tecato" (Junkie's Song) and "El apatético" [sic] (The Apathetic One), included in *Borinquen: An Anthology of Puerto Rican Literature* (1974), Jack Agüeros counters the paternalistic discourse and failings of the Great Society and urban renewal. Written in vernacular Puerto Rican Spanish, these poems give voice to those who remain invisible even to a well-meaning liberalism: in the latter poem, the speaker complains about the falling plaster and broken toilet in his house, only to be told to wait because the Model Cities Program is coming, a reference to an initiative of President Lyndon Johnson's War on Poverty widely regarded as a failure, partly for its centralization and unre-sponsiveness to the views of the poor communities it aimed to help (Epstein). While Agüeros is perhaps best known as an activist, for the 1968 hunger strike he staged protesting the lack of Puerto Ricans in Mayor John V. Lindsay's administration and for later directing El Museo del Barrio and translating the poetry of Julia de Burgos, his critiques of how Puerto Ricans, immigrants, and the poor are written out of the very fabric of their own neighborhoods by outside interests anticipate Quiñónez's and Perdo-mo's anti-gentrification texts.

In between the original and current iterations of the Nuyorican Poets Cafe there is a generation of 1980s poets working partly or wholly within the Nuyorican tradition yet also responding to the political tenor of the time: the rise of Reagan and neoliberalism in the United States. The most famous of these poets is Martín Espada, whose reflections on Chile in his 2006 book *The Republic of Poetry*, a Pulitzer Prize finalist, are analyzed by scholar Michael Dowdy in his study *Broken Souths*. Dowdy shows how poets such as Espada challenge the logics of neoliberalism and globalization through poetic counter-genealogies of resistance that invoke various global souths to disrupt hegemonic histories. Espada's "republic" spans his native Puerto Rican Brooklyn and Allende's Chile, inasmuch as both have been shaped by interventionist politics and histories of oppression, but also inasmuch as they embody legacies of struggle and alternative political imaginations.

In the case of Nancy Mercado and Lydia Cortés, two poets with long-time trajectories in the downtown poetry scene, including the Poetry Project at St. Mark's Church, poetry emerges as a critical response to the privatization and resegregation of public space in neoliberal New York, practices that David Harvey foregrounds in his influential analyses of the spatial politics of neoliberalism. Thus, in "Mother Says," a poem from Mercado's book *It Concerns the Madness* (2000) dedicated to *"los desaparecidos"* ("the disappeared"), a mother cries for her disappeared daughter while "condominium prices were negotiated on 5th Avenue" and "black nannies prepared the carriages of white children / To take a stroll along Washington Square Park" (54–55). In connecting state violence in Latin America and capital accumulation, segregation, and gentrification in New York, Mercado, who was instrumental in publishing many younger Nuyorican poets for the first time as a long-time editor of the influential post-Beat journal *Long Shot*, points to a transnational political imagination that understands Nuyorican spatial politics as a strategic site for the critique of global power. Similarly, in her poem "In Honor of a Puerto Rican-American War Hero Dead in Somalia," the diasporic Puerto Rican experience becomes a framework for understanding the limitations of a poetry of witness, inasmuch as "Memories can be replayed over & over / At no corporate expense, / Memories can easily be forgotten as such" (50).

While Mercado's poetics is partly in keeping with the lyric exploration of trauma epitomized in Carolyn Forché's anthology *Against Forgetting: Twentieth-Century Poetry of Witness* (1993), hers is not the U.S. American activist poet heading south, as in the famed Salvadoran Civil War poems from Forché's *The Country Between Us* (1981), or even the hemispheric testimonial lyrics of Chilean American poet Marjorie Agosín, with their insistence on the "persistent tenacity / of remembrance" (67). As a 1980s poet informed by poetics of witness, Mercado summons the political power of memory, but as a poet steeped in the Nuyorican tradition she understands memory itself in the context of the struggle for public space that has defined the Puerto Rican diaspora.

Significantly, neither poet is from Loisaida – Mercado is from Atlantic City, New Jersey, while Cortés is from Williamsburg, Brooklyn – yet both have long poetic and activist trajectories in and around Loisaida that predate the publication of their respective debut collections in the early 2000s. Thus, their cases, along with those of others such as the influential Massachusetts-based poet/performer Magdalena Gómez, reveal how Loisaida- (and East Harlem–) centered Nuyorican histories fail to account for a diversity of poetics, as well as how the emerging male-dominated canon of Nuyorican poetry books in the 1980s failed to account for the historical (and ongoing) marginalization of women poets. (Esteves, by far the most nationally visible woman poet from the original *Nuyorican Poetry* anthology, did not publish a book with Arte Público until *Bluestown Mockingbird Mambo* in 1990 and has mostly self-published since, whereas Laviera, Piñero, and Algarín benefited from publishing multiple books with the press during its 1980s heyday.) At the same time, the spatial and temporal differences that animate Mercado and Cortés's work testify to the richness and complexities of Nuyorican poetry's routes and roots.

Cortés's *Lust for Lust* (2002) works against abject and sexualized stereotypes of Puerto Ricans as "perpetrators" (17) that can arguably be dated at least as far back as the film *West Side Story* (1961), while working through the ironies of supposed assimilation, as in the pointedly titled "All American," which ends "But somewhere along the way, perdí algo" (20). The very system that produces Puerto Ricans as perpetrators also produces women as objects, as cleverly depicted in the poem "Más Cara," which plays on the resonances between "mascara" and "más cara" (meaning both "more expensive" and "more face" in addition to "mask" or a black coating for eyelashes). The system sends Puerto Ricans to Vietnam (as was the case with Cortés's friend Pietri) and drugs them into submission "so they wouldn't be afraid to die" (64) and, in the poem "Cool Retro," it makes them fetishize digital technology just as an earlier generation had yearned for the "wrap-around sectional couches" (70) that signaled the idealized, upwardly mobile nuclear family. Faced with a digital generation obsessed with e-mail, cell phones, and "declaring their geographical whereabouts to whomever has answered or called" (71), the speaker of the poem highlights the porous geography of the Nuyorican complexion, much as Cortés does in her 2009 collection *Whose Place*.

With its lack of a question mark, the title *Whose Place* works both as declaration and open-ended rhetorical question, at once affirming and questioning, in the spirit of Pietri, New York Puerto Rican spatial logics. Pietri, who died in 2004, is everywhere in *Whose Place*. He is the subject of two moving poems: "Black Was Pedro" – a prose poem that underscores his eccentric performances and radical approach to the politics of representation ("black" here stands for death, but also for Pietri's trademark all-black wardrobe, for his black humor, his somber, all-black paintings, and for his appeal to strategic invisibility) – and "To Pedro Pietri, Traffic Misinterpreter, Mr. Interpreter, Ms. Interpreter, Misinterpietri. . . The Reverendo," which uses Pietrian wordplay to locate Pietri within a radical Nuyorican genealogy alongside street poet Jorge Brandon, a grandfather figure for Nuyorican poets whom Pietri had celebrated in his poem "Traffic Misdirector" (from 1983's *Traffic Violations*). By remixing Pietri's remix of Brandon, Cortés claims a lineage of experimental downtown resistance as her own, and inserts herself into a tradition of political and poetic misdirection and urban dissidence poised against an increasingly policed and corporate post–9/11 New York City. Just as Pietri's misdirections and wordplay "speak claridad" (71) or clarity to the programmatic logic of neoliberalism, Cortés poems such as *Whose Place*'s "Guerrulona" eccentrically perform the encroachment of digital space and the militarization of global space, from Vietnam to the Cuban embargo to Afghanistan, a microhistory that links U.S. imperial pasts and the neoliberal present. With its bilingual flood of slashes and at-signs, "Guerrulona" embodies the post–9/11 "Netlish" described by Emily Apter as a schizophrenic "postmedia form of expressionism" (239) shaped by the tension between digital entropy and universal translatability. Similarly, the poem "MTA Terrorism: Signs of The Times" echoes Pietri's found-text subway poems, insofar as Cortés's builds the whole text around bilingual wordplay on the ubiquitous subway warning – "If you see something, say something" – a hallmark of the policing of public space in post–9/11 New York.

Although published just before 9/11, Mercado's *It Concerns the Madness* already diagnoses the neoliberal war machine in the Middle East in the ironically titled poem "No Vietnam Here," which understands wars in faraway desert lands as media-driven and as sustaining consumer culture: the "we" in the poem refers both to Christmas shoppers on 34th Street and to soldiers who "annihilate each other" in order to "help the nation's cash flow problem" (66) by boosting the stock market (67). Perhaps echoing Pietri's play *Illusions of a Revolving Door*, collected in his 1992 book of the same name, Mercado, whose book also includes a heartfelt poem for Pietri, concludes her poem "The Master Pedro Albizu Campos" with "A group of travelers /

through revolving doors" (63). Thus, the poem locates the Puerto Rican diaspora in and against the vicious cycle of colonialism that fueled Albizu Campos's revolutionary nationalism and that unites Puerto Ricans on and off the island. Both firmly rooted in Nuyorican poetic and social histories and attuned to what Jorge Duany has called the "Puerto Rican nation on the move," Mercado's work, like that of Cortés, Pietri, and so many other Nuyorican poets, understands liminal New York Puerto Rican space as disruptions of the imperial logic of North-South geographies, as a Thirdspace where "sounds are unheard and voices disappearing" (Mercado 39).

Although Nuyorican literature has traveled far beyond the barrio, contemporary works often return to Loisaida (or East Harlem) to reflect on contemporary realities from a critical, revisionist, or irreverent perspective. Such is the case of Edgardo Vega Yunqué in his 2004 novel *The Lamentable Journey of Omaha Bigelow into the Impenetrable Loisaida Jungle*. Vega Yunqué, a onetime director of the Lower East Side's Clemente Soto Vélez Cultural Center and an essential Nuyorican fiction writer since the publication of his novel *The Comeback* in 1985, often interrupts the narrative of the down-and-out protagonist Bigelow with metafictional games and asides and commentary, including his opening observation that "Loisaida is a gallant and quixotic cultural attempt to dominate the geography even though renting is not the same as owning" (1). With characteristic irony, Vega Yunqué both affirms and parodies the urban activist idealism that inspired Rivas and García's Loisaida. Whereas Rivas and Jorge Brandon eccentrically adapted *Don Quijote* for their Loisaida street theater as a quixotic affirmation of beauty amid decay (Ševčenko 299), Vega Yunqué's acid punch lines serve as a grim if oblique meditation on post-gentrification Loisaida, where CHARAS / El Bohío is a target for real-estate developers, and the Nuyorican Poets Cafe is surrounded by luxury developments.

A more recent term that encapsulates and expands upon the performative spatial politics of Loisaida and Nuyorican Thirdspace is *Nuyorico*. The term already appears in a 1980s painting by Martin Wong called *La Vera de Nuyorico: Miguel Piñero Recita La Poesía de Loisaida Para Martin Wong Corner of Ridge Street and Stanton*. As the subtitle suggests, the painting depicts Piñero reading his poetry on the Lower East Side, and the text of his "A Lower East Side Poem" is written along the borders of the painting. Significantly, the address mentioned in the subtitle is in the heart of the historical Lower East Side yet just outside of Loisaida proper as defined in Piñero's poem, so in fact Wong locates Piñero's outsider performance at *la vera* ("the edge" or "the border") of Nuyorico, and, given the poem's inscription at the painting's edges, Nuyorico itself is at the border. The intersection of violence and love defines this border, as evident from the silhouette of a gun shooting at a heart-shaped moon made of bricks above the urban skyline. But the affect here is publicly intimate, as Piñero is reading his poetry aloud for Wong, an openly gay Chinese American artist (and legendary Loisaidan) with whom Piñero lived for a time. Wong, then, was not culturally Nuyorican, but his painting embodies Nuyorico as an urban borderlands where the struggle over public space that has long defined Loisaida is embedded with queer affects and uneasy intimacies, and where Asian-Latino affective geographies can be mapped in the contact zones between and beyond Loisaida and nearby Chinatown.

In his book *Queer Ricans*, Lawrence La Fountain-Stokes explores how the term *Nuyorico* figures in the performances of queer Bronx performers such as Arthur Avilés and Elizabeth Marrero, highlighting the inherent queerness of "Nuyorico" as it is deployed in their "neighborhood-based, transgressive performances and local interventions [that] offer new social visions and spaces for Puerto Ricans and other queer people of color" (132). La Fountain-Stokes emphasizes the at-once pragmatic and utopian (132) dimension of their Nuyorico, as transgressive as it is locally rooted, and while he does not refer to Wong or Piñero in his discussion, it is hard not to find echoes of their transgressive queer borderlands.

The strategically utopian politics of Nuyorico are also emphasized by Patricia Herrera in her analysis of Caridad De La Luz "La Bruja"'s performance of her one-woman-show *Brujalicious*, which took place at the Bronx Academy of Arts and Dance (BAAD!), co-founded by Avilés and writer Charles Rice-González in 1998. Herrera emphasizes De La Luz's use of the term "Nuyorico" as well as her affirmation that "Todos somos amigos en Nuyorico" ("We are all friends in Nuyorico"). Herrera's reading locates De La Luz's performance in the Nuyorican tradition and emphasizes her references to Pietri (164). Although, as Herrera, suggests, De La Luz's "we" is informed by the Afro-diasporic utopianism of the hip-hop nation, it also arguably echoes the radical insideness of Pietri's "Obituary."

Recent scholarship has also summoned *Nuyorico* to map the spatial politics of older writers and artists far removed from the queer and feminist ferment of the past two decades. For instance, in his reading of Edward Rivera's celebrated autobiographical novel *Family Installments* (1982), literary critic Juan José Cruz emphasizes how Nuyorico functions as a "conceptual border"

(81) that defines the politics of Rivera's book less in terms of any explicit commentary than in its depiction of "people who try to survive ethnocide, whether as landless peasants in the Caribbean or as immigrants in the cities of the North" (81). For Cruz, theorizing Nuyorico becomes a way to unpack the translocal working-class logic in Rivera's book as it bridges the struggle of the rural island peasants (or *jíbaros*) and that of their diasporic progeny, as both confront the crisis of the union left and the casualization of labor (82). Elsewhere, musicologist Malena Kuss argues that Willie Colón's concept album *El Baquiné de Angelitos Negros* (1977), an experimental take on an Afro-Puerto Rican religious celebration, is set in "urban Nuyorico" and she foregrounds "the heterogeneity of its Afro-Caribbean styles" (176). Nuyorico here correctly marks Bronx-native Colón's seminal version of salsa as a translocal project; its exploratory cosmopolitanism inspired Algarín, who has a poem in his book *Mongo Affair* (1978) about Colón's "salsa ballet," and for whose *Nuyorican Poetry* anthology Colón provided a back-cover blurb.

Understood translocally, Nuyorico is not unproblematic, inasmuch as it is subject to appropriation by corporate elites: a promotional website for De La Luz boasts that her poem "Nuyorican" was "featured in a Levi's print ad in magazines featured across the globe" (Sphinxmg.com). At the same time, the trajectory of poets such as Luivette Resto – born in Puerto Rico, raised in the Bronx and living in California, and the author of books such as *Ascension* (2013) – points to what poet and scholar Li Yun Alvarado, also a California-based Nuyorican, calls in her 2013 chapbook of the same name, *Nuyorico, CA*. To be sure, Resto and Alvarado are by no means the first Nuyorican poets to call California home: Cruz did much of his most radical work while living in the San Francisco Bay Area, while Jesús Papoleto Meléndez – a foundational Nuyorican poet and author of important early 1970s books such as *Street Poetry & Other Poems* (1972) – spent years living and writing in San Diego, where he published his volume *Concertos on Market Street* (1993) and inspired younger Chicano poets such as Tomás Riley, a core member of the famed 1990s poetry and performance collective Taco Shop Poets. What is true is that increasing Puerto Rican mobility and dispersal, accentuated by technology and further complicated by the gentrification of New York City and by the last decade's exodus from the island due to its difficult economic situation, is once again challenging what diaspora looks like, from above and from below, in northern cities such as Chicago and Philadelphia and in sunbelt destinations such as Orlando. How does twenty-first century Nuyorico relate to the rich tradition of Chicago Puerto Rican poetry epitomized by the late David Hernandez (1946–2013) – author of several books of poetry, long-time leader of the band Street Sounds, and editor of the 1977 *Nosotros anthology*, a special issue of *Revista Chicano-Riqueña* devoted to Latina/o Chicago writers –, or to works such as Quiara Alegría Hudes's Pulitzer-winning play *Water by the Spoonful* (2011), which depicts the struggles of a Puerto Rican family in Philadelphia across urban and digital spaces marked by the scars of war? How does Nuyorico fit into the broader "enclave of the scattered 'DiaspoRico'" (*Bomba* 187) that Flores finds in Fernández's "Ode to the Diasporican" or into the stateless ironies and furies of Abraham Rodríguez's *The Boy without a Flag: Tales of the South Bronx* (1992)? These are some of the questions that need to be asked to continue mapping Nuyorican poetry's legacies.

Both Pietri's "Puerto Rican Obituary" and Piñero's "A Lower East Side Poem" reference Long Island Cemetery; in the latter, the speaker states not wanting to be buried there (nor in Puerto Rico) but rather wanting to remain amid the violence and vitality of the Lower East Side, while the former proclaims that it is "a long ride / from Spanish Harlem / to long island cemetery where they were buried" (3). Both poems seek to interrupt the logic of assimilation and its death-drive, and to affirm the difficult beauty of the diaspora's struggle by mapping the evolving geography of its complexions.[1]

WORKS CITED

Agosin, Marjorie. *Among the Angels of Memory / Entre los ángeles de la memoria*. Trans. Laura Rocha Nakazawa. San Antonio, TX: Wings, 2006.

Agüeros, Jack. "Canción del tecato." *Borinquen: An Anthology of Puerto Rican Literature*. Ed. María Teresa Babín and Stan Steiner. New York: Knopf, 1974. 451.

"El apatético." *Borinquen: An Anthology of Puerto Rican Literature*. Ed. María Teresa Babín and Stan Steiner. New York: Knopf, 1974. 452.

Algarin, Miguel. "Afterword." "Introduction: Nuyorican Language." *Nuyorican Poetry*. Ed. Algarín and Piñero. 9–20.

Mongo Affair. New York: Nuyorican Press, 1978.

"Nuyorican Literature." *MELU.S.* 8.2 (1981): 89–92. JSTOR. Accessed May 30, 2015.

Survival Supervivencia. Ed. Marc Newell. Houston, TX: Arte Público, 2009.

Algarín, Miguel, and Bob Holman, eds. *Aloud: Voices from the Nuyorican Poets Cafe*. New York: Holt, 1994.

Algarín, Miguel, and Miguel Piñero, eds. *Nuyorican Poetry: An Anthology of Puerto Rican Words and Feelings*. New York: Morrow, 1975.

Alvarado, Li Yun. *Nuyorico. CA*. N.p., 2013.

---

[1] For a fuller analysis of Nuyorican poetry, see my book *In Visible Movement*, upon which parts of this essay are based.

Aparicio, Frances R. "From Ethnicity to Multiculturalism: An Historical Overview of Puerto Rican Literature in the United States." *Handbook of Hispanic Cultures in the United States: Literature and Art.* Ed. Francisco Lomeli. Houston: Arte Público, 1993. 19–39.

"La vida es un Spanglish disparatero: Bilingualism in Nuyorican Poetry." *European Perspectives on Hispanic Literature of the United States.* Ed. Genevieve Fabre. Houston, TX: Arte Público, 1988. 147–60.

"Salsa, Maracas, and Baile: Latin Popular Music in the Poetry of Victor Hernâández Cruz." *MELU.S.* 16.1 (1989–1990): 43–58. JSTOR. Accessed May 30, 2015.

Aparicio, Frances R., and Susana Chavez-Silverman. *Tropicalizations: Transcultural Representations of Latinidad.* Hanover, NH: Dartmouth University Press, 1997.

Apter, Emily. *The Translation Zone: A New Comparative Literature.* Princeton, NJ: Princeton University Press, 2006.

Carlson, Jen, "Photos: The 1970s, When Central Park Was Flooded with Music & Loose Joints." Gothamist.com.

Colón, Willie. *El Baquiné de Angelitos Negros.* 1977. Fania. LP.

Cortés, Lydia. *Lust for Lust.* New York: Ten Pell, 2002.

Whose Place. Philadelphia: Straw Gate, 2009.

Cruz, Juan José. "Edward Rivera and American Mythology: A Reading of *Family Installments.*" *Nor Shall Diamond Die: American Studies in Honour of Javier Coy.* Ed. Carme Manuel and Paul Scott Derrick. Valencia: Universitat de València, 2003.

Cruz, Victor Hernández. *Snaps.* 1968. New York: Vintage, 1969.

Tropicalization. New York: Reed, 1976.

DeCosta-Willis, Miriam. "Sandra María Esteves's Nuyorican Poetics: The Signifying Difference." *Afro-Hispanic Review* 23.2 (2004): 3–12. JSTOR. Accessed May 30, 2015.

De la Luz, Caridad [La Bruja], perf. *Brujalicious.* 2006. De la Luz. CD.

Dowdy, Michael. *Broken Souths: Latina/o Poetic Responses to Neoliberalism and Globalization.* Tucson: University of Arizona Press, 2013.

Duany, Jorge. *The Puerto Rican Nation on the Move: Identities on the Island and in the United States.* Chapel Hill: University of North Carolina Press, 2002.

Epstein, William M. *Democracy without Decency: Good Citizenship and the War on Poverty.* University Park: Pennsylvania State University Press, 2010.

Espada, Martín. *The Republic of Poetry.* New York: Norton, 2006.

Esteves, Sandra María, perf. "Aguacero." Democracy Now! Youtube channel. Accessed May 30, 2015.

Undelivered Love Poems. New York: No Frills, 1997.

Yerba Buena: Dibujos y poemas. Greenfield Center, NY: Greenfield Review, 1980.

Fernández, María Teresa Mariposa. "Ode to the Diasporican." Stavans, *Norton* 2424.

Figueroa, José-Angel. *East 110th Street.* Detroit, MI: Broadside, 1973.

Flores, Juan. *The Diaspora Strikes Back: Caribeño Tales of Learning and Turning.* New York: Routledge, 2009.

Divided Borders: Essays on Puerto Rican Identity. Houston, TX: Arte Público, 1993.

From Bomba to Hip-Hop: Puerto Rican Culture and Latino Identity. New York: Columbia University Press, 2000.

"Nueva York, Diaspora City: Latinos Between and Beyond." *Bilingual Games: Some Literary Investigations.* Ed. Doris Sommer. New York: Palgrave, 2003. 69–76.

Flores, Juan, and Mayra Santos-Febres, eds. *Open Mic / Micrófono Abierto: Nuevas literaturas puerto/neorriqueñas / New Puerto/Nuyorican Literatures*. Spec. issue of *Hostos Review* 2 (2005). Bronx, NY: Latin American Writers Institute, 2005.

Forché, Carolyn, ed. *Against Forgetting: Twentieth-Century Poetry of Witness*. New York: Norton, 1993.

The Country Between Us. New York: Harper, 1981.

Gilroy, Paul. *The Black Atlantic: Modernity and Double Consciousness*. Cambridge, MA: Harvard University Press, 1993.

González, Bobby. *The Last Puerto Rican Indian*. New York: Cemi, 2006.

Harvey, David. *Spaces of Global Capitalism: Towards a Theory of Uneven Geographical Development*. New York: Verso, 2006.

Hernández, Carmen Dolores. *Puerto Rican Voices in English: Interviews with Writers*. Westport, CT: Praeger, 1997.

Hernandez, David, ed. *Nosotros: A Collection of Latino Poetry and Graphics from Chicago*. Spec. issue of *Revista Chicano-Riqueña* 5.1 (1977).

Herrera, Patricia. "Nuyoriqueñas in the House: Performing Identity through Hip Hop, Poetry, and Theatre." Diss. CUNY, 2007.

Hudes, Quiara Alegría. *Water by the Spoonful*. New York: Theatre Communications Group, 2012.

Jiménez Román, Miriam, and Juan Flores, eds. *The Afro-Latin@ Reader: History and Culture in the United States*. Durham, NC: Duke University Press, 2010.

Kuss, Malena. *Music in Latin America and the Caribbean: An Encyclopedic History. Vol. 2. Performing the Caribbean Experience*. Austin: University of Texas Press, 2006.

La Fountain-Stokes, Lawrence. *Queer Ricans: Cultures and Sexualities in the Diaspora*. Minneapolis: University of Minnesota Press, 2009.

Laviera, Tato. *AmeRícan*. 2nd ed. Houston, TX: Arte Público, 2003.

Enclave. Houston, TX: Arte Público, 1985.

La Carreta Made a U-Turn. 2nd ed. Houston, TX: Arte Público, 1992.

Mainstream Ethics. Houston, TX: Arte Público, 1988.

Lewis, Oscar. *La Vida; A Puerto Rican Family in the Culture of Poverty – San Juan and New York*. New York: Random House, 1966.

Luciano, Felipe. "Jibaro, My Pretty Nigger." *Puerto Rican Poetry: An Anthology from Aboriginal to Contemporary Times*. Ed. and trans. Roberto Márquez. Amherst: University of Massachusetts Press, 2007. 410–11.

perf. "Jibaro/My Pretty Nigger." *Live at Sing Sing*. By Eddie Palmieri. 1972. Tico, n.d. CD.

perf. "Jibaro/My Pretty Nigger." *Right On! The Original Last Poets*. 1970. Collectables, 1991. CD.

Medina, Tony, and Louis Reyes Rivera, eds. *Bum Rush the Page: A Def Poetry Jam*. New York: Three Rivers, 2001.

Meléndez, Jesús Papoleto. *Concertos on Market Street*. San Diego, CA: Kemetic Images, 1993.

Hey Yo! Yo Soy! 40 Years of Nuyorican Street Poetry, A Bilingual Edition. New York: 2 Leaf, 2012.

Street Poetry & Other Poems. New York: Barlenmir House, 1972.

Mercado, Nancy. *It Concerns the Madness*. Hoboken, NJ: Long Shot, 2000.

Morales, Ed. *Living in Spanglish: The Search for Latino Identity in America*. New York: St. Martin's, 2003.

"Places in the Puerto Rican Heart: Eddie Figueroa and the Nuyorican Imaginary." *Voices*. New York: Center for Puerto Rican Studies at Hunter College. n.d. Accessed May 2, 2016.

Moreno Vega, Marta. "The Yoruba Orisha Tradition Comes to New York City." Jiménez Román and Flores, eds. *The Afro-Latin@ Reader*. 245–51.

Noel, Urayoán. *In Visible Movement: Nuyorican Poetry from the Sixties to Slam*. Iowa City: University of Iowa Press, 2014.

Perdomo, Willie, perf. "Nigger-Reecan Blues." *Def Poetry*. Season 5, Episode 4. HBO, 2006. DVD.

Smoking Lovely. New York: Rattapallax, 2003.

Where a Nickel Costs a Dime. New York: Norton, 1996.

Pietri, Pedro, perf. *Aqui Se Habla Español: Pedro Pietri en Casa Puerto Rico*. 1971. Discos Coquí. LP.

Illusions of a Revolving Door: Plays. Ed. Alfredo Matilla Rivas. Río Piedras: University of Puerto Rico Press, 1992.

Puerto Rican Obituary. New York: Monthly Review, 1973.

Traffic Violations. Maplewood, NJ: Waterfront, 1983.

Piñero, Miguel. *La Bodega Sold Dreams*. Houston, TX: Arte Público, 1980. Rpt. in *Outlaw: The Collected Works of Miguel Piñero*. Ed. Nicolas Kanellos and Jorge Iglesias. Houston: Arte Público, 2012. 3–40.

Short Eyes. New York: Hill and Wang, 1975.

Quiñónez, Ernesto. *Bodega Dreams*. New York: Vintage, 2000.

Ramírez, Yasmin. "Nuyorican Visionary: Jorge Soto and the Evolution of an Afro-Taíno Aesthetic at Taller Boricua." *Centro: Journal of the Center for Puerto Rican Studies* 17.2 (2005): 22–41. REDALYC. Accessed May 30, 2015.

Relph, E. C. *Place and Placelessness*. London: Pion, 1976.

Resto, Luivette. *Ascension: Poems*. Los Angeles, CA: Tia Chucha, 2013.

Rivas, Bimbo [Bittman Rivas]. "Loisaida." Algarin and Holman 359–60.

Rivera, Edward. *Family Installments: Memories of Growing up Hispanic*. New York: Morrow, 1982.

Rivera, Louis Reyes. "Inside the River of Poetry." *In Motion*. May 19, 2002. Accessed May 30, 2015.

"Introduction: By Way of Sharing Perspective." Sandra María Esteves, *Yerba Buena* xiii–xvii.

Who Pays the Cost. New York: Shamal, 1977.

Rodriguez, Jr., Abraham. *The Boy without a Flag: Tales of the South Bronx*. Minneapolis, MN: Milkweed, 1992.

Ševčenko, Liz. "Making Loisaida: Placing Puertorriqueñidad in Lower Manhattan." *Mambo Montage: The Latinization of New York City*. Ed. Arlene M. Dávila and Agustin Laó-Montes. New York: Columbia University Press, 2001. 293–318.

Soja, Edward. *Postmetropolis: Critical Studies of Cities and Regions*. Malden, MA, 2000.

Sommer, Doris. "AmeRícan Accents Syncopate the State." *The Ends of Performance*. Ed. Peggy Phelan and Jill Lane. New York: New York University Press, 1998. 169–77.

Bilingual Aesthetics: A New Sentimental Education. Durham, NC: Duke University Press, 2004.

Sphinxmg.com. Accessed May 30, 2015.

Stanchich, Maritza. "Towards a Post-Nuyorican Literature." *Sargasso*. 2005–2006 (II): 113–24.

Stavans, Ilan, ed. *The Norton Anthology of Latino Literature*. New York: Norton, 2011.

Sutton, Lorraine. *SAYcred LAYdy*. New York: Sunbury, 1975.

Thomas, Piri. *Down These Mean Streets*. New York: Knopf, 1967.

Vega Yunqué, Edgardo. *The Comeback*. Houston, TX: Arte Público, 1985.

   The Lamentable Journey of Omaha Bigelow into the Impenetrable Loisaida Jungle. New York: Overlook, 2004.

Wong, Martin. *La Vera de Nuyorico: Miguel Piñero Recita la Poesía de Loisaida Para Martin Wong Corner of Ridge Street and Stanton. A Day in the Life: Tales from the Lower East Side: An Anthology of Writings from the Lower East Side, 1940–1990*. Ed. Alan Moore and Josh Gosciak. New York: Evil Eye, 1990.

Xavier, Emanuel, ed. *Bullets & Butterflies: Queer Spoken Word Poetry*. San Francisco: Suspect Thoughts, 2005.

Zentella, Ana Celia. "'Chiquitafication' of U.S. Latinos and their Languages, or Why We Need an *Anthro-Political Linguistics*." *SALSA III: Proceedings of the Symposium about Language and Society at Austin*. Austin: University of Texas at Austin Department of Linguistics, 1995. 1–18.

   Growing Up Bilingual: Puerto Rican Children in New York. Malden, MA: Blackwell, 1997.

20

Cuban American Counterpoint

*The Heterogeneity of Cuban American Literature,
Culture, and Politics*[1]

WILLIAM LUIS

Para CeCe. Por nuestras conversaciones.

Juan Felipe Herrera's appointment as the Library of Congress's twenty-first Poet Laureate should dispel any notion that Latino literature is just another fad or that it is a marginal literature. Herrera joins a list of distinguished world-class Latino authors, including Cuban American Oscar Hijuelos, the first Cuban American and Latino Pulitzer Prize winner for 1990, and most recently, poet Richard Blanco, the first Cuban American Latino to address the nation at President Obama's second inauguration in 2013.[2]

Cuban or Cuban American writing in the United States is not new. It can be traced to the early to mid-nineteenth century, when Cubans traveled abroad to escape Spanish colonial control over its most lucrative colony. Writers like José María Heredia, Cirilo Villaverde, Félix Varela, Martín Morúa Delgado, José Martí, and others wrote about their birthplace from the US mainland. Although these and other writers form an integral part of Cuba's national literature, I propose that their works were also influenced by the society in which they lived – the United States – and they can be considered under a broader concept of Cuban American or Latino literature.[3]

Indeed, there was an exchange of ideas between liberal supporters of Cuba's emerging national culture and the expanding United States, as events

---

[1] I want to thank Adriana Méndez Rodenas for reading the essay and making valuable comments and suggestions.
[2] Other award recipients include Junot Díaz, Pulitzer Prize winner for 2007 and a MacArthur Genius Grant winner for 2008. These and other Latino authors are changing the literary scape not only in the United States, but also in their parents' country of origin.
[3] See my *Dance Between Two Cultures*, Chapter 1.

of the island also reached the mainland. The atrocities of the Ladder Conspiracy of 1844, in which and freed blacks were tied to a ladder and whipped
into confessing their alleged participation, fueled the abolitionist movement
in the neighboring country. Information about the conspiracy circulated in
abolitionist publications, as did the works of the Cuban slave poet Juan
Francisco Manzano and the free mulatto poet Gabriel de la Concepción
Valdés, also known as Plácido.[4] Oddly, the names of the two poets were
fused into one, and life and works of Juan Plácido circulated among interested readers.[5] The United States' presence on the island became a permanent fixture with the Spanish–American War of 1898 and the insertion of the
Platt Amendment into Cuba's constitution allowed the neighboring country
to intervene in the island's internal affairs.

Fidel Castro's revolution of 1959 produced the largest exodus ever in
distinct waves. The first one, from 1959 to 1961, comprised mainly of professionals, included writers of the stature of Lino Novás Calvo and Lydia
Cabrera, and others of lesser standing like José Sánchez Boudy. Like their
earlier nineteenth-century counterparts, these writers believed in their imminent return home and their works denounced the present social and political
conditions on the island. Many of these works were gathered in an early
bibliography compiled by Fernández and Fernández.[6] Other exile writers
soon followed. Some lived and wrote in other countries; Jesús Díaz and
César Leante lived in Spain, Mayra Montero in Puerto Rico, and Zoé Valdés
in France, but most like Antonio Benítez Rojo made the United States their
new home. Unlike the first wave of exiles, the most recent ones remained in
Cuba; some even supported government ideology but later voted themselves
off the island.

The Mariel Boatlift of 1980 produced the most concentrated group of
Cuban exiles in two concurrent events: In the first, 10,000 Cubans sought
asylum in the Peruvian embassy and, in the second, 125,000 fled through the
port of Mariel, from April to October of that year. If the first wave of Cubans
dissented from the newly created communist government, these other exiles
were sons and daughters of the revolution, the children for whom the
government came to power, and they too fled their country of provenance.
Though much has been said about the delinquency of these exiles, for some

---

[4] Plácido was wrongly accused of masterminding the plot. See Francisco Calcagno, *Poetas de Color*.
[5] John Whittier, *The Stranger in Lowell*.
[6] *Índice bibliográfico de autores cubanos: Diáspora, 1959–1979*.

were hardened criminals, the overwhelming majority were young, decent individuals and families looking to better their lives. This aspect of Cuban history has been captured by Reinaldo Arenas, himself a Marielito, in his short story "Termina el desfile" (1981) about the crowded and inhumane conditions asylum seekers endured in the Peruvian embassy, and *Antes que anochezca* (1992), a memoir about his life in Cuba and, after he escaped through the Mariel boatlift, in the United States; he died of AIDS in New York City.[7] Arenas denounced the Castro dictatorship, but he also wrote about life in the United States. *El portero* (1987) takes place in New York and describes the life of an exile whose ultimate goal is to seek freedom. Mirta Ojito, also a Marielito, authored *Finding Mañana: A Memoir of a Cuban Exodus* (2005), about her experiences during her riveting voyage of survival, but she and others of her generation narrate their accounts in English, as we shall see later.

The Mariel boatlift pointed to a fissure within Cuban society, as intellectuals abandoned the revolution they once supported. Two notable writers include Heberto Padilla, a renowned poet accused as an enemy of the state, and Antonio Benítez Rojo, who held a high position in Cuba's premier cultural institution, Casa de las Américas. A member of the controversial literary supplement *Lunes de Revolución* (1959–1961),[8] Padilla was outspoken against the government's monolithic control of life in Cuba. He was critical of the Partido Socialista Popular's (Cuba's Communist Party) control over cultural institutions. His collection of poems, *Fuera del juego* (1968), denounced the lack of freedom of expression on the island, won the UNEAC poetry prize, and was published with a defamatory note from officials.[9] Two years later Padilla was detained, and his arrest precipitated an international scandal about the lack of liberty in Cuba.[10] In the United States, Padilla published *En mi jardín pastan los heroes* (1981) and *La mala memoria* (1989), about his interpretation of events in the revolution. He and his wife, Belkis Cuza Malé, edited *Linden Lane Magazine* and publicized Cuban literature and art abroad. Arenas, a member of the editorial board, broke with Padilla and

---

[7] *Julian Schnabel* made Arenas's autobiography into a full-featured film, *Before Night Falls*, in 2000.

[8] See my *Lunes de Revolución*. [9] See Lourdes Casal, *El caso Padilla*.

[10] An open letter to Castro, signed by numerous intellectuals in *LeMonde*, led to Padilla's release. Padilla was then made to confess his crimes against the state. A second letter followed denouncing the forced confession, creating another major crisis among those who once supported the government, now opposed to its draconian tactics. See *El caso Padilla*.

founded his own literary magazine, *El Mariel*, which gave additional space to dissident voices.

Known as a writer of the revolution, with such works as *Tute de reyes* (1967) and *El mar de las lentejas* (1979), Benítez Rojo was the director of the Caribbean section of Casa de las Américas. Unbeknownst to many of his colleagues, he sought exile while traveling in Europe and made his way to the United States. He taught at major US universities and for many years at his home institution, Amherst College. Benítez Rojo contributed to Cuban literature from the United States with his historical novel *Mujer en traje de batalla* (2001) and to Caribbean and Latin American literary criticism with his much celebrated *La isla que se repite* (1989), which underscores chaos theory to understand the plantation system in the Caribbean. The United States allowed Benítez Rojo and other writers to envision their subject without the fear of censorship or political retribution.

Though all these writers are Cuban-born, there is a distinction between a Reinaldo Arenas and a Mirta Ojito; they narrate similar themes, but the former writes in Spanish and the latter in English. The tendency is to read Arenas alongside Cuban literature, even though he wrote in the United States, and Ojito, next to Cuban American or Latino literature written in English. Latino literature emerges in the decades of the sixties and seventies out of the social, political, and racial conditions of Chicanos living in the Southwest and Puerto Ricans in Chicago and New York City. These writers expressed the marginal conditions in which they live in a society that treats them as foreigners, and Cuban Americans did the same. During the decade of the seventies, a small group of the sons and daughters of Cuban exiles distanced themselves from their parents' conservative position, broke with the old anti-Castro paradigm, and voiced their concerns in the journal *Areíto*.[11]

Indebted greatly to Lourdes Casal's leadership and vision, *Areíto* represented an independent position from US and exile politics as its members sought a new understanding of the island and the government their parents left behind. These early voices proclaimed in the journal were developed into a testimonial, *Contra viento y marea* (1978), about their experiences in the adopted country, and a film, *55 hermanos*, about their historic three-week trip to the island in December of 1977. Although written in Spanish, *Contra viento y marea* documents the life these marginalized young Cuban Americans

---

[11] See, for example, Terri Shaw's "Lively Exile Magazine Is Target for Bombers." *Washington Post*, May 23, 1976.

experienced in the United States. Their approach to Cuba was in line with those of other peripheral and dissenting groups, like the Black Panthers and Young Lords Party, who also protested the war in Vietnam and supported the civil rights and women's movements. A significant number of members of *Areíto*, some of whom participated in the first contingent of the Brigada Antonio Maceo, went on to occupy influential positions in US institutions of higher learning and help set the foundation for what became a Cuban American literary history. Casal was a narrator and poet in her own right, and wrote openly about her blackness and lesbianism, but her lasting contribution entailed creating a space for a new Cuban American voice in *Areíto*.[12] Not all the members of this generation visited the island or welcomed a new approach to US–Cuba relations. On the contrary, some vowed to maintain a hostile position defined, by their parents' politics. In recent years there would be other Latino journals that responded to changing political circumstances, such as *generation ñ*, self-described as a "Latin thing, but with more cowbell."[13] The online publication featured Cuban American writers like Richard Blanco, born in Madrid and raised in the United States around the time of the Padilla Affair.

Writers of the earlier generations, those who were born and educated in their country of origin, expressed themselves in their native language, and those of the younger generations, born or raised and educated in the United States, members of Gustavo Pérez Firmat's 1.5 generation, narrate their experiences in their parents' language but also in English, the language of their adopted country. Their position is best expressed by Carolina Hospital's *Cuban American Writers: Los atrevidos* (1989), published by Linden Lane Press, which gathers the voices of young Cuban Americans who began to spread their wings in their new, increasingly more permanent, environment. Some,

---

[12] Consider *Los fundadores: Alfonso y otros cuentos*, and the poetry collections *Cuadernos de agosto* and *Palabras juntan revolución*, which was published posthumously and won the 1981 Casa de las Américas poetry prize for poetry. Also see www.cintasfoundation.org/index.php/fellows/creative-writers/114-lourdes-casal#sthash.oJ3RuoOz.dpuf. Casal also wrote about race matters in Cuba with her contribution on "Race Relations in Contemporary Cuba." For a thorough discussion of Casal's importance and contributions, see Laura Lomas's "In-Between States: Lourdes Casal's Critical Interdisciplinary and Intersectional Feminism." I want to thank Lomas for sending me a copy of her essay.

[13] "We are the folks for whom being latino has never been a chore. Not trapped between two identities, we embrace our roots while enjoying our American identity with fervor. Buying into the American dream in every broadband, Blu Ray, HD kinda way. Rather than feel divided, we're feelin' kinda doubled." See http://generation-ntv.com/about-2/all-bout-n.

like Gustavo Pérez Firmat, Roberto Fernández, and Ricardo Pau-Llosa, among others, represented this new generational voice.

It would be a mistake, one often made by literary critics and social commentators, to group all Cuban Americans or Cuban American literature under one rubric. For example, Rafael Rojas refers to Cuba as a post-diasporic nation, but he homogenizes the exile experience.[14] Just as there is a distinction between the members of *Areíto* and those who chose to support their parents' anti-Castro position, there are significant differences between Cuban Americans who fled Cuba with the first wave of exiles and those who left during the Mariel Boatlift, between those who live in Miami and those who reside in other cities like New York, Chicago, Philadelphia, and Los Angeles. Furthermore, differences are noticeable among Miami Cubans living in the same city. There is no one singular Cuban American experience or literature; rather it is rich, varied, and nuanced. And even when authors write about exile, they express this painful subject in different perspectives. The pain of the past, for some like Hospital, in her poem "Dear Tía," comes not from nostalgia but from the fact that she has no memory at all.[15] Cuban American writers, whose parents lived in the United States when Castro came to power, tell a different story from those who fled the island during the same historic event. I should also say something about exiles and migrants. Though they do represent different diasporic subjects, not everyone leaving Cuba does so for political reasons, and not all migrants departing their country do so willingly. Nevertheless, this important discussion goes beyond the purview of this essay.

Oscar Hijuelos is the most recognized writer of Cuban American heritage. Some Cuban Americans claim that he does not embody the exile way of life, yet the Cuban American experience cannot and should not be reduced to one or two themes, characteristics, or perspectives, and these continue to evolve. Making his debut with *Our House in the Last World* (1983), winner of the Rome Prize of the Academy of Arts and Letters, Hijuelos became the first Latino to win the much-coveted Pulitzer Prize with *The Mambo Kings Play Songs of Love* (1989). The novel was adapted into a movie of the same name in 1992 and a musical in 2005. Two brothers, Néstor and César Castillo, leave Cuba for New York during the heyday of the Mambo era and succeed with Néstor's nostalgic song "Beautiful María of My Soul." Each brother represents a different version of the Cuban immigrant experience. If César looks

---

[14] See Rojas, "Diaspora y literatura: Indicios de una ciudadanía postnacional," 136–47.
[15] For an analysis of "Dear Tía," see *Dance Between Two Cultures*, 173–74.

forward to finding his American Dream in his blond American girlfriend Vana Vane, Néstor never separates himself from María, a symbol of his Cuban past. Néstor's accidental death or suicide changes César's life and transforms him into a version of his brother; he takes care of his brother's wife and children and, like Néstor, engages in a slow suicide and drinks himself to death.

Hijuelos wrote other novels – *The Fourteen Sisters of Emilio Montez O'Brien* (1993), *Empress of the Splendid Season* (1999), *Dark Dude* (2008) – that in one way or the other touch upon the exile's adjustment to the US environment. However, before his premature death in 2013, Hijuelos returned to the theme of his prize-winning novel with *Beautiful María of My Soul* (2010), telling the early story from María's point of view. María, who migrates from her home in Pinar del Río to Havana, later becomes a Miami exile, and her Cuban-born daughter raised in the United States is Cuban American, with little recollection of her mother's place of birth. If the mother focuses on traditional concepts of womanhood, the daughter's comport corresponds more to the culture of the adopted country. Hijuelos, cleverly, makes an appearance in his own novel and his characters disagree with him, thus recalling other Hispanic literary traditions that serve as subtext for many Cuban American writers.[16]

Cristina García, whose parents became exiles when she was two years old, was raised in New York City. Like Hijuelos she provides a balanced, albeit womanly, perspective of the exile experience. García made her literary entrance with *Dreaming in Cuban* (1992), about the Castro revolution's breakup of the Cuban family. Pilar's conflict with her mother, and her desire to identify with her grandmother and her vision of Cuba and the revolution, mirrors closely the complex sentiments of many Cuban Americans who visited the island with the first contingent of the Antonio Maceo Brigade. García shows that Cuban culture exists as much in New York as it does in Cuba, and Santería plays an important role for the characters both at home and abroad. If Pilar rejects her mother's assimilation into US culture, represented by the Yankee Doodle Bakery, and her rebellion reflects a generational voice (she provides an unorthodox drawing of the Statue of Liberty), in Cuba she undergoes a profound change; she betrays her grandmother and conspires with her mother to help her cousin, Ivanito, escape by seeking refuge in the Peruvian embassy.

---

[16] For example, in *Niebla*, Miguel de Unamuno's Agusto Pérez speaks to the author. Also, Guillermo Cabrera Infante makes an appearance in his *Tres tristes tigres*.

In *The Agüero Sisters* (1997), García narrates the lives of Constancia and Reina who were also divided by the Cuban revolution. Each preserves a distinct memory of their parents' past. The father, Ignacio, was born into the republic and prefigures life during that period of Cuban history, dominated by corruption. Thus, the novel shows that Cuba's problems did not begin with the revolution but were present generations before and can be traced to the events leading up to the Spanish–American War. Only in exile do the two sisters reconcile the different interpretations of their mother's death and family past.

Perhaps more than any other Cuban American writer, García experimented with the many facets of Cuba's diverse culture. *The Agüero Sisters* unfolds over a carefully constructed vision of Santería, one of Cuba's notable African religions. Ignacio represents Orula (St. Francis of Assisi), Blanca (Oshún), and Blanca's lover is Changó (St. Barbara).[17] The novel also provides an allegorical reading of the maternal body and an ecological understanding of the Cuban past.[18] In *Monkey Hunting* (2003), the author searches into Cuba's past, to the nineteenth century, when Chinese indentured servants were brought to Cuba to supplement slave labor. The narration describes three generations of the family of Cheng Peng and his African slave wife, and how their lives also contributed to Cuban culture. They too flee the revolution and live in the United States.

García continues to branch out geographically in *A Handbook to Luck* (2007), with characters from Cuba, El Salvador, and Iraq, for they belong to a larger diaspora and all have reasons to live outside of their parents' homeland. However, with *King of Cuba* (2013) she returns to the topic closest to her, the exile experience. In this most recent novel, García narrates the mirrored life of two octogenarians, Fidel Castro and the Cuban exile Goyo Herrera, between island despotism and exile obsession.

More in line with the dominant narrative of Cuban American Miami exile culture is Gustavo Pérez Firmat's *Next Year in Cuba* (1995), a memoir in which the character internalizes his father's exile traumas. While Pérez Firmat has little or no recollection of Cuba, he relives his father's exiled existence.

---

[17] See William Luis, "Hurricanes, Magic, Science, and Politics in Cristina García's *The Agüero Sisters*" in Lyn Di Iorio Sandín and Richard Perez's *Contemporary U.S. Latino/a Literary Criticism*, 144–64.

[18] These ideas are discussed in Nivia Montenegro's "*The Agüero Sisters*: Disremembering the Cuban Past," 267–85, and Adriana Méndez Rodena's "En búsqueda del paraíso perdido: La historia natural como imaginación diaspórica en Cristina García," 392–418, respectively.

However, the protagonist is a refugee, not from Cuba but from Miami, a city to which he desires to return. If Hijuelos's Néstor looked to the past and César to the future, like Ricky Ricardo with Lucy, Pérez Firmat's narrator finds his American Dream in Mary Ann, his second wife. Even though Pérez Firmat's memoir suggests that he takes on his father's identity, he cannot hide that he does not get along with his parents and certainly not with his siblings, and each follows a different Cuban American lifestyle. In the Pérez Firmat household, the family problems predate their exile; and in the United States, his brothers and sister have elected to pursue their own destinies.

Hijuelos's *The Mambo Kings Play Songs of Love* is centered on the *I Love Lucy Show*; similarly Pérez Firmat's *A Cuban in Mayberry: Looking Back at America's Hometown* (2014) is a beautiful recollection and analysis of the highly popular Andy Griffith Show. Living in North Carolina, the TV sitcom TAGS takes place not too far from where Pérez Firmat still owns a home. Yet, unlike the show's characters who never left their home, and in which nothing happened, Pérez Firmat's life was marked by displacement and constant change.

Consistent with members of Pérez Firmat's 1.5 generation, who feel comfortable writing in both Spanish and English, Roberto G. Fernández began his literary career in Spanish prose, authoring *La vida es un special* (1982) and *La montaña rusa* (1985), among others, and provides a nostalgic view of Cuba and Miami. However, he is better known for his works mainly in English (with some Spanish grammar), *Raining Backwards* (1988) and *Holy Radishes!* (1995). Roberto Fernández is more critical than other writers of the tension present in the exile community in general and in the family in particular. While the press has correctly trumpeted the success of the hardworking Cuban community, it has been at a great cost, at least in terms of how that community imagines its life at home and abroad. If the island provided a blueprint of Cuban culture and customs, in the adopted country the scheme is disarticulated and rearranged. In *Raining Backwards*, Mima Rodríguez succeeds in her plantain-chip business, but her children, Connie and Keith, are caught in a no man's land and fail to adapt to either Cuban or US cultural expectations; one of her sons becomes involved in drugs, and the daughter in a superficial glamour of dating the captain of the football team, who later kills her. Her son Quinn, the most successful of the three, becomes a religious leader of the exile community, but he also fails to successfully adapt to his new environment. The lack of social adaptability undermines the economic success of Cubans, and in some respects brings them closer to the struggles of other Latino groups, even though most white

Cuban exiles do not experience the racial concerns of their dark-skinned counterparts.

If *Raining Backwards* focuses on the fate of Cubans in Florida, *Holy Radishes!* presents the other side of the coin: how US nationals view and resent Cuban arrivals. Whereas the U.S. government warmly welcomes Cuban exiles, the newly arrived neighbors are a threat to many people considered locals to the area. The Cuban presence in Miami has negatively impacted the lives of mainstream South Floridians like Mr. Olson, who come to feel like outsiders in their own geographic space. He and others do not hesitate to express their displeasure at the continual invasion of Cuban exiles and lash out at them. Each holds on to what he or she knows: Mr. Olson, to life prior to the onset of Cuban exiles; Mirta Vergara, to her romantic Cuban past; and Eloy, in the words of the Nuyorican poet, Tato Laviera, to his in-betweenness, "nideaquinideallá" (neitherfromherenorfromthere).

Like Hijuelos, García, and Pérez Firmat, Fernández is aware that Cuban problems are not new and were in place before Castro came to power, which the revolution and exile exacerbate. If Pérez Firmat draws a distinction between Cuban American writers who were marked by their parents' exile (Miami) experience and those who were not, the Cuban American way is not a one-sided conversation about separation from the island. In the United States, Nellie and Ms. B understand they share common experiences: abusive husbands transcend linguistic, geographic, and cultural differences. *En la Ocho y la Doce* (2001) is a collection of stories that continues to parody life in Miami, but in this work Fernández returns to writing for a Spanish-speaking public, which means that he is reaffirming his linguistic roots. Jorge Febles identifies certain recurring themes in Fernández's work, including the presence of Mirta Vergara in different manifestations.[19]

Pablo Medina's *Exiled Memories: A Cuban Childhood* (1990) is an autobio-graphical account of the idea he poeticizes so well in "The Exile."[20] In both he captures the memories of a Cuban exile, and of a Cuban child of exiles, but also presents memories as a form of exile, writing from the position of one who has been ejected from paradise to which he must return.[21] The journey of collective memories of the past has been lost in time and in a different language, Spanish. Its recovery is scriptural, in another language and

---

[19] Febles, "Am I your worst nightmare?" *Cuban American Literature and Art*, 77–92.

[20] For a study of this poem, see my *Dance Between Two Cultures*, 165–67.

[21] In the second edition, Medina adds a new final chapter, "The Winds that Came" about his return to Cuba in 1999.

from another time and location, the place of exile. Autobiography, memoir, or any other first-person account is always a looking back from the present, for the present dictates how we imagine or reconstruct the past. The past is a function of the present and the present of the past. Yet each narrating subject must come to terms with that real or inventive past, to reckon with it and accept his/her present reality. Pérez Firmat best expresses the duality, double identity or fragmented self to which I refer as he recounts his departure from Cuba as a departure from himself:

> I have replayed our departure from Cuba in my mind hundreds, perhaps thousands of times ... As the ferry lurches away from the pier, I look back and see a small boy waving good-bye to me. He's my age, or perhaps a year or two younger, dressed as I would have been dressed ... I realize that this boy on the dock is me. Somehow, in my dream, I'm in two places at once. I'm on the dock and I'm waving; I'm on the ferry and I'm waving. The last image in my dream is of me on the ferry, with my hands gripping the deck railing and my head barely above it, looking toward the shore and seeing the Cuban boy I was, the Cuban boy I am no longer, fade to a point and then to nothing. Finally, the only kid is the one on the ferry, which has also sailed out into the open sea.[22]

The exile is estranged from himself. He views himself as other, and he will always be himself and his other.

Medina conveys the same idea: "Thus it was that I became two persons, one creature of warmth, the other the snow swimmer. The first would be forever a child dancing to the beat of waves; the second was the adult, striving to emerge from the river of cold ... without hope of reconciliation."[23] For Medina the creation of this New Man is antithetical to what revolutionary Cuba and Cubans represent.[24]

The idea of disillusionment is continued in Medina's *The Marks of Birth* (1994), *The Return of Felix Nogara* (2000), produced by the revolution and magnified by the exile subject, and *The Cigar Roller* (2006), whose protagonist in the period of the republic migrated to Ybor City. Therefore, when Medina or Pérez Firmat revisits the past, the present circumstances allow him to do so, not as himself but as other, as a Cuban or Cuban American. This different subject attempts to understand the past from the same and different perspectives, to accept and reject it and move forward. Pérez Firmat's work is significant here in different manners. When referring to his brother Carlos's

---

[22] *Next Year in Cuba*, 20–21.   [23] *Exiled Memories*, 113.
[24] Also see Méndez, "Identity and Diaspora," 143–44.

theft of his identity and credit cards, Pérez Firmat does not act like a Cuban, who would protect the image of his family at all costs, but as a US citizen seeking justice and retribution.[25] However, what I want to emphasize is the idea of the stolen identity, because an exile feels that he must borrow or steal another's identity to replace his own. He wants to be the person he is not. The exile lives with borrowed or stolen identities.

Medina's *The Marks of Birth* contains three parts – Antón's family during the period of the Cuban revolution, the devastation brought about by the revolution and the reasons for exile, and a desire to recover a childhood past – and can be read as a continuation of *Exiled Memories*. *The Marks of Birth* deals not necessarily with the memory of a bygone era but with the experience of exile itself. Similar to García's early novels, Medina chronicles the lives of three generations of the García-Turner family, thus providing a continuity of actions from which to understand the present.

In essence, the present exists as part of the past, and in all the mentioned works the revolution is responsible for fragmenting the Cuban family, although problems existed before the tragic exodus. Felicia's silence and later writing, as a form of therapy and a way of recovering the past, show that Cubans who are silenced or silence themselves do have a story to tell, and they must reveal it to heal the past. Felicia's actions recall Rosario Ferré's Isabel Monfort, and her challenge to write a woman's version of the unfolding of historical events in Puerto Rico, but in Medina's case, within the context of the Cuban exile experience.[26] In fact, Felicia's writings include the lives of others and therefore become a collective voice of those who suffered under the Castro dictatorship.

Antón's section describes the all-too-familiar conflict of many Cuban Americans who are lost between two cultures, two languages, and two lifestyles, between the stories of the past and the reality of the present, and he is doomed to a life of despair. Reading his grandmother's writings allows him to revisit the family's traditions, and they provide the necessary liberation he needs to face and accept his current situation. The flight to the United States affords him the possibility to follow and free himself from the mark of the family, but also to return to it when the protagonist travels to the island.

Medina's *The Return of Felix Nogara* continues to explore the dimension of the exile identity seen in his previous works. Despite the social and economic

---

[25] *Next Year in Cuba.*   [26] Ferré, *House on the Lagoon.*

privileges the earliest wave of Cuban exiles enjoyed in the home country, they are not exempt from the consistent indignation, prejudice, discrimination, and exclusion suffered by other members of the broader Latino communities. Terra, in *The Cigar Roller*, is not an exile but an immigrant who left Cuba in the nineteenth century to work in the tobacco industry. Because of his present deteriorating conditions, he idealizes the past. With this text, Medina explores another important dimension of the Cuban American experience many decades before the advent of the revolution, but whose perspective is not so different from that of his exile counterpart.

New voices continue to emerge, such as Carlos Eire's *Waiting for Snow in Havana* (2003), a beautifully written account of the protagonist's life before and during Castro's coming to power, of a bygone era full of innocence and dreams of someone who belonged to a privileged class of grandeur and splendor. The narrative voice associated with Eire assumes his father's fascination with the privileges of the European aristocracy; Eire imagines himself to have been of French royalty, enjoying the comfort of maids and servants. The lifestyle exists in contrast to the mundane activities all children experience regardless of class, such as the recurrent cruelty to living forms when the young Eire and his buddies kill lizards. However, this lifecycle comes to an end with the change in government, sending Eire's aspirations into a tailspin. Eire narrates a specific portion of a history he was forced to experience; he was one of 14,000 children who were airlifted to Miami in what was known as Operation Pedro Pan. The act was both a salvation and a condemnation, since he and his brother had to leave his family behind. After almost four years of living with foster parents, he was reunited with his mother, while his father chose to stay behind. Exile physically rips the family apart. Yet his privileged background and the rupture of the family force him to excel and become a successful professor. Nonetheless, the exile relives his condition; just as he waited for snow in Havana, he waits for sunshine in United States, for the exile subject is internally trapped between two geographic and cultural spaces.

In *Dance Between Two Cultures*, I study the poetry of Cuban American writers and announce two currents.[27] The men are fixed on their exile condition, and the women celebrate their newfound sexual liberties denied

---

[27] *Dance Between Two Cultures*. Also see Iraida H. López's "Reading Lives in Installments: Autobiographical Essays of Women from the Cuban Diaspora," in *Cuban American Literature and Art*, 61–75, which surprisingly excludes Obejas's narrative from her analysis.

to them by Cuban macho culture (even though Cubans were experiencing a sexual revolution of their own during the early Castro years). The gay experience in Cuba, but also in the United States, is best addressed by Arenas's *Antes que anochezca*, which narrates the obvious political differences between the two countries and their similarities in the treatment of gays. Though the narrator denounces vehemently the Castro government, he yearns for his homosexual activities back home, because he does not find them in a free and democratic country. Yet it is precisely this freedom that, ironically, produces his premature death. Richard Blanco's *The Prince of Los Cocuyos: A Miami Childhood* (2014), whose title recalls Severo Sarduy's *Cocuyo* (1990) but also his uncle's Miami bodega El Cocuyito, comes out of his cocoon and explores his homosexuality within the interstices of Cuban and US cultures.

Achy Obejas's perspective is a welcome addition in light of the lack of frank literary representation of lesbian sexuality that Lourdes Casal mentions briefly in her early *Los fundadores: Alfonso y otros cuentos*. If writers like Mercedes Limón and Iraida Iturralde poeticize their newly discovered sexuality,[28] Obejas does the same but as a consequence of lesbian love. The theme of exile is present in her collection of stories *We Came All the Way from Cuba So You Could Dress like This?* (1994), but it appears in passing and focuses on the present. It is as if the protagonist is a lesbian who happens to be Cuban rather than a Cuban lesbian. For the present overpowers the past, even though the initial exile escape to Key West in 1963 figures in detail. Despite the exile experience, the difference in language and culture, it would be difficult to imagine coming to terms with one's sexuality in a society that did not create a space for lesbianism, in the same fashion that her parents opposed it. In the title story, the protagonist challenges her father's reasons for leaving the island, and becomes independent of him. For this protagonist and other women poets, exile is a liberation of sorts from the sexual trappings of the traditional culture of origin. The United States becomes an opportunity to start a new life and a way of inventing a new future.

In *Memory Mambo* (1996), the mambo in the title refers to a Cuban musical composition of the fifties that also impacted the various Latino communities in Chicago and other parts of the United States, as suggested by Hijuelos's *The Mambo Kings* and by Pérez Firmat's chapter interludes entitled "Mambos" in *Life on the Hyphen*. The mambo is also a rhythmic and dynamic instability

---

[28] *Dance Between Two Cultures*, Chapter 4.

of instruments and music, of memory, narrative creation, and identity formation. This is particularly the case with Juani, her sister, and cousins, who venture out into the new culture and explore their sexuality. *Memory Mambo* also provides a frame for the protagonist's introspection into the family past and the self, where memory is fluid and nothing is certain. The novel exposes the historically inventive past, and racial and homophobic actions of Juani's parents, Alberto and Xiomara. It pits men against women; men cheat, lie and molest women, who are weak and untrustworthy. Juani mediates her identity somewhere between the extreme positions of her cousins and sisters, between submissiveness and rebellion, to improvise a unique and individualized identity different from the rest of the family.

Yet in the end she gives into inventive memory, and recreates the past to resolve in the present a fight with her lover, Gina, by accepting an exilic, fictive, memory that is also hers. Obejas's novel precedes Julia Alvarez's treatment of Camila's lesbian love *In the Name of Salomé* (2001), when her mother, Salomé, warns her unborn child of macho behavior. In the present, it draws Camila closer to her companion Marion. In each of these two cases, as well as with other women poets and writers, the US context is fundamental for uncovering other aspects of sexuality in ways that would not have been possible in the culture and place of their parents' origin. If many male writers are stuck in the repetitive cycle of exiled memory, women writers like Obejas find freedom of expression in the adopted environment.

Other women authors such as Mirta Ojito, but also Ana Menéndez (*Loving Che*, 2004 and *Adios Happy Homeland*, 2011), Teresa Dovalpage (*A Girl Like Che* and *Posesas de La Habana*, both in 2004, *Muerte de un murciano en La Habana*, 2006, *¡Por culpa de Candela!*, 2008), Andrea O'Reilly Herrera (*The Pearl of the Antilles* and *ReMembering Cuba: Legacy of a Diaspora*, both in 2001), and also literary critics such as Eliana Rivero, Adriana Méndez Rodenas, Isabel Álvarez Borland, and Iraida H. López[29] are joining other Latina writers and with them addressing issues of sexuality, whether heterosexual or homosexual. They are consolidating a counterdiscourse to a traditional, patriarchal culture that dominates at home and continues to thrive in the adopted homeland.

As I have argued, Cuban American literature is not one-dimensional and cannot be defined exclusively by the Miami experience. On the contrary, it is rich in how topics such as exile are addressed. Within the context of Latino

[29] I refer to these critics who contribute to *Cuban American Literature and Art*. See also Iraida López, *Impossible Returns: Narratives of the Cuban Diaspora* (2015).

literature, the Cuban American experience is traumatic; it produces displacement, fragmentation, linguistic, and cultural schizophrenia already evident in the works of other Latino writers. However, because of the types of Cubans who have migrated – mainly white, of high social and economic standing, as defined by the first wave of exiles –, the black perspective has been less apparent. This should come as a surprise since Cuba has a highly visible Afro-Cuban population and culture. It exists in the Cuban music of the son, rumba, mambo, cha-cha-chá, charanga, and rap played in cities across the country, but also in the ever-popular botánicas that carry all the ingredients necessary to practice Santería, Regla de Ocha, Ifá, and Palo Monte. It is especially present in the religious music of Afro-Cuban rituals.

Blacks and their culture, practically invisible from the lives of the early Cuban exiles and their descendants, make appearances in Cristina García's *Dreaming in Cuban* and *The Agüero Sisters*, mentioned in the first novel and woven into the structure of the second one. The racial aspect of the Cuban American experience is openly addressed in Evelio Grillo's *Black Cuban Black American* (2000). In this work, situated in the first half of the twentieth century, the narrator describes his experiences as a tobacco roller in Ybor City, where Cubans worked together but lived in segregated neighborhoods. Certainly Cuban racism, but also its manifestation in the United States, impacted Grillo's daily life. Yet, he shares with other Afro-Latinos a welcoming invitation from the African-American community, who provide them with a sense of belonging. This racial aspect is also visible in Lourdes Casal's "Memories of a Black Cuban Childhood,"[30] where she explores her blackness within the racial constraints of US culture. In *Cantos to Blood and Honey* (1997), Adrián Castro's poems are steeped in Afro-Cuban and Afro-Caribbean history, myth, and music. This will become an important trend among black (but also white) Cubans as more of them identify with the African contribution to Cuban culture.

An integral part of Latino literature, Cuban American literature will continue to evolve in the direction of Cuban and Cuban American traditions, but also of US society and cultural mores. It will also incorporate their in-betweenness and develop new forms. As more Cubans leave the island and travel to the mainland, and mainland Cuban Americans return to the place of their parents' provenance, new experiences and ways of recounting them will enrich the literary landscape. But these will also vary according to the cities in

---

[30] Casal, "Memories of a Black Cuban Childhood," 61–62.

which the writer resides, whether it be in one location or another, or even in an in-between, hybrid space, defined by the mixtures of cultures, languages, time periods, experiences, memories, genders, races, and so on. The Cuban American experience also welcomes those who may not be Cuban American by birth, but by belief, association, friendship, or culture. Joy Castro, who was adopted by a Cuban family in Key West and believed her mother to be Cuban, but was mistaken, indeed is Cuban and has begun to define a new direction of the Cuban American experience.[31]

[31] See Falconer, Blas, and Lorraine López, eds. *The Other Latin@*.

21

Latina/o Theatre and Performance in the Context of Social Movements

RICARDO L. ORTÍZ

Before the middle of the twentieth century, the spaces of performance culture and performance practice that could be termed "Latino theatre" in the United States operated primarily in isolation from one another, and in modes that were highly idiosyncratic to those locations and their unique political, social, and cultural histories. From the middle of the nineteenth through to the early and mid-twentieth centuries, such theatrical and performance communities originated and developed in mostly heterogeneous and uneven ways in population centers as dissimilar, variegated, and far-flung as Mexican California (from Monterey, eventually to both Los Angeles and San Francisco), Arizona (Tucson) and Texas (San Antonio) to primarily Cuban and Puerto Rican locations on the East Coast (from Cuban Tampa to a more pan-Caribbean New York City). Over these many decades, the prehistory of what would eventually become a more consolidated, national Latino theatrical and performance cultural movement was characterized by a number of important struggles and challenges: these included negotiating language usage (that is, the shift in dominant or majority usage of Spanish to the same in English), transitioning from more characteristically immigrant practices retaining direct and living connections to countries and cultures of origin to practices more fully inscribed within (and assimilated into) dominant North American modes and contexts, choosing among a wide variety of available forms and genres (including "minor" forms such as *revistas, zarzuelas,* and *actos,* as well as the conventional "major" form of the *obra,* or play, including the musical play), operating across all the available modes of (in-)formality and (non-)professionalism, and, finally, emerging out of primarily localized and heterogeneous contexts of practice, into something even loosely resembling a singular national formation that, as recently as the early twenty-first century, refuses to let go entirely of its roots in local cultures and trans- and subnational practices, values, themes, interests, and movements.

By the 1950s and certainly into the 1960s, the seeds of what would become recognizable by century's end as a national Latino theatrical and performance culture, and perhaps even a theatrical and performance *project*, were already becoming evident in the form of a number of important if apparently unrelated events with highly different yet equally relevant connections to the signature social and cultural movements of the times. For example, the arrival in New York City in 1953 of the young (and eventually legendary) Puerto Rican actress Miriam Colón, coinciding with the first production in the same city of Puerto Rican playwright René Márques's play *La Carreta*, set an early stage for what would in the decades to come emerge as a vital and growing mainland Puerto Rican (or Nuyorican) influence on New York's theatrical culture, on-, off- and off-off-Broadway, and in ways that would, thanks to New York City's centrality to U.S. theatre, shine a national spotlight on many performers, writers, and other theatrical figures of Puerto Rican descent. Such a cultural history would both parallel and interact with the political history of Puerto Rico's complicated colonial relationship with the United States, a history with a very direct impact upon the formation of a mainland Puerto Rican identity and the sociopolitical movement that would make significant contributions to the U.S. civil rights movement unfolding across the same decades. As the 1950s and 1960s saw the emergence of performers like Chita Rivera and Rita Moreno as major stars of both theatre and film, they also saw the continuing interest in both Spanish- and English-language productions of *La Carreta*, arguably the first play to represent the Puerto Rican experience as simultaneously encompassing life both on and off the island. The establishment in 1967 by Colón and Roberto Rodríguez of The Puerto Rican Traveling Theatre saw the arrival of an influential New York City-based cultural institution that still operates successfully well into the twenty-first century.

Over the same decades, American theatrical culture would also begin to feel the impact and influence of another, quite distinct artist of Hispanic-Latina descent, the Cuban-born avant-garde playwright and director, María Irene Fornés. In 1957, Fornés returned to New York City after living for years in Paris, inspired by continental artistic and intellectual cultures, and especially by her encounter with the work of Samuel Beckett, to contribute her own unique, experimental innovations to (and radical deconstructions of) conventional theatrical practice and playwriting, which, by the 1965 appearance of pieces like *The Successful Life of 3* and *Promenade*, commanded the attention of off-Broadway audiences and began her long streak of winning Obie Awards. Readers looking for explicitly legible Latino social or political themes in Fornés work might be frustrated by her highly abstract, strategically antirealist pieces, but across her career Fornés devoted a great deal of sustained attention to the explosively patriarchal gender politics of canonical theatre and cinema, producing some of the most inventive and subversive representations of women's experiences and capacities in the North American theatrical tradition, highlighted in particular by her 1977 masterwork, *Fefu and Her Friends*. In addition, Fornés secured her theatrical legacy for future generations by teaching and mentoring some of the more prominent and influential Latina/o writers and artists to follow her into the world of U.S. theatre, and well beyond the confines of off-Broadway and New York; they include such notable artists as Eduardo Machado, Cherríe Moraga, Carmelita Tropicana, and Nilo Cruz. And while Machado, Tropicana, and Cruz, all artists (like Fornés) of Cuban descent, have produced considerable and important work that more accessibly explores what readers will recognize as a more conventional account of "Cuban-American" experience, Fornés's own work, and the impressive narratives of her career and her life, are suggestive of the larger possibilities open to imaginative expression that refuses literal conformity to the admittedly compelling, and urgent, representational logics of American immigrant art and politics.

The 1960s and 1970s also saw a polar formation, on the opposite coast of the United States, and in a rural rather than an urban setting, and with a quite distinct relationship to the emerging politics of immigrant- and racial-minority themed movements for civil rights: the theatre-based cultural "arm" of César Chávez's California-based, and primarily Mexican American or Chicano, United Farm Worker movement. Over the same years that Colón and her collaborators were enlivening Puerto Rican theatre in New York, and that Fornés was helping to recast and expand the reaches of dramatic and theatrical art from the same urban base, the Mexican American playwright and director Luis Valdez was beginning to realize a version of the Brechtian dream of a radically political theatre through his collaborations with Chávez, and in the service of educating, inspiring, and mobilizing the recently organized populations of Chicana/o seasonal and migrant farm workers laboring in the fields of California's Central Valley. Himself the child of migrant farm workers, Valdez eventually attended San Jose State College (later San Jose State University), majoring in English and composing his earliest dramatic works, from one-acts to his first full-length play. By 1965, Valdez had returned to the valley of his youth, and committed himself to working with Chávez, by writing and producing mostly shorter pieces in the mode of agitprop, a highly political form of theatrical practice with roots in communist Russia and a long history of influence in both Europe and the United States through the mid-twentieth century. In the following years, Valdez and his collaborators would establish *El Teatro Campesino*, perhaps the most politically and historically influential Latina/o theatrical project of the latter twentieth century. That project would both extend and develop from Valdez's early one-act, agitprop work to produce longer and eventually full-length dramatic pieces that covered an even wider scope of Mexican-American and Chicana/o life and culture, and at the same time serve as a template for the numerous local Chicana/o theater companies that would sprout and often thrive across the United States from the 1965 onward (including Seattle's Teatro del Piojo, El Paso's Teatro de los Pobres, Denver's Su Teatro, and eventually Teatro Nacional de Aztlán, or TENAZ). Valdez can also be credited with articulating the vision shaping both his own career and the larger movement he helped to inaugurate, in his influential 1970 essay, "Notes on Chicano Theatre." While Valdez's career would eventually take him away from the valley where *Teatro Campesino* would establish its permanent and lasting home base, he would maintain direct ties with it even into the twenty-first century, returning often to both it and the central California region where his career began.

Regardless of all of his admittedly important impact across the long and (in 2017) ongoing course of his career, Luis Valdez's primary contribution to the history of Latina/o theatre in the United States remains his extraordinary semi-musical, semi-mytho-graphic, pseudo-epic, documentary-historical play, *Zoot Suit*, which enjoyed its first and signature production at Los Angeles's Mark Taper Forum in 1978. The 1970s had, however, already seen the rise to public prominence of theatre artists like the Nuyorican playwright Miguel Piñero, whose play *Short Eyes* (1974) began its life in a prison drama workshop before the productions at Joseph Papp's Public Theater and eventually Broadway would command national and international attention. Valdez's chief contributions through *Zoot Suit* were multiple, but they include: wrenching the focus of the U.S. theatrical consciousness away from New York City and to the West Coast; composing a piece whose ambitious use of music and dance to analyze critically the class- and racial-political causes of urban youth gangs and their criminalization responds directly to and corrects Broadway's own canonical attempt at a similar depiction in *West Side Story*; and (among other techniques) basing his own narrative so closely on the actual historical details of the Sleepy Lagoon Murder and Zoot Suit

Riots (which had occurred in the Los Angeles of the early 1940s) that audiences could not help but experience the kind of productively alienating, consciousness-raising shocks to their established worldviews that Bertolt Brecht (among others) demanded of the most politically engaged kind of theatre. Although the first New York production of *Zoot Suit* failed to reproduce the critical and commercial success of the debut run in Los Angeles, the 1981 film adaptation (also written and directed by Valdez) stands as a vivid testament to the inherent strengths of the piece, and the success of the Los Angeles run served as a watershed moment for the future prolifer-ation of a Chicana/o and Latina/o-based theatrical culture in California's largest city. In the course of the following two decades, metropolitan Los Angeles would see the emergence of a robust infrastructure to cultivate local Chicana/o and Latina/o theatrical and performance projects, support-ing artists as varied in their practices as the performance troupe Culture Clash, the solo performance artist and all-around theatre impresario Luis Alfaro, the playwright and producer Josefina López, and the actor and performance artist Marissa Chibás; these artists and many others would enjoy a rich variety of popular and institutional support from community projects and professional spaces like the Mark Taper Forum, the Los Angeles Theatre Center, the Hispanic Playwrights Project at the South Coast Reper-tory, Casa 0101 in Boyle Heights, and the Highways Performance Space in Santa Monica.

If Valdez's accomplishments from the 1960s into the 1980s can stand, even in 2015, as a kind of inaugural moment for a larger national Latina/o theatre movement that would no longer need to rely on the influence and authority of the New York "scene" to determine what could succeed and thrive beyond New York, much was also occurring from within to complicate the tenor and character of that scene over the same period. It would be difficult to imagine a more distinct trajectory of struggle and accomplishment to the one mod-eled by Valdez than the one that marks the career of Nuyorican playwright, poet, and actor Miguel Piñero. Having moved as a child from Puerto Rico to Manhattan in the early 1950s, Piñero spent much of his adolescence and early adult life fighting extreme poverty and the kind of profound social precarity that understandably leads to substance abuse and other forms of criminal behavior. It was actually while incarcerated for theft in the early 1970s that Piñero composed the first draft of what would become his one major play, the explosive prison drama *Short Eyes* (also adapted into a fine film by Robert Young in 1977). As the title suggests, the narrative focuses primarily on the fate of one prisoner whose charge of pedophilia marks him as the inevitable target of violence for all of his fellow inmates; but it also exploits that central conceit to explore the more extreme facets of raced, gendered, and classed power by making that pedophile character (like most of the guards) white, and by making most of the other prisoners either Latino or African American. Set as it is in the confines of a single setting, and populated as it is by a single-sex cast of characters, *Short Eyes* plays in spite of its brutal realism more like one of Fornés's inventions of theatrical abstraction than like Valdez's more directly representational and accessible modes of treating the politics of culture and identity. But, in many ways, the aesthetic commitments and strategic deployments of these three major figures, so foundational of the Latina/o theatrical world that would follow them, do neatly position them on a spectrum that begins with the more uncompromisingly formal interventions that we find in Fornés's work from the early 1960s onward, through Piñero's attempts to push at those modes of formal abstraction at least toward something more legibly allegorical, and finally toward the more variegated, full-bodied, and politically committed modes of theatrical and dramatic practice found in *Zoot Suit* and much of Valdez's later work, especially but not only in film. Piñero, like Valdez, also had a hand in establishing an important cultural institution (the Nuyorican Poets Café, in 1973) supporting his particular community, and, also like Valdez, took serious advantage of the surrounding culture-industry infrastructure to pursue (in his case) a career in television acting. But Piñero finally could not overcome the tendencies toward self-destruction that haunted him much of his life; in 1988, he died of cirrhosis in New York City at the age of 41. As a legacy, however, Miguel Piñero has also left behind him both the play and film adaptation of *Short Eyes*, a collection of striking verse pieces in his inimitably poetic voice, some unfinished dramatic work, the inspiration for *Piñero*, a fine 2001 film by Leon Ichaso, and the ongoing life of the Nuyorican Poets' Café, where succeeding generations of writers, artists, performers, and poets continue to find a space for their work, and audiences for their voices.

As the progressive and left-wing civil rights, labor, and third-world nationalist movements of the 1960s and 1970s gave way in the 1980s to the late–Cold War age of Ronald Reagan and the national conservative political and cultural backlash he embodied, the heart of the Latina/o theatrical and performance cultures in the United States of the same period also shifted, expanded and variegated in response to, and sometimes even helping to drive, the changes emerging over that differently turbulent decade. Admittedly, while figures like Fornés, Piñero, and Valdez all in their own ways resisted as much as they flirted with the canonical modes of formal and professional theatre, the fact that all of their reputations rest in some part on works of theirs that enjoyed considerable success in those formal, professional circles, suggests that work remained to be done to forge modes of theatre and performance practice that could more effectively subvert and even explode the structures of hierarchy and exclusion that kept so many artists, especially those from the most excluded and vulnerable populations, from finding audiences for their work, and from securing the resources, and spaces, for the very production of that work. The 1980s figure, therefore, as the decade when previous modes of alternative, underground and avant-garde theatrical practice began to coalesce more visibly around a mode of practice that came to be known as performance art, and which in turn provoked the formation of a new scholarly and critical discipline that could produce a viable alternative knowledge about such practices, a discipline that eventually came to call itself performance studies. Performance art originates in and covers a bracingly wide array of modes of expressive practice, with as viable roots in, and links to, stand-up comedy, folk ritual, cabaret, drag, highly abstract modes of body- and gesture-oriented conceptual and installation art (bleeding more than occasionally into modes of experimental dance), as in and to all the conceivable modes of complex multimedia platforming (including film, television, and digital media) that the most inventive performer or performance group can throw onto whatever space can serve as a stage and for whatever grouping of gathered bodies can serve as an audience.

From the 1980s onward, performance art by Latina/o-identified practitioners and/or engaging Latina/o themes has taken root across the U.S. cultural landscape, including but not only in those metropolitan spaces that also serve as centers of more conventional theatrical practice as New York and Los Angeles. As represented by artists and collectives as varied as Harry Gamboa, Guillermo Gómez-Peña, Luis Alfaro, Marga Gómez, Carmelita Tropicana, Vaginal Davis, Mónica Palacios, Culture Clash, El Vez, Coco Fusco, Adelina Anthony, and the Butchlalis de Panochtitlán, the post-1980 Latina/o American performance art project has for almost four decades now explored and exploded, rethought and un-thought, recovered and invented anew, all of the salient conditions and challenges of Latina/o experience as they shifted and evolved over that period, from the politics of gender and sexuality, to the failure of U.S. immigration policy (and its impact both for undocumented immigrants and for everyone else living in "border spaces" that far exceed the literal U.S.–Mexican political border), to the crisis of AIDS in all the U.S. queer and ethnic minority communities it ravaged, to the ongoing and increasingly pervasive Latina/o-ization of North American cultural, social, and political life in general. If the career of a performer like John Leguizamo can stand as perhaps the most spectacular example of someone's rise from roots in this performance culture to the kind of "mainstream" success to which his three decades of work in film, television, and theatre can attest, we should also be mindful that often quite successful lifelong careers in theatre and performance do not rise as manifestly to popular consciousness. Luis Alfaro, for example, who has been working with consistent success as long as Leguizamo has, may not enjoy his peer's public celebrity, but he has over the course of a thirty-plus-year career developed a body of work, from early solo performances coming right out of his experiences as a queer Chicano man living in an AIDS-ravaged community to differently ambitious theatrical projects, like the Latina/o-izing adaptations of Aeschylus' *Electra* (*Electricidad*), Sophocles' *Oedipus* (*Oedipus el Rey*) and Euripides' *Medea* (*Mojada*) he developed in the early 2010s, that can stand on its own as a transformative contribution to U.S. theatre.

By the beginning of the 1990s, much of the infrastructural, foundational work that had characterized Latina/o theatre and performance practice in preceding decades began to coalesce in powerful ways. Alongside those developments in living culture, scholarly practices began at the same moment to both catch up with and parallel what was happening on the nation's stages and performance spaces; major studies of both the long pre-history and exciting contemporary unfolding of Latina/o theatre and performance started to appear, in book form, in scholarly collections in major journals, as well as in a series of important, influential standalone articles by a growing population of scholars specializing in the fields in question. From Nicolás Kanellos's *A History of Hispanic Theatre in the United States: Origins to 1940* (1990), to David Román's *Acts of Intervention: Performance, Gay Culture, and AIDS* (1998), to Alberto Sandoval-Sánchez's *José, Can You See: Latinos On and Off Broadway* (1999), to José Muñoz's *Disidentifications: Queers of Color and the Performance of Politics* (1999), to Jorge Huerta's *Chicano Drama: Performance, Society, Myth* (2000), to Alicia Arrizón and Lillian Manzor-Coats's *Latinas on Stage: Practice and Theory* (2000), and to Arrizón's own *Latina Performance: Traversing the Stage* (1999), the 1990s proved to be as much a watershed moment for Latino theatre and performance studies as the 1970s and 1980s had been for Latina/o theatre and performance practice. Three exemplary threads proceeding from this larger process of cultural proliferation can together take the measure of the importance of the last decade of the twentieth century for setting the stage for what would happen after the turn to the twenty-first. These include: the proliferation of a new generation of twenty-first century Latina/o playwrights and theatre artists like the Pulitzer Prize-winners Nilo Cruz (in 2003, for *Anna in the Tropics*) and Quiara Alegría Hudes (in 2012, for *Water by the Spoonful*), but also counterparts of theirs like the Washington, DC-based Karen Zacarías, Ricardo Abreu Bracho (based in California and New York), Jorge Ignacio Cortiñas (New York) and Melinda Lopez (Boston), as well as solo performance artists like Quique Avilés (Washington, DC) and Adelina Anthony (San Antonio); the unprecedented critical and commercial success of the "Nuyorican" Broadway impresario Lin Manuel Miranda, especially thanks to his two major theatrical projects, the hip-hop inflected musical plays, *In the Heights* (2008) and *Hamilton* (2015); and the ongoing infrastructural, institutional work of projects like INTAR in New York City and the Latino Theater Company in Los Angeles.

The historical "turn" into the twenty-first century saw U.S. Latino life, and U.S. Latino theatre practice, dominated by a handful of compelling themes. Following the Immigration Reform and Control Act signed by Ronald Reagan in 1986, and through the series of aggressive anti-immigrant ballot propositions in California in the 1990s, and through the conversion of the Immigration and Naturalization Service into the Immigration and Customs Enforcement (ICE) agency in the wake of the September 11, 2001 terrorist attacks and the establishment of a new Department of Homeland Security (which houses ICE), through to the controversy surrounding (among others) Arizona's own anti-immigrant SB 1070 legislation of 2010 and finally to DACA, Barack Obama's 2012 executive order for Deferred Action for Childhood Arrivals, the dynamics of both federal and state-specific forms of immigrant legislation, and immigration policy more generally, have directly and indirectly conditioned most Latinos' sense of legitimate political and cultural belonging to U.S. life, and this without any single necessary relationship to any given family's or individual's actual legal status in the United States. By the run-up to the presidential elections of 2016, the national discourse around immigration tends to conflate not only "immigrant" with "illegal," but also "immigrant" with "Latino"; for this reason, a large majority of U.S. Latinos support comprehensive immigration reform with a path toward citizenship for the many millions of people living in the United States without proper documentation, and this without any direct reference to their own legal status. In addition, early twenty-first century U.S. Latinos also face in their own unique ways many of the other economic, social, and political challenges that have colored life in the United States in that volatile era, encompassing: the 2001 terrorist attacks and the ensuing "Wars," on Terror, on Drugs, and in Afghanistan and Iraq; the financial, cultural, and community damage inflicted by the economic meltdown of 2008 and 2009 and the increases in income and opportunity inequality that followed; the violently negative and disproportional impacts of both mass incarceration and mass deportation on Latino communities and families across the United States; the ongoing harm of persistent structural and institutional biases regarding race, class, gender, and gender expression, sexuality and physical ability that disproportionally impact the most vulnerable members of society; and, at the same time, a measure of positive social, political, and economic mobility for those Latinos fortunate enough to be able to seize upon opportunities, especially but not exclusively through higher education, to access forms of material and symbolic "capital" that can lead to greater political enfranchisement, and increasing cultural influence.

One significant indication of this increasing cultural influence can be found in the two Pulitzer Prize–winning theatrical works written by Latina/o playwrights and spanning the near-decade between 2003 and 2012. It would be difficult to imagine two more dissimilar plays than Nilo Cruz's *Anna in the Tropics* (2003) and Quiara Alegría Hudes's *Water by the Spoonful* (2012), but together these two remarkable pieces suggest everything about the rich complexity of Latino life in the United States, and far beyond the quality of that life in the decade (and even century) of their appearance. Of the two, *Anna in the Tropics* might seem superficially to be the more conservative or perhaps more conventional. Like its predecessors *Short Eyes* (by Miguel Piñero) and *Real Women Have Curves* (by Josefina López), Cruz's *Anna* also benefits from the effect of dramatic compression that can come from setting almost all of the play's action in one space, here a 1920s cigar factory in Tampa, Florida's, Ybor City, and over a brief span of time. Unlike its predecessors, however, *Anna in the Tropics* features characters of both genders, and indeed makes gender and sexuality politics one prominent thematic axis, the other being the combustion of cultural and material politics as they play out in the larger context of the U.S. immigrant narrative. By setting his play as distantly in the past as the Roaring Twenties and the ensuing Great Depression, and by devoting much of its action to a debate between tradition and modernity in the conduct of both a business's manufacture of its product (cigars) and the cultural practices overlaying that manufacture (the Cuban use of "lectores," or readers, to entertain and inform workers as they rolled those cigars), Cruz can be charged with indulging a certain degree of uncritical nostalgia for a romanticized past that might predictably appeal to a "mainstream" theatre audience's predilection for an exoticized and sentimentalized latinidad. Cruz, however, clearly has other concerns in mind as his story and his stagecraft unfold. Setting his tale well before the 1959 Cuban Revolution, for example, Cruz can sidestep any direct reference to or engagement with the defining political tension in post-revolution and post-exile Cuban American life, at the same time that his play is deeply concerned with the spiritual and ethical demands, as well as the spiritual and ethical costs, of sacrificing everything to the brutal materialism of capitalist ambition in its most nakedly greedy mode. At the same time, the performance-within-the-performance of the "lector" character Juan Julián's reading of Tolstoy's *Anna Karenina* to the factory workers, and the corollary depiction of the workers' readerly consumption of Tolstoy's story, replete with their attempts to make sense of their own modest but complicated lives in terms of those of *Anna*'s tragic Russian aristocrats, tells us that we are in the hands of a playwright who knows how to exploit the impressive resources of postmodern literary inter-textuality in the handling of artistic material. Layer over this the almost didactic passages where characters inform one another, and the play's audience, of the deep indigenous ritual powers of cigar-smoking, and Cruz fully rehearses in the complexity of his own stagecraft the contemporary tensions between (post) modernity and tradition, tensions that analogously drive the conflicts between characters, and the dialectic of themes, coursing through *Anna*'s story.

A decade later, the Philadelphia-born, Puerto Rican-descended playwright Quiara Alegría Hudes opened for her audience a new world of alternative imaginative possibilities by setting a significant amount of the "action" in 2012's Pulitzer Prize–winning *Water by the Spoonful* in cyberspace, namely in a sobriety chat room managed by one of her characters and inhabited by several others. If Cruz's play finds its home in the tension between cultural tradition and capitalist modernity, Hudes's play lands squarely in the vexed space of its own contemporaneity. The second installment in a masterful trilogy of plays centering on the character of Elliot Ortiz (a Philadelphia-born, Puerto Rican-descended Iraq War vet and aspiring actor loosely based on one of Hudes's own relatives), *Water by the Spoonful* tackles by turns and through effective strategies of dramatic synthesis issues as alive in the second decade of the twenty-first century as: the massive harm, and possible recovery and survival, from substance abuse and addiction experienced by all sectors of U.S. society; the negative legacies of the wars in Afghanistan and Iraq for the service members, many of them working-class young people of color, who fought them and returned to suffer afterward, often from both physical and psychological injury; and the stakes and wages of identity, certainly for traditional immigrant communities with ambiguous and often precarious relationships with more stable and official forms of political and cultural citizenship, but also for anyone who has ever ventured online into spaces where virtual anonymity and virtual play allow for an infinite variety of opportunities for self-reinvention and alternative social interaction, and in settings where that interaction can include participants scattered over the entire globe even as they "meet" in virtual spaces like Recovertogether.com. While one of *Water*'s narrative axes involves a set of familial tensions that set the character Elliot, his cousin Yazmin, and their mothers Ginny and Odessa on a course to come to terms with the tragic fallout of Odessa's crack addiction, a difficult process of forgiveness and near-redemption that will require the two cousins coming to a moment of crisis and breakthrough on the island, the other axis hovers in cyberspace, and because of that can reach beyond Philadelphia, where the recovering Odessa manages her sobriety chatroom using the alias "haikumom," and can include members as far-flung and anonymous as "chutes&ladders" (an African-American man who works for the IRS in San Diego) and "orangutan" (a young Japanese-American woman searching for her birth mother in Japan). All three plays in what is called the "Elliot Trilogy" can stand alone as independent pieces, and across them Hudes manages to employ quite startlingly different kinds of narrative structure and to explore a vast range of thematic obsessions, but they also work together to form one of the more ambitious projects of dramatic storytelling on the part of a Latina/o artist since the Cuban-American playwright Eduardo Machado's quartet of *Floating Island Plays* from the late 1980s and early 1990s.

A similarly "monumental" ambition can be found in the career projects of two additional prize-winning Latina/o theatre artists who have arguably hit their stride or indeed just come into prominence in the early decades of the twenty-first century: the MacArthur "Genius" Grant recipients Luis Alfaro (1997) and Lin-Manuel Miranda (2015). Roughly a generation apart in age, Alfaro (born 1963) and Miranda (born 1980) together can help us appreciate the challenge and the necessary complexity of approach that confront any attempt to summarize Latina/o theatre practice in the United States in the mid 2010s as anything coalescing toward a coherent national project. While Alfaro's roots in theatre practice go back to the 1980s and remain more or less anchored on the West Coast, primarily in Los Angeles, the queer Chicano performance artist, playwright, and theatre impresario has forged an important career primarily by fusing his creative enterprise with an activist practice that both turns to local communities of color across the country to find inspiration and to serve as laboratories for his work, and takes the opportunity of his collaborations with established theatre companies across the country to connect them more directly with their own local communities of color. This can be seen most starkly in the development of Alfaro's monumental trilogy of Chicano-themed theatre pieces based on some of the most canonical tragedies of Greek antiquity: *Electricidad* (2004, based on Aeschylus' *Electra*), *Oedipus el Rey* (2010, based on Sophocles' *Oedipus the King*), and *Mojada* (2015, based on Euripides' *Medea*). In each of these pieces, Alfaro demonstrates how the primal human urgency driving such challenging issues in contemporary Latino life as gang violence, mass incarceration, and undocumented immigration can find compelling translation in the terms of ancient, equally primal, equally violent, equally human tragedy. In *Oedipus el Rey*, for example, Alfaro alternates his narrative between the gang-dominated neighborhoods of East Los Angeles and the state prison in California's Central Valley that houses many male inmates from the kin and gang networks of the civilian characters in Los Angeles. Struggles for power, declarations and betrayals of family and gang loyalty, and the twists of narrative and existential fate that befall the piece's main characters all propel Alfaro's rendition toward the same tragic, bloody outcomes that befell the more famous characters in Sophocles' work. Transposing onto the brutal contemporary realism of Alfaro's depictions of gang and prison life some of the formal elements of classical tragedy, especially, for example, the use of a chorus of tattooed and uniformed male prisoners who recite verse lines in a hypnotic, staccato rhythm, and the dispensation of historically realistic stage settings at times in favor of more abstract, hallucinatory uses of stage design, costuming, and props, *Oedipus el Rey* fuses the present and the past, reality and myth, stereotype and archetype, in ways that contribute directly to the piece's overall effect on its audience, an effect that refuses any easy dissociation of the chaotic force of contemporary violence from the anything-but-chaotic, ritual, ceremonial and even stylized, aesthetic intensity of lives so materially, erotically, and spiritually constrained.

More than a decade into the twenty-first century, Latino theatrical practice and Latino theatrical culture in the United States have made important strides toward at least establishing a more prominent national status thanks to the contribution of artists as dispersed and mobile on the national scene as Cruz, Hudes, and Alfaro, as well as many of their contemporaries. If these creative, cultural, and institutional practices have yet to coalesce meaningfully into anything one might want to characterize as a focused, coherent, and organized national project, signs at least exist into 2017 that U.S. Latino theatre's best days lie ahead of it. Perhaps the most prominent example of such hope-inspiring work looms in the successful Broadway-based career of the actor, singer, composer, and all-around theatrical impresario Lin-Manuel Miranda, whose two major productions, the Tony- and Pulitzer-winning *In the Heights* (2008, with a book by Hudes) and the explosively successful and transformational *Hamilton* (2015) have not only made their mark thanks to unprecedented critical and commercial success, but have done so while adhering uncompromisingly (each in its own way) to a vision of U.S. political, social, and cultural life within which Latinos and other people of color figure not just prominently but centrally. Miranda's achievements, already well documented but still mostly unfolding in the early stages of what promises to be a long and storied career, open the door to whatever comes next in the process of forging a robust and inclusive theatrical culture in the United States. That future U.S. theatrical culture, thanks to the contributions of the many figures cited in the present and now closing discussion, will undoubtedly embrace an American life, and an American world, where Spanish will sound as familiar as English, where hip-hop and salsa will orchestrate a musical score as legitimately as pop and swing, and where performers, writers, and all other workers in theatre will find their rightful place, onstage or backstage, thanks to their talent, their vision, their *ganas* and their commitment to political, social, and cultural change.

WORKS CITED

Arrizón, Alicia. *Latina Performance: Traversing the Stage*. Bloomington: Indiana University Press, 1999.

Queering Mestizaje: Transculturation and Performance. Ann Arbor: University of Michigan Press, 2006.

Arrizón, Alicia and Lillian Manzor, eds. *Latinas on Stage: Practice and Theory*. Berkeley, CA: Third Woman Press, 2000.

Herrera, Brian. *Latin Numbers: Playing Latino in Twentieth Century U.S. Popular Performance*. Ann Arbor: University of Michigan Press, 2015.

Huerta, Jorge. *Chicano Drama: Performance, Society and Myth*. Cambridge: Cambridge University Press, 2000.

Chicano Theater: Themes and Forms. Tempe, AZ: Bilingual Press. 1981.

Kanellos, Nicolás. *A History of Hispanic Theatre in the United States: Origins to 1940*. Austin: University of Texas Press, 1990.

Muñoz, José Esteban. *Disidentifications: Queers of Color and the Performance of Politics*. Minneapolis: University of Minnesota Press, 1999.

Ramos-García, Luis A., ed. *The State of Latino Theater in the United States*. New York and London: Routledge, 2002.

Rivera-Servera, Ramón. *Performing Queer Latinidad: Dance, Sexuality, Politics*. Ann Arbor: University of Michigan Press, 2012.

Sandoval-Sánchez, Alberto. *José, Can You See?: Latinos On and Off Broadway*. Madison: University of Wisconsin Press, 1999.

Taylor, Diana and Juan Villegas, eds. *Negotiating Performance: Gender, Sexuality and Theatricality in Latin/o America*. Durham, NC: Duke University Press, 1994.

PART IV

★

LITERARY MIGRATIONS ACROSS THE AMERICAS, 1980–2017

22

Undocumented Immigration in Latina/o Literature

MARTA CAMINERO-SANTANGELO

In recent decades, undocumented immigrants have gradually woven themselves into the fabric of many Latina/o communities in the United States, including in areas of the country that were not historically destinations for immigrant migrant routes. Deportations and raids have affected entire communities as neighbors and family members are detained and removed, with serious psychological impact on those that remain. As a result, literary representations of undocumented characters and of undocumented immigration, with all of the politics and dangers surrounding it, have begun to figure prominently in the work of U.S. Latina/o and Chicana/o writers. The growing prominence of undocumented characters in this body of literature, particularly by authors who are not themselves undocumented, suggests that Latina/o authors are coming to see the treatment of complicated immigration issues as integral to the ethical and social framework of their writing. Alberto Ledesma, one of the very first Latina/o literary scholars to write about the theme of unauthorized immigrants in U.S. Latina/o literature beginning in the late 1990s (who had himself been undocumented) insists that undocumented existence *is* a significant aspect of Latina/o existence; consequently, for Ledesma, "the voices of undocumented immigrant subjects present in Chicana and Chicano narratives should be read, understood, and discussed as a fundamental part of Chicano experience" ("Undocumented Crossings" 92). Yet he has also acknowledged that Chicana/o writers themselves have frequently obscured issues of undocumented immigration (88). Nonetheless, increasingly since the 1990s, Chicana/o literary production as well as Latina/o literature more generally has made the experience of undocumented immigrants an ethical focus demanding attention and has represented this experience as fundamental to a larger history connecting the United States to Latin America and the Caribbean.

The criminalization of undocumented immigrants from Latin America and the Caribbean to the United States arguably has its origins in the second half of the twentieth century. In the nineteenth century, and for much of the twentieth, migration back and forth across the U.S.–Mexico border was largely unregulated; between 1910 (the beginning of the Mexican Revolution) and 1930, roughly one-tenth of the Mexican population migrated to the United States for reasons ranging from political upheaval to labor demand (De Genova, "Production" 162). As Nicholas De Genova points out, there were no numerical caps on Mexican immigrants until 1965, although immigrants could be and were barred or deported for other reasons and in ways that largely corresponded to the management of labor demand (163). But in 1965, the Hart-Celler Act placed quantitative restrictions on numbers of immigrants from the Western Hemisphere – restrictions that did not correlate to existing and long-established migration patterns or to demands for cheap labor from Mexico in particular. In effect, the 1965 immigration law created the category of "illegal immigration" as it is currently understood.

The long-standing effects of this legislation on U.S. public discourse can be witnessed in the vitriolic and racist rhetoric that has developed around the topic of illegal immigration. Several scholars in the social sciences, most prominently Leo Chavez in *The Latino Threat* (2008) and *Covering Immigration* (2001), have documented the power of images, metaphors, and a generalized discourse about so-called "illegal immigrants" to dehumanize and demonize undocumented immigrants, characterizing them as criminals, disease carriers, drug dealers, breeders, and – after the September 11 terrorist attacks – as terrorists, potential invaders, and a threat to national "homeland security." Simultaneously, prominent narratives of national identity in the media and in books such as Samuel Huntington's *Who Are We* (2004) have excluded undocumented immigrants especially, and Latina/o immigrants as a whole, from any possible understanding of collective "American" identity. While Chicanos and Puerto Ricans in particular had long-standing experience as marginalized ethnic "minority" populations in the United States, the creation of a recognizable category of person referred to as "illegal" had effects on the inclusion of even U.S. citizen Latina/os in the national imaginary. As Nicholas De Genova has argued, the construction of our current concept of "illegal immigrants" has involved a pervasive racialization of the category, such that illegal immigrants are assumed to be predominantly Mexican, and Mexicans are similarly assumed to be largely "illegal." Witness, for instance, the pejorative term "wetback," referring technically to those who waded across the Río Grande in order to enter the United States from Mexico, but applied much more broadly and loosely. Because the category of "illegality" is created and reified in large part by powerful stories about what it means to be an "American," what "Americanness" is, and who constitutes a threat to "America," the late twentieth and twenty-first centuries have given rise to a multitude of counter-narratives about migration and unauthorized status that critique and challenge these categorizations.

Historicizing the U.S.-Mexico Border

Gloria Anzaldúa's foundational Chicana text *Borderlands / La Frontera* (1987), known for its crossing and blending of genre borders including memoir, personal essay, history, and poetry, takes a posture of explicit challenge to the border's existence. Anzaldúa extends the history of "illegal" crossing backward, to put late twentieth-century migration north in a much longer context of U.S. conquest. The "illegal crossing" that *Borderlands* targets is thus not that of migrant Mexicans north, but of U.S. colonial expansion southward and westward under the principles of Manifest Destiny:

> In the 1800s Anglos migrated illegally into Texas, which was then part of Mexico, in greater and greater numbers ... their illegal invasion forced Mexico to fight a war to keep its Texas territory... The land established by the treaty [of Guadalupe Hidalgo in 1848] as belonging to Mexicans was soon swindled away from its owners. The treaty was never honored and restitution, to this day, has never been made. (6–7)

Anzaldúa positions more recent waves of migration within this larger post-colonial understanding of how legality and illegality are constructed categories defined by the colonial power, noting that while undocumented laborers are particularly vulnerable, employers benefit from their cheap and exploitable labor.[1] Further, she narrates the personal impact of the history of perceived illegality of Mexicans and Mexican Americans, recalling how Pedro (presumably a cousin) was rounded up by "la migra" (even though he was a U.S. citizen) and deported to Guadalajara because he was *"sin papeles"* – he did not carry his birth certificate with him when working in the fields (4).

The thrust of Anzaldúa's counter-narrative critique lies not only in the deportation of a citizen, but also in her use of the trope of translation to render a story *differently*. Literally, *"sin papeles"* would translate as "without papers," that is, "undocumented." However, Anzaldúa *re*translates it to the

---

[1] See Mae Ngai's *Impossible Subjects* on the deportation of Mexican American US citizens in the 1930s, the long-standing pattern of US agribusiness dependence on Mexican labor, as well as the ramifications of the Hart-Celler Act of 1965, which for the first time placed a numerical ceiling on migration from Mexico, on the category of "illegality."

MARTA CAMINERO-SANTANGELO

equivalent of "he did not carry his papers with him." The structure of Anzaldúa's sentence, with its switch from Spanish to English, also uses this translation effect to render synonymous the condition of being undocumented and the circumstance of not having one's proof (papers, documentation) on one's body. That is, Pedro's legal status is precarious not because he is not a citizen (he is) but because he is racialized as Mexican and therefore "illegal." Agents of the border patrol "la migra" simply assume this status in the absence of "proof" otherwise. While translation is embedded in many Latina/o narratives of migration, it is also often used in ways that critique dominant discourses of Americanness and belonging. Anzaldúa herself insists both on her right to presence in the U.S. Southwest, as the land of her Aztec ancestors, and on her right *not to have to translate* for the dominant U.S. culture. Indeed, these two things go hand in hand, since for Anzaldúa it is the dominant U.S. culture that engaged in "illegal" conquest, and its linguistic hegemony is a manifestation of this.

Some classic texts of Chicano/a letters depict migration across the southern U.S. border and into the United States in a much more matter-of-fact way than Anzaldúa does, as part of the story of arrival rather than as a counter-narrative critique. These novels, while they historicize the larger contexts of border crossing, tend to be less focused on the nature of undocumented and "underground" existence in the United States than on the representation of communities that still bear strongly the shape of their Mexican cultural heritage. Both *Pocho* (1959) by José Antonio Villarreal and *The Rain God* (1984) by Arturo Islas, for instance, depict migration north as a product of the Mexican Revolution beginning in 1910; this flow precedes by several decades the 1965 legislation that turned these migration patterns into "illegal" ones. The title of *Pocho* refers in a pejorative manner to the central character who, as an Americanized Mexican, has lost his facility with Spanish (165). The term thus points in a derogatory way to the loss of culture via the loss of language; characters are lost, as it were, in translation. "Pocho" is a slur that precedes by several decades the label "illegal," however; and the label refers to cultural differences, rather than legal ones. Islas's *The Rain God* takes great care to point out that the Mexican American family living on the Texas–Mexico border has held American citizenship for two generations, establishing a history of presence and belonging for the clan. The main characters are rooted in the United States, even if those they employ are sometimes unauthorized immigrants who travel back and forth over the border between their home and workplace.

Tomas Rivera's classic story cycle, *Y no se lo tragó la tierra*... (1971; translated as *And the Earth Did Not Devour Him*...), about migrant workers, is particularly notable in that the workers, though unmarked in terms of their status, are U.S. citizens by default. When undocumented characters appear in the work, they are specifically marked as "illegal" and regarded as outsiders to the migrant community. In the story "Hand in his Pocket" ("La mano en la bolsa"), an old couple provides room and board for a young boy for three weeks while he finishes school in the absence of his migrant family. The old couple is clearly an integral part of the community – the boy's father leaves him with them, and "even the Anglos liked them so much" (101) – but the woman is apparently making money on the side as a prostitute having sex with a "wetback" (in the original Spanish, "mojadito," or *little* wetback). Eventually the couple kill the "wetback" for his money after telling each other that "it would be so easy" because there is "not even anyone to worry about him... That boss could care less, he darn sure knows that he's a wetback and if something happens to him, you think he'll be concerned about him? Nobody knows that he comes here" (100). The couple enlist the young boy narrator to help bury the body. Reading metaphorically, the presence of undocumented migrants in the community is "killed off," repressed, buried, and yet haunts and hovers at the edges of this story about farmworkers. No one in the community misses the so-called "wetback" or mourns his absence; and he is killed so that respected and recognized community members can profit financially. Yet the story also suggests that the real threat is not the "wetback" himself, but rather the old couple's willingness to kill and bury him, which makes them appear quite sinister. In this way, Rivera gestures toward a profound ugliness at the heart of communal identity: the foreign "other" that must be hidden/expelled but the sign of which remains visible: "In the yard you could see the mound of dirt" (101). The larger socioeconomic context of Rivera's novel, of course, is the Chicano farmworkers' movement; in order for this labor movement to gain momentum in the mid to late 1960s, the looming threat of deportation over a significant percentage of workers needed to be removed. Thus it becomes clear that, from a labor perspective, the economic interests of Chicano farmworkers did not align with those of non-U.S.-citizen Mexican migrants (see Mae Ngai 163). Rivera's story thus gestures, albeit implicitly, toward the Chicano movement's willingness to sacrifice Mexican foreign nationals for the financial security of the Chicanos themselves. A foundational text of the Chicano/a literary canon, *And the Earth Did Not Devour Him...* suggests a problematic and perhaps even deeply skeptical view of the "connection" among Chicanos and Mexican migrants in the mid-twentieth century.

Helena María Viramontes's story "The Cariboo Café," from her debut short-story collection, *The Moths and Other Stories* (1985), interweaves the perspectives of four people at the very margins of U.S. society: a working class cook at a diner that serves a largely undocumented clientele, who are occasionally rounded up for deportation in front of his eyes; an undocumented Central American woman who flees the violence in her home country, where her son has been "disappeared" by government forces; and two small children, probably Mexican, who, terrified of "la migra," become lost and disoriented on the streets of Los Angeles one evening while their parents, also undocumented immigrants, are working. This story is remarkable for foregrounding issues of what Peter Orner has called a "culture of anxiety" (10) in the underground existence of undocumented immigrants, as well as for its gesture toward connections or parallels among immigrant groups of *differing* Latin American origin.

Helena María Viramontes's subsequent novel, *Under the Feet of Jesus* (1995), revisits Tomás Rivera's subject matter, migrant workers, but foregrounds the possibility of a much more fluid boundary between the "legal" and "illegal" workers than Rivera's work. An obvious heir to Anzaldúa's notions of a transnational Chicano/Mexican group identity, *Under the Feet of Jesus* suggests the possibility of transnational communities comprised of both U.S. citizens of Mexican descent and undocumented Mexican immigrants – communities that are constituted by a pervasive sense of "illegality" and vulnerability *regardless* of citizenship status. The novel reflects a profound understanding of the mechanisms by which the category "illegal immigrant" is racialized, such that the identifiers of legal status are utterly blurred. The generalized sense of vulnerability due to racialization as "illegal" is conveyed in an early scene in which Estrella, the thirteen-year-old protagonist, stops on her way home from work in the fields to watch a baseball game. But she is frightened when the game's high-wattage floodlights turn on in the early evening hours: "The border patrol, she thought, and she tried to remember which side she was on and which side of the wire mesh she was safe in. . . . Where was home?" (59–60). As one of the reader's early encounters with the issue of legal status, the scene seems to strongly suggest that Estrella is nervous about being "seen" and caught by border patrol. Passages like this one blur the lines of belonging, home, and nation (Estrella is in fact a U.S. citizen, as readers find out near the novel's conclusion), so that the migrant community as a whole is positioned by its lived experiences in the shadows of belonging, rather than being divided into lines of "us" and "them," citizens and "illegals."

Central American Immigration of the 1980s

Arguably, one of the first means by which undocumented immigration began to register prominently in the work of U.S. Latina/o writers was via the issue of Central American immigration in the 1980s. *Mother Tongue* (1994), by Chicana writer Demetria Martínez, is notable (like Viramontes's "The Cariboo Cafe") for the connections it interweaves between undocumented Central Americans escaping possible torture, death, and disappearance, and Mexican American communities in the United States. Set in New Mexico, the novel fictionalizes the sanctuary movement, in which U.S. citizens provided material aid to Central American migrants and offered a visible platform by which they could testify to the conditions in their home countries. Martínez herself participated in the sanctuary movement and was indicted on charges of conspiring against the U.S. government for her alleged role in transporting two pregnant Salvadoran women across the border, but she was ultimately acquitted on First Amendment grounds as a journalist. Also as with "The Cariboo Cafe," the novel implicates U.S. policies in Central American migration flows. It has in addition received attention for issues of culture and cultural translation between the male Salvadoran migrant, José Luis, and the somewhat unrooted female Mexican American narrator, Mary/María. Mary imagines the two as deeply and even essentially connected and assumes easy cultural familiarity with José Luis's world, even though the structure and format of the novel take great pains to emphasize the *difficulties* of translating across vastly different experiences and to underscore Mary's relatively privileged perspective.

Other novels followed which also explored the migration flows northward from Mexico and Central America. Graciela Limón's *The River Flows North* (2009) conveyed this "flow" metaphorically through its title, suggestive of the natural tendency to migrate and of the power and force of continued movement north when migration patterns are already well established: "the flow of people moves to where jobs wait" (2). As one character from southern Mexico comments with regard to the inexorable flow of migration, "I saw that the river of our lives had reversed its course and that it now flowed back to its original source because it is natural to return to where one begins" (101). The characters exchange their stories on their journey in a fashion reminiscent of *The Canterbury Tales*, revealing the personal histories and push/pull factors driving them north from Mexico as well as El Salvador.

Very recent novels about migration from Central America share Limón's multinational tapestry of characters and depict the tentative formation of immigrant communities in the United States, even while suggesting the ways in which these new, broad formulations of community are fragile and exist uneasily alongside deep transnational connections to countries of origin. Several works, further, bring overt attention to the ways in which migration flows from Central America were stimulated, in large part, by Cold War–era U.S. foreign policy. Salvadoran author and long-time U.S. resident Mario Bencastro's *Odyssey to the North* (1998) depicts characters from various Central American nations as a sort of chorus of undocumented immigrants, some of whom are fleeing the repressive governments of their home countries. It is, however, the current status of the characters as "illegal" in the United States and therefore vulnerable to raids and deportations, rather than the specifics of their original cultures, that weaves together their voices and experiences. Guatemalan-American writer Hector Tobar's novel *The Tattooed Soldier* (1998), likewise, represents a multitude of diverse-origin Latina/o immigrants who have converged in Los Angeles (pre–Rodney King riots). The novel traces the histories of two of these migrants: a former university student from Guatemala whose radicalized wife and small child were murdered by a death squad, and the soldier who killed them. Like so many novels with Central American conflict as part of their story, *The Tattooed Soldier* makes very explicit its critique of U.S. involvement in the Guatemalan repression via the vicious training of the titular soldier in military training grounds such as Ft. Bragg in North Carolina and the "School of the Americas" at Ft. Benning, Georgia.[2] But the novel is also highly interested in its exploration of the U.S. late-twentieth-century (circa 1992) urban landscape in which immigrants don't need to "translate" on a daily basis because they can continue to speak Spanish within their own communities, and in which new communities are formed by the experience of marginality. *The Tattooed Soldier* attempts (following Anzaldúa) a rearticulation and more complex imagining of forms of "illegality" by implicating U.S. policies and training in government-sponsored murder and by touching upon the "illegal" activity of the riots as a collective and even predictable response to deep-seated marginality, deprivation, and frustration. In Francisco Goldman's *The Ordinary Seaman* (1997), characters from various Central American countries are recruited to work abroad a ship in the Brooklyn Navy yard under Panamanian registry. The crew labor to repair the nonfunctional ship but receive no wages and are forbidden by their captain to disembark; thus they evoke enslaved

---

[2] The latter, commonly referred to as the "School of the Assassins" by its critics, was renamed the "Western Hemisphere Institute for Security Cooperation" in 2001; critics, however, claim that the name change was merely cosmetic rather than a reflection of changed mission or practices.

laborers in the ship's hold. Again, a fragile and tentative transnational community is constructed under the present circumstances of immigrant liminality – the crew cannot set foot on land without risking detention and deportation as "illegal." The novel in this way points to how the larger structures of transnational labor recruitment create an exploitable and exploited workforce, which becomes visible here as the truer measure of illegality.

Magical Realism, Humor, and the Picaresque

Though it is unusual to see the theme of undocumented immigration treated in a style other than realism or in other than a high seriousness of tone, some alternative modes have emerged. Oregon-based Peruvian-American writer Eduardo González Viaña's collection of stories *American Dreams* (2005) delivers a humorous and magical realist treatment of themes of migration. In "Porfirio's Book," the title character is a donkey, which functions as a device through which many of the common and even pedestrian aspects of undocumented immigration are rehearsed in a magnified form. As the narrator – who speaks primarily in the first person plural "we," emphasizing a collective sensibility understood generally by the undocumented, but alien to others – explains,

> The truth is we all wish we could have brought the donkey, the house, the town clock, the pub, and our friends, but coming to this country is like dying and all you can take with you, besides your hopes and sorrows, are the clothes on your back... We all must make ourselves invisible when the Migra comes to call, but it's difficult to imagine how the Espinos could make Porfirio invisible. (2–3)

The donkey is an exaggerated figure for the necessity to render oneself unseeable, unnoticeable, despite the obvious and practical impossibility of doing so; simultaneously he represents what must, of necessity, be tragically left behind. The story's humor functions through exaggeration to underscore aspects of undocumented existence that are disturbing or ridiculous, and thus to magnify the preposterousness of the real, as in Wendy Faris's theorization of magical realism (168). "Frontier Woman," also from *American Dreams*, suggests the development of a new pan-ethnic and trans-American Latina/o sensibility; the story's cast of characters in the United States includes a Peruvian family, an Ecuadorian master of healing arts, an Argentine singer, and a Venezuelan woman known as "The Magical Lady of the Caribbean," thus extending the scope of South to North migration in a manner that is congruent with González Viaña's own Peruvian origins. "Frontier Woman" again employs magical realism to explore themes related to illegal immigration: Doña Asunción brings her son Doroteo across the border in order to secure the best possible medical treatment for his brain tumor, but the task becomes increasingly Herculean given that Doroteo, even while seeking treatment, is pronounced already clinically dead. Like the collection's title, *American Dreams*, this short story thus encapsulates the blind hope that propels migrants, who imagine a better life in the North despite the possibility that the United States is not the magical solution for life's problems.

The novel *Into the Beautiful North* (2009) by Chicano novelist and journalist Luis Alberto Urrea – while suggesting the very serious theme of familial loss and disappearance and the impact on Mexican communities of heavy male migration north – also incorporates the trope of border crossing as a form of picaresque adventure, with a ragtag assembly of friends leaving Mexico on a quest to bring back seven men (dubbed the "Magnificent Seven" [57]) from the United States in order to repopulate and re-masculinize their small village, which has been decimated by the exodus of men northward that the community has suffered.[3]

Border Crossing and Collective Trauma

Substantial attention to the actual journey of illegal migration began to appear in the literature of Latina/o writers after the implementation of Operation Gatekeeper in 1994 and similar enforcement strategies that escalated militarization tactics. The impact of the increased enforcement was to drive crossers to greater degrees of subterfuge, to create more reliance on a black market guided by notoriously unscrupulous "coyotes," and to drive crossing routes through significantly more hazardous desert landscapes. The number of deaths and disappearances rose dramatically, with annual death rates roughly doubling from the late 1990s to 2005. In *Migrant Imaginaries*, Alicia Schmidt Camacho discusses these disappearances as a form of

---

[3] As Rubén Martínez notes in *Crossing Over*, male out-migration is so pervasive in some rural areas of Mexico that "There are towns in the highlands whose population decreases by 60 to 70 percent during the spring and summer months, when the majority of able-bodied men . . . between the ages of seventeen and forty-five go north" (31). In recent decades the numbers of women migrants entering the United States from Mexico as well as Central America have also increased dramatically. The growing female out-migration is represented in recent Latina/o literature that depicts women (as well as men) who migrate north, including *Into the Beautiful North*, Ana Castillo's *The Guardians*, and Alvarez's *Return to Sender* (to give just a few examples) as well as narrative journalism such as Sonia Nazario's *Enrique's Journey*.

national trauma for Mexican sending communities (34, 310). Luis Alberto Urrea brought significant attention to the issue with his work of narrative journalism *The Devil's Highway* (2004), about the deaths of fourteen migrants, known as the "Yuma 14," from dehydration and hyperthermia in the Sonoran Desert as they attempted to enter the United States. Urrea's narrative is notable for the ways in which it portrays the debates surrounding immigration from multiple perspectives often considered incompatible with each other (border patrol, humanitarian organizations, vigilante groups, the migrants themselves) while stylistically opening the text to invite connections between undocumented immigrants and U.S. citizens, including readers.

Some novels followed suit by focusing attention on lost and disappeared border crossers. In Ana Castillo's *The Guardians* (2007), one of the central characters is an undocumented teenage boy named Gabriel, or "Gabo," who lives with his U.S.-citizen aunt after his father's disappearance, presumably while crossing the border. This novel tackles in broad strokes the general crisis of deaths and disappearances in the borderlands, including by heat stroke, dehydration, bandits, unscrupulous coyotes, vigilantes, and drug smugglers. Castillo implicates U.S. immigration policies in these many border hazards, including the escalation of demand for human smuggling; similarly, her character Regina observes that drug smuggling across the border would not thrive without the demand for those drugs on the U.S. side. Likewise, Alicia Gaspar de Alba's novel *Desert Blood: The Juárez Murders* (2005), also speculates about deaths and disappearances as a result of other forms of illegal trafficking along the border, including in human organs and snuff pornography. In Chicana writer Reyna Grande's novel, *Across a Hundred Mountains* (2006), the father figure's disappearance while trying to reach the United States has such a profound effect on the loved ones he leaves behind that the family unit disintegrates, as debt and the mother's turn to addiction and prostitution force his surviving daughter to migrate. These novels by Grande, Castillo, Gaspar de Alba, and others suggest that the cumulative impact on Latina/o communities of border disappearances is the formation of cultural trauma and the interruption of both individual and collective identities (Caminero-Santangelo, "The Lost Ones").

Life Narrative and Illegal Immigration

A new phenomenon, life narratives of the undocumented, emerged in the 1990s and early 2000s. These narratives have, in various ways, contested both stock narratives of the "Latino Threat" and dominant national narratives about the United States. *Diario de un mojado*, translated as *Diary of an Undocumented*

Immigrant (1991), described Ramon "Tianguis" Pérez's experiences as a migrant farmworker, including his disinterest in applying for amnesty and his return to Mexico. This text challenges the narrative of the "American Dream" by suggesting that the undocumented worker sees himself as a temporary migrant who does not see the United States as the promised land and in fact always intends to return home. Increasing border enforcement efforts in the mid 1990s would dramatically decrease "revolving door" migration; the collection *The Border Patrol Ate My Dust* (2004; first published in Spanish as *La migra me hizo los mandados*, 2002) attests to this more recent history. The collection originated in a question asked on the air by radio host Alicia Alarcón to her largely Latina/o immigrant listeners, and presents a series of vignettes about unauthorized migration to the United States that challenge "American" narratives by exposing the illusory nature of the dream. The insouciance of the title (in both its English and Spanish versions) turns the act of migration itself into a heroic and defiant act that mocks U.S. state authority, a defiance that the narratives themselves, however, generally lack.

Reyna Grande's memoir *The Distance Between Us* (2012) details how her mother left her and her two siblings in Mexico to follow their father to the United States. In Grande's depiction, "El Otro Lado" (literally "the other side") is rendered not specifically as a geopolitical locale but rather as a nebulous zone where others go and do not return, as a place that "had already taken my father away" (4) and now takes her mother, as well. In this rendering, El Otro Lado is active, not passive; indeed, Grande compares it to the Mexican folklore figure of La Llorona, the murdering mother who kidnaps children to replace her own, except that El Otro Lado "is something more powerful than La Llorona – a power that takes away parents, not children" (3). Grande's memoir powerfully delineates the sense of betrayal that sending families can feel in the wake of the migration of a primary caregiver: "I was too young to know about the men who leave for El Otro Lado and never return. Some of them find new wives, start a new family. Others disappear completely, reinventing themselves as soon as they arrive, forgetting about those they've left behind" (8). The memoir details the children's abandonment when their mother leaves and does not keep her promises to return within a year.

Testimony and Solidarity

The themes of testimony and solidarity across ethnic and citizenship lines are salient both in novels that represent earlier waves of Central American migration in response to repressive regimes as well as novels that are concerned with the contemporary, post–Operation Gatekeeper landscape of immigration. Demetria Martínez's *Mother Tongue* plays out the theme of testimony rather explicitly, since one function of the sanctuary movement of the 1980s in which Martínez herself participated was to provide a forum by which refugees could raise awareness for U.S. audiences about the government-sponsored repression, torture, and mass killing in Guatemala and El Salvador. Certainly, as *Mother Tongue* depicts, *testimonio* played a crucial role in mobilizing the sanctuary movement (unnamed but strongly alluded to in the novel) and transforming public opinion about U.S. military support to right-wing dictatorships. Thus the Chicana narrator of *Mother Tongue* learns to understand the depths of human-rights violations in El Salvador by listening to the testimony of the man who becomes her lover, as well as to that of other refugees. Nonetheless, *Mother Tongue* displays a certain skepticism about the testimonial project, as the narrator correctly anticipates ways in which the mainstream U.S. media will report the testimony of refugees to undermine its truth value.

Bencastro's *Odyssey to the North* and Cuban American writer Cristina García's *A Handbook to Luck* (2007) similarly suggest a concern with the limits of testimony, despite its vital and necessary functions in solidarity building. In the former, a Salvadoran refugee, Teresa, must give legal testimony during an asylum hearing about the situation in El Salvador that has driven her own migration to the United States. Her request for asylum is denied, however, because the judge cannot understand how her testimony fits into the criteria of U.S. asylum law; she is returned to El Salvador and presumably murdered. In García's *A Handbook to Luck*, testimony about the Salvadoran situation seems likewise thwarted; the character who most explicitly witnesses the atrocities of the government (and is driven North because of them) is deported back to his home country without, apparently, being able to give voice to the violence he has seen.

Very recently, in response to the human rights crisis posed by raids, deportations, and deaths and disappearances at the border, some Latina/o writers have responded by foregrounding themes of testimony and/or cross-ethnic or cross-status solidarity in works that address more recent undocumented migration. The emergence of this body of writing, in both nonfiction and fiction, suggests that Latina/o writers in the United States see the issue of contemporary undocumented immigration as an ethical one that demands practices of solidarity.

Urrea's *The Devil's Highway* employs a trope of testimony by having various sections written from the point of view of those who would have been interviewed or interrogated about the events surrounding the abandoning of a group of undocumented migrants by their coyote and the death of fourteen of these men from dehydration and hyperthermia. Strikingly, *The Devil's Highway* suggests that testimony is always and inevitably contradictory; that memory, especially in extremis, is faulty, and that human interest shapes memory differently, so that, for instance, the coyote gives a different account of what happened than do the surviving men, who in any case cannot agree with one another about the details. Urrea's text raises the question of how readers might consider ethical interventions in the face of unreliable testimony. Who should be held accountable, in the final analysis, for the tragedies surrounding undocumented immigration?

Julia Alvarez's *Return to Sender* (2009), a young-adult novel, is perhaps one of the most striking examples of U.S. Latina/o writers engaging in a politics of cross-ethnic solidarity; Alvarez and her family came from the Dominican Republic and entered the United States legally on visas, and Alvarez herself was born a U.S. citizen. In *Return to Sender*, Alvarez clearly means to be pedagogical in her approach, teaching young adults to understand and reframe immigration issues differently than through the dominant U.S. position of xenophobic, anti-immigrant narrative. The novel's title is strongly suggestive of the unwanted and rejected position of undocumented immigrants within the boundaries of the "American" nation; as with mail returned to sender, the nation seeks to expel them from its boundaries. Indeed, "Operation Return to Sender" was the name given to a strategic series of raids that arrested tens of thousands of undocumented immigrants beginning in 2006.[4] In *Return to Sender*, Tyler, an adolescent farm boy in Vermont, befriends Mari, the Mexican daughter of laborers working on his family's farm; the ethical thrust of the novel is that Tyler must learn, through his friendship with Mari, to reconfigure his understanding of "patriotism" (without abandoning it) so that it is flexible enough to allow for the possibility that specific U.S. laws should be changed to become more inclusive about who is permitted to become "American." Alvarez's rather didactic style in this text can be understood as one means of shaping a rhetorical strategy specifically calculated to respond to the very strong cultural pressures to adopt a nativist endorsement of raids and deportations.

Rick Rivera's novel *Stars Always Shine* (2001) enacts a vision of cross-status, cross-citizenship solidarity; even while the status of Mexican American labor is clearly understood to be different than that of undocumented labor in this

---

[4] ICE claimed the operation targeted the most dangerous criminals and known gang members, although this contention has been challenged.

novel, Chicanos are tied to a larger community of Mexicans by deep cultural bonds that incur obligation and cannot be ignored. The novel follows a married couple, Michelle ("Mitch") and Plácido (a Mexican-American man, nicknamed "Place") who are hired to work as ranch managers. A Mexican ranch-hand, Salvador, who was previously employed by the former owners, still lives on the ranch, although the new owners want him off the property. As it turns out, Salvador is undocumented. Place struggles early on to pinpoint and reify Salvador's "status" in relation to his own; it is no coincidence that Plácido's nickname is "Place," suggesting his more stable and recognized claim to "belonging" than Salvador's, his right to occupy this "place" and benefit from its social, economic, and political meanings. But Salvador's name is also heavily symbolic; he is the "Savior" who can reconnect "Place" to the cultural ties that emanate from Mexican peoplehood rather than a specific, geographically bounded "place." Place, reciprocally, helps Salvador to acquire a secure geographical grounding through a green card.

Most recently, the issue of testimony is one that is foregrounded in the life narratives of DREAMers, undocumented youth who came to the United States as children and who see their life possibilities as severely restricted by their inability to obtain legal status in the only country that many of them know. Youth who are activists for the passage of the DREAM Act (Development, Relief, and Education for Alien Minors, proposed legislation that would provide a path to legalization for many immigrants who arrived as children) have placed emphasis on the telling of their life stories as a form of testimony intended to increase understanding of and solidarity with their condition; many of those most engaged in activist testimony are high-achieving students, civically involved, and otherwise model "citizens." Collections such as *Underground Undergrads* (2008) and *Papers: Stories by Undocumented Youth* (2012), as well as a recently published memoir, *Undocumented: A Dominican Boy's Odyssey from a Homeless Shelter to the Ivy League* (2015), by Princeton graduate and DREAM activist Dan'el Padilla Peralta – not to mention numerous stories on blogs and on YouTube – give testimony to the life ambitions and sense of thwarted potential experienced by DREAMers, as well as, in many cases, to the aspirations of their parents for a better life for their children, which brought them to the United States.

Directions for Future Scholarship

Scholarship specifically addressing the topic of representations of illegal immigration in Latina/o literature is still quite scant, although growing.

Aside from Ledesma's early work on this topic, my own book *Documenting the Undocumented: Latino/a Narrative and Social Justice in the Era of Operation Gatekeeper* (2016) is, to date, the only full-length treatment on literary representations of the undocumented, making the case that increasingly, Latina/o writing – and writing by the undocumented themselves – represents illegal migration and underground existence as forms of *testimonio* that make ethical claims on readers. Maya Socolovsky, in *Troubling Nationhood in U.S. Latina Literature* (2013), discusses how rhetorics of illegality have played a part in shaping notions of national belonging, and argues that some Chicana writers have engaged in a narrative remapping of geopolitical boundaries such that Mexico and the United States are imagined as inextricably imbricated within each other.

Other directions in scholarship on literature of the undocumented are imaginable. The work of Peruvian writer González Viaña, for instance, opens the door to inquiry about how this issue is represented in forms other than strict realism, such as humor, parody, and magical realism. A further direction in emerging scholarship turns attention to unauthorized immigration from the Spanish-speaking Caribbean. A large unauthorized Dominican population resides in Puerto Rico, either as the point of destination or en route to the continental United States; Cubans in significant numbers have traveled without state authorization to the United States by "balsas," or makeshift rafts and boats, although on arrival they have benefited (until 2017) from the "Wet Foot, Dry Foot" policy which privileged Cuban immigrants by creating a path to legalization, a benefit not extended to immigrants from other nations. Scholars such as Marisel Moreno and myself are beginning to explore literary representations of unauthorized Caribbean migration and the convergences with other undocumented experience.

Likewise, literary scholarship on the intersections of queer and undocumented identities – building on the work of scholars such as Eithne Luibhéid and Lionel Cantú Jr., which unpacks the interrelations between the policing of borders and the policing of heteronormativity and explores the impact of the presence of LGBTQ immigrants on wider migrant communities – is still in its early stages. The important research currently being done on queer migrations suggests the need to interrogate further the representation of queer undocumented identity in Latina/o cultural production[5]. Some DREAMer *testimonios*, for instance, have also drawn heavily on the

---

[5] See also the Queer Migrations Research Network website, established in 2010 by Karma R. Chávez and Eithne Luibhéid.

intersections of status and non-normative sexualities, and the movement as a whole has adopted the "coming out" metaphor from the LGBTQ Movement.

As I have suggested, scholars approach literature of the undocumented largely through fundamental questions of inclusion and exclusion. Linda Bosniak has pointed out in *The Citizen and the Alien: Dilemmas of Contemporary Membership* that the category of illegality both depends upon and reinforces the "sovereign authority" of the nation state to "maintain [its] boundaries" (37); yet, under other concepts of "citizenship" with long-standing intellectual traditions, undocumented immigrants would well be considered American "citizens." And indeed, recent fiction and nonfiction by Latina/os forces a reconsideration of the criteria for "American" identity and presents alternative narratives of belonging and Americanness to that of legal citizenship. Consider especially, here, Ana Castillo's novel *The Guardians*, which makes the undocumented part and parcel of a larger U.S. Latina/o community, as well as the collection of testimonies included in *Underground Undergrads* or *Underground America*, both of which draw upon the myth of the "American Dream" in making the case for the "Americanness" of their subjects, regardless of legal status. Further, both of the above collections include undocumented voices from nations of origin outside of Latin America: from the Philippines, China, Vietnam, South Korea, India, Pakistan, Iran, and South Africa. The grouping of these stories together, despite the specificities of experience, is one indication of how Latina/o cultural production has laid important groundwork for a broader understanding of undocumented experience and emergent global literatures in the United States. In general, the last two decades of Latina/o literary production about/by the undocumented increasingly reflects the paradox of a population that is, in crucial ways, becoming intermeshed with the fabric of American life, although it has yet to be recognized as an integral part of that life.

WORKS CITED

Alarcón, Alicia. *La migra me hizo los mandados.* Houston, TX: Arte Público Press, 2002.
   The Border Patrol Ate My Dust. Houston, TX: Arte Público Press, 2004.
Alvarez, Julia. *Return to Sender.* New York: Alfred A. Knopf, 2009.
Anaya, Rodolfo. *Bless Me Ultima.* 1972. New York: Warner Books, 1994.
Anzaldúa, Gloria. *Borderlands/La Frontera.* San Francisco: Aunt Lute Books, 1987. 2nd ed. 1999.
Bosniak, Linda. *The Citizen and the Alien: Dilemmas of Contemporary Membership.* Princeton, NJ: Princeton University Press, 2006.
Caminero-Santangelo, Marta. "The Lost Ones: Post-Gatekeeper Border Fiction and the Construction of Cultural Trauma." *Latino Studies* 8.3 (2010): 304–27.

Documenting the Undocumented: Latino/a Narrative and Social Justice in the Era of Operation Gatekeeper. Gainesville: University Press of Florida, 2016.

Castillo, Ana. *The Guardians*. New York: Random House, 2007.

Chavez, Leo R. *Covering Immigration: Popular Images and the Politics of the Nation.* Berkeley: University of California Press, 2001.

The Latino Threat: Constructing Immigrants, Citizens, and the Nation. Stanford, CA: Stanford University Press, 2008.

De Genova, Nicholas. *Working the Boundaries: Race, Space, and "Illegality" in Mexican Chicago.* Durham, NC: Duke University Press, 2005.

Faris, Wendy B. "Scheherazade's Children: Magical Realism and Postmodern Fiction." *Magical Realism: Theory, History, Community.* Eds. Lois Parkinson Zamora and Wendy B. Faris. Durham, NC: Duke University Press, 1995. 163–90.

García, Cristina. *A Handbook to Luck.* New York: Alfred A. Knopf, 2007.

Gaspar de Alba, Alicia. *Desert Blood: The Juárez Murders.* Houston, TX: Arte Público Press, 2005.

Goldman, Francisco. *The Ordinary Seaman.* New York: Grove Press, 1997.

Grande, Reyna. *Across a Hundred Mountains.* New York: Atria, 2006.

The Distance between Us. New York: Washington Square Press, 2012.

Islas, Arturo. *The Rain God.* New York: Avon Books, 1984.

Ledesma, Alberto. "Narratives of Undocumented Mexican Immigration as Chicana/o Acts of Intellectual and Political Responsibility." *Decolonial Voices: Chicana and Chicano Cultural Studies in the 21st Century.* Ed. Arturo J. Aldama and Naomi H. Quiñonez. Bloomington: Indiana University Press, 2002.

"Undocumented Crossings: Narratives of Mexican Immigration to the United States." *Culture Across Borders: Mexican Immigration and Popular Culture.* Ed. David R. Maciel and María Herrera-Sobek. Tucson: University of Arizona Press, 1998. 67–98.

Limón, Graciela. *The River Flows North.* Houston, TX: Arte Público Press, 2009.

Luibhéid, Eithne and Lionel Cantú Jr., eds. *Queer Migrations: Sexuality, US Citizenship, and Border Crossings.* Minneapolis: University of Minnesota Press, 2005.

Madera, Gabriela, Angelo A. Mathay, Armin M. Najafi, Hector H. Saldívar, Stephanie Solis, Alyssa Jame M. Titong, Gaspar Rivera-Salgado, Janna Shadduck-Hernández, Kent Wong, Rebecca Frazier, and Julie Monroe, eds. *Underground Undergrads: UCLA Undocumented Immigrants Speak Out.* Los Angeles: UCLA Center for Labor Research and Education, 2008.

Manuel, José, Cesar Pineda, Anne Galisky, and Rebecca Shine, eds. *Papers: Stories by Undocumented Youth.* Portland, OR: Graham Street Productions, 2012.

Martínez, Demetria. *Mother Tongue.* New York: Ballantine Books, 1994.

Martínez, Rubén. *Crossing Over: A Mexican Family on the Migrant Trail.* New York: Picador, 2002.

Moreno, Marisel. "Bordes líquidos, fronteras y espejismos: El dominicano y la migración intra-caribeña en *Boat People* de Mayra Santos Febres." *Revista de estudios hispánicos* 34.1 (2007): 17–32.

Nazario, Sonia. *Enrique's Journey: The Story of a Boy's Dangerous Odyssey to Reunite with His Mother.* New York: Random House, 2007.

Ngai, Mae M. *Impossible Subjects: Illegal Aliens and the Making of Modern America.* Princeton, NJ: Princeton University Press, 1994.

Orner, Peter. "Introduction: Permanent Anxiety." *Underground America: Narratives of Undocumented Lives.* Ed. Peter Orner. San Francisco: McSweeney's Books, 2008. 5–13.

Padilla Peralta, Dan'el. *Undocumented: A Dominican Boy's Odyssey from a Homeless Shelter to the Ivy League.* New York: Penguin Press, 2015.

Pérez, Ramón "Tianguis". *Diary of an Undocumented Immigrant.* Trans. Dick J. Reavis. Houston, TX: Arte Público Press, 1991.

"Queer Migrations Research Network." http://queermigration.com.

Rivera, Rick. *Stars Always Shine.* Tempe, AZ: Bilingual Press, 2001.

Rivera, Tomás. *. . .y no se lo tragó la tierra / . . .And the Earth Did Not Devour Him.* Trans. Evangelina Vigil-Piñón. 1971 (orig. Spanish). Houston, TX: Arte Público Press, 1992.

Schmidt Camacho, Alicia. *Migrant Imaginaries: Latino Cultural Politics in the US-Mexico Borderlands.* New York: New York University Press, 2008.

Tobar, Héctor. *The Tattooed Soldier.* New York: Penguin, 1998.

Urrea, Luis Alberto. *Into the Beautiful North.* Boston, MA: Little, Brown and Company, 2009.

The Devil's Highway. Boston, MA: Little, Brown and Company, 2004.

Villarreal, José Antonio. *Pocho.* New York: Anchor Books, 1959.

Venegas, Daniel. *The Adventures of Don Chipote: Or, When Parrots Breast-Feed.* Trans. Ethriam Cash Brammer. 1928. Houston, TX: Arte Público Press, 2000.

Viramontes, Helena María. "The Cariboo Cafe." *The Moths and Other Stories.* Houston, TX: Arte Público Press, 1985.

The Moths and Other Stories. Houston, TX: Arte Público Press, 1985.

Under the Feet of Jesus. New York: Penguin, 1995.

23

Latina Feminist Theory and Writing

VANESSA PÉREZ-ROSARIO

Latina feminist writing has for decades provided critical concepts to innovate and transform feminist theory in the United States and beyond. While Latina literature has proliferated over the past forty years, this essay looks at key writers beginning from the 1980s to the present whose work has intervened in the field of feminist theory although their contributions to the field are not always recognized.[1] In the 1970s and 1980s, women of color were in the process of defining themselves, asserting their agency, and building their own intellectual traditions. The publication of Cherríe Moraga and Gloria Anzaldúa's *This Bridge Called My Back* (1981) and Gloria Hull, Patricia Bell Scott, and Barbara Smith's *All the Women Are White, All the Blacks Are Men, but Some of Us Are Brave* (1982) set out to expand the definition of *feminist* to make this analysis relevant to women of color in the United States. These texts sought a signifier, a self-representation that would underscore women's multiple subjectivities of race, class, sexuality, and gender, generating a theoretical space to critique sexism, homophobia, a gendered analysis of history, politics, institutionalized racism, and economic exploitation. Out of their subordination as Latinas and their exclusion from both the male-dominated ethnic-studies movements and the white-dominated women's movements, Chicanas and Latinas sought to create spaces to articulate a feminist consciousness as members of diverse national groups, and as pan-ethnic Latinas, while also articulating political solidarity between third world women in the United States and women activists south of the border.[2] This chapter looks

---

[1] Important Latina authors such as Julia Alvarez, Cristina García, Helena Viramontes, Judith Ortiz Cofer, Angie Cruz, and Nelly Rosario are covered in other chapters of this collection. This chapter looks specifically at writers whose work is the basis of Latina feminist theory.

[2] For more on Latina feminist self-representation in the 1980s, see Edna Acosta-Belén, "Beyond Island Boundaries: Ethnicity, Gender, and Cultural Revitalization in Nuyorican Literature" and Edna Acosta-Belén and Christine Bose, "US Latina and Latin American

specifically at Latina and Chicana writers whose writings, essays, poetry, and theatre are the foundation of Latina feminist theoretical interventions.

Writing by Latinas surged in the 1980s with the publication of key anthologies that opened spaces for Latinas of various ethnic and national backgrounds, including Nuyorican, Chicana, Brazilian, Dominican, Cuban, and Puerto Rican. Anthologies such as Alma Gómez, Cherríe Moraga, and Mariana Romo-Carmona's *Cuentos: Stories by Latinas* (1983) and Juanita Ramos's *Compañeras: Latina Lesbians* (1987) as well as a book of criticism, *Breaking Boundaries: Latina Writing and Critical Readings* (1989), edited by Asunción Horno-Delgado, Eliana Ortega, Nina M. Scott, and Nancy Saporta Sternbach, signaled the emergence of literary voices that transcended a single national identification. Speaking from a hemispheric perspective coalescing under the unifying (and often contested) term "Latina," these authors align themselves with third world women's struggles in countries across Latin America.[3] Latina writers were conscious of writing for and about their communities, which are defined by national and colonized cultures, as well as interethnically, extending support to all women writers. Edna Acosta-Belén notes that

> while these groups challenge the cultural and socioeconomic hegemony that promotes an unfulfilled American dream, they affirm a distinctive collective identity which preserves, rejects, modifies or transforms elements taken from the culture of origin, from the surrounding world of the oppressor, and from their interaction with other subordinate groups with whom they share cultural and racial affinities or a similar structural position.   (986–87)

This essay explores how Latina feminist theory and writing emerged around an oppositional political consciousness and highlights its role in developing "third world feminism" from the 1980s through the twenty-first century.

Cherríe Moraga and Gloria Anzaldúa redefined the feminist movement in the United States offering a critical challenge to conventional U.S. feminist theorizing with the publication of *This Bridge*, an anthology that broke new ground by bringing together women of color and "third world" feminists

---

Feminisms: Hemispheric Encounters." For more on feminism across borders, see Sonia Saldívar-Hull *Feminism on the Border: Chicana Gender Politics and Literature.*

[3] These anthologies include writings by authors such as Rosario Morales, Aurora Levins Morales, Denise Chavez, Scherezade "Chiqui" Vicioso, Helena Viramontes, Bessy Reyna, Nicholasa Mohr, and Sandra María Esteves, just to name a few. These writers represent a wide range of ethnic and national backgrounds. For more on the limitations of the term "Latina," see Frances Aparicio, "Jennifer as Selena: Rethinking Latinidad in Media and Popular Culture" and "(Re)constructing Latinidad: The Challenge of Latina/o Studies." See Sonia Saldívar-Hull for Latina writers aligning with third world women's struggles south of the border.

from diverse ethnic and racial, economic, sexual, and national backgrounds.[4] *This Bridge* opened a space for Latina, Chicana, African American, Asian American, Native American, Afro-Caribbean, Puerto Rican, and Nuyorican writers to challenge the feminist movement to rethink the privileged term "woman" by bringing together a multiplicity of voices in a collection of poetry, *testimonios*, short fiction, and essays that had not been audible in literary and academic publishing. This collection demonstrates "the transformative possibilities that arise when we theorize in multiple genres and modes" (Keating 9) and it recenters this radical feminist subjectivity by suggesting that these women hold together disparate masses, across which their bodies form a bridge.

Moraga and Anzaldúa met at a national feminist writers' organization where they were the only two Chicanas in the group. Disillusioned with a collective that refused to address its privilege, they left the organization and began working on *This Bridge* (Moraga and Anzaldúa, xliii). In the original proposal for the anthology, they wrote:

> We want to express to all women – especially to white middle-class women – the experiences which divide us as feminists; we want to examine incidents of intolerance, prejudice and denial of differences within the feminist movement. We intend to explore the causes and sources of, and solutions to, these divisions. We want to create a definition that expands what "feminist" means to us. (xliii)

The anthology is a reminder that feminism has never belonged solely to "white," middle-class women and calls for new feminist communities and practices. In remarkably direct language, the passage problematizes the denial of differences and the long-standing presence of intolerance and prejudice within the prevailing culture of women's movements in the 1970s.

Anticipating the concept of intersectionality, Moraga and Anzaldúa began writing the essays that congealed a woman-of-color, *tercermundista* critique of dominant feminist discourse by calling attention to the way discourses of

---

[4] After Anzaldúa's passing, Moraga reflected on their relationship and their separation shortly after the publication of *This Bridge*. She tells how Anzaldúa was ill with uterine cancer and relinquished much of the organization and editing of the anthology to Moraga, who at the time felt it reflected their shared vision and only later realized that perhaps it did not, as there were important ideological differences between them. For more on their intellectual friendship, see "The Salt that Cures" in *A Xicana Codex of Changing Consciousness*. For more on the significance of *This Bridge*, see Norma Alarcón's excellent exposition in "The Theoretical Subject(s) of this Bridge Called My Back and Anglo-American Feminism."

gender intersect with domination along the lines of sexuality, class, race, religion, nationality, and language. Moraga's *Loving in the War Years* (1983) and Anzaldúa's *Borderlands/La Frontera: The New Mestiza* (1987), launched a hybrid genre that exposed the limits of conventional academic writing by juxtaposing *testimonio*, legend, music, poetry, and critical analysis.

Moraga's groundbreaking autobiography *Loving in the War Years* explores the contradictory experience of being a Chicana and a lesbian, grapples with the legacy of *familia*, the tensions in the mother-daughter relationship, and in the Chicano movement, while offering a critique of racism and sexism.[5] Through this multigenre autobiography, Moraga asserts that the personal is always political, as "political oppression is always experienced personally by someone" (iv). Inspired by the Combahee River Collective, a black feminist organization, she argues that Chicanas, like all women of color, experience oppressions simultaneously.[6] Moraga's text gives expression to a third world feminism that attempts to fully integrate the concept of the "simultaneity of oppression" as the paradigm for understanding the social position of Chicanas and Latinas (119). She critiques the tercermundista movement because it works to annihilate the concept of white supremacy, without acknowledging the importance of male supremacy (99). Similarly, she notes that "Radical Feminism" focused on men's oppression of women as the root of all other forms of oppression and was unable (or unwilling) to see its own position of privilege (119). Both take a single-issue approach to feminism and fail to acknowledge their complicity with reproducing racism, sexism, and other forms of oppression.

Lesbian disillusionment with the racism and classism of women's and gay movements, and the sexism and homophobia of third world movements, led to their organizing as third world feminists. Moraga notes that a political commitment to women must involve a commitment to lesbians, because "to refuse to allow the Chicana lesbian the right to free expression of her own sexuality, and her politicization of it, is in the deepest sense to deny one's self the right to the same" (130). For Moraga, feminism and the search for freedom from oppression should satisfy all hungers, including desire and sexuality. She argues that Latinas' hungers and desires are the source of their power:[7]

---

[5] See Mary Pat Brady and Juanita Heredia, "Coming Home: Interview with Cherríe Moraga," *Mester* 22 (2) Fall, 1993: 149–64.

[6] The Combahee River Collective, "A Black Feminist Statement," in *But Some of Us Are Brave: Black Women's Studies*, eds. Gloria T. Hull, Patricia Bell Scott, and Barbara Smith (Old Westbury, NY: The Feminist Press, 1982).

[7] For an excellent critique of the centrality of sexuality in Moraga, see Sonia Saldívar-Hull *Feminism on the Border: Chicana Gender Politics and Literature*.

To the extent to which our sexuality and identity as Chicanas have been distorted both within our culture and by the dominant culture is the measure of how great a source of our potential power it holds. We have not been allowed to express ourselves in specifically female and Latina ways or even to explore what those ways are. As long as that is held in check, so is much of the rest of our potential power.

I cannot stomach the twists sexual repression takes in the Latina. It makes us too-hot-to-handle. Like walking fire hazards, burning bodies in our paths with the singe of our tongues, or the cut of our eyes. Sex turned manipulation, control – which ravages the psyche, rather than satisfies the yearning body and heart. (127)

A central voice in sexuality studies and Latina feminism, Moraga makes sexuality and desire central to her feminism, a legacy that is still in need of further theorization by Chicana/Latina feminists. The distortion of Latina sexuality is ever present in society and seems to expand as Latinas become more visible in popular culture and mass media. Figures like Sofia Vergara flaunt the stereotype of the spitfire Latina. Moraga notes that if "the spirit and sex have been linked in our oppression, then they must also be linked in the strategy toward our liberation"(123).

A precursor to both intersectionality, queer, and postcolonial theory, Anzaldúa explores the themes of self-representation, and lesbian experience making significant contributions to Latino studies, queer theory, critical race theory, and women and gender studies. *Borderlands/La Frontera* was eagerly awaited by the emerging field of Chicana feminism, still in its early stages in the 1980s. In the late 1970s, Chicana/o literature was still not considered a legitimate subject of study. Anzaldúa grew frustrated with the doctoral program at the University of Texas at Austin that would not allow her to pursue Chicana/o literature and left Texas for California in 1977.[8] In 2005 she was posthumously awarded a doctorate from the University of California, Santa Cruz. In *Borderlands*, Anzaldúa uses the geography of home, the place of her birth, the lower Rio Grande Valley carved open by the U.S.–Mexico border in South Texas, as a site of theory making. For Anzaldúa, theory begins with the body; the body and its feelings become a valid framework for theorizing from a situated location and from a previously unacknowledged point of view. Bringing these ideas together, *Borderlands* offers recurring images of the Chicana, queer, and brown body as border:

[8] See Norma Élia Cantú and Aída Hurtado, "Introduction to the Fourth Edition" of *Borderlands/La Frontera: The New Mestiza* (2012).

I am a border woman. I grew up between two cultures, the Mexican (with heavy Indian influence) and the Anglo (as a member of a colonized people in our own territory). I have been straddling that tejas-Mexican border, and others, all my life. It's not a comfortable territory to live in, this place of contradictions. Hatred, anger and exploitation are the prominent features of this landscape. (19)

For Anzaldúa, learning through the experiences of the body, pain, violence, and oppression foment forms of knowledge that develop as survival tactics that promote the recognition and the expansion of an oppositional consciousness. Oppression and pain occasion the cultivation of a keen sense of awareness if the choice is made to grow, change, develop, and become "more of who we are" (68). These moments of discomfort and distress can generate the making of meaning and theory that might become a catalyst for change in the individual and in the world around her.

Hybridity and bicultural identity are fashionable trends in the academy today as markers of inclusivity and resilience, and as political and theoretical correctives to essentialism. Anzaldúa's concept of mestizaje has been used to support the celebration of hybridity, although her treatment of it has been far more complex. Anzaldúa's mestiza consciousness is quite different from José Vasconcelos's mestizaje and the idea of a cosmic race that he proposed in the 1930s, which appears to be a facetious celebration of mixed-race people into the formation of a new race, *una raza cósmica*. Anzaldúa argues for the creation of a new consciousness that might arise out of mental and emotional perplexity, internal strife, and psychic restlessness. For Anzaldúa, being mixed race is a dilemma that tears at the psychic borders, and "the positive articulation of mestiza identity is a project to be undertaken, rather than something that already exists" (Martín Alcoff 257).[9] Further theorization of Anzaldúa's concept of mestizaje is critical for helping us to evaluate and asses the demographic shift unfolding in the United States today, driven by immigration and intermarriage. In 2011 the *New York Times* published an article titled "Black? White? Asian? More Young Americans Choose All of the Above," that reports an increased claim to mixed race, and hybridity, by young people in college. This trend is also apparent in television ads and marketing campaigns such as L'Oreal's, where celebrities such as Beyoncé and Jennifer Lopez choose a foundation

---

[9] For a more extended discussion on Anzaldúa's concept of mestizaje, see Linda Martín Alcoff "The Unassimilated Theorist" *PMLA* 121, (1), Jan. 2006: 255–59. See also Sonia Saldívar-Hull, *Feminism on the Border: Chicana Gender Politics and Literature*, pages 59–80.

to match their skin while listing the various races and ethnicities that make up their complexion. A return to Anzaldúa's work may help us grapple with questions such as: What does it mean to claim mixed race or hybridity today without accounting for the pain, violence, history, and forms of oppression experienced differently by different groups?

Anzaldúa suggests the possibility of creating a new consciousness, one that does not react, but rather acts, one that holds various positions in balance, lives with ambiguity and contradictions, creates a new reality, one that is pluralist, one that pushes the boundaries, and questions established ways of being and knowing. This new consciousness offers the opportunity of being a mediator, and a bridge, that can heal, disrupt, question, and bring about social change. It is a way to fight against all forms of oppression without ranking them, which is both innovative and radical in the fight for social justice.

Malintzin, Malinche, La Chingada, or La Vendida, as she is commonly known, represents feminine subversion and the treacherous victimization of her people. Latina feminist theorist Norma Alarcón traces this archetypal figure in her essay "Traddutora, Traditora: A Paradigmatic Figure of Chicana Feminism" (1989) from the colonial period to the present as a symbol in Mexican culture that has been revised and appropriated by Chicanas from Mexican hetero-masculinist narratives and Chicano oral tradition in an attempt to recover their experience and their language. Malintzin Tenepal was the indigenous female slave who was transformed into Guadalupe's monstrous double and also "aided and abetted in the nation-making process or, at least, in the creation of nationalistic perspectives" (58). She was seen as Cortés's whore, and compared to Eve, "especially when she is viewed as the originator of the Mexican people's fall from grace and the procreator of a 'fallen' people" (58). She comes to be known as "la lengua," the metaphor used by Cortes and the chroniclers to refer to Malintzin as translator between Nahuatl and Spanish (59). Because she is viewed as a woman who speaks for herself and not for the community, she is seen as having betrayed her primary community role of mother. Alarcón theorizes the way that Chicana feminists such as Anzaldúa, Moraga, and Lorna Dee Cervantes reinvent Malintzin, who as a historical subject "remains shrouded in preternatural silence, and as object she continues to be on trial for speaking and bearing the enemy's children and continues to be a constant source of revision and appropriation – indeed, for articulating our modern and postmodern condition" (85). During and after the Chicana/o movement, Chicanas who spoke out against patriarchy within the community, and theorized their oppression as women, were seen as assuming an individualized non-maternal voice and labeled as Malinchistas by the men and leaders of the movement. Through revision of tradition and the myth of Malintzin, Chicanas radically reenvisioned and reinvented their possibilities as women and Chicanas. They grounded their discourse in the Chicano community through their engagement with the myth of Malintzin, posing a challenge to dominant forms of first-world feminisms, while simultaneously launching a critique of patriarchy within the community and the Chicano movement.

Just as Chicana feminists revised and reinvented the myth of Malintzin as a way to root themselves in Chicano culture while simultaneously imagining new possibilities for themselves and their community, Caribbean Latina feminists looked to early Latina feminist writers within their cultures such as anarchist Luisa Capetillo, poet Julia de Burgos and political activist Lolita Lebrón. Luisa Capetillo is remembered as one of the most important writers and union organizers for the cigar industry, a lector and anarchist who articulated a critique of how the ideal of bourgeois marriage did not serve working-class women because of how the institution permitted men freedom to pursue extramarital relationships while constraining women. Capetillo herself was born to a couple that never married and she did not marry the father of her children. Today she is celebrated as an early Puerto Rican feminist who courageously affirmed female sexual liberation in the early twentieth century, and who famously was arrested for wearing pants in public in Havana.[10] Written on the eve of her departure for the United States, Capetillo's *Mi opinión sobre las libertades, derechos, y deberes de la mujer* (My Opinion on the Freedoms, Rights, and Duties of Women, 1911) was the first Puerto Rican book dedicated exclusively to questions of gender and women's rights. From Tampa, she significantly revised and expanded this work to write about the condition of women more generally, publishing the new edition in Florida in 1913. Lisa Sánchez González notes that Capetillo left the island after being "harassed by both colonial regimes she had experienced in Puerto Rico and becoming discontented with the workers' movement" there (23). As an early feminist who left the island in search of greater freedoms from a patriarchal society, her work anticipates later generations of writers who similarly saw migration as way to escape masculinist provincialism. Literary works abound with Caribbean women

---

[10] See Julio Ramos, introduction to Capetillo, *Amor y anarquía*. The book opens with a picture of Capetillo dressed in a man's suit in Havana.

characters whose sexuality is seen as transgressive or deviant and who are ostracized by their communities. It is important to understand the role that gender similarly played in Julia de Burgos's decision to leave Puerto Rico and in her inability to make a home for herself in Cuba or New York. Social circumstances beyond her control repeatedly thwarted her ambitions.[11] In the next section, we will see examples of how Caribbean Latinas grapple with the legacy of these early feminist figures in their work in the twenty-first century.

New Directions of Latina Feminist Writing in the Twenty-First Century

The twenty-first century has seen the renewed backlash against immigrants in the United States and an increased anxiety around the U.S.-Mexico border. Latinas find themselves and their communities subject to violence and media representations that distort and dehumanize. Contemporary Latina feminist writings move in new directions such as disability studies and the Afro-Latina movement while continuing to expand the use of genres such as *testimonio* that incorporate orality into the text. At the turn of the century, the Latina Feminist Group began to meet to discuss their concerns as Latina feminists in higher education, and published their "papelitos" as *Telling to Live: Latina Feminist Testimonio* (2001), an important anthology that includes writings by eighteen women of diverse Latina backgrounds from regions across the country.[12] Their work foregrounds the tradition of using *testimonios* to reveal the complexity of Latina identities in the United States and highlights the connection between life experience and new knowledge creation. They use autobiographical texts to theorize latinidades at the intersection of racism, sexism, and heterosexism and to rethink feminism, women's, Latino, American, and cultural studies by centering *testimonio* or life-writing as "a crucial means of bearing witness and inscribing into history those lived realities that would otherwise succumb to the alchemy of erasure" (2). The Latina Feminist Group's life-writing has an intellectual depth that is used as a springboard for theorizing latinidades in the academy, and their communities, to create their own social and discursive spaces, to document silenced histories, and for feminist consciousness raising.

---

[11] See Vanessa Pérez-Rosario, *Becoming Julia de Burgos: The Making of a Puerto Rican Icon*.
[12] To learn more about the collective, see "Introduction. *Papelitos Guardados*: Theorizing *Latinidades* through *Testimonio*" in *Telling to Live: Latina Feminist Testimonio*.

Latina Feminism and Disability Studies

An important figure of Latina and third-world feminism, Aurora Levins Morales is a contributor to both *This Bridge Called My Back* and *Telling to Live*, and is still writing today. Levins Morales's writing generates theory from her physical body and experience. Born in Puerto Rico to a Puerto Rican mother and a Jewish father, Levins Morales was raised on the island and since 1970 has lived in Berkeley, California, and Cambridge, Massachusetts. She is the author of several books, including *Remedios: Stories of Earth and Iron from the History of Puertorriqueñas* (1998), *Medicine Stories: History, Culture and the Politics of Integrity* (1999), and *Kindling: Writings on the Body* (2013). Levins Morales describes herself as "an activist, a healer, a revolutionary. I tell stories with medicinal powers. Herbalists who collect wild plants to make medicine call it wildcrafting. I wildcraft the details of the world, of history, of people's lives, and concentrate them through art in order to shift consciousness, to change how we think about ourselves, each other and the world."[13] Through the power of the personal and storytelling, Levins Morales weaves a narrative that makes meaning of the social, historical, and political fragments of the world around her.

Remedios is a powerful account of Puerto Rican women's history written in an innovative mix of prose and verse, first- and third-person accounts. Drawing on both memory and history, *Remedios* begins in Africa and ends in New York in 1954, the year of the author's birth. Levins Morales draws on the lives of African, indigenous, Spanish, and Jewish women, including women who were stolen and sold and the everyday women who kept communities together. The remarkable women in the book who used their voices to speak out against injustice across the decades include: Francisca Brignoni, who spoke out for Puerto Rican independence during the Grito de Lares; Ida B. Wells, who advocated against lynching; Lola Rodríguez de Tió, who called for the release of prisoners during the fight for Puerto Rican independence from Spain; anarchist Luisa Capetillo, who was a labor organizer; and poet Julia de Burgos, who advocated for better living conditions for Puerto Ricans in New York while calling for the independence of the island. Levins Morales weaves her own story/history into the narrative of this intellectual feminist genealogy. Writing about Julia de Burgos,

---

[13] See the "About Me" page on Aurora Levins Morales's website (www.auroralevinsmor ales.com/about-me.html).

Sylvia Plath, and Sylvia Rexach, Levins Morales reflects on the deadly mid-twentieth-century cult of domesticity:

> Literary men will write about these women's sadness and suicide as if it were the greatest poetic achievement of their lives, a glorious celebration of women's inevitable suffering, an accomplishment that merely living women must strive to emulate. They will poke among the lyrics looking for evidence that nothing could have been done to save them.

> Their fingerprints are everywhere, but I proclaim that these women did not die by their own hands, that their fingers were in captivity, that death was prepared for them by others. That they fell in a brutal decade, murdered in the gender wars, unable to imagine there was solace to be found in the collective rage of women if they could have only waited five or six years, that they were not alone, that there could have been another ending to the song. (*Remedios* 203)

By remembering, writing, and revising history, *Remedios* seeks to expand collective memory and demonstrates that literature is a powerful antidote to historical amnesia. This powerful paragraph also constructs connections between writers and their readers, between the sense of isolation or desperation and a transformative "collective rage of women." Thus, Levins Morales proposes the power of poets to leave their fingerprints on history.

Levins Morales's most recent book *Kindling* intervenes in the growing field of disability studies. The book is comprised of essays, poems, and blog posts she wrote while living in Cuba where she received treatment for chronic pain, fatigue, and migraines that had confined her to a wheelchair. After two months of socialist medical care that involved intense physical therapies lasting two to three hours a day, she left the island nation on her own two feet, and even danced on her way out as she had promised to do upon her arrival. Her text bears witness to the way that the medical-industrial complex, the use of pesticides in farming, and the uncontrolled industrial developments of late capitalist countries are responsible for epidemics and chronic illnesses, specifically of the autoimmune variety that leave thousands literally fighting for their lives. She notes, however, that these illnesses are often viewed as psychosomatic:

> If there was widespread recognition that many people are depressed because oppression makes us miserable and that large numbers of people are getting sick because of the reckless use of toxic chemicals for profit, more of us might become inspired to organize, and resist the policies that make us sick and sad. (64)

Levins Morales intervenes in the field of disability studies by looking at the way that sufferers of environmental and chronic illness intersect with the experiences of those with physical disabilities. Although both groups have often come together to fight the same oppression, persons with physical disabilities have a limitation that is visible to those around them, but they are not sick. Suffers of chronic illnesses often have no known cause or cure, and as a result are met with disbelief by family, friends, and loved ones, leaving many who live with environmental illnesses in isolation and with no support system. In the Cuba blog section of *Kindling*, Levins Morales poetically records her recovery back to health at the CIREN, the International Center for Neurological Restoration, while implicitly offering a comparison between capitalist and socialist societies like Cuba where "the primary commitment is to the wellbeing of people, not corporations" (98).

Continuing with the theme of state and economic exploitation, Irene Vilar interrogates both nationalism and the effects of U.S.-sponsored forced sterilization on Puerto Rican women's bodies in her memoirs *The Ladies' Gallery* (2009) and *Impossible Motherhood: Testimony of an Abortion Addict* (2011). *The Ladies' Gallery* tells the story of three generations of women grappling with the legacy of suicide. Lolita Lebrón, Vilar's grandmother, was one of four Puerto Rican nationalists who, on March 1, 1954, stormed the U.S. Capitol with pistols demanding independence for the island. [14] Vilar recounts the event as a suicide mission, as the nationalists had no escape plan and did not expect to survive the attack (*Ladies Gallery*, 85–95). As a result of this political act, Lolita Lebrón became the most public female embodiment of heroic self-sacrifice in Puerto Rico. [15] Anyone who spoke out against this sacrificial role is seen as having betrayed her primary community role of mother, much like Malintzin in Chicana/o culture.

In both memoirs, Vilar excavates Puerto Rican women's designated role as mother of the nation beginning with the 1930s Puerto Rican nationalist party leader Pedro Albizu Campos, who glorified the myth of "la gran familia puertorriqueña" and maternity. [16]

---

[14] Lebrón, along with Rafael Cancel Miranda, Andres Figueroa Cordero, and Irving Flores, shot thirty rounds from semiautomatic pistols from the Ladies' Gallery (a balcony for visitors) of the House of Representatives chamber in the US Capitol. They were later tried, convicted, and served long prison sentences in federal penitentiaries, but were pardoned by President Jimmy Carter.

[15] For more on Lolita Lebrón as symbolic mother of the nation, see Jossianna Arroyo, "Living the Political: Julia de Burgos and Lolita Lebrón."

[16] Albizu Campos argued that birth control on the island was part of a US federal policy of genocide, while Puerto Rican feminists who supported the cause of independence

The brazenness of the Yankee invaders has reached the extreme of trying to profane Puerto Rican motherhood; of trying to invade the very insides of nationality. When our women lose the transcendental and divine concept that they are not only mothers of their children but mothers of all future generations of Puerto Rico, if they come to lose that feeling, Puerto Rico will disappear within a generation. The Puerto Rican mother has to know that above all she is a mother, and that motherhood is the greatest privilege God has given the human species. That there is oppression, that there is pain, that there is hunger, that there is death, we know all that; but neither pain nor hunger nor death is cured by murdering nationality in its very insides.   (Albizu Campos qtd. in Vilar, *Ladies Gallery* 45)

This statement by the nationalist leader was made as a reaction to the debates around birth control on the island in the early part of the twentieth century. Many Puerto Rican feminists advocated for safe birth control for women as a way to protect their health, and to offer them control of their bodies and lives by choosing when and how many children to bear, while simultaneously calling for the independence of the island. These women were seen as traitors of the nation for speaking out for themselves rather than preserving perceived community interests and values.

Several years later, on the eve of the anniversary of Lolita Lebrón's 1954 attack on Congress, Vilar's mother committed suicide by throwing herself out of a moving car while the eight-year-old Vilar sat in the back seat. She died the next morning in a hospital, her suicide motivated at least in part as an act of revenge against her philandering husband. Vilar struggled with the legacy of suicide, sacrifice, and politics, as she wrestled to define herself against these two mother figures. In the closing chapters of the memoir, Vilar chooses to delay motherhood by aborting when she discovers she is pregnant. Perhaps the most daring of all is her resolution to break with tradition and save her own life, redefining for herself her relationship to the past. Vilar examines what the women and men of her family have made of these recurrent themes and reinvents them for herself.

never relied on the mother-is-nation paradigm. They argued for both birth control and independence. To read more about these debates, see Laura Briggs "Discourses of 'forced sterilization' in Puerto Rico: the problem with the speaking subaltern." *differences: A Journal of Feminist Cultural Studies* 10(2), summer 1998: 30–66. For more on the role of "la gran familia puertorriqueña" in literary studies, see Marisel Moreno, *Family Matters: Puerto Rican Women Authors on the Island and the Mainland* (Charlotte: University of Virginia Press, 2012) and in literary and cultural studies, see Vanessa Pérez-Rosario *Becoming Julia de Burgos: The Making of a Puerto Rican Icon* (Urbana-Champaign: University of Illinois Press, 2014).

In *Impossible Motherhood: Testimony of an Abortion Addict*, Vilar explores how abortion can become an addiction when it takes on a repetitive pattern, through her own personal experience of having fifteen abortions in as many years. Vilar attended college in Syracuse, New York, at the age of sixteen, still a minor and dealing with the pain of family trauma. She became sexually and romantically involved with a male professor who was thirty-four years her senior, a relationship that would eventually lead to a fifteen-year marriage. Vilar took a sacrificial position before him, like her grandmother in service of the nation and her mother before her husband. Her death wish manifested itself in the imbalance of power in their relationship, "the more of a wolf he became, and the more I wished I could be a lamb" (45). She became entangled in a self-destructive pattern of pregnancies, abortions, and suicide attempts that lasted sixteen years. Her husband, who didn't want children, reminded her that she should also reject motherhood if she were to be a successful writer. In a relationship where she had relinquished all control, the pattern of pregnancies was a way of defying her husband, of asserting herself, and having power over him:

> I know that I'm destined to be misunderstood, that many will see my nightmare as a story of abusing a right, of using abortion as a means of birth control. It isn't that. My nightmare is part of the awful secret, and the real story is shrouded in shame, colonialism, self-mutilation, and a family history that features a heroic grandmother, a suicidal mother, and two heroin-addicted brothers (5).

The Ladies' Gallery was written at her lover's encouragement; he was her editor, guiding and shaping her story. In *Impossible Motherhood*, Vilar tells the story of this oppressive relationship, multiple pregnancies, abortions, suicide attempts, and hospitalizations, which is mostly left out of her first memoir. Through *Impossible Motherhood*, she finally writes the story she needed to write. Vilar does not propose a political solution beyond learning to take care of herself and her family in the face of generations of self-destruction, neglect, and abuse; her critique of women as sacrifice to the nation in Puerto Rico opens spaces for theorizing about subordination and for imagining alternative forms of political engagement.

Redefining Identities

In the twenty-first century, Afro-Latina writers gave voice to a new political identity as they affirmed their blackness. In the United States, blackness/Afro- and Latinidad/Latino are often thought of as distinct and mutually exclusive. One is either black or Latina/o but not both. The term "Afro-Latina/o" gained currency in the United States in the 1990s to describe those of African descent whose origins are in Latin America and the hispanophone Caribbean. In this formulation, blackness and Latinidad are not mutually exclusive concepts, and the Latino concept itself is inadequate to describe this heritage. Juan Flores notes in the introduction to *The Afro-Latin@ Reader* that "in their quest for a full and appropriate sense of social identity, Afro-Latin@s are thus typically pulled in three directions at once" (Flores and Jiménez Román 14). He describes this "three-pronged web of affiliations" as a "triple-consciousness," taking a cue from W. E. B. Du Bois in *The Souls of Black Folk* (1903). The Afro-Latina/o is constantly aware of his/her three-ness – Latina/o, black, and American, "three souls, three thoughts, three unreconciled strivings; three warring ideals in one dark body, whose dogged strength alone keeps it from being torn asunder" (15).

Nuyorican poet, Mariposa (María Teresa Fernández), pushes Flores's definition of Afro-Latinidad to also consider gender adding a fourth prong to the web of affiliations. The complicated relationships among blackness, Latinidad, and gender are exemplified in Mariposa's "Poem for My Grifa-Rican Sistah."[17] In this poem, she invokes Julia de Burgos, as do several Nuyorican women poets, as a way to claim their Puerto Ricanness, their blackness, and their presence.[18] The poem's title evokes an Afro-Latina identity as well as refers to Burgos's "Ay, ay, ay de la grifa negra" (Oh My, Oh My, Oh My, of the Nappy-Haired Negress, 1938). *Grifa* refers to a woman of African descent with coarse hair; *Rican* signals a Puerto Rican identity; and *Sistah*, with its phonetic spelling, educes an African-American identity with a gesture to African-American Vernacular English. The poem revolves around the external pressures to suppress blackness through the act of hair straightening, a common ritual among women of African descent

---

[17] Different versions of this poem exist. I quote from the version included in *The Afro-Latin@ Reader*, ed. Jiménez Román and Flores, 280–81. For more on the importance of blackness in Mariposa's work, see Vanessa Pérez-Rosario "Affirming an Afro-Latin@ Identity: An Interview with Poet María Teresa 'Mariposa' Fernández," *Latino Studies Journal* 12(3), fall 2014: 1–8.

[18] Mariposa has acknowledged the importance of Burgos as a literary influence, and that influence is also evident from the multiple references to Burgos in her work. For more on the significance of Julia de Burgos as a figure in Nuyorican women's poetry, see Vanessa Pérez Rosario, *Becoming Julia de Burgos: The Making of a Puerto Rican Icon* (Urbana-Champaign: University of Illinois Press, 2014).

with curly hair. In a world where female beauty is associated with long, flowing locks and European features, women of African descent feel pressured to engage in practices that will help them approximate these images of beauty: "Pinches y ribbons / to hold back and tie / oppressing baby naps / Never to be free"(280). The stress to conform to these images appears in the mother's intimate act of fixing her child's hair, suggesting how racism and a colonized mentality are internalized by the oppressed and taught to the next generation: "It hurts to be beautiful, 'ta te quieta. / My mother tells me" (280). In Africa and in the diaspora, the ritual of braiding women's hair is an intimate bonding activity. In this poem, the bonding practice has been subverted to involve cultural, psychic, and personal alienation. In this case, the mother sends the powerful message that the daughter's hair needs to be "fixed" through the practice of hair straightening.

> Chemical relaxers to melt away the shame
> Until new growth reminds us
> That it is time once again
> For the ritual and the fear of
> Scalp burns and hair loss
> And the welcoming
> Of broken ends
> And broken
> Promises.   (281)

The hair straightening products mentioned in the poem hold false promises of assimilation to white standards of beauty. The ritual is never-ending as new hair growth reveals the underlying hair textures that can never be completely or permanently straightened to approximate European standards of beauty. The final stanza suggests that freedom will come only through self-acceptance and the affirmation of blackness, not the suppression of it.

Mariposa's signature poem, "Ode to the Diasporican," famously expresses a Nuyorican identity. Writing in English and Spanish, Mariposa claims the Puerto Rican heritage she learned on the streets of New York. Her free verse features an intense language, passion, and imagination. The poem opens with the speaker's unassimilable physical qualities that mark her difference in American society. She has dark skin, curly hair, and an attachment to another place, Puerto Rico. As Mariposa performs the poem, she often touches her hair and holds out her hands when they are mentioned, commanding audiences' attention to her body and its physical features. Stanzas in Spanish open and close the poem. The poem contrasts the New York cityscape with the Puerto Rican landscape in a reference to Julia de Burgos's canto to Puerto Rico's river, "Río Grande de Loíza":

> Some people say that I'm not the real thing
> Boricua, that is
> Cause I wasn't born on the enchanted island
> Cause I was born on the mainland
> North of Spanish Harlem
>
> Cause I was born in the Bronx
> Some people think that I'm not bonafide
> Cause my playground was a concrete jungle
> Cause my Río Grande de Loíza was the Bronx River
> My Luquillo, Orchard Beach
> And summer nights were filled with city noises
> Instead of coquíes
> And Puerto Rico
> Was just some paradise
> That we only saw in pictures.
>
> What does it mean to live in between
> What does it take to realize
> That being Boricua
> Is a state of mind
> A state of heart
> A state of soul. (Fernández, 2424)

The third stanza raises the island's ambivalent political status and the bicultural identity of those who live outside of the island. With a play on words, the speaker suggests that Puerto Rico's collective identity is defined by the features of diaspora: a history of dispersal, memories of a homeland, and alienation in the host country. As a stateless nation, Puerto Rico is a state of mind. Although the desire for return often defines diaspora, Mariposa's poem rejects this idea. The connection to that other place, an elsewhere, is clear in her work. But her poem articulates how she has made New York her own, affirming her existence and her right to be here.

Performance artist, writer, and poet Josefina Báez theorizes the dual marginality of black Dominicanyork's women as living in "El Nié," in her book *Levente no. yolayorkdominican york* and explores the complexities inherent in inhabiting transnational spaces, transnational lives and living as a body formed of these colonial and diasporic junctures. El Nié is a colloquial way of saying neither here nor there in Caribbean Spanish and in its most vulgar definition means perineum. In this way Báez queers the idea of living on the border.

In classic Báez style, *Levente no.* challenges the boundaries of form in a text she refers to as a "performance theatre text." With no page numbers or chapters it moves fluidly between speakers and linguistic expressions set in a building in the historically Dominican neighborhood of Washington Heights in Manhattan.

> El Ni e' es un edificio que aparece en cada barrio. En muchos barrios. Se podría decir que es un edificio con alas. Que aterriza . . .que se crea cuando se juntan las Niensas. El edificio y el barrio aparecen. Eso es lo de menos. Lo importante son las inquilinas. Viviendo muchos mapas simultáneamente. (NP)

> (The Ni e' is a building that appears in each neighborhood. In many neighborhoods. You could say that it is a building with wings. That lands . . .that is created when the Nienses gather. The building and the neighborhood appear. That is the least of it. The important thing are the renters. Living multiple maps simultaneously.)[19]

Báez makes clear that what creates El Nié in the end is not the building but the women, the residents of El Nié who create this space out of their physical bodies. El Nié is made up of women, "this building is full of strong, sometimes sad, lonely women and fatherless children" who find companionship and solidarity in each other (NP). As Lorgia García-Peña notes in *The Borders of Dominicanidad*, the symbolic space of El Nié expands our understanding of borders; it displaces the location and polarity of the nation-border and rather proposes the body as the site that absorbs, accommodates, holds and displays national exclusions across time and space, history and generations, race and gender (191–97).

Among the more recent Latina feminist voices who gives expression to new identities is Daisy Hernández, a Cubana-Colombiana raised in New Jersey. She is former executive editor of *Color Lines Magazine*, and her writing has appeared in the *New York Times*, NPR's *All Things Considered*, and *Ms. Magazine*. Almost twenty years after the publication of *This Bridge*, she coedited *Colonize This!: Young Women of Color on Today's Feminism* (2002), an important anthology that continues the tradition of bringing together a diversity of voices of women of color in the United States. Her book *A Cup of Water Under My Bed: A Memoir* (2014), explores immigration, family, and her bisexual identity, by looking at the various cultural lessons that make her who she is as she writes of the porous border that

---

[19] My translation.

fades in the spaces between the Queens borough of New York and Colombia. She draws from the U.S. feminist movement and her family heritage to fashion her bisexual and feminist identity, while affirming a group identity that maintains, discards, and transforms aspects of the culture of origin and her surrounding world.

A Cup of Water puts pressure on notions of "normal" sexuality and desire. At the core of the text is the author's bisexual identity that she describes as a love without boundaries. In her search for love she becomes involved with men, women, and some who are transgender. Hernández struggles for the words to describe what it feels like to love both men and women:

> Generally speaking, gay people come out of the closet, straight people walk around the closet, and bisexuals have to be told to look for the closet. We are too preoccupied with shifting.
>
> . . .
>
> At twenty-four, I am eager to share my findings about bisexuality with everyone, including a woman with a mane of curly hair who picks me up at a bar in Provincetown. After a few hours of clumsy sex, while still lying naked in bed with her, I decide it's important to tell her that I'm bisexual. She listens patiently, then closes her eyes, and sighs, "Why can't I meet a normal lesbian?"
>
> I smile sympathetically. As much as she wants to date a normal lesbian, I would like to be one, not a lesbian but normal, the kind of story where you know what's going to happen next.   (93)

The desire to love and be loved, find a tribe, find a home, and belong are central to the story. Hanging like a shadow over this love without a shore is a constant state of fear: fear of persecution, that someone will discover that her partners are transgender. Woven in her story is the story of Gwen Araujo, a transgender, who was beaten to death by two college football players when they discovered her story. The defendants' lawyers spun a story around the killing to justify it, and argued that the defendants experienced "transpanic," and this panic of discovering they had been attracted to a transgender was considered normal (103). They killed to keep their narrative intact; to insist they are straight, hetero-men, not gay, but *normal*.

A Cup of Water is an important contribution to Latina feminist writing, expanding on Moraga's and Anzaldúa's work on sexuality as central to Latina identity. During the 1980s, lesbianism was for Moraga the supreme trope in the quest for newer gender identities, for anything that epitomizes difference in the face of hetero gender norms. Hernández explores bisexuality and transgender identity as a way to interrogate the idea of "normal" and a future that is impossible to predict.

Latina feminist writing has been central to the articulation of women of color feminist theory in the United States and beyond, exploring the way that gender intersects with sexuality, class, race, religion, nationality, and language. Latina feminists set out to expand the definition of "feminist" and "woman" creating new spaces to articulate a political consciousness, that both defines national groups as well as interethnic solidarity. Just as Chicana writers revise Malinche's scanty biography, the figures of writers and political activists such as Luisa Capetillo, Lolita Lebrón, and Julia de Burgos are recovered and commemorated by Puerto Rican women writers. Latina feminist writing creates spaces to remember the past and, through the imagination, explore new possibilities for Latinas in the twenty-first century. Latina feminist theory and writing continues to explore new mediums, push boundaries, and expand our understanding of what it means to be Latina and feminist, by contributing to the expression of women of color feminist theory.

WORKS CITED

Acosta-Belén, Edna. "Beyond Island Boundaries: Ethnicity, Gender, and Cultural Revitalization in Nuyorican Literature." *Callaloo* 15.4 (Autumn 1992): 979–98.

Acosta-Belén, Edna and Christine Bose. "U.S. Latina and Latin American Feminisms: Hemispheric Encounters." *Signs* 25.4 (Summer 2000): 1113–19.

Alarcón, Norma. "The Theoretical Subject(s) of *This Bridge Called My Back* and Anglo-American Feminism." In Anzaldúa, ed., *Making Face, Making Soul/Haciendo Caras*. San Francisco: Aunt Lute Foundation, 1990. 356–69.

"Traddutora, Traditora: A Paradigmatic Figure of Chicana Feminism." *Cultural Critique* 13, The Construction of Gender and Modes of Social Division (Autumn 1989): 57–87.

Anzaldúa, Gloria. *Borderlands/La Frontera: The New Mestiza*. San Francisco: Aunt Lute Books, 1987.

Arroyo, Jossianna. "Living the Political: Julia de Burgos and Lolita Lebrón." *Centro Journal* 26.2 (Fall 2014): 128–55.

Báez, Josefina. *Levente no. Yolayorkdominicanyork*. New York: I Om Be Press, 2011.

Brady, Mary Pat and Juanita Heredia. "Coming Home: Interview with Cherríe Moraga." *Mester* 22.2 (Fall 1993): 149–64.

Briggs, Laura. "Discourses of 'Forced Sterilization' in Puerto Rico: the Problem with the Speaking Subaltern." *differences: A Journal of Feminist Cultural Studies* 10.2 (Summer 1998): 30–66.

Burgos, Julia de. *Song of the Simple Truth: Obra poética completa/the complete poems of Julia de Burgos*. Ed and trans. Jack Agüeros. Willimantic, CT: Curbstone Press, 1997.

Capetillo, Luisa. *Amor y anarquía: Los escritos de Luisa Capetillo*. Ed. and intro. Julio Ramos. San Juan, Puerto Rico: Huracán, 1992.

A Nation of Women: An Early Feminist Speaks Out/ Mi opinion sobre las libertades, derechos, y deberes de la mujer. Ed. and intro. Félix V. Matos Rodríguez. Trans. Alan West-Durán. Houston, TX: Arte Público Press, 2004.

Fernández, María Teresa. "Ode to a Diasporican." *The Norton Anthology of Latino Literature*. Eds. Ilan Stavans, Edna Acosta-Belén, and Harold Augenbraum. New York: W. W. Norton and Co., 2010.

Flores, Juan and Miriam Jiménez Román, eds. *The Afro-Latin@ Reader: History and Culture in the United States*. Durham, NC: Duke University Press, 2010.

García-Peña, Lorgia. *The Borders of Dominicanidad: Race, Nation, and Archives of Contradiction*. Durham, NC: Duke University Press, 2016.

Gómez, Alma; Cherríe Moraga, and Mariana Romo-Carmona, eds. *Cuentos: Stories by Latinas*. New York: Kitchen Table Women of Color Press, 1983.

Hernández, Daisy. *A Cup of Water Under My Bed: A Memoir*. Boston, MA: Beacon Press, 2014.

Hernández, Daisy and Bushra Rehman, eds. *Colonize This! Young Women of Color on Today's Feminism*. Berkeley, CA: Seal Press, 2002.

Horno-Delgado, Asunción, Eliana Ortega, Nina M. Scott, and Nancy Saporta Sternbach, eds. *Breaking Boundaries: Latina Writing and Critical Readings*. Amherst: University of Massachusetts Press, 1989.

Hull, Gloria T., Patricia Bell Scott, and Barbara Smith, eds. The Combahee River Collective, "A Black Feminist Statement," in *All the Women Are White, All the Blacks Are Men, but Some of Us Are Brave*. Old Westbury, NY: The Feminist Press, 1982.

Keating, AnaLouise. *The Gloria Anzaldúa Reader*. Durham, NC: Duke University Press, 2009.

Levins Morales, Aurora. *Remedios: Stories of Earth and Iron from the History of Puertorriqueñas*. Cambridge, MA: South End Press, 1998, 2001.

Kindling: Writings on the Body. Cambridge, MA: Palabrera Press, 2013.

Medicine Stories: History, Culture and the Politics of Integrity. Boston, MA: South End Press, 1998.

"Review of *A Message from God in the Atomic Age*, by Irene Vilar." Trans. Gregory Rabassa. *Women's Review of Books* 14.8 (May 97): 10–12.

Martín Alcoff, Linda. "The Unassimilated Theorist." *PMLA* 121.1 (Jan. 2006): 255–59.

Moraga, Cherríe. *Loving in the War Years: lo que nunca pasó por sus labios*. Expanded second edition. Cambridge, MA: South End Press, (1983) 2000.

A Xicana Codex of Changing Consciousness: Writings, 2000-2010. Durham, NC: Duke University Press, 2011.

Moraga, Cherríe and Gloria Anzaldúa, eds. *This Bridge Called My Back: Writings by Radical Women of Color*. Fourth Edition. Albany: State University of New York Press, 2015.

Moreno, Marisel. *Family Matters: Puerto Rican Women Authors on the Island and the Mainland*. Charlotte: University of Virginia Press, 2012.

Negrón-Muntaner, Frances. "Bridging Islands: Gloria Anzaldua and the Caribbean." *PMLA* 121.1 (Jan 2006): pp. 272–78.

Pérez-Rosario, Vanessa. *Becoming Julia de Burgos: The Making of a Puerto Rican Icon*. Urbana-Champaign: University of Illinois Press, 2014.

"Affirming an Afro-Latin@ Identity: An Interview with Poet María Teresa (Mariposa) Fernández." *Latino Studies Journal* 12:3 (Fall 2014).

Ramos, Juanita, ed. *Compañeras: Latina Lesbians*. New York: Latina Lesbian History Project, 1987. (New York: Routledge, 1994.)

Saldívar-Hull, Sonia. *Feminism on the Border: Chicana Gender Politics and Literature*. Berkeley: University of California Press, 2000.

Sánchez González, Lisa. *Boricua Literature: A Literary History of the Puerto Rican Diaspora*. New York: New York University Press, 2001.

Saulny, Susan. "Black? White? Asian? More Young Americans Choose All of the Above." *The New York Times*. January 29, 2011. Accessed March 22, 2016. www.nytimes.com/2011/01/30/us/30mixed.html?pagewanted=all. Online.

The Latina Feminist Group. *Telling to Live: Latina Feminist Testimonios*. Durham, NC: Duke University Press, 2001.

Vasconcelos, José. *The Cosmic Race/La raza cósmica*. Trans. and annotated Didier T. Jaén. Baltimore, MD: The Johns Hopkins University Press, 1997.

Vilar, Irene. *The Ladies' Gallery*. Trans. Gregory Rabassa. New York: Other Press, 2009.

Impossible Motherhood: Testimony of an Abortion Addict. New York: Other Press, 2009.

"Addicted to Pregnancy Highs; The American Author Irene Vilar Has Caused an Outcry with Her Book about Being an 'Abortion Addict'. Here She Explains the Reasons behind Her 15 Terminations in 16 Years." *Times* [London, England] October 24, 2009: 44. *Academic OneFile* Web. Accessed Nov. 8, 2015.

24

Invisible No More

U.S. Central American Literature Before and
Beyond the Age of Neoliberalism

ANA PATRICIA RODRÍGUEZ

In *A Brief History of Neoliberalism*, David Harvey mentions, almost in passing, that for the United States, Central America has long served as a testing ground for liberal and neoliberal economic programs. Repeatedly, the U.S. govern-ment has intervened economically, politically, and militarily in the Central American isthmus in order to ensure the flow of global capital. It has protected its interests in Central America through Dollar Diplomacy, covert and overt military interventions, and, in the twenty-first century, new regional trade agreements and international development policies such as the Domin-ican Republic-Central American Free Trade Agreement (DR-CAFTA, 2007) and the Alliance for Prosperity (2016), which ultimately strengthen the eco-nomic and security presence of the United States in the region. According to Harvey, the U.S. government implemented in Central America "a more open system of imperialism without colonies during the twentieth century" (27) through its support of military dictatorships and right-wing regimes up through the civil wars in Guatemala, Nicaragua, and El Salvador in the last half of the twentieth century.

With the signing of the Peace Accords in El Salvador (1992) and Guatemala (1996), the region was also formally opened to neoliberal economic reforms, which mandated that, "if markets do not exist (in areas such as land, water, education, health care, social security, or environmental pollution) then they must be created, by state action if necessary" (Harvey 2). In his book *Transnational Conflicts: Central America, Social Change and Globalization*, William I. Robinson shows as well how transnational agents in and outside of the region were quick to capitalize on newly forced open markets in Central America, creating in their wake greater scarcity, poverty, and hard-ships for large sectors of the population. The social violence that is commonplace today throughout the region is a product of neoliberal economic and political agendas, enforcing the privatization of Central American assets, resources, and bodies, including those of more than 3 million Central American immigrants living, working, and generating remittance capital in the United States and across the world ("Remittances Received by El Salvador"). Given state-run neoliberal policies and socioeconomic conditions forcing people to leave their homelands in search of economic and physical security, Central Americans continue to migrate to the United States, becoming a more pronounced presence in the cultural imaginary of the nation as shown by their increasing representation in Latina/o literature.

Mapping out the Central American diaspora through its literary representations, this chapter examines a corpus of U.S. Central American literary texts, which critically reflect on the legacy of violence, war, and the struggle for social justice in the region.[1] Highly referential and historically contextualized, these texts draw from the rich literary traditions of Central America, such as social justice/protest literature, testimonial discourse, and *exteriorista* poetry, which is characterized by its references to history, use of colloquial language, and concrete imagery associated with the work of T. S. Eliot, Ezra Pound, and others.[2] Today, these traditions inform the production of new literary texts produced under and beyond the far-reaching neoliberal influences and conditions of Central America and its diasporas. Indeed, in *The Art of Transition: Latin American Culture and Neoliberal Crisis*, Francine Masiello has studied the art and literature produced at the end of the dirty wars in Chile and Argentina as reactions to rising neoliberal forces, while Michael Dowdy, in *Broken South: Latina/o Poetic Responses to Neoliberalism and Globalization*, surveys a number of contemporary transnational Latina/o texts as discursive "responses" to the "abject violence" of neoliberalism (Dowdy ix). Likewise, this chapter examines a corpus of U.S. Central American literary texts grounded in Central American history, particularly the period before and beyond the civil wars, U.S. interventions, forced displacements, and neoliberalism in the region, all of which have historically produced migration and diaspora in and from Central America. Resisting the historical aphasia

---

[1] In this chapter, US Central American literature includes texts produced by Central American first-generation immigrants and US-born-and-raised Central American writers.

[2] As practiced by Central American poets like Ernesto Cardenal, Claribel Alegría, Roque Dalton, and others, *exteriorista* or concrete poetry references the "exterior" world, alludes to "concrete" historical events, people, and places, focuses on social issues and themes, and uses local colloquial language. This genre has been an important discursive vehicle of protest and social critique, especially during the Central American armed conflicts.

associated with globalization in literary production that Elena Machado Sáez draws our attention to in *Market Aesthetics*, U.S. Central American literature is grounded in acts of historical remembrance and referentiality, as will be shown in this chapter. I suggest that it is in these literary acts of historical retelling, or "un-silencing" (Padilla 99) that the Central American diaspora resists its own erasure and challenges the trope of Central American invisibility by making visible and audible what Arturo Arias calls the "unrepresentable" acts and narratives of Central America (*Taking Their Word* 215).

De/constructing Foundational Fictions from the Diaspora

The foundational liberal nation-building narratives of Central America almost always begin with coffee production in the mid nineteenth century. As in other regions of Latin America, the burgeoning *criollo* elites of Central America desired to break into international markets and to break with Spain's export restrictions barring commerce by its colonies with other nations or with more proximate economic centers (Anna 1987; Lynch 1987). These national elites sought independence from Spain in order to consolidate their power over land, people, and economic expansion. For the Central American isthmus, independence from Spain came hand-in-hand with mass-scale production and exportation of coffee – the golden crop that fueled nation-building projects and the founding narratives of Central America (Lauria-Santiago 1999; Paige 1997; Gudmundson and Lindo-Fuentes 1995). First introduced to the nations of Costa Rica, Guatemala, and El Salvador in the 1820s and 1830s, coffee production required intense labor in small-scale family-based *fincas* and/or large-scale plantations (Paige 1997; Roseberry, Gudmundson, and Samper Kutschbach 1995). Replacing indigo as a primary export crop, the production and export of coffee generated great capital for landowners, known as *caficultores*. In countries with large populations of laborers such as Guatemala and El Salvador, the oligarchic elite class used extreme measures to exploit, repress, and force local indigenous and mestizo peasants to work in coffee production. In El Salvador, for example, *ejidos* (collective land grants) were formally abolished by the 1880s, and anti-vagrancy laws were established and enforced in the 1870s to put "landless peasants to work on coffee plantations" (Booth, Wade, and Walker 138). Eventually, the landowning elite in concert with military forces resorted to genocidal practices to subject peasants to forced labor. In 1932, the dictator Maximiliano Hernández Martínez carried out one of the worst massacres in the history of the Americas. Known as *La Matanza* in El Salvador, almost 30,000 peasants, mostly indigenous people, perished in a massacre that lasted a few weeks in the western coffee-producing region of the country, leaving deep and long-lasting scars in Salvadoran cultural memory (Lindo-Fuentes, Ching, and Lara-Martínez 2007). Early on, coffee production became the subject of nation building and local-color literature throughout the Central American countries. It also figures as the backdrop of Marcos McPeek Villatoro's diasporic foundational novel, *A Fire in the Earth*, which I discuss in the next section.

Set in the coffee-producing regions of El Salvador, Villatoro's *A Fire in the Earth*, like Sandra Benítez's *Bitter Grounds*, and Mario Bencastro's *Mansión del olvido* (Mansion of Oblivion), uses La Matanza as a narrative trope to represent the (neo)liberal coffee republic divided by class interests leading up to the civil war of the 1980s and more current remittance-producing labor migrations. From nation-building literature to these diasporic Latina/o novels, coffee production serves as a synecdoche of labor exploitation that ties subjects to liberal and neoliberal economic systems of oppression – from forced labor on coffee plantations to labor migrations for transnational remittance production. While Bencastro's novel represents the return of a native son to the mythical Ausolia, *la tierra de infancia* (childhood land) that recalls Claudia Lars's novel of the same name,[3] Benítez's novel follows the lives of women born into wealth and poverty under the patriarchal regime of coffee production in the family plantation. In similar fashion, Villatoro's family saga represents the rise and downfall of the Colonez (Colonial) family, who build their wealth literally making bricks for the coffee-producing elite – the caficultura. The novel begins as Patricio Colonez, the family patriarch, arrives from his studies abroad in rural El Salvador to work as an English–Spanish translator and general manager for the International Railroad of Central America (Villatoro, *A Fire*, 98–99). Upon arrival, Colonez meets Romilia Vazquez, a local peasant woman, whom he marries shortly thereafter. Over a span of five decades, the couple amasses great wealth and property, almost brick by brick, building a brick-house factory to supply materials for the growing coffee-industrial complex in the region around the fictional town of *El Comienzo* – the beginning. The accumulation of wealth by the Colonez family is tied to the liberal market economy that determines the

---

[3] Claudia Lars is a Salvadoran writer and poet, best known for her memoir, *Tierra de infancia*, based on her childhood memories of growing up in the coffee-producing region of western El Salvador during La Matanza.

price of coffee and the social condition of the Salvadoran citizenry. At the start of the novel, Patricio Colonez comments on the "thousands and thousands of coffee trees," which before his eyes are transformed into "a field of money" (101).

Coffee production permits the Colonez family's entry into the liberal export-based economy vis-à-vis the exchange of commodities and acquisition of luxury items, foreign language and customs, and relationships with "gringo" friends (108). Early on, the novel shines light on the liberal (materialistic) values of the Salvadoran industrializing class: "So much is coming in and out of the city, exporting and importing. A trainload of goods comes in twice a week from La Libertad" (99). While products enter the country at a rapid pace, coffee production exposes the Colonez family to travel and possible migration to places in the United States, which with time will become poles of attraction for Central American elites and others (Córdova 2005; Mahler 1995). At one point, Colonez's brother and business partner comments: "With my ideas and your English, we could end up living in San Francisco, California, or perhaps New York!" (Villatoro 1996, 100). Heavily tied to the coffee-market economy, however, Colonez begins to lose his wealth to land speculators as coffee production begins its decline in El Salvador in the latter half of the twentieth century. The arc of the story of the Colonez family, thus, rises and falls with the transition from a liberal to a neoliberal economy in El Salvador. The novel tells us:

> Science had spread quickly by then throughout their developing little country. It gobbled up tradition in their cities and towns, and it showed them the modern life. Science and technology came on the trains, whose tracks wrapped about the tiny nation like a tight metal cocoon, yanking it out of hiding from beneath the rest of the American republics and hurling it into the mainstream. Progress had come to his doorstep, had shown him how to develop his business. Science had brought him a new machine to his brick factory. (*A Fire*, 105–106)

While the novel represents the economic and cultural shift toward the positivist ideals of science, technology, and industry, it also highlights the violence that makes this shift possible and leads to the extreme political repression of La Matanza and the violence thereafter during the civil war in the 1980s. The workers who had made bricks by hand in the Colonez brick factory find that "work awaited them in the coffee fields" along with heightened forms of labor exploitation (106), signaling the cyclical systemic nature of oppression in Central America. Although the novel culminates and ends with the fall of the house of the Colonez as the civil war approaches,

A Fire in the Earth falls short of deconstructing El Salvador as the nostalgic homeland – the land of infancy.

Like Benítez's, and Bencastro's novels, Villatoro's family saga is embedded in what I have called elsewhere an internalized "neocolonialist nostalgia" (A. P. Rodríguez 396), the gaze of diasporic subjects yearning for homeland memories of "the idyllic countryside" (396), or the land of infancy left behind, which far from ever having existed or providing safe haven, was built on historical erasure and silencing of other voices, which Yajaira Padilla highlights in her work and whose *un-silencing* will be discussed later in this chapter. Indeed in *Culture and Truth: The Remaking of Social Analysis*, the anthropologist Renato Rosaldo talks about a "nostalgia for colonized culture as it was 'traditionally'" (69), upon which is founded a great part of early ethnographic literature by insiders and outsiders, alike, as well as, by extension, the foundational literature discussed by Doris Sommer in *Foundational Fictions: The National Romances of Latin America*. As Sommer and Rosaldo would have it, foundational and ethnographic literature is often premised on representing past and present cultures through the lens of nostalgia and loss. Although in his U.S. Central American neo-foundational novel Villatoro calls attention to the conditions of violence, marginalization, and exploitation upon which Salvadoran society was built and sustained from its colonial foundations through its neo/liberal reconstructions, he also leaves untouched and unrepresented other histories that challenged and collided with the foundational narratives of the coffee plantation, so to speak. Like Bencastro and Benítez, Villatoro's *Fire from the Mountain* remains silent on the *hidden figures* such as Prudencia Ayala, who clamored behind the scenes, and whose story will be told by new generations of U.S.-born-and-raised Central American writers and poets discussed at the end of this chapter.

Reimagining the Transition from Civil War to Postwar

Calling attention to the civil war, Salvadoran first-generation immigrant writers like Mario Bencastro, Horacio Castellanos Moya, and Martivón Galindo, among others, who fled the region in the 1980s and 1990s as war-displaced migrants (if not recognized refugees), began to write from their new diasporic (dis)locations. Aligned or identified with the social movements of the 1980s, they were forced into exile as a consequence of their political activism. During that period, more than 2 million Central Americans were displaced due to civil unrest in their countries (García and Gomáriz 101).

Although many of them sought refuge primarily in the United States, most were denied political asylum in the country,[4] except for refugees from countries such as Nicaragua under Sandinista rule, with which the U.S. government was not on "friendly terms" in the 1980s. At the height of the civil wars in El Salvador, Guatemala, and Nicaragua, the classification and status of "refugee" was denied to most Central Americans fleeing to the United States, as it applied only to those who could prove persecution in countries of origin, and this proof was difficult to gain.

In her collection of short stories *Retazos* (Pieces) and more recently in *Para amaestrar un trigre* (To Tame a Tiger) and *La tormenta rodando por la cuesta: Impresiones El Salvador 1979–1981* (The Storm Moving through the Mountain: Impressions El Salvador 1979–1981), Martivón Galindo recounts her personal migration to San Francisco, California, following her capture and torture by military personnel, her incorporation into the solidarity community in the San Francisco Bay Area, and, years later, her coming to terms with the effects of war in her life. Like Galindo, Horacio Castellanos Moya, also writes numerous texts from diasporic locations and focuses on post/war violence, impunity, and subjectivity in Central America. In his novel, *El sueño del retorno* (The Dream of Return), Castellanos Moya reflects upon the predicament of a Salvadoran man incapable of moving on or moving back to his country when the opportunity presents itself. Through his metaphysical impasse, the novel seems to interrogate the return narrative of the diasporic subject. In these texts, El Salvador for the diasporic subject becomes a place of no return, as Castellanos Moya reminds his readers throughout his oeuvre, including his most cited works to date: *La diáspora, El asco, El arma en el hombre, La diabla en el espejo, Insensatez, Tirana memoria,* and *El sueño del retorno.*

In his 2010 collection of short stories and poems, *Paraíso portátil / Portable Paradise*, published by Arte Público Press in both Spanish and English in the same volume, Mario Bencastro likewise represents the lives of Salvadoran first-generation immigrants forced to leave their country during the civil war and to live in its aftermath away from their homeland. Casting light on a new postwar era of impunity, crisis, violence, and fear, Bencastro's stories

---

[4] As designated by the UNHCR (United Nations High Commission of Refugees) at the 1951 Convention of Refugees, the category and status of refugee refers to any person who flees her/his country of origin for fear of persecution because of racial, religious, nationality, group affiliations, or political opinions, and is forced to reside outside of the country of origin because s/he fears further persecution (*Los refugiados centroamericanos*).

represent scenarios in the life of Salvadoran postwar transnational society. His stories represent an array of neoliberal postwar diasporic subjectivities, including a Salvadoran immigrant woman living in Australia who encounters her family's killer in an online chat room ("De Australia con amor / From Australia with Love"); a political asylee living in Switzerland who returns to El Salvador to take premeditated revenge on his former victimizers ("El Plan / The Plan"); a private security guard hired to protect the home of absentee migrants living in the United States ("El vigilante / The Watchman"); and an orphaned glue-sniffer living and working as a fire-eater on the streets of San Salvador ("El niño dragon / Dragon Boy"). Representing a variety of new transnational social actors, Bencastro's characters demonstrate the growing socioeconomic inequities and physical and psychical traumas shaping Central American nations, communities, families, and individuals under neoliberal market forces. Bencastro's stories call attention to the production of new neoliberal subjectivities tied to and shaped by the flows of the market economy, including security agents, gang members, glue-sniffers, and would-be migrants.

In diaspora, Bencastro's characters yearn for a past that ceased to exist with the war, and in the different stories, they play out various contradictory narrative resolutions. Some break with the past, others attempt to avenge it, and some reconcile with it, coming ambivalently to terms with their diasporic condition. In the title poem of the collection, "Paraíso portátil / Portable Paradise," featured at the end of the book, Bencastro describes the paradoxical position of the Central American diasporic subject and writer. He writes,

> In the land I come from I am / loved and hated / the faraway brother and the one close by / good and bad / the one who left and returns / the one who never went away nor came back / the one who saves the homeland from ruin / the one who sinks it into chaos . . . hero and undesirable / the unknown exile / the respected compatriot. . . .
>
> (Bencastro, *Portable Paradise*, 213; translation in original collection)

In his reference to the "faraway brother [sic sister]," Bencastro alludes to what the Salvadoran state has called *el hermano lejano*, or *Departmento 15* (Baker-Cristales 2004), namely an imaginary political and cultural entity created by the constant stream of immigrants who remain largely undocumented but yet contribute more than $4 billion annually in remittances to the economy of El Salvador ("Remittances Received by El Salvador"), far surpassing the capital generated from coffee production to the gross national product of El Salvador. Whereas coffee had been a high-yielding item in the

GNP of the liberal economies, in the neoliberal era, migrants as human capital drive the economy, as seen in this post–civil war diasporic literature concerned with Central American migration and migrants.

In "Las ilusiones de Juana / Juana's Dream," Bencastro, like Galindo and Castellanos Moya in their respective texts, deconstructs the diasporic nostalgic narrative of return. He tells the story of a divorced middle-age woman named Juana, who immigrated with her family to Virginia during the civil war and had long since attained legal residency in the United States. Every year she visits El Salvador for the August festivals. Returning home from one such trip, she smuggles three avocados, which she prunes, nurtures, and replants in her garden in the hope of recreating a bit of her homeland in her backyard. The one surviving Salvadoran avocado plant, however, withers in the summer heat, as does Juana's dream of returning to El Salvador. Representing, perhaps, first-generation migration nostalgia and estranged affiliations, the avocado seedlings in Bencastro's story show the transnational divide between Salvadoran migrants and nationals to be considerable, and perhaps insurmountable, in the twenty-first century as migrants and families are separated by the need to produce remittance capital. In these postwar narratives, Central American neoliberal subjects almost always represent potential immigrants made to produce capital and mediate between the homeland and host states, while, on the other hand, U.S.-Central American writers born or raised in the United States, such as those discussed in the next section, in the void of firsthand experiences of homeland invent their own secondhand memories, histories, and images of Central America.

Re/making History and Memories

In their respective texts, Tanya María Barrientos, Francisco Goldman, Cristina Henríquez, Sandra Rodríguez Barron, Sylvia Sellers-García, Héctor Tobar, Marcos McPeek Villatoro, and other writers born and/or raised in the United States return to, what are for them, originating moments of earlier generations' dispersions from Central America. For many of these U.S. Central American writers, the civil wars or more recent postwar crises associated with natural disasters, poverty, unemployment, food scarcity, violence, extortion, and death threats serve as the originating moments of the Central American diaspora. In re/making histories and memories to which they have no direct link or context, these writers produce fictions of origins, so to speak, and spaces of diasporic memory for new and emerging generations of the Central American diaspora.

Originally published in 1998, Héctor Tobar's *The Tattooed Soldier* can be described as a watershed text not only for U.S. Central American literature but also for Latina/o literature as a whole, as it was one of the first diasporic novels about Central America/ns written by a U.S.-born Guatemalan and published by a U.S. mainstream press. As such, *The Tattooed Soldier* prompted long-overdue conversations on Central America/ns in the U.S. Latina/o cultural imaginary. It is telling that in his analysis of Tobar's novel for the inaugural issue of the *Latino Studies* journal, the critic Arturo Arias launches his discussion on the invisibility of Central America/ns in the United States and introduces the term "'Central American-American' as a dissonance ... that opens up the possibility for recognition of this as-yet unnamed segment of the U.S. population" ("Central American-Americans," 170–71). In this piece, Arias discusses not only the novel's recreation of Guatemalan history and the role of the U.S. government in training Guatemalan military surrogates to commit extreme acts of violence on their own people, but also the re/construction of post/war Central American diasporic subjectivities as represented by the main characters – Guillermo Longoria and Antonio Bernal – both forced to leave Guatemala and their former identities and to assume new ones in the United States. But, as they quickly learn, they cannot leave behind nor forget the histories that travel with them to the north.

Set in Guatemala during its long civil war (1954–1996), when more than 250,000 people were killed, disappeared, or forcefully displaced, *The Tattooed Soldier* tells the story of two Guatemalan refugees, the soldier Longoria and his victim, the student, Antonio, who flee the violence of the civil war only to reencounter one another in Los Angeles during the riots in 1992. In a reversal of the original violence inflicted by Longoria on Antonio and his family, Antonio kills the soldier in a dead-end tunnel in Los Angeles, California, following the LA Riots. In similar fashion, in *The Long Night of White Chickens*, Francisco Goldman uses the noir genre to grapple with the violence, disappearances, and massacres in Guatemala during the civil war. Following up with *The Art of Political Murder: Who Killed the Bishop?*, Goldman narrates his own behind-the-scenes investigative work documenting the trial of assassinated Bishop Juan José Gerardi Conedera (1922–1998). Killed by unknown assailants on the heels of the publication of the *Guatemala Never Again! Recovery of Historical Memory Project (REMHI)* report in 1998, Bishop Gerardi was known to have denounced human-rights abuses by the Guatemalan government and armed forces. In *The Ordinary Seaman*, Goldman further explores the fate of Central American labor migrants held captive on a stateless boat in the New York harbor. Delving into the new illicit markets and policing tactics brought about by neoliberalism in the Americas, Marcos McPeek Villatoro, in his series of crime novels, titled *Homekillings, Minos, Venom Beneath the Skin,* and *Blood Daughters,* introduces readers to Romilia Chacón. The daughter of Salvadoran civil war immigrants and Nashville police-officer-turned-FBI-agent in Los Angeles, Chacón fights transnational crime. Throughout Villatoro's series, Chacón's nemesis is a shadowy figure named Rafaél Murillo (aka *Tecún Umán*), who is a former Kaibil soldier-turned-drug-trafficker in the United States. Both detective Chacón and drug trafficker Murillo not only share a common history of war, violence, and displacement in Central America, but also represent the diasporic transference of war trauma across generations, migrations, and hemispheric translocations of the Central American diaspora.

In what I have called "postmemorial texts" by U.S. Central American writers who may not have directly experienced the violence in Central America, Tanya Maria Barrientos, Sylvia Sellers-García, and Sandra Rodríguez Barron, in their respective novels, *Family Resemblance, When the Ground Turns in Its Sleep,* and *The Heiress of the Water,* search for their personal and national histories, which have remained buried, silenced, and inaccessible to them through their parents' silences and omissions. Never having lived in their parents' homelands, the protagonists of these novels engage in the production of vicarious secondhand memories in order to grapple with the ghosts of historical calamities, a process that Marianne Hirsch has called postmemory in the context of post-Holocaust generations (Hirsch 4–6). In their novels, Rodríguez Barron, Sellers-García, and Barrientos produce memories (where there were perhaps none) out of secondary materials such as family photos, letters, newspaper clippings, books, and media representations, among other archives of a traumatic past. In this act of creation, if not recuperation of memories, they participate in what Yajaira Padilla has also called the "historical act of un-silencing" (99), to which I will return in the last section of this chapter.

In *Family Resemblance,* Barrientos, for example, tells the story of Nita (Juanita) DeLeon, a young woman of Guatemalan descent born and raised in the United States, whose parents fled Guatemala under mysterious circumstances. Nita DeLeon grows up in the United States in her parents' shadows and silences, never knowing much about her parents' family, homeland, or history, until the day her father, Diego DeLeon, a retired professor of Latin American literature in Texas, suffers a massive stroke that leaves him partially paralyzed due to an "emboli" and experiencing "global aphasia" (Barrientos 3). Fearing disclosure of his past involvement with the leftist opposition front supporting Guatemalan president Jacobo Guzmán Arbenz, Nita's father keeps silent about the reasons why the family had to leave Guatemala. Instead, he severs all ties to his family and country. It is a great shock, then, to Nita that upon searching among her father's papers, she finds a mysterious letter from Guatemala, dated July 2, 1976, and a phonebook with names and numbers from her parents' past. The letter from her father's long-presumed-dead sister Francisca (Pancha) DeLeon and Nita's deceased mother's phonebook shatter Nita's family narrative as she knows it, forcing her to confront the family history hidden from her by her parents' silence on the matter. Suddenly, Nita learns that her parents weren't the people she thought she knew and that her memory of them is filled with omissions and silences, just like her parents' wedding album filled with images of people unknown to her and for whom she had made up stories, "pieced together in [her] imagination" (16).

What Nita excavates in the shards and pieces of her family history is that her father had been an ardent supporter of President Jacobo Arbenz, whom the U.S. government overthrew in a 1954 CIA-sponsored coup d'état to protect the economic interests of the United Fruit Company. Part of the making of national history, and unbeknownst to Nita, her father had been affiliated with the Communist Party and to the end had supported Arbenz. His sister Pancha DeLeon, on the other hand, had joined the *right-wing* opposition guerrilla movement that aided in the coup d'état to topple Arbenz. Divided by political ideologies, Nita's father and pregnant mother fled to the United States, while Nita's aunt Pancha and grandmother remained in Guatemala, never to mend their differences or communicate with Nita's parents, until the arrival of Pancha DeLeon's mysterious letter, dated July 2, 1976, addressed to Nita's mother in an attempt to reestablish contact with the extended family. On a collision course with history, Nita not only learns about her family's divided allegiances in the 1954 coup, which forced her family to migrate, but also that it was the right-wing Pancha who helped her communist brother to escape certain death in Guatemala. Her father and mother never knew of the life-saving assistance provided by Pancha when they cut off all ties to Guatemala and Pancha, and silenced the past for Nita. In the end, Nita must piece together and "unsilence" her family's history in order to reconnect with her Guatemalan heritage. She must shatter the well-intentioned silences and "false memories" that her mother and father created for her and begin to produce her own Guatemalan narrative, incorporating a new understanding of her family and her country's history as a diasporic subject. Perhaps a constant in these texts by U.S.-born-and-raised Central American writers is the search for memory, history, and heritage, which can only be filled in through the power of fiction and storytelling.

Mixing It Up and Saying It Loud

Like the aforementioned writers, U.S. Central American poets including the California-based Epicentro spoken-word collective and others like William Archila, Mario Escobar, Karina Oliva Alvarado, Quique Avilés, Maya Chinchilla, Lorena Duarte, Leticia Hernández-Linares, Raquel Gutiérrez, Harold Terezón, among others, from their respective borderlands create other stories for the Central American diaspora. Inspired by the theorizing of Chicana/Latina feminists, particularly Gloria Anzaldúa, Hernández-Linares, Duarte, and Chinchilla, whose work is discussed in this section, speak and write (out) of their own matrix of hybrid Central American experiences, voices, histories, and struggles, while adhering to the larger tenets of Latina feminisms. Often, they speak and theorize from personal experiences, call attention to intersecting forms of oppression, challenge patriarchy and heteronormative structures of power, and build solidarity or "broader communal ground among Latinas/os" and across difference (Anzaldúa 109). In this context, these U.S. Central American poets use their voices to disarticulate the narrative of silence or invisibility that has been ascribed to Central Americans through disappearing physical actions and speech acts induced by war, violence, and migration, as Arias first theorizes in his work ("Central American-Americans," 170). Breaking silences and speaking explicitly about the particular struggles of Central Americans in the United States, Hernández-Linares, Duarte, and Chinchilla strategically deploy the voice of the *hocicona* – the outspoken mestiza women armed with a critical consciousness and articulating a feminist critique of nationalism and transnational neoliberalism, which regulate the lives, subjectivities, and representations of Central American women across trans/national location. In her superb analysis of transnational Salvadoran women's narratives, and in particular the work of Hernández-Linares, Yajaira Padilla reminds us of the need to deconstruct "the patriarchal underpinnings of the process of Salvadoran transnational community building and construction of new identities" (99), as exemplified by the work of the poets discussed in this section.

Born in Hollywood, California, to Salvadoran immigrant parents, and residing in San Francisco, California, Leticia Hernández-Linares has performed her spoken-word poems in public venues throughout the United

States and El Salvador. In her signature poem, "La sibila, la cigua y la poetisa (Conversaciones)" from her first book of poetry titled *Razor Edges of My Tongue*, Hernández-Linares pays homage to Prudencia Ayala (1885–1936) – early Salvadoran feminist, suffragist, labor leader, presidential candidate, and poet born under the sign of La Ciguanaba, also a figure of female resistance in Salvadoran oral history and tradition.[5] Aligning herself with Central American female resistance figures, Hernández-Linares also writes about Prudencia Ayala as "hocicona e imprudente," an imprudent woman with a loud voice, a hollering woman, as Sandra Cisneros writes in her own revision of La Llorona. Like La Malinche of Chicana history, Prudencia commands a presence in Hernández-Linares's revisioning: "hocicona e imprudente / ese día el domingo veintitrés / caminó hacia la alcadía y pidió en voz alta / su ciudadanía / con un paso, una pregunta / se declara esclava, muda / no más" (34). Born April 28, 1885, in Sonzacate in the Department of Sonsonate, El Salvador, of indigenous parents, Ayala achieved a second grade education, yet by 1914 had published her poetry and articles on feminist issues and on Central American unionism in newspapers in El Salvador and Guatemala ("Prudencia Ayala"). She published the book *Inmortal, amores de loca* (1925) and *Payaso literario en combate* (1928), while denouncing the dictatorship of Manuel Estrada Cabrera in Guatemala and the U.S. Marine invasion of Nicaragua of 1912–1933, and expressing her support of Augusto C. Sandino's revolution in that country. In 1930, Ayala announced her candidacy for presidency in the first free elections in El Salvador in two decades and ran against the oligarch Arturo Araujo, who won the elections. By December 1931, however, General Maximiliano Hernández Martínez had overthrown the elected president, and, in 1932, ordered *La Matanza*, the massacre of 30,000 campesinos in a

---

[5] According to Nahua-Pipil legend, La Ciguanaba, also known as Segua, is a post-conquest figure of pre-Colombian Mesoamerican origins. In ancient times, she was a beautiful Pipil/nahuatl woman named Sihuehuet, who was impregnated by the son of the rain god Tlaloc and who gave birth to a boy known as el Cipitío, who is big-bellied from eating ashes and whose two feet face backwards. Punished for neglecting her child Cipitío, La Ciguanaba wanders at night by waterways and approaches men. US Salvadoran and Central American feminist writers and critics like Leticia Hernández-Linares, Yajaira Padilla, and Karina O. Alvarado recuperate and resignify La Ciguanaba as a figure of resistance, resilience, and empowerment in the context of misogyny and patriarchy. Padilla and Alvarado lucidly construct what Alvarado calls a "gynealogy of Cigua resistance," which includes the legendary Ciguanaba, the historic Prudencia Ayala, the poet Hernández-Linares, and other US Central American women in the long line of resistance against "colonization, colonialism, gendered violence, gendered exile, and dehumanization" (Alvarado 98).

period of few weeks as well as the execution of communist leader Farabundo Martí ("Prudencia Ayala").

Against the backdrop of military dictatorship, phallocratic order, and political repression, Prudencia Ayala not only ran for president but also dared to voice her dissent with the political order, for which at times she was incarcerated and tortured, forced to stand upright for days in a small cell. Hernández-Linares invokes and honors this early Salvadoran feminist and working-class activist: "Prudencia Ayala / escritora, política, sibila / candidata presidencial en mil novecientos treinta / desafió / con letra y advinanza sobre páginas / que enterraron bajo el concreto y que ya no se publican /... Sabia, Prudencia, deshaciendo las cadenas con sus poemas / siembra flores en el polvo que se acumula en las esquinas / del suelo" (Prudencia Ayala / writer, politician, sibyl / presidential candidate in nineteen thirty / challenged / with word and prophecy on the pages / that they buried in concrete and did not publish /... Sage, Prudencia, tears apart the chains with her poems / sows flowers in the dust that gathers in the corners / of the floor) (Hernández-Linares 34–35; my translation).

In her ode to Ayala, Hernández-Linares pays homage to the woman born into the exploitative world that coffee production wrought. She was "descalza" (bare-foot) most of her life, yet protected by the spirit of "Sihuán / mujer, espíritu del agua" (Sihuán / woman, water spirit) (34). Establishing a culturally specific feminine genealogy, or "gynealogy" in the poem (Alvarado 98), Hernández-Linares imagines La Ciguanaba visiting Ayala in prison, telling her "no te preocupes porque a todas nos castigan / pero con nuestra persistencia continuaremos siendo chingonas!" (do not worry because we are all punished / but we go on being chingonas with our persistence!) (35; my translation). In a self-reflexive moment, the implied narrator of the poem pauses to reflect on the use of the word "chingona" (badass woman), which gives protagonical power to the woman who rather than receiving sexual violence exercised her agency: "¡¿Pero, qué pasa aquí, estas palabras no son salvadoreñas?!" (But what is happening here, these words are not Salvadoran?!) (36), calling attention to the mestiza consciousness of Hernández-Linares, who was raised in the Chicana/Latina borderlands of California and who respects "ninguna lengua, ninguna patria" (no language, no fatherland). Hernández-Linares, like other intersectional feminist borderland poets, can no more speak in one language than lay claim to one national identity or cultural heritage (Padilla 110–14). Instead these *Salvi* or U.S.-made Salvadoran and other Central American writers engage in an intersectional dialogue drawing from feminist critiques of masculinist heteronormative nationalism and invoking feminine figures such as la Ciguanaba, Prudencia Ayala, and others.

The poem ends thus by reclaiming the Salvadoran / Central American tradition of outspoken women: "No era monstrua, ni mala / nada, nada de esas pendejadas que definen y trauman [las mujeres] / era naba / era cigua / mujer de espíritu y agua / que inspiró espirales de palabras / revelaciones como tales" (She was not a monster, nor bad / none of that nonsense that defines and traumatizes [women] / she was naba / she was cigua / woman of spirit and water / who inspired spirals of words and revelations) (Hernández-Linares 36; my translation). In other words, Prudencia Ayala, like the poets discussed here, lay claim to the power of words that they now "un-silence." In spoken-word poems recorded on her CD *Mucha muchacha: Too much girl* and compiled in her book by the same title, Hernández-Linares goes on to sing praise to Latina women's unleashed experiences, stories, and voices claiming that her stories "wrestle the truth, cut it up, and paste it back together with letters that want to be sung and spoken aloud" (CD jacket cover). As "la cuchillera" (knife-wielder) in one of her more recent spoken-word poems, Leticia Hernández-Linares is part of a new generation of U.S. Salvadoran and Central American writers not afraid to speak, sample, and mix genres, traditions, and languages, to borrow-in-solidarity from the artistic practices of Chicana and other feminists, and to write anew the narratives of U.S. Central Americans.

Like Hernández-Linares, Lorena Duarte is a second-generation writer of Salvadoran descent born in the United States. She has published her award-winning work in a number of anthologies, including *Kalina: Theatre Under My Skin*, gathering the voices of Salvadoran poets born in the last quarter of the twentieth century in El Salvador and in the United States (Pleitez Vela 67–86). Her poem "Flint Tongue" speaks from the Latina borderlands that recall Anzaldúa's struggle with oppressive monolingualisms on both sides of English and Spanish. Like Anzaldúa, Duarte reflects on learning to speak to survive. The persona of the poem begins the text by telling readers: "When I was four / I nearly cut off my own tongue / Slipped and neatly pierced it with my teeth... If you don't believe me, kiss me and you will feel the scar" (Pleitez Vela 226). Since Anzaldúa's *Borderlands/La frontera*, the borderlands has been associated with the metaphor of the open wound, produced by the grating proximity of nations, cultures, languages, and belief systems, among all other things, represented by the U.S.–Mexico border. Taking up this metaphor, Duarte's poetic persona has internalized the wound of living in-between and thus she is conscious at all times of her "flint tongue, / A split and shattered tongue, / A patched up, miracle tongue / A survivor tongue / A grateful tongue, aware of its nearly mute destiny / An urgent tongue" (226).

Whereas Anzaldúa's injured tongue sought healing and voice in the Chicana/o Spanish articulated throughout her book *Borderlands/La frontera*, Duarte's flint tongue, like a pointed obsidian object lodged inside her mouth maintains a constant state of injury: "a bloody mouth" that causes injury as well. As the poet says, her tongue is double-edged like a sword. Hers is "a biting tongue, a bitten tongue," that lashes and likes causing pain and feeling pleasure all at once: "This, this, this – is a battling tongue / A honey tongue – / A tongue ready to renounce traitors and fools / Or to mediate peaceful ending" (228). Throughout the poem, the tongue represents the tortured flesh of the speaking subject and the ambivalent site of contradictions, conflicts, and intersecting discourses of Central American war-induced diasporas, borrowing from feminist scholars of theory in the flesh. Against the historical silencing of Central American subjects, Duarte's tongue in this poem is always in action, bleeding, piercing, biting, sharpening, suffocating, crushing, grabbing, battling, renouncing, mediating, silencing, screaming, weeping, holding back, forgetting, unrolling, unfurling, unhinging, twisting, teasing, tasting, and loving. It is even "tied up in knots" (228), "dumb and frozen / by the world's weeping" (230), and "chopped up and fried" (232). This is the tongue of the Central American *hocicona*, who rejects and talks over the narrative of injury of war inherited by the 1.5 and successive generations of U.S. Central Americans.

Finally, in her collection of poems, *The Cha Cha Files: A Chapina Poética*, Maya Chinchilla offers readers a cycle of poems that ponder the construction of Central American identities, histories, and memories in the United States and gives voice to hybrid queer Central American subjects. Organized into four parts, respectively titled "Solidarity Babies," "Central American Unicorns," "Homegirls and Dedications," and "Cha Cha Files," Chinchilla's collection of poems bridges the past and present, the historical and the imaginary, the poetic and the testimonial, and the Central American and the diasporic, posing these terms not as binaries but as continuums. In the first section, she reflects on a childhood spent in between cultures, countries, histories, and geopolitics that give shape and purpose to her consciousness, especially in her poem, "Solidarity Baby," in which she recounts attending marches and rallies in "a yellow baby backpack with a metal frame" atop the backs of her parents, silently watching "the Central American

Underground Railroad" run "thru [her] living room," and "listening to proud
Maya woman / mujer de maíz / using the conquerors language to testify /
while Mami interprets" ("Solidarity Baby," 3–4). Witness to the history of the
civil wars but not quite the subject of it, the solidarity baby and others of
successive Central American diasporic generations resist essentialist notions
of Central Americanness, for there is no way to "know what it's really like"
to be Central American. Instead, in Chinchilla's poems, what matters is not
getting *it* right, but knowing one's place in the "long line of resilience" and
resistance.

Hence, throughout Chinchilla's work, all things Central American –
names, places, persons, history, identity, among other things – are always
uncertain. She assumes a position of unreliability because of her attenuated
location: "I'm just a solidarity baby / don't know what it's really like" (3).
In her account, dictators, revolutionaries, and solidarity workers like her
parents made plans, took actions, and told truths, while the solidarity baby
was left "looking for [her] place" and asking "am I a CENTRAL American?"
(4) The questions as to what is Central America and who are Central
Americans appear recurrently throughout Chinchilla's poems. The "Solidarity Baby" comes to the realization that though the diaspora (including
the solidarity babies) may not share the same history and experiences as
Central Americans in the isthmus, diasporic Central Americans have created
their own space of belonging in diaspora. The persona of the poem, thus,
undoes the history of Central American marginalization or invisibility and
locates herself at the center of creative enunciations: "soy del epicentro,"
the imaginary site of poetic creations, political actions, and diasporic
(dis)locations.

In the Epicentro, Maya Chinchilla's solidarity baby (a metaphor for U.S.-
born-and-raised Central American diasporic subjects with a critical interpretation of the legacy of empire and neoliberalism in the region) wages battles,
makes secret plans, takes action, practices "storyteller strategies," translates
languages, observes "what is not obvious," reports "truths untold," and
documents that which has been rendered invisible, especially in the case of
Central American women. Chinchilla's poem, like those by Hernández-
Linares and Duarte discussed in this section, give voice and visibility to
Central American diasporic subjects and articulate the discursive crossings
of latinidades. Their works also lay claim to a shared history of feminist
resistance. Merging U.S. Latina/Chicana mestiza consciousness and a long
history of Central American resistance, these outspoken (*hocicona*) poets
cloak themselves, moreover, with the radical courage of Central American

women such as the Co-MADRES speaking on behalf of their disappeared children, María Teresa Tula denouncing her torturer on Salvadoran national TV, Nora Astorga and her Nicaraguan *compatriotas* speaking back to the power of the Somoza and Daniel Ortega regimes, Rigoberta Menchú giving testimony of her people's suffering at the hands of the Guatemalan government, Berta Cáceres fighting and dying for environmental justice and human rights, and many other Central American *cuchilleras*. Not short on words, the U.S. Central American poets discussed in this last section shatter the silence and invisibility ascribed to Central America/ns struggling in and outside of the isthmus against normative orders and neo/liberal forces that erase differences.

Conclusion

Drawing from a growing corpus of U.S. Central American literature, this chapter has attempted to examine the "un-silencing" and making visible of diverse Central American diasporic subjectivities in a variety of U.S. Central American texts of the neo/liberal era and beyond. As analyzed here, the body of U.S. Central American literature published to date makes visible what Arias once called the "un[re]presentablility" of Central America and Central Americans in certain "topographical site[s] of migration" ("Central American-American" 169), and, by extension, within Latina/o literature at large. Through a reading of a hybrid mix of U.S. Central American literary texts – from novels to poetry and from neo-foundational fictions to post/ memorial narratives – this chapter brings to the fore new diasporic subjectivities and voices, especially in the more eclectic, intersectional works by queer and feminist poets of the Central American diaspora. Time and time again, as shown here, Central American immigrant writers like Mario Bencastro, Horacio Castellanos Moya, and Martivón Galindo, to name only an exemplar few, and U.S. Central American writers born and/or raised in the United States like Tanya Maria Barrientos, Francisco Goldman, Héctor Tobar, Marcos McPeek Villatoro, Maya Chinchilla, Lorena Duarte, and Leticia Hernández-Linares confront the ghosts of past wars and the pervasive violence of neoliberal regimes through the creation of Central American narratives, deeply grounded in historical contexts yet unbound by place and borders. By "un-silencing" the past and producing new narratives out of the shards of civil war, displacement, and ever-morphing forms of violence *in situ* and in diasporic sites, U.S. Central American literature comes out of the shadows and is invisible and silent no more.

WORKS CITED

Alvarado, Karina O. "A Gynealogy of Cigua Resistance: La Ciguanaba, Prudencia Ayala, and Leticia Hernández-Linares in Conversation." *US Central Americans: Reconstructing Memories, Struggles, and Communities of Resistance*. Ed. Karina O. Alvarado, Alicia Ivonne Estrada, and Ester E. Hernández. Tucson: University of Arizona Press, 2017. 98–121.

Transverse: Altar de Tierra, Altar de Sol. Los Angeles, CA: Izote Press, 2009.

Anna, Timothy. "The Independence of Mexico and Central America." *The Independence of Latin America*, vol. 3. Ed. Leslie Bethell. Cambridge and New York: Cambridge University Press, 1987. 49–94.

Anzaldúa, Gloria. *Borderlands/La frontera: La nueva mestiza*. San Francisco: Spinsters/Aunte Lute, 1987.

Archila, William. *The Gravedigger's Archaeology*. Pasadena, CA: Red Hen Press, 2015.

The Art of Exile. Tempe, AZ: Bilingual Press/Editorial Bilingüe, 2009.

Arias, Arturo. *Taking Their Word: Literature and the Signs of Central America*. Minneapolis and London: University of Minnesota Press, 2007.

"Central American-Americans: Invisibility, Power and Representation in the US Latino World." *Latino Studies* 1.1 (2003): 168–87.

Baker-Cristales, Beth. *Salvadoran Migration to Southern California: Redefining El Hermano Lejano*. Gainesville: University of Florida Press, 2004.

Barrientos, Tanya Maria. *Family Resemblance*. New York: NAL/Penguin Group, 2003.

Bencastro, Mario. *Mansión del olvido*. Port Saint Lucy, FL: Ediciones Puerto Santa Lucia, 2015.

Paraíso Portátil/Portable Paradise. Houston, TX: Arte Público Press, 2010.

Benítez, Sandra. *Bitter Grounds*. New York: Hyperion, 1997.

Booth, John A., Christine J. Wade, and Thomas W. Walker. *Understanding Central America: Global Forces, Rebellion, and Change*. Boulder, CO: Westview Press, 2010.

Castellanos Moya, Horacio. *El sueño del retorno*. Mexico, DF: Tusquets Editores, 2013.

Chinchilla, Maya. *The Cha Cha Files: A Chapina Poética*. San Francisco: Kórima Press, 2014.

Chinchilla, Maya and Karina Oliva Alvarado, eds. *Desde el EpiCentro: An Anthology of US Central American Poetry*. Oakland: n.p., 2007.

Cohen, Robin. *Global Diasporas: An Introduction*. London and New York: Routledge, 2008.

Córdova, Carlos B. *The Salvadoran Americans*. Westport, CT: Greenwood Press, 2005.

Dowdy, Michael. *Broken South: Latina/o Poetic Responses to Neoliberalism and Globalization*. Tucson: The University of Arizona Press, 2013.

Duarte, Lorena. "Flint Tongue." *Theater Under My Skin: Contemporary Salvadoran Poetry/Teatro Bajo mi piel: Poesía salvadoreña contemporánea*. Ed. Tania Pleitez Vela. San Salvador: Editorial Kalina, 2014.

Dunkerley, James. *The Pacification of Central America: Political Change in the Isthmus 1987–1993*. New York and London: Verso, 1994.

Escobar, Mario. *Paciente 1980*. Turlock, CA: Orbis Press, 2012.

Galindo, Martivón. *La tormenta rodando por la cuesta: Impresiones El Salvador, 1979–1981*. San Francisco: n.p., 2015.

Para Amaestrar un tigre: Cuentos. San Francisco: n.p., 2012.

Retazos. San Francisco: Editorial Solaris, 1996.

García, Ana Isabel and Enrique Gomáriz. *Efectos del conflicto.* Vol. 2 *Mujeres centroamericanas ante la crisis, la guerra y el proceso de paz.* San José, Costa Rica: FLACSO, 1989.

Goldman, Francisco. *The Art of Political Murder: Who Killed the Bishop?* New York: Grove, 2007.

The Ordinary Seaman. New York: Grove, 1997.

The Long Night of White Chickens. New York: Atlantic Monthly, 1992.

Gudmundson, Lowell and Héctor Lindo-Fuentes. *Central America, 1821–1871: Liberalism before Liberal Reform.* Tuscaloosa: University of Alabama Press, 1995.

Harvey, David. *A Brief History of Neoliberalism.* Oxford and New York: Oxford University Press, 2005.

Henríquez, Cristina. *The Book of Unknown Americans.* New York: Vintage, 2014.

Hernández-Linares, Leticia. *Mucha muchacha, Too Much Girl: Poems.* Sylmar, CA: Tía Chucha Press, 2015.

Mucha muchacha /Too Much Girl. San Francisco: San Francisco Arts Commission, 2010. CD.

Razor Edges of My Tongue. San Diego, CA: Calaca Press, 2002.

Hirsch, Marianne. *The Generation of Postmemory: Writing and Visual Culture after the Holocaust.* New York: Columbia University Press, 2012.

Lars, Claudia. *Tierra de infancia.* 9th ed. San Salvador: UCA Editores, 2000.

Lauria-Santiago, Aldo. *An Agrarian Republic: Commercial Agriculture and the Politics of Peasant Communities in El Salvador, 1823–1914.* Pittsburgh, PA: University of Pittsburgh Press, 1999.

Lindo-Fuentes, Héctor, Erik Ching, and Rafael A. Lara-Martínez. *Remembering a Massacre in El Salvador: The Insurrection of 1932, Roque Dalton, and the Politics of Historical Memory.* Albuquerque: University of New Mexico Press, 2007.

Los refugiados centroamericanos. Heredia, Costa Rica: Universidad Nacional & Editores Universidad para la Paz, 1987.

Lynch, John. "The Origins of Spanish American Independence." *The Independence of Latin America*, vol. 3. Ed. Leslie Bethell. Cambridge and New York: Cambridge University Press, 1987.

Machado Sáez, Elena. *Market Aesthetics: The Purchase of the Past in Caribbean Diasporic Fiction.* Charlottesville and London: University of Virginia Press, 2015.

Mahler, Sarah J. *Salvadorans in Suburbia: Symbiosis and Conflict.* Boston, MA: Allyn and Bacon, 1995.

Masiello, Francine. *The Art of Transition: Latin American Culture and Neoliberal Crisis.* Durham, NC and London: Duke University Press, 2001.

Padilla, Yajaira M. *Changing Women, Changing Nation: Female Agency, Nationhood, and Identity in Trans-Salvadoran Narratives.* Albany: State University of New York Press, 2012.

Paige, Jefferey M. *Coffee and Power: Revolution and the Rise of Democracy in Central America.* Cambridge, MA: Harvard University Press, 1997.

Pew Research Center. "Remittances Received by El Salvador." Nov. 14, 2013. Accessed March 15, 2017. Web. www.pewhispanic.org/2013/11/15/remittances-to-latin-america-recover-but-not-to-mexico/ph-remittances-11–2013-a-08/.

Pleitez Vela, Tania, ed. *Theater Under My Skin: Contemporary Salvadoran Poetry/Teatro Bajo mi piel: Poesía salvadoreña contemporánea.* San Salvador: Editorial Kalina, 2014.

"Prudencia Ayala." Museo de la Palabra y la Imagen (MUPI). Nov. 22, 2010. Accessed March 15, 2017. Web. http://museo.com.sv/2010/11/biografia-prudencia-ayala-la-hija-de-la-centella/.

Concertación Feminista Prudencia Ayala. Accessed April 21, 2015. Web. http://colectivafeminista.org.sv/2013/05/12/concertacion-feminista-prudencia-ayala/.

Robinson, William I. *Transnational Conflicts: Central America, Social Change, and Globalization.* New York and London: Verso, 2003.

Rodríguez, Ana Patricia. "Refugees of the South: Central Americans in the US Latino Imaginary." *American Literature* 73.2 (2001): 385–412.

Rodriguez Barron, Sandra. *The Heiress of Water.* New York: Rayo/HarperCollins Books, 2006.

Rosaldo, Renato. *Culture and Truth: The Remaking of Social Analysis.* Boston, MA: Beacon Press, 1989.

Roseberry, William, Lowell Gudmundson, and Mario Samper Kutschbach, eds. *Coffee, Society, and Power in Latin America.* Baltimore, MD: The Johns Hopkins University Press, 1995.

Sellers-García, Sylvia. *When the Ground Turns in Its Sleep.* New York: Riverhead Books/Penguin Group, 2007.

Sommer, Doris. *Foundational Fictions: The National Romances of Latin America.* Berkeley and Los Angeles: University of California Press, 1991.

Soto Hall, Máximo. *La sombra de la Casa Blanca.* Buenos Aires: Ateneo, 1927.

El problema. 1899. San José: Editorial de la Universidad de Costa Rica, 1999.

Tobar, Héctor. *The Tattooed Soldier.* New York: Penguin Group, 2000.

Tula, María Teresa. *Hear My Testimony: Maria Teresa Tula, Human Rights Activist of El Salvador.* Ed. and trans. Lynn Stephen. Cambridge, MA: South End Press, 1994.

Villatoro, Marcos McPeek. *Blood Daughters: A Romilia Chacón Novel.* Pasadena, CA: Red Hen Press, 2011.

A Venom Beneath the Skin: A Romilia Chacón Novel. Boston, MA: Kate's Mystery Books/Justin, Charles & Co., Publishers, 2005.

Minos: A Romilia Chacón Novel. New York: Bantam Dell/Random House, 2003.

Home Killings: A Romilia Chacón Novel. New York: Bantam Dell/Random House, 2001.

A Fire in the Earth. Houston, TX: Arte Público Press, 1996.

25

Latina/o Life Narratives

Crafting Self-Referential Forms in the Colonial Milieu of the Americas

CRYSTAL M. KURZEN

Classically, in the Western literary tradition, autobiography appears as a retrospective prose narrative articulating the truthful events of the individual life of a man of some fame through the first-person point of view. Definitions surrounding this complicated genre, or "umbrella concept," as contemporary autobiography critics Sidonie Smith and Julia Watson prefer to call it, certainly have evolved with time; however, one cannot overlook the special challenges of narrating a life and subjectivity as it emerges within the colonial milieu of the Americas wherein negotiations of race, ethnicity, class, gender, sexuality, religion, region, nation, language, and culture must occur simultaneously and continuously. As I have mentioned elsewhere, autobiography scholars such as Timothy Dow Adams, Laura J. Beard, G. Thomas Couser, Paul John Eakin, Susanna Egan, Leigh Gilmore, Nancy K. Miller, and Julie Rak, among many others, generally assert that current scholarship in this interdisciplinary field should focus on discourses of identity and the self-conscious formulation of self-representation.[1] Smith and Watson locate us in the third wave of autobiography criticism characterized by "a subject that is in process, a subject in context (historical, social, geographical), a subject whose self-knowing is always implicated, discursively and dialogically" and who uses the concepts of performativity, positionality, and relationality to define this moment in life writing (218).[2]

---

[1] See Kurzen, "Towards a Native American Women's Autobiographical Tradition: Genre as Political Practice," *The Oxford Handbook of Indigenous American Literature*, eds. James H. Cox and Daniel Heath Justice (New York: Oxford UP, 2014) 202–14.

[2] In Chapters 7 and 8 of the second edition of *Reading Autobiography*, Smith and Watson identify and describe three waves of autobiography criticism, with the third wave occurring since the 1990s (Minneapolis: U of Minnesota P, 2010).

Arguably the tradition of Latina/o life narrative begins as early as Álvar Núñez Cabeza de Vaca's *La Relación* (1542)[3] and continues with Spanish letters and chronicles through the end of the sixteenth century. Critics such as Genaro M. Padilla, in his book-length study *My History, Not Yours: The Formation of Mexican American Autobiography* (1993), and Juan Velasco in his work on *automitografias* detail the fact that Latina/os, Mexican Americans in particular, have put their lives to paper – and grito – prior to the twentieth century through diaries, official documents, speeches, personal correspondence, and *corridos*, among other generic forms.[4] In his essay on "The Latino Autobiography," Silvio Torres-Saillant discusses the transnational formation of Latina/o identity and the autobiographical literature that arises out of a "diasporic uprooting and the sense of living outside the dominant realm of the receiving society" (63). While Mexicans, Puerto Ricans, Cubans, Dominicans, and many Central American and South American peoples became and become ethnic communities in the United States through incredibly different routes, they are "bound by political imperatives to see themselves as one" (63). He traces the emergence of autobiographical traditions within specific Latina/o contexts – Mexican Americans, Cuban Americans, Puerto Rican, Dominican Americans, Central and South Americans – and refers his readers to a variety of sources while ultimately arguing that although the Latina/o autobiographer's ideology "will always be individual, ... it will have complications at a collective level" (76). He offers an incredible overview of each tradition of self-life-writing and connects them historically, socially, and culturally to nuanced Latina/o forms.

Specifically focusing her concerns on gender and multiple marginalities, Lourdes Torres addresses the construction of the self in Latina autobiographies discussing the identity fragmentation she sees Latina/os confront and engage in their texts. Although she looks specifically at the multigeneric works of Cherríe Moraga, *Loving in the War Years: lo que nunca pasó por sus labios* (1983), Aurora Levins Morales and Rosario Morales, *Getting Home Alive* (1986), and Gloria Anzaldúa, *Borderlands/La Frontera: The New Mestiza* (1987),

---

[3] The full title of this edition is *La relación y comentarios del Governador Alvar Núñez Cabeça de Vaca, de lo acaescido en las dos jornadas que hizo a las Indias.*

[4] See Padilla, *My History, Not Yours: The Formation of Mexican American Autobiography* (Madison: University of Wisconsin Press, 1993) and Velasco, "*Automitografias*: The Border Paradigm and Chicana/o Autobiography," *Biography* 27.2 (2004): 313–38. I also use grito here to represent the ways in which Latinas/os have participated in oral tradition generally and more specifically vocalized opposition to power through self-articulation and storytelling.

her observations certainly extend to other life narratives within the larger context of Latina/o literature. Like Torres-Saillant, she examines the complications of identity development for these three Latina/os and comes to the conclusion that "[n]o existing discourse is satisfactory because each necessitates the repression of different aspects of the self" (279). She asserts that writers in these kinds of multiply informed and minoritized positions must then craft forms that exist in a borderland and "reject prescript[ions]" while "creat[ing] radical personal and collective identities" to challenge the systems of power that subjugate them and other people of color (279).

In a similar way, in her essay on memoir, autobiography, and testimonio in *The Routledge Companion to Latino/a Literature* (2013), Norma E. Cantú describes her own expectations of these genres to render a person's life on the page, to situate the story in a time and space/place, to communicate the cultural or ethnographic aspects of the life being told, to explore the "intersections of oppressions in Latino/a communities [, and . . .] to offer a glimpse into someone's life that will illuminate [her] own" (310). She references her fictional autobioethnographic work, which she says emerges out of a "theorizing and assessing [of] knowledge formation from the author's exploration of a self-folklore" (310). Tracing immigrant stories to fictionalized autobiographies to oral narratives and as-told-to testimonios to Latina and Chicana feminist life writing, Cantú ultimately concludes that self-referential works coming out of the Latina/o consciousness "offer a myriad of experiences and are rooted in the poetry of indigenous peoples that stretches back to pre-conquest times and comes into its own in the mid-nineteenth century with Mexico's losing of the U.S.–Mexico war and ceding more than half its territory to the U.S." (321). She also cites the collection *Telling to Live: Latina Feminist Testimonios* (2001) by The Latina Feminist Group – which I will return to later – as an important and hard-won assemblage featuring the coming together of a variety of women across Latina differences to find commonality to affect cultural change and impel social action as the form of testimonio demands.

Rather than rehearse or duplicate the historical and archival work of these scholars, I add to what they offer us by analyzing the specific genre innovations employed by Latina/o authors to render visible both individuals in the United States and communities with transnational ties to Latin America and the Caribbean as they employ various autobiographical strategies to establish a self-narrated tradition that ultimately leads to the making and remaking of an entire corpus of particularized identity discourses. I proceed, then, with a case study on formal evolutions in Chicana/o autobiographical discourses as informed by previously discussed frameworks to show how reimagined self-referential genres negotiate entry into global modernity via modern capitalism, the nation-state, and the diasporas that resulted from these conjunctions.

Genre and Convention

Before and throughout the years of the Chicano civil rights movement, during the 1960s and early 1970s approximately, Mexican American male authors began employing both semi-autobiographical and autobiographical modes to document their life experiences. The Chicano self-writing tradition, like el movimiento itself, was born out of an urgency to represent oneself, to authorize self and community. Those authors who voice their selves immediately before and after the Chicano movement, unlike some of their predecessors who Padilla examines, initiate a different kind of tradition that relies heavily on Western autobiographical forms. Authors like José Antonio Villarreal in *Pocho* (1959), Ernesto Galarza in *Barrio Boy* (1971), and Richard Rodriguez in *Hunger of Memory: The Education of Richard Rodriguez* (1982), in their efforts to represent self and multiple narrative selves, wrote what many see as the foundational texts that speak to or enliven Mexican American experiences during this formative period.[5] Upon closer consideration, we see the ways in which these early texts initiate and create ongoing conversations about form, fiction, identity, and truth. Rather than establishing a kind of literary nationalism that rejected Anglo literary conventions, particularly in the field of autobiography, Villarreal, Galarza, and Rodriguez mirror many of the Western, male, heteronormative, autobiographical conventions in their texts, ones they read and admired while growing up as Mexican Americans in the 1950s and 1960s. Because all are preoccupied with assimilation, it is, therefore, no mistake that they replicate these dominative forms. In contrast to these earlier Chicano and Mexican American writers, Chicanas such as Cherríe Moraga, Gloria Anzaldúa, and Norma Elia Cantú offer alternative, multigeneric models of life narrative to better articulate their fragmented and multiply marginalized selves in flux, such as the autohistoria-teoría and fictional autobioethnography.

Published in 1959, *Pocho* offers readers an epic narrative that depicts the lives of Mexicans and first-generation Mexican Americans such as Richard

---

[5] See Rodriguez, "An American Writer," *The Invention of Ethnicity*, ed. Werner Sollors (New York: Oxford University Press, 1989), 3–13.

Rubio, the main character, as they come up against racisms and forced assimilations in their California home. Like Richard, José Antonio Villarreal was born and grew up in California, the son of a Mexican migrant worker, who fought with Pancho Villa in the Mexican Revolution of 1910–1920. In an interview, Villarreal states, "[Pocho] was an attempt to share my experiences of growing up in an old country traditional way, breaking away from that culture and going on to a new way of life, yet still holding on to the traditional ways that were good and adding to them the new things I liked in the Anglo-American society" (Jiménez 67). Villarreal uses Pocho to work out his conflicted identities; he is both Mexican and American, living in the United States. In his own words, Villarreal describes his life as a new construction, holding onto traditional values he saw reflected in his community while at the same time taking from his new culture what appealed to him. Villarreal reports the truths of war, hard labor, and poverty, among other things, as he and others growing up Mexican in Northern California during the 1930s and 1940s experienced them.

In this way, Villarreal creates an ethnographic narrative in Pocho, describing the real-world conditions of Mexicans and Mexican Americans in fictional circumstances. He discusses his first published piece and the complications surrounding its generic category: "Everything I wrote was truth: it was fiction, but it was truth ... In Pocho it was very important to me to show things that I had seen" (Sedore 78, 82).[6] While many critics such as Ramón Eduardo Ruiz, who wrote the introduction to the Doubleday paperback edition, disagree about the value of Pocho as a novel, Villarreal is often credited with the esteemed title of "Founder of Chicano Literature" for this semiautobiographical account of his life; however, by his own admission, it appears that he is actually one of the first Chicanos to publish a life narrative or autobiography. Nothing needs to be invented; names are simply changed.

Rather than form, what makes this novel contentious is its ultimate support of assimilation. Over the course of the text, Richard vacillates between belonging to multiple communities, such as his gang of boyhood friends, the pachuco zoot-suiters, newly arrived Mexican migrants, and liberal intellectuals, and isolating himself in books or with his Anglo

[6] For further information about Pocho's contribution to literature and Chicano literature specifically, see Saldívar's "Paredes, Villarreal, and the Dialectics of History," *Chicano Narrative: The Dialectics of Difference* (Madison: University of Wisconsin Press, 1990) 47–73 and Bruce-Novoa, "Pocho as Literature," *Aztlán* 7.1 (1977): 65–78.

girlfriend Mary. Although Richard struggles with self-identification throughout, he ultimately rejects the identity of his Mexican and Mexican American family while yet not being fully accepted by Anglos. Richard finally arrives at self-determination near the end of the novel, realizing his power to live for himself alone. Richard belongs to no group, denying his first language of Spanish and the community offered to him by his home and neighborhood. In the end, he chooses flight, leaving his family to enlist to defend a country that has not yet recognized him as one of its full citizens during the Second World War. As the last line of the text reminds him, "he knew that for him there would never be a coming back" (187). He breaks from his family to start out alone in the world, embracing an American individualism that has seemingly bought him his freedom.

As a result of Richard's becoming an assimilated man who has rejected his Mexican culture in favor of American individualism, Villarreal received much criticism from those involved more politically in the Chicano movement. When asked about his literary influences, Villarreal replies, "My greatest influence ... has been English literature, specifically I acknowledge the influence of James Joyce, William Faulkner, and when I was young, Thomas Wolfe. When writing *Pocho* I was very much aware of these three" (Jiménez 70). Also citing *Huck Finn* as a favorite book, Villarreal writes in a Western, male tradition that has been willing to see him and those who look like him in only a very limited way. Villarreal initiates a particular kind of Chicano life narrative tradition, one strongly influenced by fiction but that is also epic and multigenerational like many of Faulkner's works, that embraces the coming-of-age narrative, not unlike Joyce's *Portrait of an Artist*, and that showcases the adventures of childhood, like *Huck Finn*. Although he does not call the main character José Antonio Villarreal, he bases his narrative on the truths of real-life experiences and the styles of authors that he read while pursuing his studies in school. He particularizes his efforts to create characters that make Mexicans and Mexican Americans visible in a landscape where they had previously been overlooked.

Following in the Western tradition that Villarreal replicates in *Pocho*, Ernesto Galarza published *Barrio Boy: The Story of a Boy's Acculturation* in 1971. Like many other immigrant Mexicans living in California during the early 1900s, Galarza finds himself in a country where race and class deeply affect the access he has to work and education. He discovers that he must acculturate to have any success in his new home. This text is a retrospective, coming-of-age narrative that describes Galarza's own childhood in Jalcocotán, Mexico, living with his extended family in a peaceful mountain community.

Unrest comes to his village, though, and causes young Ernesto and his family to journey north, which he eventually realizes is a journey to the United States. Galarza was born at the beginning of a very difficult period in Mexico that resulted in the Mexican Revolution. After settling in Sacramento, California, Galarza begins the process of acculturation he alludes to in the subtitle of the book. Somewhat more fortunate than other Mexican immigrant children in his ability to assimilate to the American public school system, Galarza becomes a successful student. Encountering teachers who supported his continued use of Spanish and "roasted racial hatred out" of their pupils, Galarza learns to speak English and succeeds as an official translator for his multiethnic and multilingual barrio community. The text closes with Galarza's impending entrance into high school.

In both its content and construction, *Barrio Boy* follows the more traditional Anglo forms of autobiography talking about a life retrospectively from youth to manhood. At times *Barrio Boy* takes on the characteristics of nostalgic ethnography, a type of writing about a society done by an outsider or a participant observer, specifically to record the practices of that community for the purpose of cultural study or preservation. The text details a perfect past as Galarza informs his audience about the traditions of his home in Jalcocotán, Mexico, including exhaustive accounts of daily life, such as work duties as well as food preparation techniques. Critic and anthropologist Renato Rosaldo defines classic ethnography as "a genre of social description," an account "usually moved upward from environment and subsistence through family and kinship to religion and spiritual life" (31). Alternatively, autoethnography, a form crafted by a cultural insider that more accurately describes the genre of *Barrio Boy*, explains a shared worldview and the author's sense of community. This form could even be defined generally as a written self-reflection of a social past. This last definition though does not leave it very far from the generic conventions of autobiography.

In these generic categories complicated issues arise about who can speak for whom and how to construct the self. Cultural anthropologist Deborah E. Reed-Danahay writes, "[Autoethnography] synthesizes both a postmodern ethnography, in which the realist conventions and objective observer position of standard ethnography have been called into question, and a postmodern autobiography, in which the notion of the coherent, individual self has been similarly called into question" (2). Galarza takes up the conventions of this genre; he reports a collective self, a layered self made up of multiple members of the many communities in which he dwells, by informing his reader about the specific roles of his mother, his aunt, his uncles, and even his own chores around the home and the rituals of his village. He takes great pride in describing his home and the animals the family owns. Later he continues this practice in regards to his barrio life in California. As Reed-Danahay claims, "[T]he autoethnographer is a boundary-crosser, and the role can be characterized as that of a dual identity" (3). Galarza acts as a boundary-crosser in this text, offering an insider's view into the daily lives of his family and other Mexican American/Chicano families who have migrated to the United States. Galarza's work serves as a foundational text in both form and approach.

Although published eleven years after Galarza's account, Richard Rodriguez's *Hunger of Memory: The Education of Richard Rodriguez* (1982) adds to the corpus of Mexican American assimilation life narratives by offering readers an intellectual autobiography of how a scholarship boy becomes a writer and professor of English Renaissance literature.[7] As an autobiography, this text, like *Barrio Boy*, begins with a subject at a young age and follows him into adulthood. Rodriguez enters school in Sacramento, California, knowing only fifty words of English, and he proceeds to complete his graduate studies, writing his dissertation in the reading room of the British Museum. Rodriguez stresses the losses associated with social and cultural assimilation, and specifically how his educational opportunities have separated him from his working-class family. He gives up Spanish and the comforts of a private life for public success in the United States. As Ellie D. Hernández argues, "The autobiography of Richard Rodriguez thus corresponds to the withdrawal of the 'I' that he associates with his Mexican family and his private life and the designation of his public 'I,' which is capable of renouncing his past" (149). Like Villarreal and Galarza before him, he claims a uniquely individual subject position in this text, rejecting a communal subjectivity in order to focus on the self. While he reaps academic success as well as financial gain using this strategy, he loses his family, culture, and native language. Rodriguez uses the life narrative tradition initiated by Villarreal and Galarza to heal the breaks in his discontinuous past. Rodriguez puts the pieces of his life back together; he discovers a sense of continuity through the repair work he attempts during the autobiographical process.

Speaking about his cultural influences, Rodriguez states, "I have come to this lecture room, to face a room full of strangers, to say that I am an American like you. Thomas Jefferson is my cultural forefather, not Benito

---

[7] See Limón, "Editor's Note on Richard Rodriguez," *Texas Studies in Literature and Language* 40.4 (Winter 1998): 389–96.

Juárez. I claim Martin Luther King. And Walt Disney. And Lucille Ball. And Elvis Presley. And Benjamin Franklin. And Sister Mary Regis" (5). In this statement, Rodriguez stakes his claim as an American; he no longer maintains a Mexican American worldview. In the prologue to *Hunger*, Rodriguez writes, "I have become notorious among certain leaders of America's Ethnic Left. I am considered a dupe, an ass, the fool – Tom Brown, the brown Uncle Tom, interpreting the writing on the wall to a bunch of cigar-smoking pharaohs" (4). Regardless of how he wants his audience to see him in this text, Rodriguez has succeeded in adding to the corpus of Mexican American self-writing, following in the tradition established first by Anglo writers and then taken up by proto-Chicanos like Villarreal and Galarza.

Innovation and Identity Discourses

In response to the growing frustration with their lack of representation in the works of their Chicano predecessors and white feminists, both who often claimed to speak for them, Cherríe Moraga and Gloria Anzaldúa coedited a collection in 1981 called *This Bridge Called My Back: Writings by Radical Women of Color*. Along with the various writers and activists in their anthology, Moraga and Anzaldúa, through their abilities to push generic boundaries, find their own creative language of self-expression and ways to represent themselves textually foregrounding a political articulation of the everyday. In imagining this text, they demand a different kind of representation that did not yet exist in the early 1980s. Texts like *Pocho* or even *Hunger of Memory*, which was published within a year of this anthology, did not represent issues of racism, sexism, and classism in the same ways that Moraga and Anzaldúa would in their collection. In order to take control of their own representations, Moraga and Anzaldúa work hard to offer their fellow third world women a space to voice their realities in their own words. A text like this pushes generic boundaries – even rejects them – and offers something entirely different to readers. These women create complex generic configurations, combining poetry, essay, songs, prayers, to name a few, that challenge traditional categories of form while demanding to be visible and taken seriously. They create theories of identity and form in direct contrast to all who came before by telling their personal and political stories in radically altered forms that recognize and reflect fractured and fragmented lived experiences.

Two years later, Cherríe Moraga publishes her own autobiography, a stream-of-consciousness, life narrative called *Loving in the War Years: lo que nunca pasó por sus labios.* In this text she continues to struggle with generic representation that can accommodate her experience and identity as the lesbian daughter of a Chicana mother and an Anglo father. Her anxiety about its legibility as such suggests she is aware she needs to speak in a language readers can follow, acknowledging the tenets of the "autobiographical contract" Lejeune originally identified years before:

> What does it mean that the Chicana writer if she truly follows her own voice, she may depict a world so specific, so privately ours, so full of "foreign" language to the anglo reader, there will be no publisher. . . . The combining of poetry and essays in this book is the compromise I make in the effort to be understood. (vi)[8]

Moraga finds her drive to write in personal experience and is moved to record her life as she has lived it, or as she has wished to live. She divides her poetry and essays into sections to better aid her reader, but mostly she has chosen a form for herself. Like in the collection she edited with Anzaldúa, she rejects traditional genres like poetry, novel, short story, and essay for a form that accommodates and accentuates her particular lived experiences. Even in the quotation above, she does not apologize for the form she chooses; instead she laments only that it will be difficult to find a publisher as a result of her writing technique.

Like Moraga, Gloria Anzaldúa is compelled to craft a theory of Chicana identity construction and adds to the ongoing conversation by publishing her own personal life narratives in a form that challenges the theory of conventional autobiography. Four years after *Loving in the War Years,* Anzaldúa published *Borderlands/La Frontera: The New Mestiza* (1987), naming it an autohistoria.[9] While others struggle with form, Anzaldúa names it, authorizing it and giving it power. *Borderlands* as an autohistoria contradicts the form (and content) found in the pieces of self-writing examined earlier, *Pocho, Barrio Boy,* and *Hunger of Memory.* In *Borderlands,* Anzaldúa draws on personal experiences to carve out an activist-subject that takes her life in the Borderlands, on the fringes of multiple cultures, and turns it back on itself, taking up a new consciousness – the New Mestiza Consciousness – to recreate the

---

[8] See Lejeune, *On Autobiography* (Minneapolis: University of Minnesota Press, 1989).

[9] Anzaldúa defines autohistoria in this way: *"Autohistoria* is a term I use to describe the genre of writing about one's personal and collective history using fictive elements, a sort of fictionalized autobiography or memoir; an autohistoria-teoría is a personal essay that theorizes" (578). See Anzaldúa, "now let us shift . . . the path of conocimiento . . . inner work, public acts," *This Bridge We Call Home: Radical Visions for Transformation,* eds. Gloria E. Anzaldúa and Analouise Keating (New York: Routledge, 2002), 540–78.

Borderlands as a place of empowerment where subjects (not objects) of multiple identities thrive. Through this theory of the new mestiza consciousness, Anzaldúa crafts a form of her own, one that unsurprisingly fails to "fit" into the hegemonic model of life narrative and thus reveals the limitations of the genre outside of its parent culture.

What she needs to say as a Chicana living in the Borderlands, she cannot say in a genre that has historically served a Western, male, hierarchical, and heteronormative society. Anzaldúa is not visible as a subject in Western society; therefore, why would her writings about her own life take on those generic conventions? In her article "now let us shift ... the path of conocimiento ... inner work, public acts," Anzaldúa discusses her theory of form: "it's not enough to denounce the culture's old account – you must provide new narratives embodying alternative potentials. You're sure of one thing: the consciousness that's created our social ills (dualistic and misogynist) cannot solve them . . ... The new stories must partially come from outside the system of ruling powers" (560). Anzaldúa, like Moraga and the women of color who came before her, helps other Chicanas and marginalized communities to step outside of generic confines and write something that expresses who they are within the context of their own cultures, even if they exist in the Borderlands, as many Chicana/o writers do. While Chicana/o authors since this time have added greatly to the conversation about radical generic forms, Anzaldúa does important work in this text, mixing personal narrative, political essays, and poetry.

With the publishing of their groundbreaking, multigeneric theories on Chicana/o lesbian identity construction, Moraga and Anzaldúa carve out space for other Chicanas/os to narrate not only themselves, but fictional characters as well. In 1984, Sandra Cisneros published the first piece of fiction showcasing an adolescent Chicana narrator living in urban Chicago. Esperanza offers the voice of a younger generation growing up in the city as she tries to understand the forces that operate upon her life in the crowded barrio that she inhabits with her family. Formally, Cisneros weds Tomás Rivera's vignette style in . . .y no se lo tragó la tierra/. . .And the Earth Did Not Devour Him (1971) to José Antonio Villarreal's coming-of-age narrative in Pocho (1959). Cisneros melds these styles together, creating a new voice in fiction to reveal particularized aspects of one year in a girl's life. The following year, Helena María Viramontes published The Moths and Other Stories (1985), showcasing a multiplicity of women's voices, both young and old, and of different class positions. Viramontes chooses short stories to appeal to her readers, demonstrating the social and cultural conventions that shape these women's lives while offering a sharp critique of institutions such as the Roman Catholic Church. Adding to the growing corpus of Chicana literature, in 1993 Ana Castillo published *So Far from God*, introducing yet another new form. In contrast to this literary translation of form, from novela to telenovela and back again, Castillo's revision of the genre outlines different possibilities for women, rewarding those who find solace outside of traditional gender roles. Within the larger trajectory of the Chicano self-writing tradition, I see these women as key players in the movement to represent female voices and concerns through genres that not only challenge traditional forms but also give rise to entirely different modes of expression.

Norma Elia Cantú's *Canícula: Snapshots of a Girlhood en la frontera*, published in 1995 and classified as both fiction and memoir on the back cover, shifts the genre conversation in a different direction, affirming that the Chicana/o experience is one of multiple identifications, becoming both collective and fictitious at times. While Moraga and Anzaldúa first initiate this Chicana/o feminist response to earlier Chicano assimilationist texts, and authors like Cisneros, Viramontes, and Castillo offer complicated representations in fiction, Cantú's work signifies another phase in the evolution of this genre conversation. This fictional autobioethnography, as Cantú has named it, introduces a protagonist who does not, at first glance, have the same name as the author, and it includes personal photographs and documentation papers that appear to be the author's own. The book begins with a hand-drawn map and an introduction that explains the origin of the project. The description seems to imply a work of nonfiction; however, the reader begins to suspect manipulations of "truth" when Cantú comments, "As in most fiction, many of the characters and situations in these three works originate in real people and events, and become fictionalized" (xi). It seems that Cantú writes strategically, playing with generic conventions and invoking notions of truth in fiction and fiction in truth.

Recognizing the vexed nature of her own project, Cantú builds on the ideas of Roland Barthes and Susan Sontag in order to prove her place in the ongoing conversation surrounding the relationship between truth and photography. She describes the experiences from the photographs in short vignettes, filled with what appears to be personal, autobiographical, and/or biographical narratives. Sometimes, corresponding photographs accompany these vignettes and, at times, if the reader looks carefully, he or she recognizes the discrepancies between the visual image and the written word. Cantú writes in her Introduction, "In *Canícula*, the story is told through the photographs, and so what may appear to be autobiographical is not always so. On the other hand, many of the events are completely fictional, although they may be true in a historical context" (xi). Cantú changes the rules of the game with this text, mixing her own life with that of the main character's, creating a narrative palimpsest.

For example, the ambiguous relationship between the author and the narrator begins with the first photograph in the text, captioned "May," which is accompanied by this description, "Dahlia, Bueli, Tino, cousin Lalo, and I pose one balmy May evening in front of the four-room frame house on San Carlos Street" (4). Even though the photograph does show all of these people in front of a house, the "factual" effect of the image is undermined by the small detail of the photograph's backward reproduction, evidenced by the reversed date at the bottom. Cultural critic Marianne Hirsch asserts that "familial looking can ... function as a screen; the identifications it engenders can be too easy .... As it automatically places individuals into familial relation within a field of vision, familial looking is a powerful, if slippery and often deceptive, instrument of cultural dialogue and cultural memory" (xiii). A simple scanning of the photographs in this collection tells one story; however, the stories they tell when examined closely are entirely different.

As in *Loving in the War Years* and *Borderlands*, the form presented in *Canícula* reveals how Chicana/os must reinvent and revise autobiographical conventions to contain or accommodate their multiple identities. Cantú writes in the introduction that "although it may appear that these stories are my family's, they are not precisely, and yet they are" (xi). While situating her work in the first sentence as the second part of a trilogy that seems to be tracing a "real" family, she challenges the reader to join her in the journey to discover the facts mixed with the fictions on this journey toward subjectivity. Cantú continues in her introduction by referencing Pat Mora, who claims that "life en la frontera is raw truth, and stories of such life, fictitious as they may be, are even truer than true" (xi). This is the tradition in which she writes. Cantú, like Moraga and Anzaldúa, offers a generic model to others who both reside in the Borderlands and desire to offer a mirror to those like themselves. Cantú names this genre fictional autobioethnography, a discourse that gives form to the new mestiza consciousness that Anzaldúa posits, by creating something innovative that employs multiple languages, varied subject positions, and photographs. This genre innovation finds a way to represent that unique consciousness of the Borderlands that is in constant motion. Cantú theorizes the everyday life of her Chicana experience (or an imagined experience), forging a space for survival of subjects, not objects.

Although her text resists genre, in many ways, she asks the reader to continue to contemplate those categories and their larger implications in how texts are both constructed and read.

Ultimately, Moraga, Anzaldúa, and Cantú are consciously writing back to the master narratives that have ruled the genre of autobiography; however, they, as Chicana feminists, have authored and authorized an alternative generic tradition of self-narration and self-conscious formulation of texts. Moraga, Anzaldúa, and Cantú, in their cultural production, challenge readers to accept a different kind of truth. Together these writers fashion new storytelling practices rooted in autobiographical discourses, remaking genre in order to participate in the larger literary tradition of life narrative.

Legacies

In conversation with the generic interventions made by Chicanas/os, we also see a specific reconfiguration of the testimonio by The Latina Feminist Group as we move into the twenty-first century. Rather than tell a personal or even collective story, testimonio, as a genre, allows the speaker(s) to act as a witness to state- or nation-sanctioned violence. Whereas the other self-referential forms mentioned up to this point allow for articulation of one's identity and communities broadly, this form acts as an alternative history, always engaging questions of survival in an environment that is overtly hostile and oppressive. A variety of testimonios come to publication (and translation into English) between the late 1970s and the 1990s articulating context-specific atrocities against embattled communities who dared to speak against power structures throughout Latin America such as Domitila Barrios de Chungara's *Let Me Speak! Testimony of Domitila, a Woman of the Bolivian Mines* (1978), Rigoberta Menchú's famous *I, Rigoberta Menchú: An Indian Women in Guatemala* (1983), Alicia Partnoy's *The Little School: Tales of Disappearance and Survival* (1986), and María Teresa Tula's *Hear My Testimony: María Teresa Tula, Human Rights Activist of El Salvador* (1994). The eighteen women who make up The Latina Feminist Group came together across differences of all kinds – which remain important during their collaboration – to work toward greater visibility in the environments they encounter every day. Sharing their narratives from memory aloud and then transcribing them, the members follow a common practice of testimonio production and hope that their "collective bearing witness conveys [their] outrage at multiple forms of violence toward women" and acknowledge that their collectivity "nurtures utopian visions of social formation . . . that are formed on the basis

CRYSTAL M. KURZEN

of equality, respect, and open negotiation of difference" (20). Speaking specifically about their genre decisions, they theorize their "unique praxis within testimonio traditions, as [they] have made [themselves] the subjects and objects of [their] own inquiry and voice" (21). Reimagining testimonio for their twenty-first century needs, these Latinas assemble to use the privilege they have gained – in large part from those genre innovators who came before them – to call for further agency and equality in the creative and professional spaces they currently inhabit.

Additionally, as we move further into the twenty-first century, we see a proliferation of writings by Latina/o lesbian, gay, and queer writers who, like The Latina Feminist Group, use genre to theorize issues of intersectionality and negotiate the power structures that keep their voices from being heard. Lourdes Torres explores the gaps and silences in the memoirs of Antonia Pantoja's, *Memoir of a Visionary* (2002), and Luisita López Torregrosa's, *The Noise of Infinite Longing* (2004), as she examines the specificity of the Puerto Rican woman's experience around gender, sexual, racial, national, and class dynamics and suggests that "shame implicitly and explicitly conditions the articulation of Puerto Rican identity" (84). While neither of these authors position themselves as queer, Torres encourages us to see them in the contexts in which they move and acknowledge the ways in which they see their intersectional identities as significant.

As we venture further into the twenty-first century, we find authors such as Richard Blanco, the first Latino and openly gay inaugural poet of the United States, who published his memoir *The Prince of Los Cocuyos* in 2014. It chronicles his experiences growing up in a family of Cuban exiles in Miami during the 1970s and 1980s while grappling with intersectional identities. Like some of the authors writing before him, he, too, contends with truth and fiction. In his author's note, he says that "these pages are emotionally true, though not necessarily or entirely factual ... I've bent time and space in the way that the art of memory demands" (n.p.). In the same year, Daisy Hernández published *A Cup of Water Under My Bed*, a lyrical, coming-of-age memoir, that traces the lives of women in her Cuban Colombian family as they teach her about love and men but also the consequences of migration and colonization and racial difference in the United States. She opens the text with a short piece entitled "Condemned" wherein she talks about her role to testify to the truth of her family life but also to the larger historical context in which she grew up and fashioned her own queer life. She puts her hands in other people's stories and says: "Nothing is more vulnerable than the words in our mouths, because nothing has more power" (xii). Blanco and

Hernández write and find publishers in the twenty-first century because of the persistency of those genre innovator-activists who came before them, those who were willing to look across racial, cultural, sexual, and class boundaries to examine the relationality of their intersectional identities while arguing for their rightful insertion into our (trans)national American master narratives.

WORKS CITED

Adams, Timothy Dow. "Case History: Sheila Ortiz Taylor and Sandra Ortiz Taylor." *Light Writing & Life Writing: Photography in Autobiography*. Chapel Hill: The University of North Carolina Press, 2000. 57–78.

"'Heightened by Life' Vs. 'Paralyzed by Fact': Photography and Autobiography in Norma Elia Cantú's *Canícula*." *Biography* 24.1 (2001): 57–72.

Anzaldúa, Gloria. *Borderlands/La Frontera: The New Mestiza*. San Francisco: Spinsters/Aunt Lute, 1987.

"now let us shift. . .the path of conocimiento. . .inner work, public acts." *This Bridge We Call Home: Radical Visions for Transformation*. Eds. Gloria Anzaldúa and Ana Louise Keating. New York: Routledge, 2002. 540–78.

Blanco, Richard. *The Prince of Los Cocuyos: A Miami Childhood*. New York: HarperCollins, 2014.

Cantú, Norma Elia. *Canícula: Snapshots of a Girl en la Frontera*. Albuquerque: University of New Mexico Press, 1995.

"Memoir, Autobiography, Testimonio." *The Routledge Companion to Latino/a Literature*. London and New York: Routledge, 2013. 310–22.

"The Writing of *Canícula*: Breaking Boundaries, Finding Forms." *Chicana Feminisms: A Critical Reader*. Eds. Aída Hurtado, Norma Klahn, Olga Nájera-Ramírez, and Patricia Zavella. Durham, NC: Duke University Press, 2003. 97–108.

Galarza, Ernesto. *Barrio Boy: The Story of a Boy's Acculturation*. South Bend, IN: University of Notre Dame Press, 1971.

Hernández, Daisy. *A Cup of Water Under My Bed*. Boston, MA: Beacon Press, 2014.

Hernández, Ellie D. "Performativity in the Chicana/o Autobiography." *Postnationalism in Chicana/o Literature and Culture*. Austin: University of Texas Press, 2009. 125–54.

Hirsch, Marianne. "Introduction: Familial Looking." *The Familial Gaze*. Ed. Marianne Hirsch. Hanover, NH: University Press of New England, 1999. xi–xxv.

Jiménez, Francisco. "An Interview with José Antonio Villarreal." *The Bilingual Review* 3.3 (Jan.–Apr. 1976): 66–72.

Lejeune, Philippe. *On Autobiography*. Minneapolis: University of Minnesota Press, 1989.

Moraga, Cherríe. *Loving in the War Years: lo que nunca pasó por sus labios*. Boston, MA: South End, 1983.

Moraga, Cherríe and Gloria E. Anzaldúa, eds. *This Bridge Called My Back: Writings by Radical Women of Color*. Watertown, MA: Persephone Press, 1981.

Padilla, Genaro M. *My History, Not Yours: The Formation of Mexican American Autobiography*. Madison: University of Wisconsin Press, 1993.

Reed-Danahay, Deborah. "Introduction." *Auto/Ethnography: Rewriting the Self and the Social*. Oxford: Berg, 1997. 1–17.

Rodriguez, Richard. *Hunger of Memory: The Education of Richard Rodriguez*. New York: Bantam, 1982.

Rosaldo, Renato. *Culture and Truth: The Remaking of Social Analysis*. Boston, MA: Beacon Press, 1989.

Sedore, Timothy S. "'Everything I Wrote Was Truth': An Interview with José Antonio Villarreal." *Northwest Review* 39.1 (2001): 77–89.

Smith, Sidonie and Julia Watson. *Reading Autobiography: A Guide for Interpreting Life Narratives*. 2001. Minneapolis: University of Minnesota Press, 2010.

Torres, Lourdes. "The Construction of the Self in US Latina Autobiographies." *Third World Women and the Politics of Feminism*. Eds. Chandra Talpade Mohanty, Ann Russo, and Lourdes Torres. Bloomington: Indiana University Press, 1991. 276–87.

"Queering Puerto Rican Women's Narratives." *Meridians: Feminism, Race, Transnationalism* 9.1 (2009): 83–112.

Torres-Saillant, Silvio. "The Latino Autobiography." *Latino and Latina Writers*. 2 Vols. Ed. Alan West. New York: Charles Scribner's Sons, 2004. 61–79.

Velasco, Juan. "*Automitografías*: The Border Paradigm and Chicana/o Autobiography." *Biography* 27.2 (2004): 313–38.

Villarreal, José Antonio. *Pocho*. New York: Anchor, 1959.

26

Poetics of the "Majority Minority"

NORMA ELIA CANTÚ

My mother taught me to do laundry when I was a child in South Texas. To hang the clothes of our large family on a line, a *soga*, out on the yard to dry in the hot Texas sun. The color and size of the pieces dictated how and where on the line I was to pin them with the wooden *horquillas*, clothespins. I thought that such a skill would serve me for the rest of my life. But that was not to be. I have not hung clothes on a line in decades, and my friend tells me that now computer programs perform the calculations for analyses that only ten years ago had to be done by calculators and earlier than that by hand! As is often the case, we have moved on, and the old ways are no longer viable or needed. It is so with many of the skills that we learned fifty years ago, and for sure it will be so of what we are learning now in fifty years' time. It is not our parents' poetry, or our grandparents' for that matter. We have come a long way, but we have a long way to go. Yet, the future looks bright. Due to our growing numbers and our growing stature in the arts in the United States, we will integrate into the fabric of the literary fabric of this country. But it is this threat that incites much of the reactionary politics at this juncture almost twenty years into the twenty-first century. The Latina/o community in the United States is currently experiencing considerable antipathy from much of the nation as it is poised, by virtue of demographic trends, to form the numerically largest population group by 2050. Having surpassed the African American population to become the largest minority group in the early 2000s, Latinas/os have only slowly gained visibility as something other than a secondary, "pathological" population but nonetheless are still plagued by accusations of illegality and criminality in an atmosphere charged by twenty-first century fears of terrorism. The poetry of our times reflects this situation and offers surcease as it points forward. In this brief paper, I explore the past, the present, and the future of our poetics and offer a grounding of the vision that poets offer us as we grapple with our contemporary realities.

The selection of gay Cuban American poet Richard Blanco to write the occasional poem "One Today" for Barack Obama's second inaugural in 2013 and the selection of Chicano poet Juan Felipe Herrera as the nation's poet laureate in 2015 marked key moments in the newly visible prominence of Latinas/os on the cultural landscape of the United States. Blanco and Herrera are two of many contemporary Latina/o poets, some who have been poeting – yes, I am coining a verb – for a long time, such as Martín Espada, Sandra Maria Esteves, Tino Villanueva, Lucha Corpi, Victor Hernández Cruz, Willie Perdomo, Marisela Norte, Rigoberto González, Cecilia Vicuña, Johnny Lorenz, Mónica de la Torre, and others who are new to the terrain but whose work continues along a path that extends back to the nineteenth century when our *antepasados* published their poetry in newspapers and broad sheets.

To explore the shifting terms upon which Latina/o communities have been characterized within the U.S. national imaginary and to explore our resistance, too, we need to turn to our poets. Often refiguring those terms with their formal innovations in poetic structure, popular allusions, and bilingual code-switching, Latina/o poets offer a trans-American vision of latinidad that asserts a national presence while maintaining strong linguistic and cultural ties to Mexico, Latin America, and the land that was once Mexico and is now part of the United States, or what folklorist Américo Paredes called Greater Mexico. Contemporary Latina/o poetry anticipates, in its formal characteristics, the future cultural landscape of the United States. This essay offers an overview of the literary history focusing on the collective literary movements, eschewing the more traditional manner of narrating our history through the roll call of luminaries. In addition, I also discuss the Spanish-language poets and their role in maintaining the poetic integrity of our literature. Finally, I delve into a perfunctory analysis of themes following threads that I see in form and content of contemporary Latina/o poetics.

Past and Current Landscape

Various scholars have pointed out the origins of our literary production in the Americas. Nicholás Kanellos most notably cites the existence of our literature in the oral tradition and in the early texts. In his introduction to the anthology *Herencia*, he notes that our literary output since the nineteenth century has been characterized as belonging to three main kinds of expressions: native, immigrant, or exile (4). He describes the literary output from colonial times to the present (1–32). He further explores key components in Chicano and Puerto Rican poetic output in his essay "An Overview of Latino Poetry: The Iceberg below the Surface." Most recently, Latino/a poetry has appeared in anthologies such as *Angels of the Americlypse: An Anthology of New Latin@ Writing*, edited by Carmen Giménez Smith and John Chávez and in the surge of publications of poetry books and chapbooks in English, Spanish, and Spanglish.

The current state of poetry in the United States cannot be assessed without including an overview of certain trends in our literary history such as the landmarks or change points marked by the establishment of certain institutions. The founding of the Bay Area's Centro Chicano de Escritores (CCE) by Barbara Brinson Curiel, Francisco Alarcón, Juan Felipe Herrera, and Lucha Corpi in the early 1970s is a case in point.[1] CCE poets and writers worked together with many others throughout the San Francisco Bay Area and in California as a whole to establish a visible and activist presence of Chicana/o poets.[2] In Sacramento, The Royal Chicano Air Force (originally the Rebel Chicano Air Force) led by poet José Montoya established a presence in support of the farmworker movement. Literary groups such as the Mission Poets included Latino poets such as Alejandro Murguía, Nicaraguan Roberto Vargas, Salvadoran Nina Serrano, who published in venues such as *El Tecolote*. Poets such as Cecilio Garcia Camarillo, Reymundo "Tigre" Pérez, raul r. salinas, Ricardo Sánchez, Evangelina Vigil, Inés Hernández Ávila (at the time Hernández Tovar), Lalo Delgado, Sabine Ulibarri, Dorinda Moreno, and Bernice Zamora were publishing in small Chicano movement grassroots publications in the 1960s and 1970s in Texas, Arizona, New Mexico, and Colorado. In Texas specifically, the activity was concentrated in El Paso, Austin, and San Antonio; Inés Hernández Ávila (Hernández Tovar at the time), Carmen Tafolla, Raymundo "Tigre" Pérez,

---

[1] Throughout the next twenty years or so, various writers joined the group. Among them were Victor Martínez (fiction), Rodrigo Reyes (playwright and other theater arts), Juan Pablo Gutiérrez (poetry and arts), Elba Sánchez (poet), Odilia Rodríguez Galván (poet), Martivon Galindo (poet and memoirist), and Ana Castillo (poet, fiction writer, and scholar).

[2] Centro Chicano de Escritores merged with Aztlán Cultural (AC), an arts-service organization so they could use the latter's 501(c)(3) status to obtain grants to expand and connect with the smaller towns and cities in California; the idea was for the poets and writers to travel to the smaller Mexican and Latin American communities. Lucha Corpi became director of AC/CCE, and the group applied to NEA and received a grant to rent vans and transport six poets/writers at a time to visit and read at communities such as Marysville, Guadalupe, Salinas Valley, Santa Maria, and other small towns in Southern California. Although the program was a great success, the group could not sustain the demands of the organization as everyone had day jobs and was involved in a number of other activities.

Cecilio García Camarillo, and Lalo Delgado were publishing in small regional venues such as *El Caracol* and *Tejidos*.

The New York City-based Nuyorican Poets Café brought together Tato Laviera, Miguel Algarín, Sandra María Esteves, and other poets on the East Coast. In some cases, there were exchanges and communications among the poets, but it was sporadic and there was no concentrated effort or institution that functioned for poets the same way that the Teatros Nacionales de Aztlán (TENAZ) functioned for theater groups across the United States and indeed across the continent. Yet, the poets along the East Coast, according to Kanellos, also sought to establish a sense of solidarity.

In the late twentieth century, the work of Latina/o and Chicana/o poets were known only to a very limited local circle, for the most part; in effect the poets and their work remained silenced and isolated. It was precisely this silencing, this erasure, that was the impetus to establish a national network of support for Latina/o poets across latinidades. We sought to create a space that would accommodate all of our languages, all of our class statuses, all of our skin colors, all of our ways of being in the world. Thus, we established CantoMundo, a summer workshop for Latina/o poets that nurtures and supports poetry even as it creates a community of poets. It was not the first time that we had attempted to establish connections, to gather as a tribe, as it were. Chicana poets Carmen Tafolla and Theresa Palomo Acosta had attempted to unite Chicana poets in the 1980s, but failed as there were scarce resources and little support from institutions.

Again, in the 1990s, Latina/o writers sought ways to come together in community. CantoMundo exists because of these earlier attempts, most directly due to Macondo, the space created by Sandra Cisneros. When Pablo Miguel Martínez, Celeste Mendoza, Deborah Paredez, Carmen Tafolla, and I met, we envisioned what CantoMundo needed to be for us, and we modeled the existing spaces for poets of color, namely, Cave Canem for African American and Kundiman for Asian American poets. CantoMundo's vision statement explicitly calls for a space where we can be Latina/o poets, where we can do our thing, as it were. Through workshops, symposia, and public readings, CantoMundo provides a space for the creation, documentation, and critical analysis of Latina/o poetry. We have formed a community of support. When Sandra Cisneros founded Macondo, and thus offered a space for Latina/o and other writers of color to come together for workshops – including poetry – and to form a community of writers similar to what exits for the mainstream writing community, she envisioned a similar space; all of us Macondistas felt a sense of being in the world as writers of color.

CantoMundo began as an offshoot of Macondo as some of us poets would go off and hold our own writing retreats. When several of us Macondistas founded the CantoMundo poetry workshop, we had hopes and ideas of what we wanted it to be, but were unsure if the climate was right, if the funding would be there, if poets would indeed heed the call. Our first successful attempt to bring together poets across the latinidades occurred in 2009, and, every summer since, the CantoMundo workshop hosts poets from across the United States. The inaugural workshop, held at the National Hispanic Cultural Center in Albuquerque, featured Demetria Martinez and Martin Espada as faculty. Subsequent workshops have continued this tradition of having Chicana/o and Latina/a faculty and holding a public reading by fellows and faculty that is open to the community. Recently, the CantoMundo Poetry Prize was announced by the University of Arkansas Press, furthering the goals of the CantoMundo founders who sought to celebrate Latina/o and Chicana/o poetry, and thus fulfilling one of our goals for CantoMundo to continue to expand and support poetry by Latina/o poets in the United States. Thus, CantoMundo continues the work of the earlier gatherings, the Floricantos and poetry festivals.

A brief overview tracing the key moments along the trajectory of poetry's history in Latina/o literature must include a brief overview of the literary journals that have published Latina/o poetry. The 1970s and 1980s brought interest in Latina/o literature and scholarship and the establishment of various academic journals. Quinto Sol Publications, an independent publisher founded by Octavio I. Romano-V., Nick C. Vaca, and Andres Ybarra began publishing *El Grito: A Journal of Contemporary Mexican-American Thought* in 1967. With the advent of Latino studies and Chicano studies on university campuses across the country came numerous publications, often under student editorships and due to the efforts of student activists. In 1970, the Department of Chicano Studies and the Chicano Studies Research Center at the University of California, Los Angeles, began publishing *Aztlán: A Journal of Chicana/o Studies*. In 1974, Gary Keller began publishing *Bilingual Review* through the Bilingual Review Press; the press and the journal were initially housed at Eastern Michigan State University and subsequently moved to the University of Arizona. In San Jose, California, in 1976, Lorna Dee Cervantes established Mango Publications, where Sandra Cisneros first published her poetry. In the 1980s, Tino Villanueva began publishing *Imagine: International Chicano Poetry Journal* in Boston. One of the latest venues is *Palabra: A Magazine of Chicano & Latino Literary Art*, founded and edited by Elena Minor. One of the predominantly Spanish-language publications that opened a space for writers of Spanglish is *Ventana Abierta* published by the Chicano Studies Institute at the University of California, Santa Barbara, originally under the direction of Luis Leal and Victor Fuentes. In 1986, El Centro de Estudios Puertorriqueños at Hunter College began publishing *El Centro Journal*, but its focus has been mostly on research in the social sciences.

At the University of Indiana, Bloomington, key players planted seeds that are still bearing fruit. In 1973, Luis Dávila and Nicolás Kanellos, both at Indiana University, published *La Revista Chicano-Riqueña*, which subsequently became *Americas Review* after moving to the University of Houston with Kanellos as editor. Under the direction of Dávila, the interdisciplinary Chicano-Riqueño Studies Program began in 1976 with the study of Puerto Rican, Chicano, and other Spanish-speaking communities in the United States as its aim. In 1976, the first issue of *Chiricú*, focused on **Chi**cano-**Ri**queño-**Cu**bano experience, was published as a multilingual journal of Latina/o literature and literary criticism; the journal continues to be published annually and is now under the auspices of Latina/o Studies at the University of Indiana. As the journal's website states, it seeks to serve "as a linguistic and cultural bridge for fraternal exchange published in Spanish, English, and Portuguese." Also at Indiana, in 1979, Norma Alarcón founded Third Woman Press and began publishing the feminist Latina literary journal *Third Woman*. In the 1980s, when Alarcón moved to the University of California, Berkeley, the press went with her, and she continued to publish feminist works of literature, including poetry collections, by Chicanas, Latinas and other women of color until 2004. The press was revived by Sara Ramírez and a collective editorship in 2011 with a similar mission.

As we have seen, the 1960s and 1970s saw a flourishing of venues both grassroots and academic for Latina/o and Chicana/o writers. Most recently we have a similar flourishing in electronic journals. In the 1960s and 1970s, poets would gather at conferences like Floricanto.[3] Now they attend poetry festivals and publish in mainstream journals as well as the ones discussed above. The number of poets who are active and engaged in the art of poetry has also increased; more than 150 Latina/o poets are listed in the Poetry Foundation's website, although relatively few poets who write exclusively in Spanish are included.

---

[3] Floricanto festivals were held mostly in the Southwest and many Chicana/o poets presented their work at these venues. I recall the one held in Corpus Christi, Texas, in the late 1970s where poets such as Dorinda Moreno and Lorna Dee Cervantes read their work.

Festivals and Poetry in Spanish

Another important aspect in examining Latina/o poetry in the United States is the existence of poetry festivals across the country that celebrate Latina/o poetry, such as the Floricanto festivals that began in the 1970s. One of the most recently founded is the annual Flor de Nopal Literary Festival housed at the Mexican American Cultural Center in Austin, Texas, established by CantoMundo fellow ire'ne lara silva and her brother Moises. In addition to regularly scheduled festivals, there have also been several occasional events such as the Marathón de Poesía del Teatro de la Luna held in Washington, DC, in 2007 under the leadership of Rei Berroa. As a result of the latter, an annual event is now held at De Paul University. In 2016, they will hold the ninth annual event. The organizer, Juana Iris Goergen, shared with me in an e-mail that she attended the event in DC and then got the idea of hosting the annual *Poesía en abril* festival at De Paul University where she teaches Spanish in the Department of Modern Languages. She explained that the aim of the poetry festival was to show that "Latin America is one and that the Latinos in the United States are an integral part of that América ... that we are adding to the culture all the time but especially in the area of poetry" (my translation). She continued by highlighting that there are many poets writing in Spanish in the United States who are renowned poets admired throughout the continent. She then listed almost fifty poets who attended from nine countries and Puerto Rico. Among them are many of the poets who were included in the special issue on poetry of De Paul University's journal, *Diálogo*,[4] with over thirty Latina/o poets from the Americas, and critical essays on contemporary issues such as the emergence of poetry by indigenous poets in Mexico. Indeed the very active Latina/o poetic world exists at the national level and in small local groups like the Latino Writers Collective in Kansas City, or the spontaneously created groups like Undocupoets, founded in 2015, that find that there is indeed strength in numbers.

---

[4] Among the poets included in this list are: Eduardo Chirinos, Roger Santibáñez, and Mariela Dreyfus (Peru), Zulema Moret, Gladys Ilarregui, and Ezequiel Zaidenwerg (Argentina); Javier Ávila, Aurea María Sotomayor, and Johanny Vázquez Paz (Puerto Rico); Aurora Arias, Rei Berroa, Josefina Báez, René Rodríguez Soriano, Medar Serrata, and Rebeca Castellanos (Dominican Republic); Xánath Caraza, Arturo Dávila S., Olivia Maciel, Jorge Montiel, Febronio Zataráin, Gerardo Cárdenas, Jorge Ortega, and Elizabeth Narváez Luna (Mexico/USA); Silvia Goldman and Marquesa Macadar (Uruguay); Natalia Gómez, Ana Merino, Fernando Operé, and Eduardo Urios (Spain); Andrea Cote Botero, Marta Cecilia Rivera, and Armando Romero (Colombia), Verónica Lucuy Alandia and Miguel Marzana (Bolivia); Jorge García de la Fe, Jesús Barquet, and José Kozer (Cuba).

They come together to work on their craft, publish their work, and insure that Latina/o poetry is not subsumed, or erased, by the larger world of poetry in the United States. In the lower Rio Grande Valley of South Texas, the group Border Poets, in what is commonly called El Valle, have come together, as poets during the 1930s did, including a young Américo Paredes.

Geography impacts the proliferation of site-based poetry, and contemporary poets may no longer be bound to a particular space, fluidly existing in various spaces. Poets like Rosebud Ben Oni, a Latina from South Texas based in New York, or Puerto Rican poet Denice Frohman, who now resides in Denver, as well as a number of poets from California or the East Coast whose Central American origins brings them to that liminal location of being reterritorialized. While we may still talk of Puerto Rican poets like Urayoán Noel or Edwin Torres whose experimental aesthetics transcend their identitarian location as Puerto Rico, we must see beyond the geographic to the poetic identity. Yet, some poets may remain grounded in a particular location, deploying a Borderlands sensitivity for analysis as well as for poetic expression. Poets like Emmy Pérez, comes to mind; although she grew up in California, her recent work focused on the U.S.–Mexico border exemplifies the *transfrontera* nature of a border poetics that was there with Américo Paredes and Gloria Anzaldúa and that continues with Pat Mora, Benjamin Alire Saénz, Alberto Rios, Rigoberto González, Raquel Valle Senties, and Lauren Espinoza. Amalia Ortiz, whose outstanding spoken-word performances earned her notoriety in that poetic space, is also based in the lower Rio Grande Valley, combining border poetics with that of the oral performance and weaves in, as many other Chicanas and Latinas do, themes of sexuality and gender. Her book *Rant, Chant, Chisme*, published by Wings Press, includes satire and cutting critiques of the racist and sexist world that Latinas face. She and Emmy Pérez are influencing students, and in the Creative Writing Program at the University of Texas – Rio Grande Valley, training more Latina/o and Chicana/o poets.

Topics, Themes, Trends

As we turn to look at the topics and themes that recur in the poetry by Latinas/os, I highlight three salient areas that correspond to our literary history. In the oral contests, we have traditional poetry such as *declamación* and the sung poems or ballads known as *corridos*. Not surprisingly, the earliest poetry reflected the topics and forms of the period; so the nineteenth-century poets such as Sara Estela Ramírez or Jose Martí wrote rhymed poems that dealt with the politics of the time even as most of their contemporaries were engaged in romantic poetry modeled after that of Spain or Latin America. In like fashion, contemporary poets do slam poetry or spoken word, addressing contemporary political issues even as some poets remain rooted to the more traditional celebration of cultural mores. But, what are those topics? What are the themes that emerge as the subject for poets whether they are using traditional forms or experimental? As several scholars have noted, the often anthologized and taught epic poem *Yo Soy Joaquín* by Rodolfo "Corky" Gonzales established a collective narrative of the history of Chicanos in poetic form.

As Rafael Pérez-Torres argues in *Movements in Chicano Poetry: Against Myths, Against Margins*, Chicano poetry, and I would say all of Latino poetry, develops "in the borderlands of our contemporary postmodern migratory society... [and] represents a new means of engagement and understanding, one that suggests the formation of new and more fluid epistemologies" (3). Writing in 1995, Pérez-Torres examines the contemporary poetic production at the end of the millennium as he lays out a format that still holds true. The "new and more fluid epistemologies" include new bridges across latinidades. While the social turmoil of the mid-twentieth century cuts loose in the poetry of Nuyorican and Chicano poets, the beginning of the twenty-first century elicits poetry that responds to the social realities of a post–9/11 country with its anti-immigrant sentiments. Themes that existed then, such as language, identity, and cultural resistance to hegemonic popular culture and practices remain but are framed differently. Contemporary poets still focus on unifying themes of solidarity, including the search for linguistic freedom and a self-defined social reality while producing work that speaks of the political struggles of DREAMers and DACA students.[5] The Undocupoets co-founders Javier Zamora, Christopher Soto, and Marcelo Hernández Castillo work to force literary contests to rethink their citizenship requirements.

At various times in Latina/o literary history, poets have answered the need for a poetry that speaks of resistance, for poetry that is political and

---

[5] DREAMers are undocumented youth who meet the general requirements of the Development, Relief, and Education for Alien Minors (DREAM) Act: they came to the United States as children, have lived in the country continuously, and are in school. DACA applies to individuals who fall within the guidelines of Deferred Action for Childhood Arrivals. Through DACA, individuals who came to the United States as children and meet several guidelines may request deferred action for a period of two years, subject to renewal, and they are eligible for work authorization even though it does not grant lawful status.

relevant. In my estimation, three critical times have given birth to a decidedly political poetry: at the end of the nineteenth century and the beginning of the twentieth century in response to the devastation wreaked upon Latinas/os and Mexicans by the U.S.–Spanish War and the Mexican Revolution, respectively; during the struggle for civil rights in the 1960s and 1970s; and the current moment in the twenty-first century as we respond to the onslaught of racist and xenophobic attacks upon Latinas/os and Chicanas/os. The most salient of these has been the effort by San Francisco Bay Area poet Francisco X. Alarcón (1954–2016) who pioneered the use of social media to instigate a poetic reaction to the oppressive laws passed in Arizona against immigrants. His "Poets responding to HB 1070" – on Facebook, blogs, and e-mail – has resulted in a poetic movement that united the many Latino poets who responded to the call for poetry. The group eventually gathered these poems into an anthology, *Poetry of Resistance: Voices for Social Justice*, coedited by Francisco X. Alarcón and Odilia Galván Rodríguez.

Contemporary Chicana/o and Latina/o poets navigate different waters than did their *antepasados*, those who came before to engage the realities of their time. Along with feminist poetics, as exemplified by the poetry of poets like Rosebud Ben-Oni and Carmen Giménez Smith, contemporary Latina/o poets tackle the topics of health and illness, of sexuality and gender, of immigrant rights and police brutality, of the nature of poetry itself. In ire'ne lara silva's *Blood Sugar Canto*, the poet tackles the difficult encounter with diabetes and explores the physical reality of illness, including the legacies and alchemies that have impacted her body. In like fashion, Emmy Pérez looks at the physical reality of the border and dissects the kind of life lived under surveillance.

A contemporary poetics of transition, demanding flexibility and accommodation by the larger hegemonic poetics that Pérez-Torres described in 1995 has occurred with the new emergent epistemologies; these allow poets of color, and especially Latina/o poets, to express themselves in numerous poetic expressions with a poetics that is inclusive and expansive both formally and linguistically, allowing for Spanish and indigenous languages. Xanath Caraza's work comes to mind with its mixture of Náhuatl, English, and Spanish. Like the early Chicano movement poets like Alurista who reclaimed lost languages, poets are exploring the multilinguality of expression and a defiance of the traditional poetic forms. In her latest collection, *A Crown for Gumecindo*, Laurie Ann Guerrero sets the sonnet on its head. She breaks down the traditional form and takes command of it with strong engagement with death, in this case her grandfather Gumecindo's death.

Latina/o poetry has organically developed to its current exciting and dynamic state; we can claim that Latina/o poets exist across the United States writing in English and in Spanish, as well as in Spanglish and in various forms from the traditional sonnet or villanelle to the invented forms that bring together the rhythms of rap and *son jarocho*. Experimenting with form and language is at the core of some of the experimental work by Roberto Tejeda and Valerie Martínez, as well. Latina/os who write and publish poetry in the United States include the varying languages of Spanish and English, such as Marjorie Agosín's Chilean Spanish, or Alicia Partnoy's Argentine Spanish, or Lucha Corpi's Mexican Spanish alongside Xanath Caraza's or Liliana Valenzuela's, or Leticia Hernandez's unique blend of Salvadoran and Mexican Spanish of her California home. All these poets writing in the Spanish of their home regions fuse the English and Spanglish of Chicana/os and third- or fourth-generation immigrants who have embraced English as their poetic tool, such as Sandra Cisneros or Eduardo Corral. Searching for an identity through the language of their poetry becomes a running motif celebrating their group's identity; the Portuguese American Amy Sayre's work comes to mind. The themes that Latina/o poets have embraced include the tension and celebration of the varied and various languages that are at their disposal as wordsmiths. It is an issue that Pérez-Torres explored as well; it remains true in contemporary poetics. While he focused on the poets who use Spanglish or Tex-Mex or interlingualism, a process that allows for the use of two or more languages, he nevertheless points to issues faced by any Latina/o poet writing in the United States.

Conclusion

When Juan Felipe Herrera assumed the post of Poet Laureate of the United States in 2015, he initiated a campaign to bring poetry to the people; he called his initiative Casa de Colores, a metaphorical home of many colors that is a place for all of us in this country, of any ethnic or racial background. Such a monumental effort has been taken up by a number of groups. Every April, when we celebrate National Poetry Month, I envision the many colors of poetry coming together under one roof to celebrate poetry, all our poetries. Noted Chicano poet Rigoberto González has called for a celebration of our diverse latinidades and of our poetic output. CantoMundo fellow Francisco Aragón, who heads Letras Latinas, has been a promoter of our poetry and our poets as well. Having Latina/o poets as state and city poet laureates, also contributes to the visibility of our poetry. The presence of Latina/o poetry resides in leading journals and literary anthologies as well as the prominence of poetry in spaces like the annual meeting of the Association of Writing Programs (AWP) and at festivals like Split this Rock in Washington, DC. As our institutions – including journals like the aforementioned *Diálogo*, *Aztlán*, and *Chiricú* – recommit to publishing poetry, and as new spaces like *Palabra* and *Chicana/Latina Studies*, the journal of Mujeres Activas en Letras y Cambio Social, emerge where poets can find a home for their art, we can rest assured that Latina/o poetry is alive and well. Highlighting the cutting-edge work of Latina/o poets in contemporary spaces, I affirm that they are posed to take up the challenges of this century and go forth armed with the same desires and passions as Latina/o poets of earlier generations; they seek to explore new directions and to leave their mark. In my view, they will face new technologies, but these new technologies are not only limited to the obvious technological advances that will facilitate dissemination of our work to a general public but also the technologies of oppression that the current political climate has fostered. The content and the forms of our poems must respond to that future that consistently eludes us but that also confronts us constantly and relentlessly. The challenges remain: How do we engage with other poets of color? How do we form coalition? Is community possible? How do we become more visible? More responsive to our community? These are some of the questions that will certainly emerge as we move forward. My prediction? Based on the record already established by Canto-Mundo and other spaces, we will continue to link and network and to realize that there is strength in numbers, that together we can do more than by remaining isolated. That together, doing work that matters, as Gloria Anzaldúa urged, we can transform this historical reality, we can effect change, we can bring about social change and prove that the word is indeed powerful, que *sí se puede*, that yes, we can!

WORKS CITED

Kanellos, Nicolas. "Introduction" in *Herencia: The Anthology of Hispanic Literature*. New York: Oxford University Press, 2002. 1–32.
　"An Overview of Latino Poetry: The Iceberg below the Surface." *Americas Review* 24.1 (Nov–Dec 2002).
Pèrez-Torres, Rafael. *Movements in Chicano Poetry: Against Myths, against Margins*. Cambridge: Cambridge University Press, 1995.
Torres, Lourdes. "In the Contact Zone: Code-switching Strategies by Latino/a Writers." *MELUS* 32.1 (Spring 2007).

27

The Quisqueya Diaspora

The Emergence of Latina/o Literature from Hispaniola

SOPHIE MARÍÑEZ

This essay explores aspects of the literary production of Haitian and Dominican writers primarily located in the United States. As these authors belong to a diaspora comprised of two populations of intertwined African and European descents, their combined inclusion here aims at challenging critical traditions in Latino/a studies that have tended to exclude Haitian-American literary production. For, if the much-contested term "Hispanics" refers primarily to a Spanish-speaking population, the more progressive term "Latina/o" should open up the umbrella to include people with a cultural background originating in *all* nations in the Americas whose primary language is derived from Latin, including French, and its own American derivation, Haitian Creole. Yet critical volumes of Latina/o studies have consistently excluded Haitian-Americans, many of whom write in English, seasoned with dashes of French or Haitian Creole. Considering that recent definitions of latinidad have expanded the concept to include Portuguese-speaking authors as well as writers who sprinkle their English-based works with indigenous languages, the exclusion of Haitian authors is egregious, especially considering the crucial historical role Haiti took in the independence of Bolivarian nations.[1] Further, as Latino/a literary criticism has expanded to include Dominican-American authors, the exclusion of their

---

[1] For recent discussions of latinidad, see Suzanne Bost and Francis R. Aparicio, eds., *The Routledge Companion to Latino/a Literature*. London; New York: Routledge, 2012; and Frederick Luis Aldama, ed., *The Routledge Concise History of Latino/a Literature*. London; New York: Routledge, 2013. For an exception to this normalized exclusion of Haitian authors, see Ricardo Ortíz's "Edwidge Danticat's 'Latinidad': *The Farming of Bones* and the Cultivation (of Fields) of Knowledge," in Marcus Bullock and Peter Y. Paik eds., *Aftermaths: Exile, Migration, and Diaspora Reconsidered*. New Brunswick, New Jersey and London: Rutgers University Press, 2009, pp. 150–72. Although Ortíz does not argue for an inclusion of Haitian-American authors in the Latino/a canon, he sustains that Danticat's novel challenges overall notions of latinidad as it denounces the 1937 massacre of Haitians in the Dominican Republic as well as dominant notions of "Hispanidad" in official discourses of Dominican national identity.

Haitian counterparts prevents offering a larger, more complex perspective on Dominicans as a group. It also misses the potential offered by reading this unique diaspora from a Caribbean island whose multiple names (Quisqueya, Haiti, Saint-Domingue, Santo Domingo, Española, and Hispaniola) stand as residues of its colonial history and of the inextricable relationship of the two peoples that share its geographical space, blurring the line that divides them into the Hispanophone/Dominican, on the one hand, and the French/Creolophone/Haitian on the other. Certainly, few studies of anything Dominican can stand on their own without mention of Haiti and of the relationship between both nations, be it of their "conflict" or the very real collaboration that has permeated their histories for centuries between progressives of both sides and between the reactionaries as well. To be sure, efforts have been made to explore Haitian and Dominican diasporic literary production in tandem, but much remains to be done in comparing the effects of their condition as immigrants or second generation on their works. Except for Lucía Suárez (2006), Silvio Torres-Saillant (2006b), and, Manuel A. Victoriano-Martínez (2014), few have offered new insights on how these combined productions reveal the tangled dynamics of the island.[2]

This essay attempts partially to address these gaps by focusing on the relationship of these diasporic subjectivities to the homeland and to the "other side" of the island. In this sense, I argue that their shared condition as immigrants opens new, potential avenues of understanding between the two nations. I also contend that the diasporic condition of many Dominican writers has been crucial in developing an empathy toward Haitian immigrants that the normalization of anti-Haitian sentiments prevailing in the Dominican Republic would seldom promote. Thus, this essay begins with a brief review of the intertwined history of both nations, the construction of Haiti as the "primitive Other" (Valerio-Holguín, n.d.) in the Dominican

---

[2] Critics who have recently examined Haitian and Dominican literary production in tandem include Elissa Lister (2013), who focuses on the literature dealing with the 1937 massacre; Manuel A. Victoriano-Martínez (2014) who explores the concept of the "rayano" or subjectivity standing at the intersection of the Haiti-Dominican Republic border, and includes a discussion of Danticat's *The Farming of Bones*; and Maria Cristina Fumagalli (2015), who focuses on literary and cultural productions from the island, as well as Danticat's *The Farming of Bones* (1998) and Junot Díaz's "Monstro" (2012). The few critics who include various diasporic authors from both sides are Lucía Suárez (2006), who examines works by Danticat, Jean-Robert Cadet, Julia Alvarez, and Loyda Maritza Pérez; and Myriam Chancy (2012), who discusses Caribbean women writers including Alvarez, Pérez, and Danticat, among others. See also the epilogue of Silvio Torres-Saillant's *An Intellectual History of the Caribbean* (2006) for further discussions of Haitian and Dominican diasporic authors.

national imagination, and the great distance that, especially after the 1937 massacre of tens of thousands of Haitians and Afro-Dominicans, characterized relations between both peoples. To be sure, after the fall of Haitian dictator Jean-Claude "Baby Doc" Duvalier in 1986, a gradual rapprochement emerged, but this culminated in renewed tensions from 2005 onward. Given this context, I borrow a term employed by Haitian writer Marie-Helène Laforest in her reflection on her own migratory experience, and I expand it to argue that the diasporic condition functions as an "equalizer" on these two collectivities who, largely unknown to each other, share similar experiences as immigrants in the United States. Finally, I maintain that a combined reading of these works suggests that this diasporic condition offers potential for both groups to shed stereotypes about each other in order to develop new perspectives on the island's tensions.

Indeed, the diasporic condition of Haitian and Dominican immigrants brings them together in sharing a similar predicament. While Haitians and Dominicans living on the island are separated by a linguistic barrier and geopolitical border, there is potential for their respective diasporas to be united by their migratory experience and the use of English, the *lingua franca* of immigrants. As many other immigrants, Haitian and Dominican immigrants also face similar racial discrimination and are confronted with new identity categories. If Haitians saw themselves as Haitians, and Dominicans as Dominicans, as immigrants they learn they are equalized and lumped together with "Blacks," a category that erases the specificity of their national historical past and ethnicities, and leads them to learn from, adopt, or join forces with others in a heterogeneous African diaspora. Light-skinned Dominicans, too, are lumped together in a larger category –"Hispanics" or "Latino/as" –, which also has an unintended effect of effacing historical and ethnic specificities. As I explain below, they also share a state of precariousness as to the perceived authenticity of their cultural identity and sense of belonging to the homeland.

A brief history of a tormented relationship

As scholars have amply documented, official discourses of national identity in the Dominican Republic have been marred by an anti-Haitian ideology that can be traced to the revolution of Saint-Domingue, when its first outbursts in 1791 prompted French and Spanish ideologues to construct both colonies as the two opposite sides of a binary system easily recognizable in Western epistemology and colonial discourses (Franco Pichardo,

2013; Torres-Saillant, 1999a; 1999b, 2003; Valerio-Holguín, n.d.). Briefly recounted, the history of the two nations begins as follows: shortly after the arrival of the Spaniards on the island they baptized as La Española, Spain prioritized Mexico and Peru in its conquest and colonization agenda, and gradually abandoned Española. The so-called "Devastaciones de Osorio" (1606–1607) prohibited the population from settling the northern coasts of the island as a measure to prevent them from establishing trade exchange with other European nations. As a result, French buccaneers and filibusters gradually populated the deserted lands and, in 1665, requested the French king's recognition of their territory as a colony. In 1697, France and Spain signed the treaty of Ryswick, which established a first border between the two colonies. A new Treaty of Bale, signed in 1795 between Spain and the French revolutionary regime, ceded the Spanish colony to France, thus making it technically "French". During the same period, black rebellions that had been taking place in Saint-Domingue since 1791, culminated into a full-fledged revolution that led to the first abolition of slavery in the Americas and the first black republic on the hemisphere. Its first leader, Toussaint Louverture attempted to claim Santo Domingo under the Treaty of Bale, brought his troops and proclaimed the abolition of slavery, but was repelled by the local Spanish-descended, *criolla* elite, who would only accept French authorities to make the Treaty effective. In 1805, Dessalines, too, marched on Santo Domingo in an unsuccessful effort to free the entire island from the French. In 1809, Spanish creoles fought the French but only to restore their colonial status under the Crown of Spain. Then, in 1822, Haiti responded to the call from other, progressive sectors of the Spanish side who wanted to abolish slavery and unified the island under one regime. During this Unification period, which lasted until 1844, Haitian authorities abolished slavery permanently; confiscated lands from the Catholic Church and redistributed them among the peasants; and modernized the legal system by establishing civil marriage and the Napoleon Code. This relationship turned sour when, in 1826, France decided to recognize Haiti as a sovereign nation in exchange for an indemnity for its "losses" and Haitian authorities imposed new taxes on the Spanish side to help pay this debt. Finding this taxation unjust, the Spanish creoles rallied against the Haitian regime, proclaiming the Separation from Haiti and the birth of the Dominican Republic in 1844.[3]

---

[3] Cassá, 2001. See also Franklyn Franco Pichardo, *Historia del Pueblo Dominicano*. Santo Domingo: Sociedad Editorial Dominicana, 1992, especially p. 185. For details on the

Ever since 1804, slave-owning powers throughout the world and especially in the hemisphere represented Haiti as a nation of primitive, evil,
cannibalistic creatures – an image in stark contrast to the one used to define
its Spanish neighbors: white, Catholic, civilized and obedient.[4] Toward the
end of the nineteenth century and the beginning of the twentieth, conservative elites revived this dichotomy to define their nation in opposition to
everything Haiti represented in their eyes. Despite the presence of progressive voices expressing a vision of both peoples as "brothers" as well as an
admiration among foundational leaders Juan Pablo Duarte, José Maria
Imbert, and Gregorio Luperón toward Haiti for having resisted and defeated
the European colonial power, to this day, a negro-phobic, anti-Haitian
ideology has always been available to serve the ruling elite's political and
economic interests, sometimes even justifying extreme violence, such as the
1937 massacre.[5]

Still, despite all this, Haitians and Dominicans have not always lived in
a state of "fatal conflict," as some observers have characterized them.[6]
Certainly, important aspects of the history of the island have been determined by the capitalist interests of the region, leading, in the twentieth
century, to the importation of Haitian workers to sugar plantations on
Dominican soil, a practice imposed by the United States during its occupation

dynamics between both nations between 1843 and 1865, see Anne Eller, *We Dream
Together: Dominican Independence, Haiti, and the Fight for Caribbean Freedom*. Durham:
Duke University Press, 2016.

[4] For details on early European narratives see Ginetta Candelario, *Black Behind the Ears:
Dominican Racial Identity from Museums to Beauty Shops*. Durham: Duke University Press,
2007, and Carlos Jáuregui, "El 'Negro Comegente': Terror, colonialism y etno-política."
Afro-Hispanich Review 28:1 (2009): 45–79. For a study on the construction of Haiti as the
"primitive Other," see Fernando Valerio-Holguín, "Nuestros vecinos, los primitivos."
Academia.edu.

[5] For details on Duarte's, Luperón's and Imbert's views on Haiti, see Quisqueya Lora H.,
"La construcción de Haití en el imaginario dominicano del siglo XIX," in "República
Dominicana y Haití: El derecho a vivir." Santo Domingo: Fundación Juan Bosch, 2014,
pp. 171–204. For Francisco del Rosario Sánchez's relationship with Haiti and Haitian
president Geffrard, whose help he requested in 1863, see Franco Pichardo, *Historia del
pueblo dominicano*, pp. 249–265. For details on how anti-Haitian ideology was used in the
aftermath of the 1937 massacre to justify it *ad posteriori*, see Robyn Derby and Richard
Turrits, "Historias de terror y los terrores de la historia: la masacre haitiana de 1937 en la
República Dominicana," in *Estudios Sociales*, XXVI: 92 (1993): 65–76.

[6] See journalist Michele Wucker's controversial *Why the Cock Fights? Dominicans, Haitians
and the Struggle for Hispaniola* (2000), which argues that both nations are stuck in an
inevitable, territorial, "fatal conflict," an argument that has been dismantled by Samuel
Martínez (2003) and Manuel A. Victoriano-Martínez (2014), who have condemned the
essentialist tenets of such argument, not to mention the reduction of the complex
dynamics between these nations to a primitive, animalistic fight.

of both sides of the island between 1916 and 1924.[7] As infrastructures were built on the Dominican Republic, Haiti became the main source of cheap labor. This economic model continued throughout the U.S.-backed regimes of Trujillo (1930–1961) and Joaquín Balaguer (1966–1978), until it was replaced, in the 1980s, by a model of services and manufacture – tourism, free zones, and telecommunications – that served the interests of multinational corporations and local ruling elites. To be sure, the last two decades are also a period in which the growing presence of Haitians in the Dominican Republic has met great resistance on the part of those who still operate under anti-Haitian ideology. Yet, as sociologists Guy Alexandre (2013) and Rubén Silié (2014) clearly demonstrate, both countries initiated a stage of "rapprochement" due, in part, to these structural changes in the Dominican economy, which led to a diversification of Haitian migrants, who from then on, were not relegated to the plantations but were rather hired to work in the construction and agricultural industries. This rapprochement was also a result of the fall of Duvalier in 1986, a change in political dynamics that corresponded, on the Dominican side, to an era of relative respect for civil liberties. During this period between 1986 and 2005, the media, professional, intellectual, and artistic circles of both sides begin to display mutual interest and respect. Further, as Alexandre has maintained, the embargo imposed on Haiti by the United Nations and the Organization of American States (OAS) to penalize those who had overthrown democratically elected President Jean-Bertrand Aristide provoked an emergence of a commercial relationship between the two nations never seen in the modern history of the island, causing an "explosion" of exports of Dominican products to Haiti (Alexandre, 91–95). This "rapprochement" ended in 2005, as Leonel Fernández's government began a new wave of neo-nationalistic discourses and discriminatory state practices that culminated, under his successor Danilo Medina's regime, with court ruling 168-13, effective retroactively to 1929, which, in clear violation of their human rights, deprived hundreds of thousands of Afro-Dominicans and Dominicans of Haitian descent from their citizenship. Against this backdrop, the murder of a Dominican businesswoman in Hatillo Palma, a town in the province of Montecristi near the border with Haiti, was attributed (though never proven) to local Haitian residents, prompting a veritable witch hunt in the area (Alexandre 95; Coupeau, 154; Yacou, 122).

---

[7] For a detailed discussion of the imposition of the sugar-cane industry to serve US interests, see Bernardo Vega, *Trujillo y Haití*. Santo Domingo: Fundación Cultural Dominicana, 1988.

Then again, in the aftermath of the 2010 earthquake, animosities were put aside to give way to massive solidarity toward Haiti, creating perhaps what Lorgia García-Peña (2013) identified as a "rupture" in official anti-Haitian narratives. This rupture, I might add, was short-lived, however, as court ruling 168–13 fueled, again, the fans of anti-Haitianism.

Dominican Diasporic Literary Production

Since until recently much of Dominican literary and cultural production has been in the hands of conservative sectors of the ruling elite, it is not surprising to see references to Haiti or Haitians marred by stereotypes that reproduce earlier vilifications. Rare early dissident voices include those of Ramón Marrero Aristy (1913–1959) and Juan Bosch (1909–2001), who denounced the mistreatment of Haitian workers in the sugar plantations in the novel *Over* (1939) and the short story "Luis Pie" (1946), respectively. Only in the twenty-first century and mostly in the works of writers living abroad does a significant denunciation of this mistreatment emerge in Dominican literary and cultural production.

The presence of Dominican writers in the United States can be traced to the early twentieth century, with the arrival of politicians, scholars, and writers who left the country for political reasons.[8] However, massive migration of Dominicans to the United States begins in the 1960s, creating the conditions for the emergence of a "diaspora," that is, a collectivity of immigrants bonded by their common national origin, whose numbers and geographical proximity allow them to develop political awareness of their social and economic impact in both the country of origin and the host country.[9] Most of these Dominicans relocated primarily to New York, New Jersey, Florida, and Massachusetts. To be sure, this diaspora is not homogeneous. As critic Silvio Torres-Saillant (2012) has noted, its literary production is split between those who, having arrived as adults, write in

---

[8] During the first half of the century, most of these writers belonged to the upper class, and included José M. Bernard, Fabio Fiallo Cabral, Manuel Florentino Cestero, Gustavo Bergés Bordas, Angel Rafael Lamarche, Virginia de Peña, and Andrés Francisco Requena (Cocco and Gutiérrez, 2001). Torres-Saillant (2012) classifies these individuals as "before the diaspora" as they wrote from an exilic position, in Spanish, and perceived themselves "away from home," even when the fantasized return to the Dominican Republic after the end of the Trujillo dictatorship never took place (424–25).

[9] For a thought-provoking discussion on diasporas' heterogeneous condition, especially those from the Caribbean, see Jana Evans Braziel, "Diasporic Disciplining of Caliban? Haiti, the Dominican Republic, and Intra-Caribbean Politics," in *Small Axe 26*, 12: 2 (2008): 149–159.

Spanish, and those who, born or raised in the United States, write in English. The first group includes, among others, Norberto James Rawlings, Marianela Medrano, Yrene Santos, Virginia Moore, Julio Alvarado, Diógenes Abreu, César Sánchez Beras, Raquel Virginia Cabrera, José de la Rosa, Eduardo Lantigua, Dagoberto López, Juan Tineo, Osiris Mosquea, Kianny Antigua, Keiselim Montás, and Rey Andújar. Recently arrived writers belonging to this group include Aurora Arias and Rita Indiana Hernández, both of whom were already established in their careers when they moved to the United States.

Dominican writers who publish in English include Junot Díaz, author of the short story collections *Drown* (1997) and *This is How You Lose Her* (2012), as well as of the acclaimed novel *The Brief and Wondrous Life of Oscar Wao* (2008), winner of the 2008 National Book Critics Circle Award and the 2008 Pulitzer Prize, and Julia Alvarez, author of the novels *How the García Girls Lost Their Accent* (1991), *In the Time of the Butterflies* (1994), *Yo!* (1997), *In the Name of Salomé* (2000), *Saving the World* (2006), the essay collection *Something to Declare* (1998), the poetry collections *The Other Side/El Otro Lado* (1995), *Homecoming* (1996), and *The Woman I Kept to Myself* (2004), and several children's and young adult books. Alvarez has also received numerous honors and awards, including the 2013 National Medal of the Arts. This category also includes Rhina Espaillat, a recipient of numerous poetry awards and the author of eight poetry collections, including *Lapsing to Grace* (1992), *Where Horizons Go* (1998), *Rehearsing Absence* (2001), *Mundo y Palabra/The World and the Word* (2001), *The Shadow I Dress In* (2004), *The Story-Teller's Hour* (2004), and *Playing at Stillness* (2003), winner of the 2003 National Poetry Book Award. Other writers in this category include Annecy Báez, author of *My Daughter's Eyes and Other Stories* (2007); Angie Cruz, author of the novels *Soledad* (2001) and *Let It Rain Coffee* (2005), a finalist in the 2007 International IMPAC Dublin Literary Award; Ana-Maurine Lara, whose debut novel *Erzulie's Skirt* (2007) was a Lambda Literary Award finalist; Loida Maritza Pérez, author of the novel *Geographies of Home* (2000); Nelly Rosario, author of *Songs of the Water Saints: A Novel* (2002), winner of a 2002 PEN/Open Book Award; and Alan Cambeira, author of *Azúcar: The Story of Sugar* (2001), *Azúcar's Sweet Hope..: Her Story Contiues* (2004), and *Tattered Paradise: Azúcar's Trilogy Ends!* (2008), a trilogy denouncing the exploitation of Haitian and Dominican workers in sugar plantations in the Dominican Republic.

A third category of Dominican diasporic authors includes those who alternate between English and Spanish, either by making substantial switches from one language to the other within a text or by writing entire pieces in either language. This category includes Josefina Báez, author of several texts for performance, including *Dominicanish* (2000), *Comrade Bliss Ain't Playing* (2008), and *Levente no. Yolayorkdominicanyork* (2011); Juan Dicent, author of the collections *Summertime* (2007), *Poeta en Animal Planet* (2007), *My Uncle's First Jeans y otros tíos* (2009), *Winterness* (2012), and *Monday Street* (2013); and Francis Mateo, author of the poetry collection *Ubre Urbe* (2013).

These three groups of diasporic authors most often address themes typical of the migration experience, including loss and separation from the home country, nostalgia, the difficulties of adaptation to the new culture, life in inner-city poverty, fragmentation and dysfunction of families, complicated racial and gendered identities, and feelings of ambivalence toward the home culture. Some writers also explore historical figures or events in the Dominican Republic, including dictator Rafael Trujillo, the Mirabal sisters, Camila and Salomé Ureña, or the 1916–1924 U.S. occupation. While most scholarly attention has been devoted to works by Julia Alvarez, Junot Díaz, and, to a lesser extent, Nelly Rosario, Angie Cruz, Josefina Báez, and Rita Indiana Hernández, much remains to be explored in the production of Rhina Espaillat, Alan Cambeira, Ana-Maurine Lara, Juan Dicent, and the numerous authors who publish primarily in Spanish.

Haitian Diasporic Literary Production

The Haitian diaspora is equally diverse and heterogeneous. Although its history can be traced from 1804 onward, two important moments are 1957, when Haitians began to leave the island as political refugees from the Duvalier dictatorship, and the 1990s, as a result of instability provoked by the coup against Aristide.[10] The first wave of exiles included upper- and middle-class French-educated individuals who moved to France, Canada, and French-speaking African countries. The second wave comprised hundreds of thousands of working-class, Creole-speaking Haitians who chose the Dominican Republic, Cuba, and other Caribbean islands, but also major cities in the

---

[10] For a detailed history of Haitian migration in the nineteenth and twentieth centuries, see Richard Laguerre, *Diasporic Citizenship: Haitian Americans in Transnational America*. New York: Palgrave MacMillan, 1998. In addition, for a study on Haitian literary production in the United States between 1940 and 1986, see Jean Jonassaint "Des productions littéraires haïtiennes aux États-Unis (1948–1986)." *Journal of Haitian Studies*, Vol. 5/6 (1999–2000), pp. 4–19. Jonassaint indicates that in the 1940s and 1950s, this migration was small, since Haiti enjoyed a period of relative prosperity and stability. The few Haitian writers who either wrote or published their works, or had them translated into English during this period include Philippe Toby-Marcelin, Marie Vieux Chauvet, and Jacques Roumain.

United States, including New York, Miami, and Boston. Still others relocated to Chicago, Los Angeles, Washington, DC, and New Orleans (Laguerre 75–76).

As with Dominican authors, who can be divided by their choice of language, Haitian writers can be split between those who write in French and those who prefer English.[11] The first group is located primarily in Canada or France, and includes, among many others, Robert Berrouët-Oriol, Gérard Bloncourt, Louis-Phillipe Dalembert, René Depestre, Joel Des Rosiers, Danny Laferriere, Jean Métellus, Rodney Saint-Eloi, and Anthony Phelps. Other French-speaking authors include Paul Laraque, who also writes in Creole, Michèle Voltaire Marcelin, who also writes in Spanish and English, and Jean-Pierre Richard Narcisse.[12] Among those who write in English, the best-known is Edwidge Danticat, author of acclaimed novels and short-story collections *Breath, Eyes, Memory* (1994), *Krik? Krak!* (1996), *The Farming of Bones* (1998), *The Dew Breaker* (2004), *Claire of the Sea Light* (2013), and several young-adult books, essay collections, and edited anthologies. She too has received numerous awards and prizes, including the 2007 National Book Critics Circle Award and the National Book Award for her memoir *Brother, I'm Dying* (2007).

Curiously, except for Danticat's work, literary production in English by Haitian-American writers has escaped scholarly attention, as they are studied neither under the rubric of Francophone Haitian authors nor under that of Caribbean or Latino/a writers. In contrast to the scholarship on diasporic Dominicans, which devotes most of its attention to English-speaking authors, scholars specializing in Haitian literature have ignored the production of Anglophone Haitian diaspora writers. One possible cause for exclusion might be the compartmentalization of literary studies in U.S. academia, where literary productions are often categorized by language and national origin, thus unwittingly reproducing much of the colonial legacy of a fragmented Caribbean. In addition, the role of African-American literature and scholarship might have fallen short, as Haitian critic Jean Jonassaint suggested, to recognize the contributions of Haitian-American production. Further, as Jonassaint pointed out, the type of questions and issues raised by Haitian-American productions may not have been the same as the ones raised in mainstream African-American

[11] Although some writers, including Lyonel Trouillot and others, have chosen Haitian Creole as a language of literary expression, most of their works have been published in Haiti, not the United States or other host countries.
[12] Jonassaint, ibid.

literary production.[13] In fact, the much and rightly-deserved attention lavished upon Edwidge Danticat may have had the unintended consequence of keeping the works of other Haitian-American authors in her shadow, despite her own laudable efforts in editing their works into three notable anthologies.[14]

In addition to Danticat, English-speaking Haitian-American writers include Roxane Gay, author of the essay collections *Ayiti* (2011) and *Bad Feminist* (2014), and of *An Untamed State* (2014), a remarkable novel about a young Haitian-American woman who is kidnapped as she visits her wealthy family in Haiti; Boston Poet Laureate Danielle Legros Georges, author of *Maroon* (2001); Marilène Phipps-Kettlewell, who published *Crossroads and Unholy Water* (2000), winner of the Grolier Poetry Prize and the Crab Orchard Poetry Prize, and *The Company of Heaven: Stories from Haiti* (2010), winner of the Iowa Short Fiction Award; Marie-Helène Laforest, author of the short-story collection *Foreign Shores* (2002); Myriam Chancy, who has published several scholarly books on Caribbean women writers as well as the novels *Spirit of Haiti* (2003), *The Scorpion's Claw* (2005), and *The Loneliness of Angels* (2010), which won the 2011 Guyana Prize for Literature; Jean-Robert Cadet, author of the memoir *Restavek: From Haitian Slave Child to Middle Class American* (1998), and Lily Dauphin, author of the novel *I will Fly Again: A Restavek* (2007), both of which are haunting accounts of the horrors of child slavery in Haiti; and Joanne Hyppolite, author of the children's books *Seth and Samona* (1995) and *Ola Shakes It Up* (1998). In addition, the work of these authors and others, such as Francie Latour, Jean-Pierre Benoit, Katya Ulysse, Babette Wainwright, and Ibi Zoboi, has also appeared in anthologies of other Anglophone Caribbean, African-American and African diasporic authors.[15] Last but not least, Gina Athena Ulysse, a poet, performance artist, activist, and professor of Anthropology at Wesleyan University has recently drawn international attention for her *Why Haiti Needs New Narratives: A Post-Quake Chronicle* (2015).

---

[13] Jonassaint, ibid, p. 12.
[14] Indeed, without these anthologies, it would have been far more difficult to identify these works. See Edwidge Danticat, *The Butterfly's Way, Voices from the Haitian Dyaspora in the United States.* New York: Soho Press, 2001; *Haiti Noir.* New York: Akashic Books, 2011; and *Haiti Noir 2.* New York: Akashic Books, 2014.
[15] See Marion Rohrleitner, and Sarah E. Ryan, *Dialogues across Diasporas: Women Writers, Scholars, and Activists of Africana and Latina Descent in Conversation.* Lanham: Lexington Books, 2013.

The Diasporic Condition: An Equalizing Moment

Haitian-American authors address questions similar to those tackled by their Dominican counterparts, including feelings of loss, nostalgia, and ambivalence for the homeland, difficulties of adaptation to and inclusion in the new culture, race and/or class issues, stereotypes, and historical figures and events. For instance, Joanne Hyppolyte's "Dyaspora" (2001) reveals the negotiations an immigrant child must make between the world inside her home, filled with Haitian food, music, and culture, and the world outside, filled with stereotypes about Haitians. Her account and that of Katya Ulysse in "Mashe Petion" (2001) poignantly reflect on the losses migration entails, evoking Julia Alvarez's *How the García Girls Lost Their Accent*, Junot Díaz's *Drown*, Angie Cruz's *Soledad*, and Josefina Baez's *Dominicanish*, all of which deal with the negotiations that children of immigrants must make in the host country. But, as Hyppolite decries, Haitian Americans must also contend with common stereotypes constantly reproduced by pervasive images of Haiti in mainstream media, including images of "boat people" arriving on Florida's shores and narratives linking Haitians to stigmatized diseases such as AIDS, tuberculosis, and, most recently, cholera. Hyppolite's lament echoes those of Francie Latour in "Made Outside" (2001) on how established images of misery and suffering as well as television series or Hollywood movies on zombies have contributed to an overall negative construction of Haiti. They and other Haitian writers rightly argue that poverty, disease, and natural catastrophe are not the only stories Haiti has to offer.

Both Dominican and Haitian authors also contend with questions of race, as they emerge in the homeland and in the new home. For instance, Myriam Chancy notes in "Lazarus Rising: An Open Letter to My Daughter" (2001), "it was in Winnipeg, a prairie city in the middle of the country, that I was to find out categorically what it meant to be black in a country not your own" (226). She also comments on her offended dignity as a Haitian woman, when she discovers how blacks are expected to behave in certain areas of the United States: "How dare a young, brown woman walk down the street and hold up her head high, and smile, and look people in the eye? This is what I did, not knowing I was meant to look down and away, and step aside" (226). In contrast, in "Vini Nou Bèl" (2001), Annie Grégoire refers to the internalized racism she experienced as a Haitian child growing up in Brooklyn, as when she

> heard and saw some students being teased about the darkness of their skin, a few still compared the tint of the inner surface of their forearms to determine their true hue ... I thought about the irony of Haitian history:

the first independent black nation to successfully revolt against oppression and yet, among some of us feelings of inferiority still lurk, keeping Haitians of different classes and skin tones divided. (161)

Grégoire's observation evokes Marie-Helène Laforest's perception, as when, in "Homelands" (2001), she notes the shock that U.S. racism provoked in her family, who "had not been black before leaving the Caribbean," since, in Haiti, their lighter skin and wealth made them "white" (23). Her remark on how exile in the United States became an "equalizer" in terms of race and class evokes observations made by Silvio Torres-Saillant, who noted the "epistemic shift" many Dominicans experience in racial self-perception when they confront the dominant racial paradigm in the United States (2003). Then again, Laforest and Saillant's remarks echo those made by Frantz Fanon in *Peau noire, masques blancs* (1952), in reference to the Antilleans (from Martinique and other French Caribbean islands) who think of themselves as "Antillais" and are shocked to "discover" their blackness in social interactions in France. Indeed, the often-criticized concerns of Dominicans who obsess with "whitening" the race are similar to Laforest's mother, who "had an obsession with her lower lip and consequently with mine, reminding me all the time to pull it in" (30). Later on, as she comes of age during the civil-rights movement, Laforest realizes her need to identify with the black community, becoming part of the African-American revolution. As she states: "Exile had made me black" (30).

Laforest, who grew up between New York City and San Juan, Puerto Rico, and is currently a professor of postcolonial literature at the University of Naples, Italy, also explores questions of class. In her short story collection *Foreign Shores* (2002), especially "The Wish Book," "Marguerite's Flowers," and "Ma's Household," she addresses the deeply intricate racial and class relations of Haitian society. A similar emphasis on class permeates Marie-Ketsya Theodore-Pharel in "Haiti: A Cigarette Burning at Both Ends" (2001) and Jean-Robert Cadet, in *Restavek: From Haitian Child Slave to Middle Class American* (1998). Poets of both sides of the island, such as Julia Alvarez and Marilene Phipps-Kettlewell, who, coincidentally, belong to the upper class and received elite educations in the United States, also offer a lens informed by class awareness. Indeed, Alvarez comes from a family able to send her to boarding school in the States, after which she earned a degree in English at Middlebury College, an MFA at Syracuse University, and has been a professor and a writer-in-residence at Middlebury College for the past thirty years. Similarly, Haitian poet, painter, and short-story writer Marilene

Phipps-Kettlewell comes from a middle-class family in Haiti and has lived in France and the United States. She earned a degree in anthropology at the University of California, Berkeley, an MFA at the University of Pennsylvania, and has won fellowships from the Guggenheim Foundation and Harvard's W. E. B. DuBois Institute. Many of Alvarez's and Phipps-Kettlewell's stories and poems resemble one another in style and content, as they insert words in French and Creole (Phipps-Kettlewell) or Spanish (Alvarez) into mostly-English poems and also discuss the presence of nannies, cooks, and other staff who populated their childhood.

Haitian and Dominican diasporic writers also address national identity constructs and what can be termed as the anxiety of authenticity, or the need and desire to be accepted or perceived as fully Haitian or Dominican, even when exile or the migratory experience leads them to contest or resist some of the constructs that make up this identity. For instance, in "Made Outside" (2001), Haitian-American Francie Latour reflects on her hyphenated condition and recounts her anxiety about not being "Haitian enough," of not belonging to Haiti, of not being "authentically" Haitian because she was "made outside," which is how those who "abandoned" Haiti to its fate seem to be perceived in Latour's work (131). As she states:

> Like many children of immigrants born and raised in the United States, I have skated precariously along the hyphen of my Haitian-American iden-tity. On one side, I bask in the efficiencies of American life: mail-order catalogs, direct-deposit checking, and interoffice envelopes. From the other side, I take the comfort food of Haitian oatmeal and tap into the ongoing debate Haitians love more than any other: politics. It's an endless menu of traits and qualities that I access and draw from, mixing and matching to fit the situation. But I knew that my return to Haiti wouldn't allow me to pick and choose as I pleased. My identity would no longer be defined by me; it would be defined by the Haitians around me. (125)

As Latour adds, the only authentic measure of Haitian-ness derives from having lived and suffered with the population in Haiti. Seen through this lens, suffering becomes synonymous with Haitian identity. As she observes, "for Haitians who have struggled through the poverty and terror of daily life, there is no room for hyphens in a person's identity. Because I have not suffered with them, I can never be of them" (131). The diasporic subject is thus seen either as a "traitor" or as an opportunity for money, food, and water since her credentials as Haitian are insufficient or inadequate (127). "I am still a stranger" (127), she laments, using a term that evokes the French "étranger" (foreigner) and "étrange" (strange).

The anxiety of, and questioning of, this alleged lack or inadequacy also appears in the works of Dominican diasporic writers, especially Julia Alvarez, who, in "With your Permission, Doña Aída," (1998) defends her right to write in English and still be accepted as Dominican; Josefina Baez, whose *Dominicanish* calls into question dominant constructs of national identity (Maríñez, 2005); and, to a broader extent, Dominican writers and scholars whose works have denounced official constructs that glorify a Hispanic ancestry, a white race, and a Catholic religion at the expense of a vilified African background (Torres-Saillant 1999a, 1999b; Candelario 2007; Díaz 2007; Rodríguez 2003). Some of these scholars and writers have seen their Dominican credentials questioned by conservative sectors that, in the Dominican Republic, attempt to de-authorize their views on the grounds that diasporic authors write in English or live abroad and are thus inadequately prepared to understand or critique social and political dynamics in the homeland (López 2013).

Finally, although friendship and solidarity between both peoples have always existed on the island, the diasporic condition has also allowed a closer relationship between the two groups. As Rubén Silié has noted, in the 1970s and 1980s when both nations were still isolated from each other, it was usually in exile or at foreign universities that Dominican and Haitian professionals met for the first time (2014, 101). And while significant bonds between writers and scholars of both diasporas still need to be nurtured, from the diaspora have emerged some of the most adamant voices condemning the mistreatment of Haitians in the Dominican Republic. This is especially the case in activist forums denouncing terrorizing migratory policies and the nefarious Dominican court ruling 168-13, vigorously protested by the New York-based group *We Are All Dominicans*, and writers Julia Alvarez, Junot Díaz, and Edwidge Danticat, who published a collective letter in *The New York Times* denouncing the ruling (Alvarez et al., 2013). Indeed, of all Haitian and Dominican diasporic writers, Díaz and Danticat have most openly and consistently professed mutual admiration and friendship. In addition to sharing the same literary agent for over twenty years, they have joined efforts many times to condemn Dominican anti-Haitian policies and ideologies.

This activism and ethic of collaboration to condemn divisive policies on the island has also emerged, to varying degrees, in recent writings by Dominican diasporic authors writing in both English and Spanish. Over the past decade, it has appeared in the story "La Sangre de Philippe" (2005) and novel *Candela* (2007), by Rey Andújar; the stories "Eyeless" and "No Excuses" in Juan Dicent's collection *Poeta en Animal Planet* (2007), and the novel

Nombres y Animales (2013) by Rita Indiana Hernández (Bustamante 2014). Junot Díaz's *The Brief and Wondrous Life of Oscar Wao* (2007) and Marianela Medrano's poem "El Corte" (2015) also make numerous references to the mistreatment of Haitians and the 1937 massacre. In addition, Alan Cambeira's *Azúcar: The Price of Sugar* (2001) and Ana-Maurine Lara's *Erzulie's Skirt* (2007) are two novels entirely devoted to the plight of Haitian immigrants in the Dominican Republic. On the Haitian side, the most renowned text on this subject is Danticat's *The Farming of Bones* (1998). Although not all diasporic authors have adopted a position of dissent from state-sponsored anti-Haitianism, those who have may have been compelled to do so as a result of their own experience as immigrants, their access to debates on racial discrimination, and an overall autonomy from political strictures imposed on writers and intellectuals in the homeland.

By contrast, as critic Leon-François Hoffman (2008) observed in his study of the presence of Dominicans in Haitian literature, except for the 1937 massacre and the reproduction of stereotypes of Dominican women as prostitutes in Haiti, Dominicans are rarely the focus of attention in Haitian literature. This may be due in part to what Rubén Silié (2014) identified as an indifference that developed as a response to recurrent news about the mistreatment of Haitians (105). The lack of references to, or interest in, Dominican issues other than the mistreatment of Haitians seems to be the case in the works of diasporic writers as well, except for Myriam Chancy, who also claims partial Dominican ancestry and whose scholarship on racial and gender identities in the Caribbean (2012) has included works by Julia Alvarez and Loida Maritza Pérez. She also collaborated with Dominican scholar Ginetta Candelario in producing the first-ever roundtable between two Haitian women writers, Edwidge Danticat and herself, and two Dominican writers, Nelly Rosario and Loida Maritza Pérez, in the journal *Meridians* (2004). As the introduction of this collective interview states, "the authors sought to provide a forum for the productive exchange of imagined and real Dominican/Haitian realities and to celebrate women's voices from the beleaguered island by representing a small but forceful coalition of contemporary women writers from Hispaniola" (69). Their roundtable addresses subjects ranging from the relationship with the homeland to racial and gender issues, history, politics, and the relations between both nations.

Interestingly, the works of Dominican and Haitian authors also appear together, among other diasporic authors, in anthologies such as *The Beacon Best of 1999: Creative Writing by Women and Men of All Colors*, edited by Ntozake Shange, with works by Marilene Phipps, Junot Díaz, and Danielle

Legros Georges; *The Beacon Best of 2001: Great Writing by Women and Men of All Colors and Cultures*, edited by Junot Díaz, with works by Edwidge Danticat, Myriam Chancy, Josefina Baez, and Rhina Espaillat; and *Dialogues across Diasporas: Women Writers, Scholars, and Activists of Africana and Latina Descent in Conversation* (2015), edited by Marion Rohrleitner and Sarah E. Ryan, with works by Myriam Chancy, Angie Cruz, Ana-Maurine Lara, and Nelly Rosario. This joint attention confirms the view that the diasporic condition can eliminate, to a certain extent, the nationalistic barriers that trouble Haitian and Dominican relations on the island.

Indeed, some Dominican diasporic authors have begun to "cross the border," reaching out to Haiti itself, and getting to know this neighboring country, which Julia Alvarez depicts as that "sister that I hardly knew." In *A Wedding in Haiti* (2011), Alvarez recounts her experience as she travels to Haiti for the first time to attend the wedding of Piti, a young Haitian man she hired to work in her coffee farm in the Dominican Republic and for whom she developed such affection that she agreed to sponsor the wedding party as "madrina" or godmother. The account evokes her mixed feelings of affection, curiosity, and apprehension as she travels to Haiti, an act that is particularly laudable considering the heavy taboo that crossing to "the other side" has become in the Dominican psyche. It is perhaps due to this strong psychological and political barrier that, despite the abundance of critical and literary works about the presence of Haiti in the Dominican Republic, so few have genuinely attempted to represent Haitian geography and culture, and very few do so without the usual clichés and stereotypes. Alvarez repeated her gesture with the publication of the poem "There are Two Countries" (2013), which rewrites the celebrated poem "Hay un país en el mundo," by Dominican National Poet Pedro Mir, to inscribe the presence of Haiti as a sibling nation with whom Dominicans share an island home.

Another gesture in this direction is the novel *Marassá y la Nada* (2013) by Berlin-based Alanna Lockward, a Dominican journalist and art curator who was one of the first to venture into Haiti in the 1990s to cover various political and social events, notably the accession of Aristide, the coup that overthrew him, and the presence of Dominican immigrants in Haiti. A recent compilation of these articles titled *Un Haití dominicano* (2014) offers an insider's perspective on Haitian-Dominican relations devoid of traditional fatalist narratives about Haiti or the relations between the two nations. The significance of *Marassá y la Nada* resides in the importation of the term *Marassá*, the Sacred Twins of the voudoun pantheon. As I have argued elsewhere (Maríñez 2016), the figure of Marassa carries significant symbolic import by offering an alternative paradigm for modeling a new relation between both nations. Rather than reproducing old cannibalistic constructs of Haiti in the Dominican imagination, Marassa could provide a foundational narrative representing both nations as twins born of the same mother (island), who become empowered when united and in harmony. Within this paradigm, the Dossou or Dossa, the child born after the twins (a possible figure for the diasporic subject), could reinforce the strength of its symbolic siblings.

In sum, the literary production of both diasporic groups potentially opens avenues of understanding between the two nations. Their immigrant status has yielded perspectives that could enrich mutual debate and interest in the sibling nation on their shared island. As Haitian-Dominican studies continue to grow, comparative studies of this diasporic production will also enrich Latina/o literary history. Incorporating the writings of both Haitian and Dominican diasporic authors introduces two new languages–French, Kreyol, and combinations of these with English–into the heterolingualism that Latina/o and African-diasporic literary histories are uniquely positioned to theorize. Careful study of the literary texts from the sibling nations and their diasporas will illuminate future discussions about multilingualism, race, class, and colonialism in scholarly research and literary history.

WORKS CITED

Aldama, Frederick Luis, ed. *The Routledge Concise History of Latino/a Literature*, London and New York: Routledge, 2013.

Alexandre, Guy. *Pour Haïti. Pour la République Dominicaine: Interventions, positions et propositions pour une gestion responsable des relations bilatérales*. Pétion-Ville, Haiti: C3 Editions, 2013.

"Algunos aspectos de evolución del Estado dominicano entre 1918 y 2011. Materiales para un análisis," in *Haití y República Dominicana: Miradas desde el siglo XXI*. André Corten., ed Pétion-Ville, Haiti: C3 Editions, 2013, pp. 81–100

Alvarez, Julia, Junot Díaz, Edwidge Danticat and Mark Kurlanksy. "Two Versions of One Tale," *The New York Times*, October 31, 2013.

Alvarez, Julia. "There are Two Countries," *Afro-Hispanic Review* 32.2 (2013): 145–48.

A Wedding in Haiti. New York: Penguin, 2011.

Saving the World. Chapel Hill: Algonquin, 2006.

The Woman I Kept to Myself. Chapel Hill: Algonquin, 2004.

In the Name of Salomé. Chapel Hill: Algonquin, 2000.

Something to Declare. Chapel Hill: Algonquin, 1998.

"Doña Aída, with Your Permission," in *Brújula/Compass* 28 (Winter 1998), reprinted in *Something to Declare*. New York: Algonquin, 1998, pp. 171–76.

Yo! Chapel Hill: Algonquin, 1997.

Homecoming: New and Collected Poems. New York: Plume, 1996.

The Other Side/El Otro Lado. New York: Dutton, 1995.

In the Time of the Butterflies. Chapel Hill: Algonquin, 1994.

How the García Girls Lost Their Accent. Chapel Hill: Algonquin, 1991.

Baez, Annecy. *My Daughter's Eyes and Other Stories*. Willimanctic: Curbstone Press, 2007.

Baez, Josefina. *Levente no. Yolayorkdominicanyork*. New York: Ay Ombe Theatre, 2011.

Comrade Bliss Ain't Playing. New York: Ay Ombe Theatre/I Om Be Press, 2008.

Dominicanish. New York: I Ombe, 2000.

Bosch, Juan. "Luis Pie," *Cuentos*. Havana: Casa de las Américas, 1983, pp. 10–17.

Bost, Suzanne, and Francis R. Aparicio, eds., *The Routledge Companion to Latino/a Literature*. London and New York: Routledge, 2012.

Bustamante, Fernanda. "Representar el «problema de lo haitiano» o el problema de representar lo haitiano: una lectura de textos literarios dominicanos del 2000." *452 °F Revista Electrónica de teoría de la literatura y literatura comparada* 11 (2014): 125–41. www.452f.com/pdf/numero11/11_452f-mis-fernanda-bustamante-orgnl.pdf.

Cambeira, Alan. *Azúcar! The Story of Sugar*. Belecam & Associates, Inc, 2001.

Candelario, Ginetta. *Black behind the Ears: Dominican Racial Identity from Museums to Beauty Shops*. Durham: Duke University Press, 2007.

Cassá, Roberto. *Historia social y económica de la República Dominicana*, Santo Domingo, Dominican Republic: Editora Alfa y Omega, 2001.

Chancy, Myriam. *From Sugar to Revolution: Women's Visions of Haiti, Cuba, and the Dominican Republic*. Waterloo: Wilfrid Laurier University Press, 2012.

The Loneliness of Angels. Leeds: Peepal Tree, 2010.

The Scorpion's Claw. Leeds: Peepal Tree Press, 2005.

Spirit of Haiti. London: Mango Publications, 2003.

Lazarus Rising: An Open Letter to My Daughter," *The Butterfly's Way, Voices from the Haitian Dyaspora in the United States* in Edwidge Danticat, ed. New York: Soho Press, 2001, pp. 223–40.

Framing Silence: Revolutionary Novels by Haitian Women. New Brunswick: Rutgers University Press, 1997.

Cocco de Filippis, Daisy, and Franklyn Gutiérrez, eds. *Literatura dominicana en los Estados Unidos: Presencia temprana 1900–1950*. Santo Domingo, Dominican Republic: Editora Búho, 2001.

Coupeau, Steeve, *The History of Haiti*. Wesport: Greenwood Press, 2008.

Cruz, Angie. *Let It Rain Coffee*. New York: Simon & Schuster, 2005.

Soledad, New York: Simon & Schuster, 2001.

Danticat, Edwidge. *Haiti Noir 2*. New York: Akashic Books, 2014.

Haiti Noir 2. New York: Akashic Books, 2014.

Claire of the Sea Light. New York: Knopf, 2013.

Haiti Noir. New York: Akashic Books, 2011.

Brother, I'm Dying. New York: Knopf, 2007.

The Dew Breaker. New York: Knopf, 2004.

The Butterfly's Way, Voices from the Haitian Dyaspora in the United States. New York: Soho Press, 2001.

The Farming of Bones. New York: Soho Press, 1998.

Krik? Krak! New York: Soho Press, 1995.

Breath, Eyes, Memory. New York: Vintage Books, 1994.

Díaz, Junot. *This Is How You Lose Her*. New York: Riverhead Books, 2012.

The Brief and Wondrous Life of Oscar Wao. New York: Riverhead Books, 2007.

The Beacon Best of 2001: Great Writing by Women and Men of All Colors and Cultures. Boston, MA: Beacon Press, 2001.

Drown. New York: Riverhead Books, 1996.

Dicent, Juan, *Monday Street.* San José, Costa Rica: Editorial Germinal, 2013.

Winterness. Santo Domingo, Dominican Republic: Ediciones de a poco, 2012.

My Uncle's First Jeans y otros tíos. Córdoba, Argentina: Textos de Cartón, 2009.

Summertime. Buenos Aires, Argentina: Santiago Arcos, 2007.

Poeta en Animal Planet. Buenos Aires, Argentina: Ediciones Vox 7 y 13, 2007.

Eller, Anne. We *Dream Together: Dominican Independence, Haiti, and the Fight for Caribbean Freedom* Durham: Duke University Press, 2016.

Espaillat, Rhina. *Her Place in These Designs.* Kirksville: Truman State University Press, 2008.

Playing at Stillness. Kirksville: Truman State University Press, 2005.

Story-Teller's Hour. Louisville: Scienter Press, 2004.

The Shadow I Dress In: Poems. Cincinnati: David Robert Books, 2004.

Greatest Hits, 1942–2001. Johnstown: Pudding House Publications, 2003.

Mundo y Palabra / The World and the Word. Durham: Oyster River Press, 2001.

Rehearsing Absence: Poems. Evansville: University of Evansville Press, 2001

Where Horizons Go: Poems. Kirksville: New Odyssey Press, 1998.

Lapsing to Grace. East Lansing: Bennett and Kitchel, 1992.

Evans Braziel, Jana. "Diasporic Disciplining of Caliban? Haiti, the Dominican Republic, and Intra-Caribbean Politics," in Small Axe 26, 12: 2 (2008): 149–159.

Fanon, Frantz, *Peau noire, masques blancs.* Paris: Seuil, 1952

Franco Pichardo, Franklyn. *Du racisme et de l'anti-haïtianisme.* Pétion-Ville, Haiti: C3 Editions, 2013.

Historia del Pueblo Dominicano. Santo Domingo: Sociedad Editorial Dominicana, 1992.

García-Peña, Lorgia. "Un-bordering Hispaniola: David Pérez's Performance Actions of Haitian-Dominican Solidarity. *Afro-Hispanic Review.* 32.2 (2013): 57–70.

Gay, Roxane. *An Untamed State.* New York: Black Cat, 2014.

Bad Feminist: Essays. New York: Harper Perennial, 2014.

Ayiti. Phoenix, AZ: Artistically Declined Press, 2011.

González, Raymundo. "El Comegente, una rebelión campesina al final del periodo colonial." *En Homenaje a Emilio Cordero Michel.* Santo Domingo: Academia Dominicana de la Historia, 2004, pp. 175–224.

Grégoire, Annie. "Vini Nou Bèl," *The Butterfly's Way: Voices from the Haitian Dyaspora in the United States* in Edwidge Danticat, ed. New York: Soho Press, 2001, pp. 156–63.

Hoffman, Léon-Francois. "La République dominicaine dans la fiction haïtienne," *The Caribbean Writer as Warrior of the Imaginary: L'ecrivain Caribéen, guerrier de l'imaginaire* in Kathleen Gyssels and Bénédicte Ledent, eds. Amsterdam: Rodopi, 2008, pp. 345–57.

Hyppolite, Joanne. "Dyaspora," *The Butterfly's Way: Voices from the Haitian Dyaspora in the United States* in Edwidge Danticat, ed. New York: Soho Press, 2001, pp. 7–11.

Ola Shakes It Up. New York: Delacorte Press, 1998.

Seth and Samona: New York: Delacorte Press, 1995.

Jáuregui, Carlos. "El 'Negro Comegente': Terror, colonialismo y etno-política." *Afro-Hispanich Review* 28.1 ((2009): 45–79.

Johnson, Sarah E. *The Fear of French Negroes: Transcolonial Collaboration in the Revolutionary Americas.* Berkeley and Los Angeles: University of California Press, 2012.

Jonassaint, Jean. "Des productions littéraires haïtiennes aux États-Unis (1948–1986)." *Journal of Haitian Studies* 5.6 (1999–2000): 4–19.

Laforest, Marie-Hélène. *Foreign Shores*. Montreal: CIDIHCA, 2002.

"Homelands," *The Butterfly's Way: Voices from the Haitian Dyaspora in the United States* in Edwidge Danticat, ed. New York: Soho Press, 2001, pp. 23–30.

Laguerre, Richard. *Diasporic Citizenship: Haitian Americans in Transnational America*. New York: Palgrave MacMillan, 1998.

Lara, Ana-Maurine. *Erzulie's Skirt*. Washington, DC: RedBone Press, 2006.

Latour, Francie. "Made Outside," *The Butterfly's Way: Voices from the Haitian Dyaspora in the United States* in Edwidge Danticat, ed. New York: Soho Press, 2001, pp. 125–31.

Legros Georges, Danielle. *Maroon*. Willimantic: Curbstone Press, 2001.

Lister, Elissa L. *Le Conflit haïtiano-dominicain dans la littérature caribéenne (El conflicto domínico-haitiano en la literatura caribeña)*. Pétion-Ville, Haiti: C3 Editions, 2013.

Lockward, Alanna. *Un Haití dominicano*. Santo Domingo, Dominican Republic: Santuario, 2014.

Marassá y la Nada. Santo Domingo, Dominican Republic: Santuario, 2013.

Lopez, Oscar. "Is Junot Diaz Dominican Enough? Writers Question His Loyalty and Think He's 'Offensive,'" *Latintimes.com*, December 2, 2013.

Lora H., Quisqueya. "La construcción de Haití en el imaginario dominicano del siglo XIX," in *República Dominicana y Haití: El derecho a vivir*. Santo Domingo: Fundación Juan Bosch, 2014, pp. 171–204.

Maeseneer, Rita De. "The Contemporary Dominican Literature in the Caribbean Perspective," *Caribbean Interfaces* in Lieven d' Hulst, et al., eds. Amsterdam and New York: Rodopi, 2007, pp. 349–51.

Encuentro con la narrativa dominicana contemporánea. Madrid and Frankfurt: Iberoamericana/Vervuert, 2006.

Maríñez, Sophie. "Mito y feminismo en *Marassá y la Nada* de Alanna Lockward,". *Revista Canadiense de Estudios Hispánicos* 42.2 (2016): 437–454.

"Poética de la Relación en *Dominicanish* de Josefina Báez,". *La Torre, Revista de la Universidad de Puerto Rico* 10.35 (Jan–March 2005): 149–60.

Marrero, Aristy R. *Over: Novela*. Ciudad Trujillo, Dominican Republic: Imp. La Opinión, 1939.

Martínez, Samuel. "Not a Cockfight: Rethinking Haitian-Dominican Relations,". *Latin American Perspectives* 30.3, Popular Participation against Neoliberalism (May 2003): 80–101.

Mateo, Francis. *Ubre Urbe*. New York: Dioccus, 2013.

Matibag, Eugenio. *Haitian-Dominican Counterpoint: Nation, Race, and State on Hispaniola*. New York: Palgrave-MacMillan, 2003.

Medrano, Marianela. "El Corte." *The Black Scholar: Journal of Black Studies and Research* 45.2: 67–68.

Ortíz, Ricardo. "Edwidge Danticat's 'Latinidad': *The Farming of Bones* and the Cultivation (of Fields) of Knowledge," *Aftermaths: Exile, Migration, and Diaspora Reconsidered* in Marcus Bullock and Peter Y Paik, eds. New Brunswick: Rutgers University Press, 2009, pp. 150–72.

Pérez, Loida Maritza. *Geographies of Home*. New York: Viking, 1999.

Phipps-Kettlewell, Marilène. *The Company of Heaven: Stories from Haiti*. Iowa City: University of Iowa Press, 2010.

Crossroads and Unholy Water. Carbondale: Southern Illinois University Press, 2000.

Prestol Castillo, Freddy. *El masacre se pasa a pie*. Santo Domingo, Dominican Republic: Editora Taller, 1973.

Rodríguez, Néstor. *La isla y su envés: representaciones de lo nacional en el ensayo dominicano contemporáneo*. San Juan: Instituto de Cultura Puertorriqueña, 2003.

Rohrleitner, Marion, and Sarah E. Ryan. *Dialogues across Diasporas: Women Writers, Scholars, and Activists of Africana and Latina Descent in Conversation*. Lanham: Lexington Books, 2013.

Rosario, Nelly. *Song of the Water Saints*. New York: Pantheon Books, 2002.

Silié, Rubén. "Haití y República Dominicana ¿países en conflicto o construyendo una nueva amistad?" *Conjonction: La revue franco-haïtienne de l'Institut Français en Haïti*. 2014 (226): 99–111.

Suárez, Lucía M. *The Tears of Hispaniola: Haitian and Dominican Diaspora Memory*. Gainsville: University Press of Florida, 2006.

Theodore-Pharel, Marie-Ketsya. "Haiti: A Cigarette Burning at Both Ends," *The Butterfly's Way, Voices from the Haitian Dyaspora in the United States* in Edwidge Danticat, ed. New York: Soho Press, 2001, pp. 83–88.

Torres-Saillant, Silvio. "Dominican-American Literature," *The Routledge Companion to Latino/a Literature*. in Suzanne Bost and Francis R. Aparicio, eds. London and New York: Routledge, 2012, pp. 423–35.

An Intellectual History of the Caribbean. New York: Palgrave Macmillan, 2006.

"Blackness and Meaning in Studying Hispaniola: A Review Essay." En *Small Axe*, 19 (Vol. 10:1) (March 2006), pp. 180–188.

"The Tribulations of Blackness: Stages in Dominican Racial Identity." *Calalloo* 23.3 (2003): 1086–111.

El retorno de las yolas: Ensayos sobre diáspora, democracia y dominicanidad. Santo Domingo, República Dominicana: Librería La Trinitaria, 1999.

"Introduction to Dominican Blackness," in *Dominican Studies Working Papers Series*, No. 1, New York: CUNY Dominican Studies Institute, 1999.

Ulysse, Gina A. *Why Haiti Needs New Narratives: A Post-Quake Chronicle*. Middletown: Wesleyan University Press, 2015.

Ulysse, Katya. "Mashe Petion," *The Butterfly's Way, Voices from the Haitian Dyaspora in the United States* in Edwidge Danticat, ed. New York: Soho Press, 2001, pp. 109–14.

Valerio-Holguín, Fernando. "Nuestros vecinos, los primitivos." www.academia.edu/4869993/ Nuestros_vecinos_los_primitivos_-Fernando_Valerio-Holguin. Accessed June 25, 2014.

Victoriano-Martínez, Ramón Antonio. *Rayanos y Dominicanyorks: La dominicanidad del siglo XXI*. Pittsburgh: Instituto Internacional de Literatura Iberoamericana, 2014.

Wucker, Michelle. *Why the Cock Fights? Dominicans, Haitians and the Struggle for Hispaniola*. New York: Hill and Wang, 2000.

Yacou, Alain, ed. *De l'île espagnole à la République dominicaine d'aujourd'hui*. Paris: Editions Karthala; Pointe-à-Pitre (Guadeloupe): CERC, 2010.

28

Listening to Literature

Popular Music, Voice, and Dance in the Latina/o Literary Imagination, 1980–2010

LORENA ALVARADO

In his *La Carreta Made a U-Turn* (1979), poet Tato Laviera declares himself "nothing but a historian" ("para ti, mundo bravo"). His poetry, rhythmic and resonant, chronicles the unheard and overheard in neighborhoods like El Barrio (or Spanish Harlem) and Loisaida (New York's Lower East Side). In particular, the poetry encodes the thunder of its congueros, the echoes of jíbaro *le lo lais*, the repetition of questions in the unemployment line. He proclaims to the exacting world: "I am nothing but a historian / who took your actions / and jotted them on paper" (3). His self-description challenges us to reconsider the subjects of history as sounds, voices, and music that are typically absent from the archive. The "actions" here are the everyday acts of walking or dancing, the preaching of a high priest, the rituals in honor of Santa Barbara, or Changó. His poetry engages the orality of the everyday, the sounds heard and gone, laced with the "crusty cries of ghetto hearts" and turnstiles. His attention to music and nonmusical sounds, voices, and vernacular auralities produces a radical archive of the unheard and overhead. Frances Aparicio, borrowing a term from sound studies, considers Laviera an "earwitness," foregrounding Laviera's masterful sense of hearing the diasporic Boricua and indeed, Latina/o soundscapes more broadly.[1]

---

[1] Composer and writer R. Murray Schafer coined the term "earwitness" in devising a methodology for historians interested in investigating sounds from the past that were never recorded sonically. In using Schafer's method, historians would rely on literary "earwitness accounts" in their exploration of unheard sonic phenomenon from the past. For Schafer, reliable "earwitness accounts" derive from writers that have personally and directly experienced the sonic phenomenon they document in writing (*Hearing History*, 7). Mark M. Smith assesses Schafer's criteria as limiting, given it dismisses the ways sounds are imagined and mediated regardless of direct experience, an equally necessary perspective in studying how sound is perceived and interpreted in historically

In this chapter, I consider how Latina/o writers of prose and poetry since the 1980s listen to and encode popular musical practice into their literary efforts. The making of sound (and music is part of the sonic) consists of an "interrelation of materiality and metaphor" (Novak and Sakakeeny 1), that is, music and sound are not only vibration and pulse moving through air, bodies, and other matter, but also how we express ourselves about it, be it in writing or other methods of expression. The literary texts here discussed document politics of the sonic and musical latinidad that demonstrate how the musical, as part of the sonic world, is "a basic part of how people frame their knowledge about the world" (2). How do the authors discussed in this chapter, as earwitnesses to sounds, music, or other non-logocentric forms, modulate mambo, the singing or speaking voices of fans, or the body dancing to salsa? If, as Victor Hernández Cruz asserts in his title "Listening to the music of Arsenio Rodríguez is moving closer to knowledge," what knowledge is derived from the act of listening? How are these sounds central, if not indispensable, in the development of Latina/o literature? Moreover, when Latina/o music circulates as a current of hypersexuality and tropicalization across mainstream platforms, what role does writing play in enforcing or contesting these tropes on the page? More than objects to describe, the musical constitutes a field of knowledge that yields methods of rewriting obsolete notions of Latina/o music and sound. To engage music is to engage dancing bodies or fan subcultures. The subject of analysis implies a spectrum of other popular productions, like telenovelas or the graphic novel, that intersect with the literary works I address.

Here, I consider how texts by Marta Moreno Vega, Mary Helen Ponce, Achy Obejas, Oscar Hijuelos, Sandra Cisneros, Terri de la Peña, Denise Chavez, Amina Gautier, and Cristy C. Road encode a variety of genres and voices in prose and poetry. Their works represent a diverse, though by no means absolute, range of styles and tones, of commercial visibility and independent publishing histories. In sounding out the written verb that apprehends Lavoe's soneo, Pérez Prado's grunt, or the imagined

and culturally contingent conditions. As a poet deeply attuned to the Nuyorican musical and oral vernacular, Laviera anticipates this discourse of sound studies in his documentation of noise and sounds, in addition to and beyond music. Moreover, many Latina/o authors, including those discussed in this chapter, have written as "earwitnesses" not of a faraway time necessarily, but of their contemporary moment. Latina/o literature, in this sense, has been attentive to the sonic and the musical elements of a community as a "gesture of resistance" (Aparicio 2013), as their writing also defies the silences, ineffability, and unintelligibility that has too often framed Latina/o sound in the national imaginary.

"salsa-flavored rock" of a Chicana music band, I tackle thematic and theoretical concerns ranging from dance and embodiment to listening and fan cultural practices within diaspora. As crucial listeners of Latina/o music (and critics of what Latina/o music constitutes), these authors produce, in concert, a sheet score replete with counterpoint and contradiction. This chapter explores four primary themes that emerge in engaging and mediating the musical in these texts: dance, the vocal gesture, affect and melodrama, and listening practices. These concerns are discussed in the context of romantic, familial or generational tensions, of patriarchal desire and its dissolution, of the secretive, the unspeakable, and of the ecstasy of fan subcultures. These questions of power, violence, and pleasure intertwine within the dynamics of gender and sexuality, ethnicity and race, class, as well as diaspora and geography. I begin with the mambo as historically resonant of racialized latinidad. The bolero as romantic effervescence follows. Finally, I engage publics and fan subcultures from salsa to alternative rock, as they reframe musical icons and their material and affective impacts in the intimacy of the listener's life, often defying tropes associated with latinidad in the process.

Mambo Choreographies from the Zenda to the Palladium

The mambo, as music and metaphor, often appears in the Latina/o literary landscape of the late 1980s and 1990s, from Sandra Maria Estevez's *Bluestown Mockingbird Mambo* (1990) to Achy Obejas's *Memory Mambo* (1996). The mambo's sound and emergence do not develop within a single location, not Cuba, where it does have "some of its roots" as critic Gustavo Pérez Firmat affirms, not New York, nor Mexico City, where the great Damaso Pérez Prado achieved success. The literary geographies where the mambo flourishes, from Mary Helen Ponce's Southern California fictional town of Taconos to Marta Moreno Vega's Spanish Harlem, reflect mambo and other Afro-Latino musical forms' transnational appeal and influence.

In Mary Helen Ponce's *The Wedding* (1989), set in 1950s Los Angeles, the mambo is the driving force in the wedding of Cricket and Blanca, two young, working-class pachucos. Ponce constructs the mambo's fervent reception among Mexican Americans in Southern California, and the skill that those Angeleno dancers developed, particularly in places like the Zenda Ballroom. The novel nods at the historical embrace of Afro-Caribbean and East Coast Latina/o dance practices in the West Coast. Ponce's fiction resonates with

Anthony Macia's research on mid-twentieth-century dance cultures in Los Angeles: "Los Angeles produced many skilled dancers, just as the Latin scene provided spaces for Mexican Americans and other Latinos to express a non-Anglo sexuality and sensibility, it also allowed them to claim visibility in the public sphere" (278). *The Wedding* imagines how these skills constituted forms of gendered power.

Dancing know-how bestows cultural and economic capital. Cricket disavows the mambo publicly for racist reasons – "this aint Africa" – and, moreover, feels insecure about his ability to excel on the dance floor. Unlike those of his rival-gang leader Skippy, Cricket's moves are clumsy and sloppy. More than the desire to dance with his wife Blanca on their wedding day, his attempts at the mambo are a means to claim his territory and authority. The mambo's sound is a calling to establish masculine leadership, his moving body attuned more to power than recreational pleasure, directed at his male companions more than at his wife. Blanca is a much more skilled dancer, one who enjoys her moves, "fast on her feet ... she rarely tired and could out-dance most of the Tacones" (172). Her endurance and satisfaction compete with that of the men, who eventually turn the wedding dance floor into a fight between the Tacones and their rival gang. The skill of these Los Angeles dancers serves to negotiate gendered roles and tensions between factions.

The dancing mambo body is central, as well, in Marta Moreno Vega's account of mid-twentieth-century life in El Barrio in her semi-autobiographical novel, *When the Spirits Dance Mambo* (2004). The narrator Cotito's older brother, Chachito, is an exquisite and confident dancer who frequents Hunts Point Palace, the Park Place, and the legendary Palladium ballroom. During the 1950s, the Palladium was a "social and artistic force," eventually becoming an institution of salsa and mambo that featured musicians such as Tito Puente, Frank Grillo "Machito" and his Afro-Cubans, and Miguelito Valdés, "Mr. Babalú."

The Palladium was and continues to be a site of mambo authenticity for many dancers. Before it featured Latino music, however, the Palladium was a waning foxtrot and tango club. To avoid the economic and cultural decline of the ballroom, the manager decided to open doors, for the first time, to nonwhites. In particular, he featured Afro-Cuban bands, drawing Latinos to the audience, largely working-class Puerto Rican, like Chachito. Before heading out, Chachito practices choreographies with Cotito in the family's living room to achieve smooth, impeccable, and seemingly effortless moves on the dance floor. A part-time student and worker at a dry-cleaning establishment, Chachito meticulously prepares his Palladium style. Crucial details are important to attend to before heading out the door:

> Once dressed, Chachito refused to sit or bend, lest he wrinkle his clothes and lose the all-important crisp, just-pressed look. His preparation for Palladium nights was extra special. He sent his shirts to be starched and pressed at the Chinese laundry, insisting that the launderer place them on hangers rather than folding them. Walking through the door with a bundle of plastic-wrapped clothes from the neighborhood dry cleaner's, he would hang each item up and then carefully select his outfit for the evening. . . With his newly buffed, manicured nails, he refused to do any task that would destroy his look. (119)

More than a look, his demeanor signifies a fantasy and a desire. He was a member of the young Palladium royalty by night that, as Cotito notes, by day "were just regular people like [Cotito] who lived in [her] neighborhood" (121). The preparation and performance of what dance scholar Cindy Garcia calls "sequined coporealities," dancing Latina/o bodies whose flawless glamour, impeccable outfits, and refined dance moves not only prepare them for unforgettable nights but also "mask the socioeconomic status of their daily lives [while accumulating] salsa club capital" (68). Garcia's discussion focuses on contemporary salsa practices among Central American and Mexican American dancers in Los Angeles. Yet, these politics of working-class dance emerge in the mid-century memory and contemporary memoir of a New York Puerto Rican woman. The sequined salsero corporealites in Garcia's ethnography strive to embody a deterritorialized, ahistorical, hyper-eroticized and de-Mexicanized latinidad. In 1950s New York, a young Afro-Boricua like Chachito may not be attempting to revoke his racial background in dancing mambo, but he does pivot and swing to the fantasy that "the best dances drew the prettiest women, those who were worthy of his looks, fashion sense and dancing prowess" (118). Garcia's theorization of un/sequined corporealities insist on the power and fantasy inherent in dance and the moves we make on dance floors charged with sweat, class, and racial anxieties.

Details of Latina/o Music

An aural zoom into this musical landscape is a gesture that African American studies and music studies scholar Alexandra Vazquez, through her theory of the musical detail, suggests we perform. There are many such details in the music that concerns us, particularly those that are wordless, nearly anti-literary. There are the *gritos* of rancheras, the "ay ay ays" in "Cielito Lindo" that young Lala from Sandra Cisneros's *Caramelo* (2004) so despises. In mambo, one of these may constitute Damaso Pérez Prado's guttural accent. Pérez Prado's vocal interjection evokes something akin to "dale!" or "dilo!" (say it!) while it simultaneously transgresses this logocentric interpretation. Obejas's *Memory Mambo*, despite its title, does not dedicate pages, chapters or the entire text to the music in the title. However, Pérez Prado's signature is another way to engage the mambo and, simultaneously, say the unspeakable in the diegetic text. Pérez Prado's grunt illuminates how certain musical and vocal characteristics of the genre (and sound itself) defy normative modes of telling the story, be it mambo history or Obejas's novel.

Pérez Prado's signature grunt (*"Unngh!"*) is too much for Juani, the protagonist. Juani is a young Cuban lesbian who lives in Chicago and works in her family's laundry. She comes of age in the midst of exile politics and family secrets. As she recovers from a grueling emotional and physical altercation with her last lover, she decides to leave for a few days and pay her sister Nena a visit in Miami. She yearns for this trip, to reconnect with Nena, to confide and connect again. Amid a complicated conversation with Nena, she selects a Pérez Prado record and plays it. But an inconvenience arises as she begins to listen: "The hyper-happy sound filled the room. Trumpets struggled against saxes, saxes against trombones. 'Unnngh!', grunted Prado. I couldn't take it" (191). Disturbed, she replaces it with a Beny Moré album, "with his smooth as brandy voice." Prado's music and its brassy, joyous arrangement disrupt Juani, perhaps enhancing her anxiety about the unspeakable. Moré's fluid tenor inspires ease and pleasure with his singing: Viiiidaaaaa! Soon after, Juani asks her sister Nena how she talks to her new partner about their family's history when "everybody in our family's a liar" (194). When Nena responds that she simply says what's true for her and acknowledges other people's versions, Juani dismisses the approach:

I shook my heard. "Very relative," I said. "It must take forever to tell all those stories."

"Hey we're into communicating, okay?" She said with a chuckle. It's sort of like singing 'Guantanamera,' everybody gets their chance to make up their own verse."

"Memory Mambo," I said… "one step forward, two steps back, unngh!" (194)

The grunts and vocal interjections cause anxiety at the same time they enable Juani to think through her family's dynamics, to, as Vazquez suggests, "reveal the method to her family's madness" (162). Appearing just once, the "unngh" calls attention to the extra-musical within the musical, as well as the noise, word, or instruments that puzzle us at the same time we claim them as ours. Caught for a moment in a literary landscape, Pérez Prado's grunt is not subsumed to explanation or reasoning. Vazquez offers that the grunt is key to the book. Obejas's story requires this sound's inclusion; only then is the literary resolution accomplished.

Intonations of Maria: The Bolero

The bolero, its lyrics and interpretation, recall melodrama, sensuality, romanticism, all dominant discourses of latinidad. The genre appears across the books discussed here, from Achy Obejas to Moreno Vega. It was the bolero, just as much as the mambo, that dominated in the prose of the first Latino work of fiction to win the Pulitzer Prize, Oscar Hijuelos's *The Mambo Kings Play Songs of Love* (1989). Curiously, or perhaps not surprisingly, it was a novel centered on the Latino music scene in 1950s New York that, according to Juan Flores, ushered in the "entry of 'Latino literature' onto the landscape of mainstream American letters" (*From Bomba to Hip Hop*, 167). In the afterword of the twentieth-anniversary edition, Hijuelos mentions that the reception of his 1989 novel "made a difference in the way mainstream publishers view novels by our own homegrown Latino authors" (429).

The role that music, particularly music closely identified with racialized affect, may play in the exuberant debut of the novel is intriguing. The invention of "Latin music" in the first half of the twentieth century created a commodity of exotic rhythms and imagery that catered to audiences attuned to and craving, among other clichés, fantasies of Latina/o hypersexuality and sensuality. *The Mambo Kings* continues this legacy of fascination with the "Latin," with prose that renders the female body a series of (musical) parts at the mercy of phallic dominion. These familiar tropes prevail in the text backboned not only by the mambo, but by the bolero written as part of the novel, "Beautiful Maria of My Soul."

The bolero is the foremost romantic ballad of the Americas. It emerged in Cuba in the 1880s and subsequently spread throughout the hemisphere. This decade also marked the emergence of the literary phenomenon of modernismo, which featured a turn to romantic and lush embellishments in language. According to Irma Zavala, modernity's sensual, idealizing vocabulary and symbolism influence the bolero's lavish romantic lexicon.

In the ballad tradition, women surface as divine and unreachable, as disembodied objects of desire, the source of unrequited love.

The novel's featured bolero "Beautiful Maria of My Soul" – "a song about wanting a woman even when she has abandoned you" – is an example of the bolero's ornateness grounded in feminine archetypes, most notably "the betrayer." Below is a sample of the featured song included in the text:

> What delicious pain love has brought to me
> In the form of a woman
> My torment and ecstasy,
> Maria, my life. . .
> Beautiful Maria of my soul,
>
> Why did she finally mistreat me so?
> Tell me, why is it that way?
> Why is it always so? (125)

The song addresses an absent lover and glorifies unrequited love and its painful outcome. In the process, it renders "Maria" an unattainable, diffuse, disembodied memory that simultaneously causes great pain. This writing and signing to the bewitching seductress, both virtuous and poisonous, is, as Frances Aparicio notes, "closely linked to patriarchy and to is male-gendered voices and lyrics" (*Listening to Salsa*, 128). The writing itself seems infused with the politics of lavish romanticism and graphic objectification, celebrated by critic Margo Jefferson as "rich and sorrowful . . . the language of everyday and the language of longing" ("Dancing into the Dream").

"Beautiful Maria" emulates the bolero at the same time as it fascinates in the mainstream literary marketplace. It participates in two representational genealogies – that of courtly love and masculinity in the bolero, and of domesticated, tropicalized, and hypersexual latinidad in television, film, literature and other realms of representation. The musical cameo in the text by Desi Arnaz, foundational Latino entertainment figure, upholds a particular sentimentality in regard to the latter. Arnaz is the respectable Latino musician and Cuban immigrant, whose success Hijuelos' brothers admire and whose endorsement opens doors for them. "Beautiful Maria" debuts to a national audience on his show. As Alberto Sandoval-Sanchez notes, Arnaz laid the foundations for contemporary stereotypes of Latinos in the U.S. cultural imaginary. The text capitalizes on this master icon as Cesar and Nestor Castillo emerge as palatable literary and musical figures. The novel caters to American nostalgia for romantic and virile latinidad of a golden age, using the lexicon of the bolero as primary muse, a move that simplifies the possibilities of the bolero and exaggerates the "Latin" macho in the figure of Cesar, in the name of seducing the gaze of the reader and listener. Hijuelos translates the bolero in a version that fits the traditional trope of virile and uncontrollable Latino libido.

The bolero as a translated articulation of romance, from Spanish to English, also appears in Sandra Cisneros's *Caramelo* to different effect. In this Mexican-American generational saga, Lala, a Chicana from the Midwest, narrates the story of her family, from the youth of her great-grandparents to her own coming of age between Chicago and Mexico City. The first part of the narrative, "Recuerdo de Acapulco" (Memory of Acapulco) begins precisely with a *recuerdo*, a souvenir: a photograph of the family in the beaches of the Guerrero resort when Lala was a young girl. These first pages are prefaced with an epigraph with the lyrics of Agustín Lara's celebrated bolero "Maria Bonita" (Pretty Maria):

> Acuérdate de Acapulco
> De aquellas noches
> María Bonita, María del alma
> Recuerda que en la playa
> Con tus manitas
> Las estrellas enjuagabas

> Remember Acapulco
> Remember those nights
> Pretty Maria, Maria of the Soul!
> Remember that on the beach
> With your small hands
> the stars you rinsed (3, my translation)

The source explains the author and title, as well as the following depiction: "sung by the composer while playing the piano and accompanied by a sweet, but very, very sweet violin" (3). The epigraph sets the tone for the rest of this first section consisting of the childhood narrative. Although it takes place partly in Chicago before a big family drive south of the border, this part of the novel occurs mostly in Lala's childhood Mexico City, with its different colors and smells and sounds ("Honk, say the cars at home, here they say *tán-tán-tán,*" 17).

One of Lara's many musical tributes to his wife, iconic actress María Félix, "María Bonita" is an often covered song, not unlike his "Solamente una Vez (You Belong in My Heart)". The adjective in the epigraph, that insistence on the "sweet, but very, very sweet violin," makes the reader aware of forthcoming excess and hyperbole in the narrative. Cisneros's modulation of "María Bonita" magnifies the extraordinary mawkishness of the song, and perchance of the bolero itself. Or, she reminds us of the artifice of the bolero, the surplus that it relies upon, the plastic of the pedestal upon which Maria stands, or for that matter, in this book, upon which her family memories stand, not real but malleable, exchangeable, recyclable. The melodrama of Mexican music in *Caramelo*, from Lara to Lola Beltrán to Pedro Infante's "Las Mañanitas" (comically rebaptized as "Little Mornings") are presented as works of artifice, as processed as any telenovela.

Consider the epigraph to another chapter, "Que Elegante": "Pouring out from the windows, 'Por un amor,' from the hi-fi, the version by Lola Beltrán, that queen of Mexican country, with tears in the throat and a group of mariachis cooing, – but don't cry Lolita, and Lola replying – I'm not crying, it's just ... that I remember" (10). Soon afterward, we are introduced to Aunty Licha, Uncle Fat-Face's spouse, a woman "as beautiful as a Mexican Elizabeth Taylor". We learn she is the jealous type, according to Lala's mother, Zoila, who observes, "Mexican women are just like Mexican songs, *locas* for love"(11). This statement is followed by an anecdote that seemingly proves Zoila's observation:

> Once Aunty almost tried to kill herself because of Uncle Fat-Face. "My own husband! What a barbarity! A prostitute's disease from my own husband. Imagine! *Ay*, get him out of here! I don't even want to see you again. *Lárgate!* You disgust me, *me das asco*, you *cochino*! ... I'm going to kill myself, kill myself!!!" Which sounds so much more dramatic in Spanish – *Me mato! Me maaaaaaaatooooooo*!! The big kitchen knife, the one Aunty dips in a glass of water to cut the boy's birthday cakes, pointed toward her own sad heart. (11)

The painful memory of betrayal is conveyed by Lala in the hyperbolic rhetoric of the telenovela. Aunty Licha's exclamations are intertwined with Lola Beltrán's, one of *ranchera* music's foremost artists, and her "tears in the throat," both the narrative (memory) and the song relying on the same device of heightened artifice.

This descriptive passage both gives a sense of exaggeration to the music, and sets the tone of excess and parody in the novel. To cry (to sing, to affect, to perform, to write) is to remember. Cisneros uses Lola Beltrán's method of emotional artifice for her own literary retelling, borrows her song and its subterfuge. If *Caramelo* is the result of Cisneros's effort to translate the telenovela into a literary genre, as Amara Graf contends, the bolero and ranchera are objects of pleasure, memory and discourse essential to this literary effort. *Caramelo's* engagement with melodrama, visual and sonic, is as much an historical as a contemporary trend. *Caramelo* as well as recent works like Nina Marie Rodriguez's *Caramba!* (2011) play with similar sensibilities of Latina/o aesthetics and musicality, raising the question of the possibilities and limits of the genre of telenovelas and the aesthetics of affect as Latina/o cultural expressions.

That Voice!: Radical Timbres in the Latina/o Literary Imaginary

That voice . . . This is the expression that marks a surrender and a recognition. Not only do we recognize the style of a writer, a writer can also reinvent the voice of the performers we already know or don't know. How is it that voices are heard through visual imaginaries? How is it that the writer can sing? "Her voice comes out of her knees / her fingernails are full of sound" begins Victor Hernández Cruz's tribute to La Lupe, "la Yiyiyi," a riddle that proposes voices don't come out only from the mouth, which they don't. Sound can and must emerge from other spaces, from the forehead, across the skin and keratin, as any classical singing instructor will tell you. Marta Moreno Vega likened Machito's voice to a roar of thunder, still powerful across telephone wires.

In the middle of *Caramelo*, an elusive character, Panfila Palafox, appears as part of a circus entourage in a coastal village of the Isthmus of Tehuantepec, where Lala's grandfather worked in his youth. With his mistress, Exaltación, he goes to the circus and witnesses Panfila's performance. She has "that voice. Like the quivering grief of a guitar . . . Everyone cried. Everyone was overjoyed. Panfila sang *con ganas*, as they say. . . it gave everything she sang authenticity, and authenticity of emotions engendered admiration and admiration – love" (178). That lighting effect on the singer seduces the listener, and in particular Exaltación, who later runs off with the performer. What occurs there between singer and listener is a Sapphonic instance, a vocal phenomenon that is developed in Terri de la Peña's novel *Latin Satins* (1989).

Terri de la Peña's novel does not refer to any living performer in particular, but imagines them. It introduces the reader to the four members of the fictitious queer band Latin Satins from Santa Monica: Chic, Rita, Cindy, and Jessica. Musically, the Latin Satins configure a "salsa-flavored rock" fusion sound. This band is emblematic of the syncretic sound that popular Latina/o performers have developed since the twentieth century. In imagining a lesbian Chicana band from late 1980s Southern California, the novel invokes popular performers and syncretic practices from the 1970s through the 1990s, notably Linda Ronstadt and Selena (Quintanilla).

Jess, the songwriter of the band, is the most developed of the four characters, the one with the most intriguing voice. Although de la Peña's prose provides a limited sonic identity to Jess's voice, her novel is a provocative proposal to remember singers like Chavela Vargas or Myrta Silva and acknowledge histories like Chicana punk rocker Alice Bag's punk grito. Jess, with her romantic femme demeanor, embodies a vocal legacy of lesbian desire. She is a powerful, versatile contra-alto, having background in ranchera performance and a concurrent membership in the Sapphonic Feminist Choir ensemble whose specialty are "suffragist hymns, peace anthems, and feminist standards," and the Latin Satins. Jess has a Sapphonic effect, in particular, during one night with the Feminist Choir.

Sapphonics is both a listening space and singing voice, a noun and adjective. According to Elizabeth Wood, it is a mode of articulation, "a way of describing a space of lesbian possibility, for a range of erotic and emotional relationships among women who sing and women who listen" (27). That is, Sapphonics privilege listening and the listener who is attentive and sensitive to the queer voice. This brings us to the lesbian singing voice. Wood continues, "I also call sapphonic a particular voice that thrills or excites me . . . if this trained female singing voice is no longer audible as material sound, it is visible and resonant as presence in historical contexts and imaginary representations that once shaped and projected it" (28). Jess Tamayo projects a Sapphonic voice in the Latina/o literary imaginary, both historical and fictional. She both sings and writes material of queer erotic impact. Outside of it, she constitutes that imaginary of Chicana and Latina singing bodies across genres.

An erotic moment of aurality occurs during one of Jessica's solos with the choir during a community "multicultural fair." She sings "Beautiful Soul," a mellow voice and piano piece by Margie Adam from the women's music movement, "singing the lesbian standard in a bluesy voice" (108). De la Peña's reference to this genre links Jessica Tamayo to a musical culture aesthetically distant from the rancheras she grew up listening to. She sings the first stanza, "I wonder where you are, lovable lady," alone, joined by the chorus afterward.

Audience member Andrea Romano is enraptured by Jess. At a post-performance meeting, a chorus member notes that "Jess's ballad caused at least one heart to flutter . . . my friend Andrea twisted my arm, bugging me for the scoop on you. Seems you had her floating when you sang 'Beautiful

Soul' ... you sent her... into orbit" (164). While Jess captivates several listeners, the chorus has also alienated a section of those in attendance, as Jess had feared. Several leave halfway through their performance. Their politics had been fully revealed, after all, with a preface by the director, "Being gay or lesbian in this society also means being a part of another culture. This next piece is a love song written by Margie Adam to a woman she once loved" (155). Their performance that night is met by some listeners with disappointment at their inclusion into the festival. The lesbian singing voice and body causes both frisson and frenzy in the listener, both fans and anti-fans.

Critical Latina/o Fandom

As the concept of Sapphonics reminds us, there is no music without listeners. There are no celebrities without their fans, and fans are not merely consumers. "We, the fans, make her. Not the radio, not the newspaper, not the TV – it was us," contends Gerardo Rodriguez, a Jenni Rivera fan. Deborah Vargas, writing about alternative ways of making music, quotes Rodriguez to insist on the various practices of musical "play." Fans are prominent in these literary pursuits as well; their devotion to, appreciation of, singing alongside their favorites reveal another way that song and dance is mediated in the text. Fandom studies and new-media studies are growing fields within popular-music studies, with scholars like Melissa Hidalgo and Michelle Rivera proposing exciting directions in this field. In the following examples, a novel by Denise Chávez, a short story by Amina Gautier, and a graphic novel by Cristy C. Road, the artist is rendered as secondary, albeit still essential, while the practice of fandom looms central. From these works, a series of concerns emerge, namely: female homosociality, celebrity as kin, *sucio* aesthetics, and non-Latina/o musical subjects of desire.

Loving Pedro Infante

In *Loving Pedro Infante*, Teresina "Tere" Avila's fervent identification with Infante is not an isolated activity, but a socially engendered pleasure. Tere is a thirty-something-year-old divorceé living in the fictional border town of Cabritoville, between El Paso and Las Cruces. For her, Infante's music is a text that she and her close friend Irma scrutinize as a method to approach their own lives as Chicanas dealing with quotidian prejudice and sexism. From inside the packed, humid Colon theater on a July night featuring a Pedro Infante film, Tere introduces her companions: "It is here that I prefer to dream, seated in the middle of people I call family. To my right is my comadre, Irma 'La Wirma' Granados, and next to her is her mother, Nyvia Ester Granados" (3). The only "real" family Tere has is her girlfriend Irma and the members of the Pedro Infante Club de Admiradores Norteamericanos #256, "and the characters in Pedro's movies, whom Irma and I know . . . better than we do our own kin" (48). The singer / celebrity as family is a common thread that I shall revisit in discussing Amina Gautier's "Aguanile."

Tere's thorough knowledge of Infante's songs and films becomes a domain of agency and power. Through this domain, Tere gains the power she lacks with respect to those who consider her a disposable woman, including her lover. Tere has an affair with a married, condescending man, Lucio Vasquez. During one of their surreptitious encounters at the Sands Motel, Tere listens to and sings along to Infante's rendition of "Mi Tenampa." The Tenampa is the legendary cantina in Mexico City. Here, with its possessive (*My Tenampa*), it points as much to the physical as to the metaphoric space of Mexicano masculinity. This ranchera by Mexican songwriter José Alfredo Jiménez is a declaration of pride, an ownership of the "parranda y tenampa, mariachi y canciones" lifestyle. Written from the masculine perspective, it chides the listening woman: "what do you know about life? / Of life between drinks? / For you to be my darling / you need many things" ("Mi Tenampa," José Alfredo Jiménez).

This partiality for "la vida entre copas" is more than a preference, and typifies a lifestyle and world outside bourgeois comportment. Tere's musical tastes, in the eyes of her lover, align her to a life considered poor and dirty. As Tere washes her hair, Lucio asks who's singing, and if she "can turn that crap down" (169), reinforcing a stereotypical attitude toward her, as if she were in fact a phillistine *puta*. His request comes as he reads through Roget's Thesaurus. His reading activity and her listening and singing along illuminate the tension in their relationship. His notion of status and success is incompatible with Mexicana / o popular border culture, Spanglish, and theaters like the Colon ("Only poor Mexicans see movies there," 78). Lucio expresses his distaste once more, and Tere ignores him, singing loudly with what Lucio calls her "ugly Mexican voice" (171). The "crap" she enjoys, her popular tastes, the "dirty" spaces she patronizes, the revolting singing, position her as surplus, as sucia. Deborah Vargas proposes lo sucio as a Latina / o queer analytic to consider how "the dirty and obscene of surplus holds some potentiality of sustainability and persistence for queer sex and sexuality" (715). Tere, as a working-class woman of color, young divorceé, and "mistress," embodies non-normativity. Her fan practices and musical tastes link her to a suciedad that she claims as an exercise of nonconformity.

Lucio hates Tere's gritos, the heartfelt, wordless, spontaneous cries (again, the detail) that pepper mariachi performances. In addition, he dislikes that she knows all the Mexican songs "he's never heard of." Tere, with passionate exaggeration, sings, "Mi Tenampa." While drying her hair and performing femininity, Tere revels in her knowledge of Infante's rancheras. She claims mastery and her Mexicanidad, at the same time using "Mi Tenampa" to critique Lucio's shortcomings: "What do you know about life / about life between bottles?" Tere's singing exerts knowledge derived from living dangerously, far from standards of feminine sexual and social propriety.

"Aguanile": Dissolving the Diasporic Grudge

In Gautier's short story "Aguanile," a similar dynamic of idol-as-family develops between the narrator's grandfather and the great Boricua salsero, Hector Lavoe (1946–1993). Héctor Juan Pérez Martínez, better known as Hector Lavoe (which roughly translates to "the voice") was an electrifying performer, an icon of Puerto Rican pride that helped define modern salsa in the 1960s and 1970s. The grandfather, who remains nameless, has a complicated relationship with his granddaughter, whom he calls "Nena." Nena is the daughter of the family he abandoned in the United States when he left for Puerto Rico to start a new life. Nena is the only connection the grandfather has to his first wife and children, who resent him deeply. In the years of her adolescence, he would call her whenever one of his favorite salsa musicians died, beginning with Charlie Palmieri, "announcing the passing as if it were that of a family member or someone we had actually known" (1). While he is a fan of Palmieri, Rubén Blades, Willie Colon, Tito Puente, Grandfather's favorite of the salsa greats is Lavoe.

Salsa dura performers, and Lavoe in particular, are like surrogate family to the grandfather. For example, he feels chided when his son, from his second family, refuses to play the singer at his wedding ("my grandfather announced this as if it were a personal affront, something his son had done out of spite," 10). In another instance, when he calls Nena soon after Lavoe dies, "a man who was no relation to him at all, a man who had never even known my grandfather existed," Nena is aghast at Grandfather's gall to mourn his death and not that of his former wife, gone some years before.

The grandfather treats this painful fissure between his first family and himself through Nena, with whom he shares salsa dura's musical notes. He teaches her about salsa's timing, its instruments, and what he calls the demons of Lavoe, which make him late to concerts, and which drive him eventually to jump off a high-rise hotel balcony. Speaking about Lavoe and salsa enables the sharing of unspeakables and opens the doors for a legacy beyond rancor and spite. His sharing of salsa dura and his idol is also a way, she muses in the coda, to absolve himself. Lavoe's song "Aguanile" is the centerpiece of this absolution, as they both listen to it on her last night in Puerto Rico.

> [The song] began as if it were in a jungle or a forest ... with the sounds of birds cawing, chirping, tittering and screeching. Elephants trumpeted. In the distance, drums spoke, and voices changed, putting me in the mind of what I guessed African music sounded like ... a man's voice singing one lone word, stretching it to its limit, repeating it and pulling everything and more from the word he sang over and over. (14)

That word is "Aguanile." The recorded version, as Nena recounts, evokes the sounds of wildlife, which gradually fuse with the instruments. The music is somewhat foreign to Nena. Her grandfather clarifies that the clanging that is mere noise to her is the clave, "the key, the rhythm, the heartbeat of all salsa" (14). Just as popular cultural forms like salsa have been for Latinos a source of and practice of autonomy and identity, here we see how salsa functions affectively in a space of difficult intimacy due to torn family relations; this music pumps away the bad blood. Nena, as part of the family Grandfather has abandoned, must not only witness but listen to and through the music, that is, his surrogate, his sensibility, to hear what inscribes his humanity and not his cruelty. Lavoe facilitates the vulnerability. Because his estranged children now eschew "all things Puerto Rican," Nena's listening to "Aguanile" after her grandfather dies marks this scene as a dialogue between herself and the icon she never knew about. The music dissolves the diasporic grudge.

Green Music: Synesthetic Pairings of Fan Love

Sometimes, it takes an unknown sound, distinct from the familiar rhythms of home, to fulfill a connection. Latina/o literature does not exclusively encode salsa, ranchera, mambo, merengue and other genres. An example of trans-cultural fandom, as Bertha Chin and Lori Morimoto call the affective relationship between the fan and the border-crossing object, is the Latina/o and especially Chicana/o connection with Steven Patrick Morrissey's music. This relationship is exemplified in Brando Skyhorse's *The Madonnas of Echo Park* (2010). In a fashion analogous to that of the grandfather in "Aguanile," the teenager Aurora adores Morrissey, whom she admires as a paternal figure. After her father Hector abandons their family, she pastes Morissey's image over her father's: "I pasted in Morrissey's picture because he was the kind of man who would never leave my mother, or abandon a child" (155).

In Cristy C. Road's graphic novel "Spit and Passion," the pop-punk band Green Day make music that provides solace and hope in violent milieus: "having grown up around salsa and Latin Pop, I wanted something foreign, because fuck, I felt foreign – like an alien from gay space." (33) Road's graphic novel departs from the tropes of tropicalization that may appear in the musico-literary. The music that "moves her mountain of self-hate" (99) – the consequence of casual homophobia in her everyday life as a queer, working-class U.S. Cubana – is Queen, punk, rock, "the devil's music" (35). Her text and visuals depict Green Day most prominently. This was the band that, upon listening to for the first time as an alienated, disaffected teen, transforms her: "I felt protected and warm – alive and in love" (41). Their punk rock was that more tortured, more remote sonicity than Oro Solido's merengue or Madonna's early 1990s pop. The attraction here, despite mainstream media's treatment of Green Day, is not Billy Joe Armstrong's "done up" face. His looks, and the band's overall visual aesthetics, matter for other reasons. Blemished and ungroomed, with "chipped teeth, shape-shift hair, and makeshift clothing," they embody an unruly whiteness – although Road, practicing her fan knowledge, acknowledges that for many in the punk community, they were sell-outs (107).

Nevertheless, their seemingly rebellious masculinity resonates with her own gender nonconformity, something she portrays in her panel: her unshaven legs, loose clothing, a single, long "butch" braid, her full waist bulging from her shorts. The graphic is essential to note here, as her work visualizes the sound more dramatically than the typical prosaic insertion of lyrics into the text. Black and white panels where bodies' waste, sweat, and spit are often part of each person's semblance, where bodies, rather than hypersexualized, are unfiltered with under-eye circles and pimples or armpit hair. The body is re-covered and queerly living, rather than frozen in cisgender fantasy. In a scene of a Green Day concert where Road imagines swaying alongside her crush, lyrics become Billy Joe Armstrong's spit, which reaches their skin, their closed eyes and mouths ajar, finger inside, evoking pleasure. This image inspires the title, and the matter of fan reciprocity: "spit and passion."

In addition to transcultural fandom studies, Road's graphic novel asks us to consider the relationship between the sonic, the textual, and the visual, In particular, the book's incarnation shifts from the tangible to the digital. Music remains a concern about representation, but not solely as it is "replayed" with words or descriptions in prose and poetry. In exploring how popular modes traditionally rebuffed as serious objects of study relate to the culture of the book, the novel, and other literary modes, music tenses the page. It puzzles the temporality of reading, a linear silent development, with the chaos of musical experience and pleasure.

The contemporary graphic novel by Road tells us as much about the transformation of the ways gender, sexuality, and love are configured in the act of music making, listening, and writing. Between the celebration of patriarchal romance in Hijuelos's text (also a product of the Cuban diaspora) and Road's visual and textual ecstasy of queer love, there is no direct reference or discussion. And yet they trouble each other – Road's text in particular is a fierce awakening to other ways of experiencing the euphoria of love and music as a Latina subject. While their presentations differ in terms of publisher and format, Road's work is a testament to the alternatives to mainstream publication and a type of desired (sonic) latinidad.

The Latina/o authors discussed in this chapter have written as earwitnesses to sound and music, not of a faraway time but of their contemporary moment. Latina/o literature, in this sense, has been attentive to the sonic and the musical elements of a community as a "gesture of resistance" (Aparicio 2013), as their writing is also an act of defiance to the silences, ineffability and unintelligibility that has too often constituted Latina/o sound in the national imaginary. Sound and music and published text work jointly as crucial devices that enable exploration of methods of survival: moving the body in dance, listening through and to sung secrets, tuning in to and singing the forbidden, making life in a cisgender world perhaps more bearable. Or, conversely, some of these works rehearse latinidad as merely musical and sonic, informing its mainstream ubiquity as celebratory, ludic, carnal – the written language a key method to transfer and create this knowledge. Popular music is very much present in Latina/o literature, as representation. But beyond this relationship where literature seems to merely capture the sonic, both constitute and depend on one another. Both catalyze questions about latinidad in the process. At the intersection of popular music and literature, latinidad is constituted in the intersecting sensory fields of performance and soundscape and in the discursive domains of the literary.

WORKS CITED

Aparicio, Frances. *Listening to Salsa: Gender, Latin Music and Puerto Rican Cultures.* Hanover, NH: Wesleyan University Press, 1998.

"The Poet as Earwitness: Reading Sound, Voice and Music in Tato Laviera's Poetry." *The AmeRican Poet: Essays on the Work of Tato Laviera.* New York: Center for Puerto Rican Studies, 2014.

"Popular Music." *The Routledge Companion to Latina/o Literature.* New York: Routledge, 2013.

Chavez, Denise. *Loving Pedro Infante*. New York: Washington Square Press, 2001.

Chin, Berta and Lori Morimoto. "Towards a Theory of Transcultural Fandom." *Participants: The Journal of Audience and Reception Studies* 10.1 (2013).

Cisneros, Sandra. *Caramelo*. New York: Alfred A. Knopf, 2002.

De la Peña, Terri. *Latin Satins*. Berkeley, CA: Seal Press, 1989.

Flores, Juan. *From Bomba to Hip Hop: Puerto Rican Culture and Latino Identity*. New York: Columbia University Press, 2000.

Garcia, Cindy. *Salsa Crossings: Dancing Latinidad in Los Angeles*. Durham, NC: Duke University Press, 2013.

Gautier, Amina. "Aguanile." *Now We Will Be Happy*. Lincoln: University of Nebraska Press, 2014.

Graf, Amara. "Mexicanized Melodrama: Sandra Cisneros' Literary Translation of the Telenovela." *Label Me Latina/o: Journal of Twentieth and Twenty First Centuries Latina/o Literary Production* (Fall 2014): 1–20.

Hernández-Cruz, Victor. "Listening to Arsenio Rodriguez is Moving Closer to Knowledge." *The Shadow of Al-Andalus*. Minneapolis, MN: Coffee House Press, 2011.

"La Lupe." *Maracas: New and Selected Poems: 1966–2000*. Minneapolis, MN: Coffee House Press, 2001.

Hijuelos, Oscar. *The Mambo Kings Play Songs of Love*. New York: Hyperion, 1989.

Jefferson, Margo. "Dancing into the Dream." *New York Times*. August 1989. www.nytimes.com/books/99/02/21/specials/hijuelos-mambo.html, Accessed December 2015.

Laviera, Tato. *Bendicion: The Complete Poetry of Tato Laviera*. Houston, TX: Arte Public Press, 2014.

Macias, Anthony. *Mexican-American Mojo: Popular Music, Dance and Urban Culture in Los Angeles, 1935–1968*. Durham, NC: Duke University Press, 2008.

Martinez, Nina Marie. *Caramba!* New York: Anchor Books, 2004.

Moreno Vega, Marta. *When the Spirits Dance Mambo*. New York: Three Rivers Press, 2004.

Murray Schafer, R. "Soundscapes and Earwitnesses." *Hearing History: A Reader*. Athens: University of Georgia Press, 2004.

Novak, David and Matt Sakakeeny. "Introduction." *Keywords in Sound*. Durham, NC: Duke University Press, 2015.

Obejas, Achy. *Memory Mambo*. Berkeley, CA: Cleis Press, 1996.

Ponce, Mary Helen. *The Wedding*. Houston, TX: Arte Public Press, 1989.

Road, Cristy C. *Spit and Passion*. New York: The Feminist Press, 2012.

Sandoval Sanchez, Alberto. *José, Can You See?: Latinos on and off Broadway*. Madison: University of Wisconsin Press, 1999.

Skyhorse, Brando. *The Madonnas of Echo Park*. New York: Free Press, 2010.

Smith, Mark M. "Introduction: Onward to Audible Pasts." *Hearing History: A Reader*. Athens: University of Georgia Press, 2004.

Vargas, Deborah. "Ruminations on Lo Sucio as a Latino Queer Analytic." *American Quarterly* 66.3 (2014): 715–26.

"Un Desmadre Positivo: Notes on How Jenni Rivera Played Music." *Contemporary Latina/o Media: Production, Circulation, Politics*. New York: New York University Press, 2014.

Vasquez, Alexandra. *Listening in Detail: Performances of Cuban Music*. Durham, NC: Duke University Press, 2014.

Wood, Elizabeth. "Sapphonics." *Queering the Pitch: New Gay and Lesbian Musicology*. New York: Routledge, 2006.

29

Brazuca Literature

Old and New Currents, Countercurrents, and Undercurrents

LUZ ANGÉLICA KIRSCHNER

The publication of *Luso-American Literature: Writing by Portuguese-Speaking Authors in North America* (2011), edited by Roberto Henry Moser and Antonio Luciano de Andrade Tosta, can be considered a watershed moment for Portuguese-speaking communities in the Unites States and Canada. Expanding the historical meaning of the terms Luso and Luso-American, the anthology brings together for the first time Portuguese, Brazilian, *Brazuca*, and Cape Verdean authors and includes a substantial number of texts (e.g., short stories, letters, memoirs, and poems) translated from Portuguese into English. The desire to affirm the presence of the Luso-American tradition in the multicultural and multilingual literary landscape of the United States and Canada, and to display that the literary traditions of the American hemisphere are in conversation with one another and with the rest of the world, are rationales that the editors put forward to justify the compilation of writing not only by Lusophone immigrants and their descendants but also by itinerant exiles and temporary visitors to the United States. More recently (2013), in "On the Shoulders of Giants: The Study of Portuguese and Luso-Brazilian Literature in the United States," Earl E. Fitz writes with a sense of jubilation about Portuguese, the world's sixth most widely spoken language, and the positive impact that the ascension of Brazil as an economic global player has had on the institutionalization of Luso-Brazilian studies in universities of the United States: "We are living in very a propitious time for the study of the Portuguese language as well as the history, culture and literature of the Luso-Brazilian world. With the growing international visibility of Brazil, Portuguese is increasingly recognized as one of the languages of global power and the international market."[1] Taking these important statements as points of departure,

---

[1] Earl E. Fitz, "On the Shoulders of Giants," *Luso-Brazilian Review* 50.2 (2013): pp. 1–12; p. 1. My translation.

this essay critically discusses the intricate position of *Brazuca* (Brazilian American) literature within long-standing nationalist, literary, and identity discourses in Latin America and the United States. Initially written largely in Portuguese and published in Brazil by short-term residents in the United States, today this literature is increasingly written by members of a numerically underestimated migrant community, which in the U.S. context has been considered "invisible,"[2] and is often identified as Latina/o or Hispanic, but whose position within the Latina/o community has been contested by Brazilians and Brazilian Americans arguing that Latin/a/o or Hispanic identities obscure their distinctive Lusitanian heritage and Brazilian national origins. Along these lines, this essay also explores the possibilities and challenges that the field of *Brazuca* literature opens for the field of Latina/o literary studies in particular and Latina/o studies in general, as well as our understanding of latinidad in the context of an unevenly globalized world ruled by colorblind racism in the age of migration.

To understand the position of *Brazuca* literature and its authors in the United States, it is necessary to be aware of hegemonic intellectual traditions, originating in Latin America where Spanish American histories, cultures, and literatures traditionally, in the best of cases, have been studied as distinct from Brazil, the only Portuguese-speaking country in the region.[3] Not unfrequently, Brazilian cultural traditions and literatures have been simply ignored or reduced to a gracious afterthought even by recognized scholars of Latin American literature.[4] Until recently, differences in colonial histories of discovery, conquest, political independence, and national recognition of Spanish America and Brazil, along with differences in language, have been posited as insurmountable barriers that preclude the study of parallels and commonalities in the historical and cultural developments of their respective literatures. From a U.S. perspective, the historical invisibility of Brazil in the Americas can be linked to the country's geographical location in an ostensibly Spanish-speaking and culturally uniform hazy batch of nations known as Latin America. The traditional compartmentalized training imparted to prospective scholars in departments of Spanish and Portuguese, romance languages, and comparative iterature in the United States has equally

---

[2] Maxine L. Margolis, *An Invisible Minority: Brazilians in New York City*, Revised and Expanded Edition (Miami: University Press of Florida, 2009), p. 7.

[3] Bernardo Subercaseaux, Mónica González Gracía, and Horst Nitschack, "Introducción," *Revista Chilena de Literatura* 88 (2014): pp. 5–6; p. 5.

[4] Earl E. Fitz, "Internationalizing the Literature of the Portuguese-Speaking World," *Hispania* 85.3 (2002): pp. 439–48; p. 440.

contributed to a sense of incommensurability between Spanish America and Brazil.[5] The same observation applies to English departments that, at the dawn of the globalized twenty-first century, recognize the existence of other Americas besides the United States in the western hemisphere and train bilingual doctoral students in English and Spanish, seeking to create a hemispheric or transamerican space "of improved literary and cultural relations."[6] Unfortunately, perhaps because, in the United States, Latin America refers to a region of Spanish speakers or those of Spanish-speaking descent, or because the nation is witnessing a "Spanish-centered 'Latinization,'"[7] the same intellectuals who promote the cultivation of Spanish for hemispheric literary dialogue "totally ignore Brazil, the largest nation in Latin America."[8]

It is likewise noteworthy that the claiming of Brazil by Pedro Álvares Cabral for the Kingdom of Portugal in 1500 has equally impelled Brazilians to set themselves "apart from the rest of Latin America" where Christopher Columbus's 1492 voyage is commemorated.[9] Furthermore, even if compounded with anxiety about acculturation (i.e., "Americanization"), Brazil's attempts to define its national identity and the national quest for suitable development models has often led Brazilians, attracted by "the image of the United States as the home of democracy, wealth, and social equity," to favor the adoption of U.S. values.[10] Brazil's vastness and its human diversity frequently have led Brazilians and non-Brazilian outsiders alike to recognize more similarities in the nation's historical development with the United States than with other Latin American countries. We are reminded that the process of colonization in both countries resulted in the usurpation of huge dominions requiring the dispossession of indigenous peoples and the subsequent importation of a significant number of Africans that enabled the

---

[5] Ibid., p. 440.

[6] Earl E. Fitz, *Brazilian Narrative Traditions in a Comparative Context* (New York: The Modern Language Association of America, 2005), p. 3.

[7] Helen B. Marrow, "Who Are the *Other* Latinos, and Why?," in José Luis Falconi and José Antonio Mazzotti (eds.), *The Other Latinos: Central and South Americans in the United States* (Cambridge, MA: Harvard University Press, 2007), pp. 125–39; p. 56.

[8] Earl E. Fitz, "Spanish American and Brazilian Literature in an Inter-American Perspective: The Comparative Approach," in Sophia McClennen and Earl E. Fitz (eds.), *Comparative Cultural Studies and Latin America* (West Lafayette, IN: Purdue University Press, 2004), pp. 69–88; p. 78.

[9] Robert E. Levine and John C. Crocitti, "Introduction," in *The Brazil Reader: History, Culture, Politics* (Durham, NC: Duke University Press, 1999), pp. 1–9; p. 6.

[10] Renato Cordeiro Gomes et al. "Historic Displacements in Twentieth-Century Brazilian Literary Culture" in Mario J. Valdés and Djelal Kadir (eds.), *Literary Cultures in Latin America: A Comparative History*, Vol. 3, (New York: Oxford University Press, 2004), pp. 473–502; p. 489.

emergence of "the two largest slave societies of modern times."[11] Until the economic recession of the mid 1980s, comparable to the United States, Brazil was known as a country of immigrants from all over the world. Both countries managed to fashion "multicultural societies with substantial indigenous, African, Italian, German, Japanese, Slavic, Arab, and Jewish (Ashkenazi and Sephardi) populations and influences."[12] More recent studies indicate that unemployment, underemployment, and social stagnation in the face of slower economic growth and the restructuring of the global labor market have pushed sizeable numbers of middle-class, and increasingly middle-lower class and poor Brazilians, to immigrate to countries as diverse as the United States, Spain, Portugal, Italy, Japan, Paraguay, and Venezuela.[13] The United States has been a preferred target country for emigration where the prospect of higher wages, in even menial jobs that migrants would never perform back home, have enabled some to achieve the social mobility and the "middle-class levels of consumption" that are unfeasible even for educated professionals in Brazil.[14] The predilection of the United States as a country for emigration, however, is also linked to the fascination embedded in the Brazilian imagination with "all [U.S.] American 'things'," from idealized patterns of consumption and behavior to music, technology, and fashion consolidated during the twentieth century through the media that circulated idealized representations of the good life in the United States.[15]

As immigration studies in the United States become increasingly aware of Brazilian communities, Latina/o scholars have called attention to the ambiguous position, if not absence, of Brazil and Brazilians within discourses of latinidad. Addressing some of the multiple incongruities and contradictions posed by a unified Latina/o "cultural identity," for instance, Juana María Rodríguez queries geographical and linguistic latinidad and the discursive non-spaces it assigns, among others, to Haitians who share the same island with Dominicans, the South and Central American English- and Creole-speaking nations of Guyana, Surinam, and Belize, but also the

---

[11] Robert Stam, "Brazilian Cinema: Reflections on Race and Representation," in Stephen Hart and Richard Young (eds.), *Contemporary Latin American Cultural Studies* (London: Oxford University Press, 2003), pp. 203–14; p. 203.

[12] Ibid., p. 203.

[13] Maxine L. Margolis, *Goodbye, Brazil: Émigrés from the Land of Soccer and Samba* (Madison: The University of Wisconsin Press, 2013), pp. 16–42.

[14] Ibid., p. 20.

[15] Leticia J. Braga and and Clémence Jouët-Pastré (eds.), "Introduction: Interdisciplinary Perspectives on Becoming Brazuca," in *Becoming Brazuca: Brazilian Immigration to the United States* (Cambridge, MA: Harvard University Press, 2008), pp. 1–21; p. 7.

Portuguese-speaking giant Brazil.[16] Silvio Torres-Saillant has discussed how sympathetic historical relations between the political elites of Brazil and the United States reveal further affinities between these two countries that greatly profited financially from the transatlantic slave trade, and whose societies were heavily influenced "by the dynamics of plantation society."[17] However, problematizing the absence of Brazilians in conversations about the community in Latina/o studies, Torres-Saillant points out commonalities based on the shared Latin American background of Brazilian and other Latin American immigrants. The scholar reminds us of their similar immigrant experience that historically often has been the outcome of U.S. foreign policy in the region, but also of the modality of interaction of these groups with their countries of origin, and the processes of incorporation of these communities into U.S. society.[18] Yet, we also need to remember that the discursive marginalization of Brazilians in the United States is partly linked to the fact that, although Brazilians are Latin Americans, they do not match the common sense of what an emblematic Latin American is supposed to be according to mainstream U.S. imagination. In addition, Brazilians themselves reject the official umbrella term "Hispanic," which, unlike Latina/o, "excludes the possibility of affirming Brazilian identity."[19] A further complication is Brazil's colonial history of struggle against Spanish supremacy which, in the popular imagery, may entail historical sound bites that reach back to disputes over the newly discovered lands in the Americas that the Treaty of Tordesillas sought to solve, or to the Portuguese Restoration War (1668) that ended the sixty-year rule of the Spanish Habsburgs in Portugal.[20] Their inconspicuousness is likewise a product of the reluctance of some Brazilians to self-identify as Latinas/os. This hesitation is somewhat a reaction to the ignorance about the historical, linguistic, and cultural distinctiveness of Brazil in the U.S. context, where the nation and its diaspora are figured in simplistic exoticized terms and average people do not distinguish between *Brazucas* and other Latinas/os. More often, however, subscribing to racist Anglo-Saxon discourse about Latinas/os (Hispanics) and the hierarchies

---

[16] Juana María Rodríguez, *Queer Latinidad: Identity, Practices, Discursive Spaces* (New York: New York University Press, 2003), p. 13.

[17] Silvio Torres-Saillant, "The Unlikely Latinas/os: Brazilians in the United States," *Latino Studies* 6.4 (2008): pp. 466–77; p. 468.

[18] Ibid., p. 474.

[19] Ana Cristina Braga Martes, "Neither Hispanic, nor Black: We're Brazilian," in José Luis Falconi and José Antonio Mazzotti (eds.), *The Other Latinos: Central and South Americans in the United States* (Cambridge, MA: Harvard University Press, 2007), pp. 125–39; p. 231.

[20] Ibid., pp. 241–42.

of power predominant in the United States, Brazilians, especially first-generation immigrants, seek to distance themselves from the Latina/o community, reject the "black" category "in which they are often placed,"[21] underscore their distinctive ethnicity, deny their own "latinidade" or define it in terms that delink them from the inferiority of stigmatized latinidad.[22] And yet, it is notable that, in the United States, "brasilidade" (Brazilianness) has often been built on the idea that "we're not like them,"[23] which besides promoting the homogeneous ethnic demotion of Latinas/os likewise targets other Brazilians who, based on their perceived inferior "social class,"[24] are marginalized and avoided by their middle- and upper-class compatriots.[25] The use of class to regulate social distance among Brazilians in the U.S. context reflects the obsession with class and color distinctions that have characterized Brazil, where "Blacks and the poor are in fact interchangeable categories"[26] while the myth of the nation as a racial paradise remains current, and "whiteness and 'European' features are valued and are associated with the higher social classes."[27] According to Maxine L. Margolis, the Brazilian immigrant population to the United States has tended to be "lighter than the nation as a whole" and the probable future diversification in terms of social class of this diaspora "will be reflected in more racially diverse Brazilian communities."[28]

As already stated, the tendency among Brazilians to differentiate themselves from other Latin Americans or peoples with Latin American heritages is not a gesture that emerges exclusively in the U.S. context. This predisposition, also a result of "feelings of cultural pride,"[29] traces its origins back to Brazil and the nation's unique Lusitanian heritage and, according to Margolis, has induced Brazilians to perceive themselves as "distinct from Spanish-speaking Latin America" and display indifference "to the common Iberian

---

[21] Braga and Jouët-Pastré, "Introduction," p. 1.
[22] Bernadete Beserra, *Brazilian Immigrants in the United States: Cultural Imperialism and Social Class* (New York: LFB Scholarly Publishing LLC, 2003), p. 63.
[23] Margolis, *Goodbye, Brazil*, p. 191. [24] Ibid., p. 191.
[25] Beserra, *Brazilian Immigrants in the United States*, p. 16; p. 75.
[26] Anani Dzidzienyo, "The Changing World of Brazilian Race Relations," in Suzanne Oboler and Anani Dzidzienyo (eds.), *Neither Enemies nor Friends: Latinos, Blacks, Afro-Latinos* (New York: Palgrave, 2005), pp. 137–55; p. 140.
[27] Ana Cristina Braga Martes, *New Immigrants, New Land: A Study of Brazilians in Massachusetts* (Miami: University Press of Florida, 2011), p. 205.
[28] Margolis, *Goodbye, Brazil*, p. 53.
[29] Maxine L. Margolis, "Becoming *Brazucas*: Brazilian Identity in the United States," in José Luis Falconi and José Antonio Mazzotti (eds.), *The Other Latinos: Central and South Americans in the United States*, pp. 213–56; p. 218.

roots they share with their Latin neighbors."[30] But in the context of the diasporas in the western hemisphere, Brazilian and Latina/o identities are intertwined with the Iberian Peninsula in more complex ways than we may initially suspect. For instance, discussions over the reductive ethnic moniker that would officially name the communities now known as "Hispanics" ultimately emphasized the Spanish and not the "Iberian origin or culture"[31] of the dissimilar groups. As a result, even though during a conference organized (1973) by committed Portuguese community leaders at Harvard University "an absolute majority" voiced the aspiration to have the Portuguese share the minority status imparted to Hispanics, the Portuguese and Portuguese-descent people were eventually excluded from the Hispanic category.[32] At a time when the Brazilian diaspora was essentially absent from the Boston area and Brazilians were not even mentioned in the decision process, the legislators involved in the vote declared that since "Hispanic" stands for "Spanish-speaking Latin Americans," it precluded the inclusion of "Portuguese" under the rubric.[33] Had the Portuguese been officially defined as non-white Hispanics, Helen B. Marrow writes, "Brazilians and immigrants from other Portuguese-speaking countries would likely be considered U.S. Hispanics/Latinos today."[34] The experience of the Portuguese diaspora and its exclusion from latinidad, as well as the decision to emphasize the Spanish rather than the Iberian background of Hispanics and Latinas/os, reveal and alert us as to how institutional factors, decisions, and interventions beyond a heterogeneous community control can contribute to manipulate and regulate interaction of minority groups, create resentments, advance social segmentation, or restrain intergroup relations.

We are reminded that despite important differences, Brazilians do have much in common with Latinas/os, according to Alberto Sandoval-Sánchez: "Any attempt at mapping the politics of representation of Latinos/as on Broadway and Hollywood must have as its foundation two artistic figures: Carmen Miranda and Desi Arnaz."[35] Although Sandoval-Sánchez points out that the first-generation Miranda and Arnaz "had no consciousness of being a minority solely defined by race and ethnicity," the scholar affirms that, in the process of revising what it means to be Latina/o, Miranda and Arnaz

---

[30] Ibid., p. 218.   [31] Marrow, "Who Are the *Other* Latinos, and Why?," p. 42.
[32] Luz Angélica Kirschner, "Re: Academic Question," e-mail message to Professor Oné-simo T. Almeida, Brown University, Oct. 8, 2015.
[33] Ibid.   [34] Marrow, "Who Are the *Other* Latinos, and Why?," p. 42.
[35] Sandoval-Sánchez, Alberto, *José, Can You See? Latinos on and off Broadway* (Madison: University of Wisconsin Press, 1999), p. 21.

are crucial "components of the history of 'Latinidad'" in the United States.[36] A native of Portugal, the Broadway and Hollywood singer and actress Carmen Miranda, neé Maria de Carmo Miranda da Cunha, became cultural ambassador and emblem of Brazilian national identity, and authentic icon of Latin Americanness in the context of Franklin D. Roosevelt's Good Neighbor Policy during the 1930s and the Second World War. Mixing languages, musical genres, and elements from Cuban, Mexican, and Argentine traditions in her shows, Miranda actively contributed to advance the lasting perception and representation of "Latin America" as an undifferentiated linguistic and cultural space. Her exuberant and eclectic performances of "negritude"[37] confirmed all "dominant Anglo-American stereotypes of Latin American and Latin Americans."[38] The tropical and comical imitation of Miranda's iconic Lady in the Tutti-Frutti Hat – the artist's personal adaptation of the costume of Bahian women – widely disseminated through "Chiquita Banana" during the 1940s, similarly substantiated sociocultural notions that objectified and commodified Latin America and Latin American women as available commodities in the U.S. popular imagination.[39] To this day, not only Brazilian women in the United States but also contemporary Latina artists and performers struggle with Miranda's legacy.[40]

Furthermore, Spanish American nations and Brazil equally share a colonial past connected to the Iberian Peninsula that includes, for instance, Roman Catholicism, the Inquisition and its doubts about "purity of blood,"[41] economies based on slavery, the development of "complex forms of racial taxonomy,"[42] and legacies of the massive colonial accumulation of land by the Spanish and Portuguese, and the concomitant exploitation of labor (read: indigenous and black populations) that it necessitated. The emergence of the Americas in the European awareness and imagination prompted the ideological stratification of humanity, i.e., the "complex 'racial' matrix"[43] of colonial human classification that survived colonialism, abolition, and

---

[36] Ibid., p. 22.
[37] Walter Aaron Clark, "Doing the Samba on Sunset Boulevard," in Walter Aaron Clark (ed.), *From Tejano to Tango: Latin American Popular Music* (New York: Routledge, 2002), pp. 252–76; p. 263.
[38] Sandoval-Sánchez, *José, Can You See?*, p. 57.   [39] Ibid., p. 29.
[40] Beserra, *Brazilian Immigrants in the United States*, p. 42; Torres-Saillant, "The Unlikely Latinas/os," p. 467.
[41] Stuart B. Schwartz, *All Can Be Saved: Religious Tolerance and Salvation in the Iberian Atlantic World* (New Haven, CT: Yale University Press, 2008), p. 52.
[42] Francisco Bethencourt, *Racisms: From the Crusades to the Twentieth Century* (Princeton, NJ: Princeton University Press, 2013), p. 173.
[43] Walter Mignolo, *The Idea of Latin America* (Malden, MA: Blackwell, 2005), p. 17.

independence of young Latin American nations. We are reminded that in order to come to terms with the challenges posed by heterogeneous populations constituted by large segments of impoverished indigenous communities, peoples of African descent, and other poor dark-skinned and mixed-raced peoples, post-independence Creole and mestizo elites and analysts subscribed to the modern discourse of unifying latinidad "in the figure of the *mestizo* or *mulatto*."[44] Focusing their efforts on the productive elaboration of heterosexual *mestizaje/mestiçagem* for unifying national projects, but not necessarily on the eradication of socioeconomic inequity, the all-encompassing credo of Latin American racial and cultural hybridity, which for the purpose of this essay includes the Caribbean too, promised the democratic celebration of the amalgamation of European, indigenous, and African races and traditions. However, since the *mestizaje/mestiçagem* ideology is committed to western European "whiteness,"[45] signified by its inclusionary driving force called *"blanqueamiento/branqueamento"* (read: whitening), instead reinforced prevailing social relations and colonial racial hierarchies of power and continues to do so to the present day.[46] Manifestations of *mestizaje/mestiçagem* have never been uniform across Latin America and have depended on the racial composition of individual national populations and their particular historical and sociopolitical specificities at a given time. Every nation developed a distinctive version of the white supremacist doctrine that rapidly became "symbolic of racial harmony"[47] in a region where "'race' per se" is seldom acknowledged "as an important historical signifier of experience"[48] despite the glaring socioeconomic inequality and political marginalization that nowadays continue to affect black people, indigenous communities, and diverse peoples of color throughout the region.

This state of affairs belies the problematic common sense across the Americas that proposes that "'race' (rather than class or wealth) is *the* fundamental

[44] Peter Wade, *Race and Sex in Latin America* (London: Pluto P, 2009), p. 115.
[45] Luz Angélica Kirschner, "Expanding *Latinidad*: An Introduction," in Kirschner (ed.), *Expanding Latinidad: An Inter-American Perspective* (Tempe: Bilingual Press, Arizona State University, 2012), pp. 1–56; p. 9.
[46] David Theo Goldberg, *The Threat of Race: Reflections on Racial Neoliberalism* (Malden, MA: Blackwell, 2008), p. 219.
[47] Peter Wade, "Race and Nation: An Anthropological View" in Nancy P. Appelbaum, Anne S. Macpherson, and Karin Alejandra Rosemblatt (eds.), *Race and Nation in Modern Latin America* (Chapel Hill: University of North Caroline Press, 2003), pp. 263–81; p. 263.
[48] Suzanne Oboler and Anani Dzidzienyo, "Flows and Counterflows: Latinas/os, Blackness, and Racialization in Hemispheric Perspective," in Oboler and Anani Dzidzienyo (eds.), *Neither Enemies Nor Friends: Latinos, Blacks, Afro-Latinos* (New York: Palgrave, 2005), pp. 3–35; p. 9, original emphasis.

'American' (i.e., U.S.) paradox or dilemma ... while issues of 'class' and poverty – rather than race – are the 'real' problems in Latin America."[49] Even if unspoken, race, ethnicity, pigmentation, and phenotype are indeed barriers to full democratic participation in social life in the lands of the *mestizo/mestico* race. If there is a truly indisputable commonality between Spanish America and Brazil, and throughout the Americas, it is the unambiguous predilection for "whiteness" as Suzanne Oboler and Anani Dzidzienyo articulate,

> "Freedom" has always had a different meaning for Black and other "people of color" through the Americas when they censure their movements on the streets and in areas where people of white-European descent live; when the hemisphere's indigenous populations know that they take a chance by leaving their towns, villages, or reservations, or when African Americans, Blacks, Afro-Latinas/os, Afro-Latin Americans, dark skinned mestizos, and people of Asian descent are discriminated against in terms of employment and denied access to political and other institutions in the societies of the Americas.[50]

Given the elusiveness but lethality of racial classification and stratification in Latin America, coupled with the fast growth of the U.S. Latina/o diasporic population, the United States is becoming more racially and ethnically diverse; the black-white racial binary is evolving into a "postracial" order that very much resembles that of many Latin American countries, leading scholars to express their apprehension about the prospect of the "Latin Americanization"[51] of race relations in the United States.

In the U.S. context, colorblind *mestizaje/mestiçagem* is advanced as "an antidote to racial difference and hierarchy"[52] despite the complicated relationship that Latinas/os have with blackness, as revealed by the segregation of Afro-Latinos and Afro-Brazilians, the stereotyping of indigenous people, and the reluctance to identify as indigenous. These realities challenge the harmonious veneer of the ideology of Latin Americanization that proclaims the irrelevance of race and ethnicity by declaring "We all have Indian blood," "We are all 'Latinoamericanos,'" "we are all mestizos," "*aquí todos somos café con leche; unos más café, otros más leche,*"[53] "We're Brazilian,"[54] and

[49] Ibid., pp. 9–10.   [50] Ibid., p. 6.
[51] Eduardo Bonilla-Silva, *Racism without Racists: Color-Blind Racism and the Persistence of Racial Inequality in the United States* (New York: Rowman & Littlefield Publishers, Inc., 2010), p. 183.
[52] Wade, *Race and Sex in Latin America*, p. 238.
[53] Kirschner, "Expanding *Latinidad*: An Introduction," p. 10
[54] Braga Martes, "Neither Hispanic, nor Black," p. 231.

last but not least, as U.S. president Barrack Obama proclaimed during his visit to Chile in 2011, "We are all Americans. Todos somos Americanos" in postracial times.[55] Moreover, since indigenous populations in Latin America have been considered *the* matter of ethnicity *par excellence* and blacks of racism, little attention has been paid to the cultures of Latin Americans who trace their ancestries to "the Middle East, Asia, or Eastern Europe, or those whose ancestors were characterized as non-Catholics,"[56] which the discourse of *mestizaje/mestiçagem* has managed to "silence" or minimize in mainstream historic accounts of the region.[57] Too often, scholars approach the experiences of these communities as "foreign" to the continent "and thus outside of the national experience," although their presences have been essential to the histories and sociocultural landscapes of Latin American nations.[58] In the U.S. context, this historic exclusion becomes evident in the reluctance of Latinas/os to recognize Latinas/os with the aforementioned heritages as rightful representatives of diverse latinidad or to conceive these experiences as relevant to latinidad.[59]

Brazuca Literature: Challenges and Possibilities

This theoretical excursion not only makes us aware of nationalist, cultural, intellectual, and racial currents, countercurrents, and undercurrents that help us locate the intricate position of contemporary *Brazuca* literature, it similarly begins to unravel the challenges and possibilities that the consolidation of the Brazilian American diaspora (with approximately 350,000 largely undocumented immigrants already forming 1.5 and second generations)[60] and its literature opens for Latina/o literary history and theorizations of latinidad(es). *Brazuca* literature has been produced by Brazilians who have lived and worked not only in the United States, but also countries such as Japan, Portugal, Spain, and Paraguay. Similar to other Latina/o literatures, most of the texts were published in Brazil and have been written in Portuguese by

---

[55] Kirschner, "Expanding *Latinidad*," p. 29.
[56] Jeffrey Lesser and Raanan Rein (eds.), "Introduction," in *Rethinking Jewish-Latin Americans* (Albuquerque: University of New Mexico Press, 2008), pp. 1–40; p. 23.
[57] Kirschner, "Expanding *Latinidad*," p. 12.
[58] Jeffrey Lesser, *Immigration, Ethnicity, and National Identity in Brazil, 1808 to the Present* (New York: Cambridge University Press, 2013), p. 197.
[59] Kirschner, "Expanding *Latinidad*," pp. 19–28.
[60] Robert Henry Moser and Antonio Luciano de Andrade Tosta, "Brazilian Voices: Brazilian American Literature," in Moser and Andrade Tosta de (eds.), *Luso-American Literature: Writing by Portuguese-Speaking Authors in North America* (New Brunswick, NJ: Rutgers University Press, 2011), pp. 167–71; p. 167.

first-generation immigrants, exiles, or visitors who lived, worked, or traveled to other countries; this literature includes letters, diaries, novels, poetry, short stories, *crônicas*, and critical essays. In the context of the Americas, the writing has attempted to represent the complex and ambivalent relations between Brazil and the United States during the twentieth century and to creatively map a definition of a Brazilian national identity; these texts "mark the starting point of a Brazilian-American literature."[61] To mention some *Brazuca* sojourners would be to include, for instance, the poet and journalist Joaquim de Sousa Andrade, better known as Sousândrade (1832–1902), whose forms and techniques made him a marginal figure during his lifetime. Misunderstood by his conservative contemporaries, more recent literary critics have celebrated Sousândrade as "modernist before his time,"[62] "Pound's precursor,"[63] forerunner of Marinetti's "futurism,"[64] and "the epitome of a late experimental romanticism."[65] Today Sousândrade is also hailed as the patron of the writers of the literature of the Brazilian diaspora.[66] While working in New York City as a journalist in the 1870s, the abolitionist Sousândrade published the epic poem *Guesa errante* (Guesa the Errant). In thirteen cantos the classic represents the pan-American and transatlantic journey from the Andes through the Amazon, Brazil, Senegal, the Caribbean, Central America, and New York of *Guesa*, the mythological sacrificial victim of the Muysca Indians of the great plain Bogotá, Colombia,[67] on his mission to restore humanity. The political and poetically radical poem criticizes the brutality of the conquest and the devastation it brought upon subjugated peoples, foreshadowing Pablo Neruda's New World epic *Canto general*, 1930–1950.[68] Sousândrade's

---

[61] Antonio Luciano de Andrade Tosta, "American Dream, *Jeitinho Brasileiro*: On the Crossroads of Cultural Identities in Brazilian-American Literature," in Carlota Caulfield and Darién J. Davis (eds.), *A Companion to US Latino Literatures* (Woodbridge: Tamesis, 2007), pp. 140–57; p. 144.

[62] Rachel L. Price, *The Objects of the Atlantic: Concrete Aesthetics in Cuba, Brazil, and Spain, 1868–1968* (Evanston, IL: Northwestern University Press, 2014), p. 79.

[63] Ignacio Infante, *After Translation: The Transfer and Circulation of Modern Poetics across the Atlantic* (New York: Fordham University Press, 2013), p. 133.

[64] Domício Coutinho, "O patron, profeta e precursor Sousândrade," unpublished paper prepared for the "*III Encontro Mundial de Escritores Brasileiros no Exterior*," CLACS Center for Latin American and Caribbean Studies at NYU, Sept. 2–3, 2015.

[65] "Sousândrade from *O Guesa Errante: The Wall Street Inferno*," in Jerome Rothenberg and Jeffrey C. Robinson (eds.), *Poems for the Millennium: Book of Romantic and Postromantic Poetry, Volume Three* (Berkeley: University of California Press, 2009), pp. 655–63; p. 662.

[66] Coutinho, "O patron, profeta e precursor Sousândrade."

[67] Infante, *After Translation*, pp. 121–22.

[68] Haroldo de Campos, "The Trans-American Pilgrimage of Sousândrade's *Guesa*," in Antonio Sergio Bessa and Odile Cisneros (eds.), *Novas: Selected Writings of Haroldo de Campos* (Evanston, IL: Northwestern University Press, 2007), pp. 194–200; p, 199.

apocalyptic episode "The Wall Street Inferno" from Canto X reveals the poet's ambivalence toward the rise of monopoly capitalism and its concomitant culture of speculation, which was becoming the driving force of world economy during the second half of the nineteenth century. Comparative readings of Sousândrade and his contemporary, the Cuban José Martí (1853–1895), interpret the authors as concrete poets whose verses reveal a common commitment to "non-linear, antidevelopmentalist time"[69] while engaging geopolitical concerns of imperial change and racial economic inequality in their nations of origin and the American hemisphere. More recently, Domício Coutinho interprets Sousândrade's poem as a literary event that anticipates historical events of worldwide relevance such as the Wall Street Crash of 1929 and the destruction of the Twin Towers on September 11, 2001.[70]

Another noteworthy *Brazuca* intellectual is the accomplished essayist, poet, translator, critic, and visiting professor at Yale and the University of Texas at Austin, Haroldo de Campos (1929–2003). With his brother Augusto de Campos, the intellectual rescued Sousândrade from literary oblivion in *ReVisão de Sousândrade* (1964, Revision of Sousândrade) as part of their revision of the Brazilian literary tradition that rehabilitated writers excluded from the national canon. In the 1950s, with his brother and Décio Pignarati (1927–2012), Campos launched the Concrete poetry movement called *Noigrandes*, after a word in one of Ezra Pound's *Cantos*, and projected it internationally. The development demonstrated "the validity and originality of Brazilian culture," placing its literature on equal standing, and in competition with, literatures from the United States and western European nations.[71] Another famed *Brazuca* who decisively contributed to the definition of Brazil's cultural identity was the sociologist and cultural critic Gilberto Freyre (1900–1987), a student of Franz Boas at Columbia University during the 1920s. His candid analysis of the patriarchal slave-plantation world in *Casa Grande e Senzala* (1933, in English *The Masters and the Slaves*), vindicated Brazil's "racial peculiarities" that were often made responsible for Brazil's underdevelopment by European and U.S. observers.[72] Despite Freyre's expressed endeavor to correct interpretations of the role of blacks and indigenous people in Brazilian society, however, *Casa Grande e Senzala* does

---

[69] Price, *The Objects of the Atlantic*, pp. 77–78.
[70] Coutinho, "O patron, profeta e precursor Sousândrade."
[71] Fitz, *Brazilian Narrative Traditions*, p. 83.
[72] Zita Nunez, *Cannibal Democracy: Race and Representation in the Literature of the Americas* (Minneapolis: University of Minnesota Press, 2008), p. 64.

not advance "a union or mixture of 'contradictory elements' or of different races equally apprehended."[73] Although his persuasive narrative of Brazilian identity formation promotes racial mixture as an antidote to racism, Freyre upholds a racial blending in which black and indigenous people ideally dissolve into the white race. His assimilationist account ultimately focuses "on the partnering of black and indigenous women with white men" in a benevolent movement toward *"enbranquecimento"* (whitening) in the formation of Brazil.[74]

More recently, as *Brazuca* literature addresses the struggles of the transnational Brazilian diaspora with the dilemmas of their cultural identity in the U.S. context and the sense of displacement produced by the categories Latina/o or Hispanic, occasionally this writing reveals "underlying prejudices" against Latinas/os.[75] It also true, however, that the majority of texts display dynamic intercultural relationships and exchanges. Authors belonging to the 1.5 and second Brazilian-American generations, such as Roberto DaMatta, Regina Rheda, Johnny Lorenz, and Claudia Nogueira, write literature in both Portuguese and English. The literary history of contemporary *Brazuca* literature also includes the award-winning first-generation Adriana Lisboa, who currently resides in Boulder, Colorado. Lisboa's writing includes novels, short stories, flash fiction, poetry, and books for children penned in Portuguese that often document intercultural and polyglot interactions; her widely acclaimed works *Sinfonia im branco* (2001) and *Azul corvo* (2010), which respectively engage the unarticulated horrors of the military dictatorship in Brazil and problematize ideas of home, have been translated into English as *Symphony in White* (2010) and *Crow Blue* (2014).

Due to space constraints, I will now discuss literary pieces written in English by Luana Monteiro and Kathleen de Azevedo in some detail. Born in Recife, Brazil, Monteiro moved to the United States in 1993, where she now lives, in Madison, Wisconsin; her work *Little Star of Bela Lua: Stories from Brazil* was first published in 2005. Like other Latina/o authors, Monteiro's collection of lyrical prose has been acclaimed for her skillful use of magical realism in which the natural and unnatural intersect flawlessly. Case in point is "The Whirling Dove," the closing short story of the collection, which moves back and forth between Brazil and the United States while addressing, I suggest, transgressive and non-tragic female sexuality. Inflected with words in Portuguese and Spanish, the account narrates Cloé's life struggle with her

---

[73] Ibid., p. 63.   [74] Ibid., p. 73.
[75] Moser and de Andrade Tosta, "Brazilian Voices: Brazilian American Literature," p. 170.

non-normative sex life as a consequence of the character's possession of a *pomba gira*, the whirling dove of the story, a well-known figure in Brazil also recognized by the name of Maria Padilha. In the Afro-Brazilian spirit world, *pomba gira* stands for the sexually independent and childless woman, the opposite of "the docile, domestic, and maternal female."[76] At the age of thirteen, the account reveals, sensuous Cloé is formally familiarized with the world of *pomba gira* through the unabashed sexual content of the Brazilian adaptation of Georges Bizet's tragic opera *Carmen* that used to be broad-casted on television at midnight. But Monteiro's narrative likewise displays how the sexually active Cloé would have to experience two failed marriages, conflict-ridden experiences with Catholicism and Pentecostalism, many years of bad conscience, and recurrent bouts of depression to finally come to terms with her non-normative female sexuality and life prospects. In Monteiro's account, Cloé's proud return to Bahia at the end of the story signalizes the character's guiltless acceptance of having a non-tragic *pomba gira;* her aware-ness that, in "a man's world," possessing the spirit of the polyvalent, syncre-tic, and morally ambivalent Maria Padilha "isn't necessarily bad" as long as she knows how to strategically deal with the liminal spirit within the terms of the dominant patriarchal order that seeks to label her, denigrate her emo-tional life, and frame her threatening sexuality.[77]

The 1.5 literary generation also includes *Samba Dreamers* (2006), the first *Brazuca* novel written in English by Kathleen de Azevedo, born in Rio de Janeiro to a Brazilian mother and a Jewish-American father. A teacher of English at Skyline College, Azevedo currently lives in San Francisco; a writer of short fiction, poetry, and nonfiction, she focuses her research on the history of Brazilian Jews. The replica of Desi Arnaz playing the conga on the cover of the book, along with the name of her fictional character Carmen Socorro, a controversial Brazilian bombshell, displays Azevedo's awareness of the cen-trality of Desi Arnaz and Carmen Miranda in the construction of clichéd latinidad including tropical Brazilianness, Cubanness, and Latin Americanness in the Hollywood imaginary. The destiny of the main character, the Brazilian American Rosea Socorro Katz – Carmen Miranda's literary daughter – in Azevedo's novel, however, reveals that, despite Rosea's struggles to problem-atize the typecasting of Brazilians, Brazilian Americans, Latinas/os, and Latin

---

[76] Kelly E. Hayes, "The Dark Side of the Feminine: Pomba Gira Spirits in Brazil," in Chima J. Korieh and Philomina Okeke-Ihejirika (eds.), *Gendering Global Transformation: Gender, Culture, Race, and Identity* (New York: Routledge, 2009), pp. 119–32; p. 123.

[77] Luana Monteiro, "The Whirling Dove," in *Little Star of Bela Lua: Stories from Brazil* (New York: Harper Perennial, 2006), pp. 187–225; p. 211.

Americans while simultaneously seeking to vindicate and control the image of her legendary mother who contributed to said stereotyping, the character eventually fails to achieve either goal. Although disparaging ethnic stereotypes resulting from racialized cultural hierarchies and sexism injure Rosea, ultimately, it is unquestioned power structures based on the "inevitable need for dominance" that converge to bring about her tragic end.[78] She remains unaware that the struggle "for empowerment and recognition is a complex and probably never-ending process, a dynamic state of constant transition, ambiguity, and contradiction that requires our ongoing 'search for nonessentialist forms of cultural politics.'"[79] Rosea's suicide, I suggest, results from her failure to see herself as more than a victim – i.e., as a social actor who can protest the hierarchical structures that oppress her and cause her unbearable despair – with the result that the narrative leaves the reader with the lingering image of an incoherent Jewish Catholic Brazilian-American woman, that is, with a helpless Latina who remains a disastrously unarticulated minority member. Azevedo's valuable novel enables us to understand the sources of Rosea's misery and to become more sensitive to the dangers of an ontological understanding of ethnicity; rather, the novel encourages viewing ethnicity as a social construct created within a racial context in which the ruling class and / or minority elites make "the system of racial categories, hierarchies, and politiculture."[80] These observations redirect us to the defining moments in the 1970s, when arbitrarily Iberianness and the Portuguese were excluded from latinidad and which, yet again, should remind Latina/o scholars of the artificiality yet material violence of ethnic categories.

Strictly speaking, ethnic groups usually do not name themselves in the United States. Their *"characterization,"* i.e., stereotyping, and *"naming"* occur in a racialized context and are the results of the power of dominant segments to control "the ethnoracial landscape" of the nation which, by maintaining a socially and economically stratified society, preserves the racial status quo that protects the position of the dominant groups.[81] And though ethnic groups not always can regulate their labeling and construction, they do have agency in the way they participate "in the politics of race,"[82] act in the face of

---

[78] Luz Angélica Kirschner, *"Samba Dreamers*; or, the Tenuousness of a 'Perfect Ending,'"
in Kirschner (ed.), *Expanding Latinidad: An Inter-American Perspective*, pp. 133–52; p. 148.

[79] Ibid., p. 150; emphasis added.

[80] Vilna Bashi Treitler, *The Ethnic Project: Transforming Racial Fiction into Ethnic Factions* (Stanford, CA: Stanford University Press, 2013), p. 176.

[81] Ibid., pp. 8–9; original emphases.

[82] Arlene Dávila, *Latino Spin: Public Image and the Whitewashing of Race*, (New York: New York University Press, 2008), p. 1.

antagonisms resulting from the manipulation of ethnic struggles, and respond to the racialization that takes place as they perform their race and ethnicity. We need to remember, Arlene Dávila writes, that ethnic groups can be "co-opted" into larger projects of "whitening, which, far from welcoming them to the rungs of whiteness,"[83] participate in the lethal racialization and subjugation of blacks, indigenous peoples, and other people of color. In this sense, *Brazuca* literature and Latina/o literary history are called to not only limit themselves to highlight the instability and fluidity of cultures and/ or their transnational nature; they are advised to never lose sight of the deeply engrained colonial legacy of racism and its gendered hierarchical power structures that historically have informed subjection, despite being deleted from official discourses by the ideology of *mestizaje/mestiçagem*. *Brazuca* and Luso-American literatures and literary criticism can "help dismantle the intellectual paradigms that have historically condoned oppression against specific groups."[84] Cases in point are, for instance, Alexandra Isfahani-Hammond's *White Negritude: Race, Writing, and Brazilian Cultural Identity* (2008), whose approach to Brazil's racial democracy as "a speech act"[85] contributes to extricate the workings of the ideology through the analysis of white-authored prefaces of black writing and of diverse genres of black poetry to unravel the texts' complicity with the erasure of blackness. The theorization of the "remainder" by Zita Nunez in *Cannibal Democracy: Race and Representation in the Literature of the Americas* (2008) critically approaches the discourse of cannibalism in Gilberto Freyre's *Casa Grande e Senzala* and other narratives of identity formation in Brazil and the United States in order to extricate their compromise with genetic whitening. In *Colonialism and Race in Luso-Hispanic Literature* (2006), Jerome C. Branche tackles racially injurious texts written by white colonizers to "challenge the racist archive and the imagination that feeds it"[86] as part of the transformational impulse to explore the meaning of race "articulated under the aesthetic cover of the literary."[87]

---

[83] Ibid., p.18.

[84] Silvio Torres-Saillant, "Racism in the Americas and the Latino Scholar," in Suzanne Oboler and Anani Dzidzienyo (eds.), *Neither Enemies Nor Friends: Latinos, Blacks, Afro-Latinos* (New York: Palgrave, 2005), pp. 281–304; p. 282.

[85] Alexandra Isfahani-Hammond, *White Negritude: Race, Writing, and Brazilian Cultural Identity* (New York: Palgrave, 2008), p. 5.

[86] Jerome C. Blanche, *Colonialism and Race in Luso-Hispanic Literature*, (Columbia: University of Missouri Press, 2006), p. 253.

[87] Ibid., p. 249.

The ethnic diversity of Brazil and the Americas, with immigrants from Europe, Africa, Asia, the Middle East,[88] and the understanding that latinidad is a global phenomenon may help Latina/o scholars become more sensitive to the ethnic, religious, and cultural diversity, even if to different degrees, of other Latin American nations and therefore Latinas/os in the United States. These recognitions demand "a new historical consciousness"[89] that will of necessity disrupt the Christian and non-Catholic Christian paradigms that govern substantial sectors of Latina/o cultural and identity discourses. *Brazuca* literature, after all, inherits the aforesaid religious plurality (as the discussed works of Luana Monteiro and Kathleen de Azevedo reveal) but also the religious imaginaries present in the writing of other renowned *Brazuca* authors such as Moacyr Scliar or Milton Hatoum, who from Jewish Ashkenazic and Arab immigrant sensibilities respectively have addressed the fallacy of the Brazilian racial paradise and narrated tensions between Judaism, Christianity, and Islam in the western hemisphere and elsewhere.[90] Along these lines, we should remember Latina writers such as Demetria Martínez, Denise Chávez, Kathleen Alcalá, and Achy Obejas, who have emphasized Sephardic history as integral to the Latina/o communities,[91] a growing number of Latin Americans who express appreciation of "their Morisco or Sephardi *converso* lineage,"[92] and Latina/o Muslims retrieving the silenced heritage of "Muslim Spain"[93] to find a voice and affirm their latinidad. Latest readings of Freyre's work indeed reveal the importance that the intellectual gave "to the Moorish-Sephardic cultural history of Portugal as actively

---

[88] Nelson H. Vieira, ed., *Contemporary Jewish Writing in Brazil: An Anthology* (Lincoln: University of Nebraska Press, 2009); Zelideth María Rivas, "Narrating Japaneseness through World War II: The Brazilianization, Peruvianization, and U.S. Americanization of Immigrants," in Kirschner (ed.), *Expanding Latinidad: An Inter-American Perspective*, pp. 109–122.

[89] Hjamil A. Martínez-Vázquez, in Ada María Isasi-Díaz and Eduardo Mendieta (eds.), "The Act of Remembering: The Reconstruction of U.S. Latina/o Identities by U.S. Latina/o Muslims," *Decolonizing Epistemologies: Latina/o Theology and Philosophy* (New York: Fordham University Press, 2012), pp. 127–50; p. 128.

[90] Daniela Birman, "Orientalism in Milton Hatoum's Fiction," in Paul Amar (ed.), *The Middle East and Brazil: Perspectives on the New Global South* (Bloomington: Indiana University Press, 2014), pp. 308–21; Stefania Chiarelli, "Images of Displacement in Brazilian Literature," in Kirschner (ed.), *Expanding Latinidad: An Inter-American Perspective*, pp. 87–94.

[91] Kandiyoti, Dalia, "Sephardism in Latina Literature," in Yael Halevi-Wise (ed.), *Sephardism: Spanish Jewish History and the Modern Literary Imagination*, (Stanford, CA: Stanford University Press, 2012), pp. 235–55; p. 235.

[92] Ella Shohat and Robert Stam, "Tropical Orientalism: Brazil's Race Debates and the Sephardi-Moorish Atlantic," in Paul Amar (ed.), *The Middle East and Brazil: Perspectives on the New Global South*, pp. 119–61; p. 123.

[93] Martínez-Vázquez, "The Act of Remembering," p. 138.

shaping Brazilian customs and practices";[94] Freyre invokes Islam and the Orient to theorize "a cultural synthesis based on eroticized systems of domination."[95] Despite the fact that Spain and Spanish Americans remain largely marginal to discourses of latinidad, María DeGuzmán shows that not only Latina/o Muslims and Jewish Latinas/os approach Spain as a source of identity and a means to come to terms with marginalization in the U.S. context. Queer Latina/o writers and cultural critics who do not view Spain "as a fixed entity"[96] claim Federico García Lorca and the "multicultural Indo-Afro-Arabic-Jewish-Andalusia and Southern Spain" to work through experiences of marginalization, alienation, sexism, and heterosexism in Anglo and Latina/o contexts.[97] In the meantime, as Latina/o scholars acknowledge meaningful differences and equally establish "meaningful commonalities,"[98] we will expand our critical understanding of latinidad(es), *Brazuca*, Brazilian-American, Brazilian, Spanish-American, Spanish, and Luso-American literatures, identities, and cultures as part of a broader Latina/o culture in the United States, while avoiding complicity in the ranking of humanity, the reinforcement of color-lines between blacks and non-blacks, the perpetuation of silence about racism in purported raceless times, and the predisposition "to put a worth on human differences."[99]

[94] Shohat and Stam, "Tropical Orientalism," p. 123.
[95] Alexandra Isfahani-Hammond, "Slave Barracks Aristocrats: Islam and the Orient in the Work of Gilberto Freyre," in Paul Amar (ed.), *The Middle East and Brazil: Perspectives on the New Global South*, pp. 162–81; p. 177.
[96] María DeGuzmán, *Spain's Long Shadow: The Black Legend, Off-Whiteness, and Anglo-American Empire*, (Minneapolis: University of Minnesota Press, 2005), p. xxv.
[97] Ibid., p. 299.
[98] Elizabeth Russ, "Transnationalism," in Suzanne Boost and Frances R. Aparicio (eds.), *The Routledge Companion to Latina/o Literature*, (New York: Routledge, 2013), pp. 172–81; p. 172.
[99] Bashi Treitler, *The Ethnic Project*, p. 11.

30

Staging Latinidad and Interrogating Neoliberalism in Contemporary Latina/o Performance and Border Art

LAURA G. GUTIÉRREZ

On August 27, 2005, David Smith captured mainstream media's attention with an unusual cannonball stunt. Playing the role of a cannonball while human, Smith was launched over the border that divides Mexico and the United States, Tijuana and San Ysidro to be specific. As a form of popular entertainment, this particular spectacle has a long historical trajectory going back to the 1800s. But there were two key things that made this human cannonball performance different from others. First of all, it occurred on the border that divides two nation-states, and marked the first time that a cannon had catapulted a human across such a divide. As Smith flew over the border, he flashed his U.S. passport in order to prove that he had the proper documentation on hand to enter the United States. Secondly, the context in which this stunt took place also stood outside the conventions of human cannonball performance. Smith's performance was part of a broader artistic piece by the artist Javier Téllez entitled *One Flew over the Void* (Bala perdida), which in itself was part of inSite 2005, a bi-national art series of events and interventions that had taken place since 1992 sporadically, every two to three years.[1]

Téllez, a Venezuelan-born artist currently residing in New York City, was one of the twenty-five-plus artists, collectives, and curators who participated in this last instantiation of inSite. As in previous years, and perhaps more

---

[1] I should note that this was last time inSite took place, in 2005. For a full appreciation of the projects that were part of inSite 2005, I invite the reader to examine the catalogue *[Situational] Public*, edited by Osvaldo Sánchez and Donna Conwell. In addition to the inSite catalogs, some of which are held at the University of California, San Diego, there is some scant scholarship on the subject. See chapters in the following: George Yúdice's *The Expediency of Culture*, Ila Nicole Sheren's *Portable Borders*, and Amy Sara Carroll's forthcoming *ReMex* (University of Texas Press).

emphatically so, inSite 2005 had several elements to it, but at its heart was the creation of a series of conversations between the invited artists and the local communities. A number of these, if not all, resulted in public interventions. Téllez's *One Flew over the Void* is an example of such an artistic and collaborative process. After sustained conversations with patients from a mental health center in Las Playas, Tijuana, Mexico, the members of this one-time collective led a parade to the northwestern corner of Mexico, delimited by the border fence and the ocean. Once they had arrived at the site, those who had been part of the parade engaged with the public at large in the tradition of a town fair. This event involved music and dancing, but the event's climatic moment was the catapulting of Smith across the border. Using the tropes associated with fairs, parades, and other forms of popular entertainment, and through the artistic and collaborative process described above, this public performative intervention explored the limits and the porosity of mental and spatial borders.

One Flew over the Void's multifaceted deployment of artistic production – process, collaboration, public intervention, and public engagement – can be read from different angles.[2] However, for the purposes of this essay that centers the concept of performance through the discourses of latinidad and neoliberalism, I want to focus on this intervention's intention, to call into question borders and how they are constructed or upheld by neoliberal economic and social regimes. Yet, I want to also be mindful of the ways in which a critique of economic restructuring on a global scale might also be circumscribed by it. In other words, a significant number of performative artistic practices produced by Latinas/os, or from within the discourse of critical Latina/o studies, interrogate neoliberalism. This should not be a surprise to anyone; these are often alternative (read non-mainstream) artistic interventions that are responding to the ways in which economic restructuring has affected the working poor around the globe in disproportionate numbers, and this includes Latinas/o in this country.

An example of this is the dismantling of the unions in the United States has had grave consequences for Latinas/os as the possibilities for employment with (semi-) decent living wages were eroded with this practice, one of the principal characteristics of neoliberal tactics. And yet another neoliberal tactic has been the relaxation of tariffs for commercial trade across nation-states that has also facilitated the entry of products and companies into Latin

___

[2] For the most extensive academic study of *One Flew over the Void*, see Ila Nicole Sheren's *Portable Borders: Performance Art and Politics on the U. S. Frontera since 1984*.

American countries, mostly from the United States, but also from other so-called first-world countries. Both of these tactics have had grave effects for Latinas/os as modes of employment have become more precarious, numerous people from Latin America have had to leave their country in search of a better way of living, many of whom decide to cross into the United States without proper documentation. As David Harvey has argued in *A Brief History of Neoliberalism*, neoliberalism is a political philosophy that argues – and has convinced states, corporations, and individuals – that freedom of the market translates into human freedom; he writes: "The assumption that individual freedoms are guaranteed by freedom of the market and of trade is a cardinal feature of neoliberal thinking, and it has long dominated the U.S. stance towards the rest of the world" (7). This reconceptualization of freedom has, however, mostly benefitted the corporations and the states that support them.

However, I would be remiss if I did not attend to some of the ways in which contemporary artistic interventions come to exist precisely because of a neoliberal cultural apparatus (i.e., funding structures for the arts, particularly from the private corporate sector); that is, we can identify within neoliberalism moments in which the simultaneous presence of other discourses has ironically provided a space for artistic interventions that critique neoliberalism.[3] In *The Expediency of Culture*, George Yúdice has argued that culture – including so-called alternative culture – has been used by and/or benefitted the neoliberal state. My analysis of Téllez's intervention is not as critical of contemporary cultural production as Yúdice's, even as I agree with his argument. Or, as a form of clarification, I want to highlight that despite the trappings of neoliberal logic and how institutions are permeated by this logic, we need to account for the important function that Latina/o cultural production has had in its critique of neoliberalism since the 1990s, if not before. This is the main objective of this essay.

Having said that, here I emphasize the ways in which three operative rubrics for understanding contemporary cultural production and criticism weave in and out of each other at different key moments in the last thirty years: performance, latinidad, and neoliberalism. By no means a comprehensive examination of the ways in which these three analytics function jointly, this essay simply aims to introduce the reader to some work – just to reiterate, Latina/o performance that interrogates neoliberalism – that can

---

[3] I wish to thank Ramón Rivera-Servera for pushing me to think further on this point.

be understood via these three categories of analysis. As Ramón Rivera-Servera writes in *Performing Queer Latinidad*: "Latinidad cannot be properly addressed without attending to the political economies that have shaped both the living conditions of Latinas/os living in the United States and their available strategies for making sustainable and pleasurable lives" (22). Thus, latinidad as a process of becoming for people of a shared Latin American heritage living in the United States finds in performance (here widely understood) a perfect stage from which to continue to perform identities in a critical and complex way. And, depending on the performance, it could either question or exalt the conditions that make Latina/o life bearable or pleasurable. However, while we may be better able to identify less progressive understandings or expressions of Latina/o identity in other expressive cultures, particularly in mass or popular culture, in performance art and other forms of experimental expression, the latinidad that is staged is in a sense more oppositional. It is contesting dominant forms of oppression, including what can be discerned as either or both epistemic and material violence brought about by a new economic model.

On the (Performance of the) Exhaustion of Neoliberalism

During the session "Kill the Keyword?" at the 2014 American Studies Association conference in Los Angeles, the audience had the opportunity to nominate keywords that they felt were no longer necessary for the field of American studies. Among the different keywords nominated to receive the death sentence, and after much debate among the panelists and the audience, the only one that was not granted immunity was neoliberalism. While the experimental and open-format conversation between the panelists and the audience members considered that other key terms for American studies still had some significance, as long as they were rethought or further complicated (ironically, even the concept "to complicate" was saved from the death sentence), the final consensus on neoliberalism was that it had become evacuated of any specificity due to its being so overused in academic discourse. Something that I both fully agree with but also feel persuaded to argue that, in regard to Latina/o studies, it may still be a useful concept, if, for nothing else, to historicize.

But, as the reader has already come to appreciate from the opening of this essay, I want to propose that we, as Latina/o studies scholars, have not done the adequate historical work of thinking about the ways in which Latina/o thought and the discourse of neoliberalism are more than two points of contact on the timeline of historical developments of the last twenty-five to thirty years. Thus, I acknowledge the current conversations in academia, such as the one during ASA 2014 where I find myself agreeing with those who believe that "neoliberalism" as a critical term for examining culture and society has been evacuated due to its overuse. Yet, at the same time, I want to offer the following provocation: considering the vast amount of work produced by some Latina/o contemporary artists where they have used their critical voice and artistic practice to challenge the ways in which excessive forms of capitalism, deregulation, privatization, and free-trade accords have impacted Latina/o social life, we have not done sufficient research, thinking, and writing about it.

Coupled with the above, there is something else that needs to be considered. Against the backdrop of the development of Latina/o studies and the presence of neoliberal discourses and practices, there is also a predominance of Latina/o performance since the decade of the 1990s that has been understudied and that came into existence because of or despite the neoliberalization of the world economy. In other words, I simply ask: can we begin to assess what the 1990s meant in terms of both Latina/o performance practices and the significant amount of production and the scholarly inquiries around them? This essay also aims to do that, open up the possibility to say that we are at a point in which we can begin thinking about what the past thirty years has meant and to evaluate where we are now, and continue to do research and produce knowledge and theorize around the intersection of latinidad, performance, and neoliberalism.

To further push the conversation, as I have been mostly focusing on border performance, I now want to think through another site for or of performance that is also staging latinidad as it interrogates neoliberalism: the gendered body. I am particularly interested in embodied performances that can also be described as feminist and queer interrogations of neoliberalism and that move within and through a transnational circuit. In a sense it continues with the previous idea in this essay, the ways in which site-specific work on and about the border, serves as a stage for pushing our understanding of latinidad, which is not solely constituted through the experiences of Latinas/os in the United States, but always in relation to what is happening across borders and throughout the hemisphere.

I aim, in other words, to (re)introduce the reader to my previous scholarly work on Latina performance at the same time that it actualizes it by bringing to the fore – in an attempt to historicize – the ways in which a number of artists from different disciplinary and artistic formations interrogate neoliberalism from a feminist and queer vantage point. In the remainder of this essay, I will focus on feminist and queer interrogations of neoliberalism to think about the ways in which different artists and/or collectives who are situated within a transnational circuit of performance and exhibition respond (directly or subtly) to the ways society and culture have been restructured under this "new" economic regime. Lastly, in pondering about the valence of the concept of "performance" to critically examine feminist and queer experimental art, public interventions, political cabaret, and mass-mediated representations, this essay also serves as a way to further think about and expand the capaciousness of the field of Latina/o cultural studies.

Bala perdida and Border Performance Art

Taking the above into consideration, let us now turn to Téllez's *One Flew over the Void* once again for a closer look. I suggest that this performance intervention – as others that I will discuss in more detail in this essay – offers us an opportunity to be capacious in our understanding of both latinidad and performance. I should point out, however, that I am less interested in naming latinidad for who is creating the piece – although Téllez's own biography offers that possibility to be expansive – than for the themes and strategies that it addresses: migration, border crossing, transnationalism. Likewise, performance here is being used in an ample way, an artistic, social, and cultural embodied practice. Border performance art has been, in some ways, bourgeoning alongside and in conversation with the critical academic concept of latinidad. However, if we look at the scholarly attention that, let us say, the Border Arts Workshop/Taller de Arte Fronterizo and one of its members, Guillermo Gómez-Peña, have received, we may begin to think that this is what constitutes border performance. I am thus trying to insist that we push not just the way in which we think about border performance through the analytics of latinidad and neoliberalism, but also the site-specific work other artists and performers are and have been doing.

To put it more succinctly, Latina/o studies methods and the advances in the field in terms of identifying and expanding on our objects of study and themes provide us with the opportunity to recognize the political possibilities of a performance intervention like *One Flew over the Void*. Thus, despite the centrality and almost exclusivity that the actual performance of the catapulting of a human across a geo-political border in the media, the overall performative intervention – from the dialogic collaboration between Téllez and the mental health patients to the parade (and use of theatrical conventions to stage it) – question the logic that drives much of the art market. The creative collaboration between the different people involved across days if not weeks highlights process over product, eliding some aspects of the art market. Additionally, this piece is definitely adhering to one of the most salient precepts of Latina/o studies, a commentary on the uneven historical and economic power relations between the United States and Mexico, or, in more general terms, Latin America. The power of the critique resides in the ways in which embodied practices defy the maxim that there is an artistic product that has value and can be bought, sold, or traded. Additionally, and similarly to the bulk of Latina/o performance and border art, *One Flew over the Void* calls attention to the contemporary disparities that were created by the colonial and capitalist system of power. Although colonialism and capitalism are hardly new, I would venture to say that these disparities have become even more salient in the last forty years as privatization and free trade have expanded, and social welfare responsibilities began to rest on the individual under neoliberalism.

It could be said that a significant number of the public interventions that were part of inSite 2005, eleven years after the North American Free Trade Agreement (NAFTA) had been signed and implemented, were also actively interrogating neoliberalism, in particular in the ways in which it was affecting labor, migration, and border relations. Another example of a public intervention that had several layers of process and production is the creation of a line of cross-trainer, low-top sneakers by New York-based Argentine-born Judi Werthein. Werthein's line of *Brinco* shoes generated a massive amount of discussion and controversy because they were manufactured in China, but were distributed in two locations. On the Mexican side of the U.S.–Mexico border, they were distributed for free to would-be border-crossers, the part of the intervention that provoked controversy because, as conservative news pundits posed, the artist was enabling illegality. On the U.S. side the shoes were sold in a high-end boutique in San Diego at over $200 a pair, which highlights the question of commodity fetishism. In short, this intervention had, at the very least, the intention of making a commentary on "illegal" immigration, global labor, and consumer culture.[4] However, as I suggested

---

[4] For an analysis of another inSite 2005 see my article "Sneaking into the Media: Judi Werthein's *Brinco* Shoes and Post-Border Art, Illegal Immigration, Global Labor and Mass Media." It discusses the public reception to the Brinco shoes that Werthein conceived and manufactured for inSite 2005. See also: www.reintentionexhibition.com/brincos/.

above, these types of interventions are not exclusive to 2005. In fact, this bi-national performance and collaborative art series of events have been using the location – the U.S.–Mexico border – to stage the concerns related to the restructuring of the economy and the effect this would have or was having on working people since the early 1990s. And, while the materiality of the border is unquestionable, what border art and performative interventions have been demonstrating is that there are moments in which the border becomes porous. Furthermore, what I am suggesting is that in the border's porosity – whether this is tangible or discursive – we find the inimitable stage where latinidad is created, represented, debated, performed, and lived.

Neoliberal Interrogations and the Female Body in *Stuff*

In previous writings I have examined the ways in which Chicana perform-ance and conceptual artist Nao Bustamante's video performance *The Chain Goes South* (1996) can be read as a critique of a U.S.-based multinational company and its neocolonial or imperialist tendencies to conquer the world, in particular here the country south of the U.S.–Mexico border. *The Chain Goes South* documents a cross-border public intervention wherein Busta-mante, dressed as Ronaldo McDonaldo, demanded free meals from every McDonald's chain restaurant on a road trip from San Francisco to Mexico City, and, as I have stated, "the maniacal characteristics of transnational capital and the ways in which through it and because of it the United States and Mexico are historically and economically bound: A chain, allegorized here by McDonald's binds the two countries" (*Performing Mexicanidad* 150). In this essay I would like to focus my attention on a performance in which Bustamante collaborated with Cuban American performance and conceptual artist Coco Fusco, the same year, to make a similar commentary about North and South relations through their performance play *Stuff*. And while it may also bring in the question of food and travel, it does so differently. But what is important to mention is that, as opposed to the border performance *One Flew over the Void* from the previous sections, the interrogation and critique of neoliberalism that these two Latina feminist performers offer us in *Stuff* is more direct.

The performance *Stuff* uses humor to think about the cultural myths that link Latinas and "food to the erotic in the Western popular imagination" (Fusco, 111). To be more precise, Bustamante and Fusco spoof North and South relations where the West's understanding of Latin America as a cannibalist Other is satirized through the use of food as a stand-in for sex. Again, in Fusco's words, *"Stuff* is our commentary on how globalization and its accompanying versions of cultural tourism are actually affecting women of color both in the third world, and in Europe and North America, where hundreds of thousands of [Latinas] are currently migrating to satisfy consumer desires for 'a bit of the other'" (Fusco, 111). The performance piece's premise revolves around the idea that consumers no longer have to travel beyond the comforts of their own Northern location to consume the Other, it is delivered to them. In a more structural way, *Stuff* "consists of a series of five sketches loosely connected by the premise that they are being brought to us by 'The Institute of Southern Hemispheric Wholeness' – a tourism company promising 'ritual without revolution' and 'sweat without heat' to Northern vacationers" (Weatherson, 516). Of all of the characters that traverse the stage I want to briefly mention Marta, from the Mexican state of Chiapas, who stands before us, the audience, ready to sell the Zapatista dolls that her mother crafts in the likeness of important Zapatistas struggling for indigenous rights in her home state. Although other important "events" were taking place in Latin America, particularly in Cuba, as sexual tourism to the island in the mid 1990s is also presented to be critiqued, I want to argue that the simultaneous insurrection of the Zapatistas and the implementation of NAFTA on January 1, 1994 was highly influential in the ways in which Latina feminist artists were aiming to amplify their critique; they were understanding very well the ways in which gender and sexuality are not isolated from the political and economic systems that govern us and our bodies. There is, of course, nothing new here as we can go back to the 1970s and find ample evidence of this, but I do want to emphasize the 1990s as another important moment in which accelerated forms of capitalism, the growth of performance as a legitimate locus of enunciation and denunciation, and transnational circuits of movement brought about a kind of work that needs to be examined. And although in some instances there already is scholarship on this issue, it needs to be reevaluated in a broader context.

At this point I need to mention that the above gesture also applies to my own scholarly production. In my book *Performing Mexicanidad*, the primary analytics are gender and sexuality in relationship to the ways in which embodied performances unsettle heterosexist and nationalist culture. However, and although it may not be evident as it is not framed in such a way, one of the aims there is "to develop methodological and theoretical strategies to understand the dynamics of subjectivity under the neoliberal political and economic systems; that is, I am interested in exploring the imbrication of sexuality, gender, and race with economic, political and informational processes on national and transnational scales" (150). Thus, if we can temporarily refer back to Bustamante's *The Chain Goes South* and the end of that video performance, Ronaldo McDonaldo's entry into Mexico is both literal and symbolic. On one level, this incursion could both be symbolic and literal as there is no denying that since the late 1990s Mexico has seen more U.S.-based transnational corporations set up shop there, not only fast food chains, but also other companies such as Walmart and Home Depot that do their fair share of obliterating existing small-scale businesses. Yet, on another level, I want to take this image of Ronaldo traveling to Mexico as both the easy movement of capital across borders but also the ways in which Latina performers (and I want to be expansive here and include some artists that may not reside in the United States, at least full time) and their works also move transnationally.

The Women of the Port: Body-Nation-Body

In an attempt to be more expansive here, as in *Performing Mexicanidad*, I examine a performance genre that might have been considered minoritarian as it was, particularly during the decade of the 1990s, a mostly independent and at times clandestine form of expression: political cabaret, a mixture of song and dance numbers combined with political satirical sketches that has been thriving in Mexico since that decade, primarily because the first generation of political cabareteros – Jesusa Rodríguez, Liliana Felipe, Astrid Hadad, Tito Vasconcelos, and Regina Orozco – have been working incessantly challenging all forms of hegemonic power, such as the state, the church, the World Bank, and the International Monetary Fund. And one of the things that I argue, and in fact push as an important point to consider, is that the genre does not in any way limit its capaciousness for critique. That is, while we may often think about scantily clad women, sexual puns, and social satire as part and parcel of political cabaret, and it is all of those things (and there is so much delight in watching the *cabareteros* revel in their own pleasure), the work that originated on the independent theater stages in Mexico City and then traveled transnationally, does a great deal with regard to rethinking notions of perversity. That is, and I quote from the book, "I contend that in the cultural production by these Mexican political cabareteras, representations of so-called deviant sexualities are also used deliberately for another purpose: to dislodge the concept of the 'perverse' from the queer female body and displace (or transfer) it to the national or supranational body politic" (12). Astrid Hadad's reappropriation of the figure of the prostitute, embodied by the woman of the port who awaits the arrival of a sailor whom she will service, and her reworking her to invoke Lady Liberty with all of the recognizable symbols of the Statue of Liberty, although with a flashlight instead of a torch, signals the ways in which humor can function as critique. In a fashion similar to *Stuff*, Hadad's use of Lady Liberty to stand-in for the prostitute figure/woman of the port illuminates that sexual tourism within a highly accelerated capitalist system needs to be understood as functioning alongside other forms of transactions that also put the body, however symbolic, at the center.

It should be noted that this strategy for critique among Mexican performers is not exclusive terrain of political *cabareteros*, although the majority of my work may focus on that. Stepping outside of the genre (or subgenre), and perhaps because of the fact that the 1990s were so charged politically, socially, and economically (something that has not exactly left us, I want to argue), artists who used other media were also thinking about this moment and producing work that challenged all forms of dominance. One such person is conceptual artist and activist Lorena Wolffer, who is perhaps better known for her performative interventions as billboard displays at ten different points of Mexico City – I'm referring here to her *Soy totalmente de hierro* (I am made completely of iron) from the beginning of the new millennium (2000). A literal critique of, if not attack upon, the Mexican Palacio de Hierro department store, the billboards highlight advertising campaigns that target women specifically. Wolffer's *Soy totalmente de hierro* mimicked the department store's campaign ("Soy totalmente palacio" / I am completely palace) in order to draw attention to the ways in which women are perceived to be commodities to be sold or traded as the property of men.

Prior to *Soy totalmente de hierro*, and while living in the United States and working as an artist in San Francisco in the mid to late 1990s, Wolffer, who had already been using her body to stage performance interventions, used the tropes associated with female modeling to make a statement about Mexico's precariousness vis-à-vis more powerful entities. Using her body as an allegory of the nation, Wolffer strutted on the catwalk as a model, while wearing nationalist colors and symbols but also showing bruises, cuts, and blood in *If She Is Mexico, Who Beat Her Up?* (1997–1998). The title of the performance did much of the work to allegorize the abuse that nation has endured, particularly if we think about transnational relations. As Wolffer traversed the stage incorporating movements and gestures associated with the endurance of physical and psychic pain and suffering, the accompanying soundtrack was a mash-up of the 1988 U.S. Senate hearings that attempted to decertify Mexico as an ally in the war against drugs and rap music. In my reading of the performance piece, through its different elements, from the title to the use of the physical violence of the woman, from the colors and references to the Mexican nation and the use of audio of the hearings, the pathology of the interpersonal relationship of, let's say couples involved in domestic violence, is displaced and tagged onto the relationship between two nation-states, one that has the power to certify or decertify the other as a good ally in the war on drugs, but also must thread a fine line to not upset the weaker one as it is still an important trading "partner." The context is of course important, if not ironic here, at the moment of the hearings we were still within a few years of the signing and implementation of NAFTA, while the performance took place after 1994.

Wolffer's provocation, which also functions in a similar way to the ways in which the previously mentioned political cabaret artists use the body (often cisgendered female) to think about the national and supranational body politic, helps us think not only about the artistic work that was taking place in the decade of the 1990s, but also how it is connected to the present moment. That is, the neoliberal policies, then and now, have placed marginalized people in even more precarious situations. And, as I skirt around what has happened in Mexico in the last nine years or so, first with Felipe Calderón as president from 2006 to 2012 and now during the Enrique Peña Nieto administration, knowing full well that my page limit does not even allow me to scratch at the surface of what has been happening there, much less artistic responses, I want to continue pushing the idea that we need to reassess the 1990s in order to understand not only neoliberal economic policies, but the ways in which Latina/o performance artists were working and collaborating with each other to bring attention to the issues that were affecting (and even afflicting) them across borders.

Lorena Wolffer, in addition to *Soy totalmente palacio* and *If She Is Mexico, Who Beat Her Up?*, was also one of the first artists to begin to draw attention to the working conditions of women in maquiladoras and how they began to disappear in unfathomable numbers during the 1990s. This, by the way, is still perhaps the issue at the heart of her artistic interventions: violence against women. And as a way of circuiting back to U.S.-based Latina artists, and while there has been much cultural work regarding the feminicides[5]

---

[5] Although I am unable to delve more in-depth into a discussion of feminicide along the US–Mexico border and the cultural responses to this phenomenon, I want to briefly

in Ciudad Juárez, I want to return to the work of Coco Fusco. Her one-act play, *The Incredible Disappearing Woman* (performed 2000–2003) not only takes up the question of the female body as disposable under these economic and political regimes of government, but also makes a meta-statement about the art world that also profits from the violence enacted on women of color and other minoritarian subjects. Set in 1998, the play's story occurs in a Southern California contemporary art museum. The cast consists of three Latina migrants (one Chilean, one Salvadoran, and the other Mexican) to the United States, all of whom have roles as custodial employees of the museum, two of them as cleaners and the third as a security guard. The projected mediated screen introduces us to other characters, mainly the artist whose work will be exhibited at the museum and the curator of the show/space. While an extensive analysis of the performance is not possible here, what is important to mention is that these women have to help with an exhibit ("Making a Scene: Art in LA in the 1970s") by participating in a diorama of a particular piece that had been important/controversial in the 1970s; the artist ("an American artist in his late 40s"), Donald Horton, had a piece, "Live Male Seeks Dead Female" that necessitated a female corpse, but, as he recounts in his conversations with the curator on the projected screen, he had trouble finding a dead female in the United States during the development of the piece and therefore had to travel to Mexico to locate one. One of these custodial employees has to perform the role of the dead woman in the diorama. Fusco's critique not only of the ways in which the female body's worth is null, especially once dead, and the uneven North–South relations and the presumptuousness of the United States in terms of locating the macabre south of the border, is here coupled with her critique of the contemporary art world. This meta-commentary of course gives us some pause in terms of the ways in which we can potentially understand the body of artistic work that has surfaced in the NAFTA and post-NAFTA era[6]. How can we do so ethically without jumping on the first bandwagon that

mention my use of feminicide versus the femicide concept that is longer-standing. Since its reformulation by Mexican scholar and activist Marcela Lagarde, feminicide, which extends femicide – the killing of women because they are women – into a political term that attempts to hold the state and its institutions accountable for their misogyny, has become a more apt term to characterize the situation of women in Mexico, Guatemala and other Central American countries, and along the US–Mexico border and, in some cases, into the United States' territory.

[6] By post-NAFTA era I do not mean to imply that we are beyond a NAFTA-era moment; in fact, I would argue quite the contrary, we are only now fully experiencing the effects of the signing of this free trade agreement between the three North American countries, most specially between Mexico and the United States.

comes along – whether feminicides or the war on drugs – in order to think about artistic performances that actually aim to challenge the structural causes of these human tragedies? In a way I am asking questions similar to those of Deborah Paredez, whose seminal work around the performance of Selena and the Tejana artist's afterlives in *Selenidad* proposes that we pair performance studies and Latina feminism in order to think about not just the specter of Selena's body, but think about it alongside "the material consequences for actual Latina bodies" (28). For Paredez, in other words, "Latina feminism enables the acknowledgement and examination of the relationship between the frequently appropriated, once glamorous dead Latina bodies of Evita, Frida, and Selena and other, more quotidian though no less significant Latina deaths that have occurred as the result of welfare reform, border militarization, and the post-NAFTA economy" (28).

Conclusion

In this essay I have used two specific sites, the border and the female body, to argue that, for better or worse, they have been the key locations from which to explore the ways in which a latinidad that questions neoliberalism is staged. The performance interventions that I describe above – those that were part of inSite 2005 – as well as other site-specific border performance art pieces like those of BAW/TAF and the work of Latina performers that exists along a transnational circuit, both in terms of the performance itself but also thematically, do much of the necessary labor to question an important axiom of neoliberalism. In *A Brief History of Neoliberalism*, David Harvey writes:

> Neoliberalism is in the first instance a theory of political economic practices that proposes that human well-being can best be advanced by liberating individual entrepreneurial freedoms and skills within an institutional framework characterized by strong property rights, free markets, and free trade (2).

I return to my initial discussion of Téllez's *One Flew over the Void* as the human cannonball that interrupted into mid-air and across the U.S.–Mexico geopolitical divide serves as spectacularized rendition of the above quote. The freedom for a certain kind of mobility is afforded to only a few with the logics of neoliberal political and economic regimes. For others, working people, women, people of color, the idea of freedom, if it has ever existed, has been further eroded. Instead, as the other performances analyzed in this essay, the Latina body has become a site where these sort of economic experimentations are carried through. But in a similar way, Bustamante, Fusco, Hadad, and Wolffer are also aware that it is through corporeal or embodied performances that they can push back and enact a critique of the uneven ways in which neoliberalism affects Latinas (as other women of color) perhaps more than any other group.

WORKS CITED

Bustamante, Nao and Coco Fusco. "Stuff." *The Bodies that Were Not Ours and Other Writings*. London and New York: Routledge, 2001: 111–27.

Bustamante, Nao and Miguel Calderón. *The Chain Goes South*. Video performance, 1996.

Fusco, Coco. "The Incredible Disappearing Woman." *The Bodies that Were Not Ours and Other Writings*. London and New York: Routledge, 2001: 201–20.

Gutiérrez, Laura G. *Performing Mexicanidad: Vendidas y Cabareteras on the Transnational Stage*. Austin: The University of Texas Press, 2010.

"Sneaking into the Media: Judi Werthein's *Brinco* Shoes and Post-Border Art, Illegal Immigration, Global Labor and Mass Media." *Building Walls in a Borderless World: Media and Human Mobility across Divided Spaces*. Ed. Jaime J. Nasser. *Spectator* 29.1 (Spring 2009): 11–22.

Harvey, David. *A Brief History of Neoliberalism*. Oxford: Oxford University Press, 2005.

Paredez, Deborah. *Selenidad: Selena, Latinos, and the Performance of Memory*. Durham, NC: Duke University Press, 2009.

Rivera-Servera, Ramón H. *Performing Queer Latinidad: Dance, Sexuality, Politics*. Ann Arbor: The University of Michigan Press, 2012.

Sheren, Ila Nicole. *Portable Borders: Performance Art and Politics on the US Frontera since 1984*. Austin: The University of Texas Press, 2015.

Weatherson, Rosemary. "*Stuff* (Performance Review)." *Theatre Journal* 49.4 (1997): 516–18.

Yúdice, George. *The Expediency of Culture: Uses of Culture in the Global Era*. Durham, NC: Duke University Press, 2003.

31

Trans-American Popular Forms
of Latina/o Literature

Genre Fiction, Graphic Novels, and Digital Environments

WILLIAM ORCHARD

The late twentieth and early twenty-first century witnessed a surge in writing by Latinos and Latinas in popular genres. To speak of popular fiction is to evoke a disparate array of fictional categories: some established, like the detective novel and science fiction, and some emergent, such as the horror story and "chica lit." Each of these types of popular writing is governed not only by a familiar set of conventions but is also embedded in specific histories that constrain and enable the exploration of distinct content or modes of thinking. If the term "genre" points to a seemingly inchoate mass of convention-bound writing, the term "popular" is equally fraught. As Juan Flores demonstrates, labeling a body of cultural production "popular" often suggests a series of spatial metaphors that places popular work either below or at the periphery of some normative "center," but this may obscure how work that is "socially peripheral is so frequently *symbolically* central" (Flores 17).[1] As we shall see, the centrality of Latina/o popular fiction emerges from the way this work actively critiques official literary cultures and how it has served as a resource for literary writers who want to explore new political content or give voice to subjects who have been historically excluded from canonical Latina/o literature.[2]

If critics have remained suspicious of popular writing by Latinos, it is in part because of how this body of writing is closely aligned with the marketplace. Indeed, it is difficult speak about Latina/o popular fiction without discussing the larger Latino market that came into being in the late 1990s and 2000s. This

---

[1] Flores is here quoting from the important work of Peter Stallybrass and Allon White on transgression. See Stallybrass and White, 3.

[2] In *Hybrid Cultures: Strategies for Entering and Leaving Modernity*, anthropologist Nestor García Canclini refers to the fluidity between popular and official forms of cultural production as "reconversion" (171–73).

period was also marked by the ascent of neoliberal governance, which saw a retraction of state investment in the public sphere as resources became increasingly privatized as well as a scaling back of regulations and commercial boundaries, perhaps best exemplified in the 1994 North American Free Trade Agreement (NAFTA), that allowed for the transnational circulation of goods and capital. These global economic and political developments produced conditions for imagining and maintaining transnational connections while also foreclosing the opportunities for resource redistribution that would satisfy the social-justice demands of Latinos from a previous generation. While some have seen the growth of a Latino market presence as a sign that the group is increasingly recognized in the economic and political spheres, others have noted how that recognition has often come at the cost of de-politicizing Latinos and rendering them simple commodities ripe for exchange and manipulation. In her ethnographic study of Latino markets and marketing, Arlene Dávila challenges us to consider how marketing is "constitutive of Latinidad" (*Latinos* 3), which requires that critics look beyond representation to consider how production, consumption, and distribution illuminate the ways and ends to which "Latino" is produced in a given instantiation. This resonates with Flores's view that the "popular" should not be considered in spatial metaphors but as "a system of relations" that could suggest the multitudinous and contradictory ways in which politics and power operate.

However, as Raphael Dalleo and Elena Machado Sáez note in their examination of post-1960s Latina/o canon formation, literary critics have been reluctant to see the marketplace in these terms, often separating more contemporary writing (1975–2002) from that which coincided with the social-movement era (1960–1975).[3] On this account, writers of the Civil Rights era – who often identified with a particular nation of origin rather than with the broader Latino category – faced a literary marketplace that marginalized them and that was unreceptive to their commitments to social justice. As a result, this earlier generation not only produced work that scholars continue to regard as properly political but also built institutions, like Arte Público Press or Third Woman Press, to publish and distribute writing when mainstream publishers rejected it.

---

[3] Dalleo and Machado Sáez label the critics who hold this view "anticolonialist" and differentiate them from a group of "multiculturalist" critics and book reviewers who laud post-1960s work for increasing representation and translating Latina/o culture for diverse audiences. While the multiculturalist group is best exemplified by the work of Ilan Stavans, the anticolonialist critics grow out of "broader Caribbean and even hemispheric movements" and include such figures as Juan Flores, Silvio Torres-Saillant, and Frances Negrón-Muntaner (4–6).

In contrast, writers of the next generation – which includes such stalwart figures as Cristina García and Julia Alvarez, who are staples of most contemporary Latina/o literature syllabi – are sometimes regarded with suspicion because they have been published by mainstream publishing houses. On this reading, such writers produce an easily consumable – rather than contestatory – account of cultural difference, translating culture while also abandoning the political demands of the previous generation. According to Dalleo and Machado Sáez, literary critics have tended to "[conceive] of a politics of social justice as incompatible with market popularity" (3). If this suspicion of the market has tainted critical assessment of more recent *literary* fiction, it is compounded for genre fiction, which gravitates toward the commercial rather than the aesthetic and academic ends of the publishing spectrum. Yet, as Dalleo and Machado Sáez argue, and in a way that parallels what Dávila suggests about analyzing the market and Flores about popular culture, scholars must "avoid succumbing to reductive ways of reading the relationship of culture, politics, and the market" (9). Latina/o popular genres have proven unusually responsive to recent shifts in global economic organization and political relations, quickly inventing new protagonists and forms of representation that react to these changes.

Attending to the complicated interplay between politics, culture, and the market requires a set of methodologies and approaches that may differ from those that we bring to mainstream literary works. In addition to being dismissed for its proximity to the market, popular fiction is often discounted for being "genre driven" – which here means being rigidly bound by narrative conventions that render the work a formulaic product rather than an aesthetic achievement. Although genre criticism is often viewed as staid and antiquated, versions of it, particularly those informed by the Frankfurt School, remain powerfully generative. On these accounts, genre narratives are escapist products that interpellate the masses into society's norms, providing a sense of relief that the contradictions of capitalism can be magically resolved by happy endings that are both expected and delivered. However, more recent scholars have come to regard genre in different ways. Lauren Berlant, for instance, notes how genres merit our attention because they are sites of mutual collective recognition: that is, they are sites where certain kinds of unnoticed beings materialize.[4] Insofar as genres provide the

---

[4] Although often not seen in these terms, recent critical considerations have emphasized Berlant's affiliation with genre criticism (see Jackson 2015; also Ducschinsky and Wilson 2014). Her criticism is most distinctly oriented around genre in *The Female Complaint*, but also takes on this cast in *Cruel Optimism*, linking genre in productive ways to a critique of neoliberalism.

conditions of legibility in an environment of erasure, the happy endings derided by those who pursue ideology critique might give way to a critical attention to moments in a text in which, in Berlant's terms, subjects try to "adjust" or imagine worlds that would free them from generic constraints, even if the narrative propels them forward toward an inevitable conclusion (Jackson, n.p.). Read this way, genre fictions reveal how the desire for recognition is often undergirded with a muted but real desire that the world be otherwise.

This view of genre accords with Ramón Saldívar's recent writing on speculative realism and "postrace aesthetics." Saldívar notes how contemporary writers of literary fiction turn to speculative and fantasy modes associated with popular genres in order to produce new racial imaginaries. These writers, most of whom were born after the social movement era or have no personal memory of it, turn away from some of the social realist modes of the previous generation in search of an aesthetic in which "the representation of social justice requires a formal medium incorporating states of fantasy that occupy and override previous attempts to represent the real" (594). These "states of fantasy" often involve deploying the repertoires of popular fiction: Junot Díaz, for instance, draws upon comic book conventions and science fiction tropes in *The Brief Wondrous Life of Oscar Wao* (2007), while Sesshu Foster combines science fiction and counterfactual history in *Atomik Aztex* (2005). If writers like Díaz and Foster – who enjoy wide acclaim – draw on some of the signal features of genre fiction, it is important to note that they are also products of what Mark McGurl terms "the Program Era," a period dating from World War II in which literary fiction writers emerged from or were affiliated with MFA programs in creative writing. According to McGurl, these programs foster "systematic creativity," which is his phrase for creative work that maintains the aura of the "aesthetic" while also formulaically emulating the short stories studied in the workshop environment (72). The Program Era institutionalized fiction writers in the university, bringing them into close proximity with scholars of literature and sometimes creating a feedback loop about what constituted legitimate aesthetic achievement in narrative form. Ethnic American writers were incorporated into this system comparatively late, during a time that overlaps with the development of a Latina/o literary marketplace.[5] In the run-up to the institutionalization of the

---

[5] McGurl's account of the MFA program's rise in significance begins with the establishment of the Iowa Writer's Workshop in 1936, an institution that flourishes in the post–World War II period. If this is the historical framework in which the creative-writing

university-credentialed ethnic fiction writer, scholars of Latina/o literature devoted themselves to securing a place for Latina/o literature in the academy, an endeavor that often meant turning away from popular genres and toward literary objects that conformed to the norms of the discipline. Simultaneously, these scholars worked to define a Latina/o subject who was congruent with those imagined in social movements of the Civil Rights Era and who would provide the field with a necessary coherence as it was establishing itself. The institutionalization of Latina/o literature thus required both a narrowing of Latina/o literary aesthetics, which in narrative often centered on social realist modes of representation, and of the Latina/o subject, often figured as working-class and resistant.

Popular fiction remained a space where alternate aesthetics and neglected subjects found expression. It is no wonder, then, that "postrace" writers of the Program Era have turned to popular genres as they attempt to represent new protagonists of Latina/o literature and to adjust the Latina/o canon's desire for social justice with the altered circumstances caused by globalization and neoliberalism. In contrast to contemporary *literary* writers, most writers of popular Latina/o fiction do not emerge from MFA programs, though they often possess college or graduate degrees in other fields. Indeed, several of these writers actively contest the kinds of representations circulated in literary fiction, but, despite these disavowals, they also share with the "postrace" writers a confidence that genres are ways of bypassing forms of realist representation that are perceived as either exclusionary, stale, or incapable of portraying new social formations and political circumstances. If these dimensions of popular fiction render it an important resource for Latina/o literary production and criticism, one must also recognize the bargains with the market that popular writers must make in order to represent these subjectivities. Insofar as popular works are more heavily mediated by the publishing industry than their more traditional literary counterparts, popular Latina/o fiction must also be seen as a node in a wider Latina/o media industry, which, as Arlene Dávila notes in her recent work on Latina/o media, is a "product of transnational processes" that are rooted

program came to influence the shape of American fiction generally, the same historical frame does not apply to writers of color. Although a few notable Latina/o writers, such as Sandra Cisneros and Helena María Viramontes, attended MFA programs in the late 1970s and 1980s, it is not until the late 1990s and early 2000s that we begin to see a generation of writers of color emerge from these programs. The work of this generation of writers often nimbly negotiated the publishing marketplace and was quick to earn acclaim and secure places on university syllabi.

as much in Latin America as in centers of publishing like New York City (*Media* 2). In order to attend to this aspect of media, Dávila urges us to move beyond simply analyzing representation by turning our "attention to issues of production, circulation, distribution, and consumption" (1). Interpreting popular fiction, then, requires a critical balancing act that is attuned to the history and ideological bent of particular genres like chica lit, science fiction, the detective novel, or horror story, while also remaining alive to the ways in which works contradict genre conventions and provide glimpses of life that could be lived otherwise. Additionally, critics must consider the way in which a given writer situates herself or himself in relation to not only the literary marketplace but also cultural capital, and how readers and publishers respond to or shape the literary output that results from all of these complex negotiations. When we begin to turn a critical eye toward Latina/o popular fiction that emerged in the last twenty years, we also begin to scrutinize forms that were produced but ignored as a Latina/o canon was taking shape, most notably the graphic novel. This, in turn, draws our attention to do-it-yourself work in print and digital media that shares with popular fiction the habit of seizing existing infrastructures to experiment with new content. In this way, popular fiction and the authors who produce it are not simply sellouts who profit from their art and community but rather are continuous with the utopian impulses and institution building that has characterized Latina/o cultural production writ large.

No genre of popular Latina/o fiction demonstrates these interpretive challenges more than chica lit, which, among the genres discussed in this essay, is the most recent to emerge. The story of chica lit's emergence begins with Alisa Valdes-Rodriguez's *The Dirty Girls Social Club* (2003). Educated at the Berklee College of Music and Columbia University School of Journalism, Valdes-Rodriguez had been a reporter for the *Boston Globe* and *Los Angeles Times* before she ventured into fiction writing. Her novel about six Latinas from various national, racial, and class backgrounds who meet at a Boston-area college and are beginning to navigate various professional worlds was eagerly received by a publishing industry that longed for a work that would break into a rising Latina marketplace in the same way that Terry McMillan's *Waiting to Exhale* (1992) and *How Stella Got Her Groove Back* (1996) succeeded with African American women readers. *Dirty Girls* did not disappoint: it was the first novel by a U.S. Latina to debut on the *New York Times* bestseller list. While publishers saw *Dirty Girls* as the latest profitable ethnic incarnation of the established chick lit genre, Valdes-Rodriguez saw her work as a response to an absence in Latina/o literature, telling one interviewer that she "wrote the book that I wanted to read for years . . .. Many of the established Latino writers – Sandra Cisneros, Gabriel García Márquez – spoke more to my grandparents' generation than to mine" (qtd. in Morrison 326). *Dirty Girls* and the chica lit genre emerge, as Catherine Ramírez argues, at the intersection of two crises, one in feminism and the other in Latina representation.

Chick lit develops as a part of a "postfeminist" reevaluation of second-wave feminism, which was criticized in the late twentieth century for making heterosexual men impotent and rendering women frustrated in their desires to find fulfillment in both the domestic and professional spheres (Ramírez 6). In novels like Helen Fielding's *The Bridget Jones Diaries* (1996) and Lauren Weisberger's *The Devil Wears Prada* (2003) and television shows like *Ally McBeal* and *Sex and the City*, a postfeminist response to the second wave constructed women as "subjects of neoliberalism," which is to say "subjects only to the extent that they consume," and was overwhelmingly "concerned with the possible consequences of female independence, such as the emotional isolation often associated with being single and the difficulty of balancing career and romance" (Ramírez 7, 8). For Valdes-Rodriguez and other chica lit authors, this genre provided a vehicle for exploring the lives of upwardly mobile, college-educated Latinas who were emerging as not only potent figures in their respective professions but also in a marketplace where they could exercise tastes that proclaimed their achieved mobility. Yet, the genre's construction of women as "subjects of neoliberalism" often traded consumption for political action, which is most seen in the characters' tendency to respond to racism as something remedied through individual will rather than systemic struggle (Hurt 137).

While *Dirty Girls* is reluctant to engage in the forms of protest apparent in fiction and politics of the preceding generation, it vehemently protests representations *within* Latino/a cultural production, viewing them as stale, outdated, or incapable of addressing the experience of young professional Latinas. Indeed, the narrative blames the stereotypes that characters encounter not on the dominant culture but on Latina/o writing. In the introductory chapter, Lauren, a *Boston Globe* reporter who many readers see as a stand-in for the author's views, asserts her difference by distancing herself from a Latino canon:

> In reality, we *sucias* are all professionals. We're not meek maids. Or cha-cha hookers. We're not silent women playing to the Virgin of Guadalupe with lace *mantillas* on our heads. We're not even like those downtrodden chicks in the novels of those old-school, Chicana writers, you know the ones. (11)

By positioning the experience of the *sucias* against the women represented in the fiction of writers like Sandra Cisneros, Ana Castillo, and Denise Chavez, the narrator Lauren (and the novel) promote a pan-Latina program as a more cosmopolitan advancement on a Chicana politics that is seen as both inaccessibly radical and out of date (Ramírez 16, Morrison 316). In her interview in which she mentions Cisneros, Valdes-Rodriguez also distinguishes her work from that of Garcia Marquez, a rebuke of magical realism that Lauren repeats when she declares that the stories of the *sucias* will not portray "something really super Latina, you know, like . . . a treasured recipe from a short, fat wrinkled old *abuelita* who works erotic magic with *chocolate* and all her secret herbs and spice," a veiled reference to Laura Esquivel's magical realist novel *Like Water for Chocolate* (5). Here, we detect a critique that extends beyond the writers themselves to a literary marketplace that understands "Latino" transnationally and insists that Latina/o writers produce work that repeats the figuration of life presented in the best-known U.S. Latino and Latin American literary works. By turning away from forms of representation that seem stale and instead showing a world that is un-magical, chica lit can lay claim to being realist despite indulging romance conventions.

Chica lit thus negotiates a complex and contradictory set of imperatives: it critiques both the market that enables it and the literary tradition that is its antecedent. Although it mobilizes a popular genre to bring a new identity into the discursive fold, it also is bound by that genre's conventionality to bring the stories its sets loose into formulaic endings. In her analysis of *Dirty Girls*, Debra Castillo notes how each character "must work their way through some ellipsis in identity, to a fuller, more powerful Latina self" (53). The conventional ending may be a sign that the characters are still in ellipsis, and may be one reason why critics often speak about the genre's "ambivalence." Erin Hurt, for instance, sees the genre as producing "an ambivalent Latinidad that argues for a common American sameness, but also insists on a distinct ethnicity" (134), while Tace Hedrick sees chica lit narratives as oscillating between the question of "how to 'do' a recognizable ethnicity while clearly embodying the requirements for being 'American' in the early twenty-first century" (11).

Although this ambivalence often seems connected to an unspoken equation of wealth with Americanization, another strain of ambivalence emanates from the readers themselves. Catherine Ramírez, for instance, notes how, despite her critical reservations, she still finds herself attracted to these narratives because "for better or worse, I, like many of her fans, see a bit of myself in it" (31). Ramírez's comment registers both the pleasures that genre can generate by providing collective recognition for a group that has been ignored, as well as the ongoingness of adjusting these identities to new circumstances – the "ellipsis" that Castillo notes. Although chica lit is required by the marketplace to produce conventional endings and these endings seem to correlate with ideological statements, readers do not necessarily surrender to these conclusions. Many chica lit authors foster fan communities. Valdes-Rodriguez, for instance, submitted three plans for a new novel to her Yahoo Internet community, and discovered not only that they rejected her preferred narrative but that they endorsed her least favorite, which she committed to writing based on fan responses (McCracken 19).

The work of continuing to negotiate and adjust the depiction of affluent, professional Latinas to current social, political, and economic realities continues not only in Valdes-Rodriguez's oeuvre, in the form of sequels such as *Dirty Girls on Top* (2006) and *Lauren's Saints of Dirty Faith* (2011), but also in the similarly themed work of a host of other writers who explore the issues *Dirty Girls* raises in different ways. Dominican-Puerto Rican writer Sofia Quintero draws on her experiences as a community activist to fashion more politically minded and socially progressive narratives in her chica lit novel *Divas Don't Yield* (2006) and in short stories that she contributed to the collections *Names I Call My Sister* (2009) and *Friday Night Chicas* (2005).[6] In those anthologies, Quintero's work appears alongside that of established chica lit writers like Mary Castillo (the Hot Tamara series) and Berta Platas (*Cinderella Lopez* and *Lucky Chica*). Novels like Lisa Wixon's *Dirty Blonde and Half Cuban* (2009) and Lara Rios's *How to Become Latina in 10 Easy Steps* (2013) attempt to imagine ways of coordinating affluent identities with ethnic pasts that protagonists are only beginning to understand. In this way, as Hedrick notes, chica lit novels perform pedagogical or didactic work that place them in a long tradition of women's domestic fiction. At the "literary" end of the spectrum, a writer like Nina Marie Martínez deconstructs the commodity fetishism and romance conventions that undergird chica lit in her novel *¡Caramba!* (2004), set in a working-class California border town but similarly concerned with beauty and fashion, female relationships, and social mobility. The profusion of writing that engages the themes that *Dirty Girls* inaugurated demonstrates not only a market for stories about groups of Latinas who have

---

[6] Under the pen name "Black Artemis," Quintero has also authored the hip-hop novels *Explicit Content* (2004) and *Burn* (2006). While these novels center on strong female protagonists, they offer a corrective to the misogyny of hip-hop culture rather than representing the lives of upwardly mobile Latinas.

received little representation in earlier literature but also suggests that the work of thinking through the implications of these representations is ongoing.

Chica lit contains several subgenres, including the paranormal romance. In part, the popularity of paranormal romances was spurred by the mainstream success of Stephenie Meyer's *Twilight* (2005). Paranormal romances combine romance and horror-story conventions, a hybridization that expands the work's market appeal. In Latina/o popular fiction, Marta Acosta's *Happy Hour at Casa Dracula* (2006) and its sequels are the most successful in this subgenre and provide an occasion for considering the ways in which horror conventions have been taken up Latina/o writers. *Happy Hour* centers on the protagonist Milagro de los Santos, who is an aspiring writer and alumna of Fancy University. Milagro also seeks romantic fulfillment after a string of "boyfriends who were like beach reads, momentary fun but nothing you'd ever buy in hardcover" (5). Frustrated in romance and in her career, she fears that she "was only a beach read as well," but really aspires to be a "deep and serious character" like the heroines she admires in nineteenth-century novels like *Pride and Prejudice* and *Middlemarch* (5). The horror element of the story is introduced when a man who's later revealed to be a vampire accidentally infects her during an awkward kiss. Sequestered in a vampire lair in order to recover, Milagro learns the ways of vampires and becomes embroiled in a plot involving a secret society called Corporate America for the Conservation of America (excrementally abbreviated CACA) that wants to extract the vampires' DNA in order to profit from immortality. CACA provides Acosta the opportunity to comment upon the ways in which corporations, rather than the government, police hegemonic forms of national identity, and how these corporations mine difference as a resource while excluding and destroying those marginal populations that they exploit in order to maintain the nation.

Latina/o horror fiction is situated at the intersection of two genealogies. On the one hand, there is a long gothic tradition in European and American literatures that evokes fear and terror by representing the return of the repressed – typically an abject "other" – in the form of a monster, a revenant, or a ghost. The abject other could symbolize an excluded population or elided history, among other things, but is something that the dominant social order has expelled in order to produce its identity. In this way, the gothic can be seen as a mode of resistance because it forces the dominant social imaginary to encounter those that it has excluded, cast out, or dispossessed (González 47). Gothic traditions fit easily with Latina/o writing because both share Catholic locales and Latino fiction's deployment of magical realist tropes gesture toward the supernatural (González 46). In *Happy Hour*, Milagro de los Santos's name ("miracle of the saints") invokes this tradition, as even the baroquely named vampire Oswald Krakatoa remarks on its excessiveness. Although the novel lacks the quality of fear associated with the gothic, instead retaining the romantic comedy tone associated with chica lit, *Happy Hour* discovers in the vampire not a monster but rather a milieu that is able to tolerate and appreciate aspects of Milagro's Mexicanness – from her body to her manners – that U.S. culture figures as threatening to normative constructions of national identity that hinge upon whiteness, bourgeois comportment, and regulated sexuality.

Seeing the "monster" as something not to be feared but rather as an agent of cultural critique is something that is prevalent in the second tradition in which we can understand Latina/o horror writing: the horror film. As Jesse Alemán notes in his study of Chicano/a horror cinema, the modern horror film traces its origins to a Latino production: George Romero's *Night of the Living Dead* (1968), a film that arrived at an important moment in the history of U.S. civil rights activism and global anticolonial struggle. The film both marked the sense of social disorder prevailing at this historical juncture and demonstrated how horror was adept at responding to contemporary social issues. James Baldwin writes that horror movies are finally about property rights (122).[7] In Latina/o horror, the concern for property rights is, as Alemán notes, more specifically figured in terms of the effects of U.S. and European colonialism, the ways that neoliberal governance and economic relations between the United States and Latin America have dispossessed Latinos, and how racism combines with these to inhibit opportunities in labor and education. Latino horror draws on a familiar set of figures like vampires, zombies, and werewolves, but also may draw on folkloric figures like La Llorona, El Cucuy, or chupacabras. Although mainstream horror films may sometimes figure Latinos as a menacing threat, Latina/o horror more often sees the monster as a vehicle for returning a repressed past to the U.S. consciousness or as a way of embodying "people who have endured an entire history of dispossession" (Alemán 65).

---

[7] In his analysis of *The Exorcist* (1973), Baldwin notes that the film "is not the least concerned with damnation, an abysm far beyond the confines of its imagination, but with property, with safety, tax shelters, stocks and bonds, rising and falling markets, the continued invulnerability of a certain class of people, and the continued sanctification of a certain history" (122). Extending this logic, one sees how stories that hinge on haunting or return may be about competing claims on property.

Some of this is present in *Happy Hour*: the vampire represents a way of being in the world that doesn't have to experience excess as failure; the conflict with CACA exposes a resistance to contemporary attempts to profit from cultural difference through the unwilling exploitation of marginalized bodies. Among the other Latino writers who have achieved acclaim in the horror fiction is the Puerto Rican writer Pedro Cabiya, who has authored three novels: *La cabeza* (2005), *Trance* (2007), and *Malas hierbas* (2011). While the first two novels tilt more toward fantasy and science fiction, the last, translated in English as *Wicked Weeds*, centers on a zombie with a university education. As Alemán notes, zombies are "uncanny figurations of the working class" (59), but, in Cabiya's imaginings, they become figures for the Caribbean subject under the thrall of neoliberal capitalism.

Just as Acosta combined chica lit with the horror story in the Casa Dracula series, Mario Acevedo combines the horror story with the detective novel in his six Felix Gomez novels, which begin with *The Nymphos of Rocky Flats* (2006). Acevedo's novels are centered on Gomez, a veteran of the first Iraq war who returns as a vampire and becomes a private investigator. In contrast to the zombie's affiliation with the working classes, the vampire is, as Alemán notes, "well dressed, aristocratic, and sexual," an undead person who stands apart from the masses. As such, the vampire is an ideal figure for the detective genre, which centers on a protagonist who is alienated, separate from but still connected to the community that he or she investigates. As an outsider, the detective defamiliarizes what is known in the community by asking questions and using methods that produce new ways of knowing. In his study of Chicana/o detective fiction, Ralph Rodriguez notes how the "driving force behind these narratives is a quest for knowledge," a pursuit that has both epistemological and ontological consequences, since the result of these pursuits is often an enlarged understanding of what it means to be Latina/o (8).

Although the detective story could trace its origins to Edgar Allan Poe's tales of ratiocination or Arthur Conan Doyle's Sherlock Holmes mysteries in the nineteenth century, which were similarly concerned with discovering new epistemologies, Rodriguez locates the immediate antecedents of Chicana/o and Latina/o detective fiction in the feminist and African American writing of such authors as Sara Paratesky and Walter Moseley. These writers demonstrated not only the market viability of detective novels that did not center on white male sleuths but also showed how issues related to crises in identity and cultural difference could be woven into the genre (4). For Rodriguez, Rolando Hinojosa's *Partners in Crime* (1985), which features the detective Rafe Buenostro, inaugurates the detective form in Latina/o letters as well as its concern with searching for new ways of thinking about identity. In the case of Hinojosa's novel, Mexican American identity in the U.S.–Mexican borderlands is thrown into disarray by a number of economic, political, and social alterations to the order of things. In this way, popular genres prove nimble in commencing the process of either adjusting to new historical circumstances or allowing a new collectivity to be recognized.

On the latter score, one of the most significant and celebrated detective series written by a Latino is Michael Nava's Henry Rios series, whose protagonist is a gay Chicano lawyer and occasional private investigator. Of the seven novels published in the series, which began with *A Little Death* (1986) and ended with *Rag and Bone* (2001), six won Lambda Literary Awards for achievement in gay and lesbian writing. Significantly, Nava's first novels in the series were issued by Alyson Books, a niche publisher that promotes gay and lesbian literature. As Rodriguez notes, much genre fiction that is produced by large publishing houses quickly goes out of print as it is replaced by newer titles that need to be sold. This is yet another reason why popular fiction has remained marginal in Latina/o literary studies: it is difficult to teach or research work that isn't readily available. Yet, smaller presses like Alyson and Arte Público, which published Hinojosa's detective novels and Chicana writer Lucha Corpi's Gloria Damasco series, keep these works in press for a longer period of time. Smaller presses, though, have a limited reach, and few of these writers penetrate large reading publics commensurate with those achieved by writers like Alisa Valdes-Rodriguez. Nava, however, has enjoyed a substantial reading public, so much so that Ballantine and G. P. Putnam published the later novels in the series (Rodriguez 10). True to the detective genre's affinity for exploring new ways of knowing and examining new ways of being, Nava's Henry Rios pursues "the question of how to negotiate and know Chicano and gay spaces" at a historical moment marked, on the one hand, by the AIDS crisis and, on the other, by a gay male Chicano community reluctant to assert its identity, despite a concurrent flowering of writing by out lesbian Chicanas (Stenger 300).[8] Indeed, Nava's work wasn't even legibly Latino or Chicano to many: Raymund Paredes declared him "Chicano in name only" and Alan West-Duran did not include an entry for Nava in his multivolume reference work

---

[8] For more on this seeming asymmetry between the flowering of Chicana lesbian cultural expression in this period and the reticence of Chicano gay male writers and artists to discuss their sexuality, see Viego.

on Latina/o writers (Stenger 305). That such dismissals or omissions seem strange to the contemporary reader indicate that Nava's detective fiction was successful in its search for news ways of being Chicano. Beyond this, the work also performs a procedural pedagogy, often informing readers about the U.S. justice system and drawing attention to flaws in public policy and corruption within the institutions that the public trusts.

Other Latina/o detective fiction also confronts the new identities that are emerging in the present and demanding recognition and assessment. Manuel Ramos's Luis Montez mysteries, like Lucha Corpi's novels, display nostalgia for Chicano movement-era constructions of identity but recognize the obsolescence of those formations as society changes (Rodriguez 12). While Chicana/o writers have formed the preponderance of Latina/o mystery writers to date, Latinos from other groups have made important contributions and remind us that the genre not only connects with work done by feminist and ethnic American writers but also with a tradition of Latin American crime fiction that "has been at the vanguard of social protest and political critique" (Rodríguez, "Latina Body" 246). Cuban American writer Carolina García-Aguilera's Lupe Solano series is largely set in Cuban Miami and registers some of the adjustments to identity that occur in the 1.5 generation who were, like the author and her character, born in Cuba but raised in the United States. Salvadoran American writer Marcos McPeek Villatoro writes the Romilia Chacón mysteries, a series that documents a history of Central American migration to the U.S. South, explains the effects of that migration on identity construction, and shows how both of these processes are haunted by the violence associated with civil war, the military, and a hemispheric drug trade (Padilla 376, 380).

While Latina/o writers have authored scores of novels in the detective genre, they have produced relatively few science-fiction ones. Lázaro Lima believes that this is because Latina/o writing has been preoccupied with history and consequently Latina/o writers and scholars "depoliticize the possibility for a viable Latino future" (qtd. in Maguire 351). However, as Emily Maguire counters, such a sentiment is anchored by a misguided belief that science fiction is primarily oriented toward the future (351). The genre of sci-fi, in fact, opens up a set of intriguing questions about the representation of the past, present, and future in Latina/o cultural production. Ramón Saldívar contends that Latina/o literature has been motivated by both social protest and utopian longings (Orchard and Padilla 195). If social protest keeps literature in a realist present that explains what has happened, different forms of fantasy express the wish for a future that is clearly not connected to an intolerable present. Sci-fi most often represents a world that might be, and, in this connection, that world frequently emerges in Latina/o cultural production in dystopian rather than utopian terms: Latina/o writers imagine a calamitous future that is the outgrowth of present conditions that have been deemed intolerable (Maguire 352). This is the case in the best known Latina/o science-fiction work, Alex Rivera's film *Sleep Dealer* (2007), which imagines a future in which the anti-immigrant sentiment and the exploitation of undocumented labor converge in a system in which Mexicans perform labor remotely via robots that use Mexican bodies contained in Mexico. Similarly, Rosaura Sánchez and Beatrice Pita's *Lunar Braceros, 2125–2148* (2009) imagines a future in which contemporary social and economic struggles have continued unchecked, resulting in a dystopia in which corporations control the earth and moon and where workers are confined to reservations where they are exploited.

Sánchez and Pita, of course, are also accomplished literary critics, which corresponds with sci-fi's tendency to attract more literary and theoretically inclined writers – more so than in other popular genres. For instance, the Cuban-born novelist Daína Chaviano, author of *Fábulas de una abuela extraterrestre* (1988), helped establish the Oscar Hurtado Writers' Workshop in Cuba, which not only cultivated a number of Cuban and Latin American science-fiction writers but also brought U.S. and Soviet-era science fiction into contact with each other. Among the writers to emerge out of that workshop was Yoss (the pen name of José Miguel Sánchez), Cuba's most celebrated science-fiction writer, whose novel, *Se alquila una planeta* (2001, translated by David Frye in 2015 as *Planet for Rent*), displaces some of the problems that faced Cuba in the 1990s to a colonized planet in the near future.

Another set of literary-minded writers have been less interested in the future than in the relationship of Latinos to technology. Often, these writers play on the rhyme between "tech" and "Aztec," such as in performance artist Guillermo Gomez-Pena's cyberpunk character El Naftazteka, Ernest Hogan's *High Aztech* (1992), or Sesshu Foster's *Atomik Aztex* (2005), a novel that plots a counterfactual history in which the Aztecs conquered their Spanish invaders. Catherine Ramírez has termed work in this vein "Chicanofuturist" because of the way in which it challenges stereotypes that assign Chicanos and Latinos to the rural, the undeveloped, or the traditional and instead shows the ways in which modern technologies infiltrate Latina/o lives.[9]

---

[9] This discussion of science fiction has emphasized more recent work of the last twenty years. However, it is important to acknowledge pioneering works of Latina/o science fiction such as Isabel Ríos's *Victuum* (1976) and Arthur Tenorio's *Blessing from Above* (1971), both of which imagine immigration anxieties in terms of extraterrestrial alien encounters.

Arguably the best known science-fiction work by a Latino is one that doesn't exist: Oscar De Leon's lost opus in Junot Díaz's *The Brief Wondrous Life of Oscar Wao*. Critics have often remarked upon Oscar's devotion to the "genres," which comprise an archive of fantasy that allows him to imagine other possible ways of living in the world, ones that exceed those offered by the norms of diasporic Dominican culture. As a result of *Oscar Wao*'s universal acclaim, critics have also been more confident in considering popular genres and their relation to Latina/o literature. However, in *Oscar Wao*, the popular genres that Oscar turns to in order to discover ways of coordinating his "ghetto nerd" self with Dominican identity are rarely Latino. This archive consists of anime, *Lord of the Rings*, *X-Men*, and *The Fantastic Four*. One Latino work that Díaz's text directly alludes to is the Hernandez Brothers' long-running comic book *Love and Rockets* (1982–present). In interviews, Díaz says that he learned how to craft narrative by reading the work of Gilbert and Jaime Hernandez (Barrios). Díaz's comment suggests that the work of Los Bros has a decidedly literary cast even though it appears as graphic narrative, a form that has often been deemed popular. Scholars of literature have often praised the brothers' for their achievement in comic art and storytelling. In a 1993 special issue of *The Americas Review* devoted to cartooning and the graphic arts, Rosaura Sánchez and Beatrice Pita single out *Love and Rockets* as one of the most important Latino achievements in graphic art, while José David Saldívar ends his entry on postmodern realism in *The Columbia History of the American Novel* by declaring *Love and Rockets* "narrative for the next century" (541). In histories of the graphic novel, *Love and Rockets* is seen as a signal achievement in the form, comparable to such works as Art Spiegelman's *Maus* (1986) and Alan Moore and Dave Gibbons's *Watchmen* (1986). Indeed, though the Hernandez Brothers' work coincides with the period in which the graphic novel became an esteemed object of study, *Love and Rockets* received comparably little attention in Latina/o literary criticism. While part of this is attributable to Latina/o studies' anxiety about producing recognizably literary objects as the field was establishing itself in the 1980s and 1990s, it is also attributable to the ways in which the Hernandez Brothers' work, like the work of writers in other popular genres, threw into relief subjects who were at the fringes of Chicana/o and Latina/o identity. Although there are recognizably Chicano characters in the Hernandez Brothers' world, they don't sit easily with contemporaneous pictures of Chicano life. Gilbert's Heartbreak Soup series is set in Palomar, a town "south of the border" that experiences many of the forms of political violence and upheaval that plagued Central American nations in the post–World War II period. Jaime's Locas series is set in contemporary Southern California and includes Chicano characters as well as characters of other racial and ethnic backgrounds participating in a world in which a punk sensibility reigns. Both brothers featured queer characters as well as women who were frankly and unapologetically sexual. Of the writers of Latina/o popular fiction discussed in this essay, the Hernandez Brothers had by far the largest and most mixed readership and continue to have an immense impact on fiction writers and other comic artists.

The Hernandez Brothers are pioneers in alternative comics, a tradition of comic art that follows the Underground Comix movement (late 1960s to early 1980s) and that, like the underground, traffics in mature content while using established small presses to distribute their work. Alternative comics are often auteur productions, written and drawn by the same person. The world of Latina/o alternative comics includes figures like Wilfred Santiago, a Puerto Rican comic artist who has written a comic biography of Robert Clemente, *21*, as well as *In My Darkest Hour*, a novel whose protagonist battles bipolar depression as the United States advances toward its second war with Iraq. Much as the Hernandez Brothers make spaces for queer subjects, Latina writers Erika Lopez (*Lap Dancing for Mommy* and *Flaming Iguanas*) and Cristy Road (*Indestructible*) produce do-it-yourself works that combine text and image while exploring queer feminisms, mixed-race identities, and punk sensibilities.

Latina/o artists have been instrumental in mainstream superhero comics as well, albeit in less conspicuous ways. Several Latino artists produce the illustrations for the mass market works published by DC or Marvel.[10] Although this work may be invisible to many, it occasionally reaches the attention of the mainstream such as when the half-Mexican, half-Puerto Rican hero Araña entered the Marvel Comics universe or when the Afro-Dominican character Miles Morales succeeded Peter Parker as Spiderman. One of the best-known artists and pencillers is Phil Jimenez, who worked on *Wonder Woman* from 2000 to 2003 and on *The New X-Men*. Some Latinos have created the superheroes outside of the major publishers. Among these are Javier Hernandez's El Muerte and Judge Garza's Relampago. Because most of these alternative heroes are produced independently, they often have

---

[10] An important early example of such an illustrator is José Cuahtémoc "Bill" Melendez who illustrated *Peanuts* and key Disney films. *Peanuts* creator Charles Schulz entrusted him to animate the comic strip's television specials. Melendez also voiced the Snoopy and Woodstock characters in these specials.

short and irregular runs. One notable success is *Blood Syndicate*, a comic in part produced by Puerto Rican artist Ivan Velez for Milestone Comics, a comic publisher founded in 1993 to increase minority representation. Velez established his reputation with *Tales of the Closet* (1987), a comic about gay and lesbian teens that he produced in collaboration with the Hetrick-Martin Institute to use as an instructional tool in New York City area schools.

Latinos have also been active as producers of cartoon strips, which, unlike graphic novels or comic books, are published serially in magazines or newspapers. Gus Arriola produced the syndicated comic strip *Gordo*, which ran in newspapers largely in the Southwest from 1950 to 1984. *Gordo* chronicled the comic adventures of its titular hero, a bean farmer who later becomes a tour guide in Mexico. Other notable strips include Hector Cantú and Carlos Castellanos's *Baldo* (2000–present), a strip about a Latino teen who is obsessed with women and cars, and Lalo Alcaraz's *La Cucaracha*, a daily politically oriented strip that began syndication in 2002 and continues through the present. As newspapers have shifted from being print publications to being multiplatform content providers that readers interface with on the Internet or via mobile devices, comic strips increasingly appear on the Web. Both *Baldo* and *La Cucaracha* enjoy robust presences on the Internet, and Alcaraz has been a prime mover – what he calls "the jefe-in-chief" – of the Latina/o humor website Pocho.com.

The internet and various forms of new media have emerged as an important, if sometimes anarchic, site for cultural production by Latinos. In addition to serving as a vehicle for distributing content that would have been accessible in print forms – like comic strips – the Internet provides Latinos opportunities for self-publishing that bypass the demands of the publishing industry. The challenge for authors who write in these modes is attracting a reading public that discusses, considers, and shapes the work. Self-published blogs have helped create spaces for Latina/o literary culture, such as La Bloga, a blog that reviews Latina/o literature of all types and includes informative interviews with contemporary writers. Established authors also use these tools, such as Lorna Dee Cervantes, who has vocally contested the ways in which anthologies frequently excerpt from her first book of poetry, *Emplumada* (1981) while ignoring the issues and themes taken up in later works like *From the Cables of Genocide* (1991) and *Drive* (2006) and inadvertently producing a distorted picture of her career and of Latina/o literature. Latinos have also been at the forefront of marshalling the powers of digital technology to develop platforms for exploring popular culture and politics. Cuban American Mario Lavandeira achieved fame with his celebrity blog

PerezHilton.com, while Mexican American Gwendolyn Zepeda, an author of chica lit and Houston's first poet laureate, was one of the cofounders of the television fan site Television Without Pity. In the realm of politics, Salvadoran American Markos Moulitsas Zúniga founded the influential left-leaning political blog DailyKos.[11]

Despite these successes, it is also worth noting that Latino access to digital technologies is highly uneven. Latina/o youth access digital media more than rest of the general population does and far more than their parents do, but they are also less likely to have broadband access at home, relying either on cellular phone networks or access provided at public locations. These factors will no doubt affect the kinds of content produced by Latinos in new media, but we are already seeing emergent Latina/o groups inventively harnessing the powers of digital media. For instance, DREAMers have used social-media sites such as YouTube, Tumblr, Facebook, and Twitter to create "an alternative public sphere, generating online content that speaks to an imagined public of both allies and adversaries" (Beltrán 246). In 2010's "Coming Out of the Shadows" campaign, undocumented youth, adopting strategies from the queer movement, "came out" as undocumented in videos that articulated forms of citizenship that ranged from the radical to the normative. As political scientist Cristina Beltrán notes, "by refusing the politics of innocence, questioning the state-centered logics of citizenship, and reconfiguring the criteria for political membership, DREAMers are queering the movement in ways that can't be 'delimited in advance'" (250). Seizing new technologies and producing themselves as legible subjects in the genre of the coming out narrative, these young activists demonstrate how DIY work in new media performs several of the same functions as writing in popular genres. Their work also reminds us of the activist origins of Latina/o literature itself, which so often had to build its own institutions as it produced work that reshaped and remade our sense of what literature in the Americas could look like.

---

[11] Lavandeira began his celebrity gossip blog PerezHilton.com in 2001. Television Without Pity was founded in the late 1990s and provided witty recaps of popular television series. The site was sold to NBC Universal in 2007, but ceased production in 2014. Although he was a registered Republican in his youth, Markos Moulitsas became increasingly liberal after serving in the US military from 1989 to 1992. In 2002, he started the liberal political blog DailyKos, which took its name from his online handle and former military nickname, "Kos." In addition to running this blog, Moulitsas is also a columnist for the Washington, DC, newspaper *The Hill* and cofounded SB Nation (Sports Blog Nation), a website devoted to sports reporting.

WORKS CITED

Acosta, Marta. *Happy Hour at Casa Dracula*. New York: Pocket Star, 2006.

Aldama, Frederick Luis. *Your Brain on Latino Comics: From Gus Arriola to Los Bros Hernandez*. Austin: University of Texas Press, 2009.

Alemán, Jesse. "Days of the (Un)Dead: Vampires, Zombies, and Other Forms of Chicano/a Horror in Film." *Latinos and Narrative Media: Participation and Portrayal*. Ed. Frederick Luis Aldama. New York: Palgrave-Macmillan, 2013. 49–70.

Baldwin, James. *The Devil Finds Work*. 1976. New York: Vintage, 2011.

Barrios, Gregg. "Guest Interview: Junot Diaz." *LaBloga*, labloga.blogspot.com, Oct. 21, 2007. Web. Accessed March 10, 2015.

Beltrán, Cristina. "'No Papers, No Fear': DREAM Activism, New Social Media, and the Queering of Immigrant Rights." *Contemporary Latina/o Media: Production, Circulation, Politics*. Ed. Arlene Dávila and Yeidy M. Rivero. New York: New York University Press, 2014. 245–66.

Berlant, Lauren. *The Female Complaint: The Unfinished Business of Sentimentality in American Culture*. Durham, NC: Duke University Press, 2008.

Castillo, Debra. "Impossible Indian." *Chasqui* 35.2 (2006): 42–57.

Dalleo, Raphael and Elena Machado Sáez. *The Latino/a Canon and the Emergence of Post-Sixties Literature*. New York: Palgrave-Macmillan, 2007.

Dávila, Arlene. *Latinos, Inc.: The Marketing and Making of a People*. Berkeley: University of California Press, 2001.

"Introduction." *Contemporary Latina/o Media: Production, Circulation, Politics*. Ed. Arlene Dávila and Yeidy M. Rivero. New York: New York University Press, 2014. 1–20.

Duschinsky, Robbie and Emma Wilson. "Flat Affect, Joyful Politics, and Enthralled Attachments: Engaging with the Work of Lauren Berlant." *International Journal of Politics, Culture, and Society* 28 (2014): 1–12.

Flores, Juan. *From Bomba to Hip Hop: Puerto Rican Culture and Latino Identity*. New York: Columbia University Press, 2000.

García Canclini, Néstor. *Hybrid Cultures: Strategies for Entering and Leaving Modernity*. Trans. Christopher L. Chiappari and Silvia L. López. Minneapolis: University of Minnesota Press, 1995.

González, Christopher. "Latino Sci-Fi: Cognition and Narrative Design in Alex Rivera's *Sleep Dealer*." *Latinos and Narrative Media: Participation and Portrayal*. Ed. Frederick Luis Aldama. New York: Palgrave-Macmillan, 2013. 211–23.

González, Tanya. "The (Gothic) Gift of Death in Cherríe Moraga's *The Hungry Woman*." *Chicana/Latina Studies* 7.1 (2007): 44–77.

Hedrick, Tace. *Chica Lit: Popular Latina Fiction and Americanization in the Twenty-First Century*. Pittsburgh, PA: University of Pittsburgh Press, 2015.

Hurt, Erin. "Trading Cultural Baggage for Gucci Luggage: The Ambivalent Latinidad of Alisa Valdes-Rodriguez's *The Dirty Girls Social Club*." *MELUS* 34.3 (2009): 133–53.

Jackson, Virginia. "The Function of Criticism at the Present Time." *Los Angeles Review of Books*. Lareviewofbooks.org. April 12, 2015. Web. Accessed July 5, 2015.

Maguire, Emily A. "Science Fiction." *The Routledge Companion to Latino/a Literature*. Ed. Suzanne Bost and Frances R. Aparicio. New York: Routledge, 2013. 351–60.

McCracken, Ellen. "From Chapbooks to *Chica Lit*: US Latina Writers and the New Literary Identity." *International Perspectives on Chicana/o Studies: "This World Is My Place."* Ed. Catherine Leen and Niamh Thornton, New York: Routledge, 2014. 11–23.

McGurl, Mark. *The Program Era: Postwar Fiction and the Rise of Creative Writing.* Cambridge, MA: Harvard University Press, 2011.

Morrison, Amanda Maria. "Chicanas and 'Chica Lit': Contested *Latinidad* in the Novels of Alisa Valdes-Rodriguez." *Journal of Popular Culture* 43.2 (2010): 309–29.

Nava, Michael. *Rag and Bone.* New York: Putnam, 2001.

Orchard, William, and Yolanda Padilla. "You Choose Your Place and You Fight There: An Interview with Ramón Saldívar." *Bridges, Borders, and Breaks: History, Narrative, and Nation in Twenty-First Century Chicana/o Literary Criticism.* Pittsburgh, PA: University of Pittsburgh Press, 2016. 177–200.

Padilla, Yajaira M. "Sleuthing Central American Identity and History in the New Latino South: Marco McPeek Villatoro's *Home Killings.*" *Latino Studies* 6 (2008): 376–97.

Ramírez, Catherine. "Afrofuturism/ Chicanofuturism: Fictive Kin." *Aztlán* 33 (2008): 185–94.

"End of *Chicanismo*: Alisa Valdes-Rodriguez's *Dirty Girls.*" Research Report no. 2. Los Angeles: University of California, Los Angeles, Chicano/Latino Research Center, n.d.: 1–41.

Rodríguez, Ana Patricia. "The Body in Question: The Latina Detective in the Lupe Solano Mystery Series." *From Bananas to Buttocks: The Latina Body in Popular Film and Culture.* Ed. Myra Mendible. Austin: University of Texas Press, 2007. 243–61.

Rodriguez, Ralph. *Brown Gumshoes: Detective Fiction and the Search for Chicana/o Identity.* Austin: University of Texas Press, 2005.

Saldívar, José David. "Postmodern Realism." *The Columbia History of the American Novel.* Ed. Emory Elliot and Cathy Davidson. New York: Columbia University Press, 1991. 521–541.

Saldívar, Ramón. "Historical Fantasy, Speculative Realism, and Postrace Aesthetics in Contemporary American Fiction." *American Literary History* 23.3 (2011): 574–99.

Sánchez, Rosaura, and Beatrice Pita, "Cartooning and Other Graphic Arts: An Introduction." *The America's Review* 22 (Fall–Winter 1994): 7–27.

Stallybrass, Peter and Allon White. *The Politics and Poetics of Transgression.* Ithaca, NY: Cornell University Press, 1986.

Valdes-Rodriguez, Alisa. *The Dirty Girls Social Club.* New York: St. Martin's Press, 2003.

Viego, Antonio. "The Place of the Gay Male Chicano in Queer Chicana/o Cultural Work." *Gay Latino Studies.* Ed. Michael Hames-García and Ernesto Javier Martínez. Durham, NC: Duke University Press, 2011. 86–104.

32

Trauma, Translation, and Migration in the Crossfire of the Americas

The Intersection of Latina/o and South American Literatures

JUANITA HEREDIA

To speak of a group of authors of South American descent, born or living in the United States, is to undertake no small task in disseminating the complexity of their literary worlds in diverse historical contexts that are often unknown or unrecognized by U.S. literary scholars. Yet, if one looks more closely at the commonalities as well as the differences that unite this disparate group of writers, one should consider a shared history of colonization and immigration *to* and *from* the South American homeland and heritage to the United States. In the nineteenth century, when colonial Spain lost the last of its colonies to the South American independence movements led by *criollos*, various republics were created: Argentina, Bolivia, Chile, Colombia, Ecuador, Paraguay, Peru, Uruguay, and Venezuela. In the case of Portugal, Brazil emerged. The political independence that these nation-states experienced from Spain and Portugal, however, did not translate into human freedom for all citizens within the national parameters because class differences, racial division, and gender inequality continued to plague each nation state. Furthermore, in the twentieth century, many South American nations underwent civil wars due to economic disparities that resulted in internal migrations, usually from the small towns and cities in the countryside to the greater metropolis. If economic and political strife continued, disempowered groups of people emigrated to the United States, not only for better economic opportunities, but also for human survival due to political violence. As will be discussed in this chapter, military governments, many of which were supported by U.S. intervention, swarmed various nations from the 1960s through the 1990s. This legacy of colonialism and neoliberal dictatorship extends into the twenty-first century not only in these ten nations of South America, but in the diasporas of these communities, many of which are found throughout the United States as a consequence of migrations.

As a result of geographic movements, be they economic migrations or political relocations from South America to the United States, people of these diasporic communities experienced various cultures and languages simultaneously. Some authors in this essay left their homeland in South America as adults, forming a new residence in the United States but longing for the familiarity of their South American culture through nostalgia. Others came as young children and could arguably pertain to a 1.5 generation, as Pérez-Firmat has observed for the Cuban exile experience in his *Life on the Hyphen*. Yet, another group can be said to be "in between" two cultures and two frames of mind, switching between Spanish and English and other languages with ease. This essay addresses diverse South American experiences and their points of contact between the homeland and the United States, or, the interstices of what it means to live and *think* at the border of two nations, two languages, and at least two cultures.

Another element that the writers in this chapter share is the notion of translation, be it linguistic, cultural, or social, as they cross transnationally between South America and the United States. Whether the authors are Spanish or Portuguese-dominant, they may be interpreting U.S. experiences in their fiction for a South America–based audience. Similarly, those authors who are trained formally in English may also be denizens of translating an "imaginary" homeland in South America for audiences in the United States, as Salman Rushdie has commented in reference to his India as a postcolonial subject.

The writers in this essay also reflect on the experience of trauma because many underwent physical or psychological torture as they experienced a dictatorship or a civil war that stripped them of their literary voices through censorship, exile, or immigration. In terms of gender, women and LGBTQ communities had to confront discriminatory treatment in theory and practice that have disabled them from participating as full citizens in their homeland or heritage of South America or as people of color in the United States. Trauma takes on the form of the emotional and psychological pain of the effects of war as well as the physical violence against women's bodies, queers, youth, marginalized ethnic groups, and political groups contesting military dictatorships.

Many authors in this essay often present an alternative history of South America and its diaspora, due to periods of exile in response to dictatorship, dirty wars, and civil unrest of the 1970s, 1980s, and 1990s in Argentina, Brazil, Chile, Colombia, Peru, and Uruguay. At times, their works engage the relative class privilege of displaced intellectuals who landed positions in academic institutions in the United States. At other times the texts may speak to a position of negotiating marginality from the center. Some authors search for ways to convey the melancholy of tango, inexpressible longing of *saudade*, human trafficking for capital, Andean scenes of civil conflict, torture, or massacres, in which the U.S. government was often complicit. Due to the memory of these traumatic experiences, the writers in this essay find themselves as mediators between the United States and South America. In order to understand these transnational experiences, I outline a map in my discussion of the writers and their texts by nationality and national heritage.

The Dictatorship in Chile and Exile

In the case of Chile, texts by Isabel Allende, Marjorie Agosín, and Ariel Dorfman examine the role of language, culture, and literature as a response to repression and censorship. Originally writing in Spanish, these aforementioned authors seek refuge in the Spanish language and, through this medium, translate the horrors of violence they lived under a dictatorship. Relocating upon the arrival of the Pinochet dictatorship in her native Chile during the early 1970s, Isabel Allende and her family became exiled in Venezuela, where she began her career as a novelist and led the boom of Latin American women writers with her successful novel *The House of the Spirits* (1982), which was later translated into numerous languages, including English. This first novel covers three generations of women who struggle against patriarchal oppression, especially a dictatorship that alludes to the Pinochet regime. Her interest in the South American presence in the United States, however, became apparent when she published *Daughter of Fortune* (1999) and its sequel *Portrait in Sepia* (2000), which chronicle the presence of Chilean immigrants in contact with multiethnic California during the gold rush period in the mid nineteenth century, and in particular with Chinese immigrants. By employing the trope of genealogy, Allende reconfigures the role of women as central to these two novels in which the heroines must resist long-standing patriarchy. More recently, Allende takes a transnational perspective in her novel *Maya's Notebook* (2011), which tracks the trials and tribulations of a Chilean-descent teenager caught in a whirlwind of misfortunes as she travels between Berkeley, California, and Chiloé, an island off the coast of Chile. While Allende began her career as a journalist, and then became an internationally acclaimed novelist, she never abandoned her chronicling of women's perspectives on turbulent history or the pursuit of social justice in the face of human-rights violations.

Likewise, fellow Chilean native Marjorie Agosín and Argentine Chilean Ariel Dorfman have also committed themselves to seek social justice and to advocate for human rights in the face of dictatorships such as the Pinochet regime that affected Chile for sixteen years (1973–1989). In particular, they have confronted an additional oppression for their religious and cultural background as Jewish Latinas/os, be it in the United States or in South America. Dorfman's *Heading South, Looking North: A Bilingual Journey* (1999) has been hailed as a classic memoir of negotiating multiple displacements across generations between Chile, Europe, and the United States. After his family fled the pogroms in Eastern Europe and Russia in the early twentieth century, his parents escaped the dictatorship in Chile in the 1970s. A prolific scholar in the field of Latin American cultural and literary studies, Dorfman publishes another memoir called *Feeding on Dreams: Confessions of an Unrepentant Exile* (2011) about the trauma of his exile experience from Chile and the consequences for his wife and children.

A prolific writer, scholar, and activist, Marjorie Agosín is considered one of the foremost champions of human rights, especially oppression affecting women, children, Jewish communities, and other marginalized groups. As a poet, Agosín has recuperated the silenced voices of victims of the Holocaust such as that of Anne Frank, of Chilean women artisans of *arpilleras* – brightly colored patchwork depictions of life of the oppressed under the dictatorship – and of women who have denounced femicides in Juárez. As an editor, she has participated in various collections dedicated to the struggles of Latin American and Latina women of Jewish descent of various generations. She is also interested in the motif of travel; she chronicles the voyages of Latin American women since the nineteenth century, especially those from South America. Through genealogy and gender, Agosín and her family suffered double migrations as her grandparents escaped the horrors of the Holocaust before and during the Second World War and then again when her parents were forced to migrate when the Pinochet dictatorship emerged in Chile in the 1970s. In "South American Latino/a Writers in the United States," I explain that Agosín identifies as a Latina in the United States in her memoirs because she experiences discrimination based on language and ethnicity. While her earlier poetry and activist collections expressed her concern for human rights, her more recent young-adult novel *I Lived on Butterfly Hill* (2014) traces the emotional trauma of a young girl who must flee from Chile as the country enters a dictatorship that pursues intellectuals of dissent, something that directly affects the protagonist's parents' due to their leftist political position. This narrative also explores the dilemmas of a young

Jewish girl who grows up in a predominantly Catholic community in Valparaíso, Chile, and who later becomes an immigrant, foreigner, and outsider; she is forced to live with her exiled aunt in a small town in Maine in the United States to escape torture and violence, psychological as well as physical, plaguing many Chilean exiles in the 1970s. At one point, the character's aunt reminds her bilingually, "Oh, Celeste. Por eso, se llama exilio. That's why they call it exile. You belong everywhere and nowhere at the same time" (280). Since the young protagonist has been displaced from her home due to political circumstances, she must reflect on what it means to be removed from her homeland temporarily, but eventually returns when political matters have stabilized.

The Effects of the Dirty War in Argentina and Its Diaspora

The Dirty War in Argentina (1976–1983) sent many writers into exile from Argentina to the United States, particularly Luisa Valenzuela, María Negroni, and Sergio Waisman. Although this group varies generationally and stylistic-ally, all have in common the experience of writing from the North to the South, as critic and writer Sergio Waisman points out in his essay, "Argentine Writers in the U.S.: Writing South, Living North," particularly if they made their permanent residence in the United States. Argentine politics, history, and culture during the Dirty War have made these authors serve as transla-tors of the trauma of censorship and violence in their literary texts, not only for an Argentine audience in Spanish but also for a U.S. readership in English as they cross nations through translations.

Born in Buenos Aires, Argentine journalist and novelist Luisa Valenzuela has been hailed as a writer who denounces the military dictatorship in her country as well as an outspoken defender of human rights, especially crimes committed against women, globally. Earning fellowships such as a Fulbright, Valenzuela was able to travel to France to work as a journalist and translator and then to the United States to continue her education. Once the Dirty War began in the 1970s, Valenzuela moved as an exiled writer to New York City where she taught at Columbia University and New York University as a visiting professor. In her short fiction and novels she uses memory to recover the silenced voices of victims (i.e. women, opponents to the dictatorship) during internal civil conflicts in Argentina. In novels such as *Como en la Guerra* (1977) and *The Lizard's Tail* (1983), Valenzuela critiques the patriarchal form of government during the civil conflict in Argentina, especially the gender inequality that led to the violent abuse and sexual exploitation against women. Known for her mixture of fantasy with reality, Valenzuela's short fiction collection *Other Weapons* (1985) is especially attentive to the role of women whose bodies and minds were tortured during the military dictatorship. During her residency in the United States for almost a decade, Valenzuela developed an interest in crime fiction with her *Black Novel with Argentines* (1992). Situated in New York City, this narrative looks at Argentine exiles who are haunted by the violent past of the Dirty War.

A poet, essayist, novelist, and translator, Argentine María Negroni is concerned with displacement, nostalgia, and poetic experimentation in her reflection of the Dirty War in her works. She has made a career as a university professor and a home for herself in the United States after having received a doctoral degree in Latin American literature from Columbia University. In her essay "Cultura latinoamericana en Nueva York" in the collection *Ciudad gótica* (1994), Negroni calls attention to the need to be able to define one's culture and its aesthetics rather than play into an exoticism dominated by U.S. standards. In *Night Journey* (2002), the poetic voice explores the topics of travel and exile as she searches for a home. Negroni has also created a Buenos Aires trilogy where she addresses Argentine history of the Dirty War in a variety of genres. In collaboration with Jorge Macchi in *Buenos Aires Tour* (2006), she provides a visual poetic guide to the capital, and to its internationally renowned dance form, tango. In the novel *La anunciación* (2007), Negroni examines the effects of the dictatorship of the 1970s on civilians. Finally in the poetry collection *Andanza* (2009), also translated in English as *Tango Lyrics* (2013), she experiments with the tango form in verse by taking the eight basic steps in the dance and translating them into eight stanzas in her poems. The poetic voice also explores the transnational aspect of living between cities as well as nations, especially between Buenos Aires and New York, having the music of tango as an instrumental symbol of nostalgia for the homeland. Negroni's published works in Spanish have been well-received in Spanish-speaking nations, but the English translations of her works have broadened her readership in the United States.

Sergio Waisman, a critic, novelist, professor, and translator, offers a different perspective from the previous authors of Argentine background because he actually came of age in both Argentina and the United States. Born in New York City in 1967, he lived in France one year as a child learning basic French and then spent his earlier formative years in Buenos Aires, where he attended school until the age of nine and became familiar with Argentine culture and history and was completely immersed in the Spanish language. When the Dirty War broke out in 1976, Waisman and his family could no longer remain safe in Argentina under the military dictatorship and were forced to leave to the United States where he continued his formal education in English until he received his doctoral degree in Hispanic Languages and Literatures at the University of California, Berkeley. In his first novel, *Leaving* (2004), published originally in English, Waisman captures a semiautobiographical transnational genealogy that can be traced back to his grandparents, who escaped violent anti-Semitism in Poland in the 1930s by immigrating to Argentina, at a moment in time when a vibrant Yiddish community flourished culturally with newspapers and other cultural practices to preserve the Jewish heritage. Waisman's novel also chronicles his parents' assimilation to Argentine culture through involvement with leftist politics, the Spanish language, musical tastes in tango and folklore, and soccer fever. In the protagonist's generation, he, himself, becomes a migrant in the United States when he travels numerous times as an adult from San Diego to Berkeley to Colorado and Rhode Island to name a few locales. In the Spanish version of this novel, *Irse* (2010), Waisman translates his own work and restores many characters to their original environs in Argentina.

History and Memory in Uruguay and Beyond

Uruguay is another Southern Cone nation that suffered repression and migratory displacement under a dictatorship that lasted from 1973 to 1984. Of Uruguayan parentage and raised in the United States from the age of ten, Carolina De Robertis captures crucial events in Uruguayan history from European immigration and internal migration to the capital city of Montevideo in the early twentieth century, exile during Peronismo in the mid-twentieth century, and, finally, the turbulent period of the dictatorship in her internationally bestselling novel *The Invisible Mountain* (2009). A novelist, editor, and literary translator, she examines the effects of the Dirty War on the children of the disappeared victims of the dictatorship in her second novel *Perla* (2012). In her award-winning third novel, *The Gods of Tango* (2015), De Robertis depicts a multicultural Buenos Aires as her characters travel from there to Montevideo; the formation of ethnic communities and gender relationships in the early twentieth century contributes to the making of the revered musical and dance genre of tango on both sides of the River Plate border. An advocate of immigrant, LGBTQ, and women's rights, De Robertis does not refrain from critiquing various forms of social injustice in her fiction and nonfiction. In 2017, she edited the epistolary collection *Radical*

Hope: Letters of Love and Dissent in Dangerous Times, bringing together a wide array of writers, many of whom are U.S. Latinas/os, to reflect on the past, current, and future political climate in the United States.

Peruvian (Im)migration to the United States

In texts by Peruvian and Peruvian American authors with residences and migrations to the United States during different periods in the twentieth century, diversity pervades as well. Immigration is a common factor for most authors in this group at different levels. Some moved with their families before the Immigration Act of 1965 while others left for the United States during the civil war that tore the nation into fragmented political factions and culminated with the Shining Path years (1980–1992). Nonetheless, it is worth mentioning that a colonial mentality has existed in Peru since the Spanish Conquest until the twenty-first century. Walter Ventosilla and Fredy Roncalla, who were born and raised primarily in Peru, immigrated to the United States as young adults. The experiences they capture in their narratives reflect another complicated portrait of migration as they represent the social inequalities that affect Andean indigenous people who originate from the *sierra* (Peruvian Andes) and must often migrate to the capital of Lima and then, as immigrants to the United States, specifically to New York City.

A short-fiction writer, novelist, playwright, and theatre director/producer, Walter Ventosilla began his career in the arts as an actor at the age of fourteen with the theatre group *Yego* in Lima, Peru, his birthplace. As a young adult, he became a founder of his own theatre group, *Septiembre*, before studying literature formally at the Universidad Nacional de San Marcos in Lima. Prior to settling in New York City, he lived and studied in France while working with local theatre groups. He has published fiction extensively in Peru as well as directed and produced plays in New York City. The short-fiction collection *Cuentos de tierra y eucaliptos* (1999) takes place in the Andean region of Peru and critiques the neocolonial modes that still influence the native people in their everyday lives. By contrast, the collection of short fiction *Asunción* (1995) addresses relationships among Peruvians who must negotiate gender and race matters in urban as well as Andean contexts. While his novel *Luis, Bandolero, Luis* (2005) follows the trials and tribulations of an Andean protagonist resembling Robin Hood in search of social justice by helping the disempowered at the expense of the wealthy, his short-fiction collection *A quien corresponda* (2008) crosses national borders into the United States by demonstrating how Peruvian immigrants must confront an aggressive New York metropolis by trying to practice their art while facing discrimination from other immigrants. Ventosilla exemplifies a unique voice that spans internal migrations within Peru as well as the immigrant experiences that move from the Andes or Lima to the United States.

A cultural commentator, fiction writer, and scholar, Fredy Amilcar Roncalla represents a distinctive example of the Peruvian diaspora in the United States as a trilingual speaker who incorporates his three languages – Quechua, Spanish, and English – into his writing. Living in the United States from a young age, Roncalla has become a transnational ambassador across cultures, languages, and nations. In the autobiographical essay, "Fragments for a Story of Forgetting and Remembrance" (2000), Roncalla reveals his personal experiences in traveling between languages by learning a formal Spanish in school and an oral Quechua in the community of Chalhuanca, a small provincial capital and his birthplace in the Peruvian Andes. As a critic of Andean culture and literature, he engages the Quechua-speaking world in his scholarship with works such as *Escritos mitimaes: hacia una poética andina postmoderna* (1998) by emphasizing that the culture is constantly shifting and transforming. In *Hawansuyo ukun words* (2014), Roncalla demonstrates how Andean culture has been affected by modernization, globalization, and immigration. Whether it is economics or politics, many Andean people have been forced to leave their homes in Peru to travel not only to the United States, but globally to Europe, Asia, and elsewhere. Roncalla also views technology such as the Internet and Youtube as important resources in disseminating Andean cultural practices such as music (e.g., huayno) throughout the world. At the same time, Andean migrants and culture undergo their own transformations in their new places of residence. The trilingual Roncalla recuperates and remembers his mother tongue, Quechua, to theorize about Andean culture, exemplifying his role as a cultural activist.

In the twenty-first century, Peruvian American writers who were educated formally in English in U.S. institutions have intervened in U.S. national literary circles beginning in 2001 with the publication of Marie Arana's memoir, *American Chica* and followed by two other important Peruvian American writers, Daniel Alarcón and Carmen Giménez Smith. These authors recover experiences within Peruvian and U.S. social and historical contexts to give their narratives, essays, and poetry a transnational quality by crossing as hybrid authors writing from the North to the South as others in this essay do as well. By doing so, they entertain a wider reading publics across nations and borders as cultural translators who render South American history in short direct English sentences, instead of as literary translations of texts marked by Spanish's more effusive sentence structure and different grammar.

Critic, journalist, historian, and author Marie Arana was born and raised during her childhood in Peru and then moved with her family to the United States where she was educated. Due to these circumstances, she holds a unique position in bridging two very different cultures by writing in English about her Peruvian heritage. In her memoir *American Chica* (2001), Arana focuses on the coming of age of a bicultural female protagonist whose family migrated from Peru to the United States in 1959 when she was ten years old. In addition to mapping a transnational genealogy, Arana provides context on Peruvian history and U.S.–Peruvian relations that led to her Peruvian father's academic studies and residence in the United States in the 1940s. During this time, he met her American mother before embarking on a decade-long journey back to his homeland in Peru, where their daughter/narrator Marisi Arana was born. This narrative vividly portrays the emotional trauma of living between two worlds, two languages, and two ways of thinking. The protagonist must also negotiate gender roles between her father's Peruvian side and her mother's American ways of fiercely practicing independence and asserting women's rights. Arana has also published two novels: *Cellophane* (2006) and *Lima Nights* (2008), an award-winning historical biography *Bolívar: American Liberator* (2013), and scholarly introductions to various cultural books about Peru. While the novels focus on family relationships in various historical contexts from the rubber boom to the Shining Path period, it is in her biography of Simón Bolívar where Arana finds the heart and soul, not only of the liberator, but also of the geographical landscape of South America, a continent that gave birth to six republics, including Peru, and consequently, to the migrations and formations of diasporas in the United States. In this important biography, I suggest that Arana is translating South American history for an English readership. Furthermore, Arana's role as an editor of "Book World" at *The Washington Post* has also enabled her to introduce other Latina/o authors since the 1990s.

Following in similar footsteps, the Peruvian-born author Daniel Alarcón emigrated with his family at the age of three to Birmingham, Alabama, at the dawn of the Shining Path civil war in 1980. Alarcón's fiction originally written in English has been translated into Spanish and numerous languages. When his collection of short fiction *War by Candlelight* (2005) was published, he received praise in both the United States and Peru for representing the migratory experiences of Peruvians in the United States and Peru during the Shining Path years as is evidenced by his short stories, "July 28, 1980, Lima, Peru" and "War by Candlelight." More poignantly, Alarcón captures the emotional trauma of civil war and its effects on the civilians caught in the crossfire of fighting enemies, be it in the Andean regions or in the coastal capital, Lima. Alarcón has developed a greater following after the publication of his novels, *Lost City Radio* (2007) and *At Night They Walk in Circles* (2013), both of which take place exclusively in Peru and translate the effects of war and migrations on the families of its victims within the Peruvian context. Since Alarcón publishes in English about Peruvian experiences that do not necessarily involve crossing national borders, Alarcon's consciousness as a U.S. Latino author does. Alarcón has also developed an audio podcast called *Radio Ambulante*, launched in 2012, to continue with transnational and translational storytelling but on a greater scale. In this narrative form of social media, Alarcón and a team of journalists and translators collect stories predominantly from the Spanish-speaking world, including the United States, to transmit via podcast to a global audience. Essentially, anyone who has access to Internet can participate in listening to the stories and educate themselves on various cultural or social matters. The issues discussed range from immigration to transgender identity to nostalgia for the homeland exemplified in one story by the Peruvian waltz, "Todos vuelven." In this last narrative innovation, Alarcón unites his training in journalism with fiction writing.

Another important author of the Peruvian diaspora in the United States, Carmen Giménez Smith adds a refreshing voice to the genres of poetry and the essay. She reconfigures questions of gender, place, and poetic aesthetics by challenging representations of women, be it in historical contexts or mythologies. Born in New York City in 1971, Giménez Smith advances a feminist consciousness that is in dialogue as much with American women's poetry of the 1960s and 1970s as with Latin American vanguard poetry of the 1920s and 1930s. While her hybrid poetic voice jumps through various time periods and landscapes in her earlier poetry collections *The City She Was* (2011) and *Goodbye, Flicker* (2012), her memoir *Bringing Down the Little Birds: On Mothering, Art, Work, and Everything Else* (2010) displays an unsentimental look at women's roles in everyday life, especially negotiating the tasks of mothering and writing. She interrogates the myths, the glorification, and realities in an intimate voice by complicating the politics of being a mother, conscientious of the fact that gender does matter. Unapologetic and direct, Giménez Smith brings an unflinching perspective to her role as a woman poet who transcends various historical periods to incorporate female arche-types such as the Virgin of Guadalupe and Malinche in her collection *Milk and Filth* (2013). At one point, the poetic voice reflects, "I want my problems to be Wallace Stevens, but they're Anne Sexton" (36). This confession shows that she is constantly reformulating her aesthetics and feminism. In the coedited anthology *Angels of the Americlypse* (2014), Giménez Smith and John Chávez present an array of new Latina/o texts that constitute an innovative direction in Latina/o poetry through global influences, genre crossings, and gender in the twenty-first century.

Colombia's Civil and Intimate Wars

Similar to the civil war in Peru, Colombia also experienced a turbulent past of political violence in the 1980s that left an exodus of migrations to the United States. The writers of the Colombian diaspora reflect on how politics in public and in private can play a significant role in the everyday lives of individuals and their families. An essayist, novelist, and poet, Jaime Manrique is not only a pioneer author of Colombian American literature, but also at the vanguard of redefining gender roles and expectations in his historical fiction and autobiographies across transnational lines. In "South American Latino/a Authors," I situated Manrique's novels, *Latin Moon in Manhattan* (1992) and *Twilight at the Equator* (1997), as pioneer novels in understanding the Colombian diaspora in the United States, especially in New York City in the 1980s. In this chapter, I expand on Manrique as a significant voice for gay Latino writing who disrupts the patriarchal domination of the Latin American and Latino literary canons. In *Eminent Maricones: Arenas, Lorca, Puig and Me* (1999), he examines the biographies of gay writers of the Spanish-speaking world such as Cuban Reinaldo Arenas, Argentine Manuel Puig, and Spaniard Federico García Lorca. Similar to Manrique, all of these writers lived at various times of their lives, as exiles or immigrants, in New York City. By constructing this literary tradition of gay writing in the Americas in relationship to himself, Manrique reveals his identity as a gay Latino writer who dialogues openly with other gay authors before him in letters and rejects any form of censorship and oppression against people of color's sexual orientation. Manrique also provides an alternative perspective regarding gender roles and marginalized women in history when he recreates a fictional account of the Ecuadorian freedom fighter Manuela Sáenz in the novel *Our Lives Are the Rivers* (2006). Throughout South American history, official textbooks uniformly praise male figures such as the South American liberator Simón Bolívar of Venezuela. Manrique, however, recovers and credits Bolívar's great love, Manuela Sáenz, who actually saved his life on many occasions during the liberation wars in the nineteenth century. Manrique revitalizes this great romance in South American history to demonstrate that women were thinkers and activists who fought for South

American independence not with physical violence, but with their intelligence and resourcefulness. Yet, they have not always been recognized as such. Similar to his work on gay Latino writing, Manrique explores the possibilities of expanding literary history by focusing on marginal groups such as women who hardly receive their dues for their efforts, especially in South American culture, history, and politics.

Belonging to a younger generation of women writers in Colombian American literature, Patricia Engel was born to Colombian parents and raised in New Jersey. She received much critical acclaim for her first major literary work of fiction, *Viva* (2010), which crosses genres between a short-fiction collection and a novel. In this narrative, Engel subtly refers to Colombia's civil war of the 1980s to understand the context behind drug dealers, prostitution transactions, and illicit deals that involve the governments of the United States as well as Colombia. More importantly, Engel excavates how patriarchal domination and censorship in these spaces have detrimental effects for individuals, especially immigrant women from Colombia, a significant number of whom are violently kidnapped and sold into prostitution as if they were commodities. Once again, women's bodies and minds suffer torture and trauma beyond their control. Rather than entertain a melodrama of corruption and violence, Engel focuses on the intimacy of female friendship between two women, a Colombian immigrant and a Colombian American, to show that transnational alliances are possible at the grassroots levels among individuals to combat the physical and sexual violence against women enforced by drug dealers and corrupt officials. In her first novel, *It's Not Love, It's Just Paris* (2013), Engel traverses national boundaries from the perspective of a female protagonist who is educated and raised in the United States by Colombian immigrant parents. Different from her first fiction, Engel's protagonist travels to live abroad in Paris, France, for a year before settling back in the United States to return to her family. Instead of presenting the romance and idealization of Paris, Engel shows the complicated realities of living in this multiethnic global city of exiles and immigrants in the twenty-first century. In both works of fiction, Engel brings to the forefront the effects of civil wars and migration that the Colombian diaspora, especially women, experience in the United States and beyond.

Unlike Manrique and Engel, Colombian-Cuban American author Daisy Hernández engages a dual heritage from the Caribbean as well as South America to explore the interstices of gender/bisexuality, migration, and translation in her memoir *A Cup of Water Under My Bed* (2014). In this narrative, Hernández unsettles the representation of a single national heritage as the daughter of a Colombian mother and Cuban father as she unravels her bisexual/queer identity from the local home context of North Bergen, New Jersey, to the Americas. Hernández further demonstrates how Latinas of multiple cultures and sexual orientations seek community and a sense of belonging as they negotiate their situational identities. Even though Daisy Hernández was born in the United States in 1975, I suggest that she is a hybrid product of various national belongings, including Colombia and Cuba. While she learned spoken Spanish at home from her Colombian mother and Cuban father, she also became immersed in the English language in the U.S. school system at the age of five, making her a bilingual heritage speaker. Despite this gradual process of assimilation into U.S. culture, Hernández maintained cultural practices such as the Spanish language, storytelling, and spirituality of Santería from her national heritages. As the daughter of working-class South American and Caribbean immigrants who met in the United States, Hernandez also became a linguistic and cultural translator for her Spanish-speaking parents and the English-speaking bureaucracy of school, social services, and other institutions at various moments in her life. In the essay, "Las lesbianas are on the Other Side" (2000), Hernández reflects on the role of languages in her life: "English had given me freedom but it had also alienated me from my family . . .. I say very little in Spanish about my career, my dreams, my lovers . . .. For my parents there will always be sides of me that exist only in translation" (141). Upon learning English, Hernández's world splits temporally/spatially between the past associated with Spanish and certain limitations concerning sexual orientation and goals and the present/future in English which brings her sexual independence but also causes emotional fragmentation between her and her parents. She realizes that she cannot share all the intimate parts of her life with them.

In conclusion, the South American-descent writers in this chapter unite in bringing a new vision to transnational American literature and contemporary world literature with stories/narratives to challenge the limited representation of South American culture, history, and politics and its diaspora that circulate via media in the United States. Within this tradition, I further suggest that South American Latina/o authors, those educated during their formative years in the United States, contest and revise authoritative perspectives from the government or patriarchal systems in both their homelands because they belong to multiple national belongings as they travel across nations. They are broadening the canon of North American literature from the United States to include a fuller version of their South American cultural heritage in English. In addition, some of their texts are also in dialogue with a South American readership if they are translated into Spanish, giving them a wider audience because their texts will serve as bridges across the Americas. As part of a larger tradition of the South American exile and im/migrant writings, these authors add another dimension of heterogeneity to the current Latina/o literary discourse.

WORKS CITED

Agosín, Marjorie. *Cartographies: Meditations on Travels.* Trans. Nancy Abraham Hall. Foreword by Isabel Allende. Athens: University of Georgia Press, 2007.

Dear Anne Frank: Poems. Trans. Richard Schaaf. Washington, DC: Azul Editions, 1994.

I Lived on Butterfly Hill. Trans. E. M. O'Connor. New York: Atheneum Books for Young Readers, 2014.

Inhabiting Memory: Essays on Memory and Human Rights in the Américas. San Antonio, TX: Wings Press, 2011.

Secrets in the Sand: The Young Women of Juárez. Trans. Celeste Kostopulos Cooperman. Buffalo, NY: White Pine Press, 2006.

Writing Toward Hope: The Literature of Human Rights in Latin America. New Haven, CT: Yale University Press, 2006.

Agosín, Marjorie and Julie H. Levison, eds. *Magical Sites: Women Travelers in 19th Century Latin America.* Buffalo, NY: White Pine Press, 1999.

Alarcón, Daniel. *At Night We Walk in Circles.* New York: Riverhead Books, 2013.

Lost City Radio: A Novel. New York: Harper Collins, 2007.

War by Candlelight. New York: Harper Collins, 2005.

Allende, Isabel. *Daughter of Fortune.* Trans. Margaret Sayers Peden. New York: Harper-Collins, 1999.

Portrait in Sepia. Trans. Margaret Sayers Peden. New York: HarperCollins, 2001.

Maya's Notebook. Trans. Anne McLean. New York: Harper, 2013.

The House of the Spirits. Trans. Magda Bogin. New York: A. A. Knopf, 1985.

Arana, Marie. *American Chica: Two Worlds, One Childhood.* New York: Dial Press, 2001.

Bolívar: American Liberator. New York: Simon and Schuster, 2013.

Cellophane. New York: Dial Press, 2006.

Lima Nights. New York: Dial Press, 2008.

De Robertis, Carolina. *Perla.* New York: Knopf, 2012.

The Gods of Tango. New York: Knopf, 2015.

The Invisible Mountain. New York: Knopf, 2009.

ed. *Radical Hope: Letters of Love and Dissent in Dangerous Times.* New York: Vintage, 2017.

Dorfman, Ariel. *Feeding on Dreams: Confessions of an Unrepentant Exile.* (1998). Boston, MA: Houghton Mifflin Harcourt, 2011.

Heading South, Looking North: A Bilingual Journey. New York: Farrar, Straus, and Giroux, 1998.

Engel, Patricia. *It's Not Love, It's Just Paris.* New York: Grove Press, 2013.

Vida. New York, Black Cat, Distributed by Publishers Group West, 2010.

Falconi, José Luis and José Antonio Mazzotti, eds. *The Other Latinos: Central and South Americans in the United States*. Cambridge, MA: David Rockefeller Center for Latin American Studies, Harvard University Press, 2008.

Giménez Smith, Carmen. *Bring Down the Little Birds: On Mothering, Art, Work,* and *Everything Else*. Tucson: University of Arizona Press, 2010.

Goodbye, Flicker: Poems. Amherst: University of Massachusetts Press, 2012.

Milk and Filth. Tucson: University of Arizona Press, 2013.

The City She Was: Poems. Fort Collins: The Center for Literary Publications/Colorado State University, 2011.

Giménez Smith, Carmen and John Chávez, eds. *Angels of the Americlypse: New Latin@ Writings*. Denver, CO: Counterpath, 2014.

Heredia, Juanita. "South American Latino/a Writers in the United States." *The Routledge Companion to Latino/a Literature*. Ed. Suzanne Bost and Frances Aparicio. New York and London: Routledge, 2012. 436–44.

Transnational Latina Narratives in the Twenty-First Century: The Politics of Gender, Race and Migrations. New York: Palgrave Macmillan, 2009.

"The Task of the Translator: An Interview with Daniel Alarcón." *Latino Studies* 10.3 (Autumn 2012): 395–409.

Hernández, Daisy. *A Cup of Water Under My Bed: A Memoir*. Boston, MA: Beacon Press, 2014.

Manrique, Jaime. *Eminent Maricones: Arenas, Lorca, Puig, and Me*. Madison: University of Wisconsin Press, 1999.

Latin Moon in Manhattan. New York: St. Martin's Press, 1992.

Our Lives Are the Rivers. New York: Harper Collins, 2006.

Twilight at the Equator. Boston, MA: Faber and Faber, 1997.

Negroni, María. *Andanza*. Valencia: Pre-textos Poesía, 2009.

Buenos Aires Tour. México, DF: Conaculta-Fonca: Aldus, 2006.

Ciudad gótica. Rosario-Buenos Aires: Bajo La Luna Nueva, 1994.

La anunciación. Buenos Aires: Seix Barral, 2007.

Night Journey. Trans. Anne Twitty. Princeton, NJ: Princeton University Press, 2002.

Tango Lyrics. Trans. Michelle Gil-Montero. Toronto: Quattro Books, 2013.

Pérez Firmat, Gustavo. *Life on the Hyphen: The Cuban-American Way*. Austin: University of Texas Press, 1994.

Roncalla, Fredy Amilcar. *Escritos mitimaes: hacia una poética andina postmoderna*. Barro Editorial Press, 1998.

"Fragments for a Story of Forgetting and Remembrance." *Languages Crossings: Negotiating the Self in a Multicultural World*. Ed. Karen Ogulnick. New York: Teachers College Press, 2000. 64–70.

Hawansuyo ukun words. Lima, Peru: Grupo Pakarina, 2014.

Rushdie, Salman. *Imaginary Homelands: Essays and Criticism, 1981–1991*. New York: Viking, 1991.

Valenzuela, Luisa. *Black Novel with Argentines*. Trans. Toby Talbot. New York: Simon & Schuster, 1992.

Como en la Guerra. Buenos Aires: Editorial Sudamericana, 1977.

Other Weapons. Trans. Deborah Bonner. Hanover, NH: Ediciones del Norte, 1985.

The Lizard's Tail. Trans. Gregory Rabassa. New York: Farrar, Straus, Giroux, 1983.

Ventosilla, Walter. *A quien corresponda*. Lima, Peru: Urpi Editores, 2008.

Asunción. Lima, Peru: Lluvia Editores, 1995.

Cuentos de tierra y eucalpitos. Lima, Peru: Chiripaq, Centro de Culturas Indias, 1999.

Luis, Bandolero, Luis. Lima, Peru: Paloma Ediciones, 2005.

Waisman, Sergio. "Argentine Writers in the U.S.: Writing South, Living North." Ed. Carlota Caulfield and Darién Davis. *A Companion to US Latino Literature*. Woodbridge, UK: Tamesis, 2007. 158–76.

Irse. Buenos Aires: Bajo la Luna, 2010.

Leaving. Hurricane, 2004.

33

The Mesoamerican Corridor, Central American Transits, and Latina/o Becomings

CLAUDIA MILIAN

In a podcast interview with the online project Radio Ambulante, spearheaded by Daniel Alarcón, the novelist spoke with Salvadoran journalist Óscar Martínez about his acclaimed book, *The Beast: Riding the Rails and Dodging Narcos on the Migrant Trail.* Martínez characterized Central Americans' perilous movements through Mexico – as they travel up toward the United States on freight trains – as a crossing "through the most unknown Mexico, the Mexico of public lands, of small towns, but never the Mexico of resources. The Mexico of traintracks, not of highways" (Alarcón, 2014).[1] Alarcón queried Martínez about *The Beast*'s title in Spanish – *Los migrantes*

---

[1] Alarcón's question is: "'The book is called in Spanish 'The Migrants that Don't Matter,' which I think is a title that has much more anger. *The Beast* is a more poetic title. Tell me about some of that change and what is the ... Am I misinterpreting it? That title has a rage and a denunciation? The original title, I mean." Martínez's response follows:
"Yes, look. I've always described it, I think it's difficult, as a journalist, to be an optimistic person in this world. The Migrants that Don't Matter had meaning. When we were traveling, seeing that territory, you realized that there is not a concentration camp, rather, there is hostels where they eventually stay. They travel through the most unknown Mexico, the Mexico of public lands, of small towns, but never the Mexico of resources. The Mexico of traintracks, not of highways. They do not vote, obviously. They are not a political asset that interests anyone. And, above all, they do not press charges, and it's become so ingrained that anyone could understand why a migrant does not register complaints, it's like asking a soldier to get water from the enemy garrison. A migrant will never press charges, to him the local police and the Zetas are hardly distinguishable. So it's a population that will generate few costs. It's a population that Central American governments have reused to raise the voice because they are interested in remittances continuing to represent about 31 percent of the income of the domestic product from Honduras, El Salvador, and Guatemala. ... And evidently the only thing that interests the United States is that these people cross the border infrequently. They find themselves at a crossroads where, as they say in Mexico, valen completamente madre [they don't give a fuck about them], no? There's no one who has more of an interest than certain altruistic Mexicans who raffle off their lives dealing with these migrants. Literally, and yes, the book 'The Migrants that Don't Matter,' is more of thicker title for me, it has much anger" (Alarcón, 2014).
All translations in this essay are mine, unless specified otherwise.

que no importan (2010) – and how the original heading, "The Migrants that Don't Matter," "has much more anger … a rage and a denunciation" (Alarcón, 2014). *The Beast*, Alarcón gauged, is "more poetic" (ibid).

Something is amiss in Alarcón's interpretation. Anger and poetic sensibility aside, *Los migrantes que no importan* cannot be equivalently translated into English as "The Migrants that Don't Matter." The train, in this geography, has shifted in meaning. Whereas the freight train was once made and used for the carrying of commodities that were packaged for delivery to other places, it is now Central American people who have become commodities themselves. This industrial and efficient mode of transporting goods is the only viable option for the movement of many Central Americans from the "Northern Triangle" of Guatemala, Honduras, and El Salvador. The urgency of the matter at hand – why as Martínez told National Public Radio (NPR), "Central America is bleeding" and "what it is that so many [Central Americans] are fleeing from" – would be lost in the United States, collapsed with mainstream perceptions on the threatening, brown tide of undocumented Latino and Latina migration (NPR, October 24, 2013). As Mae Ngai has shown, the production of the illegal alien depends on "*a new legal and political subject*, whose inclusion within the nation [is] simultaneously a social reality and a legal impossibility" (4). Needless to add, I do not minimize the magnitude of what is happening with regard to U.S. undocumented Latino migrations, the separation of families, social and national hierarchies, human rights violations, and, in Saskia Sassen's general overview, "the unsettlements of daily life" (2009, 228).

My impetus, instead, draws from other formalized exclusions of political being: to the nearly 140,000 Central Americans who annually cross the Mexico–Guatemala border, their main gateway to the United States (Melimopoulos, 2012). I veer toward illegality and citizenship from Mexico and Central America, a Mesoamerican site that, from a different terrain, anthropologists John and Jean Comaroff define as "ID-ology," wherein "various sorts of identity struggle express themselves in the politics of everyday life" (35). The affixed "ID" to ideology links it to "identity" and "identification"; to individuals who may identify over and against other persons; and to barriers of existence posed through the official need for authorized, federal, state, or local ID cards – the ultimate confirmation of legality and national citizenship. But ID-ology can be reconstituted with new political actors and affiliations that bring about other forms of "becoming," mainly for those whose construction arises from a lack of identity documents (one's "papers"), an ontological otherness traced through the Central American map, or, in vernacular shorthand, "where the wild things are."

This undertaking pores through the contemporary events of "other" Latinos in the making through the Mesoamerican corridor, alongside the inception of an ever-expanding latinidad to other regional spaces in the twenty-first century. Martínez yields to the off-site production of subaltern Central American-American subjects as subjects of news stories – distant news stories, "crisis moments," about other alien others interrupting American myths.[2] *The Beast* illuminates how migrants trying to find a place in the world become the abject signifiers of indignities, rurality, crushing poverty, underdevelopment, and instability – a projection of an iconic, peripheral Central Americanness whose derogatory status within a Global South parallels the social configurations of unwanted Latino migrants in the U.S. public sphere. What concerns me is "Latino" as a conceptual and political affiliation gesturing toward another narration: that of Central American-American deracinated constituencies who do not neatly usher in a commensurate U.S. Americanness. Questions of minoritarian status away from the habitus of the United States arise, as do notions of being and the understanding of Latino as a rubric with multiple points of entry and alternative names: invader, immigrant, "refugee, deportee, foreigner, 'illegal,' criminal" (Rubin and Melnick, 10). Analogous contours are present in Chiapas, the southern Mexican state bordering Guatemala, which is "fed up with Central American migrants. . . . They are poorer than Mexicans, and they are seen as backward and ignorant. People think they bring disease, prostitution, and crime and take away jobs" (Nazario, 79).

The ethnoracial Latino label is attended to as a "Latino/a" grammar moving with and operating in the world, though often through nonexistence.[3] But this analysis does not presume a universal through this U.S.

---

[2] I follow Lázaro Lima's lead on "crisis moments": "The term 'crisis' is meant to call attention to the cultural manifestations of historical conflict that have resulted in publicly rendered and redressed modes of being both American and Latino through narratives, images, and other sign systems" (6). The Latino and American crisis, dating back to the Mexico–US War, is unresolved. "Ever since the war, the various conceits associated with American democratic participation and the unfulfilled promise of equality have created crisis moments where competing forms of cultural citizenship have vied for legitimacy and access to cultural capital" (6–7).

[3] Nonexistence becomes a methodology, paradigm, or a motif running through recent publications from Central America. This logic of not mattering is punctuated in Martínez's *Los migrantes que no importan* and *El Faro.net*'s *Crónicas Negras: desde una región que no cuenta* ("Dark Chronicles: From a Region that Doesn't Count"). These works depict quotidian worlds of violence, socioeconomic hierarchies, and subhuman

categorization. It seeks to understand the sociopolitical experience of Latina/ o as a "modern processes of identification" in the Global South, "albeit in different forms and with different intensities," as Boaventura de Sousa Santos asserts (2014, 28). The Mesoamerican corridor is yoked to an order of double displacement, political life, and conflict. It is a differential space whose genealogy is added to Latino thought for philosophical thinking about Latino likeness and what it means to be from a remote, unrecognized space at a time when a remarkable conception of Central American-Americans is taking place.[4] Martínez's in-depth reporting orients us to subjects without human and equal epistemic value, prompting other conceptualizations of transient Latino citizenship – or, the "thingness" of discardable being that Central American mutilated migrations have become.

Given the marginal location of Central America within a discursive Latin American "community," I do not pursue a comparative Latin American hemispherist framework grappling with what goes into the making of the idea of "America" as well as "Latin America" (although the formation "Central American-American," soon to be explored, ineluctably invites further conversations). This essay's pointed yet open-ended preoccupation is how Latino otherness appears and functions in transit, before it is "delivered" and takes on life as U.S. Latino. This interrogative impulse dialogues with David Palumbo-Liu's *The Deliverance of Others*, where he contends that "the aim of [modern] literature is precisely to deliver to us 'others' whose lives are unlike our own" (1). Readers must cope with this core issue: "if we still adhere to the modern valorization of literature as bringing the lives of others in a vivid way, once we admit 'others' into 'our' world and place

conditions whose nothingness and invisibility spark forms of nonbeing – "being," as they are, overpowered by their own pathological Central Americanness, one that could metamorphose, vis-à-vis the Beast, into Central American-Americanness. Central American invisibility is not a facile, naturally given state, but one that acknowledges and renounces the excess under which "Central America" comes to be recognized, misrecognized, or absent. If for Frantz Fanon, *black* invisibility gives rise to "the Negro," one needs to consider the kind of Central American humanity and the different lines of contact that come into play aboard the Beast (see Goldberg, 1997). What is the logic behind the in/visibility (a visibility that has an "in" – a means of inclusion – but that may be hidden) of how the Central American comes to be visualized and socially accepted, especially through the frontier of drug trafficking?

[4] My book, *Latining America: Black-Brown Passages and the Coloring of Latino/a Studies*, broadly framed geographic, cultural, and epistemological insignificance as "Guatepeorianness." This state connotes a regional inconsequentiality, or "the presumed inevitable state of Central American calamitousness" (132). "Central America tinkers on the margins of epistemological and research abandon – no one's business," registers Shaun Grech (14). Arguably, what happens on the Mesoamerican corridor is no one's business, too.

value in the difference they bring into our lives, where do we set the limit of *how much* otherness is required, as opposed to how much is excessive, disruptive, disturbing, in ways that damage us, rather than enhance our lives" (2)? *The Beast*, as a journalistic enterprise, demands craft and narrative skills that cast light on extraordinary despair and the now "normative" recognition of Central American transit-migrants as "second-class citizens" who are "maimed, shot, or hacked to death" (Martínez, 43). Whereas "the tragedy of the migrants is what editors call a 'non-story'" in the United States (Goldman, xv), Martínez, as a first respondent, so to speak, of the crises behind Central American vulnerability, gives an idea of the incipience of collectivities that as Lily Cho determines, are "borne out of the losses of dislocation" – the very sets of deracinated otherness that delivers us to Latino contingencies (109).

Ellen Moodie styles accounts of conflict and violence in postwar El Salvador – fragmented anecdotes that do not focus on peace or war, but that are "something else, something somehow more sinister, less knowable" – as "crime stories" occurring "at the intersection of self and other, citizen and state, the powerful and powerless" (2). These sketches, drawn from personal experiences and not police authorities, need deliberation "within a larger narrated/narrative world" (5). The storytellers imagine "a common shape of their world": their narratives have patterns and convey information possible in postwar Central America (14). Their play-by-play gives word to their adeptness, know-how, "convictions, social facts, structures of feelings, senses of reality that [have] effects. Consciousness cannot be false in that sense" (ibid.). Crime stories, as Moodie devises them, are not exclusively about war, horror, suffering, and ongoing violence. They transmit "strength, resilience, and survival" (17). Yet Martínez's tableau can be conjured as oral autobiographies of migrants' lives, "say[ing] things for which our vernaculars have not prepared us" (Mendieta, 19). How, one might ask, do these lives take shape and how do these voices fit in extant Latina/o processes of life writing and histories with disparate lives: common, uncommon, or extraordinary?

The Be(a)st Option

The Beast is "a compilation of dispatches published over two years" in El Salvador's online publication, *ElFaro.net*. As novelist and journalist Francisco Goldman noted, Martínez's endeavor "has the organic coherence, development, and narrative drive of a novel" (viii–ix). Goldman appraised this volume as one of "the most impressive nonfiction books I've read in years," adding, "it should be required reading for any migrant setting out across Mexico" (ix, x). In postwar Central America, these journeys disorder our terms of engagement around the guiding principles of migration. A revised word that more accurately captures contemporary movements along the U.S.–Mexico and the Mexico–Guatemala borders "is not migration, but escape," Martínez registers (1). What could operate as the ameliorated designation for these transit-migrants in Mexico, or would-be American migrants: refugees, escapees, deserters, fugitives, runaways, or, through the optic of a more affectively-laden phrase, "upchucked Central Americans," as Martínez tags the disaggregated bodies spat out and vomited by the isthmus (19)?

Nausea and the ejection of bile are the first affect, a means of access into the experience of deracination for Central American outsiders in Central America. The Northern Triangle has produced what sociologist Zygmunt Bauman qualifies as "'human waste,' or more correctly wasted humans (the 'excessive' and 'redundant,' that is the population of those who either could not or were not wished to be recognized or allowed to stay)" (5). These "excessive and redundant" outliers turn into a major symptomatic cavalcade from Central America. Central American-Americans thus come into view through what Lauren Berlant pegs as *touchy* subjects" (Berlant 2014). This is "a word for the delicacy of manner that people develop while trying not to incite unwonted violence," one that spreads to those who have been violently spewed out, signaling a crisis in Central American citizenship (ibid.). Social prestige and economic accomplishment come through migration, as a prosperous and consumptive citizenship is enacted abroad. Martínez reflected:

> When you're 18, you don't think about going to college, but about migrating. . . . I think, in a sense, it's a sham: you have to be successful when you migrate, the one who migrates isn't raped, the one who migrates doesn't fall from a train or goes hungry, the one who migrates dresses with Lakers shirts and returns [to Central America] with a plasma TV. You don't talk about the [Mexican journey]. Even among families you don't talk about the migration route. For purposes of moving, of executing the verb "migrate," people are not going to stop, people have to come and see for themselves that [the United States] is not what they think it is. How are you going to dispose of an idea that's been in a person's head for 10 years, or for 20 years, saying, "no, don't go, it's not so easy." The person will tell you, "No, I wanna see. I may screw myself later, but I wanna see." (Alarcón, 2014)

Martínez's "seeing" alludes to the collective memory of migration, and a past and present that orbit around U.S. and Central American relations.

But migrant memory needs to backtrack and widen the two-way street, for although the United States has been haunting Central American imaginations, Mexican involvement in these journeys and existing traumas are obfuscated. The irony is that, in U.S. immediate thinking, the bodies behind these Southern passages are lumped together as "Mexican," even as these individuals are christened as "*cachuco*, a derogatory term used for Central Americans in Mexico [that] roughly translates to 'dirty pig'" (Vogt, 764). It is easier, perhaps, for the empire to admit Central American bodies as part of a larger "horde" that presumably takes over jobs. It is simpler to see "Mexico" as a "'body' country" arsenal while the Northernness of the United States remains a "'brain' country," or the brains behind the harvest of empire, meaning, the architect behind current waves of Latina/o becoming through menial labor (Brennan, 6). "In countries with high rates of out-migration like El Salvador and Honduras," anthropologist Wendy A. Vogt reminds us, "labor migration has become a process of 'exporting people and recruiting remittances' ..., a 'transnational proletarianization,' whereby the value derived from migrant workers is split, albeit highly unevenly, between the U.S. economy and home economies" (Vogt, 770).

The éclat of a greatly valorized Central American citizen is one where the individual is unmarked by the process of migration and remittances, the so-called migradollars. El Salvador, as a case in point,

> depends on emigration and on maintaining emotional and cultural connections with ... "Salvadorans abroad" as a strategy for encouraging or even guaranteeing the flow of remittances and nostalgic links to the home country. Migrant aspirations and portrayals of the "American Dream" in the media, consumption in shopping malls, and service work (such as bilingual call centers) are facets of Salvadoran transnationalism.   (Rivas, 5)

Those aboard the Beast are "persons that, paradoxically, cannot yet act as citizens" at home (Berlant, 2005, 5). Just as Berlant has assessed that the right in the United States "has attempted to control the ways questions of economic survival are seen as matters of citizenship" so too, one might say, has this transpired in Central America (2005, 8). There, "people rendered expendable in their home communities – through chronic unemployment, violence, and death – strive to sell their labor power abroad and join the global reserve army" (Vogt, 770). The confounding part is that if these are the migrants that do not matter – considering that their acts of citizenship are premised on a devaluation of a Central Americanness that is reduced to Central Americanness in Mexico, while also being denied a national citizenship for "the common good" in their home countries due to sociopolitical and economic marginalization – they end up becoming the "ID-alized" migrants that do matter. In Vanessa Núñez Handal's words, "the only migrants that matter are those that guarantee remittances" (Díaz, May 22, 2014). These Mesoamerican journeys evince Central American-American dehumanization and signal the promise of a flourishing self-made (Central American) citizen, a subject who thrives in and through terror. Berlant's scholarly architecture from *The Queen of America Goes to Washington City* resonates here:

> citizenship is a status whose definitions are always in process. It is continually being produced out of a political, rhetorical, and economic struggle over who will count as "the people" and how social membership will be measured and valued. It must, then, be seen as more than a patriotic category. ... Citizenship provides an index for appraising domestic national life, and for witnessing the process of valorization that make different populations differently legitimate socially and under the law.   (2005, 20)

Present-day Central Americans, the "last in line" to cross over, are principally targeted (143). They tend to get land-locked in Mexico, under what Clifford Shearing and Jennifer Wood specify as "a multi-layered world of governing auspices" (102). Coyotes charge migrants from the isthmus an extra $600 for their northern odyssey (175). *The Beast* is a record of the neglected life in Central America and a seemingly endless border along the way, a Mexican trek populated by wastelands, heat, bandits, and *narcos* – a "systemization of kidnapping, smuggling, and extortion" otherwise called as "the cachuco industry" (Vogt, 765).[5] A specific language attests to the different circumstances these Central American-Americans undergo in this pilgrimage for "greener pastures." The coyotes are no longer coyotes. They are now *guías*, since there has been a change in their occupational function and they must pay dues to Mexican paramilitary groups like Los Zetas, who, as journalist

---

[5] A *New Yorker* article annotated the large-scale profits of the cachuco industry. The commercial enterprise transcends Mexico, becoming "America's migrant-extortion market" and remaining "in the shadows of our fierce immigration debate" (Stillman 2015). The magazine explains:
"'The Zetas' strategy, it's classic wholesale,'" Marta Sánchez Soler, the director of the Mesoamerican Migrant Movement and the trip's coordinator, told me. "'When organized crime kidnaps somebody rich, the media and police mobilize. Then the criminals feel the heat. So they realized that, rather than doing one big, flashy kidnapping of someone rich and powerful, it would be better to do a hundred small kidnappings of migrants whom nobody pays attention to.'" Together, we did the arithmetic: by recent estimates, at least eighteen thousand migrants are seized in Mexico each year. If a third of their families pay a lowball ransom of four thousand dollars, that's twenty-four million dollars, with minimal risk or labor" (ibid.).

Alfredo Corchado declares, are "terrorists without a political agenda" (4). *Cuerpomátic* is the term for "the transformation of the migrant's body" (73). Bodies become "a credit card, a new platinum-edition 'bodymatic' which buys you a little safety, a little bit of cash and the assurance that your travel buddies won't get killed. Your bodymatic, except for what you get charged, buys a more comfortable ride on the train" (ibid.). Central American women, sometimes human trafficking victims, are turned into an everyday material product. Sexual assault "has lost its terror," and some women "knew they'd be raped on this journey . . . they feel it's a sort of tax that must be paid" (72). As Alma Guillermoprieto has it, "Rape is such a common part of the journey for women that before they start out on their trek, they start taking contraceptive pills" (Guillermoprieto, 2012). Rape is the price of the ticket in what Sassen diagrams as "the feminization of survival" through "survival circuits that have emerged in response to the deepening misery of the global south" (2006, 30). This feminization "restores features of oppressive feudal relations, such as indentured servitude, servile relations, political disenfranchisement, and sexual slavery" (Hawkesworth, 24).

Murder, rape, and robbery cease to be "serious crimes," as the weightiest offense is drug trafficking (39). These are quotidian transgressions, jobs performed on a daily basis, with unshaken sangfroid. "The bandits leave their houses in the morning just like everybody leaves their houses in the morning, on their way to work," Martínez recounts. "They leave from the ranches and farms, and they station themselves waiting to do their business: rape and robbery. And at the end of the day they haul in their booty and go back home and rest, until the next day of work," when a "narco-hired rapist will demand his daily fuck" (42–43). Bra trees are indigenous in this topography: "It's a desert tree literally draped with the bras and panties of migrant women who are raped by bandits along this border. Their underwear is kept as trophies. The rape of migrant women is a border-wide practice. ... Bra trees grow everywhere" (164). The scenery ceases to be merely green, spiritual, and harmonious.[6] It is a degraded landscape in tune with what Levi R. Bryant propositions as a black ecology,

---

[6] As a 2014 article in the *Guardian* announced, Mexican narco-traffickers, who have extended their influence in Central America through local gangs, are responsible for a "little-known phenomenon of 'narco-deforestation' that is destroying huge tracts of rainforest" in Honduras, Guatemala, and Nicaragua (Saliba, 2014). Per the *Guardian*: "Narco-deforestation enables cartels to occupy territory to the detriment of their competitors. If that continues, the entire Mesoamerican biological corridor, which stretches from Panama to Mexico, will be affected by tree felling." The exploitation of Mesoamerica's nature also punctuates the exploitation of humankind.

a view of nature that conforms to an environment's circumstances, abandoning "spiritualized conceptions of nature as a warm and inviting place outside [a] culture to which hominids can go" (291). Bryant's tenebrific ecology emphasizes "race, minoritization, and second- and third-world countries" (ibid.). On this part of Mexico's countryside we encounter a destructive, polluting, relationship to "nature": the ultimate "unnatural." This environment underlines an extralegal, man-made landscape constructed around the sexual violence of Central American-American gendered bodies, with trees being the new public memory of a different type of mob action and "southern horrors" (cf., Simien, 2013; Feimster, 2011; Gilmore, 1996; and Wells, 1996). To recall Nicole Guidotti-Hernández's observation: "Subjugated identities are produced through spatial configurations of power that literally turn a landscape against its inhabitants" (8). In this instance, the Mesoamerican transit-migrants are people who have "no intention of staying, traveling through Mexico as fast as they possibly [can]. Trying, in fact, to leave, not even a shadow behind them" (Guillermoprieto, 2012).

The border is burdened and has its limits. It admits and prioritizes – with limits. "We began to understand that even a border this long doesn't have space for everyone, much less for those who are last in line," writes Martínez (143). And so begins, yet again, the continuous reproduction of borders: new borders replacing old borders (161–162). This spatial reproduction suggests the reproduction of piracy, bandits, and conquerors. While there is no nation-state attached to Central American-American rape – or, the *cuerpomátic* that the Central American-American body has become – sexual aggression and terror are institutionalized and systematic. Yet, as Anabel Hernández discusses, Mexicans are not altogether exempt from their nation's criminal economy of the *narco* system, an outlaw network of drug traffickers, businessmen, and politicians that has imposed "on all Mexicans their intolerable law of 'silver or lead.' Pay up or die" (7). Mesoamerica references countries that are now being dubbed as "narco-democracies," for as Hernández calls up, it was the Iran-Contra affair – "something nobody seems to remember anymore" – that "turned Mexican drug traffickers from humble marijuana and poppy farmers into sophisticated international dealers in cocaine and synthetic drugs" (5–6; cf. Scott and Marshall, 1991).

Central American-Americans' discardable bodies – or involuntary, automatic "bodymatics" – possess an illegality that begins in and runs through Mesoamerica. This Mesoamerican corridor is integrated into the modern Mexican nation. Its mortiferous landscape, without governance, logically turns into the "proper" travel route for Guatepeorians with their sui generis "backwardness," contributing to the unevenness of rugged Central Americans in North-South relations. The Mesoamerican corridor incarnates a horrifying road to the promise of inclusion somewhere: possibly in the U.S. Latina/o landscape; perhaps within a different kind of U.S. membership, or their particular Central American country; or conceivably in the Mexican nation now comprised of migrants, or in this case, of citizens "in waiting" whose location as rights-bearing subjects in this political frontier has yet to be captured. Ngai is inerrant in postulating the U.S. illegal alien as an "'impossible subject,' a person who cannot be and a problem that cannot be solved" (5). Upchucked Central American-Americans are impossible Mesoamerican subjects through Ngai's well-cogitated reasons. But they have been just as impossible to put up with from their national and migratory "origins": these Central American-Americans have not been passed through by someone (as they are undigested in the isthmus) or by something (the Mexican terrain).

The Beast, "the snake, the machine, the monster" – the human cargo container delivering an overloaded stream of labor – has produced a vivid and continuous kinship in the same northern direction (53). "The Beast is the Rio Grande's first cousin. They both flow with the same Central American blood," Martínez verbalizes (ibid). These metaphorical yet intimate blood relations flow together and replicate strangely familiar border families, even as the Beast operates as a large fence that weeds out, mutilates, and injures Central American-American undesirables. Vogt outlines the Beast's capacity to dismember and mutilate bodies as "the result of structural, state, and local economies of violence and inequality." A Central American-American's transformation

> from productive laborer to disabled subject tells us how the migrant journey has become a site of violence and commodification wherein migrants' bodies may both gain and lose value. . . . These migrants, many quite literally cut in half, physically embod[y] the brutal consequences of transnational migration and the global processes that create them. Collectively, they represent a global workforce of people whose lives teeter on the edge of disposability in an economic sense but also in an immediate embodied sense. (771–72)

The movement of the vomited Central American stock, as Martínez gives to understand, is an "overflowing of the territory by the event" (Gordillo, 228). "At a bare minimum," Richard Bellamy underscores, the qualities associated with citizenship "seek to preserve our bodies and property from physical harm by others, and provide clear and reasonably stable conditions for all the various forms of social interaction that most individuals find to some degree unavoidable – be it travelling on the roads, buying and selling goods and labour, or marriage and co-habitation" (4). The quiddity of a migrating "citizenship" elicits, to borrow from Kim Rygiel, a Central American cachuco-ness as the source for a regional body that "is also 'just' a body: it is no longer so clearly a holder of rights: the figure of the body as the subject of rights has faded out of sight" (148).

These transient Central American-Americans "do not vote, obviously," Martínez highlights, and so "they are not a political asset that interests anyone. And, above all, they do not press charges, and it's become so ingrained that anyone could understand why a migrant does not register complaints . . . . A migrant will never press charges . . . it's a population that will generate few costs" (Alarcón, 2014). The Beast allows us to move, as Clifford Shearing and Jennifer Wood advance, from citizenship to denizen-ship (101). The notion of the denizen and denizenship is linked to social spaces that are not limited to citizenship. Denizenship may be apparent through assemblages that shift over time and space, chiefly through different governmental realms that may include gated communities, neighborhood watch committees, and surveillance, or the "strategies and practices of the three 'c's' (cops, courts, and corrections) . . . the dominant paradigm of 'crimology'" (98). Shearing and Wood broaden denizenship "beyond a 'habitual visitor to a place' so that it refers to an affiliation with rights and responsibilities that applies to any auspice of government" (ibid.).

Denizenship may be temporary or more permanent, but denizens must be "situated within the regulatory domain of [the] governmental node . . . with which they are associated" (102). To insist on Central Americans as Central Americans who are only bounded to the isthmus warrants renewed para-digms for understanding, in Michaeline Crichlow's terms, "liminal move-ments within and across power relations" (78). The larger continuity of this problem – the "violent mapping" (Crichlow, 78) of the highly differentiated Central American-American migrant in Mexico – must be rehomed, as Shearing and Wood posit, to "improve the quality of their citizenship" (110). This may seem odd, considering how Central Americans are divorced from "citizenship" in the migration process. Yet there is an ethical foundation for the way people should be treated. The expected treatment of the Central American is dehumanizing. It is the beginning of a lower expectation of treatment – dismantling our conventional understanding of citizenship, and replacing it with a dehumanized functional citizenship. The prospect of rape and prostitution would be the basis of the transience of migrant women: acquiescing, for example, their corporeal rights, the thing that belongs to them, having their body being taken away from them. Such expectations of treatment are not at the level of citizenship. And just because Central American persons risk their lives does not mean they are disconnected from the very substance of civil rights and legal recognition in Mexico. Mexico's National Institute for Migration recognizes three kinds of standings: nonimmigrant, immigrant, and permanent resident status. Central Americans would fall under the "transit-migrant" classification of nonimmigrant status, as they "are migrants who stay in [a] certain country for some period of time while seeking to migrate permanently to another country" (Eche, 9). But as it has been appraised, "Some critics claim that the United States fosters this [uneven] situation because it expects Mexico to act as a filter for immigrants headed north from Central America. As a result, Mexican immigration agents are especially tough on Central Americans trying to squeeze through" (Novas, 249).

This disparity in citizenship is concretized in Mexico through the invisibility of – or, the silences that surround – the Central American problem. The Central American en route to the United States thus moves to a coeval Central American-Americanness, the conceptual theory that Arturo Arias has bequeathed to Latino/a studies, for not only do we encounter a nascent discourse on how to theorize Central Americans, but also how to recognize their odd, discursive positionings in a stigmatized Mexican terrain. Central Americans in Mexico are hardly situated as valuable newcomers. But when seen through the Central American-American lens, an awkward, lived denizenship arises. This Central American-Americanness outside the United States can be grasped as Central American-American "citizenness," as Crichlow would have it – a "limboing counterconduct of modern power" (78; cf. Arias, 2003). Citizenness connotes "the struggle for humanity, dignity, economic survival, and place in and through the world economy" (77). The Mesoamerican route sheds light on some kind of uprooted beginning that cannot be localized or grounded. Still, the Mesoamerican space yields to a kind of becoming, as the persistent presence of illicit Central American-Americans is something that can be strikingly Latino in its deracinated state, unnaturalness, and discardability. We come across the evolving shape of the demographics of Latino/a Studies by a people who strive for new lives.

Latinoness here is wide-reaching deracination. Recall the seventy-two kidnapped migrants assassinated in August 2010 after they refused to either pay a ransom for their release or take jobs as hitmen for Los Zetas in Mexico (Tuckman, 2010). They were fifty-eight men and fourteen women, mostly Central American, but there were some Brazilian migrants, too.

They constitute the "diaspora of the hemisphere's poor," as Guillermoprieto brands these migrant streams (Guillermoprieto, 2012). The lone survivor is an Ecuadoran, suggesting a particular kind of Mesoamerican, if not "The Beast Latinidad." Since then, as the *New York Review of Books* made known, a group of Mexican journalists and writers created a website and virtual altar, named 72migrantes.com, to commemorate each of the victims, some of whom have never been identified (*New York Review of Books*, September 5, 2011). The memorialization of these seventy-two murders turns into an online geography and a global site of information. And yet this globalization is visualized through deracination and death. We do not know their races, just what they look like in some cases. Many remain unidentified, bringing us back to the reality that we do not know who they are. The seventy-two migrants are just "there," but as an interference akin to a "haunting," as Avery F. Gordon sets forth. Their "ghostly matter" represents an "animated state in which a repressed or unresolved social violence is making itself known" (xvi). They have "a real presence and demand [their] due, your attention." This Latino becoming draws near to the U.S. Latino as apart and different from the U.S. terrain, and it could extend to a Central American-American "Latinoness," an "infiltration" that is hard to assimilate – take in, or absorb – in Mexico. Latino can be generalizable in its striving for – or, "taking up" of – human aspiration. This taking up is a response to, as María Lugones submits, "an appetite for moving against entrapment, being cornered, trapped, reduced, and conceptually invaded" (ix).

Modus Vivendi: Migrants and the Mega-Slum

The Central American-American space is a squalid part of Mesoamerica, a no-man's land, train tracks producing a new border of spatial inequality, a "huge farm" of migrants – past the point of no return and with great concentrations of people in search of socioeconomic survival (Mendieta, 25). Eduardo Mendieta imparts that the invention of any nonhuman animal as "the beast" is fabulated "to philosophise about our humanity" (ibid.). So too is the Beast and the tenebrific ecology serving as a memorial, or a site of Central American-American abjection. It maps the "mega-slummisation" of Central American-American humanity (ibid.). "We cannot talk about the present state of the planet's climate," Mendieta puts forward in connection to the Anthropocene and the age of mega-slums, "without talking about colonialism, imperialism, neo-imperialism, and today, global finance capitalism" – the post–Cold War ideological content, the "nature," behind the Beast's communities (23). Martínez's writing of migrants' lives describes a major event in our lifetime. *The Beast* summons a correlative interrogation of how Latino autobiographies, subject positions, citizenships, success and/or unfulfillment are narrated in moments of crisis.

WORKS CITED

Alarcón, Daniel. "Transcripción: La Bestia: Conversación con Óscar Martínez." Radio Ambulante. March 9, 2014. <http://radioambulante.org/transcripcion/transcrip cion-la-bestia-oscar-martinez>, accessed March 23, 2014.

Arias, Arturo. "Central American-Americans: Invisibility, Power, and Representation in the US Latino World." *Latino Studies* 1.1 (2003): 168–87.

Bauman, Zygmunt. *Wasted Lives: Modernity and Its Outcasts*. Malden, MA: Polity Press, 2004.

Bellamy, Richard. *Citizenship: A Very Short Introduction*. Oxford: Oxford University Press, 2008.

Berlant, Lauren. "Claudia Rankine by Lauren Berlant." *Bomb*. Fall 2014. <http://bomb magazine.org/article/10096/claudia-rankine>, accessed April 20, 2015.

   The Queen of America Goes to Washington City: Essays on Sex and Citizenship. Durham, NC: Duke University Press, 2005.

Brennan, Teresa. *Globalization and Its Terrors: Daily Life in the West*. New York: Routledge, 2003.

Bryant, Levi R. "Black." *Prismatic Ecology: Ecotheory beyond Green*. Ed. Jeffrey Jerome Cohen. Minneapolis: University of Minnesota Press, 2013: 290–310.

Comaroff, John and Jean Comaroff. "Reflections on Liberalism, Policulturalism, and ID-ology: Citizenship and Difference in South Africa." *Limits to Liberation after Apartheid: Citizenship, Governance, and Culture*. Ed. Steven L. Robins. Athens: University of Georgia Press, 2005: 33–56.

Corchado, Alfredo. *Midnight in Mexico: A Reporter's Journey through a Country's Descent into the Darkness*. New York: Penguin Press, 2013.

Crichlow, Michaeline. *Globalization and the Post-Creole Imagination: Notes on Fleeing the Plantation*. Durham, NC: Duke University Press, 2009.

de Sousa Santos, Boaventura. *Epistemologies of the South: Justice against Epistemicide*. Boulder, CO: Paradigm Publishers, 2014.

Díaz, Lilian Carolina. "En El Salvador los únicos migrantes que importan son los que garantizan una remesa." *Ethos: Blog de periodismo especializado radicado en El Salvador*. May 22, 2014. https://blogdeperio3.wordpress.com/2014/05/22/en-el-salvador-los-unicos-migrantes-que-importan-son-los-que-garantizan-una-remesa/, accessed April 23, 2015.

Eche, David. *Land Degradation, Small-Scale Farms' Development, and Migratory Flows: The Case of Tapachula/Chiapas*. Kassel, Germany: Kassel University Press, 2013.

Feimster, Crystal N. *Southern Horrors: Women and the Politics of Rape and Lynching*. Cambridge, MA: Harvard University Press, 2011.

Gilmore, Glenda Elizabeth. *Gender and Jim Crow: Women and the Politics of White Supremacy in North Carolina, 1896–1920*. Chapel Hill: University of North Carolina Press, 1996.

Goldberg, David Theo. *Racial Subjects: Writing on Race in America*. London: Routledge, 1997.

Goldman, Francisco. "Foreword." *The Beast: Riding the Rails and Dodging Narcos on the Migrant Trail*. By Óscar Martínez. Trans. Daniela Maria Ugaz and John Washington. London: Verso, 2013: vii–xvi.

Gordon, Avery F. *Ghostly Matters: Haunting and the Sociological Imagination*. Minneapolis: University of Minnesota Press, 2008 [1997].

Grech, Shaun. *Disability and Poverty in the Global South: Renegotiating Development in Guatemala*. New York: Palgrave Macmillan, 2015.

Guidotti-Hernández, Nicole. *Unspeakable Violence: Remapping US and Mexican National Imaginaries*. Durham, NC: Duke University Press, 2011.

Hawkesworth, Mary E. *Globalization and Feminist Activism*. Lanham, MD: Rowman & Littlefield Publishers, 2006.

Lugones, María. *Pilgrimages/Peregrinajes: Theorizing Coalition against Multiple Oppressions*. Lanham, MD: Rowman & Littlefield Publishers, 2003.

Martínez, Óscar. *The Beast: Riding the Rails and Dodging Narcos on the Migrant Trail*. Trans. Daniela Maria Ugaz and John Washington. London: Verso, 2013.

Los migrantes que no importan. Barcelona: Icaria Editorial, 2010.

Melimopoulos, Elizabeth. "Migrant Mothers Search for Their Lost Sons: Central American Women Hold Caravan to Search for Children who Went Missing while Crossing through Mexico to the US." *Al Jazeera*. October 26, 2012. www.aljazeera.com/indepth/features/2012/10/20121024103223936928.html, accessed April 6, 2014.

Milian, Claudia. *Latining America: Black-Brown Passages and the Coloring of Latino/a Studies*. Athens: University of Georgia Press, 2013.

Moodie, Ellen. *El Salvador in the Aftermath of Peace: Crime, Uncertainty, and the Transition to Democracy*. Philadelphia: University of Pennsylvania Press, 2012.

Nazario, Sonia. *Enrique's Journey: The Story of a Boy's Dangerous Odyssey to Reunite with His Mother*. New York: Random House, 2007.

Novas, Hilmice. *Everything You Need to Know about Latino History*. New York: Plume, 2007 [1994].

NPR. "Questions for Óscar Martínez, Author of 'The Beast.'" National Public Radio. October 24, 2013. www.npr.org/2013/10/24/240534299/questions-for-oscar-martinez-author-of-the-beast, accessed March 24, 2014.

Palumbo-Liu, David. *The Deliverance of Others: Reading Literature in a Global Age*. Durham, NC: Duke University Press, 2012.

Prieto-Rios, Enrique and Kojo Koram. "Decolonizing Epistemologies, Politicising Rights: An Interview with Eduardo Mendieta." *The Birkbeck Law Review* 3.1 (May 2015): 13–30. www.bbklr.org/volume-3-issue-1.html, accessed May 14, 2015.

Rivas, Cecilia. *Salvadoran Imaginaries: Mediated Identities and Cultures of Consumption*. New Brunswick, NJ: Rutgers University Press, 2014.

Rubin, Rachel and Jeffrey Melnick. *Immigration and American Popular Culture: An Introduction*. New York: New York University Press, 2006.

Rygiel, Kim. *Globalizing Citizenship*. Vancouver: University of British Columbia Press, 2011.

"Sacrificing Their Lives to Work: 72migrantes.com." *New York Review of Books/NYR Blog*. September 5, 2011. www.nybooks.com/blogs/nyrblog/2011/sep/05/migrants-sacrificing-lives-work-united-states, accessed April 7, 2014.

Sala Negra del Faro. *Crónicas negras: desde una región que no cuenta*. Antiguo Cuscatlán, El Salvador: Aguilar, 2013.

Saliba, Frédéric. "Deforestation of Central America Rises as Mexico's War on Drugs Moves South." *The Guardian*. April 15, 2014. www.theguardian.com/environment/ 2014/apr/15/central-america-deforestation-mexico-drugs-war, accessed April 15, 2014.

Sassen, Saskia. "Incompleteness and the Possibility of Making: Towards Denationalized Citizenship?" *Cultural Dynamics* 21.3 (November 2009): 227–54.

"Global Cities and Survival Circuits." *Global Dimensions of Gender and Carework*. Ed. Mary K. Zimmerman, Jacquelyn S. Litt, and Christine E. Bose. Stanford, CA: Stanford University Press, 2006: 30–38.

Scott, Peter Dale and Jonathan Marshall. *Cocaine Politics: Drugs, Armies, and the CIA in Central America*. Berkeley: University of California Press, 1991.

Shearing, Clifford and Jennifer Wood. "Nodal Governance, Denizenship, and Communal Space: Challenging the Westphalian Ideal." *Limits to Liberation after Apartheid: Citizenship, Governance, and Culture*. Ed. Steven L. Robins. Athens: University of Georgia Press, 2005: 97–112.

Simien, Evelyn M., ed. *Gender and Lynching: The Politics of Memory*. New York: Palgrave Macmillan, 2013.

Stillman, Sarah. "Where Are the Children? For Extortionists, Undocumented Migrants Have Become Big Business." *New Yorker*. April 27, 2015. www.newyorker.com/ magazine/2015/04/27/where-are-the-children, accessed April 20, 2015.

"Travelers in Hiding: Telling a Story of Central Americans in Mexico/Radcliffe Institute." Harvard University YouTube Channel. November 20, 2012. www.youtube.com/ watch?v=BpwnjYqbqDI, accessed April 7, 2014.

Tuckman, Jo. "Survivor Tells of Escape from Mexican Massacre in which 72 Were Left Dead." *The Guardian*. August 25, 2012. www.theguardian.com/world/2010/aug/25/ mexico-massacre-central-american-migrants, accessed April 7, 2012.

Vogt, Wendy A. "Crossing Mexico: Structural Violence and the Commodification of Undocumented Central American Migrants." *American Ethnologist* 40.4 (November 2013): 764–80.

Wells, Ida B. *Southern Horrors and Other Writings: The Anti-Lynching Campaign of Ida B. Wells, 1892–1900*. New York: Bedford/St. Martin's, 1996.

34

Differential Visions

The Diasporic Stranger, Subalternity, and the Transing of Experience in U.S. Puerto Rican Literature

RICHARD PEREZ

For Juan Flores

Foreign in a Domestic Sense: Transnational Consciousness of U.S. Puerto Rican Literature

To be "foreign in a domestic sense,"[1] as the insular cases famously defined Puerto Rican citizenship, speaks to a transnational and diasporic inheritance forged in a de/colonial imaginary and sensibility. In documenting the "repressed side of the American century,"[2] Puerto Rican writers develop and deploy a transnational consciousness that reimagines Puerto Rico as bridge and borderland between Latin America, the Caribbean, and the United States by infusing their narratives with multinational events and experiences. That the first critical work on U.S. Puerto Rican literature emerges from the island, Eugene Mohr's *The Nuyorican Experience: Literature of the Puerto Rican Minority*, demonstrates a transnational identity in dialogic formation. Mohr's text identifies a hermeneutic tension regarding the capacity of "sociological studies" with "small literary interest" to capture the rich nuance found in U.S. Latina/o fiction and poetry.[3] With Puerto Rican studies taking form through a preponderance of social science scholarship responding to the demands of "one of the most studied, researched, card-catalogued, and cross-indexed immigrants in history," the task for Mohr became how to develop alternative interpretive avenues capable of gleaning the

---

[1] For a comprehensive look at the insular cases see: Christina Duffy Burnett and Burke Marshall, eds., *Foreign in a Domestic Sense: Puerto Rico, American Expansion, and the Constitution* (Durham, NC: Duke University Press, 2001).
[2] Flores, *Divided Borders*, 143.
[3] Eugene Mohr, *The Nuyorican Experience: Literature of the Puerto Rican Minority* (Westport, CT: Greenwood Press, 1982), xv.

complex representational layers making up "one of America's richest immigrant literatures."[4] For Mohr, U.S. Puerto Rican literature adumbrated a qualitatively "different picture" chronicling the texture and fabric of "several generations of immigrant experience."[5] In this essay I not only heed Mohr's appeal to read U.S. Puerto Rican literature on its own terms, but from its transnational and interdisciplinary amplitude where race, class, gender, and sexuality inform a diasporic sensibility. Transnationalism, in U.S. Puerto Rican literature, is more than a discourse between nations. Rather, it narrates how multi-national experiences (de)ontologize the racialized body; resurrects laboring subjects from social death; discerns, in the mute violence of colonialism, the utterances of gendered subalterns; and generates utopias through queerly conceived imaginative acts. While Mohr rightly recognizes and warns against the reduction of literature to a social scientific account, his own work falls back on a structurally safe analysis, a close reading that fails to engage the deeper theoretical implications of the literature.

Indeed, close to a decade after the publication of Mohr's groundbreaking text, Juan Flores would build on Mohr's foundational commentary by introducing a transnational hermenuetic. In his transnational account, Flores performs a more nuanced second reading, as Barthes would put it, through which a text reveals its textuality, levels of consciousness, and aesthetic significance. In *Divided Borders*, Flores places Puerto Rican literature from the island in a more overt dialectical relation to the writers of the diaspora to reestablish a transnational conversation largely ignored in Mohr's work. As he argues almost defiantly, "In fact, it is Nuyorican literature's position straddling two national literatures and hemispheric perspectives that most significantly distinguishes it among American minority literatures."[6] This essay, informed by Mohr and Flores, as well as a range of theorists, weaves together the rich hermeneutic potential offered by a transnational and interdisciplinary approach, which serve as formative components of U.S. Puerto Rican narratives. By exploring exemplary moments in the history of U.S. Puerto Rican literature, this essay shows how authors such as Piri Thomas, Pedro Pietri, Esmeralda Santiago, and Justin Torres plumb important theoretical terrain that links us to our transnational and diasporic roots.[7]

---

[4] Ibid., xii.   [5] Ibid., xi–xii.

[6] Juan Flores, *Divided Borders: Essays on Puerto Rican Identity* (Houston, TX: Arte Publico Press, 1993), 143.

[7] Hereafter quotations from primary texts will be followed by page number: Piri Thomas, *Down These Mean Streets* (New York: Vintage, 1967); Juan Flores and Pedro López Adorno, eds., *Pedro Pietri: Selected Poetry* (San Francisco: City Lights Books, 2015); Esmeralda Santiago, *América's Dream* (New York: Rayo, 1996); Justin Torres, *We the Animals* (Boston, MA: Houghton Mifflin Harcourt, 2011).

The Racialized Face of U.S. Puerto Rican Literature

The Jones Act of 1917 granted Puerto Ricans U.S. citizenship, and along with the economic crisis of the 1930s, spurred the great Puerto Rican migration of the following decade. In Piri Thomas's classic account *Down These Mean Streets*, Thomas chronicles this historic episode with an autofictional narrative that documents the racially overwrought environment he experiences as a first-generation Afro-Puerto Rican in mid-century "America."[8] Piri depicts this new diasporic stranger metynomically by concentrating on the transnational dimensions of the face of the racialized subject in search of alternate forms of life and recognition. His scrupulous concern with the fungible and ungraspable nature of the face serves a heuristic function insofar as it enables him to explore the ethnic, racial, and social codes and traps a first-generation immigrant of color must learn to navigate. Piri builds a narrative from the figurative and symbolic particulars of the face in order to elude the de/possessive grip of the white colonial order. As Levinas argues, "The face resists possession, resists my powers. In its epiphany, in expression, the sensible, still graspable, turns into total resistance to the grasp. This mutation can occur only by the opening of a new dimension."[9] Thus, writing enables Thomas, and in a larger sense U.S. Puerto Rican literature, to perform this "mutation" and forge "a new dimension" found in the imaginative and hermeneutic contours of the face. Here, on the face of the diasporic stranger, negotiations of language and geography, culture and politics, race and being, find expression.[10]

Initially, however, Piri resists the expansive terms of the face. Instead, Piri adopts a hardened mask, *cara palo*, both as a defensive shield against

---

[8] For interesting and diverse readings of Piri Thomas demonstrating the scholarly interest this text inspires see, for example: Lisa Sanchez Gonzalez, *Boricua Literature: A Literary History of the Puerto Rican Diaspora* (New York: New York University Press, 2001); William Luis, *Dance Between Two Cultures: Latino Caribbean Literature Written in the United States* (Nashville, TN: Vanderbilt University Press, 1997); Michael Hames-Garcia, *Fugitive Thought: Prison Movements, Race, and the Meaning of Justice* (Minneapolis: University of Minnesota Press, 2004); Rosaura Sanchez, "*Shakin Up*" *Race and Gender: Intercultural Connections in Puerto Rican, African American, and Chicano Narratives and Culture (1965–1995)* (Austin: Texas University Press, 2005); David Vazquez, *Triangulations: Narrative Strategies for Navigating Latino Identity* (Minneapolis: University of Minnesota Press, 2011).

[9] Emmanuel Levinas, *Totality and Infinity*, trans. by Alphonso Lingis (Pittsburgh, PA: Duquesne University Press, 1969), 197.

[10] I have addressed the face in *Down These Mean Streets* in an earlier essay entitled: "Racial Spills and Disfigured Faces in Piri Thomas' Down These Mean Streets and Junot "Diaz's 'Ysrael,'" in *Contemporary U.S. Latino/a Literary Criticism* (New York: Palgrave Macmillan, 2007).

the social aggressions he encounters and as an investment in a normative hypermasculinity. Thus, in actively identifying with hypermasculinity, Piri reaches for a normative identity that conceals (and reveals) the rigid structure of race and social experience. It is as if the racial violence of Piri's familial and diaporic context, and his overinvestment in a turbulent street masculinity, accumulates like mortar subduing the iterative capacity of its features. As Lyn Di Iorio Sandín explains: "The mask, always representing pain, aggressiveness, uprootedness, hypersexuality, racial and class marginalization for Latinas and Latinos, then is also a stereotype."[11] Thus, the novel dramatizes Piri's relation to this painfully crafted mask by chronicling its formation in his family, in society, and in the institutions he enters. As the tension accrues with every social injury, an emergent hermeneutic crisis drives Piri to account for the noxious forms of masculinity and racialized identity he continually negotiates. The face, locked into this repressed state, comes up against an ontological restlessness, a jarring intensity made up of the transnational fragments that form a contradictory energy intent on releasing and experiencing a more fully formed sense of self. Therefore, the overemphasis of this *cara palo* incites a critical dimension for if *cara palo* refigures his face into a sculptural non-expressivity, it also calls attention to itself as an art object that Piri obsessively addresses, explains, and interprets throughout the text. Ultimately, the narrative attention dedicated to the face forces the reader to understand that the "face is present in its refusal to be contained" and thus cannot be, in any reductive sense, "comprehended" or "encompassed."[12] In this sense, the novel posits *cara palo* as the interrogative starting point of the narrative where race encrusts itself on the flesh and concretizes the dehumanizing treatment he experiences into a legible form. This point of intensity and presence, the "there is" of the face, launches an encounter with the transnational and multiracial aspects of his identity.

In the chapter entitled "Brothers under the Skin," Thomas recounts a domestic conflict between siblings emblematic of the identificatory tensions that posit race and ethnicity, island nativism, and diasporic identity in antithetical relation. The scene begins when the bathing Piri refuses to open the bathroom door causing José to urinate on himself. That this scene occurs

---

[11] Lyn Di Iorio Sandín, *Killing Spanish: Literary Essays on Ambivalent US Latino/a Identity* (New York: Palgrave Macmillan, 2004), 101.
[12] Levinas, *Totality and Infinity*, 194.

in the bathroom establishes the abject tenor of their encounter in which otherness presents itself, as Levinas explains, "in a mode of irresistible manifestation . . . in one's nudity, that is, in one's destitution and hunger."[13] The incident leads to a subsequent conversation about blackness within the racial economy of the family, a discussion that pits a Puerto Rican notion of ethnicity at the expense of race. For José, the rejection of blackness reduces race to animalized terms that cannot be bridged without an assault on the fragile privilege of whiteness: "I ain't black, damn you! . . . My motherfuckin lips are not like a baboon's ass. My skin is white. White Godddamit!" (144). The severe rejection of blackness triggers a short circuit in Piri who, having begun to develop a racialized consciousness in diaspora, is thrust by the conversation into a revelatory violence: "Lights began to jump into my head and tears blurred out that this was my brother before me" (146). Piri, as if falling into a violent trance, attacks his brother until his white mask meta-morphoses into a "blood-smeared face" (146). Indeed, the trance-like violence imbues the scene with a strangely rhythmic quality: he "beat beat beat" (146) his face, as if to invoke an African drum, and a reminder, as Victoria Chevalier argues following Mikkel Borch-Jacobsen, that the Afro-religious trance functions as an attempt to exit the white symbolic order, revealing a colonial and racialized subject "sick of the symbolic."[14] Thus, the "blurred confusion" (146) signals the dynamic insistence of the racialized subject to announce his presence even in the face of widespread social denial. The "blood-smeared face" (146) then functions as a veritable sign of humanity, akin to what Emma Pérez calls "blood memory," which marks the diasporic stranger as a hemispheric family member mutilated by a (domestic) history and (transnational) politics of dislocation.[15]

His blackness rejected at home, Piri finds solace in the street until he is finally arrested for armed robbery and shooting an undercover police officer. Upon his release from prison, Piri returns to his old neighborhood and finds a Spanish Harlem ravaged by poverty and drugs. Soon he returns to old habits of disavowal possessed by the "wild" life of "hustling, whoring, and hating" before he confronts a warped image of himself in the mirror:

---

[13] Ibid., 200.
[14] Victoria Chevalier, "Coaxing the Skull: Writing in Paolo Monte in Lyn Di Iorio's *Outside the Bones*," paper delivered at 2nd Biennial US Latina/o Literature and Theory Conference, April 24, 2015.
[15] Emma Pérez, *Forgetting the Alamo, or, Blood Memory* (Austin: University of Texas Press, 2009).

> My eyes were red from smoke and my face was strained from the effort of trying to be cool . . . I pulled away from the mirror and sat on the edge of my bed. My head was still full of pot, and I felt scared. I couldn't stop trembling inside. I felt as though I had a hole in my face and out of it were pouring all the different masks that my *cara-palo* face had fought so hard to keep hidden. (321)

The power of the prose lies in the way it incrementally breaks Piri down from the strain in his eyes to the dramatic encounter with himself in the mirror where the truth of his years of repression gazes back at him in a startlingly, indeed beautiful, moment of realization. This uncanny recognition incites a "pouring" or in Levinasian terms, an "overflowing" whereby "the form of a relation with the face" induces an "epiphany" that puts Piri in contact with the non-assimilatory "infinity" of his Being.[16] In this sense, Piri witnesses in the mirror an appeal for expression and manifestation unencumbered by what Fanon calls a "dark and unarguable"[17] one-dimensionality. The "hole" in Piri's face then, creates a structure of vision that calls attention to the void from which the object emerges. This void is not unfathomable nothingness, but an openness, a charged potentiality that reveals the transnational/trans-experiential "there is" of the infinity of Being. In this "openness upon Being" an "indeterminate density" or humanity manifests itself.[18] Therefore, what the hole in Piri's face reveals is potentiality stripped of the reductive stereotypes intent on minimizing the rich difference of the diasporic stranger to a series of simple and debilitating definitions.

If the novel begins with *cara palo* as a sign of a hypermasculine presence, ossified by social pressures into a hardened stoicism, it also systematically breaks this version of his face until Piri reaches a revelatory void where his face once stood, marking a nothingness rife with the promise for a future beyond the alienating limits of the street. Newly empowered, he renounces the socially and historically engineered limits of *"what I was"* (321) for a reimagined future. In the end, *Down These Mean Streets* documents the epiphanic moments that enable Piri to reassess the racial and transnational dimensions of his identity. Through a newfound complexity he may "escape" the "inhuman" trappings of the face and forge an alternative "destiny" that open "strange true becomings that get past the wall" or *cara palo* and move into a visionary "destiny" in difference.[19]

---

[16] Levinas, *Totality and Infinity*, 196–97.
[17] Frantz Fanon, *Black Skin, White Masks*, trans. by Charles Lam Markmann (New York: Grove Press, 1967), 117.
[18] Levinas, *Totality and Infinity*, 189–91.

Poetry and Performance from Below: Listening to the Dead and the Revaluation of Value

If Piri Thomas focuses on the face as a canvas of the racialized image he must shatter and reconfigure, then Pedro Pietri offers a poetics that gives performative voice to the commodified laborer. Pedro Pietri's poetry opens a hermeneutics from below by which I mean, following Juan Flores's concept of "diaspora from below," the radical reencounter of the marginalized subject with distorted racial, sexual, and class identities violently conditioned to serve the hegemonic dictates of capital and colonialism. This reencounter takes place within a diasporic context, or what Flores calls a "triadic relational field shared by diaspora, country of origin, and host society," to set in motion an expressive economy dependent on "multiple forms and trajectories of translocal cultural movement."[20] For Pietri, poetics and its performance bring to life a laboring corpse from below animated by a potentiality that begins, as Giorgio Agamben argues, in privation.[21] Pietri performs an "articulatory potential" in as much as the performance of death discloses the privative conditions and "blurred visibility of diaspora."[22] Perhaps no poem in the U.S. Puerto Rican tradition embodies these tensions and complexities more than "Puerto Rican Obituary," written and performed in 1969 at the people's church takeover and published in the Young Lord's Party newspaper as an urgent call to arouse a revolutionary consciousness.

The poem begins with a matter-of-fact description of the Sisyphean workload that characterizes the surreal life of the diasporic worker. The third person "they" in the first stanza establishes the objecthood of the workers throughout the poem. In repeating "worked" (3), Pietri stresses the drudgery of labor that captures the worker in a protracted bind that ensnares them in a cycle of poverty and social death. Their work not only subsumes their life – "They worked / and they died" (3) – it also calls attention to their diasporic condition of non-value within the economic system: "They died never knowing / what the front entrance / of the first national bank looks like" (3). Here Pietri's performance of the poem stages an alienated

[19] Gilles Deleuze and Félix Guattari, *A Thousand Plateaus: Capitalism and Schizophrenia*, trans. by Brian Massumi (Minneapolis: University of Minnesota Press, 1987), 170–71.
[20] Juan Flores, *The Diaspora Strikes Back: Caribeño Tales of Learning and Turning* (New York: Routledge, 2009), 26–30.
[21] Giorgio Agamben, *Potentialities: Collected Essays in Philosophy*, trans. by Daniel Heller-Roazen (Stanford, CA: Stanford University Press, 1999), 178–81.
[22] Urayoán Noel, *In Visible Movement: Nuyorican Poetry from the Sixties to Slam* (Iowa City: Iowa University Press, 2014), xvi.

presence, as Urayoán Noel argues, too dreadful to watch, "weirdly disembodied" and full of "eerie silences," where pain is experienced as nonreciprocal, as a revelation of death that confronts the audience.[23] On the one hand, the poem serves as an obituary for Juan, Miguel, Milagros, Olga, and Manuel, who "all died yesterday today / and will die again tomorrow" (3); on the other its performance functions as an effigy. In *Cities of the Dead: Circum-Atlantic Performance*, Joseph Roach traces the etymology of performance to a process of substitution where "voices of the dead may speak freely now only through the bodies of the living."[24] For Roach, the meaning of performance functions through a logic of conjuration – "to bring forth, to make manifest" "to transmit" and "to reinvent" – situating the poet as the uncanny replacement for "something that preexists it."[25] Pietri then embodies the socially dead laborer whose performance transforms the poet from bard to effigy image, thereby providing a representation of the dead in their absence. As a result, Pietri forces the audience, inasmuch as he stands in for Juan, Miguel, Milagros, Olga, and Manuel, to reencounter the dead laborer and confront the Real (the mutilated bodies) of capitalist exploitation. This strange engagement between performance and death produces a speaking corpse, if you will, who addresses the audience and creates what Noel calls an "encounter politics," an "intersubjective space" that invites the viewer/reader "to share death by rehearsing for it."[26] This death-in-life performance, in short, discloses the operation of capital on the diasporic body that absorbs it from abroad into a transnational network of labor in order to generate surplus value through a process of mortification. Thus, in Pietri's performance, the diasporic laborer transmutes right before our eyes into a hollow wo/man drawn into capital by the siren call of a better life. A life in labor effectively divests the worker of value and reduces his or her existence to an all-encompassing relation to work, a move that constitutes the barbarous destruction, as "Puerto Rican Obituary" tells us, of their capacity to experience.[27]

Yet, by presenting an object who speaks from the dead and of the dead, the poem generates an afterlife that aims to revive the laborers through a consciousness of their mortified place in capital. What the speaking object or

---

[23] Ibid., xix, 24.
[24] Joseph Roach, *Cities of the Dead: Circum-Atlantic Performance* (New York: Columbia University Press, 1996), xiii.
[25] Ibid., xi, 3.   [26] Noel, *In Visible Movement*, 25.
[27] I am thinking here of Giorgio Agamben's text *Infancy and History: On the Destruction of Experience* (New York: Verso, 1993), 15–71. He argues: "Estrangement, which removes

corpse expresses in "Puerto Rican Obituary" is an alternative, revolutionary theory of value. The revolutionary point of the poem insists, "death is not dumb and disable" (8). Here Pietri posits an awkward grammar that miscombines the adjective "dumb" and verb "disable" to demonstrate the negative capacity of death to engender expression. Hence, the object of death responds, speaks out, gathers from its place of social annulment a rejoinder to make us cognizant of its presence, to make us privy to its wisdom, and to warn the subjects-of-capital of their own imminent erasure. Inasmuch as objects can and do resist, as Fred Moten argues, they provoke through their unexpected utterance, an "extended movement of a specific upheaval" whose "ongoing irruption ... arranges every line" disturbing the evidently normative link between race, subjectivity, and capital.[28] In this sense, the diasporic laborer in Pietri's poem speaks from the dead to exert a "troubled and dispossessive force" that disfigures and deforms the normative subject "by the object it possesses."[29] Thus, Pietri enacts, similar to the history of black musical performance Moten describes, the resistance of the diasporic object through the interarticulation of subject and object, commodity and capital, life and (social) death. Nevertheless, Pietri neither emits the shrieks of James Brown nor the comprehensive conceits of Whitmanian optimism, but rather deadpan susurrations emblematic of the ontological exhaustion endured by diasporic laborers. In addressing the life-denying toll of capital, "Puerto Rican Obituary" accosts the audience with the commodified bodies that capital abjects and consumes. At once macabre and revelatory, the poem presents zombies subdued of their life substance to expose the obscene gap between a utopian promise of surplus and the dead laborers required for its ruthless extraction.

Hence, the effect of the poem and the affect of the performance functions to reverse, as I have been suggesting, the active entitlement of the subject and the presumed passivity of the laboring object. The commodified object, in this case the laborer, embodies a revolutionary potential. As Hardt and Negri argue: "The poor, in other words, refers not to those who have nothing but to the wide multiplicity of all those who are inserted in the mechanisms of social production regardless of social order or property. And

<hr>

from the most commonplace objects their power to be experienced, thus becomes the exemplary procedure of a poetic project which aims to make of the Inexperiencible the new 'lieu commun', humanity's new experience."

[28] Fred Moten, *In the Break: The Aesthetics of the Black Radical Tradition* (Minneapolis: University of Minnesota Press, 2003), 1.

[29] Ibid., 1.

this conceptual conflict is also a political conflict. Its productivity is what makes the multitude of the poor a real and effective menace for the republic of property."[30] In Pietri's performance, the dead object rattles the privileged subject of capital into a shocked recognition faced as it is with the traumatic content of the poem and a speaker whose being stands annulled: "They are dead / and will not return from the dead / until they stop neglecting / the art of their dialogue" (9). This reversal imbues the object (poem, perform- ance, laborer) with a disturbing force that stuns the subject (audience/ reader/cog in capitalist system) into a revelatory recognition. Like the negative grammar of "dumb and disable" the dead speaker creates a shift or "parallax view" of the diasporic laborer insofar as it exhibits the "displace- ment of an object ... by a change in observational position that provides a new line of sight."[31] The poem, then, makes it possible for Pietri's listeners and readers to perceive their own displacement through a subversive discon- tentment that warps the object so that all "died" not only "never knowing" but "hating" (10) each other and the system that determined their lives. This "hate" breathes a conflictive life into the dead object to shift our observa- tional and ideological position, converting death from a one-sided conquer- ing, to something rife with the "effective menace" of resistance.

Significantly, the poem ends on a utopian note having granted us a parallax view of the multitude from exploited other to potential revolutionary. "Juan/ Miguel/Milagros/Olga/Manuel" now steeped in a revolutionary conscious- ness emerge where "beautiful people sing/and dance and work together" (12). Pedro Pietri's performance of the poem resuscitates the materiality of the laboring body, unhinging it from the frame of capital to compel the audience to see and feel the humanity of the dead figure that speaks before us. In as much as the dead speak, the audience/reader recognize themselves mirrored in the ineffable figure, for death not only stands outside, embodied by the speaking poet to facilitate our viewing of it, but is also, we come to realize, a knowledge or logic internalized, situated within. The reader and audience are inescapably entwined with the revolutionary potential of this multitude. To quote Žizek once more: "Materialism means that the reality I see is never 'whole' – not because a large part of it eludes me, but because it contains a stain, a blind spot, which indicates my inclusion in it."[32] Pietri, in this sense, locates himself within the violent "reality" of this "materialism" and

---

[30] Michael Hardt and Antonio Negri, *Commonwealth* (Cambridge, MA: The Belknap Press of Harvard University Press, 2009), 40.

[31] Slavoj Žižek, *The Parallax View* (Cambridge, MA: MIT Press, 2006), 17.   [32] Ibid., 17.

discloses his inclusion within (and our own) as spectral "stain" and "blind spot" of capital. If "Puerto Rican Obituary" offers a utopic end, it does so by insisting on new modes of value and materialism. Thus, the poem compels us to live with the complicity of our own death and the death of the other. The utopian refiguring of the self and social begins in this traumatic witnessing of the diasporic laborer through which we are ethically reborn and open anew to our own desire, to latent forms of potential and power, making "LOVE" (12), in its deepest revolutionary sense, possible.

Engendering America: Subaltern Speech and the (Dis)Incorporation of the Puerto Rican Subject

While Thomas and Pietri gloss over the gendered particularities of colonial and capitalist violence, Esmeralda Santiago makes it the central concern of her novel *América's Dream*. How does U.S. Puerto Rican literature address the complex process of gendering that renders many Puerto Rican women subalterns, figures tied to a muted existence? The gendered subaltern, in Gayatri Spivak's sense, finds herself obstructed by social and economic conditions, which sever her capacity to be audible within hegemonic structures of power.[33] In the United States, the dependence on cheap, illegal forms of labor has been part and parcel of its (economic) history from slavery to the present. Hence, what the subaltern has to "say" fails to register, impact, or influence decision-making sectors of society, leaving the female laborer at the mercy of the market they, paradoxically, sustain by providing "cheap" forms of labor. Esmeralda Santiago's 1996 novel *América's Dream* tells the story of a domestic worker, América Gonzalez, from her early life in Vieques, where she works as a hotel housekeeper; to her volatile relationship with a controlling and violent man aptly named Correa; to her subsequent migration to the United States, where she works as a nanny for an affluent family in Westchester, New York. América Gonzalez embodies then, in her capacity as domestic worker, the exploited underside of the American Dream. It is

---

[33] See Gayatri Chakravorty Spivak, "Can the Subaltern Speak?," in *Marxism and the Interpretation of Culture*, ed. by Lawrence Grossberg and Cary Nelson (Urbana: University of Illinois Press, 1988), 271–313. Also, Gayatri Chakravorty Spivak, *A Critique of Postcolonial Reason: Toward a History of the Vanishing Present* (Cambridge, MA: Harvard University Press, 1999), 198–311. For a theoretical overview of Spivak's notion of the subaltern, see Rosalind C. Morris, ed., *Can the Subaltern Speak?: Reflections on the History of an Idea* (New York: Columbia University Press, 2010).

within this context that America the nation and América Gonzalez the transnational laborer meet in an obscene symbiotic encounter.

Indeed, the novel opens with América positioned abjectly on her "knees, scrubbing behind a toilet" at a hotel in Vieques where she is employed as a maid. Despite her abjection, América hums a romantic ballad as she works, something the "tourists" find "charming" as it signals her seeming content-ment with her job. Yet this sense of harmony between laborer and service shatters when América, "still on her knees," abruptly "catches a nail on the corner" of a tile and "tears it to the quick." (1). The scene exposes how violence informs the logic of her labor since not only does it tear at her body and psyche with a numbing regularity, but in so doing keeps tourists at a "charming" (1) distance from its distressing realities. The severing of her nail, therefore, marks an inaugural injury that precedes the possibility of a socially emergent voice. As Mary Pat Brady comments, "Even before her name appears, before she speaks, she bleeds."[34] By using the term incorporation rather than interpellation, I aim to call attention to a fundamental shift from a traditionally legal and political hailing of subjects to its replacement by the hegemonic beckoning of female bodies in capital and colonialism. This hegemonic beckoning turns to vulnerable bodies in transnational contexts. According to Mary Pat Brady: "Her labor is cut short by the wound and the wound prefigures her hailing. In this manner the opening passage warns of the battering and loss to follow, wherein América seems almost not to exist without physical violence, without her body being battered and threatened."[35] In the life of a domestic worker, therefore, violence acts as an incorporative feature insofar as it serves to discipline the worker, to acclimate it to its own psychic and corporeal disfigurement, and develop a tolerance, even a desire for, an abject positioning which gives it an identifi-able place within capitalist society.

The aberrant continuity between her life as domestic worker and her relationship to Correa demonstrates how the process of incorporation shapes the structure of her desire by inculcating a tolerance for violence. Indeed, the fact that she is drawn to Correa – his very name means belt or strap – bespeaks the disciplinary terms conferred on masculinity and the passive acceptance of abuse instilled in América. In the novel, her ingrained

[34] Mary Pat Brady, "'So Your Social is Your Real?' Vernacular Theorists and Economic Transformation," in *Contemporary U.S. Latino/a Literary Criticism*, ed. by Lyn Di Iorio Sandín and Richard Perez (New York: Palgrave Macmillan, 2007), 213.
[35] Ibid., 213.

receptivity to violence proves inseparable from a market logic of exploitation, a colonial condition that emphasizes servility and submission. In short, capital, abetted by hypermasculinity, produces a gendered "predicament," as Gayatri Spivak says of the subaltern,[36] which interrupts América's capacity to speak assertively, with frankness, in just proportion. Hence, Correa effectively functions as her heteronormative boss, a menacing figure who polices and manages her desire:

> He lives on the other side of the island, has other women, has, in fact, a legal wife and kids in Fajardo. But he always comes back to América, under the pretext of seeing his daughter. And when he does he stays in her bed. And if any other man dares get too friendly, he beats her up. In the fifteen years Correa has been in her life, no other men have dared enter it, for fear he will kill her. (25)

Estranged from her own will, this arrangement functions as an unspoken understanding between men, which not only infantilizes América by requiring her to be a "charming" participant, but effectively shuts her out from deciding who, what, or how she will desire. In this sense, the novel situates patriarchy as the fascist center, the organizing principle and binding agent, of capital and colonialism. Correa's territorial behavior then, mimics a transnational arrangement where officials set up austere overseers to manage their businesses. Ultimately, the abusive terms become intolerable for América and she makes the decision to leave Correa and the island. What she abandons is less a man or Puerto Rico, and more nearly a colonial condition that depends on the subjugation of female-gendered bodies for its fortification.

América subsequently finds that her diasporic move to the United States mirrors rather than provides an alternative to the circumscribed labor options she experienced in Puerto Rico. In New York, she secures employment as a nanny in the Leverett household, a quintessential nuclear family. While both Leveretts have their own careers, it is Karen who manages and schedules América's tasks and responsibilities, which multiply in a short time without commensurate pay increases. These class distinctions serve as a bitter reminder of the feminist compromise perpetrated by privileged white woman at the expense of working-class women of color. As Mary Pat

---

[36] For an interesting discussion of the predicament of subalternity, "the structured place from which the capacity to access power is radically obstructed," see Rosalind Morris, "Introduction," *Can the Subaltern Speak?: Reflections on the History of an Idea* (New York: Columbia University Press, 2010), 8.

Brady points out: "Not surprisingly, given the failure of feminist efforts to renarrate reproductive labor in the broader social imagination, Karen's dismissal echoes the ongoing dismissals of homeworkers' contributions to the economy."[37] In light of this, we must be careful not to read her employment with the Leveretts as a turning point in her life, where she is ostensibly saved by the market, or by benevolent, if frugal, employers. Or, to paraphrase Spivak, a white family is not saving a brown woman from a brown man.[38] For América's occupation with the Leveretts situates her within a masculine-imperialist logic despite a more sanitized, seemingly polite, and enabling work environment. The coercion of normativity reveals itself not in ostentatious displays of violence, but in the comprehensive range of daily repressions América endures. Indeed, the family achieves an obscenely structured harmony from the accumulated inventory of these repressions. In this perverse formulation, América is included through her sustained exclusion.[39] So when Correa locates América, he finds the home easy to access, as if the house itself were symbolically receptive to his patriarchal violence. He breaks into the house with the express intent to maim or kill América. He slashes her throat and face, the symbolic markers of her voice and figurative identity. However, América refuses to cower to the violent onslaught; instead, she kicks Correa and sends him smashing into a coffee table, emblematic of her awakening, where he hits his head and dies on impact.

In murdering Correa, even in self-defense, América offers a qualitatively different example of subaltern action. The potential of her murder lies in its assault of the masculinist-imperialist privilege that typifies her subaltern condition. To kill symbolically sets in motion a decolonial process of "unlearning," which is instrumental, as Spivak asserts, to the "uncoercive rearrangement of desire."[40] For Spivak, this rearrangement requires a commitment to an ethics of desire attuned to the gendered damage produced in capital and colonialism. Murder challenges the incorporative tenets of the American Dream, revealing it as a fantasmatic smoke screen that enables colonialism and normalizes subalternity by rendering América (and Puerto

---

[37] Brady, "So Your Social is Your Real?" 216.
[38] Spivak, *A Critique of Postcolonial Reason*, 283–86.
[39] I am alluding here to Giorgio Agamben's notion of *Homo Sacer: Sovereign Power and Bare Life*, trans. by Daniel Heller-Roazen (Stanford, CA: Stanford University Press, 1998).
[40] Spivak, "In Response: Looking Back, Looking Forward," in *Can the Subaltern Speak?: Reflections on the History of an Idea*, ed. by Rosalind Morris (New York: Columbia University Press, 2010), 230.

Rico) a gendered receptacle of institutional violence who must be read, represented, and spoken for. Murder, therefore, suggests a desire to be heard, if not literally then through the symbolic shifting of a gendered self-assertion that opens a revolutionary hermeneutic.

América, in the end, strikes out against and punctures the ideological assumptions of the American Dream parodied in Santiago's title. In this sense, América embodies a potentiality for democracy, a radical movement beyond an incorporated speech, to more complex forms of respresentability. Indeed, *América's Dream* refers to a gendered agency, antithetical to the mythic American Dream of capital, where the shift from subalternity to new, authoritative forms of subjecthood is facilitated by what we learn to challenge, resist, and transfigure. Ultimately, the offer of U.S. Puerto Rican literature, from Thomas to Pietri to Santiago, urges us to unlearn hegemonic and dominative traditions for something more, something gendered, racially complex and courageously queer–for utopia in difference.

"We Wanted More": Longing for a Queer Future in U.S. Latina/o Literature

The concept of utopia plays an important role in Justin Torres's novel *We the Animals*, which tells the story of three brothers growing up in a chaotic, dysfunctional, yet oddly loving household. This oddly loving dimension points to a queer version of utopia "outside the linearity of straight time" leading to revelatory forms of kinship and estrangement.[41] Indeed, the link between kinship and estrangement begins with their parents: the father of Puerto Rican descent and white mother. Their ethnic/racial difference and their warped affective states creates a disciplinary distance from the children that provides them with a strange liberty to stray unencumbered by parental oversight or heteronormative prohibitions. Thus, the chaos of the working-class household unwittingly grants the children a freedom to wander in the neighborhood unconstrained by a nuclear family's logic of protection, which would otherwise block their experience with the unfamiliar and unconventional elements that surround them. As the narrator explains at the opening of the novel, "We wanted more" (1). This expression of desire refers not to a capitalist form of wanting, but to an insatiable curiosity for experience that drives the children to continually cross familial, communal, and sexual

---

[41] José Esteban Muñoz, *Cruising Utopia: The Then and There of Queer Futurity* (New York: New York University Press, 2009), 25.

boundaries. To want more signifies a refusal of normative conditions and an insistence on the fecundity of experience, on the freedom to desire queerly as a utopian gesture in search of a differential future.

This queer potentiality signals a diversity of experience alluded to in the title's reference to animals. *We the Animals* echoes and rearticulates "We the People," the sovereign preamble to the U.S. Constitution. By substituting animals for humans, Torres privileges a non-sovereign mode of identification. Thus, the animal state the children live within functions neither in predatory nor territorial terms, but rather through a devotion to wildness, to experimental digression, and imaginative movement. To quote Michael Taussig:

> Wildness also raises the specter of death of the symbolic function itself. It is the spirit of the unknown and the disorderly, loose in the forest encircling the city and the sown land, disrupting the convention upon which meaning and the shaping function of image rests. Wildness challenges the unity of the symbol, the transcendent totalization binding the image to that which it represents. Wildness pries open this unity and its place creates slippage and a grinding articulation between signifier and signified. Wildness makes of these connections spaces of darkness and light in which objects stare out in their mottled nakedness while signifiers float by. Wildness is the death space of signification.[42]

What *We the Animals* conveys then, is a desire for the death of normative signification conducive to a sense of being lost, which comes to "critique possession" and the conformist domesticity foisted on the queer subject as "illogical."[43] This "intention to be lost" compels the queer subject to "relinquish one's role . . . in the heteronormative order" and subvert its "encroaching assimilationist ideology"[44] for what I want to call the "trans-ing" of experience, an unceasing crossing of borders, bodies, and sense. This movement across different registers, "beyond the pragmatic here and now," ushers us beyond a colonial and heterosexually dominant "present."[45]

Indeed, the narrator remains unnamed in order to suggest a futurity where a "gathering emptiness," like the hole in Piri's face at the end of *Down These Mean Streets*, is "meant to make room for other worlds of sexual possibility."[46] So when the narrator ranges through the neighborhood and finds queer sexual awakening in a bus station, a symbol of transition and

---

[42] Michael Taussig, *Shaminism, Colonialism, and the Wild Man: A Study in Terror and Healing* (Chicago: University of Chicago Press, 1987), 219.
[43] Ibid., 72–73. [44] Ibid., 72–73. [45] Ibid., 21. [46] Ibid., 42.

transport, the scene foreshadows his move away from his family and the heteronormative setting of his provincial upstate New York town. The transing of experience, in this sense, constitutes a utopian injunction that functions through what Jose Esteban Muñoz calls an "antonished contemplation" that "helps one surpass the limitations of an alienating presentness and allows one to see a different time and place."[47] For Torres, it is not just that the protagonist becomes queer and breaks from his broken family, but that his subjectivity emerges from a queer foundation marked by a wild potentiality and the (trans)values of the Puerto Rican community.

Therefore, when his stunned parents discover he was "made" in the bus station by reading his journal where he documents a burgeoning queer life, they come face to face with the wild potentiality constitutive of their home life. Their disturbed reaction attempts to reassert a tenuous heternormativity especially evident in his hypermasculine father. It is wrong, nevertheless, to see the father as simply a hetero-masculine example the son rejects. Rather, the father's hypermasculinity must be read as a repression of his own queer dimensions, as a kind of shield the son sees beyond. Indeed, the son inherits – a more nuanced reading makes clear – what the father has repressed. It is, in this sense, his father's concealed queerness that the narrator takes on, a wild potentiality present if covered over. The narrator responds "like an animal" at his family's discovery of his journal until "they retreated into their love for me," soothed by the recognition that "we were, all of us, sons of whores, mongrels, our mother fucked a beast" (118). Queer utopia begins and exists in this context of de-domesticated longings, away from a fetishized notion of a heteronormative humanity that holds at bay those animal dimensions where imagination, exploration, and queer forms of life thrive. If, as the narrator states, "Puerto Ricans have language," it is a language linked to transnational horizons that allow them to "dream" in queer ways "about their wild futures." (104). This connection to language functions as part of a queer inheritance marked and committed to difference, a formative sensibility honed in a history of colonialism and disaporic experience where there "ain't no other boys as pitiless, as new, as orphaned" (104). The narrator carries this queer and decolonial endowment with him. For the capacity to "sing the mixed breed" provides Puerto Ricans, according to the narrator, a view "into the future" where they "saw otherwise" (104). For the narrator, a transnational Puerto Rican perspective compels a language of futurity, a utopic capacity to inhabit

[47] Ibid., 5.

multilayered, multidimensional realities and garner "recognition across" identificatory "antagonisms."[48]

In the final lines of the novel, the narrator dreams of "standing upright" in a decolonial pose, attuned to the rich potential of his queerly constituted transnational identity, opening a capacity to narrate in three-dimensional difference: "I say, I slur, I vow" (125). His reference to differing forms of enunciation suggests an act of *parrhesia*, which as Foucault points out, is a kind of frankness or truthfulness that links the speaker to freedom and a queer self-sovereignty.[49] *Parrhesia*, as an utterance of truth, provides an intersubjective frankness rooted in "generosity" and a "benevolent" attention toward the other.[50] In this sense, *parrhesia* aims to "encourage, intensify, and enliven" by creating a queer "obligation to speak freely" and thereby set the terms for subjects to "save each other and be saved through each other."[51] In the spirit of *parrhesia*, the narrator of *We the Animals* asserts a diasporic voice (to say), curses in ethical response (to slur) and commits (to vow) to a future informed by queer potentiality. Torres, like Thomas, Pietri, and Santiago, stands "upright" (125) in queer resolve and with visionary force directs us into a future where "the truth, passing from one to the other in *parrhesia*, seals, ensures, and guarantees the other's autonomy, the autonomy of the person who received the speech from the person who uttered it."[52] In this sense, U. S. Puerto Rican literature compels a transnational conversation between texts, cultures, and languages giving life to a differential consciousness, a queer imaginary attuned to what is possible, a world of more to come.

WORKS CITED

Agamben, Giorgio. *Infancy and History: On the Destruction of Experience*. New York: Verso, 1993.

    Homo Sacer: Sovereign Power and Bare Life. Trans. Daniel Heller-Roazen. Stanford, CA: Stanford University Press, 1998.

    Potentialities: Collected Essays in Philosophy. Trans. Daniel Heller-Roazen. Stanford, CA: Stanford University Press, 1999.

Barthes, Roland. *S/Z: An Essay*. Trans. Richard Miller. New York: Hill and Wang Publishers, 1974.

Brady, Mary Pat. "'So Your Social Is Your Real?' Vernacular Theorists and Economic Transformation." *Contemporary US Latino/a Literary Criticism*. Ed. Lyn Di Iorio Sandín and Richard Perez. New York: Palgrave Macmillan, 2007.

---

[48] Ibid., 93.
[49] Michel Foucault, *The Hermenuetics of the Subject: Lectures at the Collége de France 1981–1982*, trans. by Graham Burchell (New York: Picador, 2005), 366, 385.
[50] Ibid., 385, 389.   [51] Ibid., 389.   [52] Ibid., 379.

Burnett, Christina Duffy and Marshall, Burke, eds. *Foreign in a Domestic Sense: Puerto Rico, American Expansion, and the Constitution*. Durham, NC: Duke University Press, 2001.

Deleuze, Giles and Guattari, Félix. *A Thousand Plateaus: Capitalism and Schizophrenia*. Trans. Brian Massumi. Minneapolis: University of Minnesota Press, 1987.

Fanon, Frantz. *Black Skin, White Masks*. Trans. Charles Lam Markmann. New York: Grove Press, 1967.

Flores, Juan. *Divided Borders: Essays on Puerto Rican Identity*. Houston, TX: Arte Público Press, 1993.

   From Bomba to Hip-Hop: Puerto Rican Culture and Latino Identity. New York: Columbia University Press, 2000.

   The Diaspora Strikes Back: Caribeño Tales of Learning and Turning. New York: Routledge, 2009.

Flores, Juan and Adorno, Pedro López, eds., *Pedro Pietri: Selected Poetry*. San Francisco: City Lights Books, 2015.

Foucault, Michel. *The Hermenuetics of the Subject: Lectures at the Collège de France 1981–1982*. Trans. Graham Burchell. New York: Picador, 2005.

Gherovici, Patricia. *The Puerto Rican Syndrome*. New York: Other Press, 2003.

González, Lisa Sánchez. *Boricua Literature: A Literary History of the Puerto Rican Diaspora*. New York: New York University Press, 2001.

Hardt, Michael and Negri, Antonio. *Commonwealth*. Cambridge, MA: The Belknap Press of Harvard University Press, 2009.

Levinas, Emmanuel. *Totality and Infinity*. Trans. Alphonso Lingis. Pittsburgh, PA: Duquesne University Press, 1969.

Márquez, Roberto, ed. *Puerto Rican Poetry: An Anthology from Aboriginal to Contemporary Times*. Amherst: University of Massachusetts Press, 2007.

Mohr, Eugene. *The Nuyorican Experience: Literature of the Puerto Rican Minority*. Westport, CT: Greenwood Press, 1982.

Morris, Rosalind C., ed. *Can the Subaltern Speak? Reflections on the History of an Idea*. New York: Columbia University Press, 2010.

Moten, Fred. *In the Break: The Aesthetics of the Black Radical Tradition*. Minneapolis: University of Minnesota Press, 2003.

Muñoz, José Esteban. *Cruising Utopia: The Then and There of Queer Futurity*. New York: New York University Press, 2009.

Negrón-Muntaner, Frances. *Boricua Pop: Puerto Ricans and the Latinization of American Culture*. New York: New York University Press, 2004.

Noel, Urayoán. *In Visible Movement: Nuyorican Poetry from the Sixties to Slam*. Iowa City: Iowa University Press, 2014.

Pérez, Emma. *Forgetting the Alamo, or, Blood Memory*. Austin: University of Texas Press, 2009.

Perez, Richard. "Racial Spills and Disfigured Faces in Piri Thomas' *Down These Mean Streets* and Junot Díaz's "Ysrael." *Contemporary US Latino/a Literary Criticism*. Ed. Lyn Di Iorio Sandín and Richard Perez. New York: Palgrave Macmillan, 2007.

Roach, Joseph. *Cities of the Dead: Circum-Atlantic Performance*. New York: Columbia University Press, 1996.

Sandín, Lyn Di Iorio. *Killing Spanish: Literary Essays on Ambivalent US Latino/a Identity*. New York: Palgrave Macmillan, 2004.

Santiago, Esmeralda. *América's Dream*. New York: Rayo, 1996.

Spivak, Gayatri Chakravorty. "In Response: Looking Back, Looking Forward." *Can the Subaltern Speak?: Reflections on the History of an Idea*. Ed. Rosalind Morris. New York: Columbia University Press, 2010.

  A Critique of Postcolonial Reason: Toward a History of the Vanishing Present. Cambridge, MA: Harvard University Press, 1999.

  "Can the Subaltern Speak?" *Marxism and the Interpretation of Culture*. Ed. Lawrence Grossberg and Cary Nelson. Urbana: University of Illinois Press, 1988.

Thomas, Piri. *Down These Mean Streets*. New York: Vintage, 1967.

Torres, Justin. *We the Animals*. Boston, MA: Houghton Mifflin Harcourt, 2011.

Vázquez, David J. *Triangulations: Narrative Strategies for Navigating Latino Identity*. Minneapolis: University of Minnesota Press, 2011.

Žižek, Slavoj. *The Parallax View*. Cambridge, MA: MIT Press, 2006.

35

Temporal Borderlands

Toward Decolonial Queer Temporality in Latinx Literature

ELIANA ÁVILA

> For me, "El Movimiento" has never been a thing of the past; it has retreated
> into subterranean uncontaminated soils awaiting resurrection in a "queerer,"
> more feminist generation.
>
> – Cherríe Moraga, *The Last Generation*

Temporality inflects all cultural perceptions within which certain lives are made to matter less than others; it is instrumental not only in defining the boundaries of reality itself, but also in naturalizing those boundaries under as innocent a force as the emblematically natural stream of time. Perceptions and knowledges that are not couched in discourses of advanced temporality tend to be figured as backward, their contemporaneity unthinkable.[1] This essay explores some ways in which the narrative of backwardness, which relegates ongoing knowledges to the past, becomes a covert mode of racialization that gains force precisely at a time deemed post-racial, when more visible forms of racism have been scrutinized and no longer hold credence. Already in 1983, Johannes Fabian argued that

> the distance between the West and the Rest . . . is by now being disputed in regard to almost every conceivable aspect (moral, aesthetic, intellectual, political). Little more than technology and sheer economic exploitation seem to be left over for the purposes of "explaining" Western superiority. It has become foreseeable that even those prerogatives may either disappear or no longer be claimed. There remains "only" the all-pervading denial of

---

[1] I have developed this argument in the context of Edwidge Danticat's revisional historiography of genocide through genre trouble in *The Farming of Bones* (Ávila 2014a); and in the context of Chican@ cyber-art countering neocolonial anachronism (Ávila 2014b). This chapter reflects part of my work as a visiting scholar in the Department of Latin American and Latino Studies and the Chicano/Latino Research Center at the University of California at Santa Cruz (2015–2016), through a research grant awarded by CAPES (Brazil's federal agency for improving higher education) and Universidade Federal de Santa Catarina, Brazil.

coevalness which ultimately is expressive of a cosmological myth of frightening magnitude and persistency. It takes imagination and courage to picture what would happen to the West ... if its temporal fortress were suddenly invaded by the Time of its Other.[2]   (35)

At the time of Fabian's writing, U.S.-bound migration from South of the borders had long been referred to as an "invasion," or "silent invasion" (Arnold 2011) – ignoring decades of U.S. state-sponsored economic and military interventions spurring waves of newly constituted underclass populations into massive deterritorialization, uprootedness, and migration from Latin American countries to the global centers.[3] Now having grown into the largest minority in the U.S. and threatening Euro-American cultural hegemony, Latinx communities have refused the homogenizing state-imposed "Hispanic" identity that operates, as Laura Lomas argues, "as the very ground upon which a new white-pluralist dominant comes into being in the U.S." (67). While "Hispanic" is placed "*in competition* with African Americans and Native Americans, and effectively launches a process of deracialization" (71), many Latinxs claiming middle-class positions in U.S. society are systematically pressed to replicate the denial of coeval economic, political, historical, and cultural ties with other groups at the bottom rungs of the racial ladder both within the U.S. and across its borders.

The fact that Latinxs are being channeled to serve as agents of the U.S. border patrol (Mariscal 97) emblematizes the drive to distance them from "other others," documented and undocumented, who are increasingly criminalized at and across the border, fed by ethnic profiling both into the expanding prison system (Ioanide 124) and, by equally pervasive recruitment programs, into the frontlines of the U.S. armed forces (Mariscal 42). According to the December 2007 survey by the U.S. Department of Defense, the militarization of Latinx youths, mainly among first-generation migrants, doubled that of white youths in wars that, as Jorge Mariscal has argued, have "less to do with the defense of the nation and more to do with the very ideologies – colonialism, racism, and Manifest Destiny – that had led to oppression in Latin@ barrios domestically and Latin American countries abroad" (49). Whereas Latinxs increasingly occupy positions codifying advanced temporality

---

[2] Throughout this essay, references to the "West" refer to Walter Mignolo's critique of the Rooseveltean transformation of the "Western Hemisphere" into the "North Atlantic" which, while marginalizing Latin America from Western civilization, "also creates the conditions for the emergence of forces that remain hidden in the Creole (Latin and Anglo) ... rearticulation of Amerindian and Afro-American forces fed by the growing migrations and techno-globalism" (2001, 51).

[3] On overt and covert U.S. state-sponsored militarism in Latin American countries, see, among others, Renda 2001 and McSherry 2005.

(for example, those of digital, financial, and military conquests), they remain stigmatized by association with the racialized sites of pre-migration, or pre-colonization. These are the baselines of anachronism, the "outer limits of Latino identity"[4] from which Latinxs must dissociate themselves – where racialization is reinstalled yet again, cementing the temporal fortress of the West within which "Latinos are subordinated even when they are supposedly joining the ranks of mainstream culture" (Dávila 2008, 13).

With the aim to propose a de-anachronizing paradigm for reading Latinx literature, criticism, and literary history, this essay will first consider some ways in which the straight time of coloniality returns insidiously even in seemingly transgressive narratives of queer temporality. The de-anachronizing paradigm I refer to is that of the temporal borderlands, a chronoqueer dimension implicit in Gloria Anzaldúa's borderlands theory that both recognizes and unhinges the geotemporal borders by which coevalness has been effectively denied.[5] Far from ignoring the existence of borders between cultural groups and their intra-group identities, this paradigm recalls and exposes those borders as the "emotional residue of an unnatural [temporal] boundary ... distinguish[ing] *us* from *them*" (Anzaldúa 3). Thus counteracting the presumption that borderlessness can be idealized into existence through the transcendence of social, cultural, geopolitical, and temporal hierarchies, this essay offers an analysis of some of the ways in which Latina/o and Latinx literature – specifically twenty-first-century novels by Daisy Hernández and Felicia Luna Lemus – bring into relational view the temporal borderlands obscured by straight temporality.

Straight Temporality's Colonial Roots

Groundbreaking queer theories have been animated by questions of time, temporality, and futurity in the so-called queer turn to temporality, which is best understood as the realization or visibilization of temporality's central relevance in queer thought, considering that "temporality has inflected queer theory from the outset" (Freeman 2010, xii). Temporality has been

---

[4] This dissociative dynamic can be related to what Kirsten Silva Gruesz calls "the vexed question at the heart of Latino studies: what are the outer limits of Latino identity? That identitarian problem ... needs to be addressed within a temporal framework that is generally either taken for granted or undertheorized" (116).

[5] I am here following Silvio Torres-Saillant's call for the need to recognize that "borders exist," and for the need to "separate Latin American from Latino identity" in order to deal with the "intra-Latino injustices" by which Dominican Americans and other Afro-Latinx groups are systematically excluded under the "better-positioned portions of the Latino population" (439).

increasingly consolidated as a point of departure for strengthening the epistemic impact of queer perspectives that, exceeding prevailing assumptions of embodiment, work to expand and transform the ways we shape history, futurity, and present reality itself.

The proliferation of queer perspectives on temporality, coupled with the articulation of queerness away from the myth of heterosexuality's prerogative on futurity, has generated an unflinching critique of tropes of the child; crucially, it has implicated the field of queer criticism in its coalitional roots – asserting, for example, as Alison Kafer does in *Feminist, Queer, Crip*, that queer temporality is always already *crip*, and that "'the future' has been deployed in the service of compulsory able-bodiedness and able-mindedness" (2013, 27).[6] It has expanded the scope of utopian politics to engage actual coalitional imaginings of futurity. Thus, in *No Future: Queer Theory and the Death Drive*, Lee Edelman argues that futurity itself is reduced to a heterosexual prerogative through the figure of the child as the "telos of the social order" (2004, 11). In *Cruising Utopia: The Then and There of Queer Futurity*, José Esteban Muñoz adds a rejoinder to Edelman's argument by reclaiming not only a future, as the politically utopian "not yet here," but also a present and a past for queer youths of color – thus refusing the prototypically universal, raceless and classless figure of the child as privileged social telos in heteronormative imaginings of the future (2009, 94). The telos of an advanced timespace has also been critiqued in *In a Queer Time and Place* by Judith (Jack) Halberstam, who proposes the term *metronormativity* to counter the normative mapping of migration from rural to urban centers onto the coming-out narrative (2005, 36–37).

While these influential writings have challenged the notions of pathology and development along a timeline culminating in the telos of heterosexually coded adulthood, the decolonial critique of anachronism still remains marginal to the queer turn to temporality.[7] A coalitional project materializing such a critique necessarily exposes and counters the intersecting ways in which racialization is updated when mobility is mapped from an anachronic, ahistorical past to an ableist, all-encompassing Euro-American present.

---

[6] As David Mitchell and Sharon Snyder have argued convincingly, "disability has undergone a dual negation – it has been attributed to all 'deviant' biologies as a discrediting feature, while also serving as the material marker of inferiority itself. One might think of disability as the master trope of human disqualification" (2000, 3).

[7] Mignolo distinguishes *decolonial* from *postcolonial* perspectives thus: "the genealogy of these [latter] are located in French post-structuralism more than in the dense history of planetary decolonial thinking" (2011, 46).

I want to articulate Halberstam's concept of metronormativity with his important mention of the "projection of sex/gender anachronism onto so-called developing nations" (38), a projection generating ethnocentric narratives that posit migration as a movement from repression to liberation across the spatiotemporal colonial/modern divide.[8] This is where entire populations are marked as belated, performatively anachronized under the ableist narrative of advanced temporality. Alongside Kafer's critique of ableism's claim over the future, the critique of metronormativity across Latin American and Latinx contexts is central to making legible temporal rework-ings of geopolitical and intragroup boundaries, boundary crossings, and intersecting relations of power. I believe that the queer turn to temporality has much to gain in engaging the juncture of queer and decolonial critiques of developmental temporality – a powerful juncture for challenging the eugenicist, developmentalist narratives of belatedness, pathology, deficit, and deficiency. The paradigm of decolonial queer temporality I propose for reading Latinx literature sees in this juncture an urgent analytical lens whose critical absence calls for legibility.

Anachronism, a Racializing Device

The neologism *Latin@* can be understood as an emblem of this emerging visibility, for the *arroba* marks an open ending where the visible and the invisible clash, so that cultural erasure becomes visible, even though who and what has been erased does not. Before I specify the significance of this conflicting in/visibility for reading temporality in Latinx writings, I must first clarify the sense in which the narrative of *straight time* shapes what Peruvian sociologist Aníbal Quijano has termed the *coloniality of power*, an ongoing division of the population of the planet along the racial lines installed by colonialism (2000; 2001–2002).

Initially paraphrasing Quijano, Latinx philosopher María Lugones high-lights the invention of "race" as a cognitive form of domination shaped by inter-locking systems of oppression that permeate the production of Western knowledge. Race is here understood as an invention masking domination such that from the colonial period on,

[T]he global population was differentiated into inferior and superior, irrational and rational, primitive and civilized, traditional and modern.

---

[8] For an introduction to such a critique, see Luibhéid 2005.

"Primitive" referred to a *prior time* in the history of the species, in terms of *[linear] evolutionary time*. . . . Thus, [non-European] human inhabitants of the planet came to be mythically conceived not as dominated through conquest, nor as inferior in terms of wealth or political power, but as an *anterior stage* in the history of the species, in this unidirectional path. (Lugones 2008, 2–4, emphases added)

Lugones thus highlights the production of *anachronism as a racializing device of the coloniality of power*. Racialization relies on anachronism, an ideology of cultural effacement naturalizing unilinear evolutionism at the root of the colonial/modern divide. However, whereas Lugones follows Quijano's critique of racialized anachronism, she crucially takes issue with his theorization of the coloniality of power because, ironically, he reiterates gender in accordance with the very Eurocentric framework he is theorizing. As she puts it,

there is an account of gender within the framework that is not itself placed under scrutiny and that is too narrow and overly biologized as it presupposes sexual dimorphism, heterosexuality, patriarchal distribution of power, and so on. . . . Quijano appears to take it for granted that the dispute over control of sex is a dispute among men, about men's control of resources who are thought to be female. (1; 5; 6)

The contradiction by which Quijano reinstalls the Eurocentric notion of gender within his conception of the coloniality of power leads Lugones to put forth a pathbreaking analysis of the *coloniality of gender*.[9] She concludes, among other things, that Western conceptions of both race and gender, differentially imbricated across the colonial/modern divide, are "tied to a persistently violent domination that marks the flesh multiply by accessing the bodies of the unfree in differential patterns devised to constitute them as the *tortured materiality of power*" (2007, 188, my emphasis).[10]

It is not only the heteronormative racially marked regime that is used to reproduce "unfree bodies . . . as the tortured materiality of power." As seen from debates on *homonationalism* and *pinkwashing*, narratives of queer sexual freedom have also become tokens of liberation justifying the sovereignty of supposedly "advanced societies" vis-à-vis purportedly backward

[9] See Lugones 2007 and 2008.
[10] The *tortured materiality of power* can be understood in reference to those whom Frantz Fanon referred to as the *damnés de la terre*, typically dismissed by Eurocentrism as *"not mattering,"* yet whose human dignity under colonization produces a differing knowledge and conception of humanity – from which emerges Fanon's decolonization theory. See Fanon 1961.

cultures coded by contrast as homophobic.[11] Pressed into this straight temporal logic, queer becomes at once polarized and doubled: if on the one hand it has historically signified a sign of premodernity, on the other hand it has become a means of reproducing anachronism even through its own coded entrance into contemporaneity. Whether coded as premodern or advanced, queer immigration to the North operates within contexts in which *homophobic* and *Latin American* tend to be conflated, assigned to a space-time of abjection in a remote, obsolete past, a site of prior immobility finally transcended in a triumphalist here and now.

Clearly, the colonial/modern structure of power contains its others in morphing ways. It is not only against but also in affiliation with this discursive field of anachronism that the term *Latin@* emerges as a coding of entrance into the advanced temporality of both the digital and the genderqueer age. As Latinx cultural critic Juana Maria Rodríguez points out, the "*@*" ending is "a linguistic convention, emerging from queer online communities, [that have] taken up the *arroba* to create terms such as Latin@ or amig@s, marking instead where someone is 'at' in terms of gender" (Rodríguez 2014, 146).[12] Notice, however, that this queer disidentification from *heteronormativity* is also a temporal identification with straight time, or *chrononormativity*.[13] In other words, *Latin@* marks where one is 'at' not only in terms of gender but also in terms of temporality, given that the symbol @ codes the emancipation of both latinidad and queerness into the advanced temporal status of digital culture.[14] Despite such coding, the notion that Latin@ cultures have transcended geopolitical power barriers through their entrance into the advanced side of the temporal divide is countered by the insidious return of anachronism precisely upon such entry into realms that symbolize the privileged sites of power militaristically metaphorized as the avant-garde (realms of aesthetic, sexual, digital, and military conquests of new frontiers). Here anachronism is projected onto *other* others, such that temporal borderlines, whitewashing, and covert racialization go hand in hand even as they thrive on the discourse of equality. As Arlene Dávila puts it,

---

[11] On *homonationalism* and *pinkwashing*, see Jasbir Puar 2007; Jin Haritaworn, Tamsila Tauqir, and Esra Erdem 2008; Sarah Schulman 2012; and Jin Haritaworn 2015, among others.

[12] See Juana María Rodríguez 2003, 126.

[13] "Chrononormativity is a mode of implantation, a technique by which institutional forces come to seem like somatic facts ... forms of temporal experience that seem natural to those whom they privilege" while "linking properly temporalized bodies to narratives of movement and change" (Freeman 2010, 3–4).

[14] See Monica deHart (2004) for an excellent analysis of the neoliberal dynamics pervading the Latino crossing of the digital divide.

> The discourse of equality ... is obviously racialized; for it is ultimately
> about sustaining unequal economic privilege while promoting whiteness
> and normativity, especially among those groups such as Latinos, who are
> considered its greatest threat. (2008, 4)

On the "modern" side of the temporal divide, the narrative of advancement
into contemporaneity must write off perspectives of coeval history experienced in different parts of the world such that the narrative's chronic (in
both senses: temporal and tortured) material effects are reproduced as
symptoms of an essential geocultural belatedness pertaining ahistorically
to those locations alone. As massive immigration to the North installs the
perceived threat of epistemic difference, mainstream discourses again performatively anachronize the South, but this time under the justification that
it is *not queer enough*. In her analysis of the legal terms on which immigration
to the U.S. was granted in 1993 to the Brazilian Marcelo Tenório, Rodríguez
exposes the temporal borderline implicit in the characterization of homophobia in his country of origin (2003, 84–113). Critiquing this metronormative
characterization underlying Brazil-U.S. relations, Rodríguez underscores the
salvationist construction of US homonationalism that "reinscribes Brazil as a
site of violence" on the anachronized side of the colonial/modern divide
by which Brazil is re-situated "as a savage counterpart to the civilized
image of the United States" (2003, 102).[15] Rodríguez thus exposes the anachronizing legal discourse by which Tenório's entry reproduces cultural
backwardness to reinstall the myth of the U.S. as a site of the ethos of
freedom for all, selectively writing off the U.S. history of overt and covert
involvement in regimes of political torture, genocide, and socioeconomic
devastation (100).[16]

In this context, it is still urgent to question any conception of temporal
inclusion that leaves those subjects constructed as immobile again rendered
anachronic, uncannily visible as abject other – to question, in other words,
"the presumption that rootless mobility is the defining feature of contemporary experience" (Ahmed et al. 2003, 2). An emancipatory move that would not

---

[15] Rodríguez asserts that "as the number of Brazilians in the United States have grown,
they are increasingly being included in the designation 'Latin@'" a term that is
untraceable to any coherent geographic or epistemic referent (2014, 146).
[16] Rodríguez refers to the "history of racialized torture and genocide ... that Brazil shares
intrinsically with the United States, well known for its own history of sexual mutilation,
brutalizing violations, and systematic murder of non-Europeans and others categorized
as threatening to the nation-state's security and interests" (2003, 100). On specific
histories of US involvement in political regimes prompting Latinx immigration to the
United States, see, for example, Renda 2001 and McSherry 2005

reproduce anachronism, or further racialize so-called immobility,[17] thus requires an eye to the coalitional bridging of perspectives of both rootedness and migrancy. In this light, recent calls for equating mobility with humanity as a strategy against the dehumanization and criminalization of immigrants,[18] while undoubtedly urgent, demand coalition with contemporary thinking from standpoints of rootedness as well.[19] This coalitional view is imbricated in the notion of temporal borderlands, unsettling the colonialist geotemporal borders within which coevalness has been effectively denied.

The temporal borderlands unsettle the markers of anachronicity that "distinguish *us* from *them*" across the "emotional residue of an unnatural boundary" (Anzaldúa 1987, 3) which, I emphasize, is also temporal. Given the real effects of such boundaries, temporal distancing is normalized in discourses of geographical and identitarian mobility that celebrate as advances the epistemic annihilation resulting from assimilation processes. Thus even Daniele Archibugi, who makes the case for a "cosmopolitical democracy" that may respond to the growing pressures for decentralization towards the democratization of an integrated transnational community, reiterates the developmentalist discourse assuming a unilinear timeline of "varying stages of development" (143) – one that elides temporal hierarchy as a matricidal framework perpetuating cultural, social, political, and economic decimation in the guise of aiding the South in its need to be rescued from belatedness. Indeed, as Arturo Escobar (1995) has demonstrated, the "varying stages of development" are real effects of networks of social and economic policies that further entrench the inequalities between North and South via "restructuring" requirements, trade agreements, and financial packages, which Wendy Brown aptly describes as "yank[ing] the chains of every aspect of Third World existence, including political institutions and social formations" (37).[20] This

---

[17] Gayatri Chakravorty Spivak (2000) and others have argued that immobility is a fallacy, considering that rooted populations inevitably develop (and resist through) consciousness of the denial of their coevalness within the dominance of global time.

[18] The urgency of such a discursive strategy seemed consensual among scholars, including myself, when articulated by Nicholas de Genova during the Q&A session at his talk, "New and Emerging Terms in Migration Studies" at the Chicano and Latino Research Center, UC Santa Cruz, April 14, 2016.

[19] This coalitional view has been put forth by Sara Ahmed et al. 2003 El-Tayeb, 2012; and Haritaworn 2015, among others.

[20] In the context of Latinx studies, the North/South dichotomy is understood as a real effect, or a lived reality, of the coloniality of power. Walter Mignolo, for example, refers to the South in the general sense that includes Central America and the Caribbean, "south of Rio Grande" in the one sense; and the Caribbean that in spite of being English or French, has more in common with the South than with the North, that is, North America (US and Canada). Briefly, the imperial/colonial history is what

apparatus of coloniality and the temporal borderlands it obscures are challenged, as we will see in the next section, by Daisy Hernández's 2014 memoir *A Cup of Water Under My Bed*.

The *Damnés*, or Condemned[21]

Daisy Hernández's 2014 memoir begins by making explicit the Latinx author's writerly challenge: "I needed to see on paper the women and the father I had loved and resisted and *betrayed*, and to write them without the *mancha* of a white man who thought our lives and our stories should be bulldozed" (1, original emphases). This challenge appears as she exposes the term used against her family's world: "Condemned," further highlighted as the title of her introductory chapter. As she introduces her memoir, she explains that this is the term used by the town official who came to examine her family's house when she was a child. Asked to translate the official's words by her Spanish-speaking mother, the child downplays the violence they convey, and later in life realizes that she had not been able to translate the word because its epistemic meaning was nonexistent in her family's way of understanding the world. Hernández explains, "I didn't have a word in our language that would say, 'this photograph on the wall, this pot of black beans, this radio we listen to each day, these stories you tell us' – he's saying none of this matters. It should be not only thrown away but bulldozed" (1). Yet, this impossible translation of the white-dominant world's attitude to the world and language of her Colombian and Cuban migrant family members has the effect of a betrayal, a lack of epistemic resistance, which her writing aims to revise.

Hernández's scrutiny of the term "condemned" recalls Fanon's critique of the violence against the *damnés de la terre* – those whose knowledge of human dignity under colonization is typically dismissed by Eurocentrism yet produces an expansive conception of humanity from which the forces of decolonization emerge. In this context, the town official's condemnation can be likened to that of her white-dominant readers' possible dismissal of her writing. Hernández's memoir can thus be situated in the context of the Latina writer's awareness of being epistemically silenced or "condemned," once her refusal to bulldoze her family's stories and meanings tends to be

is at stake rather than European or North American text-books on geography" (Mignolo 2007, 14, fn1).
[21] This section was published earlier in *Ilha do Desterro* 70.1, Jan/Apr 2017, 39–49.

reductively interpreted as an inability or unwillingness to "advance" away from so-called traditional collective roots toward a supposedly emancipating monocultural Americanism. Emphatically, then, she characterizes her refusal to silence those stories as an attachment *not to a traditional past but to an ongoing history of cultural relationality.*

Hernández thus contrasts ongoing relationality against the deadly family relations of the powerful white teachers whose self-definition begins with placing their history in the forgotten past: those teachers' "grandmothers are dead. When they mention Poland, Ireland, or Germany, it sounds like they are talking about a sock they lost in the laundry. They are white now. American. They have no history, no songs, no past" (4). After years of writing in fear of being condemned under this monocultural regime, Hernández has come to narrate her very revision of her own former silencing in relation to the expected annihilation of her family's stories, life, and worldview. She thus weaves into her memoir's introduction not only a self-critique of her monoculturalist betrayal but also her commitment to write differently, from a relational perspective that will no longer abide epistemic violence.

To challenge the assumption of an easy continuum from a traditional to an advanced culture is not to deny the struggle for access to sites of hegemonic power, but to insist instead that "nothing happens in isolation" (1). This is the claim that makes Hernández's translocal narrative one of hearing and recalling the interconnectedness between what takes place quietly in the U.S. and its torturing resonances in Colombia within coeval time:[22]

> These quiet stories were taking place when the suits in Washington were waging their private wars in Central America ... when they signed NAFTA and everyone began seeking the safety of corners. My mother and father prayed harder .... The stories arrive from Latin America. Women with missing teeth cry into microphones. Men with brown faces scream. Los niños carry younger children. Sometimes, it is only the image of men's feet in their shoes and the white sheets covering the rest of their bodies. The women wail behind the reporter, who talks about the number of dead and those left behind. (xii; 7)

That they are "left behind" is a commonplace assumption that essentializes backward economies and underdeveloped societies by ignoring the global

---

[22] *Translocality* is a simultaneous understanding of both situatedness and connectedness with various locales, what Michael Burawoy calls "global connections between [local] sites" that themselves play active roles in expanding epistemic knowledge and relationality (2000, 29).

relations in which interlocking narratives of straight time remain unquestioned. The decolonial queer temporality at the core of Hernández's narrative is a rejection of any linear evolutionist narrative that naturalizes epistemic anachronism itself in the past; to use Hernández's powerful metaphor, this dissonant temporality prevents the "bulldozing" of cultural stories and meanings deemed obsolete. In this light, the writerly challenge Hernández makes explicit in the introduction to her memoir and now in the reporter's discourse can be understood as a *complicitous critique* – Linda Hutcheon's apt term for a politics refusing the rhetoric of innocence in order to confront its own incorporation of ideology by "chip[ping] away at any confidence in the transparency of [its] conventions" (202–03). When, in *Borderlands/La frontera*, Anzaldúa asserts that "[a]ll reaction is limited by, and dependent on, what it is reacting against" (78), she is challenging the romantic, autonomist view that there might be a "pure" or unmediated politics uncontaminated by the assimilationist compulsions that press on migrant life and writing. This challenge stands in stark contrast to the translocal refusal to bulldoze el otro lado, which is frequently reduced to a refusal to advance, to move on, away from "traditional" collective roots towards personal liberation and professional success.

Thus significantly undercutting the evolutionist myth of migration to the U.S. as "a movement from repression to freedom" (Luibhéid 2005, xxv), Hernández portrays the "private wars in Central America" within the context of the signing of NAFTA, and further underlines geopolitical interconnectedness by following her mention of the signing of NAFTA with the phrase, "and everyone began seeking the safety of corners" (1). Situating herself in this geopolitical borderland, Hernández counters the narrative of straight time which relegates to the past century the concern of Latinx texts with "naming or locating themselves within a geopolitical, ethnic, psychological, or spiritual borderland, as tended to occur in Chicana lesbian texts of the 1980s and 1990s" (Cuevas ¶12).

The specific writer whose work is assumed by Jackie T. Cuevas to exemplify a "post-borderlands" temporality in Latin@ literature is Felicia Luna Lemus. In an interview with Michelle Tea, Lemus posits the relative anachronicity by which those "who aren't more assimilated … *still* play by the kind of old school rules of butch/femme" in Chican@ culture, where there's "something about it that culturally works" (Tea 178, emphasis added). This reiteration of temporal stillness, a denial of coeval time, suggests an avant-garde sexual politics essentially defined as emanating from the U.S. eventually propagating a common temporality that delivers unassimilated others from backwardness.

This anachronistic portrayal unwittingly retrenches a universalized subject whose freedom from constraints regarding borders and border crossings coincides with the trope of a liberated temporality brought on by assimilation within the lighter side of the Mexican-U.S. border.

In what follows I refute this anachronizing narrative by focusing on a twenty-first-century novel by Lemus in which the Latin@ text does locate itself in borderlands which are at once geopolitical, ethnic, psychological, spiritual – and also *temporal*.[23] I highlight this temporal dimension of the geopolitical borderlands because I want to make the point that they cannot be reduced to anachronicity – no matter how easily this reduction feeds all social markers of difference as one naturalized in an era dazzled by the certainty of its temporal superiority.

Anachronistic Transnormativity

Narrated by a second-generation female-to-male Latino whose name has shifted from Francisca to Frank, Lemus's *Like Son: A Novel* (2007) explores the relational meanings between, on the one hand, the transgender narrator's unflinching normalcy in his performance of masculinity, and, on the other hand, his troubling of the heterosexual matrix (the normative alignment of designated sex, gender, and desire).[24] This tension that both distances and approximates normative and nonnormative queer texts installs a politics working importantly to bend the binary division of fixity/fluidity used to hierarchize queer sexualities across the colonial/modern divide, thus reiterated.[25] Lemus's narrative can be understood, in this light, to engage the borderlands where "the subject of resistance is neither fixed nor fluid, but both and more. And this 'more' involves the sense that resistance is resistance to both fixity and to fluidity" (Pile 30, qtd. in Halberstam 2005, 21).

---

[23] It is important to highlight that any borderland is plural because of the epistemic proliferation that defines and marks liminality. See Anzaldúa 1987, p. 80, and the epigraph to Cuevas's article: "The brown body's ambiguity is endlessly generative" (Hiram Pérez, 2005).

[24] Drawing from Monique Wittig's notion of the "heterosexual contract" and Adrienne Rich's notion of "compulsory heterosexuality," Judith Butler formulated the concept of the *heterosexual matrix* as "the compulsory order of sex/gender/desire" (1990, 9; 194): The cultural matrix through which gender identity has become intelligible requires that certain kinds of "identities" cannot "exist" – that is, those in which gender does not follow from sex and those in which the practices of desire do not "follow" from either sex or gender. (1990, 23–24).

[25] As Abby Wilkerson has argued, "a group's sexual status tends to reflect and reinforce its broader political and social status" (35).

This bifocal view of sexual politics does not translate as inherent resistance, however, let alone as pure resistance; instead, it implies queerness as *assemblage*, in the sense that it "deprivileges a binary opposition between queer and not-queer subjects, and, instead of retaining queerness exclusively as dissenting, resistant, and alternative (all of which queerness importantly is and does), it underscores contingency and complicity with dominant formations" (Puar 2005, 121–22).

Frank himself makes explicit his contingent complicity within dominant cultural formations, as when he explains the name he has chosen for himself: "To live without the curses and consequences that crippled my family before me, to break free of a life I preferred were not mine, to pass without constraint through the world . . . as a man, a good and decent man – to this I aspired" (Lemus, 112). Notice, however, that to read Frank's aspiration "to pass without constraint" as a desire for the recognition needed to live a "livable life" (Butler 2004, 39) does not entail retrenching (or anachronizing) others who also aspire to live livable lives, nor does it entail reading them as threatening his privilege to pass.[26] In what follows, I hope to make clear that the novel's marginalized *jota* text,[27] rather than signifying an anachronic anti-assimilationist politics lagging behind the twenty-first century, actually disturbs the straight narrative of repression/liberation implied in the shift Cuevas sees from same-sex desire to genderqueerness as "the next borderlands of Chican@ identity."[28]

[26] Notice, for example, that Frank's assertion is structured in the ableist discourse David Mitchell and Sharon Snyder term "narrative prosthesis" and its use of disability as "an opportunistic metaphorical device" (47).

[27] The term *jota* is used here to emphasize the ethnic borderlands in which Consuelo-Nahui's affair is recalled. *Jota* is untranslatable as *lesbian*, being used to refer to Latinx, Chicanx, and Indigenous-identified nonnormative identity formations concerned with geopolitical, ethnic, psychological and spiritual borderlands. For Michael Hames-Garcia, "while some authors draw close comparisons with terms like *lesbian*, *gay*, *bisexual*, *trans*, and *queer*, others suggest that historical, geographic, and cultural contexts make jotería not equivalent to any of these North American terms." (139)

[28] See Nestle and Wilchins 2002. Marilyn Roxie defines *genderqueer* as "a term that may be used to describe those with nonnormative gender, either as an umbrella term or a standalone identity, typically encompassing those who are in one, or more, of these six categories:

- both man and woman (example: *androgyne*);
- neither man nor woman (*agender, neutrois, non-gendered*);
- moving between two or more genders (*gender fluid*);
- third gendered or other-gendered (includes those who prefer 'genderqueer' or 'nonbinary' to describe their gender without labeling it otherwise);
- having an overlap or blur of gender and orientation and/or sex (*girlfags* and *guydykes*);
- those who 'queer' gender, in presentation or otherwise, who may or may not see themselves as nonbinary or having a gender that is queer; this category may also include

The central narrative thread in *Like Son* is that of the growing stagnation of Frank's relationship with Nathalie, a woman who resembles "the sort [Frank's father] fell for every time" (32). The beginning of their relationship is foreshadowed at Frank's reunion with his father several years after they'd been apart. Addressing him as Francisca, his blind father tells him of his love life and hands him a birthday gift, a photograph of the "fire-eyed" (32) Nahui Olín – the radical Mexican feminist and genius poet who, in the novel, is portrayed as having kissed Frank's grandmother Consuelo in public in the 1920s:

"Nahui was a cautionary tale," he said.

Huh? "And she's exactly the sort I fell for every time," he added.

Wait, was my dad trying to talk ladies with me? I wasn't sure if I should be happy or miserably uncomfortable. Regardless, my end of the conversation would be inherently limited. . ... If I ever fell hard for a girl, if it ever felt like something big and real and lasting, if that ever happened, would it be for a fire-eyed girl like Nahui? Would I follow in what seemed to be Cruz *tradition*? (32, my emphasis)

The photograph is worshipped by Frank's father, who refers to it as a *retablo* (altarpiece), thus introducing the spiritual borderlands as an underlying trope within Frank's Latinx genderqueer narrative.[29] Found among Consuelo's belongings after her death, Nahui Olín's image as a Chicana retablo becomes an icon for Frank's trans narrative both as his father's *male* son and, less conspicuously, as his grandmother's *queer* grandson.

Frank's use of the term "tradition" is intriguing. It may first imply that the transgender subject here is radically "like son," a phrase that reads ambiguously, between queer and heterosexual, until the narrative reveals that he is not merely like *a son*; rather, he *is* a son, for he self-identifies as male – and as one who resembles his father, as we learn, in terms of the way he falls in love. Distancing queerness away from the homo/hetero coding of sexuality, this characterization emphasizes, instead, an alternative queerness based on a desire shared with his father - and with Consuelo, even though this aspect is silenced in the title and throughout the narrative: a "like grandson" desire for "a fire-eyed girl" whose identity is defined not only by the gender(s) of her object(s) of desire but also by the non-normativity of her desire.

those who are consciously political or radical in their understanding of being genderqueer," http://marilynroxie.com/projects/genderqueer-and-non-binary-identities/

[29] The bibliography on the Chicana/o/@/x spiritual borderlands is extensive; see, for example, Ana Maria Díaz-Stevens and Anthony Stevens-Arroyo 1998; Laura Pérez 2007; Theresa Delgadillo 2011.

In this light, it is crucial to note the lesbian and bisexual resonances of Olin's characterization and their overtones in the characterizations of both Frank and his father, whose constitution within Consuelo's lesbian/bisexual text is thoroughly evaded by the supposed stability of the male-centered narrative. Ironically, this constitution troubles the "like heteronormative" narrative in *Like Son*, given that the effacement of the lesbian/bisexual text is the condition of possibility for the transnormative narrative (Frank and Nathalie as a male-female couple). *Like Son* potentializes a coalition among these narratives of difference, instead of requiring the performance of any choice or hierarchy between them: just as Frank's female masculinity exceeds the male/female binary assignment of sex, his grandmother's lesbian desire – a family narrative that father and son inherit and disavow – also exceeds the straight/queer binary of sexuality. This untameable gender trouble in *Like Son* can be understood to bring Consuelo and the as yet anachronized lesbian text from the margins to the center of the narrative.

Frank's desire to narrativize his male subjectivity within a family genealogy of what he calls "freaks" (25) gains force not as a project to finally gain acceptance from his family, at least on his father's side, but, rather, as a tracing of relational connectedness *despite* the lack of external recognition. Filial identification is constructed, in other words, regardless of the lack of recognition he receives from his father concerning his transgendered *male* identity. Frank's identification with his father thus pervades the novel in unspoken ways from the outset, as the like son inherits his grandmother's retablo iconizing his similarity to his father in terms of disavowing the lesbian text in relation to tropes of desire coded as and beyond heterosexual, transgender, genderqueer, lesbian, and bisexual.

It is crucial to underscore the abject dynamics drawing on Consuelo and Nahui as the couple in the novel whose story is both overtly honored and covertly disavowed within Frank's narrative. By "talking girls" with his father upon his inheritance of Consuelo's retablo, Frank effectively reduces Nahui's *jota* text to an icon for his own transman-ciswoman relationship with the similarly "fire-eyed girl" Nathalie (whose name resonates with *Nahui*). Frank's identification with his father in adopting Olín as "object" of desire/worship may suggest his anxiety to straighten out his grandmother, and himself, by effacing the jota sexuality from which he has inherited the retablo for the performance of his own heterosexual desire. However, whereas Frank's desire is self-defined in the *heterosexual* male terms by which he would be "happy" to code his inheritance, the retablo also codes his "traditional" affiliation to the *jota* sexuality of his grandmother. Rejecting this identification yet embracing a "freak" inheritance, Frank's narrative again signals an alternative identificatory reading against the grain of his disidentification from Consuelo, thus genderqueering his relationship with Nathalie as one both assimilating and resisting binary stability. Far from drawing a linear trajectory defined by past origins, this narrative of descent constructs a genealogy of historical trajectories that meet in a *present reconstruction of relational connectedness*, disseminating and overlapping heterosexual, trans, genderqueer, lesbian, jota, and bisexual subject-positions.

Here it is worth noting that the point of genealogy is not to search for so-called 'origins' expected to essentialize a linear causality: "The search for descent is not the erecting of foundations: on the contrary, it disturbs what was previously thought immobile; it fragments what was thought unified; it shows the heterogeneity of what was imagined consistent with itself" (Foucault 1991, 82). From this genealogical perspective, the reader need not resolve sexual ambiguity within the linearity of descent, but rather, perceive the simultaneous overlapping of proliferating paradigms of sexuality connected by historical trajectories that do not converge, but conflictingly border on each other as they call attention to intragroup differences.

To the extent that the disavowed jota subtext makes way for Frank's transgender narrative, it also brings Consuelo and her silenced (jota/bi) sexuality from the margins to the center of the novel. Frank's oblique identification with his grandmother thus pervades the novel from the outset as he inherits her jota retablo now iconizing both men's similarity also in terms of their reiterative disavowal of Consuelo's and Nahui's jotería. As the condition of possibility for Frank's "like heterosexual" text, the disavowal of Consuelo's and Nahui's *jotería* raises questions concerning the autonomy of the transnormative text, potentializing a coalition among the queer intragroup differences mentioned above, and challenging any narrative of a resolution, choice, or hierarchy between them.

From this coalitional perspective, Frank's use of the word *tradition*, which initially reads as sealing father-and-son's male bonding, actually recalls the genealogical redefinition of the term articulated by Paul Gilroy as an ongoing history of contemporary differential epistemes, "a non-traditional tradition . . . that cannot be apprehended through the Manichean logic of binary coding . . . a living memory" (198). Far from constituting an outdated reality, let alone a necrophilic one (more on this soon), tradition in Hernández's and Lemus's literary texts can also be understood in the key of constitutive resonance (genealogy) rather than sequential replacement (anachronism). In other words, it is resignified in the mnemonic function of revitalizing the "significant, nodal points in [a] common history and its social memory" – a "living memory" of "borders that do not shift beneath our feet but simply grow with every step we take" (Hernández 18; 19). Under the surface text, Frank's use of the term can be read as a call for coalition – far from either a transcendence or, on the contrary, a denial of existing borders – among those rendered invisible, constrained at the junctures where difference precludes respectability (as he would later suggest in aspiring to "pass without constraint as a man, a good and decent man.") In this light, we need not subscribe to his certainty, on the surface text, when he expresses fascination for Nahui's image throughout the novel, that "[t]hose eyes, pure crystalline fire, could burn all barriers – the barriers between here and there, between what she had and what she wanted, between the past and present" (Lemus 30).

Trans-Validation and the Disavowal of Jotería

As crucial as it is in *Like Son*, the perspective of proliferating borders and of the borderlands they open up is gradually emptied toward the novel's closure. Problematically, the narrator invests in queer temporality only to the extent that it serves his project of trans-validation via his access to Nahui/Nathalie from within the normative family history's disavowal of the jota text. The retablo, in this context, is also an emblem of jota in/visibility. One year into their relationship, the couple sets up an altar in their apartment for Frank's deceased father. After placing the retablo of Nahui at its center, Nathalie asks whether it was "strange to put her on the altar"; at this, he recalls that he had felt Nahui had been "jailed inside the intentionally gaudy gold frame and its thick glass pane" six years earlier when Nathalie had framed the photograph as a gift for him: *"Nahui will stay safe this way, she'd said"* (122, original emphasis). Having "taken on the role of Nahui and brought her to life" (187), Nathalie's questioning of Frank's act of enshrining her (Nahui? Nathalie?) is just as metaphorical as it is literal, once she has possibly realized that she has become framed as well, reduced to a fetish for his male filial identification.

Grasping that her role-playing of Nahui has enshrined (and anachronized) her in a stifling (time)frame within which she herself disappears, Nathalie becomes haunted by the prospect of loss and disappearance, which she enacts literally by vanishing for days at a time. Unsurprisingly, Frank's sense of time is gradually undone; on sleeping pills, and fearing that a fire might start in the apartment from the sulfurous remains on the altar after days of mirroring their mutual abandonment, Frank characterizes the pull back into a necrophilic time of loss as a typically Mexican trait:

I'd spend the rest of my life in mourning, refusing to love again, refusing to sleep, refusing ever to eat another pear. Okay, maybe I really *was* Mexican after all. (124)

This anachronistic characterization has the effect of comic relief, for it remains unproblematized from the moment Nathalie no longer accepts her role as a fetish for Frank's transnormative identification. Now Frank's interest shifts. Problematically, it is Frank's disconnection from the *past* rather than from its *fetishization* that warrants conflict resolution toward a futurity for the couple by the end of the novel. Rather than "integrat[ing] his family's past into his own present," as Lisa Justine Hernandez posits (2007, 134), Frank's narration from this point on rigidly develops into a temporal rift: the historiography of a relational, ongoing history is reductively conflated with his being haunted by the dead icons of his family's past:

Wouldn't you freak out a little too if you suddenly realized you were necrophilic? Personally, I'd never thought that particular perversion was my cup of tea, but really, when it comes down to it, isn't retrospection, sentimental or otherwise, ultimately romancing the dead? (257)

The point Lemus's narrator tends to evade is that his earlier focus on the queer temporality of "living memory" becomes reductively conflated with the necrophilic "romancing [of] the dead" that he now mocks as obsolete Mexicanism, while effectively masking his anachronizing discourse in the most convincing terms of "getting on with [his] life" (257). Futurity is made to naturally stem from projecting "retrospection, sentimental or otherwise" onto the southern side of the border, even after the narrative had initially refused to anachronize historical connectedness, as we have seen – that is, to reduce it to a past that inappropriately lingers on in a linear framework of evolutionary time.

In the interview conducted by Tea, Lemus characterizes genderqueer in the context of her earlier novel (2003) as resembling more closely (or aspiring to) the genderqueer codings she sees in the mainstream culture constituted by assimilated "people of different ethnicities" other than the Chicana:

I don't know many androgynous Chicanas or anyone who plays that line quite like I see people of different ethnicities play it. People who are still very much in touch with their culture, who aren't more assimilated, they still play by the kind of old school rules of butch/femme. And I respect that. There's something about it culturally that works. (Tea 178)

The "more assimilated" are understood to shift from butch/femme to FTM (Female-to-Male), the newly protagonized genderqueer on the horizon of

Chicanx readability which now makes its entrance into an advanced queer temporality contrasted against "old school" queer protagonism. Rather than challenging the temporal borderline that constrains differential ethnicity, this temporally-driven contrast anachronizes jota-identified lesbian relations as well as the culture in which Lemus sees joteria as a mark of unassimilated sexuality. In this regime, Frank's transgender passing takes place as a temporal advancement over an anachronized other, a kind of liberation enacted by genderqueerness as it supposedly replaces the butch/femme imaginary. It is important to notice, however, that both the butch-femme and the FTM-femme configurations are genderqueer in the sense that they blur, rather than transcend, the boundaries between stability and fluidity. Nonetheless, in contrast to the FTM-femme couple, the butch-femme configuration and struggle at the intersection of Chicanx racial and sexual identity formation has been supposedly surpassed. In this arbitrary rendition, and unlike the coalitional text we have seen in *Like Son*, it is transgender fluidity alone rather than its coalition with other queer codings which, in the interview, Lemus renders as expanding Chicanx legibility of sexual diversity in the twenty-first century.

In this account, the FTM genderqueer protagonist is more progressive than the Chicana butch-femme "old school." However, as Halberstam pointed out already in 1998, "oppositions between FTM and butch come at the expense of a complex butch subjectivity," which is "central to any and all attempts to theorize sexual identity and its relations to gender variation" (152; 124). Anachronized, the butch-femme binary configuration – unlike the FTM-femme configuration narrated in *Like Son* (a configuration no less based on gender binarism) – comes to represent mere ethnic authenticity and solidarity relevant only to those "people who are still very much in touch with their culture."

While it is relevant to take issue with the dominance of butch-femme or other binary configurations as the only ones presumed readable within heteronormative contexts on both sides of the border, what seems to emerge instead is a deracializing (and specifically de-Mexicanizing) narrative of homonormative and transnormative queer liberation justifying and joining the sovereignty of supposedly "advanced societies" vis-à-vis purportedly backward cultures. Here, homonormativity has been updated and upgraded into genderqueernormativity, including transnormativity, against a traditional and backward queerphobia in order to code a temporal distinction between assimilated and unassimilated Latinxs.[30] This taking of temporal

---

[30] Jack Halberstam is critical of the "seemingly radical ethic of flexibility" (2005, 19) which sees in transgenderism a "patina of transgression" (21), and of the "project[ion] of

distance from Mexican culture obliterates the decolonial queering of temporality that is potentialized precisely in the transmodern text anachronized by Cuevas yet emblematized by the retablo in Lemus's *Like Son*.[31]

Decolonizing queer temporality requires countering the presumption that multi-issue politics has been superseded by the straight-temporal evolution of any single-issue politics, even when it centers around genderqueer narratives. From a decolonial perspective, the tension between conflicting political needs is one which should expand rather than repress epistemic relationality, resisting what Audre Lorde famously termed "horizontal hostility" (1984, 48): the myth of a hierarchy of oppressions which denies the coevalness of simultaneous, heterogeneous yet interconnected political struggles. Supposedly tamed into straight time, coalitional politics is prematurely anachronized and prescriptively written off. Framed as a sequence in linear time, the politics that posits temporal advancement over others is reduced to horizontal opposition between supposedly disconnected issues. This is "a method of managing threatening diversity," as Michelle Bastian puts it, noting that

> the temporalities of others are rearranged so that they join the line of western time at some point in its past, thus excluding this diversity from the "present"[;] differences between groups are understood as developmental, rather than constitutive, and the conflict between them is downplayed. (161)

Horizontal hostility is a tradition that has not been outdated but, rather, updated when genderqueer unreadability is defined as a temporal advancement beyond ethnic solidarity or epistemic coalition. Notice, then, that Lorde's remarks below can be extended in response to the "post-borderlands" argument mentioned above if we consider a coalitional analogy between overlapping race and sexuality struggles under the myth of discreet, self-contained oppressions. The terms used by Cuevas may be understood in analogy with Lorde's (here replaced in brackets):

> Within the [genderqueer] community I am [Chican@], and within the [Chican@] community I am [genderqueer]. Any attack against [Chican@

---

sex/gender anachronism onto so-called developing nations" (38); therefore, it is contradictory that he seems to define queer time only within postmodernity: "'Queer time' is a term for those specific models of temporality that emerge within the recent development of postmodern temporality, or once one has occupied and then leaves the temporal frames of bourgeois reproduction and family, longevity, risk/safety, and inheritance" (6).

[31] Maldonado-Torres explains Enrique Dussel's conception of *transmodernity* as "an invitation to think modernity/coloniality critically from different epistemic positions and according to the manifold experiences of subjects who suffer different dimensions of the coloniality of Being" (2007, 261). See Dussel 2002.

people] is a [genderqueer] issue, because I and thousands of other [Chican@s] are part of the [genderqueer] community. Any attack against [genderqueers] is a [Chican@] issue, because thousands of [genderqueers] are [Chican@s]. There is no hierarchy of oppression.   (1984, 9)[32]

In sum, Lorde's argument may be extended to the context of what is purportedly a twenty-first-century Latinx advancement over Chicana/o traditionalism. Her call for attention to the workings of horizontal hostility should problematize the cooptation of the contestatory political potential of nonconforming sexualities whenever they are deployed to reinforce discourses of modernization in supposedly progressive sites of global power, in anachronizing ways that increasingly widen the gap between racialized and non-racialized populations.

My purpose in this essay has been to counter the reduction of Latinx literature as a new venue for anachronizing otherness under the coloniality of time. I therefore propose the temporal borderlands as a decolonial parameter for a historiography of Latinx writings against the pull of straight temporality and its self-validating rewards. From this perspective, the decolonial power of the expanding field of Latinx literature, theorization, and criticism resides in its complicitous critique – in other words, its own self-implicating challenge of anachronism. The challenge of Latinx literature is therefore to expose and confront the compulsion to reproduce the anachronism inherited from colonial and eugenicist discourses in what is often euphemistically characterized as the "price" of empowerment within U.S. society: the annihilation of transmodern knowledges under coloniality's logic of Eurocentric evolutionary stages through which the migrant subject must pass on the way to being recognized as a progressive character, one who can finally speak.

WORKS CITED

Ahmed, Sara, Claudia Castañeda, Anne-Marie Fortier, and Mimi Sheller. "Introduction." *Uprootings/Regroundings: Questions of Home and Migration.* New York: Berg, 2003.
  Strange Encounters: Embodied Others in Post-Coloniality. London and New York: Routledge, 2000.
Anzaldúa, Gloria. *Borderlands / La frontera: The New Mestiza.* San Francisco: Aunt Lute Books, 1987.

---

[32] Famously, Lorde's text reads: "Within the lesbian community I am Black, and within the Black community I am a lesbian. Any attack against Black people is a lesbian and gay issue, because I and thousands of other Black women are part of the lesbian community. Any attack against lesbians and gays is a Black issue, because thousands of lesbians and gay men are Black. There is no hierarchy of oppression" (9).

Archibugi, Daniele. "Cosmopolitical Democracy," *New Left Review* 4 (July–August 2000): 137–50.

Arnold, Kathleen R., ed. *Anti-immigration in the United States: A Historical Encyclopedia.* 2 vols. Santa Barbara, CA: Greenwood, 2011.

Ávila, Eliana. "Decolonizing Straight Temporality through Genre Trouble in Edwidge Danticat's *The Farming of Bones.*" *Ilha do Desterro* 67 (June–Dec 2014a).

"Do High-Tech à Azteca: Descolonização cronoqueer na ciber-arte chicana." *Revista Estudos Feministas* 23.1 (Jan–Apr 2014b).

Bastian, Michelle. "The Contradictory Simultaneity of Being with Others: Exploring Concepts of Time and Community in the Work of Gloria Anzaldúa." *Feminist Review* 97. Religion & Spirituality (2011): 151–67.

Brown, Wendy. *Edgework: Critical Essays on Knowledge and Politics.* Princeton, NJ: Princeton University Press, 2005.

Burawoy, Michael. "Introduction: Reaching for the Global." *Global Ethnography: Forces, Connections, and Imaginations in a Postmodern World.* Ed. Michael Burawoy et al. Berkeley: University of California Press, 2000.

Butler, Judith. *Undoing Gender.* New York and London: Routledge, 2004.

Gender Trouble: Feminism and the Subversion of Identity. New York and London: Routledge, 1990.

Cuevas, T. Jackie. "Imagining Queer Chican@s in the Post-Borderlands." *Revue LISA/LISA e-journal.* International Perspectives on the Transforming U.S.A in the 21st Century. 11.2 (2013): online. Accessed April 12, 2016.

Dávila, Arlene. *Latino Spin: Public Image and the Whitewashing of Race.* New York: New York University Press, 2008.

De Genova, Nicholas. "New and Emerging Terms in Migration Studies: A Seminar," Chicano and Latino Research Center, UC Santa Cruz, April 14, 2016.

DeHart, Monica. "'Hermano Entrepreneurs!': Constructing a Latino Diaspora across the Digital Divide." *Diaspora: A Journal of Transnational Studies* 12.2/3 (Fall/Winter 2004): 253–77.

Delgadillo, Theresa. *Spiritual Mestizaje: Religion, Gender, Race, and Nation in Contemporary Chicana Narrative.* Durham, NC and London: Duke University Press, 2011.

Díaz-Stevens, Ana Maria and Anthony M. Stevens-Arroyo. 1998. *Recognizing the Latino Resurgence in US Religion: The Emmaus Paradigm.* Boulder, CO: Westview Press.

Duggan, Lisa. "The New Homonormativity: The Sexual Politics of Neoliberalism." *Materializing Democracy: Toward a Revitalized Cultural Politics.* Ed. Russ Castronovo and Dana D. Nelson. Durham, NC and London: Duke University Press, 2002. 175–94.

Dussel, Enrique. "World System and 'Trans'-Modernity. Trans. Alessandro Fornazzari. *Nepantla: Views from South* 3.2 (2002): 221–44.

Edelman, Lee. *No Future: Queer Theory and the Death Drive.* Durham, NC: Duke University Press, 2004.

El-Tayeb, Fatima. "'Gays Who Cannot Properly Be Gay': Queer Muslims in the Neoliberal European City." *European Journal of Women's Studies* 19.1 (2012): 79–95.

Escobar, Arturo. *Encountering Development: The Making and Unmaking of the Third World.* Princeton, NJ: Princeton University Press, 1995.

Fabian, Johannes. *Time and the Other: How Anthropology Makes Its Object*. New York: Columbia University Press, 1983.

Fanon, Frantz. *Les Damnés de la Terre*. Paris: François Maspero, 1961. [Published in English as *The Wretched of the Earth*. Trans. Constance Farrington. New York: Grove Press, 1965.]

Foucault, Michel. "Nietzsche, Genealogy, History." *The Foucault Reader*. Ed. Paul Rabinow. New York: Pantheon, 1991.

Freeman, Elizabeth. *Time Binds: Queer Temporalities, Queer Histories*. Durham, NC: Duke University Press, 2010.

Gilroy, Paul. *The Black Atlantic: Modernity and Double Consciousness*. London: Verso, 1993.

Gruesz, Kirsten Silva. "The Once and Future Latino: Notes Toward a Literary History *Todavía Para Llegar*." *Contemporary US Latino/a Literary Criticism*. Edited by Lyn Di Iorio Sandín and Richard Perez. New York: Palgrave Macmillan, 2007. 115–42.

Halberstam, Judith. *In a Queer Time and Place: Transgender Bodies, Subcultural Lives*. New York and London: New York University Press, 2005.

  Female Masculinity. Durham, NC: Duke University Press, 1998.

Hames-Garcia, Michael. "Jotería Studies, or The Political Is Personal." *Aztlán: A Journal of Chicano Studies* 39.1 (Spring 2014): 135–41.

Haritaworn, Jin. 2015. *Queer Lovers and Hateful Others: Regenerating Violent Times and Places*. London: Pluto Press.

Haritaworn, Jin, Tamsila Tauqir, and Esra Erdem. "Gay Imperialism: Gender and Sexuality Discourse in the 'War on Terror.'" *Out of Place: Interrogating Silences in Queerness/Raciality*. Ed. Adi Kuntsman and Esperanza Miyake. York, UK: Raw Nerve Books, 2008. 71–95.

Harvey, David. *The Condition of Postmodernity*. Oxford: Basil Blackwell, 1990.

Hernández, Daisy. *A Cup of Water Under My Bed*. Boston: Beacon Press, 2014.

Hernandez, Lisa Justine. "*Trace Elements of Random Tea Parties* and *Like Son*: The Chican@ Queer Borderlands." *Chicana/Latina Studies* 7.1 (Fall 2007): 132–34.

Ioanide, Paula. *The Emotional Politics of Racism: How Feelings Trump Facts in and Era of Colorblindness*. Stanford, CA: Stanford University Press, 2015.

Jackman, Michael Connors and Nishant Upadhyay. "Pinkwatching Israel, Whitewashing Canada: Queer (Settler) Politics and Indigenous Colonization in Canada." *Women's Studies Quarterly* 42.3–4 (Fall 2014): 195–210.

Jameson, Fredric. *Postmodernism, or, The Cultural Logic of Late Capitalism*. London and New York: Verso, 1991.

Kafer, Alison. *Feminist, Queer, Crip*. Bloomington: Indiana University Press, 2013.

Lemus, Felicia Luna. *Like Son: A Novel*. New York: Akashic Books, 2007.

Lomas, Laura. "Beyond 'Fixed' and 'Mixed' Racial Paradigms: The Discursive Production of the Hispanic and the 2000 US Census," in *Diversity and/or Difference? Critical Perspectives*. Edited by Eliana Ávila and Lianne Schneider. *Revista Ilha do Desterro*, 48 (January–June 2005): 65–93.

Lorde, Audre. *Sister Outsider: Essays and Speeches*. Berkeley, CA: The Crossing Press, 2007 [1984].

Love, Heather. *Feeling Backward: Loss and the Politics of Queer History*. Cambridge, MA and London: Harvard University Press, 2007.

Lugones, María. "Toward a Decolonial Feminism." *Hypatia* 25.4 (Fall 2010): 742–59.

  "The Coloniality of Gender." *Worlds & Knowledges Otherwise* (Spring 2008): 1–17.

"Heterosexualism and the Colonial/Modern Gender System." *Hypatia* 22.1 (Winter 2007): 186–209.

Luibhéid, Eithne. "Introduction: Queering Migration and Citizenship." *Queer Migrations: Sexuality, US Citizenship, and Border Crossings*. Ed. Eithne Luibhéid and Lionel Cantú. Minneapolis: University of Minnesota Press, 2005.

Maldonado-Torres, Nelson. "On the Coloniality of Being: Contributions to the Development of a Concept." *Cultural Studies* 21.2/3 (March/May 2007): 240–70.

Mariscal, Jorge. "Latin@s in the US Military." In *Inside the Latin@ Experience: A Latin@ Studies Reader*. Edited by Norma Cantú and María E. Fránquiz. New York: Palgrave Macmillan, 2010. 37–50.

McPherson, Alan. *A Short History of US Interventions in Latin America and the Caribbean*. Hoboken, NJ: John Wiley & Sons, 2015.

McSherry, J. Patrice. *Predatory States: Operation Condor and Covert War in Latin America*. Lanham, MD and Boulder: Rowman & Littlefield, 2005.

Mignolo, Walter. "Epistemic Disobedience and the Decolonial Option: A Manifesto." *TransModernity: Journal of Peripheral Cultural Production of the Luso-Hispanic World* (Fall 2011): 44–66.

"*Epistemic Disobedience*: The De-Colonial Option and the Meaning of Identity in Politics." *Gragoatá* 22 (10. semestre 2007): 11–41.

"Coloniality at Large: The Western Hemisphere in the Colonial Horizon of Modernity." *The New Centennial Review* 1.2 (2001): 19–54.

Mitchell, David, and Sharon Snyder. *Narrative Prosthesis: Disability and the Dependencies of Discourse*. Ann Arbor: University of Michigan Press, 2000.

Moraga, Cherríe. "Queer Aztlán: The Reformation of the Chicano Tribe." *The Last Generation: Prose and Poetry*. Boston: South End Press, 1993.

Muñoz, José Esteban. *Cruising Utopia: The Then and There of Queer Futurity*. New York and London: New York University Press, 2009.

Nestle, J., C. Howell, and R. Wilchins. *GenderQueer: Voices from beyond the Sexual Binary*. Los Angeles and New York: Alyson Books, 2002.

Ong, Aihwa. *Flexible Citizenship: The Cultural Logics of Transnationality*. Durham, NC: Duke University Press, 1999.

Pérez, Hiram. "You Can Have My Brown Body and Eat It, Too!" *Social Text* 23.3–4 (Fall–Winter 2005): 171–91.

Pérez, Laura Elisa. *Chicana Art: The Politics of Spiritual and Aesthetic Altarities*. Durham, NC: Duke University Press, 2007.

Puar, Jasbir K. *Terrorist Assemblages: Homonationalism in Queer Times*. Durham, NC: Duke University Press, 2007.

"Queer Times, Queer Assemblages." *Social Text* 84–85, 23.3–4 (Fall–Winter 2005): 121–39.

Quijano, Anibal. "Colonialidad del poder, globalización y democracia. *Revista de Ciencias Sociales de la Universidad Autónoma de Nuevo León*, Año 4, 7–8 (September 2001–April 2002).

"Colonialidade del Poder y Clasificacion Social." Festschrift for Immanuel Wallerstein. *Journal of World Systems Research* 5.2 Special issue (Summer/Fall 2000b).

Renda, Mary. *Taking Haiti: Military Occupation and the Culture of US Imperialism, 1915–1940*. Chapel Hill and London: University of North Carolina Press, 2001.

Ritchie, Jason. "Pinkwashing, Homonationalism, and Israel–Palestine: The Conceits of Queer Theory and the Politics of the Ordinary." *Antipode* 47.3 (2014): 616–34. Accessed Dec. 4, 2015.

Rodríguez, Juana Maria. "Latino, Latina, Latin@." *Keywords for American Cultural Studies*. 2nd Edition. Ed. Bruce Brugett and Glenn Hendler. New York: New York University Press, 2014.

   Queer Latinidad: Identity Practices, Discursive Spaces. New York: New York University Press, 2003.

Roxie, Marilyn. "What Is 'Genderqueer'?" http://genderqueerid.com/what-is-gq. Updated Dec. 30, 2011. Accessed March 12, 2017.

Schulman, Sarah. *The Gentrification of the Mind: Witness to a Lost Imagination*. Berkeley: University of California Press, 2012.

   Israel/Palestine and the Queer International. Durham, NC: Duke University Press, 2012b.

   "Now a Word from Our Sponsor." Paper delivered at the University of California, San Diego, January 1995.

Sedgwick, Eve K. *Tendencies*. Durham, NC: Duke University Press, 1993.

Spivak, Gayatri Chakravorty. "Translation as Culture." *Parallax* 6.1 (2000): 13–24.

Tea, Michelle. "Michelle Tea Talks with Felicia Luna Lemus." *The Believer Book of Writers Talking to Writers*. Ed. Vida Vendela San Francisco: Believer Books, 2005. 171–91.

Torres-Saillant, Silvio. "Problematic Paradigms: Racial Diversity and Corporate Identity in the Latino Community." In *Latinos: Remaking America*. Edited by Marcelo Suarez-Orozco and Mariela M. Páez. Berkeley: University of California Press, 2002.

Wilkerson, Abby. "Disability, Sex Radicalism, and Political Agency." *NWSA Journal* 14.3 (2002): 33–57.

Epilogue

Latina/o Literature: The Borders Are Burning

MARÍA JOSEFINA SALDAÑA-PORTILLO

Killing the Abuelita

The final story in Ito Romo's 2013 *The Border is Burning* ends with parallel explosions on either side of the Rio Grande, the border obliterated by the two fires making the twin cities of Laredo and Nuevo Laredo one in a conflagration of cartel retaliations. Romo's dark, powerful stories bring together crack heads, battered women, unemployed fathers, *narcos*, pimps, and prostitutes through the plot device of Interstate 35, that thriving thoroughfare of imports, exports, immigrants, and drugs, the northern branch of the Pan American Highway reaching all the way to South American cocaine country. Significantly, the racial or ethnic character of the protagonists in these stories is often indeterminate. Or more precisely, determinant but muted, appearing almost incidental to the narrative – almost. In "Killer Dog," a lesbian couple gentrifying a Mexican American neighborhood in San Antonio demand the police put down their neighbor's unleashed dog, much to the neighbor's distress. The puppy's rumbustiousness is read as a violent, deadly force by the couple, but is it the dog they find threatening or the distinct cultural mores of their new neighbors? These stories belong to the post-nationalist period in Latina/o literature, both in terms of their aesthetic form and their content. As flash fiction, the form of the narratives is at once hyperrealist and Cubist; the racial and classed violence in these short stories is inferred, telegraphed to the reader through vibrant, abrupt imaging and cryptic dialogue. Meanwhile, the content exceeds the concerns of a previous generation of writers tasked with founding a canon and distinguishing its contours through distinctly ethnic themes.

Accordingly, *The Border Is Burning* stands in stark contrast to Romo's 2001 collection of short stories, *El Puente/The Bridge*. Written in part in the literary style of magical realism and in part in the Chicana/o aesthetic of rasquachismo, *El Puente* stages fourteen vignettes around one international incident: the Rio Grande River having perplexingly turned a ruby red. As Mexican and U.S. media, environmental agencies, and militaries descend on the scene to investigate, the lives of fourteen women intersect over the course of a twenty-four-hour period on one of the international bridges spanning the red river. There are no diabolical or desperate characters in *El Puente* as in *Border*, only tender ones: broken-hearted widows, buxom waitresses, and kindly *abuelitas*; jilted lovers, abused wives, and empathetic nuns; militant Chicana activists and hard-working transvestite showgirls. Published just seven years after the passage of the North American Free Trade Agreement (NAFTA), *El Puente* offers us a vision of a border still on the cusp of the major reorganization of life that the free trade accord would bring. The incident that turns the river red is indirectly caused by the expanding *maquiladora* industry poisoning the river, but the characters respond to the incident in ways that are still folkloric and quintessentially Mexican American.[1]

Even the titles of the two collections reflect the cataclysmic transformations that occurred along the U.S.–Mexico border under the auspices of NAFTA in the intervening twelve years between their publications. However, they also reflect dramatic changes in the character of Latina/o literature at the turn of the twenty-first century. *El Puente/The Bridge* suggests congenial differences ready to be traversed: a linking of communities, an exchange of people, goods, and cultures. Even the slash in the title promises to bridge the linguistic and cultural divide for the reader. And accordingly, Romo lovingly depicts characters who crisscross the Rio Grande as if they were crossing the street, depicting in luscious detail the web of familial and familiar relations that traditionally united communities on either side of the border. By contrast, *The Border Is Burning* tolerates no translation, suggesting instead the obliteration of difference, of division, and of reciprocity. The incendiary amalgamation of cultures suggested by the title also reflects the devastation wrought by globalization and by the relentless flow of cocaine and methamphetamines set off by NAFTA. Characters living on multiple edges are depicted in terse prose, and all human interaction is tinged with

---

[1] I use folkloric here not in a pejorative way, to indicate some anachronistic or premodern tradition. Rather I use it in the more capacious sense it holds in Spanish. By *lo folclórico* in literary production, I am referring to Mexican-American authors who regularly reference Mexican traditions in their novels, short stories, and creative nonfiction, particularly those of the popular classes in Mexico and the United States; for example, those religious *dichos y costumbres de la gente* that were the thematic of Rodolfo Añaya's *Bless Me, Ultima*, or Tómas Rivera's *...y no se lo trago la tierra*, and more recently, Gloria Anzaldúa's *Borderlands/La Frontera: The New Mestiza*.

proximate danger. In an interview with John Phillips Santos for *Texas Monthly*, Romo described *El Puente* as "whimsical" and as "still [having] hope." For his second book, Romo insists, "I wanted to kill the abuelita . . . I wanted to kill the tortilla stories."[2] The distance between Romo's two collections, captured in this interview, reflects the profound transformation of the field of Latina/o literature, Latina/o literary aesthetics, and Latina/o literary criticism over the last fifty years. The geographical border between North and South has been obliterated, for both the materiality of bordered lives and for the composition of the Latina/o literary canon. Temporal boundaries have dissolved as well with the demise of nationalistic paradigms. Of equal importance, Latina/o literature (and criticism) expands beyond its previous aesthetic limits – beyond its recuperative mission and repertoire of domestic themes – beyond its ethnic moniker.

Destinies Manifested

When John Morán González and I began our careers together at Stanford University twenty-five years ago, putting together a qualifying exam list in "Latina/o" literature was a fairly straightforward task. Firstly, there was no such thing as "Latina/o" literature. Rather, primarily under the guidance of earlier graduate cohorts, we put together a list in two parts: Chicana/o authors on the one hand and Puerto Rican authors on the other, with perhaps the additions of Julia Alvarez, Oscar Hijuelos, and Dolores Prida to "represent" (!) the rest of the Hispanic Caribbean.[3] Temporally, we organized our list primarily from the nationalist period for each group through the women-of-color feminist interventions into masculinist canon formation: roughly from the early 1960s through the late 1980s. We might also have included early-twentieth-century authors who had already been recovered or whose significance had been forgotten: Américo Paredes for the Chicana/o canon and Julia de Burgos for the Puerto Rican canon. Literary criticism on the list reflected this "national" divide as well: María Herrera-Sobek's *Beyond*

---

[2] See Texas Monthly Staff, "10 Writers to Watch (and Read)" in *Texas Monthly*, October, 2015. At www.texasmonthly.com/list/the-10-writers-to-watch-and-read/. Accessed April 16, 2016.

[3] John Morán Gonzalez and I arrived at Stanford University right before Arturo Islas's brave but quick struggle with AIDS. While I was fortunate enough to work with Arturo for my MA exam, by the time of my doctoral exams, he was too ill. In the gap between the departure of Arturo and the arrival of Ramón Saldívar, who served as dissertation advisor to both John and myself, graduate students Alicia Arrizón, Nina Menedez, and others filled the void.

Stereotypes: The Critical Analysis of Chicana Literature (1985) and Ramón Saldí-var's *Chicano Narrative: The Dialectics of Difference* (1990) on one hand; Eugene V. Mohr's *The Nuyorican Experience: Literature of the Puerto Rican Minority* (1982) and Juan Flores's *Divided Borders: Essays on Puerto Rican Identity* (1993) on the other. While our lists were meant to establish a broad teaching expertise, we nevertheless expected to pursue "our" ethnic/national literature in our critical scholarship. No one told us to do so; no one pressured us indirectly. Rather, this was just the way literary criticism was done.

As *The Cambridge History of Latina/o American Literature* makes clear, however, the tidy order of such early manifestations of the field of Latina/o literature has come undone. The pretense of distinctions based on subnational canons that would be roughly analogous to an African-American or U.S. literary canon dissolves as an (im)properly *Latina/o* literature emerges. The categorical divisions between Chicana/o and Puerto Rican literary studies followed the political impetus behind the founding of ethnic studies programs and departments across the country. Under the twin banners of anticolonialism and national liberation, "Third World" student movements pushed for the establishment of ethnic studies on college and university campuses through their strikes, occupations, sit-ins, and teach-ins.[4] While coalitions *across* racial and ethnic minority organizations account for the success of these militant student movements in the 1960s and 1970s, when the institutionalization of such programs or departments transpired, it did so along identity formations congruent with the anticolonial and liberation politics of these movements: Asian-American studies, Native American studies, and Puerto Rican studies along the East Coast of the United States, while Chicano or Mexican-American studies predominated across the Southwest and Midwest. These Third World student movements were national and broadly anticolonial *liberation* movements after all, and they demanded a scholarship committed to the transformation of the social conditions (and consciousness) of their corresponding identity-based communities. Born under the sign of Third World liberation, early Puerto Rican and Chicano/Mexican-American scholarship dedicated itself to recuperating the *nationalist*

---

[4] For a history of this vibrant movement, see Rodolfo F. Acuña, *Occupied America: A History of Chicanos*; Carlos Muñoz, *Youth, Identity, Power: The Chicano Movement*; Ernesto Chavez, *¡Mi Raza Primero!: Nationalism, Identity, and Insurgency in the Chicano Movement in Los Angeles, 1966–1978*; Maylei Blackwell, *¡Chicana Power! Contested Histories of Feminism in the Chicano Movement*; Bobby Seale, *Sieze the Time: The Story of the Black Panther Party and Huey P. Newton*; Assata Shakur and Angela Davis, *Assata: An Autobiography*; Huey P. Newton and Toni Morrison, *To Die for a People*.

histories and literatures of these distinct communities. There was no "Latina/o studies" in this early period; rather it is a twenty-first century construct that we cast back onto the past, one that gathers multiple though distinct histories and traditions, but also surpasses them in the field's expanding revisions and ambitions.

As evidenced by the essays gathered in this anthology, the category of Latina/o literature and its criticism is no longer bound by the colonialist geography of the United States, which originally included the Mexican-American Southwest and Puerto Rico, but also the immigrant literatures of the Hispanic Caribbean. It is not simply that Latina/o authors in the United States now come from a wide array of Latin American countries. It is also that heuristic practices now exceed the nationalist borders of the U.S. and of American literary studies, as critics place Latina/o literature in its proper hemispheric context for interpretation. An understanding of Sor Juana Inés de la Cruz's own writing, for example, is deemed essential for understanding fully the aesthetic dimensions of Latina feminist fiction, leaving one to question why Sor Juana herself, writing in a viceroyalty that included the northern part of Mexico extending through California, Texas, and New Mexico, should not be part of the Latina/o literary canon (q.v. Vera Tudela). Meanwhile, contemporary Latina/o poetics draw from pre-Columbian indigenous iconography cosmology, and philosophy, thus requiring the well-honed historical and anthropological analysis of Inca, Mayan, and Nahuas traditions (q.v. Arias, Mazotti, Perez-Torres). However, even a hemispheric interpretative practice can be insufficient as new taxonomical concerns emerge from the stream of Latin American immigrants flowing into Europe: Do these immigrant groups form part of a "Latina/o" collectivity? And if so, should not the literature they produce also be the object of study for Latina/o literary study (q.v. Blanco)?

Temporal boundaries are implicated and expanded as well – traversed and even interdicted – for if Latina/o literature no longer conforms to the geography of the United States and its real or imagined sub-nations (Aztlán or Boriquén), then why must it conform to the time of the nation? Or to the *longue durée* of the ethnos? As new interpretative practices trace the roots and references of Latina/o poetics back to the Spanish colonial period and to the precolonial period before that, then the temporal borders of the Latina/o literary canon must recede backward to include genres, themes, and regions that differ from English-dominant American literary history (q.v. García-Caro). And thus Latina/o literary criticism must accordingly consider early indigenous systems of representation that went beyond the written word but were nevertheless narratological: codices, glyphics, weavings, performance, but also indigenous histories written after the coming of the Spaniards and the imposition of a Roman alphabet (q.v. Arias, Lazo). Moving away from national geographies of time and space also enables a focus on hetero-temporal cities like New Orleans, which, because of its four decades under Spanish colonial rule, has episodically participated in a trans-Caribbean exchange of literary expression. As a border city to the sea, it has repeatedly served as a port of entry for multilingual prose, journalism, poetry, and fiction, but has also been central to entire literary movements, like that of Latin American *modernismo* (q.v. Gruesz). Thinking time horizontally rather than teleologically allows critics to interpret Latina/o authors within global literary periods and political movements as well; to consider, for example, how Latina/o authors like William Carlos Williams or Manuel Torres contributed respectively to revolutionary political discourse, Euro-American high modernisms and liberal philosophies (q.v. García, Colón, Lazo). Once outside of the construct of national time, Latina/o literary criticism expands beyond the narrow racial or ethnic interpretations of Latina/o literary themes but without losing sight of the cultural uniqueness and historical specificity of Latina/o writerly practices. By moving us to an aesthetic register – be it that of romanticism, modernism, postmodernism, and so on – critics enable us to see how Latinas/os have often located their literary practices at the intersection of U.S., British, Spanish, and Latin American literary traditions, with bilingualism and translation playing a fundamental role in the exertion of literary influences and instances of exchange and appropriation.

Perhaps the most dramatic shift in Latina/o literature and literary studies pertains to language. As scholars examine Latina/o literature beyond the national paradigm and within the context of colonial and precolonial aesthetic practices, the difficulty in limiting Latina/o literature to English and Spanish becomes apparent. Firstly, the very colonial experience suggests we must at least expand Latina/o literature to other colonial languages, given the historical intimacies and overlap of populations colonized by the Spanish, French, Portuguese, and Dutch. All over the hemisphere and beyond there exist geographical borderlands that switched hands among these empires for decades or just a few years, or whose histories and cultural expression after independence have remained completely entangled. As but one example, Haiti and the Dominican Republic share not only an island but a history of Catholic colonialism, enslavement, independence, racism, and solidarity that is reflected in the literary traditions of both. To interpret the literary tradition of the Dominican Republic and its lettered immigrants, a scholar must analyze it in relation to the literary and cultural traditions of Haiti, and vice-versa (q.v. Mariñez, Blanco). Moreover, such scholarship requires not only a familiarity with French and Spanish, but with Kreyòl as well. One might conclude that "Latina/o" should at the very least connote its linguistic root, that of Latin and the romance languages that derive from it. One would be wrong in drawing this conclusion. The politics of language are a serious issue for the future of Latina/o studies, as the field should not replicate the colonial or national exclusions and hierarchies. After all, Kreyòl brings together various African languages with French and Spanish, just as Latin American Spanishes incorporate indigenous languages in each region. With the rise of indigenous immigrants from Latin America and long-standing Asian-Latin American communities in transit to the United States, it is only a matter of time until Zapotec-, Mixtec- or Chinese-speaking bilingual or trilingual authors add their hybridized voices, languages, and genre to the mix of "Latina/o" literature. Scholarship should anticipate and welcome these linguistic challenges, as it is certain that for the purposes of Latina/o literary history, Latinas/os no longer (and probably never did) denote a monolinguistic whole.

As a critical enterprise, Latina/o literary studies must interrogate colonialism itself as a system of knowledge production, one that has elevated the written word over other forms of cultural expression for the explicit purpose of occluding and repressing indigenous and Afro-mestizo cultural expression (q.v. Arias). In addition to the repression of these racialized groups, Latin American letters also tended to exclude the popular classes (*las clases populares*) – those members of the working class and lumpenproletariat whose narrative forms were forged on the street – from national canons. Thus as Latina/o literary critics expand the linguistic registers of latinidad, so too must they expand the genres considered proper for literary study, in order to decolonialize knowledge production and shed light on the cultures of these traditionally excluded groups. The occlusion of *afromestizos*, for example, is made visible through "sound witnessing," through elucidating the unique relationship of music to Latino/a literature. Much of Latina/o literature registers the sonic traces of Latinidad – dance, song, improvisation, and listening practices – as a mode of recuperating these narratological forms (q.v. Alvarado). And so the "time" of Latina/o literature is also the musical time of the bolero, the *corrido*; of cha cha, mambo, bomba, cumbia, tango. Literary genres must expand to include the event of Latina/o performance. *Floricantos* are evenings of musical performances and spoken-word poetry that are rarely transcribed but are nevertheless a vibrant part of Latina/o literature and cultural transmission (q.v. Pérez-Torres). The cabaret has long been another popular form of cultural expression that uses satirical song and parodic performance to critique political elites, as well as racist and sexist ideologies. The study of performance as part of Latina/o literary studies captures the critical and creative spirit of the popular classes thus expressed (q.v. Gutíerrez). Meanwhile, fictional autoethnography emerges as a feminist genre that is akin to memoir but that recognizes the importance of fiction to the recuperation of excluded histories and marginalized subjects (q.v. Kurzen). The scholars gathered in this critical anthology make clear that decolonial aesthetic practices like these defy strict generic codification and require the proliferation of flexible genres for "Latina/o literature."

And as I hope I have made equally clear, the instability of the term Latina/o becomes apparent under the weight of the multiple geographies, temporalities, languages, and histories it is meant to bear. Even as this anthology goes to press, Central American child migrants, who are set in motion by the rippling effects of free trade and the drug trade recorded in Romo's *The Border Is Burning*, add the weight of their narratives to the instability of the term, for how shall we locate their would-be latinidad? Given that these children are set in motion by forces predicated on a hemispheric drug economy that feeds the United States' insatiable consumption, one might consider them "Latina/o" from the moment they cross into Mexico. Central Americans crossing Mexico are becoming Latinas/os in transit, as no one is more so than the unrecognized, abject, and unwanted immigrant refugee (q.v. Milian). One might shift the geographical parameters yet again, if we imagine these latest refugees as the newest Latina/o citizens of a new trans-American *Narcolandia*. What if Latina/o has only ever been the tracings of a displacement? Latina/o literature only tenuously unified as serial narratives of displacement that we might trace back to 1492 (q.v. Alemán)? What if "Latina/o" is but the quintessential iteration of displacement and loss (q.v. Alemán, Saldaña-Portillo)?[5] To be Latina/o is to be displaced – be that in the United States, Canada, Mexico, Europe, or beyond. Is this the ground zero of latinidad? I suggest instead that the term Latina/o is a term under erasure, in the strictest Derridian sense. Latina/o is an inadequate term for all that it is meant to encompass, an unsuitable catachrestic sign but necessary one. As

---

[5] For a discussion of the loss of indigeneity at the heart of Chicanidad, see Maria Josefina Saldaña-Portillo, *Indian Given: Racial Geographies across Mexico and the United States*, Durham, NC: Duke University Press (2016).

Gayatri Spivak explains in her introduction to *Of Grammatology*, signifiers are "always already inhabited by the trace of another sign which never appears as such" (xxxix).[6] So we may say of the signifier "Latina/o literature," which contains multiple signs of difference, of geographies, histories, temporalities, and languages that may never appear as such, but that always leave their trace under its sign. Thus, the authors contributing to this anthology must be celebrated for commitment to recognizing and working *with* the erasure that is "Latina/o" with boldness, creativity, and wit. The authors expose the instances in which Latina/o literature betrays its own false unity, and move beyond the limits of its imagined signification by reflecting on its *différance* rather than shying away from its multiple manifested destinies with false unities and tidy histories.

Beyond Taxonomies

The cultural critic and Puerto Rican/Latino scholar Juan Flores was originally meant to write the afterword for this anthology, and so I too am an inadequate but necessary placeholder for him. I conclude by revisiting his 2009 "Thinking Diaspora from Below: Lines of Definition," as in this essay I find an analogous way of approaching the futures of Latina/o literature and literary studies.[7] Like the recent rise of all things hemispheric, "the explosion of diaspora-speak came as recently as the early 1990s, coincid[ing] with the ascendancy of postcolonial theorizing and the ubiquity of the term 'globalization' in modern-day public and academic parlance" (Flores 21). While Flores reviews several scholarly definitions of diasporic community and culture in this essay, he himself is not interested in producing another taxonomy: "Instead of aiming to state what diasporas are, more fruitful lines of inquiry are directed at determining *how* they are, where they are in time and place, and *what sets of relations condition their existence* ... diasporas are not about fixed states of social being but about process" (16, emphasis added). With Flores and as manifested in this anthology, as literary scholars we should be less interested in producing taxonomies of Latina/o literature than in "determining *how* they are," less interested in arriving at binding parameters than in recognizing that this literature configures many Latina/o

---

[6] Gayatri Spivak, in *Of Grammatology* by Jacques Derrida, Baltimore, MD: John Hopkins University Press (1977).

[7] Juan Flores, "Thinking Diaspora from Below: Lines of Definition." In Flores, *The Diaspora Strikes Back: Caribbean Latino Tales of Learning and Turning*. New York: Routledge (2009): 15–31.

communities in diaspora: some are ancient, some are new; some are reactionary in their political practices, some are progressive; some practice elite aesthetic genres, while others practice stubbornly subaltern ones. However, what mattered to Flores, and in his view should continue to guide our scholarly inquiry, were the social and material relations that condition both the displacement of diasporic communities from their places of origin and their reception in their places of arrival, because "diaspora exists in relation to power, whether national or international, whether primarily political or economic" (18). Similarly, the social and material relations that condition Latina/o literary production should guide Latina/o literary studies, not as a singular motivation of course, but as a commitment that echoes the origins of the field in the heady days of anticolonialist struggle, when Juan Flores and others struggled for institutional transformation and accountability, and helped to create pioneering interdisciplinary programs in ethnic, Africana, Puerto Rican and Latino studies.

Rather than studying Latina/o literature for its own sake, in other words, to determine its discrete characteristics in contradistinction to other discrete national or subnational literatures, Flores urges the scholar to focus on the processes of global inequality wrought by capitalism and racism that result in communal displacements across time and space, displacements that are inevitably recorded in literary narratives. Flores also suggests we focus our attention on the unequal relations of power among Latina/o diasporic populations, those racial or class forces that produce diasporic communities with relative cultural and economic power in the receiving country, and those without access to any such capital. For ultimately, Flores is advocating a scholarship from below, as scholarship he practiced throughout his academic lifetime: Latina/o literary and cultural studies in the service of these subaltern populations who remain oppressed even in displacement. These are the subjects who warrant our scholarly attention.

As an assistant professor in Stanford University's German Department in the late 1960s and early 1970s, Juan Flores became radicalized through his participation in the antiwar and Chicano movements on campus and in the broader Bay Area. Juan never abandoned the commitment to subaltern subjects and social justice that he acquired as part of his radicalization, nor did he abandon his engagement with German philosophical thought, though he did abandon Stanford's German Department for Hunter College-City University of New York, where he helped to found the field of Puerto Rican studies at the *Centro de Estudios Puertorriqueños*. As a Puerto Rican studies scholar and cultural theorist, Juan deployed the anti-humanist, contra-individualist critical strain of the Enlightenment developed from within the German tradition by such theorists as Johann Gottfried Herder and Wilhelm Dilthey (as well as Marx and Weber) to argue against economic inequality, political disenfranchisement, and racial animus.[8] Juan's commitment to a Latino literary and cultural studies from below explains why he dedicated the last decade of his intellectual life to developing Afro-Latino studies in his publications, lectures, and community forums. Juan took up this underdeveloped area of study not simply to underscore and celebrate the undeniably rich contribution of Afro-Latinos to the broader field, but to address racism within the Latino diaspora, in Latin America, and the Hispanic Caribbean, as well as to analyze and address the economic disparities between Afro-Latinos and all other Latinos.

Flores always practiced and advocated an insurrectional theorizing of diaspora, in the spirit of Edward Said's "traveling theory."[9] In his memory I suggest that an insurrectional Latina/o literary theory would take aim at the racist and exploitative forces of economic, cultural, and political power that compel people into motion by dispossessing them of their resources in the interest of capital, race, religion, and so forth, because Latina/o literary studies should always side with these agents of historical change, rather than the diasporic entrepreneurial classes. Juan was my friend, departmental colleague, and political ally, and if it fell to me to write the epitaph for his gravestone, it would simply read: "Juan Flores, he was never a liberal," and Juan would know exactly what I meant. He was in every way a radical theorist and cultural practitioner. Several scholars already called for an ethics of Latina/o literary studies.[10] With Flores, I suggest that this ethics is best expressed as a Latina/o literary studies from below.

---

[8] In one of the last conversations I had with Juan in Brooklyn, at the end of the spring semester before his untimely death, he recounted his intellectual political trajectory from John Flores the Germanist to Juan Flores the Puertorriqueñista. It was a thrilling conversation for me, and we agreed that I would formally interview him on the details of his life story when we returned to school in the fall semester. That night he e-mailed me an article in which he analyzed this transition. For a too-brief account of this formative transition in his own words, see Flores, "Reclaiming Left Baggage: Some Early Sources for Minority Studies," *Cultural Critique* 59 (2005): 187–206.

[9] See Edward Said, "Traveling Theory," in Said, *The World, the Text, and the Critic*. Cambridge, MA: Harvard University Press (1983): 226–47.

[10] Although I do not advocate the prescriptions drawn by these scholars, see Paula Moya, *The Social Imperative: Race, Close Reading, and Contemporary Latino Criticism* and Paula Moya and Michael Hames-García, *Reclaiming Identity: Realist Theory and The Predicament of Postmodernism* for examples of this call for ethics.

Bibliography

Aching, Gerard. *The Politics of Spanish American modernismo*. Cambridge: Cambridge University Press, 1997.

Adorno, Rolena. *The Polemics of Possession in Spanish American Narrative*. New Haven, CT and London: Yale University Press, 2008.

Agüeros, Jack. "Julia de Burgos: Una Introducción/Julia de Burgos: An Introduction." *Song of the Simple Truth: The Complete Poems of Julia de Burgos*. Ed. and trans. Jack Agüeros. Willimantic, CT: Curbstone Press, 1997: ii–xl.

Alarcón, Norma. "Cognitive Desires. An Allegory of/for Chicana Critics." *Chicana (W) rites: On Word and Film*. Eds. Maria Herrera-Sobek and Helena Maria Viramontes. Berkeley, CA: Third Woman Press, 1992.

  "Making *Familia* from Scratch: Split Subjectivities in the Work of Helena María Viramontes and Cherríe Moraga." *Chicana Creativity and Criticism: Charting New Frontiers in American Literature*. Eds. María Hererra-Sobek and Helena María Viramontes. Houston, TX: Arte Público Press, 1988: 14–59.

  "The Theoretical Subject(s) in *This Bridge Called My Back* and Anglo American Feminism." *Making Face, Making Soul: Haciendo Caras*. Ed. Gloria Anzaldúa. San Francisco: Aunt Lute, 1990: 356–69.

  "Traddutora, Traditora: A Paridigmatic Figure of Chicana Feminism." *Cultural Critique* 5 (1989): 57–87.

  "What Kind of Lover Have You Made Me, Mother?: Towards a Theory of Chicana's Feminism and Cultural Identity Through Poetry." *Women of Color: Perspectives on Feminism and Identity*. Ed. Audrey T. McCluskey. Bloomington: Indiana University, Women's Studies Program Occasional Papers Series, 1.1 (1985): 85–110.

Aldama, Arturo J. *Disrupting Savagism: Intersecting Chicana/o, Mexican Immigrant, and Native American Struggles for Self-Representation*. Durham: Duke University Press, 2001.

Aldama, Arturo J., Chela Sandoval, and Peter García, eds. *Performing the US Latina and Latino Borderlands*. Bloomington: Indiana University Press, 2012.

Aldama, Frederick Luis. *Postethnic Narrative Criticism: Magicorealsm in Oscar 'Zeta' Acosta, Ana Castillo, Julie Dash, Hanif Kureishi, and Salman Rushdie*. Austin: University of Texas Press, 2009.

  Your Brain on Latino Comics: From Gus Arriola to Los Bros Hernandez. Austin: University of Texas Press, 2009.

  ed. *The Routledge Concise History of Latino/a Literature*, New York: Routledge, 2013.

Alemán, Jesse. "Days of the (Un)Dead: Vampires, Zombies, and Other Forms of Chicano/ a Horror in Film." *Latinos and Narrative Media: Participation and Portrayal*. Ed. Frederick Luis Aldama. New York: Palgrave-Macmillan, 2013: 49–70.

"Introduction." *The Woman in Battle: The Civil War Narrative of Loreta Janeta Velaquez, Cuban Woman and Confederate Soldier*. Madison: University of Wisconsin Press, 2003.

Alemán, Jesse and Shelley Streeby, eds. *Empire and the Literature of Sensation: An Anthology of Nineteenth-Century Popular Fiction*. New Brunswick, NJ: Rutgers UP, 2007.

Alfau de Solalinde, Jesusa. "El barroco en la vida de Sor Juana." *Humanidades México*: Facultad de Filosofía y Letras, UNAM I. 1, 1943. (reproduced by *Claustro de SorJuana*, Cuaderno n° 8, 1981).

Alfonso, Vitalina. *Ellas hablan de la Isla*. Havana: Ediciones Unión, 2002.

Algarín, Miguel. "Afterword." "Introduction: Nuyorican Language." *Nuyorican Poetry: An Anthology of Puerto Rican Words and Feelings*. Ed. Algarín, Miguel, and Miguel Piñero. New York: Morrow, 1975: 9–20.

"Nuyorican Literature." *MELUS* 8.2 (1981): 89–92. JSTOR. Web. 30 May 2015.

Algarín, Miguel, and Bob Holman, eds. *Aloud: Voices from the Nuyorican Poets Cafe*. New York: Holt, 1994.

Algarín, Miguel, and Miguel Piñero, eds. *Nuyorican Poetry: An Anthology of Puerto Rican Words and Feelings*. New York: Morrow, 1975.

Allatson, Paul. "From 'Latinidad' to 'Latinid@des': Imagining the Twenty-First Century." *The Cambridge Companion to Latina/o American Literature*. Ed. John Morán González. New York: Cambridge University Press, 2016: 128–45.

Key Terms in Latino/a Cultural and Literary Studies. New York: Wiley-Blackwell, 2007.

"A Shadowy Sequence: Chicana Textual/Sexual Reinventions of Sor Juana." *Chasqui* 33.1 (May 2004): 3–27.

Alvarado, Li Yun. "Ambivalence and the Empire City: Julia de Burgos's New York." *Arizona Quarterly* 71.1 (2015): 53–81.

Alvarez, Stephanie, and William Luis, eds. *The AmeRícan Poet: Collected Essays on the Works of Tato Laviera*. New York: Centro de Estudios Puertorriqueños Press, 2014.

¡¿Qué qué?! Transculturation and Tato Laviera's Spanglish Poetics. *CENTRO: Journal of the Center for Puerto Rican Studies* 18.2 (2006): 25–57.

Alvarez-Borland, Isabel and Lynette M. F. Bosch, eds. *Cuban-American Literature and Art: Negotiating Identities*. Albany: State University of New York Press, 2008.

Antebi, Susan. *Carnal Inscriptions: Spanish American Narratives of Difference and Disability*. New York: Palgrave Macmillan, 2009.

Anzaldúa, Gloria. *Borderlands / La Frontera: The New Mestiza*. San Francisco: Aunt Lute Books, 1987.

"now let us shift...the path of conocimiento...inner work, public acts." *This Bridge We Call Home: Radical Visions for Transformation*. Eds. Gloria Anzaldúa and Ana Louise Keating. New York: Routledge, 2002: 540–78.

"To(o) Queer the Writer: Loca, escritora y chicana." In *In/versions: Writing by Dykes and Lesbians*. Ed. Betsy Warland. Vancouver: Press Gang, 1991: 249–59.

Aparicio, Frances R. "From Ethnicity to Multiculturalism: An Historical Overview of Puerto Rican Literature in the United States." *Handbook of Hispanic Cultures in the*

United States: Literature and Art. Ed. Francisco Lomeli. Houston: Arte Público, 1993: 19–39.

"La vida es un Spanglish disparatero: Bilingualism in Nuyorican Poetry." *European Perspectives on Hispanic Literature of the United States.* Ed. Genevieve Fabre. Houston: Arte Público, 1988: 147–60.

Listening to Salsa: Gender, Latin Music and Puerto Rican Cultures. Hanover: Wesleyan University Press, 1998.

"Salsa, Maracas, and Baile: Latin Popular Music in the Poetry of Victor Hernández Cruz." *MELUS* 16.1 (1989–1990): 43–58.

Aparicio, Frances R. and Suzanne Bost, eds. *The Routledge Companion to Latino/a Literature.* New York: Routledge, 2015: 476–84.

Aparicio, Frances R., and Susana Chavez-Silverman, eds. *Tropicalizations: Transcultural Representations of Latinidad.* Hanover: Dartmouth University Press, 1997.

Aranda, José. "Contradictory Impulses: María Amparo Ruiz de Burton, Resistance Theory, and the Politics of Chicano/a Studies." *American Literature* 70 (September 1998): 551–79.

"Recovering the US Hispanic Literary Heritage." *The Routledge Companion to Latino/a Literature.* Eds. Frances R. Aparicio and Suzanne Bost. New York: Routledge, 2015: 476–84.

When We Arrive: A New Literary History of Mexican America. Tucson: University of Arizona Press, 2003.

Ardao, Arturo. *Génesis de la idea y el nombre de América Latina.* Caracas: Centro de Estudios Latinoamericanos Rómulo Gallegos, 1993.

Arenal, Electa. "This Life Within Me Won't Keep Still." *Reinventing the Americas: Comparative Studies of Literature of the United States and Spanish America.* Eds. Bell Gale Chevigny and Gari Laguardia. Cambridge: Cambridge University Press, 2009: 158–202.

Arenal, Electa and Vincent Martin. *Sor Juana Inés de la Cruz. Neptuno alegórico.* Madrid: Cátedra 2009.

Arias, Arturo. *Taking Their Word: Literature and the Signs of Central America.* University of Minnesota Press, 2007.

"Central American-Americans: Invisibility, Power, and Representation in the US Latino World." *Latino Studies* 1.1 (2003): 168–87.

Arias, Arturo, and Claudia Milian. "US Central Americans: Representations, Agency, and Communities." *Latino Studies* 11.2 (Summer 2013): 131–49.

Arrizón, Alicia. *Latina Performance: Traversing the Stage.* Bloomington: Indiana University Press, 1999.

Queering Mestizaje: Transculturation and Performance. Ann Arbor: University of Michigan Press, 2006.

Arrizón, Alicia and Lillian Manzor, eds. *Latinas on Stage: Practice and Theory.* Berkeley: Third Woman Press, 2000.

Arroyo-Martínez, Jossianna. "Living the Political: Julia de Burgos and Lolita Lebrón." *Centro Journal* 26.2 (2014): 128–55.

"Technologies: Transculturations of Race, Gender & Ethnicity in Arturo A. Schomburg's Masonic Writings." *Centro Journal* 17.1: 4–25.

Writing Secrecy in Caribbean Freemasonry. New York: Palgrave Macmillan, 2013.

Arteaga, Alfred. *Chicano Poetics: Herotexts and Hybridities.* New York: Cambridge University Press, 1997.

Ávila, Eliana. "Decolonizing Straight Temporality through Genre Trouble in Edwidge Danticat's *The Farming of Bones." Ilha do Desterro* 67, June–Dec 2014a.

"Do High-Tech à Azteca: Descolonização cronoqueer na ciber-arte chicana." *Revista Estudos Feministas* 23.1, Jan–Apr 2014b.

Ballón, José. *Lecturas Norteamericanas de José Martí: Emerson y el socialismo contemporaneo (1880–1887).* México: Centro Coordinador y Difusor de Estudios Latinoamericanos, Universidad Nacional Autónoma de México, 1995.

Bastian, Michelle. "The Contradictory Simultaneity of Being with Others: Exploring Concepts of Time and Community in the Work of Gloria Anzaldúa." *Feminist Review* 97, Religion & Spirituality (2011): 151–67.

Bauer, Ralph. *The Cultural Geography of Colonial American Literatures: Empire, Travel, Modernity.* New York: Cambridge University Press, 2003.

Bebout, Lee. *Whiteness on the Border: Mapping the US Racial Imagination in Brown and White.* New York: New York University Press, 2016.

Belnap, Jeffrey, and Raul Fernández, eds. *José Martí's "Our America": From National to Hemispheric Cultural Studies.* Durham: Duke University Press, 1998.

Benítez-Rojo, Antonio. *The Repeating Island: The Caribbean and the Postmodern Perspective.* Durham: Duke University Press, 1996.

Bergmann, Emilie L. "Ficciones de Sor Juana: poética y biografia." *Y diversa de mí misma entre vuestras plumas ando. Homenaje internacional a Sor Juana Inés de la Cruz.* Ed. Sara Poot. Herrera, Mexico: El Colegio de México, 1993: 171–83.

Bergmann, Emile L., and Stacey Schlau. *Approaches to Teaching the Works of Sor Juana Inés de la Cruz.* New York: The Modern Language Association of America, 2007.

Beverley, John. *Essays on the Literary Baroque in Spain and Spanish America.* London: Tamesis, 2008.

Latinamericanism after 9/11. Durham: Duke University Press, 2011.

Binder, Wolfgang. *Partial Autobiographies: Interviews with Twenty Chicano Poets.* Erlangen, Germany: Palm and Enke, 1985.

Blanco, Maria del Pilar. *Ghost-Watching American Modernity: Haunting, Landscape, and the Hemispheric Imagination.* New York: Fordham University Press, 2012.

Bokser, Julia A. "Sor Juana's Rhetoric of Silence." *Rhetoric Review* 25 (2006): 5–21.

"Reading and Writing Sor Juna's Arch: Rhetorics of Belonging, Criollo Identity and Feminist Histories." *Rhetoric Society Quarterly* 42 (2012): 144–63.

Bolton, Herbert. *The Spanish Borderlands: A Chronicle of Old Florida and the Southwest.* New Haven: Yale University Press, 1921.

Bost, Suzanne. *Encarnación: Illness and Body Politics in Chicana Feminist Literature.* New York: Fordham University Press, 2009.

Mulattas and Mestizas: Representing Mixed Identities in the Americas, 1850–2000. Athens: University of Georgia Press, 2005.

Bost, Suzanne, and Francis R. Aparicio, eds. *The Routledge Companion to Latino/a Literature.* New York: Routledge, 2012.

Boyle, Catherine. "Sor Juana Inés de la Cruz. The Tenth Muse and the Difficult Freedom to Be." *The Cambridge History of Mexican Literature*. New York: Cambridge University Press, Forthcoming.

Brady, Mary Pat. *Extinct Lands, Temporal Geographies: Chicana Literature and the Urgency of Space*. Durham: Duke University Press, 2002.

"'So Your Social Is Your Real?' Vernacular Theorists and Economic Transformation." *Contemporary US Latino/a Literary Criticism*. Eds. Lyn Di Iorio Sandín and Richard Perez. New York: Palgrave Macmillan, 2007.

Brickhouse, Anna. *Transamerican Literary Relations and the Nineteenth-Century Public Sphere*. New York: Cambridge University Press, 2004.

The Unsettlement of America: Translation, Interpretation, and the Story of Don Luis de Velasco, 1560–1945. New York: Oxford University Press, 2014.

Brotherston, Gordon. *The Book of the Fourth World: Reading the Native Americas through their Literature*. New York: Cambridge University Press, 1995.

Broyles-González, Yolanda. *El Teatro Campesino: Theater in the Chicano Movement*. Austin: University of Texas Press, 1994.

Bruce-Novoa, Juan. *Chicano Poetry: A Response to Chaos*. Austin: University of Texas Press, 1982.

Retrospace: Collected Esssays on Chicano Literature. Houston: Arte Público Press, 1990.

"Shipwrecked in the Seas of Signification: Cabeza de Vaca's *Relación* and Chicano Literature." *Reconstructing a Chicano/a Literary Heritage: Hispanic Colonial Literature of the Southwest*. Ed. María Herrera-Sobek. Tucson: University of Arizona Press, 1993: 3–23.

Burkhart, Louise M. *Aztecs on Stage: Religious Theater in Colonial Mexico*. Norman: University of Oklahoma Press, 2011.

Buscaglia-Salgado, José. *Undoing Empire: Race and Nation in the Mulatto Caribbean*. Minneapolis: University of Minnesota Press, 2003.

Bustamante, Fernanda. "Representar el «problema de lo haitiano» o el problema de representar lo haitiano: una lectura de textos literarios dominicanos del 2000". *452 °F Revista Electrónica de teoría de la literatura y literatura comparada* 11 (2014): 125–41.

Cabán, Pedro. "The New Synthesis of Latin American and Latino Studies," in *Borderless Borders: US Latinos, Latin Americans, and the Paradox of Interdependence*. Eds. Frank Bonilla, Edwin Meléndez, Rebecca Morales, and María de los Angeles Torres. Philadelphia: Temple University Press, 1998: 195–215.

Calderón, Héctor. *Narratives of Greater Mexico: Essays on Chicano Literary History, Genre, and Border*. Austin: University of Texas Press, 2005.

Calderón, Héctor and José David Saldívar, eds. *Criticism in the Bordrlands: Studies in Chicano Literature, Culture and Ideology*. Durham: Duke University Press, 1991.

Calderón, Roberto, and Emilio Zamora. "Manuela Solís Sager and Emma Tenayuca: A Tribute." *Chicana Voices: Intersections of Class, Race, and Gender*. Eds. Teresa Córdova, Norma Cantú, Gilberto Cárdenas, Juan García, and Christine Sierra. Austin: University of Texas Center for Mexican American Studies, 1986.

Caminero-Santangelo, Marta. *Documenting the Undocumented: Latino/a Narrative and Social Justice in the Era of Operation Gatekeeper*. Gainesville: University Press of Florida, 2016.

"Historias Transfronterizas: Contemporary Latina/o Literature of Migration." *The Cambridge Companion to Latina/o American Literature.* Ed. John Morán González. New York: Cambridge University Press, 2016: 231–46.

On Latinidad: US Latino Literature and the Construction of Ethnicity. Gainesville: University Press of Florida, 2007.

Campa, Román de la. "Latin Americans and Latinos: Terms of Engagement." *Contemporary US Latino/a Literary Criticism.* Eds. Lyn Di Iorio Sandín and Richard Perez. New York: Palgrave Macmillan, 2007.

Candelaria, Cordelia. *Chicano Poetry: A Critical Introduction.* Westport, CT: Greenwood Press, 1986.

Cantú, Norma Elia. "Latin@ Poetics: Voices." *The Cambridge Companion to Latina/o American Literature.* Ed. John Morán González. New York: Cambridge University Press, 2016.

"Memoir, Autobiography, Testimonio." *The Routledge Companion to Latino/a Literature.* Eds. Frances R. Aparicio and Suzanne Bost. New York: Routledge, 2013: 310–22.

"The Writing of *Canícula*: Breaking Boundaries, Finding Forms." *Chicana Feminisms: A Critical Reader.* Eds. Aída Hurtado, Norma Klahn, Olga Nájera-Ramírez, and Patricia Zavella. Durham: Duke University Press, 2003: 97–108.

Castellanos, Rosario. "Asedio a Sor Juana." *Juicios Sumarios.* Xalapa: Universidad Veracruzana, 1966: 19–25.

"Otra vez Sor Juana." *Juicios Sumarios.* Xalapa: Universidad Veracruzana, 1966: 26–30.

"Lección de cocina." *Album de familia.* México: Joaquín Moniz, 1972.

Castillo, Debra. *Redreaming America: Toward a Bilingual American Culture.* Albany: State University of New York Press, 2004.

Chabram-Dernersesian, Angie. "'I Throw Punches for My Race, But I Don't Want to Be a Man.'" *Cultural Studies.* Eds. Lawrence Grossberg, Cary Nelson, and Paula Treichler. New York: Routledge, 1992: 81–96.

Chancy, Myriam. *From Sugar to Revolution: Women's Visions of Haiti, Cuba, and the Dominican Republic.* Waterloo: Wilfrid Laurier University Press, 2012.

Framing Silence: Revolutionary Novels by Haitian Women. New Brunswick, NJ: Rutgers University Press, 1997.

Chavez, Leo R. *Covering Immigration: Popular Images and the Politics of the Nation.* Berkeley: University of California Press, 2001.

The Latino Threat: Constructing Immigrants, Citizens, and the Nation. Palo Alto, CA: Stanford University Press, 2008.

Christian, Karen. *Show and Tell: Identity as Performance in US Latina/o Fiction.* Albuquerque: University of New Mexico Press, 1997.

Clamurro, William H. "Sor Juana Inés de la Cruz Reads her Portrait." *Revista de Estudios Hispánicos* 20. 1(January 1986): 27–43.

Cocco de Filippis, Daisy, and Franklyn Gutiérrez, eds. *Literatura dominicana en los Estados Unidos: Presencia temprana 1900–1950.* Santo Domingo: Editora Búho, 2001.

Colahan, Clark A. *The Visions of Sor María de Agreda: Writing Knowledge and Power.* Tucson: University of Arizona Press, 1994.

Colón, David A., ed. *Between Day and Night: New and Selected Poems, 1946–2010 by Miguel González-Gerth.* Fort Worth: Texas Christian University Press, 2013.

Contreas, Sheila Marie. *Blood Lines: Myth, Indigenism, and Chicana/o Literature*. Austin: University of Texas Press, 2008.

Cornejo Polar, Antonio. "El discurso de la armonía imposible: (el Inca Garcilaso de la Vega: discurso y recepción social)." *Revista de crítica literaruia latinoamericana* 19.38 (1993): 73–80.

Escribir en el aire. *Ensayo sobre la heterogeneidad sociocultural en las literaturas andinas*. Lima: Centro de Estudios Literarios "Antonio Cornejo Polar," Latinoamericana Editores, 2003.

Coronado, Raúl. *A World Not to Come: A History of Latino Writing and Print Culture*. Cambridge: Harvard University Press, 2013.

Cortés, Jason. *Macho Ethics: Masculinity and Self-Representation in Latino Caribbean Narrative*. Lewisburg, PA: Bucknell University Press, 2015.

Cotera, María. *Native Speakers: Ella Deloria, Zora Neal Hurston, Jovita González, and the Poetics of Culture*. Austin: University of Texas Press, 2010.

Cruz-Malavé, Arnaldo. *Queer Latino Testimonio, Keith Haring and Juanito Extravaganza: Hard Tails*. New York: Palgrave Macmillan, 2007.

Cuevas, T. Jackie. "Imagining Queer Chican@s in the Post-Borderlands." *Revue LISA/LISA e-journal*. International Perspectives on the Transforming USA in the 21st Century. 11.2 (2013).

Cutler, John Alba. *Ends of Assimilation: The Formation of Chicano Literature*. New York: Oxford University Press, 2015.

Dalleo, Raphael. *Caribbean Literature and the Public Sphere: From the Plantation to the Postcolonial*. Charlottesville: University of Virginia Press, 2011.

American Imperialism's Undead: *The Occupation of Haiti and the Rise of Caribbean Anticolonialism*. Charlottesville: University of Virginia Press, 2016.

Dalleo, Raphael and Elena Machado Sáez. *The Latino/a Canon and the Emergence of Post-Sixties Literature*. New York: Palgrave Macmillan, 2007.

Dávila, Arlene and Agustin Laó-Montes. *Mambo Montage: The Latinization of New York City*. New York: Columbia University Press, 2001.

DeCosta-Willis, Miriam. *Daughters of the Diaspora: Afra-Hispanic Writers*. Kingston, Jamaica: Ian Randle Publishers, 2003.

"Sandra María Esteves's Nuyorican Poetics: The Signifying Difference." *Afro-Hispanic Review* 23.2 (2004): 3–12.

DeGuzmán, María. *Buenas Noches, American Culture: Latina/o Aesthetics of Night*. Bloomington: Indiana University Press, 2012.

Spain's Long Shadow: *The Black Legend, Off-Whiteness, and Anglo-American Empire*. Minneapolis: University of Minnesota Press, 2005.

Delgadillo, Theresa. *Spiritual Mestizaje: Religion, Gender, Race, and Nation in Contemporary Chicana Narrative*. Durham: Duke University Press, 2011.

Díaz, Junot. "MFA vs POC." *The New Yorker* (April 30, 2014).

Dowdy, Michael. *Broken Souths: Latina/o Poetic Responses to Neoliberalism and Globalization*. Tucson: University of Arizona Press, 2013.

Dúran, Isabel. "Latina/o Life Writing: Autobiography, Memoir, *Testimonio*." *The Cambridge Companion to Latino American Literature*. Ed. John Morán González. New York: Cambridge University Press, 2016: 161–77.

Dworkin y Méndez, Kenya. "The Tradition of Hispanic Theater and the WPA Federal Theater Project in Tampa-Ybor City, Florida." *Recovering the US Hispanic Literary Heritage, Volume 2.* Eds. Erlinda Gonzales-Berry and Chuck Tatum. Houston: Arte Público Press, 1996.

"From Factory to Floodlights: Original Spanish-Language Cigar Workers' Theatre in Ybor City and West Tampa, Florida." *Recovering the US Hispanic Literary Heritage, Volume 3.* Eds. María Herrera-Sobek and Virginia Sánchez Korrol. Houston: Arte Público Press, 2000.

Esquibel, Catriona Rueda. *With Her Machete in Her Hand: Reading Chicana Lesbians.* Austin: University of Texas Press, 2006.

Falconer, Blas, and Lorraine M. López, *The Other Latin@: Writing Against a Singular Identity.* Tucson: University of Arizon Press, 2011.

Falconi, José Luis, and José Antonio Mazzotti, eds. *The Other Latinos: Central and South Americans in the United States.* Cambridge: Harvard University Press, 2007.

Fiol-Matta, Licia. *The Great Woman Singer: Gender and Voice in Puerto Rican Music.* Durham, NC: Duke University Press, 2017.

Flores, Juan. *The Diaspora Strikes Back: Caribeño Tales of Learning and Turning.* New York: Routledge, 2009.

Divided Borders: Essays on Puerto Rican Identity. Houston: Arte Público, 1993.

From Bomba to Hip-Hop: Puerto Rican Culture and Latino Identity. New York: Columbia University Press, 2000.

"The Latino Imaginary: Meanings of Community and Identity." *The Latin American Cultural Studies Reader.* Eds. Ana del Sarto, Alicia Ríos, and Abril Trigo. Durham: Duke University Press, 2004: 606–19.

"Nueva York, Diaspora City: Latinos Between and Beyond." *Bilingual Games: Some Literary Investigations.* Ed. Doris Sommer. New York: Palgrave, 2003: 69–76.

Salsa Rising: New York Latin Music of the Sixties Generation. New York: Oxford University Press, 2016.

Flores, Richard. *Remembering the Alamo: Memory, Modernity, and the Master Symbol.* Austin: University of Texas Press, 2002.

Franco, Jean. *Plotting Women: Gender and Representation in Mexico.* New York: Columbia University Press, 1989.

García, Emily. "On the Borders of Independence: Manuel Torres and Spanish American Independence in Filadelphia." *The Latino Nineteenth Century.* Eds. Rodrigo Lazo and Jesse Alemán. New York: New York University Press, 2016: 71–88.

García, Patricia M, and John Morán González, eds. "Latina/o Literature: The Trans-Atlantic and the Trans-american in Dialogue." *Symbolism: An International Annual of Critical Aesthetics.* Berlin: DeGruyter, 2017.

García-Caro, Pedro. *After the Nation: Postnational Satire in the Works of Carlos Fuentes and Thomas Pynchon.* Chicago: Northwestern University Press, 2014.

García-Peña, Lorgia. *Borders of Dominicanidad: Race, Nation, and the Archives of Contradiction.* Durham: Duke University Press, 2016.

"Un-bordering Hispaniola: David Pérez's Performance Actions of Haitian-Dominican Solidarity. *Afro-Hispanic Review.* 32:2 (2013): 57–70.

Gaspar de Alba, Alicia. *[Un]Framing the "Bad Woman": Sor Juana, Malinche, Coyolxauhqui, and Other Rebels with a Cause.* Austin: University of Texas Press, 2014.

755

Gil Amate, Virginia. *Sueños de unidad hispánica en el siglo XVIII. Un estudio de Tardes americanas de José Joaquín Granados y Gálvez*. Alicante, Spain: Centro de Estudios Mario Benedetti, Universidad de Alicante, 2012.

Glantz, Margo. *Sor Juana Inés de la Cruz: ¿Hagiografía o autobiografía?* Mexico: Grijalbo-Universidad Nacional Autónoma de México, 1995.

    ed. *Sor Juana Inés de la Cruz y sus contemporáneos*. Mexico: Facultad de Filosofía y Letras Universidad Autónoma de México, 1998.

González, Christopher. "Latino Sci-Fi: Cognition and Narrative Design in Alex Rivera's *Sleep Dealer.*" *Latinos and Narrative Media: Participation and Portrayal*. Ed. Frederick Luis Aldama. New York: Palgrave-Macmillan, 2013: 211–23.

González, John Morán. "Between Ethnic Americans and Racial Subjects: Latina/o Literature, 1936–1959." *The Cambridge Companion to Latino American Literature*. Ed. John Morán González. New York: Cambridge University Press, 2016: 36–54.

    Border Renaissance: The Texas Centennial and the Emergence of Mexican American Literature. Austin: University of Texas Press, 2009.

    The Troubled Union: Expansionist Imperatives in Post-Reconstruction American Novels. Columbus: Ohio State University Press, 2010.

    ed. *The Cambridge Companion to Latino American Literature*. New York: Cambridge University Press, 2016.

González, Juan. *Harvest of Empire. A History of Latinos in America*. New York: Viking, 2000.

González, Marcial. *Chicano Novels and the Politics of Form: Race, Class, and Reification*. Ann Arbor: University of Michigan Press, 2008.

González, Tanya. "The (Gothic) Gift of Death in Cherríe Moraga's *The Hungry Woman.*" *Chicana/Latina Studies* 7.1 (2007): 44–77.

González Acosta, Alejandro. *El enigma de Jicoténcal. Dos estudios sobre el héroe de Tlxacala*. Mexico: Instituto Tlaxcalteca de Cultura, 1997.

Gracia, Jorge J.E., Lynette M.F. Bosch, Isabel Alvarez-Borland, eds. *Identity, Memory, and Diaspora: Voices of Cuban-American Artists, Writers and Philosophers*. Albany: State University of New York Press, 2008.

Grosfoguel, Ramón. "The Epistemic Decolonial Turn: Beyond Political-Economy Paradigms." *Cultural Studies* 21.2/3 (March/May 2007).

Gruesz, Kirsten Silva. *Ambassadors of Culture. The Transamerican Origins of Latino Writing*. Princeton: Princeton University Press, 2002.

    "Alien Speech, Incorporated: On the Cultural History of Spanish in the US." *American Literary History* 25.1 (Spring 2013): 18–32.

    "Utopia Latina: *The Ordinary Seamen* in Extraordinary Times." *Modern Fiction Studies* 49.1 (2003): 54–83.

    "Unsettlers and Speculators," *PMLA* 131.3 (May 2016): 743–51.

    "What Was Latino Literature?" *PMLA* 127.2 (2012): 335–41.

Gruzinski, Serge. *La colonisation de l'imaginaire: societés indigènes et occidentalisation dans le Mexique espagnol, XVIe-XVIIe siècle*. Paris: Gallimard, 1988.

Guaman Poma de Ayala, Felipe. *El primer nueva corónica y buen gobierno*. Digital edition (revised 2004). Copenhagen, The Royal Library, GKS 2232 4°, 1615; on The Guaman Poma Website. www.kb.dk/permalink/2006/poma/info/en/frontpage.htm

Guidotti-Hernandez, Nicole. *Unspeakable Violence: Remapping US and Mexican National Imaginaries*. Durham: Duke University Press, 2011.

Gutiérrez, Laura G. *Performing Mexicanidad: Vendidas y Cabareteras on the Transnational Stage*. Austin: University of Texas Press, 2010.

Gutiérrez, Ramón. "The Politics of Theater in Colonial New Mexico: Drama and the Rhetoric of Conquest." *Reconstructing a Chicano/a Literary Heritage: Hispanic Colonial Literature of the Southwest*. Ed. María Herrera-Sobek. Tucson: University of Arizona Press, 1993: 49–67.

Gutiérrez-Jones, Carl. *Rethinking the Borderlands: Between Chicano Culture and Legal Discourse*. Berkeley: University of California Press, 1995.

Habell-Pallán, Michelle. *Loca Motion: The Travels of Chicana and Latina Popular Culture*. New York: New York University Press, 2005.

Halperin, Laura. *Intersections of Harm: Narratives of Latina Deviance and Defiance*. New Brunswick, NJ: Rutgers University Press, 2015.

Hames-García, Michael. *Fugitive Thought: Prison Movements, Race, and the Meaning of Justice*. Minneapolis: University of Minnesota Press, 2004.

Hames-García, Michael, and Ernesto Javier Martínez, eds. *Gay Latino Studies: A Critical Reader*. Durham: Duke University Press, 2011.

Hanna, Monica, Jennifer Harford Vargas and José David Saldívar, eds. *Junot Díaz and the Decolonial Imagination*. Durham: Duke University Press, 2016.

Hedrick, Tace. *Chica Lit: Popular Latina Fiction and Americanization in the Twenty-First Century*. Pittsburgh: University of Pittsburgh Press, 2015.

Henríquez Ureña, Pedro. *El Español en Santo Domingo*. 4th ed. Santo Domingo: Editora Taller, 1982.

Literary Currents in Hispanic America. Cambridge: Harvard University Press, 1945.

Las corrientes literarias en la América Hispánica. Mexico: Fondo de Cultura Económica, 1945.

Seis ensayos en busca de nuestra expresión. Obra Crítica. Ed. Emma S. Speratti Piñero. Mexico: Fondo de Cultura Económica, 1960.

La Utopía de América. Ed. Angel Rama and Rafael Giardot. Caracas: Biblioteca Ayacucho, 1978.

Heredia, Juanita and Bridget Kevane, eds. *Latina Self-Portraits: Interviews with Contemporary Women Writers*. Albuquerque: University of New Mexico Press, 2000.

"South American Latino/a Writers in the United States." *The Routledge Companion to Latino/a Literature*. Eds. Suzanne Bost and Frances Aparicio. New York: Routledge, 2012: 436–44.

Transnational Latina Narratives in the Twenty-First Century: The Politics of Gender, Race and Migrations. New York: Palgrave Macmillan, 2009.

Hernández, Carmen Dolores. *Puerto Rican Voices in English: Interviews with Writers*. Westport, CT: Praeger, 1997.

Hernández, Ellie D. *Postnationalism in Chicana/o Literature and Culture*. Austin: University of Texas Press, 2009.

Hernandez, Inés. "Sara Estela Ramirez: Sembradora." *Legacy* 6.1 (1989): 13–26.

Herrera, Brian. *Latin Numbers: Playing Latino in Twentieth Century US Popular Performance*. Ann Arbor: University of Michigan Press, 2015.

Herrera-Sobek, María. *Northward Bound: The Mexican Immigrant Experience in Ballad and Song*. Bloomington: Indiana University Press, 1993.

ed. *Reconstructing a Chicano/a Literary Heritage: Hispanic Colonial Literature of the Southwest*. Tucson: University of Arizona Press, 1993.

Hind, Emily. "Sor Juana, an Official Habit: Twentieth-Century Mexican Culture." *Approaches to Teaching the Works of Sor Juana Inés de la Cruz*. Eds. Emilie L. Bergmann and Stacey Schlau. New York: The Modern Language Association of America, 2007: 245–55.

Hoffman, Léon-Francois. "La République dominicaine dans la fiction haïtienne." *The Caribbean Writer as Warrior of the Imaginary: L'ecrivain Caribéen, guerrier de l'imaginaire*. Eds. Kathleen Gyssels and Bénédicte Ledent. Amsterdam: Rodopi, 2008: 345–57.

Hoffnung-Garskoff, Jesse. "The World of Arturo Alfonso Schomburg." *The Afro-Latin@ Reader: History and Culture in the United States*. Eds. Miriam Jiménez Román and Juan Flores. Durham: Duke University Press, 2010: 70–91.

Hoyos, Héctor. *Beyond Bolaño: The Global Latin American Novel*. New York: Columbia University Press, 2015.

Huerta, Jorge. *Chicano Drama: Performance, Society and Myth*. New York: Cambridge University Press, 2000.

Chicano Theater: Themes and Forms. Tempe, AZ: Bilingual Press. 1981.

Irrizary, Guillermo. *José Luis Gonzalez: El intelectual nómada*.Rio Piedras, Puerto Rico: Editorial Callejón, 2006.

Irrizary, Ylce. *Chicana/o and Latina/o Fiction: The New Memory of Latinidad*. Champaign: University of Illinois Press, 2016.

Jáuregui, Carlos. *Canibalia: canibalismo, calibanismo, antropofagia cultural y consumo en América Latina*. Madrid: Iberoamericana Vervuert, 2008.

Jiménez, Francisco, ed. *The Identification and Analysis of Chicano Literature*. New York: Bilingual Press, 1979.

Jiménez Román, Miriam, and Juan Flores, eds. *The Afro-Latin@Reader: History and Culture in the United States*. Durham: Duke University Press, 2010.

Jonassaint, Jean. "Des productions littéraires haïtiennes aux États-Unis (1948–1986)." *Journal of Haitian Studies* 5/6 (1999–2000): 4–19.

Kanellos, Nicolás. *Hispanic Immigrant Literature: El Sueño del Retorno*. Austin: University of Texas Press, 2012.

"El Clamor Público: Resisting the American Empire." *California History* 84.2 (2006–2007): 10–18, 69–70.

A History of Hispanic Theatre in the United States: Origins to 1940. Austin: University of Texas Press, 1990.

Kanellos, Nicolás and Helvetia Martell. *Hispanic Periodicals in the United States, Origins to 1960: A Brief History and Comprehensive Bibliography*. Houston: Arte Público Press, 2000.

et al. *Herencia: The Anthology of Hispanic Literature of the United States*. New York: Oxford University Press, 2002.

Kevane, Bridget. "Confessions of an Editor: César Andreu Iglesias and the 'Memorias de Bernardo Vega.'" *Latin American Literary Review* 27.53 (1999): 67–80.

Kirschner, Luz Angélica, ed. *Expanding Latinidad: An Inter-American Perspective*. Tempe, AZ: Bilingual Review Press, 2012.

Kutzinski, Vera M. *Against the American Grain: Myth and History in William Carlos Williams, Jay Wright, and Nicolás Guillén.* Baltimore: Johns Hopkins University Press, 1987.

La Fountain-Stokes, Lawrence. *Queer Ricans: Cultures and Sexualities in the Diaspora.* Minneapolis: University of Minnesota Press, 2009.

"Queering Latina/o Literature." *The Cambridge Companion to Latina/o American Literature.* Ed. John Morán González. New York: Cambridge University Press, 2016: 178–94.

Lamadrid, Enrique R. *Hermanitos comanchitos: Indo-Hispano Rituals of Captivity and Redemption.* Albuquerque: University of New Mexico Press, 2003.

Lamas, Carmen. "The Black Lector and Martín Morúa Delgado's *Sofía* (1891) and *La familia Unzúazu* (1901)." *Latino Studies* 13 (Spring 2015): 113–30.

Lane, Jill. *Blackface Cuba, 1840–1895.* Philadelphia: University of Pennsylvania Press, 2005.

"On Colonial Forgetting: The Conquest of New Mexico and Its *Historia*." *The Ends of Performance.* Eds. Peggy Phelan and Jill Lane. New York: New York University Press, 1998: 52–69.

Laó-Montes, Agustin. "Islands at the Crossroads: Puerto Ricanness Traveling between the Translocal Nation and the Global City." *Puerto Rican Jam: Rethinking Nationalism and Colonialism.* Eds. Frances Negrón-Muntaner and Ramón Grosfoguel. Minneapolis: University of Minnesota, 1997: 169–88.

Lazo, Rodrigo. "The Trans-American Literature of Conquest and Exile, 1823–1885." *The Cambridge Companion to Latina/o American Literature.* Ed. John Morán González. New York: Cambridge University Press, 2016: 3–16.

Writing to Cuba: Filibustering and Cuban Exiles in the United States. Chapel Hill: University of North Carolina Press, 2005.

Lazo, Rodrigo and Jesse Alemán, eds. *The Latino Nineteenth Century.* New York: New York University Press, 2016.

Leal, Luis. "Jicoténcal, primera novela histórica en castellano." *Revista Iberoamericana* 25.49 (1960): 9–31.

"Mexican American Literature: A Historical Perspective." *Modern Chicano Writers: A Collection of Essays.* Eds. Joseph Sommers and Tomás Ybarra Frausto. Englewood Cliffs, NJ: Prentice Hall, 1979: 18–30.

Ledesma, Alberto. "Undocumented Crossings: Narratives of Mexican Immigration to the United States." *Culture Across Borders: Mexican Immigration and Popular Culture.* Eds. David R. Maciel and María Herrera-Sobek. Tucson: University of Arizona Press, 1998: 67–98.

L'Hoeste, Héctor Fernández and Juan Poblete, *Redrawing the Nation: National Identity in Latin/o American Comics.* New York: Palgrave Macmillan, 2009.

Lima, Lázaro. *The Latino Body: Crisis Identities in American Literary and Cultural Memory.* New York: New York University Press, 2007.

Limón, José E. *American Encounters: Greater Mexico, the United States, and the Erotics of Culture.* Boston: Beacon, 1999.

Américo Paredes: Culture and Critique. Austin: University of Texas Press, 2013.

Dancing with the Devil: Society and Cultural Poetics in Mexican American South Texas. Madison: University of Wisconsin Press, 1994.

Mexican Ballads, Chicano Poems: History and Influence in Mexican American Social Poetry. Berkeley: University of California Press, 1992.

Lindo-Fuentes, Héctor, Erik Ching, and Rafael A. Lara-Martínez. *Remembering a Massacre in El Salvador: The Insurrection of 1932, Roque Dalton, and the Politics of Historical Memory*. Albuquerque: University of New Mexico Press, 2007.

Lister, Elissa L. *Le Conflit haïtiano-dominicain dans la littérature caribéenne*. Pétion-Ville, Haiti: C3 Editions, 2013.

Lomas, Clara. "Introduction: Revolutionary Women and the Alternative Press in the Borderlands." *The Rebel*. By Leonor Villegas de Magnón. Ed. Clara Lomas. Houston: Arte Público Press, 1994: xi-lvi.

Lomas, Laura. *Translating Empire: José Martí, Migrant Latino Subjects and American Modernities*. Durham: Duke University Press, 2008.

"Migration and Decolonial Politics in Two Afro-Latino Poets: 'Pachín' Marín and 'Tato' Laviera." *Review: Literature and Arts of the Americas* 47.2 (2014): 155–63.

"The Trans-American Literature of Empire and Revolution, 1880–1938." *The Cambridge Companion to Latina/o American Literature*. Ed. John Morán González. New York: Cambridge University Press, 2016: 17–35.

Lomelí, Francisco A. and Donaldo W. Urioste, eds. *Historical Dictionary of US Latino Literature*. Guilford: Rowman and Littlefield, 2016.

López, Antonio. *Unbecoming Blackness: The Diaspora Cultures of Afro-Cuban America*. New York: New York University Press, 2012.

López, Iraida H. *Impossible Returns: Narratives of the Cuban Diaspora*. Gainesville: University Press of Florida, 2015.

López, Marissa K. *Chicano Nations: The Hemispheric Origins of Mexican American Literature*. New York: New York University Press, 2011.

López, Tiffany Ana. "The 1980s: Latina/o Literature during the 'Decade of the Hispanic." *The Cambridge Companion to Latina/o American Literature*. Ed. John Morán González. New York: Cambridge University Press, 2016: 91–110.

López-Peláez Casellas, Milagros. *What about the Girls?: Estrategias narrativas de resistencia en la primera literatura chicana*. Oxford: Peter Lang, 2012.

Lora H., Quisqueya. "La construcción de Haití en el imaginario dominicano del siglo XIX." *República Dominicana y Haití: Derecho a vivir*. Santo Domingo: Fundación Juan Bosch, 2014: 171–204.

Lozano, Tomás. *Cantemos al alba: Origins of Songs, Sounds, and Liturgical Drama of Hispanic New Mexico*. Ed. Rima Montoya. Albuquerque: University of New Mexico Press, 2007.

Luciani, Frederick. "Recreaciones de Sor Juana en la narrativa y teatro hispano/norteamericano, 1952–1988." *Y diversa de mí misma entre vuestras plumas ando. Homenaje internacional a Sor Juana Inés de la Cruz*. Ed. Sara Poot Herrera. Mexico: El Colegio de México, 1993: 395–408.

Ludmer, Josefina. "Las tretas del débil." Eds. Patricia González and Eliana Ortega. *La sartén por el mango. Encuentro de escritoras latinoamericanas*. Río Piedras, Puerto Rico: Ediciones Huracán, 1984: 47–55.

"Una máquina para leer el siglo XIX." *Revista de la Universidad Autónoma de México* 530 (1995): 65–66.

Lugo-Ortiz, Agnes. "La antología y el archivo: Reflexiones en torno a *Herencia, En Otra Voz* y los límites del saber." *Recovering the US Hispanic Literary Heritage Project*. V. Houston: Arte Público Press, 2006: 139–68.

Identidades imaginadas: Biografía y nacionalidad en el horizonte de la guerra (Cuba 1860-1898). Río Piedras, Puerto Rico: Editorial de la Universidad de Puerto Rico, Serie Caribe, 1999.

Luis, William. *Dance Between Two Cultures: Latino Caribbean Literature Written in the United States.* Nashville: Vanderbuilt University Press, 1997.

Literary Bondage: Slavery in Cuban Narrative. Austin: University of Texas Press, 2012.

Luis-Brown, David. *Waves of Decolonization: Discourses of Race and Hemispheric Citizenship in Cuba, Mexico, and the United States.* Durham: Duke University Press, 2008.

Machado Sáez, Elena. *Market Aesthetics: The Purchase of the Past in Caribbean Diasporic Fiction.* Charlottesville: University of Virginia Press, 2015.

Maeseneer, Rita De. *Encuentro con la narrativa dominicana contemporánea.* Madrid/Frankfurt: Iberoamericana/Vervuert, 2006.

Maldonado-Torres, Nelson. "On the Coloniality of Being: Contributions to the Development of a Concept." *Cultural Studies* 21.2 (2007): 240–70.

"The Time of History, the Times of Gods, and the *Damnés de la terre.*" *Worlds & Knowledges Otherwise* (Spring 2006): 1–12.

Mangini, Shirley. *Las modernas de Madrid: Las grandes intelectuales de la vanguardia.* Barcelona: Ediciones Península, 2001.

Mann, Kristin Dutcher. *The Power of Song: Music and Dance in the Mission Communities of Northern New Spain, 1590–1810.* Palo Alto, CA: Stanford University Press, 2010.

Maríñez, Sophie. "Mito y feminismo en *Marassá y la Nada* de Alanna Lockward." *Revista Canadiense de Estudios Hispánicos* 42.2 (2016).

"Poética de la Relación en *Dominicanish* de Josefina Báez." *La Torre, Revista de la Universidad de Puerto Rico* 10.35 (January–March 2005): 149–60.

Márquez, Roberto. *A World Among these Islands: Essays on Literature, Race, and National Identity in Antillean America.* Amherst: University of Massachusetts Press, 2010.

Martínez, Ernesto Javier. *On Making Sense: Queer Race Narratives of Intelligibility.* Palo Alto, CA: Stanford University Press, 2012.

Martinez, Manuel Luis. *Countering the Counterculture: Rereading Postwar American Dissent from Jack Kerouac to Tomás Rivera.* Madison: University of Wisconsin Press, 2003.

Martínez-San Miguel, Yolanda. *Coloniality of Diasporas: Rethinking Intra-Colonial Migrations in a Pan Caribbeann Context.* New York: Palgrave, 2014.

From Lack to Excess: Minor Readings of Latin American Colonial Discourse. Lewisburg, PA: Bucknell University Press, 2008.

"Otra vez Sor Juana: leer la heterogeneidad colonial en un contexto transatlántico." *Revista de Crítica Literaria Latinoamericana* XXXI.62 (2005): 53–71.

Marzán, Julio. *The Spanish American Roots of William Carlos Williams.* Austin: University of Texas Press, 1994.

Mazzotti, José Antonio. "Criollismo, Creole and Créolité." *Critical Terms in Caribean and Latin American Thought: Historical and Institutional Trajectories.* Eds. Yolanda Martínez-San Miguel, Ben Sifuentes-Jáuregui, and Marisa Belausteguigoitia. New York: Palgrave, 2016: 87–100.

"Epic, Creoles and Nation in Spanish America." *A Companion to the Literatures of Colonial America.* Eds. Susan Castillo and Ivy Schweitzer. Oxford: Blackwell Publishing Ltd., 2005: 480–99.

McCracken, Ellen. *New Latina Narrative: The Feminine Space of Postmodern Ethnicity.* Tucson: University of Arizona Press, 1999.

McKenna, Teresa. *Migrant Song: Politics and Process in Contemporary Chicano Literature.* Austin: University of Texas Press, 1997.

McKnight, Joy, and Leo J. Garofalo, eds. *Afro-Latino Voices: Narratives from the Early Modern Ibero-Atlantic World, 1550–1812.* Indianapolis: Hackett Publishing Company, 2009.

McMahon, Marci. R. *Domestic Negotiations: Gender, Nation, and Self-Fashioning in US Mexicana and Chicana Literature and Art.* New Brunswick, NJ: Rutgers University Press, 2013.

Meléndez, A. Gabriel. *So Not All Is Lost: The Poetics of Print in Nuevomexicano Communities, 1834–1958.* Albequerque: University of New Mexico Press, 1997.

  Spanish-language Newspapers in New Mexico, 1834–1958. Tucson: University of Arizona Press, 2005.

Mendez Rodenas, Adriana. *Cuba en su imagen. Historia e identidad en la literatura cubana.* Madrid: Editorial Verbum, 2002.

Mendoza, Louis Gerard. *Historia: The Literary Making of Chicana and Chicano History.* College Station: Texas A&M Press, 2001.

Merrim, Stephanie. *Early Modern Women's Writing and Sor Juana Inés de la Cruz.* Nashville: Vanderbilt University Press, 1999.

Mignolo, Walter D. *The Darker Side of the Renaissance: Literacy, Territoriality, & Colonization.* Ann Arbor: University of Michigan Press, 1995.

  The Idea of Latin America. Oxford: Blackwell, 2005.

  Local Histories/Global Designs: Coloniality, Subaltern Knowledges, and Border Thinking. Princeton: Princeton University Press, 2000.

Milian, Claudia. *Latining America: Black-Brown Passages and the Coloring of Latino/a Studies.* Athens: University of Georgia Press, 2013.

  "Latinos and the Like: Reading Mixture and Deracination." *The Cambridge Companion to Latina/o American Literature.* Ed. John Morán González. New York: Cambridge University Press, 2016: 195–212.

Minich, Julie Avril. *Accessible Citizenships: Disability, Nation, and the Cultural Politics of Greater Mexico.* Philadelphia: Temple University Press, 2015.

Mistral, Gabriela. "Silueta de Sor Juana Inés de la Cruz." *Lecturas para mujeres.* [1923.] 1924. 2nd ed. Intro. by Sara Sefchovich. Mexico (1987): 176–79.

Mohr, Eugene. *The Nuyorican Experience: Literature of the Puerto Rican Minority.* Westport, CT: Greenwood Press, 1982.

Molloy, Sylvia. *At Face Value: Autobiographical Writing in Spanish America.* New York: Cambridge University Press, 1991.

Montero, Oscar. *José Martí: An Introduction.* New York: Palgrave Macmillan, 2004.

Montes, Amelia María de la Luz and Anne Elizabeth Goldman, eds. *María Amparo Ruiz de Burton: Critical and Pedagogical Perspectives.* Lincoln: University of Nebraska Press, 2004.

Moore, Robin. *Nationalizing Blackness: Afrocubanismo and Artistic Revolution in Havana, 1920–1940.* Pittsburgh: University of Pittsburgh Press, 1997.

Moraga, Cherríe and Gloria E. Anzaldúa, eds. *This Bridge Called My Back: Writings by Radical Women of Color.* Watertown, MA: Persephone Press, 1981.

Morales, Ed. *Living in Spanglish: The Search for Latino Identity in America*. New York: St. Martin's Press, 2003.

Moreno, Marisel C. *Family Matters: Puerto Rican Women Authors in the Island and the Mainland*. Charlottesville: University of Virginia Press, 2012.

Morrison, Amanda Maria. "Chicanas and 'Chica Lit': Contested *Latinidad* in the Novels of Alisa Valdes-Rodriguez." *Journal of Popular Culture* 43.2 (2010): 309–29.

Moya, Paula. *Learning from Experience: Minority Identities, Multicultural Struggles*. Berekely: University of California Press, 2002.

The Social Imperative: Race, Close Reading, and Contemporary Literary Criticism*. Palo Alto, CA: Stanford University Press, 2015.

Mullen, Edward J., ed. *Langston Hughes in the Hispanic World and Haiti*. Hamden, CT: Archon Books, 1977.

Muñoz, José Esteban. *Cruising Utopia: The Then and There of Queer Futurity*. New York: New York University Press, 2009.

Disidentifications: Queers of Color and the Performance of Politics*. Minneapolis: University of Minnesota Press, 1999.

Negrón-Muntaner, Frances. *Boricua Pop: Puerto Ricans and the Latinization of American Culture*. New York: New York University Press, 2004.

None of the Above: Puerto Ricans in the Global Era*. Palgrave Macmillan, 2007.

Nericcio, William Anthony. *Tex[t]-Mex: Seductive Hallucinations of the 'Mexican' in America*. Austin: University of Texas Press, 2007.

Noel, Urayoán. "For a Caribbean American Graininess: William Carlos Williams, Translator." *Small Axe: A Caribbean Journal of Criticism*, 17.3 (2013): 138–50.

In Visible Movement: Nuyorican Poetry from the Sixties to Slam*. Iowa City: University of Iowa Press, 2014.

Olavarría y Ferrari, Enrique de. *Reseña histórica del teatro en México: 1538–1911*. Vol. I. 6 vols. México, DF: Editorial Porrúa, 1961.

Olguín, B. V. *La Pinta: Chicana/o Prisoner Literature, Culture, and Politics*. Austin: University of Texas Press, 2010.

Ontiveros, Randy J. *In the Spirit of a New People: The Cultural Politics of the Chicano Movement*. New York: New York University Press, 2014.

Orchard, William, and Yolanda Padilla, eds. *Bridges, Borders, and Breaks: History, Narrative, and Nation in Twenty-First Century Chicana/o Literary Criticism*. Pittsburgh: University of Pittsburgh Press, 2016.

Ortíz, Fernando. *Contrapunteo cubano del tabaco y el azúcar*. Caracas: Biblioteca Ayacucho, 1978 (1947).

Ortíz, Ricardo. "The Cold War in the Americas and Latina/o Literature." *The Cambridge Companion to Latina/o American Literature*. Ed. John Morán González. New York: Cambridge University Press, 2016: 72–90.

Cultural Erotics in Cuban America*. Minneapolis: University of Minnesota Press, 2007.

"Edwidge Danticat's 'Latinidad': *The Farming of Bones* and the Cultivation (of Fields) of Knowledge." *Aftermaths: Exile, Migration, and Diaspora Reconsidered*. Eds. Marcus Bullock and Peter Y Paik. New Brunswick, NJ: Rutgers University Press, 2009: 150–72.

Padilla, Genaro. *The Daring Flight of My Pen: Cultural Politics and Gaspar Perez de Villagra's Historia de la Nueva Mexico*. Albuquerque: University of New Mexico Press, 2011.

My History, Not Yours: The Formation of Mexican American Autobiography. Madison: University of Wisconsin Press, 1993.

Padilla, Yajaira M. *Changing Women, Changing Nation: Female Agency, Nationhood, and Identity in Trans-Salvadoran Narratives*. Albany: State University of New York Press, 2012.

Padilla, Yolanda, and William Orchard, eds. *The Plays of Josefina Niggli: Recovered Landmarks of Literature*. Madison: University of Wisconsin Press, 2007.

Paredes, Américo. *Folklore and Culture on the Texas-Mexican Border*. Austin: University of Texas Press, 1995.

    A Texas-Mexican Cancionero: Folksongs of the Lower Border. Austin: University of Texas Press, 1995.

    With His Pistol in His Hand: A Border Ballad and Its Hero. Austin: University of Texas Press, 1958.

Paredez, Deborah. *Selenidad: Selena, Latinos, and the Performance of Memory*. Durham: Duke University Press, 2009.

Park, Stephen M. *The Pan American Imagination: Contested Visions of the Hemisphere in Twentieth-Century Literature*. Charlottesville: University of Virginia Press, 2014.

Paz, Octavio. *El laberinto de la soledad*. Mexico: Fondo de Cultura Económica, 1950.

    Sor Juana Inés de la Cruz o Las trampas de la fé. Barcelona: Seix Barral, 1982.

Perelmuter, Rosa. *Los límites de la femineidad en Sor Juana Inés de la Cruz*. Madrid: Universidad de Navarra-Iberoamericana-Vervuert, 2004.

Perez, Domino Renee. *There Was a Woman: La Llorona from Folklore to Popular Culture*. Austin: University of Texas Press, 2008.

Perez, Emma. *The Decolonial Imaginary: Writing Chicanas into History*. Bloomington: Indiana University Press, 1999.

Pérez, Hiram. *A Taste for Brown Bodies: Gay Modernity and Cosmopolitan Desire*. New York: New York University Press, 2015.

Perez, Richard. "Racial Spills and Disfigured Faces in Piri Thomas' *Down These Mean Streets* and Junot Díaz's "Ysrael." *Contemporary US Latino/a Literary Criticism*. Eds. Lyn Di Iorio Sandín and Richard Perez. New York: Palgrave Macmillan, 2007.

Pérez, Vincent. *Remembering the Hacienda: History and Memory in the Mexican American Southwest*. College Station: Texas A&M Press, 2006.

Pérez Firmat, Gustavo. *Life on the Hyphen: The Cuban-American Way*. Austin: University of Texas, 1994.

Pérez-Rosario, Vanessa. "Affirming an Afro-Latin@ Identity: An Interview with Poet María Teresa (Mariposa) Fernández." *Latino Studies Journal*, 12:3 (Fall 2014).

Pérez-Rosario, Vanessa. *Becoming Julia de Burgos: The Making of a Puerto Rican Icon*. Champaign: University of Illinois Press, 2014.

    ed. *Hispanic Caribbean Migration: Narratives of Displacement*. London: Palgrave MacMillan, 2010.

Pérez-Torres, Rafael. *Mestizaje: Critical Uses of Race in Chicano Culture*. Minneapolis: University of Minnesota Press, 2006.

    Movements in Chicano Poetry: Against Myths, Against Margins. New York: Cambridge University Press. 1995.

Pittman, Thea. "*Mestizaje* and Cyborgism on Either Side of the Line." *The Cambridge Companion to Latina/o American Literature*. Ed. John Morán González. New York: Cambridge University Press, 2016: 213–30.

Poblete, Juan. *Critical Latin American and Latino Studies*. Minneapolis: University of Minnesota Press, 2003.

Poot Herrera, Sara. "Traces of Sor Juana in Contemporary Mexicana and Chicana/Latina Writers." *Approaches to Teaching the Works of Sor Juana Inés de la Cruz*. Eds. Emilie L. Bergmann and Stacey Schlau. New York: Modern Language Association of America, 2007: 256–64.

Poyo, Gerald. *"With All, and for the Good of All: The Emergence of Popular Nationalism in the Cuban Communities of the United States, 1848–1898*. Durham: Duke University Press, 1989.

  Exile and Revolution: José D. Poyo, Key West, and Cuban Independence. Gainesville: University Press of Florida, 2014.

Pratt, Mary Louise. *Imperial Eyes: Travel Writing and Transculturation*. New York: Routledge, 1992.

Quijano, Aníbal. "Colonialidad y Modernidad/Racionalidad." *Perú Indígena* 13.29 (1991): 11–20.
  "Coloniality of Power, Eurocentrism, and Latin America." *Nepantla: Views from South* 1.3 (2000): 533–80.

Quintana, Alvina. *Home Girls: Chicana Literary Voices*. Philadelphia: Temple University Press, 1996.

Rabasa, José. *Without History: Subaltern Studies, The Zapata Insurgency, and the Specter of History*. Pittsburgh: University of Pittsburgh Press, 2010.

  Writing Violence on the Northern Frontier: The Historiography of Sixteenth Century New Mexico and Florida and the Legacy of Conquest. Durham: Duke University Press, 2000.

Rama, Angel. *La ciudad letrada*. Prólogo Hugo Achugar. Montevideo, Uruguay: Arca, 1998.
  Las Máscaras democráticas del modernismo. Montevideo, Uruguay: Fundación Angel Rama, 1985.

  "La dialéctica de la modernidad en José Martí," Estudios Martianos: Memoria del Seminario José Martí. Río Piedras: Editorial Universitaria, Universidad de Puerto Rico, 1974.

Ramírez, Catherine. "Afrofuturism/ Chicanofuturism: Fictive Kin." *Aztlán: A Journal of Chicano Studies* 33 (2008): 185–94.

  The Woman in the Zoot Suit: Gender, Nationalism, and the Cultural Politics of Memory. Durham: Duke University Press, 2009.

Ramos, Julio. *Desencuentros de la modernidad: literatura y política en América Latina*. México: Fondo de Cultura Económica, 1989.
  Divergent Modernities: Culture and Politics in Nineteenth-Century Latin America. Durham: Duke University Press, 2001.

Ramos, Peter. "Cultural Identity, Translation, and William Carlos Williams." *MELUS: Multi-Ethnic Literature of the US* 38.2 (Summer 2013): 89–110.

Ramos-García, Luis A., ed. *The State of Latino Theater in the United States*. New York: Routledge, 2002.

Rebolledo, Tey Diana. *Women Singing in the Snow: A Cultural Analysis of Chicana Literature*. Tuscon: University of Arizona Press, 1995.

  The Chronicles of Panchita Villa and Other Guerrilleras: Essays on Chicana/Latina Literature and Criticism. Austin: University of Texas Press, 2006.

Renda, Mary. *Taking Haiti: Military Occupation and the Culture of US Imperialism, 1915–1940*. Chapel Hill: University of North Carolina Press, 2001.

Riofrio, John D. *Continental Shifts: Migration, Representation, and the Struggle for Justice in Latin(o) America*. Austin: University of Texas Press, 2015.

Rivas, Cecilia. *Salvadoran Imaginaries: Mediated Identities and Cultures of Consumption*. New Brunswick, NJ: Rutgers University Press, 2014.

Rivera, John-Michael. *The Emergence of Mexican America: Recovering Stories of Mexican Peoplehood in US Culture*. New York: New York University Press, 2006.

Rivera, Luis Reyes. "Inside the River of Poetry." *In Motion*. May 19, 2002.

Rivera, Raquel. *New York Ricans from the Hip Hop Zone*. New York: Palgrave Macmillan, 2003.

Rivera-Servera, Ramón H. *Performing Queer Latinidad: Dance, Sexuality, Politics*. Ann Arbor: University of Michigan Press, 2012.

Rodríguez, Ana Patricia. "The Body in Question: The Latina Detective in the Lupe Solano Mystery Series." *From Bananas to Buttocks: The Latina Body in Popular Film and Culture*. Ed. Myra Mendible. Austin: University of Texas Press, 2007: 243–61.

Dividing the Isthmus: Central American Transnational Histories, Literatures & Cultures. Austin: University of Texas Press, 2009.

"Heridas abiertas de América Central: La salvadoreñidad de Romilia Chacón en las novelas negras de Marcos McPeek Villatoro." *Revista Iberoamericana*, 76.231 (2010): 425–42.

Rodríguez, Jaime Javier. *The Literatures of the US-Mexican War: Narrative, Time, and Identity*. Austin: University of Texas Press, 2010.

Rodríguez, Juana Maria. *Queer Latinidad: Identity Practices, Discursive Spaces*. New York: New York University Press, 2003.

Sexual Futures, Queer Gestures, and Other Latina Longings. New York: New York University Press, 2014.

Rodríguez, Néstor. *La isla y su envés: representaciones de lo nacional en el ensayo dominicano contemporáneo*. San Juan: Instituto de Cultura Puertorriqueña, 2003.

Rodriguez, Ralph. *Brown Gumshoes: Detective Fiction and the Search for Chicana/o Identity*. Austin: University of Texas Press, 2005.

Rodriguez, Richard T. "The Aesthetics of Politics: Cultural Nationalist Movements and Latina/o Literature." *The Cambridge Companion to Latina/o American Literature*. Ed. John Morán González. New York: Cambridge University Press, 2016: 57–71.

Next of Kin: The Family in Chicano/a Cultural Politics. Durham, NC: Duke University Press, 2009.

Rodríguez Castro, Malena. "De Memorias y manuscritos: César Andreu Iglesias y Bernardo Vega," *Op. Cit.* 21 (2012–2013): 99–151.

Rodríguez Pagán, Juan Antonio. *Julia en blanco y negro*. San Juan: Sociedad Histórico de Puerto Rico, 2000.

Rogelia, Lily Ibarra, "Gómez de Avellaneda's Sab: A Modernizing Project." 94.3 (2011): 385–95.

Rohrleitner, Marion, and Sarah E. Ryan, eds. *Dialogues across Diasporas: Women Writers, Scholars, and Activists of Africana and Latina Descent in Conversation*. Lanham, MD: Lexington Books, 2013.

Rojas, Rafael. "Diaspora y literatura: Indicios de una ciudadanía postnacional," *Encuentro* 12/13 (1999) : 136–47.

La invención de José Martí. Madrid: Editorial Colibrí, 2000.

Román, David. *Acts of Intervention: Performance, Gay Culture, and AIDS.* Bloomington: Indiana University Press, 1998.

Román, Elda María. *Race and Upward Mobility: Seeking Gatekeeping and Other Class Strategies in Postwar America.* Palo Alto, CA: Stanford University Press, 2017.

Rosaldo, Renato. *Culture and Truth: The Remaking of Social Analysis.* Boston: Beacon Press, 1989.

Rosenberg, Fernando J. *The Avant-Garde and Geopolitics in Latin America.* Pittsburgh: University of Pittsburgh Press, 2006.

Rosenstein, Roy. "Nicaraguan Poet as Wandering Jew: Salomón de la Selva and 'Mi primer judío.'" *Latin American Literary Review* 18.35 (1990): 59–70.

Rubiera Castillo, Daisy and Inés María Martiatu, eds. *Afrocubanas: historia, pensamiento y prácticas culturales.* Havana: Editorial de Ciencias Sociales, 2011.

Rudman, Mark. "William Carlos Williams in America." *American Poetry Review* 37.2 (2008): 53–62.

Russell, Craig H. *From Serra to Sancho: Music and Pageantry in the California Missions.* New York: Oxford University Press, 2009.

Saldaña-Portillo, María Josefina. *Indian Given: Racial Geographies across Mexico and the United States.* Durham: Duke University Press, 2016.

   The Revolutionary Imagination in the Americas and the Age of Development. Durham, NC: Duke University Press, 2003.

   "Who's the Indian in Aztlán? Re-Writing Mestizaje, Indianism, and Chicanismo from the Lacadón." *The Latin American Subaltern Studies Reader.* Ed. Ileana Rodríguez. Durham, NC: Duke University Press, 2001: 402–23.

Saldívar, José David. *Border Matters: Remapping American Cultural Studies.* University of California Press, 1997.

   Trans-Americanity: Subaltern Modernities, Global Coloniality, and the Cultures of Greater Mexico. Durham, NC: Duke University Press, 2012.

   The Dialectics of Our America: Genealogy, Cultural Critique and Literary History. Durham, NC: Duke University Press, 1991.

Saldívar, Ramón. *The Borderlands of Culture: Américo Paredes and the Transnational Imaginary.* Durham, NC: Duke University Press, 2006.

   Chicano Narrative: The Dialectics of Difference. Madison: University of Wisconsin Press, 1990.

   "Historical Fantasy, Speculative Realism, and Postrace Aesthetics in Contemporary American Fiction." *American Literary History* 23.3 (2011): 574–99.

Saldívar-Hull, Sonia. *Feminism on the Border: Chicana Gender Politics and Literature.* Berkeley: University of California Press, 2000.

Salgado, César A. *From Modernism to Neo-Baroque: Joyce and Lezama Lima.* Lewisburg, PA: Bucknell University Press, 2001.

Sánchez, Marta Ester. *Contemporary Chicana Poetry: A Critical Approach to an Emerging Literature.* Berkeley: University of California Press, 1985.

Sánchez, Rosaura. *Telling Identities: The Californio Testimonio.* Minneapolis: University of Minnesota Press, 1995.

Sánchez González, Lisa. *Boricua Literature: A Literary History of the Puerto Rican Diaspora.* New York: New York University Press, 2001.

Sandín, Lyn Di Iorio. *Killing Spanish: Literary Essays on Ambivalent US Latino/a Identity.* New York: Palgrave Macmillan, 2004.

Sandín, Lyn Di Iorio and Richard Perez, eds. *Contemporary US Latino/a Literary Criticism.* New York: Palgrave Macmillan, 2007.

Sandoval Sanchez, Alberto. *José, Can you See?: Latinos on and off Broadway.* Madison: University of Wisconsin Press, 1999.

Schmidt Camacho, Alicia R. *Migrant Imaginaries: Latino Cultural Politics in the US-Mexico Borderlands.* New York: New York University Press, 2008.

Schulman, Ivan A. *Genesis del modernismo: Martí, Nájera, Silva, Casal.* Mexico City: Colegio de México, 1966.

Seed, Patricia. *Ceremonies of Possession in Europe's Conquest of the New World, 1492–1640.* Cambridge; New York: Cambridge University Press, 1995.

Ševčenko, Liz. "Making Loisaida: Placing Puertorriqueñidad in Lower Manhattan." *Mambo Montage: The Latinization of New York City.* Eds. Arlene M. Dávila and Agustin Laó-Montes. New York: Columbia University Press, 2001: 293–318.

Sheren, Ila Nicole. *Portable Borders: Performance Art and Politics on the US Frontera since 1984.* Austin: University of Texas Press, 2015.

Socolovsky, Maya. *Troubling Nationhood in US Latina Literature: Explorations of Place and Belonging.* New Brunswick, NJ: Rutgers University Press, 2013.

Sommer, Doris. "AmeRícan Accents Syncopate the State." *The Ends of Performance.* Eds. Peggy Phelan and Jill Lane. New York: New York University Press, 1998: 169–77.

Bilingual Aesthetics: A New Sentimental Education. Durham, NC: Duke Univeristy Press, 2004.

Bilingual Games: Some Literary Investigations. New York: Palgrave Macmillan, 2003.

Soto, Sandra K. *Reading Chican@ Like a Queer: The De-Mastery of Desire.* Austin: University of Texas Press, 2011.

Sponsler, Claire. *Ritual Imports: Performing Medieval Drama in America.* Ithaca: Cornell University Press, 2004.

Stanchich, Maritza. "Towards a Post-Nuyorican Literature." *Sargasso* 2005–2006 (II): 113–24.

Stavans, Ilan, et al. *The Norton Anthology of Latino Literature.* New York: W. W. Norton, 2011.

Suárez, Lucía M., *The Tears of Hispaniola: Haitian and Dominican Diaspora Memory.* Gainsville: University Press of Florida, 2006.

"Trans-American Latina/o Literature of the 1990s: Resisting Neoliberalism." *The Cambridge Companion to Latina/o American Literature.* Ed. John Morán González. New York: Cambridge University Press, 2016: 111–27.

Taylor, Diana and Juan Villegas, eds. *Negotiating Performance: Gender, Sexuality and Theatricality in Latin/o America.* Durham, NC: Duke University Press, 1994.

Tedlock, Dennis. *2000 Years of Mayan Literature.* Berkeley: University of California Press, 2010.

Tinajero, Araceli. *El Lector: A History of the Cigar Factory Reader.* Trans. Judith E. Grasberg. Austin: University of Texas Press, 2010.

Torres, Lourdes. "The Construction of the Self in US Latina Autobiographies." *Third World Women and the Politics of Feminism*. Eds. Chandra Talpade Mohanty, Ann Russo, and Lourdes Torres. Bloomington: Indiana University Press, 1991: 276–87.

"Queering Puerto Rican Women's Narratives." *Meridians: Feminism, Race, Transnationalism* 9.1 (2009): 83–112.

Torres-Padilla, José L. and Carmen Haydee Rivera, eds. *Writing off the Hyphen: New Critical Perspectives on the Literature of the Puerto Rican Diaspora*. Seattle: University of Washington Press, 2008.

Torres-Saillant, Silvio. "Before the Diaspora: Early Dominican Literature in the United States." *Recovering the US Hispanic Literary Heritage, Volume 3*. Eds. María Herrera-Sobek and Virginia Sánchez Korrol. Houston: Arte Público Press, 2000.

"Dominican-American Literature." *The Routledge Companion to Latino/a Literature*. Eds. Suzanne Bost and Francis R. Aparicio. New York: Routledge, 2012: 423–35.

An Intellectual History of the Caribbean. New York: Palgrave Macmillan, 2006.

El retorno de las yolas: Ensayos sobre diáspora, democracia y dominicanidad. Santo Domingo: Librería La Trinitaria, 1999.

Tudela, Elisa Sampson Vera. *Colonial Angels: Narratives of Gender and Spirituality in Mexico, 1580–1750*. Austin: University of Texas Press, 2010.

Valdés, Vanessa. *Oshun's Daughters: The Search for Womanhood in the Americas*. Albany: State University of New York Press, 2014.

Valle-Ferrer, Norma. *Luisa Capetillo, Pioneer Puerto Rican Feminist*. New York: Peter Lang, 2006.

Vargas, Jennifer Harford. *Forms of Dictatorship: Power, Narrative, and Authoritarianism in the Latina/o Novel*. New York: Oxford University Press, 2017.

Vásquez, David J. *Triangulations: Narrative Strategies for Navigating Latino Identity*. Minneapolis: University of Minnesota Press, 2011.

Velasco, Juan. "*Automitografías*: The Border Paradigm and Chicana/o Autobiography." *Biography* 27.2 (2004): 313–38.

Vélez-Ibáñez, Carlos. *Border Visions: Mexican Cultures of the Southwest*. Tucson: University of Arizona Press, 1996.

Viego, Antonio. *Dead Subjects: Toward a Politics of Loss in Latino Studies*. Durham, NC: Duke University Press, 2007.

"The Place of the Gay Male Chicano in Queer Chicana/o Cultural Work." *Gay Latino Studies*. Eds. Michael Hames-García and Ernesto Javier Martínez. Durham, NC: Duke University Press, 2011: 86–104.

Villa, Raúl Homero. *Barrio-Logos: Space and Place in Urban Chicano Literature and Culture*. Austin: University of Texas Press, 2000.

Viqueira Albán, Juan Pedro. *Propriety and Permissiveness in Bourbon Mexico*. Trans. Lipsett-Rivera, Sonya and Sergio Rivera Ayala. Wilmington, DE: Scholarly Resources, 1999.

Waisman, Sergio. "Argentine Writers in the US: Writing South, Living North." *A Companion to US Latino Literature*. Eds. Carlota Caulfield and Darién Davis. Woodbridge, UK: Tamesis, 2007: 158–76.

Wald, Sarah D. *The Nature of California: Race, Citizenship, and Farming since the Dust Bowl*. Seattle: University of Washington Press, 2016.

Yarbro-Bejarano, Yvonne. *The Wounded Heart: Writing on Cherríe Moraga*. Austin: University of Texas Press, 2001.

Ybarra, Priscilla Solis. *Writing the Goodlife: Mexican American Literature and the Environment*. Tuscson: University of Arizona Press, 2016.

Yúdice, George. *The Expediency of Culture: Uses of Culture in the Global Era*. Durham, NC: Duke University Press, 2003.

Index

Abel, Jessica, 652
abject dynamics, 726–727
ableism, 715, 724n
abolitionists, 183, 207, 318–319, 379n, 380, 436,
    613–614
Abreu, Diógenes, 568
Abreu Bracho, Ricardo, 460
Abya Yala, 44n, 44, 133
Academia Brasileira de Letras (Brazilian
    Academy of Letters), 35n
Acevedo, Mario, 647
Aching, Gerard, 147–148
Acosta, José Julián, 378–379, 379–380n,
    380–381, 647
Acosta, Marta, 645
Acosta-Belén, Edna, 489
Across a Hundred Mountains (Grande 2006),
    479
actos, 452
Acuña, Rodolfo, 111n
ADÁL (Maldonado), 421
Adam, Margie, 594
Adams, John Quincy, 201
Adams, Timothy Dow, 532
Adams-Onís Treaty (1819), 101
Adorno, Rolena, 58
Adventures of Huckleberry Finn, The (Twain
    1884), 537
aesthetics
    of affect, 593
    and border gnosis, 52
    and Burgos, 369
    and Cervantes's floricanto, 405–406
    in Chacón's novellas, 225
    Chicana/o, 221
    and conquest drama, 51
    of Cosmé's *declamación*, 323
    and cultural nationalist movements, 20
    and fandom, 595

Giménez Smith on, 667–668
and Latin American cultural production,
    42
and Latina/o literature, 639–640
of Latina/o literature, 739
and Martí's antiracist politics, 267
and modernist poetics, 353–354
Negroni on, 662
and politics, 15
and popular fiction, 640
postrace, 27
and Puerto Rican poets, 556
Saldívar on, 639
"A Few Don'ts by an Imagiste" (Pound 1913),
    353
African American history, 377
African American literature, 6, 570–571
African Americans
    and Afro-Latinos, 450
    and black affirmation, 277–278
    and blackness, 277–278
    and civil rights movement, 281–282
    and Cosme's performances, 324–325
    demographics of, 20–21
    and Garifuna, 283
    and Hispanic identity, 712
    and internal colonialism, 111n
    and Jim Crow, 13
    and literary-sonic culture, 310n
    and Puerto Ricans, 11
    and Reconstruction, 288
    and Schomburg, 373
    Tenayuca on, 314
    and whiteness, 611
African diaspora, 372, 384, 612
Afro-Antillean activists, 373–374
Afro-Caribbean migrants, 381n
Afro-Caribbean rhythms, 25
Afro-Caribbean subjects, 213

Index

Aparicio, Frances, 145–146, 415, 418, 420,
422–423, 583, 590
Aparicio, Manuel, 320–321n
apparitions, 60
Appeal, The (Walker 1829), 278
APRA (Alianza Popular Revolucionaria
Americana; Popular Revolutionary
American Alliance), 131
A quien corresponda (Ventosilla 2008),
664–665
Aquí Se Habla Español (Pietri 1971), 413
Aragón, Francisco, 559
Arana, Marie, 27–28, 665–666
Aranda, José F., 234n
Arbenz, Jacobo, 188
Archibugi, Daniele, 719–720
Archila, William, 522
Archive and the Repertoire, The (Taylor 2003),
57–58
archives
and Latina/o literary history, 160–161
and translation, 107
Archivo José Martí (1943), 131n
Ardao, Arturo, 212
area studies
and archival research, 160–161
and transnational Latina/o studies,
283–284
and world literature, 154–155
Areíto, 438–440
Arenal, Electa, 87
Arenas, Reinaldo, 20, 437–438, 448, 668
Argudín, Pastor, 382–383
Arguedas, José María, 131n
Arias, Arturo, 8, 512, 519, 522
Arias, Aurora, 555n, 568
Ariel (Rodó 1900), 41, 147
Aristide, Jean-Bertrand, 566, 569
Arizona, 111
Arnaz, Desi, 26, 590, 608–609, 616
"A Roosevelt" (Darío 1904), 147–148
Arp, Hans, 353
Arriola, Gus, 653
Arrizón, Alicia, 739n
arroba (@), 715, 717
Arroyo-Martínez, Jossianna, 252n, 368,
380–381, 381n
Arte Público Press (University of Houston)
and *Astucias por heredar*, 68
and genre fiction, 648
and *Jicoténcal* (Varela 1826), 161–162n
and *La Carreta Made a U-Turn*, 420
and literary marketplace, 637

and Nuyorican poetry, 425
and Ruiz de Burton's novels, 209n
and text availability, 5
*Arthur Alfonso Schomburg: Black Bibliophile and
Collector* (Sinnette 1989), 372–373
Art of Political Murder, The (Goldman 2007),
519
Art of Transition, The (Masiello 2001), 511
*Arturo Alfonso Schomburg: A Puerto Rican's
Quest for His Black Heritage* (Piñeiro de
Rivera 1989), 377–379
Ascension (Resto 2013), 429
Asians, 115
Asociación Latinoamericana de Integración
(ALADI), 133
assimilation, 281–282
Assis, Machado de, 35n
Astorga, Nora, 527–528
*Astucias por heredar, un sobrino a un tío [Tricks
to Inherit: a Nephew and His Uncle]*, 54,
66–71, 70n
Asunción (Ventosilla 1995), 664–665
Ateneo de la Juventud (Atheneum of Youth),
42
At Night They Walk in Circles (Alarcón 2013),
666–667
Atomik Aztex (Foster 2005), 639
Augenbraum, Harold, 103–104
Aurora, 226
Aurora (Laredo, Texas), 341–342
Aurora Commercial Advertiser, 201
autobioethnography, 543–545
autobiography, 444–445, 496, 532, 543, 678
Autobiography (Williams 1951), 355
Autobiography of an Ex-Colored Man, The
(Johnson 1912), 322
auto da fe, 7
autoethnography, 538–539
automitografías, 533
Autonomous University of Santo Domingo,
298
avant-garde poets
in Europe and United States, 362
and language, 355
in Latin America, 362–363
Aves sin nido (Matto de Turner), 239–240,
239n
Ávila, Eliana, 29
Avila, Javier, 555n
Avila, Quíque, 20
Avilés, Arthur, 428
Avilés, Quique, 460, 522
Ayala, Prudencia, 515, 523–524, 523n

774

Index